8B-3 Adjusted cash balance, $8,353.68
8B-4 No key figure
8B-5 No key figure
8B-6 (a) Adjusted bank balance, $28,122.05
Bus. Dec. Prob. 8: No key figure

9A-1 (b) Net accounts receivable, $461,280
9A-2 No key figure
9A-3 No key figure
9A-4 (c) Uncollectible accounts expense, $15,699
9A-5 No key figure
9A-6 (b) Accrued interest receivable, $73.06
9B-1 (b) Net accounts receivable, $232,320
9B-2 No key figure
9B-3 (a) Probable loss, $5,116.54
9B-4 No key figure
9B-5 No key figure
9B-6 (b) Uncollectible accounts expense, $21,032
Bus. Dec. Prob. 9: (a) Net income, $17,700

10A-1 (a) Year 1, gross profit percentages, 32½%
10A-2 (a) (2) $228,750; (b) gross profit on sales (fifo), $292,175
10A-3 (a) Gross profit rate for Year 3, 25%
10A-4 (b) Cost ratio, 75%
10A-5 (c) Gross profit, $670
10A-6 (a) Net income, Year 9, $301,633
10B-1 (a) Year 1, gross profit percentage, 33%
10B-2 (a) (1) $106,100; (b) gross profit on sales (lifo), $793,000
10B-3 (a) Cost ratio, 75%
10B-4 (a) Ending inventory at cost, $19,754
10B-5 (c) Gross profit, $3,800
10B-6 (a) Year 4, net income, $150,817
Bus. Dec. Prob. 10: (a) Gross profit, $5,850

11A-1 (a) Double-declining balance, total, $135,164
11A-2 (b) Land, $90,000
11A-3 Depreciation for Year 3: (b) $25,200; (c) $18,466
11A-4 No key figure
11A-5 (b) Depreciation expense, $67,410
11A-6 (c) Corrected net income for Year 8, $99,115.20
11B-1 1978 Depreciation expense, $13,680
11B-2 (b) Land, $60,000
11B-3 Depreciation for Year 2: (b) $76,800; (c) $70,349
11B-4 (b) Depreciation expense, $127,620
11B-5 No key figure
11B-6 (c) Corrected net income for 1979, $440,512
Bus. Dec. Prob. 11: (a) Company A. $67.500, Company B, $124,088

12A-1 Year ended June 30, Year 7, depreciation expense, $20,150
12A-2 (b) Loss, $875
12A-3 No key figure
12A-4 No key figure
12A-5 (b) Total net gain, $118,690
12A-6 (b) Paid for goodwill, $97,740
12B-1 (b) Cost basis, machinery (new), $166,500
12B-2 (b) Loss, $900
12B-3 No key figure
12B-4 Amortization for Year 3, $43,750
12B-5 Inventory, $340,320
12B-6 (b) Revised earnings for Company X, $52,800; (c) price to be offered for Company X, $383,040
Bus. Dec. Prob. 12: No key figure

13A-1 (d) Total payroll expense, $12,230.40
13A-2 No key figure
13A-3 (b) $2,976.18; (c) 6.4%
13A-4 (b) $120,000
13A-5 (a) Net pay due, $4,933.30
13B-1 (d) Total payroll expense, $10,483.20
13B-2 No key figure
13B-3 (b) $4,360.38; (c) 6.5%
13B-4 (b) $80,000
13B-5 (a) Net pay due, $6,881.82
Bus. Dec. Prob. 13: No key figure

14A-1 (c) Total assets, $265,720
14A-2 No key figure
14A-3 (a) Year 3, $375,000; (c) Year 3, $505,500
14A-4 (a) Cost percentage, 60%; (b) net income, $119,980
14A-5 Net income, $26,080
14B-1 (a) Net income, cash basis, $47,900
14B-2 No key figure
14B-3 (a) Revised net income: Year 2, $121,920
14B-4 (a) Net income as revised, $157,080
14B-5 (b) Total liabilities & owner's capital, end of Year 1, sales method $37.2; production method $39.6; installment method, $31.2
Bus. Dec. Prob. 14 (b) (1) Net income, same accounting, Year 9, $72,000; (2) revised accounting, Year 9, $90,000

15A-1 (b) Total assets, $289,800
15A-2 (a) Net income, $33,760; (c) total assets, $225,760
15A-3 (c) Bonus to existing partners, $26,250
15A-4 No key figure
15A-5 (c) Capital balance for Davies, Sept. 30, $57,435
15A-6 (b) Cash to Carlos, $18,144
15A-7 (b) Cash to Fay, $12,000; Cash to May, $26,000
15B-1 (b) Total assets, $220,800

(continued on back cover)

ACCOUNTING
The Basis for Business Decisions

ACCOUNTING
The Basis for Business Decisions
Fourth Edition

Walter B. Meigs, Ph.D., C.P.A.

Professor of Accounting
University of Southern California

Charles E. Johnson, Ph.D., C.P.A.

Late Professor of Accounting
University of Oregon

Robert F. Meigs, D.B.A.

Associate Professor of Accounting
California State University, San Diego

McGraw-Hill Book Company

New York St. Louis San Francisco Auckland Bogotá Düsseldorf Johannesburg
London Madrid Mexico Montreal New Delhi Panama Paris São Paulo Singapore
Sydney Tokyo Toronto

ACCOUNTING: THE BASIS FOR BUSINESS DECISIONS

567890 KPKP 78321098

This book was set in Vega by York Graphic Services, Inc.
The editors were Donald E. Chatham, Jr., Marjorie Singer, and Edwin Hanson;
the cover was designed by Anne Canevari Green;
the cover painting was done by Glen S. Heller;
the production supervisor was Dennis J. Conroy.
New drawings were done by York Graphic Services, Inc.,
Kingsport Press, Inc., was printer and binder.

Library of Congress Cataloging in Publication Data

Meigs, Walter B
    Accounting, the basis for business decisions.

    Includes index.
    1. Accounting. I. Johnson, Charles E., joint author.
II. Meigs, Robert F., joint author. III. Title.
HF5635.M49 1977   657   76-44508
ISBN 0-07-041241-3

Contents

THE PURPOSE AND NATURE OF ACCOUNTING. A system for creating accounting information. The work of accountants. Public accounting. Private accounting. Governmental accounting. Development of accounting standards—the FASB. Two primary business objectives. Accounting as the basis for management decisions. Internal control. Forms of business organization. **FINANCIAL STATEMENTS: THE STARTING POINT IN THE STUDY OF ACCOUNTING.** The balance sheet. Assets. Liabilities. Owner's equity. The accounting equation. Effect of business transactions upon the balance sheet. Effect of business transactions upon the acounting equation. **USE OF FINANCIAL STATEMENTS BY OUTSIDERS.** Bankers and other creditors. Others interested in financial information. **KEY TERMS INTRODUCED IN CHAPTER 1. DEMONSTRATION PROBLEM FOR YOUR REVIEW. SOLUTION TO DEMONSTRATION PROBLEM. REVIEW QUESTIONS. EXERCISES. PROBLEMS. BUSINESS DECISION PROBLEM 1.**

The accounting model. The use of accounts for recording transactions. **THE LEDGER.** Debit and credit entries. Recording transactions in ledger accounts: illustration. Running balance form of ledger account. The normal balance of an account. Sequence and numbering of ledger accounts. Flow of information through the accounting system. **THE JOURNAL.** The general journal: illustration of entries. Posting. Ledger accounts after posting. **THE TRIAL BALANCE.** Uses and limitations of the trial balance. Locating errors. Dollar signs. Accounting records in perspective. **KEY TERMS INTRODUCED**

considerations of the voucher register. Presentation of the liability in the balance sheet. A "voucher system" without vouchers. Electronic funds transfer systems (EFTS). **KEY TERMS INTRODUCED OR EMPHASIZED IN CHAPTER 8. DEMONSTRATION PROBLEM FOR YOUR REVIEW. SOLUTION TO DEMONSTRATION PROBLEM. REVIEW QUESTIONS. EXERCISES. PROBLEMS. BUSINESS DECISION PROBLEM 8.**

of use. Depreciation not a process of valuation. Causes of depreciation. Methods of computing depreciation. Revision of depreciation rates. Depreciation and income taxes. Accumulated depreciation does not consist of cash. Capital expenditures and revenue expenditures. Extraordinary repairs. Inflation and depreciation. Historical cost versus replacement cost. The SEC requirement for disclosure of replacement cost. Price-level adjustments of accounting data. **KEY TERMS INTRODUCED OR EMPHASIZED IN CHAPTER 11. REVIEW QUESTIONS. EXERCISES. PROBLEMS. BUSINESS DECISION PROBLEM 11.**

Disposal of plant and equipment. Trading in used assets on new. Maintaining control over plant and equipment: subsidiary ledgers. **NATURAL RESOURCES.** Accounting for natural resources. **INTANGIBLE ASSETS.** Characteristics. Operating expenses versus intangible assets. Amortization. Goodwill. Leaseholds. Leasehold improvements. Patents. Research and development costs. Copyrights. Trademarks. Other intangibles and deferred charges. **KEY TERMS INTRODUCED OR EMPHASIZED IN CHAPTER 12. REVIEW QUESTIONS. EXERCISES. PROBLEMS. BUSINESS DECISION PROBLEM 12.**

Internal control over payrolls. Other uses of payroll records. Distinction between employees and independent contractors. Employee earnings. Deductions from earnings of employees. Social security taxes (FICA). Federal income taxes. Illustration: computation of employee's net pay. Payroll records and procedures. Payroll taxes on the employer. Combined entry for payroll and all related taxes and deductions. Accrual of payroll taxes at year-end. Presentation of payroll taxes in the financial statements. Payment of payroll taxes. **KEY TERMS INTRODUCED OR EMPHASIZED IN CHAPTER 13. REVIEW QUESTIONS. EXERCISES. PROBLEMS. BUSINESS DECISION PROBLEM 13.**

A basic objective of accounting. Generally accepted accounting principles. Authoritative support for accounting principles. The accounting environment. The accounting entity concept. The going-concern assumption. The time period principle. The monetary principle. The objectivity principle. Asset valuation: the cost principle. Measuring revenue: the realization principle. Measuring expenses: the matching principle. Recognition of gains and losses. The consistency principle. The disclosure principle. Materiality. Conservatism as a guide in resolving uncertainties. Opinion on financial statements rendered by independent CPAs. **THE SEARCH FOR BETTER FINANCIAL REPORTING.** Inflation—the greatest challenge to accounting. Profits—fact or illusion? Two approaches to "inflation accounting." General purchasing power financial statements. Current-value accounting distinguished from general purchasing power accounting. Current-value accounting—objectives and problems. Responsibility of CPA firms for replacement cost data. Comparison of current-value accounting with general purchasing power accounting. **KEY TERMS INTRODUCED OR EMPHASIZED IN CHAPTER 14. REVIEW QUESTIONS. EXERCISES. PROBLEMS. BUSINESS DECISION PROBLEM 14.**

Reasons for formation of partnerships. Significant features of a partnership. Advantages and disadvantages of a partnership. The partnership contract. Partnership accounting. Opening the accounts of a new partnership. Additional investments. Drawing accounts. Loans from partners. Closing the accounts of a partnership at year-end. Partnership profits and income taxes. The nature of partnership profits. Alternative methods of dividing profits and losses. Admission of a new partner. Retirement of a partner. Death of a partner. Liquidation of a partnership. **KEY TERMS INTRODUCED OR EMPHASIZED IN CHAPTER 15. DEMONSTRATION PROBLEM FOR YOUR REVIEW. SOLUTION TO DEMONSTRATION PROBLEM. REVIEW QUESTIONS. EXERCISES. PROBLEMS. BUSINESS DECISION PROBLEM 15.**

Definition of corporation. Advantages of the corporate form of organization. Disadvantages of the corporate form of organization. Formation of a corporation. Authorization and issuance of capital stock. Par value. Issuance of capital stock. Capital stock outstanding. Cash dividends. Preferred and common stock. The underwriting of stock issues. Market price of common stock. Stock issued for assets other than cash. No-par stock. Subscriptions to capital stock. Special records of corporations. Balance sheet for a corporation illustrated. **KEY TERMS INTRODUCED OR EMPHASIZED IN CHAPTER 16. REVIEW QUESTIONS. EXERCISES. PROBLEMS. BUSINESS DECISION PROBLEM 16.**

Extraordinary items. Discontinued operations of a segment of a business. Public misconceptions of the rate of corporate earnings. Earnings per share (EPS). Income statement for a corporation illustrated. Cash dividends. Regular and special dividends. Dividend dates. Dividends on preferred stock. Liquidating dividends. Stock dividends. Stock splits. Retained earnings. Prior period adjustments to Retained Earnings account. Appropriations and restrictions of retained earnings. Statement of retained earnings. **TREASURY STOCK.** Recording purchases and reissuance of treasury stock. Treasury stock not an asset. Restriction of retained earnings when treasury stock is acquired. **BOOK VALUE PER SHARE OF COMMON STOCK.** Book value when company has both preferred and common stock. Illustration of stockholders' equity section. **KEY TERMS INTRODUCED OR EMPHASIZED IN CHAPTER 17. REVIEW QUESTIONS. EXERCISES. PROBLEMS. BUSINESS DECISION PROBLEM 17.**

BONDS PAYABLE. Characteristics of a bond. Effect of bond financing on holders of capital stock. Management planning of the bond issue. Accounting entries for a bond issue. The concept of present value. The present value concept and bond prices. Bonds sold at a discount. Amortization of the discount. Bonds sold at a premium. Amortization of the premium. Year-end adjustments for bond interest expense. Retirement of bonds payable. Conversion of bonds payable into common stock. Bond sinking fund. Mortgages payable. Leases. Pension plans. **INVESTMENTS IN CORPORATE SECURITIES.** Securities transactions from the viewpoint of investors. Marketable securities as current assets. Valuation of marketable securities. The argument for valuation at market value. Determining the cost of investments in stocks and bonds. Acquisition of bonds at premium or discount. Gains and losses from sale of investments in securities. How should investors measure their performance? **KEY TERMS INTRODUCED OR EMPHASIZED IN CHAPTER 18. REVIEW QUESTIONS. EXERCISES. PROBLEMS. BUSINESS DECISION PROBLEM 18.**

Nature of business combinations. Consolidation at date of acquisition. Consolidation after date of acquisition. Less than 100% ownership in subsidiary. Acquisition of subsidiary stock at more (or less) than book value. Intercompany receivables and payables. Consolidated income statement. Consolidated statement of retained earnings. Unrealized profits on intercompany sales. Consolidated statements on a pooling-of-interests basis. When should consolidated statements be prepared? Who uses consolidated financial statements? **KEY TERMS INTRODUCED OR EMPHASIZED IN CHAPTER 19. REVIEW QUESTIONS. EXERCISES. PROBLEMS. BUSINESS DECISION PROBLEM 19.**

The critical importance of income taxes. The federal income tax: history and objectives. The effect of income taxes on business decisions. Classes of

Preface

The environment of accounting is changing fast, and these environmental changes, such as continued inflation and the critical financial problems of many cities, affect the goals and the content of an introductory text in accounting. In order to function intelligently as a citizen as well as in a business of any size or type, every individual needs more than ever before a clear understanding of basic accounting concepts. In this fourth edition, we have tried to reflect the impact of inflation on accounting measurements and to suggest the direction of needed changes in accounting concepts and methods. The importance of adequate disclosure in the system of financial reporting is stressed, and attention is drawn to the need for improved accounting controls in all sectors of society.

Our goal is to present accounting as an essential part of the decision-making process for the voter, the taxpayer, the government official, the business manager, and the investor. This edition, like the preceding one, is designed for the first college-level course in accounting. In this course, instructors often recognize three general groups of students: those who stand at the threshold of preparation for a career in accounting, students of business administration who need a good understanding of accounting as an important element of the total business information system, and students from a variety of other disciplines who will find the ability to use and interpret accounting information a valuable accomplishment. During the process of revision the authors have tried to keep in mind the needs and interests of all three groups.

New features of this edition

Among the many new features of this edition are:

1 A glossary at the end of each chapter, with concise explanations of key terms introduced or emphasized in that chapter.

2 An increase of about 20% in the number of exercises and problems throughout the book.

3 A discussion of the impact of inflation on the measurement of profits, on inventories, and on plant and equipment.

4 People-oriented problems which depict the hard decisions that must be made by men and women acting as administrators, owners, and investors and in other roles.

5 Increased attention to perpetual inventory systems.

6 Increased emphasis on internal control–how a small business can strengthen its system of internal control.

7 Evaluation of corporate profits. Are they adequate? Are they reasonable? What are the appropriate yardsticks?

8 Two parallel sets of Achievement Tests and Comprehensive Examinations.

9 An examination booklet, with test material arranged chapter by chapter for the entire text.

10 Attention to the increased activity of the SEC in establishing accounting standards.

11 Careful integration into the text and problems of the pronouncements of the Financial Accounting Standards Board.

12 New emphasis on replacement cost and the implied move from historical cost to present-value accounting.

13 Improved format for supplementary materials. Partially filled-in working papers and practice sets appear in a new improved format, with wider rulings and printed in color.

14 The concept of present value, presented in clear understandable terms, with application to such decisions as replacing plant assets or expanding productive resources.

Features carried forward from prior editions

Special qualities that are carried forward from prior editions include:

1 The only introductory accounting book that is part of an integrated series of introductory, intermediate, and advanced accounting textbooks with continuity of authorship. This established series concept provides assurance that students finishing the introductory course will be prepared to move readily into intermediate accounting without gaps or unnecessary overlaps.

2 Problem material developed and tested firsthand by the authors in their own classes for introductory accounting students.

3 A good blend of (*a*) the theoretical and conceptual aspects of accounting and (*b*) the realities of applying these concepts to everyday practical business situations.

4 Provocative problems that raise a variety of interesting questions and carry the student far beyond routine drill.

New and extensively revised chapters

Chapter 6, entitled Internal Control, is mostly new material. It explains the purpose and nature of internal control and illustrates methods of achieving good internal control without incurring excessive expense. Chapter 10, on the subject of inventories, contains much new material on the impact of inflation upon the measurement of cost of goods sold and the valuation of inventories. The topic of "inventory profits" is related to recent official pronouncements pointing to the need for considering replacement costs when measuring the profit realized on a sales transaction. Chapter 11, dealing with depreciation of plant and equipment, presents the problems arising from an environment of inflation. Attention is focused on the rules issued by the SEC requiring large corporations to disclose the replacement cost of plant and equipment and to show what depreciation would amount to if it were computed on the basis of the replacement cost of the assets now in use. Chapter 14, Accounting Principles, pulls together the theoretical concepts covered in the first half of the book and gives further attention to the problems created by rising prices. The dramatic change in position of many of the large international CPA firms which are now advocating current-value accounting as the wave of the future is related to the increasingly active role of the SEC. Chapter 18 contains a revised presentation of accounting for marketable securities with attention to recent pronouncements by the FASB. Chapter 22, Analysis and Interpretation of Financial Statements, is extensively revised and invites students to use the accounting expertise they have acquired to evaluate the adequacy or inadequacy of corporate profits in relation to sales volume, to total assets of the firm, to invested capital, and to other yardsticks. The significance of profits as a means of capital formation is emphasized. The last chapter in the text is almost entirely new. Chapter 28, Capital Budgeting and Other Aids to Managerial Decisions, includes such questions as the desirability of replacing plant assets or expanding productive resources. These items are considered in the framework of the concept of present value, which is treated in a simple but comprehensive manner.

Emphasis and perspective

As in the previous editions we have attempted to present a balanced coverage of accounting from both financial and managerial viewpoints. Similarly, we have given continued attention to the problem of finding an ideal relation between an understanding of accounting procedures and the ability to use accounting information effectively. The advent of electronic data processing is thoroughly recognized in the discussion of accounting systems (Chapter 7). However, students must understand, for example, how to make a journal entry by hand before they can instruct a computer to make it for them or before they can understand the journal-output of a computer. The discussion of accounting procedure throughout the book is geared to the objective of enhancing the student's grasp of the accounting process and its informational output.

Supplementary materials

A full assortment of supplementary materials accompanies this text:

1 Two parallel sets of **Achievement Tests** and **Comprehensive Examinations.**

Each set consists of six Achievement Tests with each test covering four or five chapters; each Comprehensive Examination covers one-half of the entire text and may be used as a final examination. The availability of two parallel sets of tests makes it possible for an instructor to rotate examinations from year to year or to use two different examinations of equal difficulty and coverage in a single class.

2 *An examination booklet.*   With an abundance of test questions and exercises arranged chapter by chapter for the entire text, this examination booklet will be a most useful source for instructors who prefer to assemble their own examinations. The questions in this book are printed in an $8\frac{1}{2}$ x 11 format on one side of a page. They can be torn out and copied to prepare individual examinations.

3 *A self-study guide.*   Written by Professor Robert F. Meigs, the **Study Guide** enables students to measure their progress by immediate feedback. This self-study guide includes an outline of the most important points in each chapter, an abundance of objective questions, and several short exercises for each chapter. In the back of the self-study guide are answers to questions and solutions to exercises to help students evaluate their understanding of the subject. The self-study guide will also be useful in classroom discussions and for review by students before examinations.

4 *Working papers.*   Two sets of problems for each chapter, Group A problems and Group B problems, are included in the text. The problems in the two groups are of similar difficulty and require about the same solution time. Soft-cover books of *partially filled-in working papers* are available for the Group A problems, as well as similar but separate workbooks for the Group B problems. Instructors may choose to alternate assignments, using Group A problems in one year or in one class and Group B problems in another. On these work sheets, the problem headings and some preliminary data have been entered to save students much of the mechanical pencil-pushing inherent in problem assignments. Also available are specially designed *blank accounting forms,* with a number of work sheets of each type appropriate for a course of typical assignments covering the entire book. All the working papers are in a new, improved format featuring wider money columns and the use of color.

5 *Practice sets.*   The two practice sets available with the preceding edition have been completely revised and appear in convenient bound form with improved format. The first, Sterling Company, is for use after covering the first seven chapters of the book. The second, Butler Corporation, may conveniently be used at any point after Chapter 18. Each practice set consists of a narrative of transactions and appropriate work sheets for preparing the solution.

6 *Checklist of key figures for problems.*   This list appears on the front and back inside covers of this book. The purpose of the checklist is to aid students in verifying their problem solutions and in discovering their own errors.

7 *Transparencies of problem solutions.*   This is a visual aid prepared by the publisher for the instructor who wishes to display in a classroom the complete solutions to most problems.

In the development of problem material for this book, special attention has been given to the inclusion of problems of varying length and difficulty. By referring to the time estimates, difficulty ratings, and problem descriptions in the *Solutions Manual,* instructors can choose problems that best fit the level, scope, and emphasis of the course they are offering.

8 *Additional transparencies for classroom illustrations.* Sixteen special transparencies have been produced for use in the classroom to illustrate such concepts as closing entries, the preparation of a work sheet, the use of controlling accounts and subsidiary ledgers, and the preparation of a break-even chart.

9 *A booklet of learning objectives.* This brief statement of learning objectives for each chapter is designed to focus the student's attention on key principles and procedures. A clear understanding of these points will be especially helpful in following the chapters.

Contributions by others

We want to express our sincere thanks to the many users of preceding editions who offered helpful suggestions for this edition. Especially helpful was the advice received from Professors John J. Gorman, Rider College; Larzette G. Hale, Utah State University; Nanci Lee Dummett, Marie Perino, and Glen Swanson, American River College; Robert E. Arnold, Youngstown State University; Don Scalamogna, Houston Community College; Eugene Imhoff, Syracuse University; Marcia A. Wood, University of Hawaii at Manoa; Elliott H. Puretz, Merrimack College; Wayne E. Pfingsten, Belleville Area College; Arthur A. Volk, University of South Dakota; T. A. Gavin, University of Tennessee at Chattanooga; Raymond Larson, Appalachian State University; Kenneth O. Elvik, Iowa State University; Robert Jacob, Casper College; Raymond Loester, Housatonic Community College; Beverly G. Barnes, East Texas State University; Paul Plumer, Catonsville Community College; S. James Galley, Augustana College; and Leslie R. Loschen, University of Southern California.

Special thanks go to Professor Louis Geller of Queens College and Professor John J. Gorman of Rider College for assisting us in the proof stages of this edition by reviewing the end-of-chapter problems and text examples for accuracy.

The assistance of Richard Fell, June Jensen, and Judi Takagaki was most helpful in preparation of the manuscript.

We acknowledge with appreciation permission from the American Institute of Certified Public Accountants to quote from many of its pronouncements.

Walter B. Meigs
Robert F. Meigs

1 Accounting: The Basis for Business Decisions

Accounting has often been called the "language of business." People in the business world—owners, managers, bankers, stockbrokers, attorneys, engineers, investors—use accounting terms and concepts to describe the events that make up the day-to-day existence of every business, large or small. Since a language is a man-made means of communication, it is natural that languages should change to meet the changing needs of society. Accounting, too, is a man-made art, one in which changes and improvements are continually being made in the process of communicating business information.

We live in an era of accountability. Although accounting has made its most dramatic progress in the field of business, the accounting function is vital to every unit of our society. The individual must account for his or her income. The federal government, the states, the cities, the school districts: all must use accounting as a basis for controlling their resources and measuring their accomplishments. Accounting is equally essential to the successful operation of a university, a fraternity, a church, or a city.

In every election the voters must make decisions at the ballot box on issues involving accounting concepts; therefore, some knowledge of accounting is needed by every citizen if he is to act intelligently in meeting the challenges of our society.

THE PURPOSE AND NATURE OF ACCOUNTING

The underlying purpose of accounting is to provide financial information about an economic entity. In this book the economic entity which we shall be concentrating upon is a business enterprise. The financial information provided by an accounting system is needed by managerial decision makers to help them plan and control the activities of the economic entity. Financial information is also needed by *outsiders*—owners, creditors, investors, the government, and the public—who have supplied money to the business or who have some other interest that will be served by information about its financial position and operating results.

A system for creating accounting information

In order to provide up-to-date financial information about a business, it is necessary to create a systematic record of the daily business activity, in terms of money. For example, goods and services are purchased and sold, credit is extended to customers, debts are incurred, and cash is received and paid out. These *transactions* are typical of business events which can be expressed *in monetary terms,* and must be entered in accounting records. The *recording* process may be performed in many ways: that is, by writing with pen or pencil, by printing with mechanical or electronic equipment, or by punching holes or making magnetic impressions on cards or tape.

Of course, not all business events can be measured and described in monetary terms. Therefore, we do not show in the accounting records the appointment of a new chief executive or the signing of a labor contract, except as these happenings in turn affect future business transactions.

In addition to compiling a narrative record of events as they occur, we *classify* various transactions and events into related groups or categories. Classification enables us to reduce a mass of detail into compact and usable form. For example, grouping all transactions in which cash is received or paid out is a logical step in developing useful information about the cash position of a business enterprise.

To create accounting information in a form which will be useful to the people who use the information, we *summarize* the classified information into financial reports, called *financial statements.* These financial statements are concise, perhaps only three or four pages for a large business. They summarize the business transactions of a specific time period such as a month or a year. Financial statements show the financial position of the business at the time of the report and the operating results by which it arrived at this position.

These three steps we have described—recording, classifying, and summarizing—are the means of creating accounting information. Thus one part of accounting is a system for creating financial information.

USING ACCOUNTING INFORMATION Accounting extends beyond the process of *creating* records and reports. The ultimate objective of accounting is the *use* of this information, its analysis and interpretation. Accountants are always concerned with the significance of the figures they have produced. They look for meaningful relationships between events and financial results; they study the effect of various alternatives; and they search for significant trends that may throw some light on what will happen in the future.

Interpretation and analysis are not the sole province of the accountant. If managers, investors, and creditors are to make effective use of accounting information, they too must have some understanding of how the figures were put together and what they mean. An important part of this understanding is to recognize clearly the limitations of accounting reports. A business manager, an investor, or a creditor who lacks an understanding of accounting may fail to appreciate the extent to which accounting information is based upon *estimates* rather than upon precisely accurate measurements.

THE DISTINCTION BETWEEN ACCOUNTING AND BOOKKEEPING Persons with little knowledge of accounting may also fail to understand the difference between accounting and bookkeeping. *Bookkeeping* means the recording of transactions, the record-making phase of accounting. The recording of transactions tends to be mechanical and repetitive; it is only a small part of the field of accounting and probably the simplest part. *Accounting* includes the design of accounting systems, preparation of financial statements, audits, cost studies, development of forecasts, income tax work, computer applications to accounting processes, and the analysis and interpretation of accounting information as an aid to making business decisions. A person might become a reasonably proficient bookkeeper in a few weeks or months; to become a professional accountant, however, requires several years of study and experience.

The work of accountants

Accountants tend to specialize in a given subarea of the discipline just as do attorneys and members of other professions. In terms of career opportunities, the field of accounting may be divided into three broad areas: (*1*) the public accounting profession, (*2*) private accounting, and (*3*) governmental accounting.

Public accounting

Certified public accountants are independent professional persons comparable to attorneys or physicians, who offer accounting services to clients for a fee. The *CPA certificate* is a license to practice granted by the state on the basis of a rigorous examination and evidence of practical experience. All states require that candidates pass an examination prepared and administered on a national basis twice each year by the American Institute of Certified Public Accountants. Requirements as to education and practical experience differ somewhat among the various states.

AUDITING The principal function of a CPA is auditing. To perform an audit of a business, a firm of certified public accountants makes a careful review of the accounting system and gathers evidence both from within the business and from outside sources. This evidence enables the CPA firm to express its professional opinion as to the fairness and reliability of the financial statements. Persons outside the business, such as bankers and investors who rely upon financial statements for information, attach great importance to the annual *audit report* by the CPA firm. The *independent* status of a CPA firm retained to make an annual audit is just as important as its technical competence in assuring outsiders that the financial statements prepared by management disclose all relevant information and provide a fair picture of the company's financial position and operating results.

TAX SERVICES An important element of decision-making by business executives is consideration of the income tax consequences of each alternative course of action. The CPA is often called upon for "tax planning," which will show how a future transaction such as the acquisition of new equipment may be arranged in a manner that will hold income taxes to a minimum amount. The CPA is also frequently retained to prepare the federal and state income tax returns. To render tax services, the CPA must have extensive knowledge of tax statutes, regulations, and court decisions, as well as a thorough knowledge of accounting.

MANAGEMENT ADVISORY SERVICES Auditing and income tax work have been the traditional areas of expertise for CPA firms, but the field of management advisory services has recently become a rapidly growing new area. When CPA firms during the course of an audit discovered problems in a client's business, it was natural for them to make suggestions for corrective action. In response, the client often engaged the CPA firm to make a thorough investigation of the problem and to recommend new policies and procedures needed for a solution.

Public accounting firms gradually found themselves becoming more involved in management consulting work. Although this work often concerned accounting and financial matters, sometimes it dealt with organizational structure, statistical research, and a wide variety of problems not closely related to accounting. In recent years many CPA firms have created separate management advisory service departments which are staffed with mathematicians, industrial engineers, and other specialists as well as accountants. The experience, reputation, and independence of the CPA firms have placed them in an advantageous position to render advisory services to management over a broad range of administrative and operating problems. For example, these services might include study of the desirability of a merger with another company, the creation of a pension plan for employees, or the researching of a foreign market for the company's products.

Private accounting

In contrast to the CPA in public practice who serves many clients, an accountant in private industry is employed by a single enterprise. The chief accounting officer of a medium-sized or large business is usually called the *controller,* in recognition of the fact that one of the primary uses of accounting data is to aid in controlling business operations. The controller manages the work of the accounting staff. He or she is also a part of the management team charged with the task of running the business, setting its objectives, and seeing that these objectives are met.

The accountants in a private business, large or small, must record transactions and prepare periodic financial statements from accounting records. Within this area of general accounting, or in addition to it, a number of specialized phases of accounting have developed. Among the more important of these are:

DESIGN OF ACCOUNTING SYSTEMS Although the same basic accounting principles are applicable to all types of businesses, each enterprise requires an individually tailored *financial information system.* This system includes accounting forms, records, instruction manuals, flow charts, programs, and reports to fit the particular needs of the business. Designing an accounting system and putting it into operation are thus specialized phases of accounting. With the advent of electronic data processing equipment, the problems that arise in creating an effective financial information system have become increasingly complex. However, computers compile information that would be too costly to gather by hand methods and also increase the speed with which reports can be made available to management.

COST ACCOUNTING Knowing the cost of a particular product, a manufacturing process, or any business operation is vital to the efficient management of a business. The phase of accounting particularly concerned with collecting and interpreting cost data is called *cost accounting.* Determining the cost of anything is not as simple as it appears at first glance, because the term *cost* has many meanings and different kinds of costs are useful for different purposes.

FINANCIAL FORECASTING A financial forecast (or budget) is a plan of financial operations for some future period, expressed in monetary terms. By using a forecast, management is able to make comparisons between *planned operations* and the *actual results achieved.* A forecast is thus an attempt to preview operating results before the actual transactions have taken place. A forecast is a particularly valuable tool for the controller because it provides each division of the business with a specific goal, and because it gives management a means of measuring the efficiency of performance throughout the company.

TAX ACCOUNTING As income tax rates have gone up and the determination of taxable income has become more complex, both internal accountants and independent public accountants have devoted more time to problems of taxation. Although many companies rely largely on CPA firms for tax planning and the preparation of income tax returns, larger companies also maintain their own tax departments.

INTERNAL AUDITING Most large corporations maintain staffs of internal auditors with the responsibility of seeing that company policies and established procedures are being followed consistently in all divisions of the corporation. The internal auditor, in contrast to the independent auditor or CPA, is not responsible for determining the overall fairness of the company's annual financial statements.

MANAGEMENT ACCOUNTING We have already discussed the way business organizations sometimes call upon CPA firms to render management advisory services. In larger companies, however, we can also recognize *management accounting* as a specialized field of work by the company's own accounting staff. First, we need to emphasize that the accounting system provides information for both external and internal use. The external reporting function of the accounting system has already been touched upon in our discussion of audits of annual financial statements by CPA firms. The internal reporting function of an accounting system gives managers information needed in planning and controlling day-to-day operations; it also gives managers information needed for long-range planning and for major decisions such as the introduction of a new product or the closing of an older plant.

Management accounting utilizes the techniques of both cost accounting and forecasting to achieve its goal of helping executives formulate both short-range and long-range plans, to measure success in carrying out these plans, to identify problems requiring executive attention, and to choose among the alternative methods of attaining company objectives. At every organizational level of a company, specific problems arise for which accounting information is needed to help define the problem, identify alternative courses of action, and make a choice among these alternatives.

Governmental accounting

Government officials rely on financial information to help them direct the affairs of their agencies just as do the executives of private corporations. Many governmental accounting problems are similar to those applicable to private industry. In other respects, however, accounting for governmental affairs requires a somewhat different approach because the objective of earning a profit is absent from public affairs. Universities, hospitals, churches, and other nonprofit institutions also follow a pattern of accounting that is similar to governmental accounting.

INTERNAL REVENUE SERVICE   One of the governmental agencies which perform extensive accounting work is the Internal Revenue Service (IRS). The IRS handles the millions of income tax returns filed by individuals and corporations, and frequently performs auditing functions relating to these income tax returns and the accounting records on which they are based. Also, the IRS has been called upon to administer certain temporary economic controls, such as wage and price controls. These temporary controls have involved extensive and complex financial reporting by businesses, which is then reviewed and audited by the IRS.

SECURITIES AND EXCHANGE COMMISSION   Another governmental agency greatly involved in accounting is the Securities and Exchange Commission (SEC). The SEC reviews the financial statements of corporations which offer securities for sale to the public. In addition, the SEC has the legal power to require specific accounting methods and standards of financial disclosure for these companies.

Other governmental agencies employ accountants to prepare budgets and to audit the accounting records of various governmental departments and of private businesses which hold government contracts. Every agency of government at every level (federal, state, and local) must have accountants to carry out its responsibilities.

Development of accounting standards—the FASB

Research to develop accounting principles and practices which will keep pace with changes in the economic and political environment is a major activity of professional accountants and accounting educators. In the United States four groups which have been influential in the improvement of financial reporting and accounting practices are the American Institute of Certified Public Accountants, the Financial Accounting Standards Board, the Securities and Exchange Commission, and the American Accounting Association. Of special importance in establishing accounting principles is the Financial Accounting Standards Board, known as the FASB. The FASB consists of seven full-time members, including representatives from public accounting, industry, and accounting education. In addition to conducting extensive research, the FASB issues Statements of Financial Accounting Standards, which represent authoritative expressions of generally accepted accounting principles. The contribution of the FASB and the other groups mentioned above will be considered in later chapters. At this point we merely want to emphasize that accounting is not a closed system or a fixed set of rules, but a constantly evolving body of knowledge. As we explore accounting principles and related practices in this book, you will become aware of certain problems and conflicts for which fully satisfactory answers are yet to be developed. The need for further research is apparent despite the fact that present-day American accounting practices and standards of financial reporting are by far the best achieved anywhere at any time.

Two primary business objectives

The management of every business must keep foremost in its thinking two primary objectives. The first is to earn a profit. The second is to stay solvent, that is, to have on hand sufficient funds to pay debts as they fall due. Profits and solvency are of course not the only objectives of business managers. There are many others, such as providing jobs for people, protecting the environment, creating new and improved products, and providing more goods and services at a lower cost. It is clear, however, that a business cannot hope to accomplish these things unless it meets the two basic tests of survival—operating profitably and staying solvent.

A business is a collection of resources committed by an individual or group of individuals, who hope that the investment will increase in value. Investment in any given business, however, is only one of a number of alternative investments available. If a business does not earn as great a profit as might be obtained from alternative investments, its owners will be well-advised to sell or terminate the business and invest elsewhere. A business that continually operates at a loss will quickly exhaust its resources and be forced out of existence. Therefore, in order to operate successfully and to survive, the owners or managers of an enterprise must direct the business in such a way that it will earn a reasonable profit.

Business concerns that have sufficient funds to pay their debts promptly are said to be *solvent.* In contrast, a firm that finds itself unable to meet its obligations as they fall due is called *insolvent.* Solvency must also be ranked as a primary objective of any enterprise, since a firm that becomes insolvent may be forced by its creditors to stop operations and end its existence.

Accounting as the basis for management decisions

How do business executives know whether a company is earning profits or incurring losses? How do they know whether the company is solvent or insolvent, and whether it will probably be solvent, say, a month from today? The answer to both these questions in one word is *accounting.* Accounting is the process by which the profitability and solvency of a company can be measured, and it also provides information needed as a basis for making business decisions that will enable management to guide the company on a profitable and solvent course.

Stated simply, managing a business is a matter of deciding what should be done, seeing to it that the means are available, and getting people employed in the business to do it. At every step in this process management is faced with alternatives, and every decision to do something or to refrain from doing something involves a choice. Successful managers must make the right choice when "the chips are down." In most cases the probability that a good decision will be made depends on the amount and validity of the information that the manager has about the alternatives and their consequences. It is seldom that all the information needed is either available or obtainable. Often a crystal ball in good working order would be helpful. As a practical matter, however, information which flows from the accounting records, or which can be developed by special analysis of accounting data, constitutes the basis on which a wide variety of business decisions should be made.

For specific examples of these decisions, consider the following questions. What price should the firm set on its products? If production is increased, what effect will this have on the cost of each unit produced? Will it be necessary to borrow from the bank? How much will costs increase if a pension plan is established for employees? Is it more profitable to produce and sell product A or product B? Shall a given part be made or be bought from suppliers? Should an investment be made in new equipment? All these issues call for decisions that should depend, in part at least, upon accounting information. It might be reasonable to turn the question around and ask: What business decisions could be intelligently made without the use of accounting information? Examples would be hard to find.

In large-scale business undertakings such as the manufacture of automobiles or the operation of nationwide chains of retail stores, and even in enterprises much smaller than these, the top executives cannot possibly have close physical contact with and knowledge of the details of operations. Consequently, these executives must depend to an even greater extent than the small business owner upon information provided by the accounting system.

We have already stressed that accounting is a means of measuring the results of business transactions and of communicating financial information. In addition, the accounting system must provide the decision-maker with *predictive information* for making important business decisions in a changing world.

Internal control

Throughout this book, the fact that business decisions of all types are based at least in part on accounting data is emphasized. Management, therefore, needs assurance that the accounting data it receives are accurate and dependable. This assurance is provided in large part by developing a strong system of *internal control.* A basic principle of internal control is that no one person should handle all phases of a transaction from beginning to end. When business operations are so organized that two or more employees are required to participate in every transaction, the possibility of fraud is reduced and the work of one employee gives assurance of the accuracy of the work of another.

A system of internal control comprises all the measures taken by an organization for the purpose of (1) protecting its resources against waste, fraud, and inefficiency; (2) ensuring accuracy and reliability in accounting and operating data; (3) securing compliance with company policies; and (4) evaluating the level of performance in all divisions of the company.

When a CPA firm conducts an audit of a company, it will judge the adequacy of internal control in each area of the company's operations. The stronger the system of internal control, the more confidence the CPA can place in the integrity of the company's financial statements and accounting records. Consequently, the audit work can be performed more rapidly, with less detailed investigation of transactions, when internal controls are strong. The internal auditors also regard the study of internal control as a major part of their work. If internal controls are weak, the usual consequences are waste, fraud, inefficiency, and unprofitable operations.

Forms of business organization

A business enterprise may be organized as a *single proprietorship,* a *partnership,* or a *corporation.*

SINGLE PROPRIETORSHIP   A business owned by one person is called a single proprietorship. Often the owner also acts as the manager. This form of business organization is common for small retail stores and service enterprises, for farms, and for professional practices in law, medicine, and public accounting. For an individual to start a small business of which he or she is the sole owner requires no legal formalities. From a legal viewpoint the business and its owner are not separate entities. From an accounting viewpoint, however, the business is an entity separate from the proprietor.

PARTNERSHIP   A business owned by two or more persons voluntarily associated as partners is called a partnership. The organization of a partnership requires only an agreement (written or oral) among the persons joining together as partners. (A written agreement is highly desirable in order to lessen the chance of misunderstanding and disputes.) The partnership agreement usually provides for the division of profits or losses each year and the settlement to be made upon the withdrawal or death of a partner. Partnerships, like single proprietorships, are widely used for small businesses and for professional practices. A great many CPA firms are organized as partnerships. As in the case of a single proprietorship, a partnership is not legally an entity separate from its owners; consequently, a partner is personally responsible for the debts of the partnership. From an accounting standpoint, however, a partnership is a business entity separate from the personal activities of the partners.

CORPORATION   A business incorporated under the laws of one of the 50 states, with the owners identified as stockholders, is called a corporation.

Ownership of a corporation is evidenced by shares of capital stock which can be sold by one investor to another. Persons wanting to form a corporation must file an application with state officials for a corporate charter. When the application for a charter has been approved, it is referred to as the *articles of incorporation.* After payment of an incorporation fee to the state and approval of the articles of incorporation by the designated state official, the corporation comes into existence as a *legal entity* separate from its owners. The incorporators (who are now stockholders) hold a meeting to elect a board of directors. The directors in turn appoint the officers of the corporation to serve as active managers of the business. Capital stock certificates are issued to the owners (stockholders), and the formation of the corporation is complete. Nearly all large businesses and many small ones are organized as corporations. The dominant role of the corporation in our economy is based on such advantages as the ease of gathering large amounts of money, transferability of shares in ownership, limited liability of owners, and continuity of existence.

Accounting principles and concepts of measurement apply to all three forms of business organization. In the first several chapters of this book, our study of basic accounting concepts will use as a model the single proprietorship, which is the simplest and most common form of business organization.

FINANCIAL STATEMENTS:
THE STARTING POINT IN THE STUDY OF ACCOUNTING

The preparation of financial statements is not the first step in the accounting process, but it is a convenient point to begin the study of accounting. The financial statements are the means of conveying to management and to interested outsiders a concise picture of the profitability and financial position of the business. Since these financial statements are in a sense the end product of the accounting process, the student who acquires a clear understanding of the content and meaning of financial statements will be in an excellent position to appreciate the purpose of the earlier steps of recording and classifying business transactions.

There are two major financial statements, the *balance sheet* and the *income statement.* Together, these two statements (perhaps a page each in length) summarize all the information contained in the hundreds or thousands of pages comprising the detailed accounting records of a business. In this introductory chapter and in Chapter 2, we shall explore the nature of the balance sheet, or statement of financial position, as it is sometimes called. Once we have become familiar with the form and arrangement of the balance sheet and with the meaning of technical terms such as *assets, liabilities,* and *owner's equity,* it will be as easy to read and understand a report on the financial position of a business as it is for an architect to read the blueprint of a proposed building.

The balance sheet

The purpose of a balance sheet is to show the financial position of a business at a particular date. Every business prepares a balance sheet at the end of the year, and most companies prepare one at the end of each month. A balance sheet consists of a listing of the assets and liabilities of a business and of the owner's equity. The following balance sheet portrays the financial position of the Westside Cleaning Shop at December 31.

WESTSIDE CLEANING SHOP
Balance Sheet
December 31, 19____

	Assets		Liabilities & Owner's Equity	
Balance sheet shows financial position at a specific date	*Cash*	$ 19,500	*Liabilities:*	
	Accounts receivable	9,000	*Notes payable*	$ 18,000
	Land	21,000	*Accounts payable*	12,000
	Building	45,000	*Total liabilities*	$30,000
	Office equipment	3,000	*Owner's equity:*	
	Delivery equipment	7,500	*Joe Crane, capital*	75,000
		$105,000		$105,000

Note that the heading of the balance sheet sets forth three items: (*1*) the name of the business (*2*) the name of the statement "Balance Sheet," and (*3*) the date of the balance sheet. Below the heading is the body of the balance sheet, which consists of three distinct elements: assets, liabilities, and the owner's equity. The remainder of this chapter is largely devoted to making clear the nature of these three elements.

THE BUSINESS ENTITY The illustrated balance sheet refers only to the financial affairs of the business entity known as Westside Cleaning Shop and not to the personal financial affairs of the owner, Joe Crane. Crane may have a personal bank account, a home, a car, a cattle ranch, and other property, but since these personal belongings are not a part of his cleaning shop business, they are not included in the balance sheet of this business unit.

In brief, *a business entity is an economic unit which enters into business transactions that must be recorded, summarized, and reported. The entity is regarded as separate from its owner or owners;* the entity owns its own property and has its own debts. Consequently, for each business entity, there should be a separate set of accounting records. A balance sheet and an income statement are intended to portray the financial position and the operating results of a single business entity. If the owner intermingles his or her personal affairs with the transactions of the business, the resulting financial statements will be misleading and will fail to describe the business fairly.

A person who owns two businesses, such as a drive-in theater and a drugstore, should have a completely separate set of accounting records for each. Separate financial statements should also be prepared for each business, thus providing information on the financial position and profitability of each venture.

Assets

Assets are economic resources which are owned by a business and are expected to benefit future operations. Assets may have definite physical form such as buildings, machinery, or merchandise. On the other hand, some assets exist not in physical or tangible form, but in the form of valuable legal claims or rights; examples are amounts due from customers, investments in government bonds, and patent rights.

One of the most basic, and at the same time most controversial, problems in accounting is the valuation of assets: that is, the assignment of dollar values to the assets of a business. Two kinds of assets cause little difficulty. Cash and amounts due from customers represent assets that either are available for expenditure or will be in the near future (when the customers pay their accounts). The amount of cash on hand is a clear statement of the dollars that are available for expenditure. The amount that customers owe the business (after taking into account that some receivables may prove uncollectible) represents the dollars that will be received in the near future.

THE COST PRINCIPLE Assets such as land, buildings, merchandise, and office equipment represent economic resources that will be used in producing income for the business. The prevailing point of view is that such assets should be accounted for on the basis of the dollars that have been invested in these resources, that is, the *historical cost* incurred in acquiring such property or property rights. When we record a business transaction, it is the transaction price that establishes the accounting value for the property or service received. In accounting terms, therefore, the "value" or "valuation" of an asset ordinarily means the cost of that asset to the entity owning it.

For example, let us assume that a business buys a tract of land for use as a building site, paying $40,000 in cash. The amount to be entered in the accounting records as the value of the asset will be the cost of $40,000. If we assume a booming real estate market, a fair estimate of the sales value of the land 10 years later might be $100,000. Although the market price or economic value of the land has risen greatly, the accounting value as shown in the accounting records and on the balance sheet would continue unchanged at the cost of $40,000. This policy of accounting for assets at their cost is often referred to as the *cost principle* of accounting.

In reading a balance sheet, it is important to bear in mind that the dollar amounts listed do not indicate the prices at which the assets could be sold, nor the prices at which they could be replaced. One useful generalization to be drawn from this discussion is that a balance sheet does not show "how much a business is worth."

THE GOING-CONCERN CONCEPT It is appropriate to ask *why* accountants do not change the recorded values of assets to correspond with changing market prices for these properties. One reason is that the land and building used to house the business are acquired for use and not for resale; in fact, these assets cannot be sold without disrupting the business. The balance sheet of a business is prepared on the assumption that the business is a continuing enterprise, a *going concern.* We assume that the business will not be sold or liquidated in the near future but will continue to operate and will carry out its present plans. Consequently, the present estimated prices at which the land and buildings could be sold are of less importance than if these properties were intended for sale.

THE OBJECTIVITY PRINCIPLE Another reason for using cost rather than present market values in accounting for assets is the need for a definite, factual basis. The cost of land, buildings, and many other assets purchased for cash can be rather definitely determined. Accountants use the term *objective* to describe asset valuations that are factual and can be verified by independent experts. For example, if land is shown on the balance sheet at cost, any CPA who performed an audit of the business would be able to find objective evidence that the land was actually valued at the cost incurred in acquiring it. Estimated market values, on the other hand, for assets such as buildings and specialized machinery are not factual and objective. Market values are constantly changing and estimates of what price assets could be sold for are largely a matter of personal opinion. Of course at the date of acquisition of an asset, the cost and value are usually the same because the buyer would not pay more than the asset was worth and the seller would not take less than current market value. The bargaining process which results in the sale of an asset serves to establish both the current market value of the property and the cost to the buyer. With the passage of time, however, the current market value of assets is likely to differ considerably from the cost recorded in the owner's accounting records.

ACCOUNTING FOR INFLATION Severe worldwide inflation in recent years has raised serious doubts as to the adequacy of the conventional cost basis in accounting for assets. When inflation becomes very severe, historical cost values for assets simply lose their relevance as a basis for making business decisions. Proposals for adjusting recorded dollar amounts to reflect changes in the value of the dollar, as shown by a price index, have been considered for many years.[1] However, stronger interest is being shown at present in balance sheets which would show assets at current appraised values or replacement costs rather than at historical cost. The British government recently gave basic approval to the concept of revising corporate accounting to reflect inflation. The British plan requires that year-end balance sheets show assets at their current value rather than at historical or original cost. Many companies in the Netherlands are now using some form of current-value accounting. In the United States, the Securities and Exchange Commission has proposed that companies disclose the current replacement cost of certain assets as *supplementary information* to conventional cost-based financial statements.

Accounting concepts are not as exact and unchanging as many persons assume. To serve the needs of a fast-changing economy, accounting concepts and methods must also undergo continuous evolutionary change. As of today, however, the cost basis of valuing assets is still in almost universal use.

The problem of valuation of assets is one of the most complex in the entire field of accounting. It is merely being introduced at this point; in later chapters we shall explore carefully some of the valuation principles applicable to the major types of assets.

Liabilities

Liabilities are debts. All business concerns have liabilities; even the largest and most successful companies find it convenient to purchase merchandise and supplies on credit rather than to pay cash at the time of each purchase. The liability arising from the purchase of goods or services on credit (on time) is called an *account payable,* and the person or company to whom the account payable is owed is called a *creditor.*

A business concern frequently finds it desirable to borrow money as a means of supplementing the funds invested by the owner, thus enabling the business to expand more rapidly. The borrowed funds may, for example, be used to buy merchandise which can be sold at a profit to the firm's customers. Or, the borrowed money might be used to buy new and more efficient machinery, thus enabling the company to turn out a larger volume of products at lower cost. When a business borrows money for any reason, a liability is incurred and the lender becomes a creditor of the business. The form of the liability when money is borrowed is usually a *note payable,* a formal written promise to pay a certain amount of money, plus interest, at a definite future time. An *account payable,* as contrasted with a *note payable,* does not involve the issuance of a formal written promise to the creditor, and it does not call for payment of interest. When

[1] See *Financial Statements Restated for General Price-Level Changes,* Statement No. 3 of the Accounting Principles Board, American Institute of Certified Public Accountants, June 1969, New York.

a business has both notes payable and accounts payable, the two types of liabilities are shown separately in the balance sheet. The sequence in which these two liabilities are listed is not important, although notes payable are usually shown as the first item among the liabilities. A figure showing the total of the liabilities may also be inserted, as shown by the illustrated balance sheet on page 12.

The creditors have claims against the assets of the business, usually not against any particular asset but against the assets in general. The claims of the creditors are liabilities of the business and have priority over the claims of owners. Creditors are entitled to be paid in full even if such payment should exhaust the assets of the business, leaving nothing for the owner. The issue of valuation, which poses so many difficulties in accounting for assets, is a much smaller problem in the case of liabilities, because the amounts of most liabilities are specified by contract.

Owner's equity

The owner's equity in a business represents the resources invested by the owner; it is equal to the total assets minus the liabilities. The equity of the owner is a residual claim because the claims of the creditors legally come first. If you are the owner of a business, you are entitled to whatever remains after the claims of the creditors are fully satisfied.

For example:

The Westside Cleaning Shop has total assets of	*$105,000*
And total liabilities amounting to	*30,000*
Therefore, the owner's equity must equal	*$ 75,000*

Suppose that the Westside Cleaning Shop borrows $3,000 from a bank. After recording the additional asset of $3,000 in cash and recording the new liability of $3,000 owed to the bank, we would have the following:

The Westside Cleaning Shop now has total assets of	*$108,000*
And total liabilities are now	*33,000*
Therefore, the owner's equity still is equal to	*$ 75,000*

It is apparent that the total assets of the business were increased by the act of borrowing money from a bank, but the increase in assets was exactly offset by an increase in liabilities, and the owner's equity remained unchanged. The owner's equity in a business is not increased by borrowing from banks or other creditors.

INCREASES IN OWNER'S EQUITY If you begin a small business of your own, you will probably invest cash and possibly some other assets to get the business started. Later, as the business makes payments for rent, office equipment, advertising, salaries to employees, and other items, you may find it necessary to supply additional cash to the business. Hopefully, before long, the business will become self-sustaining. Whenever, as owner of the business, you transfer cash or other personally owned assets to the business entity, your ownership equity will increase. In summary, the owner's equity in a business comes from two sources:

1 Investment by the owner
2 Earnings from profitable operation of the business

Only the first of these two sources of owner's equity is considered in this chapter. The second source, an increase in owner's equity through earnings of the business, will be discussed in Chapter 3.

DECREASES IN OWNER'S EQUITY   If you are the owner of a single proprietorship, you have the right to withdraw cash or other assets from the business at any time. Since you are strongly interested in seeing the business succeed, you will probably not make withdrawals that would handicap the business entity in operating efficiently. Once the business achieves momentum and financial strength, you may choose to make substantial withdrawals. Withdrawals are most often made by writing a check drawn on the company's bank account and payable to the owner. However, other types of withdrawals also occur, such as taking office equipment out of the business for personal use by the owner, or by causing cash belonging to the business to be used to pay a personal debt of the owner. Every withdrawal by the owner reduces the total assets of the business and reduces the owner's equity. In summary, decreases in the owner's equity in a business are caused in two ways:

1 Withdrawals of cash or other assets by the owner
2 Losses from unprofitable operation of the business

Only the first of these two causes of decrease in owner's equity is emphasized in this chapter. The second cause, a decrease in owner's equity through operating at a loss, will be considered in Chapter 3.

The accounting equation

One of the fundamental characteristics of every balance sheet is that the total figure for assets always equals the total figure for liabilities and owner's equity. This agreement or balance of total assets with total equities is one reason for calling this statement of financial position a *balance sheet.* But *why* do total assets equal total equities? The answer can be given in one short paragraph, as follows:

The dollar totals on the two sides of the balance sheet are always equal because these two sides are merely two views of the same business property. The listing of assets shows us what things the business owns; the listing of liabilities and owner's equity tells us who supplied these resources to the business and how much each group supplied. Everything that a business owns has been supplied to it by the creditors or by the owner. Therefore, the total claims of the creditors plus the claim of the owner equal the total assets of the business.

The equality of assets on the one hand and of the claims of the creditors and the owner on the other hand is expressed in the equation:

Fundamental accounting equation

Assets = Liabilities + Owner's Equity
$105,000 = $30,000 + $75,000

The amounts listed in the equation were taken from the balance sheet illustrated on page 12. A balance sheet is simply a detailed statement of this equation. To illustrate this relationship, compare the balance sheet of the Westside Cleaning Shop with the above equation.

To emphasize that the equity of the owner is a residual element, secondary to the claims of creditors, it is often helpful to transpose the terms of the equation, as follows:

Alternative form of equation

Assets − Liabilities = Owner's Equity
$105,000 − $30,000 = $75,000

Every business transaction, no matter how simple or how complex, can be expressed in terms of its effect on the accounting equation. A thorough understanding of the equation and some practice in using it are essential to the student of accounting.

Regardless of whether a business grows or contracts, this equality between the assets and the claims against the assets is always maintained. Any increase in the amount of total assets is necessarily accompanied by an equal increase on the other side of the equation, that is, by an increase in either the liabilities or the owner's equity. Any decrease in total assets is necessarily accompanied by a corresponding decrease in liabilities or owner's equity. The continuing equality of the two sides of the balance sheet can best be illustrated by taking a brand-new business as an example and observing the effects of various transactions upon its balance sheet.

Effects of business transactions upon the balance sheet

Assume that James Roberts, a licensed real estate broker, decided to start a real estate business of his own, to be known as the Roberts Real Estate Company. The operations of the business consist of obtaining listings of houses being offered for sale by owners, advertising these houses, and showing them to prospective buyers. The listing agreement signed with each owner provides that the Roberts Real Estate Company shall receive at the time of sale a commission equal to 6% of the sales price of a house sold.

The new business was begun on September 1, when Roberts deposited $60,000 in a bank account in the name of the business, the Roberts Real Estate Company. The initial balance sheet of the new business then appeared as follows:

ROBERTS REAL ESTATE COMPANY
Balance Sheet
September 1, 19___

Assets		*Owner's Equity*	
Cash	$60,000	James Roberts, capital	$60,000

Observe that the equity of the owner in the assets is designated on the balance sheet by the caption, James Roberts, capital. The word **capital** is the traditional accounting term used in describing the equity of the proprietor in the assets of the business.

PURCHASE OF AN ASSET FOR CASH   The next transaction entered into by the Roberts Real Estate Company was the purchase of land suitable as a site for an office. The price for the land was $21,000 and payment was made in cash on September 3. The effect of this transaction on the balance sheet was twofold: first, cash was decreased by the amount paid out; and second, a new asset, Land, was acquired. After this exchange of cash for land, the balance sheet appeared as follows:

ROBERTS REAL ESTATE COMPANY
Balance Sheet
September 3, 19___

Assets		*Owner's Equity*	
Cash	$39,000	James Roberts, capital	$60,000
Land	21,000		
	$60,000		$60,000

PURCHASE OF AN ASSET AND INCURRING OF A LIABILITY   On September 5 an opportunity arose to buy from OK Company a complete office building which had to be moved to permit the construction of a freeway. A price of $36,000 was agreed upon, which included the cost of moving the building and installing it upon the Roberts Company's lot. As the building was in excellent condition and would have cost approximately $60,000 to build, Roberts considered this a very fortunate purchase.

The terms provided for an immediate cash payment of $15,000 and payment of the balance of $21,000 within 90 days. Cash was decreased $15,000, but a new asset, Building, was recorded at cost in the amount of $36,000. Total assets were thus increased by $21,000 but the total of liabilities and owner's equity was also increased as a result of recording the $21,000 account payable as a liability. After this transaction had been recorded, the balance sheet appeared as shown on page 20. Notice that cash is always the first asset listed on a balance sheet.

ROBERTS REAL ESTATE COMPANY
Balance Sheet
September 5, 19___

	Assets			Liabilities & Owner's Equity	
Totals increased equally by purchase on credit	Cash	$24,000	Liabilities:		
	Land	21,000	Accounts payable	$21,000	
	Building	36,000	Owner's equity:		
			James Roberts, capital....	60,000	
		$81,000		$81,000	

Note that the building appears in the balance sheet at $36,000, its cost to the Roberts Real Estate Company. The estimate of $60,000 as the probable cost to construct such a building is irrelevant. Even if someone should offer to buy the building from the Roberts Company for $60,000 or more, this offer, if refused, would have no bearing on the balance sheet. Accounting records are intended to provide a historical record of *costs actually incurred;* therefore, the $36,000 price at which the building was purchased is the amount to be recorded.

SALE OF AN ASSET After the office building had been moved to the Roberts Company's lot, Roberts decided that the lot was much larger than was needed. The adjoining business, Carter's Drugstore, wanted more room for a parking area so, on September 10, the Roberts Company sold the unused part of the lot to Carter's Drugstore for a price of $6,000. Since the sales price was computed at the same amount per foot as the Roberts Company had paid for the land, there was neither a profit nor a loss on the sale. No down payment was required but it was agreed that the full price would be paid within three months. By this transaction a new asset, Accounts Receivable, was acquired, but the asset Land was decreased by the same amount; consequently, there was no change in the amount of total assets. After this transaction, the balance sheet appeared as follows:

ROBERTS REAL ESTATE COMPANY
Balance Sheet
September 10, 19___

	Assets			Llabilities & Owner's Equity	
No change in totals by sale of land at cost	Cash	$24,000	Liabilities:		
	Accounts receivable	6,000	Accounts payable	$21,000	
	Land	15,000	Owner's equity:		
	Building	36,000	James Roberts, capital....	60,000	
		$81,000		$81,000	

In the illustration thus far, the Roberts Real Estate Company has an account receivable from only one debtor, and an account payable to only one creditor. As the business grows, the number of debtors and creditors will increase, but the Accounts Receivable and Accounts Payable designations will continue to be used. The additional records necessary to show the amount receivable from each debtor and the amount owing to each creditor will be explained in Chapter 7.

PURCHASE OF AN ASSET ON CREDIT A complete set of office furniture and equipment was purchased on credit from General Equipment, Inc., on September 14 for $5,400. As the result of this transaction the business owned a new asset, Office Equipment, but it had also incurred a new liability in the form of Accounts Payable. The increase in total assets was exactly offset by the increase in liabilities. After this transaction the balance sheet appeared as follows:

ROBERTS REAL ESTATE COMPANY
Balance Sheet
September 14, 19___

	Assets		*Liabilities & Owner's Equity*	
Totals	*Cash*	*$24,000*	*Liabilities:*	
increased	*Accounts receivable*	*6,000*	*Accounts payable*	*$26,400*
by *acquiring*	*Land*	*15,000*	*Owner's equity:*	
asset on	*Building*	*36,000*	*James Roberts, capital.*	*60,000*
credit	*Office equipment*	*5,400*		
		$86,400		*$86,400*

COLLECTION OF AN ACCOUNT RECEIVABLE On September 20, cash of $1,500 was received as partial settlement of the account receivable from Carter's Drugstore. This transaction caused cash to increase and the accounts receivable to decrease by an equal amount. In essence, this transaction was merely the exchange of one asset for another of equal value. Consequently, there was no change in the amount of total assets. After this transaction, the balance sheet appeared as shown below:

ROBERTS REAL ESTATE COMPANY
Balance Sheet
September 20, 19___

	Assets		*Liabilities & Owner's Equity*	
Totals	*Cash*	*$25,500*	*Liabilities:*	
unchanged	*Accounts receivable*	*4,500*	*Accounts payable*	*$26,400*
by *collection*	*Land*	*15,000*	*Owner's equity:*	
of an	*Building*	*36,000*	*James Roberts, capital.*	*60,000*
account *receivable*	*Office equipment*	*5,400*		
		$86,400		*$86,400*

PAYMENT OF A LIABILITY On September 30 Roberts paid $3,000 in cash to General Equipment, Inc. This payment caused a decrease in cash and an equal decrease in liabilities. Therefore the totals of assets and equities were still in balance. After this transaction, the balance sheet appeared as follows:

ROBERTS REAL ESTATE COMPANY
Balance Sheet
September 30, 19___

	Assets		*Liabilities & Owner's Equity*	
Totals	*Cash*	*$22,500*	*Liabilities:*	
decreased *by paying*	*Accounts receivable*	*4,500*	*Accounts payable*	*$23,400*
a liability	*Land*	*15,000*	*Owner's equity:*	
	Building	*36,000*	*James Roberts, capital*	*60,000*
	Office equipment	*5,400*		
		$83,400		*$83,400*

The transactions which have been illustrated for the month of September were merely preliminary to the formal opening for business of the Roberts Real Estate Company on October 1. Since we have assumed that the business earned no commissions and incurred no expenses during September, the owner's equity at September 30 is shown in the above balance sheet at $60,000, unchanged from the original investment by Roberts on September 1. September was a month devoted exclusively to organizing the business and not to regular operations. In succeeding chapters we shall continue the example of the Roberts Real Estate Company by illustrating operating transactions and considering how the net income of the business is determined.

Effect of business transactions upon the accounting equation

A balance sheet is merely a detailed expression of the accounting equation, Assets = Liabilities + Owner's Equity. To emphasize the relationship between the accounting equation and the balance sheet, let us now repeat the September transactions of Roberts Real Estate Company to show the effect of each transaction upon the accounting equation. Briefly restated, the seven transactions were as follows:

Sept.   **1** Began the business by depositing $60,000 in a company bank account.
      3 Purchased land for $21,000 cash.
      5 Purchased a building for $36,000, paying $15,000 cash and incurring a liability of $21,000.
    10 Sold part of the land at a price equal to cost of $6,000, collectible within three months.

14 Purchased office equipment on credit for $5,400.
20 Received $1,500 cash as partial collection of the $6,000 account receivable.
30 Paid $3,000 on accounts payable.

In the table below, each transaction is identified by date; its effect on the accounting equation and also the new balance of each item are shown. Each of the lines labeled Balances contains the same items as the balance sheet previously illustrated for the particular date. The final line in the table corresponds to the amounts in the balance sheet at the end of September. Note that the equality of the two sides of the equation was maintained throughout the recording of the transactions.

	Cash	+ Accounts Receivable	+ Land	+ Building	+ Office Equipment	= Accounts Payable	+ James Roberts, Capital
			Assets			= **Liabilities**	+ **Owner's Equity**
Sept. 1	+$60,000						+$60,000
Sept. 3	−21,000		+$21,000				
Balances	$39,000		$21,000				$60,000
Sept. 5	−15,000			+$36,000		+$21,000	
Balances	$24,000		$21,000	$36,000		$21,000	$60,000
Sept. 10		+$6,000	−6,000				
Balances	$24,000	$6,000	$15,000	$36,000		$21,000	$60,000
Sept. 14					+$5,400	+5,400	
Balances	$24,000	$6,000	$15,000	$36,000	$5,400	$26,400	$60,000
Sept. 28	+1,500	−1,500					
Balances	$25,500	$4,500	$15,000	$36,000	$5,400	$26,400	$60,000
Sept. 30	−3,000					−3,000	
Balances	$22,500 +	$4,500 +	$15,000 +	$36,000 +	$5,400 =	$23,400 +	$60,000

USE OF FINANCIAL STATEMENTS BY OUTSIDERS

Through careful study of financial statements, it is possible for the outsider with training in accounting to obtain a fairly complete understanding of the financial position of the business and to become aware of significant changes that have occurred since the date of the preceding balance sheet. Bear in mind, however, that financial statements have limitations. As stated earlier, only those factors which can be reduced to monetary terms appear in the balance sheet. Let us consider for a moment some important business factors which are not set forth in financial statements. Perhaps a new competing store has just opened for business across the street; the prospect for intensified competition in the future will not be described in the balance sheet. As another example, the health, experience, and managerial skills of the key people in the management group may be extremely important to the success of a business, but these qualities cannot be measured and expressed in dollars in the balance sheet. Efforts to develop methods of accounting for the human resources of an organization presently constitute an important area of accounting research.

Bankers and other creditors

Bankers who have loaned money to a business concern or who are considering making such a loan will be vitally interested in the balance sheet of the business. By studying the amount and kinds of assets in relation to the amount and payment dates of the liabilities, a banker can form an opinion as to the ability of the business to pay its debts promptly. The banker gives particular attention to the amount of cash and of other assets (such as accounts receivable) which will soon be converted into cash; he compares the amount of these assets with the amount of liabilities falling due in the near future. The banker is also interested in the amount of the owner's equity, as this ownership capital serves as a protecting buffer between the banker and any losses which may befall the business. Bankers are seldom, if ever, willing to make a loan unless the balance sheet and other information concerning the prospective borrower offer reasonable assurance that the loan can and will be repaid promptly at the maturity date.

Another important group making constant use of balance sheets consists of the credit managers of manufacturing and wholesaling firms, who must decide whether prospective customers are to be allowed to buy merchandise on credit. The credit manager, like the banker, studies the balance sheets of customers and prospective customers for the purpose of appraising their debt-paying ability. Credit agencies such as Dun & Bradstreet, Inc., make a business of obtaining financial statements from virtually all business concerns and appraising their debt-paying ability. The conclusions reached by these credit agencies are available to business concerns willing to pay for credit reports about prospective customers.

Others interested in financial information

In addition to owners, managers, bankers, and merchandise creditors, other groups making use of accounting data include governmental agencies, employees, investors, and writers for business periodicals. Some very large corporations have more than a million stockholders; these giant corporations send copies of their annual financial statements to each of these many owners. In recent years there has been a definite trend toward wider distribution of financial statements to all interested persons, in contrast to the attitude of a generation or more ago when many companies regarded their financial statements as confidential matter. This trend reflects an increasing awareness of the impact of corporate activities on all aspects of our lives and of the need for greater disclosure of information about the activities of business corporations.

The purpose of this discussion is to show the extent to which a modern industrial society depends upon accounting. Even more important, however, is a clear understanding at the outset of your study that accounting does not exist just for the sake of keeping a record or in order to fill out social security records, income tax returns, and various other regulatory reports. These are but auxiliary functions. If you gain an understanding of accounting concepts, you will have acquired an analytical skill essential to the field of professional management. *The prime and vital purpose of accounting is to aid in the choice among alternatives that faces every decisionmaker in the business world.*

KEY TERMS INTRODUCED IN CHAPTER 1

Accounting equation   Assets equal liabilities plus owner's equity. A = L + OE.

Accounting system   A financial information system which includes accounting forms, records, instruction manuals, flow charts, programs, and reports to fit the particular needs of the business.

Accounts payable   Amounts which a company owes its creditors for goods and services purchased on credit.

Accounts receivable   Amounts which a company expects to collect from its customers for goods and services sold to them on credit.

American Institute of Certified Public Accountants (AICPA)   The national professional association of Certified Public Accountants (CPAs). Carries on extensive research and is influential in improving accounting standards and practices.

Assets   Economic resources (things of value) owned by a business which are expected to benefit future operations.

Auditing   The principal activity of a CPA. Consists of an independent examination of the accounting records and other evidence relating to a business to support the expression of an impartial expert opinion about the reliability of the financial statements.

Audit report   A report issued by a CPA expressing an independent professional opinion on the fairness and reliability of the financial statements of a business.

Balance sheet   A financial statement which shows the financial position of a business entity by summarizing the assets, liabilities, and owner's equity at a specific date.

Business entity   An economic unit that enters into business transactions that must be recorded, summarized, and reported. The entity is regarded as *separate from its owner or owners.*

Certified public accountants   Independent professional accountants licensed by a state to offer auditing and accounting services to clients for a fee.

Controller   The chief accounting officer of a business.

Corporation   A business organized as a separate legal entity and chartered by a state, with ownership divided into transferable shares of capital stock.

Cost accounting   A specialized field of accounting concerned with determining and controlling the cost of particular products or processes.

Cost principle   A widely used policy of accounting for assets at their original cost to the business.

CPA certificate   A license to practice public accounting granted by a state on the basis of educational requirements, a rigorous examination, and (in most states) evidence of practical experience.

Creditor   The person or company to whom a liability is owed.

Financial Accounting Standards Board (FASB)   An independent group which conducts research in accounting and issues authoritative statements as to proper reporting of financial information.

Financial statements   Reports which summarize the financial position and operating results of a business (balance sheet and income statement).

Going-concern concept   An assumption by accountants that a business will continue to operate indefinitely unless specific evidence to the contrary exists, as, for example, impending bankruptcy.

Internal control   All measures used by a business to guard against errors, waste, and fraud and to assure the reliability of accounting data.

Internal Revenue Service   A governmental agency charged with responsibility for collecting federal income taxes from individuals and corporations.

Liabilities   Debts or obligations of a business. The claims of creditors against the assets of a business.

Notes payable   Liabilities evidenced by a formal written promise to pay a certain amount of money plus interest at a future date. Usually arise from borrowing.

Owner's equity   The excess of assets over liabilities. The amount of an owner's net investment in a business plus profits from successful operations which have been retained in the business.

Owner's withdrawals   Amounts of cash or other assets removed from the business by the owner. Cause a decrease in owner's equity.

Partnership   A business owned by two or more persons voluntarily associated as partners.

Securities and Exchange Commission (SEC)   A government agency which reviews the financial statements and other reports of corporations which offer securities for sale to the public. Works closely with the FASB and the AICPA to improve financial reporting practices.

Single proprietorship   A business owned by one person.

Solvency   Having enough money to pay debts as they fall due.

Tax accounting   The determination of taxable income, preparation of federal and state income tax returns, and planning of operations along lines that will hold tax payments to the legal minimum.

Transactions   Business events which can be measured in money and which are entered in the accounting records.

DEMONSTRATION PROBLEM FOR YOUR REVIEW

An alphabetical list of the various items showing the financial condition of Wilson Company at September 30 appears below. Although the figure for the owner's equity is not given, it can be determined when all the items are arranged in the form of a balance sheet.

Accounts payable	$18,100	Land	$24,000
Accounts receivable	16,400	Notes payable	35,000
Building	39,200	Notes receivable	1,400
Cash	8,500	Office equipment	4,800
Delivery truck	3,000	Ralph Wilson, capital	?

On October 1, the following transactions occurred:
(1) Accounts payable of $8,000 were paid.
(2) The owner, Ralph Wilson, invested an additional $5,000 cash in the business.
(3) Office equipment was purchased at a cost of $1,000 to be paid for within 10 days. This equipment was almost new and was purchased from an attorney who had accepted a political appointment overseas. The equipment would have cost $1,500 if purchased through regular channels.
(4) One-quarter of the land was sold at cost. The buyer gave a promissory note for $6,000 due in 30 days. (Interest applicable to the note is to be ignored.)

Instructions
a Prepare a balance sheet at September 30, 19___.
b Prepare a balance sheet at October 1, 19___.

SOLUTION TO DEMONSTRATION PROBLEM

a

WILSON COMPANY
Balance Sheet
September 30, 19___

Assets		Liabilities & Owner's Equity	
Cash	$ 8,500	Liabilities:	
Notes receivable	1,400	Notes payable	$35,000
Accounts receivable	16,400	Accounts payable	18,100
Land	24,000	Total liabilities	$53,100
Building	39,200	Owner's equity:	
Office equipment	4,800	Ralph Wilson, capital	44,200
Delivery truck	3,000		
	$97,300		$97,300

b

WILSON COMPANY
Balance Sheet
October 1, 19___

Assets		Liabilities & Owner's Equity	
Cash	$ 5,500	Liabilities:	
Notes receivable	7,400	Notes payable	$35,000
Accounts receivable	16,400	Accounts payable	11,100
Land	18,000	Total liabilities	$46,100
Building	39,200	Owner's equity:	
Office equipment	5,800	Ralph Wilson, capital	49,200
Delivery truck	3,000		
	$95,300		$95,300

REVIEW QUESTIONS

1 Why is a knowledge of accounting terms and concepts useful to persons other than professional accountants?

2 In broad general terms, what is the purpose of accounting?

3 What is meant by the term *business transaction?*

4 Distinguish between bookkeeping and accounting.

5 What are financial statements and how do they relate to the accounting system?

6 Distinguish between public accounting and private accounting.

7 In general terms, what are the requirements to become a certified public accountant?

8 What is the principal function of certified public accountants? What other services are commonly rendered by CPAs?

9 Private accounting includes a number of subfields or specialized phases, of which cost accounting is one. Name five other such specialized phases of private accounting.

10 One primary objective of every business is to operate profitably. What other primary objective must be met for a business to survive? Explain.

11 Not all the significant happenings in the life of a business can be expressed in monetary terms and entered in the accounting records. List two examples of significant events affecting a business which could not be satisfactorily measured and entered in its accounting records.

12 Information available from the accounting records provides a basis for making many business decisions. List five examples of business decisions requiring the use of accounting information.

13 State briefly the purpose of a balance sheet.

14 Define assets. List five examples.

15 State briefly two proposals which have been made to enable accounting to function better during a period of inflation.

16 Define liabilities. List two examples.

17 Roger Kent, owner of the Kent Company, was offered $100,000 for the land and buildings occupied by his business. He had acquired these assets five years ago at a price of $75,000. Kent refused the offer of $100,000 but is inclined to believe that the land and buildings should be listed at the higher valuation on the balance sheet in order to show more accurately "how much the business is worth." Do you agree? Explain.

18 Explain briefly the concept of the business entity.

19 State the accounting equation in two alternative forms.

20 State precisely what information is contained in the heading of a balance sheet.

21 The owner's equity in a business arises from what two sources?

22 Why are the total assets shown on a balance sheet always equal to the total of the liabilities and the owner's equity?

23 Can a business transaction cause one asset to increase or decrease without affecting any other asset, liability, or the owner's equity?

24 If a transaction causes total liabilities to decrease but does not affect the owner's equity, what change, if any, will occur in total assets?

25 Give examples of transactions that would:

a Cause one asset to increase and another asset to decrease without any effect on the liabilities or owner's equity.

b Cause both total assets and total liabilities to increase without any effect on the owner's equity.

EXERCISES

Ex. 1-1 *a* Beach Company has total assets of $256,000, and the owner's equity amounts to $64,000. What is the amount of the liabilities?

b The balance sheet of Border Company shows that the owner's equity is $102,000; it is equal to one-third the amount of total assets. What is the amount of the liabilities?

c The assets of Corner Company amounted to $90,000 on December 31 of Year 1, but increased to $126,000 by December 31 of Year 2. During this same period, liabilities increased by $30,000. The owner's equity at December 31 of Year 1 amounted to $60,000. What was the amount of owner's equity at December 31 of Year 2? Explain the basis for your answer.

Ex. 1-2 The items included in the balance sheet of Daly Company at December 31, 19____, are listed below in random order. You are to prepare a balance sheet (including a complete heading). Arrange the assets in the sequence shown in the balance sheet illustrated on page 12. You must compute the amount for William Daly, capital.

Land	$30,000	Office equipment	$ 3,400
Accounts payable	14,600	Building	70,000
Accounts receivable	18,900	Cash	12,100
William Daly, capital	?	Notes payable	75,000

Ex. 1-3 Indicate the effect of each of the following transactions upon the total assets of a business by use of the appropriate phrase: "increase total assets," "decrease total assets," "no change in total assets."

(*a*) Investment of cash in the business by the owner.
(*b*) Collected an account receivable.
(*c*) Made payment of a liability.
(*d*) Purchased an office desk on account (on credit).
(*e*) Borrowed money from a bank.
(*f*) Sold land on account (on credit) for a price equal to its cost.
(*g*) Sold land for cash at a price equal to its cost.
(*h*) Sold land for cash at a price below its cost.
(*i*) Sold land for cash at a price above its cost.
(*j*) Purchased a delivery truck at a price of $7,000, terms $1,000 cash and the balance to be paid in 30 equal monthly installments.

Ex. 1-4 For each of the following, describe a transaction that will have the required effect on elements of the accounting equation.

a Increase an asset and increase owner's equity.
b Increase an asset and increase a liability.
c Increase one asset and decrease another asset.
d Decrease an asset and decrease a liability.
e Increase one asset, decrease another asset, and increase a liability.

Ex. 1-5 Certain transactions of Crest Company are listed below. For each transaction you are to determine the effect on total assets, total liabilities, and owner's equity. Prepare your answer in tabular form, identifying each transaction by letter and using the symbols (+) for increase, (−) for decrease, and (NC) for no change. An answer is provided for the first transaction to serve as an example. Note that some of the transactions concern the personal affairs of the owner, John Crest, rather than being strictly transactions of the business entity.

	Total Assets	Liabil-ities	Owner's Equity
a Owner invested cash in the business.	+	NC	+
b Purchased office equipment on credit			
c Purchased a delivery truck for cash			
d Owner withdrew cash from the business			
e Paid a liability of the business			
f Returned for credit some defective office equipment which had been purchased on credit but not yet paid for.			
g Obtained a loan from the bank for business use			
h Owner gave a typewriter used in the business to his son as a birthday present.			
i Owner wrote a check on company bank account to pay for vacation trip by his daughter			

Ex. 1-6 List the following four column headings on a sheet of notebook paper as follows:

Transaction	Total Assets	Liabilities	Owner's Equity

Next, you are to identify each of the following transactions by number on a separate line in the first column. Then indicate the effect of each transaction on the total assets, liabilities, and owner's equity by placing a plus sign (+) for an increase, a minus sign (−) for a decrease, or the letters (NC) for no change in the appropriate column.

(1) Purchased a typewriter on credit.
(2) Owner invested cash in the business.
(3) Purchased office equipment for cash.
(4) Collected an account receivable.
(5) Owner withdrew cash from the business.
(6) Paid a liability.
(7) Returned for credit some of the office equipment previously purchased on credit but not yet paid for.
(8) Sold land for a price in excess of cost.

As an example, transaction (1) would be shown as follows:

Transaction	Total Assets	Liabilities	Owner's Equity
(1)	+	+	NC

PROBLEMS

Group A

1A-1 The items to be included in the balance sheet of Crown Car Wash at September 30, 19___ are listed below in random order. Prepare a balance sheet using a similar sequence of assets as in the illustrated balance sheet on page 12. Include a figure for total liabilities. (The amount for George Klein, capital can be computed).

Accounts payable	$ 6,000		Delivery truck	$ 7,920
Accounts receivable	9,840		George Klein, capital	?
Land	19,200		Office equipment	6,240
Building	24,000		Cash	10,008
Notes payable	31,200			

1A-2 Five transactions of Glade Company are summarized in the table below with each transaction identified by a letter. The effect of each transaction upon the accounting equation is shown, and also the new balance of each item in the equation. For each of the transactions (*a*) through (*e*), you are to write a sentence explaining the nature of the transaction.

		Assets				=	Liabil- ities	+	Owner's Equity
	Cash	+ Accounts + Receiv- able	Land	+ Building +	Office Equip- ment	=	Accounts + Payable		T. Lee, Capital
Balances	$2,000	$7,000	$9,000	$50,000	$7,000		$8,000		$67,000
(a)					+700		+700		
Balances	$2,000	$7,000	$9,000	$50,000	$7,700		$8,700		$67,000
(b)	+600	−600							
Balances	$2,600	$6,400	$9,000	$50,000	$7,700		$8,700		$67,000
(c)	−400						−400		
Balances	$2,200	$6,400	$9,000	$50,000	$7,700		$8,300		$67,000
(d)	−300				+1,300		+1,000		
Balances	$1,900	$6,400	$9,000	$50,000	$9,000		$9,300		$67,000
(e)	+1,100								+1,100
Balances	$3,000 +	$6,400	+ $9,000 +	$50,000 +	$9,000 =		$9,300	+	$68,100

1A-3 The balance sheet shown below was prepared by the owner of the business, Ken Marsh, who had never studied accounting. Although the balance sheet appears to balance, it contains several errors in the location of items and in the headings. You are to prepare a corrected balance sheet using a similar sequence for assets as in the illustrated balance sheet on page 12. Include a figure for total liabilities.

MARSH COMPANY

For the Year Ended December 31, 19___

Cash	$ 26,112	Accounts payable	$ 34,386
Land	35,827	Accounts receivable	48,384
Building	44,836	Notes payable	77,076
Ken Marsh, capital	93,657	Notes receivable	37,611
Delivery truck	4,687	Office equipment	7,662
	$205,119		$205,119

1A-4 The transactions listed below occurred during the organization of Sub Zero Service, a refrigeration repair business. You are to show the effects of business transactions upon the balance sheet by preparing a new and separate balance sheet for Sub Zero Service at each of the four dates listed below. Each balance sheet should reflect all transactions completed to date.

(1) On May 1, Dean Simmons deposited $36,000 cash in a bank account in the name of the new business, Sub Zero Service.

(2) On May 4, land and a building were acquired at a cost of $8,400 for the land and $15,600 for the building. Full payment was made on this date.

(3) On May 11, Sub Zero Service purchased tools and equipment to do repair

work for a down payment of $1,440 cash and a final payment of $1,800 due in 30 days.

(4) On May 30, Sub Zero Service bought a delivery truck at a cost of $4,320. A cash down payment of $1,200 was made, with payment of the balance to be made within 60 days. Also on this date, the account payable incurred by the purchase of tools and equipment on May 11 was paid in full.

1A-5 A balance sheet has been constructed for Little Joe's after each transaction. By studying these successive balance sheets, you can determine the nature of each transaction. Prepare a list of these transactions. For example, the transaction leading to the balance sheet of July 1, 19____ could be described as follows: "On July 1, 19____, Joe Gennaro invested $90,000 in cash and started the business called 'Little Joe's.'"

(1)

LITTLE JOE'S
Balance Sheet
July 1, 19____

Assets		*Owner's Equity*	
Cash	$90,000	Joe Gennaro, capital	$90,000

(2)

LITTLE JOE'S
Balance Sheet
July 8, 19____

Assets		*Owner's Equity*	
Cash	$72,000	Joe Gennaro, capital	$90,000
Land	18,000		
	$90,000		$90,000

(3)

LITTLE JOE'S
Balance Sheet
July 23, 19____

Assets		*Liabilities & Owner's Equity*	
Cash	$ 55,200	Liabilities:	
Land	18,000	Accounts payable	$ 19,200
Building	36,000	Owner's equity:	
		Joe Gennaro, capital	90,000
	$109,200		$109,200

(4)

LITTLE JOE'S
Balance Sheet
August 14, 19___

Assets		Liabilities & Owner's Equity	
Cash	$ 42,000	Liabilities:	
Land	18,000	Accounts payable	$ 13,200
Building	36,000	Owner's equity:	
Equipment	7,200	Joe Gennaro, capital	90,000
	$103,200		$103,200

1A-6 From the information listed below for Riverside Campgrounds, you are to prepare a balance sheet at June 30. Also prepare a new balance sheet after the transaction on July 1 and a third balance sheet after the transaction on July 11.

Accounts payable	$12,100	Notes payable	$ 3,410
Office equipment	7,920	Cash	?
J. P. Penner, capital	58,190	Accounts receivable	16,940
Land	13,200	Building	28,600

July   1 One-half of the land was sold at a price of $6,600, which was equal to its cost. A down payment of $2,200 in cash was received and the buyer agreed to pay the balance within 10 days.

July 11 Cash in the amount of $4,400 was received from collection of an account receivable as final settlement from the buyer of the land. Also on this date a cash payment of $1,210 was made on an account payable.

1A-7 Hollywood Scripts is a service-type enterprise in the entertainment field, and its owner, Bradford Jones, has only a limited knowledge of accounting. He prepared the balance sheet below, which, although arranged satisfactorily, has defects with respect to concepts as the business entity and asset valuation.

HOLLYWOOD SCRIPTS
Balance Sheet
November 30, 19___

Assets		Liabilities & Owner's Equity	
Cash	$ 1,260	Notes payable	$ 75,000
Notes receivable	1,000	Accounts payable	18,000
Accounts receivable	4,565	Total liabilities	$ 93,000
Land	45,000		
Building	61,025	Owner's equity:	
Office furniture	6,843	Bradford Jones, capital	35,958
Other assets	9,265		
	$128,958		$128,958

In discussion with Jones and by inspection of the accounting records, you discover the following facts.

(1) One of the accounts receivable amounting to $3,000 is an IOU which Jones received in a poker game about ten years ago. The IOU bears only the initials B.K. and Jones does not know the name or address of the maker.

(2) Office furniture includes an antique desk purchased November 29 of the current year at a cost of $1,800. Jones explains that he is not required to pay

for the desk until January and therefore he has not included this debt among the liabilities.

(3) Also included in the amount for office furniture is a typewriter which cost $425 but is not on hand, because Jones gave it to his son as a birthday present.

(4) The "Other assets" of $9,265 represents the total amount of income taxes Jones has paid the federal government over a period of years. Jones explains that he considers the income tax law to be unconstitutional and that a friend who attends law school will help Jones recover the taxes paid as soon as he completes his legal education.

(5) The asset land was acquired at a cost of $25,000, but was increased to a valuation of $45,000 when a friend of Jones offered to pay that much for it if Jones would move the building off the lot.

Instructions

a Prepare a corrected balance sheet at November 30, 19____.

b For each of the five numbered items above, use a separate numbered paragraph to explain whether the treatment followed by Jones is in accord with generally accepted accounting principles.

Group B

1B-1 A list of balance sheet items in random order appears below for Sun Basin Lodge at October 31, 19____. You are to prepare a balance sheet at October 31 using a sequence for assets similar to that in the balance sheet on page 12. Include a figure for total liabilities. The figure for owner's equity must be computed.

Accounts payable	$18,750	Snowmobiles	$12,300
Thomas Rayor, capital	?	Notes payable	30,000
Buildings	78,000	Equipment	37,500
Accounts receivable	16,875	Land	37,500
Cash	14,625		

1B-2 Five transactions of Coronado Company are summarized below in equation form, with each of the five transactions identified by a letter. For each of the transactions (*a*) through (*e*), you are to write a separate sentence explaining the nature of the transaction.

	Cash	+	Accounts Receivable	Land	+	Building	+	Office Equipment	=	Accounts Payable	+	J. Winn, Capital
Balances	$3,100		$6,400	$21,000		$57,100		-0-		$9,100		$78,500
(a)	+500		-500									
Balances	$3,600		$5,900	$21,000		$57,100		-0-		$9,100		$78,500
(b)	-1,200							+1,200				
Balances	$2,400		$5,900	$21,000		$57,100		$1,200		$9,100		$78,500
(c)	+2,000											+2,000
Balances	$4,400		$5,900	$21,000		$57,100		$1,200		$9,100		$80,500
(d)								+1,600		+1,600		
Balances	$4,400		$5,900	$21,000		$57,100		$2,800		$10,700		$80,500
(e)	-400							+2,400		+2,000		
Balances	$4,000	+	$5,900	+ $21,000	+	$57,100	+	$5,200	=	$12,700	+	$80,500

Liabilities = Liabilities + Owner's Equity (Assets)

1B-3 Shown below is a list of balance sheet items in random order for Rabbit Foot Farms at September 30, 19___. You are to prepare a balance sheet by using these items and computing the amount of owner's equity. Use a similar sequence of assets as in the illustrated balance sheet on page 12. Include a figure for total liabilities.

Land	$210,000	Fences & gates	$18,650
Buildings	43,500	Irrigation system	32,180
Notes payable	295,000	Taxes payable	4,675
Accounts receivable	12,425	Cash	7,015
T. R. Wilson, capital	?	Livestock	67,100
Notes receivable	6,029	Farm machinery	23,872
Accounts payable	42,830	Wages payable	1,010

1B-4 During the period of organizing Margaret's Tennis Ranch, a balance sheet was prepared after each transaction. By studying these successive balance sheets, you can determine what transactions have occurred. You are to prepare a list of these transactions by date of occurrence. For example, the transaction leading to the balance sheet of March 1, 19___, could be described as follows: "On March 1, 19___, Margaret See invested $122,400 in cash and started the business of Margaret's Tennis Ranch."

(1)

MARGARET'S TENNIS RANCH
Balance Sheet
March 1, 19___

Assets		Owner's Equity	
Cash	$122,400	Margaret See, capital	$122,400

(2)

MARGARET'S TENNIS RANCH
Balance Sheet
March 6, 19___

Assets		Liabilities & Owner's Equity	
Cash	$ 99,000	Liabilities:	
Land	59,400	Notes payable	$ 36,000
		Owner's equity:	
		Margaret See, capital	122,400
	$158,400		$158,400

(3)

MARGARET'S TENNIS RANCH
Balance Sheet
March 16, 19___

Assets		Liabilities & Owner's Equity	
Cash	$ 81,000	Liabilities:	
Supplies	5,400	Notes payable	$ 36,000
Land	59,400	Owner's equity:	
Equipment	12,600	Margaret See, capital. . . .	122,400
	$158,400		$158,400

(4)

MARGARET'S TENNIS RANCH
Balance Sheet
March 20, 19___

Assets		Liabilities & Owner's Equity	
Cash	$ 54,000	Liabilities:	
Supplies	5,400	Notes payable	$ 29,700
Land	59,400	Owner's equity:	
Equipment	33,300	Margaret See, capital. . . .	122,400
	$152,100		$152,100

1B-5 The eight items listed below pertain to Fields Real Estate Company at September 1, 19___.

Accounts payable	$ 19,500
Buildings.	125,125
Office equipment.	26,650
Office supplies	?
June Fields, capital	239,200
Cash	11,700
Land	80,600
Automobile	7,800

Sept. 2 The land owned by Fields Real Estate Company was larger than needed by the business. Consequently, one-half of the land was sold at cost to a contractor for $40,300 which represented the cost of the land to Fields and did not involve a gain or loss. A cash down payment of $6,500 was received and the buyer agreed to pay the balance within 10 days.
Sept. 4 A cash payment of $3,250 was made on an account payable.
Sept. 9 Cash in the amount of $33,800 was received from the buyer of the land in final settlement of the Sept. 2 transaction.

Instructions Prepare a balance sheet as of September 1, 19___. Also prepare a separate balance sheet after each of the three transactions. Each balance sheet should reflect all transactions to date.

1B-6 Balance sheet items for Pineapple Hill Restaurant (arranged in alphabetical order) were as follows at October 1.

Accounts payable	$ 8,400		Land	$52,500
Accounts receivable	630		Notes payable	75,600
Building	42,000		Supplies	5,880
Cash	9,660		Ann Thomas, capital	?
Furniture	54,600			

During the next two days, the following transactions occurred:

Oct. 2 Thomas invested an additional $31,500 cash in the business. The accounts payable were paid in full. (No payment was made on the notes payable.)

Oct. 3 Furniture was purchased at a cost of $18,900 to be paid within 10 days. Supplies were purchased for $1,050 cash from a restaurant supply center which was going out of business. These supplies would have cost $1,890 if purchased through normal channels.

Instructions
a Prepare a balance sheet at October 1, 19____.
b Prepare a balance sheet at October 3, 19____.

1B-7 After several years of experience with a national firm of certified public accountants, James Lee resigned from his position on September 1, 19____, in order to begin a public accounting practice of his own. The following events occurred during September; some of these relate to the business entity, James Lee, CPA, and others are personal in nature and do not affect the business entity.

Sept. 1 Sold personal investments consisting of an apartment building and some IBM stock for a total of $98,000 cash. Deposited $75,000 of this cash in a bank account in the name of the practice, James Lee, CPA.

Sept. 2 Lee bought some gold bars for $6,000, which he placed in a safe deposit box rented under his name.

Sept. 2 Purchased land with a small office building suitable for his accounting practice. Total cost was $90,000 of which $50,000 was paid from the business bank account as a cash down payment. Lee signed a note payable for the balance calling for payment in five years or less. The county property tax assessor had indicated that the land had a current fair value 50% greater than the office building. (Divide the total cost between land and office building.)

Sept. 3 Purchased office equipment for cash of $5,200.

Sept. 5 Lee moved his personal accounting library from his home to the office with the purpose of investing this library as an asset of the business. Fair market value of the library was $850.

Sept. 5 Agreed to employ a recent college graduate as staff assistant at a monthly salary of $1,000. The staff assistant was to report for work on October 1.

Sept. 6 Lee purchased a dirt track motorcycle which he planned to use on weekend trips. He turned in an old motorcycle and paid a balance of $800 in cash.

Sept. 7 Returned a defective chair included in the September 3 purchase of office equipment for full credit of $210. Received in exchange another model chair priced at $185 and a cash refund of $25.

Sept. 8 On Sunday while visiting a friend who was going out of business and entering military service, Lee had an opportunity to buy for $600 cash some office supplies which had originally cost $1,000. Lee used a personal check to pay for the supplies.

Sept. 9 Lee brought to his office the office supplies purchased the previous day.

Instructions
a Prepare a list of those transactions which are personal in nature, do not affect the business entity, and should not be included in the balance sheet of James Lee, CPA.
b Prepare a balance sheet for the business entity, James Lee, CPA, at September 9, 19____.

BUSINESS DECISION PROBLEM 1

Adams Company and Baker Company are in the same line of business and both were recently organized, so it may be assumed that the recorded costs for assets are close to current market values. The balance sheets for the two companies are as follows at July 31, 19___.

ADAMS COMPANY
Balance Sheet
July 31, 19___

Assets			Liabilities & Owner's Equity		
Cash	$	4,800	Liabilities:		
Accounts receivable		9,600	Notes payable		
Land		36,000	(due in 60 days)	$	62,400
Building		60,000	Accounts payable		43,200
Office equipment		12,000	Total liabilities		$105,600
			Owner's equity:		
			Ed Adams, capital		16,800
		$122,400			$122,400

BAKER COMPANY
Balance Sheet
July 31, 19___

Assets		Liabilities & Owner's Equity		
Cash	$24,000	Liabilities:		
Accounts receivable	48,000	Notes payable		
Land	7,200	(due in 60 days)		$14,400
Building	12,000	Accounts payable		9,600
Office equipment	1,200	Total liabilities		$24,000
		Owner's equity:		
		Tom Baker, capital		68,400
	$92,400			$92,400

Instructions
a Assume that you are a banker and that each company has applied to you for a 90-day loan of $12,000. Which would you consider to be the more favorable prospect?

b Assume that you are an investor considering the purchase of one or both of the companies. Both Ed Adams and Tom Baker have indicated to you that they would consider selling their respective businesses. In either transaction you would assume the existing liabilities. For which business would you be willing to pay the higher price? Explain your answer fully. (It is recognized that for either decision, additional information would be useful, but you are to reach your decisions on the basis of the information available.)

2

Recording Changes in Financial Position

Many business concerns have several hundred or even several thousand business transactions each day. It would obviously be impracticable to prepare a balance sheet after each transaction, and it is quite unnecessary to do so. Instead, the many individual transactions are recorded in the accounting records, and, at the end of the month or other accounting period, a balance sheet is prepared from these records.

The accounting model

You are already familiar with the use of *models* in many fields. Just as the aerospace scientist builds a model of a spaceship or an urban planner builds a model of a new city, so shall we construct a model of an accounting system. A good model is an accurate portrayal of the real world situation it represents. However, a model usually emphasizes certain key factors and relationships, while deemphasizing details which may vary without affecting the successful working of the system. The accounting model presented in this and following chapters is a miniature portrayal of the factors and key relationships that influence the accounting process in a real-world business enterprise.

Remember that accounting systems may be maintained in some businesses by one person with pen-and-ink methods, or in other companies by hundreds of people with electric accounting machines, or by large-scale computers. By use of a model which emphasizes basic concepts, however, you can gain an understanding of accounting which will be useful in any one of the wide range of real-world business situations. The purpose of our rather simple model is to demonstrate how business transactions are analyzed, entered into the accounting system, and stored for use in preparing balance sheets and other financial statements. The model will enable us to study the interrelationships of the business enterprise; to determine what information is needed, by whom it is needed, how it can be gathered and classified, and how frequently the information in the system should be summarized and reported.

The use of accounts for recording transactions

The accounting system includes a separate record for each item that appears in the balance sheet. For example, a separate record is kept for the asset Cash, showing all the increases and decreases in cash which result from the many transactions in which cash is received or paid. A similar record is kept for every other asset, for every liability, and for owner's equity. The form of record used to record increases and decreases in a single balance sheet item is called an *account,* or sometimes a *ledger account.* All these separate accounts are usually kept in a looseleaf binder, and the entire group of accounts is called a *ledger.*

Today many businesses use computers for maintaining accounting records, and data may be stored on magnetic tapes rather than in ledgers. However, an understanding of accounting concepts is most easily acquired by study of a manual accounting system. The knowledge gained by working with manual accounting records is readily transferable to any type of automated accounting system. For these reasons, we shall use standard written accounting forms such as ledger accounts as the model for our study of basic accounting concepts. These standard forms continue to be used by a great many businesses, but for our purposes they should be viewed as conceptual devices rather than as fixed and unchanging structural components of an accounting system.

THE LEDGER

Ledger accounts are a means of accumulating information needed by management in directing the business. For example, by maintaining a Cash account, management can keep track of the amount of cash available for meeting payrolls and for making current purchases of assets or services. This record of cash is also useful in planning future operations, and in advance planning of applications for bank loans. The development of the annual cash forecast or budget requires estimating in advance the expected receipts and payments of cash; these estimates of cash flow are naturally based to some extent on the ledger accounts showing past cash receipts and payments.

In its simplest form, an account has only three elements: (*1*) a title, consisting of the name of the particular asset, or liability, or owner's equity; (2) a left side, which is called the *debit* side; and (3) a right side, which is called the *credit* side. This form of account, illustrated below, is called a *T account* because of its resemblance to the letter T. More complete forms of accounts will be illustrated later.

T account: a ledger account in simplified form

	Title of Account
Left or debit side	Right or credit side

Debit and credit entries

An amount recorded on the left or debit side of an account is called a *debit,* or a *debit entry;* an amount entered on the right or credit side is called a *credit,* or a *credit entry.* Accountants also use the words debit and credit as verbs. The act of recording a debit in an account is called *debiting* the account; the recording of a credit is called *crediting* the account. A debit to an account is also sometimes called a *charge* to the account; an account is debited or *charged* when an amount is entered on the left side of the account.

Students beginning a course in accounting often have preconceived but erroneous notions about the meanings of the terms debit and credit. For example, to some people unacquainted with accounting, the word credit may carry a more favorable connotation than does the word debit. Such connotations have no validity in the field of accounting. Accountants use *debit* to mean an entry on the left-hand side of an account, and *credit* to mean an entry on the right-hand side. The student should therefore regard debit and credit as simple equivalents of left and right, without any hidden or subtle implications.

To illustrate the recording of debits and credits in an account, let us go back to the cash transactions of the Roberts Real Estate Company as illustrated in Chapter 1. When these cash transactions are recorded in an account, the receipts are listed in vertical order on the debit side of the account and the payments are listed on the credit side. The dates of the transactions may also be listed, as shown in the following illustration:

Cash transactions entered in ledger account

			Cash		
9/1		60,000	9/3		21,000
9/20	22,500	1,500	9/5		15,000
		61,500	9/30		3,000
					39,000

Note that the total of the cash receipts, $61,500, is in small-size figures so that it will not be mistaken for a debit entry. The total of the cash payments (credits), amounting to $39,000, is also in small-size figures to distinguish it from the credit entries. These **footings,** or memorandum totals, are merely a convenient step in determining the amount of cash on hand at the end of the month. The difference in dollars between the total debits and the total credits in an account is called the **balance.** If the debits exceed the credits the account has a **debit balance;** if the credits exceed the debits the account has a **credit balance.** In the illustrated Cash account, the debit total of $61,500 is larger than the credit total of $39,000; therefore, the account has a debit balance. By subtracting the credits from the debits ($61,500 − $39,000), we determine that the balance of the Cash account is $22,500. This debit balance is noted on the debit (left) side of the account. The balance of the Cash account represents the amount of cash owned by the business on September 30; in a balance sheet prepared at this date, Cash in the amount of $22,500 would be listed as an asset.

DEBIT BALANCES IN ASSET ACCOUNTS In the preceding illustration of a cash account, increases were recorded on the left or debit side of the account and decreases were recorded on the right or credit side. The increases were greater than the decreases and the result was a debit balance in the account.

All asset accounts normally have debit balances; as a matter of fact, the ownership by a business of cash, land, or any other asset indicates that the increases (debits) to that asset have been greater than the decreases (credits). It is hard to imagine an account for an asset such as land having a credit balance, as this would indicate that the business had disposed of more land than it had acquired and had reached the impossible position of having a negative amount of land.

The balance sheets previously illustrated in Chapter 1 showed all the assets on the left side of the balance sheet. For your convenience in recalling the basic structure of a balance sheet, the fundamental accounting equation is again presented:

Assets = Liabilities + Owner's Equity

Remember that the balance sheet is simply a detailed statement of this equation, as shown by the following balance sheet.

ROBERTS REAL ESTATE COMPANY
Balance Sheet
September 30, 19____

Assets		Liabilities & Owner's Equity	
Cash	$22,500	Liabilities:	
Accounts receivable	4,500	Accounts payable	$23,400
Land	15,000	Owner's equity:	
Building	36,000	James Roberts, capital	60,000
Office equipment	5,400		
	$83,400		$83,400

The fact that assets are located on the left side of the balance sheet is a convenient means of remembering the rule that an increase in an asset is recorded on the *left* (debit) side of the account, and also that an asset account normally has a debit (*left-hand*) balance.

Asset accounts normally have debit balances	Any Asset Account	
	(Debit) *Increase*	*(Credit)* *Decrease*

CREDIT BALANCES IN LIABILITY AND OWNER'S EQUITY ACCOUNTS Increases in liability and owner's equity accounts are recorded by credit entries and decreases in these accounts are recorded by debits. The relationship between entries in these accounts and their position on the balance sheet may be summed up as follows: (*1*) liabilities and owner's equity belong on the *right* side of the balance sheet; (*2*) an increase in a liability or an owner's equity account is recorded on the *right* side of the account; and (*3*) liability and owner's equity accounts normally have credit (*right-hand*) balances.

Liability and owner's equity accounts normally have credit balances	Any Liability Account or Owner's Equity Account	
	(Debit) *Decrease*	*(Credit)* *Increase*

CONCISE STATEMENT OF THE RULES OF DEBIT AND CREDIT The rules of debit and credit, which have been explained and illustrated in the preceding sections, may be concisely summarized as follows:

	Asset Accounts	Liability & Owner's Equity Accounts
Mechanics of debit and credit	*Increases are recorded by debits* *Decreases are recorded by credits*	*Increases are recorded by credits* *Decreases are recorded by debits*

EQUALITY OF DEBITS AND CREDITS Every business transaction affects two or more accounts. The *double-entry* method, which is in almost universal use, takes its name from the fact that equal debit and credit entries are made for every transaction. If only two accounts are affected (as in the purchase of land for cash) one account, Land, is debited, and the other account, Cash, is credited for the same amount. If more than two accounts are affected by a transaction, the sum of the debit entries must be equal to the sum of the credit entries. This situation was illustrated when the Roberts Real Estate Company purchased a building for a price of $36,000. The $36,000 debit to the asset account, Building, was exactly equal to the total of the $15,000 credit to the Cash account plus the $21,000 credit to the liability account, Accounts Payable. Since every transaction results in an equal amount of debits and credits in the ledger, it follows that the total of all debit entries in the ledger is equal to the total of all the credit entries.

Recording transactions in ledger accounts: illustration

The procedure for recording transactions in ledger accounts will be illustrated by using the September transactions of the Roberts Real Estate Company. Each transaction will first be analyzed in terms of increases and decreases in assets, liabilities, and owner's equity. Then we shall follow the rules of debit and credit in entering these increases and decreases in T accounts. Asset accounts will be shown on the left side of the page; liability and owner's equity accounts on the right side. For convenience in following the transactions into the ledger accounts, the letter used to identify a given transaction will also appear opposite the debit and credit entries for that transaction. This use of identifying letters is for illustrative purposes only and is not used in actual accounting practice.

Transaction (a)   Roberts invested $60,000 cash in the business on September 1.

	Analysis	*Rule*	*Entry*
Recording an investment in the business	The asset Cash was increased	Increases in assets are recorded by debits	Debit: Cash, $60,000
	The owner's equity was increased	Increases in owner's equity are recorded by credits	Credit: James Roberts, Capital, $60,000

Cash		James Roberts, Capital	
9/1 (a) 60,000		9/1 (a) 60,000	

Transaction (b)   On September 3, the Roberts Real Estate Company purchased land for cash in the amount of $21,000.

	Analysis	*Rule*	*Entry*
Purchase of land for cash	The asset Land was increased	Increases in assets are recorded by debits	Debit: Land, $21,000
	The asset Cash was decreased	Decreases in assets are recorded by credits	Credit: Cash, $21,000

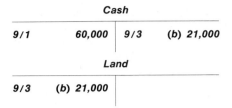

Cash

9/1	60,000	9/3	(b) 21,000	

Land

9/3	(b) 21,000

Transaction (c) On September 5, the Roberts Real Estate Company purchased a building from OK Company at a total price of $36,000. The terms of the purchase required a cash payment of $15,000 with the remainder of $21,000 payable within 90 days.

	Analysis	Rule	Entry
Purchase of an asset, with partial payment	A new asset, Building, was acquired	Increases in assets are recorded by debits	Debit: Building, $36,000
	The asset Cash was decreased	Decreases in assets are recorded by credits	Credit: Cash, $15,000
	A new liability, Accounts Payable, was incurred	Increases in liabilities are recorded by credits	Credit: Accounts Payable, $21,000

Cash

9/1	60,000	9/3	21,000
		9/5	(c) 15,000

Accounts Payable

9/5	(c) 21,000

Building

9/5	(c) 36,000

Transaction (d) On September 10, the Roberts Real Estate Company sold a portion of its land on credit to Carter's Drugstore for a price of $6,000. The land was sold at its cost, so there was no gain or loss on the transaction.

	Analysis	Rule	Entry
Sale of land on credit (no gain or loss)	A new asset, Accounts Receivable, was acquired	Increases in assets are recorded by debits	Debit: Accounts Receivable, $6,000
	The asset Land was decreased	Decreases in assets are recorded by credits	Credit: Land, $6,000

Accounts Receivable

9/10 (d) 6,000	

Land

9/3 21,000	9/10 (d) 6,000

Transaction (e) On September 14, the Roberts Real Estate Company purchased office equipment on credit from General Equipment, Inc., in the amount of $5,400.

	Analysis	Rule	Entry
Purchase of an asset on credit	A new asset, Office Equipment, was acquired	Increases in assets are recorded by debits	Debit: Office Equipment $5,400
	A new liability, Accounts Payable, was incurred	Increases in liabilities are recorded by credits	Credit: Accounts Payable, $5,400

Office Equipment

9/14 (e) 5,400	

Accounts Payable

	9/5 21,000
	9/14 (e) 5,400

Transaction (f) On September 20, cash of $1,500 was received as partial collection of the account receivable from Carter's Drugstore.

	Analysis	Rule	Entry
Collection of an account receivable	The asset Cash was increased	Increases in assets are recorded by debits	Debit: Cash, $1,500
	The asset Accounts Receivable was decreased	Decreases in assets are recorded by credits	Credit: Accounts Receivable, $1,500

Cash

9/1 60,000	9/3 21,000
9/20 (f) 1,500	9/5 15,000

Accounts Receivable

9/10 6,000	9/20 (f) 1,500

Transaction (g) A cash payment of $3,000 was made on September 30 in partial settlement of the amount owing to General Equipment, Inc.

	Analysis	Rule	Entry
Payment of a liability	The liability Accounts Payable was decreased	Decreases in liabilities are recorded by debits	Debit: Accounts Payable, $3,000
	The asset Cash was decreased	Decreases in assets are recorded by credits	Credit: Cash, $3,000

Cash					Accounts Payable			
9/1	60,000	9/3	21,000		9/30	(g) 3,000	9/5	21,000
9/20	1,500	9/5	15,000				9/14	5,400
		9/30	(g) 3,000					

Running balance form of ledger account

The T form of account used thus far is very convenient for illustrative purposes. Details are avoided and we can concentrate on basic ideas. T accounts are also often used in advanced accounting courses and by professional accountants for preliminary analysis of a transaction. In other words, the simplicity of the T account provides a concise conceptual picture of the elements of a business transaction. In formal accounting records, however, more information is needed, and the T account is replaced in many manual accounting systems by a ledger account with special rulings, such as the following illustration of the Cash account for the Roberts Real Estate Company.

Cash   Account No. /

	Date	Explanation	Ref	Debit	Credit	Balance
Ledger account with a balance column	19__ Sept. 1			60 000 00		60 000 00
	3				21 000 00	39 000 00
	5				15 000 00	24 000 00
	20			1 500 00		25 500 00
	30				3 000 00	22 500 00

The **Date** column shows the date of the transaction—which is not necessarily the same as the date the entry is made in the account. The **Explanation** column is needed only for unusual items, and in many companies it is seldom used. The **Ref** (Reference) column is used to list the page number of the journal in which the transaction is recorded, thus making it possible to trace ledger entries back to their source (a journal).

The use of a *journal* is explained later in this chapter. In the *Balance* column of the account, the new balance is entered each time the account is debited or credited. Thus the current balance of the account can always be observed at a glance.

Although we will make extensive use of this three-column running balance form of account in later chapters, there will also be many situations in which we shall continue to use T accounts to achieve simplicity in illustrating accounting principles and procedures.

The normal balance of an account

The running balance form of ledger account does not indicate specifically whether the balance of the account is a debit or credit balance. However, this causes no difficulty because we know that asset accounts normally have debit balances and that accounts for liabilities and owner's equity normally have credit balances.

The balance of any account normally results from recording more increases than decreases. In asset accounts, increases are recorded as debits, so asset accounts normally have debit balances. In liability and owner's equity accounts, increases are recorded as credits, so these accounts normally have credit balances.

Occasionally an asset account may temporarily acquire a credit balance, either as the result of an accounting error or because of an unusual transaction. For example, an account receivable may acquire a credit balance because a customer overpays his account. However, a credit balance in the Building account could be created only by an accounting error.

Sequence and numbering of ledger accounts

Accounts are usually arranged in the ledger in *financial statement order,* that is, assets first, followed by liabilities, owner's equity, revenue, and expenses. The number of accounts needed by a business will depend upon its size, the nature of its operations, and the extent to which management and regulatory agencies want detailed classification of information. An identification number is assigned to each account. A *chart of accounts* is a listing of the account titles and account numbers being used by a given business.

In the following list of accounts, certain numbers have not been assigned; these numbers are held in reserve so that additional accounts can be inserted in the ledger in proper sequence whenever such accounts become necessary. In this illustration, the numbers from 1 to 29 are used exclusively for asset accounts; numbers from 30 to 49 are reserved for liabilities; numbers in the 50s signify owner's equity accounts; numbers in the 60s represent revenue accounts and numbers from 70 to 99 designate expense accounts. The balance sheet accounts with which we are concerned in this chapter are numbered as shown in the following brief chart of accounts.

Account Title	Account No.
Assets:	
Cash	1
Accounts Receivable	2
Land	20
Building	22
Office Equipment	25
Liabilities:	
Accounts Payable	30
Owner's Equity:	
James Roberts, Capital	50

System for number-ing ledger accounts

In large businesses with many more accounts, a more elaborate numbering system would be needed. Some companies use a four-digit number for each account; each of the four digits carries special significance as to the classification of the account.

Flow of information through the accounting system

The term *transaction* was explained in Chapter 1, but a concise definition at this point may be a helpful reminder. *A transaction is a business event which can be expressed in money and must be recorded in the accounting records.* Common examples are the payment or collection of cash, a purchase or sale on credit, and the withdrawal of assets by the owner of a business. Note that a transaction has an accounting value and has an influence on the financial statements. Events such as the opening of a competing business or the retirement of an employee, although possibly of importance to the business, are not considered to be transactions and are not entered in the accounts.

Business transactions are evidenced by *business documents* such as a check, a sales ticket, or a cash register tape. These business documents are the starting point for the flow of accounting information through the accounting system into the financial statements. In our description of the accounting process thus far, emphasis has been placed on the analysis of transactions in terms of debits and credits to ledger accounts. Although transactions *could* be entered directly in ledger accounts, it is much more convenient and efficient in a manual accounting system to record the information shown on business documents first in a *journal* and later to transfer the debits and credits to ledger accounts.

Occurrence of a business trans- action

Prepa- ration of a business document

Infor- mation entered in journal

Debits and credits posted from journal to ledger

Financial statements prepared from ledger

THE JOURNAL

The *journal,* or book of original entry, is a chronological (day-by-day) record, showing for each transaction the debit and credit changes caused in specific ledger accounts. A brief explanation is also included for each transaction. At convenient intervals, the debit and credit entries recorded in the journal are transferred to the accounts in the ledger. The updated ledger accounts, in turn, serve as the basis from which the balance sheet and other financial statements are prepared. The flow chart on the left illustrates the sequence of steps by which information flows through the accounting system.

The unit of organization for the journal is the transaction, whereas the unit of organization for the ledger is the account. By making use of both a journal and a ledger, we can achieve several advantages which are not possible if transactions are recorded directly in ledger accounts:

1 *The journal shows all information about a transaction in one place and also provides an explanation of the transaction.* In a journal entry, the debits and credits for a given transaction are recorded together, but when the transaction is recorded in the ledger, the debits and credits are entered in different accounts. Since a ledger may contain hundreds of accounts, it would be very difficult to locate all the facts about a particular transaction by looking in the ledger. The journal is the record which shows the complete story of a transaction in one entry.

2 *The journal provides a chronological record of all the events in the life of a business.* If we want to look up the facts about a transaction of some months or years back, all we need is the date of the transaction in order to locate it in the journal.

3 *The use of a journal helps to prevent errors.* If transactions were recorded directly in the ledger, it would be very easy to make errors such as omitting the debit or the credit, or entering the debit twice or the credit twice. Such errors are not likely to be made in the journal, since the offsetting debits and credits appear together for each transaction. It is of course possible to forget to transfer a debit or credit from the journal to a ledger account, but such an error can be detected by tracing the entries in the ledger accounts back to the journal.

The general journal: illustration of entries

Many businesses maintain several types of journals. The nature of oper- ations and the volume of transactions in the particular business determine the number and type of journals needed. The simplest type of journal, and the one with which we are concerned in this chapter, is called a *general journal.* It has only two money columns, one for debits and the other for credits; it may be used for all types of transactions.

The process of recording a transaction in a journal is called *journalizing* the transaction. To illustrate the use of the general journal, we shall now journalize the transactions of the Roberts Real Estate Company which have previously been discussed.

General Journal

Date		Account Titles and Explanation	LP	Debit	Credit
September	**19___**				
Sept.	**1**	Cash	1	60,000	
		James Roberts, Capital	50		60,000
		Invested cash in the business.			
	3	Land	20	21,000	
		Cash	1		21,000
		Purchased land for office site.			
	5	Building	22	36,000	
		Cash	1		15,000
		Accounts Payable	30		21,000
		Purchased building to be moved to our lot.			
		Paid part cash; balance payable within 90 days			
		to OK Company.			
	10	Accounts Receivable	2	6,000	
		Land	20		6,000
		Sold the unused part of our lot at cost to			
		Carter's Drugstore. Due within three months.			
	14	Office Equipment	25	5,400	
		Accounts Payable	30		5,400
		Purchased office equipment on credit from			
		General Equipment, Inc.			
	20	Cash	1	1,500	
		Accounts Receivable	2		1,500
		Collected part of receivable from Carter's			
		Drugstore.			
	30	Accounts Payable	30	3,000	
		Cash	1		3,000
		Made partial payment of the liability to General			
		Equipment, Inc.			

September journal entries for Roberts Real Estate Company

Efficient use of a general journal requires two things: (*1*) ability to analyze the effect of a transaction upon assets, liabilities, and owner's equity; and (*2*) familiarity with the standard form and arrangement of journal entries. Our primary interest is in the analytical phase of journalizing; the procedural steps can be learned quickly by observing the following points in the illustrations of journal entries shown above.

1 The year, month, and day of the first entry on the page are written in the date column. The year and month need not be repeated for subsequent entries until a new page or a new month is begun.

2 The name of the account to be debited is written on the first line of the entry and is customarily placed at the extreme left next to the date column. The amount of the debit is entered on the same line in the left-hand money column.

3 The name of the account to be credited is entered on the line below the debit entry and is indented, that is, placed about 1 inch to the right of the date column. The amount credited is entered on the same line in the right-hand money column.

4 A brief explanation of the transaction is usually begun on the line immediately below the last account credited. The explanation need not be indented.

5 A blank line is usually left after each entry. This spacing causes each journal entry to stand out clearly as a separate unit and makes the journal easier to read.

6 An entry which includes more than one debit or more than one credit (such as the entry on September 5) is called a *compound journal entry.* Regardless of how many debits or credits are contained in a compound journal entry, all the debits are customarily entered before any credits are listed.

7 The LP (ledger page) column just to the left of the debit money column is left blank at the time of making the journal entry. When the debits and credits are later transferred to ledger accounts, the numbers of the ledger accounts are listed in this column to provide a convenient cross reference with the ledger.

Remember in journalizing transactions that the exact titles of the ledger accounts to be debited and credited should be used. For example, in recording the purchase of a typewriter for cash, *do not* make a journal entry debiting "Office Equipment Purchased" and crediting "Cash Paid Out" There are no ledger accounts with such titles. The proper journal entry would consist of a debit to Office Equipment and a credit to Cash.

Posting

The process of transferring the debits and credits from the journal to the proper ledger accounts is called *posting.* Each amount listed in the debit column of the journal is posted by entering it on the debit side of an account in the ledger, and each amount listed in the credit column of the journal is posted to the credit side of a ledger account.

The mechanics of posting may vary somewhat with the preferences of the individual. For example, the debits and credits may be posted in the sequence shown in the journal, or all the debits on a journal page may be posted first. The following sequence is commonly used:

1 Locate in the ledger the first account named in the journal entry.

2 Enter in the Debit column of the ledger account the amount of the debit as shown in the journal.

3 Enter the date of the transaction in the ledger account.

4 Enter in the Reference column of the ledger account the number of the journal page from which the entry is being posted.

5 The recording of the debit in the ledger account is now complete; as evidence of this fact, return to the journal and enter in the LP (ledger page) column the number of the ledger account or page to which the debit was posted.

6 Repeat the posting process described in the preceding five steps for the credit side of the journal entry.

ILLUSTRATION OF POSTING To illustrate the posting process, the journal entry for the first transaction of Roberts Real Estate Company is repeated at this point along with the two ledger accounts affected by this entry.

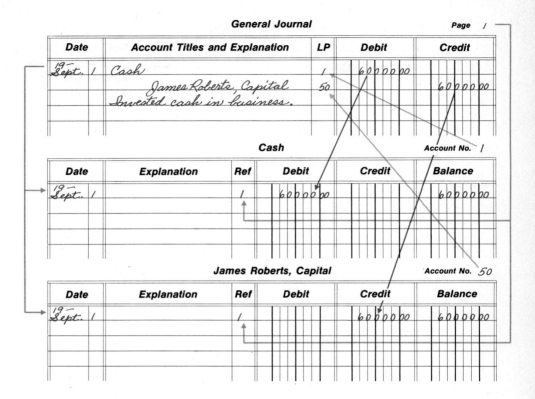

General Journal

Page /

Date	Account Titles and Explanation	LP	Debit	Credit
19— Sept. 1	Cash	1	6000000	
	James Roberts, Capital	50		6000000
	Invested cash in business.			

Cash

Account No. 1

Date	Explanation	Ref	Debit	Credit	Balance
19— Sept. 1		1	6000000		6000000

James Roberts, Capital

Account No. 50

Date	Explanation	Ref	Debit	Credit	Balance
19— Sept. 1		1		6000000	6000000

Note that the Ref (Reference) column of each of the two ledger accounts illustrated above contains the number 1, indicating that the posting was made from page 1 of the journal. Entering the journal page number in the ledger account and listing the ledger page in the journal provide a cross reference between these two records. The audit of accounting records always requires looking up some journal entries to obtain more information about the amounts listed in ledger accounts. A cross reference between the ledger and journal is therefore essential to efficient audit of the records. Another advantage gained from entering in the journal the number of the account to which a posting has been made is to provide evidence throughout the posting work as to which items have been posted. Otherwise, any interruption in the posting might leave some doubt as to what had been posted.

Journalizing and posting by hand is a useful method for the study of accounting, both for problem assignments and for examinations. The manual approach is also followed in many small businesses. One shortcoming is the opportunity for error that exists whenever information is being copied from one record to another. In businesses having a large volume of transactions, the posting of ledger accounts is performed by accounting machines or by a computer, which speeds up the work and reduces errors. In these more sophisticated applications, transactions may be recorded simultaneously in both the journal and the ledger.

Ledger accounts after posting

After all the September transactions have been posted, the ledger of the Roberts Real Estate Company appears as shown below and on page 55. The accounts are arranged in the ledger in balance sheet order, that is, assets first, followed by liabilities and owner's equity.

Cash   Account No. *1*

Ledger showing September transactions

Date	Explanation	Ref	Debit	Credit	Balance
19— Sept. 1		1	60000 00		60000 00
3		1		21000 00	39000 00
5		1		15000 00	24000 00
20		1	1500 00		25500 00
30		1		3000 00	22500 00

Accounts Receivable   Account No. *2*

Date	Explanation	Ref	Debit	Credit	Balance
19— Sept. 10		1	6000 00		6000 00
20		1		1500 00	4500 00

Land   Account No. *20*

Date	Explanation	Ref	Debit	Credit	Balance
19— Sept. 3		1	21000 00		21000 00
10		1		6000 00	15000 00

Building   Account No. *22*

Date	Explanation	Ref	Debit	Credit	Balance
19— Sept. 5		1	36000 00		36000 00

Office Equipment   Account No. *25*

Date	Explanation	Ref	Debit	Credit	Balance
19— Sept. 14		1	5400 00		5400 00

Accounts Payable   Account No. *30*

Date	Explanation	Ref	Debit	Credit	Balance
19— Sept. 5		/		2100000	210000
14		/		54000	264000
30		/	300000		234000

James Roberts, Capital   Account No. *50*

Date	Explanation	Ref	Debit	Credit	Balance
19— Sept. 1		/		6000000	6000000

THE TRIAL BALANCE

Since equal dollar amounts of debits and credits are entered in the accounts for every transaction recorded, the sum of all the debits in the ledger must be equal to the sum of all the credits. If the computation of account balances has been accurate, it follows that the total of the accounts with debit balances must be equal to the total of the accounts with credit balances.

Before using the account balances to prepare a balance sheet, it is desirable to *prove* that the total of accounts with debit balances is in fact equal to the total of accounts with credit balances. This proof of the equality of debit and credit balances is called a *trial balance.* A trial balance is a two-column schedule listing the names and balances of all the accounts *in the order in which they appear in the ledger;* the debit balances are listed in the left-hand column and the credit balances in the right-hand column. The totals of the two columns should agree. A trial balance taken from the ledger of the Roberts Real Estate Company appears below.

ROBERTS REAL ESTATE COMPANY
Trial Balance
September 30, 19____

Trial balance at month-end proves ledger is in balance

Cash	$22,500	
Accounts receivable	4,500	
Land	15,000	
Building	36,000	
Office equipment	5,400	
Accounts payable		$23,400
James Roberts, capital		60,000
	$83,400	$83,400

Uses and limitations of the trial balance

The trial balance provides proof that the ledger is in balance. The agreement of the debit and credit totals of the trial balance gives assurance that:

1 Equal debits and credits have been recorded for all transactions.
2 The debit or credit balance of each account has been correctly computed.
3 The addition of the account balances in the trial balance has been correctly performed.

Suppose that the debit and credit totals of the trial balance do not agree. This situation indicates that one or more errors have been made. Typical of such errors are: (*1*) the entering of a debit as a credit, or vice versa; (*2*) arithmetic mistakes in balancing accounts; (*3*) clerical errors in copying account balances into the trial balance; (*4*) listing a debit balance in the credit column of the trial balance, or vice versa; and (*5*) errors in addition of the trial balance.

The preparation of a trial balance does not prove that transactions have been correctly analyzed and recorded in the proper accounts. If, for example, a receipt of cash were erroneously recorded by debiting the Land account instead of the Cash account, the trial balance would still balance. Also, if a transaction were completely omitted from the ledger, the error would not be disclosed by the trial balance. In brief, *the trial balance proves only one aspect of the ledger, and that is the equality of debits and credits.*

Despite these limitations, the trial balance is a useful device. It not only provides assurance that the ledger is in balance, but it also serves as a convenient steppingstone for the preparation of financial statements. As explained in Chapter 1, the balance sheet is a formal statement showing the financial position of the business, intended for distribution to managers, owners, bankers, and various outsiders. The trial balance, on the other hand, is merely a working paper, useful to the accountant but not intended for distribution to others. The balance sheet and other financial statements can be prepared more conveniently from the trial balance than directly from the ledger, especially if there are a great many ledger accounts.

Locating errors

In the illustrations given thus far, the trial balances have all been in balance. Every accounting student soon discovers in working problems, however, that errors are easily made which prevent trial balances from balancing. The lack of balance may be the result of a single error or a combination of several errors. An error may have been made in adding the trial balance columns or in copying the balances from the ledger accounts. If the preparation of the trial balance has been accurate, then the error may lie in the accounting records, either in the journal or in the ledger accounts. What is the most efficient approach to locating the error or errors? There is no single technique which will give the best results every time, but the following procedures, done in sequence, will often save considerable time and effort in locating errors.

1 Prove the addition of the trial balance columns by adding these columns in the opposite direction from that previously followed.

2 If the error does not lie in addition, next determine the exact amount by which the schedule is out of balance. The amount of the discrepancy is often a clue to the source of the error. If the discrepancy is divisible by 9, this suggests either a *transposition* error or a *slide.* For example, assume that the Cash account has a balance of $2,175, but in copying the balance into the trial balance the figures are *transposed* and written as $2,157. The resulting error is $18, and like all transposition errors is divisible by 9. Another common error is the slide, or incorrect placement of the decimal point, as when $2,175.00 is copied as $21.75. The resulting discrepancy in the trial balance will also be an amount divisible by 9.

To illustrate another method of using the amount of a discrepancy as a clue to locating the error, assume that the Office Equipment account has a *debit* balance of $420, but that it is erroneously listed in the *credit* column of the trial balance. This will cause a discrepancy of two times $420, or $840, in the trial balance totals. Since such errors as recording a debit in a credit column are not uncommon, it is advisable, after determining the discrepancy in the trial balance totals, to scan the columns for an amount equal to exactly one-half of the discrepancy. It is also advisable to look over the transactions for an item of the exact amount of the discrepancy. An error may have been made by recording the debit side of the transaction and forgetting to enter the credit side.

3 Compare the amounts in the trial balance with the balances in the ledger. Make sure that each ledger account balance has been included in the correct column of the trial balance.

4 Recompute the balance of each ledger account.

5 Trace all postings from the journal to the ledger accounts. As this is done, place a check mark in the journal and in the ledger after each figure verified. When the operation is completed, look through the journal and the ledger for unchecked amounts. In tracing postings, be alert not only for errors in amount but also for debits entered as credits, or vice versa.

Dollar signs

Dollar signs are not used in journals or ledgers. Some accountants use dollar signs in trial balances; some do not. In this book, dollar signs are used in trial balances. Dollar signs should always be used in the balance sheet, the income statement, and other formal financial reports. In the balance sheet, for example, a dollar sign is placed by the first amount in each column and also by the final amount or total. Many accountants also place a dollar sign by each subtotal or other amount listed below an underlining. In the published financial statements of large corporations, however, the use of dollar signs is often limited to the first and last figures in a column.

When dollar amounts are being entered in the columnar paper used in journals and ledgers, commas and periods are not needed. On unruled paper, commas and periods should be used. Most of the problems and illustrations in this book are in even dollar amounts. In such cases the cents column can be left blank, or if desired, zeros or dashes may be used.

Accounting records in perspective

We have emphasized in this chapter the purpose of the journal and ledger and have explained how these accounting records are used. Now we need to consider how these records fit into the accounting process as a whole. It is important to keep in mind that accounting records are not an end in themselves. Just as the physician uses symbols and cryptic notations to write a prescription in the course of providing medical services, the accountant uses symbols and concise notations to interpret business transactions and to classify information about them. Although the prescription order written by the physician and the records created by the accountant are important and must be accurate and complete, they are only a means to an end. The goal of the physician is to restore the health of the patient. The goal of the accountant is to *communicate accounting information to persons who will use this information as a basis for business decisions.* These persons include managers, owners, investors, creditors, and governmental agencies. They want to know the financial position of the business as shown by the balance sheet. What resources (assets) does the business have and what debts (liabilities) does it owe? These persons also want to know how profitable the business has been, as shown by the income statement. Finally, they would like to know about the future prospects of the business. Looking into the future of a business involves much uncertainty, but the accumulating and interpreting of accounting information are vitally important elements of financial forecasting.

The use of journals and ledgers, along with the double-entry system and the various symbols and technical terms, has developed over a long period of time because these devices constitute an efficient *information system.* This information system absorbs each day the economic essence of many business transactions. After classifying and summarizing this mass of data, the accounting process produces concise financial statements for the use of decision-makers. Remember that your study of the accounting model in the early chapters of this book will equip you to read financial statements with understanding and to make better decisions because you are familiar with the underlying accounting concepts and processes.

KEY TERMS INTRODUCED IN CHAPTER 2

Account A record used to summarize all increases and decreases in a particular asset, such as Cash, or any other type of asset, liability, owner's equity, revenue, or expense.

Account balance The difference in dollars between the total debits and total credits in an account.

Business documents Original evidence of transactions, as for example, checks, sales tickets, and cash register tapes.

Credit An amount entered on the right-hand side of an account. A credit is used to record a decrease in an asset and an increase in a liability or owner's equity.

Credit balance The balance of an account in which the total amount of credits exceeds the total amount of debits.

Debit An amount entered on the left-hand side of an account. A debit is used to record an increase in an asset and a decrease in a liability or owner's equity.

Debit balance The balance of an account in which the total amount of debits exceeds the total amount of credits.

Double-entry method In recording transactions, the total dollar amount of debits must equal the total dollar amount of credits.

Financial statement order The usual sequence of accounts in a ledger; that is, assets first, followed by liabilities, owner's equity, revenue, and expenses.

Footing The total of amounts in a column.

Journal A chronological record of transactions, showing for each transaction the debits and credits to be entered in specific ledger accounts.

Ledger A loose-leaf book, file, or other record containing all the separate accounts of a business.

Posting The process of transferring information from the journal to individual accounts in the ledger.

Trial balance A two-column schedule listing the names and the debit or credit balances of all accounts in the ledger.

DEMONSTRATION PROBLEM FOR YOUR REVIEW

a Drill Company was organized on July 1 and carried out a number of transactions during July before opening for business on August 1. The partially filled in journal for the company appears on page 60. You are to determine the titles of the accounts to be debited and credited to complete these July journal entries.

b Post the journal entries on page 60 to the proper ledger accounts shown on pages 60 and 61. Insert the ledger account number in the LP column of the journal as each item is posted.

c Complete the following trial balance as of July 31, 19____.

DRILL COMPANY
Trial Balance
July 31, 19____

	Debit	Credit
Cash	$	
Land		
Building		
Office equipment		
Notes payable		$
Accounts payable		
Howard Drill, capital		
	$	$

General Journal

Date		Account Titles and Explanations	LP	Debit	Credit
19___					
July	1			50,000	
					50,000
		Howard Drill opened a bank account in the name of the business by making a deposit of his personal funds.			
	2			30,000	
					10,000
					20,000
		Purchased land. Paid one-third cash and issued a note payable for the balance.			
	5			12,000	
					12,000
		Purchased a small portable building for cash. The price included installation on Drill Company's lot.			
	12			2,500	
					2,500
		Purchased office equipment on credit from Suzuki & Co.			
	28			1,000	
					1,000
		Paid part of account payable to Suzuki & Co.			

Cash

Account No. *1*

Date	Explanation	Ref	Debit	Credit	Balance
19— July					

Land

Account No. *20*

Date	Explanation	Ref	Debit	Credit	Balance

Building

Account No. *22*

Date	Explanation	Ref	Debit	Credit	Balance

Office Equipment

Account No. *25*

Date	Explanation	Ref	Debit	Credit	Balance

Notes Payable

Account No. *30*

Date	Explanation	Ref	Debit	Credit	Balance

Accounts Payable

Account No. *32*

Date	Explanation	Ref	Debit	Credit	Balance

Howard Drill, Capital

Account No. *50*

Date	Explanation	Ref	Debit	Credit	Balance

SOLUTION TO DEMONSTRATION PROBLEM

a   **General Journal**

Date		Account Titles and Explanations	LP	Debit	Credit
19___					
July	1	Cash	1	50,000	
		Howard Drill, Capital	50		50,000
		Howard Drill opened a bank account in the			
		name of the business by making a deposit of			
		his personal funds.			
	2	Land	20	30,000	
		Cash	1		10,000
		Notes Payable	30		20,000
		Purchased land. Paid one-third cash and			
		issued a note payable for the balance.			
	5	Building	22	12,000	
		Cash	1		12,000
		Purchased a small portable building for cash.			
		The price included installation on Drill Com-			
		pany's lot.			
	12	Office Equipment	25	2,500	
		Accounts Payable	32		2,500
		Purchased office equipment on credit from			
		Suzuki & Co.			
	28	Accounts Payable	32	1,000	
		Cash	1		1,000
		Paid part of account payable to Suzuki & Co.			

b   **Cash**   Account No. *1*

Date		Explanation	Ref	Debit	Credit	Balance
19— July	1		1	50 000 00		50 000 00
	2		1		10 000 00	40 000 00
	5		1		12 000 00	28 000 00
	28		1		1 000 00	27 000 00

Land   Account No. 20

Date		Explanation	Ref	Debit	Credit	Balance
19— July	2		1	30 000 00		30 000 00

Building   Account No. 22

Date	Explanation	Ref	Debit	Credit	Balance
19— July 5		1	1 200 00		1 200 00

Office Equipment   Account No. 25

Date	Explanation	Ref	Debit	Credit	Balance
19— July 12		1	250 00		250 00

Notes Payable   Account No. 30

Date	Explanation	Ref	Debit	Credit	Balance
19— July 2		1		2 000 00	2 000 00

Accounts Payable   Account No. 32

Date	Explanation	Ref	Debit	Credit	Balance
19— July 12		1		250 00	250 00
28		1	100 00		150 00

Howard Drill, Capital   Account No. 50

Date	Explanation	Ref	Debit	Credit	Balance
19— July 1		1		5 000 00	5 000 00

c

DRILL COMPANY
Trial Balance
July 31, 19____

Cash	$27,000	
Land	30,000	
Building	12,000	
Office equipment	2,500	
Notes payable		$20,000
Accounts payable		1,500
Howard Drill, capital		50,000
	$71,500	$71,500

REVIEW QUESTIONS

1 What relationship exists between journals and ledgers on the one hand and financial statements on the other?

2 What is an *account* and how does it differ from a *ledger?*

3 Is it true that favorable events are recorded by credits and unfavorable events by debits? Explain.

4 What relationship exists between the position of an account on the balance sheet and the rules for recording increases in that account?

5 In its simplest form, an account has only three elements or basic parts. What are these three elements?

6 State briefly the rules of debit and credit as applied to asset and liability accounts.

7 Does the term *debit* mean increase and the term *credit* mean decrease? Explain.

8 What requirement is imposed by the double-entry method in the recording of any business transaction?

9 Explain precisely what is meant by each of the phrases listed below. Whenever appropriate, indicate whether the left or right side of an account is affected and whether an increase or decrease is indicated.
  a A debit of $200 to the Cash account
  b Credit balance
  c Credit side of an account
  d A debit of $600 to Accounts Payable
  e Debit balance
  f A credit of $50 to Accounts Receivable
  g A debit to the Land account

10 For each of the following transactions, indicate whether the account in parentheses should be debited or credited, and give the reason for your answer.
  a Purchased a typewriter on credit, promising to make payment in full within 30 days. (Accounts Payable)
  b Purchased land for cash. (Cash)
  c Sold an old, unneeded typewriter on 30-day credit. (Office Equipment)
  d Obtained a loan of $5,000 from a bank. (Cash)
  e James Brown began the business of Brown Sporting Goods Shop by depositing $20,000 cash in a bank account in the name of the business. (James Brown, Capital)

11 How does a T account differ from a three-column running balance form of ledger account?

12 For each of the following accounts, state whether it is an asset, a liability, or owner's equity; also state whether it would normally have a debit or a credit balance: (*a*) Office Equipment, (*b*) John Williams, Capital, (*c*) Accounts Receivable, (*d*) Accounts Payable, (*e*) Cash, (*f*) Notes Payable, (*g*) Land.

13 List the following five items in a logical sequence to illustrate the flow of accounting information through the accounting system:
  a Information entered in journal
  b Preparation of a business document
  c Financial statements prepared from ledger
  d Occurrence of a business transaction
  e Debits and credits posted from journal to ledger

14 Compare and contrast a *journal* and a *ledger.*

15 Which step in the recording of transactions requires greater understanding of accounting principles: (*a*) the entering of transactions in the journal, or (*b*) the posting of entries to ledger accounts?

16 What purposes are served by a trial balance?

17 Are dollar signs used in journal entries? In ledger accounts? In trial balances? In financial statements?

18 What is a *compound* journal entry?

19 State two facts about the sequence of accounts in a journal entry and the use of indentation which make it easy to distinguish between a debit and a credit.

20 A student beginning the study of accounting prepared a trial balance in which two unusual features appeared. The Buildings account showed a credit balance of $20,000, and the Accounts Payable account a debit balance of $100. Considering each of these two abnormal balances separately, state whether the condition was the result of an error in the records or could have resulted from proper recording of an unusual transaction.

21 During the first week of an accounting course, Student A expressed the opinion that a great deal of time could be saved if a business would record transactions directly in ledger accounts rather than entering transactions first in a journal and then posting the debit and credit amounts from the journal to the ledger. Student B agreed with this view but added that such a system should not be called double-entry bookkeeping since each transaction would be entered only once. Student C disagreed with both A and B. He argued that the use of a journal and a ledger was more efficient than entering transactions directly in ledger accounts. Furthermore, he argued that the meaning of double-entry bookkeeping did not refer to the practice of maintaining both a journal and ledger. Evaluate the statements made by all three students.

EXERCISES

Ex. 2-1 Analyze separately each of the following transactions:

a On August 1, Ron Mitchell organized Mitchell Travel Service by opening a bank account in the company name with a deposit of $105,000 cash.

b On August 3, land was acquired for $35,000 cash.

c On August 5, a prefabricated building was purchased at a cost of $38,500 from Custom Company. A cash down payment of $14,000 was made and it was agreed that the balance should be paid in full within 30 days.

d On August 8, office equipment was purchased on credit from Taylor Office Supply Co. at a price of $12,600. The account payable was to be paid within 60 days.

e On August 31, a partial payment of $3,500 was made on the liability to Taylor Office Supply Co.

Note: The type of analysis to be made is shown by the following illustration, using transaction (*a*) as an example.

a (1) The asset Cash was increased. Increases in assets are recorded by debits. Debit Cash, $105,000.

(2) The owner's equity was increased. Increases in owner's equity are recorded by credits. Credit Ron Mitchell, Capital, $105,000.

Ex. 2-2 Enter the following transactions in T accounts drawn on ordinary notebook paper. Label each debit and credit with the letter identifying the transaction. Prepare a trial balance at July 31.

a On July 10, Kathy Lee opened a bank account in the name of her new business, National Realty Company, by making a deposit of $56,000 cash.

b On July 13, purchased land for cash of $28,000.

c On July 18, a restored building was purchased at a cost of $33,600. A cash payment of $8,400 was made and a note payable was issued for the balance.

d On July 20, office equipment was purchased at a cost of $8,400. A cash down payment of $2,800 was made, and it was agreed that the balance should be paid within 30 days.

e On July 30, paid $2,800 of the $5,600 liability arising from the purchase of office equipment on July 20.

Ex. 2-3 The first six transactions of a newly organized company appear in the following T accounts.

Cash		Office Equipment		Accounts Payable	
(1) 57,500	(2) 30,000	(4) 11,250		(6) 11,250	(4) 11,250
	(3) 12,500				
	(5) 2,500				
	(6) 11,250				

Land		Delivery Truck		Bob Love, Capital	
(2) 30,000		(5) 10,000			(1) 57,500

Building		Notes Payable	
(3) 45,000		(3) 32,500	
		(5) 7,500	

For each of the six transactions in turn, indicate the type of accounts affected (asset, liability, or owner's equity) and whether the account was increased or decreased. Arrange your answers in the form illustrated for transaction (1), shown here as an example.

	Account Debited		Account Credited	
Transaction	Type of Account	Increase or Decrease	Type of Account	Increase or Decrease
(1)	Asset	Increase	Owner's equity	Increase

Ex. 2-4 The following accounts of Briarwood Insurance Agency at December 31, 19____, are listed below in random order. The amount for Accounts Payable has been purposely omitted. You are to prepare a trial balance with the proper heading and with the accounts listed in proper sequence. Indicate the balance for Accounts Payable.

Land	$ 25,200	Building	$52,020
Accounts payable	?	Notes payable	4,140
Terry Nelson, capital	105,120	Office equipment	7,740
Automobiles	8,820	Cash	14,040
Accounts receivable	27,540		

Ex. 2-5 Which of the following errors would cause unequal totals in a trial balance? Give a brief explanatory statement for each paragraph.

a An $870 payment for a typewriter was recorded as a debit to Office Equipment of $87 and a credit to Cash of $87.

b A check for $1,000 issued to pay an account payable was recorded by debiting Accounts Payable $1,000 and crediting Accounts Receivable $1,000.

c Collection of an account receivable in the amount of $1,200 was recorded by a debit to Cash for $1,200 and a debit to the owner's capital account for $1,200.

d A payment of $695 to a creditor was recorded by a debit to Accounts Payable of $695 and a credit to Cash of $69.

Ex. 2-6 Enter the following transactions in the two-column journal of Coast Tile Service Company. Include a brief explanation of the transaction as part of each journal entry. Do not include in the explanation any amounts or account titles since these are shown in the debit-credit portion of the entry.

Nov. 1 The owner, William Powell, invested an additional $12,000 cash in the business.

Nov. 3 Purchased an adjacent vacant lot for use as parking space. The price was $28,800, of which $4,800 was paid in cash; a note payable was issued for the balance.

Nov. 12 Collected an account receivable of $4,800 from a customer, Brad Parkman.

Nov. 17 Acquired office equipment from Tower Company for $2,040.

Nov. 21 Issued a check for $864 in full payment of an account payable to Hampton Supply Co.

Nov. 28 Borrowed $18,000 cash from the bank by signing a 90-day note payable.

Ex. 2-7 The trial balance prepared by Johnson Company at April 30 was not in balance. In searching for the error, an employee discovered that a transaction for the purchase of a typewriter on credit for $854 had been recorded by a *debit* of $854 to the Office Equipment account and a *debit* of $854 to Accounts Payable. The credit column of the incorrect trial balance had a total of $129,640.

In answering each of the following five questions, explain briefly the reasons underlying your answer and state the dollar amount of the error if any.

a Was the Office Equipment account overstated, understated, or correctly stated in the trial balance?

b Was the total of the debit column of the trial balance overstated, understated, or correctly stated?

c Was the Accounts Payable account overstated, understated, or correctly stated in the trial balance?

d Was the total of the credit column of the trial balance overstated, understated, or correctly stated?

e How much was the total of the debit column of the trial balance before correction of the error?

PROBLEMS

Group A

2A-1 The Rent-All Company was organized to rent trailers, tools, and other equipment to its customers. The organization of the business began on July 1 and the following transactions occurred in July before the company began regular operations on August 1.

a On July 1, Robert Caldwell opened a bank account in the name of his new company with a deposit of $40,000 cash.

b On July 3, the Rent-All Company bought land for use in its operations at a total cost of $25,000. A cash down payment of $15,000 was made, and a note payable (payable within 90 days without interest) was issued for the balance.

c On July 5, a movable building was purchased for $14,000 cash and installed on the lot.

d On July 10, office equipment was purchased on credit from Dell Office Equipment at a cost of $2,200. The account payable was to be paid within 30 days.

e On July 31, a cash payment of $5,000 was made in partial settlement of the note payable issued on July 3.

Instructions

a Prepare an analysis of each of the above transactions. The form of analysis to be used is as follows, using transaction (*a*) above as an example.

    a (1) The asset Cash was increased. Increases in assets are recorded by debits. Debit Cash, $40,000.

        (2) The owner's equity was increased. Increases in owner's equity are recorded by credits. Credit Robert Caldwell, Capital, $40,000.

b Prepare journal entries for the above five transactions. Include an explanation as a part of each journal entry.

2A-2 The ledger accounts of Hillside Golf Club at July 31 are shown below in an alphabetical listing.

Accounts payable	$ 4,225	Lighting equipment	$ 33,400
Accounts receivable	860	Notes payable	384,500
Building	42,100	Notes receivable	65,000
Cash	11,940	Office equipment	1,160
Fences	21,200	Office supplies	570
Golf carts	28,000	Paul Reynolds, capital	177,968
Land	369,000	Taxes payable	6,537

Instructions

a Prepare a trial balance with the ledger accounts arranged in the usual financial statement order.

b Prepare a balance sheet.

c Assume that immediately after the July 31 balance sheet was prepared, a tornado struck the golf course and destroyed the fences, which were not insured against this type of disaster. If the balance sheet were revised to reflect the loss of the fences, explain briefly what other change in the balance sheet would be required.

2A-3 William Baker organized a business, Baker Construction Company, on October 1 to perform remodeling work on homes and other buildings. After one month devoted to organizing the business and contacting prospective customers, the ledger accounts at November 30 contained the following entries:

Cash					Delivery Equipment		
Oct. 2	64,000	Oct. 3	12,224		Oct. 3	15,040	
31	1,040	19	2,000				
		29	256				

Accounts Receivable					Notes Payable		
Oct. 16	2,080	Oct. 31	1,040		Oct. 19	1,600	Oct. 3	16,000

Office Supplies					Accounts Payable		
Oct. 7	2,400	Oct. 27	32		Oct. 19	400	Oct. 7	2,400
21	288				27	32	21	288
					29	256		

Office Equipment				*William Baker, Capital*	
Oct. 3	13,184	Oct. 16	2,080	Oct. 2	64,000

Instructions

a Reconstruct the journal entries as they were probably made by the company's accountant, giving a full explanation for each transaction.

b Determine account balances and prepare a trial balance at October 31, 19____ .

c Prepare a balance sheet at October 31, 19____ .

2A-4 A new business, Apartment Management Service, was started on October 1 by Ruth Forrester to provide managerial services for the owners of apartment buildings. The organizational period extended throughout the month of October and included the transactions listed below.

The account titles and account numbers to be used are:

Cash	11		Notes payable	31
Accounts receivable	15		Accounts payable	32
Land	21		Ruth Forrester, capital	51
Building	23			
Office equipment	25			

Oct. 1 Opened a bank account in the name of the business, Apartment Management Service, by depositing personal savings in the amount of $49,000.

Oct. 4 Purchased land and an office building for a price of $70,000, of which $33,600 was considered applicable to the land and $36,400 attributable to the building. A cash down payment of $21,000 was made and a note payable for $49,000 was issued for the balance of the purchase price.

Oct. 7 Purchased office equipment on credit from Harvard Office Equipment, $3,850.

Oct. 9 A typewriter (cost $490) which was part of the October 7 purchase of office equipment proved defective and was returned for credit to Harvard Office Equipment.

Oct. 11 Sold to Regent Pharmacy at cost one-third of the land acquired on October 4. No down payment was required. The buyer promised to pay one-half the purchase price of $11,200 within 10 days and the remainder by November 12.

Oct. 18 Paid $1,400 in partial settlement of the liability to Harvard Office Equipment.

Oct. 21 Received cash of $5,600 as partial collection of the account receivable from Regent Pharmacy.

Instructions

a Prepare journal entries for the month of October.

b Post to ledger accounts of the three-column running balance form.

c Prepare a trial balance at October 31.

2A-5 High-Line Blueprints, a service-type business, provides fast production and distribution of blueprints and other drawings and documents to customers throughout the city. At September 30, the ledger accounts appeared as follows:

Cash			*Notes Payable*	
5,672.10	1,555.80		3,000.00	42,000.00
1,684.50	3,000.00			
7,395.00	1,785.00			
945.00	1,080.00			

Accounts Receivable		Accounts Payable	
11,394.00	780.00	955.80	692.05
789.00	165.00	600.00	955.80
165.00		1,080.00	2,670.00
571.50			801.00
6,315.00			1,539.05

Office Supplies		Taxes Payable	
4,500.00		795.00	4,395.00
750.00		990.00	
750.00			

Office Equipment		Edward Morris, Capital	
39,720.00			45,253.20

Delivery Equipment	
18,600.00	

Instructions

a Determine the account balances and prepare a trial balance as of September 30, 19____ .

b Prepare a balance sheet.

2A-6 Frank Brown, a certified public accountant, resigned from his position with a CPA firm in a large city in order to move to a small town and begin his own public accounting practice. The business transactions during September while the new venture was being organized are listed below.

Sept. 1 Brown opened a bank checking account in the name of his firm, Frank Brown, Certified Public Accountant, by depositing $50,400 which he had saved over a period of years.

Sept. 3 Purchased a small office building located on a large lot for a total price of $91,200, of which $48,000 was applicable to the land and $43,200 to the building. A cash payment of $45,600 was made and a note payable was issued for the balance of the purchase price.

Sept. 7 Purchased a used calculating machine for $384, paying cash.

Sept. 9 Purchased office furniture, filing cabinets, and a typewriter from Davidson Office Supply Co. at a cost of $3,960. A cash down payment of $720 was made, the balance to be paid in three equal installments due September 28, October 28, and November 28. The purchase was on open account and did not require signing of a promissory note.

Sept. 10 Three-quarters of the land purchased September 3 was sold for $36,000 to Douglass and Douglass, a law firm. The buyer made a down payment of $12,000 cash and agreed to pay the balance within 20 days. Since the land was sold at the same price per foot that Brown had paid for it, there was no gain or loss on the transaction.

Sept. 28 Paid Davidson Office Supply Co. $1,080 cash as the first installment due on the account payable for office equipment.

Sept. 30 Received $24,000 cash from Douglass and Douglass in full settlement of the account receivable created in the transaction of September 10.

Instructions

a Journalize the above transactions, then post to ledger accounts. Use the running balance form of ledger account rather than T accounts. The account titles and the account numbers to be used are:

Cash	10	Office equipment	23
Accounts receivable	16	Notes payable	32
Land	20	Accounts payable	35
Building	22	Frank Brown, capital	50

b Prepare a trial balance at September 30, 19___ .

Group B

2B-1 A trial balance of Morgan Associates at March 31 follows:

	Debit	Credit
Cash	$17,625	
U.S. government bonds	25,000	
Accounts receivable	22,840	
Office equipment	5,327	
Notes payable		$35,000
Accounts payable		18,562
Judi Morgan, capital		17,230
	$70,792	$70,792

The following transactions occurred early in April:

a On April 2, collected cash of $1,200 from accounts receivable.
b On April 3, made a payment of $922 on accounts payable.
c On April 4, Morgan invested an additional $800 in the business.
d On April 5, acquired additional office equipment on credit at a cost of $1,125.
e On April 6, bought additional office equipment for cash of $400.

Instructions

a Prepare an analysis of each of the above transactions. The form of analysis to be used is as follows, using transaction (*a*) as an example.
   a (1) The asset Cash was increased. Increases in assets are recorded by debits. Debit Cash, $1,200.
      (2) The asset Accounts Receivable was decreased. Decreases in assets are recorded by credits. Credit Accounts Receivable, $1,200.
b Prepare journal entries including explanations for the above transactions.
c Prepare a trial balance at April 6.

2B-2 Century Financial Company was organized to offer financial advisory services and to provide property management services for its clients. The account balances at March 31 are shown by the following alphabetical list.

Accounts payable	$ 9,420	Notes receivable	$ 1,200
Accounts receivable	14,132	Office furniture	4,684
Automobiles	12,640	Office supplies	381
Building	58,500	Robert Dash, capital	?
Cash	12,376	Taxes payable	6,875
Computer	36,010	Technical library	1,600
Land	45,050	U.S. government bonds (should	
Notes payable	111,200	follow Cash)	25,000

Instructions

a Prepare a trial balance with the accounts arranged in financial statement order. (Compute the balance for the owner's capital account so that the ledger will be in balance.)

b Prepare a balance sheet.

2B-3 During February while Milton Gordon was organizing a new business, Gordon Pool Maintenance, he kept only an informal record of transactions in the form of T accounts which he maintained on a large blackboard. Gordon asks you to develop from the T accounts a ledger using the standard three-column running balance form of accounts. He says that he will prepare journal entries for February from some rough notes he has kept but that he will need some assistance in establishing the running balance form of ledger accounts. The T accounts reflecting all February transactions are as follows:

	Cash			1		Office Equipment		25
2/2	18,000	2/4	10,800		2/7	3,240		
		2/8	162		2/13	450		
		2/23	450					

	Office Supplies	9		Notes Payable		30
2/8	162				2/3	37,800

	Land	20		Accounts Payable		31
2/4	12,600		2/23	450	2/7	3,240
					2/13	450

	Building	22		Milton Gordon, Capital		50
2/4	36,000				2/2	18,000

Instructions

a Transfer the information shown by the T accounts to ledger accounts of the three-column running balance form.

b Prepare a trial balance at February 28 from the ledger accounts completed in part (a).

2B-4 David McCall, a licensed real estate broker, on January 1 began the organization of his own business to be known as McCall Land Company. The following events occurred during January:

Jan. 2 David McCall opened a bank account in the name of the business by depositing personal savings of $60,000.

Jan. 3 Purchased land and a small office building at a total price of $86,400. The terms of the purchase required a cash payment of $38,400 and the issuance of a note payable for $48,000. The records of the tax assessor indicated that the value of the building was one-half that of the land.

Jan. 5 Sold one-quarter of the land at a cost of $14,400 to an adjacent business, Village Medical Clinic, which wished to enlarge its parking lot. No down payment was required. Terms of the sale called for payment of $4,800 within 10 days and the balance within 30 days.

Jan. 11 Purchased office equipment on credit from Buffington Company in the amount of $5,040.

Jan. 15 Received cash of $4,800 as partial collection of the receivable from Village Medical Clinic.

Jan. 20 Paid $2,880 as partial settlement of the liability to Buffington Company.

The account titles and account numbers to be used are:

Cash	11	Notes payable	30
Accounts receivable	15	Accounts payable	32
Land	21	David McCall, capital	50
Building	23		
Office equipment	26		

Instructions

a Prepare journal entries for the month of January.

b Post to ledger accounts of the three-column running balance form.

c Prepare a trial balance at January 31, 19____.

2B-5 The account records of King Electric at July 31 are summarized in the following T accounts.

Cash			Notes Payable	
20,436.80	21,030.40			8,000.00
2,124.80	1,329.60			
4,945.60				
1,244.80				

Accounts Receivable			Accounts Payable	
1,990.40	4,945.60		19,430.40	726.40
6,908.80				2,024.00
55,916.80				19,144.00

Land			Taxes Payable	
32,000.00			1,169.60	1,513.60

Building			Mortgage Payable	
51,200.00				44,800.00

Furniture & Fixtures			Dave Lester, Capital	
4,000.00	524.80			80,000.00
11,680.00				35,200.00

Delivery Equipment	
7,595.20	1,404.80

Instructions

a Compute the account balances and prepare a trial balance at July 31, 19____.

b Prepare a balance sheet at July 31, 19____.

2B-6 Robert Service, after several seasons of play in professional football, had saved enough money to establish his own business to be known as the Service Auto Rental Company. The business transactions during February while the new business was being organized were as follows:

Feb. 1 Using money taken from his personal savings account and from sale of securities, Service deposited $128,000 in a bank checking account in the name of the business, Service Auto Rental Company.

Feb. 3 The new company purchased land and a building at a cost of $80,000, of which $48,000 was regarded as applicable to the land and $32,000 to the building. The transaction involved a cash payment of $28,800 and the issuance of a note payable for $51,200.

Feb. 5 Purchased 20 new automobiles at $5,600 each from Swift Sales Company. Paid $32,000 cash, and agreed to pay another $32,000 by February 26 and the remaining balance by March 15.

Feb. 7 Sold an automobile at cost to Service's father-in-law, Howard Facey, who paid $2,400 in cash and agreed to pay the balance within 30 days.

Feb. 8 One of the automobiles was found to be defective and was returned to Swift Sales Company. The amount payable to this creditor was thereby reduced by $5,600.

Feb. 20 Purchased office equipment at a cost of $4,480 cash.

Feb. 26 Issued a check for $32,000 in partial payment of the liability to Swift Sales Company.

Instructions

a Journalize the above transactions, then post to ledger accounts. Use the running balance form of ledger account rather than T accounts. The account titles and the account numbers to be used are as follows:

Cash	10	Notes payable	31
Accounts receivable	11	Accounts payable	32
Land	16	Robert Service, capital	50
Buildings	17		
Office equipment	20		
Automobiles	22		

b Prepare a trial balance at February 28, 19____.

BUSINESS DECISION PROBLEM 2

Richard Fell, a college student with several summers' experience as a guide on canoe camping trips, decided to go into business for himself. To start his own guide service, Fell estimated that at least $4,800 cash would be needed. On June 1 he borrowed $3,200 from his father and signed a three-year note payable which stated that no interest would be charged. He deposited this borrowed money along with $1,600 of his own savings in a business bank account to begin a business known as Birchbark Canoe Trails. Also on June 1, Birchbark Canoe Trails carried out the following transactions:

(1) Bought a number of canoes at a total cost of $6,400, paid $1,600 cash and agreed to pay the balance within 60 days.

(2) Bought camping equipment at a cost of $3,200 payable in 60 days.

(3) Bought supplies for cash, $800.

After the close of the season on September 10, Fell asked another student, Joseph Gallal, who had taken a course in accounting, to help him determine the financial position of the business.

The only record Fell had maintained was a checkbook with memorandum notes written on the check stubs. From this source Gallal discovered that Fell had invested an additional $1,600 of his own savings in the business on July 1, and also that the accounts payable arising from the purchase of the canoes and camping equipment had been paid in full. A bank statement received from the bank on September 10 showed a balance on deposit of $3,240.

Fell informed Gallal that he had deposited in the bank all cash received by the business. He had also paid by check all bills immediately upon receipt; consequently, as of September 10 all bills for the season had been paid.

The canoes and camping equipment were all in excellent condition at the end of the season and Fell planned to resume operations the following summer. In fact he had already accepted reservations from many customers who wished to return. Gallal felt that some consideration should be given to the wear and tear on the canoes and equipment but he agreed with Fell that for the present purpose the canoes and equipment should be listed in the balance sheet at the original cost. The supplies remaining on hand had cost $40 and Fell felt that he could obtain a refund for this amount by returning them to the supplier.

Gallal suggested that two balance sheets be prepared, one to show the condition of the business on June 1 and the other showing the condition on September 10. He also recommended to Fell that a complete set of accounting records be established.

Instructions

a Use the information in the first paragraph (including the three numbered transactions) as a basis for preparing a balance sheet dated June 1.

b Prepare a balance sheet at September 10. (Because of the incomplete information available, it is not possible to determine the amount of cash at September 10 by adding cash receipts and deducting cash payments throughout the season. The amount on deposit as reported by the bank at September 10 is to be regarded as the total cash belonging to the business at that date.)

c By comparing the two balance sheets, compute the change in owner's equity. Explain the sources of this change in owner's equity and state whether you consider the business to be successful. Also comment on the cash position at the beginning and end of the season. Has the cash position improved significantly? Explain.

3

Measuring Business Income

The earning of net income, or profits, is a major goal of almost every business enterprise, large or small. If you were to organize a small business of your own, you would do so with the hope and expectation that the business would operate at a profit, thereby increasing your equity in the business. In other words, **profit is an increase in the owner's equity resulting from operation of the business.** From the standpoint of the individual firm, profitable operation is essential if the firm is to succeed, or even to survive.

Operating profitably usually leads to an increase in total assets as well as in owner's equity. From the fundamental accounting equation (A = L + OE), we know that any transaction which changes total assets must also change either total liabilities or owner's equity. For example, borrowing money from a bank increases both total assets and total liabilities. Operating profitably increases owner's equity and this increase is usually accompanied by an increase in total assets. It is possible that the increase in owner's equity from profitable operations could be accompanied by a decrease in liabilities, but in the great majority of cases, operating profitably increases total assets along with the increase in owner's equity.

Profits may be retained in the business to finance expansion, or they may be withdrawn by the owner or owners. Some of the largest corporations have become large by retaining their profits in the business and using these profits for purposes of growth. Retained profits may be used, for example, to acquire new plant and equipment, to carry on research leading to new and better products, and to extend sales operations into new territories. A satisfactory rate of business profits is generally associated with high employment, an improving standard of living, and a strong, expanding national economy.

Net income

Since the drive for profits underlies the very existence of business organizations, it follows that a most important function of an accounting system is to provide information about the profitability of a business. Before we can measure the profits of a business, we need to establish a sharp, clear meaning for **profits.** Economists define profits as the amount by which an entity becomes **better off** during a period of time. Unfortunately, how much "better off" an entity has become may be largely a matter of personal opinion and cannot be measured **objectively** enough to provide a useful definition for accountants.

For this reason, accountants usually look to actual business transactions to provide objective evidence that a business has become better off. For example, if an item which cost a business $60 is sold for $100 cash, we have objective evidence that the business has become $40 better off. Since business managers and economists use the word **profits** in somewhat different senses, accountants prefer to use the alternative term **net income,** and to define this term very carefully. **Net income is the excess of the price of goods sold and services rendered over the cost of goods and services used up during a given time period.** At this point, we shall adopt the technical accounting term **net income** in preference to the less precise term **profits.**

To determine net income, it is necessary to measure for a given time period (1) the price of goods sold and services rendered and (2) the cost of goods and services used up. The technical accounting terms for these items comprising net income are **revenue** and **expenses.** Therefore, we may state that **net income equals revenue minus expenses.** To understand why this is true and how the measurements are made, let us begin with the meaning of revenue.

Revenue

Revenue is the price of goods sold and services rendered to customers. When a business renders services to its customers or delivers merchandise to them, it either receives immediate payment in cash or acquires an account receivable which will be collected and thereby become cash within a short time. The revenue for a given period is equal to the inflow of cash and receivables from sales made in that period. For any single transaction, the amount of revenue is a measurement of the asset values received from the customer.

Not all receipts of cash represent revenue; for example, as shown in Chapter 1, a business may obtain cash by borrowing from a bank. This increase in cash is offset by an increase in liabilities in the form of a note payable to the bank. The owner's equity is not changed by the borrowing transaction.

Collection of an account receivable is another example of a cash receipt that does not represent revenue. The act of collection causes an increase in the asset, Cash, and a corresponding decrease in another asset, Accounts Receivable. The amount of total assets remains unchanged, and, of course, there is no change in liabilities or owner's equity.

As another example of the distinction between revenue and cash receipts, let us assume that a business begins operations in March and makes sales of merchandise or services to its customers in March as follows: sales for cash, $25,000; sales on credit (to be collected in April), $15,000. The revenue for March is $40,000, an amount equal to the cash received or to be received from the month's sales. When the accounts receivable of $15,000 are collected during April, they must not be counted a second time in measuring revenue for April.

Revenue causes an increase in owner's equity. The inflow of cash and receivables from customers increases the total assets of the company; on the other side of the accounting equation, the liabilities do not change, but the owner's equity is increased to match the increase in total assets. Thus revenue is the gross increase in owner's equity resulting from business activities. Bear in mind, however, that not every increase in owner's equity comes from revenue. As illustrated in Chapter 1, the owner's equity is also increased by the investment of assets in the business by the owner.

Various terms are used to describe different types of revenue; for example, the revenue earned by a real estate broker may be called *Commissions Earned;* in the professional practice of lawyers, physicians, dentists, and CPAs, the revenue is called *Fees Earned;* a person owning property and leasing it to others has revenue called *Rent Earned;* and companies selling merchandise rather than services generally use the term *Sales* to describe the revenue earned.

Expenses

Expenses are the cost of the goods and services used up in the process of obtaining revenue. Examples include salaries paid employees, charges for newspaper advertising and for telephone service, and the wearing out (depreciation) of the building and office equipment. All these items are necessary to attract and serve customers and thereby to obtain revenue. Expenses are sometimes referred to as the "cost of doing business," that is, the cost of the various activities necessary to carry on a business. Since expenses are the cost of goods and services used up, they are also called *expired costs.*

Expenses cause the owner's equity to decrease. Revenue may be regarded as the positive factor in producing net income, expenses as the negative factor. The relationship between expenses and revenue is a significant one; the expenses of a given month or other time period are incurred in order to generate revenue in that same period. The salaries earned by sales employees waiting on customers during July are applicable to July revenue and should be treated as July expenses, even though these salaries may not actually be paid to the employees until sometime in August.

As previously explained, revenue and cash receipts are not one and the same thing; similarly, expenses and cash payments are not identical. Examples of cash payments which are not expenses of the current period include the purchase of an office building for cash, the purchase of merchandise for later sale to customers, the repayment of a bank loan, and withdrawals of cash from the business by the owner. In deciding whether a given transaction should be regarded as an expense of the current period, it is often helpful to pose the following questions:

1 Was the alleged "expense" incurred in order to produce revenue in the current period?
2 Does the item in question reduce the owner's equity?

If the answer to both questions is Yes, the transaction does represent an expense.

Matching revenue and expenses

To prepare an income statement and determine the net income of a business for any particular time period, we use the *matching principle.* Revenue must be matched with the related expenses incurred in obtaining that revenue. In matching revenue and expenses in the income statement, we show first all the revenue earned during the period and then deduct from the revenue all the expenses incurred in producing that revenue.

Withdrawals by the owner

The owner of an unincorporated business (James Roberts, in our continuing example) invests money in the enterprise and devotes all or part of his time to its affairs in the hope that the business will earn a profit. The owner does not earn interest on the money he invests nor a salary for his personal services. His incentive, rather than interest or salary, is the increase in owner's equity that will result if the business earns a net income.

An owner of an unincorporated business usually makes withdrawals of cash from time to time for personal use. These withdrawals are in anticipation of profits and are not regarded as an expense of the business. The withdrawal of cash by the owner is like an expense in one respect; it reduces the owner's equity. However, expenses are incurred for the purpose of generating revenue, and a withdrawal of cash by the owner does not have this purpose. From time to time the owner may also make additional investments in the business. The investment of cash and the withdrawal of cash by the owner may be thought of as exact opposites: the investment does not represent revenue; the withdrawal does not represent an expense. Investments and withdrawals of cash affect only balance sheet accounts and are not reported in the income statement.

Since a withdrawal of cash reduces the owner's equity, it *could be* recorded by debiting the owner's capital account (James Roberts, Capital, in our example). However, a clearer record is created if a separate *drawing account* (James Roberts, Drawing) is debited to record all amounts withdrawn. The drawing account is also known as a *personal account.*

Debits to the owner's drawing account are required for any of the following transactions:

1 Withdrawals of cash.

2 Withdrawals of other assets. The owner of a clothing store, for example, may withdraw merchandise for his or her personal use. The amount of the debit to the drawing account would be for the cost of the goods which were withdrawn.

3 Payment of the owner's personal bills out of company funds.

The disposition of the drawing account when financial statements are prepared will be illustrated later in this chapter.

Relating revenue and expenses to time periods

A balance sheet shows the financial position of the business at a given date. An income statement, on the other hand, shows the results of operations over *a period of time.* In fact, the concept of income is meaningless unless it is related to a period of time. For example, if the owner of a business says, "My business produces net income of $5,000," the meaning is not at all clear; it could be made clear, however, by relating the income to a time period, such as "$5,000 a week," "$5,000 a month," or "$5,000 a year."

THE ACCOUNTING PERIOD Every business concern prepares a yearly income statement, and most businesses prepare quarterly and monthly income statements as well. Management needs to know from month to month whether revenue is rising or falling, whether expenses are being held to the level anticipated, and how net income compares with the net income of the preceding month and with the net income of the corresponding month of the preceding year. The term *accounting period means the span of time covered by an income statement.* It may consist of a month, a quarter of a year, a half year, or a year.

Many income statements cover the calendar year ended December 31, but an increasing number of companies are adopting an annual accounting period ending with a month other than December. Generally a business finds it more convenient to end its annual accounting period during a slack season rather than during a time of peak activity. Any 12-month accounting period adopted by a business is called its *fiscal year.* A fiscal year ending at the annual low point of seasonal activity is said to be a *natural business year.* The fiscal year selected by the federal government for its accounting purposes begins on October 1 and ends 12 months later on September 30.

TRANSACTIONS AFFECTING TWO OR MORE ACCOUNTING PERIODS The operation of a business entails an endless stream of transactions, many of which begin in one accounting period but affect several succeeding periods. Fire insurance policies, for example, are commonly issued to cover a period of three years. In this case, the apportionment of the cost of the policy by months is an easy matter. If the policy covers three years (36 months) and costs, for example, $360, the insurance expense each month is $10.

Not all transactions can be so precisely divided by accounting periods. The purchase of a building, furniture and fixtures, machinery, a typewriter, or an automobile provides benefits to the business over all the years in which such an asset is used. No one can determine in advance exactly how many years of service will be received from such long-lived assets. Nevertheless, in measuring the net income of a business for a period of one year or less, the accountant must estimate what portion of the cost of the building and similar long-lived assets is applicable to the current year. *Since the apportionments for these and many other transactions which overlap two or more accounting periods are in the nature of estimates rather than precise measurements, it follows that income statements should be regarded as useful approximations of annual income rather than as absolutely accurate determinations.*

If we assume a stable price level, the time period for which the measurement of net income can be most accurate is the entire life-span of the business. When a business concern sells all its assets, pays its debts, and ends its existence, it would then theoretically be possible to determine with precision the net income for the time period from the date of organization to the date of termination. Such a theoretically precise measurement of net income would, however, be too late to be of much use to the owners or managers of the business. The practical needs of business enterprise are well served by income statements of reasonable accuracy that tell managers and owners each month, each quarter, and each year the results of business operation.

Rules of debit and credit for revenue and expenses

Our approach to revenue and expenses has stressed the fact that revenue increases the owner's equity, and expenses decrease the owner's equity. The rules of debit and credit for recording revenue and expenses follow this relationship, and therefore the recording of revenue and expenses in ledger accounts requires only a slight extension of the rules of debit and credit presented in Chapter 2. The rule previously stated for recording increases and decreases in owner's equity was as follows:

Increases in owner's equity are recorded by credits.
Decreases in owner's equity are recorded by debits.

This rule is now extended to cover revenue and expense accounts:

Revenue increases owner's equity; therefore revenue is recorded by a credit.
Expenses decrease owner's equity; therefore expenses are recorded by debits.

XIET INCOME = REVENUE — EXPENSES

Ledger accounts for revenue and expenses

During the course of an accounting period, a great many revenue and expense transactions occur in the average business. To classify and summarize these numerous transactions, a separate ledger account is maintained for each major type of revenue and expense. For example, almost every business maintains accounts for Advertising Expense, Telephone Expense, and Salaries Expense. At the end of the period, all the advertising expenses appear as debits in the Advertising Expense account. The debit balance of this account represents the total advertising expense of the period and is listed as one of the expense items in the income statement.

Revenue accounts are usually much less numerous than expense accounts. A small business such as the Roberts Real Estate Company in our continuing illustration may have only one or two types of revenue, such as commissions earned from arranging sales of real estate, and commissions earned from the rental of properties in behalf of clients. In a business of this type, the revenue accounts might be called Sales Commissions Earned and Rental Commissions Earned.

RECORDING REVENUE AND EXPENSE TRANSACTIONS: ILLUSTRATION The organization of the Roberts Real Estate Company during September has already been described. The illustration is now continued for October, during which month the company earned commissions by selling several residences for its clients. Bear in mind that the company does not own any residential property; it merely acts as a broker or agent for clients wishing to sell their houses. A commission of 6% of the sales price of the house is charged for this service. During October the company not only earned commissions but also incurred a number of expenses.

Note that each illustrated transaction which affects an income statement account also affects a balance sheet account. This pattern is consistent with our previous discussion of revenue and expenses. In recording revenue transactions, we shall debit the assets received and credit a revenue account. In recording expense transactions, we shall debit an expense account and credit the asset Cash, or perhaps a liability account if payment is to be made later. The transactions for October were as follows:

Oct. 1 Paid $360 for publication of newspaper advertising describing various houses offered for sale.

	Analysis	Rule	Entry
Advertising expense incurred and paid	The cost of advertising is an expense	Expenses decrease the owner's equity and are recorded by debits	Debit: Advertising Expense, $360
	The asset Cash was decreased	Decreases in assets are recorded by credits	Credit: Cash, $360

Oct. 6 Earned and collected a commission of $2,250 by selling a residence previously listed by a client.

	Analysis	Rule	Entry
Revenue earned and collected	The asset Cash was increased	Increases in assets are recorded by debits	Debit: Cash, $2,250
	Revenue was earned	Revenue increases the owner's equity and is recorded by a credit	Credit: Sales Commissions Earned, $2,250

Oct. 16 Newspaper advertising was ordered at a price of $270, payment to be made within 30 days.

	Analysis	Rule	Entry
Advertising expense incurred but not paid	The cost of advertising is an expense	Expenses decrease the owner's equity and are recorded by debits	Debit: Advertising Expense, $270
	An account payable, a liability, was incurred	Increases in liabilities are recorded by credits	Credit: Accounts Payable, $270

Oct. 20 A commission of $3,390 was earned by selling a client's residence. The sales agreement provided that the commission would be paid in 60 days.

	Analysis	Rule	Entry
Revenue earned, to be collected later	An asset in the form of an account receivable was acquired	Increases in assets are recorded by debits	Debit: Accounts Receivable, $3,390
	Revenue was earned	Revenue increases the owner's equity and is recorded by a credit	Credit: Sales Commissions Earned, $3,390

Oct. 30 Paid salaries of $2,100 to office employees for services rendered during October.

	Analysis	Rule	Entry
Salaries expense incurred and paid	Salaries of employees are an expense	Expenses decrease the owner's equity and are recorded by debits	Debit: Office Salaries Expense, $2,100
	The asset Cash was decreased	Decreases in assets are recorded by credits	Credit: Cash, $2,100

Oct. 30 A telephone bill for October amounting to $144 was received. Payment was required by November 10.

	Analysis	Rule	Entry
Telephone expense incurred, to be paid later	The cost of telephone service is an expense	Expenses decrease the owner's equity and are recorded by debits	Debit: Telephone Expense, $144
	An account payable, a liability, was incurred	Increases in liabilities are recorded by credits	Credit: Accounts Payable, $144

Oct. 30 Roberts withdrew $1,800 cash for his personal use.

	Analysis	Rule	Entry
Withdrawal of cash by owner	Withdrawal of assets by the owner decreases the owner's equity	Decreases in owner's equity are recorded by debits	Debit: James Roberts, Drawing, $1,800
	The asset Cash was decreased	Decreases in assets are recorded by credits	Credit: Cash, $1,800

The journal entries to record the October transactions are as follows:

General Journal Page 2

	Date		Account Titles and Explanation	LP	Debit	Credit
October journal entries for Roberts Real Estate Company	Oct.	1	Advertising Expense	70	360	
			Cash	1		360
			Paid for newspaper advertising.			
		6	Cash	1	2,250	
			Sales Commissions Earned	61		2,250
			Earned and collected commission by selling residence for client.			
		16	Advertising Expense	70	270	
			Accounts Payable	30		270
			Ordered newspaper advertising; payable in 30 days.			
		20	Accounts Receivable	2	3,390	
			Sales Commissions Earned	61		3,390
			Earned commission by selling residence for client; commission to be received in 60 days.			
		30	Office Salaries Expense	72	2,100	
			Cash	1		2,100
			Paid office salaries for October.			
		30	Telephone Expense	74	144	
			Accounts Payable	30		144
			To record liability for October telephone service.			
		30	James Roberts, Drawing	51	1,800	
			Cash	1		1,800
			Withdrawal of cash by owner.			

The column headings at the top of the illustrated journal page (*Date, Account Titles and Explanation, LP, Debit,* and *Credit*) are seldom used in practice. They are included here as an instructional guide but will be omitted from some of the later illustrations of journal entries.

Sequence of accounts in the ledger

Accounts are located in the ledger in financial statement order; that is, the balance sheet accounts first (assets, liabilities, and owner's equity) followed by the income statement accounts (revenue and expenses). The usual sequence of accounts within these five groups is shown by the following listing.

Balance Sheet Accounts	Income Statement Accounts
Assets:	**Revenue:**
Cash	Commissions earned (fees earned, rent
Marketable securities	earned, sales, etc.)
Notes receivable	**Expenses:** (No standard sequence of listing
Accounts receivable	exists for expense accounts.)
Inventory (discussed in Chapter 5)	Advertising
Office supplies (unexpired insurance, prepaid	Salaries
rent, and other prepaid expenses discussed in	Rent
Chapter 4)	Telephone
Land	Depreciation
Buildings	Various other expenses
Equipment	
Other assets	
Liabilities:	
Notes payable	
Accounts payable	
Salaries payable (and other short-term liabili-	
ties discussed in Chapter 4)	
Owner's equity:	
John Smith, capital	
John Smith, drawing	

Why are ledger accounts arranged in financial statement order?

Remember that a trial balance is prepared by listing the ledger account balances shown in the ledger, working from the first ledger page to the last. Therefore, if the accounts are located in the ledger in *financial statement order,* the same sequence will naturally be followed in the trial balance, and this arrangement will make it easier to prepare the balance sheet and income statement from the trial balance. Also, this standard arrangement of accounts will make it easier to locate any account in the ledger.

Ledger accounts for Roberts Real Estate Company: illustration

The ledger of the Roberts Real Estate Company after the October transactions have been posted is now illustrated. The accounts appear in financial statement order. To conserve space in this illustration, several ledger accounts appear on a single page; in actual practice, however, each account occupies a separate page in the ledger.

Cash

Account No. 1

Date		Explanation	Ref	Debit	Credit	Balance
19—Sept.	1		1	60000 00		60000 00
	3		1		21000 00	39000 00
	5		1		15000 00	24000 00
	20		1	1500 00		25500 00
	30		1		3000 00	22500 00
Oct.	1		2		360 00	22140 00
	6		2	2250 00		24390 00
	30		2		2100 00	22290 00
	30		2		1800 00	20490 00

Accounts Receivable

Account No. 2

Date		Explanation	Ref	Debit	Credit	Balance
19—Sept.	10		1	6000 00		6000 00
	20		1		1500 00	4500 00
Oct.	20		2	3390 00		7890 00

Land

Account No. 20

Date		Explanation	Ref	Debit	Credit	Balance
19—Sept.	3		1	21000 00		21000 00
	10		1		6000 00	15000 00

Building

Account No. 22

Date	Explanation	Ref	Debit	Credit	Balance
19—Sept 5		1	36000 00		36000 00

Office Equipment

Account No. 25

Date	Explanation	Ref	Debit	Credit	Balance
19—Sept. 14		1	5400 00		5400 00

Accounts Payable
Account No. 30

Date		Explanation	Ref	Debit	Credit	Balance
19— Sept.	5		1		21000 00	21000 00
	14		1		5400 00	26400 00
	30		1	3000 00		23400 00
Oct.	16		2		270 00	23670 00
	30		2		144 00	23814 00

James Roberts, Capital
Account No. 50

Date		Explanation	Ref	Debit	Credit	Balance
19— Sept.	1		1		60000 00	60000 00

James Roberts, Drawing
Account No. 51

Date		Explanation	Ref	Debit	Credit	Balance
19— Oct.	30		2	1800 00		1800 00

Sales Commissions Earned
Account No. 61

Date		Explanation	Ref	Debit	Credit	Balance
19— Oct.	6		2		2250 00	2250 00
	20		2		3390 00	5640 00

Advertising Expense
Account No. 70

Date		Explanation	Ref	Debit	Credit	Balance
19— Oct.	1		2	360 00		360 00
	16		2	270 00		630 00

Office Salaries Expense
Account No. 72

Date		Explanation	Ref	Debit	Credit	Balance
19— Oct.	30		2	2100 00		2100 00

Telephone Expense
Account No. 74

Date		Explanation	Ref	Debit	Credit	Balance
19— Oct.	30		2	144 00		144 00

Trial balance

The trial balance at October 31 was prepared from the preceding ledger accounts.

ROBERTS REAL ESTATE COMPANY
Trial Balance
October 31, 19___

Cash	$20,490	
Accounts receivable	7,890	
Land	15,000	
Building	36,000	
Office equipment	5,400	
Accounts payable		$23,814
James Roberts, capital		60,000
James Roberts, drawing	1,800	
Sales commissions earned		5,640
Advertising expense	630	
Office salaries expense	2,100	
Telephone expense	144	
	$89,454	$89,454

Proving the equality of debits and credits

Recording depreciation at the end of the period

The preceding trial balance includes all the October expenses requiring cash payments such as salaries, advertising, and telephone service, but it does not include any depreciation expense. The term *depreciation* means the systematic allocation of the cost of an asset to expense over the accounting periods making up its useful life. Although depreciation expense does not require a monthly cash outlay, it is nevertheless an inevitable and continuing expense. Failure to make an entry for depreciation expense would result in *understating* the total expenses of the period and consequently in *overstating* the net income.

BUILDING The office building purchased by the Roberts Real Estate Company at a cost of $36,000 is estimated to have a useful life of 20 years. The purpose of the $36,000 expenditure was to provide a place in which to carry on the business and thereby to obtain revenue. After 20 years of use the building will be worthless and the original cost of $36,000 will have been entirely consumed. In effect, the company has purchased 20 years of "housing services" at a total cost of $36,000. A portion of this cost expires during each year of use of the building. If we assume that each year's operations should bear an equal share of the total cost (straight-line depreciation), the annual depreciation expense will amount to $\frac{1}{20}$ of $36,000, or $1,800. On a monthly basis, depreciation expense is $150

($36,000 cost ÷ 240 months). There are alternative methods of spreading the cost of a depreciable asset over its useful life, some of which will be considered in Chapter 11.

The journal entry to record depreciation of the building during October follows:

General Journal   Page 2

	Date		Account Titles and Explanation	LP	Debit	Credit
Recording depreciation of the building	19__ Oct.	31	Depreciation Expense: Building	76	150	
			Accumulated Depreciation: Building .	23		150
			To record depreciation for October.			

The depreciation expense account will appear in the income statement for October along with the other expenses of salaries, advertising, and telephone expense. The Accumulated Depreciation: Building account will appear in the balance sheet as a deduction from the Building account, as shown by the following illustration of a *partial* balance sheet:

Showing accumulated depreciation in the balance sheet

ROBERTS REAL ESTATE COMPANY
Partial Balance Sheet
October 31, 19__

Building (at cost).	$36,000	
Less: Accumulated depreciation	150	$35,850

The end result of crediting the Accumulated Depreciation: Building account is much the same as if the credit had been made to the Building account; that is, the net amount shown on the balance sheet for the building is reduced from $36,000 to $35,850. Although the credit side of a depreciation entry *could* be made directly to the asset account, it is customary and more efficient to record such credits in a separate account entitled Accumulated Depreciation. The original cost of the asset and the total amount of depreciation recorded over the years can more easily be determined from the ledger when separate accounts are maintained for the asset and for the accumulated depreciation.

Accumulated Depreciation: Building is an example of a *contra-asset account,* because it has a credit balance and is offset against an asset account (Building) to produce the proper balance sheet valuation for the asset.

OFFICE EQUIPMENT Depreciation on the office equipment of the Roberts Real Estate Company must also be recorded at the end of October. This equipment cost $5,400 and is assumed to have a useful life of 10 years. Monthly depreciation expense on the straight-line basis is, therefore, $45, computed by dividing the cost of $5,400 by the useful life of 120 months. The journal entry is as follows:

	General Journal			Page 2

Date		Account Titles and Explanation	LP	Debit	Credit
19___					
Oct.	*31*	*Depreciation Expense: Office Equipment* . .	*78*	*45*	
		Accumulated Depreciation: Office			
		Equipment	*26*		*45*
		To record depreciation for October.			

Recording depreciation of office equipment

No depreciation was recorded on the building and office equipment for September, the month in which these assets were acquired, because regular operations did not begin until October. Generally, depreciation is not recognized until the business begins active operation and the assets are placed in use. Accountants often use the expression "matching costs and revenues" to convey the idea of writing off the cost of an asset to expense during the time periods in which the business uses the asset to generate revenue.

The journal entry by which depreciation is recorded at the end of the month is called an *adjusting entry.* The adjustment of certain asset accounts and related expense accounts is a necessary step at the end of each accounting period so that the information presented in the financial statements will be as accurate and complete as possible. In the next chapter, adjusting entries will be shown for some other items in addition to depreciation.

The adjusted trial balance

After all the necessary adjusting entries have been journalized and posted, an *adjusted trial balance* is prepared to prove that the ledger is still in balance. It also provides a complete listing of the account balances to be used in preparing the financial statements. The following adjusted trial balance differs from the trial balance shown on page 89 because it includes accounts for depreciation expense and accumulated depreciation.

ROBERTS REAL ESTATE COMPANY
Adjusted Trial Balance
October 31, 19___

Adjusted trial balance

Cash	$20,490	
Accounts receivable	7,890	
Land	15,000	
Building	36,000	
Accumulated depreciation: building		$ 150
Office equipment	5,400	
Accumulated depreciation: office equipment		45
Accounts payable		23,814
James Roberts, capital		60,000
James Roberts, drawing	1,800	
Sales commissions earned		5,640
Advertising expense	630	
Office salaries expense	2,100	
Telephone expense	144	
Depreciation expense: building	150	
Depreciation expense: office equipment	45	
	$89,649	$89,649

FINANCIAL STATEMENTS

The income statement

When we measure the net income earned by a business we are measuring its economic performance—its success or failure as a business enterprise. The owner, the manager, and the company's banker are anxious to see the latest available income statement and thereby to judge how well the company is doing. If the business is organized as a corporation, the stockholders and prospective investors also will be keenly interested in each successive income statement. The October income statement for Roberts Real Estate Company appears as follows:

ROBERTS REAL ESTATE COMPANY
Income Statement
For the Month Ended October 31, 19___

Income statement showing results of operations for October

Sales commissions earned		$5,640
Expenses:		
Advertising expense	$ 630	
Office salaries expense	2,100	
Telephone expense	144	
Depreciation expense: building	150	
Depreciation expense: office equipment	45	3,069
Net income		$2,571

This income statement consists of the last six accounts in the adjusted trial balance on page 92. It shows that the revenue during October exceeded the expenses of the month, thus producing a net income of $2,571. Bear in mind, however, that our measurement of net income is not absolutely accurate or precise, because of the assumptions and estimates involved in the accounting process. We have recorded only those economic events which are evidenced by accounting transactions. Perhaps during October the Roberts Real Estate Company has developed a strong interest on the part of many clients who are on the verge of buying or selling homes. This accumulation of client interest is an important step toward profitable operation, but is not reflected in the October 31 income statement because it is not subject to objective measurement. Remember also that in determining the amount of depreciation expense we had to estimate the useful life of the building and office equipment. Any error in our estimates is reflected in the net income reported for October. Despite these limitations, the income statement is of vital importance, and indicates that the new business has been profitable during the first month of its operation.

Alternative titles for the income statement include **earnings statement, statement of operations,** and **profit and loss statement.** However, **income statement** is by far the most popular term for this important financial statement. In summary, we can say that an income statement is used to evaluate the performance of a business by matching the revenue earned during a given time period with the expenses incurred in obtaining that revenue.

The balance sheet

Previous illustrations of balance sheets have been arranged in the **account form,** that is, with the assets on the left side of the page and the liabilities and owner's equity on the right side. The balance sheet on page 94 is shown in **report form,** that is, with the liabilities and owner's equity sections listed below rather than to the right of the asset section. Both the account form and the report form are widely used.

The relationship between the income statement and the balance sheet is shown in the owner's equity section of the balance sheet. The owner's original capital investment of $60,000 was increased by reason of the $2,571 net income earned during October, making a total equity of $62,571. This equity was decreased, however, by the owner's withdrawal of $1,800 in cash at the end of October, leaving a final balance of $60,771.

Alternative titles for the balance sheet include **statement of financial position** and **statement of financial condition.** Although "balance sheet" may not be a very descriptive term, it continues to be the most widely used, perhaps because of custom and tradition.

In the Roberts Real Estate Company illustration, we have shown the two common ways in which the owner's equity in a business may be increased: *(1)* investment of cash or other assets by the owner, and *(2)* operating the business at a profit. There are also two ways in which the

ROBERTS REAL ESTATE COMPANY

Balance Sheet

October 31, 19___

Assets

Cash		$20,490
Accounts receivable		7,890
Land		15,000
Building	$36,000	
Less: Accumulated depreciation	150	35,850
Office equipment	$ 5,400	
Less: Accumulated depreciation	45	5,355
		$84,585

Balance sheet at October 31: report form

Liabilities & Owner's Equity

Liabilities:		
Accounts payable		$23,814
Owner's equity:		
James Roberts, capital, Oct. 1, 19___	$60,000	
Net income for October	2,571	
Subtotal	$62,571	
Less: Withdrawals	1,800	
James Roberts, capital, Oct. 31, 19___		60,771
		$84,585

owner's equity may be decreased: *(1)* withdrawal of assets by the owner, and *(2)* operating the business at a loss.

CLOSING THE ACCOUNTS

The accounts for revenue, expenses, and drawings are **temporary proprietorship accounts** used during the accounting period to classify changes affecting the owner's equity. At the end of the period, we want to transfer the net effect of these various increases and decreases into the permanent account showing the owner's equity. We also want to reduce the balances of the temporary proprietorship accounts to zero, so that these accounts will again be ready for use in accumulating information during the next accounting period. These objectives are accomplished by the use of **closing entries.**

Revenue and expense accounts are closed at the end of each accounting period by transferring their balances to a summary account called Income Summary. When the credit balances of the revenue accounts and the debit balances of the expense accounts have been transferred into one summary account, the balance of this Income Summary will be the net income or net loss for the period. If the revenue (credit balances) exceeds the expenses (debit balances), the Income Summary account will have a credit balance representing net income. Conversely, if expenses exceed revenue, the Income Summary will have a debit balance representing net loss.

As previously explained, all debits and credits in the ledger are posted from the journal; therefore, the closing of revenue and expense accounts requires the making of journal entries and the posting of these journal entries to ledger accounts. A journal entry made for the purpose of closing a revenue or expense account by transferring its balance to the Income Summary account is called a *closing entry.* This term is also applied to the journal entries (to be explained later) used in closing the Income Summary account and the owner's drawing account into the owner's capital account.

A principal purpose of the year-end process of closing the revenue and expense accounts is to reduce their balances to zero. Since the revenue and expense accounts provide the information for the income statement of *a given accounting period,* it is essential that these accounts have zero balances at the beginning of each new period. The closing of the accounts has the effect of wiping the slate clean and preparing the records for the recording of revenue and expenses during the succeeding accounting period.

It is common practice to close the accounts only once a year, but for illustration, we shall now demonstrate the closing of the accounts of the Roberts Real Estate Company at October 31 after one month's operation.

CLOSING ENTRIES FOR REVENUE ACCOUNTS Revenue accounts have credit balances. Closing a revenue account, therefore, means transferring its credit balance to the Income Summary account. This transfer is accomplished by a journal entry debiting the revenue account in an amount equal to its credit balance, with an offsetting credit to the Income Summary account. The only revenue account of the Roberts Real Estate Company is Sales Commission Earned, which had a credit balance of $5,640 at October 31. The journal entry necessary to close this account is shown on page 96.

After this closing entry has been posted, the two accounts affected will appear as shown on page 96. A few details of account structure have been omitted to simplify the illustration; a directional arrow has been added to show the transfer of the $5,640 balance of the revenue account into the Income Summary account.

General Journal Page 3

	Date		Account Titles and Explanation	LP	Debit	Credit
Closing a revenue account	19__ Oct.	31	Sales Commissions Earned . . . . Income Summary . . . . To close the Sales Commissions Earned account.	61 53	5,640	 5,640

	Sales Commissions Earned				61

Date		Exp.	Ref	Debit	Credit	Balance
Oct.	6		2		2,250	2,250
	20		2		3,390	5,640
	31	To close	3	5,640		–0–

	Income Summary				53

Date		Exp.	Ref	Debit	Credit	Balance
Oct.	31		3		5,640	5,640

CLOSING ENTRIES FOR EXPENSE ACCOUNTS Expense accounts have debit balances. Closing an expense account means transferring its debit balance to the Income Summary account. The journal entry to close an expense account, therefore, consists of a credit to the expense account in an amount equal to its debit balance, with an offsetting debit to the Income Summary account.

There are five expense accounts in the ledger of the Roberts Real Estate Company. Five separate journal entries could be made to close these five expense accounts, but the use of one *compound journal entry* is an easier, more efficient, time-saving method of closing all five expense accounts. A compound journal entry is an entry that includes debits to more than one account or credits to more than one account.

General Journal Page 3

	Date		Account Titles and Explanation	LP	Debit	Credit

Closing the various expense accounts by use of a compound journal entry	19__
	Oct.
		31	Income Summary . . . .
			    Advertising Expense . . . .
			    Office Salaries Expense . . . .
			    Telephone Expense . . . .
			    Depreciation Expense: Building . . . .
			    Depreciation Expense: Office
			        Equipment . . . .
			To close the expense accounts.
				53
				70
				72
				74
				76
				
				78
					3,069	
						630
						2,100
						144
						150
						
						45

After this closing entry has been posted, the Income Summary account has a credit balance of $2,571, and the five expense accounts have zero balances, as shown on page 97.

Income Summary
Account No. 53

Date		Explanation	Ref	Debit	Credit	Balance
19___						
Oct.	31		3		5,640	5,640
	31		3	3,069		2,571

Expense accounts have zero balances after closing entries have been posted

Advertising Expense
Account No. 70

Date		Explanation	Ref	Debit	Credit	Balance
19___						
Oct.	2		2	360		360
	16		2	270		630
	31	To close	3		630	–0–

Office Salaries Expense
Account No. 72

Date		Explanation	Ref	Debit	Credit	Balance
19___						
Oct.	30		2	2,100		2,100
	31	To close	3		2,100	–0–

Telephone Expense
Account No. 74

Date		Explanation	Ref	Debit	Credit	Balance
19___						
Oct.	30		2	144		144
	31	To close	3		144	–0–

Depreciation Expense: Building
Account No. 76

Date		Explanation	Ref	Debit	Credit	Balance
19___						
Oct.	31		2	150		150
	31	To close	3		150	–0–

Depreciation Expense: Office Equipment
Account No. 78

Date		Explanation	Ref	Debit	Credit	Balance
19___						
Oct.	31		2	45		45
	31	To close	3		45	–0–

CLOSING THE INCOME SUMMARY ACCOUNT   The five expense accounts have now been closed and the total amount of $3,069 formerly contained in these accounts appears in the debit column of the Income Summary account. The commissions of $5,640 earned during October appear in the credit column of the Income Summary account. Since the credit entry of $5,640 representing October revenue is larger than the debit of $3,069 representing October expenses, the account has a credit balance of $2,571—the net income for October.

The net income of $2,571 earned during October causes the owner's equity to increase. The *credit* balance of the Income Summary account is, therefore, transferred to the owner's capital account by the following closing entry:

General Journal   Page 3

	Date		Account Titles and Explanation	LP	Debit	Credit
Net income	**19___**					
earned	Oct.	31	Income Summary	53	2,571	
increases			James Roberts, Capital	50		2,571
the			To close the Income Summary account for			
owner's			October by transferring the net income to the			
equity			owner's capital account.			

After this closing entry has been posted, the Income Summary account has a zero balance, and the net income earned during October appears in the owner's capital account as shown below:

Income Summary   Account No. 53

19___						
Oct.	31	Revenue	3		5,640	5,640
	31	Expenses	3	3,069		2,571
	31	To close	3	2,571		–0–

James Roberts, Capital   Account No. 50

19___						
Sept.	1	Investment by owner	1		60,000	60,000
Oct.	31	Net income for October	3		2,571	62,571

In our illustration the business has operated profitably with revenue in excess of expenses. Not every business is so fortunate; if the expenses of a business are larger than its revenue, the Income Summary account will have a debit balance. In case of a loss, the closing of the Income Summary account will require a debit to the owner's capital account and an offsetting credit to the Income Summary account. The owner's equity will, of course, be reduced by the amount of the loss debited to the capital account.

Note that the Income Summary account is used only at the end of the period when the accounts are being closed. The Income Summary account has no entries and no balance except during the process of closing the accounts at the end of the accounting period.

CLOSING THE OWNER'S DRAWING ACCOUNT As explained earlier in this chapter, withdrawals of cash or other assets by the owner are not considered as an expense of the business and, therefore, are not a factor in determining the net income for the period. Since drawings by the owner do not constitute an expense, the owner's drawing account is closed not into the Income Summary account but directly to the owner's capital account. The following journal entry serves to close the drawing account in the ledger of the Roberts Real Estate Company at October 31.

General Journal   *Page 3*

	Date		Account Titles and Explanation	LP	Debit	Credit
Drawing account is closed to owner's capital account	19___ Oct.	31	James Roberts, Capital . . . . James Roberts, Drawing . . . . To close the owner's drawing account.	50 51	1,800	1,800

After this closing entry has been posted, the drawing account will have a zero balance, and the amount withdrawn by Roberts during October will appear as a deduction or debit entry in his capital account, as shown below:

James Roberts, Drawing   51

One account now shows total equity of owner	19___ Oct.	30 31	Withdrawal To close	2 3	1,800	1,800	1,800 –0–

James Roberts, Capital   50

	19___ Sept. Oct.	1 31 31	Investment by owner Net income for October From owner's drawing account	1 3 3	1,800	60,000 2,571	60,000 62,571 60,771

SUMMARY OF CLOSING PROCEDURE Let us now summarize briefly the procedure of closing the accounts:

1 Close the various revenue and expense accounts by transferring their balances into the Income Summary account.

2 Close the Income Summary account by transferring its balance into the owner's capital account.

3 Close the owner's drawing account into the owner's capital account. (The balance of the owner's capital account in the ledger will now be the same as the amount of capital appearing in the balance sheet.)

The closing of the accounts may be illustrated graphically by use of T accounts as follows:

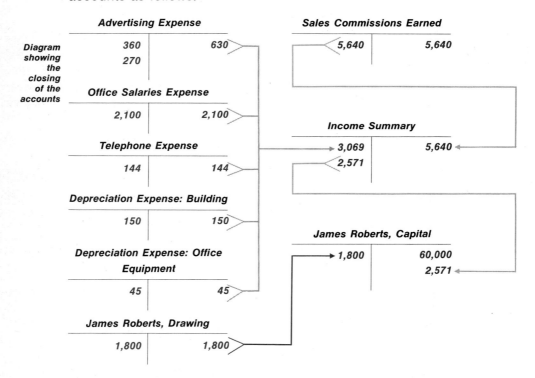

Diagram showing the closing of the accounts

After-closing trial balance

After the revenue and expense accounts have been closed, it is desirable to prepare an **after-closing trial balance,** which of course will consist solely of balance sheet accounts. There is always the possibility that an error in posting the closing entries may have upset the equality of debits and credits in the ledger. The after-closing trial balance, or **post-closing trial balance** as it is often called, is prepared from the ledger. It gives assurance that the accounts are in balance and ready for the recording of the transactions of the new accounting period. The after-closing trial balance of the Roberts Real Estate Company follows:

ROBERTS REAL ESTATE COMPANY
After-Closing Trial Balance
October 31, 19____

Only the Cash	$20,490	
balance Accounts receivable	7,890	
sheet accounts Land	15,000	
remain Building	36,000	
open Accumulated depreciation: building		$ 150
Office equipment	5,400	
Accumulated depreciation: office equipment		45
Accounts payable		23,814
James Roberts, capital		60,771
	$84,780	$84,780

Sequence of accounting procedures

The accounting procedures described to this point may be summarized in eight steps, as follows:

1 Journalize transactions Enter all transactions in the general journal, thus creating a chronological record of events.

2 Post to ledger accounts Post debits and credits from the general journal to the proper ledger accounts, thus creating a record classified by accounts.

3 Prepare a trial balance Prove the equality of debits and credits in the ledger.

4 Make end-of-period adjustments Draft adjusting entries in the general journal, and post to ledger accounts. Thus far we have illustrated only one type of adjustment: the recording of depreciation at the end of the period.

5 Prepare an adjusted trial balance Prove again the equality of debits and credits in the ledger.

6 Prepare financial statements An income statement is needed to show the results of operation for the period. A balance sheet is needed to show the financial position of the business at the end of the period.

7 Journalize and post closing entries The closing entries clear the revenue, expense, and drawing accounts, making them ready for recording the events of the next accounting period. The closing entries also transfer the net income or loss of the completed period to the owner's capital account.

8 Prepare an after-closing trial balance This step ensures that the ledger remains in balance after posting of the closing entries.

Accrual basis of accounting versus cash basis of accounting

We now want to consider whether revenue should be recorded in the accounting period in which it is earned or in the period in which it is collected in cash. A parallel question is whether expenses should be recorded in the accounting period in which they are incurred or in the period in which they are paid. A business which recognizes revenue in the period in which it is earned and which deducts in the same period the expenses incurred in generating this revenue is using the *accrual basis of accounting.*

Net income has meaning only when it is related to a specific period of time. Since net income is determined by offsetting expenses against revenue, both the expenses and the revenue used in the calculation must relate to the same time period. This matching or offsetting of related revenue and expenses gives a realistic picture of the profit performance of the business each period. The positive economic effect which revenue has on the business should be recognized at the time the revenue is earned (that is, at the time the services are rendered to customers). The negative economic effect of expenses (that is, using up goods and services) should be recognized at the time these goods and services are consumed. The accrual basis is thus essential to income determination, and as we have already indicated, the measurement of income is a major objective of the whole accounting process.

The alternative to the accrual basis of accounting is the *cash basis.* Under cash basis accounting, revenue is not recorded until received in cash; expenses are assigned to the period in which cash payment is made. Most business concerns use the accrual method of accounting, but individuals and professionals (such as physicians and lawyers) usually maintain their accounting records on a cash basis.

The cash basis of accounting does not give a good picture of profitability. For example, it ignores uncollected revenue which has been earned and expenses which have been incurred but not paid. Throughout this book we shall be working with the accrual basis of accounting, except for that portion of Chapter 20 dealing with the income tax returns of individuals.

KEY TERMS INTRODUCED OR EMPHASIZED IN CHAPTER 3

Accounting period   The span of time covered by an income statement. One year is the accounting period for much financial reporting, but financial statements are also prepared by most companies for each quarter of the year and also for each month.

Accrual basis of accounting   Calls for recording revenue in the period in which it is earned and recording expenses in the period in which they are incurred. The effect of events on the business is recognized as services are rendered or consumed rather than when cash is received or paid.

Accumulated depreciation   A contra-asset account shown as a deduction from the related asset account in the balance sheet. Depreciation taken throughout the useful life of an asset is accumulated in this account.

Adjusted trial balance   A listing of all ledger account balances after the amounts have been changed to include the adjusting entries made at the end of the period.

Adjusting entries   Entries required at the end of the period to update the accounts before financial statements are prepared. Adjusting entries serve to apportion transactions properly between the accounting periods affected and to record any revenue earned or expenses incurred which have not been recorded prior to the end of the period.

After-closing trial balance A trial balance prepared after all closing entries have been made. Consists only of accounts for assets, liabilities, and owner's equity.

Cash basis of accounting Revenue is recorded when received in cash and expenses are recorded in the period in which cash payment is made. Fails to match revenue with related expenses and therefore does not lead to a logical measurement of income. Use is limited mostly to individual income tax returns and to accounting records of physicians and other professional firms.

Closing entries Journal entries made at the end of the period for the purpose of closing temporary accounts (revenue, expense, and drawing accounts) and transferring balances to the owner's capital account.

Contra-asset account An account with a credit balance which is offset against or deducted from an asset account to produce the proper balance sheet valuation for the asset.

Depreciation The systematic allocation of the cost of an asset to expense during the periods of its useful life.

Drawing account The account used to record the withdrawals of cash or other assets by the owner. Closed at the end of the period by transferring its balance to the owner's capital account.

Expenses The cost of the goods and services used up in the process of obtaining revenue. Sometimes referred to as *expired costs.*

Financial statement order Sequence of accounts in the ledger: balance sheet accounts first (assets, liabilities, and owner's equity), followed by income statement accounts (revenue and expenses).

Fiscal year Any 12-month accounting period adopted by a business.

Income statement A report used to evaluate the performance of a business by matching its revenue and related expenses for a particular accounting period. Shows the net income or net loss.

Income Summary account The summary account in the ledger to which revenue and expense accounts are closed at the end of the period. The balance (credit balance for a net income, debit balance for a net loss) is transferred to the owner's capital account.

Matching principle The revenue earned during an accounting period is matched with the expenses incurred in generating this revenue.

Net income The excess of revenue earned over the related expenses for a given period.

Report form balance sheet A balance sheet in which the sections for liabilities and owner's equity are listed below the section for assets.

Revenue The price of goods sold and services rendered by a business. Equal to the inflow of cash and receivables in exchange for services rendered or goods delivered during the period.

Temporary proprietorship accounts The accounts for revenue, expenses, and withdrawals, used during the accounting period to classify changes affecting the owner's equity.

DEMONSTRATION PROBLEM FOR YOUR REVIEW

Lane Insurance Agency began business on April 1, 19___. Assume that the accounts are closed and financial statements prepared each month. The company occupies rented office space but owns office equipment estimated to have a useful life of 10 years from date of acquisition, April 1. The trial balance for Lane Insurance Agency at June 30, 19___, is shown on page 104.

Cash	$ 1,275	
Accounts receivable	605	
Office equipment	6,000	
Accumulated depreciation: office equipment		$ 100
Accounts payable . . . . : . .		1,260
Richard Lane, capital, May 31, 19___		6,500
Richard Lane, drawing	1,000	
Commissions earned		3,710
Advertising expense	500	
Rent expense	370	
Telephone expense	120	
Salaries expense	1,700	
	$11,570	$11,570

Instructions

a Prepare the adjusting journal entry to record depreciation of the office equipment for the month of June.

b Prepare an adjusted trial balance at June 30, 19___.

c Prepare an income statement for the month ended June 30, 19___, and a balance sheet in report form at June 30, 19___.

SOLUTION TO DEMONSTRATION PROBLEM

a Adjusting journal entry:

Depreciation Expense: Office Equipment	50	
Accumulated Depreciation: Office Equipment		50
To record depreciation for June ($6,000 ÷ 120 months).		

b

LANE INSURANCE AGENCY
Adjusted Trial Balance
June 30, 19___

Cash	$ 1,275	
Accounts receivable	605	
Office equipment	6,000	
Accumulated depreciation: office equipment		$ 150
Accounts payable		1,260
Richard Lane, capital		6,500
Richard Lane, drawing	1,000	
Commissions earned		3,710
Advertising expense	500	
Rent expense	370	
Telephone expense	120	
Salaries expense	1,700	
Depreciation expense: office equipment	50	
	$11,620	$11,620

c

LANE INSURANCE AGENCY
Income Statement
For the Month Ended June 30, 19___

Commissions earned		$3,710
Expenses:		
Advertising expense	$ 500	
Rent expense	370	
Telephone expense	120	
Salaries expense	1,700	
Depreciation expense: office equipment	50	2,740
Net income		$ 970

LANE INSURANCE AGENCY
Balance Sheet
June 30, 19___

Assets

Cash		$1,275
Accounts receivable		605
Office equipment	$6,000	
Less: Accumulated depreciation	150	5,850
		$7,730

Liabilities & Owner's Equity

Liabilities:		
Accounts payable		$1,260
Owner's equity:		
Richard Lane, capital, May 31, 19___	$6,500	
Net income for June	970	
Subtotal	$7,470	
Less: Withdrawals	1,000	
Richard Lane, capital, June 30, 19___		6,470
		$7,730

REVIEW QUESTIONS

1 What is the meaning of the term *revenue?* Does the receipt of cash by a business indicate that revenue has been earned? Explain.

2 What is the meaning of the term *expenses?* Does the payment of cash by a business indicate that an expense has been incurred? Explain.

3 The Milan Company, owned by Robert Gennaro, completed its first year of operation on December 31, 1979. State the proper heading for the first annual income statement.

4 Does a well-prepared income statement provide an exact measurement of net income for the period, or does it represent merely an approximation of net income? Explain.

5 How does depreciation expense differ from other operating expenses?

6 Assume that a business acquires a delivery truck at a cost of $4,800. Estimated life of the truck is four years. State the amount of depreciation expense per year and per month. Give the adjusting entry to record depreciation on the truck at the end of the first month, and explain where the accounts involved would appear in the financial statements.

7 Explain the rules of debit and credit with respect to transactions recorded in revenue and expense accounts.

8 Supply the appropriate term (debit or credit) to complete the following statements.

    a The owner's equity account, income summary account, and revenue accounts are increased by _____ entries.

    b Asset accounts and expense accounts are increased by _____ entries.

    c Liability accounts and owner's equity accounts are decreased by _____ entries.

9 Supply the appropriate term (debit or credit) to complete the following statements.

    a When a business is operating profitably, the journal entry to close the Income Summary account will consist of a _____ to that account and a _____ to the owner's capital account.

    b When a business is operating at a loss, the journal entry to close the Income Summary account will consist of a _____ to that account and a _____ to the owner's capital account.

    c The journal entry to close the owner's drawing account consists of a _____ to that account and a _____ to the owner's capital account.

10 All ledger accounts belong in one of the following five groups: asset, liability, owner's equity, revenue, and expense. For each of the following accounts, state the group in which it belongs. Also indicate whether the normal balance would be a debit or credit.

    a Fees Earned   **e** Building

    b Notes Payable   **f** Depreciation Expense

    c Telephone Expense   **g** Accumulated Depreciation: Building

    d William Nelson, Drawing

11 A service enterprise performs services in the amount of $500 for a customer in May and receives payment in June. In which month is the $500 of revenue recognized? What is the journal entry to be made in May and the entry to be made in June?

12 Which of the following accounts should be closed by a debit to Income Summary and a credit to the account listed?

    James Harris, Drawing   Salaries Expense

    Fees Earned   Accounts Payable

    Advertising Expense   Depreciation Expense

    Accounts Receivable   Accumulated Depreciation

13 Supply the appropriate terms to complete the following statements. _____ and _____ accounts are closed at the end of each accounting period by transferring their balances to a summary account called _____ _____ . A _____ balance in this summary account represents net income for the period; a _____ balance represents a net loss for the period.

14 Which of the ten accounts listed below and on page 107 are affected by closing entries at the end of the accounting period?

    Cash   James Miller, Drawing

    Fees Earned   James Miller, Capital

Income Summary   Accumulated Depreciation
Accounts Payable   Accounts Receivable
Telephone Expense   Depreciation Expense

15 How does the accrual basis of accounting differ from the cash basis of accounting? Which gives a more accurate picture of the profitability of a business? Explain.

EXERCISES

Ex. 3-1 Label each of the following statements as true or false. Explain the reasoning underlying your answer and give an example of a transaction which supports your position.

a Every transaction that affects a balance sheet account also affects an income statement account.

b Every transaction that affects an income statement account also affects a balance sheet account.

c Every transaction that affects an expense account also affects an asset account.

d Every transaction that affects a revenue account also affects another income statement account.

e Every transaction that affects an expense account also affects a revenue account.

Ex. 3-2 Determine the amount of the missing figure for each of the following five independent cases.

a Net income for the year . . . . $ 61,200

Owner's equity at beginning of year   300,000

Owner's equity at end of year . . . .   _____

Owner's drawings during the year   46,500

b Owner's equity at end of year $233,700

Owner's drawings during the year   37,200

Net income for the year   49,800

Owner's equity at beginning of year . . . .   _____

c Net income for the year . . . . $ _____

Owner's equity at end of year   96,300

Owner's equity at beginning of year   79,500

Owner's drawings during the year   31,200

d Owner's drawings during the year . . . . $ _____

Owner's equity at end of year   130,200

Net income for the year   35,400

Owner's equity at beginning of year   142,500

e Owner's equity at beginning of year $155,100

Owner's equity at end of year   180,600

Additional investment by owner during the year   30,000

Net income for the year . . . .   _____

Owner's drawings for the year   24,300

Ex. 3-3 The following transactions were carried out during the month of June by K. Davis and Company, a firm of real estate brokers. Which of these transactions represented revenue to the firm during the month of June? Explain.

a Borrowed $12,800 from Century Bank to be repaid in three months.

b Collected cash of $2,400 from an account receivable. The receivable originated in May from services rendered to a client.

c Arranged a sale of an apartment building owned by a client, Stephen Roberts. The commission for making the sale was $14,400, but this amount would not be received until August 20.

d Collected $480 rent for June from a dentist to whom K. Davis and Company rented part of its building.

e K. Davis invested an additional $6,400 cash in the business.

Ex. 3-4 During July the Columbus Company carried out the following transactions. Which of these transactions represented expenses for July? Explain.

a Paid a garage $640 for automobile repair work performed in May.

b The owner withdrew $1,600 from the business for personal use.

c Paid $6,400 in settlement of a loan obtained three months earlier.

d Purchased a typewriter for $960 cash.

e Paid $192 for gasoline purchases for the delivery truck during July.

f Paid $960 salary to a salesman for time worked during July.

Ex. 3-5 The income statement prepared by University Mile Company for the month of August showed a net income of $30,456. In recording August transactions, however, certain transactions were incorrectly recorded. Study the following list of selected August transactions, and identify any which were incorrectly recorded. Also give the journal entry as it should have been made, and compute the correct amount of net income for August.

a Made an error in computing depreciation on the building for August. Recorded as $30. The correct amount of depreciation was $300.

b Recorded the withdrawal of $4,800 by the owner, Ruth Davis, by debiting Salaries Expense and crediting Cash.

c Earned a commission of $3,000 by selling a residence for a client. Commission to be received in 60 days. Recorded by debiting Commissions Earned and crediting Accounts Receivable.

d A payment of $300 for newspaper advertising was recorded by debiting Advertising Expense and crediting Accounts Receivable.

e Received but did not pay a bill of $342 for August telephone service. Recorded by debiting Telephone Expense and crediting Commissions Earned.

Ex. 3-6 Madison Company maintains a ledger with accounts arranged in *financial statement order,* so that a trial balance prepared from the ledger will show the accounts in a convenient sequence for preparing the financial statements. Rearrange the following random list of account titles in the order in which they are located in the ledger of Madison Company.

(1) Notes Payable	(12) Advertising Expense
(2) Stanley Orr, Capital	(13) Accounts Payable
(3) Depreciation Expense: Buildings	(14) Interest Payable
(4) Rent Expense	(15) Marketable Securities
(5) Buildings	(16) Depreciation Expense:
(6) Accounts Receivable	Office Equipment
(7) Land	(17) Electricity Expense
(8) Notes Receivable	(18) Commissions Earned
(9) Telephone Expense	(19) Stanley Orr, Drawing
(10) Accumulated Depreciation: Buildings	(20) Salaries Expense
(11) Accumulated Depreciation:	(21) Office Equipment
Office Equipment	(22) Cash

Ex. 3-7 An employee of Service Company prepared the following closing entries from the ledger accounts for the year of 19____ .

a .Identify any errors which the employee made.
b Prepare correct closing entries for the business.

Entry 1

Lawn Service Revenue	124,800	
Accumulated Depreciation	12,800	
Accounts Payable	43,200	
Income Summary		180,800

To close accounts with credit balances.

Entry 2

Income Summary	116,800	
Salaries Expense		89,600
J. Doe, Drawing		17,600
Advertising Expense		6,400
Depreciation Expense		3,200

To close accounts with debit balances.

Entry 3

J. Doe, Capital	64,000	
Income Summary		64,000

To close Income Summary account.

PROBLEMS

Group A

3A-1 The transactions during October for Niles Plumbers included the following:
(*1*) On October 1, paid $320 cash for the month's rent.
(*2*) On October 3, made repairs for First National Bank and collected in full the charge of $507.
(*3*) On October 8, performed repair work for American Home Builders. Sent bill for $666 for services rendered.
(*4*) On October 15, placed an advertisement in the *Tribune* at a cost of $155, payment to be made within 30 days.
(*5*) On October 21, Jack Niles, owner of Niles Plumbers, withdrew $528 from the business for his personal use.
(*6*) On October 30, received a check for $666 from American Home Builders.
(*7*) On October 31, sent check to the *Tribune* in payment of liability incurred on October 15.

Instructions
a Write an analysis of each transaction. An example of the type of analysis desired is as follows:
(*1*) (*a*) Rent is an operating expense. Expenses are recorded by debits. Debit Rent Expense, $320.
(*b*) The asset Cash was decreased. Decreases in assets are recorded by credits. Credit cash, $320.
b Prepare a journal entry (including explanation) for each of the above transactions.

3A-2 Shown on page 110 in alphabetical order are the ledger accounts and dollar balances required to prepare an adjusted trial balance for Anderson Insurance Agency at November 30, 19____ .

Accounts payable	$ 1,242	Depreciation expense:		
Accounts receivable	1,011	building	$	165
Accumulated depreciation:		Depreciation expense:		
building	495	office equipment		150
Accumulated depreciation:		Land		37,125
office equipment	450	Lighting expense		534
Advertising expense	594	Notes payable		30,300
Bob Anderson, capital	111,000	Office equipment		18,000
Building	79,200	Salaries expense		3,462
Cash	14,100	Telephone expense		300
Commissions earned	11,154			

Instructions
a Prepare an adjusted trial balance with the accounts arranged in the *customary sequence* of ledger accounts.
b Prepare an income statement for the month ended November 30, 19____.
c Prepare a balance sheet in report form.

3A-3 During the month of June, 19____, John Trent organized and began to operate an air taxi service to provide air transportation from a major city to a number of small towns not served by scheduled airlines. Transactions during the month of June were as follows:

June 1 John Trent deposited $480,000 cash in a bank account in the name of the business, Trent Air Service.
June 2 Purchased an aircraft for $356,400 and spare parts for $42,000, paying cash.
June 4 Paid $540 cash to rent a building for June.
June 10 Cash receipts from passengers for the first 10 days amounted to $10,320.
June 14 Paid $750 to Motor Maintenance Service for maintenance and repair service for June.
June 15 Paid $2,880 to employees for services rendered during first half of June.
June 20 Cash receipts from passengers for the second 10 days amounted to $12,480.
June 30 Cash receipts from passengers for the last 10 days of June amounted to $20,100.
June 30 Paid $2,880 to employees for services rendered during the second half of June.
June 30 Trent withdrew $1,920 from business for his personal use.
June 30 Received a fuel bill from Phillips Oil Company amounting to $4,548 to be paid before July 10.

The account titles and numbers used by Trent Air Service are as follows:

Cash	11	Fares revenue	51
Spare parts	14	Maintenance expense	61
Aircraft	21	Fuel expense	62
Accounts payable	31	Salaries expense	63
John Trent, capital	41	Rent expense	64
John Trent, drawing	42		

Instructions Based on the foregoing transactions
a Prepare journal entries. (Number journal pages to permit cross reference to ledger.)
b Post to ledger accounts. (Number ledger accounts to permit cross reference to

journal.) Enter ledger account numbers in the LP column of the journal as the posting work is done.

c Prepare a trial balance at June 30, 19 ___ .

3A-4 Plaza Parking System was organized on March 1 for the purpose of operating an automobile parking lot. Included in the company's ledger are the following ledger accounts and their identification numbers.

Cash	11	*Howard Ward, drawing*	42
Land	21	*Parking fees earned*	51
Notes Payable	31	*Advertising expense*	61
Accounts Payable	32	*Utilities expense*	63
Howard Ward, capital	41	*Salaries expense*	65

The business was organized and operations were begun during the month of March. Transactions during March were as follows:

Mar. 1 Howard Ward deposited $102,000 cash in a bank account in the name of the business, the Plaza Parking System.

Mar. 2 Purchased land for $90,000, of which $54,000 was paid in cash. A short-term note payable (without interest) was issued for the balance of $36,000.

Mar. 2 An arrangement was made with the Century Club to provide parking privileges for its customers. Century Club agreed to pay $660 monthly, payable in advance. Cash was collected for the month of March.

Mar. 7 Arranged with Times Printing Company for a regular advertisement in the *Times* at a monthly cost of $114. Paid for advertising during March by check, $114.

Mar. 15 Parking receipts for the first half of the month were $1,836, exclusive of the monthly fee from Century Club.

Mar. 31 Received bill for light and power from Pacific Power Company in the amount of $78, to be paid before April 10.

Mar. 31 Paid $720 to the parking attendant for services rendered during the month. (Payroll taxes are to be ignored.)

Mar. 31 Parking receipts for the second half of the month amounted to $1,682.

Mar. 31 Ward withdrew $1,080 for his personal use.

Mar. 31 Paid $12,000 cash on the note payable incurred with the purchase of land.

Instructions
a Journalize the March transactions.
b Post to ledger accounts.
c Prepare a trial balance at March 31.
d Prepare an income statement and a balance sheet in report form.

3A-5 Shortly after completing his medical education, John Lawson established his own medical practice in his home town on October 1. A trial balance at October 1, 19 ___ is shown on page 112. Some related information follows.

The useful life of the medical equipment was estimated to be 5 years (60 months), and of the office equipment 8 years (96 months).

Instructions
a Prepare adjusting entries at October 31 to record depreciation for October of the medical equipment and the office equipment.
b Prepare an adjusted trial balance at October 31.
c Prepare an income statement and a balance sheet in report form.
d Prepare closing entries.
e Prepare an after-closing trial balance.

JOHN LAWSON, M.D.
Trial Balance
October 31, 19____

	Debit	Credit
Cash	$ 4,752	
Accounts receivable	1,368	
Medical equipment	31,320	
Office equipment	1,728	
Notes payable		$30,384
Accounts payable		563
John Lawson, capital		9,000
John Lawson, drawing	1,710	
Professional fees earned		5,220
Rent expense	540	
Medical supplies expense	666	
Electricity expense	32	
Salaries expense	2,934	
Insurance expense	117	
	$45,167	$45,167

3A-6 On June 1, 19____, Scott Miller organized Coast Moving Company to provide long-distance moving of household furniture. The transactions shown below and on page 113 occurred during June and were recorded in the following ledger accounts.

Cash	1	Accounts payable		30
Accounts receivable	3	Scott Miller, capital		50
Land	5	Scott Miller, drawing		51
Buildings	7	Income summary		60
Accumulated depreciation:		Moving service revenue		62
Buildings	8	Salaries expense		70
Trucks	10	Gasoline expense		72
Accumulated depreciation:		Repairs expense		74
Trucks	11	Depreciation expense:		
Office equipment	13	buildings		76
Accumulated depreciation:		Depreciation expense:		
Office equipment	14	trucks		78
		Depreciation expense:		
		office equipment		80

June 1 Miller deposited $240,000 cash in a bank account in the name of the business, Coast Moving Company.

June 3 Purchased land and building for a total price of $146,400, of which $60,000 was applicable to the land, and $86,400 to the building. Paid cash for full amount.

June 5 Purchased three trucks from Dawson Motors at a cost of $34,560 each. A cash down payment of $48,000 was made, the balance to be paid by July 12.

June 6 Purchased office equipment for cash, $5,760.

June 6 Moved furniture for Mr. and Mrs. David Hart from San Diego to Boston for $4,044. Collected $1,164 in cash, balance to be paid within 30 days (credit Moving Service Revenue).

June 11 Moved furniture for various clients for $7,764. Collected $4,404 in cash, balance to be paid within 30 days.

June 15 Paid salaries to employees for first half of the month, $3,624.

June 24 Moved furniture for various clients for a total of $6,480. Cash collected in full.

June 30 Salaries expense for the second half of month amounted to $3,180.

June 30 Received a gasoline bill for the month of June from Atlantic Oil Company in the amount of $4,200, to be paid before July 10.

June 30 Received bill of $300 for repair work on trucks during June by Century Motor Company.

June 30 The owner, Scott Miller, withdrew $1,440 cash for his personal use.

Miller estimated a useful life of 20 years for the building, 4 years for the trucks, and 10 years for the office equipment.

Instructions

a Prepare journal entries. (Number journal pages and enter the proper journal page number in the "Ref" column of the ledger accounts as each debit or credit is posted.)

b Post to ledger accounts. (As each journal entry is posted to the ledger, enter the identification number of the ledger account debited or credited in the "LP" column of the journal. This will show that the amount has been posted and will provide a cross reference between journal and ledger.)

c Prepare a trial balance as of June 30, 19____.

d Prepare adjusting entries and post to ledger accounts.

e Prepare an adjusted trial balance.

f Prepare an income statement for June, and a balance sheet at June 30, 19____, in report form.

g Prepare closing entries and post to ledger accounts.

h Prepare an after-closing trial balance.

Group B

3B-1 The transactions during July for Cross Travel Service included the following:

(*1*) On July 1, paid $450 for office rent for July.

(*2*) On July 2, Cross Travel Service placed an advertisement in the Travel section of the *New York News,* payment to be made in 30 days in the amount of $297.

(*3*) On July 4, fly-now, pay-later Pacific tours were arranged for several clients. Far-East Airlines agreed to pay Cross Travel Service $675 as a commission for arranging the tours, payment to be made as soon as client travel agreements were confirmed.

(*4*) On July 11, Louise Johnson, owner of Cross Travel Service, withdrew $225 from the business for personal use.

(*5*) On July 22, cash in the amount of $675 was collected from Far-East Airlines.

(*6*) On July 31, an invoice in the amount of $78 was received, payable August 10, for telephone service during July.

Instructions

a Write an analysis of each transaction. The following example will illustrate an *analysis* of a transaction using (*1*) above as an example.

   (*1*) (*a*) Rent is an operating expense. Expenses are recorded by debits. Debit Rent Expense, $450.

      (*b*) The asset Cash was decreased. Decreases in assets are recorded by credits. Credit Cash, $450.

b Prepare a journal entry (including explanation) for each of the above transactions.

3B-2 The Three Knights, a musical group, was organized as a partnership on September 1 to provide music at various functions. The three partners were Paul Knight, James Lee, and Carl Day. During September the following transactions occurred.

Sept. 1 Knight, Lee, and Day each deposited $1,600 (a total of $4,800) in a bank account in the name of the business, the Three Knights. (Use three separate capital accounts.)

Sept. 2 Three Knights purchased musical instruments from Webster Music, Inc., for $3,200. A cash down payment of $1,600 was made, the balance to be paid in 60 days.

Sept. 6 Purchased a used automobile for $2,000, paying cash.

Sept. 8 Retained Music Ltd. as exclusive agents for the Three Knights. The arrangement called for a flat $120 monthly retainer fee plus 10% of gross fees earned, to be paid on last day of every month. The $120 fee was paid on this date (debit Promotion Expense).

Sept. 10 Fees from appearances before various organizations for the first ten days of September amounted to $1,320. Cash was collected.

Sept. 18 Signed an agreement with Coral Tree Racquet Club to provide music for the regular Saturday dances and also at other parties (not to exceed two per month) scheduled by the club. The agreement covered a period of four months, beginning October 1, and provided for a maximum cost to the club of $5,760.

Sept. 20 Fees from appearances for the second ten days of September amounted to $960. Cash was collected.

Sept. 30 Paid gasoline bill for month, $64.

Sept. 30 Fees from appearances for last ten days of September amounted to $840. Cash was collected.

Sept. 30 Paid Music, Ltd., 10% of the gross fees earned during the month.

Sept. 30 Each partner withdrew $800 for personal use. (Use a separate drawing account for each partner.)

Instructions

a Journalize the above transactions. (Number journal pages to permit cross reference to ledger.)

b Post to ledger accounts. (Number accounts consecutively, beginning with no. 8, and enter account number in "LP" column of journal as each posting is made.)

c Prepare a trial balance as of September 30, 19____.

3B-3 John Adams, after several years of employment in the television industry, resigned from his job and invested his time and money in a new business, Adams TV Repair. The new business opened its doors to customers for the first time on July 1, 19____. The accounting policy followed by Adams was to close the accounts and prepare financial statements at the end of each month. A trial balance prepared at September 30, 19____ is shown on page 115.

Depreciation of the building was based on an estimated useful life of 25 years. Useful life of the equipment was estimated to be 5 years.

Instructions

a Prepare journal entries at September 30 to record depreciation for the month of September.

b Prepare an *adjusted* trial balance at September 30, 19____.

c Prepare an income statement for the month ended September 30, 19____, and a balance sheet in report form.

d If the company had overlooked the need for recording depreciation for September, what effect, if any, would this oversight have had upon the income statement and the balance sheet?

e Adams wants to compare the earnings from the business with what he earned when working as a salaried employee. Before starting his own business, Adams

ADAMS TV REPAIR
Trial Balance
September 30, 19___

Cash	$ 2,528	
Accounts receivable	1,456	
Land	29,400	
Building	50,400	
Accumulated depreciation: building		$ 336
Repair equipment	6,720	
Accumulated depreciation: repair equipment		224
Notes payable		28,000
Accounts payable		840
John Adams, capital		58,800
John Adams, drawing	1,414	
Repair service revenue		8,520
Advertising expense	154	
Repair parts expense	728	
Utilities expense	140	
Wages expense	3,780	
	$96,720	$96,720

had earned a monthly salary of $1,500 and had on deposit in a bank the amount of $58,800 which paid interest at an annual rate of 5%. Explain how the results of operations for September compare with the income (salary and interest) Adams would have received if he had continued work as a salaried employee and had kept his $58,800 of savings in an interest-bearing bank account rather than investing it to start his own business.

3B-4 Listed below are the balance sheet accounts at March 1, Year 5, and the adjusted trial balance at March 31, Year 5, for Blue Mountain Resort.

	March 1		March 31	
Cash	$ 18,600		$ 21,480	
Accounts receivable	40,020		33,600	
Supplies on hand	3,180		2,640	
Equipment	20,760		22,800	
Accumulated depreciation: equipment		$ 4,320		$ 4,560
Accounts payable		2,580		660
Notes payable		19,200		4,200
Ruth Park, capital		56,460		56,460
Ruth Park, drawing			9,600	
Revenue				52,800
Operating expenses			28,200	
Depreciation expense: equipment			240	
Interest expense			120	
	$82,560	$82,560	$118,680	$118,680

All revenue is recorded in Accounts Receivable. No supplies were purchased in March.

Instructions

a Prepare journal entries without dates to summarize the events that occurred during the month of March. Use one entry for all transactions of a particular type; for example, the first entry should be to summarize all revenue earned during March. This entry will consist of a debit to Accounts Receivable and a credit to Revenue for $52,800. This entry will account in full for the increase in the balance of the Revenue account during March and in part for the change in Accounts Receivable during the month. In a similar manner, one entry can be prepared to record all cash collections of accounts receivable during March. Do not use any accounts that do not appear in the adjusted trial balance at March 31.

b Prepare an after-closing trial balance at March 31, Year 5.

3B-5 The operations of Bayview Realty consist of obtaining listings of houses being offered for sale by owners, advertising these houses, and showing them to prospective buyers. The company earns revenue in the form of commissions. The building and office equipment used in the business were acquired on January 1 of the current year and were immediately placed in use. Useful life of the building was estimated to be 30 years and that of the office equipment 8 years. The company closes its accounts monthly; on March 31 of the current year, the trial balance is as follows:

BAYVIEW REALTY

Trial Balance

March 31, 19____

	Debit	Credit
Cash	$ 6,480	
U.S. government bonds	8,784	
Accounts receivable	5,160	
Land	22,800	
Building	64,800	
Accumulated depreciation: building		$ 360
Office equipment	23,040	
Accumulated depreciation: office equipment		480
Notes payable		72,000
Accounts payable		10,374
Ellen Norton, capital		45,191
Ellen Norton, drawing	1,800	
Commissions earned		19,344
Advertising expense	600	
Automobile rental expense	540	
Salaries expense	13,356	
Telephone expense	389	
	$147,749	$147,749

Instructions   From the trial balance and supplementary data given, prepare the following as of March 31, 19____.

a Adjusting entries for depreciation of building and of office equipment (building $64,800 ÷ 30 years × $\frac{1}{12}$).

b Adjusted trial balance.

c Income statement for the month of March and a balance sheet at March 31 in report form.

d Closing entries.

e After-closing trial balance.

3B-6 Richard Lund, M.D., after completing his medical education, established his own practice on May 1. The following transactions occurred during the first month.

May   1 Lund opened a bank account in the name of his practice, Richard Lund, M.D., by making a deposit of $7,800.

May   1 Paid office rent for May, $455.

May   2 Purchased office equipment for cash, $2,496.

May   3 Purchased medical equipment from Niles Instruments, Inc., at a cost of $10,530. A cash down payment of $1,430 was made and a note payable was signed which required a payment of $4,550 on July 3 of the current year and a final payment of $4,550 on September 2.

May   3 Retained by Brandon Merchandising, Inc., to be on call for emergency service at a monthly fee of $195. The fee for May was collected in cash.

May 15 Excluding the retainer of May 3, fees earned during the first 15 days of the month amounted to $813, of which $137 was in cash and $676 was in accounts receivable.

May 15 Paid Mary Hester, R.N., her salary for the first half of May, $585.

May 16 Dr. Lund withdrew $975 for his personal use.

May 19 Treated Michael Tracy for injuries received in an accident during his employment at Brandon Merchandising, Inc. Completed medical portions of insurance and industrial accident reports.

May 27 Treated Cynthia Knight, who paid $13 cash for an office visit and who agreed to pay $31 on June 1 for laboratory medical tests completed May 27.

May 31 Excluding the treatment of Cynthia Knight on May 27, fees earned during the last half of month amounted to $1,378, of which $273 was in cash and $1,105 was in accounts receivable.

May 31 Paid Mary Hester, R.N., $585 salary for the second half of month.

May 31 Received a bill from McGraw Medical Supplies in the amount of $312, representing the amount of medical supplies used during May. (Debit Medical Supplies Expense.)

May 31 Paid utilities bill for the month, $43.

Other information Dr. Lund estimated the useful life of medical instruments at 9 years and of office equipment at 8 years. The account titles to be used and the account numbers are as follows:

Cash	10	*Richard Lund, capital*	40
Accounts receivable	13	*Richard Lund, drawing*	41
Medical instruments	20	*Income summary*	45
Accumulated depreciation:		*Fees earned*	49
medical instruments	21	*Medical supplies expense*	50
Office equipment	22	*Rent expense*	51
Accumulated depreciation:		*Salaries expense*	52
office equipment	23	*Utilities expense*	53
Notes payable	30	*Depreciation expense:*	
Accounts payable	31	*medical instruments*	54
		Depreciation expense:	
		office equipment	55

Instructions
a Journalize the above transactions. (Number journal pages to permit cross reference to ledger.)
b Post to ledger accounts. (Use running balance form of ledger account. Number ledger accounts to permit cross reference to journal.)
c Prepare a trial balance at May 31, 19____.
d Prepare adjusting entries and post to ledger accounts. (Round amounts to nearest dollar.)
e Prepare an adjusted trial balance.
f Prepare an income statement and a balance sheet in report form.
g Prepare closing entries and post to ledger accounts.
h Prepare an after-closing trial balance.

BUSINESS DECISION PROBLEM 3

Tom Doyle, owner of a small business called Lawn Service Company, has accepted a salaried position overseas and is trying to interest you in buying his business. He describes the operating results of the business as follows: "The business has been in existence for only 18 months, but the growth trend is very impressive. Just look at these figures."

	Cash Collections from Customers
First six-month period	$30,000
Second six-month period	40,000
Third six-month period	45,000

"I think you'll agree those figures show real growth," Doyle concluded.
   You then asked Doyle whether sales were made only for cash or on both a cash and credit basis. He replied as follows:
   "At first we sold both for cash and on open account. In the first six months we made total sales of $50,000 and 70% of those sales were made on credit. We had $20,000 of accounts receivable at the end of the first six-month period.
   "During the second six-month period, we tried to discourage selling on credit because of the extra paper work involved and the time required to follow up on slow-paying customers. Our sales on credit in that second six-month period amounted to $17,500, and our total accounts receivable were down to $15,000 at the end of that period.
   "During the third six-month period we made sales only for cash. Although we prefer to operate on a cash basis only, we did very well at collecting receivables. We collected in full from every customer to whom we ever sold on credit and we don't have a dollar of accounts receivable at this time."

Instructions
a Do you consider Doyle's explanation of the "growth trend" of cash collections to be a well-founded portrayal of the progress of his business? Explain fully any criticism you may have of Doyle's line of reasoning.
b To facilitate your reaching a decision, it is suggested that you compile data for each of the three six-month periods under review, using the following column headings for the analysis:

(1) Sales on Credit	(2) Collections on Accounts Receivable	(3) Ending Balance of Accounts Receivable	(4) Sales for Cash	(5) Total Cash Collections from Customers	(6) (1) + (4) Total Sales
First six months					
Second six months					
Third six months					

4

Completion of the Accounting Cycle

Accounting periods and financial statements

For the purpose of making accounting measurements and preparing financial statements, the life of a business is divided into accounting periods of equal length. Since accounting periods are equal in length, we can fairly compare the revenue and expenses of the current period with the revenue and expenses of prior periods and determine whether our operating results are improving or declining. Accounting thus provides a scorekeeping service. If this year's operations set a new record, the accounting system will tell us so.

As explained in Chapter 3, the term *accounting period* means the span of time covered by an income statement. The usual accounting period for which complete financial statements are prepared and distributed to public investors, bankers, and government agencies is one year. The measurement and reporting of taxable income to the Internal Revenue Service by corporations and individuals is also on an annual basis. However, most businesses also prepare quarterly and monthly financial statements so that management will be currently informed on the profitability of the business from month to month.

At the end of an accounting period, adjustments of some of the account balances in the ledger must be made before financial statements are prepared. Adjusting entries are necessary, for example, because the recorded costs of buildings and office equipment are gradually expiring with the passage of time. Before financial statements are prepared, the accounts must be brought up to date with respect to depreciation and several other items.

To serve the needs of management, investors, bankers, and other groups, financial statements must be as complete and accurate as possible. The balance sheet must contain all the assets and liabilities at the close of business on the last day of the period. The income statement must contain all the revenue and expenses applicable to the period covered but must not contain any revenue or expenses relating to the following period. In other words, a precise *cutoff* of transactions at the end of the period is essential to the preparation of accurate financial statements.

Apportioning transactions between accounting periods

Some business transactions are begun and completed within a single accounting period, but many other transactions are begun in one accounting period and concluded in a later period. For example, a building purchased this year may last for 25 years; during each of those 25 years a fair share of the cost of the building should be recognized as expense. The making of *adjusting entries* to record the depreciation expense applicable to a given accounting period was illustrated in the preceding chapter. Let us now consider all types of transactions which overlap two or more accounting periods and therefore require adjusting entries.

PRINCIPAL TYPES OF TRANSACTIONS
REQUIRING ADJUSTING ENTRIES

The various kinds of transactions requiring adjusting entries at the end of the period may be classified into the following groups:

1 Recorded costs which must be apportioned between two or more accounting periods. Example: the cost of a building.
2 Recorded revenue which must be apportioned between two or more accounting periods. Example: commissions collected in advance for services to be rendered in future periods.
3 Unrecorded expenses. Example: wages earned by employees after the last payday in an accounting period.
4 Unrecorded revenue. Example: commissions earned but not yet collected or billed to customers.

To demonstrate these various types of adjusting entries, the illustration of the Roberts Real Estate Company will be continued for November. We shall consider in detail only those November transactions relating to adjusting entries. The routine operating transactions during November such as the earning of sales commissions and payment of expenses are not considered individually, but their overall effect is shown in the November 30 trial balance included in the work sheet on page 130.

Recorded costs apportioned between accounting periods

When a business concern makes an expenditure that will benefit more than one period, the amount is usually debited to an asset account. At the end of each period which benefits from the expenditure, an appropriate portion of the cost is transferred from the asset account to an expense account.

PREPAID EXPENSES Payments in advance are often made for such items as insurance, rent, and office supplies. At the end of the accounting period, a portion of the services or supplies probably will have expired or will have been consumed, but another portion will be unexpired or unused. That portion of the economic benefits from the expenditure which *has expired or has been consumed is an expense of the current period.* However, the *unexpired or unused portion of the economic benefits from the expenditure represents an asset* at the balance sheet date which will not become expense (expired cost) until a later accounting period.

INSURANCE On November 1, the Roberts Real Estate Company paid $540 for a three-year fire insurance policy covering the building. This expenditure was debited to an asset account by the following journal entry:

Expenditure for insurance policy recorded as asset

Unexpired Insurance	540	
Cash		540
Purchased three-year fire insurance policy.		

Since this expenditure of $540 will protect the company against fire loss for three years, the cost of protection each year is $\frac{1}{3}$ of $540, or $180. The insurance expense applicable to each month's operations is $\frac{1}{12}$ of the annual expense, or $15. In order that the accounting records for November show insurance expense of $15, the following adjusting entry is required at November 30:

Portion of asset expires (becomes expense)

Insurance Expense	15	
Unexpired Insurance		15
To record insurance expense for November.		

This adjusting entry serves two purposes: (1) it apportions the proper amount of insurance expense to November operations and (2) it reduces the asset account so that the correct amount of unexpired insurance will appear in the balance sheet at November 30. What would be the effect on the income statement for November if the above adjustment were not made? The expenses would be understated by $15 and consequently the net income would be overstated by $15. The balance sheet would also be affected by failure to make the adjustment: the assets would be overstated by $15 and so would the owner's equity. The overstatement of the owner's equity would result from the overstated amount of net income transferred to Roberts' capital account when the accounts were closed at November 30.

OFFICE SUPPLIES On November 2, the Roberts Real Estate Company purchased a sufficient quantity of stationery and other office supplies to last for several months. The cost of the supplies was $720, and this amount was debited to an asset account by the following journal entry:

Expendi-
ture for
office
supplies
recorded
as asset

Office Supplies	*720*	
Cash		*720*
Purchased office supplies.		

No entries were made during November to record the day-to-day usage of office supplies, but on November 30 a careful count was made of the supplies still on hand. This count, or physical inventory, showed unused supplies with a cost of $600. It is apparent, therefore, that supplies costing $120 were used during November. An adjusting entry is made on the basis of the November 30 count, debiting an expense account $120 (the cost of supplies consumed during November), and reducing the asset account by $120 to show that only $600 worth of office supplies remained on hand at November 30.

Portion of
supplies
used
represents
expense

Office Supplies Expense	*120*	
Office Supplies		*120*
To record consumption of office supplies in November.		

The Office Supplies account will appear in the balance sheet as an asset; the Office Supplies Expense account will be shown in the income statement. How would failure to make this adjustment affect the financial statements? In the income statement for November, the expenses would be understated by $120 and the net income overstated by the same amount. Since the overstated amount for net income in November would be transferred into the owner's capital account in the process of closing the accounts, the owner's equity section of the balance sheet would be overstated by $120. Assets would also be overstated because Office Supplies would be listed at $120 too much.

When payments for insurance, office supplies, and rent are expected to provide economic benefits for more than one accounting period, the advance payment is usually recorded by a debit to an asset account such as Unexpired Insurance or Office Supplies, as shown in the preceding examples. However, the advance payment *could* be recorded by debiting an expense account such as Insurance Expense. At the end of the period, the adjusting entry would then consist of a debit to Unexpired Insurance and a credit to Insurance Expense. This alternative method would lead to the same amounts in the balance sheet and income statement as the method previously illustrated. Under both procedures, we would be treating as an expense of the current period the cost of the economic benefits consumed, and carrying forward as an asset the cost of the economic benefits applicable to future periods.

DEPRECIATION OF BUILDING   The November 30 journal entry to record depreciation of the building used by the Roberts Real Estate Company is exactly the same as the October 31 entry explained in Chapter 3.

Cost of building is gradually converted to expense

Depreciation Expense: Building *150*
       Accumulated Depreciation: Building *150*
To record depreciation for November.

This allocation of depreciation expense to November operations is based on the following facts: the building cost $36,000 and is estimated to have a useful life of 20 years (240 months). Using the straight-line method of depreciation, the portion of the original cost which expires each month is $\frac{1}{240}$ of $36,000, or $150.

The Accumulated Depreciation: Building account now has a credit balance of $300 as a result of the October and November credits of $150 each. The book value of the building is $35,700, that is, the original cost of $36,000 minus the accumulated depreciation of $300. The term *book value* means the net amount at which an asset is shown in the accounting records, as distinguished from its market value. *Carrying value* is an alternative term, with the same meaning as book value.

DEPRECIATION OF OFFICE EQUIPMENT   The November 30 adjusting entry to record depreciation of the office equipment is the same as the entry for depreciation a month earlier, as shown in Chapter 3.

Cost of office equipment gradually converted to expense

Depreciation Expense: Office Equipment *45*
       Accumulated Depreciation: Office Equipment *45*
To record depreciation for November.

Original cost of the office equipment was $5,400, and the estimated useful life was 10 years (120 months). Depreciation each month under the straight-line method is therefore $\frac{1}{120}$ of $5,400, or $45. What is the book value of the office equipment at this point? Original cost of $5,400 minus accumulated depreciation of $90 for two months leaves a book value of $5,310.

What would be the effect on the financial statements if the adjusting entries for depreciation of the building and office equipment were omitted at November 30? In the income statement the expenses would be understated by $195 ($150 depreciation of building and $45 depreciation of office equipment), and net income for the month would be overstated by $195. In the balance sheet the assets would be overstated by $195, the owner's equity would be overstated the same amount because of the $195 overstatement of the net income added to the capital account. If depreciation had not been recorded in either October or November, the overstatement in the balance sheet at November 30 would, of course, amount to $390 with respect both to assets and to owner's equity.

Recorded revenue apportioned between accounting periods

On November 1, James Fortune, a client of the Roberts Real Estate Company, asked Roberts to accept the responsibility of managing a considerable amount of rental properties. The duties consisted of keeping the buildings rented, arranging for repairs, and collecting rents which were to be deposited in Fortune's bank account. It was agreed that $300 a month would be a reasonable fee to the Roberts Real Estate Company for its services. Since Fortune was leaving the country on an extended trip, he paid the company for six months' service in advance at the time of signing the agreement. The journal entry to record the transaction on November 1 was as follows:

Commission collected but not yet earned

Cash	1,800	
Unearned Rental Commissions		1,800
Collected in advance six months' commissions for management of Fortune properties.		

Note that no service had been performed for the customer at the time the $1,800 was received. As emphasized in Chapter 3, not every receipt of cash represents revenue. In this case the receipt of cash represented an advance payment by the customer which obligated the Roberts Real Estate Company to render services in the future. Revenue is earned only by the *rendering* of services to customers, or the *delivering* of goods to them. A portion of the agreed services (one-sixth, to be exact) will be rendered during November, but it would be unreasonable to regard the entire $1,800 as revenue in that month. The commission is earned gradually over a period of six months as the Roberts Real Estate Company performs the required services. The $1,800 collected in advance is therefore credited to an *unearned revenue* account at the time of its receipt. Some accountants prefer the alternative term *deferred revenue.* At the end of each month, an amount of $300 will be transferred from unearned revenue to an earned revenue account by means of an adjusting entry. The first in this series of transfers will be made at November 30 as follows:

Entry to recognize earning of a part of commission

Unearned Rental Commissions	300	
Rental Commissions Earned		300
Commission earned from Fortune property management in November.		

The $1,500 credit balance remaining in the Unearned Rental Commissions account represents an obligation to render $1,500 worth of services in future months; therefore, it belongs on the balance sheet in the liability section. An unearned revenue account differs from other liabilities since it will ordinarily be settled by the rendering of services rather than by making a cash payment, but it is nevertheless a liability. The Rental Commissions Earned account is shown in the income statement as revenue for the month.

Unrecorded expenses

Adjusting entries are necessary at the end of each accounting period to record any expenses which have been incurred but not recognized in the accounts. Salaries of employees and interest on borrowed money are common examples of expenses which accumulate day by day but which may not be recorded until the end of the period. These expenses are said to *accrue,* that is, to grow or accumulate.

ACCRUAL OF INTEREST   On November 1, the Roberts Real Estate Company borrowed the sum of $3,000 from a bank. Banks require every borrower to sign a *promissory note,* that is, a formal, written promise to repay the amount borrowed plus interest at an agreed future date. (Various forms of notes in common use and the accounting problems involved will be discussed more fully in Chapter 9.) The note signed by Roberts, with certain details omitted, is shown below. A 6% annual interest rate is used in this illustration to make the calculations simple. Banks are currently charging interest rates considerably above 6%.

Note payable issued to bank

$3,000 Los Angeles, California November 1, 19——	
Three months .... *after date* .... I .... *promise to pay*	
to the order of .... American National Bank	
————Three thousand and no/100———— .... *dollars*	
for value received, with interest at .... 6 per cent	
Roberts Real Estate Company	
By .... *James Roberts*	

The note payable is a liability of the Roberts Real Estate Company, similar to an account payable but different in that a formal written promise to pay is required and interest is charged on the amount borrowed. A Notes Payable account is credited when the note is issued; the Notes Payable account will be debited three months later when the note is paid. Interest accrues throughout the life of the note payable, but it is not payable until the note matures on February 1. To the bank making the loan, the note signed by Roberts is an asset, a note receivable. The revenue earned by banks consists largely of interest charged to borrowers.

The journal entry made on November 1 to record the borrowing of $3,000 from the bank was as follows:

Entry when bank loan is obtained

Cash	*3,000*	
Notes Payable		*3,000*
Obtained from bank three-month loan with interest at 6% a year.		

No payment of interest was made during November, but one month's interest expense, or $15 ($3,000 × 0.06 × $\frac{1}{12}$), was incurred during the month. The following adjusting entry is made at November 30 to charge November operations with one month's interest expense and also to record the amount of interest owed to the bank at the end of November.

<table>
<tr><td>*Entry for*</td><td>Interest Expense</td><td>. . . . .</td><td>*15*</td><td></td></tr>
<tr><td>*interest*</td><td></td><td>Interest Payable . . . .</td><td></td><td>*15*</td></tr>
<tr><td>*expense*</td><td></td><td></td><td></td><td></td></tr>
<tr><td>*incurred*</td><td colspan="4">To record interest expense applicable to November.</td></tr>
<tr><td>*in*</td><td></td></tr>
<tr><td>*November*</td><td></td></tr>
</table>

The debit balance in the Interest Expense account will appear in the November income statement; the credit balances in the Interest Payable and Notes Payable accounts will be shown in the balance sheet as liabilities. These two liability accounts will remain in the records until the maturity date of the loan, at which time a cash payment to the bank will wipe out both the Notes Payable account and the Interest Payable account.

ACCRUAL OF SALARY On November 20, Roberts hired Carl Nelson as a part-time salesman whose duties were to work evenings calling on property owners to secure listings of property for sale or rent. The agreed salary was $225 for a five-evening week, payable each Friday; payment for the first week was made on Friday, November 24.

Assume that the last day of the accounting period, November 30, fell on Thursday. Nelson had worked four evenings since being paid the preceding Friday and therefore had earned $180($\frac{4}{5}$ × $225). In order that this $180 of November salary expense be reflected in the accounts before the financial statements are prepared, an adjusting entry is necessary at November 30. Personal income taxes and other taxes relating to payroll are ignored in this illustration.

<table>
<tr><td>*Salaries*</td><td>Sales Salaries Expense</td><td>. . . . .</td><td>*180*</td><td></td></tr>
<tr><td>*expense*</td><td></td><td>Sales Salaries Payable . . . .</td><td></td><td>*180*</td></tr>
<tr><td>*incurred*</td><td></td><td></td><td></td><td></td></tr>
<tr><td>*but unpaid*</td><td colspan="4">To record salary expense and related liability to salesman for last</td></tr>
<tr><td>*at Novem-*</td><td colspan="4">four evenings' work in November.</td></tr>
<tr><td>*ber 30*</td><td></td></tr>
</table>

The debit balance in the Sales Salaries Expense account will appear as an expense in the November income statement; the credit balance in the Sales Salaries Payable account is the amount owing to the salesman for work performed during the last four days of November and will appear among the liabilities on the balance sheet at November 30.

The next regular payday for Nelson will be Friday, December 1, which is the first day of the new accounting period. Since the accounts were adjusted and closed on November 30, all the revenue and expense accounts have zero balances at the beginning of business on December 1. The payment of a week's salary to Nelson will be recorded by the following entry on December 1:

Payment of salaries incurred in two accounting periods

Sales Salaries Payable	180	
Sales Salaries Expense	45	
Cash		225

Paid weekly salary to salesman.

Note that the net result of the November 30 accrual entry has been to split the salesman's weekly salary expense between November and December. Four days of the work week fell in November, so four days' pay, or $180, was recognized as November expense. One day of the work week fell in December so $45 was recorded as December expense.

No accrual entry is necessary for office salaries in the Roberts Real Estate Company because Roberts regularly pays the office employees on the last working day of the month.

Unrecorded revenue

The treatment of unrecorded revenue is similar to that of unrecorded expenses. Any revenue which has been earned but not recorded during the accounting period should be recognized in the accounts by means of an adjusting entry, debiting an asset account and crediting a revenue account. *Accrued revenue* is a term often used to describe revenue which has been accumulating during the period but which has not been recorded prior to the closing date.

On November 16, the Roberts Real Estate Company entered into a management agreement with Henry Clayton, the owner of several office buildings. The company agreed to manage the Clayton properties for a commission of $240 a month, payable on the fifteenth of each month. No entry is made in the accounting records at the time of signing the contract, because no services have yet been rendered and no change has occurred in assets or liabilities. The managerial duties were to begin immediately, but the first monthly commission would not be received until December 15. The following adjusting entry is therefore necessary at November 30:

Entry for commissions earned but uncollected

| Rental Commissions Receivable . . . . | 120 | |
| Rental Commissions Earned . . . . | | 120 |

To record revenue accrued from services rendered Henry Clayton during November.

The debit balance in the Rental Commissions Receivable account will be shown in the balance sheet as an asset. The credit balance of the Rental Commissions Earned account, including earnings from both the Fortune and Clayton contracts, will appear in the November income statement.

The collection of the first monthly commission from Clayton will occur in the next accounting period (December 15, to be exact). Of this $240 cash receipt, half represents collection of the asset account, Rental

Commissions Receivable, created at November 30 by the adjusting entry. The other half of the $240 cash receipt represents revenue earned during December; this should be credited to the December revenue account for Rental Commissions Earned. The entry on December 15 is as follows:

Commis-
sion
applicable
to two
account-
ing
periods

Cash	240	
Rental Commissions Receivable		120
Rental Commissions Earned		120

Collected commission for month ended December 15.

The net result of the November 30 accrual entry has been to divide the revenue from managing the Clayton properties between November and December in accordance with the timing of the services rendered.

Adjusting entries and the accrual basis of accounting

Adjusting entries help make accrual basis accounting work successfully. By preparing adjusting entries, we can recognize revenue in the accounting period in which it is earned and also bring into the accounts any unrecorded expenses which helped to produce that revenue. For example, an adjusting entry to record revenue which has been earned but has not been recorded or collected prior to the end of the period helps achieve our goal of an income statement which includes all the revenue earned in a given time period. Other adjusting entries cause expenses to be recorded in the accounting period in which the benefits from the expenditures are received, even though cash payment is made in an earlier or later period.

THE WORK SHEET

The work necessary at the end of an accounting period includes construction of a trial balance, journalizing and posting of adjusting entries, preparation of financial statements, and journalizing and posting of closing entries. So many details are involved in these end-of-period procedures that it is easy to make errors. If these errors are recorded in the journal and the ledger accounts, considerable time and effort can be wasted in correcting them. Both the journal and the ledger are formal, permanent records. They may be prepared manually in ink, produced on accounting machines, or created by a computer in a company utilizing electronic data processing equipment. One way of avoiding errors in the permanent accounting records and also of simplifying the work to be done at the end of the period is to use a **work sheet.**

A work sheet is a large columnar sheet of paper, especially designed to arrange in a convenient systematic form all the accounting data required at the end of the period. The work sheet is not a part of the permanent accounting records; it is prepared in pencil by accountants for their own convenience. If an error is made on the work sheet, it may be erased and corrected much more easily than an error in the formal accounting records. Furthermore, the work sheet is so designed as to minimize errors by automatically bringing to light many types of discrepancies which might otherwise be entered in the journal and posted to the ledger accounts. Dollar signs, decimal points, and commas are not used with the amounts entered on work sheets.

The work sheet may be thought of as a testing ground on which the ledger accounts are adjusted, balanced, and arranged in the general form of financial statements. The satisfactory completion of a work sheet provides considerable assurance that all the details of the end-of-period accounting procedures have been properly brought together. After this point has been established, the work sheet then serves as the source from which the formal financial statements are prepared and the adjusting and closing entries are made in the journal.

Preparing the work sheet

A commonly used form of work sheet with the appropriate headings for the Roberts Real Estate Company is illustrated on page 130. Note that the heading of the work sheet consists of three parts: (*1*) the name of the business, (*2*) the title Work Sheet, and (*3*) the period of time covered. The body of the work sheet contains five pairs of money columns, each pair consisting of a debit and a credit column. The procedures to be followed in preparing a work sheet will now be illustrated in five simple steps.

1 Enter the ledger account balances in the Trial Balance columns The titles and balances of the ledger accounts at November 30 are copied into the Trial Balance columns of the work sheet, as illustrated on page 130. In practice these amounts may be taken directly from the ledger. It would be a duplication of work to prepare a trial balance as a separate schedule and then to copy this information into the work sheet. As soon as the account balances have been listed on the work sheet, these two columns should be added and the totals entered.

2 Enter the adjustments in the Adjustments columns The required adjustments for the Roberts Real Estate Company have been explained earlier in this chapter; these same adjustments are now entered in the Adjustments columns of the work sheet. (See page 132.) As a cross reference, the debit and credit parts of each adjustment are keyed together by placing a key letter to the left of each amount. For example, the adjustment debiting Insurance Expense and crediting Unexpired Insurance is identified by the key letter (a). The use of the key letters makes it easy to match a debit entry in the Adjustments columns with its related credit. The identifying letters also key the debit and credit entries in the Adjustments columns to the brief explanations which appear at the bottom of the work sheet.

ROBERTS REAL ESTATE COMPANY
Work Sheet
For the Month Ended November 30, 19___

	Trial Balance		Adjustments		Adjusted Trial Balance		Income Statement		Balance Sheet	
	Dr	Cr	Dr	Cr	Dr	Cr	Dr	Cr	Dr	Cr
Cash	25,800									
Accounts receivable	6,990									
Unexpired insurance	540									
Office supplies	720									
Land	15,000									
Building	36,000									
Accumulated depreciation: building		150								
Office equipment	5,400									
Accumulated depreciation: office equipment		45								
Notes payable		3,000								
Accounts payable		23,595								
Unearned rental commissions		1,800								
James Roberts, capital		60,771								
James Roberts, drawing	1,500									
Sales commissions earned		5,484								
Advertising expense	1,275									
Office salaries expense	1,200									
Sales salaries expense	225									
Telephone expense	195									
	94,845	94,845								

Trial balance is entered in first pair of columns on work sheet

The titles of any accounts debited or credited in the adjusting entries but not listed in the trial balance are written on the work sheet below the trial balance. For example, Insurance Expense does not appear in the trial balance; it is written on the first available line below the trial balance totals. After all the adjustments have been entered in the Adjustments columns, this pair of columns must be totaled. Proving the equality of debit and credit totals tends to prevent arithmetical errors from being carried over into other columns of the work sheet.

3 Enter the account balances as adjusted in the Adjusted Trial Balance columns The work sheet as it appears after completion of the Adjusted Trial Balance columns is illustrated on page 133. Each account balance in the first pair of columns is combined with the adjustment, if any, in the second pair of columns, and the combined amount is entered in the Adjusted Trial Balance columns. This process of combining the items on each line throughout the first four columns of the work sheet requires horizontal addition or subtraction. It is called *cross footing,* in contrast to the addition of items in a vertical column, which is called *footing* the column.

For example, the Office Supplies account is seen to have a debit balance of $720 in the Trial Balance columns. This $720 debit amount is combined with the $120 credit appearing on the same line in the Adjustments column; the combination of a $720 debit with a $120 credit produces an adjusted debit amount of $600 in the Adjusted Trial Balance debit column. As another example, consider the Office Supplies Expense account. This account had no balance in the Trial Balance columns but shows a $120 debit in the Adjustments debit column. The combination of a zero starting balance and $120 debit adjustment produces a $120 debit amount in the Adjusted Trial Balance.

Many of the accounts in the trial balance are not affected by the adjustments made at the end of the month; the balances of these accounts (such as Cash, Land, Building, or Notes Payable in the illustrated work sheet) are entered in the Adjusted Trial Balance columns in exactly the same amounts as shown in the Trial Balance columns. After all the accounts have been extended into the Adjusted Trial Balance columns, This pair of columns is totaled to prove that no arithmetical errors have been made up to this point.

4 Extend each amount in the Adjusted Trial Balance columns into the Income Statement columns or into the Balance Sheet columns Assets, liabilities, and the owner's capital and drawing accounts are extended into the Balance Sheet columns; revenue and expense accounts are extended to the Income Statement columns. The process of extending amounts horizontally across the work sheet should begin with the account at the top of the work sheet, which is usually Cash. The cash figure is extended to the Balance Sheet debit column. Then the accountant goes down the work sheet line by line, extending each account balance to the appropriate Income Statement or Balance Sheet column. The likelihood of error is

ROBERTS REAL ESTATE COMPANY
Work Sheet
For the Month Ended November 30, 19____

	Trial Balance Dr	Trial Balance Cr	Adjustments* Dr	Adjustments* Cr	Adjusted Trial Balance Dr	Adjusted Trial Balance Cr	Income Statement Dr	Income Statement Cr	Balance Sheet Dr	Balance Sheet Cr
Cash	25,800									
Accounts receivable	6,990									
Unexpired insurance	540			(a) 15						
Office supplies	720			(b) 120						
Land	15,000									
Building	36,000									
Accumulated depreciation: building		150		(c) 150						
Office equipment	5,400									
Accumulated depreciation: office equipment		45		(d) 45						
Notes payable		3,000								
Accounts payable		23,595								
Unearned rental commissions		1,800	(e) 300							
James Roberts, capital		60,771								
James Roberts, drawing	1,500									
Sales commissions earned		5,484								
Advertising expense	1,275									
Office salaries expense	1,200									
Sales salaries expense	225		(g) 180							
Telephone expense	195									
	94,845	94,845								
Insurance expense			(a) 15							
Office supplies expense			(b) 120							
Depreciation expense: building			(c) 150							
Depreciation expense: office equipment			(d) 45							
Rental commissions earned				(e) 300						
				(h) 120						
Interest expense			(f) 15							
Interest payable				(f) 15						
Sales salaries payable				(g) 180						
Rental commissions receivable			(h) 120							
			945	945						

Explanatory footnotes keyed to adjustments

*Adjustments:
(a) Portion of insurance cost which expired during November
(b) Office supplies used during November
(c) Depreciation of building during November
(d) Depreciation of office equipment during November
(e) Earned one-sixth of the commission collected in advance on the Fortune properties
(f) Interest expense accrued during November on note payable
(g) Salesman's salary for last four days of November
(h) Rental commission accrued on Clayton contract in November

ROBERTS REAL ESTATE COMPANY
Work Sheet
For the Month Ended November 30, 19___

	Trial Balance		Adjustments *		Adjusted Trial Balance		Income Statement		Balance Sheet	
	Dr	Cr	Dr	Cr	Dr	Cr	Dr	Cr	Dr	Cr
Cash	25,800				25,800					
Accounts receivable	6,990				6,990					
Unexpired insurance	540			(a) 15	525					
Office supplies	720			(b) 120	600					
Land	15,000				15,000					
Building	36,000				36,000					
Accumulated depreciation: building		150		(c) 150		300				
Office equipment	5,400				5,400					
Accumulated depreciation: office equipment		45		(d) 45		90				
Notes payable		3,000				3,000				
Accounts payable		23,595				23,595				
Unearned rental commissions		1,800	(e) 300			1,500				
James Roberts, capital		60,771				60,771				
James Roberts, drawing	1,500				1,500					
Sales commissions earned		5,484				5,484				
Advertising expense	1,275				1,275					
Office salaries expense	1,200				1,200					
Sales salaries expense	225		(g) 180		405					
Telephone expense	195				195					
	94,845	94,845								
Insurance expense			(a) 15		15					
Office supplies expense			(b) 120		120					
Depreciation expense: building			(c) 150		150					
Depreciation expense: office equipment			(d) 45		45					
Rental commissions earned				(e) 300 (h) 120		420				
Interest expense			(f) 15		15					
Interest payable				(f) 15		15				
Sales salaries payable				(g) 180		180				
Rental commissions receivable			(h) 120		120					
			945	945	95,355	95,355				

Enter the adjusted amounts in columns 5 and 6 of work sheet

* Explanatory notes relating to adjustments are the same as on page 132.

much less when each account is extended in the order of its appearance on the work sheet, than if accounts are extended in random order.

The extension of amounts horizontally across the work sheet is merely a sorting of the accounts making up the Adjusted Trial Balance into the two categories of income statement accounts and balance sheet accounts. The work sheet as it appears after completion of this sorting process is illustrated on page 135. Note that each amount in the Adjusted Trial Balance columns is extended to one and only one of the four remaining columns.

5 Total the Income Statement columns and the Balance Sheet columns. Enter the net income or net loss as a balancing figure in both pairs of columns, and again compute column totals The work sheet as it appears after this final step is shown on page 136.

The net income or net loss for the period is determined by computing the difference between the totals of the two Income Statement columns. In the illustrated work sheet, the credit column total is the larger and the excess represents net income:

Income Statement credit column total (revenue)	*$5,904*
Income Statement debit column total (expenses)	*3,420*
Difference: net income for period	*$2,484*

Note on the work sheet that the net income of $2,484 is entered in the Income Statement *debit* column as a balancing figure and also on the same line as a balancing figure in the Balance Sheet *credit* column. The caption Net Income is written in the space for account titles to identify and explain this item. New totals are then computed for both the Income Statement columns and the Balance Sheet columns. Each pair of columns is now in balance.

The reason for entering the net income of $2,484 in the Balance Sheet credit column is that the net income accumulated during the period in the revenue and expense accounts causes an increase in the owner's equity. If the balance sheet columns did not have equal totals after the net income had been recorded in the credit column, the lack of agreement would indicate that an error had been made in the work sheet.

Let us assume for a moment that the month's operations had produced a loss rather than a profit. In that case the Income Statement debit column would exceed the credit column. The excess of the debits (expenses) over the credits (revenue) would have to be entered in the credit column in order to bring the two Income Statement columns into balance. The incurring of a loss would decrease the owner's equity; therefore, the loss would be entered as a balancing figure in the Balance Sheet *debit* column. The Balance Sheet columns would then have equal totals.

SELF-BALANCING NATURE OF THE WORK SHEET Why does the entering of the net income or net loss in one of the Balance Sheet columns bring this

ROBERTS REAL ESTATE COMPANY
Work Sheet
For the Month Ended November 30, 19___

Account	Trial Balance Dr	Cr	Adjustments Dr	Cr	Adjusted Trial Balance Dr	Cr	Income Statement Dr	Cr	Balance Sheet Dr	Cr
Cash	25,800				25,800				25,800	
Accounts receivable	6,990				6,990				6,990	
Unexpired insurance	540			(a) 15	525				525	
Office supplies	720			(b) 120	600				600	
Land	15,000				15,000				15,000	
Building	36,000				36,000				36,000	
Accumulated depreciation: building		150		(c) 150		300				300
Office equipment	5,400				5,400				5,400	
Accumulated depreciation: office equipment		45		(d) 45		90				90
Notes payable		3,000				3,000				3,000
Accounts payable		23,595				23,595				23,595
Unearned rental commissions		1,800	(e) 300			1,500				1,500
James Roberts, capital		60,771				60,771				60,771
James Roberts, drawing	1,500				1,500				1,500	
Sales commissions earned		5,484				5,484		5,484		
Advertising expense	1,275				1,275		1,275			
Office salaries expense	1,200				1,200		1,200			
Sales salaries expense	225		(g) 180		405		405			
Telephone expense	195				195		195			
	94,845	94,845								
Insurance expense			(a) 15		15		15			
Office supplies expense			(b) 120		120		120			
Depreciation expense: building			(c) 150		150		150			
Depreciation expense: office equipment			(d) 45		45		45			
Rental commissions earned				(e) 300 (h) 120		420		420		
Interest expense			(f) 15		15		15			
Interest payable				(f) 15		15				15
Sales salaries payable				(g) 180		180				180
Rental commissions receivable			(h) 120		120				120	
			945	945	95,355	95,355				

Extend each adjusted amount to columns for income statement or balance sheet

*Explanatory notes relating to adjustments are the same as on page 132.

ROBERTS REAL ESTATE COMPANY
Work Sheet
For the Month Ended November 30, 19___

Completed work sheet

	Trial Balance		Adjustments*		Adjusted Trial Balance		Income Statement		Balance Sheet	
	Dr	Cr	Dr	Cr	Dr	Cr	Dr	Cr	Dr	Cr
Cash	25,800				25,800				25,800	
Accounts receivable	6,990				6,990				6,990	
Unexpired insurance	540			(a) 15	525				525	
Office supplies	720			(b) 120	600				600	
Land	15,000				15,000				15,000	
Building	36,000				36,000				36,000	
Accumulated depreciation: building		150		(c) 150		300				300
Office equipment	5,400				5,400				5,400	
Accumulated depreciation: office equipment		45		(d) 45		90				90
Notes payable		3,000				3,000				3,000
Accounts payable		23,595				23,595				23,595
Unearned rental commissions		1,800	(e) 300			1,500				1,500
James Roberts, capital		60,771				60,771				60,771
James Roberts, drawing	1,500				1,500				1,500	
Sales commissions earned		5,484				5,484		5,484		
Advertising expense	1,275				1,275		1,275			
Office salaries expense	1,200				1,200		1,200			
Sales salaries expense	225		(g) 180		405		405			
Telephone expense	195				195		195			
	94,845	94,845								
Insurance expense			(a) 15		15		15			
Office supplies expense			(b) 120		120		120			
Depreciation expense: building			(c) 150		150		150			
Depreciation expense: office equipment			(d) 45		45		45			
Rental commissions earned				(e) 300 (h) 120		420		420		
Interest expense			(f) 15		15		15			
Interest payable				(f) 15		15				15
Sales salaries payable				(g) 180		180				180
Rental commissions receivable			(h) 120		120				120	
			945	945	95,355	95,355	3,420	5,904	91,935	89,451
Net income							2,484			2,484
							5,904	5,904	91,935	91,935

*Explanatory notes relating to adjustments are the same as on page 132.

pair of columns into balance? The answer is short and simple. All the accounts in the Balance Sheet columns have November 30 balances with the exception of the owner's capital account, which still shows the October 31 balance. By bringing in the current month's net income as an addition to the October 31 capital, the capital account is brought up to date as of November 30. The Balance Sheet columns now prove the familiar proposition that assets are equal to the total of liabilities and owner's equity.

Uses for the work sheet

PREPARING FINANCIAL STATEMENTS   Preparing the formal financial statements from the work sheet is an easy step. All the information needed for both the income statement and the balance sheet has already been sorted and arranged in convenient form in the work sheet. The income statement shown below contains the amounts listed in the Income Statement columns of the work sheet.

ROBERTS REAL ESTATE COMPANY
Income Statement
For the Month Ended November 30, 19____

Data taken from Income Statement columns of work sheet

Revenue:		
Sales commissions earned		$5,484
Rental commissions earned		420
Total revenue		$5,904
Expenses:		
Advertising	$1,275	
Office supplies	120	
Office salaries	1,200	
Sales salaries	405	
Telephone	195	
Insurance	15	
Depreciation: building	150	
Depreciation: office equipment	45	
Interest	15	
Total expenses		3,420
Net income		$2,484

Balance sheet and statement of owner's equity   The balance sheets previously illustrated have shown in the owner's equity section the changes during the month caused by the owner's withdrawals and by the net income or loss from operation of the business. A separate statement, illustrated below, is sometimes used to show the changes in the owner's equity during the period. When a separate statement is used, only the ending amount of the owner's capital account is shown in the balance sheet. The separate statement showing changes in the owner's equity may be used with either the account form or the report form of balance sheet. In this illustration, the report form of balance sheet is used.

ROBERTS REAL ESTATE COMPANY
Statement of Owner's Equity
For the Month Ended November 30, 19___

Net in-
come James Roberts, capital, Nov. 1, 19___ $60,771
exceeded Net income for November 2,484
with- Subtotal $63,255
drawals by
owner Less: Withdrawals 1,500
James Roberts, capital, Nov. 30, 19___ $61,755

ROBERTS REAL ESTATE COMPANY
Balance Sheet
November 30, 19___

Assets

Compare Cash $25,800
these
amounts Accounts receivable 6,990
with Rental commissions receivable 120
figures
in Unexpired insurance 525
Balance Office supplies 600
Sheet
columns Land 15,000
of Building $36,000
work
sheet Less: Accumulated depreciation 300 35,700
Office equipment . . . . $ 5,400
Less: Accumulated depreciation 90 5,310
$90,045

Liabilities & Owner's Equity

Liabilities:
Notes payable . . . . $ 3,000
Accounts payable 23,595
Interest payable 15
Sales salaries payable 180
Unearned rental commissions 1,500
Total liabilities $28,290
Owner's equity:
James Roberts, capital 61,755
$90,045

RECORDING ADJUSTING ENTRIES IN THE ACCOUNTING RECORDS After the financial statements have been prepared from the work sheet at the end of the period, the ledger accounts are adjusted to bring them into agreement with the financial statements. This is an easy step because the adjustments have already been computed on the work sheet. The amounts appearing in the Adjustments columns of the work sheet and the related explanations at the bottom of the work sheet provide all the necessary information for the adjusting entries, as shown on page 140, which are first entered in the journal and then posted to the ledger accounts.

RECORDING CLOSING ENTRIES When the financial statements have been prepared from the work sheet, the revenue and expense accounts have served their purpose for the current period and should be closed. These accounts will then have zero balances and will be ready for the recording of revenue and expenses during the next fiscal period.

The journalizing and posting of closing entries were illustrated in Chapter 3. The point to be emphasized now is that the completed work sheet provides in convenient form all the information needed to make the closing entries. The preparation of closing entries from the work sheet may be summarized as follows:

1 To close the accounts listed in the Income Statement credit column, debit the revenue accounts and credit Income Summary.

2 To close the accounts listed in the Income Statement debit column, debit Income Summary and credit the expense accounts.

3 To close the Income Summary account, transfer the balancing figure in the Income Statement columns of the work sheet ($2,484 in the illustration) to the owner's capital account. A profit is transferred by debiting Income Summary and crediting the capital account; a loss is transferred by debiting the capital account and crediting Income Summary.

4 To close the owner's drawing account, debit the capital account and credit the drawing account. Note on the work sheet that the account, James Roberts, Drawing, is extended from the Adjusted Trial Balance debit column to the Balance Sheet debit column. It does not appear in the Income Statement columns because a withdrawal of cash by the owner is not regarded as an expense of the business.

The closing entries at November 30 are shown on page 141.

Sequence of accounting procedures when work sheet is used

In any business which maintains a considerable number of accounts or makes numerous adjusting entries, the use of a work sheet will save much time and labor. Since the work sheet includes a trial balance, adjusting entries in preliminary form, and an adjusted trial balance, the use of the work sheet will modify the sequence of accounting procedures given in Chapter 3 as follows:

1 Record all transactions in the journal as they occur.

2 Post debits and credits from the journal entries to the proper ledger accounts.

3 Prepare the work sheet. (The work sheet includes a trial balance of the ledger and all necessary adjustments.)

General Journal

Adjust-ments on work sheet are entered in general journal	19___ Nov.				
		30	Insurance Expense	15	
			Unexpired Insurance		15
			Insurance expense for November.		
		30	Office Supplies Expense	120	
			Office Supplies		120
			Office supplies used during November.		
		30	Depreciation Expense: Building	150	
			Accumulated Depreciation: Building .		150
			Depreciation for November.		
		30	Depreciation Expense: Office Equipment . .	45	
			Accumulated Depreciation: Office		
			Equipment		45
			Depreciation for November.		
		30	Unearned Rental Commissions	300	
			Rental Commissions Earned		300
			Earned one-sixth of commission collected in advance for management of the properties owned by James Fortune.		
		30	Interest Expense	15	
			Interest Payable		15
			Interest expense accrued during November on note payable.		
		30	Sales Salaries Expense	180	
			Sales Salaries Payable		180
			To record expense and related liability to salesman for last four evenings' work in November.		
		30	Rental Commissions Receivable	120	
			Rental Commissions Earned		120
			To record the receivable and related revenue earned for managing properties owned by Henry Clayton.		

General Journal   *Page 6*

Date		Account Titles and Explanation	LP	Debit	Credit
Closing *entries* *derived* *from work* *sheet* **Nov.** 19__ 30		Sales Commissions Earned		5,484	
		Rental Commissions Earned		420	
		Income Summary			5,904
		To close the revenue accounts.			
	30	Income Summary		3,420	
		Advertising Expense			1,275
		Office Salaries Expense			1,200
		Sales Salaries Expense			405
		Telephone Expense			195
		Insurance Expense			15
		Office Supplies Expense			120
		Depreciation Expense: Building			150
		Depreciation Expense: Office Equip-			
		ment			45
		Interest Expense			15
		To close the expense accounts.			
	30	Income Summary		2,484	
		James Roberts, Capital			2,484
		To close the Income Summary account.			
	30	James Roberts, Capital		1,500	
		James Roberts, Drawing			1,500
		To close the owner's drawing account.			

4 Prepare financial statements, consisting of an income statement, a statement of owner's equity, and a balance sheet.

5 Using the information shown on the work sheet as a guide, enter the adjusting and closing entries in the journal. Post these entries to ledger accounts.

6 Prepare an after-closing trial balance to prove that the ledger is still in balance.

Note that the first two procedures, consisting of the journalizing and posting of transactions during the period, are the same regardless of whether a work sheet is to be used at the end of the period.

The accounting cycle

The above sequence of accounting procedures constitutes a complete accounting process, which is repeated in the same order in each accounting period. The regular repetition of this standardized set of procedures is often referred to as the *accounting cycle.*

In most business concerns the accounts are closed only once a year;

for these companies the accounting cycle is one year in length. For purposes of illustration in a textbook, it is convenient to assume that the entire accounting cycle is performed within the time period of one month. The completion of the accounting cycle is the occasion for closing the revenue and expense accounts and preparing financial statements.

Preparing monthly financial statements without closing the accounts

Many companies which close their accounts only once a year nevertheless prepare *monthly* financial statements for managerial use. These monthly statements are prepared from work sheets, but the adjustments indicated on the work sheets are not entered in the accounting records and no closing entries are made. Under this plan, the time-consuming operation of journalizing and posting adjustments and closing entries is performed only at the end of the fiscal year, but the company has the advantage of monthly financial statements. Monthly and quarterly financial statements are often referred to as *interim statements,* because they are in between the year-end statements. The annual or year-end statements are usually audited by a firm of certified public accountants; interim statements are usually unaudited.

KEY TERMS INTRODUCED OR EMPHASIZED IN CHAPTER 4

Accounting cycle   The sequence of accounting procedures performed during an accounting period. The procedures include journalizing transactions, posting, preparation of a work sheet and financial statements, adjusting and closing the accounts, and preparation of an after-closing trial balance.

Accrued expenses   Expenses such as salaries of employees and interest on notes payable which have accumulated but are unpaid and unrecorded at the end of the period.

Accrued revenue   Revenue which has been earned during the accounting period but has not been collected or recorded prior to the closing date. Also called *unrecorded revenue.*

Book value   The net amount at which an asset is shown in accounting records. For depreciable assets, book value equals cost minus accumulated depreciation. Also called *carrying value.*

Carrying value   See book value.

Deferred revenue   An obligation to render services or deliver goods in the future because of advance receipt of payment.

Interim statements   Financial statements prepared at intervals of less than one year. Usually quarterly and monthly statements.

Prepaid expenses   Advance payments for such expenses as rent and insurance. The portion which has not been used up at the end of the accounting period is included in the balance sheet as an asset.

Promissory note   A formal written promise to repay an amount borrowed plus interest at a future date.

Unearned revenue   See deferred revenue.

Unrecorded expenses   See accrued expenses.

Work sheet A large columnar sheet designed to arrange in convenient form all the accounting data required at the end of the period. Facilitates preparation of financial statements.

REVIEW QUESTIONS

1 Which of the following statements do you consider most acceptable?
   a Adjusting entries affect balance sheet accounts only.
   b Adjusting entries affect income statement accounts only.
   c An adjusting entry may affect two or more balance sheet accounts or two or more income statement accounts, but cannot affect both a balance sheet account and an income statement account.
   d Every adjusting entry affects both a balance sheet account and an income statement account.

2 The recording of depreciation involves two ledger accounts: Depreciation Expense and Accumulated Depreciation. Explain the purpose of each account; indicate whether it normally has a debit balance or a credit balance; and state where it appears in the financial statements.

3 At the end of the current year, the adjusted trial balance of the Midas Company showed the following account balances, among others:

Building, $31,600

Depreciation Expense: Building, $1,580

Accumulated Depreciation: Building, $11,060

Assuming that straight-line depreciation has been used, what length of time do these facts suggest that the Midas Company has owned the building?

4 The net income reported by Haskell Company for the year was $21,400, and the capital account of the owner, J. B. Haskell, stood at $36,000. However, the company had failed to recognize that interest amounting to $375 had accrued on a note payable to the bank. State the corrected figures for net income and for the owner's equity. In what other respect was the balance sheet of the company in error?

5 Office supplies on hand in the Melville Company amounted to $642 at the beginning of the year. During the year additional office supplies were purchased at a cost of $1,561 and charged to the asset account Office Supplies. At the end of the year a physical count showed that supplies on hand amounted to $812. Give the adjusting entry needed at December 31.

6 The X Company at December 31 recognized the existence of certain unexpired costs which would provide benefits to the company in future periods. Give examples of such unexpired costs and state where they would be shown in the financial statements.

7 In performing the regular end-of-period accounting procedures, does the preparation of the work sheet precede or follow the posting of adjusting entries to ledger accounts? Why?

8 The Adjustments columns of the work sheet for Davis Company contained only three adjustments, as follows: depreciation of building, $3,600; expiration of insurance, $500; and salaries accrued at year-end, $4,100. If the Trial Balance columns showed totals of $600,000, what would be the totals of the Adjusted Trial Balance columns?

9 Should the Adjusted Trial Balance columns be totaled before or after the adjusted amounts are carried to the Income Statement and Balance Sheet columns? Explain.

10 In extending adjusted account balances from the Adjusted Trial Balance columns to the Income Statement and Balance Sheet columns, is there any particular sequence to be followed in order to minimize the possibility of errors? Explain.

11 Do the totals of the balance sheet ordinarily agree with the totals of the Balance Sheet columns of the work sheet?

12 Is a work sheet ever prepared when there is no intention of closing the accounts? Explain.

EXERCISES

Ex. 4-1 On Friday of each week, Lake Company pays its sales personnel weekly salaries amounting to $45,000 for a five-day work week.
   a Draft the necessary adjusting entry at year-end, assuming that December 31 falls on Tuesday.
   b Also draft the journal entry for the payment by Lake Company of a week's salaries to its sales personnel on Friday, January 3, the first payday of the new year.

Ex. 4-2 Stone Company adjusts and closes its accounts at the end of the calendar year. Prepare the adjusting entries required at December 31, based on the following information:
   a A six-month bank loan in the amount of $160,000 had been obtained on October 1 at an annual interest rate of 9%. No interest has been paid as yet and no interest expense has been recorded.
   b Depreciation on office equipment is based on the assumption of a 10-year life and no scrap value. The balance in the Office Equipment account is $26,400; no changes have occurred in this account during the current year.
   c Interest receivable on U.S. government bonds owned is $1,920.
   d On December 31, an agreement was signed to lease a truck for 12 months beginning January 1 at a rate of 24 cents a mile. Usage is expected to be 1,500 miles per month and the contract specifies a minimum payment equivalent to 10,000 miles a year.

Ex. 4-3 On September 1, Key Company purchased a three-year fire insurance policy and recorded the payment of the full three-year premium of $4,320 by debiting Unexpired Insurance. The accounts were not adjusted or closed until the end of the calendar year. Give the necessary adjusting entry at December 31.

Ex. 4-4 For each of the following items relating to Glenwood Speedway, write first the journal entry (if one is required) to record the external transaction and secondly, the adjusting entry, if any, required on March 31, the end of the fiscal period.
   a On March 1, paid rent for the next four months at $22,500 per month.
   b On March 2, sold season tickets for a total of $600,000. The season includes 60 racing days: 15 in March, 25 in April, and 20 in May.
   c On March 3, an agreement was reached with Snack-Bars, Inc., allowing that company to sell refreshments at the track in return for 10% of the gross receipts from refreshment sales.
   d On March 5, schedules for the 15 racing days in March and the first 10 racing days in April were printed at a cost of $10,000.
   e On March 31, Snack-Bars, Inc., reported that the gross receipts from refreshment sales in March had been $135,000 and that the 10% owed to Glenwood Speedway would be remitted on April 10.

Ex. 4-5 The Property Management Company manages office buildings and apartment buildings for various owners who wish to be relieved of this responsibility. The revenue earned for this service is credited to Management Fees Earned. On December 1, the company received a check for $10,800 from a client, David

Howell, who was leaving for a six-month stay abroad. This check represented payment in advance for management of Howell's real estate properties during the six months of his absence. Explain how this transaction would be recorded, the adjustment, if any, to be made at December 31, and the presentation of this information in the year-end financial statements.

Ex. 4-6 The following amounts are taken from consecutive balance sheets of Raymond Company.

	Year 1	Year 2
Unexpired insurance	$ –0–	$ 900
Unearned rental revenue	3,000	1,500
Interest payable	100	875

The income statement for Year 2 of the Raymond Company shows the following items:

Insurance expense	$ 700
Rental revenue	18,000
Interest expense	1,000

Instructions Determine the following amounts of cash:
a Paid during Year 2 on insurance policies.
b Received during Year 2 as rental revenue.
c Paid during Year 2 for interest.

PROBLEMS

Group A

4A-1 The accounting records of Green Mountain Lodge are maintained on the basis of a fiscal year ending June 30. The following facts are to be used as a basis for making adjusting entries at June 30, 19____.
(1) Depreciation on the buildings for the year ended June 30 amounted to $14,125.
(2) A 36-month fire insurance policy had been purchased on June 1. The premium of $1,440 for the entire life of the policy had been paid on June 1 and recorded as Unexpired Insurance.
(3) A portion of the land owned had been leased on June 16 of the current year to a service station operator at a yearly rental rate of $4,800. One year's rent was collected in advance at the date of the lease and credited to Unearned Rental Revenue.
(4) A small bus to carry guests to and from the airport had been rented on June 19 from Truck Rentals, Inc., at a daily rate of $21. No rental payment had yet been made.
(5) Among the assets owned by Green Mountain Lodge were government bonds in the face amount of $25,000. Accrued interest receivable on the bonds at June 30 was computed to be $975.
(6) A three-month bank loan in the amount of $100,000 had been obtained on June 1 at an annual interest rate of 9%. No interest expense has been recorded.
(7) The company signed an agreement on June 30 to lease a truck from Hill Motors for a period of one year beginning July 1 at a rate of 18 cents a mile and with a clause providing for a minimum monthly charge of $300.
(8) Salaries earned by employees but not paid amounted to $3,300.

4A-2 Listed on page 146 are six transactions of Community Playhouse for the month of June. Among the accounts used by Community Playhouse are Unearned Admissions Revenue, Performers' Compensation Expense, and Performers' Compensation Payable.

(1) On June 1, purchased a public address system for $4,320. The useful life was estimated at five years. (Debit Stage Equipment.)

(2) On June 1, purchased a three-year fire insurance policy for $1,152.

(3) On June 2, Community Playhouse sold tickets for $9,600 cash for a Drama Subscription Series consisting of five different plays, to be presented as follows: Play A, June 10–17; play B, June 20–27; play C, July 4–10; play D, July 14–20; and play E, July 24–30.

(4) On June 4, an agreement was reached with Debra Williams to give six solo performances, June 28 to July 3, inclusive. Compensation was arranged at 15% of total box office receipts for the six performances, to be paid in one lump sum after the sixth performance. Box office receipts for three performances ending June 30 amounted to $6,080. (Note: No entry is needed on June 4.) Give entry for the cash receipts and for the compensation owed to Williams.

(5) On June 5, purchased makeup supplies for $1,104. A physical count on June 30 showed unused supplies amounting to $560.

(6) On June 15, borrowed $12,800 from the First National Bank, to be repaid six months later, plus interest at 9% per year. A promissory note was signed.

Instructions Prepare a journal entry to record each transaction at the transaction date followed by an adjusting entry at June 30, the end of the fiscal period.

4A-3 Shown below is a four-column schedule consisting of the trial balance and the adjusted trial balance of Meadows Realty Company at June 30, 19___, the end of the fiscal year. The pair of Adjustments columns which would normally appear between the Trial Balance columns and the Adjusted Trial Balance columns has purposely been omitted.

	Trial Balance		Adjusted Trial Balance	
	Debit	Credit	Debit	Credit
Cash	42,000		42,000	
Commissions receivable	12,780		24,780	
Office supplies	2,700		660	
Office equipment	79,200		79,200	
Accumulated depreciation: office equipment		17,280		17,940
Notes payable		60,000		60,000
Accounts payable		7,800		7,800
Salaries payable				6,600
Interest payable				900
Unearned commissions		5,100		3,900
Fred Chapman, capital		39,000		39,000
Commissions earned		14,100		27,300
Salaries expense	6,600		13,200	
Interest expense			900	
Office supplies expense			2,040	
Depreciation expense: office equipment			660	
	143,280	143,280	163,440	163,440

Instructions Prepare six adjusting entries which will explain the changes from the amounts in the Trial Balance columns to the amounts in the Adjusted Trial Balance columns. Include an explanation as part of each journal entry.

4A-4 On January 1, 19____, Howard Shell organized Shell Storage Company for the purpose of leasing a large vacant building and renting space in this building to others for storage of various industrial materials. The accounting policies of the company call for making adjusting entries and closing the accounts each month. Shown below is a trial balance and other information needed in making adjusting entries at January 31.

SHELL STORAGE COMPANY

Trial Balance

January 31, 19____

Cash	$ 8,105	
Unexpired insurance	4,080	
Office supplies	405	
Office equipment	7,200	
Notes payable		$ 3,000
Unearned storage fees		1,350
Howard Shell, capital		11,795
Howard Shell, drawing	450	
Storage fees earned		8,850
Rent expense	1,800	
Telephone expense	135	
Salaries expense	2,820	
	$24,995	$24,995

Other data

(a) The monthly insurance expense amounted to $255.

(b) The amount of office supplies on hand, based on a physical count on January 31, was $195.

(c) A $3,000 one-year note payable was signed on January 1, with interest at 10% a year.

(d) The useful life of office equipment was estimated at 8 years.

(e) Certain clients chose to pay several months' storage fees in advance. It was determined that $480 of such fees was still unearned as of January 31.

(f) Several clients neglected to send in storage fees amounting to $330 for the month of January. These amounts have not been recorded but are considered collectible.

(g) Salaries earned by employees but not yet paid amounted to $240.

Instructions Based on the above trial balance and other information, prepare the adjusting entries (with explanations) needed at January 31.

4A-5 A four-column schedule consisting of the first four columns of a 10-column work sheet to be prepared for Zenith Service Company for the month ended September 30, 19____ is shown on page 148. It is assumed that the company adjusts and closes its accounts each month. (The completed Adjustments columns have been included to minimize the detail work involved.) These adjustments were derived from the following information available at September 30.

Data

(a) Monthly rent expense, $1,050.

(b) Insurance expense for the month, $53.

(c) Advertising expense for the month, $525.
(d) Cost of supplies on hand, based on physical count on September 30, $1,365.
(e) Depreciation expense on equipment, $455 per month.
(f) Accrued interest expense on notes payable, $123.
(g) Salaries earned by employees but not yet paid, $613.
(h) Services amounting to $1,400 were rendered during September for customers who had paid in advance. This portion of the Unearned Revenue account should be regarded as earned as of September 30.

	Trial balance		Adjustments	
	Dr	Cr	Dr	Cr
Cash	34,475			
Prepaid rent	3,150			(a) 1,050
Unexpired insurance	893			(b) 53
Prepaid advertising	2,065			(c) 525
Supplies	2,205			(d) 840
Equipment	40,950			
Accumulated depreciation: equipment		3,640		(e) 455
Notes payable		26,250		
Unearned revenue		4,200	(h) 1,400	
Dan Morehead, capital		43,803		
Dan Morehead, drawing	1,750			
Revenue from services		14,473		(h) 1,400
Salaries expense	6,878		(g) 613	
Rent expense			(a) 1,050	
Insurance expense			(b) 53	
Advertising expense			(c) 525	
Supplies expense			(d) 840	
Depreciation expense: equipment			(e) 455	
Interest expense			(f) 123	
Accrued interest payable				(f) 123
Salaries payable				(g) 613
	92,366	92,366	5,059	5,059

Instructions Prepare a 10-column work sheet utilizing the trial balance and adjusting data provided. Include at the bottom of the work sheet a legend consisting of a brief explanation keyed to each adjusting entry.

4A-6 Lakeside Golf Course adjusts and closes its accounts at the end of each calendar year. Revenue is obtained from greens fees and also from a contract with a concessionaire who sells refreshments on the premises. At December 31, 19 ____, the information for adjustments was gathered and a work sheet was prepared. The first four columns of the work sheet contained the account balances and adjustments shown on page 149.

Instructions Using the data on page 149, complete the work sheet by listing the appropriate amounts in the remaining six columns of the work sheet as illustrated on page 136.

	Trial Balance		Adjustments*	
	Dr	Cr	Dr	Cr
Cash	10,920			
Unexpired insurance	2,520			(a) 840
Prepaid advertising	1,200			(b) 360
Land	450,000			
Equipment	57,600			
Accumulated depreciation: equipment		9,600		(f) 4,800
Notes payable		72,000		
Unearned revenue from concessions		9,000	(d) 6,000	
Walter Nelson, capital		321,600		
Walter Nelson, drawing	18,000			
Revenue from greens fees		269,400		
Advertising expense	6,600		(b) 360	
Water expense	12,480			
Salaries expense	94,680		(e) 1,320	
Repairs and maintenance expense	21,000			
Miscellaneous expense	6,600			
	681,600	681,600		
Insurance expense			(a) 840	
Interest expense			(c) 480	
Interest payable				(c) 480
Revenue from concessions				(d) 6,000
Salaries payable				(e) 1,320
Depreciation expense: equipment			(f) 4,800	
			13,800	13,800

* Adjustments:
(a) $840 insurance expired during year.
(b) $360 prepaid advertising expired during year.
(c) $480 accrued interest expense on notes payable.
(d) $6,000 concession revenue earned during year.
(e) $1,320 of salaries earned but unpaid at Dec. 31, 19___.
(f) $4,800 depreciation expense for year.

4A-7 A trial balance and supplementary information needed for adjustments at September 30 are shown below and on page 150 for Golden Gate Theater. The company follows a policy of adjusting and closing its accounts at the end of each month.

Other data
(a) Advertising expense for the month, $9,375.
(b) Film rental expense for the month, $42,125.
(c) Depreciation expense on building, $875 per month; on projection equipment, $1,500 per month.
(d) Accrued interest on notes payable, $250.
(e) The company's share of revenue from concessions for September, as reported by concessionaire, $8,125. Check should be received by October 6.
(f) Salaries earned by employees but not paid, $3,750.

GOLDEN GATE THEATER
Trial Balance
September 30, 19___

Cash	$ 65,500	
Prepaid advertising	15,500	
Prepaid film rental	65,000	
Land	75,000	
Building	210,000	
Accumulated depreciation: building		$ 4,375
Projection equipment	90,000	
Accumulated depreciation: projection equipment		7,500
Notes payable		37,500
Accounts payable		8,500
Brian Davis, capital		415,375
Brian Davis, drawing	10,625	
Revenue from admissions		87,375
Salaries expense	21,250	
Light and power expense	7,750	
	$560,625	$560,625

Instructions   Prepare
a A work sheet for the month ended September 30.
b An income statement.
c A statement of proprietor's capital.
d A balance sheet.
e Adjusting and closing entries.

Group B

4B-1 Wasatch Ski Bowl maintains its accounting records on the basis of a fiscal year ending March 31. Based on the information shown below, you are to prepare all necessary adjusting entries at March 31, 19___.
   (1) A one-year fire insurance policy had been purchased and paid for in full at a total premium of $1,800 on March 1 of the current year.
   (2) On March 31, Wasatch Ski Bowl signed an agreement to lease a truck from Olympic Rentals for the period of one year beginning April 1 at a rate of 24 cents per mile, with a minimum monthly charge of $240.
   (3) Depreciation on the building for the period ended March 31 was $3,600.
   (4) A portion of the land owned had been leased to an amusement park at a yearly rental of $14,400. One year's rent had been collected in advance at the date of the lease (March 17) and credited to Unearned Rental Revenue.
   (5) Another portion of the land owned had been rented on March 1 to a service station operator at an annual rate of $2,880. No rent had as yet been collected from this tenant.
   (6) Accrued wages payable, $5,520.
   (7) Interest receivable on U.S. government bonds owned, $990.
   (8) A six-month bank loan in the amount of $72,000 had been obtained on January 31 at an annual interest rate of 10%. No interest had been paid and no interest expense recorded.
   (9) Accrued property taxes, $3,470.

Instructions   From the information given above, draft the adjusting entries (including explanations) required at March 31.
4B-2 Listed on page 151 in paragraphs (*1*) through (*6*) are transactions which occurred

during June for the Southern Music Festival. The company recognizes two types of revenue: Admissions Revenue and Concessions Revenue.

(*1*) On June 1, paid rent for six months at $1,350 per month.

(*2*) On June 2, sold season tickets to the Southern Music Festival for a total of $15,600. Four different programs were included in the festival, scheduled to be presented as follows: Program no. 1, June 15–16; program no. 2, June 29–30; program no. 3, July 5–6; and program no. 4, July 19–20. (Credit Unearned Admissions Revenue.)

(*3*) On June 6, an agreement was reached with Harvey Lynn, allowing him to sell refreshments in the theater. In return for the privilege, Lynn agreed to pay 5% of his gross receipts to the management within three days after the conclusion of each program.

(*4*) On June 7, four program notes, one for each of the four programs, were printed at a total cost of $1,260. Cash was paid.

(*5*) On June 19, cash in the amount of $96 was received from Lynn, representing 5% of refreshment sales of $1,920 during program no. 1. (Credit Concessions Revenue.)

(*6*) On June 30, Lynn reported that total refreshment sales at program no. 2 amounted to $2,160.

Instructions For each of the numbered paragraphs, you are to write first the journal entry (if one is required) to record the event, and secondly the related adjusting entry, if any, required at June 30, the end of the fiscal period.

4B-3 The trial balances of Miles Advertising Agency before and after the posting of adjusting entries are shown below:

MILES ADVERTISING AGENCY
Trial Balances
January 31, 19____

	Before Adjustments		After Adjustments	
	Dr	Cr	Dr	Cr
Cash	$18,720		$18,720	
Commissions receivable			360	
Prepaid rent	6,000		4,800	
Office supplies	1,960		1,280	
Office equipment	25,920		25,920	
Accumulated depreciation: office equipment		$ 1,200		$ 1,440
Notes payable		4,920		4,920
Accounts payable		16,000		16,000
Salaries payable				360
Interest payable				80
Unearned commissions		1,520		1,040
George Adams, capital		27,000		27,000
George Adams, drawing	3,600		3,600	
Commissions earned		12,480		13,320
Salaries expense	6,920		7,280	
Rent expense			1,200	
Office supplies expense			680	
Depreciation expense: office equipment			240	
Interest expense			80	
	$63,120	$63,120	$64,160	$64,160

Instructions The differences between the amounts in the "Before Adjustments" columns and the amounts in the "After Adjustments" columns are the result of seven adjusting entries. You are to prepare the seven adjusting entries indicated. Include an explanation as part of each journal entry.

4B-4 Pacific Pension Consultants is a new firm organized January 1, 19____, to help other companies to develop employee pension plans which will meet the complex legal and accounting requirements imposed by federal regulations for all pension plans. Some clients of the company pay in advance for advisory services; others are billed after the services have been rendered. The company adjusts and closes its accounts each month. At May 31, the trial balance appeared as follows:

PACIFIC PENSION CONSULTANTS
Trial Balance
May 31, 19____

Cash	$19,747	
Prepaid rent	4,425	
Office supplies	1,485	
Office equipment	9,396	
Accumulated depreciation: office equipment		$ 348
Accounts payable		1,425
Unearned revenue		18,900
Kay Brett, capital		16,000
Kay Brett, drawing	675	
Fees earned		14,250
Telephone expense	840	
Travel expense	1,020	
Salaries expense	13,335	
	$50,923	$50,923

Other data
(a) The monthly rent was $885.
(b) Office supplies on hand May 31 amounted to $975.
(c) The office equipment was purchased on January 1. The useful life was estimated at 9 years.
(d) Services rendered during the month and chargeable to Unearned Revenue (subscription basis) amounted to $4,350.
(e) Pension advisory services (nonsubscription basis) rendered during the month but not yet billed amounted to $840 (debit Pension Service Receivables).
(f) Salaries earned by employees during the month but not yet paid amounted to $345.

Instructions
a Prepare adjusting entries.
b Prepare an adjusted trial balance.

4B-5 North Slope Engineering Consultants was organized January 1, 19____, to provide technical services to various oil companies in Alaska. The trial balance on page 153 was prepared at June 30 after six months of operations. The accounts are to be adjusted and closed for the first time at June 30.

NORTH SLOPE ENGINEERING CONSULTANTS
Trial Balance
June 30, 19___

Cash	$ 61,000	
Prepaid office rent	72,000	
Supplies	14,400	
Instruments	79,200	
Notes payable		$ 60,000
Unearned fees		156,000
Ronald Moulton, capital		131,200
Ronald Moulton, drawing	51,240	
Fees earned		127,440
Salaries expense	194,400	
Miscellaneous expense	2,400	
	$474,640	$474,640

Other data
(1) Office rent for one year was paid on January 1, when the lease was signed.
(2) Supplies on hand on June 30 amounted to $2,880.
(3) Instruments were purchased on January 1. The useful life was estimated at 10 years.
(4) Accrued interest expense on notes payable was $600 as of June 30.
(5) A number of clients obtained during the first six months of the company's operations had made advance payments for services to be rendered over a considerable period. As of June 30, value of services rendered and chargeable against Unearned Fees was $114,000.
(6) Services rendered and chargeable to other clients amounted to $44,400 as of June 30. No entries had yet been made to record the revenues earned by performing services for these clients.
(7) Salaries earned by staff personnel but not yet paid amounted to $6,000 on June 30.

Instructions
a Prepare adjusting entries as of June 30, 19___ .
b Prepare an adjusted trial balance. (Note: You may find the use of T accounts helpful in computing the account balances after adjustments.)
c Prepare an income statement for the six-month period ended June 30, 19___, a statement of owner's equity, and a balance sheet.

4B-6 Financial Research Associates is in the business of performing investigations and preparing financial analyses for business organizations and government agencies. Much of its work is done through a computer service center for which payment is made on an hourly basis. The company adjusts and closes its accounts monthly. At October 31, 19___, the account balances were as follows before adjustments were made.

Cash	$ 71,760
Research fees receivable	
Prepaid office rent	28,800
Prepaid computer rental expense	42,960
Office supplies	4,200

Office equipment	$25,200
Accumulated depreciation: office equipment	600
Notes payable	24,000
Accounts payable	8,760
Interest payable	
Salaries payable	
Unearned research fees	114,600
Greg Green, capital	83,820
Greg Green, drawing	2,400
Research fees earned	16,200
Office salaries expense	5,040
Research salaries expense	58,320
Telephone expense	2,640
Travel expense	6,660
Office rent expense	
Computer rental expense	
Office supplies expense	
Depreciation expense: office equipment	
Interest expense	

Other data
(a) The amount in the Prepaid Office Rent account represented office rent for eight months paid in advance on October 1, 19___ when the lease was renewed.
(b) During October, 220 hours of computer time were used at a cost of $180 an hour.
(c) Office supplies on hand October 31 were determined by count to amount to $840.
(d) Office equipment was estimated to have a useful life of 7 years from date of purchase.
(e) Accrued interest on notes payable amounted to $96 on October 31.
(f) Services to clients amounting to $76,440 performed during October were chargeable against the Unearned Research Fees account.
(g) Services to clients who had not made advance payments and had not been billed amounted to $35,280 at October 31.
(h) Salaries earned by research staff but not paid amounted to $5,160 on October 31.

Instructions
a Prepare a work sheet for the month ended October 31, 19___.
b Prepare an income statement and a balance sheet that contains the details of changes in owner's equity.

4B-7 Trade Winds Airline provides passenger and freight service among some Pacific islands. The accounts are adjusted and closed each month. At June 30, 19___, the trial balance on page 155 was prepared from the ledger.

Other data
(a) Monthly rent amounted to $3,000.
(b) Insurance expense for June was $3,900.
(c) All necessary maintenance work was provided by Ryan Air Service at a fixed charge of $7,500 a month. Service for three months had been paid for in advance on June 1.
(d) Spare parts used in connection with maintenance work amounted to $3,750 during the month.

(e) At the time of purchase, the remaining useful life of the airplanes, which were several years old, was estimated at 5,000 hours of flying time. During June, total flying time amounted to 160 hours.

(f) The Chamber of Commerce purchased 2,000 special tickets for $60,000. Each ticket allowed the holder one flight normally priced at $45. During the month 400 tickets had been used by the holders.

(g) Salaries earned by employees but not paid amounted to $3,300 at June 30.

TRADE WINDS AIRLINE

Trial Balance

June 30, 19___

Cash	$ 190,500	
Prepaid rent expense	54,000	
Unexpired insurance	46,800	
Prepaid maintenance expense	22,500	
Spare parts	57,000	
Airplanes	810,000	
Accumulated depreciation: airplanes		$ 76,950
Unearned passenger revenue		60,000
John Morgan, capital		977,760
John Morgan, drawing	12,000	
Passenger revenue earned		183,990
Gasoline expense	13,800	
Salaries expense	86,700	
Advertising expense	5,400	
	$1,298,700	$1,298,700

Instructions

a Prepare a work sheet for the month ended June 30, 19___.

b Prepare an income statement and a balance sheet that includes the details of changes in owner's equity.

c Prepare adjusting and closing entries.

BUSINESS DECISION PROBLEM 4

Windy Point Marina rents 50 slips in a large floating dock to owners of small boats in the area. The marina also performs repair services on small craft.

Dave Hands, a friend of yours, is convinced that recreational boating will become increasingly popular in the area and he has entered into negotiations to buy Windy Point Marina.

Dave does not have quite enough cash to purchase the business at the price the owner has demanded. However, the owner of the marina has suggested that Dave might purchase the marina with what cash he does have, and turn the net income of the business over to the retiring owner until the balance of the purchase price has been paid. A typical month's income for Windy Point Marina is determined as shown on page 156.

Dave is concerned about turning the whole net income of the business over to the former owner for the next several months, because he estimates that he and his family will need to keep at least $1,500 a month to meet their living expenses. In coming to you for advice, Dave explains that all revenue of Windy Point Marina is collected when earned, and both wages and "other" expenses are paid when incurred. Dave does not understand, however, when depreciation expense must be paid, or why there is any insurance expense when the insurance policies of the business have more than two years to run before new insurance must be purchased.

Revenue:

Slip rentals		$ 3,750
Repairs		7,000
Total revenue		$10,750
Operating expenses:		
Wages	$3,500	
Insurance	75	
Depreciation expense: docks	2,000	
Depreciation expense: equipment	250	
Other expenses	250	6,075
Net income		$ 4,675

Instructions

a Advise Dave as to how much cash the business will generate each month. Will this amount of cash enable Dave to withdraw $1,500 per month to meet his living expenses and pay $4,675 per month to the former owner?

b Explain why insurance expense appears on the income statement of the business if no new policies will be purchased within the next two years.

5

Accounting for Purchases and Sales of Merchandise

The preceding four chapters have illustrated step by step the complete accounting cycle for Roberts Real Estate Company, a business rendering personal services. Service-type companies represent an important part of our economy. They include, for example, airlines, railroads, motels, theaters, golf courses, ski resorts, and professional football clubs. In contrast to the service-type business, there are a great many companies whose principal activity is buying and selling merchandise. The term **merchandise** means goods acquired by a business for the purpose of resale to customers. In other words, merchandise consists of the goods in which a business regularly deals. Merchandising companies may be engaged in either the retail or wholesale distribution of goods. The accounting concepts and methods we have studied for a service-type business are also applicable to a merchandising concern; however, some additional accounts and techniques are needed in accounting for the purchase and sale of merchandise.

Income statement for a merchandising business

An income statement for a merchandising business consists of three main sections: (1) the revenue section, (2) the cost of goods sold section, and (3) the operating expenses section. This sectional arrangement is illustrated in the income statement for a retail sporting goods store on page 158. We shall assume that the business of the Campus Sports Shop consists of buying sports equipment from manufacturers and selling this merchandise to college students and others. To keep the illustration reasonably short, we shall use a smaller number of expense accounts than would generally be used in a merchandising business.

ANALYZING THE INCOME STATEMENT   How does this income statement compare in form and content with the income statement of the service-type business presented in the preceding chapters? The most important change is the inclusion of the section entitled Cost of Goods Sold. Note how large the cost of goods sold is in comparison with the other figures on the statement. The cost of the merchandise sold during the year amounts to $120,000, or 60% of the year's sales of $200,000. Another way of looking at this relationship is to say that for each dollar the store receives by selling goods to customers, the sum of 60 cents represents a recovery of the cost of the merchandise. This leaves a *gross profit* of 40 cents from each sales dollar, out of which the store must pay its operating expenses. In our illustration the operating expenses for the year were $50,000, that is, 25% of the sales figure of $200,000. Therefore, the gross profit of 40 cents contained in each dollar of sales was enough to cover the operating expenses of 25 cents and leave a net income of 15 cents from each dollar of sales.

CAMPUS SPORTS SHOP

Income Statement

For the Year Ended December 31, Year 10

Note distinction between cost of goods sold and operating expenses	*Sales*		*$200,000*
	Cost of goods sold:		
	Inventory, Jan. 1	*$ 25,000*	
	Purchases	*125,000*	
	Cost of goods available for sale	*$150,000*	
	Less: Inventory, Dec. 31	*30,000*	
	Cost of goods sold		*120,000*
	Gross profit on sales		*$ 80,000*
	Operating expenses:		
	Salaries	*$ 36,000*	
	Advertising	*8,000*	
	Telephone	*1,000*	
	Depreciation	*4,000*	
	Insurance	*1,000*	
	Total operating expenses		*50,000*
	Net income		*$ 30,000*

Of course the percentage relationship between sales and cost of goods sold will vary from one type of business to another, but, in all types of merchandising concerns, the cost of goods sold is one of the largest elements in the income statement. Accountants, investors, bankers, and businessmen in general have the habit of mentally computing percentage relationships when they look at financial statements. Formation of this habit will be helpful throughout the study of accounting, as well as in many business situations.

In analyzing an income statement, it is customary to compare each item in the statement with the amount of sales. These comparisons are easier to make if we express the data in percentages as well as in dollar amounts. If the figure for sales is regarded as 100%, then every other item or subtotal on the statement can conveniently be expressed as a percentage of sales. The cost of goods sold in most types of business will be between 60 and 80% of sales. Conversely, the **gross profit on sales** (sales minus cost of goods sold) will usually vary between 40 and 20% of sales. Numerous exceptions may be found to such a sweeping generalization, but it is sufficiently valid to be helpful in visualizing customary relationships on the income statement.

APPRAISING THE ADEQUACY OF NET INCOME The income statement for the Campus Sports Shop shown on page 158 shows that a net income of $30,000 was earned during the year. Should this be regarded as an excellent, fair, or mediocre performance? Before reaching a conclusion, let us consider what this item of net income represents in an unincorporated business.

First, let us make the reasonable assumption that the owner of the Campus Sports Shop, Robert Riley, works full time as manager of the business. It is not customary, however, to include any compensation for the personal services of the owner among the expenses of the business. One reason for not including among the expenses a salary to the owner-manager is the fact that he would be in a position to set his own salary at any amount he chose. The use of an arbitrarily chosen, unrealistic salary to the owner would tend to destroy the significance of the income statement as a device for measuring the earning power of the business. Another reason may be that in the owner's own thinking he is not working for a salary when he manages his own business but is investing his time in order to make a profit. The net income of the Campus Sports Shop must, therefore, be considered in part as the equivalent of a salary earned by the owner. If we assume that the owner, Robert Riley, could obtain employment elsewhere as a store manager at a salary of $20,000 a year, then we can reasonably regard $20,000 of the net income earned by the Campus Sports Shop as compensation to Riley for his personal services during the year.

Secondly, it is necessary to recognize that Riley, as owner of this small business, has invested his own savings, amounting to, say, $50,000. If, as an alternative to starting his own business, he had invested this $50,000 capital in high-grade securities, he might be receiving investment income of perhaps $4,000 a year.

After deducting from the $30,000 reported net income of the Campus Sports Shop an assumed yearly salary of $20,000 to the owner and an estimated return on invested capital of $4,000, we have left a "pure profit" of $6,000. In judging the adequacy of this amount, we must bear in mind that this residual element of profit is the all-important incentive which induced Riley to risk his savings in a new business venture. The residual profit may also be regarded as the reward for the time and effort which an owner must spend in planning, financing, and guiding a business, apart from the routine aspects of day-to-day management. Moreover, the earning of $30,000 net income in one year provides no assurance that a similar profit, or for that matter any profit, will be forthcoming in another year. It would be somewhat rash to form an opinion about the adequacy of earning power of a business on the basis of such a short period of operating experience.

Economists often use the word *profit* to mean the residual pure profit remaining after deducting from the net income the estimated amounts needed to compensate the proprietor for his personal services and the use of his capital. Confusion over the meaning of technical terms is a major difficulty faced by accountants in conveying to economists and business executives the results of their analysis of business operations.

Accounting for sales of merchandise

If merchandising companies are to succeed or even to survive, they must, of course, sell their goods at prices higher than they pay to the vendors or suppliers from whom they buy. The selling prices charged by a retail store must cover three things: (1) the cost of the merchandise to the store; (2) the operating expenses of the business such as advertising, store rent, and salaries of the sales staff; and (3) a net income to the business.

When a business sells merchandise to its customers, it either receives immediate payment in cash or acquires an account receivable which will soon become cash. As explained in Chapter 3, the inflow of cash and receivables from sales of the current period is equal to the revenue for that period. The entry to record the sale of merchandise consists of a debit to an asset account and a credit to the sales account, as shown by the following example:

Journal entry for cash sale

Cash	*100*	
Sales		*100*

To record the sale of merchandise for cash.

If the sale was not a cash transaction but called for payment at a later date, the entry would be:

Journal entry for sale on credit

Accounts Receivable	*100*	
Sales		*100*

To record the sale of merchandise on credit; payment due within 30 days.

Revenue from the sale of merchandise is considered as earned in the period in which the merchandise is delivered to the customer, even though payment in cash is not received for a month or more after the sale. Consequently, the revenue earned in a given accounting period may differ considerably from the cash receipts of that period.

The amount and trend of sales are watched very closely by management, investors, and others interested in the progress of a company. A rising volume of sales is evidence of growth and suggests the probability of an increase in earnings. A declining trend in sales, on the other hand, is often the first signal of reduced earnings and of financial difficulties ahead. The amount of sales for each year is compared with the sales of the preceding year; the sales of each month may be compared with the sales of the preceding month and also with the corresponding month of the preceding year. These comparisons bring to light significant trends in the volume of sales. The financial pages of newspapers regularly report on the volume and trend of sales for corporations with publicly owned stock.

Accounting for the cost of goods sold

In the illustrated income statement of Campus Sports Shop on page 158, the cost of goods sold for the year was computed as follows:

Computing cost of goods sold **Inventory of merchandise at beginning of year**	**$ 25,000**
Purchases	**125,000**
Cost of goods available for sale	**$150,000**
Less: Inventory at end of year	**30,000**
Cost of goods sold	**$120,000**

Every merchandising business has *available for sale* during an accounting period the merchandise on hand at the beginning of the period *plus* the merchandise purchased during the period. If all these goods were sold during the period, there would be no ending inventory, and cost of goods sold would be equal to the cost of goods available for sale. Normally, however, some goods remain unsold at the end of the period; *cost of goods sold is then equal to the cost of goods available for sale minus the ending inventory of unsold goods.*

The cost of goods sold is an important concept which requires careful attention. To gain a thorough understanding of this concept, we need to consider the nature of the accounts used in determining the cost of goods sold.

The Purchases account

The cost of *merchandise purchased for resale* to customers is recorded by debiting an account called Purchases, as illustrated on page 162.

Journal
entry for
purchase
of mer-
chandise

Purchases *10,000*

    Accounts Payable (or Cash) *10,000*

Purchased merchandise from ABC Supply Co.

The Purchases account *is used only for merchandise acquired for resale;* assets acquired for use in the business (such as a delivery truck, a typewriter, or office supplies) are recorded by debiting the appropriate asset account, not the Purchases account. The Purchases account does not indicate whether the purchased goods have been sold or are still on hand.

At the end of the accounting period, the balance accumulated in the Purchases account represents the total cost of merchandise purchased during the period. This amount is used in preparing the income statement. The Purchases account has then served its purpose and it is closed to the Income Summary account. Since the Purchases account is closed at the end of each period, it has a zero balance at the beginning of each succeeding period.

Inventory of merchandise

An inventory of merchandise consists of the goods on hand and available for sale to customers. In the Campus Sports Shop, the inventory consists of golf clubs, tennis rackets, and skiing equipment; in a pet shop the inventory might include puppies, fish, and parakeets. Inventories are acquired through the purchase of goods from wholesalers, manufacturers, or other suppliers. The goods on hand at the beginning of the period are referred to as the *beginning inventory;* the goods on hand at the end of the period are referred to as the *ending inventory.* Thus in our example of a year's operations of Campus Sports Shop, the beginning inventory on January 1 was $25,000 and the ending inventory on December 31 was $30,000. The ending inventory of one accounting period is, of course, the beginning inventory of the following period. For the following year, Campus Sports Shop would have a beginning inventory of $30,000—the amount determined to be on hand at the close of business on December 31 of the current year.

Inventory of merchandise and cost of goods sold

The cost of the merchandise sold during the year appears in the income statement as a deduction from the sales of the year. The merchandise which is *available for sale but not sold* during the year constitutes the inventory of merchandise on hand at the end of the year. The inventory is included in the year-end balance sheet as an asset.

How can the manager determine, at the end of a year, a month, or other accounting period, the quantity and the cost of the goods remaining on hand? How can management determine the cost of the goods sold during the period? These amounts must be determined before either a balance sheet or an income statement can be prepared. In fact, the determination of inventory value and of the cost of goods sold may be the most important single step in measuring the profitability of a business. There are two alternative approaches to the determination of inventory and of cost of goods sold, namely, the *perpetual inventory method* and the *periodic inventory method.*

THE PERPETUAL INVENTORY SYSTEM Business concerns which sell merchandise of high unit value, such as automobiles or television sets, generally use a perpetual inventory system. An automobile dealer or a television store makes only a few sales each day. For such a small number of sales transactions, it is possible to look in the records to determine the cost of the individual automobile or television set being sold. This cost figure can easily be recorded as the *cost of goods sold* for each sales transaction. Under this system, records are maintained showing the cost of each article in stock. Units added to inventory and units sold are recorded on a daily basis—hence the name "perpetual inventory system." At the end of the accounting period when financial statements are to be prepared, the total cost of goods sold during the period is easily determined by adding the costs recorded from day to day for the units sold.

Although the perpetual inventory system is definitely worthwhile for a business selling merchandise of high unit value, it is not practicable in a business such as a drugstore which may sell a customer a bottle of aspirin, a candy bar, and a tube of toothpaste. The sales price of this merchandise can quickly be recorded on a cash register, but it would not be practical to look up in the records at the time of each sale the cost of such small items. Instead, stores which deal in merchandise of low unit cost usually wait until the end of the accounting period to determine the cost of goods sold. They rely upon the periodic inventory system rather than maintain perpetual inventory records. In this chapter we shall concentrate upon the periodic inventory system. The perpetual inventory system is discussed in Chapter 10.

THE PERIODIC INVENTORY SYSTEM A great many businesses do not maintain perpetual inventory records; they rely instead upon a periodic inventory (a count of merchandise on hand) to determine the inventory at the end of the accounting period and the cost of goods sold during the period. The periodic inventory system may be concisely summarized as follows:

1 A physical count of merchandise on hand is made at the end of each accounting period.

2 The cost value of this inventory is computed by multiplying the quantity of each item by an appropriate unit cost. A total cost figure for the entire inventory is then determined by adding the costs of all the various types of merchandise.

3 The *cost of goods available for sale* during the period is determined by adding the amount of the inventory at the beginning of the period to the amount of the purchases during the period.

4 The *cost of goods sold* is computed by subtracting the inventory at the end of the period from the cost of goods available for sale. In other words, the difference between the cost of goods available for sale and the amount of goods remaining unsold at the end of the period is presumed to have been sold.

A simple illustration of the above procedures for determining the cost of goods sold follows:

Using the periodic inventory method **Beginning inventory (determined by count)**	**$ 25,000**
Add: Purchases	**125,000**
Cost of goods available for sale	**$150,000**
Less: Ending inventory (determined by count)	**30,000**
Cost of goods sold	**$120,000**

Because of the importance of the process for determining inventory and cost of goods sold, we shall now consider in more detail the essential steps in using the periodic inventory system.

Taking a physical inventory When the periodic inventory system is in use, there is no day-to-day record of the cost of goods sold. Neither is there any day-to-day record of the amount of goods unsold and still on hand. At the end of the accounting period, however, it is necessary to determine the cost of goods sold during the period and also the amount of unsold goods on hand. The figure for cost of goods sold is used in determining the net income or loss for the period, and the value of the merchandise on hand at the end of the period is included in the balance sheet as an asset.

To determine the cost of the merchandise on hand, a physical inventory is taken. The count of merchandise should be made if possible after the close of business on the last day of the accounting period. It is difficult to make an accurate count during business hours while sales are taking place; consequently, the physical inventory is often taken in the evening or on Sunday. After all goods have been counted, the proper cost price must be assigned to each article. The assignment of a cost price to each item of merchandise in stock is often described as *pricing the inventory.*

The Inventory account After the amount of the ending inventory has been computed by counting and pricing the goods on hand at the end of the period, this amount is entered in the records by *debiting the Inventory account and crediting Income Summary.* (This entry will be illustrated and explained more fully later in this chapter.) Entries are made in the Inventory account only at the end of the accounting period. During the period, the Inventory account shows only the cost of the merchandise which was on hand at the beginning of the current period.

Inflation and the cost of replacing inventories

Inventories have traditionally been valued at their original cost for accounting purposes. However, the rapid inflation of recent years has made original cost figures less relevant in many cases than current value or replacement cost. Consequently, large corporations are now required by the SEC to disclose in their financial statements the current replacement cost as well as the original cost for both inventories and cost of goods sold. The difference in the resulting income figures may be substantial. During a period of rising prices, a company's reported income will be less if the cost of goods sold is expressed in terms of replacement cost rather than original cost. This issue will be discussed more fully along with other aspects of accounting for inventories in Chapter 10.

Other accounts included in cost of goods sold

In the income statement of Campus Sports Shop illustrated earlier, the cost of goods sold was derived from only three items: beginning inventory, purchases, and ending inventory. In most cases, however, some additional accounts will be involved. These include the Purchase Returns and Allowances account and the Transportation-in account.

Purchase Returns and Allowances account

When merchandise purchased from suppliers is found to be unsatisfactory, the goods may be returned, or a request may be made for an allowance on the price. A return of goods to the supplier is recorded as follows:

Journal | *Accounts Payable* *1,200*
entry for | *Purchase Returns and Allowances* *1,200*
return of
goods to | *To charge Marvel Supply Co. for the cost of goods returned.*
supplier

Sometimes when a company after purchasing merchandise finds the goods not entirely satisfactory, it may agree to keep the goods in consideration for a reduction or allowance on the original price. The entry to record such an allowance is essentially the same as that for a return.

The use of a Purchase Returns and Allowances account rather than the recording of returns by direct credits to the Purchases account is advisable because the accounts then show both the total amount of the purchases and the amount of purchases which required adjustment or return. Management is interested in the percentage relationship between goods returned and goods purchased, because the returning of merchandise for credit is a time-consuming, costly process. Returning merchandise enables the purchaser to get back the price paid to the supplier, but this is only a partial recovery of the costs incurred. The time and effort spent in buying merchandise, in receiving and inspecting it, and in arranging for its return represent a costly procedure. To hold these costs to a minimum, management should be kept aware of the amount of returns and allowances. Excessive returns suggest that the purchasing department should look for more dependable sources of supply.

The Transportation-in account

The cost of merchandise acquired for resale logically includes any transportation charges necessary to place the goods in the purchaser's place of business. In some lines of business it is customary for the manufacturer to pay the cost of shipping merchandise to the retailer's store. In this case the manufacturer tries to set the price of the goods high enough to cover the transportation charges as well as all its other costs. Consequently, the cost of merchandise to the purchasing company normally includes the cost of transporting the goods, regardless of whether it pays the freight charges directly to the railroad or other carrier, or merely pays the seller a sufficiently high price to cover the cost of delivering the goods.

Transportation costs on inbound shipments *could* be debited to the Purchases account, but a more useful plan in most cases is to use a separate ledger account to accumulate the transportation charges on merchandise purchased. The journal entry to record the payment of transportation charges on inbound shipments of merchandise is as follows:

Journaliz-ing trans-portation charges on purchases of mer-chandise

Transportation-in	*125*	
Cash (or Accounts Payable)		*125*

Air freight charges on merchandise purchased from Miller Brothers, Kansas City.

Since transportation charges are part of the **delivered cost** of merchandise purchased, the Transportation-in account is combined with the Purchases account in the income statement in determining the cost of goods available for sale.

One reason for using a separate ledger account for Transportation-in rather than debiting these charges directly to the Purchases account is to provide management with a clear record of the amount expended each period for inbound transportation. A knowledge of the amount and trend of each significant type of cost is a necessary first step if management is to control costs effectively. For example, detailed information concerning transportation costs would be important to management in making decisions between rail and air transportation, or in deciding whether to order in carload lots rather than in smaller quantities.

Transportation charges on inbound shipments of merchandise must not be confused with transportation charges on outbound shipments of goods to customers. Freight charges and other expenses incurred in making deliveries to customers are regarded as selling expenses; these outlays are debited to a separate account entitled Transportation-out, and are not included in the cost of goods sold.

F.O.B. shipping point and F.O.B. destination

The agreement between the buyer and seller of merchandise includes a provision as to which party shall bear the cost of transporting the goods.

The term *F.O.B. shipping point* means that the seller will place the merchandise "free on board" the railroad cars or other means of transport, and that the buyer must pay transportation charges from that point. Many people in negotiating for the purchase of a new automobile have encountered the expression "F.O.B. Detroit," meaning that the buyer must pay the freight charges from the manufacturer's location in Detroit, in addition to the basic price of the car. In most merchandise transactions involving wholesalers or manufacturers, the buyer bears the transportation cost. Sometimes, however, as a matter of convenience, the seller prepays the freight and adds this cost to the amount billed to the buyer.

F.O.B. destination means that the seller agrees to bear the freight cost. If the seller prepays the truckline or other carrier, the agreed terms have been met and no action is required of the buyer other than to pay the agreed purchase price of the goods. If the seller does not prepay the freight, the buyer will pay the carrier and deduct this payment from the amount owed the seller when making payment for the merchandise.

Illustration of accounting cycle using periodic inventory method

An annual income statement for the Campus Sports Shop was presented on page 158. Transactions of the Campus Sports Shop for the following year, Year 11, will now be used to illustrate the accounting cycle for a business using the periodic inventory system of accounting for merchandise.

RECORDING SALES OF MERCHANDISE   All sales of sports equipment during the year were for cash, and each sales transaction was rung up on a cash register. At the close of each day's business, the total sales for the day were computed by pressing the total key on the cash register. As soon as each day's sales were computed, a journal entry was prepared and posted to the Cash account and to the Sales account in the ledger. The following journal entry is typical:

Cash *600*
   Sales *600*
To record today's sales of merchandise.

The daily entering of cash sales in the journal tends to minimize the opportunity for errors or dishonesty by employees in handling the cash receipts. In Chapter 7 a procedure will be described which provides a daily record of sales and cash receipts yet avoids the making of an excessive number of entries in the Cash and Sales accounts.

RECORDING SALES RETURNS AND ALLOWANCES   Customers of retail stores are generally permitted to return any merchandise which they find to be unsatisfactory and obtain a cash refund or credit on their accounts. Sometimes the store may agree that the customer may keep the merchandise and be allowed a reduction in the sales price. Management needs to keep informed on the amount of sales returns and allowances and the relationship of these amounts to the volume of sales. To provide such information, a return of merchandise or a price allowance is recorded in a Sales Returns and Allowances account, as shown by the following journal entry:

Sales Returns and Allowances *150*

    Cash (or Accounts Receivable) *150*

Made refund for merchandise returned by customer.

OTHER OPERATING TRANSACTIONS DURING THE YEAR Other routine transactions carried out by Campus Sports Shop during Year 11 included the purchase of merchandise, the return of goods to suppliers, payment of charges for transportation-in, payment of accounts payable, and payment of operating expenses, such as salaries, telephone, and advertising. To conserve space in this illustration, these transactions are not listed individually but are included in ledger account balances at December 31.

WORK SHEET FOR A MERCHANDISING BUSINESS After the year's transactions of the Campus Sports Shop had been posted to ledger accounts, the work sheet illustrated on page 169 was prepared. The first step in the preparation of the work sheet was, of course, the listing of the balances of the ledger accounts in the Trial Balance columns. In studying this work sheet, note that the Inventory account in the Trial Balance debit column still shows a balance of $30,000, the cost of merchandise on hand at the end of the prior year. No entries were made in the Inventory account during the current year despite the various purchases and sales of merchandise. The significance of the Inventory account in the trial balance is that it shows the amount of merchandise with which the Campus Sports Shop began operations on January 1 of the current year.

Adjustments on the work sheet Salaries to employees and interest on the notes payable were paid to date on December 31; consequently adjustments were not necessary for accrued salaries or accrued interest at year-end. Only two adjustments were necessary at December 31: one to record depreciation of the building and the other to record the insurance expense for the year. The Adjustments columns were then totaled to prove the equality of the adjustment debits and credits.

Omission of Adjusted Trial Balance columns In the work sheet previously illustrated in Chapter 4, page 136, the amounts in the Trial Balance columns were combined with the amounts listed in the Adjustments columns and then extended into the Adjusted Trial Balance columns. When there are only a few adjusting entries, many accountants prefer to omit the Adjusted Trial Balance columns and to extend the trial balance figures (as adjusted by the amounts in the Adjustments columns) directly to the Income Statement or Balance Sheet columns. This procedure is used in the work sheet for the Campus Sports Shop.

CAMPUS SPORTS SHOP
Work Sheet
For the Year Ended December 31, Year II

	Trial Balance Dr	Trial Balance Cr	Adjustments* Dr	Adjustments* Cr	Income Statement Dr	Income Statement Cr	Balance Sheet Dr	Balance Sheet Cr
Cash	8,000						8,000	
Inventory, Jan. 1	30,000				30,000			
Unexpired insurance	4,000			(b) 1,000			3,000	
Land	30,000						30,000	
Building	60,000						60,000	
Accumulated depreciation: building		12,000		(a) 3,000				15,000
Notes payable		42,000						42,000
Accounts payable		19,000						19,000
Robert Riley, capital		54,000						54,000
Robert Riley, drawing	26,000						26,000	
Sales		215,000				215,000		
Sales returns and allowances	5,000				5,000			
Purchases	128,000				128,000			
Purchase returns and allowances		2,000				2,000		
Transportation-in	4,000				4,000			
Advertising expense	9,000				9,000			
Salaries expense	37,000				37,000			
Telephone expense	1,100				1,100			
Interest expense	1,900				1,900			
	344,000	344,000						
Depreciation expense: building			(a) 3,000		3,000			
Insurance expense			(b) 1,000		1,000			
			4,000	4,000				
Inventory, Dec. 31						34,000	34,000	
					220,000	251,000	161,000	130,000
Net income					31,000			31,000
					251,000	251,000	161,000	161,000

*Adjustments: (a) Depreciation of building during the year.
(b) Insurance premium expired during the year.

Note the treatment of the beginning inventory

Note the treatment of the ending inventory

Recording the ending inventory on the work sheet The key points to be observed in this work sheet are (1) the method of recording the ending inventory and (2) the method of handling the various accounts making up the cost of goods sold.

After the close of business on December 31, Riley and his assistants took a physical inventory of all merchandise in the store. The cost of the entire stock of goods was determined to be $34,000. This ending inventory, dated December 31, does not appear in the trial balance; it is therefore written on the first available line below the trial balance totals. The amount of $34,000 is listed in the Income Statement credit column and also in the Balance Sheet debit column. By entering the ending inventory in the Income Statement *credit* column, we are in effect deducting it from the total of the beginning inventory, the purchases, and the transportation-in, all of which are extended from the trial balance to the Income Statement *debit* column.

One of the functions of the Income Statement columns is to bring together all the accounts involved in determining the cost of goods sold. The accounts with debit balances are the beginning inventory, the purchases, and the transportation-in; these accounts total $162,000. Against this total, the two credit items of purchase returns, $2,000 and ending inventory, $34,000, are offset. The three merchandising accounts with debit balances exceed in total the two with credit balances by an amount of $126,000; this amount is the cost of goods sold, as shown in the income statement on page 171.

The ending inventory is also entered in the Balance Sheet debit column, because this inventory of merchandise on December 31 will appear as an asset in the balance sheet bearing this date.

Completing the work sheet When all the accounts on the work sheet have been extended into the Income Statement or Balance Sheet columns (and the ending inventory has been entered), the final four columns should be totaled. The net income of $31,000 is computed by subtracting the Income Statement debit column from the Income Statement credit column. This same amount of $31,000 can also be obtained by subtracting the Balance Sheet credit column from the Balance Sheet debit column. To balance out the four columns, the amount of the net income is entered in the Income Statement debit column and on the same line in the Balance Sheet credit column. (The proof of accuracy afforded by the self-balancing nature of the work sheet was explained in Chapter 4.) Final totals are determined for the Income Statement and Balance Sheet columns, and the work sheet is complete.

Financial statements

The work to be done at the end of the period is much the same for a merchandising business as for a service-type firm. First, the work sheet is completed; then, financial statements are prepared from the data in the work sheet; next, the adjusting and closing entries are entered in the journal and posted to the ledger accounts; and finally, an after-closing trial balance is prepared. This completes the periodic accounting cycle.

INCOME STATEMENT The income statement below was prepared from the work sheet on page 169. Note particularly the arrangement of items in the cost of goods sold section of the income statement; this portion of the income statement shows in summary form most of the essential accounting concepts covered in this chapter.

CAMPUS SPORTS SHOP

Income Statement

For the Year Ended December 31, Year 11

This	*Revenue from sales:*		
income	*Sales*	*$215,000*	
statement			
consists	*Less: Sales returns and allowances*	*5,000*	
of	*Net sales*		*$210,000*
three			
major	*Cost of goods sold:*		
sections	*Inventory, Jan. 1*	*$ 30,000*	
	Purchases	*$128,000*	
	Transportation-in	*4,000*	
	Delivered cost of purchases	*$132,000*	
	Less: Purchase returns and allowances	*2,000*	
	Net purchases	*130,000*	
	Cost of goods available for sale	*$160,000*	
	Less: Inventory, Dec. 31	*34,000*	
	Cost of goods sold		*126,000*
	Gross profit on sales		*$ 84,000*
	Operating expenses:		
	Advertising	*$ 9,000*	
	Salaries	*37,000*	
	Telephone	*1,100*	
	Interest	*1,900*	
	Depreciation	*3,000*	
	Insurance	*1,000*	
	Total operating expenses		*53,000*
	Net income		*$ 31,000*

STATEMENT OF OWNER'S EQUITY The statement of owner's equity shows the increase in owner's equity from the year's net income and the decrease from the owner's withdrawals during the year.

CAMPUS SPORTS SHOP
Statement of Owner's Equity
For the Year Ended December 31, Year 11

Which figure for owner's equity appeared on the work sheet? Robert Riley, capital, Jan. 1, 19___		$54,000
Net income for the year		31,000
Subtotal		$85,000
Less: Withdrawals		26,000
Robert Riley, capital, Dec. 31, 19___		$59,000

BALANCE SHEET   In studying the following balance sheet, note that all items are taken from the Balance Sheet columns of the work sheet, but that the amount for Robert Riley, Capital is the December 31 balance of $59,000, computed as shown in the preceding statement of owner's equity.

CAMPUS SPORTS SHOP
Balance Sheet
December 31, Year 11

Assets

Cash		$ 8,000
Inventory		34,000
Unexpired insurance		3,000
Land		30,000
Building	$60,000	
Less: Accumulated depreciation	15,000	45,000
Total assets		$120,000

Liabilities & Owner's Equity

Liabilities:		
Notes payable		$ 42,000
Accounts payable		19,000
Total liabilities		$ 61,000
Owner's equity:		
Robert Riley, capital, Dec. 31		59,000
Total liabilities & owner's equity		$120,000

CLOSING ENTRIES   The entries used in closing revenue and expense accounts have been explained in preceding chapters. The only new elements in this illustration of closing entries for a merchandising business are the entries showing the elimination of the beginning inventory and the recording of the ending inventory. The beginning inventory is cleared out of the Inventory account by a debit to Income Summary and a credit to Inventory. A separate entry could be made for this purpose, but we can save time by making one compound entry which will debit the Income Summary account with the balance of the beginning inventory and with the balances of all temporary proprietorship accounts having debit balances. The **temporary proprietorship accounts** are those which appear in the income statement. As the name suggests, the temporary proprietorship accounts are used during the period to accumulate temporarily the increases and decreases in the proprietor's equity resulting from operation of the business. The entry to close out the beginning inventory and temporary proprietorship accounts with debit balances is illustrated below.

Closing	*Dec. 31 Income Summary* *220,000*	
temporary	*Inventory (Jan. 1)*	*30,000*
proprietor-	*Purchases*	*128,000*
ship	*Sales Returns and Allowances*	*5,000*
accounts	*Transportation-in*	*4,000*
with debit	*Advertising Expense*	*9,000*
balances	*Salaries Expense*	*37,000*
	Telephone Expense	*1,100*
	Interest Expense	*1,900*
	Depreciation Expense	*3,000*
	Insurance Expense	*1,000*
	To close out the beginning inventory and the temporary	
	proprietorship accounts with debit balances.	

Note that the above entry closes all the operating expense accounts as well as the accounts used to accumulate the cost of goods sold, and also the Sales Returns and Allowances account. Although the Sales Returns and Allowances account has a debit balance, it is not an expense account. In terms of account classification, it belongs in the revenue group of accounts because it serves as an offset to the Sales account and appears in the income statement as a deduction from Sales.

To bring the ending inventory into the accounting records after the stocktaking on December 31, we could make a separate entry debiting Inventory and crediting the Income Summary account. It is more convenient, however, to combine this step with the closing of the Sales account and any other temporary proprietorship accounts having credit balances, as illustrated in the following closing entry.

Closing	*Dec. 31 Inventory (Dec. 31)* *34,000*	
temporary	*Sales* *215,000*	
proprietor-	*Purchase Returns and Allowances* *2,000*	
ship	*Income Summary*	*251,000*
accounts	*To record the ending inventory and to close all temporary*	
with	*proprietorship accounts with credit balances.*	
credit		
balances		

The remaining closing entries serve to transfer the balance of the Income Summary account to the owner's capital account and to close the drawing account, as follows:

Closing
the Income
Summary
account
and owner's
drawing
account
Dec. 31 Income Summary   31,000

               Robert Riley, Capital   31,000

        To close the Income Summary account.

Dec. 31 Robert Riley, Capital   26,000

               Robert Riley, Drawing   26,000

        To close the drawing account.

Summary of merchandising transactions and related accounting entries

The transactions regularly encountered in merchandising operations and the related accounting entries may be concisely summarized as follows:

	Transactions during the Period	Related Accounting Entries	
		Debit	Credit
Customary journal entries relating to mer-chandise	Purchase merchandise for resale	Purchases	Cash (or Ac-counts Payable)
	Incur transportation charges on merchandise purchased for resale	Transportation-in	Cash (or Ac-counts Payable)
	Return unsatisfactory merchandise to sup-plier, or obtain a reduction from original price	Cash (or Ac-counts Payable)	Purchase Re-turns and Allowances
	Sell merchandise to customers	Cash (or Ac-counts Receiva-ble)	Sales
	Permit customers to return merchandise, or grant them a reduction from original price	Sales Returns and Allowances	Cash (or Ac-counts Receiva-ble)
	Inventory Procedures at End of Period		
	Transfer the balance of the beginning in-ventory to the Income Summary account	Income Summary	Inventory
	Take a physical inventory of goods on hand at the end of the period, and price these goods at cost	Inventory	Income Summary

Classified financial statements

The financial statements illustrated up to this point have been rather short and simple because of the limited number of transactions and accounts used in these introductory chapters. Now let us look briefly at a more comprehensive and realistic balance sheet for a merchandising business. A full understanding of all the items on this balance sheet may not be possible until our study of accounting has progressed further, but a bird's-eye view of a fairly complete balance sheet is nevertheless useful at this point.

In the balance sheet of the Graham Company illustrated on page 176, the assets are classified into three groups: (1) current assets, (2) plant and equipment, and (3) other assets. The liabilities are classified into two types: (1) current liabilities and (2) long-term liabilities. This classification of assets and liabilities, subject to minor variations in terminology, is virtually a standard one throughout American business. The inclusion of captions for the balance sheet totals is an optional step.

THE PURPOSE OF BALANCE SHEET CLASSIFICATION   The purpose underlying a standard classification of assets and liabilities is to aid management, owners, creditors, and other interested persons in understanding the financial position of the business. Bankers, for example, would have a difficult time in reading the balance sheets of all the companies which apply to them for loans, if each of these companies followed its own individual whims as to the sequence and arrangement of accounts comprising its balance sheet. Standard practices as to the order and arrangement of a balance sheet are an important means of saving the time of the reader and of giving a fuller comprehension of the company's financial position. On the other hand, these standard practices are definitely not iron-clad rules; the form and content of a well-prepared balance sheet today are different in several respects from the balance sheet of 25 years ago. No two businesses are exactly alike and a degree of variation from the conventional type of balance sheet is appropriate for the individual business in devising a clear presentation of its financial position. Standardization of the form and content of financial statements is a desirable goal; but if carried to an extreme, it might prevent the introduction of new improved methods and the constructive changes necessary to reflect changes in business practices.

The analysis and interpretation of financial statements is the subject of Chapter 22. At this point our objective is merely to emphasize that classification of the items on a balance sheet aids the reader greatly in appraising the financial position of the business. Some of the major balance sheet classifications are discussed briefly in the following section.

CURRENT ASSETS   Current assets include cash, government bonds and other marketable securities, receivables, inventories, and prepaid expenses. To qualify for inclusion in the current asset category, an asset must be capable of being converted into cash within a relatively short period without interfering with the normal operation of the business. The period is usually one year, but it may be longer for those businesses having an operating cycle in excess of one year. The sequence in which current assets are listed depends upon their liquidity; the closer an asset is to becoming cash the higher is its liquidity. The total amount of a company's

THE GRAHAM COMPANY
Balance Sheet
December 31, 19____

Assets

Current assets:

Cash			$ 14,500
U.S. government bonds			10,000
Notes receivable			2,400
Accounts receivable		$26,960	
Less: Allowance for doubtful accounts		860	26,100
Inventory			45,200
Prepaid expenses			1,200
Total current assets			$ 99,400

Plant and equipment:

Land		$10,000	
Building	$24,000		
Less: Accumulated depreciation	1,920	22,080	
Store equipment	$ 9,400		
Less: Accumulated depreciation	1,880	7,520	
Delivery equipment	$ 2,800		
Less: Accumulated depreciation	700	2,100	
Total plant and equipment			41,700

Other assets:

Land (future building site)			16,500
Total assets			$157,600

Liabilities & Owner's Equity

Current liabilities:

Notes payable		$ 11,500
Accounts payable		19,040
Accrued expenses payable		1,410
Deferred revenue		1,100
Total current liabilities		$ 33,050

Long-term liabilities:

Mortgage payable (due 1980)		25,000
Total liabilities		$ 58,050

Owner's equity:

George Graham, capital, Dec. 31		99,550
Total liabilities & owner's equity		$157,600

Note: A new item introduced in this balance sheet is the Allowance for Doubtful Accounts of $860, shown as a deduction from Accounts Receivable. This is an estimate of the uncollectible portion of the accounts receivable and serves to reduce the valuation of this asset to the net amount of $26,100 that is considered collectible.

current assets and the relative amount of each type give some indication of the company's short-run, debt-paying ability.

The term **operating cycle** is often used in establishing the limits of the current asset classification. Operating cycle means the average time period between the purchase of merchandise and the conversion of this merchandise back into cash. The series of transactions comprising a complete cycle often runs as follows: (*1*) purchase of merchandise, (*2*) sale of the merchandise on credit, (*3*) collection of the account receivable from the customer. The word **cycle** suggests the circular flow of capital from cash to inventory to receivables to cash again. This cycle of transactions in a merchandising business is portrayed in the following diagram.

The operating cycle repeats continuously

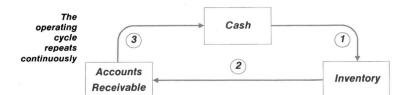

In a business handling fast-moving merchandise (a supermarket, for example) the operating cycle may be completed in a few weeks; for most merchandising businesses the operating cycle requires several months but less than a year.

CURRENT LIABILITIES Liabilities that must be paid within one year or the operating cycle (whichever is longer) are called **current liabilities.** Current liabilities are paid out of current assets, and a comparison of the amount of current assets with the amount of current liabilities is an important step in appraising the ability of a company to pay its debts in the near future.

CURRENT RATIO Many bankers and other users of financial statements believe that for a business to qualify as a good credit risk, the total current assets should be about twice as large as the total current liabilities. In studying a balance sheet, a banker or other creditor will compute the **current ratio** by dividing total current assets by total current liabilities. The current ratio is a convenient measure of the short-run debt-paying ability of a business.

In the illustrated balance sheet of The Graham Company, the current assets of $99,400 are approximately three times as great as the current liabilities of $33,050; the current ratio is therefore 3 to 1, which would generally be regarded as a very strong current position. The current assets could shrink by two-thirds and still be sufficient for payment of the current liabilities. Although a strong current ratio is desirable, an extremely high current ratio (such as 4 to 1 or more) may signify that a company is holding too much of its resources in cash, marketable securities, and other current assets and is not pursuing profit opportunities as aggressively as it might.

WORKING CAPITAL   The excess of current assets over current liabilities is called *working capital;* the relative amount of working capital is another indication of short-term financial strength. In the illustrated balance sheet of the Graham Company, working capital is $66,350, computed by subtracting the current liabilities of $33,050 from the current assets of $99,400. The importance of solvency (ability to meet debts as they fall due) was emphasized in Chapter 1. Ample working capital permits a company to buy merchandise in large lots, to carry an adequate stock of goods, and to sell goods to customers on favorable credit terms. Many companies have been forced to suspend business because of inadequate working capital, even though total assets were much larger than total liabilities.

CLASSIFICATION IN THE INCOME STATEMENT   A new feature to be noted in the illustrated income statement of the Graham Company (page 179) is the division of the operating expenses into the two categories of selling expenses and general and administrative expenses. Selling expenses include all expenses of storing merchandise, advertising and sales promotion, sales salaries and commissions, and delivering goods to customers. General and administrative expenses include the expenses of operating the general offices, the accounting department, the personnel office, and the credit and collection department.

This classification aids management in controlling expenses by emphasizing that certain expenses are the responsibility of the executive in charge of sales, and that other types of expenses relate to the business as a whole. Some expenses, such as depreciation of the building, may be divided between the two classifications according to the portion utilized by each functional division of the business. The item of Uncollectible Accounts Expense listed under the heading of General and Administrative Expenses is an expense of estimated amount. It will be discussed fully in Chapter 9.

Another feature to note in the income statement of the Graham Company is that interest earned on investments is placed after the figure showing income from operations. Other examples of such *nonoperating revenues* are dividends on shares of stock owned, and rent earned by leasing property not presently needed in the operation of the business. Any items of expense not related to selling or administrative functions may also be placed at the bottom of the income statement after the income from operations. Separate group headings of Nonoperating Revenue and Nonoperating Expenses are sometimes used.

THE GRAHAM COMPANY
Income Statement
For the Year Ended December 31, 19___

Gross sales			$310,890
Sales returns & allowances		$ 3,820	
Sales discounts		4,830	8,650
Net sales			$302,240
Cost of goods sold:			
Inventory, Jan. 1		$ 30,040	
Purchases	$212,400		
Transportation-in	8,300		
Delivered cost of purchases	$220,700		
Less: Purchase returns & allowances	$2,400		
Purchase discounts	5,100	7,500	
Net purchases		213,200	
Cost of goods available for sale		$243,240	
Less: Inventory, Dec. 31		35,200	
Cost of goods sold			208,040
Gross profit on sales			$ 94,200
Operating expenses:			
Selling expenses:			
Sales salaries		$ 38,410	
Advertising		10,190	
Depreciation: building		840	
Depreciation: store equipment		940	
Depreciation: delivery equipment		700	
Insurance		1,100	
Miscellaneous		820	
Total selling expenses		$ 53,000	
General and administrative expenses:			
Office salaries		$ 19,200	
Uncollectible accounts		750	
Depreciation: building		120	
Insurance		100	
Miscellaneous		930	
Total general and administrative expenses		21,100	
Total operating expenses			74,100
Income from operations			$ 20,100
Interest earned on investments			300
Net income			$ 20,400

Condensed income statement

The income statements prepared by different companies vary considerably in the amount of detail shown. Often the income statement is greatly

condensed because the public is presumably not interested in the details of operations. A condensed income statement usually begins with *net sales*. The details involved in computing the cost of goods sold are also often omitted and only summary figures are given for selling expenses and general and administrative expenses. A condensed income statement for the Graham Company follows:

THE GRAHAM COMPANY
Income Statement
For the Year Ended December 31, 19____

A	*Net sales*		*$302,240*
condensed income statement	*Cost of goods sold*		*208,040*
	Gross profit on sales		*$ 94,200*
	Expenses:		
	Selling	*$53,000*	
	General and administrative	*21,100*	*74,100*
	Income from operations		*$ 20,100*
	Interest earned on investments		*300*
	Net income		*$ 20,400*

The statement of owner's equity for the Graham Company would not differ significantly from the form illustrated earlier in this chapter.

KEY TERMS INTRODUCED OR EMPHASIZED IN CHAPTER 5

Beginning inventory   Goods on hand and available for sale to customers at the beginning of the accounting period.

Cost of goods sold   A computation appearing as a separate section of an income statement showing the cost of goods sold during the period. Computed by adding net delivered cost of merchandise purchases to beginning inventory to obtain cost of goods available for sale, and then deducting from this total the amount of the ending inventory. Usually equal to between 60 and 80% of net sales.

Current assets   Cash and other assets that can be converted into cash within one year or the operating cycle (whichever is longer) without interfering with the normal operation of the business.

Current liabilities   Any debts that must be paid within one year or the operating cycle (whichever is longer).

Current ratio   Current assets divided by current liabilities. A measure of short-run debt-paying ability.

Ending inventory   Goods still on hand and available for sale to customers at the end of the accounting period.

F.O.B. destination   The seller bears the cost of shipping goods to the buyer's location.

F.O.B. shipping point   The buyer of goods bears the cost of transportation from the seller's location to the buyer's location.

General and administrative expenses   Expenses of the general offices, accounting department, personnel office, credit and collection department and activities other than the selling of goods. A subdivision of operating expenses.

Gross profit on sales   Revenue from sales minus cost of goods sold.

Inventory (merchandise)   Goods acquired and held for sale to customers.

Merchandise   Goods which a business buys for the purpose of selling to customers.

Operating cycle   The average time period from the purchase of merchandise to its sale and conversion back into cash.

Operating expenses   Include both selling expenses and general and administrative expenses. Deducted from gross profit on sales to determine net income.

Periodic inventory system   A system of accounting for merchandise in which inventory at the balance sheet date is determined by counting and pricing the goods on hand. Cost of goods sold is computed by subtracting the ending inventory from the cost of goods available for sale.

Perpetual inventory system   A system of accounting for merchandise that provides a continuous record showing the quantity and cost of all goods on hand.

Physical inventory   The process of counting and pricing the merchandise on hand at a given date, usually the end of the accounting period.

Pricing the inventory   The assignment of an appropriate dollar value to each item of merchandise determined to be on hand at the time of taking a physical count of inventory.

Purchases   An account used to record the cost of merchandise purchased for the purpose of sale to customers.

Purchase Returns and Allowances   An account used by the buying company to record the cost of unsatisfactory merchandise returned to the supplier. Also used for a downward adjustment of the purchase price of merchandise because of some defect in the goods.

Replacement cost   The estimated current cost of replacing goods in inventory or goods sold during the period. Large corporations must disclose in financial statements both historical cost and current replacement cost of inventories and cost of goods sold.

Sales   The revenue account credited with the sales price of goods sold during the accounting period.

Sales Returns and Allowances   An account used by the selling company to record the sales price of goods returned by customers. Also used for a downward adjustment of the sales price allowed to the customer because of some defect in the goods.

Selling expenses   Expenses of marketing the product, such as advertising, sales salaries, and delivery of merchandise to customers. A subdivision of operating expenses.

Working capital   Current assets minus current liabilities.

DEMONSTRATION PROBLEM FOR YOUR REVIEW

In this demonstration problem for a merchandising company, note that operations for the year result in a net loss. Since the revenue for the year is less than the expenses, the Income Summary account has a debit balance. The closing of the Income Summary account into the owner's capital account therefore causes a decrease in the amount of the owner's capital.

The trial balance of Stone Supply Company at December 31, 19___ appears

below. An inventory taken on December 31, 19___ amounted to $32,440. The following adjustments should be made:
(*1*) Depreciation of buildings, $4,100; of delivery equipment, $1,500.
(*2*) Accrued salaries: office, $845; sales, $950.
(*3*) Insurance expired, $250.
(*4*) Store supplies used, $1,000.

STONE SUPPLY COMPANY
Trial Balance
December 31, 19___

Cash	$ 9,310	
Accounts receivable	10,380	
Inventory, Jan. 1, 19___	28,650	
Store supplies	1,270	
Unexpired insurance	610	
Land	89,700	
Buildings	100,000	
Accumulated depreciation: buildings		$ 17,650
Delivery equipment	45,000	
Accumulated depreciation: delivery equipment		14,800
Accounts payable		22,450
Accrued salaries payable		
John Stone, capital		285,165
John Stone, drawing	40,000	
Sales		171,220
Sales returns & allowances	2,430	
Purchases	138,900	
Purchase returns & allowances		1,820
Sales salaries expense	25,050	
Delivery expense	2,800	
Depreciation expense: delivery equipment		
Office salaries expense	19,005	
Depreciation expense: buildings		
Insurance expense		
Store supplies expense		
	$513,105	$513,105

Instructions
a Prepare a 10-column work sheet at December 31, 19___, with pairs of columns for Trial Balance, Adjustments, Adjusted Trial Balance, Income Statement, and Balance Sheet.
b Prepare an income statement for the year.
c Prepare a statement of owner's equity for the year.
d Prepare a classified balance sheet at December 31, 19___
e Prepare closing journal entries.

SOLUTION TO DEMONSTRATION PROBLEM

STONE SUPPLY COMPANY
Work Sheet
For the Year Ended December 31, 19___

	Trial Balance		Adjustments*		Adjusted Trial Balance		Income Statement		Balance Sheet	
	Dr	Cr	Dr	Cr	Dr	Cr	Dr	Cr	Dr	Cr
Cash	9,310				9,310				9,310	
Accounts receivable	10,380				10,380				10,380	
Inventory, Jan. 1, 19___	28,650				28,650		28,650			
Store supplies	1,270			(4) 1,000	270				270	
Unexpired insurance	610			(3) 250	360				360	
Land	89,700				89,700				89,700	
Buildings	100,000				100,000				100,000	
Accum. depr.: buildings		17,650		(1) 4,100		21,750				21,750
Delivery equipment	45,000				45,000				45,000	
Accum. depr.: del. eqpt.		14,800		(1) 1,500		16,300				16,300
Accounts payable		22,450				22,450				22,450
Accrued salaries payable				(2) 1,795		1,795				1,795
John Stone, capital		285,165				285,165				285,165
John Stone, drawing	40,000				40,000				40,000	
Sales		171,220				171,220		171,220		
Sales returns & allowances	2,430				2,430		2,430			
Purchases	138,900				138,900		138,900			
Purchase returns & allowances		1,820				1,820		1,820		
Sales salaries expense	25,050		(2) 950		26,000		26,000			
Delivery expense	2,800				2,800		2,800			
Depr. expense: del. eqpt.			(1) 1,500		1,500		1,500			
Office salaries expense	19,005		(2) 845		19,850		19,850			
Depr. expense: buildings			(1) 4,100		4,100		4,100			
Insurance expense			(3) 250		250		250			
Store supplies expense			(4) 1,000		1,000		1,000			
	513,105	513,105	8,645	8,645	520,500	520,500				
Inventory, Dec. 31, 19___								32,440	32,440	
							225,480	205,480	327,460	347,460
Net loss								20,000	20,000	
							225,480	225,480	347,460	347,460

*Adjustments: (1) To record depreciation expense for the year.
                (2) To record accrued salaries payable at Dec. 31, 19___.
                (3) To record insurance expired.
                (4) To record store supplies used.

a

b

STONE SUPPLY COMPANY
Income Statement
For the Year Ended December 31, 19___

Sales			$171,220
Less: Sales returns & allowances			2,430
Net sales			$168,790
Cost of goods sold:			
Inventory, Jan. 1, 19___		$ 28,650	
Purchases	$138,900		
Less: Purchase returns & allowances	1,820	137,080	
Cost of goods available for sale		$165,730	
Less: Inventory, Dec. 31, 19___		32,440	
Costs of goods sold			133,290
Gross profit on sales			$ 35,500
Operating expenses:			
Sales salaries expense		$ 26,000	
Delivery expense		2,800	
Depreciation expense: delivery equipment		1,500	
Office salaries expense		19,850	
Depreciation expense: buildings		4,100	
Insurance expense		250	
Store supplies expense		1,000	
Total operating expenses			55,500
Net loss			$ 20,000

c

STONE SUPPLY COMPANY
Statement of Owner's Equity
For the Year Ended December 31, 19___

John Stone, capital, Jan. 1, 19___		$285,165
Less: Net loss	$20,000	
Drawings	40,000	60,000
John Stone, capital, Dec. 31, 19___		$225,165

d

STONE SUPPLY COMPANY
Balance Sheet
December 31, 19___

Assets

Current assets:

Cash		$ 9,310
Accounts receivable		10,380
Inventory		32,440
Store supplies		270
Unexpired insurance		360
Total current assets		$ 52,760

Plant and equipment:

Land		$ 89,700	
Buildings	$100,000		
Less: Accumulated depreciation	21,750	78,250	
Delivery equipment	$ 45,000		
Less: Accumulated depreciation	16,300	28,700	
Total plant and equipment			196,650
Total assets			$249,410

Liabilities & Owner's Equity

Current liabilities:

Accounts payable	$ 22,450
Accrued salaries payable	1,795
Total current liabilities............	$ 24,245

Owner's equity:

John Stone, capital	225,165
Total liabilities & owner's equity	$249,410

e

			Closing Entries		
19___					
Dec.	31		Income Summary	225,480	
			Inventory, Jan. 1, 19___		28,650
			Sales Returns & Allowances.........		2,430
			Purchases		138,900
			Sales Salaries Expense.............		26,000
			Delivery Expense.................		2,800
			Depreciation Expense: Delivery Equipment		1,500
			Office Salaries Expense		19,850
			Depreciation Expense: Buildings		4,100
			Insurance Expense		250
			Store Supplies Expense		1,000
			To close the beginning inventory account and all temporary proprietorship accounts having debit balances.		

31	Sales	171,220	
	Inventory, Dec. 31, 19___	32,440	
	Purchase Returns & Allowances	1,820	
	Income Summary		205,480
	To set up the ending inventory and close all		
	temporary proprietorship accounts having credit		
	balances.		
31	John Stone, Capital	20,000	
	Income Summary		20,000
	To close the Income Summary account.		
31	John Stone, Capital	40,000	
	John Stone, Drawing		40,000
	To close the drawing account.		

REVIEW QUESTIONS

1 During the current year, Green Bay Company made all sales of merchandise at prices in excess of cost. Will the business necessarily report a net income for the year? Explain.

2 Hi-Rise Company during its first year of operation had cost of goods sold of $90,000 and a gross profit equal to 40% of sales. What was the dollar amount of sales for the year?

3 In accounting for an unincorporated business, is it customary to include a salary to the owner as an expense of the business if he or she works full time for the business? Why or why not?

4 In appraising the adequacy of the net income of a small business in which the owner works on a full-time basis, the net income may be regarded as including three separate elements. What are these three elements?

5 Which of the following expenditures by Southside Drugstore should be recorded by a debit to the Purchases account?
a Purchase of a new delivery truck
b Purchase of a three-year insurance policy
c Purchase of drugs from drug manufacturer
d Purchase of advertising space in local newspaper
e Payment in advance for three months' guard service by Security Patrol, Inc.

6 Supply the proper terms to complete the following statements:
a Net sales − cost of goods sold = _?_
b Net purchases + beginning inventory + transportation-in = _?_
c Cost of goods sold + ending inventory = _?_
d Cost of goods sold + gross profit on sales = _?_
e Net income + operating expenses = _?_

7 During the current year, Davis Corporation purchased merchandise costing $200,000. State the cost of goods sold under each of the following alternative assumptions:
a No beginning inventory; ending inventory $40,000
b Beginning inventory $60,000; no ending inventory
c Beginning inventory $58,000; ending inventory $78,000
d Beginning inventory $90,000; ending inventory $67,000

8 Zenith Company uses the periodic inventory method and maintains its accounting records on a calendar-year basis. Does the beginning or the ending inventory figure appear in the trial balance prepared from the ledger on December 31?

9 Compute the amount of cost of goods sold, given the following account balances: beginning inventory $25,000, purchases $84,000, purchase returns and allowances $4,500, transportation-in $500, and ending inventory $36,000.

10 Explain the terms *current assets, current liabilities,* and *current ratio.*

11 The Riblet Company has a current ratio of 3 to 1 and working capital of $60,000. What are the amounts of current assets and current liabilities?

12 Why is it advisable to use a Purchase Returns and Allowances account when the same end result may be achieved by crediting the Purchases account when goods purchased are returned to the suppliers?

13 Which party (seller or buyer) bears the transportation costs when the terms of a merchandise sale are (*a*) F.O.B. shipping point; (*b*) F.O.B. destination?

14 Where does the account Transportation-in appear in the financial statements?

15 Is the normal balance of the Sales Returns and Allowances account a debit or credit? Is the normal balance of the Purchase Returns and Allowances account a debit or credit?

16 In which columns of the work sheet for a merchandising company does the ending inventory appear?

17 State briefly the difference between the *perpetual* inventory system and the *periodic* inventory system.

18 If cost of goods sold amounts to 65% of the sales of a merchandising business and net income amounts to 5% of sales, what percentage of sales is represented by operating expenses? What percentage of gross profit is included in each dollar of sales?

19 When the periodic inventory method is in use, how is the amount of inventory determined at the end of the period?

20 What is the purpose of a closing entry consisting of a debit to the Income Summary account and a credit to the Inventory account?

21 Define a *condensed income statement* and indicate its advantages and possible shortcomings.

22 What disclosure requirements concerning the cost of inventories have been imposed on large corporations by the Securities and Exchange Commission as a result of continued inflation? Explain.

EXERCISES

Ex. 5-1 Use the following data as a basis for computing the amount of the beginning inventory.

Purchase returns and allowances	$ 7,360
Transportation-in	3,840
Cost of goods sold	67,040
Purchases	104,000
Ending inventory	61,520

Ex. 5-2 Compute the amount of *total* purchases for the period, given the following data:

Sales	$219,180
Ending inventory	46,200

Purchase returns and allowances	$ ⁻2,580
Beginning inventory	⁺52,368
Transportation-in	⁺2,268
Cost of goods sold	⁻151,680

Ex. 5-3 During September, Mills Company made sales of merchandise on credit amounting to $203,200, of which $174,400 remain uncollected at September 30. Sales for cash during September amounted to $48,000 and an additional $158,400 was received from customers in payment for goods sold to them in prior months. Also during September, the Mills Company borrowed $57,600 cash from the Second National Bank. What was the total revenue for September?

Ex. 5-4 The balance sheet of Rivers Company contained the following items, among others:

Cash	$137,600
Accounts receivable	48,000
Inventory	198,400
Store equipment (net)	192,000
Other assets	28,800
Mortgage payable (due in 3 years)	48,000
Notes payable (due in 10 days)	115,200
Accounts payable	38,400
Bob Rivers, capital	220,800

Instructions
a From the above information compute the amount of current assets and the amount of current liabilities.
b How much working capital does Rivers Company have?
c Compute the current ratio.
d Assume that Rivers Company pays the notes payable of $115,200, thus reducing cash to $22,400. Compute the amount of working capital and the current ratio after this transaction.

Ex. 5-5 Key figures taken from the income statement of Blue Spring Company for two successive years are shown below:

	Year 5	Year 4
Sales	$320,000	$240,000
Cost of goods sold	240,000	168,000
Selling expenses	40,000	35,000
General and administrative expenses	16,000	17,800

Instructions
a The net income increased from $ _____ in Year 4 to $ _____ in Year 5.
b The net income as a percentage of sales was _____ % in Year 4 and decreased to _____ % of sales in Year 5.
c The gross profit on sales decreased from _____ % in Year 4 to _____ % in Year 5.

Ex. 5-6 Indicate whether each of the following events would increase, decrease, or have no effect upon (1) the current ratio and (2) the working capital of a business with current assets greater than its current liabilities. Example: An account payable is paid in cash.
  (1) Increase current ratio.
  (2) No effect on working capital.
a Merchandise is purchased on account.
b An adjusting entry is made to accrue salaries earned by employees but not yet paid.

c An account receivable is collected.
d An adjusting entry is prepared to record depreciation for the period.
e Land is purchased by making a small cash down payment and signing a long-term mortgage payable.

Ex. 5-7 A portion of the ledger account balances of Green Bay Company at December 31 are listed below in random order.

Delivery equipment	$ 31,552
Accrued interest on notes payable	1,024
Advance payments from customers	5,760
Notes payable (due in 90 days)	64,000
U.S. government bonds	19,200
Accounts receivable	90,560
Accounts payable	59,200
Accrued interest receivable	192
Inventory	244,640
Accumulated depreciation: delivery equipment	3,155
Accrued salaries payable	2,560
Cash	43,040

Instructions $25 = NI$ $\frac{1}{2}G = NI$
a Compute the amount of *working capital* by arranging the *appropriate* items in the usual balance sheet sequence. A complete balance sheet is not required.
b Compute the current ratio and state whether you regard the company as being in a strong or a weak current position.

Ex. 5-8 During its first year of operation, Clarington Company earned net income equal to 5% of net sales. The selling expenses were twice as large as net income but only one-half as large as general and administrative expenses, which amounted to $240,000. Prepare a condensed income statement for the first year of operation, which ended June 30, 19___.

Ex. 5-9 Village Shop prepared a work sheet at December 31, Year 5. Shown below is the Income Statement pair of columns from that work sheet. To keep this exercise short, expense accounts have been combined. Use these work sheet data to prepare an income statement for the year ended December 31, Year 5.

	Income Statement	
	Debit	**Credit**
Inventory, Dec. 31, Year 4	90,000	
Sales		120,300
Sales returns & allowances	672	
Purchases	97,200	
Purchase returns & allowances		7,200
Transportation-in	2,400	
Selling expenses	20,000	
General and administrative expenses	8,320	
Inventory, Dec. 31, Year 5		108,000
	218,592	235,500
Net income	16,908	
	235,500	235,500

PROBLEMS

Group A

5A-1 The periodic system of inventory is used by Eastern Products, which adjusts and closes its accounts annually on December 31. The company completed the following transactions among others during the month of August.

Aug. 1 Paid rent on building for August, $1,020.

Aug. 2 Purchased merchandise on credit from Lowell Company, $1,074.

Aug. 4 Sold merchandise for cash, $2,322.

Aug. 5 Purchased equipment (for use in business) on account from Hoover Company, $2,004.

Aug. 6 Sold merchandise on credit to Yeager Construction Company, $3,414.

Aug. 8 Returned $528 worth of defective equipment purchased on August 5 from Hoover Company.

Aug. 12 Purchased merchandise for cash, $2,400.

Aug. 14 Agreed to cancel the account receivable of $3,414 from Yeager Construction Company in exchange for their services in erecting a garage on the property of Eastern Products. Garage completed today.

Aug. 18 Sold merchandise on credit to Howard and Sons, $2,976.

Aug. 19 Granted an allowance of $102 to Howard and Sons because of minor defects discovered in the merchandise sold them on August 18.

Aug. 26 Paid the balance due Hoover Company. (See transactions of August 5 and 8.)

Aug. 31 Paid $1,122 to Al's Service Station for gasoline and oil used by delivery trucks during the month. No prior entry had been made for these purchases, which occurred on a daily basis.

Instructions Prepare a separate journal entry (including an explanation) for each of the above transactions.

5A-2 The following items appeared in the income statement of Hayashi Nurseries for the year ended December 31, 19____. The company is engaged in the retail sale of trees, shrubs, and plants, and relies on a periodic inventory system.

Ending inventory	$ 62,814	Advertising expense	$ 11,275
Purchases	258,071	Sales returns & allowances	20,196
Salaries expense	47,113	Purchase returns &	
Beginning inventory	?	allowances	15,730
Sales	405,240	Gross profit on sales	134,765
Transportation-in	6,248	Delivery expense	14,010
Depreciation expense	18,242	Utilities expense	8,860
Insurance expense	2,800		

Instructions

a Compute the amount of net sales.

b Compute the gross profit percentage.

c What percentage of net sales represents the cost of goods sold?

d Prepare an income statement utilizing all the accounts listed above, including the determination of the amount of the beginning inventory.

5A-3 Norfleet Company uses the periodic inventory system and closes its accounts annually at December 31. After all adjustments had been made at December 31, Year 8, the adjusted trial balance appeared as on page 191.

NORFLEET COMPANY
Adjusted Trial Balance
December 31, Year 8

Cash	$ 41,800	
Accounts receivable	74,800	
Inventory (Dec. 31, Year 7)	63,580	
Unexpired insurance	1,540	
Supplies	2,640	
Furniture and fixtures	44,000	
Accumulated depreciation: furniture and fixtures		$ 2,640
Notes payable		18,260
Accounts payable		15,400
Anthony Baldwin, capital		113,256
Sales		644,600
Sales returns and allowances	8,800	
Purchases	421,355	
Purchase returns and allowances		3,399
Transportation-in	22,000	
Salaries and wages expense	91,080	
Rent expense	18,480	
Depreciation expense: furniture and fixtures	2,640	
Supplies expense	3,080	
Insurance expense	1,760	
	$797,555	$797,555

The inventory on December 31, Year 8, as determined by count, amounted to $78,936.

Instructions

a Prepare an income statement for Norfleet Company for the year ended December 31, Year 8.

b Prepare the necessary journal entries to close the accounts on December 31, Year 8.

5A-4 After working in a managerial position for several years with a large retail business, John Warren bought a retail store, Blue Ridge Imports, on October 1, 1978. Warren had saved $30,000 over a period of years and had received an inheritance of $72,000, all of which he invested in the new business. Before taking this step, Warren had given considerable thought to the alternative of continuing in his present position, which paid him a salary of $23,400 a year, and investing his capital in high-grade securities, which he estimated would provide an average return of 4% on the amount invested.

The trial balance on page 192 was taken from the records at September 30, 1979, after one year of operations.

BLUE RIDGE IMPORTS
Trial Balance
September 30, 1979

Cash	$ 6,000	
Accounts receivable	21,000	
Inventory (Oct. 1, 1978)	42,780	
Supplies	1,704	
Unexpired insurance	648	
Land	24,000	
Building	60,000	
Equipment	14,400	
Accounts payable		$ 33,972
John Warren, capital		102,000
John Warren, drawing	9,000	
Sales		233,580
Sales returns & allowances	2,580	
Purchases	139,452	
Purchase returns & allowances		3,408
Transportation-in	5,784	
Selling commissions expense	7,506	
Delivery expense	2,100	
Salaries and wages expense	35,538	
Property taxes	468	
	$372,960	$372,960

The September 30, 1979, inventory by physical count was $34,800.

Other data
(a) Accrued property taxes, $1,044.
(b) Supplies on hand, $684.
(c) Insurance expired during year, $216.
(d) Depreciation rates: 4% on building; 12½% on equipment.

Instructions
a Prepare an eight-column work sheet at September 30, 1979. (Omit columns for an adjusted trial balance.)
b Prepare a schedule comparing the adequacy of net income from the business for the fiscal year ended September 30, 1979, with net income Warren would have received by continuing as a salaried manager and investing his capital in securities. State your opinion based on this comparative schedule.

5A-5 Midwest Wood Products sells merchandise to retail stores and uses the periodic inventory system. An *adjusted* trial balance at December 31, 19___, is shown on page 193. The inventory taken on this date amounted to $75,320. The following adjustments have been made to the *original* trial balance figures.
(a) Depreciation of buildings, $10,080; depreciation of delivery equipment, $3,780.
(b) Accrued salaries: office, $2,366; salespersons, $2,660.
(c) Insurance expired, $504.
(d) Store supplies used, $2,128.

MIDWEST WOOD PRODUCTS
Adjusted Trial Balance
December 31, 19____

Cash	$ 23,380	
Accounts receivable	34,440	
Inventory, Jan. 1	59,920	
Store supplies	742	
Unexpired insurance	1,008	
Land	111,160	
Buildings	210,000	
Accumulated depreciation: buildings		$ 60,900
Delivery equipment	42,000	
Accumulated depreciation: delivery equipment		17,640
Accounts payable		34,860
Accrued salaries payable		5,026
Robert Chapman, capital		360,668
Robert Chapman, drawing	16,520	
Sales		451,416
Sales returns & allowances	6,804	
Purchases	332,920	
Purchase returns & allowances		5,096
Sales salaries expense	44,800	
Delivery expense	7,840	
Depreciation expense: delivery equipment	3,780	
Office salaries expense	27,580	
Depreciation expense: buildings	10,080	
Insurance expense	504	
Store supplies expense	2,128	
	$935,606	$935,606

Instructions

a Prepare a 10-column work sheet. List the figures given above in columns 5 and 6 as a first step.

b Prepare financial statements, consisting of an income statement, a statement of owner's equity, and a properly classified balance sheet. (On the income statement classify operating expenses into the subgroups of selling expenses and general and administrative expenses.) Depreciation expense on the buildings should be considered as 70% selling expense and 30% general and administrative. Insurance expense should also be divided in a 70–30 ratio. In dividing insurance expense, round the amounts to the nearest dollar.

c Prepare adjusting journal entries and closing journal entries.

Group B

5B-1 Madison Hardware relies on the periodic inventory system and closes its accounts annually on June 30. A partial list of the company's transactions during May is shown on page 194.

May 1 Purchased merchandise on 30-day credit from Pecos Baldy Company, $1,773.

May 1 Paid rent on building for May, $540.

May 3 Cash sale of merchandise, $2,700.

May 6 Purchased office equipment on account from Steele Company for use in the business, $2,777.

May 9 Sold merchandise on account to Trent Construction Company, $3,960.

May 11 Purchased merchandise for cash, $324.

May 12 Returned defective equipment which cost $540 to Steele Company for credit.

May 16 Sold merchandise on account to S. W. Hardy, $2,250.

May 17 Granted a $90 allowance to S. W. Hardy on merchandise delivered on May 16, because of minor defects discovered in the merchandise.

May 23 Agreed to cancel the account receivable from Trent Construction Company in exchange for their services in erecting a garage on our property. Construction completed today.

May 28 Paid balance due Steele Company. (See transactions of May 6 and 12).

Instructions Prepare a separate journal entry (including an explanation) for each of the above transactions.

5B-2 Merrimac Company is in the retail merchandise field and relies on the periodic inventory system. The income statement of the company for the first year ended June 30, 19___, contained the following items.

Gross profit on sales	$286,253	Sales	$874,800
Depreciation expense	23,600	Transportation-in	6,176
Utilities expense	11,420	Purchases	555,659
Beginning inventory	109,760	Ending inventory	?
Sales returns &		Salaries expense	80,312
allowances	32,880	Insurance expense	3,700
Purchase returns &		Miscellaneous expense	10,920
allowances	3,768		
Advertising expense	16,400		

Instructions

a Compute the amount of net sales.

b Compute the gross profit percentage.

c What percentage of net sales represents the cost of goods sold?

d What percentage of net sales is represented by net income? Round your answer to the nearest percentage.

e Prepare an income statement utilizing all the accounts listed above, including the determination of the amount of the ending inventory.

5B-3 Shown below and on page 195 is an alphabetical listing of the account balances of Santa Barbara Flower Shop at the end of its third year of operations. All necessary adjustments at December 31 have been made and are reflected in these balances.

Accounts payable	$ 19,200	Prepaid insurance	$ 624
Accounts receivable	32,000	Property tax expense	960
Accrued property taxes		Purchases	207,736
payable	928	Purchase returns and	
Accumulated depreciation:		allowances	6,848
equipment	3,640	Rent expense	11,520
Cash	13,312	Salaries & wages expense . .	60,104

Delivery expense	$ 3,288	Sales	$338,912
Depreciation expense	2,080	Sales returns and	
Equipment	12,736	allowances	9,312
Insurance expense	2,560	Selling commissions	
Inventory, Jan. 1	42,848	expense	12,800
Bob Johnson, capital	65,744	Supplies	1,144
Bob Johnson, drawing	8,960	Supplies expense	928
Notes receivable	5,600	Transportation-in	6,760

The inventory, determined by count at December 31, was $31,296.

Instructions

a Prepare the income statement for the year ended December 31. Operating expenses are not to be subdivided between selling expenses and general and administrative expenses.

b Prepare all necessary journal entries to close the accounts at December 31.

5B-4 Outrider Supplies, a successful small merchandising business, was purchased as a going concern by Roberta Conway on April 1, 1978. After one year of operation, the following trial balance was prepared:

OUTRIDER SUPPLIES
Trial Balance
March 31, 1979

Cash	$ 12,800	
Accounts receivable	54,400	
Inventory (Apr. 1, 1978)	115,200	
Supplies	4,544	
Unexpired insurance	1,728	
Land	64,000	
Buildings	160,000	
Equipment	38,400	
Accounts payable		$ 90,592
Roberta Conway, capital		272,000
Roberta Conway, drawing	24,000	
Sales		624,800
Sales returns & allowances	12,800	
Purchases	371,200	
Purchase returns & allowances		9,088
Transportation-in	15,424	
Selling commissions expense	20,016	
Delivery expense	5,600	
Salaries and wages expense	94,768	
Property taxes expense	1,600	
	$996,480	$996,480

A physical inventory was taken at the close of business March 31, 1979; this count showed merchandise on hand in the amount of $92,800.

Other data
(a) Property taxes accrued but not yet recorded, $2,880.
(b) A physical count showed supplies on hand of $1,344.
(c) The cost of insurance which had expired during the year was $896.
(d) Depreciation rates: 4% on buildings and 10% on equipment.

Instructions
a Prepare an eight-column work sheet at March 31, 1979. (Omit columns for an adjusted trial balance.)
b Prepare the necessary adjusting journal entries at March 31, 1979.
c Prepare the journal entries required to close the accounts as of March 31, 1979.

5B-5 Shown below is a trial balance prepared from the ledger of Bridge Company at December 31, Year 4.

BRIDGE COMPANY
Trial Balance
December 31, Year 7

Cash	$ 29,816	
Accounts receivable	38,816	
Inventory (Jan. 1, Year 7)	59,584	
Unexpired insurance	1,152	
Office supplies	808	
Land	17,024	
Buildings	60,800	
Accumulated depreciation: buildings		$ 14,592
Equipment	15,360	
Accumulated depreciation: equipment		2,560
Accounts payable		51,264
Jerry Wilson, capital		82,512
Jerry Wilson, drawing	8,000	
Sales		319,576
Sales returns & allowances	5,264	
Purchases	191,888	
Purchase returns & allowances		3,432
Transportation-in	4,744	
Salaries and wages expense	39,584	
Property taxes expense	1,096	
	$473,936	$473,936

Other data
(a) The buildings are being depreciated over a 25-year useful life and the equipment over a 12-year useful life.
(b) Accrued salaries payable as of December 31, Year 7, were $5,024.
(c) Examination of policies showed $608 unexpired insurance on December 31.
(d) Supplies on hand at December 31 were estimated to amount to $376.
(e) Inventory of merchandise on December 31, Year 7, was $44,656.

Instructions
a Prepare an eight-column work sheet at December 31, Year 7. (Omit columns for an adjusted trial balance.)
b Prepare an income statement, a statement of owner's equity, and a classified balance sheet.

c Prepare adjusting entries.
d Prepare closing entries.
e Compute the current ratio and the amount of working capital. Explain whether Bridge Company appears to be an acceptable short-term credit risk.

BUSINESS DECISION PROBLEM 5

Jane Miller, an experienced engineer, is considering buying the Eastern Engineering Company from its current owner, Jack Peterson. Eastern has been a profitable business, earning about $54,000 each year. Miller is certain she could operate the business just as profitably. Miller comes to you with the following balance sheet of Eastern Engineering Company and asks your advice about buying the business.

EASTERN ENGINEERING COMPANY

Balance Sheet

December 31, 19___

Assets		Liabilities & Owner's Equity	
Cash	$ 36,000	Notes payable	$ 54,000
U.S. government contract		Accounts payable	16,200
receivable	90,000	Wages payable	5,400
Other contracts receivable .	25,200	J. Peterson, capital	210,600
Equipment			
(net of depreciation)	81,000		
Patents	54,000		
	$286,200		$286,200

Miller immediately points out, as evidence of the firm's solvency, that the current ratio for Eastern Engineering is 2 to 1. In discussing the specific items on the balance sheet, you find that the patents were recently purchased by Eastern, and Miller believes them to be worth their $54,000 cost. The notes payable consists of one note to the manufacturer of the equipment owned by Eastern, which Peterson had incurred five years ago to finance the purchase of the equipment. The note becomes payable, however, in February of the coming year. The accounts payable all will become due within 30 to 60 days.

Since Miller does not have enough cash to buy Peterson's equity in the business, she is considering the following terms of purchase: (1) Peterson will withdraw all the cash from the business, thus reducing his equity to $174,600, (2) Peterson will also keep the $90,000 receivable from the U.S. government, leaving his equity in the business at $84,600, and (3) by borrowing heavily, Miller thinks she can raise $84,600 in cash, which she will pay to Peterson for his remaining equity. Miller will assume the existing liabilities of the business.

Instructions
a Prepare a classified balance sheet for Eastern Engineering Company as it would appear immediately after Miller acquired the business, assuming that the purchase is carried out immediately on the proposed terms.
b Compute the current ratio and the working capital position of Eastern Engineering Company after Miller's purchase of the business.
c Write a memorandum to Miller explaining what problems she might encounter if she purchases the business as planned.

6 Internal Control

The meaning of internal control

Our discussion of a merchandising business in Chapter 5 emphasized the steps of the accounting cycle, especially the determination of cost of goods sold and the preparation of financial statements. In the present chapter we shall round out this discussion by considering the system of internal control by which management maintains control over the purchasing, receiving, storing, and selling of merchandise. Strong internal controls are needed not only for purchases and sales transactions, but for all other types of transactions as well. It is particularly important to maintain strong internal controls over transactions involving cash receipts and cash payments. In fact, the concept of internal control is so important that it affects all the assets of a business, all liabilities, the revenue and expenses, and every aspect of operations. *The purpose of internal control is to aid in the efficient operation of a business.*

As defined in Chapter 1, the system of internal control includes all the measures taken by an organization for the purpose of (*1*) protecting its resources against waste, fraud, and inefficiency; (*2*) ensuring accuracy and reliability in accounting and operating data; (*3*) securing compliance with company policies; and (*4*) evaluating the level of performance in all divisions of the company.

Internal control and business decisions

Although many people think of internal control as a means of preventing embezzlement and other types of fraud, internal control has many important purposes other than the prevention of fraud. Almost all business decisions are based at least in part upon accounting data. Examples of these decisions range from such minor daily actions as the authorizing of overtime work or the purchase of office supplies to such major actions as a change in product lines or a choice between leasing or buying a new building. The fact that business decisions are based on accounting data explains the importance of internal control, because *the system of internal control provides assurance of the dependability of the accounting data relied upon in making decisions.*

Internal control as a two-way communication system

The decisions made by management become company policy. To be effective, this policy must be communicated throughout the company and followed consistently. The results of the policies—the consequences of managerial decisions—must be reported back to management so that the soundness of company policies can be evaluated and a continuous updating process carried on.

Among the means of communication included in the system of internal control are organization charts, manuals of accounting policies and procedures, flow charts, forecasts, internal audit reports, job descriptions, purchase orders, interim financial statements, operating reports, and many other types of documentation. The term *documentation* refers to all the charts, forms, reports, and other business papers that guide and describe the working of a company's system of accounting and internal control.

In summary, a system of internal control extends throughout the organization. Like the nerves and nerve centers of a person, the internal control system provides direction to all activity and monitors the working of all units comprising a business organization.

Objectives in the study of internal control

Our study of internal control at this point has two principal objectives: first, to explain the nature and importance of internal control; and second, to indicate the specific steps required to establish and maintain good internal control.

This chapter will not include detailed study of internal control measures applicable to specific topics such as cash, receivables, or inventories. Consideration of the internal controls needed for these and similar areas will appear in later chapters devoted to selected financial statement topics. Before reviewing in depth the internal controls over specific segments of a business, we need first to acquire an understanding of the principles underlying the entire system of internal control.

Administrative controls and accounting controls

Internal controls are often viewed as falling into two major classes: administrative controls and accounting controls. *Administrative controls* are measures that apply principally to operational efficiency and compliance with established policies in all parts of the organization. For example, an administrative control may be a requirement that traveling salespersons submit reports showing the number of calls made on customers each day. Another example is a directive requiring airline pilots to have an annual medical examination, and another example, the requirement that factory employees wear identification badges. These internal administrative controls have no direct bearing on the reliability of the financial statements and other accounting reports. Consequently, administrative controls are not of direct interest to accountants and independent auditors.

Internal accounting controls are measures that relate to protection of assets and to the reliability of accounting and financial reports. An example is the requirement that a person whose duties involve handling cash shall not also maintain accounting records. More broadly stated, the accounting function must be kept separate from the custody of assets. Another accounting control is the requirement that checks, purchase orders, and other documents be serially numbered. Still another example is the requirement that the person who issues a purchase order to acquire merchandise shall not have authority to approve for payment the supplier's invoice covering the merchandise, and the person who approves the invoice for payment shall not be authorized to sign the check to be sent to the supplier.

When certified public accountants perform an audit of a company, they always study and evaluate the system of internal control. However, this work is concentrated on accounting controls rather than administrative controls, because the objective of the CPA is to form an opinion of the company's financial statements and it is the accounting controls which assure reliability in financial statements. An *internal auditor,* on the other hand, is interested in the operational efficiency of the company rather than the annual financial statements and will therefore study both administrative and accounting controls.

Reliance by the CPA upon internal control

Before expressing an opinion on a company's financial statements, a CPA firm must gather evidence which supports each item in the balance sheet and income statement. This evidence includes the ledgers, journals, and all kinds of business documents. The strength of the internal controls in force determines the reliability of the accounting records and of the entire accounting process. Therefore, a CPA firm encourages its clients to maintain strong internal control and makes recommendations for improvements in the system of internal control. A weakness in internal control does not necessarily mean that the accounting records are erroneous, but it does suggest to the CPA the *possibility* that the records supporting the financial statements may be in error.

GUIDELINES TO STRONG INTERNAL CONTROL

Organization plan to establish responsibility for every function

An organization plan should indicate clearly the departments or persons responsible for such functions as purchasing, receiving incoming shipments, maintaining accounting records, approving credit to customers, and preparing the payroll. One person should be clearly responsible for each function. To illustrate the need for fixing responsibility, assume that all employees were given authority to make purchases for a business. The probable result would be duplication of orders, overstocking of some goods, and shortages of others. It would be difficult if not impossible, to determine who was at fault.

When an individual or department is assigned responsibility for a function, it is imperative that authority to make decisions also be granted. The assignment of responsibilities and all accounting and internal control policies should be in writing so that responsibility for poor performance cannot be shifted. The lines of authority and responsibility can conveniently be shown on an organization chart; a portion of an organization chart of a manufacturing company is illustrated on page 202.

As indicated in this organization chart, the direction of operations and custody of assets should be separate from the accounting function. An individual charged with the custody of assets or with the direction of operations may make errors or commit improper actions; consequently, such individuals should not be involved in the accounting function because this would enable them to conceal such errors and irregularities.

Control of transactions

If management is to direct the activities of a business according to plan, every transaction should go through four steps: It should be *authorized, approved, executed,* and *recorded.* These steps may be illustrated by the example of the sale of merchandise on credit. The top management of the company may *authorize* the sale of merchandise on credit to customers who meet certain standards. The manager of the credit and collection department may *approve* a sale of given dollar amount to a particular

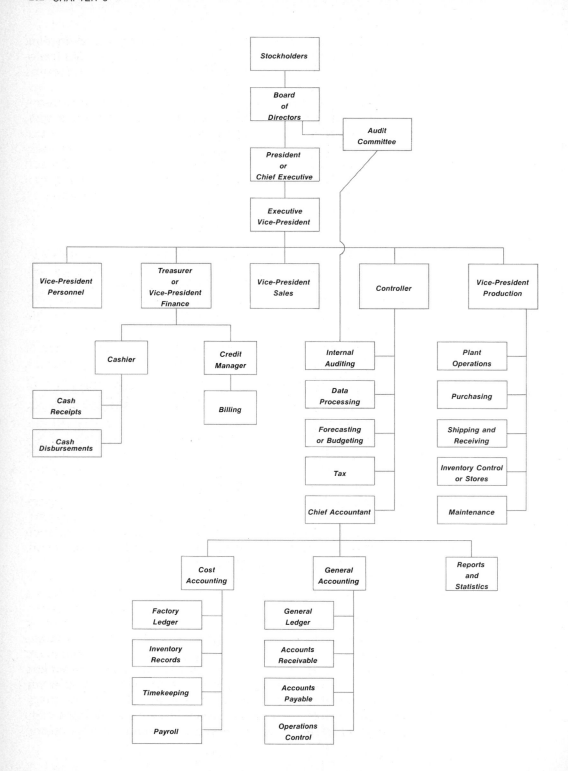

customer. The sales transaction is *executed* by preparing a sales invoice and delivering the merchandise to the credit customer. The sales transaction is *recorded* in the accounting department by debiting Accounts Receivable and crediting Sales.

Consider for a moment the losses that would probably be incurred if this internal control of transactions did not exist. Assume, for example, that all employees in a store were free to sell on credit any amount of merchandise to any customer, and responsibility for recording the sales transactions was not fixed on any one person or department. The result no doubt would be many unrecorded sales; of those sales transactions that were recorded, many would represent uncollectible receivables.

Subdivision of duties strengthens internal control

Procedures for controlling the purchase and sale of merchandise emphasize the subdivision of duties within the company so that no one person or department handles a transaction completely from beginning to end. When duties are divided in this manner, the work of one employee serves to verify that of another and any errors which occur tend to be detected promptly.

To illustrate the development of internal control through subdivision of duties, let us review the procedures for a sale of merchandise on account by a wholesaler. The sales department of the company is responsible for securing the order from the customer; the credit department must approve the customer's credit before the order is filled; the stock room assembles the goods ordered; the shipping department packs and ships the goods; and the accounting department records the transaction. Each department receives written evidence of the action of the other departments and reviews the documents describing the transaction to see that the actions taken correspond in all details. The shipping department, for instance, does not release the merchandise until after the credit department has approved the customer as a credit risk. The accounting department does not record the sale until it has received documentary evidence that (*1*) the goods were ordered, (*2*) the extension of credit was approved, and (*3*) the merchandise has been shipped to the customer.

SEPARATION OF ACCOUNTING AND CUSTODY OF ASSETS An employee who has custody of an asset or access to an asset should not maintain the accounting record of that asset. The person having custody of an asset will not be inclined to waste it, steal it, or give it away if he or she is aware that another employee is maintaining a record of the asset. The employee maintaining the accounting record does not have access to the asset and therefore has no incentive to falsify the record. If one person has custody of assets and also maintains the accounting records, there is both opportunity and incentive to falsify the records to conceal a shortage. The following diagram illustrates how separation of duties creates strong internal control.

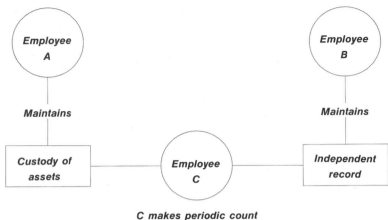

C makes periodic count
of assets held by A and
compares with record of B

In this diagram Employee A has custody of assets and Employee B maintains an accounting record of the assets. Employee C periodically counts the assets and compares the count with the record maintained by B. This comparison should reveal any errors made by either A or B unless the two have collaborated to conceal an error or irregularity.

SEPARATION OF RESPONSIBILITY FOR RELATED TRANSACTIONS When merchandise is sold to a customer on credit, the act of delivering the merchandise to the customer is closely related to the recording of the account receivable and to the later collection of the receivable. Responsibility for these related transactions should be assigned to different individuals or departments and documentary evidence should be created to record the action taken by each.

Assume for a moment, as an example of unsatisfactory internal control, that one employee was permitted to take the customer's order, approve the credit terms, get the merchandise from the stock room, deliver the goods to the customer, prepare the invoice, enter the transaction in the accounting records, and collect the account receivable. If this employee made errors, such as selling to poor credit risks, forgetting to enter the sale in the accounting records, or perhaps delivering more merchandise to the customer than was charged for, no one would know the difference. By the time such errors came to light, substantial losses would have been incurred.

PREVENTION OF FRAUD If one employee is permitted to handle all aspects of a transaction, the danger of fraud is increased. Studies of fraud cases suggest that many individuals may be tempted into dishonest acts if given complete control of company property. Most of these persons, however, would not engage in fraud if doing so required collaboration with another employee. Losses through employee dishonesty occur in a variety of ways: merchandise may be stolen; payments by customers may be withheld; suppliers may be overpaid with a view to kickbacks to employees; and lower prices may be allowed to favored customers. The opportunities for fraud are almost endless if all aspects of a sale or purchase transaction are concentrated in the hands of one employee.

ROTATION OF EMPLOYEES To the extent practicable, rotation of employees from one job assignment to another may strengthen internal control. When employees know that other persons may soon be taking over their duties, they are more likely to maintain records with care and to follow established procedures. The rotation of employees may also bring to light any errors or irregularities that have occurred. This same line of reasoning indicates that all employees should be required to take annual vacations and all their duties should be performed by others during such vacation periods.

Serially numbered documents—another control device

Another method of achieving internal control, in addition to the subdivision of duties, consists of having the printer include serial numbers on such documents as purchase orders, sales invoices, and checks. The use of serial numbers makes it possible to account for all documents. In other words, if a sales invoice is misplaced or concealed, the break in the sequence of numbers will call attention to the discrepancy.

Competence of personnel

Even the best-designed system of internal control will not work satisfactorily unless the people assigned to operate it are competent. Each person involved must have a level of competence sufficient for the work assigned and a willingness to assume responsibility for performance. Competence and integrity of employees are in part developed through training programs, but they are also related to the policies for selection of personnel, the adequacy of supervision, and the complexity of the system.

Financial forecasts

A financial forecast, as defined in Chapter 1, is a plan of operations for a future period. Specific goals are set for each division of the business as, for example, the expected volume of sales, the amounts of expenses, and the planned cash balance. Actual results achieved month by month can then be compared with the planned results and management's attention is promptly directed to any areas of substandard performance. The system of internal control is strengthened by the use of forecasts because errors or irregularities which cause actual results to differ from planned results will be identified and fully investigated.

Internal auditing

In all large organizations an important element of internal control is the internal auditing staff. Internal auditors are professional-level employees with the responsibility of investigating throughout the company the efficiency of operations in every department or other organizational unit. They are continuously studying both administrative and accounting controls and reporting to top management on compliance with company standards and on problems which require strengthening of internal controls.

Continuing review of the system of internal control

Business policies, products, and operating methods are in a constant state of change. Consequently, the system of internal control must continually be reviewed and updated if it is to continue to function effectively. In the large corporation, the internal auditing staff devotes full time on a year-round basis to reviewing internal control and recommending changes. In all businesses, large or small, one major reason to retain a CPA firm to perform an annual audit is to benefit from a thorough independent evaluation of the system of internal control by competent professionals.

Limitations of internal control

Although internal control is highly effective in increasing the reliability of accounting data and in protecting against fraud, no system of internal control is foolproof. Two or more dishonest employees working in collusion can defeat the system. Carelessness by employees and misunderstanding of instructions can cause a breakdown in controls. The much-publicized Equity Funding management fraud case demonstrated that top management can circumvent the system of internal control if it is determined to do so.

Internal control in the small business

Satisfactory internal control is more difficult to achieve in a small business than a large one because, with only a few employees, it is not possible to arrange extensive subdivision of duties. However, in many small businesses, internal control is unnecessarily weak because management does not understand the basic principles of internal control or neglects to give attention to the problem.

Some internal controls are suitable for even the smallest business, with only one or two employees. An example is the use of serial numbers on checks, sales invoices, and other documents to ensure that no document is misplaced and forgotten. Another example is insistence that documentary evidence be created to verify an invoice before it is paid, and that documents supporting the issuance of a check be marked paid when the check is issued.

An essential element in maintaining a reasonable degree of internal control in the small business is active participation by the owner-manager in strategic control procedures. These procedures will be considered in later chapters dealing with such topics as cash and receivables.

Internal control in perspective

A description of internal control solely in terms of the prevention of fraud and the detection of errors represents too narrow a concept of this managerial technique. The building of a strong system of internal control is an accepted means of increasing operational efficiency.

In appraising the merits of various internal control procedures, the question of their cost cannot be ignored. Too elaborate a system of internal control may entail greater operating costs than are justified by the protection gained. For this reason the system of internal control must be tailored to meet the requirements of the individual business. In most organizations, however, proper subdivision of duties and careful design of accounting procedures will provide a basis for adequate internal control and at the same time will contribute to economical operation of the business.

Fidelity bonds

Since no system of internal control can provide absolute protection against losses from dishonest employees, many companies require that employees handling cash or other negotiable assets be bonded. A *fidelity bond* is a type of insurance contract in which a bonding company agrees to reimburse an employer up to agreed dollar limits for losses caused by fraud or embezzlement by bonded employees.

Fidelity bonds are not a substitute for internal control; they do little or nothing to assure reliable accounting data, to prevent wasteful inefficient use of company assets, or to encourage compliance with company policies. However, they are a useful supplement in protecting a company from losses due to embezzlement. Particularly in a small business with too few employees to permit much subdivision of duties, fidelity bonds may be very appropriate. It is often the most trusted employee who turns out to be an embezzler. The very fact that an employee is trusted completely explains why he or she is given full access to cash and accounting records and assigned a combination of duties which makes large-scale embezzlement an easy matter.

INTERNAL CONTROLS OVER THE PURCHASE AND SALE OF MERCHANDISE

Business documents and procedures

Carefully designed business documents and procedures for using them are necessary to ensure that all transactions are properly authorized, approved, and recorded. We have already considered the waste and confusion that would arise if every employee in a large department store were authorized to purchase merchandise for the store and no standard forms or procedures had been provided to keep track of these purchases. The opportunity for fraud by dishonest employees, as well as for accidental errors and waste of resources, would be unlimited under such a haphazard method of operation.

Each step in ordering, receiving, and making payment for merchandise purchases should be controlled and recorded. A similar approach is necessary to establish control over the sales function.

Purchasing procedures

In small retail businesses, the owner or manager may personally perform the purchasing function by placing orders with sales representatives of wholesalers and manufacturers. These sales representatives make regular visits to the store and may carry catalogs and samples to illustrate the products offered.

The owner-manager of a small store is sufficiently familiar with the stock of merchandise to know what items need to be replenished. A notebook record of items to be ordered may be maintained by writing down each day any items which the owner observes to be running low. A sales representative of a wholesaler or manufacturer who visits the store will write up the order in an order book. A copy of the order, showing the quantities and prices of all items ordered, is left with the store owner.

Purchase orders

In many businesses and especially in large organizations, the buying company uses its own purchase order forms. A purchase order of the Zenith Company issued to Adams Manufacturing Company is illustrated on page 209.

In large companies in which the functions of placing orders, receiving merchandise, and making payment are lodged in separate departments, several copies of the purchase order are usually prepared, each on a different color paper. The original is sent to the supplier; this purchase order is an authorization to deliver the merchandise and to submit a bill based on the prices listed. Carbon copies of the purchase order are usually routed to the purchasing department, accounting department, receiving department, and finance department.

	PURCHASE ORDER		Order No.

ZENITH COMPANY

10 Fairway Avenue, San Francisco, California   **999**

Serially numbered purchase order

To: Adams Manufacturing Company   **Date** Nov. 10, 19___

        19 Union Street   **Ship via** Jones Truck Co.

        Kansas City, Missouri   **Terms:** 2/10, n/30

Please enter our order for the following:

Quantity	Description	Price	Total
15 sets	Model S irons	$60.00	$900.00
50 dozen	X3Y Shur—Par golf balls	7.00	350.00

                                        Zenith Company

                                By *D. D. McCarthy*

Note that the illustrated purchase order bears a serial number, 999. When purchase orders are serially numbered, there can be no doubt as to how many orders have been issued. Each department authorized to receive copies of purchase orders should account for every number in the series, thus guarding against the loss or nondelivery of any document.

When merchandise is ordered by telephone, a formal written purchase order should nevertheless be prepared and sent to the supplier to confirm the verbal instructions. Orders for office equipment, supplies, and other assets as well as merchandise should also be in writing to avoid misunderstanding and to provide a permanent record of the order.

The issuance of a purchase order does not call for any debit or credit entries in the accounting records of either the prospective buyer or seller. The company which receives an order does not consider (for accounting purposes) that a sale has been made until the merchandise is delivered. At that point ownership of the goods changes, and both buyer and seller should make accounting entries to record the transaction.

Invoices

The supplier (vendor) mails an invoice to the purchaser at the time of shipping the merchandise. An invoice contains a description of the goods being sold, the quantities, prices, credit terms, and method of shipment. The illustration on page 210 shows an invoice issued by Adams Manufacturing Company in response to the previously illustrated purchase order from Zenith Company.

Invoice is basis for accounting entry	

INVOICE

ADAMS MANUFACTURING COMPANY

19 Union Street

Kansas City, Missouri

Sold to Zenith Company

Invoice no. 777

10 Fairway Avenue

Invoice date Nov. 15, 19___

San Francisco, Calif.

Your order no. 999

Shipped to Same

Date shipped Nov. 15, 19___

Terms 2/10, n/30

Shipped via Jones Truck Co.

Quantity	Description	Price	Amount
15 sets	Model S irons	$60.00	$ 900.00
50 dozen	X3Y Shur-Par golf balls	7.00	350.00
			$1,250.00

From the viewpoint of the seller, an invoice is a **sales invoice;** from the buyer's viewpoint it is a **purchase invoice.** The invoice is the basis for an entry in the accounting records of both the seller and the buyer because it evidences the transfer of ownership of goods. At the time of issuing the invoice, the selling company makes an entry debiting Accounts Receivable and crediting Sales. The buying company however, does not record the invoice as a liability until after making a careful verification of the transaction, as indicated in the following section.

VERIFICATION OF INVOICE BY PURCHASER Upon receipt of an invoice, the purchasing company should verify the following aspects of the transaction:

1 The invoice agrees with the purchase order as to prices, quantities, and other provisions.

2 The invoice is arithmetically correct in all extensions of price times quantity and in the addition of amounts.

3 The goods covered by the invoice have been received and are in satisfactory condition.

Evidence that the merchandise has been received in good condition must be obtained from the receiving department. It is the function of the receiving department to receive all incoming goods, to inspect them as to quality and condition, and to determine the quantities received by counting, measuring, or weighing. The receiving department should prepare a serially numbered report for each shipment received; one copy of this *receiving report* is sent to the accounting department for use in verifying the invoice.

The verification of the invoice in the accounting department is accomplished by comparing the purchase order, the invoice, and the receiving report. Comparison of these documents establishes that the goods described in the invoice were actually ordered, have been received in good condition, and were billed at the prices specified in the purchase order. To ensure that this comparison of documents is made in every case and that the arithmetical accuracy of the invoice is proved, it is customary to require an invoice approval sheet such as that shown below to be at-

Several employees participate in verification of a purchase invoice

---

Invoice Approval Form

Invoice no. 777	**Date** Nov. 15, 19
Purchase order no. 999	**Date** Nov. 10, 19
Vendor Adams Manufacturing Company	

Invioce compared with purchase order as to:

Description of goods .... *L.B.Q.*

Quantities .... *L.B.Q.*

Prices .... *L.B.Q.*

Discount terms .... *L.B.Q.*

Transportation charges .... *L.B.Q.*

Receiving report compared with purchase order and invoice as to quantities .... *D.L.W.*

Invoice verified as to:

Extensions .... *R.A.*

Footings .... *R.A.*

Approved for payment .... *J.R.K.*

Paid by check no. 2116 **Date** Nov. 25, 19

tached to each invoice and initialed by the employees performing each step in the verification work. Some companies prefer to use a rubber stamp imprint of this form to place the verification data directly on the vendor's invoice.

When these verification procedures have been completed, *the invoice* is recorded as a liability by an entry debiting the Purchases account and crediting Accounts Payable.

Debit and credit memoranda

The verification procedures just described usually give the purchaser of merchandise assurance that the invoice should be paid. Sometimes, however, the verification procedures disclose irregularities which require adjustment. For example, there may be arithmetical errors in the invoice, a shortage of goods received as compared with those billed, damaged merchandise, goods received that were not ordered, or various other discrepancies. If the invoice contains an arithmetical error, the purchasing company can easily compute the correct amount. Other situations such as defects in merchandise or improper quantities may require negotiation with the seller. In all cases when the buying company makes an adjustment, it must notify the seller of the details. The buying company provides this notification by sending the seller a *debit memorandum* or a *credit memorandum.*

A debit memorandum informs the supplier that its account is being debited (reduced) in the records of the buyer and explains the circumstances. A credit memorandum issued by the buyer has the opposite effect of informing the supplier that its account is being credited (increased) on the buyer's records. Since an error in a purchase invoice may cause the total amount to be either overstated or understated, it is clear that the purchasing company may need to issue either a debit memorandum or a credit memorandum to correct the error.

To illustrate the use of a debit memorandum, let us assume that Zenith Company receives another shipment of merchandise from Adams Manufacturing Company and a related invoice dated November 18 in the amount of $1,000. However, some of the goods with a value of $450 were badly damaged when received and cannot be accepted. Zenith Company therefore wishes to return the damaged goods and to pay only $550 of the $1,000 amount billed. One method would be to record the purchase as $550 and send a check for that amount to the supplier accompanied by a letter explaining the situation. To record the transaction as a $550 purchase, however, would not provide a clear and complete picture of the events. A better procedure is to record the invoice in its full amount and to make a second entry recording the return of the damaged merchandise. The debit memorandum shown on page 213 should be prepared in two or more copies and the original sent to the vendor.

The duplicate copy of the debit memorandum serves as a source

<table>
<tr><td colspan="2">ZENITH COMPANY</td><td>Debit</td></tr>
<tr><td colspan="2">10 Fairway Avenue</td><td>memorandum</td></tr>
<tr><td colspan="2">San Francisco, California</td><td>no. 42</td></tr>
</table>

ZENITH COMPANY **Debit**
10 Fairway Avenue **memorandum**
San Francisco, California **no. 42**

To: Adams Manufacturing Company **Date:** Nov. 20, 19___

19 Union Street

Kansas City, Missouri

We debit your account as follows:

Return of merchandise. Fifty DLX gloves arrived
badly damaged and are being returned via Jones
Truck Co. Your invoice no. 825, dated
November 18, 19___ $450.00

Debit mem-
orandum
reduces
liability
to vendor

document supporting an entry in the buyer's accounting records showing
the return of the goods and a corresponding reduction in the liability to
the vendor. The two entries to record the purchase invoice and the debit
memorandum are as follows:

Entries | Nov. 18 Purchases .... | 1,000 |
for | Accounts Payable..................... | | 1,000
purchase | To record invoice from Adams Manufacturing Company. | |
and | | |
purchase | | |
return | Nov. 20 Accounts Payable........................ | 450 |
| Purchase Returns and Allowances .... | | 450
| To record return of damaged merchandise to Adams | |
| Manufacturing Company. See our debit memo no. 42. | |

The supplier, upon being informed of the return of the damaged
merchandise, will issue the **credit memorandum** shown below as evidence
that the account receivable from the purchaser is being credited (reduced).

The entry on the part of Adams Manufacturing Company at the time of
issuing this credit memorandum would be as follows:

Entry | Nov. 22 Sales Returns and Allowances .... | 450 |
recording | Accounts Receivable .... | | 450
credit | To record return by Zenith Company of damaged mer- | |
memo | chandise. See our credit memo no. 102. | |

This credit memorandum, when received by the Zenith Company, will
be filed with the original invoice and the carbon copy of the debit memorandum. These documents represent evidence supporting the entries in
the accounts.

```
┌─────────────────────────────────────────────────────────────────────────┐
│              ADAMS MANUFACTURING COMPANY            Credit                │
│                     19 Union Street              memorandum               │
│                    Kansas City, Missouri            no. 102               │
│                                                                           │
│   To: Zenith Company........................  Date: Nov. 22, 19__ .....   │
│                                                                           │
│        10 Fairway Avenue                                                  │
│        ...................................                                │
│                                                                           │
│        San Francisco, Calif.                                              │
│        ....................................                               │
│                                                                           │
│   We credit your account as follows:                                      │
│   ─────────────────────────────────────────────────────────────────────  │
│                                                                           │
│   Merchandise returned, 50 DLX gloves,                                    │
│   our invoice no. 825.........................................$450.00     │
└─────────────────────────────────────────────────────────────────────────┘
```

Credit memorandum issued by seller of goods

As a separate example, assume that Zenith Company, while verifying a purchase invoice, discovered an error that caused the purchase invoice to be understated by $100. To correct the error, Zenith Company would issue a *credit memorandum.* If the error were discovered before the invoice was recorded, a copy of the credit memorandum would be attached to the purchase invoice and the accounting entry debiting Purchases and crediting Accounts Payable would be for $100 more than the erroneous amount on the invoice.

Thus, a debit memorandum or a credit memorandum may be issued by either the buying or selling party in a transaction. When the buying company issues a debit memorandum, it is debiting (reducing) a liability; when it issues a credit memorandum, it is crediting (increasing) its liability to the seller. On the other hand, when the selling company issues a debit memorandum, it is debiting (increasing) an account receivable from the buyer; and when it issues a credit memorandum, it is crediting (reducing) the receivable from the buyer.

Trade discounts

Many manufacturers and wholesalers publish annual catalogs in which their products are listed at retail prices. Substantial reductions from the *list prices* (listed retail prices) are offered to dealers. These reductions from list prices (often as much as 30 or 40%) are called *trade discounts.* As market conditions change, the schedule of discounts is revised. This is a more convenient way to revise actual selling prices quickly than by publishing a new catalog.

Trade discounts are not recorded in the accounting records of either the seller or the buyer. A sale of merchandise is recorded at the actual selling price and the trade discount is merely a device for computing the actual sales price. From the viewpoint of the company purchasing goods, the significant price is not the list price but the amount which must be paid, and this amount is recorded as the cost of the merchandise.

For example, if a manufacturer sells goods to a retailer at a list price of $1,000 with a trade discount of 40%, the transaction will be recorded by the manufacturer as a $600 sale and by the retailer as a $600 purchase. Because trade discounts are not recorded in the accounts they should be clearly distinguished from the cash discounts discussed below.

Cash discounts

Manufacturers and wholesalers generally offer a cash discount to encourage their customers to pay invoices. For example, the credit terms may be "2% 10 days, net 30 days"; these terms mean that the authorized credit period is 30 days, but that the customer company may deduct 2% of the amount of the invoice if it makes payment within 10 days. On the invoice these terms would appear in the abbreviated form "2/10, n/30"; this expression is read "2, 10, net 30." The selling company regards a cash discount as a *sales discount;* the buyer calls the discount a *purchase discount.*[1]

To illustrate the application of a cash discount, assume that Adams Manufacturing Company sells goods to the Zenith Company and issues a sales invoice for $1,000 dated November 3 and bearing the terms 2/10, n/30. If Zenith Company mails its check in payment on or before November 13, it is entitled to deduct 2% of $1,000, or $20, and settle the obligation for $980. If Zenith Company decides to forego the discount, it may postpone payment for an additional 20 days until December 3 but must then pay $1,000.

REASONS FOR CASH DISCOUNTS From the viewpoint of the seller, the acceptance of $980 in cash as full settlement of a $1,000 account receivable represents a $20 reduction in the amount of revenue earned. By making this concession to induce prompt payment, the seller collects accounts receivable more quickly and is able to use the money collected to buy additional goods. A greater volume of business can be handled with a given amount of invested capital if this capital is not tied up in accounts receivable for long periods. There is also less danger of accounts receivable becoming uncollectible if they are collected promptly; in other words, the older an account receivable becomes, the greater becomes the risk of nonpayment by the customer.

Is it to the advantage of the Zenith Company to settle the $1,000 invoice within the discount period and thereby save $20? The alternative is for Zenith to conserve cash by postponing payment for an additional 20 days. The question may therefore be stated as follows: Does the amount of $20

---

[1] Some companies issue invoices payable 10 days after the end of the month in which the sale occurs. Such invoices may bear the expression "10 e.o.m."

represent a reasonable charge for the use of $980 for a period of 20 days? Definitely not; this charge is the equivalent of an annual interest rate of about 36%. (A 20-day period is approximately $\frac{1}{18}$ of a year; 18 times 2% amounts to 36%.)[2] Although interest rates vary widely, most businesses are able to borrow money from banks at an annual interest rate of 10% or less. Well-managed businesses, therefore, generally pay all invoices within the discount period even though this policy necessitates borrowing from banks in order to have the necessary cash available.

RECORDING SALES DISCOUNTS Sales of merchandise are generally recorded at the full selling price without regard for the cash discount being offered. The discount is not reflected in the seller's accounting records until payment is received. Continuing our illustration of a sale of merchandise by Adams Manufacturing Company for $1,000 with terms of 2/10, n/30, the entry to record the sale on November 3 is as shown by the following:

Sale	*Nov. 3 Accounts Receivable. . . . .*	*1,000*	
entered	*Sales . . . .*		*1,000*
at full			
price	*To record sale to Zenith Company, terms 2/10, n/30.*		

Assuming that payment is made by Zenith Company on November 13, the last day of the discount period, the entry by Adams to record collection of the receivable is as follows:

Sales	*Nov. 13 Cash . . . .*	*980*	
discounts	*Sales Discounts . . . .*	*20*	
recorded	*Accounts Receivable. . . . .*		*1,000*
at time of			
collection	*To record collection from Zenith Company of invoice*		
	of Nov. 3 less 2% cash discount.		

As previously explained, the allowing of a cash discount reduces the amount received from sales. On the income statement, therefore, sales discounts appear as a deduction from sales, as shown below:

Partial Income Statement

Treatment	*Sales . . . .*		*$189,788*
of sales	*Less: Sales returns & allowances . . . .*	*$4,462*	
discounts			
on the	*Sales discounts . . . .*	*3,024*	*7,486*
income	*Net sales. . . . .*		*$182,302*
statement			

RECORDING PURCHASE DISCOUNTS In the accounts of the Zenith Company, the purchase of merchandise on November 3 was recorded at the gross amount of the invoice, as shown by the following entry:

[2] A more accurate estimate of interest expense on an annual basis can be obtained as follows: ($20 × 18) ÷ $980 = 36.7%.

Purchase entered at full price

| Purchases | 1,000 | |
| Accounts Payable | | 1,000 |

To record purchase from Adams Manufacturing Company, terms 2/10, n/30.

When the invoice was paid on November 13, the last day of the discount period, the payment was recorded as follows:

Purchase discounts recorded when payment made

Accounts Payable	1,000	
Purchase Discounts		20
Cash		980

To record payment to Adams Manufacturing Company of invoice of Nov. 3, less 2% cash discount.

The effect of the discount was to reduce the cost of the merchandise to the Zenith Company. The credit balance of the Purchase Discounts account should therefore be deducted in the income statement from the debit balance of the Purchases account.

Since the Purchase Discounts account is deducted from Purchases in the income statement, a question naturally arises as to whether the Purchase Discounts account is really necessary. Why not reduce the amount of purchases at the time of taking a discount by crediting Purchases rather than crediting Purchase Discounts? The answer is that management needs to know the amount of discounts taken. The Purchase Discounts account supplies this information. Any decrease in the proportion of purchase discounts to purchases carries the suggestion that the accounts payable department is becoming inefficient. That department has the responsibility of paying all invoices within the discount period, and management should be informed of failure by any department to follow company policies consistently. If management is to direct the business effectively, it needs to receive from the accounting system information indicating the level of performance in every department.

ALTERNATIVE METHOD: RECORDING INVOICES AT NET PRICE As previously stated, most well-managed companies have a firm policy of taking all purchase discounts offered. These companies may prefer the alternative method of recording purchase invoices at the net amount after discount rather than at the gross amount as previously described. For example, in our illustration of a $1,000 invoice bearing terms of 2/10, n/30, the entry for the purchase could be made as follows:

Entry for purchase: net price method

| Nov. 3 Purchases | 980 | |
| Accounts Payable | | 980 |

To record purchase invoice from Adams Manufacturing Company less 2% cash discount available.

Assuming that the invoice is paid within 10 days, the entry for the payment is as follows:

Entry for payment: net price method

Nov. 13 Accounts Payable	980	
Cash		980
To record payment of $1,000 invoice from Adams		
Manufacturing Company less 2% cash discount.		

Through oversight or carelessness, the purchasing company may occasionally fail to make payment of an invoice within the 10-day discount period. If such a delay occurred in paying the invoice from Adams Manufacturing Company, the full amount of the invoice would have to be paid rather than the recorded liability of $980. The journal entry to record the late payment on, say, December 3, is as follows:

Entry for payment after discount period: net price method

Dec. 3 Accounts Payable	980	
Purchase Discounts Lost	20	
Cash		1,000
To record payment of invoice and loss of discount by		
delaying payment beyond the discount period.		

Under this method the cost of goods purchased is properly recorded at $980, and the additional payment of $20 caused by failure to pay the invoice promptly is placed in a special expense account designed to attract the attention of management. The gross price method of recording invoices previously described shows the amount of purchase discounts *taken* each period; the net price method now under discussion shows the amount of purchase discounts *lost* each period. The latter method has the advantage of drawing the attention of management to a breakdown in prescribed operating routines. The fact that a purchase discount has been taken does not require attention by management, but a discount lost because of inefficiency in processing accounts payable does call for managerial investigation.

As previously suggested, inefficiency and delay in paying invoices should not be concealed by adding the penalty of lost discount to the cost of merchandise purchased. The purchases should be stated at the net price available by taking cash discounts; the Purchase Discounts Lost account should be shown in the income statement as an operating expense.

Both the gross price method and the net price method are acceptable and commonly used. In working problems the student should be alert for an indication of which method is to be used.

MECHANICS OF HANDLING APPROVED INVOICES The procedures for proper verification of a purchase invoice were described earlier in this chapter. After a purchase invoice has been approved for payment, it should be filed in a manner which assures that the required payment date will not be overlooked. For example, the invoice of November 3 from Adams Manufacturing Company could be placed in a "tickler file," a file with index cards bearing dates. Since this invoice must be paid by November 13 to take advantage of the cash discount, the invoice is filed in front of the index card for November 13. On that date the invoice is removed from the tickler file and sent to the cashier. The cashier prepares a check for $980 payable to Adams Manufacturing Company, enters the check number on the invoice approval form, and forwards both documents to the treasurer. The treasurer signs the check, mails it, and marks the invoice "Paid." The invoice and the attached approval sheet are then returned to the accounting department and placed in an alphabetical file of paid invoices.

Sales procedures

The procedures for controlling and recording sales will necessarily vary from one business to another, depending upon the nature and size of the business. The following description of sales procedures should therefore be regarded as a generalized pattern subject to many variations.

Most orders in retail stores are received orally from customers, but in manufacturing and wholesaling companies written orders are customary. These written sales orders come through the mail from the company's staff of traveling salespeople and directly from customers. The first step in processing the order usually is to obtain the approval of the credit department as to the customer's credit rating. If credit approval is obtained, a sales invoice may be prepared in three or more copies.

The first carbon copy of the sales invoice is sent to the stock room; there the merchandise ordered is assembled and sent with this copy of the invoice to the shipping department. When the shipping department has finished packing and shipping the merchandise, the employee in charge signs the invoice, records the date of shipment, and sends the invoice to the accounting department. As an alternative, the data identifying the shipment may be placed on a separate document to accompany the invoice to the accounting department.

While this assembling, packing, and shipping of goods is taking place, a second carbon copy of the invoice is being carefully examined in the accounting department to make sure that the prices, credit terms, and all extensions and footings are correct. This copy of the invoice is also compared with the customer's order to determine that these two documents are in agreement as to quantities, prices, and other details.

When the first carbon of the sales invoice arrives from the shipping department showing that the goods have been sent to the customer, the accounting department places this invoice in a file called a *shipping record.* Now that the accounting department has written evidence that the goods have been shipped, it places its own verified copy of the invoice in a sales binder or register and makes a journal entry debiting the account receivable from the customer and crediting Sales. The original copy of the invoice is mailed to the customer promptly after the goods have been shipped. As previously mentioned, the set of procedures which has been described represents merely one of many alternative methods of processing sales orders.

Monthly statements to customers

In addition to sending an invoice to the customer for each separate sales transaction, some companies send each customer a monthly statement at the end of the month. The statement shows the balance receivable at the beginning of the month, the charges for sales during the month, the credits for payments received or goods returned, and the balance receivable from the customer at the end of the month. A statement sent by Zenith Company to one of its customers at the end of November appears in the illustration below.

		Statement			
		ZENITH COMPANY			
		10 Fairway Avenue			
		San Francisco, California			

Monthly statement summarizing transactions with customer

In account with: ***Date:*** Nov. 30, 19___

John D. Gardner
210 Moranda Lane
Santa Barbara, Calif.

Date	Our Invoice No.	Charges	Credits	Balance Due
Oct. 31	Balance forwarded			125.40
Nov. 8	4127	81.00		206.40
10			125.40	81.00
21	4352	62.50		143.50

Accounts are payable on tenth of month following purchase

Upon receipt of a monthly statement from a vendor, the customer company should make a detailed comparison of the purchases and payments shown on the statement with the corresponding entries in its accounts payable records. Any differences in the invoiced amounts, payments, or balance owed should be promptly investigated. Frequently the balance shown on the statement will differ from the balance of the customer's accounts payable record because shipments of merchandise and letters containing payments are in transit at month-end. These in-transit items will have been recorded by the sender but will not yet appear on the other party's records.

Cycle billing

Large department stores and other businesses with large numbers of accounts receivable may use *cycle billing* to avoid concentration of work at the end of the month. The customers' accounts are divided into alphabetical groups, and each group is billed regularly on a given day of the month. Thus, customers whose names fall in the L–M group might be billed on the seventeenth of each month, and those in the N–P block might be billed on the nineteenth. This procedure spreads the work of preparing customers' statements more evenly throughout the month. It also results in a more uniform inflow of cash from customers.

Sales taxes

Sales taxes are levied by many states and cities on certain retail sales. Usually certain classes of sales are exempt, notably food and some commodities, such as gasoline and cigarettes, already subject to special excise taxes. To restrict the practice of purchasing outside the state to avoid the tax, some states levy a supplementary *use tax,* applicable to goods purchased outside the state and brought in.

Typically a sales tax is imposed on the consumer, but the seller must collect the tax, file tax returns at times specified by law, and remit a percentage of the reported sales. The actual tax collected by the selling company from its customers may be greater or less than the amount paid to the government because no tax is collected on sales under a certain amount, and due to rounding of pennies, the tax collected on a given sale may be slightly more than the specified percentage.

ACCOUNTING FOR SALES TAXES A sales tax may be collected when a cash sale is made or it may be included in the charge to the customer's account on a credit sale. The liability to the governmental unit for sales taxes may be recorded at the time the sale is made as follows:

Sales tax recorded at time of sale	Accounts Receivable (or Cash) 1,050	
	Sales Tax Payable	50
	Sales	1,000

To record sale of $1,000 subject to 5% sales tax.

Instead of recording the sales tax liability at the time of sale, some businesses prefer to credit the Sales account with the entire amount collected, including the sales tax, and to make an adjustment at the end of each period to reflect sales tax payable. For example, suppose that the total recorded sales for the period under this method were $315,000. Since the Sales account includes both the sales price and the sales tax (say, 5%), it is apparent that $315,000 is 105% of the actual sales figure. Actual sales are $300,000 ($315,000 ÷ 1.05) and the amount of sales tax due is $15,000. (Proof: 5% of $300,000 = $15,000.) The entry to record the liability for sales taxes would be:

Sales tax recorded as adjustment of sales

Sales	*15,000*	
Sales Tax Payable		*15,000*

To remove sales taxes of 5% on $300,000 of sales from the Sales account, and reflect as a liability.

Any discrepancy between the tax due and the amount actually collected from customers, under this method, would be automatically absorbed in the net sales figure. If certain of the products being sold (such as food) are not subject to the tax, it is necessary to keep a record of taxable and nontaxable sales.

KEY TERMS INTRODUCED OR EMPHASIZED IN CHAPTER 6

Cash discount A reduction in price (usually 2% or less) offered by manufacturers and wholesalers to encourage customers to pay invoices within a specified discount period.

Credit memorandum A document issued to show a reduction in the amount owed by a customer because of goods returned, a defect in the goods or services provided, or an error.

Cycle billing A system of billing customers at various dates during the month to avoid concentration of work at month-end.

Debit memorandum A document issued by a buyer to show a decrease in the amount previously recorded as owing to a seller. May also be issued by a seller to increase the amount previously recorded as receivable from a customer.

Documentation All the charts, forms, tapes, reports, and other business papers that guide and describe the working of a company's system of accounting and internal control.

Embezzlement Theft by a person of assets entrusted to him or her.

Fidelity bond A form of insurance contract in which a bonding company agrees to reimburse an employer for losses caused by theft by bonded employees.

Financial forecast A plan of operations for a future period with expected results expressed in dollars.

Fraud Dishonest acts intended to deceive, often involving the theft of assets and falsification of accounting records and financial statements.

Gross price method A policy of recording invoices at the gross amount before cash discounts and of recording cash discounts taken in accounts called Purchase Discounts and Sales Discounts.

Internal accounting controls Measures that relate to protection of assets and to the reliability of accounting information and financial statements.

Internal administrative controls A subcategory of internal controls which apply principally to operational efficiency and compliance with company policy and which do not bear directly on the dependability of financial statements.

Internal auditing An activity carried on in large organizations by a professional staff to investigate and evaluate the system of internal control on a year-round basis. Also to evaluate the efficiency of individual departments within the organization.

Internal control All measures used by a business to guard against errors, waste, or fraud and to assure the reliability of accounting data. Designed to aid in the efficient operation of a business and to encourage compliance with company policies.

Invoice An itemized statement of goods being bought or sold. Shows quantities, prices, and credit terms. Serves as the basis for an entry in the accounting records of both seller and buyer because it evidences the transfer of ownership of goods.

Net price method A policy of recording purchase invoices at amounts net of (reduced by) cash discounts.

Organization chart A diagram showing organizational lines of authority and responsibility, with emphasis on separation of functions.

Purchase order A serially numbered document sent by the purchasing department of a business to a supplier or vendor for the purpose of ordering materials or services.

Receiving report An internal form prepared by the receiving department for each incoming shipment showing the quantity and condition of goods received.

Sales tax A tax levied by most states and many cities on certain retail sales. Typically the seller must collect the tax and file returns with the taxing agency.

Serial numbering of documents The assignment of an unbroken sequence of numbers to a given class of documents, such as checks or invoices, so that the omission or loss of a document will be readily apparent.

Statement of account A monthly statement sent by a company to a customer showing charges for sales during the month, credits for payments received or goods returned, and the balance receivable from the customer at the end of the month.

Trade discount A percentage reduction from the list price of merchandise allowed to dealers by manufacturers and wholesalers; not recorded in the accounts because the net price is regarded as the actual sales price.

REVIEW QUESTIONS

1 What is the purpose of a system of internal control? List four groups of measures included in a system of internal control.

2 Criticize the following statement: "Internal control may be defined as all those measures which a business uses to prevent fraud."

3 Ross Corporation is a medium-sized business with 20 office employees. State two or three guidelines or principles which should be followed in assigning duties to the various employees so that internal control will be as strong as possible.

4 State a general principle to be observed in assigning duties among employees with respect to the purchase of merchandise so that strong internal control will be achieved.

5 Suggest a control device to protect a business against the loss or nondelivery of invoices, purchase orders, and other documents which are routed from one department to another.

6 Criticize the following statement: "In our company we get things done by requiring that a person who initiates a transaction follow it through in all particulars. For example, an employee who issues a purchase order is held responsible for inspecting the merchandise upon arrival, approving the invoice, and preparing the check in payment of the purchase. If any error is made, we know definitely whom to blame."

7 If a company obtains a fidelity bond protecting it against loss from dishonest actions on the part of any of its officers or employees, would it still be necessary for the company to maintain a system of internal control? Explain.

8 What is the principal difference between an audit by independent public accountants and the work done by internal auditors?

9 Explain why the operations and custodianship functions should be separate from the accounting function.

10 A system of internal control is often said to include two major types of controls: administrative controls and accounting controls. Explain the nature of each group and give an example of each.

11 A CPA makes a study and evaluation of internal controls as part of an annual audit. Is the CPA equally concerned with administrative controls and accounting controls? Explain.

12 For an invoice dated October 21, what is the last day of the credit period if the credit terms are **(a)** 2/10, n/30? **(b)** 10 e.o.m.?

13 Blair Manufacturing Company sells appliances on both a wholesale and a retail basis and publishes an annual catalog listing products at retail prices. At what price should the sale be recorded when an item listed in the catalog at $400 is delivered to a wholesaler entitled to a 30% trade discount?

14 What is meant by the expressions **(a)** 2/10, n/30; **(b)** 10 e.o.m.; **(c)** n/30?

15 A company which has received a shipment of merchandise and a related invoice from the supplier sometimes finds it necessary to issue a debit memorandum. List three examples of situations that would justify such action by the purchasing company.

16 A cash discount affects both seller and buyer. What term describes a cash discount from the viewpoint of the seller? From the viewpoint of the buyer?

17 Distinguish between a trade discount and a cash discount.

18 What accounting entry, if any, is required on the part of the company issuing a purchase order? On the part of the company receiving the purchase order?

19 Under what circumstances is cycle billing of customers likely to be used? State two advantages which may be gained from cycle billing.

20 Name three documents (business papers) which are needed by the accounting department to verify that a purchase of merchandise has occurred and that payment of the related liability should be made.

EXERCISES

Ex. 6-1 A CPA firm performing an audit of a company's financial statements always begins with a study and evaluation of the internal controls in force. List several *documents* which a CPA firm would expect to find at the business which would be helpful in the study and evaluation of internal control.

Ex. 6-2 A strong system of internal control serves to protect a company's assets against waste, fraud, and inefficient use. Fidelity bonds provide a means by which a company may recover losses caused by dishonest acts of employees. Would it be reasonable for a company to maintain a strong system of internal control and also pay for a fidelity bond? Explain.

Ex. 6-3 Jet Auto Supply Store received from a manufacturer a shipment of 200 gasoline cans. Harold Abbott, who handles all purchasing activities, telephoned the manufacturer and explained that he had ordered only 100 cans. The manufacturer replied that two separate purchase orders for 100 cans each had recently been received from Jet Auto Supply Store. Harold Abbott is sure that the manufacturer is in error and is merely trying to justify an excess shipment, but he has no means of proving his point. What is the missing element in internal control over purchases by Jet Auto Supply Store?

66800
9200
2200
78200

134,800
78200
56600

83890
56600
27260

INTERNAL CONTROL **225**

Ex. 6-4 Robert Hale, owner of Hale Equipment, a merchandising business, explains to you how he has assigned duties to employees. Hale states: "In order to have clearly defined responsibility for each phase of our operations, I have made one employee responsible for the purchasing, receiving, and storage of merchandise. Another employee has been charged with responsibility for maintaining the accounting records and for making all collections from customers. I have assigned to a third employee responsibility for maintaining personnel records for all our employees and for timekeeping, preparation of payroll records, and distribution of payroll checks. My goal in setting up this organization plan is to have a strong system of internal control."

You are to evaluate Hale's plan of organization and explain fully the reasoning underlying any criticism you may have.

Ex. 6-5 James Company sold merchandise to Bay Company on credit. On the next day, James Company received a telephone call from Bay Company stating that one of the items delivered was defective. James Company immediately issued credit memorandum no. 163 for $100 to Bay Company.

    a Give the accounting entry required in James Company's records to record the issuance of the credit memorandum.

    b Give the accounting entry required on Bay Company's accounting records when the credit memorandum is received. (Assume that Bay Company had previously recorded the purchase at the full amount of the seller's invoice and had not issued a debit memorandum.)

Ex. 6-6 Taft Company received purchase invoices during July totaling $42,000, all of which carried credit terms of 2/10, n/30. It was the company's regular policy to take advantage of all available cash discounts, but because of employee vacations during July, there was confusion and delay in making payments to suppliers, and none of the July invoices were paid within the discount period.

    a Explain briefly two alternative ways in which the amount of purchases might be presented in the July income statement.

    b What method of recording purchase invoices can you suggest that would call to the attention of the Taft Company management the inefficiency of operations in July?

Ex. 6-7 Hudson Company sold merchandise to River Company for $3,000; terms 2/10, n/30. River Company paid for the merchandise within the discount period. Assume that both companies record invoices at the gross amounts.

    a Give the journal entries by Hudson Company to record the sale and the subsequent collection.

    b Give the journal entries by River Company to record the purchase and the subsequent payment.

Ex. 6-8 From the following information, determine the amount of the beginning inventory.

Ending inventory	$ 66,800	*Transportation-in*	$4,800
Purchases	130,000	*Purchase returns & allowances* .	9,200
Cost of goods sold	83,800	*Purchase discounts*	2,200

Ex. 6-9 The Hasagami General Store operates in an area in which a 6% sales tax is levied on all products handled by the store. On cash sales, the salesclerks include the sales tax in the amount collected from the customer and ring up the entire amount on the cash register without recording separately the tax liability. On credit sales, the customer is charged for the list price of the merchandise plus 6%, and the entire amount is debited to Accounts Receivable and credited to the Sales account. On sales of less than one dollar, the tax collected is rounded to the nearest cent.

Sales tax must be remitted to the government quarterly. At March 31 the Sales account showed a balance of $152,360 for the three-month period ended March 31.

a What amount of sales tax is owed at March 31? (Round to nearest dollar.)
b Give the journal entry to record the sales tax liability on the books.

Ex. 6-10 Give the journal entry, if any, to be prepared for each of these events:
  a Received a telephone order from a customer for $1,800 worth of merchandise.
  b Issued a purchase order to Mack Company for merchandise costing $2,500.
  c Received the merchandise ordered from Mack Company and an invoice for $2,500; credit terms 2/10, n/30. (Record at gross amount.)
  d Delivered the $1,800 of merchandise ordered in (*a*) above to the customer and mailed an invoice; credit terms 10 e.o.m.
  e Mailed check to Mack Company in full settlement of amount owed after taking allowable discount.
  f Customer returned $400 of goods delivered in (*d*) above, which were unsatisfactory. A credit memorandum was issued for that amount.

PROBLEMS

Group A

6A-1 At the Boulevard Theater, the cashier is located in a box office at the front of the building. The cashier receives cash from customers and operates a ticket machine which ejects serially numbered tickets. The serial number appears on each end of the ticket. The tickets come from the printer in large rolls which fit into the ticket machine and are removed at the end of each cashier's working period.

After purchasing a ticket from the cashier, in order to be admitted to the theater a customer must hand the ticket to a doorman stationed some 50 feet from the box office at the entrance to the theater lobby. The doorman tears the ticket in half, opens the door for the customer, and returns the ticket stub to the customer. The other half of the ticket is dropped by the doorman into a locked box.

Instructions
a Describe the internal controls present in the Boulevard Theater's method of handling cash receipts.
b What steps should be taken regularly by the theater manager or other supervisor to make these internal controls work most effectively?
c Assume that the cashier and the doorman decided to collaborate in an effort to abstract cash receipts. What action might they take?
d On the assumption made in (*c*) of collaboration between the cashier and the doorman, what features of the control procedures would be most likely to disclose the embezzlement?

6A-2 After spending several years as an executive for a large nationwide finance company, Howard Lee resigned in order to open his own finance business, which he called Friendly Loan Company. The business consists of four very small offices in four cities a few miles apart. The activity of each office consists of making small loans to individual borrowers. The borrowers agree to repay the amount borrowed plus interest in monthly installments over a period of 36 months or less.

Howard Lee has his own office at one of the four loan offices and he makes fairly frequent trips to the other offices to provide general supervision and to perform some internal auditing work. Early in the current year Lee called upon a firm of certified public accountants and explained that he was worried about the honesty of his employees. He made the following statement: "In the large nationwide loan company where I worked before starting my own business, we had over 500 offices scattered over 10 states. The system of accounting and internal control in that company made fraud absolutely impossible. I can describe the system to you in detail and I want you to install that system in my own company."

Instructions

a Explain how the CPA firm would probably respond to Lee's request that it install the large finance company's system of internal control in his new business.

b Comment on Lee's statement that the new system would make fraud absolutely impossible.

6A-3 Jay Winkler, long-time office manager of Western Building Materials, prepares all purchase orders for merchandise in which the company deals. Winkler personally owns a large waterfront lot and during the current year he was having a marina constructed on this lot. The construction plans included boat slips, a large dock, a restaurant, and a marine supply store.

To obtain building materials for this project, Winkler fraudulently issued purchase orders in the name of Western Building Materials and instructed the suppliers to deliver the materials at his waterfront site. The suppliers did not question the propriety of these orders since they were accustomed to receiving from Western Building Supplies purchase orders signed by Winkler. When purchase invoices from the suppliers relating to these materials reached Western Building Materials, Winkler entered them in the accounting records as debits to Purchases and credits to Accounts Payable. On the appropriate dates, he prepared company checks payable to the suppliers and presented them to the treasurer of Western Building Materials for signature. Since the checks were payable to suppliers from whom Western Building Materials regularly made purchases, the treasurer signed and mailed the checks without question.

The accounting system used by Western Building Materials required that duplicate copies of purchase orders be attached to the related receiving reports and purchase invoices, and then filed alphabetically by vendor. Since there were no receiving reports for the materials that Winkler diverted to his marina, he removed from the files the purchase orders and related purchase invoices for these materials and concealed these documents in his desk. During the year, the billed price of the materials which Winkler ordered and diverted to his marina totaled $110,000. Of this total, all but $10,000 had been paid for at year-end by Western Building Materials and cash discounts of $2,000 had been taken. The remaining $10,000 in unpaid invoices were included in the year-end balance of accounts payable at the gross amount.

Western Building Materials uses the periodic inventory system. A complete physical inventory was taken on December 31. In an effort to prevent the theft of materials from having a conspicuous effect on the year's reported earnings, Winkler changed figures on the inventory count sheets, thereby causing the ending inventory to be overstated by $100,000.

Condensed financial statements for the company at December 31 of the current year appeared as follows:

WESTERN BUILDING MATERIALS

Balance Sheet

December 31, 19____

Assets		Liabilities & Owner's Equity	
Cash	$ 32,000	Notes payable	$320,000
Accounts receivable	280,000	Accounts payable	260,000
Inventory	625,000	Accrued salaries	20,000
Office equipment (net)	5,000	Total liabilities	$600,000
Trucks (net)	36,000	Ralph West, capital	378,000
	$978,000		$978,000

WESTERN BUILDING MATERIALS
Income Statement
For the Year Ended December 31, 19____

Net sales				$3,661,000
Cost of goods sold:				
Beginning inventory			$ 520,000	
Purchases		$3,225,000		
Less: Purchase ret. & all.	$72,000			
Purchase discounts	60,000	132,000	3,093,000	
Cost of goods available for sale			$3,613,000	
Less: Inventory, Dec. 31, 19____			625,000	
Cost of goods sold				2,988,000
Gross profit on sales				$ 673,000
Operating expenses:				
Selling			$ 385,000	
General and administrative			265,000	650,000
Net income				$ 23,000

At an office party on New Year's Eve, Jay Winkler became somewhat intoxi-cated and confided to a secretary how he had acquired "free materials" to build a marina. The secretary reported this information to Ralph West, who immediately demanded an explanation from Winkler. Jay Winkler confessed to his dishonest actions and returned the purchase orders and purchase invoices he had removed from the files. Also on New Year's Eve, the marina being constructed by Winkler was completely destroyed by fire. There was no insurance in force, and Winkler had no other assets. Ralph West discharged Winkler and he left town without any forwarding address. Western Building Materials did not have a fidelity bond for its employees. Ralph West considers that the entire problem was caused by his failure to establish a satisfactory system of internal control. He does not attach any blame to the suppliers.

Instructions
a Compute the loss to Western Building Materials from Jay Winkler's dishonest actions. Show how you arrived at this amount.
b Prepare a corrected balance sheet and income statement. Delete from the Cost of Goods Sold section of the income statement the purchased materials which in fact were never in the possession of the company. Include as a separate, nonoperating item, Loss from Material Shortages.
c Explain the weaknesses in the system of internal control which made possible concealment of the thefts by Winkler and recommend any appropriate im-provements in the system.

6A-4 The Pickett Company completed the following transactions relating to the pur-chase of merchandise during the month of August 19____. It is the policy of the company to record all purchase invoices at the net amount and to pay invoices within the discount period.

Aug. **1** Purchased merchandise from Rallis Company, $24,000; terms 2/10, n/30.

Aug. **8** Purchased merchandise from Thomas Company, $36,000; terms 2/10, n/30.

Aug. **8** Merchandise with a list price of $3,600 purchased from Rallis Company on August 1 was found to be defective. It was returned to the supplier accompanied by debit memorandum no. 118.

Aug. 18 Paid Thomas Company's invoice of August 8, less cash discount.

Aug. 25 Purchased merchandise from Thomas Company, $22,800; terms 2/10, n/30.

Aug. 30 Paid Rallis Company's invoice of August 1, taking into consideration the return of defective goods on August 8.

The inventory of merchandise on August 1 was $98,880; on August 31, $93,780.

Instructions

a Journalize the above transactions, recording invoices at the net amount.

b Prepare the cost of goods sold section of the income statement.

c What is the amount of accounts payable at the end of August? What would be the amount of accounts payable at the end of August if the Pickett Company followed the policy of recording purchase invoices at the gross amount?

6A-5 During November, the following transactions relating to the purchase of merchandise for resale were carried out by Nelson Company.

Nov. 1 Purchased merchandise from Westport Landing, Inc., $12,000; terms, 2/10, n/30.

Nov. 7 Purchased merchandise from Border Corporation, $18,000; terms 2/10, n/30.

Nov. 8 Merchandise having a list price of $1,800 purchased from Westport Landing, Inc., was found to be defective. It was returned to the seller, accompanied by debit memorandum no. 263.

Nov. 17 Paid Border Corporation invoice of November 7, less cash discount.

Nov. 24 Purchased merchandise from Border Corporation, $11,400; terms 2/10, n/30.

Nov. 30 Paid Westport Landing, Inc., invoice of November 1.

Assume that the merchandise inventory on November 1, was $55,200; on November 30, $47,040.

Instructions

a Journalize the above transactions, recording invoices at the gross amount.

b Prepare the cost of goods sold section of the income statement.

c What is the amount of accounts payable at the end of November? What would the amount of accounts payable be at the end of November if Nelson Company followed the policy of recording purchase invoices at the net amount?

6A-6 Baker Company completed the following merchandising transactions during May. The company's policy calls for taking advantage of all cash discounts available to it from suppliers; purchase invoices are recorded at the net amount. In making sales, the company grants credit terms of 2/10, n/30 and strictly enforces the 10-day limitation. The amounts listed as cash sales below are net of sales discounts.

May 3 Sold merchandise to Rich Company for cash, $32,880.

May 16 Sold merchandise on account to Riverside Company, $14,820.

May 16 Purchased merchandise from Hilton Supply Company, $18,900; terms 2/10, n/30 (to be recorded at the *net* amount).

May 17 Paid transportation charges on goods received from Hilton Supply Company, $726.

May 18 Issued credit memorandum no. 102 to Riverside Company for allowance on damaged goods, $420.

May 24 Purchased merchandise from Pete Construction Co., $17,100, terms 1/10, n/30 (to be recorded at the net amount).

May 25 Returned defective goods with invoice price of $900 to Pete Construction Co., accompanied by debit memorandum no. 122.

May 26 Received cash from Riverside Company in full payment of account.

May 26 Paid Hilton Supply Company account in full.

Instructions

a Record the above transactions in three-column running balance ledger accounts (Cash, Accounts Receivable, Accounts Payable, Sales, etc.). Journal entries are not required.

b Prepare a partial income statement for May showing sales and cost of goods sold (in detail), and gross profit on sales. Assume the inventory at Apr. 30 to be $11,400 and the inventory at May 31 to be $13,920.

c What is the amount of accounts payable at May 31? What would be the amount of accounts payable at May 31 if the company followed a policy of recording purchase invoices at the gross amount?

6A-7 When the in-charge accountant for Ventura Company suddenly became ill in late December, the recently employed assistant was called upon to complete the year-end accounting work. The assistant, whose knowledge of accounting was rather limited, prepared the following financial statements. All dollar amounts (except the balance sheet totals) are correct, although numerous errors exist in the location of accounts in the financial statements.

VENTURA COMPANY

Loss Statement

December 31, 19___

Sales	$734,400	
Purchase returns & allowances	5,472	
Purchase discounts	10,606	
Interest earned on investments	1,368	
Increase in inventory	7,387	$759,233
Purchases	$545,256	
Sales returns & allowances	12,931	
Sales discounts	6,682	
Transportation-in	34,178	
Interest expense	2,405	
Uncollectible accounts expense	3,053	
Depreciation expense: building	2,520	
Depreciation expense: store equipment	3,218	
Depreciation expense: delivery equipment	2,650	
Insurance expense	2,304	
Office salaries expense	22,320	
Executive salaries expense	59,040	
Sales salaries expense	87,660	
Miscellaneous selling expense	1,339	
Miscellaneous general expense	2,261	787,817
Net loss for year		$ 28,584

VENTURA COMPANY
Balance Sheet
December 31, 19___

Current assets:

Notes receivable.	$ 14,400	
Accounts receivable	36,720	
Cash	23,616	
Rent collected in advance	1,152	
Land	28,800	$104,688

Plant and equipment:

Inventory	$ 77,047	
Store equipment	27,504	
Building	69,120	
Delivery equipment	20,880	194,551

Other assets:

Marketable securities held as temporary investments	$ 12,960	
Land held as future building site	18,000	30,960
Total assets		$330,199

Liabilities:

Accounts payable	$ 40,702	
Accrued salaries payable	3,145	
Short-term prepayments	1,152	
Notes payable	21,600	
Mortgage payable	72,000	
Allowance for doubtful accounts	2,362	
Accumulated depreciation: building	22,464	
Accumulated depreciation: store equipment	17,280	
Accumulated depreciation: delivery equipment	16,704	
Total liabilities		$197,409

Owner's equity:

Steven Riles, capital	$144,000	
Less: Drawings	11,210	132,790
Total liabilities & owner's equity		$330,199

Instructions

a Prepare in acceptable form an income statement for the year ended December 31, 19___. (Allocate to selling expense 60% of building depreciation and $720 of insurance expense.) The remaining portions of these two expense accounts should be classified under the General and Administrative Expenses heading. The Uncollectible Accounts Expense of $3,053 should also be listed under General and Administrative Expenses.

b Prepare a balance sheet as of December 31, 19___, properly classified. Show the Allowance for Doubtful Accounts as a deduction from Accounts Receivable in the current asset section of the balance sheet.

c What was the balance in the owner's capital account at the beginning of the current year?

Group B

6B-1 Edward Garvey, manager of Theater & Parks, Inc., made the following statement: "We consider the regular rotation of employee assignments to be an important element of a strong system of internal control. Consequently, we have our accounts receivable employee take over the work of our cashier every day from 11:30 to 12:30. Then the cashier takes over the position of the accounts receivable employee from 12:30 to 1:30 while that employee is given an hour off for lunch.

"We follow the same procedure with respect to the admission of customers to our theaters. The ticket seller in the box office will occasionally change places with the ticket taker at the door. This rotation policy also has the advantage of giving employees a better understanding of our system as a whole."

Evaluate Garvey's rotation of employees from the standpoint of maintaining strong internal control.

6B-2 Madison Company retained a firm of certified public accountants to devise a system of internal control especially suited to its operations. Assuming that the CPA firm has finished its work and the newly designed system of internal control is in use, answer fully the following questions:

a Will it be possible for any type of fraud to occur without immediate detection once the new system of internal control is in full operation?

b Describe two limitations inherent in any system of internal control that will prevent it from providing absolute assurance against inefficiency and fraud.

6B-3 Roger Banning, an employee of Ames Company, is responsible for preparing checks to suppliers in payment for purchases of merchandise. Before submitting the checks to the treasurer for signature, Banning receives a copy of the purchase order, the receiving report, and the supplier's invoice. After determining that all three documents are in agreement and that no arithmetical errors exist, he fills in an invoice approval form. He then prepares a check complete except for the treasurer's signature. Banning files the documents (purchase order, purchase invoice, receiving report, and invoice approval form) alphabetically by supplier. As a final step, he forwards the check to the treasurer for signature.

While trying to finish his work early on Friday, December 31, Banning accidentally prepared for the treasurer's signature a check payable to Miller Company, a regular supplier, for $9,642, although the invoice and other documents indicated the amount payable was actually $6,942. Banning had previously made another error in recording the invoice. He had debited the Purchases account, but the debit should have been to Office Equipment because the invoice was for typewriters and other equipment to be used in the business and not to be sold to customers. The amount of this accounting entry agreed with the invoice but not with the check. The entry was as follows:

Purchases *6,942*

    Accounts Payable *6,942*

To record purchase invoice from Miller Company. Terms,

cash upon delivery.

The check for $9,642 was forwarded to the treasurer, promptly signed, and entered in the accounting records as a debit to Accounts Payable and a credit to Cash in the amount of $9,642. The treasurer mailed the check to the supplier. The supplier did not notice the overpayment and deposited the check.

A physical inventory was taken at the close of business Dec. 31, and financial statements were prepared by Ames Company without discovery of the error. Net income for the year was $100,000 and the owner's capital at December 31 appeared in the balance sheet as $204,000.

On January 20, Banning was processing another invoice from Miller Company and discovered the previous overpayment error. Banning processed the new invoice in a normal manner and then informed Miller Company by telephone of the December overpayment. He requested that a refund check be mailed and the envelope marked for his attention. After receiving the refund check for $2,700, Banning went to a nearby town, opened a new bank account in the name of Ames Company and deposited the check. A short time later he withdrew the amount deposited, closed the bank account, and moved out of town leaving no forwarding address. Ames Company does not carry a fidelity bond on its employees.

Instructions
a Were the figures for net income and owner's equity correct as shown in the financial statements? Explain fully. If you consider these amounts incorrect, compute corrected amounts.
b Assuming that the facts about the overstated check, the refund, and the theft by Banning all came to light late in January, prepare the necessary adjusting entry or entries. Include a full explanation as part of such entries.
c Identify any weaknesses in the system of internal control indicated by the above events and make recommendations for improvements.

6B-4 The following items were included in the income statement of Amazon Company for the year ended June 30, 19____.

Sales	$1,105,200	Gross profit on sales	$367,542
Purchase discounts	11,580	Purchases	703,830
Beginning inventory	?	Sales discounts	13,920
Sales returns &		Transportation-in	17,040
allowances	41,160	Purchase returns &	
Ending inventory	171,312	allowances . . . . ˙	31,320

Instructions
a Compute the amount of net sales.
b Compute the gross profit percentage.
c What percentage of net sales represents the cost of goods sold?
d Prepare a partial income statement utilizing all the accounts listed above, including the determination of the amount of the beginning inventory. Use the columnar arrangement illustrated on page 179.

6B-5 The following transactions were completed by Tolstad Company during the month of November 19____.

Nov. 1 Purchased merchandise from Hayes Company, $8,000; terms 2/10, n/30.

Nov. 7 Purchased merchandise from Joseph Corporation, $12,000, terms 2/10, n/30.

Nov. 8 Merchandise having a list price of $1,200, purchased from Hayes Company, was found to be defective. It was returned to the seller, accompanied by debit memorandum no. 382.

Nov. 17 Paid Joseph Corporation's invoice of November 7, less cash discount.

Nov. 24 Purchased merchandise from Joseph Corporation, $7,600, terms 2/10, n/30.

Nov. 30 Paid Hayes Company's invoice of November 1, taking into consideration the return of goods on November 8.

Assume that the merchandise inventory on November 1 was $32,960; on November 30, $31,260.

Instructions

a Journalize the above transactions, recording invoices at the net amount.

b Prepare the cost of goods sold section of the income statement.

c What is the amount of accounts payable at the end of November? What would the amount of accounts payable be at the end of November if Tolstad Company followed the policy of recording purchase invoices at the gross amount?

6B-6 Fargo Company completed the following transactions relating to the purchase of merchandise during the month of April.

Apr. 2 Purchased merchandise from Hart Corporation, $42,000; terms 2/10, n/30.

Apr. 8 Purchased merchandise from Tillman, Inc., $63,000; terms 2/10, n/30.

Apr. 9 Merchandise with a list price of $6,300, purchased from Hart Corporation on April 2, was found to be defective. It was returned to the supplier accompanied by debit memorandum no. 515.

Apr. 18 Paid Tillman, Inc., invoice of April 8, less cash discount.

Apr. 25 Purchased merchandise from Tillman, Inc., $39,900; terms 2/10, n/30.

Apr. 30 Paid Hart Corporation's invoice of April 2.

The inventory of merchandise on April 1 was $193,200; on April 30, $164,640.

Instructions

a Journalize the above transactions, recording invoices at the gross amount.

b Prepare the cost of goods sold section of the income statement.

c What is the amount of accounts payable at the end of April? What would the amount of accounts payable be at the end of April if Fargo Company followed the policy of recording purchase invoices at the net amount?

6B-7 The merchandising transactions of Bothwell Wholesale Company for the month of July are detailed below. The company's policy is to take advantage of all cash discounts offered by suppliers; purchase invoices are recorded at the net amount. In making sales the company grants credit terms of 2/10, n/30, and strictly enforces the 10-day limitation for granting discounts. The amounts listed as cash sales are net of sales discounts.

July 2 Sold merchandise to Fitch Co. for cash, $164,400.

July 15 Sold merchandise on account to Ryan Furniture Co., $74,100.

July 16 Purchased merchandise from Walden Supply Co., $94,800, terms 2/10, n/30 (to be recorded at net amount).

July 16 Paid transportation charges on goods received from Walden Supply Co., $3,630.

July 18 Issued credit memorandum no. 361 to Ryan Furniture Co. for allowance on damaged goods, $2,100.

July 24 Purchased merchandise from Potter Manufacturing Co., $85,500; terms 1/10, n/30 (to be recorded at net amount).

July 25 Returned defective goods with invoice price of $4,500 to Potter Manufacturing Co., accompanied by debit memorandum no. 85.

July 25 Received cash from Ryan Furniture Co. in full payment of account.

July 26 Paid Walden Supply Co. account in full.

Instructions

a Record the above transactions in three-column, running balance ledger accounts. (Cash, Accounts Receivable, Accounts Payable, Sales, etc.) Journal entries are not required.

b Prepare a partial income statement for July showing sales and cost of goods sold (in detail), and gross profit on sales. Assume the inventory at June 30 to be $57,000 and at July 31 to be $69,600.

c What is the amount of accounts payable at July 31? What would be the amount of accounts payable at July 31 if the company followed a policy of recording purchase invoices at the gross amount?

BUSINESS DECISION PROBLEM 6

Martin Company and Winter Company are both merchandising companies applying for nine-month bank loans in order to finance the acquisition of new equipment. Both companies are seeking to borrow the amount of $210,000 and have submitted the following balance sheets with their loan applications:

MARTIN COMPANY

Balance Sheet

August 31, 19____

Assets

Current assets:				
Cash			$	57,000
Accounts receivable				153,000
Inventories				162,000
Short-term prepayments				6,000
Total current assets			$	378,000
Plant and equipment:				
Land	$150,000			
Building	$600,000			
Less: Accumulated depreciation	90,000	510,000		
Store equipment	$180,000			
Less: Accumulated depreciation	45,000	135,000		
Total plant and equipment				795,000
Total assets				$1,173,000

Liabilities & Owner's Equity

Current liabilities:		
Accounts payable	$	135,000
Accrued wages payable		45,000
Total current liabilities	$	180,000
Long-term liabilities:		
Mortgage payable (due in 13 months)		330,000
Total liabilities	$	510,000
Owner's equity:		
Steven Martin, capital		663,000
Total liabilities & owner's equity		$1,173,000

WINTER COMPANY
Balance Sheet
August 31, 19___

Assets

Current assets:		
Cash		$ 384,000
U.S. government bonds		210,000
Accounts receivable		603,000
Inventories		567,000
Total current assets		$1,764,000
Plant & equipment:		
Land	$ 180,000	
Building and equipment	$1,230,000	
Less: Accumulated depreciation	180,000	1,050,000
Total plant & equipment		1,230,000
Total assets		$2,994,000

Liabilities & Owner's Equity

Current liabilities:		
Notes payable		$ 600,000
Accounts payable		480,000
Miscellaneous accrued liabilities		180,000
Total current liabilities		$1,260,000
Long-term liabilities:		
Mortgage payable (due in 10 years)		420,000
Total liabilities		$1,680,000
Owner's equity:		
Jack Winter, capital		1,314,000
Total liabilities & owner's equity		$2,994,000

Along with its balance sheet and loan application, Winter Company submitted to the bank a report issued by a national firm of certified public accountants. The report indicated that early in the year the CPA firm had been retained by Winter Company to make a special investigation of its system of internal control; the study resulted in a number of recommendations, all of which the company had promptly adopted.

Instructions

a Compute the current ratio and amount of working capital for each company as of August 31, 19___.

b Compute the current ratio and amount of working capital that each company would have after obtaining the bank loan and investing the borrowed cash in new equipment (assuming no other transactions affecting current accounts).

c From the viewpoint of a bank loan officer, to which company would you prefer to make a $210,000 nine-month loan? Explain. Include in your answer a discussion of the ability of each company to meet its obligations in the near future and also explain what bearing the CPA firm's report on internal control would have on your decision-making process as a bank loan officer.

7

Accounting Systems: Manual and EDP

In the early chapters of an introductory accounting book, basic accounting principles can most conveniently be discussed in terms of a small business with only a few customers and suppliers. This simplified model of a business has been used in preceding chapters to demonstrate the analysis and recording of the more common types of business transactions.

The recording procedures illustrated thus far call for recording each transaction by an entry in the general journal, and then posting each debit and credit from the general journal to the proper account in the ledger. We must now face the practical problem of streamlining and speeding up this basic accounting system so that the accounting department can keep pace with the rapid flow of transactions in a modern business.

Accounting systems in common use range from manual systems, which use special journals to streamline the journalizing and posting processes, to sophisticated computer systems which maintain accounting records on magnetic tape. The accounting system in use in any given company will be specially tailored to the size and information needs of the business.

MANUAL ACCOUNTING SYSTEMS

In a large business there may be hundreds or even thousands of transactions every day. To handle a large volume of transactions rapidly and efficiently, it is helpful to group the transactions into like classes and to use a specialized journal for each class. This will greatly reduce the amount of detailed recording work and will also permit a division of labor, since each special-purpose journal can be handled by a different employee. The great majority of transactions (perhaps as much as 90 or 95%) usually fall into four types. These four types and the four corresponding special journals are as follows:

Type of Transaction	Name of Special Journal
Sales of merchandise on credit	Sales journal
Purchases of merchandise on credit	Purchases journal
Receipts of cash	Cash receipts journal
Payments of cash	Cash payments journal

In addition to these four special journals, a *general journal* will be used for recording transactions which do not fit into any of the above four types. The general journal is the same book of original entry illustrated in preceding chapters; the adjective "general" is added merely to distinguish it from the special journals.

Sales journal

Illustrated below is a sales journal containing entries for all sales on account made during November by the Seaside Company. Whenever merchandise is sold on credit, several copies of a sales invoice are prepared. The information listed on a sales invoice usually includes the date of the sale, the serial number of the invoice, the customer's name, the amount of the sale, and the credit terms. One copy of the sales invoice is used by the seller as the basis for an entry in the sales journal.

<table>
<tr><td colspan="6" align="center">Sales Journal</td><td align="right">Page 1</td></tr>
<tr><td colspan="2">Date</td><td>Account Debited</td><td>Invoice No.</td><td>√</td><td>Amount</td></tr>
<tr><td>19__
Nov.</td><td>2</td><td>John Adams</td><td>301</td><td>√</td><td>450</td></tr>
<tr><td></td><td>4</td><td>Harold Black</td><td>302</td><td>√</td><td>1,000</td></tr>
<tr><td></td><td>5</td><td>Robert Cross</td><td>303</td><td>√</td><td>975</td></tr>
<tr><td></td><td>11</td><td>H. R. Davis</td><td>304</td><td>√</td><td>620</td></tr>
<tr><td></td><td>18</td><td>C. D. Early</td><td>305</td><td>√</td><td>900</td></tr>
<tr><td></td><td>23</td><td>John Frost</td><td>306</td><td>√</td><td>400</td></tr>
<tr><td></td><td>29</td><td>D. H. Gray</td><td>307</td><td>√</td><td>1,850</td></tr>
<tr><td></td><td></td><td></td><td></td><td></td><td>6,195</td></tr>
<tr><td></td><td></td><td></td><td></td><td></td><td>(5) (41)</td></tr>
</table>

Entries for sales on credit during November

Note that the illustrated sales journal contains special columns for recording each of these aspects of the sales transaction, except the credit terms. If it is the practice of the business to offer different credit terms to different customers, a column may be inserted in the sales journal to show the terms of sale. In this illustration it is assumed that all sales are made on terms of 2/10, n/30; consequently, there is no need to write the credit terms as part of each entry. *Only sales on credit are entered in the sales journal.* When merchandise is sold for cash, the transaction is recorded in a cash receipts journal, which is illustrated later in this chapter.

ADVANTAGES OF THE SALES JOURNAL Note that each of the above seven sales transactions is recorded on a single line. Each entry consists of a debit to a customer's account; the offsetting credit to the Sales account is understood without being written, because sales on account are the only transactions recorded in this special journal.

An entry in a sales journal need not include an explanation; if more information about the transaction is desired it can be obtained by referring to the file copy of the sales invoice. The invoice number is listed in the sales journal as part of each entry. The one-line entry in the sales journal requires much less writing than would be required to record a sales transaction in the general journal. Since there may be several hundred or several thousand sales transactions each month, the time saved in recording transactions in this streamlined manner becomes quite important.

Every entry in the sales journal represents a debit to a customer's account. Charges to customers' accounts should be posted daily so that each customer's account will always be up-to-date and available for use in making decisions relating to collections and to the further extension of credit. A check mark ($\sqrt{}$) is placed in the sales journal opposite each amount posted to a customer's account, to indicate that the posting has been made.

Another advantage of the special journal for sales is the great saving of time in posting credits to the Sales account. Remember that every amount entered in the sales journal represents a credit to Sales. In the illustrated sales journal above, there are seven transactions (and in practice there might be 700). Instead of posting a separate credit to the Sales account for each sales transaction, we can wait until the end of the month and make one posting to the Sales account for the total of the amounts recorded in the sales journal.

In the illustrated sales journal for November, the sales on account totaled $6,195. On November 30 this amount is posted as a credit to the Sales account, and the ledger account number for Sales (41) is entered under the total figure in the sales journal to show that the posting operation has been performed. The total sales figure is also posted as a debit to ledger account no. 5, Accounts Receivable. To make clear the reason for this posting to Accounts Receivable, an explanation of the nature of controlling accounts and subsidiary ledgers is necessary.

Controlling accounts and subsidiary ledgers

In preceding chapters all transactions involving accounts receivable from customers have been posted to a single account entitled Accounts Receivable. Under this simplified procedure, however, it is not easy to look up the amount receivable from a given customer. In practice, nearly all businesses which sell goods on credit maintain a separate account receivable with each customer. If there are 4,000 customers, this would require a ledger with 4,000 accounts receivable, in addition to the accounts for other assets, and for liabilities, owner's equity, revenue, and expense. Such a ledger would be cumbersome and unwieldy. Also, the trial balance prepared from such a large ledger would be a very long one. If the trial balance showed the ledger to be out of balance, the task of locating the error or errors would be most difficult. All these factors indicate that it is not desirable to have too many accounts in one ledger. Fortunately, a simple solution is available; this solution is to divide up the ledger into several separate ledgers.

In a business which has a large number of accounts with customers and creditors, it is customary to divide the ledger into three separate ledgers. All the accounts with *customers* are placed in alphabetical order in a separate ledger, called the *accounts receivable ledger.* All the accounts with *creditors* are arranged alphabetically in another ledger called the *accounts payable ledger.* Both of these ledgers are known as *subsidiary ledgers,* because they support and are controlled by the general ledger.

After thus segregating the accounts receivable from customers in one subsidiary ledger and placing the accounts payable to creditors in a second subsidiary ledger, we have left in the original ledger all the revenue and expense accounts and also all the balance sheet accounts except those with customers and creditors. This ledger is called the *general ledger,* to distinguish it from the subsidiary ledgers.

When the numerous individual accounts with customers are placed in a subsidiary ledger, an account entitled Accounts Receivable continues to be maintained in the general ledger. This account shows the total amount due from all customers; in other words, this single controlling account in the general ledger takes the place of the numerous customers' accounts which have been removed to form a subsidiary ledger. The general ledger is still in balance because the controlling account, Accounts Receivable, has a balance equal to the total of the customers' accounts which were removed from the general ledger. Agreement of the controlling account with the sum of the accounts receivable in the subsidiary ledger also provides assurance of accuracy in the subsidiary ledger.

A controlling account entitled Accounts Payable is also kept in the general ledger in place of the numerous accounts with creditors which have been removed to form the accounts payable subsidiary ledger. Because the two controlling accounts represent the total amounts receivable from customers and payable to creditors, a trial balance can be prepared from the general ledger alone. The following illustration shows the relationship of the subsidiary ledgers to the controlling accounts in the general ledger:

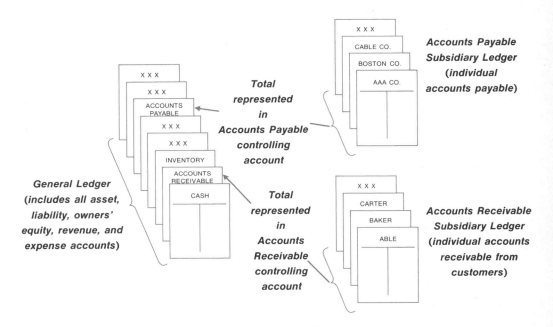

POSTING TO SUBSIDIARY LEDGERS AND TO CONTROL ACCOUNTS To illustrate the posting of subsidiary ledgers and of control accounts, let us refer again to the sales journal illustrated on page 238. Each debit to a customer's account is posted currently during the month from the sales journal to the customer's account in the accounts receivable ledger. The accounts in this subsidiary ledger are usually kept in alphabetical order and are not numbered. When a posting is made to a customer's account, a check mark (√) is placed in the sales journal as evidence that the posting has been made to the subsidiary ledger.

At month-end the sales journal is totaled. The total sales for the month, $6,195, are posted as a credit to the Sales account and also as a debit to the controlling account, Accounts Receivable, in the general ledger. The controlling account will, therefore, equal the total of all the customers' accounts in the subsidiary ledger.

The diagram on page 242 shows the day-to-day posting of individual entries from the sales journal to the subsidiary ledger. The diagram also shows the month-end posting of the total of the sales journal to the two general ledger accounts affected, Accounts Receivable and Sales. Note that the amount of the monthly debit to the controlling account is equal to the sum of the debits posted to the subsidiary ledger.

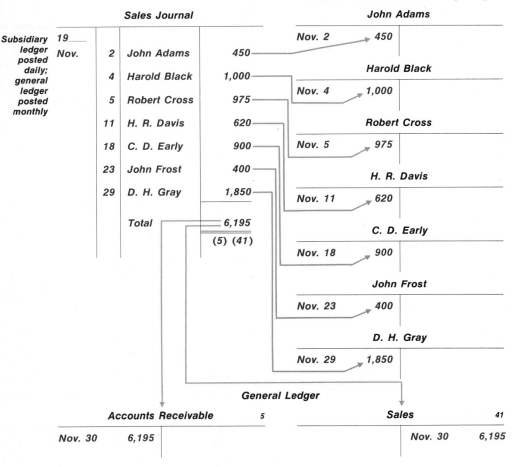

Accounts Receivable Subsidiary Ledger

Sales Journal

Subsidiary ledger posted daily; general ledger posted monthly

19__			
Nov.	2	John Adams	450
	4	Harold Black	1,000
	5	Robert Cross	975
	11	H. R. Davis	620
	18	C. D. Early	900
	23	John Frost	400
	29	D. H. Gray	1,850
		Total	6,195
			(5) (41)

John Adams

Nov. 2	450

Harold Black

Nov. 4	1,000

Robert Cross

Nov. 5	975

H. R. Davis

Nov. 11	620

C. D. Early

Nov. 18	900

John Frost

Nov. 23	400

D. H. Gray

Nov. 29	1,850

General Ledger

Accounts Receivable		5
Nov. 30	6,195	

Sales		41
	Nov. 30	6,195

Purchases journal

The handling of purchase transactions when a purchases journal is used follows a pattern quite similar to the one described for the sales journal.

Assume that the purchases journal illustrated on page 243 contains all purchases of merchandise on credit during the month by the Seaside Company. The invoice date is shown in a separate column because the cash discount period begins on this date.

The five entries are posted as they occur during the month as credits to the creditors' accounts in the subsidiary ledger for accounts payable. As each posting is completed a check mark (✓) is placed in the purchases journal.

At the end of the month the purchases journal is totaled and ruled as

Purchases Journal

	Date		Account Credited	Invoice Date		√	Amount
Entries for purchases on credit during November	19____ Nov.	2	Alabama Supply Co.	19____ Nov.	2	√	3,325
		4	Barker & Bright		4	√	700
		10	Canning & Sons		9	√	500
		17	Davis Co.		16	√	900
		27	Excelsior, Inc.		25	√	1,825
							7,250
							(50) (21)

shown in the illustration. The total figure, $7,250, is posted to two general ledger accounts as follows:

1 As a debit to the Purchases account
2 As a credit to the Accounts Payable controlling account

The account numbers for Purchases (50) and for Accounts Payable (21) are then placed in parentheses below the column total of the purchases journal to show that the posting has been made.

Under the particular system being described, the only transactions recorded in the purchases journal are purchases of merchandise on credit. The term *merchandise* means goods acquired for resale to customers. If merchandise is purchased for cash rather than on credit, the transaction should be recorded in the cash payments journal, as illustrated on pages 248 and 249.

The diagram on page 244 illustrates the day-to-day posting of individual entries from the purchases journal to the accounts with creditors in the subsidiary ledger for accounts payable. The diagram also shows how the column total of the purchases journal is posted at the end of the month to the general ledger accounts, Purchases and Accounts Payable. One objective of this diagram is to emphasize that the amount of the monthly credit to the control account is equal to the sum of the credits posted to the subsidiary ledger.

When assets other than merchandise are being acquired, as, for example, a delivery truck or an office desk for use in the business, the journal to be used depends upon whether a cash payment is made. If assets of this type are purchased for cash, the transaction should be entered in the cash payments journal; if the transaction is on credit, the general journal is used. The purchases journal is not used to record the acquisition of these assets because the total of this journal is posted to the Purchases account and this account (as explained in Chapter 5) is used in determining the cost of goods sold.

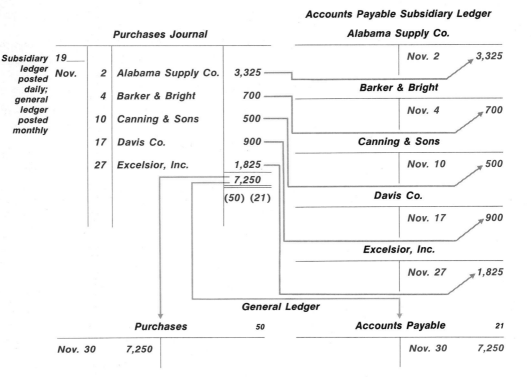

Cash receipts journal

All transactions involving the receipt of cash are recorded in the cash receipts journal. One common example is the sale of merchandise for cash. As each cash sale is made, it is rung up on a cash register. At the end of the day the total of the cash sales is computed by striking the total key on the register. This total is entered in the cash receipts journal, which therefore contains one entry for the total cash sales of the day. For other types of cash receipts, such as the collection of accounts receivable from customers, a separate journal entry may be made for each transaction. The cash receipts journal illustrated on pages 246 and 247 contains entries for selected November transactions, all of which include the receipt of cash.

Nov. 1 R. B. Jones invested $25,000 cash to establish the Seaside Company.
    4 Sold merchandise for cash, $300.
    5 Sold merchandise for cash, $400.
    8 Collected from John Adams invoice of Nov. 2, $450 less 2% cash discount.
    10 Sold portion of land not needed in business for a total price of $7,000, consisting of cash of $1,000 and a note receivable for $6,000. The cost of the land sold was $5,000.

12 Collected from Harold Black invoice of Nov. 4, $1,000 less 2% cash discount.

20 Collected from C. D. Early invoice of Nov. 18, $900 less 2% cash discount.

27 Sold merchandise for cash, $125.

30 Obtained $4,000 loan from bank. Issued a note payable in that amount.

Note that the cash receipts journal illustrated on pages 246 and 247 has three debit columns and three credit columns as follows:

Debits:

1 Cash. This column is used for every entry, because only those transactions which include the receipt of cash are entered in this special journal.

2 Sales discounts. This column is used to accumulate the sales discounts allowed during the month. Only one line of the cash receipts book is required to record a collection from a customer who takes advantage of a cash discount.

3 Other accounts. This third debit column is used for debits to any and all accounts other than cash and sales discounts, and space is provided for writing in the name of the account. For example, the entry of November 10 in the illustrated cash receipts journal shows that cash and a note receivable were obtained when land was sold. The amount of cash received, $1,000, is entered in the Cash debit column, the account title Notes Receivable is written in the Other Accounts debit column and the amount of the debit to this account, $6,000. These two debits are offset by credit entries to Land, $5,000, and to Gain on Sale of land, $2,000, in the Other Accounts credit column.

Credits:

1 Accounts receivable. This column is used to list the credits to customers' accounts as receivables are collected. The name of the customer is written in the space entitled Account Credited to the left of the Accounts Receivable column.

2 Sales. The existence of this column will save posting by permitting the accumulation of all sales for cash during the month and the posting of the column total at the end of the month as a credit to the Sales account (41).

3 Other accounts. This column is used for credits to any and all accounts other than Accounts Receivable and Sales. In some instances, a transaction may require credits to two accounts. Such cases are handled by using two lines of the special journal, as illustrated by the transaction of November 10, which required credits to both the Land account and to Gain on Sale of Land.

POSTING THE CASH RECEIPTS JOURNAL It is convenient to think of the posting of a cash receipts journal as being divided into two phases. The first phase consists of the daily posting of individual amounts throughout the month; the second phase consists of the posting of column totals at the end of the month.

Posting during the month Daily posting of the Accounts Receivable credits column is desirable. Each amount is posted to an individual customer's account in the accounts receivable subsidiary ledger. A check mark (✓) is placed in the cash receipts journal alongside each item posted to a

Cash Receipts Journal

			Debits				
					Other Accounts		
Date		**Explanation**	**Cash**	**Sales Discounts**	**Name**	**LP**	**Amount**
19___ Nov.	1	Investment by owner	25,000				
	4	Cash sales	300				
	5	Cash sales	400				
	8	Invoice Nov. 2, less 2%	441	9			
	10	Sale of land	1,000		Notes Receivable	3	6,000
	12	Invoice Nov. 4, less 2%	980	20			
	20	Invoice Nov. 18, less 2%	882	18			
	27	Cash sales	125				
	30	Obtained bank loan	4,000				
			33,128	47			6,000
			(1)	(43)			(X)

Includes all transactions involving receipt of cash

customer's account to show that the posting operation has been performed. When debits and credits to customers' accounts are posted daily, the current status of each customer's account is available for use in making decisions as to further granting of credit and as a guide to collection efforts on past-due accounts.

The debits and credits in the Other Accounts sections of the cash receipts journal may be posted daily or at convenient intervals during the month. If this portion of the posting work is done on a current basis, less detailed work will be left for the busy period at the end of the month. As the postings of individual items are made, the number of the ledger account debited or credited is entered in the LP column of the cash receipts journal opposite the item posted. Evidence is thus provided in the special journal as to which items have been posted.

Posting column totals at month-end At the end of the month, the cash receipts journal is ruled as shown on pages 246 and 247. Before posting any of the column totals, it is first important to prove that *the sum of the debit column totals is equal to the sum of the credit column totals.*

After the totals of the cash receipts journal have been crossfooted, the following column totals are posted:

1 Cash debit column. Posted as a debit to the Cash account.
2 Sales Discounts debit column. Posted as a debit to the Sales Discounts account.
3 Accounts Receivable credit column. Posted as a credit to the controlling account, Accounts Receivable.

Page 1

	Credits				
	Accounts Receivable			**Other Accounts**	
Account Credited	√	**Amount**	**Sales**	**LP**	**Amount**
R. B. Jones, Capital				30	25,000
			300		
			400		
John Adams	√	450			
Land				11	5,000 ⎫
Gain on Sale of Land				40	2,000 ⎭
Harold Black	√	1,000			
C. D. Early	√	900			
			125		
Notes Payable				20	4,000
		2,350	825		36,000
		(5)	(41)		(X)

4 Sales credit column. Posted as a credit to the Sales account.

As each column total is posted to the appropriate account in the general ledger, the ledger account number is entered in parentheses just below the column total in the special journal. This notation shows that the column total has been posted and also indicates the account to which the posting was made. The totals of the Other Accounts columns in both the debit and credit sections of the special journal are not posted, because the amounts listed in the column affect various general ledger accounts and have already been posted as individual items. The symbol (X) may be placed below the totals of these two columns to indicate that no posting is made.

Cash payments journal

Another widely used special journal is the cash payments journal, sometimes called the cash disbursements journal, in which all payments of cash are recorded. Among the more common of these transactions are payments of accounts payable to creditors, payment of operating expenses, and cash purchases of merchandise.

The cash payments journal illustrated on pages 248 and 249 contains entries for all November transactions of the Seaside Company which required the payment of cash.

Nov. **1** Paid rent on store building for November, $800.

2 Purchased merchandise for cash, $500.

8 Paid Barker & Bright for invoice of Nov. 4, $700 less 2%.

9 Bought land, $15,000, and building, $35,000, for future use in business. Paid cash of $20,000 and signed a promissory note for the balance of $30,000. (Land and building were acquired in a single transaction.)

17 Paid salesmen's salaries, $600.

26 Paid Davis Co. for invoice of Nov. 16, $900 less 2%.

27 Purchased merchandise for cash, $400.

28 Purchased merchandise for cash, $650.

29 Paid for newspaper advertising, $50.

29 Paid for three-year insurance policy, $720.

Note in the illustrated cash payments journal that the three credit columns are located to the left of the three debit columns; any sequence of columns is satisfactory in a special journal as long as the column headings clearly distinguish debits from credits. The Cash column is often placed first in both the cash receipts journal and the cash payments journal because it is the column used in every transaction.

Good internal control over cash disbursements requires that all payments be made by check. The checks are serially numbered and as each transaction is entered in the cash payments journal, the check number is listed in a special column provided just to the right of the date column. An unbroken sequence of check numbers in this column gives assurance that every check issued has been recorded in the accounting records.

The use of the six money columns in the illustrated cash payments journal parallels the procedures described for the cash receipts journal.

Cash Payments Journal

| | | | | | | Credits | | | |
| | | | | | | | Other Accounts | | |
Date	Check No.	Explanation		Cash	Purchase Discounts	Name	LP	Amount
19___								
Nov. 1	101	Paid November rent		800				
2	102	Purchased merchandise		500				
8	103	Invoice of Nov. 4, less 2%		686	14			
9	104	Bought land and building		20,000		Notes Payable	20	30,000
17	105	Paid sales salaries		600				
26	106	Invoice of Nov. 16, less 2%		882	18			
27	107	Purchased merchandise		400				
28	108	Purchased merchandise		650				
29	109	Newspaper advertisement		50				
29	110	Three-year ins. policy		720				
				25,288	32			30,000
				(1)	(52)			(X)

Includes all transactions involving payment of cash

POSTING THE CASH PAYMENTS JOURNAL The posting of the cash payments journal falls into the same two phases already described for the cash receipts journal. The first phase consists of the daily posting of entries in the Accounts Payable debit column to the individual accounts of creditors in the accounts payable subsidiary ledger. Check marks (✓) are entered opposite these items to show that the posting has been made. If a creditor telephones to inquire about any aspect of his account, information on all purchases and payments made to date is readily available in the accounts payable subsidiary ledger.

The individual debit and credit entries in the Other Accounts columns of the cash payments journal may be posted daily or at convenient intervals during the month. As the postings of these individual items are made, the page number of the ledger account debited or credited is entered in the LP column of the cash payments journal opposite the item posted.

The second phase of posting the cash payments journal is performed at the end of the month. When all the transactions of the month have been journalized, the cash payments journal is ruled as shown on pages 248 and 249, and the six money columns are totaled. The equality of debits and credits is then proved before posting.

After the totals of the cash payments journal have been proved to be in balance, the totals of the columns for Cash, Purchase Discounts, Accounts Payable, and Purchases are posted to the corresponding accounts in the general ledger. The numbers of the accounts to which these postings are made are listed in parentheses just below the respective column totals in the cash payments journal. The totals of the Other

Page 1

		Debits			
		Accounts Payable			**Other Accounts**
Account Debited	**✓**	**Amount**	**Purchases**	**LP**	**Amount**
Store Rent Expense				54	800
Purchases			500		
Barker & Bright	✓	700			
Land				11	15,000 ⎫
Building				12	35,000 ⎬
Sales Salaries Expense				53	600
Davis Co.	✓	900			
Purchases			400		
Purchases			650		
Advertising Expense				55	50
Unexpired Insurance				6	720
		1,600	1,550		52,170
		(21)	(50)		(X)

Accounts columns in both the debit and credit section of this special journal are not to be posted, and the symbol (X) may be placed below the totals of these two columns to indicate that no posting is required.

The general journal

When all transactions involving cash or the purchase and sale of merchandise are recorded in special journals, only a few types of transactions remain to be entered in the general journal. Examples include the purchase or sale of plant and equipment on credit, the return of merchandise for credit to a supplier, and the return of merchandise by a customer for credit to his account. The general journal is also used for the recording of adjusting and closing entries at the end of the accounting period.

The following transactions of the Seaside Company during November could not conveniently be handled in any of the four special journals and were therefore entered in the general journal.

Nov. 25 A customer, John Frost, was permitted to return for credit $50 worth of merchandise that had been sold to him on Nov. 23.

28 The Seaside Company returned to a supplier, Excelsior, Inc., for credit $300 worth of the merchandise purchased on Nov. 27.

29 Purchased for use in the business office equipment costing $1,225. Agreed to make payment within 30 days to XYZ Equipment Co.

General Journal   Page 1

	Date		Account Titles and Explanation	LP	Dr	Cr
	19___					
Transactions which do not fit any of the four special journals	Nov.	25	Sales Returns and Allowances..........................	42	50	
			Accounts Receivable, John Frost..........	5/ √		50
			Allowed credit to customer for return of merchandise from sale of Nov. 23.			
		28	Accounts Payable, Excelsior, Inc....................	21/ √	300	
			Purchase Returns and Allowances......	51		300
			Returned to supplier for credit a portion of merchandise purchased on Nov. 27.			
		29	Office Equipment..	14	1,225	
			Accounts Payable, XYZ Equipment Co.	21/ √		1,225
			Purchased office equipment on 30-day credit.			

Each of the above entries includes a debit or credit to a controlling account (Accounts Receivable or Accounts Payable) and also identifies by name a particular creditor or customer. When a controlling account is debited or credited by a *general journal entry,* the debit or credit must be posted twice: one posting to the controlling account in the general ledger and another posting to a customer's account or a creditor's account in a subsidiary ledger. This double posting is necessary to keep the controlling account in agreement with the subsidiary ledger.

For example, in the illustrated entry of November 25 for the return of merchandise by a customer, the credit part of the entry is posted twice:

1 To the Accounts Receivable controlling account in the general ledger; this posting is evidenced by listing the account number (5) in the LP column of the general journal.

2 To the account of John Frost in the subsidiary ledger for accounts receivable; this posting is indicated by the check mark (√) placed in the LP column of the general journal.

Showing the source of postings in ledger accounts

When a general journal and several special journals are in use, the ledger accounts should indicate the book of original entry from which each debit and credit was posted. An identifying symbol is placed opposite each entry in the reference column of the account. The symbols used in this text are as follows:

S1   meaning page 1 of the sales journal
P1   meaning page 1 of the purchases journal
CR1   meaning page 1 of the cash receipts journal
CP1   meaning page 1 of the cash payments journal
J1   meaning page 1 of the general journal

Subsidiary ledger accounts

The following illustration shows a customer's account in a subsidiary ledger for accounts receivable.

Name of Customer

Date			Ref	Debit	Credit	Balance
19___						
July	*1*		*S1*	*400*		*400*
	20		*S3*	*200*		*600*
Aug.	*4*		*CR7*		*400*	*200*
	15		*S6*	*120*		*320*

Subsidiary ledger: account receivable

The advantage of this three-column form of account is that it shows at a glance the present balance receivable from the customer. The current amount of a customer's account is often needed as a guide to collection activities, or as a basis for granting additional credit. In studying the above illustration note also that the Reference column shows the source of each debit and credit.

Accounts appearing in the accounts receivable subsidiary ledger are assumed to have debit balances. If one of these customers' accounts should acquire a credit balance by overpayment or for any other reason, the word *credit* should be written after the amount in the Balance column.

The same three-column form of account is also generally used for creditors' accounts in an accounts payable subsidiary ledger, as indicated by the following illustration:

Name of Creditor

Date			Ref	Debit	Credit	Balance
Subsidiary ledger: account payable *19___*						
July	*10*		*P1*		*625*	*625*
	25		*P2*		*100*	*725*
Aug.	*8*		*CP4*	*725*		*0*
	12		*P3*		*250*	*250*

Accounts in the accounts payable subsidiary ledger normally have credit balances. If by reason of payment in advance or accidental overpayment, one of these accounts should acquire a debit balance, the word *debit* should be written after the amount in the Balance column.

As previously stated, both the accounts receivable and accounts payable subsidiary ledgers are customarily arranged in alphabetical order and account numbers are not used. This arrangement permits unlimited expansion of the subsidiary ledgers, as accounts with new customers and creditors can be inserted in proper alphabetical sequence.

Ledger accounts

THE GENERAL LEDGER The general ledger accounts of the Seaside Company illustrated on pages 253–255 indicate the source of postings from the various books of original entry. The subsidiary ledger accounts appear on pages 255–256. To gain a clear understanding of the procedures for posting special journals, the student should trace each entry in the illustrated special journals into the general ledger accounts and also to the subsidiary ledger accounts where appropriate. The general ledger accounts are shown in T-account form in order to distinguish them more emphatically from the accounts in the subsidiary ledgers.

Note that the Cash account contains only one debit entry and one credit entry, although there were many cash transactions during the month. The one debit, $33,128, represents the total cash received during the month and was posted from the cash receipts journal on November 30. Similarly, the one credit entry of $25,288 was posted on November 30 from the cash payments journal and represents the total of all cash payments made during the month.

Cash 1

General ledger accounts	19__					19__				
	Nov.	30		CR1	33,128	Nov.	30		CP1	25,288

Notes Receivable 3

19__									
Nov.	10		CR1	6,000					

Accounts Receivable 5

19__					19__				
Nov.	30		S1	6,195	Nov.	25		J1	50
						30		CR1	2,350

Unexpired Insurance 6

19__									
Nov.	29		CP1	720					

Land 11

19__					19__				
Nov.	9		CP1	15,000	Nov.	10		CR1	5,000

Building 12

19__									
Nov.	9		CP1	35,000					

Office Equipment 14

19__									
Nov.	29		J1	1,225					

Notes Payable 20

					19__				
					Nov.	9		CP1	30,000
						30		CR1	4,000

Accounts Payable 21

19__					19__				
Nov.	28		J1	300	Nov.	29		J1	1,225
	30		CP1	1,600		30		P1	7,250

R. B. Jones, Capital   30

				19___				
				Nov.	1		CR1	25,000

Gain on Sale of Land   40

				19___				
				Nov.	10		CR1	2,000

Sales   41

				19___				
				Nov.	30		CR1	825
					30		S1	6,195

Sales Returns and Allowances   42

19___								
Nov.	25		J1	50				

Sales Discounts   43

19___								
Nov.	30		CR1	47				

Purchases   50

19___								
Nov.	30		CP1	1,550				
	30		P1	7,250				

Purchase Returns and Allowances   51

				19___				
				Nov.	28		J1	300

Purchase Discounts   52

				19___				
				Nov.	30		CP1	32

Sales Salaries Expense   53

19___								
Nov.	17		CP1	600				

Store Rent Expense   54

19___								
Nov.	1		CP1	800				

Advertising Expense   55

19___										
Nov.	29		CP1	50						

ACCOUNTS RECEIVABLE LEDGER The subsidiary ledger for accounts receivable appears as follows after the posting of the various journals has been completed.

John Adams

Customers'	19___						
accounts	Nov.	2		S1	450		450
		8		CR1		450	0

Harold Black

19___						
Nov.	4		S1	1,000		1,000
	12		CR1		1,000	0

Robert Cross

19___					
Nov.	5		S1	975	975

H. R. Davis

19___					
Nov.	11		S1	620	620

C. D. Early

19___						
Nov.	18		S1	900		900
	20		CR1		900	0

John Frost

19___						
Nov.	23		S1	400		400
	25		J1		50	350

D. H. Gray

19___					
Nov.	29		S1	1,850	1,850

ACCOUNTS PAYABLE LEDGER The accounts with creditors in the accounts payable subsidiary ledger are as follows:

Alabama Supply Co.

Creditors' accounts	19__						
	Nov.	2		P1		3,325	3,325

Barker & Bright

	19__						
	Nov.	4		P1		700	700
		8		CP1	700		0

Canning & Sons

	19__						
	Nov.	10		P1		500	500

Davis Co.

	19__						
	Nov.	17		P1		900	900
		26		CP1	900		0

Excelsior, Inc.

	19__						
	Nov.	27		P1		1,825	1,825
		28		J1	300		1,525

XYZ Equipment Co.

	19__						
	Nov.	29		J1		1,225	1,225

Proving the ledgers

At the end of each accounting period, proof of the equality of debits and credits in the general ledger is established by preparation of a trial balance, as illustrated in preceding chapters. When controlling accounts and subsidiary ledgers are in use, it is also necessary to prove that each subsidiary ledger is in agreement with its controlling account. This proof is accomplished by preparing a schedule of the balances of accounts in each subsidiary ledger and determining that the totals of these schedules agree with the balances of the corresponding control accounts.

Variations in special journals

The number of columns to be included in each special journal and the number of special journals to be used will depend upon the nature of the particular business and especially upon the volume of the various kinds of transactions. For example, the desirability of including a Sales Discounts column in the cash receipts journal depends upon whether a business

SEASIDE COMPANY
Trial Balance
November 30, 19___

General ledger trial balance	Cash	$ 7,840	
	Notes receivable	6,000	
	Accounts receivable (see schedule below).	3,795	
	Unexpired insurance	720	
	Land	10,000	
	Building	35,000	
	Office equipment	1,225	
	Notes payable		$34,000
	Accounts payable (see schedule below)		6,575
	R. B. Jones, capital		25,000
	Gain on sale of land.		2,000
	Sales		7,020
	Sales returns and allowances	50	
	Sales discounts	47	
	Purchases	8,800	
	Purchase returns and allowances		300
	Purchase discounts		32
	Sales salaries expense	600	
	Store rent expense	800	
	Advertising expense	50	
		$74,927	$74,927

Schedule of Accounts Receivable
November 30, 19___

Subsidiary ledgers in balance with control accounts	Robert Cross	$ 975
	H. R. Davis	620
	John Frost	350
	D. H. Gray	1,850
	Total (per balance of controlling account)	$3,795

Schedule of Accounts Payable
November 30, 19___

Alabama Supply Co.	$3,325
Canning & Sons	500
Excelsior, Inc.	1,525
XYZ Equipment Co.	1,225
Total (per balance of controlling account).	$6,575

offers discounts to its customers for prompt payment and whether the customers frequently take advantage of such discounts.

A retail store may find that customers frequently return merchandise for credit. To record efficiently this large volume of sales returns, the store may establish a sales returns and allowances journal. A purchase returns and allowances journal may also be desirable if returns of goods to suppliers occur frequently.

Special journals should be regarded as laborsaving devices which may be designed with any number of columns appropriate to the needs of the particular business. A business will usually benefit by establishing a special journal for any type of transaction that occurs quite frequently.

Direct posting from invoices

In many business concerns the efficiency of data processing is increased by posting sales invoices directly to the customers' accounts in the accounts receivable ledger rather than copying sales invoices into a sales journal and then posting to accounts in the subsidiary ledger. If the sales invoices are serially numbered, a file or binder of duplicate sales invoices arranged in numerical order may take the place of a formal sales journal. By accounting for each serial number, it is possible to be certain that all sales invoices are included. At the end of the month, the invoices are totaled on an adding machine, and a general journal entry is made debiting the Accounts Receivable controlling account and crediting Sales for the total of the month's sales invoices.

Direct posting may also be used in recording purchase invoices. As soon as purchase invoices have been verified and approved, credits to the creditors' accounts in the accounts payable ledger may be posted directly from the purchase invoices.

The trend toward direct posting from invoices to subsidiary ledgers is mentioned here as further evidence that accounting records and procedures can be designed in a variety of ways to meet the individual needs of different business concerns.

MECHANICAL ACCOUNTING SYSTEMS

The processing of accounting data may be performed manually, mechanically, or electronically. The term *data processing* includes the preparation of documents (such as invoices and checks) and the flow of the data contained in these documents through the major accounting steps of recording, classifying, and summarizing. A well-designed system produces an uninterrupted flow of all essential data needed by management for planning and controlling business operations.

Unit record for each transaction

Our discussion has thus far been limited to a manual accounting system. One of the points we have emphasized is that an immediate record should be made of every business transaction. The *medium* used to make this record is usually a document or form, such as an invoice or a check. This concept of a unit record for each transaction is an important one as we consider the alternatives of processing these media by accounting machines, by punched cards, or by a computer. Regardless of whether we use mechanical or electronic equipment, the document representing a single transaction is a basic element of the accounting process.

Use of office equipment in a manual data processing system

Manually kept records are a convenient means of demonstrating accounting principles, and they are also used by a great many small businesses. Strictly defined, a manual system of processing accounting data would call for handwritten journals, ledgers, and financial statements. Even in a small business with some handwritten records, however, the use of office machines and laborsaving devices such as cash registers, adding machines, desk calculators, and multicopy forms has become standard practice.

Simultaneous preparation of documents, journals, and ledgers

Traditionally, each business transaction was recorded, copied, and recopied. A transaction was first evidenced by a document such as a sales invoice, then copied into a journal (book of original entry), and later posted to a ledger. This step-by-step sequence of creating accounting records is time-consuming and leaves room for the introduction of errors at each step. Whenever a figure, an account title, or an account number is copied, the danger of introducing errors exists. This is true regardless of whether the copying is done with pen and ink or by punching a machine keyboard. The copying process is subject to human errors. From this premise it follows that if several accounting records can be created by writing a transaction only once, the recording process will be not only faster but also more accurate.

Accounting machines

The development of accounting machines designed to create several accounting records with a single writing of a transaction has progressed at a fantastic rate. Machines with typewriter keyboards and computing mechanisms were early developments useful in preparing journals, invoices, payrolls, and other records requiring the typing of names and the computation of amounts. *Accounting machines* is a term usually applied to mechanical or electronic equipment capable of performing arithmetic functions and used to produce a variety of accounting records and reports.

Punched cards and tabulating equipment

Punched cards are a widely used medium for recording accounting data. Information such as amounts, names, account numbers, and other details is recorded by punching holes in appropriate columns and rows of a standard-sized card, usually by means of a *key-punch machine.* The information punched on the cards can then be read and processed by a variety of machines, including computers.

Every business receives original documents such as invoices and checks in many shapes and sizes. By punching the information on each such document into a card, we create a document of standard size which machines and computers can use in creating records and reports. For example, once the information on sales invoices has been punched into cards, these cards can be run through machines to produce a schedule of accounts receivable, an analysis of sales by product, by territory, and by each salesman, and a listing of commissions earned by salesmen.

Processing accounting data by means of punched cards may be viewed as three major steps, with specially designed machines for each step. The first step is that of recording data; a machine often used for this purpose is an electrically operated *key punch* with a keyboard similar to that of a typewriter.

The second major step is classifying or sorting the data into related groups or categories. For this step a machine called a *sorter* is used. The sorter reads the information on each punched card and then arranges the cards in a particular order, or sorts a deck of cards into groups based on the relationship of the data punched into the cards.

The third major step is summarizing the data. This step is performed by a *tabulating machine,* which has an *output* of printed information resulting from the classifying and totaling of the data on the cards.

EDP ACCOUNTING SYSTEMS

The term *electronic data processing* (EDP) refers to the processing of data by electronic computers. A computer-based accounting system processes data in basically the same manner as does a manual or mechanical system. Transactions are initially recorded manually on source documents. The data from these source documents are then keypunched into punched cards which can be read by the computer. The computer processes the information and performs such routine tasks as printing journals (called transaction summaries), posting to ledger accounts, determining account balances, and printing financial statements and other reports.

The primary advantage of the computer is its incredible speed. The number of computations made by an electronic computer is measured in millions per second. In one minute, an electronic printer can produce as much printed material as the average clerk typist in a day. Because of this speed, ledger accounts may be kept continually up-to-date and current reports may be quickly prepared at any time to assist executives in making decisions.

Elements of an EDP system

An electronic data processing system includes a computer, also called a *central processing unit* (CPU), and a number of related machines, which are often called *peripheral equipment.* The computer is the heart of the system; it performs the processing function which includes the storage of information, arithmetic computations, and control. The other two major elements are (*1*) *input* devices which prepare and insert information into the computer and (*2*) *output* devices which transfer information out of the computer to the accountant or other user. Both input and output devices perform the function of *translation.* The machines used to feed information into a computer translate the data into computer language; the output devices translate the processed data back into the language of written words, or of punched cards, paper tape, or magnetic tape.

The relationship of the control unit, the arithmetic unit, the storage unit, and the devices for input and output are portrayed in the diagram on page 262.

HARDWARE AND SOFTWARE   The machines and related equipment used in an EDP system are called *hardware.* All the other materials utilized in selecting, installing, and operating the system (except the operating personnel) are called *software.* Software includes not only the *computer programs* (the sequence of instructions given to the computer), but also feasibility studies, training materials such as films and manuals, studies of equipment requirements, and everything about the EDP system other than the hardware.

Input devices

Among the input devices used to transfer instructions and accounting data into a computer are card readers, punched-paper-tape readers, magnetic-tape readers, character readers, and terminals. The card-reading device will either transmit information from punched cards into the memory unit of the computer or convert the information to paper or magnetic tape. Punched cards will be read by the card-reading devices at rates of several hundred or even several thousand per minute.

EDP
system
illustrated

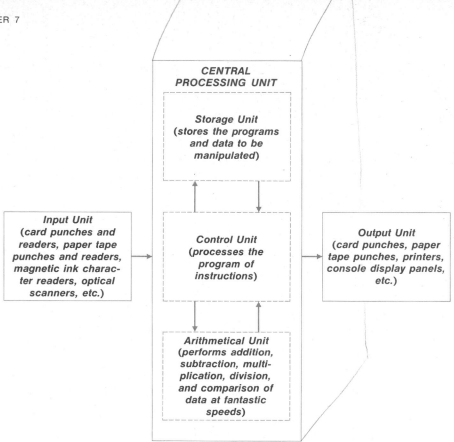

Punched-paper tape can be created as part of the process of recording transactions on cash registers or adding machines. This type of input medium is inexpensive to create and easy to use, but it does not permit the insertion of additional data or the making of corrections after the tape has been punched. Punched-tape readers deliver the data to the computer at high speeds. Both punched-card readers and paper-tape readers are usually connected directly to the computer and are described as part of the *on-line* (direct access) system. They offer the advantage of compatibility with nonelectronic equipment utilizing punched cards or tape.

Magnetic tape is a far faster means of feeding information into a computer and has the advantage of being easily stored. Corrections are also easily made on magnetic tape. Magnetic-tape reels are, however, more expensive than paper tape.

Character-reading machines are perhaps best known in the banking field. They read the account numbers printed in magnetic ink on checks and deposit tickets and convert these data into codes acceptable to the computer. Another type of character-reading device is the optical scanner, with a photoelectric cell which can read a printed document and convert the characters into computer language. This device makes unnecessary the costly step of translating printed matter into punched-card form.

Terminals are keyboard devices which make it possible to enter limited amounts of data into an EDP system without punching the information into cards or tape as a preliminary step. Terminals are extremely slow in comparison with the operating capacity of the computer because they are manually operated. However, terminals have the advantage of allowing the various departments of a business to enter data directly into the accounting system, without having to send their source documents to an EDP department to be keypunched and read into the computer. Some retail stores use terminals in the sales departments to instantly adjust customers' accounts receivable and record each sale in the accounting records. Terminals are also equipped with a printing device which permits output from the computer to be delivered immediately to the user of the terminal.

Output devices

The *printer* is the most important output device. It interprets the computer code and prints several hundred lines per minute, either at the computer center or at remote locations. The printer might be used to produce payroll checks, customers' statements, and many types of accounting reports.

Card-punching machines and paper-tape-punching machines can transfer data from the computer into punch cards and paper tape which later may be used as input data for subsequent analysis or processing.

Processing operations in the computer

The processing operations performed by a computer include storage of information, arithmetic manipulation of data, and control. The computer receives and stores instructions and data; it calls this information from the memory or storage unit as required by the processing routine; it goes through arithmetic operations, makes comparisons of numbers, and takes the action necessary to produce the required output of information.

The term *control* describes the ability of the computer to guide itself through the processing operations utilizing detailed lists of instructions concerning the work to be done.

PROGRAM A *program* is a series of steps planned to carry out a certain process, such as the preparation of a payroll. Each step in the program is a command or instruction to the computer. A program for payroll might be compared with a very detailed written set of instructions given to an inexperienced employee assigned to the payroll function in a manual accounting system. A most important attribute of the computer is its ability to receive and store a set of instructions which controls its behavior.

The preparation of a computer program is a complicated and costly task. A company may employ its own programmers or may rely on outside organizations which specialize in such services.

Differences between mechanical and electronic data processing systems

Mechanical data processing equipment such as electric calculators, mechanical accounting machines, and key-punch machines is extremely slow when compared with electronic equipment. The processing of data in the electronic system is accomplished by electric impulses traveling through electronic circuits. Such equipment functions hundreds of times faster than mechanical devices.

Another point of contrast is that the units of equipment comprising an EDP system are interconnected so that the processing of data is a continuous operation from the point of reading input data to the point of printing the report or other final result. On the other hand, a mechanical data processing system employs separate machines which do not communicate directly with each other. After each machine, such as a key punch, has performed its function, the output media (punched cards or paper tape) must be transported manually to another machine.

Reliability of EDP systems

EDP equipment itself is highly reliable, and the possibility of errors caused by the hardware is very small. However, the use of reliable equipment does not entirely eliminate the possibilities of errors in the accounting records. Errors may still be made in the preparation of source documents. The process of keypunching data into punched cards is comparable to using a typewriter, and making errors is quite possible. Also, the computer program may contain errors which may cause the data to be processed improperly. To reduce the possibility of these types of errors, an EDP system should include both *input controls* and *program controls.*

INPUT CONTROLS Input controls are the precautions taken to ensure that the data being entered into the computer are correct. One important input control is the manual preparation of *control totals,* representing the total dollar amount of all source documents sent to the EDP department for processing. The computer will add up the total dollar amount of all data processed and print this total as part of the computer output. The manually prepared control totals may then be compared to the total printed by the computer to ensure that all source documents sent to the EDP department have been processed.

Another input control is the use of a *verifier key punch.* When data are keypunched into punched cards, there is always the possibility of striking the wrong key, causing a keypunching error. A verifier key punch is used to keypunch the source data into the punched cards a second time; any differences between the first and second keypunching cause the machine to signal that an error has been made.

PROGRAM CONTROLS Program controls are error-detecting measures built into the computer program. An example of a program control is a *limit test,* which compares every item of data processed by the computer to a specified dollar limit. In the event an amount exceeds the dollar limit, the computer does not process that item and prints out an *error report.* A limit test is particularly effective in such computer applications as preparing paychecks, when it is known that none of the paychecks should be for more than a specified amount, such as $1,000.

Another example of a program control is an *item count.* The total number of punched cards to be processed by the computer is determined, and that total is entered as part of the input to the computer. The computer then counts the number of cards it processes, and if this number differs from the predetermined total, an error report is printed. This item count ensures that all the punched cards are actually processed by the computer.

Accounting applications of the computer

The use of electronic data processing equipment is possible for virtually every phase of accounting operations. Even a CPA firm, in conducting an annual audit, may use the computer as an audit tool. For this purpose the auditors may employ specially written computer programs to aid in their work of sampling and analyzing data to determine the fairness of the financial statements.

The most common application of the computer, however, is to process large masses of accounting data relating to routine repetitive operations such as accounts receivable, accounts payable, inventories, payrolls, and posting to ledger accounts.

PAYROLLS In a manual accounting system the preparation of payroll checks is usually separate from the maintenance of records showing pay rates, positions, time worked, payroll deductions, and other personnel data. An EDP system, however, has the capability of maintaining all records relating to payroll as well as turning out the required paychecks. Payroll processing is usually one of the first accounting operations to be placed on the computer.

The payroll procedure consists of determining for each employee the gross earnings, making deductions, computing net pay, preparing the payroll check, and maintaining a record of each individual's earnings. Also, the company needs a payroll summary for each period and usually a distribution of payroll costs by department, by product, or classified by the various productive processes. The payroll function has become increasingly complex and time-consuming in recent years because of the advent of social security taxes, income tax withholding, and other payroll deductions. Each employee must receive not only a payroll check but a statement showing the gross earnings, deductions, and net pay. The company's records must be designed to facilitate filing with the federal and state governments regular payroll reports showing amounts withheld for income taxes, unemployment insurance, and social security. The time and the expense required to prepare payrolls has risen in proportion to the need for more information. The demands by governments, labor unions, credit unions, and other outside agencies have added to the problem.

An EDP payroll system will not only maintain the necessary records, print the checks, and print these reports, but it can also keep management informed of the costs of various functions within the business. For example, data can be produced showing the work-hours and labor costs on each job, labor cost by department for each salesclerk, or the time required by different employees to perform similar work. In other words, much current information can be developed without significant extra expense that will provide management with a detailed breakdown of labor costs. The comparison below and on page 267 illustrates the efficiency of processing payrolls by EDP rather than manually:

Function	Payroll Prepared Manually	Payroll Prepared by EDP
1 Timekeeping	Fill in new set of records each period, making extensions manually.	Enter raw data on appropriate forms.
2 Computation of gross pay	Compute gross pay for each employee, perhaps with desk calculator, and enter manually in records.	Performed electronically.
3 Calculation of deductions	For each employee, refer to charts and make computations; enter manually in records.	Performed electronically.
4 Preparation of checks, earnings statements, and payroll register	Write by hand or type checks. Proofread and maintain controls.	Performed electronically.
5 Bank reconciliation	Reconcile payroll bank account per accounting records with monthly bank statement.	Performed electronically.
6 Reports to government	Prepare quarterly reports showing for each employee and in total amounts earned, deducted, and paid. Reconcile individual data with controls.	Performed electronically.

Payroll may be prepared either manually or by EDP

7 Managerial control data	*Prepare distribution of hours and labor cost by department or by job. Other analyses may be needed.*	*Performed electronically.*

COMPUTER-BASED JOURNALS AND LEDGERS As mentioned earlier in this chapter, computers may also be used to maintain the journals and ledgers and to prepare financial statements. Transactions and end-of-period adjustments must still be analyzed by persons possessing a knowledge of accounting principles. However, after these transactions have been analyzed and prepared in computer input form, the computer can be used to print the journals, post to the ledger accounts, and print the financial statements and other financial reports. The advantage of maintaining accounting records by computer is that the possibility of mathematical errors is greatly reduced, and the speed of the computer permits the records to be kept continuously up-to-date.

Other accounting applications of computers include forecasting the profit possibilities inherent in alternative courses of action, analyzing gross profit margins by department or by product line, and determining future cash requirements long in advance. Recent developments of accounting applications of the computer provide much more information about business operations than was available to management in the past.

Computer service centers and time-sharing

A computer and related hardware are costly to buy or rent. The employment of personnel qualified to operate the equipment is also a major expense, especially for a small business. One way in which a small business can avoid investing large sums yet gain the operating efficiencies of EDP is to turn over its raw data to a bank, an accounting firm, or a computer center that offers EDP services on a fee basis. The small business may either keypunch its data and send the punched cards to the service center for processing or write the data on special forms and let the service center do the keypunching.

Another method of using EDP services without owning a computer is called *time-sharing.* Time-sharing refers to using a large central computer by means of a portable terminal, which is both an input and output device. Through these terminals, hundreds of businesses may make use of the same central computer. The company which owns the central computer sends each of these users a monthly bill, including a fixed monthly charge plus a per-minute charge for the actual time spent using the computer. Since the portable terminals communicate with the central computer using ordinary telephone lines, the terminals may be thousands of miles away from the central computer.

An advantage of time-sharing is the convenience of direct access to the computer through a portable terminal. A disadvantage, however, is that a terminal enters data into the computer using a manual keyboard. This is a relatively slow way of entering large quantities of data into a computer. If large quantities of data must be processed, a computer service center may be less expensive than time-sharing.

Do computers make decisions?

Computers can do only what they have specifically been told to do. Computers cannot make decisions in the sense of exercising judgment. They can choose among alternatives only by following the specific instructions contained in the program. When a computer encounters a situation for which it has not been programmed, it is unable to act. Computer programs must therefore be carefully tested to determine that they provide the computer with adequate instructions for all aspects of the data processing.

Information systems

The automation of an accounting system speeds up the production and transmission of information. The term *integrated data processing* (IDP) describes the current trend of providing attachments for typewriters, accounting machines, cash registers, and other conventional equipment which will, as a by-product, produce perforated tape or cards acceptable to a computer. The typewriter, for example, when equipped with such attachments can be used not only to prepare conventional business documents but simultaneously to provide the same information in a form compatible with input requirements of a computer. The *integration* of processes for recording information in conventional form and concurrently providing input media for an EDP system eliminates the intermediate work of transferring information from invoices, checks, and other documents to the tape or cards acceptable for processing by the computer.

The integration of an accounting system requires that forms and procedures be designed not for the needs of a single department but rather as part of a complete *information system* for the entire business. To create such an integrated system, the accounting systems specialist tries to coordinate paper work and procedures in a manner that will provide a rapid and uninterrupted flow of all information needed in the conduct of the business as an entity.

KEY TERMS INTRODUCED OR EMPHASIZED IN CHAPTER 7

Accounts receivable ledger A subsidiary ledger containing an account with each credit customer. The total of the ledger agrees with the general ledger controlling account, Accounts Receivable.

Arithmetic unit The section of a computer which performs addition, subtraction, multiplication, division, and comparison of data.

Cash payments journal   A special journal used to record all payments of cash.

Cash receipts journal   A special journal used to record all receipts of cash.

Central processing unit (CPU)   Main section of a computer, including the storage unit, control unit, and arithmetic unit.

Computer   A machine which performs arithmetic and processes accounting and other data through use of electronic circuits.

Control (or controlling) account   A general ledger account which is supported by detailed information in a subsidiary ledger.

Control unit   One of three major sections of a computer; it processes the program of instructions.

Data processing   The preparation of documents and the flow of data contained in these documents through the major accounting steps of recording, classifying, and summarizing.

Electronic data processing (EDP)   A system for processing data by use of electronic computers.

Hardware   The machines and related equipment used in an EDP system.

Input controls   Measures to ensure accuracy of data entered into a computer (such as control totals, the total dollar amount of documents to be processed).

Input devices   An element of a computer used to prepare and insert information into the computer.

Key punch   An electrically operated machine used for recording data on punched cards.

Magnetic tape   An input device consisting of metal covered tape on which information is stored in the form of magnetic spots.

Output devices   An element of a computer which transfers information out of the computer to the accountant or other user.

Program   Instructions to a computer consisting of a series of steps planned to carry out a certain process (such as payroll preparation).

Program controls   Error-detecting measures built into a computer program (such as a limit test setting a maximum dollar amount, or item counts specifying the number of cards to be processed).

Punched cards   An input device on which accounting data are recorded by using holes in columns and rows to represent numerical and alphabetical data.

Purchases journal   A special journal used exclusively to record purchases of merchandise on credit.

Sales journal   A special journal used exclusively to record sales of merchandise on credit.

Software   All materials (except hardware) utilized in selecting, installing, and operating an EDP system.

Sorter   A machine used in a mechanical data processing system which arranges punched cards in an alphabetical or numerical sequence.

Subsidiary ledger   A supplementary record used to provide detailed information for a control account in the general ledger. The total of accounts in a subsidiary ledger equals the balance of the related control account in the general ledger.

Tabulating machine   A machine used in a mechanical data processing system which makes calculations and prints reports. Utilizes moving parts, not electronic circuits.

Terminals   Keyboard devices for entering information into a computer without first punching the information into punched cards or tape.

Time-sharing   Use of a central computer through a terminal upon payment of a monthly fee by the subscriber.

REVIEW QUESTIONS

1 What advantages are offered by the use of special journals?

2 Pine Hill General Store makes about 500 sales on account each month, using only a two-column general journal to record these transactions. What would be the extent of the work saved by using a sales journal?

3 When accounts receivable and accounts payable are kept in subsidiary ledgers, will the general ledger continue to be a self-balancing ledger with equal debits and credits? Explain.

4 Explain how, why, and when the cash receipts journal and cash payments journal are crossfooted.

5 During November the sales on credit made by the Hardy Company actually amounted to $41,625, but an error of $1,000 was made in totaling the amount column of the sales journal. When and how will the error be discovered?

6 Considerable copying work may be performed in preparing a sales invoice, a sales journal, and a receivables ledger. Is this step-by-step sequence, with its related opportunity for errors, a characteristic of all types of accounting systems? Explain.

7 What are the principal advantages of electronic data processing in the accounting department of a company?

8 In which phases or areas of accounting can EDP equipment be used to advantage? Which phases can most conveniently and advantageously be converted to electronic data processing?

9 What avenues are open to a small business interested in gaining the efficiencies of electronic data processing, but lacking funds for purchase or rental of a computer and not having employees familiar with computer operations?

10 Evaluate the following quotation: "The computer will ultimately replace both accountants and will be able to make many of the decisions now made by top management."

11 Distinguish between *hardware* and *software* as these terms are used in data processing systems.

12 Explain the meaning of the term *computer program.*

13 What are the principal elements of an electronic data processing system?

14 Explain the meaning of the term *input control* and give an example.

15 Explain the meaning of the term *program control* and give an example.

EXERCISES

Ex. 7-1 Fall River Company uses a cash receipts journal, a cash payments journal, a sales journal, a purchases journal, and a general journal. Indicate which journal should be used to record each of the following transactions.
a Adjusting entry to record depreciation
b Purchase of delivery truck for cash
c Purchase of merchandise on account
d Return of merchandise by a customer company for credit to its account
e Payment of property taxes
f Purchase of typewriter on account
g Sale of merchandise on account
h Sale of merchandise for cash
i Refund to a customer who returned merchandise
j Return of merchandise to a supplier for credit

Ex. 7-2 The accounting system used by Adams Company includes a general journal and also four special journals for cash receipts, cash payments, sales, and purchases of merchandise. On January 31, the Accounts Receivable control account in the general ledger had a debit balance of $160,000, and the Accounts Payable control account had a credit balance of $48,000.

During February the sales journal included transactions which totaled $96,000. The purchases journal included transactions totaling $56,000. In the cash receipts journal the Accounts Receivable column showed a credit total for February of $76,800. In the cash payments journal, the Accounts Payable column showed a debit total of $67,200.

a What posting would be made of the total of the $76,800 Accounts Receivable column total in the cash receipts journal at February 28?

b What posting would be made of the $96,000 total of the sales journal at February 28?

c What posting would be made of the $56,000 total of the purchases journal at February 28?

d Based on the above information, state the balances of the Accounts Receivable control account and the Accounts Payable control account in the general ledger after completion of posting at February 28.

Ex. 7-3 The Island Company uses a cash receipts journal, a cash payments journal, a sales journal, a purchases journal, and a general journal.

a In which of the five journals would you expect to find the smallest number of transactions recorded?

b At the end of the accounting period, the total of the sales journal should be posted to what account or accounts? As a debit or credit?

c At the end of the accounting period, the total of the purchases journal should be posted to what account or accounts? As a debit or credit?

d Name two subsidiary ledgers which would probably be used in conjunction with the journals listed above. Identify the journals from which postings would normally be made to each of the two subsidiary ledgers.

e In which of the five journals would adjusting and closing entries be made?

Ex. 7-4 Collins Company uses a sales journal to record all sales of merchandise on credit. At July 31 the transactions in this journal were as follows:

Sales Journal

Date		Account Debited	Invoice No.	Amount
July	6	Robert Baker		3,600
	15	Minden Company		8,610
	17	Pell & Warden		1,029
	26	Stonewall Corporation		17,500
	27	Robert Baker		3,000
				33,739

Entries in the general journal during July include one for the return of merchandise by a customer, as follows:

July	18	Sales Returns and Allowances		500	
		Accounts Receivable, Minden Company			500
		Allowed credit to customer for return of merchandise from sale of July 15			

a Prepare a subsidiary ledger for accounts receivable by opening a T account for each of the four customers listed above. Post the entries in the sales journal to these individual customers' accounts. From the general journal, post the credit to the account of Minden Company.

b Prepare general ledger accounts in T form as follows: a controlling account for Accounts Receivable, a Sales account, and a Sales Returns and Allowances account. Post to these accounts the appropriate entries from the sales journal and general journal.

c Prepare a schedule of accounts receivable at July 31 to prove that this subsidiary ledger is in agreement with its controlling account.

Ex. 7-5 A check for $13,230 was received from a customer within 10 days from the date of sending a sales invoice for $13,500, with terms of 2/10, n/30. In recording the receipt of the check, Robert Hall, the employee maintaining the cash receipts journal, entered $13,230 in the Cash column and $13,500 in the Accounts Receivable column. He made no entry in the Sales Discounts column. What procedure should bring this error to light?

Ex. 7-6 Jason Company maintains its sales journal and accounts receivable subsidiary ledger by EDP. Each day the accounting department prepares a control total of total credit sales and sends the sales invoices to the EDP department. The sales data are keypunched in the EDP department, and the punched cards and a control figure representing the total number of sales transactions (per the invoices) are entered into the computer.

The computer prepares the sales journal, posts to the accounts receivable ledger (maintained on magnetic tape), and performs an item count. Any discrepancy in the item count is printed out on an error report. A copy of the sales journal for each day is sent back to the accounting department for comparison with the daily control totals.

What control procedure will first detect the following independent errors?

a A sales invoice of $760 is accidentally keypunched as $7,600.

b A sales invoice is lost on the way from the accounting department to the EDP department.

c Several punched cards are lost before being processed by the computer.

PROBLEMS

Group A

7A-1 The accounting system used by Fremont Company, a small business, includes a two-column general journal and four special journals. The four special journals are:

1 A one-column sales journal

2 A one-column purchases journal

3 A six-column cash receipts journal

4 A six-column cash payments journal

Fremont Company maintains a general ledger, an accounts receivable subsidiary ledger, and an accounts payable subsidiary ledger. All the ledgers are in the three-column, running balance form.

At September 30, the subsidiary ledger for accounts receivable consisted of the accounts with customers shown on page 273.

Instructions You are to make all appropriate entries in the general ledger controlling account, Accounts Receivable, for the month of September. Use a three-column, running balance form of ledger account. Include the balance at August 31, the transactions during September in chronological order, and the running balance of the account after each entry. The dates and sources of each entry (name of journal and journal page number) should all be entered in the controlling account. Use the symbols shown on page 251 to identify the various journals. Only one posting is required for all sales during the month.

A. Anderson

Date	Explanation	Ref	Debit	Credit	Balance
19—					
Sept. 3		S4	560		560
9		S4	1040		1600
27		CR2		960	640

B. Brown

Date	Explanation	Ref	Debit	Credit	Balance
19—					
aug. 31	Balance				5184
Sept. 8		CR1		3200	1984
8		J1		640	1344
28		CR2		1344	-0-

C. Cathway

Date	Explanation	Ref	Debit	Credit	Balance
19—					
aug. 31	Balance				3520
Sept. 10		J1		800	2720
11		S4	2000		4720
30		CR2		2560	2160

D. Davis

Date	Explanation	Ref	Debit	Credit	Balance
19—					
Sept. 4		S4	7040		7040
29		S4	1920		8960
29		CR2		7040	1920

7A-2 The Crest Corporation, a small retail store, uses a general journal and four special journals for daily recording of transactions. Information in these journals is posted to a general ledger and two subsidiary ledgers. One subsidiary ledger contains accounts receivable and the other accounts payable. All three ledgers are in the three-column, running balance form.

At May 30, the subsidiary ledger for accounts payable contained the accounts with creditors shown on page 274.

Instructions Prepare a general ledger controlling account for Accounts Payable. Use the three-column, running balance form. Include the beginning balance at April 30 and all appropriate entries for May in chronological order. Use only one entry to record May purchases. Show the date and source of each entry (that is, the name and page number of the journal from which posted). Use the symbols shown on page 251 to identify the various journals.

J. Johnson

Date		Explanation	Ref	Debit	Credit	Balance
19—						
Apr.	30	Balance				1440
May	14		CP2	1440		-0-
	25		P3		4000	4000
	28		P3		6400	10400

K. Kelly

Date		Explanation	Ref	Debit	Credit	Balance
19—						
Apr.	30	Balance				20160
May	2		J1	1600		18560
	10		P3		8000	26560
	25		CP2	18560		8000

L. Lewis

Date		Explanation	Ref	Debit	Credit	Balance
19—						
May	11		P3		1920	1920
	14		P3		3200	5120
	30		CP2	1920		3200

M. McKay

Date		Explanation	Ref	Debit	Credit	Balance
19—						
May	9		P3		2880	2880
	12		P3		3840	6720
	14		J1	320		6400

7A-3 Hill Corporation has a chart of accounts which includes the following accounts, among others.

Cash 10	Accounts payable 30
Office supplies 18	Purchases 50
Land 20	Purchase returns & allowances 52
Building 22	Purchase discounts 53
Notes payable 28	Salaries expense 60

The December transactions relating to the purchase of merchandise for resale and to accounts payable are listed below along with selected other transactions.

Dec. 1 Purchased merchandise from Duncan Company at a cost of $3,120. Invoice dated today; terms 2/10, n/30.

Dec. **4** Purchased merchandise from Collins Company for $10,080. Invoice dated December 3; terms 2/10, n/30.

Dec. **5** Returned for credit to Duncan Company defective merchandise having a list price of $960.

Dec. **6** Received shipment of merchandise from Maverick Co. and their invoice dated December 5 in amount of $6,840. Terms net 30 days.

Dec. **8** Purchased merchandise from Russell Brothers, $8,160. Invoice dated today with terms 1/10, n/60.

Dec. 10 Purchased merchandise from Queen Corporation, $9,960. Invoice dated December 9; terms 2/10, n/30.

Dec. 10 Issued check to Duncan Company in settlement of balance resulting from purchase of December 1 and purchase return of December 5.

Dec. 11 Issued check to Collins Company in payment of December 3 invoice.

Dec. 18 Issued check to Queen Corporation in settlement of invoice dated December 9.

Dec. 20 Purchased merchandise for cash, $360.

Dec. 21 Bought land, $21,600, and building, $48,000, for expansion of business. Paid cash of $12,000 and signed a promissory note for the balance of $57,600. (Land and building were acquired in a single transaction from L. J. Douglas.)

Dec. 23 Purchased merchandise for cash, $300.

Dec. 26 Purchased merchandise from Busch Company for $10,800. Invoice dated December 25, terms 2/10, n/30.

Dec. 28 Paid cash for office supplies, $90.

Dec. 29 Purchased merchandise for cash, $630.

Dec. 31 Paid salaries for December, $2,640.

Instructions

a Record the transactions in the appropriate journals. Use a single-column purchases journal, a six-column cash payments journal, and a two-column general journal. Foot and rule the special journals. Make all postings to the proper general ledger accounts and to the accounts payable subsidiary ledger. Round all amounts to the nearest dollar.

b Prepare a schedule of accounts payable at December 31 to prove that the subsidiary ledger is in balance with the controlling account for accounts payable.

7A-4 The accounting records of the Midas Company include multiple-column journals for cash receipts and cash payments similar to those illustrated on pages 246–247 and 248–249. During July the cash transactions were as follows:

July **1** The owner, Pete Townsend, invested additional cash of $21,600 in the business.

July **1** Purchased U.S. government bonds, $3,600.

July **2** Paid July rent, $1,620.

July **2** Cash sales of merchandise, $4,183.

July **4** Purchased fixtures, $5,760, making a down payment of $720 and issuing a note payable for the balance.

July **9** Received $1,080 as partial settlement of Bee Co. invoice of $3,240 and 60-day, 10% note for the balance.

July 10 Paid gas and oil bill, $281, for automobile belonging to Mrs. Townsend. (Car is not used in business.)

July 12 Paid Arrow, Inc., invoice, $4,500 less 2% discount.

July 13 Sold land costing $5,400 for $6,570.

July 15 Received $2,117 in full settlement of Sattler Brothers invoice after allowing 2% discount.

July 19 Cash purchase of merchandise, $4,039.

July 20 Paid note due today, $4,320, and accrued interest amounting to $86.

July 21 Sold U.S. government bonds costing $1,800 for $1,739.

July 23 Paid installment on note payable due today, $720, of which $335 represented interest expense.

July 25 Cash sales of merchandise, $7,222.
July 25 Paid Carlsbad Company invoice, $5,760 less 2% discount.
July 26 Purchased three-year fire insurance policy, $670.
July 28 Cash purchase of merchandise, $3,398.
July 30 Received payment in full settlement of Jones Company invoice, $4,320 less 2% discount.
July 31 Paid monthly salaries, $4,342.

Instructions
a Enter the above transactions in a six-column journal for cash receipts and a six-column journal for cash payments. Round all amounts to the nearest dollar.
b Compute column totals and rule the journals. Determine the equality of debits and credits in column totals.

7A-5 Spring Company purchases and sells merchandise only on a credit basis. The accounting records include special journals for purchases, sales, cash receipts, and cash payments. During October all sales and purchases of merchandise were recorded in the special journals; no entries were made in the general journal.

Shown below is the after-closing trial balance at September 30 and the trial balance before adjustments a month later. By careful study of these trial balances, you can trace the flow of figures through the accounts. For example, you can determine the amount added to receivables from October sales on account, the amount of cash received from collections of accounts receivable, and cash received from any other source. In the same way you can determine cash payments for various purposes.

	After-closing Trial Balance, September 30		Trial Balance, October 31	
Cash	$ 78,320		$ 58,960	
Accounts receivable	105,600		114,840	
Inventory	110,880		110,880	
Equipment	154,000		161,920	
Accumulated depreciation:				
equipment		$ 33,000		$ 33,000
Accounts payable		85,800		57,200
Robert Franklin, capital		330,000		374,000
Sales				74,800
Purchases			55,000	
Salaries expense			17,600	
Advertising expense			4,400	
Supplies expense			3,300	
Property tax expense			5,500	
Miscellaneous expense			6,600	
	$448,800	$448,800	$539,000	$539,000

Instructions
a Prepare a schedule showing all sources of cash receipts during October.
b Prepare a schedule showing the purpose of all cash payments made during October.
c Prepare one compound journal entry (general journal form) summarizing all

October transactions involving the receipt of cash. The entry should include a debit to Cash and credits to other accounts for the amounts indicated in *a*.

d Prepare one compound journal entry (general ledger form) summarizing all October transactions involving the payment of cash. The entry should include a credit to Cash and debits to other accounts for amounts indicated in *b*.

7A-6 The October transactions of Lane Company, which began business on October 1, are shown below.

Oct.   1 The owner, Ruth Lane, deposited $81,000 in a bank account under the name, Lane Company.

Oct.   4 Purchased land and building on contract, paying $18,000 cash and signing a mortgage for the remaining balance of $27,000. Estimated value of the land was $14,400.

Oct.   6 Sold merchandise to Brad Parks, $6,840. Invoice no. 1, terms 2/10, n/60.

Oct.   7 Purchased merchandise from Lakeview Company, $12,780. Invoice dated today; terms 2/10, n/30.

Oct.   7 Sold merchandise for cash, $1,332.

Oct.   7 Paid $486 for a two-year fire insurance policy.

Oct. 10 Paid freight charges of $369 on Lakeview Company purchase.

Oct. 12 Sold merchandise to ABC Corporation, $8,820. Invoice no. 2; terms 2/10, n/60.

Oct. 13 Purchased merchandise for cash, $2,556.

Oct. 15 Received payment in full from Brad Parks. Invoice no. 1, less 2% discount.

Oct. 15 Purchased land for $4,680 cash.

Oct. 16 Issued credit memorandum no. 1 to ABC Corporation, $720, for goods returned today.

Oct. 17 Paid Lakeview Company invoice of October 7, less discount.

Oct. 18 Purchased merchandise from Baker Company, $6,660. Invoice dated today; terms 2/10, n/30.

Oct. 20 A portion of merchandise purchased from Baker Company was found to be substandard. After discussion with the vendor, a price reduction of $180 was agreed upon and debit memorandum no. 1 was issued in that amount.

Oct. 22 Received payment in full from ABC Corporation. Invoice no. 2, less return and discount.

Oct. 23 Purchased merchandise from Lakeview Company, $7,560. Invoice dated today; terms 2/10, n/60.

Oct. 25 Sold for $4,356 the land purchased on October 15.

Oct. 27 Sold merchandise for cash, $927.

Oct. 28 Borrowed $5,400 from bank, issuing a 60-day, 10% note payable as evidence of indebtedness.

Oct. 28 Paid Baker Company invoice of October 18, less allowance and discount.

Oct. 30 Paid first installment on mortgage, $900. This payment included interest of $162.

Oct. 30 Purchased merchandise for cash, $1,656.

Oct. 31 Paid monthly salaries of $3,807.

Oct. 31 Sold merchandise to Frank Sullivan, $4,950. Invoice no. 3; terms 2/10, n/60.

The following ledger accounts are used by Lane Company.

Cash	10	Building	21
Notes receivable	14	Furniture and fixtures	24
Accounts receivable	15	Notes payable	30
Merchandise inventory	17	Accounts payable	32
Unexpired insurance	19	Mortgage payable	36
Land	20	Ruth Lane, capital	40

Ruth Lane, drawing	42	Rent expense	70
Income summary	45	Salaries expense	72
Sales	50	Taxes expense	74
Sales returns & allowances	52	Supplies expense	76
Sales discounts	54	Insurance expense	78
Purchases	60	Interest earned	80
Purchase returns & allowances	62	Interest expense	83
Purchase discounts	64	Loss on sale of land	.84
Transportation-in	66		

Instructions

a Enter the October transactions in the following journals:
Two-column general journal
One-column sales journal
One-column purchases journal
Six-column cash receipts journal
Six-column cash payments journal
Round all amounts to the nearest dollar.
b Foot and rule all special journals.
c Show how posting would be made by placing the ledger account numbers and
check marks in the appropriate columns of the journals.

Group B

7B-1 A manual accounting system similar to the one illustrated in Chapter 7 is used by
Hastings Company. Transactions are recorded in a general journal or in one of
the four special journals (sales journal, purchases journal, cash receipts journal,
and cash payments journal).

The ledgers in use consist of a general ledger, an accounts receivable subsidiary ledger, and an accounts payable subsidiary ledger. All three of the ledgers
are in the three-column, running balance form. At October 31, the subsidiary
ledger for accounts receivable included the following accounts with individual
customers.

A. Adams

Date	Explanation	Ref	Debit	Credit	Balance
19—					
Sept. 30	Balance				100 00
Oct. 3		J4		19 20	80 80
18		CR6		80 80	—0—
28		S6	1 477 20		1 477 20

B. Bowman

Date	Explanation	Ref	Debit	Credit	Balance
19—					
Oct. 2		S5	21 20		21 20
27		CR6		16 00	5 20
27		S6	6 72		11 92

C. Christopher

Date	Explanation	Ref	Debit	Credit	Balance
19—					
Sept. 30	Balance				7424
Oct. 5		J4		640	6784
10		S5	2000		8784
23		CR6		3200	5584

D. Dunbar

Date	Explanation	Ref	Debit	Credit	Balance
19—					
Oct. 8		S5	1040		1040
12		S5	1760		2800
31		CR6		1040	1760

Instructions Prepare the general ledger controlling account, Accounts Receivable, for the month of October, in the three-column running balance form. Include the balance at September 30, all entries during October, and the running balance of the account after each posting. When completed, the controlling account should reflect in summary form the information shown above in the subsidiary ledger accounts. Be sure that entries in the controlling account are in chronological order. Only one posting is needed to record sales for September. The dates and sources of each entry (name of journal and journal page number) should be entered in the controlling account. Use the symbols shown on page 251 to identify the various journals.

7B-2 The accounting system used by Orange Corporation includes a general journal and four special journals for daily recording of transactions. Information recorded in these journals is posted to a general ledger and two subsidiary ledgers: one of the subsidiary ledgers contain accounts receivable and the other accounts payable. All three ledgers are in the three-column, running balance form. At September 30, the subsidiary ledger for accounts payable contained the accounts with creditors shown below and on page 280.

Instructions You are to prepare the general ledger controlling account, Accounts Payable, corresponding to the following subsidiary ledger accounts. Use a three-column running balance form. Include the beginning balance at August 31, and make all September entries in chronological order. Use only one posting for September purchases. Include for each entry the date and source (journal and page number) of the item. Use the symbols shown on page 251 to identify the individual journals.

R. Rodin

Date	Explanation	Ref	Debit	Credit	Balance
19—					
Sept. 1		P1		16000	16000
20		P1		12800	28800
21	Returned mdse.	J2	800		28000
28		CP3	15200		12800

S. Smith

Date	Explanation	Ref	Debit	Credit	Balance
19—					
Sept. 22		P1		1376 0	1376 0

T. Thorton

Date	Explanation	Ref	Debit	Credit	Balance
19—					
Aug. 31	Balance				960
Sept. 15		CP3	960		-0-
16		P1		3840	3840
20		P1		4800	8640

U. Ullman

Date	Explanation	Ref	Debit	Credit	Balance
19—					
Aug. 31	Balance				3520 0
Sept. 5	Returned mdse.	J2	1920		3328 0
20		CP3	2400 0		928 0
25		P1		1600	1088 0

7B-3 The accounting system of Morro Bay Company includes a general journal, four special journals, a general ledger and two subsidiary ledgers. The chart of accounts includes the following accounts among others.

Cash	10	Sales		50
Notes receivable	15	Sales returns & allowances		52
Accounts receivable	17	Sales discounts		54
Land	20	Purchases		60
Office equipment	25	Purchase returns & allowances		62
Notes payable	30	Interest revenue		82
Accounts payable	32	Gain on sale of land		85

Transactions in June involving the sale of merchandise and the receipt of cash are shown below, along with certain other selected transactions.

June 1 Sold merchandise to Williams Company for cash, $2,472.

June 4 Sold merchandise to Bravo Company, $8,480. Invoice no. 618; terms 2/10, n/30.

June 5 Returned $1,088 of merchandise to a supplier for cash refund.

June 8 Sold merchandise to Bradley Company for $4,320. Invoice no. 619; terms 2/10, n/30.

June 9 Received a check from Kamtex Company in payment of a $2,400 invoice, less 2% discount.

June 11 Received $1,120 from Olympus Company in payment of a past-due invoice.

June 13 Received check from Bravo Company in settlement of invoice dated June 4, less discount.

June 16 Sold merchandise to XYZ Company, $4,160. Invoice no. 620; terms 2/10, n/30.

June 16 Returned $960 of merchandise to supplier, King Company, for reduction of account payable.

June 18 Purchased office equipment at a cost of $3,040, signing a 9%, 90-day note payable for the full amount.

June 20 Sold merchandise to Armstrong Co. for $7,680. Invoice no. 621; terms 2/10, n/30.

June 21 XYZ Company returned for credit $640 of merchandise purchased on June 16.

June 23 Borrowed $24,000 cash from a local bank, signing a 10%, six-month note payable.

June 25 Received payment in full from XYZ Company in settlement of invoice dated June 16, less return and discount.

June 29 Sold land costing $30,400 for $11,200 cash and a 9% two-year note receivable for $33,600. (Credit Gain on Sale of Land for $14,400.)

June 30 Collected from Armstrong Co. amount of invoice dated June 20, less 2% discount.

June 30 Collected $12,992 in full settlement of a $12,800, 9%, 60-day note receivable held since May 1. (No interest revenue has yet been recorded.)

June 30 Received a 60-day, non-interest-bearing note from Bradley Company in settlement of invoice dated June 8.

Instructions Record the above transactions in the appropriate journals. Use a single-column sales journal, a six-column cash receipts journal, and a two-column general journal. Foot and rule the special journals and indicate how postings would be made by placing ledger account numbers and check marks in the appropriate columns of the journals. Round all amounts to the nearest dollar.

7B-4 Copper Kettle uses an accounting system that includes multicolumn special journals for cash receipts and cash payments. These journals are similar to those illustrated on pages 246–247 and 248–249. All the cash transactions during September are described below.

Sept. 1 Cash purchase of merchandise, $6,848.

Sept. 1 Paid Spalding Company invoice, $2,560 less 1% discount.

Sept. 2 Cash sales of merchandise, $5,504.

Sept. 2 Paid freight charges on Watkins Company invoice, $326.

Sept. 4 Purchased fixtures, $5,120, making a down payment of $1,280 and issuing a 90-day, 9% note payable for the balance.

Sept. 5 Received $960 as partial payment of National Co. invoice of $3,840 and 60-day, 10% note for the $2,880 balance.

Sept. 6 Paid Newcomb Company invoice, $4,480 less 2% discount.

Sept. 7 Paid note due today, $9,600, and accrued interest amounting to $192.

Sept. 10 Sold land costing $8,960 for $7,872. Debit Loss on Sale of Land, $1,088.

Sept. 10 The owner, B. W. Hamilton, invested additional cash of $32,000 in the business.

Sept. 12 Cash sales of merchandise, $4,243.

Sept. 15 Paid September rent, $2,080.

Sept. 15 Purchased U.S. government bonds, $6,400.

Sept. 18 Cash purchase of merchandise, $4,640.

Sept. 19 Paid gas and oil bill, $176, for automobile belonging to Mrs. B. W. Hamilton. (Car is not used in the business.)

Sept. 20 Received $1,882 in full settlement of Mesa Company invoice after allowing 2% discount.

Sept. 21 Paid Mammoth Co. invoice, $5,120 less 2% discount.
Sept. 23 Paid sales commissions of $2,528.
Sept. 30 Received payment in full settlement of Presley Company invoice, $5,440 less 2% discount.
Sept. 30 Paid monthly salaries, $6,000.

Instructions
a Enter the above transactions in cash receipts and cash payments journals. Round all amounts to the nearest dollar.
b Foot and rule the journals.

7B-5 The accounting records of Portage Company include special journals for sales, purchases, cash receipts, and cash payments. All sales and all purchases are made on a credit basis. All transactions during September were recorded in the special journals; there were no entries in the general journal. The events of the month are reflected in summary form below by the after-closing trial balance of August 31 and the trial balance before adjustments a month later on September 30.

By close study of these trial balances, it is possible to determine the total amount of cash collected from customers during the month and the amount of cash received from other sources. Similarly, it is possible to determine the total amount of cash payments against accounts payable and the cash payments for other purposes such as acquisition of equipment, salaries, and other expenses.

	After-closing Trial Balance August 31		Trial Balance September 30	
Cash	$ 56,960		$ 42,880	
Accounts receivable	76,800		83,520	
Inventory	80,640		80,640	
Equipment	112,000		117,760	
Accumulated depreciation:				
equipment		$ 24,000		$ 24,000
Accounts payable		62,400		41,600
Patrick Lewis, capital		240,000		272,000
Sales				54,400
Purchases			40,000	
Salaries expense			12,800	
Advertising expense			3,200	
Supplies expense			2,400	
Property tax expense			4,000	
Miscellaneous expense			4,800	
	$326,400	$326,400	$392,000	$392,000

Instructions
a Prepare a schedule showing all sources of cash receipts during September.
b Prepare a schedule showing the purpose of all cash payments made during September.
c Prepare one compound journal entry (general journal form) summarizing all September transactions involving the receipt of cash. The entry should include a debit to Cash and credits to other accounts for the amounts indicated in *a*.
d Prepare one compound journal entry (general journal form) summarizing all September transactions involving the payment of cash. The entry should include a credit to Cash and debits to other accounts for amounts indicated in *b*.

7B-6 Reno Company, a successful retail business, had the following transactions during November.

Nov. 2 Purchased merchandise on account from Dunlop Co., $12,960. Invoice was dated today with terms of 2/10, n/30.

Nov. 3 Sold merchandise to Filmore Company, $8,280. Invoice no. 428; terms 2/10, n/30.

Nov. 4 Purchased supplies for cash, $315.

Nov. 5 Sold merchandise for cash, $2,016.

Nov. 7 Paid the Dunlop Co. invoice dated November 2.

Nov. 10 Purchased merchandise from Burton Company, $11,700. Invoice dated November 9 with terms of 1/10, n/30.

Nov. 10 Collected from Filmore Company for invoice no. 428.

Nov. 12 Sold merchandise to Payless, Inc., $7,830. Invoice no. 429; terms 2/10, n/30.

Nov. 14 Paid freight charges of $738 on goods purchased November 9 from Burton Company.

Nov. 14 Sold equipment for $3,240, receiving cash of $540 and a 30-day, 9% note receivable for the balance. The equipment cost $7,200 and accumulated depreciation was $4,680. Debit Accumulated Depreciation, $4,680, credit Gain on Sale of Equipment, $720.

Nov. 15 Issued credit memorandum no. 38 in favor of Payless, Inc., upon return of $360 of merchandise.

Nov. 18 Paid for one-year fire insurance policy, $1,413.

Nov. 18 Purchased merchandise for cash, $2,745.

Nov. 19 Paid the Burton Company invoice dated November 9.

Nov. 20 Sold merchandise on account to Peat Brothers, $7,074; invoice no. 430. Required customer to sign a 30-day, non-interest-bearing note. (Record this sale by a charge to Accounts Receivable, then transfer from Accounts Receivable to Notes Receivable by means of an entry in the general journal.)

Nov. 22 Purchased merchandise for cash, $1,458.

Nov. 22 Sold merchandise for cash, $1,800.

Nov. 22 Received payment from Payless, Inc., for invoice no. 429. Customer made deduction for credit memorandum no. 38 issued November 15.

Nov. 25 Purchased merchandise from Amber Company, $9,540. Invoice dated November 24, with terms 2/10, n/60.

Nov. 26 Issued debit memorandum no. 42 to Amber Company in connection with merchandise returned today amounting to $360.

Nov. 27 Purchased equipment having a list price of $21,600. Paid $3,600 down and signed a promissory note for the balance of $18,000.

Nov. 30 Paid monthly salaries of $5,328 for services rendered by employees during November.

Nov. 30 Paid monthly installment on mortgage, $1,260, of which $367 was interest.

The following ledger accounts are used by Reno Company:

Cash	10	Mortgage payable	40
Notes receivable	14	C. Irwin, capital	50
Accounts receivable	16	C. Irwin, drawing	52
Supplies	17	Sales	60
Unexpired insurance	18	Sales returns & allowances	62
Equipment	26	Sales discounts	64
Accumulated depreciation:		Purchases	70
equipment	28	Purchase returns & allowances	72
Notes payable	30	Purchase discounts	74
Accounts payable	32	Transportation-in	76

Salaries expense.	80	Depreciation expense:		
Supplies expense	84	equipment	88
Insurance expense	86	Gain on sale of equipment.	90
		Interest expense	92

Instructions

a Record the November transactions in the following journals:
   General journal—2 columns
   Sales journal—1 column
   Purchases journal—1 column
   Cash receipts journal—6 columns
   Cash payments journal—6 columns
   Round all amounts to the nearest dollar.
b Foot and rule all special journals.
c Show how postings would be made by placing ledger account numbers and check marks in the appropriate columns of the journals.

BUSINESS DECISION PROBLEM 7

Custom Clothing is a mail-order company which sells clothes to the public at discount prices. Recently Custom Clothing initiated a new policy allowing a 10-day free trial on all clothes bought from the company. At the end of the 10-day period, the customer may either pay cash for his purchase or return the goods to Custom Clothing. The new policy caused such a large boost in sales that, even after considering the many sales returns, the policy appeared quite profitable.

The accounting system of Custom Clothing includes a sales journal, purchases journal, cash receipts journal, cash payments journal, and a general journal. As an internal control procedure, an officer of the company reviews and initials every entry in the general journal before the amounts are posted to the ledger accounts. Since the 10-day free trial policy has been in effect, hundreds of entries recording sales returns have been entered in the general journal each week. Each of these entries has been reviewed and initialed by an officer of the firm, and the amounts have been posted to Sales Returns & Allowances and to the Accounts Receivable control account in the general ledger, and also to the customer's account in the accounts receivable subsidiary ledger.

Since these sales return entries are so numerous, it has been suggested that a special journal be designed to handle them. This could not only save time in journalizing and posting the entries, but also eliminate the time-consuming individual review of each of these repetitious entries by the officer of the company.

Instructions

a How many amounts are entered in the general journal to describe a single sales return transaction? Are these amounts the same?
b Explain why these transactions are suited to the use of a special journal. Explain in detail how many money columns the special journal should have, and what postings would have to be done either at the time of the transaction or at the end of the period.
c Assume that there were 3,000 sales returns during the month. How many postings would have to be made during the month if these transactions were entered in the general journal? How many postings would have to be made if the special journal you designed in **b** were used? (Assume a one-month accounting period.)
d Assume that a general journal entry requires 40 seconds to write and a special journal entry can be written in 15 seconds. Also assume that each posting requires an average of 20 seconds and that the officer of the company averages

20 seconds to review and initial a general journal entry for a sales return. The officer estimates the entire sales return special journal could be reviewed in 10 minutes. How much time (expressed in hours, minutes, and seconds) would be required to journalize, review, and post 3,000 entries in (1) general journal form and (2) special journal form? What is the time savings resulting from using the special journal?

e If the estimated cost of designing a sales returns journal and training employees in its use were $800, would you recommend adopting such a journal? Present a case to support your decision, assuming that the labor cost of operating either system averages $8 per hour.

8

The Control of Cash Transactions

CASH

Accountants use the word *cash* to include coins, paper money, checks, money orders, and money on deposit with banks. However, cash does not include postage stamps, IOU's, or postdated checks.

In deciding whether a particular item comes within the classification of cash, the following rule is a useful one: *Any medium of exchange which a bank will accept for deposit is included in cash.* As an example, checks and money orders are accepted by banks for deposit and are considered as cash. Postage stamps and postdated checks are not acceptable for deposit at a bank and are not included in the accountant's definition of cash.

Balance sheet presentation

Cash is a current asset. In fact, cash is the most current and most liquid of all assets. In judging whether other types of assets qualify for inclusion in the current assets section of the balance sheet, we consider the length of time required for the asset to be converted into cash.

The banker, credit manager, or investor who studies a balance sheet critically will always be interested in the total amount of cash as compared with other balance sheet items, such as accounts payable. These outside users of a company's financial statements are not interested, however, in such details as the number of separate bank accounts, or in the distinction between cash on hand and cash in banks. A business that carries checking accounts with several banks will maintain a separate ledger account for each bank account. On the balance sheet, however, the entire amount of cash on hand and cash on deposit with the several banks will be shown as a single amount. One objective in preparing financial statements is to keep them short, concise, and easy to read.

Some bank accounts are restricted as to their use, so that they are not available for making payments to meet normal operating needs of the business. An example (discussed in Chapter 18) is a bond sinking fund, consisting of cash being accumulated by a corporation for the specific purpose of paying off bonded indebtedness at a future date and not available for any other use. A bank account located in a foreign country may also be restricted if monetary regulations prevent the transfer of funds between the two countries. Restricted bank accounts are not regarded as current assets because they are not available for use in paying current liabilities.

Management responsibilities relating to cash

Efficient management of cash includes measures that will:

1 Prevent losses from fraud or theft
2 Provide accurate accounting for cash receipts, cash payments, and cash balances
3 Maintain a sufficient amount of cash at all times to make necessary payments, plus a reasonable balance for emergencies
4 Prevent unnecessarily large amounts of cash from being held idle in bank accounts which produce no revenue

Internal control over cash is sometimes regarded merely as a means of preventing fraud or theft. A good system of internal control, however, will also aid in achieving management's other objectives of accurate accounting for cash transactions and the maintenance of adequate but not excessive cash balances.

Basic requirements for internal control over cash

Cash is more susceptible to theft than any other asset. Furthermore, a large portion of the total transactions of a business involve the receipt or disbursement of cash. For both these reasons, internal control over cash is of great importance to management and also to the employees of a business. If a cash shortage arises in a business in which internal controls are weak or nonexistent, every employee is under suspicion. Perhaps no one employee can be proved guilty of the theft, but neither can any employee prove his or her innocence.

On the other hand, if internal controls over cash are adequate, theft without detection is virtually impossible except through the collusion of two or more employees. To achieve internal control over cash or any other group of assets requires first of all that *the custody of assets be clearly separated from the recording of transactions.* Secondly, the recording function should be subdivided among employees, so that the work of one person is verified by that of another. This subdivision of duties discourages fraud, because collusion among employees would be necessary to conceal an irregularity. Internal control is more easily achieved in large companies than in small companies, because extensive subdivision of duties is more feasible in the larger business.

The major steps in establishing internal controls over cash include the following:

1 Separate the function of handling cash from the maintenance of accounting records. The cashier should not maintain the accounting records and should not have access to the records. Accounting personnel should not have access to cash.

2 Separate the function of receiving cash from that of disbursing cash. The same person should not handle cash receipts and also make cash disbursements.

3 Require that all cash receipts be deposited daily in the bank, and that all cash payments be made by check. Keep cash on hand under lock.

The application of these principles in building an adequate system of internal control over cash can best be illustrated by considering separately the topics of cash receipts and cash disbursements.

Cash receipts

Cash receipts consist of two major types: cash received over the counter at the time of a sale, and cash received through the mail as collections on accounts receivable.

USE OF CASH REGISTERS   Cash received over the counter at the time of a sale should be rung up on a cash register, so located that the customer will see the amount recorded. If store operations can be so arranged that two employees must participate in each sales transaction, stronger internal control will be achieved than when one employee is permitted to handle a transaction in its entirety. In some stores this objective is accomplished by employing a central cashier who rings on a cash register the sales made by all clerks.

At the end of the day, the store manager or other supervisor should compare the cash register tape, showing the total sales for the day, with the total cash collected.

USE OF PRENUMBERED SALES TICKETS   Internal control may be further strengthened by writing out a prenumbered sales ticket in duplicate at the time of each sale. The original is given to the customer and the carbon copy retained. At the end of the day an employee computes a total sales figure from these duplicate tickets, and also makes sure that no tickets are missing from the series. The total amount of sales as computed from the duplicate sales tickets is then compared with the total sales recorded on the cash register.

CASH RECEIVED THROUGH THE MAIL The procedures for handling checks and currency received through the mail are also based on the internal control principle that two or more employees should participate in every transaction.

The employee who opens the mail should prepare a list of the checks received. In order that this list shall represent the total receipts of the day, the totals recorded on the cash registers may be added to the list. One copy of the list is forwarded with the cash (currency and checks) to the cashier, who will deposit in the bank all the cash received for the day. Another copy of the list is sent to the accounting department, which will record the amount of cash received.

The total cash receipts recorded each day in the accounting records should agree with the amount of the cashier's deposit, and also with the list of total cash receipts for the day.

CASH OVER AND SHORT In handling over-the-counter cash receipts, a few errors in change making will inevitably occur. These errors will cause a cash shortage or overage at the end of the day, when the cash is counted and compared with the reading on the cash register.

For example, assume that the total cash sales for the day as recorded by the cash register amount to $500, but that the cash in the drawer when counted amounts to only $490. The following entry would be made to record the day's sales and the cash shortage of $10.

Recording cash shortage

Cash	*490*	
Cash Over and Short	*10*	
Sales		*500*

The account entitled Cash Over and Short is debited with shortages and credited with overages. If the cash shortages during an entire accounting period are in excess of the cash overages, the Cash Over and Short account will have a debit balance and will be shown as a miscellaneous expense in the income statement. On the other hand, if the overages exceed the shortages, the Cash Over and Short account will show a credit balance at the end of the period and should be treated as an item of miscellaneous revenue.

Cash disbursements

An adequate system of internal control requires that each day's cash receipts be deposited intact in the bank and that all disbursements be made by check. Checks should be prenumbered. Any spoiled checks should be marked "Void" and filed in sequence so that all numbers in the series can be accounted for.

The official designated to sign checks should not be given authority to approve invoices for payment or to make entries in the accounting records. When a check is presented to a company official for signature, it should be accompanied by the approved invoice and voucher showing that the transaction has been fully verified and that payment is justified. When the check is signed, the supporting invoices and vouchers should be perforated or stamped "Paid" to eliminate any possibility of their being presented later in support of another check. If these rules are followed, it is almost impossible for a fraudulent cash disbursement to be concealed without the collusion of two or more persons.

BANK CHECKING ACCOUNTS

Opening a bank account

When a depositor first opens a bank account, he must sign his name on a signature card, exactly as he will sign checks. The signature card is kept on file by the bank, so that any check bearing a signature not familiar to bank employees may be compared with the depositor's signature card. When a corporation opens a bank account, the board of directors will pass a resolution designating the officers or employees authorized to sign checks. A copy of this resolution is given to the bank.

Making deposits

The depositor fills out a *deposit ticket* (usually in duplicate) for each deposit. The deposit ticket includes a listing of each check deposited and the code number of the bank on which it is drawn. Space is also provided for listing the amounts of coin and currency deposited.

The bank statement

Each month the bank will provide the depositor with a statement of his or her account, accompanied by the checks paid and charged to the account during the month. The bank statement illustrated on page 291 shows the balance on deposit at the beginning of the month, the deposits, the checks paid, any other debits and credits during the month, and the new balance at the end of the month. Certain items in the bank statement of The Parkview Company warrant explanation and are discussed in the following paragraphs.

NSF CHECKS Deposits made by a business include checks received from customers. Occasionally a customer's check may not clear because the customer's bank balance is less than the amount of the check. For example, on July 12 The Parkview Company received a check for $50.25

STATEMENT OF ACCOUNT WITH

WESTERN NATIONAL BANK

PERIOD ENDING
July 31, 1979

ACCOUNT NO.
7 00532

The Parkview Company
19101 Parkview Road
Los Angeles, Calif. 90018

FOLD HERE

CHECKS—LISTED IN ORDER OF PAYMENT—READ ACROSS					DEPOSITS	DATE	NEW BALANCE
					300 00	7–1–79	5329 30
100 00					250 00	7–2–79	5479 30
415 20	10 00					7–3–79	5054 10
25 00	90 00	36 50			185 10	7–5–79	5087 70
					60 00	7–7–79	5147 70
96 00	400 00					7–10–79	4651 70
500 00					147 20	7–12–79	4298 90
425 00						7–15–79	3873 90
50 25M					200 00	7–18–79	4023 65
85 00					101 19	7–21–79	4039 84
150 27					83 25	7–24–79	3972 82
95 75					500 00M	7–28–79	4377 07
2 00S					625 10	7–31–79	5000 17

SUMMARY OF ACTIVITY

BALANCE FORWARD	DEBITS		CREDITS		SERVICE CHARGE		NEW BALANCE
	NUMBER	AMOUNT	NUMBER	AMOUNT	ITEMS	AMOUNT	
5 029 30	14	2 478 97	10	2 451 84	1	2 00	5 000 17

Please examine this statement at once. If no error is reported in ten days the account will be considered correct. All items are credited subject to final payment.

EXPLANATION OF SYMBOLS

S SERVICE CHARGE   M MISCELLANEOUS ENTRY

from J. B. Ball, and the check was included in the bank deposit made on that day. The Ball check was returned to Western National Bank by the bank on which it was drawn marked NSF (Not Sufficient Funds), indicating that Ball did not have a sufficient balance on deposit to cover the check. Western National Bank therefore charged the NSF check against The Parkview Company's account as shown by the July 18 item of $50.25. (The letter M alongside this entry stands for Miscellaneous Entry.)

Upon receipt of the NSF check returned by the bank, The Parkview Company should remove this item from the cash classification by a journal entry debiting an account receivable from J. B. Ball and crediting Cash.

The NSF check is thus regarded as a receivable until it is collected directly from the drawer and redeposited, or is determined to be worthless.

BANK SERVICE CHARGES Under the date of July 31 on the illustrated bank statement is a debit for $2 accompanied by the symbol S. This symbol means Service Charge, a charge made by the bank to cover the expense of handling the account. The amount of the service charge is based upon such considerations as the average balance of the account and the number of checks and deposits. Most banks would probably not make a service charge on The Parkview Company's account because the balance is substantial and the activity is low. However, a service charge is shown here for the purpose of illustrating its use. When the bank sends the monthly statement and paid checks to the depositor, it will include debit memoranda for service charges and any other charges not represented by checks.

MISCELLANEOUS CHARGES Other charges which may appear on the bank statement include rental fees for safe deposit boxes, charges for printing checks, collection charges on notes left with the bank for collection, and interest charges on borrowing from the bank.

Reconciling the bank account

The balance shown on the monthly statement received from the bank will usually not agree with the balance of cash shown by the depositor's accounting records. Certain transactions recorded by the depositor will not yet have been recorded by the bank. The most common examples are:

1 Outstanding checks. These are checks written by the depositor and deducted on the depositor's records but not yet presented to the bank for payment and deduction.
2 Deposits in transit. Deposits mailed to the bank are usually not received by the bank and not entered on the bank's records until a day or two later than the entry on the depositor's accounting records.

Transactions which may appear on the bank statement but which have not yet been recorded by the depositor include:

1 Service charges
2 Charges for NSF checks
3 Miscellaneous bank charges and credits

In some cases the bank reconciliation will be complete after such items as outstanding checks, deposits in transit, and miscellaneous bank charges have been taken into account. Other cases may require the correction of errors by the bank or by the depositor to complete the reconciliation. When a company maintains accounts in several banks, one possible type of error is to record a check drawn on one bank as a payment from another bank account. Similar errors may occur in recording deposits.

Procedures for preparing a bank reconciliation

Preparing a bank reconciliation means determining those items which make up the difference between the balance appearing on the bank statement and the balance of cash according to the depositor's records. By listing and studying these discrepancies, it is possible to determine the correct figure for cash to appear on the balance sheet. Specific steps to be taken in preparing a bank reconciliation are:

1 Compare the deposits listed on the bank statement with the deposits shown in the company's records. Place check marks in the company's cash records and on the bank statement beside the items which agree. Any unchecked item in the company's records of deposits will be deposits not yet recorded by the bank, and should be added to the balance reported by the bank. Determine that any deposits in transit listed in last month's bank reconciliation are included in the current month's bank statement.

2 Arrange the paid checks in numerical order and compare each check with the corresponding entry in the cash payments journal. (In the case of personal bank accounts for which the only record maintained is the checkbook, compare each paid check with the check stub.) Place a check mark in the depositor's cash payments journal opposite each entry for which a paid check has been returned by the bank. The unchecked entries should be listed in the bank reconciliation as outstanding checks to be deducted from the balance reported by the bank. Determine whether the checks listed as outstanding in the bank reconciliation for the preceding month have been returned by the bank this month. If not, such checks should be listed as outstanding in the current reconciliation.

3 Deduct from the balance per the depositor's records any debit memoranda issued by the bank which have not been recorded by the depositor. In the illustrated bank reconciliation on page 294, examples are the NSF check for $50.25 and the $2 service charge.

4 Add to the balance per the depositor's records any credit memoranda issued by the bank which have not been recorded by the depositor. An example in the illustrated bank reconciliation on page 294 is the credit of $500 collected by the bank in behalf of The Parkview Company.

5 Prepare a bank reconciliation, reflecting the preceding steps, similar to the illustration on page 294.

6 Make journal entries for any items on the bank statement which have not yet been recorded in the depositor's accounts.

ILLUSTRATION The July bank statement prepared by the bank for The Parkview Company was illustrated on page 291. This statement shows a balance of cash on deposit at July 31 of $5,000.17. We shall assume that The Parkview Company's records at July 31 show a bank balance of $4,172.57. Our purpose in preparing the bank reconciliation is to identify the items that make up this difference and to determine the correct cash balance.

Assume that the specific steps to be taken in preparing a bank reconciliation have been carried out and that the following reconciling items have been discovered:

1 A deposit of $310.90 mailed to the bank on July 31 does not appear on the bank statement.

2 A credit memorandum issued by the bank on July 28 in the amount of $500 was returned with the July bank statement and appears in the Deposits column of that statement. This credit represents the proceeds of a note receivable left with the bank by The Parkview Company for the purpose of collection. The collection of the note has not yet been recorded by The Parkview Company.

3 Four checks issued in July or prior months have not yet been paid by the bank. These checks are:

Check No.	Date	Amount
801	June 15	$100.00
888	July 24	10.25
890	July 27	402.50
891	July 30	205.00

4 A debit memorandum issued by the bank on July 31 for a $2 service charge was enclosed with the July bank statement.

5 Check no. 875 was issued July 20 in the amount of $85 but was erroneously listed on the check stub and in the cash payments journal as $58. The check, in payment of telephone service, was paid by the bank, returned with the July bank statement, and correctly listed on the bank statement as an $85 charge to the account. The Cash account is overstated because of this $27 error ($85 − $58).

6 No entry has as yet been made in The Parkview Company's accounts to reflect the bank's action on July 18 of charging against the account the NSF check for $50.25 drawn by J. B. Ball.

The July 31 bank reconciliation for The Parkview Company follows:

THE PARKVIEW COMPANY
Bank Reconciliation
July 31, 19___

Bank statement and depositor's records must be reconciled

Balance per depositor's records, July 31, 19___			$4,172.57
Add: Note receivable collected for us by bank			500.00
			$4,672.57
Less: Service charge	$ 2.00		
NSF check of J. B. Ball	50.25		
Error on check stub no. 875	27.00	79.25	
Adjusted balance			$4,593.32
Balance per bank statement, July 31, 19___			$5,000.17
Add: Deposit of July 31 not recorded by bank			310.90
			$5,311.07
Less: Outstanding checks			
No. 801	$100.00		
No. 888	10.25		
No. 890	402.50		
No. 891	205.00	717.75	
Adjusted balance (as above)			$4,593.32

The adjusted balance of $4,593.32 is the amount of cash owned by The Parkview Company and is, therefore, the amount which should appear as cash on the July 31 balance sheet.

Note that the adjusted balance of cash differs from both the bank statement and the depositor's records. This difference is explained by the fact that neither set of records is up-to-date as of July 31, and also by the existence of an error on The Parkview Company's records.

ADJUSTING THE RECORDS AFTER THE RECONCILIATION To make The Parkview Company's records up-to-date and accurate, four journal entries affecting the Cash account are necessary for the four items that make up the difference between the $4,172.57 balance per the depositor's records and the adjusted balance of $4,593.52. These four reconciling items call for the following entries:

Cash	*500.00*	
Notes Receivable		*500.00*
To record the note receivable collected for us by the bank.		

Miscellaneous Expense	*2.00*	
Cash		*2.00*
To record the service charge by the bank.		

Accounts Receivable, J. B. Ball	*50.25*	
Cash		*50.25*
To record as a receivable from J. B. Ball the amount of the NSF check returned to us by the bank.		

Telephone Expense	*27.00*	
Cash		*27.00*
To correct the error by which check no. 875 for an $85 payment for telephone service was recorded as $58 ($85 − $58 = $27).		

Instead of making four separate journal entries affecting the Cash account, one compound journal entry can be made to record all four of the above items. The journal entry (in general journal form) is as follows:

Miscellaneous Expense	*2.00*	
Accounts Receivable, J. B. Ball	*50.25*	
Telephone Expense	*27.00*	
Cash	*420.75*	
Notes Receivable		*500.00*
To record a service charge by the bank, the return of an NSF check, the correction of an error in recording check no. 85, and the collection by the bank of a note receivable left by us for collection.		

Petty cash

As previously emphasized, adequate internal control over cash requires that all receipts be deposited in the bank and all disbursements be made by check. However, every business finds it convenient to have a small amount of cash on hand with which to make some minor expenditures. Examples include payments for postage stamps, collect telegrams, and taxi fares. Internal control over these small cash payments can best be achieved through a petty cash fund.

ESTABLISHING THE PETTY CASH FUND To create a petty cash fund, a check is written for a round amount such as $50 or $100, which will cover the small expenditures to be paid in cash for a period of two or three weeks. This check is cashed and the money kept on hand in a petty cash box or drawer in the office.

The entry for the issuance of the check is:

Creating the petty cash fund

Petty Cash	100	
Cash		100
To establish a petty cash fund.		

MAKING DISBURSEMENTS FROM THE PETTY CASH FUND As cash payments are made out of the petty cash box, the custodian of the fund is required to fill out a *petty cash voucher* for each expenditure. A petty cash voucher shows the amount paid, the purpose of the expenditure, the date, and the signature of the person receiving the money. A petty cash voucher should be prepared for every payment made from the fund. The petty cash box should, therefore, always contain cash and/or vouchers totaling the exact amount of the fund.

The petty cash custodian should be informed that occasional surprise counts of the fund will be made and that he or she is personally responsible for the fund being intact at all times. Careless handling of petty cash has often been a first step toward large thefts; consequently, misuse of petty cash funds should not be tolerated.

REPLENISHING THE PETTY CASH FUND Assume that a petty cash fund of $100 was established on June 1 and that payments totaling $89.75 were made from the fund during the next two weeks. Since the $100 originally placed in the fund is nearly exhausted, the fund should be replenished. A check is drawn payable to Petty Cash for the exact amount of the expenditures, $89.75. This check is cashed and the money placed in the petty cash box. The vouchers totaling that amount are perforated to prevent their reuse and filed in support of the replenishment check. The journal entry to record the issuance of the check will debit the expense accounts indicated by inspection of the vouchers, as follows:

Replenish-	*Postage Expense*. *60.60*	
ment of *petty cash*	*Telephone & Telegraph Expense* *4.80*	
fund	*Freight-in* *6.00*	
	Gasoline Expense *5.25*	
	Miscellaneous Expense. *13.10*	
	Cash	*89.75*

To replenish the petty cash fund.

In studying the procedures for operation of a petty cash fund, emphasis should be placed on the fact that the Petty Cash account *is debited only when the fund is first established. Expense accounts will be debited each time the fund is replenished.* There will ordinarily be no further entries in the petty cash fund after it is established, unless the fund is discontinued or a decision is made to change the size of the fund from the original $100 amount.

The petty cash fund is usually replenished at the end of an accounting period, even though the fund is not running low, so that all vouchers in the fund are charged to expense accounts before these accounts are closed and financial statements prepared. If through oversight the petty cash fund were not replenished at the end of the period, expenditures from petty cash could still be reflected in the income statement for the period in which these expenditures occurred, by an entry debiting the expense accounts and crediting Petty Cash. The result would be an unintentional reduction in the Petty Cash fund, which would presumably need to be restored in the following period.

THE VOUCHER SYSTEM

Control over expenditures

Closely related to our discussion of the control of cash transactions is the problem of ensuring that expenditures are properly authorized and that payments to liquidate liabilities are legitimate. In every business, large or small, a considerable number of expenditures must be made each month for goods and services. Handling these transactions requires such steps as the following:

1 Purchase orders or other authorization for expenditures must be given.
2 Goods and services received must be inspected and approved.
3 Invoices from suppliers must be examined for correctness of prices, extensions, shipping costs, and credit terms.
4 Checks must be issued in payment.

In a very small business it may be possible for the owner or manager to perform all these steps for every transaction. By doing this work personally, the owner may be assured that the business is getting what it pays for, and that funds are not being disbursed carelessly or fraudulently. As a business grows and the volume of daily transactions increases, it becomes impossible for the owner or manager to give personal attention to each expenditure. When this work is assigned to various employees, a well-designed accounting system is needed to guard against waste and fraud.

Some businesses take great pains to safeguard cash receipts and cash on hand, but quite inconsistently permit a number of employees to incur liabilities by ordering goods or services without any record being made of their actions. When an invoice is received, the absence of any record of the purchase makes it difficult to determine whether the invoice is a proper statement of an amount owed. In this confused situation, invoices are apt to be paid without adequate verification. The opportunity exists for a dishonest employee to collaborate with an outsider to arrange for duplicate payments of invoices, for payment of excessive prices, or for payment for goods and services never received.

Fraud is particularly likely when an employee has authority to incur expenses and to issue checks in payment as well. In larger organizations, the work of placing orders, verifying invoices, recording liabilities, and issuing checks should be divided among several employees in such a manner that the work of each person serves to prove that of the others. A chain of documentary evidence should be created for each transaction, consisting of written approvals by key employees for the phases of the transaction for which each is responsible.

One method of establishing control over the making of expenditures and the payment of liabilities is the *voucher system.* This system requires that every liability be recorded as soon as it is incurred, and that *checks be issued only in payment of approved liabilities.* A written authorization called a *voucher* is prepared for each expenditure, regardless of whether the expenditure covers services, merchandise for resale, or assets for use in the business. The voucher system is widely used, and it is particularly common in large organizations which have given serious study to the problem of internal control. Perhaps the greatest single advantage of the voucher system is the assurance that every expenditure of the business is systematically reviewed and verified before payment is made.

Essential characteristics of a voucher

A voucher (as illustrated on page 299) is attached to each incoming invoice and given an identification number.

The voucher has spaces for listing the data from the invoice and the ledger accounts to be debited and credited in recording the transaction. Space is also provided for approval signatures for each step in the verification and approval of the liability. A completed voucher provides a description of the transaction and also of the work performed in verifying

Use of
voucher
ensures
verification
of invoice

BROADHILL CORPORATION
Chicago, Illinois

Voucher No. ....241........

Pay to ....Black Company........
Date ....May 1, 19—....
........3160 Main Street........
Date due ....May 10, 19—....
........Hilldale, Indiana........

Date of invoice ....April 30, 19—....   Gross amount $ ....1,000.00....

Invoice number ....847........   Less: Cash discount ....20.00....

Net amount $ ....980.00....

Approval

	Dates	Approved by
Extensions and footings verified	May 1, 19—	R.G.
Prices in agreement with purchase order	May 1, 19—	R.G.
Quantities in agreement with receiving report	May 1, 19—	R.G.
Credit terms in agreement with purchase order	May 1, 19—	R.G.
Account distribution & recording approved	....William Cross.... (For Accounting Dept.)	
Approved for payment	....Judith Davis.... (For Treasurer's Dept.)	

Reverse
side of
voucher

Voucher No. ....241........

Account distribution

	Amount	
Purchases	$ ....1,000.00....	
Transportation-in		Date ....May 1, 19—....
Repairs		
Heat, light, and power		Date due ....May 10, 19—....
Advertising		Payee ....Black Company....
Delivery expense		....3160 Main Street....
Misc. general expense		....Hilldale, Indiana....
Telephone and telegraph		Amount of invoice $ ....1,000.00....
Sales salaries		Less: Cash discount ....20.00....
Office salaries		Net amount $ ....980.00....
		Paid by check no. ....632....
		Date of check ....May 10, 19—....
		Amount of check $ ....980.00....
Credit vouchers payable (total) $ ....1,000.00....		
Account distribution by ....KRD....		Entered in voucher register by....A.J.....

the liability and approving the cash disbursement. Regardless of the specific form of the voucher, the following features are usually present:

1 A separate voucher for every incoming invoice
2 Consecutive numbering of vouchers
3 Name and address of creditor listed on voucher

4 Description of the liability, including amount and terms of payment
5 Approval signatures for
   a Verification of invoice
   b Recording in accounts
   c Payment of liability
6 Date of check and check number listed on voucher

In preceding chapters the payment of expenses such as the monthly telephone bill was handled by an entry debiting Telephone Expense and crediting Cash. However, when a voucher system is in use the receipt and payment of the monthly telephone bill will be recorded by these entries:

1 Upon receipt of the invoice: Debit Telephone Expense; credit Vouchers Payable.
2 At time of payment: Debit Vouchers Payable; credit Cash.

These two separate entries would be made even though the bill was paid immediately upon receipt. It is fundamental to the successful operation of a voucher system that no cash payment be made except in payment of an approved and recorded voucher. Rigorous compliance with this rule gives assurance that expenditures are recorded in the proper period, and that disbursements are made only after appropriate review by the individuals responsible for the various phases in the verification of a transaction.

Voucher Register

Voucher No.	Date (19___)		Creditor	Payment Date (19___)	Check No.	Vouchers Payable, Cr	Pur- chases, Dr	Transpor- tation-in, Dr
241	May	1	Black Company	May 10	632	1,000	1,000	
242		2	Midwest Freight	3	627	50		50
243		4	Ames Company	4	628	125		
244		5	1st Natl. Bank	5	629	8,080		
245		5	Rathco, Inc.	6	631	1,200	1,200	
246		5	Midwest Freight	6	630	110		110
286		30	O. K. Supply Co.			70		
287		30	J. Jones	30	665	210		
288		30	Black Company			1,176	1,176	
289		31	Midwest Freight	31	666	90		90
290		31	Payroll	31	667	1,865		
						25,875	9,220	640
						(21)	(51)	(52)

Preparing a voucher

To illustrate the functioning of a voucher system, let us begin with the receipt of an invoice. A voucher is prepared by filling in the appropriate blanks with information taken from the invoice, such as the invoice date, invoice number, and amount, and the creditor's name and address. The voucher with invoice (and possibly receiving report) attached is then sent to the employees responsible for verifying the extensions and footings on the invoice and for comparing prices, quantities, and terms with those specified in the purchase order and receiving report. When completion of the verification process has been evidenced by approval signatures of the persons performing these steps, the voucher and supporting documents are sent to an employee of the accounting department, who indicates on the voucher the accounts to be debited and credited.

The voucher is now reviewed by an accounting official to provide assurance that the verification procedures have been satisfactorily completed and that the liability is a proper one. After receiving this executive approval, the voucher is entered in a journal called a *voucher register.*

The voucher register

The voucher register replaces the purchases journal described in Chapter 7. It may be thought of as an expanded purchases journal with additional debit columns for various types of expense and asset accounts.

Adver-tising, Dr	Sup-plies, Dr	Repairs, Dr	Accrued Payroll, Dr	Other General Ledger Accounts			
				Account Name	LP	Debit	Credit
		125					
				Notes Payable	25	8,000 ⎫	
				Interest Expense	79	80 ⎭	
	70						
		210					
			1,865				
510	470	335	3,800			10,900	
(61)	(14)	(74)	(24)			(x)	

In comparing the voucher register with a purchases journal, it should be emphasized that the purchases journal is used *only* to record purchases of merchandise on account. Consequently, every entry in a purchases journal consists of a debit to Purchases and a credit to Accounts Payable. The voucher register, on the other hand, is used to record *all types of expenditures:* for plant and equipment, expenses, and payroll as well as for purchases of merchandise. Every entry in the voucher register will consist of a credit to Vouchers Payable, but the debits may affect various asset and expense accounts. Occasionally the entry may require a debit to a liability account; for example, when a voucher is prepared to authorize the issuance of a check in payment of an existing mortgage or note payable.

A typical form of voucher register was shown on pages 300 and 301. Note that columns are provided for the voucher number, the date of entry, the name of the creditor, and the date and number of the check issued in payment. The first money column is a credit column and has the heading of Vouchers Payable; the amount of every voucher is entered in this column. All the other money columns in the voucher register are debit columns, with the exception of one credit column in the Other General Ledger Accounts section. Separate columns are provided for accounts frequently debited, such as Purchases and Transportation-in. At the extreme right of the register, a debit column and a credit column are provided for Other General Ledger Accounts, meaning accounts infrequently used for which special columns are not provided. In this section the account title must be written opposite the amount of each debit and credit. The entries in this section of the voucher register are posted individually and a ledger page (LP) column is provided in which the account number is listed when the individual posting is made.

Each voucher is entered in the voucher register in numerical order as soon as it is prepared and approved. When payment is made the number and date of the check are entered in the columns provided for this purpose. The total amount of unpaid vouchers may be determined from the register at any time merely by listing the "open" items, that is, vouchers for which no entry has yet been made in the Payment columns. The total of the unpaid vouchers appearing in the voucher register should agree with the total of the vouchers in the unpaid vouchers file at the same date.

POSTING FROM THE VOUCHER REGISTER All columns of the voucher register are totaled at the end of the month; the equality of debit and credit entries is proved by comparing the combined totals of the two credit columns with the sum of the totals of the various debit columns. After the register has been proved to be in balance, the posting to ledger accounts is begun.

The individual items listed in the Other General Ledger Accounts section are posted as debits and credits to the various accounts indicated, but the totals of these columns are not posted. The totals of the other debit columns, such as Purchases, Transportation-in, and Advertising, are posted as debits to the accounts named, and the total of the Vouchers Payable column is posted as a credit to the ledger account, Vouchers Payable. The posting of each column total is evidenced by listing the ledger account number in parentheses just below the column total in the voucher register. In the ledger accounts, the letters VR are entered to show that the posting came from the voucher register.

The balance of the general ledger account, Vouchers Payable, should be reconciled at the end of the month with the total of the unpaid vouchers shown in the voucher register and also with the total of the vouchers in the unpaid vouchers file.

PAYING THE VOUCHER WITHIN THE DISCOUNT PERIOD After the voucher has been entered in the voucher register, it is placed (with the supporting documents attached) in a tickler file according to the date of required payment. The voucher system emphasizes the required *time for payment* of liabilities rather than the identity of the creditors; for this reason, vouchers are filed by required date of payment. In computing future cash requirements of a business, the amount of a liability and the required date of payment are of basic significance; the identity of the creditor has no bearing on the problem of maintaining a proper cash position.

Cash discount periods generally run from the date of the invoice. Since a voucher is prepared for each invoice, the required date of payment is the last day on which a check can be prepared and mailed to the creditor in time to qualify for the discount.

When the payment date arrives, the voucher is removed from the unpaid file and sent to the cashier, who draws a check for signature by the treasurer. The cashier fills in the check number, amount, and date of payment on the voucher and presents the check and voucher to the treasurer. The treasurer examines the documents, especially the approval signatures, and authorizes the payment of the liability by signing the voucher in the space labeled "Approved for payment." The treasurer also signs the check and mails it to the creditor. (Note that the check does not come back into the possession of the employee who prepared it.) The voucher is forwarded to the accounting department, which will record the issuance of the check and also note in the voucher register the payment of the voucher.

The check register

A check register is merely a simplified version of the cash payments journal illustrated in Chapter 7. When a voucher system is in use, checks are issued only in payment of approved and recorded vouchers. Consequently, every check issued is recorded by a debit to Vouchers Payable and a credit to Cash. The check register therefore contains a special

Check Register

	Check No.	Date (19___)		Payee	Voucher No.	Vouchers Payable, Debit	Purchase Discounts, Credit	Cash, Credit
Checks issued only in payment of approved vouchers	627	May	3	Midwest Freight	242	50		50
	628		4	Ames Company	243	125		125
	629		5	1st National Bank	244	8,080		8,080
	630		6	Midwest Freight	246	110		110
	631		6	Rathco, Inc.	245	1,200		1,200
	632		10	Black Company	241	1,000	20	980
	665		30	J. Jones	287	210		210
	666		31	Midwest Freight	289	90		90
	667		31	Payroll	290	1,865		1,865
						23,660	240	23,420
						(21)	(53)	(1)

column for debits to Vouchers Payable and a Cash credit column. The only other money column needed in this compact record is for credits to Purchase Discounts when invoices are paid within the cash discount period. In this illustration we are assuming that the company records purchase invoices at the gross amount. Shown above is a check register with entries corresponding to the payments listed in the voucher register on pages 300 and 301.

To record the payment of a voucher, an entry is made in the check register, and a notation of the check number and date is placed on the appropriate line in the voucher register. At the end of the month the column totals of the check register are posted as for other special journals; this posting consists of a debit to the Vouchers Payable account for the total of the vouchers paid during the month, a credit to the Purchase Discounts account, and a credit to the Cash account. The symbol CkR is placed in the ledger accounts to indicate that a posting came from the check register.

ILLUSTRATION OF USE OF VOUCHER REGISTER AND CHECK REGISTER
The use of the voucher register and the check register in handling typical transactions may be further clarified by the following examples:

June 2 Paid *Morning Times* for advertising.

Voucher Register	*Check Register*

Some sample entries	Advertising Expense xxx	
	Vouchers Payable	xxx
	(Also enter check number	
	and date in Payment	
	column.)	

Vouchers Payable . xxx	
Cash	xxx

June 3 Received shipment of merchandise from Cross Company, terms 2/10, n/30.

Voucher Register		*Check Register*	
Purchases . . . . *xxx*		*(No entry until payment is made.)*	
Vouchers Payable . .	*xxx*		

June 12 Paid Cross Company invoice of June 3; took discount.

Voucher Register		*Check Register*	
(Enter check number and		Vouchers Payable . . . . . . *xxx*	
date in Payment column.)		Purchase Discounts	*xxx*
		Cash	*xxx*

June 13 Replenished petty cash fund.

Voucher Register		*Check Register*	
Various expense accounts . *xxx*		Vouchers Payable . . . . *xxx*	
Vouchers Payable . .	*xxx*	Cash	*xxx*
(Enter check number and			
date in Payment column.)			

FILING PAID VOUCHERS   After the payment has been recorded in the check register and noted in the voucher register, the paid voucher is placed in numerical order in a paid vouchers file. Many companies prepare a duplicate copy of the check and remittance advice for filing with the paid voucher. The paid vouchers file then contains a complete set of documents describing and supporting every disbursement of cash.

Special considerations of the voucher register

AS A SUBSIDIARY LEDGER   When a voucher system is used to control liabilities and cash disbursements, there is no need to maintain an accounts payable subsidiary ledger such as the one described in Chapter 7. Since the traditional form of accounts payable ledger contains a separate account with every creditor, it requires a great deal of detailed posting and recording work. The elimination of this costly subsidiary ledger is one of the major savings to be achieved by adopting a voucher system.

Each line of the voucher register represents a liability account with an individual creditor. This liability account comes into existence when an invoice is received and a voucher is prepared and recorded, describing the amount owed under the terms of that invoice. When a voucher is paid, the check number and date are entered on the line for that voucher to show that the liability is ended. Inspection of the voucher register reveals which items have not been paid. A list of unpaid vouchers corresponds to a trial balance prepared from an accounts payable subsidiary ledger.

The voucher register thus serves a dual purpose; it is primarily a journal, but it also serves as the equivalent of a subsidiary ledger of liability accounts. However, the voucher register does not classify invoices by creditors; it does not show the total amount owed to a given creditor with several invoices outstanding. Neither does it show the total purchases from a given supplier over a period of time.

HANDLING PURCHASE RETURNS AND ALLOWANCES The following example illustrates one of the several common methods for handling purchase returns and allowances under a voucher system.

Assume that on October 2 an invoice in the amount of $2,800 was received from a supplier, Barnard Company. Voucher no. 621 was prepared and recorded in the voucher register, as illustrated below. Shortly thereafter some of the merchandise was returned to Barnard Company, and on October 8 a credit memorandum for $800 was received.

A new voucher (no. 633) was prepared in the amount of $2,000, and the original voucher (no. 621 for $2,800) was canceled, marked with a reference to the replacement voucher, and placed in the paid vouchers file.

Voucher Register

	Voucher No.	Date (19___)		Creditor	Payment		Vouchers Payable, Cr
					Date (19___)	Check No.	
Note handling of purchase returns	621	Oct.	2	Barnard Co.	See vou. no. 633		2,800
	633	Oct.	8	Barnard Co.			2,000
							4,800
							(12)

Vouchers Payable (21)			
Oct. 8	2,800	Oct. 31	4,800

Purchases (51)	
Oct. 31	2,800

Purchase Returns & Allowances (53)	
	Oct. 8	800

In the voucher register the new voucher is recorded as a credit of $2,000 to Vouchers Payable in the Vouchers Payable column and as a debit of $2,800 to Vouchers Payable in the Other General Ledger Accounts section. A credit of $800 to Purchase Returns and Allowances is also recorded in the Other General Ledger Accounts section. In the Payment column of the register, a notation is entered on the line for the old voucher, "See voucher no. 633." To make this procedure clear, the illustrated voucher register on pages 306 and 307 contains only the transactions with the Barnard Company; posting to the ledger accounts is also shown.

MAKING PARTIAL PAYMENTS If it is known at the time an invoice is received that payment will be made in two or more installments, a separate voucher should be prepared for each installment. However, if the use of partial payments is decided upon after a single voucher for the entire amount of the invoice has been recorded, the original voucher should be canceled and new vouchers prepared for each expected installment payment.

CORRECTING ERRORS IN THE VOUCHER REGISTER If an error in the voucher register is discovered *before* the posting work is performed at the end of the month, the erroneous entry may be canceled by drawing a line

Purchases, Dr	Transpor- tation-in, Dr	Other General Ledger Accounts			
		Account Name	LP	Debit	Credit
2,800					
		Vouchers Payable	21	2,800	
		Purchase Returns			
		& Allowances	53		800
2,800				2,800	800
(51)				(x)	(x)

through it and a new voucher prepared and recorded. The original voucher should be marked with the word "Canceled" and a reference to the number of the replacement voucher.

If an error in the voucher register is not discovered until after the register has been posted, a general journal entry may be made to reverse the erroneous entry. A reference to the adjusting journal entry should be made in the payment column of the voucher register. A new voucher can then be prepared and recorded in the voucher register.

Presentation of the liability in the balance sheet

Although the liability account title Vouchers Payable occasionally appears on a balance sheet, it is better practice to use the more widely understood term Accounts Payable.

A "voucher system" without vouchers

One interesting variation of the system described in this chapter is to use a voucher register, but not to prepare vouchers. Invoices are assigned consecutive numbers as they are received, and entered in the voucher register, which is usually given the name of invoice register. As each invoice is verified as to quantities, prices, extensions, and other aspects of the transaction, *approvals are noted on the invoice itself.* At the time of payment, the invoice is transferred from an unpaid invoices file to a paid invoices file. The invoice register is footed and posted at the end of the month in the same manner as a voucher register. The use of a check register follows the pattern previously described, and the review of documents by executives before approving an invoice or issuing a check may correspond to the control procedures described for the voucher system.

Electronic funds transfer systems (EFTS)

Our discussion of cash transactions and bank accounts would be incomplete without mention of the many new systems for transferring funds electronically rather than by delivery of physical documents. In the banking field, for example, automated clearing houses may eliminate the need for banks to exchange bundles of customers' checks each day. If you pay your telephone bill by a check written on Bank A, the telephone company traditionally has deposited your check in its bank (Bank B). Bank B would then deliver your check and others like it to Bank A in order to collect. At the same time Bank A would be presenting a bundle of checks deposited with it but drawn on Bank B. In reality many banks, not just Bank A and Bank B, would be involved in this "clearing house" activity. Since the number of checks written each day is roughly 50 million, this exchange of paper represents a great opportunity for saving through electronic transfer of funds. Electronic equipment now exists for banks to transfer funds from the account of one depositor to the account of another among banks without all this cumbersome exchange of paper. The updating of all customers' accounts is, of course, much faster. Instead of writing checks the depositor will authorize a payment through a computer terminal.

Many other applications of electronic funds transfer are now in use. For example, a company may pay all its employees (if they agree) by delivering payroll information to its bank on magnetic tape. The bank's computer debits the employer's account and credits the bank account of each employee without any paper changing hands.

POINT-OF-SALE (POS) TERMINALS Supermarkets and other stores cash more checks than banks do. To cut down on paper work, a bank can issue plastic identification cards to its depositors. The depositor when shopping can have the store's employees use this card at a computer terminal to obtain cash or to make a deposit. The terminal is connected to the bank's computer which will approve the transaction and transfer funds immediately from the customer's account to the store's account. In the case of a deposit, the transfer would be from the store's account to the customer's account.

The further development of electronic funds transfer systems seems to be impeded more by government regulations, legislative barriers, and public attitudes than by lack of technology. A considerable portion of the public appears to be reluctant to move into a "checkless society."

KEY TERMS INTRODUCED OR EMPHASIZED IN CHAPTER 8

Bank reconciliation   A statement listing the items which make up the difference between the balance shown on the bank statement and the balance of cash according to the depositor's records.

Bank service charge   An amount deducted from a depositor's checking account by the bank to cover the expense of maintaining a checking account or for special handling of such items as NSF checks.

Bank statement   A monthly statement provided by the bank to the depositor, along with paid checks and notices of any bank charges and credits.

Cash   Currency, coins, checks, money orders, and any other medium of exchange which a bank will accept for deposit and immediate credit to the depositor's account.

Cash over and short   A ledger account used to accumulate the amounts by which actual cash receipts differ from the amount recorded on cash registers.

Cash receipts   The inflow of cash to a business.

Check register   A simplified version of the cash payments journal (see Chapter 7) used for recording cash payments when a voucher system is in use.

Deposit ticket   A form filled out by the depositor listing the checks and currency being deposited. Each check is listed separately and identified by the code number of the bank on which it is drawn.

Deposits in transit   Cash receipts which have been entered in the depositor's accounting records and mailed to the bank or left in the bank's night depository, but which reached the bank too late to be credited to the depositor's current monthly bank statement.

Electronic funds transfer system   The electronic transfer of funds from the bank account of one depositor to the account of another without the delivery of checks. Many related applications are in use to reduce paper work in cash transactions.

NSF check   A customer's check which was deposited but returned because of a lack of funds (Not Sufficient Funds) in the account on which the check was drawn.

Outstanding checks   Checks issued by a business to suppliers, employees, or other payees but not yet presented to the bank for payment.

Petty cash fund   A small amount of cash set aside for making minor cash payments for which writing of checks is not practicable.

Petty cash voucher   A document prepared for each payment made from the petty cash fund. Serves as a receipt for the expenditure.

Point-of-sale (POS) terminals   Computer terminals located in retail stores with direct access to a bank's computer. Permits store customers to pay for purchases, obtain cash, or to make deposits without making a trip to the bank.

Voucher A document prepared to authorize and describe an expenditure.

Voucher register A special journal used to record all liabilities which have been approved for payment.

Voucher system A method of controlling expenditures and the payment of liabilities. Requires that every liability be recorded as soon as it is incurred, and that checks be issued only in payment of approved liabilities.

DEMONSTRATION PROBLEM FOR YOUR REVIEW

The information listed below is available in reconciling the bank statement for the White River Company on November 30, 19____.

(1) The ledger account for Cash showed a balance at November 30 of $7,766.64, including a $100 petty cash fund. Petty cash should be transferred to a separate account. The bank statement at November 30 indicated a balance of $9,734.70.

(2) The November 30 cash receipts of $5,846.20 had been mailed to the bank on that date and did not appear among the deposits on the November bank statement. The receipts include a check for $4,000 from a brokerage house for the sale of 150 shares of stock of the Axe Co. which cost $6,270. Neither the proceeds on the sale of stock nor the collections on accounts receivable ($1,846.20) has been recorded in the accounts of the White River Company.

(3) Included with the November bank statement was an NSF check for $220 signed by a customer, James Ruddock. This amount had been charged against the bank account on November 30.

(4) Of the checks issued in November, the following were not included among the paid checks returned by the bank:

Check No.	Amount	Check No.	Amount
924	$136.25	944	$ 95.00
940	105.00	945	716.15
941	11.46	946	60.00
943	826.70		

(5) A service charge for $340 by the bank had been made in error against the White River Company account.

(6) A non-interest-bearing note receivable for $690 owned by the White River Company had been left with the bank for collection. On November 30 the company received a memorandum from the bank indicating that the note had been collected and credited to the company's account after deduction of a $5 collection charge. No entry has been made by the company to record collection of the note.

(7) A debit memorandum for $7.50 was enclosed with the paid checks at November 30. This charge covered the printing of checkbooks bearing the White River Company name and address.

Instructions

a Prepare a bank reconciliation at November 30, 19____.

b Prepare journal entries required as of November 30, 19____, to bring the company's records up to date.

SOLUTION TO DEMONSTRATION PROBLEM

a

WHITE RIVER COMPANY
Bank Reconciliation
November 30, 19___

Balance per depositor's records, Nov. 30		$ 7,766.64
Add: Proceeds on sale of stock	$4,000.00	
Collection on accounts receivable.	1,846.20	
Note receivable collected by bank, $690, less col-		
lection charge, $5	685.00	6,531.20
		$14,297.84
Less: Petty cash fund reported separately	$ 100.00	
NSF check, James Ruddock	220.00	
Charge by bank for printing checks	7.50	327.50
Adjusted balance.		$13,970.34
Balance per bank statement, Nov. 30		$ 9,734.70
Add: Deposit of Nov. 30 not recorded by bank	$5,846.20	
Service charge made by bank in error	340.00	6,186.20
		$15,920.90
Less: Outstanding checks on Nov. 30:		
No. 924	$ 136.25	
No. 940	105.00	
No. 941	11.46	
No. 943	826.70	
No. 944	95.00	
No. 945	716.15	
No. 946	60.00	1,950.56
Adjusted balance (as above)		$13,970.34

b

General Journal

19___

Nov. 30	Cash	6,531.20	
	Loss on Sale of Marketable Securities	2,270.00	
	Miscellaneous Expense	5.00	
	Investment in Marketable Securities		6,270.00
	Notes Receivable		690.00
	Accounts Receivable		1,846.20
	To record increase in Cash account as indicated by bank reconciliation.		

Nov. 30 *Petty Cash*	*100.00*	
Miscellaneous Expense	*7.50*	
Accounts Receivable, James Ruddock	*220.00*	
Cash		*327.50*

To record cash disbursements as indicated by bank rec-
onciliation and to record petty cash in a separate account.

REVIEW QUESTIONS

1 Does the expression "efficient management of cash" mean anything more than procedures to prevent losses from fraud or theft? Explain.

2 If a company has checking accounts in three banks, should it maintain a separate ledger account for each? Should the company's balance sheet show the amount on deposit in each of the three checking accounts as a separate item? Explain.

3 Mention some principles to be observed by a business in establishing strong internal control over cash receipts.

4 Explain how internal control over cash transactions is strengthened by compliance with the following rule: "Deposit each day's cash receipts intact in the bank, and make all disbursements by check."

5 List two items often encountered in reconciling a bank account which may cause cash per the bank statement to be larger than the balance of cash shown in the accounts.

6 In the reconciliation of a bank account, what reconciling items necessitate a journal entry in the depositor's accounting records?

7 Pico Stationery Shop has for years maintained a petty cash fund of $75, which is replenished twice a month.
   a How many debit entries would you expect to find in the Petty Cash account each year?
   b When would expenditures from the petty cash fund be entered in the ledger accounts?

8 A check for $455 issued in payment of an account payable was erroneously listed in the cash payments journal as $545. The error was discovered early in the following month when the paid check was returned by the bank. What corrective action is needed?

9 It is standard accounting practice to treat as cash all checks received from customers. When a customer's check is received, recorded, and deposited, but later returned by the bank marked NSF, what accounting entry or entries would be appropriate?

10 Ringo Store sells only for cash and records all sales on cash registers before delivering merchandise to the customers. On a given day the cash count at the close of business indicated $10.25 less cash than was shown by the totals on the cash register tapes. In what account would this cash shortage be recorded? Would the account be debited or credited?

11 Classify each of the numbered reconciling items listed below under one of the following headings: *(a)* an addition to the balance per depositor's records; *(b)* a deduction from the balance per depositor's records; *(c)* an addition to the balance per bank statement; *(d)* a deduction from the balance per bank statement.
   (1) Deposits in transit
   (2) Outstanding checks
   (3) Customer's check deposited but returned by bank marked NSF

(4) Bank service charges

(5) Collection by bank of note receivable left with bank for collection in behalf of depositor

12 Name three internal control practices relating to cash which would be practicable even in a small business having little opportunity for division of duties.

13 With respect to a *voucher system,* what is meant by the terms *voucher, voucher register,* and *check register?*

14 What is the greatest single advantage of the voucher system?

15 Randall Company uses a voucher system to control its cash disbursements. With respect to a purchase of merchandise, what three documents would need to be examined to verify that the voucher should be approved?

16 Assume that a company using a general journal, a cash receipts journal, a cash payments journal, a sales journal, and a purchases journal decides to adopt a voucher system. Which of the five journals would be changed or replaced? Explain.

17 In May, R Company recorded voucher no. 106 to X Company for $1,500, covering the purchase of equipment. The voucher remained unpaid at the end of May, and in June it was discovered that the invoice had been incorrectly priced; the amount should have been $1,750. Explain how this error should be straightened out in the accounting records.

18 Explain how the following would be handled in a voucher system:
  a Return of merchandise to supplier in the same month as purchase but after original invoice has been entered in voucher register.
  b Return of merchandise to supplier in the month following purchase.

19 The following column totals appear in a voucher register at the end of the month: transportation-in, $1,280; selling expense, $6,020; general expense, $4,210; vouchers payable, $61,750; accrued payroll, $15,640; purchases, $18,440; other general ledger accounts, $16,160 (notes payable, $16,000 and interest expense, $160). Prepare in general journal form an entry summarizing the voucher transactions for the month.

20 The following column totals appear in a check register at the end of the month: cash, $11,710; vouchers payable, $11,390; cash discounts not taken, $320. Prepare a general journal entry to summarize cash disbursements for the month. Explain how the company handles cash discounts on purchases.

21 Under traditional banking practices you might be able to cash a check at a retail store for more than the balance in your bank account, and then make a deposit in your bank within a day or two to "cover" the check before it was presented to your bank for payment. Would this use of "float" or hidden borrowing be possible if the store had a point-of-sale terminal and if an electronic funds transfer system was in use by banks? Explain.

EXERCISES

Ex. 8-1 At July 31 the Cash account in the ledger of Martin Company showed a balance of $27,600. The bank statement, however, showed a balance of $34,800 at the same date. If the only reconciling items consisted of a $2,400 deposit in transit, a bank service charge of $4, and 30 outstanding checks, what was the total amount of the outstanding checks?

Ex. 8-2 At the end of the month Davis Company received a bank statement showing a balance of $30,000 on deposit. Among the reconciling items were outstanding checks totaling $5,800, bank service charges of $6, a deposit in transit of $4,400, and a memorandum showing that a $2,400 note receivable owned by Davis

Company and left with the bank for collection had been collected and credited to the company's account.

a What is the adjusted amount of cash which should appear on the Davis Company's balance sheet?

b What was the balance per the depositor's records before making adjusting entries for any of the reconciling items?

Ex. 8-3 John Cross, a trusted employee of Wilson Company, found himself in personal financial difficulties and carried out the following plan to steal $1,000 from the company and to conceal his fraud.

Cross removed $1,000 in currency from the cash register. This amount represented the bulk of the cash received in over-the-counter sales during the three business days since the last bank deposit. Cross then removed a $1,000 check from the day's incoming mail; this check had been mailed in by a customer, Larry Jansen, in full payment of his account. Cross made no entry in the cash receipts journal for the $1,000 collection from Jansen but deposited the check in Wilson Company's bank account in place of the $1,000 of over-the-counter cash receipts he had stolen. In order to keep Jansen from protesting when his month-end statement reached him, Cross made a general journal entry debiting Sales Returns and Allowances and crediting Accounts Receivable—Larry Jansen. Cross posted this entry to the two general ledger accounts affected and also to Jansen's account in the subsidiary ledger for accounts receivable.

a Did these actions by Cross cause the general ledger to be out of balance or the subsidiary ledger to disagree with the control account? Explain.

b Several weaknesses in internal control apparently exist in the Wilson Company. Indicate the corrective actions needed.

Ex. 8-4 The Warren Company established a petty cash fund of $150 on June 1. On June 20 the fund was replenished for the payments made to date as shown by the following petty cash vouchers: freight-in, $9.50; postage, $46; telephone expense, $3.20; repairs, $31.70; miscellaneous expense, $22. Prepare journal entries in general journal form to record the establishment of the fund on June 1 and its replenishment on June 20.

Ex. 8-5 Cheviot Company maintains a petty cash fund of $400. At December 31, the end of the company's fiscal year, the fund contained the following:

Currency and coins	$278.82
Expense vouchers:	
Flowers for funeral of deceased customer	20.80
Box of cigars for purchasing agent of the Powell Co.	14.18
Office supplies expense	46.20
Salary advance to employee	40.00
Total	$400.00

a Since there is a substantial amount of cash in the petty cash fund, is there any reason to replenish it at December 31? Explain.

b Prepare the entry (in general journal form) to replenish the petty cash fund.

Ex. 8-6 Mable Company uses a voucher system. You are to record the following transactions in **general journal form** (without explanations). Also indicate after each entry the journal in which the transaction would in practice be recorded.

(*a*) Voucher no. 100 prepared to purchase office equipment at cost of $6,000 from Franklin Textile Co.

(*b*) Check no. 114 issued in payment of voucher no. 100.

(*c*) Voucher no. 101 prepared to establish a petty cash fund of $225.

(*d*) Check no. 115 issued in payment of voucher no. 101.

(*e*) Voucher no. 102 prepared to replenish the petty cash fund which contained

$60 cash, and receipts for postage $57, miscellaneous expense $81, and delivery service $27.

(f) Check no. 116 issued in payment of voucher no. 102. Check cashed and proceeds placed in petty cash fund.

PROBLEMS

Group A

8A-1 The information necessary for preparing a bank reconciliation for Blue Marlin Company at November 30, 19____, appears below.

(1) As of November 30, cash per the accounting records was $16,248; per bank statement $13,877.

(2) Cash receipts of $3,122 on November 30 were not deposited until December 1.

(3) Among the paid checks returned by the bank was a stolen check for $504 paid in error by the bank after Blue Marlin Company had issued a "stop payment" order to the bank.

(4) The following memoranda accompanied the bank statement:
   (a) A debit memo for service charges for the month of November, $7.
   (b) A debit memo attached to a $389 check of Frank Miller, marked NSF.

(5) The following checks had been issued but were not included in the canceled checks returned by the bank: no. 921 for $782, no. 924 for $482, and no. 925 for $387.

Instructions Prepare a bank reconciliation for Blue Marlin Company at November 30, 19____, in the form illustrated on page 294.

8A-2 Lakeside Company reports the following information concerning cash balances and cash transactions for the month of September.

(1) Cash balance per bank statement as of September 30 was $8,793.25.

(2) Two debit memoranda accompanied the bank statement: one for $4 was for service charges for the month; the other for $64.60 was attached to an NSF check from A. Jones.

(3) The paid checks returned with the September bank statement disclosed two errors in the cash records. Check no. 832 for $456.30 had been erroneously recorded as $465.30 in the cash payments journal, and check no. 851 for $77.44 had been recorded as $44.77. Check no. 832 was issued in payment for a store display counter; check no. 851 was for telephone expense.

(4) A collection charge for $126.00 (not applicable to Lakeside Company) was erroneously deducted from the account by the bank.

(5) Cash receipts of September 30 amounting to $585.25 were mailed to the bank too late to be included in the September bank statement.

(6) Checks outstanding as of September 30 were as follows: no. 860 for $151.93, no. 867 for $82.46, and no. 869 for $123.61.

(7) The Cash account showed the following entries during September:

				Cash					*111*
Sept.	*1*	Balance		*6,341.82*	Sept.	*30*		CD7	*11,514.63*
	30		CR5	*14,411.58*					

Instructions
a Prepare a bank reconciliation at September 30.
b Prepare the necessary adjusting entries in general journal form.

8A-3 The cash transactions and cash balances of The Blueprinters for July were as follows:

(1) The ledger account for Cash showed a balance at June 30 of $12,301.65.

(2) The cash receipts journal for July showed total cash received of $45,216.18.

(3) The credit to the Cash account posted from the cash payments journal at July 31 was $35,750.88.

(4) The cash received on July 31 amounted to $4,017.15. It was left at the bank in the night depository chute after banking hours on July 31 and was therefore not recorded by the bank on the July statement.

(5) The July bank statement showed a closing balance of $23,928.12.

(6) Also included with the July bank statement was a debit memorandum from the bank for $7.65 representing service charges for July.

(7) A credit memorandum enclosed with the July bank statement indicated that a non-interest-bearing note receivable for $4,545 from Rene Manes, left with the bank for collection, had been collected and the proceeds credited to the account of The Blueprinters.

(8) Comparison of the paid checks returned by the bank with the entries in the cash payments journal revealed that check no. 821 for $835.02 issued July 15 in payment for office equipment had been erroneously entered in the cash payments journal as $853.02.

(9) Examination of the paid checks also revealed that three checks, all issued in July, had not yet been paid by the bank: no. 811 for $861.12; no. 814 for $640.80; no. 823 for $301.05.

(10) Included with the July bank statement was a $180 check drawn by Howard Williams, a customer of The Blueprinters. This check was marked NSF. It had been included in the deposit of July 27 but had been charged back against the company's account on July 31.

Instructions

a Prepare a bank reconciliation for The Blueprinters at July 31. (Suggestion: As a first step compute the cash balance per the accounting records at July 31.)

b Prepare journal entries (in general journal form) to adjust the accounts at July 31. Assume that the accounts have not been closed.

c State the amount of cash which should appear on the balance sheet at July 31.

8A-4 Augusta National Company maintains a petty cash fund to control small cash expenditures. The company does not use a voucher system. The operation of the fund during September, the last month of the company's fiscal year, is shown below.

Sept. 1 A check for $660 was issued and cashed to establish a petty cash fund.

Sept. 22 A count of the fund showed petty cash vouchers and cash on hand as follows:

Office supplies expense	$100.43
Postage expense	73.92
Telephone and telegraph expense	23.10
Miscellaneous expense	66.44
Currency and coin	396.11

In view of the fact that the fund was less than half depleted after the first three weeks, management decided to reduce the fund permanently to the amount of $440. A check was issued in the amount necessary to replenish the fund and establish it at the new authorized level.

Sept. 30 At September 30 the fund comprised the following items. However, through oversight, the fund was not replenished.

Office supplies expense	$ 79.20
Postage expense	105.60

Telephone and telegraph expense	**27.50**
Miscellaneous expense	**75.24**
Currency and coin	**152.46**

Instructions
a Prepare entries in general journal form to record the above information. Include an entry at September 30 to record the expenditures to that date even though the fund was not replenished.
b What is the amount of the asset account, Petty Cash, at the close of business on September 30? Explain the circumstances which led to this balance, and indicate the action management will probably take early in the next fiscal year.

8A-5 Cash payments made by Glacier Company are controlled through the use of a voucher system. Selected transactions from the current month's operation are shown below.
   (*1*) Issued a check to replenish the petty cash fund. All the expenditures from petty cash are chargeable to the Miscellaneous Expense account.
   (*2*) Purchased equipment from S Company on 30-day open account.
   (*3*) Made a partial payment on the equipment purchased from S Company, and gave a six-month note for the balance.
   (*4*) Paid S Company note plus accrued interest.
   (*5*) Purchased merchandise from T Company, terms net 60 days.
   (*6*) Purchased merchandise from P Company, terms 2/10, n/30, and paid invoice within 10 days.
   (*7*) Received credit memorandum from P Company for the cost of merchandise returned after invoice had been paid. Glacier Company will treat this as an account receivable from P Company.

Instructions Following the format shown in the following example, indicate how the transactions given above would be recorded by the company.

Example Purchased supplies from X Company; paid invoice in full.

Voucher Register	*Check Register*	*General Journal*
Supplies on Hand . . . . . *xx*	*Vouchers Payable* . *xx*	*No entry*
Vouchers Payable . *xx*	*Cash* . . . . . *xx*	
Enter check number and		
date of payment.		

8A-6 The cash receipts journal and the cash payments journal maintained by Sun Valley Company showed transactions during September as listed on page 318. On October 1, Sun Valley Company received from its bank a bank statement covering the month of September. Enclosed with the bank statement were 23 checks paid by the bank during September and a $4.25 debit memorandum for service charges. The September bank statement appears on page 319.

Instructions
a Prepare a bank reconciliation at September 30. (The balance of the general ledger account for Cash at August 31 was in agreement with the ending balance shown on the bank statement for August.)
b Prepare a general journal entry to adjust the Cash account at September 30.

Cash Receipts				Cash Payments			
Date		**Cash Dr**		**Date**		**Ck. No.**	**Cash Cr**
Sept.	1	72.80		Sept.	1	65	130.00
	3	361.00			1	66	90.00
	6	280.00			1	67	35.48
	8	510.00			2	68	31.15
	10	205.60			4	69	60.00
	13	180.14			4	70	70.00
	15	345.00			5	71	515.00
	17	427.50			9	72	62.50
	20	90.00			10	73	13.30
	22	360.00			10	74	28.00
	24	625.00			13	75	650.00
	27	130.25			19	76	125.06
	29	280.50			19	77	40.00
	30	315.25			19	78	85.00
		4,183.04			20	79	24.10
					21	80	38.60
					22	81	65.00
					22	82	162.40
					23	83	150.00
					26	84	15.00
					28	85	270.00
					28	86	105.20
					28	87	225.00
					28	88	355.00
					30	89	25.00
					30	90	45.00
					30	91	155.00
							3,570.79

SUN VALLEY COMPANY
4200 Badger Road
Sun Valley, California

THE FIRST NATIONAL BANK
OF SUN VALLEY

Vouchers Returned   24

Checks			Deposits	Date	Balance
				Sept. 1	7,658.75
31.15	35.48	130.00	72.80	Sept. 2	7,534.92
60.00			361.00	Sept. 5	7,835.92
70.00	515.00		280.00	Sept. 7	7,530.92
90.00				Sept. 8	7,440.92
13.30	62.50		510.00	Sept. 9	7,875.12
28.00			205.60	Sept. 12	8,052.72
650.00			180.14	Sept. 14	7,582.86
			345.00	Sept. 16	7,927.86
85.00			427.50	Sept. 19	8,270.36
24.10	125.06			Sept. 20	8,121.20
40.00	65.00		90.00	Sept. 21	8,106.20
162.40			360.00	Sept. 23	8,303.80
15.00			625.00	Sept. 26	8,913.80
355.00	270.00	225.00	130.25	Sept. 28	8,194.05
155.00	25.00	4.25S	280.50	Sept. 30	8,290.30

Group B

8B-1 Prepare a bank reconciliation for Tavern Company at July 31, 19___, from the information listed below. Use the form of reconciliation illustrated on page 294.
  (1) Cash per the accounting records at July 31 amounted to $29,834; the bank statement at this date showed a balance of $25,684.
  (2) The cash receipts of $5,464 on July 31 were mailed to the bank but not received by the bank during July.
  (3) The paid checks returned by the bank included a stolen check for $882 which had been paid in error by the bank after the Tavern Company had issued a "stop payment" order to the bank.
  (4) The following memoranda accompanied the bank statement:
    (a) A debit memo of $13 for service charges for July.
    (b) A debit memo attached to a $680 check of a customer, Albert Davis, marked NSF.
  (5) The following checks had been issued by Tavern Company but were not included among the paid checks returned by the bank: no. 167 for $1,369, no. 174 for $844, and no. 179 for $676.
8B-2 Information necessary for the preparation of a bank reconciliation and related journal entries for the Twin Peaks Company at March 31 is listed below.
  (1) The balance per records of the Twin Peaks Company is $16,604.02.
  (2) The bank statement shows a balance of $20,638.29 as of March 31.
  (3) Accompanying the bank statement was a check of Dale Tegard for $186.00, which was marked NSF by the bank.

(4) Checks outstanding as of March 31 were as follows: no. 84 for $1,841.02; no. 88 for $1,323.00; no. 89 for $16.26.
(5) Also accompanying the bank statement was a debit memorandum for $44.80 for safe deposit box rent; the bank had erroneously charged this item to the account of the Twin Peaks Company.
(6) On March 29, the bank collected a non-interest-bearing note for Twin Peaks Company. The note was for $2,963; the bank charged a collection fee of $8.40.
(7) A deposit of $2,008.50 was in transit; it had been mailed to the bank on March 31.
(8) In recording a $160 check received on account from a customer, Ross Company, the accountant for the Twin Peaks Company erroneously listed the collection in the cash receipts journal as $16. The check appeared correctly among the deposits on the March bank statement.
(9) The bank service charge for March amounted to $5.31; a debit memo in this amount was returned with the bank statement.

Instructions
a Prepare a bank reconciliation at March 31.
b Prepare the necessary journal entries.

8B-3 The cash transactions and cash balances of Fairway Equipment for April, 19____, are summarized below.
(1) As of April 30, cash per accounting records was $7,059.12; per bank statement, $6,678.67.
(2) Cash receipts of $2,187.03 on April 30 were not deposited until May 1.
(3) The following memoranda accompanied the bank statement:
　(a) A debit memo for service charges for the month of April, $7.56.
　(b) A debit memo attached to a check of G. Herron, marked NSF, for $149.88.
　(c) A credit memo for $1,452, representing the proceeds of a non-interest-bearing note collected by the bank for Fairway Equipment. The note was for $1,464; the bank deducted a collection fee of $12.
(4) The following checks had been issued but were not included in the canceled checks returned by the bank: no. 348 for $302.40, no. 351 for $124.32, and no. 356 for $85.30.

Instructions
a Prepare a bank reconciliation as of April 30.
b Draft in general journal form the journal entries necessary to adjust the accounts.
c State the amount of cash which should appear in the balance sheet at April 30.

8B-4 In order to handle small cash disbursements in an efficient manner, Greensboro Company established a petty cash fund on July 1, 19____. Greensboro Company does not use a voucher system. The following transactions occurred relating to petty cash.
July 1 A check for $250 was issued and cashed to establish a petty cash fund.
July 15 The fund was replenished after a count which revealed the following cash and petty cash vouchers for disbursements:

Office supplies expense	$39.25
Postage expense	65.00
Travel expense	78.12
Miscellaneous expense	21.00
Telephone and telegraph expense	31.75
Currency and coin	14.88

July 31 A count of the fund at month-end disclosed the following:

Office supplies expense	*$59.40*
Postage expense	*60.00*
Travel expense	*59.38*
Miscellaneous expense	*40.62*
Currency and coin	*30.60*

A check was issued on July 31 to replenish the petty cash fund and to increase the amount of the fund to $375.

Instructions
a Prepare entries in general journal form to record the above transactions.
b Explain why the petty cash fund should be replenished at the end of the accounting period even though the fund contains considerable cash.

8B-5 A voucher system is used by Summit Corporation to record and control its expenditures. A few of the transactions for October are presented below. At September 30, just prior to the listed transactions, one voucher, no. D99, was outstanding.
  (1) Issued a 90-day, 8% note payable in settlement of voucher no. D99.
  (2) Drew a check to establish a petty cash fund.
  (3) Paid a note, plus accrued interest, to Uptown Bank.
  (4) Purchased merchandise from M Company, terms 2/15, n/30.
  (5) Purchased equipment, making a down payment and agreeing to pay the balance in 60 days.
  (6) Received a credit memorandum from M Company for the return of a portion of the merchandise purchased from them.
  (7) Made several small cash payments from the petty cash fund; all are chargeable to Office Expense.
  (8) Advanced (by check) travel expenses to officer making a business trip.
  (9) Paid invoice from M Company, taking the discount.
  (10) Reimbursed officer by check for trip expenses incurred by him in excess of the amount advanced.
  (11) Drew check to reimburse petty cash fund for office expenses and delivery expenses.

Instructions Using the format illustrated in the example below, indicate how the transactions would be recorded by the company in the voucher register, the check register, and the general journal.

Example Purchased supplies from X Company; paid invoice in full.

Voucher Register	*Check Register*	*General Journal*
Supplies on Hand . . . . . *xx*	*Vouchers Payable* .*xx*	*No entry*
Vouchers Payable . *xx*	*Cash* . . . . . *xx*	
Enter check number and date of		
payment.		

8B-6 Grandview Company had never given much attention to internal control concepts and the internal controls over cash transactions were not adequate. Lee Merril, the cashier-bookkeeper, handled cash receipts, made small disbursements from the cash receipts, maintained accounting records, and prepared the monthly reconciliations of the bank account.
    At April 30, the statement received from the bank showed a balance on deposit of $30,510. The outstanding checks were as follows: no. 7062 for $371.16, no. 7183 for $306, no. 7284 for $470.61, no. 8621 for $315.34, no. 8623 for $613.80, and no. 8632 for $311.04. The balance of cash shown by the Grandview Company ledger account for Cash was $35,474.96, which included the cash on hand. The

bank statement for April showed a credit of $360 arising from the collection of a note left with the bank; the company's accounts did not include an entry to record this collection.

Recognizing the weakness existing in internal control over cash transactions, Merril removed all the cash on hand in excess of $6,025.14, and then prepared the following reconciliation in an attempt to conceal this theft.

Balance per accounting records, Apr. 30		*$35,474.96*
Add: Outstanding checks:		
No. 8621	*$315.34*	
No. 8623	*613.80*	
No. 8632	*311.04*	*1,060.18*
		$36,535.14
Less: Cash on hand		*6,025.14*
Balance per bank statement, Apr. 30		*$30,510.00*
Less: Unrecorded credit		*360.00*
True cash, Apr. 30		*$30,150.00*

Instructions

a Determine how much cash Merril took and explain how he attempted to conceal his theft. Prepare a bank reconciliation in a form which first shows the balance per the accounting records after adding the cash from collection of the note and, second, shows an adjusted bank balance after deducting the proper amount for all outstanding checks. The two adjusted balances will not agree; the difference is the amount of undeposited cash which should be on hand. Comparison of the undeposited cash which should be on hand with the actual amount on hand of $6,025.14 will indicate the amount of the cash shortage.

b Suggest some specific internal control devices for the Grandview Company.

BUSINESS DECISION PROBLEM 8

John Pigeon inherited a highly successful business, Rock Corporation, shortly after his twenty-second birthday and took over the active management of the business. A portion of the company's business consisted of over-the-counter sales for cash, but most sales were on credit and were shipped by truck. Pigeon had no knowledge of internal control practices and relied implicitly upon the bookkeeper-cashier, J. K. Wiley, in all matters relating to cash and accounting records. Wiley had been with the company for many years. He maintained the accounting records and prepared all financial statements with the help of two assistants, made bank deposits, signed checks, and prepared bank reconciliations.

The monthly income statements submitted to Pigeon by Wiley showed a very satisfactory rate of net income; however, the amount of cash in the bank declined steadily during the first 18 months after Pigeon took over the business. To meet the company's weakening cash position, a bank loan was obtained and a few months later when the cash position again grew critical, the loan was increased.

On April 1, two years after Pigeon assumed the management of the company, Wiley suddenly left town, leaving no forwarding address. Pigeon was immediately deluged with claims of creditors who stated their accounts were several months past due and that Wiley had promised all debts would be paid by April 1. The bank telephoned to notify Pigeon that the company's account was overdrawn and that a number of checks had just been presented for payment.

In an effort to get together some cash to meet this emergency, Pigeon called on two of the largest customers of the company, to whom substantial sales on account had recently been made, and asked if they could pay their accounts at once. Both customers informed him that their accounts were paid in full. They produced paid checks to substantiate their payments and explained that Wiley had offered them reduced prices on merchandise if they would pay within 24 hours after delivery.

To keep the business from insolvency, Pigeon agreed to sell at a bargain price a half interest in the company. The sale was made to Roger Smith, who had had considerable experience in the industry. One condition for the sale was that Smith should become the general manager of the business. The cash investment by Smith for his half interest was sufficient for the company to meet the demands on it and continue operations.

Immediately after Smith entered the business, he launched an investigation of Wiley's activities. During the course of this investigation the following irregularities were disclosed:

(1) During the last few months of Wiley's employment with the company, bank deposits were much smaller than the cash receipts. Wiley had abstracted most of the receipts and substituted for them a number of worthless checks bearing fictitious signatures. These checks had been accumulated in an envelope marked "Cash Receipts—For Deposit Only."

(2) Numerous legitimate sales of merchandise on account had been charged to fictitious customers. When the actual customer later made payment for the goods, Wiley abstracted the check or cash and made no entry. The account receivable with the fictitious customer remained in the records.

(3) When checks were received from customers in payment of their accounts, Wiley had frequently recorded the transaction by debiting an expense account and crediting Accounts Receivable. In such cases Wiley had removed from the cash receipts an equivalent amount of currency, thus substituting the check for the currency and causing the bank deposit to agree with the recorded cash receipts.

(4) More than $3,000 a month had been stolen from petty cash. Fraudulent petty cash vouchers, mostly charged to the Purchases account, had been created to conceal these thefts and to support the checks cashed to replenish the petty cash fund.

(5) For many sales made over the counter, Wiley had recorded lesser amounts on the cash register or had not rung up any amount. He had abstracted the funds received but not recorded.

(6) To produce income statements that showed profitable operations, Wiley had recorded many fictitious sales. The recorded accounts receivable included many from nonexistent customers.

(7) In preparing bank reconciliations, Wiley had omitted many outstanding checks, thus concealing the fact that the cash in the bank was less than the amount shown by the ledger.

(8) Inventory had been recorded at inflated amounts in order to increase reported profits from the business.

Instructions

a For each of the numbered paragraphs, describe one or more internal control procedures you would recommend to prevent the occurrence of such fraud.

b Apart from specific internal controls over cash and other accounts, what general precaution could John Pigeon have taken to assure himself that the accounting records were properly maintained and the company's financial statements complete and dependable? Explain fully.

9 Receivables and Payables

One of the key factors underlying the tremendous expansion of the American economy has been the trend toward selling all types of goods and services on credit. The automobile industry has long been the classic example of the use of retail credit to achieve the efficiencies of large-scale output. Today, however, in nearly every field of retail trade it appears that sales and profits can be increased by granting customers the privilege of making payment a month or more after the date of sale. The sales of manufacturers and wholesalers are made on credit to an even greater extent than in retail trade.

ACCOUNTS RECEIVABLE

The credit department

No business concern wants to sell on credit to a customer who will prove unable or unwilling to pay his or her account. Consequently, most business organizations include a credit department which must reach a decision on the credit worthiness of each prospective customer. The credit department investigates the debt-paying ability and credit record of each new customer and determines the maximum amount of credit to be extended.

If the prospective customer is a business concern as, for example, a retail store, the financial statements of the store will be obtained and analyzed to determine its financial strength and the trend of operating results. The credit department will always prefer to rely upon financial statements which have been audited by certified public accountants.

Regardless of whether the prospective customer is a business concern or an individual consumer, the investigation by the credit department will probably include the obtaining of a credit report from a local credit agency or from a national credit-rating institution such as Dun & Bradstreet, Inc. A credit agency compiles credit data on individuals and business concerns, and distributes this information to its clients. Most companies that make numerous sales on credit find it worthwhile to subscribe to the services of one or more credit agencies.

Uncollectible accounts

A business that sells its goods or services on credit will inevitably find that some of its accounts receivable are uncollectible. Regardless of how thoroughly the credit department investigates prospective customers, some uncollectible accounts will arise as a result of errors in judgment or because of unanticipated developments. As a matter of fact, a limited amount of uncollectible accounts is evidence of a sound credit policy. If the credit department should become too cautious and conservative in rating customers, it might avoid all credit losses but, in so doing, lose profitable business by rejecting many acceptable accounts.

Reflecting uncollectible accounts in the financial statements

One of the most fundamental principles of accounting is that *revenue must be matched with the expenses incurred in securing that revenue.*

Uncollectible accounts expense is caused by selling goods on credit to customers who fail to pay their bills; such expenses, therefore, are incurred in the year in which the sales are made, even though the accounts are not determined to be uncollectible until the following year. An account receivable which originates from a sale on credit in the year 1979 and is determined to be uncollectible sometime during 1980 represents an expense of the year 1979. Unless each year's uncollectible accounts expense is *estimated* and reflected in the year-end balance sheet and income statement, both of these financial statements will be seriously deficient.

To illustrate, let us assume that Arlington Corporation began business on January 1, 1979, and made most of its sales on credit throughout the year. At December 31, 1979, accounts receivable amounted to $200,000. On this date the management reviewed the status of the accounts receivable, giving particular study to accounts which were past due. This review indicated that the collectible portion of the $200,000 of accounts receivable amounted to approximately $190,000. In other words, management estimated that uncollectible accounts expense for the first year of operations amounted to $10,000. The following adjusting entry should be made at December 31, 1979:

Uncollectible Accounts Expense	10,000	
Allowance for Doubtful Accounts		10,000
To record the estimated uncollectible accounts expense for the year 1979.		

The Uncollectible Accounts Expense account created by the debit part of this entry is closed into the Income Summary account in the same manner as any other expense account. The Allowance for Doubtful Accounts which was credited in the above journal entry will appear in the balance sheet as a deduction from the face amount of the accounts receivable. It serves to reduce the accounts receivable to their *realizable value* in the balance sheet, as shown by the following illustration:

ARLINGTON CORPORATION
Partial Balance Sheet
December 31, 1979

Assets

Current assets:		
Cash		$ 75,000
Accounts receivable	$200,000	
Less: Allowance for doubtful accounts	10,000	190,000
Inventory		100,000
Total current assets		$365,000

The allowance for doubtful accounts

There is no way of telling in advance which accounts receivable will be collected and which ones will prove to be worthless. It is therefore not possible to credit the account of any particular customer to reflect our overall estimate of the year's credit losses. Neither is it possible to credit the Accounts Receivable control account in the general ledger. If the Accounts Receivable control account were to be credited with the estimated amount of uncollectible accounts, this control account would no longer be in balance with the total of the numerous customers' accounts in the subsidiary ledger. The only practicable alternative, therefore, is to credit a separate account called Allowance for Doubtful Accounts with the amount estimated to be uncollectible.

In the preceding chapters accounts have repeatedly been classified into five groups: (1) assets, (2) liabilities, (3) owner's equity, (4) revenue, and (5) expense. In which of these five groups of accounts does the Allowance for Doubtful Accounts belong? The answer is indicated by the position of the Allowance for Doubtful Accounts on the balance sheet. It appears among the assets and is used to reduce an asset (Accounts Receivable) from a gross value to a net realizable value. From the standpoint of account classification, the Allowance for Doubtful Accounts is, therefore, included in the asset category.

The Allowance for Doubtful Accounts is sometimes described as a **contra-asset** account, an **offset** account, an **asset reduction** account, a **negative asset** account, and most frequently of all, a **valuation** account. All these terms are derived from the fact that the Allowance for Doubtful Accounts is an account with a credit balance, which is offset against an asset account to produce the proper balance sheet value for an asset.

Alternative titles for the Allowance for Doubtful Accounts are Allowance for Bad Debts and Allowance for Uncollectible Accounts. Bad Debts Expense is also commonly used as an alternative title for Uncollectible Accounts Expense.

Other valuation accounts

The Allowance for Doubtful Accounts has a good deal in common with the Accumulated Depreciation (or Allowance for Depreciation) account, which appears on the balance sheet as a deduction from depreciable asset accounts such as buildings or office equipment. Both the Allowance for Doubtful Accounts and the Accumulated Depreciation account are created by adjusting entries and are based on estimates rather than on precisely determined amounts. In each case the debit side of the adjusting entry affects an expense account (Uncollectible Accounts Expense or Depreciation Expense).

In some respects, however, these two valuation accounts perform quite different functions. The Allowance for Doubtful Accounts serves to reduce the accounts receivable to net realizable value. The Accumulated Depreciation account is **not** intended to reduce the building to realizable value but merely to show what portion of the original cost has expired and has been recorded as expense. Realizable value is not a significant concept in accounting for plant and equipment, because these properties are not intended to be sold but are to be used in the operation of the business.

Estimating uncollectible accounts expense

Before the accounts are closed and financial statements are prepared at the end of the accounting period, an estimate of uncollectible accounts expense must be made. This estimate will usually be based upon past experience, perhaps modified in accordance with current business conditions.

Since the allowance for doubtful accounts is necessarily an estimate and not a precise calculation, the factor of personal judgment may play a considerable part in determining the size of this valuation account.

There is a fairly wide range of reasonableness within which the amount may be set. Most companies intend that the allowance shall be adequate to cover probable losses. The term *adequate,* when used in this context, suggests an amount somewhat larger than the minimum probable amount.

CONSERVATISM AS A FACTOR IN VALUING ACCOUNTS RECEIVABLE The larger the allowance established for doubtful accounts, the lower the net valuation of accounts receivable will be. Some accountants and some business executives tend to favor the most conservative valuation of assets that logically can be supported. Accountants necessarily make decisions under conditions of uncertainty. Conservatism in the preparation of a balance sheet implies a tendency to resolve uncertainties in the valuation of assets by reporting assets at the lower end of the range of reasonable values rather than by establishing values in a purely objective manner. From a theoretical point of view, the doctrine of balance sheet conservatism is difficult to support, but from the viewpoint of bankers and others who use financial statements as a basis for granting loans, conservatism in valuing assets has long been regarded as a desirable policy.

In considering the argument for balance sheet conservatism, it is important to recognize that the income statement is also affected by the estimates made of uncollectible accounts expense. The act of providing a relatively large allowance for uncollectible accounts involves a correspondingly heavy charge to expense. Setting asset values at a minimum in the balance sheet has the related effect of stating the current year's net income at a minimum amount.

Assume that the balance sheet of Company A presents optimistic, exaggerated values for the assets owned. Assume also that this "unconservative" balance sheet is submitted to a banker in support of an application for a loan. The banker studies the balance sheet and makes a loan to Company A in reliance upon the values listed. Later the banker finds it impossible to collect the loan and also finds that the assets upon which he had based the loan were greatly overstated in the balance sheet. The banker will undoubtedly consider the overly optimistic character of the balance sheet as partially responsible for the loss. Experiences of this type have led bankers as a group to stress the desirability of conservatism in the valuation of assets.

In considering the argument for balance sheet conservatism, it is important to recognize that the income statement is also affected by the estimates made of uncollectible accounts expense. The act of providing a relatively large allowance for uncollectible accounts involves a correspondingly heavy charge to expense. Setting asset values at a minimum in the balance sheet has the related effect of stating the current year's net income at a minimum amount.

Two methods of estimating uncollectible accounts expense

The provision for uncollectible accounts is an estimate of expense to be sustained. Two alternative approaches are widely used in making the annual estimate for uncollectible accounts. One method consists of adjusting the valuation account to a new balance equal to the estimated uncollectible portion of the existing accounts receivable. This method is referred to as the **balance sheet** approach and rests on an **aging of the accounts receivable.** The adjusting entry takes into consideration the existing balance in the Allowance for Doubtful Accounts.

The alternative method requires an adjusting entry computed as a percentage of the year's net sales. This method may be regarded as the **income statement** approach to estimating uncollectible accounts. This **percentage of sales** method emphasizes the expense side of the adjustment and leaves out of consideration any existing balance in the valuation account. If any substantial balance should accumulate in the allowance account, however, a change in the percentage figure being applied to sales might be appropriate. These two methods are explained below.

AGING THE ACCOUNTS RECEIVABLE A past-due account is always viewed with some suspicion. The fact that an account is past due suggests that the customer is either unable or unwilling to pay. The analysis of accounts by age is known as aging the accounts, as illustrated by the schedule below.

Analysis of Accounts Receivable by Age

December 31, 19____

	Customer	Total	Not Yet Due	1–30 Days Past Due	31–60 Days Past Due	61–90 Days Past Due	Over 90 Days Past Due
If you	A. B. Adams	$ 500	$ 500				
were credit	B. L. Baker	150			$ 150		
man-	R. D. Carl	800	800				
ager . . . ?	H. V. Davis	900				$ 800	$ 100
	R. M. Evans	400	400				
	Others	32,250	16,300	$10,000	4,200	200	1,550
	Totals	$35,000	$18,000	$10,000	$4,350	$1,000	$1,650
	Percentage	100	51	29	12	3	5

This analysis of accounts receivable gives management a useful picture of the status of collections and the probabilities of credit losses. Almost half of the total accounts receivable are past due. The question "How long past due?" is pertinent, and is answered by the bottom line of the aging analysis. About 29% of the total receivables are past due from 1 to 30 days; another 12% are past due from 31 to 60 days; about 3% are past due from 61 to 90 days; and 5% of the total receivables consist of accounts past due more than three months. If an analysis of this type is prepared at the end of each month, management will be continuously informed of the trend of collections and can take appropriate action to ease or tighten credit policy. Moreover a yardstick is available to measure the effectiveness of the persons responsible for collection activities.

The further past due an account receivable becomes, the greater the likelihood that it will not be collected in full. In recognition of this principle, the analysis of receivables by age groups can be used as a stepping-stone in determining a reasonable amount to add to the Allowance for Doubtful Accounts. To make this determination it is desirable to estimate the percentage of probable expense for each age group of accounts receivable. This percentage, when applied to the dollar amount in each age group, gives a probable expense for each group. By adding together the probable expense for all the age groups, the required balance in the Allowance for Doubtful Accounts is determined. The following schedule lists the group totals from the preceding illustration and shows how the total probable expense from uncollectible accounts is computed.

Accounts Receivable by Age Groups

		Amount	*Percentage Considered Uncollectible*	*Allowance for Doubtful Accounts*
Estimate of probable uncollectible accounts expense	Not yet due	*$18,000*	*1*	*$ 180*
	1–30 days past due	*10,000*	*3*	*300*
	31–60 days past due	*4,350*	*10*	*435*
	61–90 days past due	*1,000*	*20*	*200*
	Over 90 days past due	*1,650*	*50*	*825*
	Totals	*$35,000*		*$1,940*

This summary indicates that an allowance for doubtful accounts of $1,940 is required. Before making the adjusting entry, it is necessary to consider the existing balance in the allowance account. If the Allowance for Doubtful Accounts presently has a credit balance of, say, $500, the adjusting entry should be for $1,440 in order to bring the account up to the required balance of $1,940. This entry is as follows:

Increasing allowance for doubtful accounts	*Uncollectible Accounts Expense . . . .*	*1,440*	
	Allowance for Doubtful Accounts		*1,440*

To increase the valuation account to the estimated
probable expense of $1,940, computed as follows:

Present credit balance of valuation account	*$ 500*
Current provision for doubtful accounts	*1,440*
New credit balance in valuation account	*$1,940*

On the other hand, if the Allowance for Doubtful Accounts contained a *debit* balance of $500 before adjustment, the adjusting entry would be made in the amount of $2,440 ($1,940 + $500) in order to create the desired credit balance of $1,940.

ESTIMATING UNCOLLECTIBLE ACCOUNTS AS A PERCENTAGE OF NET SALES An alternative approach to providing for uncollectible accounts preferred by some companies consists of computing the charge to uncollectible accounts expense as a percentage of the net sales for the year. The question to be answered is not "How large a valuation allowance is needed to show our receivables at realizable value?" Instead, the question is stated as "How much uncollectible accounts expense is associated with this year's volume of sales?" This method may be regarded as the *income statement* approach to estimating uncollectible accounts.

As an example, assume that for several years the expense of uncollectible accounts has averaged 1% of net sales (sales minus returns and allowances and sales discounts). At the end of the current year, before adjusting entries, the following account balances appear in the ledger:

	Dr	*Cr*
Sales		$1,060,000
Sales returns and allowances	$40,000	
Sales discounts	20,000	
Allowance for doubtful accounts		1,500

The net sales of the current year amount to $1,000,000; 1% of this amount is $10,000. The existing balance in the Allowance for Doubtful Accounts **should be ignored in computing the amount of the adjusting entry,** because the percentage of net sales method stresses the relationship between uncollectible accounts expense and net sales rather than the valuation of receivables at the balance sheet date. The entry is:

Provision for un- collectible accounts based on percentage of net sales

Uncollectible Accounts Expense	10,000	
Allowance for Doubtful Accounts		10,000

To record uncollectible accounts expense of 1% of the year's net sales (.01 × $1,000,000).

If a concern makes both cash sales and credit sales, it may be desirable to exclude the cash sales from consideration and to compute the percentage relationship of uncollectible accounts expense to credit sales only.

Writing off an uncollectible account receivable

Whenever an account receivable from a specific customer is determined to be uncollectible, it no longer qualifies as an asset and should immediately be written off. To write off an account receivable is to reduce the balance of the customer's account to zero. The journal entry to accomplish this consists of a credit to the Accounts Receivable control account in the general ledger (and to the customer's account in the subsidiary ledger), and an offsetting debit to the Allowance for Doubtful Accounts.

Referring again to the example of the Arlington Corporation as shown on page 326, the ledger accounts were as follows after the adjusting entry for estimated uncollectible accounts had been made on December 31, 1979:

Accounts receivable	$200,000
Less: Allowance for doubtful accounts	10,000

Next let us assume that on January 27, 1980, a customer by the name of William Benton became bankrupt and the account receivable from him in the amount of $1,000 was determined to be worthless. The following entry should be made by the Arlington Corporation:

<table>
<tr><td>*Writing off an uncol- lectible account*</td><td>Allowance for Doubtful Accounts . . . . *1,000*</td><td></td></tr>
<tr><td></td><td>   Accounts Receivable, William Benton . . . .</td><td>*1,000*</td></tr>
<tr><td></td><td colspan="2">To write off the receivable from William Benton as uncollectible.</td></tr>
</table>

The important thing to note in this entry is that the debit is made to the Allowance for Doubtful Accounts and **not** to the Uncollectible Accounts Expense account. The estimated expense is charged to the Uncollectible Accounts Expense account at the end of each accounting period. When a particular account receivable is later ascertained to be worthless and is written off, this action does not represent an additional expense but merely confirms our previous estimate of the expense. If the Uncollectible Accounts Expense account were first charged with estimated credit losses and then later charged with proved credit losses, we would be guilty of double counting of uncollectible accounts expense.

After the entry writing off William Benton's account has been posted, the Accounts Receivable control account and the Allowance for Doubtful Accounts appear as follows:

Both accounts reduced by write-off of worthless receivable

Accounts Receivable

1979			*1980*	
Dec. 31		200,000	Jan. 27 (Benton write-off)	1,000

Allowance for Doubtful Accounts

1980			*1979*	
Jan. 27 (Benton write-off)		1,000	Dec. 31	10,000

Note that the **net** amount of the accounts receivable was unchanged by writing off William Benton's account against the Allowance for Doubtful Accounts.

Net value of re- ceivables un- changed by write- off

Before the Write-off		After the Write-off	
Accounts receivable	$200,00	Accounts receivable	$199,000
Less: Allowance for		Less: Allowance for	
doubtful accounts	10,000	doubtful accounts	9,000
Net value of receivables . . .	$190,000	Net value of receivables . . .	$190,000

The fact that writing off an uncollectible receivable against the Allowance for Doubtful Accounts does not change the net carrying value of accounts receivable shows that no expense is entered in the accounting records when an account receivable is written off. This example bears out the point stressed earlier in the chapter: *Credit losses belong in the period in which the sale is made, not in a later period in which the account is discovered to be uncollectible.*

WRITE-OFFS SELDOM AGREE WITH PREVIOUS ESTIMATES The total amount of accounts receivable written off in a given year will seldom, if ever, be exactly equal to the estimated amount previously credited to the Allowance for Doubtful Accounts.

If the amounts written off as uncollectible turn out to be less than the estimated amount, the Allowance for Doubtful Accounts will continue to show a credit balance. If the amounts written off as uncollectible are greater than the estimated amount, the Allowance for Doubtful Accounts will acquire a debit balance, which will be eliminated by the adjustment at the end of the period.

Recovery of an account previously written off

Occasionally an account which has been written off as worthless will later be collected in full or in part. Such collections are often referred to as *recoveries* of bad debts. Collection of an account previously written off is evidence that the write-off was an error; the write-off entry should therefore be reversed.

Let us assume, for example, that a past-due account receivable in the amount of $400 from J. B. Barker was written off by the following entry:

Barker account considered uncollectible

Allowance for Doubtful Accounts	400	
Accounts Receivable, J. B. Barker		400

To write off the receivable from J. B. Barker as uncollectible.

At some later date the customer, J. B. Barker, pays his account in full. The entry to restore Barker's account will be:

Barker account reinstated

Accounts Receivable, J. B. Barker	400	
Allowance for Doubtful Accounts		400

To reverse the entry writing off J. B. Barker's account.

A separate entry will be made in the cash receipts journal to record the collection from Barker. This entry will debit Cash and credit Accounts Receivable.

Direct charge-off method of recognizing uncollectible accounts expense

Instead of making adjusting entries to record uncollectible accounts expense on the basis of estimates, some concerns merely charge uncollectible accounts to expense at the time such receivables are determined to be uncollectible. This method makes no attempt to match revenue and related expenses. Uncollectible accounts expense is recorded in the period in which the individual accounts are determined to be worthless rather than in the period in which the sales were made.

When the direct charge-off method is in use, the accounts receivable will be listed in the balance sheet at their gross amount, and no valuation allowance will be used. The receivables, therefore, are not stated at their probable realizable value.

In the determination of taxable income under present federal income tax regulations, both the direct charge-off method and the allowance method of estimating uncollectible accounts expense are acceptable. From the standpoint of accounting theory, the allowance method is much the better, for it enables expenses to be matched with related revenue and thus aids in making a logical measurement of net income.

Credit balances in accounts receivable

Customers' accounts in the accounts receivable subsidiary ledger normally have debit balances, but occasionally a customer's account will acquire a credit balance. This may occur because of overpayment, payment in advance, or the return of merchandise. Any credit balances in the accounts receivable subsidiary ledger should be accompanied by the notation "Cr" to distinguish them from accounts with normal debit balances.

Suppose that the Accounts Receivable controlling account in the general ledger has a debit balance of $9,000, representing the following individual accounts with customers in the subsidiary ledger:

49 accounts with debit balance	$10,000
1 account with a credit balance	1,000
Net debit balance of 50 customers' accounts	$ 9,000

One of the basic rules in preparing financial statements is that assets and liabilities should be shown at their gross amounts rather than being netted against each other. Accordingly, the amount which should appear as accounts receivable in the balance sheet is not the $9,000 balance of the controlling account, but the $10,000 total of the receivables with debit balances. The account with the $1,000 *credit balance is a liability* and should be shown as such rather than being concealed as an offset against an asset. The balance sheet presentation should be as follows:

Current assets:			*Current liabilities:*	
Accounts receivable	$10,000		Credit balances in customers'	
			accounts	$1,000

Credit card sales

Many retailing businesses avoid the risk of uncollectible accounts by making credit sales to customers who use well-known credit cards, such as American Express, BankAmericard, or Master Charge. When a customer makes a purchase using one of these credit cards the retailer acquires an account receivable from the credit card company, rather than from the customer. The credit card company promptly pays the retailer and redeems the sales invoice. At the end of each month, the credit card company bills the credit card holder for all the invoices it has redeemed during the month. If the credit card holder fails to pay the amount owed, it is the credit card company which sustains the loss.

By making credit sales through credit card companies, retailers receive cash more quickly from credit sales and avoid uncollectible accounts expense. Also, the retailers avoid the expense of investigating customers' credit, maintaining subsidiary ledgers for accounts receivable, and making collections from customers. Credit card companies, however, do not redeem sales invoices at the full sales price. The agreement between the credit card company and the retailer allows the credit card company a substantial discount (usually between 3 and 7% of the amount of the sales invoice).

When a retailer makes sales to credit card customers, it may record the receivables from the credit card company at the net amount and debit an expense account for the amount of the credit card fee. These two debits will offset the credit to the Sales account for the retail price of the goods or services. To illustrate this procedure, assume Bradshaw Camera Shop sells a camera for $200 to a customer who uses a Quick Charge credit card. The entry would be:

Receivable is from the credit card company	*Accounts Receivable, Quick Charge* 190	
	Credit Card Discount Expense 10	
	Sales	200

To record a sale to a customer using a Quick Charge credit card and the discount expense of 5% charged by Quick Charge.

Bradshaw Camera Shop may then mail the sales invoice to Quick Charge and receive an immediate cash payment of $190. The expense account, Credit Card Discount Expense, should be included among the selling expenses on the income statement of Bradshaw Camera Shop.

An alternative accounting procedure leading to the same end result is to record the receivable from the credit card company at the full amount of the sale ($200 in the above example). When payment of $190 is received from the credit card company, the collection would be recorded by debiting Cash for $190 and debiting Credit Card Discount Expense for $10, offset by a credit to Accounts Receivable, Quick Charge for $200.

Analysis of accounts receivable

What dollar amount of accounts receivable would be reasonable for a business making annual credit sales of $1,200,000? Comparison of the average amount of accounts receivable with the sales made on credit during the period indicates how long it takes to convert receivables into cash. For example, if annual credit sales of $1,200,000 are made at a uniform rate throughout the year and the accounts receivable at year-end amount to $200,000, we can see at a glance that the receivables represent one-sixth of the year's sales, or about 60 days of uncollected sales. Management naturally wants to make efficient use of the available capital in the business, and therefore is interested in a rapid "turnover" of accounts receivable. If the credit terms offered by the business in the above example were, say, 30 days net, the existence of receivables equal to 60 days' sales would warrant investigation. The analysis of receivables is considered more fully in Chapter 22.

Receivables from installment sales

The importance of *installment sales* is emphasized by a recent annual report of Sears, Roebuck and Co., which shows about $4 billion of "customer installment accounts receivable." Nearly all of the company's receivables call for collection in periodic installments.

An installment sale may or may not require a down payment; substantial interest charges are usually added to the "cash selling price" of the product in determining the total dollar amount to be collected in the series of installment payments. The seller usually has the right to repossess the merchandise if installments are not collected according to the terms of the installment contract. Repossessed merchandise is recorded at its current value rather than at its original cost or at the uncollected portion of the installment receivable.

Although the collection period for an installment sale often runs as long as 24 to 36 months, such installment receivables are regarded as current assets if they correspond to customary terms of the industry.

Installment basis accounting for income tax purposes

Current provisions of the federal income tax law permit a dealer in personal property to spread the profit from installment sales over the years in which collections are received. The result is to defer the recognition of taxable income and the payment of income tax.

Assume, for example, that Cross Company sells an article for $3,000 which cost $1,800. No down payment is received, but the buyer promises to make 30 monthly payments of $100 each. The gross profit on the sale is 40% of the $3,000 total price, or $1,200; therefore 40% of each installment collected is regarded for tax purposes as profit realized. If three $100 monthly collections were received in the year in which the sale occurred, the profit reported for tax purposes would be only $120 (that is, 40% × $300). In following years the same 40% rate would be applied to all collections on this installment contract.

The installment basis of measuring income is acceptable for income tax purposes, but not for financial statements. The Accounting Principles Board of the AICPA in *Opinion No. 10* reaffirmed that "revenues should ordinarily be accounted for at the time a transaction is completed, with appropriate provision for uncollectible accounts."[1] Thus in our example of a $3,000 sale on a 30-month installment plan, proper accounting (for all purposes other than tax returns) would require a $3,000 debit to Accounts Receivable and a $3,000 credit to Sales. The entire gross profit of $1,200 ($3,000 − $1,800) would be regarded as earned in the year of the sale.

The basic accounting principle of matching revenue with related expenses will usually best be accomplished by recognizing the entire gross profit in the period of sale, and by charges to expense to establish an adequate allowance for doubtful accounts. There are a number of other more complex issues relating to installment sales; these are covered in *Modern Advanced Accounting* by the authors.

NOTES RECEIVABLE

Definition of a promissory note

A promissory note is an unconditional promise in writing to pay on demand or at a future date a definite sum of money.

The person who signs the note and thereby promises to pay is called the *maker* of the note. The person to whom payment is to be made is called the *payee* of the note. In the illustration below, G. L. Smith is the maker of the note and A. B. Davis is the payee.

Simplified form of promissory note

$1,000 ...... Los Angeles, California .... July 10, 19—	
.... One month .... **after date** .... I .... **promise to pay**	
to the order of .... A. B. Davis	
.... ─────One thousand and no/100──────── .... **dollars**	
payable at .... First National Bank of Los Angeles	
for value received, with interest at 10%	
G. L. Smith	

[1] "Omnibus Opinion—1966," Opinion No. 10 of the Accounting Principles Board, AICPA (New York: 1967), p. 149.

From the viewpoint of the maker, G. L. Smith, the illustrated note is a liability and is recorded by crediting the Notes Payable account. However, from the viewpoint of the payee, A. B. Davis, this same note is an asset and is recorded by debiting the Notes Receivable account. The maker of a note expects to pay cash at the maturity date; the payee expects to receive cash at that date.

Nature of interest

Interest is a charge made for the use of money. To the borrower (maker of a note) interest is an expense; to the lender (payee of a note) interest is revenue.

COMPUTING INTEREST A formula used in computing interest is as follows:

Principal × Rate of Interest × Time = Interest

(Often expressed as

P × R × T = I)

Interest rates are usually stated on an annual basis. For example, the interest on a $1,000, one-year, 12% note is computed as follows:

$1,000 × 0.12 × 1 = $120

If the term of the note were only four months instead of a year, the interest charge would be $40, computed as follows:

$1,000 × 0.12 × $\frac{4}{12}$ = $40

If the term of the note is expressed in days, the exact number of days must be used in computing the interest. As a matter of convenience, however, it is customary to assume that a year contains 360 days. Suppose, for example, that a 75-day, 12% note for $1,000 is drawn on June 10. The interest charge could be computed as follows:

$1,000 × 0.12 × $\frac{75}{360}$ = $25

The principal of the note ($1,000) plus the interest ($25) equals $1,025, and this amount (the **maturity value**) will be payable on August 24. The computation of days to maturity is as follows:

Days remaining in June (30 − 10)	20
Days in July	31
Days in August to maturity date	24
Total days called for by note	75

PREVAILING INTEREST RATES Interest rates, like the prices of goods and services, are always in a process of change. The Federal Reserve Board has a policy of deliberately causing interest rates to rise or fall in an effort to keep our economy running at a reasonable level of activity. At present, you can earn 5% to 6% a year interest on money deposited in a bank savings account. If you obtain a long-term mortgage loan on a residence, you will probably pay about 9% or 10% as an annual interest rate. For a six-month personal loan from a bank, you may pay an annual interest rate of perhaps 9% to 12% depending upon whether you provide collateral to secure payment of the loan and depending upon your personal credit rating. On an unsecured bank loan payable in monthly installments, the annual interest rate is now about 16%. Many retail stores charge interest on installment accounts at $1\frac{1}{2}$% a month, which is equivalent to 18% a year. On the other hand, the largest and strongest corporations borrow millions of dollars in bank loans at interest rates of perhaps 7% to 9%. In brief, interest rates vary widely depending upon the nature of the loan and the financial strength of the borrower.

SIXTY-DAY, 6% METHOD FOR COMPUTING INTEREST Considerable saving of time is often possible by using the 60-day, 6% method of computing interest. If the interest rate is 6% a year, the interest for 60 days on any amount of money may be determined merely by *moving the decimal point two places to the left.* For example,

The interest at 6% for 60 days on $1,111.00 is $11.11
The interest at 6% for 60 days on $9,876.43 is $98.76

The reasoning underlying the 60-day, 6% shortcut may be summarized as follows:

Since interest on $1.00 for one year is $0.06
And 60 days is $\frac{1}{6}$ of a year
Interest on $1.00 for 60 days is $0.01 ($\frac{1}{6}$ of $0.06)

If the interest on $1.00 at 6% for 60 days can be computed by moving the decimal point two places to the left, then the interest on any amount at 6% for 60 days can be computed in the same manner.

The 60-day, 6% method can be used for time periods other than 60 days. The time of the note can be stated as a fraction or a multiple of 60 days and the interest quickly computed. For example, assuming an annual interest rate of 6%, what is the interest on $8,844 for 15 days?

Interest for 60 days on $8,844 is $88.44
Interest for 15 days on $8,844 is $\frac{1}{4}$ of $88.44, or $22.11

The 60-day, 6% method can also be applied when the interest rate is higher or lower than 6%. If the interest rate is something other than 6%, the interest is first computed at 6%, and an adjustment is then made for the difference between 6% and the actual rate. For example, what is the interest at 8% on $963 for 60 days?

Interest at 6% on $963 for 60 days is $ 9.63
Interest at 2% on $963 for 60 days is   3.21 ($\frac{1}{3}$ × $9.63)
Interest at 8% on $963 for 60 days is $12.84

Although this shortcut method of computing interest can be used for almost any rate and any time period, not much time is saved by using it in cases in which elaborate computations are required.

Accounting for notes receivable

In some lines of business, notes receivable are seldom encountered; in other fields they occur frequently and may constitute an important part of total assets. Business concerns that sell high-priced durable goods such as automobiles and farm machinery often accept notes receivable from their customers. Many companies obtain notes receivable in settlement of past-due accounts.

All notes receivable are usually posted to a single account in the general ledger. A subsidiary ledger is not essential because the notes themselves, when filed by due dates, are the equivalent of a subsidiary ledger and provide any necessary information as to maturity, interest rates, collateral pledged, and other details. The amount debited to Notes Receivable is always the face amount of the note, regardless of whether or not the note bears interest. When an interest-bearing note is collected, the amount of cash received will be larger than the face amount of the note. The interest collected is credited to an Interest Earned account, and only the face amount of the note is credited to the Notes Receivable account.

ILLUSTRATIVE ENTRIES Assume that a 6%, 90-day note receivable is acquired from a customer, Marvin White, in settlement of an existing account receivable of $2,000. The entry for acquisition of the note is as follows:

Note received to replace account receivable	Notes Receivable 2,000	
	Accounts Receivable, Marvin White	2,000
	Accepted 6%, 90-day note in settlement of account receivable.	

The entry 90 days later to record collection of the note will be:

Collection of principal and interest	Cash 2,030	
	Notes Receivable	2,000
	Interest Earned	30
	Collected 6%, 90-day note from Marvin White.	

When a note is received from a customer at the time of making a sale of merchandise on account, two entries should be made, as follows:

Sale may be run through accounts receivable when note is received from customer	Accounts Receivable, Russ Company 1,500	
	Sales	1,500
	To record sale of merchandise on account.	
	Notes Receivable 1,500	
	Accounts Receivable, Russ Company	1,500
	To record receipt of note from customer.	

When this procedure is employed, the account with a particular customer in the subsidiary ledger for accounts receivable provides a complete record of all transactions with that customer, regardless of the fact that some sales may have been made on open account and others may have involved a note receivable. Having a complete history of all transactions with a customer on a single ledger card may be helpful in reaching decisions as to collection efforts or further extensions of credit.

WHEN THE MAKER OF A NOTE DEFAULTS A note receivable which cannot be collected at maturity is said to have been *dishonored* by the maker. Failure by the maker to pay interest or principal of a note at the due date is also known as *defaulting* on the note. Immediately after the dishonor or default of a note, an entry should be made by the holder to transfer the amount due from the Notes Receivable account to an account receivable from the debtor.

Assuming that a 60-day, 6% note receivable from Robert Jones is not collected at maturity, the following entry would be made:

Default of note receivable

Accounts Receivable, Robert Jones	1,010	
Notes Receivable		1,000
Interest Earned		10

To record dishonor by Robert Jones of a 6%, 60-day note.

The interest earned on the note is recorded as a credit to Interest Earned and is also included in the account receivable from the maker. The interest receivable on a defaulted note is just as valid a claim against the maker as is the principal of the note; if the principal is collectible, then presumably the interest too can be collected.

By transferring past-due notes receivable into Accounts Receivable, two things are accomplished. First, the Notes Receivable account is limited to current notes not yet matured and is, therefore, regarded as a highly liquid type of asset. Secondly, the account receivable ledger card will show that a note has been dishonored and will present a complete picture of all transactions with the customer.

RENEWAL OF A NOTE RECEIVABLE Sometimes the two parties to a note agree that the note shall be renewed rather than paid at the maturity date. If the old note does not bear interest, the entry could be made as follows:

Renewal of note should be recorded

| Notes Receivable | 1,000 | |
| Notes Receivable | | 1,000 |

A 60-day, non-interest-bearing note from Ray Bell renewed today with new 60-day, 6% note.

Since the above entry causes no change in the balance of the Notes Receivable account, a question may arise as to whether the entry is necessary. The renewal of a note is an important transaction requiring managerial attention; a general journal entry is needed to record the action taken by management and to provide a permanent record of the transaction. If journal entries were not made to record the renewal of notes, confusion might arise as to whether some of the notes included in the balance of the Notes Receivable account were current or dishonored.

ADJUSTMENTS FOR INTEREST AT END OF PERIOD Notes receivable acquired in one accounting period often do not mature until a following period. Interest is being earned throughout the life of the note, and this revenue should be apportioned between the two accounting periods on a time basis. At the end of the accounting period, interest earned to date on notes receivable should be accrued by an adjusting entry debiting the asset account, Interest Receivable, and crediting the revenue account, Interest Earned. When the note matures and the interest is received in the following period, the entry to be made consists of a debit to Cash, a credit to Interest Receivable for the amount of the accrual, and a credit to Interest Earned for the remainder of the interest collected.

Discounting notes receivable

Many business concerns which obtain notes receivable from their customers prefer to sell the notes to a bank for cash rather than to hold them until maturity. Selling a note receivable to a bank or finance company is often called *discounting* a note receivable. The holder of the note signs his name on the back of the note (as in endorsing a check) and delivers the note to the bank. The bank expects to collect the *maturity value* (principal plus interest) from the maker of the note at the maturity date, but if the maker fails to pay, the bank can demand payment from the endorser.

When an executive endorses a note and turns it over to a bank for cash, he or she is promising to pay the note if the maker fails to do so. The endorser is therefore contingently liable to the bank. A *contingent liability* may be regarded as a potential liability which either will develop into a full-fledged liability or will be eliminated entirely by a future event. The subsequent event in the case of a discounted note receivable is the payment (or dishonoring) of the note by the maker. If the maker pays, the contingent liability of the endorser is thereby ended. If the maker fails to pay, the contingent liability of the endorser becomes a real liability. In either case the period of contingent liability ends at the maturity date of the note.

The discounting of notes receivable with a bank may be regarded by a company as an alternative to borrowing by issuing its own note payable. To issue its own note payable to the bank, would, of course, mean the creation of a liability; to obtain cash by discounting a note receivable creates only a contingent liability.

COMPUTING THE PROCEEDS The amount of cash obtained by discounting a note receivable is called the *proceeds* of the note. In some instances the bank may compute the proceeds merely by applying an interest rate to the face amount of the note for the period of time remaining before the note matures. This approach is logical when a non-interest-bearing note is discounted, because the face amount of the note and the maturity value are identical. If the note bears interest, however, the banker will surely give consideration to the rate of interest specified in the note and to any interest accrued as of the date of discounting. After considering these factors, the bank may set its own interest charge (discount) by applying to the face of the note a lower rate than it would require to discount a non-interest-bearing note. A more precise method of computing the discount charge to be made by the bank consists of the following steps:

1 Determine the maturity value of the note. The maturity value is the amount (including interest) which the holder of the note will be entitled to collect when the note matures. For a non-interest-bearing note, the maturity value is the face amount. For an interest-bearing note, the maturity value is the face amount plus the interest.

2 Determine the length of the discount period by counting the exact number of days from the date of discount to the date of maturity. In counting the number of days, exclude the date of discount but include the maturity date. The discount period is usually shorter than the life of the note; occasionally it equals the life of the note, but obviously, it can never exceed the life of the note.

3 Compute the discount by applying the discount rate (interest rate) charged by the bank to the maturity value of the note for the discount period.

4 Deduct the discount from the maturity value. The resulting amount represents the cash received from the bank, or the proceeds of the note.

To illustrate the application of the above steps, assume that on July 1 Roger Barnes receives a 75-day, 6% note for $8,000 from Raymond Kelly. The note will mature on September 14 (30 days in July, 31 days in August, and 14 days in September). On July 16, Roger Barnes discounts this note receivable with his bank, which charges a discount rate of 6% a year. How much cash does Barnes receive? The computation is as follows:

Face of the note	*$8,000*
Add: Interest from date of note to maturity ($8,000 × .06 × $\frac{75}{360}$)	*100*
Maturity value	*$8,100*
Less: Bank discount at 6% for the discount period of 60 days	
(July 16 to Sept. 14) ($8,100 × .06 × $\frac{1}{6}$)	*81*
Proceeds (cash received from bank)	*$8,019*

The entry made by Barnes to record his discounting of the Kelly note would be as follows:

Cash	*8,019*	
Notes Receivable		*8,000*
Interest Earned		*19*
Discounted Raymond Kelly note at bank at 6%.		

In this illustration, the cash of $8,019 received from the bank was greater than the $8,000 face amount of the note. The proceeds received from discounting a note may be either more or less than the face amount of the note, depending upon the interest rates and time periods involved. The difference between the face amount of the note being discounted and the cash proceeds is usually recorded as either Interest Earned or Interest Expense. If the proceeds exceed the face value, the difference is credited to Interest Earned. However, if the proceeds are less than the face value of the note, the difference is debited to Interest Expense.

DISCOUNTED NOTE RECEIVABLE PAID BY MAKER Before the maturity date of the discounted note, the bank will notify the maker, Raymond Kelly, that it is holding the note. Kelly will therefore make payment directly to the bank.

DISCOUNTED NOTE RECEIVABLE DISHONORED BY MAKER If Kelly should be unable to pay the note at maturity, the bank will give notice of the default to the endorser, Roger Barnes. Barnes immediately becomes obligated to pay, and will make the following entry to record the payment:

Accounts Receivable, Raymond Kelly *8,100*
       Cash *8,100*
To record payment to bank of discounted Kelly note, dishonored by maker.

Under these assumptions Barnes's contingent liability to the bank has become a real liability and has been discharged by a cash payment. Barnes now has an account receivable from the maker of the defaulted note for the amount which he was compelled to pay to the bank.

Classification of receivables in the balance sheet

Accounts receivable from customers will ordinarily be collected within the operating cycle; they are therefore listed among the current assets on the balance sheet. Receivables may also arise from miscellaneous transactions other than the sale of goods and services. These miscellaneous receivables, such as advances to officers and employees, and claims against insurance companies for losses sustained, should be listed separately on the balance sheet and should not be merged with trade accounts receivable. If an account receivable from an officer or employee originates as a favor to the officer or employee, efforts at collection may await the convenience of the debtor. Consequently, it is customary to exclude receivables of this type from the current asset category.

Notes receivable usually appear among the current assets; however, if the maturity date of a note is more than a year distant and beyond the operating cycle of the business, it should be listed as noncurrent under a heading such as Investments. Any accrued interest receivable at the balance sheet date is a current asset but may be combined on the balance sheet with other accrued items such as accrued rents receivable or royalties receivable.

Contingent liabilities should be reflected in the balance sheet, because they have a considerable bearing on the credit rating of the person or firm contingently liable. A business concern with large contingent liabilities may encounter greater difficulties in obtaining bank loans than would otherwise be the case. The contingent liability arising from the discounting of notes receivable is usually disclosed by a **footnote** to the balance sheet. The following footnote is typical: "Note: At December 31, 19____, the company was contingently liable for notes receivable discounted in the amount of $250,000."

CURRENT LIABILITIES

Current liabilities are obligations that must be paid within the operating cycle or one year (whichever is longer). Comparison of the amount of current liabilities with the amount of current assets is one means of appraising the financial position of a business. In other words, a comparison of the amount of current liabilities with the amount of current assets available for paying these debts helps us in judging a company's short-run debt-paying ability.

In accounting for current liabilities, we are especially interested in making certain that all such obligations are included in the balance sheet. Fraud may be concealed by deliberate understatement of a liability. The omission or understatement of a liability will usually be accompanied by an overstatement of owner's equity or else by an understatement of assets. Depending on the nature of the error, the net income of the business may also be overstated.

Among the more common current liabilities are notes payable, accounts payable, and accrued or estimated liabilities, such as wages, interest, and taxes. An **estimated** liability is an obligation known to exist but for which the dollar amount is uncertain. In this chapter we shall consider the accounting problems relating to notes payable; the liabilities arising from payrolls will be considered in Chapter 13.

NOTES PAYABLE

Notes payable are issued whenever bank loans are obtained. Other transactions which may give rise to notes payable include the purchase of real estate or costly equipment, the purchase of merchandise, and the substitution of a note for a past-due open account. The use of notes payable in each of these situations is illustrated in the following pages.

Notes payable issued to banks

Assume that John Caldwell, the sole proprietor of a retail business, applies to his bank for a 90-day, unsecured loan of $10,000. In support of the loan application Caldwell submits a balance sheet and income statement.

After studying the financial statements, reading the auditor's report, and making inquiries about Caldwell's credit rating, the bank indicates its willingness to lend the $10,000 requested, at an interest rate of 12%. The note which Caldwell signs will read as shown below, if we omit some of the minor details.

<table>
<tr><td>*Interest stated separately*</td><td>Los Angeles, California   June 15, 19--

.............Ninety days............. **after date I promise to pay to Security National**

Bank the sum of $ ....10,000............. **with interest at the rate of 12% per**

annum.

John Caldwell</td></tr>
</table>

The journal entry in Caldwell's accounts to record this borrowing from the bank is:

<table>
<tr><td>*Face amount of note*</td><td>Cash .... 10,000</td><td></td></tr>
<tr><td></td><td>   Notes Payable ....</td><td>10,000</td></tr>
<tr><td></td><td colspan="2">*Borrowed $10,000 for 90 days at 12% per year.*</td></tr>
</table>

No interest expense is recorded at the time of issuing the note. When the note is paid on September 13, the entry to be made is:

<table>
<tr><td>*Payment of principal and interest*</td><td>Notes Payable .... 10,000</td><td></td></tr>
<tr><td></td><td>Interest Expense .... 300</td><td></td></tr>
<tr><td></td><td>   Cash ....</td><td>10,300</td></tr>
<tr><td></td><td colspan="2">*Paid bank at maturity date of loan.*</td></tr>
</table>

ALTERNATIVE FORM OF NOTES FOR BANK LOANS Instead of stating the interest separately as in the preceding illustration, the note payable to the bank could have been so drawn as to include the interest charge in the *face amount* of the note, as shown below:

<table>
<tr><td>*Interest included in face amount of note*</td><td>Los Angeles, California   June 15, 19--

On ....September 13, 19--.......... **the undersigned promises to pay to**

Security National Bank or order the sum of ....$10,300.......

John Caldwell</td></tr>
</table>

When the note is drawn in this manner the entry in Caldwell's accounts is:

Notes payable credited for face amount of note

Cash	*10,000*
Discount on Notes Payable	*300*
Notes Payable	*10,300*
Borrowed $10,000 for 90 days at 12%.	

Notice that the amount borrowed ($10,000) was less than the face amount of the note ($10,300). The borrower's liability at this time is only $10,000; the other $300 of the face amount of the note represents *future interest expense.* As this interest expense is incurred over the life of the note, the borrower's liability will grow to $10,300, just as in the previous illustration.

The entry to record borrowing $10,000 from the bank might have been recorded by crediting Notes Payable for only $10,000 and gradually recording a liability for Accrued Interest Payable. However, standard practice is to credit the Notes Payable account for the face amount of the note. It is then necessary to debit a *contra-liability* account for the amount of the future interest expense. This contra-liability account, called *Discount on Notes Payable,* is listed in the balance sheet as a deduction from the Notes Payable account. The result is $10,300 minus $300, or a net liability of $10,000.

On September 13, the maturity date of the note, Caldwell will hand the bank a check for $10,300 in payment of the note and will make the following journal entries:

Payment of note and interest expense

Notes Payable	*10,300*
Cash	*10,300*
Paid bank at maturity date of loan.	
Interest Expense	*300*
Discount on Notes Payable	*300*
To record interest expense on matured note.	

Adjustments for interest at end of period

When a note is issued in one accounting period and matures in a later period, the interest expense must be apportioned. Adjusting entries for interest-bearing notes were illustrated in Chapter 4.

A different type of adjustment is necessary at the end of the period for notes payable to banks in which the interest has been included in the face amount of the note. For example, assume that Baker Company borrows $20,000 from its bank on November 1 on a 12%, six-month note with interest of $1,200 included in the face of the note. The entry for the borrowing on November 1 would be:

Interest	*Cash*	20,000	
included	*Discount on Notes Payable*	1,200	
in face			
of note	*Notes Payable*		21,200
and . . .	Issued to bank a 12%, six-month note payable with interest		
	included in face amount of note.		

At December 31, the adjusting entry required is:

. . . related	*Interest Expense*	400	
adjusting	*Discount on Notes Payable*		400
entry	To record interest expense incurred to end of year on 12%, six-month		
	note dated Nov. 1.		

On May 1, when the six-month note matures and the Baker Company pays the bank, the entry is as follows:

Two-thirds	*Notes Payable*	21,200	
of interest	*Interest Expense*	800	
applicable			
to second	*Cash*		21,200
year	*Discount on Notes Payable*		800
	To record payment to bank of 12%, six-month note dated		
	Nov. 1, with interest included in face of note.		

Discount on Notes Payable should be classified as a contra-liability account and deducted from the face value of notes payable in the current liability section of the balance sheet. This treatment results in showing as a liability at statement date the principal of the debt plus the accrued interest payable at that time.

Prepaid interest

Discount on notes payable is sometimes called *prepaid interest* and classified as a current asset, a practice which has little theoretical justification. To prepay interest on a loan has the effect of reducing the amount of money borrowed and increasing the effective rate of interest. Assume that on July 1 you borrow $1,000 from a bank for a period of $1\frac{1}{2}$ years at an annual interest rate of 12%. Assume also that you pay the bank the full 18 months' interest of $180 ($1,000 × 12% × 1.5) at the date of borrowing the $1,000. Under this procedure you have increased your cash position by only $820. A more realistic view of the transaction is to say you have incurred a liability of $820 which will increase to $1,000 during the next year and one-half.

Current income tax regulations recognize the concept of prepaid interest. A taxpayer on the cash basis (and this includes most individuals) may deduct interest when it is paid, even though paid in advance. Thus, in the example of borrowing $1,000 and concurrently paying $1\frac{1}{2}$ years' interest in advance, you could deduct the entire interest charge of $180 for income tax purposes in the year paid. At present, however, tax regulations do not permit the deduction of prepaid interest for more than one year beyond the year in which the payment occurs.

Imputed interest on notes payable and notes receivable

Notes are often issued in connection with the acquisition of plant assets. If a realistic interest rate is not specified in the note, a portion of the face value of the note must be assumed to represent a charge for interest. Recognizing the economic reality that a portion of such a note represents an interest charge is termed *imputing* the interest. If the buyer fails to impute interest on a note payable which has an interest charge included in the face amount, the result will be to overstate the cost of the asset acquired and the amount of the related liability. It is equally important for the seller to impute interest on a note receivable containing an element of interest in the face amount. This interest charge represents *future interest revenue* to the holder of the note, and *is not part of the sale price of the asset.* If the seller fails to impute interest, the current sales revenue and notes receivable will both be overstated.

For example, assume that on July 1 Tru-Tool Company sells a large metal lathe to Everts Company for $15,000. In payment for the lathe, Everts Company issues a one-year note payable with a face amount of $16,200. The additional $1,200 included in the face amount of the note represents an interest charge of 8%. Tru-Tool Company should record the sale as follows:

Interest is	*Accounts Receivable, Everts Company* 15,000	
not included	*Sales*	*15,000*
in sales		
revenue	*To record sale of lathe.*	

Notes Receivable 16,200		
Discount on Notes Receivable	*1,200*	
Accounts Receivable, Everts Company	*15,000*	
Obtained note receivable from Everts Company with one-year		
interest charge included in face amount of note.		

Note that the sale is recorded at the price of the lathe, *not* at the face amount of the note receivable. The future interest revenue included in the face amount of the note is credited to Discount on Notes Receivable. As this revenue is earned, the balance of the Discount on Notes Receivable account will be transferred to Interest Earned. At December 31, the adjusting entry to recognize interest earned to the year-end will be:

Interest	*Discount on Notes Receivable* 600	
revenue	*Interest Earned*	*600*
recognized		
when	*To record interest earned to end of year on Everts Company*	
earned	*8% note dated July 1.*	

On June 30, of the following year, when the note receivable is collected from Everts Company, the entry required will be:

Collection of note receivable	*Cash*	*16,200*	
	Discount on Notes Receivable	*600*	
	Notes Receivable		*16,200*
	Interest Earned		*600*

To record collection of Everts Company note.

Discount on Notes Receivable is a contra-asset account which is deducted from the face amount of notes receivable on the balance sheet. Had Tru-Tool Company failed to impute interest on the Everts Company note, the financial statements for the year ended December 31 would contain the following errors: (1) sales revenue would be overstated by $1,200, (2) interest revenue would be understated by $600, and (3) notes receivable would be overstated by $600.

Failure to impute adequate interest on long-term notes receivable has occasionally resulted in large overstatements of sales revenue, especially by real estate development companies. In recognition of this problem, the Accounting Principles Board issued *Opinion No. 21* which requires imputing interest on long-term notes receivable (and also notes payable) which do not bear adequate stated rates of interest.

KEY TERMS INTRODUCED OR EMPHASIZED IN CHAPTER 9

Accounts receivable Amounts receivable from customers and others which are not supported by formal written promises to pay.

Aging the accounts receivable The process of classifying accounts receivable by age groups such as current, past due 1–30 days, past due 31–60 days, etc. A step in estimating the uncollectible portion of the accounts receivable.

Allowance for Doubtful Accounts A valuation account or contra account relating to accounts receivable and showing the portion of the receivables estimated to be uncollectible.

Bad debts expense (See uncollectible accounts expense)

Contingent liability A potential liability which either will develop into a full-fledged liability or will be eliminated entirely by a future event.

Contra account A ledger account which is deducted from or offset against a related account in the financial statements, for example, Allowance for Doubtful Accounts.

Credit agency An organization which gathers credit data on individuals and business concerns, and distributes this information to its clients for a fee, for example, Dun & Bradstreet, Inc.

Credit balances in accounts receivable A liability arising when a customer pays in advance or pays an excessive amount.

Current assets Cash and other assets expected to be converted into cash within one year or the current operating cycle (whichever is longer).

Current liabilities Debts that must be paid within one year or the operating cycle (whichever is longer).

Default Failure to pay interest or principal of a promissory note at the due date.

Direct charge-off method A method of accounting for uncollectible receivables in which no expense is recognized until individual accounts are determined to be worthless. At that point the account receivable is written off with an offsetting debit to uncollectible accounts expense. Fails to match revenue and related expenses.

Discount   The amount charged by a bank or other purchaser who buys a note prior to its maturity. Maturity value minus proceeds equals discount.

Discount period   Number of days from date of discounting a note to the maturity date.

Discounting notes receivable   Selling a note receivable prior to its maturity date.

Dishonored note receivable   A note receivable which cannot be collected at maturity (see also *Default*).

Installment basis of accounting   A method of recognizing income from installment sales in proportion to collections rather than at date of sale. Acceptable for income tax purposes but ordinarily not for other accounting purposes.

Installment sales   Sales on credit in which the customer agrees to make a series of installment payments, including substantial interest charges. Seller retains title to merchandise until the final installment is collected.

Interest   A charge made for the use of money. The formula for computing interest is Principal × Rate of Interest × Time = Interest ($P \times R \times T = I$).

Interest earned   Amount earned (revenue) by the lender from lending money.

Interest expense   The cost to a borrower (debtor) of borrowing money.

Maker   A person who signs a promissory note promising to pay the stated amount.

Maturity date   The date on which a note becomes due and payable.

Maturity value   The value of a note at its maturity date, consisting of principal plus interest.

Notes payable   A liability evidenced by issuance of a formal written promise to pay a certain amount of money, usually with interest, at a future date.

Notes receivable   A receivable (asset) evidenced by a formal written promise to pay a certain amount of money, usually with interest, at a future date.

Payee   The person named in a promissory note to whom payment is to be made (the lender).

Principal   The face amount of a promissory note.

Proceeds   The amount received from selling a note receivable prior to its maturity. Maturity value minus discount equals proceeds.

Promissory note   An unconditional promise in writing to pay on demand or at a future date a definite sum of money.

Recovery of account receivable   The collection of an account receivable previously written off as worthless.

Uncollectible accounts expense   The expense caused by failure of customers to pay the amounts they owe the company. Also, the ledger account used to show the estimated uncollectible credit sales for the year.

Valuation account   An account, such as Allowance for Doubtful Accounts, with a credit balance, which is offset against an asset account to produce the proper balance sheet value for an asset.

Writing off an account receivable   The removal of an account receivable from the accounting records because it is considered uncollectible and therefore is no longer regarded as an asset. The offsetting debit is to the Allowance for Doubtful Accounts.

DEMONSTRATION PROBLEM FOR YOUR REVIEW

General Contractors Supply Co. is short of cash and regularly discounts the notes receivable obtained from customers. Banks apply a discount rate to the maturity value of the notes which varies depending on the quality of the note and the level of interest rates. The company makes some sales on 30-day open account, but any customer who does not pay in full within 30 days is asked to substitute an interest-bearing note for the past-due account. Some customers are required to sign promissory notes at the time of sale.

The company uses the allowance method in accounting for uncollectible accounts.

A partial list of transactions for the six months ended December 31, 19____ , is given below.

July 1 Sale of merchandise to P. Linn on account, $1,545. It was agreed that Linn would submit a 60-day, 8% note upon receipt of the merchandise, and should deduct any freight he paid on the goods.

July 3 Received from Linn a letter stating that he had paid $45 freight on the shipment of July 1. He enclosed a 60-day, 8% note dated July 3 for $1,500.

July 18 Sold merchandise on account, $2,200, to Baxter Company; terms 2/10, n/30.

July 27 Discounted Linn note at bank and received $1,508 in cash.

July 28 Baxter Company paid account in full.

Aug. 8 Sold merchandise to E. Jones on account, $1,200; terms 2/10, n/30.

Sept. 1 Received notice from the bank that Linn had defaulted on his note due today. The bank charged the company's account for $1,520, the maturity value of the note.

Sept. 7 Received a 60-day note receivable from E. Jones in settlement of $1,200 open account. The note was drawn to include 60 days' interest computed at 8% per annum on the face amount.

Sept. 10 It was ascertained that an account receivable from K. L. Treff amounting to $120 cannot be collected and was written off.

Oct. 15 An account receivable of $300 from Allen Blaine had been written off in June; full payment was unexpectedly received from Blaine.

Oct. 25 Received cash from P. Linn in full settlement of his account due today, including interest of 8% on $1,520 from September 1, maturity date of defaulted note.

Nov. 6 E. Jones paid his note due today.

Dec. 31 As a result of substantial write-offs, the Allowance for Doubtful Accounts has a *debit* balance of $200. Aging of the accounts receivable (which amount to $80,000) indicates that a credit balance of $1,200 in the Allowance for Doubtful Accounts is required.

Instructions Prepare general journal entries to record the transactions and adjustments listed above.

SOLUTION TO DEMONSTRATION PROBLEM

General Journal

19____

July 1	Accounts Receivable, P. Linn	1,545.00	
	Sales		1,545.00
	Sale of merchandise on account.		

3	Notes Receivable	1,500.00	
	Freight-out Expense	45.00	
	Accounts Receivable, P. Linn		1,545.00

To record credit to P. Linn for freight paid by him and
receipt of 60-day, 8% note for balance of account owed.

18	Accounts Receivable, Baxter Company	2,200.00	
	Sales		2,200.00

Sale of merchandise on account, terms 2/10, n/30.

27	Cash	1,508.00	
	Interest Earned		8.00
	Notes Receivable		1,500.00

Discounted note from P. Linn at bank.

28	Cash	2,156.00	
	Sales Discounts	44.00	
	Accounts Receivable, Baxter Company		2,200.00

Received payment from Baxter Company within discount
period.

Aug. 8	Accounts Receivable, E. Jones	1,200.00	
	Sales		1,200.00

Sale of merchandise on account, terms 2/10, n/30.

Sept. 1	Accounts Receivable, P. Linn	1,520.00	
	Cash		1,520.00

To record payment to bank on dishonored note, and to
charge this amount to maker of note.

7	Notes Receivable	1,216.00	
	Discount on Notes Receivable		16.00
	Accounts Receivable, E. Jones		1,200.00

Received 60-day note with interest included in face
amount in settlement of open account.

10	Allowance for Doubtful Accounts	120.00	
	Accounts Receivable, K. L. Treff		120.00

Wrote off uncollectible account from K. L. Treff.

Oct. 15	Accounts Receivable, Allen Blaine	300.00	
	Allowance for Doubtful Accounts		300.00

To reverse the entry writing off Blaine's account.

15	Cash	300.00	
	Accounts Receivable, Allen Blaine		300.00

To record collection of Blaine's account which was
written off in June.

25	Cash	1,538.24	
	Accounts Receivable, P. Linn		1,520.00
	Interest Earned		18.24

Collected Linn account in full plus interest @ 8% for 54
days as follows: $1,520 \times 8\% \times \frac{54}{360}$, or $18.24.

Nov. 6	Cash	1,216.00	
	Discount on Notes Receivable	16.00	
	Notes Receivable		1,216.00
	Interest Earned		16.00
	Received payment on note from E. Jones dated Sept. 7.		
Dec. 31	Uncollectible Accounts Expense	1,400.00	
	Allowance for Doubtful Accounts		1,400.00

To provide for estimated uncollectibles as follows:

Balance required	$1,200
Present balance (debit)	200
Required increase in allowance	$1,400

REVIEW QUESTIONS

1 Adams Company determines at year-end that its Allowance for Doubtful Accounts should be increased by $6,500. Give the adjusting entry to carry out this decision.

2 In making the annual adjusting entry for uncollectible accounts, a company may utilize a **balance sheet approach** to make the estimate or it may use an **income statement approach.** Explain these two alternative approaches.

3 At the end of its first year in business, Baxter Laboratories had accounts receivable totaling $148,500. After careful analysis of the individual accounts, the credit manager estimated that $146,100 would ultimately be collected. Give the journal entry required to reflect this estimate in the accounts.

4 In February of its second year of operations, Baxter Laboratories (question 3 above) learned of the failure of a customer, Sterling Corporation, which owed Baxter $800. Nothing could be collected. Give the journal entry to recognize the uncollectibility of the receivable from Sterling Corporation.

5 What is the **direct charge-off method** of handling credit losses as opposed to the **allowance method?** What is its principal shortcoming?

6 Morgan Corporation has decided to write off its account receivable from Brill Company because the latter has entered bankruptcy. What general ledger accounts should be debited and credited, assuming that the allowance method is in use? What general ledger accounts should be debited and credited if the direct charge-off method is in use?

7 Mill Company, which has accounts receivable of $309,600 and an allowance for doubtful accounts of $3,600, decides to write off as worthless a past-due account receivable for $1,500 from J. D. North. What effect will the write-off have upon total current assets? Upon net income for the period? Explain.

8 Describe a procedure by which management could be informed each month of the status of collections and the overall quality of the accounts receivable on hand.

9 The A Corporation has in its ledger an account entitled Allowance for Bad Debts; B Corporation uses an account entitled Allowance for Doubtful Accounts; and C Corporation maintains an account called Reserve for Uncollectible Accounts. Does this information indicate that the three companies follow different methods of accounting for the expense arising from uncollectible accounts? Into which of the five major groups of accounts would you classify the three accounts listed?

10 Magnum Corporation had accounts receivable of $100,000 and an Allowance

for Doubtful Accounts of $3,500 just prior to writing off as worthless an account receivable from Standard Company in the amount of $1,000. State the net realizable value of the accounts receivable before and after the write-off of this receivable from Standard Company.

11 What are the terms used to describe the two parties to a promissory note? What is the title of the ledger account in which each of the parties would record the note?

12 In order to obtain a bank loan, Baker Company signs a 90-day note payable to the bank in the amount of $1,000 plus interest at the annual rate of 8%. Prepare the journal entry used by Baker to record this borrowing. Did Baker Company incur a contingent liability? Explain.

13 Does a contingent liability appear on a balance sheet? If so, in what part of the balance sheet?

14 Determine the maturity date of the following notes:
a A three-month note dated March 10
b A 30-day note dated August 15
c A 90-day note dated July 2

15 X Company acquires a 9%, 60-day note receivable from a customer, Robert Waters, in settlement of an existing account receivable of $4,000. Give the journal entry to record acquisition of the note and the journal entry to record its collection at maturity.

16 Jonas Company issues a 90-day, 12% note payable to replace an account payable to Smith Supply Company in the amount of $8,000. Draft the journal entries (in general journal form) to record the issuance of the note payable and the payment of the note at the maturity date.

17 Distinguish between
a Current and long-term liabilities
b Estimated and contingent liabilities

18 Howard Benson applied to the City Bank for a loan of $20,000 for a period of three months. The loan was granted at an annual interest rate of 12%. Write a sentence illustrating the wording of the note signed by Benson if:
a Interest is stated separately in the note.
b Interest is included in the face amount of the note.

19 With reference to question 18 above, give the journal entry required on the books of Howard Benson for issuance of each of the two types of notes.

EXERCISES

Ex. 9-1 The general ledger control account for accounts receivable shows a balance of $64,000 at the end of the year. An aging analysis of the individual customers' accounts indicates doubtful accounts totaling $5,440. Draft the year-end adjusting entry for uncollectible accounts under each of the following independent assumptions:
a The Allowance for Doubtful Accounts had a credit balance of $1,760.
b The Allowance for Doubtful Accounts had a debit balance of $592.

Ex. 9-2 The unadjusted trial balance for Muir Corporation at the end of the current year includes the following accounts:

	Debit	Credit
Accounts receivable	$144,000	
Allowance for doubtful accounts		$ 1,092
Sales (25% represent cash sales)		576,000

Compute the uncollectible accounts expense for the current year, assuming that uncollectible accounts expense is determined as follows:
a 1% of total sales.
b 1½% of credit sales.
c Allowance for doubtful accounts is increased to equal 3% of gross accounts receivable.

Ex. 9-3 Green Scene, Inc., reported the following amounts on its balance sheet at the end of last year:

Notes receivable from customers	$12,000
Accrued interest on notes receivable	240
Accounts receivable	50,400
Less: Allowance for doubtful accounts	1,200

You are to record the following events of the current year in general journal entries:
a Accounts receivable of $1,152 are written off as uncollectible.
b A customer's note for $330 on which interest of $18 has been accrued in the accounts is deemed uncollectible, and both balances are written off against the Allowance for Doubtful Accounts.
c An account receivable for $156 previously written off is collected.
d Aging of accounts receivable at the end of the current year indicates a need for a $1,800 allowance to cover possible failure to collect accounts currently outstanding.

Ex. 9-4 Milroy Company has accounts receivable from 100 customers; the controlling account shows a debit balance of $960,000. The subsidiary ledger shows that 99 customers' accounts have debit balances and one has a credit balance of $36,000. How should these facts be shown in the balance sheet? Give the reason for the treatment you recommend.

Ex. 9-5 Use the 60-day, 6% method to compute interest on the following notes:
a $6,501 at 6% for 60 days
b $11,838 at 6% for 90 days
c $21,372 at 6% for 30 days
d $25,245 at 8% for 60 days
e $37,908 at 12% for 120 days
f $13,878 at 18% for 90 days

Ex. 9-6 Dale Motors, an automobile dealer, sold three trucks to Zoro Truck Lines on April 1, Year 1, for a total price of $68,000. Under the terms of the sale, Dale Motors received $20,000 cash and a promissory note due in full 18 months later. The face amount of the note was $53,760, which included interest on the note for the 18 months.
Prepare all entries (in general journal form) for Dale Motors relating to the sales transaction and to the note for the fiscal year ended September 30, Year 1. Include the adjusting entry needed to record interest earned to September 30.

Ex. 9-7 Three notes receivable, each in the amount of $20,000, were discounted by a company at its bank on May 10. The bank charged a discount rate of 6%, applied to the maturity value. From the following data, compute the proceeds of each note. (Answers should be rounded to the nearest cent wherever necessary.)

Date of Note	Interest Rate, %	Life of Note
a Apr. 10	6	3 months
b Mar. 31	10	60 days
c Mar. 11	8	90 days

Ex. 9-8 On November 1, Ward Corporation borrowed $100,000 from a local bank, agree-

ing to repay that amount plus 9% interest (per annum) in six months. Show the presentation of the bank loan on Ward Corporation's December 31 balance sheet, assuming that the company signed a note as follows:

a For $100,000, interest payable at maturity.

b With the interest charge included in the face amount of the note.

PROBLEMS

Group A

9A-1 The balance sheet prepared by Milagros Santos at December 31 last year included $504,000 in accounts receivable and an allowance for doubtful accounts of $26,400. During January of the current year selected transactions are summarized as follows:

(1) *Sales on account*	$368,000
(2) *Sales returns & allowances*	7,360
(3) *Cash payments by customers (no cash discounts)*	364,800
(4) *Account receivable from Acme Company written off as worthless*	9,280

After a careful aging and analysis of all customers' accounts at January 31, it was decided that the allowance for doubtful accounts should be adjusted to a balance of $29,280 in order to reflect accounts receivable at net realizable value in the January 31 balance sheet.

Instructions

a Give the appropriate entry in general journal form for each of the four numbered items above and the adjusting entry at January 31 to provide for uncollectible accounts.

b Show the amounts of accounts receivable and the allowance for doubtful accounts as they would appear in a partial balance sheet at January 31.

c Assume that three months after the receivable from Acme Company had been written off as worthless, Acme Company won a large award in the settlement of patent litigation and immediately paid the $9,280 debt to Milagros Santos. Give the journal entry or entries (in general journal form) to reflect this recovery of a receivable previously written off.

9A-2 In the fiscal year ended October 31, the Huron Corporation engaged in the following transactions involving promissory notes:

June 6 Issued a 45-day 8% note to a long-time employee, C. W. Jones, as evidence of a loan in the amount of $6,000.

July 13 Purchased office equipment from New Company. This invoice amount was $9,000 and the New Company agreed to accept as full payment an 8% three-month note for the invoiced amount.

July 21 Paid the Jones note plus accrued interest.

Sept. 1 Borrowed $126,000 from Security Bank at an interest rate of 8% per annum; signed a 90-day note with interest included in the face amount of the note.

Oct. 1 Purchased merchandise in the amount of $5,400 from Pyles Co. Gave in settlement a 90-day note bearing interest at 6%.

Oct. 13 The $9,000 note payable to New Company matured today. Paid the interest accrued and issued a new 30-day, 8% note to replace the maturing note.

Instructions

a Prepare journal entries (in general journal form) to record the above transactions.

b Prepare the adjusting entries needed at October 31, prior to closing the accounts.

9A-3 Leather Products sells to retail stores on 30-day open account, but requires customers who fail to pay invoices within 30 days to substitute promissory notes for their past-due accounts. No sales discount is offered. Among recent transactions were the following:

Oct. 17 Sold merchandise to S. R. Davis on account, $72,000, terms n/30.

Nov. 16 Received a 60-day, 9% note from Davis dated today in settlement of his open account of $72,000.

Dec. 26 Discounted the Davis note at the bank. The bank discount rate was 6% applied to the maturity value of the note for the 20 days remaining to maturity.

Jan. 15 Received notice from the bank that the Davis note due today was in default. Paid the bank the maturity value of the note. Since Davis has extensive business interests, the management of Leather Products is confident that no loss will be incurred on the defaulted note.

Jan. 25 Made a $48,000 loan to John Raymond on a 30-day, 9% note.

Instructions

a Prepare in general journal form the entries necessary to record the above transactions.

b Prepare the adjusting journal entry needed at January 31, the end of the company's fiscal year, to record interest accrued on the two notes receivable. (Accrue interest at 9% per annum from date of default on the maturity value of the Davis note.)

9A-4 The balance sheet prepared by Arrowhead Associates at December 31, Year 6, included accounts receivable of $380,640, and an allowance for doubtful accounts of $9,720. The company's sales volume in Year 7 reached a new high of $2,562,000 and cash collections from customers amounted to $2,478,768. Among these collections was the recovery in full of a $4,680 receivable from Anthony Walker, a customer whose account had been written off as worthless late in Year 6. During Year 7, it was necessary to write off as uncollectible customers' accounts totaling $10,098.

On December 1, Year 7, Arrowhead Associates sold for $216,000 a tract of land acquired as a building site several years earlier at a cost of $144,000. The land was now considered unsuitable as a building site. Terms of sale were $60,000 cash and a 6%, six-month note for $156,000. The buyer was a large corporation and the note was regarded as fully collectible.

At December 31, Year 7, the accounts receivable included $60,174 of past-due accounts. After careful study of all past-due accounts, the management estimated that the probable loss contained therein was 20% and that, in addition, 2% of the current accounts receivable might prove uncollectible.

Instructions

a Prepare journal entries in general journal form, for all transactions in Year 7 relating to accounts and notes receivable.

b Prepare the necessary adjusting entries at December 31, Year 7. Round amounts to the nearest dollar for uncollectible accounts expense.

c What amount should appear in the income statement for Year 7 as uncollectible accounts expense?

d Prepare a partial balance sheet at December 31, Year 7, showing the accounts indicated above.

9A-5 During the fiscal year ending June 30, Valley Builders had the following transactions relating to notes payable.

Feb. 6 Borrowed $10,000 from L. W. Smith and issued a 45-day, 8% note payable as evidence of the debt.

Mar. 12 Purchased office equipment from E-Z Company. The invoice amount was $15,000 and the E-Z Company agreed to accept as full payment a 6%, three-month note for the invoiced amount.

Mar. 23 Paid the note made out to L. W. Smith plus accrued interest.

May 1 Borrowed $200,000 from First Bank at an interest rate of 7% per annum; signed a 90-day note with interest included in the face amount of the note.

May 31 Purchased merchandise in the amount of $7,500 from Patten Co. Gave in settlement a 90-day note bearing interest at 8%.

June 12 The $15,000 note payable to E-Z Company matured today. Paid in cash the interest accrued and issued a new 30-day note bearing interest at 7% to replace the maturing note.

Instructions

a Prepare journal entries (in general journal form) to record the above transactions.

b Prepare the adjusting entries needed at June 30, prior to closing the accounts.

9A-6 During a period of rapid expansion, Greystone Builders was faced with a shortage of cash. A policy was therefore established of obtaining notes receivable from customers whenever possible. These notes receivable were endorsed by Greystone Builders and discounted with its bank as a means of speeding up the inflow of cash. The bank applies a discount rate of 6% to the maturity value of the notes on these transactions. The company makes some sales on a 30-day open account, but any customer who does not pay in full within 30 days is asked to substitute an interest-bearing note for the past-due account. Some customers are required to sign promissory notes at the time of sale. When a note receivable is discounted, the company's policy calls for crediting the Notes Receivable account. A memorandum record of contingent liabilities is maintained.

A partial list of transactions for the six months ended December 31 is given below.

July 3 Sale of merchandise to B. Dawson on account, $52,195. It was agreed that Dawson would submit a 60-day, 6% note upon receipt of the merchandise and would deduct any freight he paid on the goods.

July 5 Received from Dawson a letter stating that he paid $195 freight on the shipment of July 3. He enclosed a 60-day, 6% note dated July 5 for $52,000, the net amount owed.

Aug. 4 Discounted Dawson's note at bank. (Bank discount rate 6%.) Round amounts to the nearest dollar.

Aug. 23 Sold merchandise to S. L. Adams on account, $3,900; terms 2/10, n/30.

Sept. 3 Received notice from the bank that Dawson dishonored his note due today. Made payment to bank for maturity value of note.

Sept. 22 Received a 60-day, 6% note from S. L. Adams in settlement of open account.

Oct. 2 Sold merchandise on account, $4,680, to Samson, Inc; terms 2/10, n/30.

Nov. 1 Received a 90-day, 6% note as settlement of the $4,680 account receivable from Samson, Inc.

Nov. 2 Received cash from B. Dawson in full settlement of his account due today, including interest of 6% from September 3 on maturity value of the note.

Nov. 21 S. L. Adams was unable to pay his note due today. Received a new 60-day, 6% note in settlement of old note and interest.

Instructions

a Prepare journal entries (in general journal form) to record the transactions listed above.

b Prepare any necessary adjusting entries for interest at December 31.

c Prepare a partial balance sheet at December 31 showing the notes and interest resulting from the above transactions.

Group B

9B-1 The balance sheet of Canyon Corporation at December 31 of last year showed $252,000 in accounts receivable and a credit balance of $13,200 in the allowance for doubtful accounts. The following summary shows the totals of certain types of transactions occurring during January of the current year.

(1) *Sales on account* *$180,000*

(2) *Sales returns & allowances* *3,600*

(3) *Cash payments by customers (no cash discounts)* *177,600*

(4) *Account receivable from Dan King written off as worthless following*

     the failure of his business *3,840*

At January 31, after a careful aging and analysis of all customers' accounts, the company decided that the allowance for doubtful accounts should be adjusted to the amount of $14,640 in order to reflect accounts receivable at net realizable value in the January 31 balance sheet.

Instructions
a Give the appropriate entry in general journal form for each of the four numbered items above and the adjusting entry at January 31 to provide for uncollectible accounts.
b Show the amounts of accounts receivable and the allowance for doubtful accounts as they would appear in a partial balance sheet at January 31.
c Assume that six months after the receivable from Dan King had been written off as worthless, he won $120,000 in a lottery and immediately paid the $3,840 owed to Canyon Corporation. Give the journal entry or entries to reflect this collection in Canyon Corporation's accounts. (Use general journal form.)

9B-2 The transactions relating to accounts payable and notes payable shown below were carried out by the Martin Company during the four months ended June 30:
Mar.   **6** Purchased merchandise from A. B. Hayes on open account, $25,200.
Apr.   **8** Informed A. B. Hayes that it was unable to make payment as agreed. Hayes accepted a 7%, 60-day note in settlement of account.
Apr. **20** Borrowed $48,000 from Third National Bank today and signed a 30-day, 8% note as evidence of indebtedness. The interest was included in the face amount of the note.
May **15** Purchased merchandise from Birmingham, Incorporated, on 30-day open account, $19,200.
May **20** Paid note due today at Third National Bank.
June **7** Paid note due today to A. B. Hayes.

Instructions Prepare all necessary journal entries (in general journal form) to record the above transactions in the Martin Company's accounts. Show all supporting computations. Adjusting entries are not required.

9B-3 Snow Company, owned by Linda Snow, has for the past three years been engaged in selling paper novelty goods to retail stores. Sales are made on credit and the company has regularly estimated its uncollectible accounts expense as a percentage of net sales. The percentage used has been $\frac{1}{2}$ of 1% of net sales. However, it appears that this provision has been inadequate, because the Allowance for Doubtful Accounts has a debit balance of $2,693.90 at May 31 prior to making the annual provision. Snow has therefore decided to change the method of estimating uncollectible accounts expense and to rely upon an analysis of the age and character of the accounts receivable at the end of each accounting period.

At May 31, the end of the company's fiscal year, the accounts receivable totaled $178,816. This total amount included past-due accounts in the amount of $36,982. None of these past-due accounts was considered hopeless; all accounts regarded as worthless had been written off as rapidly as they were determined to be uncollectible. These write-offs had totaled $5,113.90 during the year. After careful investigation of the past-due accounts at May 31, Linda Snow decided that the probable loss contained therein was 10%, and that in addition she should anticipate a loss of 1% of the current accounts receivable.

Instructions

a Compute the probable loss contained in the accounts receivable at May 31, based on the analysis by the owner.

b Prepare the journal entry necessary to carry out the change in company policy with respect to providing for uncollectible accounts expense.

9B-4 Several transactions involving notes payable were carried out by Glenbar Corporation during the fiscal year ended October 31.

June 6 Borrowed $11,200 from T. Hutchins, issuing to him a 45-day, 6% note payable.

July 13 Purchased office equipment from Harper Company. The invoice amount was $16,800 and the Harper Company agreed to accept as full payment a 6%, three-month note for the invoiced amount.

July 21 Paid the Hutchins note plus accrued interest.

Sept. 1 Borrowed $235,200 from Sun National Bank at an interest rate of 6% per annum; signed a 90-day note with interest included in the face amount of the note.

Oct. 1 Purchased merchandise in the amount of $2,520 from Kramer Co. Gave in settlement a 90-day note bearing interest at 7%.

Oct. 13 The $16,800 note payable to Harper Company matured today. Paid the interest accrued and issued a new 30-day, 6% note to replace the maturing note.

Instructions

a Prepare journal entries (in general journal form) to record the above transactions.

b Prepare the adjusting entries needed at October 31, prior to closing the accounts.

9B-5 J. Roberts, controller of Walnut Cabinets, became concerned over the company's weak cash position. To improve this situation, Roberts decided to minimize the amount tied up in receivables by discounting at the bank the notes receivable from customers. The bank applies a discount rate to the maturity value of the notes, which varies with the quality of the note and the general level of interest rates.

Walnut Cabinets makes some sales on 30-day open account, but any customer who does not pay in full within 30 days is asked to substitute an interest-bearing note for the past-due account. Some customers are required to sign promissory notes at the time of sale. The company uses the allowance method of accounting for uncollectible accounts.

A partial list of transactions for the six months ended December 31 is given below.

July 1 Sale of merchandise to G. Adler on account, $3,863. It was agreed that Adler would submit a 60-day, 8% note upon receipt of the merchandise and would deduct any freight he paid on the goods.

July 3 Received from Adler a letter stating that he had paid $113 freight on the shipment of July 1. He enclosed a 60-day, 8% note dated July 3 for $3,750.

July 18 Sold merchandise on account, $5,500, to Ward Company; terms 2/10, n/30.

July 27 Discounted Adler note at bank and received $3,770 in cash.

July 28 Ward Company paid account in full.

Aug. 8 Sold merchandise to W. Patrick on account, $3,000; terms 2/10, n/30.

Sept. 1 Received notice from the bank that Adler had dishonored his note due today. The bank charged the company's account for $3,800, the maturity value of the note.

Sept. 7 Received a 60-day, 7% note from W. Patrick in settlement of open account.

Sept. 10 It was ascertained that an account receivable from H. B. Gilkes amounting to $300 could not be collected and it was written off.

Oct. 15 An account receivable of $750 from Elaine Anderson had been written off in June; full payment was unexpectedly received from Anderson.

Oct. 25 Received cash from G. Adler in full settlement of his account due today, including interest of 8% on $3,800 from September 1, maturity date of note.

Nov. 6 W. Patrick paid his note due today.

Dec. 31 As a result of substantial write-offs, the Allowance for Doubtful Accounts has a *debit* balance of $500. Aging of the accounts receivable (which amount to $200,000) indicates that a credit balance of $3,000 in the Allowance for Doubtful Accounts is required.

Instructions Prepare journal entries (in general journal form) to record the transactions and adjustments listed above.

9B-6 Classic Furniture Company, a manufacturer, sells furniture to wholesalers and also to retail stores. All sales are made on credit, but there have been few credit losses of consequence. The policy of the company is to provide for uncollectible accounts expense as a percentage of net sales rather than by aging accounts receivable to determine the estimated uncollectible portion. The company's experience has been that an annual provision for uncollectible accounts expense of $\frac{1}{4}$ of 1% of net sales is adequate.

In April of the current year, Classic Furniture Company decided to open a new sales territory in another country. Sales of $482,800 were achieved in this new territory during the year, but some of the sales were made to customers of questionable credit standing. Classic Furniture Company estimated that during the period of development of the new territory the provision for uncollectible accounts for sales made should be 3% of net sales.

During the latter part of the year, the anticipated credit losses became apparent. The European Desk Company, which owed $4,080, notified Classic Furniture Company that it had been forced to suspend operations and was unable to pay any of its existing debts. Further collection efforts proved futile, and on September 12 the account was written off as worthless.

Another new customer, Maple Furniture House, entered receivership. On October 10, the receiver sent Classic Furniture Company a check for $2,074 and stated that nothing further could be paid. The balance of the account prior to this compromise settlement had been $5,219. The uncollected balance of the account was worthless.

On October 15, receivables of $2,224 from the Redwood Furniture Co., and $3,849 from the Heidelberg Co. were written off as uncollectible after extensive collection efforts had failed. On November 2, however, both of these accounts were collected in full.

Total sales during the year amounted to $3,102,160, including sales in the new territory. At the beginning of the year, the credit balance in the Allowance for Doubtful Accounts had amounted to $24,888. In addition to the credit losses in the new sales territory, accounts receivable aggregating $5,763 had been written off as worthless during the year in the company's old territory.

Instructions

a Prepare journal entries (in general journal form) for all the indicated transactions. Use one entry to summarize the sales, all of which were credit transactions. Also, use one entry to summarize all write-offs of receivables during the year.

b Open general ledger accounts for Uncollectible Accounts Expense and for the Allowance for Doubtful Accounts. Post the entries called for in *a* to the accounts.

c Compute the uncollectible accounts expense for the year, make the adjusting entry and closing entry needed at December 31, and post these entries to the ledger accounts required in *b*.

BUSINESS DECISION PROBLEM 9

Music Box and Memphis Sound are two companies engaged in selling stereo equipment to the public. Both companies sell equipment at a price 50% greater than cost. Customers may pay cash, purchase on open 30-day accounts, or make installment payments over a 36-month period. The installment receivables include a three-year interest charge (which amounts to 30% of the sales price) in the face amount of the contract. Condensed income statements prepared by the companies for their first year of operations are shown below:

	Music Box	Memphis Sound
Sales	$387,000	$288,000
Cost of goods sold	210,000	192,000
Gross profit on sales	$177,000	$ 96,000
Operating expenses	63,000	60,000
Operating income	$114,000	$ 36,000
Interest earned	–0–	10,800
Net income	$114,000	$ 46,800

When Music Box makes a sale of stereo equipment on the installment plan, it immediately credits the Sales account with the face amount of the installment receivable. In other words, the interest charges are included in sales revenue at the time of the sale. The interest charges included in Music Box's installment receivables originating in the first year amount to $72,000, of which $59,100 is unearned at the end of the first year. Music Box uses the direct charge-off method to recognize uncollectible accounts expense. During the year, accounts receivable of $2,100 were written off as uncollectible, but no entry was made for $37,200 of accounts estimated to be uncollectible at year-end.

Memphis Sound imputes interest on its installment receivables and recognizes the interest *earned during the year* as interest revenue. Memphis Sound provides for uncollectible accounts by the allowance method. The company recognized uncollectible accounts expense of $11,100 during the year and this amount appeared to be adequate.

Instructions

a Prepare a condensed income statement for Music Box for the year, using the same methods of accounting for installment sales and uncollectible accounts as were used by Memphis Sound. The income statement you prepare should contain the same seven items shown in the illustrated income statements. Provide footnotes showing the computations you made in revising the amount of sales and any other figures you decide to change.

b Compare the income statement you have prepared in part *a* to the one originally prepared by Music Box. Which income statement do you believe better reflects the results of the company's operations during the year? Explain.

c What do you believe to be the key factor responsible for making one of these companies more profitable than the other? What corrective action would you recommend be taken by the less profitable company to improve future performance?

10   **Inventories**

Some basic questions relating to inventory

In earlier sections of this book the procedures for recording inventory at the end of the accounting period have been illustrated. The use of the inventory figure in both the balance sheet and the income statement has been demonstrated, and particular emphasis has been placed on the procedure for computing the cost of goods sold by deducting the ending inventory from the cost of goods available for sale during the period.

In all the previous illustrations, the dollar amount of the ending inventory has been given with only a brief explanation as to how this amount was determined. The valuation of inventory, as for most other types of assets, has been stated to be at cost, but the concept of *cost* as applied to inventories of merchandise has not been explored or defined.

In this chapter we shall consider some of the fundamental questions involved in accounting for inventories. Among the questions to be considered are these:

1 What goods are to be included in inventory?
2 How is the amount of the ending inventory determined?
3 What are the arguments for and against each of several alternative methods of inventory valuation?
4 What are the advantages of a perpetual inventory system?

Inventory defined

One of the largest assets in a retail store or in a wholesale business is the inventory of merchandise, and the sale of this merchandise at prices in excess of cost is the major source of revenue. For a merchandising company, *the inventory consists of all goods owned and held for sale in the regular course of business.* Merchandise held for sale will normally be converted into cash within less than a year's time and is therefore re-garded as a current asset. In the balance sheet, inventory is listed imme-diately after accounts receivable, because it is just one step further removed from conversion into cash than are the accounts receivable.

In manufacturing businesses there are three major types of inventories: *raw materials, goods in process of manufacture,* and *finished goods.* All three classes of inventories are included in the current asset section of the balance sheet.

To expand our definition of inventory to fit manufacturing companies as well as merchandising companies, we can say that inventory means "the aggregate of those items of tangible personal property which (*1*) are held for sale in the ordinary course of business, (*2*) are in process of produc-tion for such sale, or (*3*) are to be currently consumed in the production of goods or services to be available for sale."[1]

Inventory valuation and the measurement of income

In measuring the gross profit on sales earned during an accounting period, we subtract the *cost of goods sold* from the total *sales* of the period. The figure for sales is easily accumulated from the daily record of sales transactions, but in many businesses no day-to-day record is maintained showing the cost of goods sold.[2] The figure representing the cost of goods sold during an entire accounting period is computed at the end of the period by separating the *cost of goods available for sale* into two elements:

1 The cost of the goods sold
2 The cost of the goods not sold, which therefore comprise the ending inventory

This idea, with which you are already quite familiar, may be concisely stated in the form of an equation as follows:

Finding cost of goods sold

$$\text{Cost of Goods Available for Sale} - \text{Ending Inventory} = \text{Cost of Goods Sold}$$

Determining the amount of the ending inventory is the key step in establishing the cost of goods sold. In separating the *cost of goods availa-*

---

[1] American Institute of Certified Public Accountants, *Accounting Research and Terminology Bulletins,* Final Edition (New York: 1961), p. 28.

[2] As explained in Chap. 5, a company that maintains perpetual inventory records will have a day-to-day record of the cost of goods sold and of goods in inventory. Our present discussion, however, is based on the assumption that the periodic system of inventory is being used.

ble for sale into its components of *goods sold* and *goods not sold,* we are just as much interested in establishing the proper amount for cost of goods sold as in determining a proper figure for inventory. Throughout this chapter you should bear in mind that the procedures for determining the amount of the ending inventory are also the means for determining the cost of goods sold. The valuation of inventory and the determination of the cost of goods sold are in effect the two sides of a single coin.

The American Institute of Certified Public Accountants has summarized this relationship between inventory valuation and the measurement of income in the following words: "A major objective of accounting for inventories is the proper determination of income through the process of matching appropriate costs against revenues."[3] The expression "matching costs against revenues" means determining what portion of the cost of goods available for sale should be deducted from the revenue of the current period and what portion should be carried forward (as inventory) to be matched against the revenue of the following period.

Importance of an accurate valuation of inventory

The most important current assets in the balance sheets of most companies are cash, accounts receivable, and inventory. Of these three, the inventory of merchandise is usually much the largest. Because of the relatively large size of this asset, an error in the valuation of inventory may cause a material misstatement of financial position and of net income. An error of 20% in valuing the inventory may have as much effect on the financial statements as would the complete omission of the asset cash.

An error in inventory will of course lead to other erroneous figures in the balance sheet, such as the total current assets, total assets, owner's equity, and the total of liabilities and owner's equity. The error will also affect key figures in the income statement, such as the cost of goods sold, the gross profit on sales, and the net income for the period. Finally, it is important to recognize that *the ending inventory of one year is also the beginning inventory of the following year.* Consequently, the income statement of the second year will also be in error by the full amount of the original error in inventory valuation.

ILLUSTRATION OF THE EFFECTS OF AN ERROR IN VALUING INVENTORY
Assume that on December 31, 1979, the inventory of the Hillside Company is actually $100,000 but, through an accidental error, it is recorded as $90,000. The effects of this $10,000 error on the income statement for the year 1979 are indicated in the first illustration on page 367, showing two income statements side by side. The left-hand set of figures shows the inventory of December 31, 1979, at the proper value of $100,000 and represents a correct income statement for the year 1979. The right-hand

---

[3] AICPA, *op. cit.,* p. 28.

set of figures represents an incorrect income statement, because the ending inventory is erroneously listed as $90,000. Note the differences between the two income statements with respect to net income, gross profit on sales, and cost of goods sold.

HILLSIDE COMPANY
Income Statement
For the Year Ended December 31, 1979

		With Correct Ending Inventory		With Incorrect Ending Inventory
Effect of error in inventory	*Sales*		$240,000	$240,000
	Cost of goods sold:			
	Beginning inventory, Jan. 1, 1979 . . .	$ 75,000		$ 75,000
	Purchases	210,000		210,000
	Cost of goods available for sale . . .	$285,000		$285,000
	Less: Ending inventory, Dec. 31, 1979	100,000		90,000
	Cost of goods sold		185,000	195,000
	Gross profit on sales		$ 55,000	$ 45,000
	Operating expenses		30,000	30,000
	Net income		$ 25,000	$ 15,000

HILLSIDE COMPANY
Income Statement
For the Year Ended December 31, 1980

		With Correct Beginning Inventory		With Incorrect Beginning Inventory
Effect on succeeding year	*Sales*		$265,000	$265,000
	Cost of goods sold:			
	Beginning inventory, Jan. 1, 1980 . . .	$100,000		$ 90,000
	Purchases	230,000		230,000
	Cost of goods available for sale . . .	$330,000		$320,000
	Less: Ending inventory, Dec. 31, 1980	120,000		120,000
	Cost of goods sold		210,000	200,000
	Gross profit on sales		$ 55,000	$ 65,000
	Operating expenses		33,000	33,000
	Net income		$ 22,000	$ 32,000

This illustration shows that an understatement of $10,000 in the ending inventory for the year 1979 caused an understatement of $10,000 in the net income for 1979. Next, consider the effect of this error on the income statement of the following year. The ending inventory of 1979 is, of course, the beginning inventory of 1980. The preceding illustration is now continued to show side by side a correct statement and an incorrect statement for 1980. The ending inventory of $120,000 for the year 1980 is the same in both statements and is to be considered correct. Note that the $10,000 error in the beginning inventory of the right-hand statement causes an error in the cost of goods sold, in gross profit, and in net income for the year 1980.

COUNTERBALANCING ERRORS The illustrated income statements for the years 1979 and 1980 show that an understatement of the ending inventory in 1979 caused an understatement of net income in that year and an offsetting overstatement of net income for 1980. Over a period of two years the effects of an inventory error on net income will counterbalance, and the total net income for the two years together is the same as if the error had not occurred. Since the error in reported net income for the first year is exactly offset by the error in reported net income for the second year, it might be argued that an inventory error has no serious conse-quences. Such an argument is not sound, for it disregards the fact that accurate yearly figures for net income are a primary objective of the accounting process. Moreover, many actions by management and many decisions by creditors and owners are based directly on the annual financial statements. To produce dependable annual statements, inven-tory must be accurately determined at the end of each accounting period. The counterbalancing effect of an inventory error is illustrated below:

	With Inventory Correctly Stated	With Inventory at Dec. 31, 1979, Understated	
		Reported Net Income Will Be	Reported Net Income Will Be Overstated (Understated)
Counter- Net income for 1979	$25,000	$15,000	($10,000)
balancing Net income for 1980	22,000	32,000	10,000
effect			
on net Total net income for two years	$47,000	$47,000	–0–
income			

RELATION OF INVENTORY ERRORS TO NET INCOME The effects of errors in inventory upon net income may be summarized as follows:

1 When the *ending* inventory is understated, the net income for the period will be understated.

2 When the *ending* inventory is overstated, the net income for the period will be overstated.

3 When the *beginning* inventory is understated, the net income for the period will be overstated.

4 When the *beginning* inventory is overstated, the net income for the period will be understated.

Taking a physical inventory

At the end of each accounting period the ledger accounts will show up-to-date balances for most of the assets. For inventory, however, the balance in the ledger account represents the **beginning** inventory, because no entry has been made in the Inventory account since the end of the preceding period. All purchases of merchandise during the present period have been recorded in the Purchases account. The ending inventory does not appear anywhere in the ledger accounts; it must be determined by a physical count of merchandise on hand at the end of the accounting period.

Establishing a balance sheet valuation for the ending inventory requires two steps: (1) determining the quantity of each kind of merchandise on hand, and (2) multiplying the quantity by the cost per unit. The first step is called **taking the inventory;** the second is called **pricing the inventory.** Taking inventory, or more precisely, taking a physical inventory, means making a systematic count of all merchandise on hand.

In most merchandising businesses the taking of a physical inventory is a year-end event. In some lines of business an inventory may be taken at the close of each month. It is common practice to take inventory after regular business hours or on Sunday. By taking the inventory while business operations are suspended, a more accurate count is possible than if goods were being sold or received while the count was in process.

PLANNING THE PHYSICAL INVENTORY Unless the taking of a physical inventory is carefully planned and supervised, serious errors are apt to occur which will invalidate the results of the count. To prevent such errors as the double counting of items, the omission of goods from the count, and other quantitative errors, it is desirable to plan the inventory so that the work of one person serves as a check on the accuracy of another.

There are various methods of counting merchandise. One of the simplest procedures is carried out by the use of two-member teams. One member of the team counts and calls the description and quantity of each item. The other person lists the descriptions and quantities on an inventory sheet. (In some situations, a tape recorder is useful in recording quantities counted.) When all goods have been counted and listed, the items on the inventory sheet are priced at cost, and the unit prices are multiplied by the quantities to determine the valuation of the inventory.

To assure the accuracy of the recorded counts, a representative number of items should be recounted by supervisors. Some businesses make a practice of counting all merchandise a second time and comparing the quantities established by the different teams. The initials of the persons making both the first and the second counts should be placed on an inventory tag attached to each lot of merchandise counted. Once it is known that all merchandise has been tagged and that the counts are accurate, the tags are gathered and sent to the accounting office so that all the information can be summarized and the dollar valuation of inventory can be computed.

INCLUDING ALL GOODS OWNED All goods to which the company has title should be included in the inventory, regardless of their location. Title to merchandise ordinarily passes from seller to buyer at the time the goods are delivered. No question arises as to the ownership of merchandise on the shelves, in stock rooms, or in warehouses. A question of ownership does arise, however, for merchandise en route from suppliers but not yet received on the last day of the year. A similar question of ownership concerns goods in the process of shipment to customers at year-end.

Goods in transit Do goods in transit belong in the inventory of the seller or of the buyer? If the selling company makes delivery of the merchandise in its own trucks, the merchandise remains its property while in transit. If the goods are shipped by rail, air, or other public carrier, the question of ownership of the goods while in transit depends upon whether the public carrier is acting as the agent of the seller or of the buyer. If the terms of the shipment are *F.O.B.* (free on board) *shipping point,* title passes at the point of shipment and the goods are the property of the buyer while in transit. If the terms of the shipment are *F.O.B. destination,* title does not pass until the shipment reaches the destination, and the goods belong to the seller while in transit. In deciding whether goods in transit at year-end should be included in inventory, it is therefore necessary to refer to the terms of the agreements with vendors (suppliers) and customers.

At the end of the year a company may have received numerous orders from customers, for which goods have been segregated and packed but not yet shipped. These goods should generally be included in inventory. An exception to this rule is found occasionally when the goods have been prepared for shipment but are being held for later delivery at the request of the customer.

Passage of title to merchandise The debit to the customer's account and the offsetting credit to the Sales account should be made when title to the goods passes to the customer. It would obviously be improper to set up an account receivable and at the same time to include the goods in question in inventory. Great care is necessary at year-end to ensure that all last-minute shipments to customers are recorded as sales of the current year and, on the other hand, that no customer's order is recorded as a sale until the date when the goods are shipped. Sometimes, in an effort to meet sales quotas, companies have recorded sales on the last day of the accounting period, when in fact the merchandise was not shipped until early in the next period. Such practices lead to an overstatement of the year's earnings and are not in accordance with generally accepted principles of accounting.

Merchandise in inventory is valued at *cost,* whereas accounts receivable are stated at the *sales price* of the merchandise sold. Consequently, the recording of a sale prior to delivery of the goods results in an unjustified increase in the total assets of the company. The increase will equal the difference between the cost and the selling price of the goods in question. The amount of the increase will also be reflected in the income statement, where it will show up as additional earnings. An unscrupulous company, which wanted to make its financial statements present a more favorable picture than actually existed, might do so by treating year-end orders from customers as sales even though the goods were not yet shipped.

Pricing the inventory

One of the most interesting and widely discussed problems in accounting is the pricing of inventory. Even those business executives who have little knowledge of accounting are usually interested in the various methods of pricing inventory, because inventory valuation has a direct effect upon reported net income. Federal income taxes are based on income, and the choice of inventory method may have a considerable effect upon the amount of income taxes payable. Federal income tax authorities are therefore much interested in the problem of inventory valuation and have taken a definite position on the acceptability of various alternative methods of pricing inventory.

In approaching our study of inventory valuation, however, it is important that we do not overemphasize the income tax aspects of the problem. It is true that in selected cases one method of inventory valuation may lead to a substantially lower income tax liability than would another method, but there are other important considerations in pricing inventory apart from the objective of minimizing the current income tax burden.

Proper valuation of inventory is one part of a larger undertaking, that is, to measure net income accurately and to provide all those persons interested in the financial position and operating results of a business with accounting data which are dependable and of maximum usefulness as a basis for business decisions.

Accounting for inventories involves determination of cost and of current fair value or replacement cost. An understanding of the meaning of the term *cost* as applied to inventories is a first essential in appreciating the complexity of the overall problem of inventory valuation.

Cost basis of inventory valuation

''The primary basis of accounting for inventory is cost, which has been defined generally as the price paid or consideration given to acquire an asset. As applied to inventories, cost means in principle the sum of the applicable expenditures and charges directly or indirectly incurred in bringing an article to its existing condition and location."[4]

TRANSPORTATION-IN AS AN ELEMENT OF COST The starting point in determining the cost of an article of merchandise is the price paid, as shown by the vendor's invoice. This acquisition cost is then increased by adding to it the cost of transportation incurred in bringing the merchandise to the location where it is to be offered for sale.

The logic of treating *transportation-in* as part of the cost of goods purchased is indicated by the following example. A Los Angeles appliance dealer orders 10 refrigerators from a Chicago manufacturer. The manufacturer pays the cost of shipping the refrigerators to Los Angeles and submits an invoice in the amount of $2,000. This is the total amount to be paid by the Los Angeles merchant, so the cost of the goods is clearly $2,000. Now assume that the appliance dealer places a second order for another 10 identical refrigerators. On this second order the invoice from the Chicago manufacturer is for only $1,800; under the terms of this purchase, however, the Los Angeles merchant is required to pay the railroad for the freight charges of $200 applicable to the shipment. On both of these identical shipments the total cash paid by the Los Angeles merchant was $2,000, so clearly the charge for transportation is part of the cost of merchandise purchased.

At the end of the year when a physical inventory is taken, the cost of each kind of merchandise is multiplied by the quantity on hand to determine the dollar amount of the ending inventory. The price paid for an article may readily be found by referring to the invoice from the supplier, but often there is no convenient method of determining how much transportation cost may have been incurred on specific types of merchandise. This is particularly true when certain shipments have included various kinds of merchandise and the freight charge was for the shipment as a whole. For reasons of convenience and economy, therefore, a merchandising business may choose to determine inventory cost at year-end by listing each item in stock at the purchase invoice price, and then adding to the inventory as a whole a reasonable proportion of the transportation charges incurred on inbound shipments during the year.

In many lines of business it is customary to price the year-end inventory without giving any consideration to transportation charges. This practice may be justified by the factors of convenience and economy, even though it is not theoretically sound. If freight charges are not material in amount, it may be advisable in terms of operating convenience to treat the entire amount as part of the cost of goods sold during the year. Accounting textbooks stress theoretical concepts of cost and of income determination; the student of accounting should be aware, however, that in many business situations an approximation of cost will serve the purpose at hand. In other words, the extra work involved in computing more precise cost data must be weighed against the benefits to be obtained.

[4] *Ibid.*, p. 28.

OTHER COSTS RELATING TO ACQUISITION OF MERCHANDISE If transportation-in is part of the cost of merchandise purchased, what about the other incidental charges relating to the acquisition of merchandise, such as the salary of the purchasing agent, insurance of goods in transit, cost of receiving and inspecting the merchandise, etc.? Although in theory these incidental charges should be identified and apportioned among the various items of merchandise purchased, the expense of computing cost on such a precise basis would usually outweigh the benefits to be derived. The costs of operating the purchasing department and the receiving department are customarily treated as expense of the period in which incurred, rather than being carried forward to another period by inclusion in the balance sheet amount for inventory.

PURCHASE DISCOUNTS AS A FACTOR IN INVENTORY VALUATION When a company purchases merchandise for resale, it often has the opportunity of saving 1 to 2% of the invoiced amount by making payment within a specified period, usually 10 days. Since purchase discounts are shown as a deduction from purchases in the income statement, they should logically be deducted from the invoice price of the items comprising the year-end inventory. Often, however, it is impracticable to compute the precise amount of discount applicable to each item in inventory. One reasonable alternative is to deduct from the invoice cost of the entire ending inventory an amount representing the estimated purchase discounts applicable to these goods. If purchase discounts are not significant in amount, they may be ignored for the purpose of inventory pricing.

Inventory valuation methods

The prices of many kinds of merchandise are subject to frequent change. When identical lots of merchandise are purchased at various dates during the year, each lot may be acquired at a different cost price.

To illustrate the several alternative methods in common use for determining which purchase prices apply to the units remaining in inventory at the end of the period, assume the data shown below.

	Number of Units	Cost per Unit	Total Cost
Beginning inventory	10	$ 800	$ 8,000
First purchase (Mar. 1)	5	900	4,500
Second purchase (July 1)	5	1,000	5,000
Third purchase (Oct. 1)	5	1,200	6,000
Fourth purchase (Dec. 1)	5	1,300	6,500
Available for sale	30		$30,000
Units sold	18		
Units in ending inventory	12		

This schedule shows that 18 units were sold during the year and that 12 units are on hand at year-end to make up the ending inventory. In order to establish a dollar amount for cost of goods sold and for the ending inventory, we must make an assumption as to which units were sold and which units remain on hand at the end of the year. There are several acceptable assumptions on this point; four of the most common will be considered. Each assumption made as to the cost of the units in the ending inventory leads to a different method of pricing inventory and to different amounts in the financial statements. The four assumptions (and inventory valuation methods) to be considered are known as: (*1*) specific identification, (*2*) average cost, (*3*) first-in, first-out, and (*4*) last-in, first-out.

Although each of these four methods will produce a different answer as to the cost of goods sold and the cost of the ending inventory, the valuation of inventory in each case is said to be at "cost." In other words, *these methods represent alternative definitions of inventory cost.*

SPECIFIC IDENTIFICATION METHOD If the units in the ending inventory can be identified as coming from specific purchases, they *may* be priced at the amounts listed on the purchase invoices. Continuing the example already presented, if the ending inventory of 12 units can be identified as, say, five units from the purchase of March 1, four units from the purchase of July 1, and three units from the purchase of December 1, the cost of the ending inventory may be computed as follows:

Specific	*Five units from the purchase of Mar. 1 @ $900*	*$ 4,500*
identifica-	*Four units from the purchase of July 1 @ $1,000*	*4,000*
tion		
method	*Three units from the purchase of Dec. 1 @ $1,300*	*3,900*
and . . .	*Ending inventory (specific identification)*	*$12,400*

The cost of goods sold during the period is determined by subtracting the ending inventory from the cost of goods available for sale.

. . . cost	*Cost of goods available for sale*	*$30,000*
of goods	*Less: Ending inventory*	*12,400*
sold com-		
putation	*Cost of goods sold (specific identification method)*	*$17,600*

A business may prefer not to use the specific identification method even though the cost of each unit sold could be identified with a specific purchase. The flow of cost factors may be more significant than the flow of specific physical units in measuring the net income of the period.

As a simple example, assume that a coal dealer purchased 100 tons of coal at $60 a ton and a short time later made a second purchase of 100 tons of the same grade coal at $80 a ton. The two purchases are in separate piles and it is a matter of indifference as to which pile is used in making sales to customers. Assume that the dealer makes a retail sale of one ton of coal at a price of $100. In measuring the gross profit on the sale, which cost figure should be used, $60 or $80? To insist that the cost depended on which of the two identical piles of coal was used in filling the delivery truck is an argument of questionable logic.

A situation in which the specific identification method is more likely to give meaningful results is in the purchase and sale of such high-priced articles as boats, automobiles, and jewelry.

AVERAGE-COST METHOD   Average cost is computed by dividing the total cost of goods available for sale by the number of units available for sale. This computation gives a **weighted-average unit cost,** which is then applied to the units in the ending inventory.

Average-	*Cost of goods available for sale*	*$30,000*
cost method	*Number of units available for sale*	*30*
and . . .	*Average unit cost*	*$ 1,000*
	Ending inventory (at average cost, 12 units @ $1,000)	*$12,000*

Note that this method, when compared with the specific identification method, leads to a different amount for cost of goods sold as well as a different amount for the ending inventory.

. . . cost of goods sold computation	*Cost of goods available for sale*	*$30,000*
	Less: Ending inventory	*12,000*
	Cost of goods sold (average-cost method)	*$18,000*

When the average-cost method is used, the cost figure of $12,000 determined for the ending inventory is influenced by all the various prices paid during the year. The price paid early in the year may carry as much weight in pricing the ending inventory as a price paid at the end of the year. A common criticism of the average-cost method of pricing inventory is that it attaches no more significance to current prices than to prices which prevailed several months earlier.

FIRST-IN, FIRST-OUT METHOD   The first-in, first-out method, which is often referred to as *fifo,* is based on the assumption that the first merchandise acquired is the first merchandise sold. In other words, each sale is made out of the oldest goods in stock; the ending inventory therefore consists of the most recently acquired goods. The fifo method of determining inventory cost may be adopted by any business, regardless of whether or not the physical flow of merchandise actually corresponds to this assumption of selling the oldest units in stock. Using the same data as in the preceding illustrations, the 12 units in the ending inventory would be regarded as consisting of the most recently acquired goods, as follows:

First-in, first-out method and . . .	*Five units from the Dec. 1 purchase @ $1,300*	*$ 6,500*
	Five units from the Oct. 1 purchase @ $1,200	*6,000*
	Two units from the July 1 purchase @ $1,000	*2,000*
	Ending inventory, 12 units (at fifo cost)	*$14,500*

During a period of rising prices the first-in, first-out method will result in a larger amount ($14,500) being assigned as the cost of the ending inventory than would be assigned under the average-cost method. When a relatively large amount is allocated as cost of the ending inventory, a relatively small amount will remain as cost of goods sold, as indicated by the following calculation:

. . . cost of goods sold computation	*Cost of goods available for sale*	*$30,000*
	Less: Ending inventory	*14,500*
	Cost of goods sold (first-in, first-out method)	*$15,500*

It may be argued in support of the first-in, first-out method that the inventory valuation reflects recent costs and is therefore a realistic value in the light of conditions prevailing at the balance sheet date.

LAST-IN, FIRST-OUT METHOD   The title of this method of pricing suggests that the most recently acquired goods are sold first, and that the ending inventory consists of "old" merchandise acquired in the earliest purchases. Such an assumption is, of course, not in accord with the actual physical movement of goods in most businesses, but there is nevertheless a strong logical argument to support this method. As merchandise is sold, more goods must be purchased to replenish the stock on hand. Since the making of a sale necessitates a replacement purchase of goods, the cost of replacement should be offset against the sales price to determine the gross profit realized.

The supporters of last-in, first-out, or *lifo,* as it is commonly known, contend that the accurate determination of income requires that primary emphasis be placed on the **matching of current costs of merchandise against current sales prices,** regardless of which physical units of merchandise are being delivered to customers. Keeping in mind the point that the **flow of costs** may be more significant than the **physical movement** of merchandise, we can say that, under the lifo method, the cost of goods sold consists of the cost of the most recently acquired goods, and the ending inventory consists of the cost of the oldest goods which were available for sale during the period.

Using the same data as in the preceding illustrations, the 12 units in the ending inventory would be priced as if they were the oldest goods available for sale during the period, as follows:

Last-in, first-out method and . . .	*Ten units from the beginning inventory @ $800*	*$8,000*
	Two units from the purchase of Mar. 1 @ $900.	*1,800*
	Ending inventory, 12 units (at lifo cost)	*$9,800*

Note that the lifo cost of the ending inventory ($9,800) is very much lower than the fifo cost ($14,500) of ending inventory in the preceding example. Since a relatively small part of the cost of goods available for sale is assigned to ending inventory, it follows that a relatively large portion must have been assigned to cost of goods sold, as shown by the following computation:

<table>
<tr><td>*... cost
of goods
sold com-
putation*</td><td>*Cost of goods available for sale* . . . .</td><td>*$30,000*</td></tr>
<tr><td></td><td>*Less: Ending inventory* . . . .</td><td>*9,800*</td></tr>
<tr><td></td><td>*Cost of goods sold (last-in, first-out method)* . . . .</td><td>*$20,200*</td></tr>
</table>

COMPARISON OF THE ALTERNATIVE METHODS OF PRICING INVENTORY

We have now illustrated four common methods of pricing inventory at cost; the specific identification method, the average-cost method, the first-in, first-out method, and the last-in, first-out method. By way of contrasting the results obtained from the four methods illustrated, especially during a period of rapid price increases, let us summarize the amounts computed for ending inventory, cost of goods sold, and gross profit on sales under each of the four methods. Assume that sales for the period amounted to $27,500.

		Specific Identifi- cation Method	Average- Cost Method	First-in, First-out Method	Last-in, First-out Method
Four methods of deter- mining inventory cost compared	*Sales*	*$27,500*	*$27,500*	*$27,500*	*$27,500*
	Cost of goods sold:				
	Beginning inventory	*$ 8,000*	*$ 8,000*	*$ 8,000*	*$ 8,000*
	Purchases	*22,000*	*22,000*	*22,000*	*22,000*
	Cost of goods available for sale .	*$30,000*	*$30,000*	*$30,000*	*$30,000*
	Less: Ending inventory	*12,400*	*12,000*	*14,500*	*9,800*
	Cost of goods sold	*$17,600*	*$18,000*	*$15,500*	*$20,200*
	Gross profit on sales	*$ 9,900*	*$ 9,500*	*$12,000*	*$ 7,300*

This comparison of the four methods makes it apparent that during periods of *rising prices,* the use of lifo will result in lower profits being reported than would be the case under the other methods of inventory valuation. Perhaps for this reason many businesses have adopted lifo. Current income tax regulations permit virtually any business to use the last-in, first-out method in determining taxable income.

During a period of *declining prices,* the use of lifo will cause the reporting of relatively large profits as compared with fifo, which will hold reported profits to a minimum. Obviously, the choice of inventory method becomes of greatest significance during prolonged periods of drastic changes in price levels.

WHICH METHOD OF INVENTORY VALUATION IS BEST?

All four of the inventory methods described are regarded as acceptable accounting practices and all four are acceptable in the determination of taxable income. Although no one method of inventory valuation can be considered as the "correct" or the "best" method, the inflation of recent years is a strong argument for the use of lifo. In the selection of a method, consideration should be given to the probable effect upon the balance sheet, upon the income statement, upon the amount of taxable income, and upon such business decisions as the establishment of selling prices for goods.

When prices are rising drastically, the most significant cost data to use as a guide to sales policies are probably the *current replacement costs* of the goods being sold. The lifo method of inventory valuation comes closer than any of the other methods described to measuring net income in the light of current selling prices and current replacement costs.

On the other hand, the use of lifo during a period of rising prices is apt to produce a balance sheet figure for inventory which is far below the current replacement cost of the goods on hand. The fifo method of inventory valuation will lead to a balance sheet valuation of inventory more in line with current replacement costs.

Some business concerns which adopted lifo more than 30 years ago now show a balance sheet figure for inventory which is less than half the present replacement cost of the goods in stock. An inventory valuation method which gives significant figures for the income statement may thus produce misleading amounts for the balance sheet, whereas a method which produces a realistic figure for inventory on the balance sheet may provide less realistic data for the income statement.

The search for the "best" method of inventory valuation is rendered difficult because the inventory figure is used in both the balance sheet and the income statement, and these two financial statements are intended for different purposes. In the income statement the function of the inventory figure is to permit a matching of costs and revenue. In the balance sheet the inventory and the other current assets are regarded as a measure of the company's ability to meet its current debts. For this purpose a valuation of inventory in line with current replacement cost would appear to be more significant.

The environment of inflation

The inflationary policies and high income tax rates of recent years have stimulated the interest of business management in the choice of inventory methods. Most business executives and government officials expect the trend of rising prices to continue; in other words, an environment of inflation has come to be considered as normal. The lifo method of inventory valuation causes reported net income to reflect the increasing cost of replacing the merchandise sold during the year and also tends to avoid basing income tax payments on an exaggerated measurement of taxable income. Therefore, the existence of inflation is an argument for the lifo method of inventory.

The SEC rules on replacement cost

The Securities and Exchange Commission in 1976 adopted disclosure requirements to spotlight the effect of inflation on the nation's largest corporations. The Commission required the 1,000 largest nonfinancial corporations to disclose what it would cost to replace their inventories at current prices and what their cost of sales would be if computed by using replacement cost of inventories. The disclosure of replacement costs can be in a special section of the financial statements or in a footnote. This information will thus supplement rather than do away with the use of historical cost as a basis of accounting for inventories and cost of goods sold.

It is expected that the rules requiring the disclosure of cost of goods sold computed on the basis of replacement cost will reveal that most large companies have been much less profitable than their financial statements of recent years have indicated. In other words, net income tends to be overstated and fictitious profits reported when companies rely solely on historical cost values during a period of inflation. The SEC action to adopt replacement cost accounting may prove to be one of the most significant changes in accounting practice in many years. Some accountants view it as a major step away from cost-based accounting toward "current value" accounting.

Inventory profits

Many accountants believe that the use of fifo or of average cost during a period of inflation results in the reporting of fictitious profits and consequently in the payment of excessive income taxes. A portion of the reported profits are considered to be fictitious because under both the fifo and average-cost methods, the gross profit is computed by subtracting old inventory costs rather than current replacement costs from sales revenue. These old costs are relatively low, resulting in a high reported gross profit. However, the company must pay the higher current cost in order to replenish its inventory.

To illustrate this concept, assume that TV Sales Shop has an inventory of 20 television sets which were acquired at an average cost of $270. During the current month, 10 television sets are sold for cash at a sales price of $350 each. Using the average-cost method to value inventory, the company will report the following gross profit for the month:

Sales (10 × $350)	$3,500
Cost of goods sold (10 × $270)	2,700
Gross profit on sales	$ 800

However, TV Sales Shop must replace its inventory of television sets to continue in business. Because of inflation, TV Sales Shop can no longer buy 10 television sets for $2,700. Let us assume that the current replacement cost of television sets is $325 each; TV Sales Shop must pay $3,250 to replenish its inventory. Thus, TV Sales Shop is able to keep only $250 ($3,500 − $3,250) of the reported $800 gross profit; the remaining $550 has to be reinvested in inventory because of the increasing cost of television sets. This $550 would be considered a fictitious profit, or an *inventory profit,* by many accountants and business executives.

In periods of rapid inflation, a significant portion of the reported net income of companies using fifo or average cost may actually be inventory profits. The net income of companies using lifo will include much less inventory profit because lifo causes more current costs to be included in the cost of goods sold.

The lower-of-cost-or-market rule

Although cost is the primary basis for valuation of inventories, circumstances may arise under which inventory may properly be valued at less than its cost. If the *utility* of the inventory has fallen below cost by reason of physical deterioration, obsolescence, or decline in the price level, a loss has occurred. This loss may appropriately be recognized as a loss of the current period by reducing the accounting value of the inventory from cost to a lower level designated as market. The word *market* as used in this context *means current replacement cost.* For a merchandising company, *market* is the amount which the concern would have to pay at the present time for the goods in question, purchased in the customary quantities through the usual sources of supply and including transportation-in. To avoid misunderstanding, the rule might better read "lower of cost or replacement cost."

In the early days of accounting when the principal users of financial statements were creditors and attention was concentrated upon the balance sheet, conservatism was a dominant consideration in asset valuation. The lower-of-cost-or-market rule was then considered justifiable because it tended to produce a "safe" or minimum value for inventory. The rule was widely applied for a time without regard for the possibility that although replacement costs had declined, there might be no corresponding and immediate decline in selling prices.

As the significance of the income statement has increased, considerable dissatisfaction with the lower-of-cost-or-market rule has developed. If ending inventory is written down from cost to a lower market figure but the merchandise is sold during the next period at the usual selling prices, the effect of the write-down will have been to reflect a fictitious loss in the first period and an exaggerated profit in the second period. Arbitrary application of the lower-of-cost-or-market rule ignores the historical fact that selling prices do not always drop when replacement prices decline. Even if selling prices do follow replacement prices downward, they may not decline by a proportionate amount.

Because of these objections, the lower-of-cost-or-market rule has

undergone some modification and is now qualified in the following respects. If the inventory can probably be sold at prices which will yield a
normal profit, the inventory should be carried at cost even though current
replacement cost is lower. Assume, for example, that merchandise is
purchased for $1,000 with the intention of reselling it to customers for
$1,500. The replacement cost then declines from $1,000 to $800, but it is
believed that the merchandise can still be sold to customers for $1,450. In
other words, the normal anticipated profit has shrunk by $50. The carrying
value of the inventory could then be written down from $1,000 to $950.
There is no justification for reducing the inventory to the replacement cost
of $800 under these circumstances.

Another qualification of the lower-of-cost-or-market rule is that inventory should never be carried at an amount greater than *net realizable value,*
which may be defined as prospective selling price minus anticipated
selling expenses. Assume, for example, that because of unstable market
conditions, it is believed that goods acquired at a cost of $500 and having
a current replacement cost of $450 will probably have to be sold for no
more than $520 and that the selling expenses involved will amount to
$120. The inventory should then be reduced to a carrying value (net
realizable value) of $400, which is less than current replacement cost.

APPLICATION OF THE LOWER-OF-COST-OR-MARKET RULE The lower
of cost or market for inventory is often computed by determining the cost
and the market figures for each item in inventory and using the lower of
the two amounts in every case. If, for example, item A cost $100 and
market is $90, the item should be priced at $90. If item B cost $200 and
market is $225, this item should be priced at $200. The total cost of the
two items is $300 and total market is $315, but the total inventory value
determined by applying the lower-of-cost-or-market rule to each item in
inventory is only $290. This application of the lower-of-cost-or-market rule
is illustrated by the tabulation shown below.

Application of Lower-of-Cost-or-Market Rule, Item-by-Item Method

	Item	Quantity	Unit Price Cost	Unit Price Market	Lower of Cost or Market
Pricing inventory at lower of cost or market	A	10	$100	$ 90	$ 900
	B	8	200	225	1,600
	C	50	50	60	2,500
	D	80	90	70	5,600
	Total				$10,600

If the lower-of-cost-or-market rule is applied item by item, the carrying
value of the above inventory would be $10,600. However, an alternative
and less rigorous version of the lower-of-cost-or-market rule calls for

applying it to the total of the entire inventory rather than to the individual items. If the above inventory is to be valued by applying the lower-of-cost-or-market rule to the total of the inventory, the balance sheet amount for inventory is determined merely by comparing the total cost of $12,300 with the total replacement cost of $11,300 and using the lower of the two figures. Still another alternative method of using the lower-of-cost-or-market concept is to apply it to categories of the inventory rather than item by item. These alternative methods of applying the lower-of-cost-or-market rule are appropriate when no loss of income is anticipated, because the decline in replacement costs of certain goods is fully offset by higher replacement costs for other items.

Gross profit method of estimating inventories

The taking of a physical inventory is a time-consuming and costly job in many lines of business; consequently, a physical inventory may be taken only once a year. Monthly financial statements are needed, however, for intelligent administration of the business, and the preparation of monthly statements requires a determination of the amount of inventory at the end of each month. In many cases this dilemma may be solved satisfactorily by estimating the inventory each month by using the *gross profit method.*

The gross profit method of estimating the inventory is based on the assumption that the rate of gross profit remains approximately the same from year to year. This assumption is a realistic one in many fields of business. The first step in using the gross profit method is to obtain from the ledger the figures for beginning inventory, net purchases, and net sales. *Cost of goods sold is then computed by reducing the sales figure by the usual gross profit rate.* The difference between the cost of goods available for sale and the cost of goods sold represents the estimated ending inventory.

To illustrate, let us assume that the beginning inventory is $25,000, the net purchases of the period $70,000, and the net sales $100,000. The gross profit rate is assumed to have approximated 40% of net sales for the past several years. This information is now assembled in the customary form of an income statement as follows:

Gross *profit* *method* *. . .*	*Net sales*	*$100,000* *(100%)*
	Beginning inventory	*$25,000*
	Net purchases	*70,000*
	Cost of goods available for sale	*$95,000*
	Less: Ending inventory	*?*
	Cost of goods sold	*60,000* *(60%)*
	Gross profit on sales (40% × $100,000)	*$ 40,000* *(40%)*

Customarily, in preparing an income statement, the ending inventory is deducted from the cost of goods available for sale to determine the cost of goods sold. In this case our calculation to determine the ending inventory consists of deducting the estimated cost of goods sold from the cost of goods available for sale.

... to Cost of goods available for sale	$95,000
estimate *ending* Less: Cost of goods sold (60% of $100,000 of sales)	60,000
inventory Ending inventory (estimate)	$35,000

The gross profit method of estimating inventory has several uses apart from the preparation of monthly financial statements. This calculation may be used after the taking of a physical inventory to confirm the overall reasonableness of the amount determined by the counting and pricing process. In the event of a fire which destroys the inventory, the approximate amount of goods on hand at the date of the fire may also be computed by the gross profit method.

The retail method of inventory valuation

The retail method of estimating ending inventory is somewhat similar to the gross profit method. It is widely used by chain stores, department stores, and other types of retail business. Goods on sale in retail stores are marked at the retail prices; it is therefore more convenient to take inventory at current retail prices than to look up invoices to find the unit cost of each item in stock. After first determining the value of the inventory at retail price, the next step is to convert the inventory to cost price by applying the ratio prevailing between cost and selling price during the current period. This method of approximating an inventory may also be carried out by using data from the accounts without taking any physical count of the goods on hand. The underlying basis for the **retail method** of inventory valuation is the percentage of markup for the **current period,** whereas the **gross profit method** of estimating inventory rests on the rate of gross profit experienced in **preceding periods.**

When the retail method of inventory is to be used, it is necessary to maintain records of the beginning inventory and of all purchases during the period in terms of selling price as well as at cost. Goods available for sale during the period can then be stated both at cost and at selling price. By deducting the sales for the period from the sales value of the goods available for sale, the ending inventory at selling price may be determined without the need for a physical count. The ending inventory at selling price is then converted to a cost basis by using the percentage of cost to selling price for the current period.

In practice, the application of this method may be complicated because the originally established sales prices are modified by frequent price markups and markdowns. These frequent changes in retail price present some difficulties in determining the correct rate to use in reducing the inventory from selling price to cost. The following illustration shows the calculation of inventory by the retail method, without going into the complications which would arise from markups and markdowns in the original retail selling price.

		Cost Price	Selling Price
Used by many department stores	*Beginning inventory*	*$20,000*	*$30,000*
	Net purchases during the month	*11,950*	*15,000*
	Goods available for sale	*$31,950*	*$45,000*
	Less: Net sales for the month		*20,000*
	Ending inventory at selling price		*$25,000*
	Cost ratio ($31,950 ÷ $45,000)		*71%*
	Ending inventory at cost (71% × $25,000)	*$17,750*	

Consistency in the valuation of inventory

A business has considerable latitude in selecting a method of inventory valuation best suited to its needs; once a method has been selected, however, that method should be followed consistently from year to year. A change from one inventory method to another will ordinarily cause reported income to vary considerably in the year in which the change occurs. Frequent switching of methods would therefore make the income statements quite undependable as a means of portraying operating results.

The need for consistency in the valuation of inventory does not mean that a business should *never* make a change in inventory method. However, when a change is made, the approval of tax authorities must be obtained, and full disclosure of the nature of the change and of its effect upon the year's net income should be included in the financial statements or in a footnote to the statements. Even when the same method of inventory pricing is being followed consistently, the financial statements should include a disclosure of the pricing method in use.

Perpetual inventory system

Throughout our discussion thus far we have emphasized the periodic inventory system. Under that system, we have demonstrated that acquisitions of merchandise are recorded by debits to a Purchases account and that no entry is made to record the cost of goods sold at the date of a sales transaction. Under the periodic system, the Inventory account is brought up to date only at the end of the accounting period when all the goods on hand are counted and priced.

However, as explained earlier in Chapter 5, companies which deal in merchandise of high unit cost, such as television sets or outboard motors, find a perpetual inventory system worthwhile and efficient. Since inventory may be one of the largest assets in a business and has a rapid rate of turnover, strong internal control is especially important. A perpetual inventory system can provide the strongest possible internal control over the inventory of merchandise.

The information required for a perpetual inventory system can be processed electronically or manually. In a manual system a subsidiary record card, as shown below, is used for each type of merchandise on hand. If the company has in stock 100 different kinds of products, then 100 inventory record cards will make up the subsidiary inventory record. Shown below is an inventory record card for item XL-2000.

Perpetual inventory record card

Item	XL-2000						Maximum	20	
Location	Storeroom 2						Minimum	8	

	PURCHASED			SOLD			BALANCE		
Date	Units	Unit Cost	Total	Units	Unit Cost	Total	Units	Unit Cost	Balance
Jan. 1							12	$50.00	$600.00
7				2	$50.00	$100.00	10	50.00	500.00
9	10	$55.00	$550.00				10	50.00	
							10	55.00	1,050.00
12				8	50.00	400.00	2	50.00	
							10	55.00	650.00
13				2	50.00	100.00			
				1	55.00	55.00	9	55.00	495.00

On this card, the quantity and cost of units received will be listed at the date of receipt; the quantity and cost of units sold will be recorded at the date of sale; and after each purchase or sales transaction, the balance remaining on hand will be shown. This running balance will be shown in number of units, cost per unit, and total dollar amount.

The information on the illustrated inventory record shows that the first-in, first-out basis of pricing the inventory is being used. After the sale of two units on January 7, the remaining inventory consisted of 10 units at a cost of $50 each. The purchase on January 9 of 10 units carried a unit cost of $55, rather than $50, hence must be accounted for separately. The balance on hand after the January 9 purchase appears on two lines: 10 units at $50 and 10 units at $55. When eight units were sold on January

12, they were treated as coming from the oldest stock on hand and therefore had a cost of $50 each. The balance remaining on hand then consisted of two units at $50 and 10 units at $55. When three units were sold on January 13, the cost consisted of two units at $50 and one unit at $55. The remaining inventory of nine units consists of the most recently acquired units with a cost of $55 each.

Perpetual inventory records may also be maintained on a last-in, first-out basis or on an average-cost basis, but these systems involve some complexities which are considered in advanced accounting courses.

Control over the amount invested in inventory can be strengthened by listing on each inventory card the maximum and minimum quantities that should be kept in stock. By maintaining quantities within these limits, overstocking and out-of-stock situations can be avoided.

GENERAL LEDGER ENTRIES FOR A PERPETUAL INVENTORY SYSTEM The general ledger control account entitled *Inventory* is continuously (perpetually) updated when a perpetual inventory system is in use. This Inventory account controls the many subsidiary record cards discussed above. A continuously updated Cost of Goods Sold account is also maintained in the general ledger.

The purchase of merchandise by a company using a perpetual inventory system requires a journal entry affecting general ledger control accounts as follows:

Inventory *550*
     Accounts Payable, Lake Company *550*
To record purchase of merchandise on credit.

This purchase transaction would also be recorded in the subsidiary ledger (the perpetual inventory cards) showing the quantity of each kind of merchandise purchased. The $550 purchase from Lake Company might affect only one or perhaps a dozen of the subsidiary records, depending on how many types of merchandise were included in this purchase transaction.

For every sales transaction, we can determine the cost of the goods sold by referring to the appropriate perpetual inventory card record. Therefore, at the time of a sale, we can record both the amount of the selling price and the *cost* of the goods sold, as illustrated in the following pair of related entries.

Accounts Receivable, J. Williams *140*
     Sales *140*
To record the sale of merchandise on credit.

Cost of Goods Sold *100*
     Inventory *100*
To record the cost of goods sold and the related
decrease in inventory.

To avoid making a large number of entries in the general journal, a special column can be entered in the Sales Journal to show the cost of the goods involved in each sales transaction. At the end of the month the total of this "Cost" column can be posted as a debit to Cost of Goods Sold and a credit to Inventory.

A company maintaining perpetual inventory records will also conduct a physical count of all merchandise once a year and compare the amount of the physical inventory with the perpetual inventory records. An adjusting entry can be made to bring the inventory records into agreement with the physical inventory. For example, if shoplifting or other factors have caused an inventory shortage, the adjusting entry will consist of a debit to the expense account, Inventory Shortage, and a credit to Inventory.

When a perpetual inventory system is in use, the Inventory account is increased by purchases of merchandise. It is decreased by the cost of goods sold, by purchase returns and allowances, and by purchase discounts. At the end of the year the dollar balances of all the subsidiary inventory record cards should be added to see that the total is in agreement with the general ledger control account. The only adjustment necessary at year-end will be to correct the Inventory control account and the subsidiary records for any discrepancies indicated by the taking of a physical inventory.

The advantages of a perpetual inventory system as indicated in the preceding discussion include:

1 Stronger internal control. By comparing the physical inventory with the perpetual records, management will be made aware of any shortages or errors and can take corrective action.

2 A physical inventory can be taken at dates other than year-end, or it can be taken for different products or different departments at various dates during the year, since the perpetual records always show the amounts which *should* be on hand.

3 Quarterly or monthly financial statements can be more readily prepared because of the availability of dollar amounts for inventory and cost of goods sold in the accounting records.

KEY TERMS INTRODUCED OR EMPHASIZED IN CHAPTER 10

Average-cost A method of inventory valuation. Weighted-average unit cost is computed by dividing the total cost of goods available for sale by the number of units available for sale.

Consistency in inventory valuation An accounting standard that calls for the use of the same method of inventory pricing from year to year, with full disclosure of the effects of any change in method. Intended to make financial statements comparable.

Cost of inventory The price paid for the inventory plus the costs of bringing the goods to the point where they are offered for sale.

First-in, first-out (fifo) A method of computing the cost of inventory and the cost of goods sold based on the assumption that the first merchandise acquired is the first merchandise sold, and that the ending inventory consists of the most recently acquired goods.

F.O.B. destination A term meaning the seller bears the cost of shipping goods to the buyer's location. Title to the goods remains with the seller while the goods are in transit.

F.O.B. shipping point The buyer of goods bears the cost of transportation from the seller's location to the buyer's location. Title to the goods passes at the point of shipment and the goods are the property of the buyer while in transit.

Gross profit method A method of estimating the cost of the ending inventory based on the assumption that the rate of gross profit remains approximately the same from year to year.

Inventory Goods acquired or produced for sale in the regular operation of a business. Goods in which a business deals.

Inventory profits That portion of reported net income considered to be fictitious because the cost of goods sold (under fifo or average cost) is less than replacement cost. A consequence of inflation.

Last-in, first-out (lifo) A method of computing the cost of goods sold by use of the prices paid for the most recently acquired units. Ending inventory is valued on the basis of prices paid for the units first acquired.

Lower-of-cost-or-market A method of inventory pricing in which goods are valued at original cost or replacement cost (market), whichever is lower.

Net realizable value The prospective selling price minus anticipated selling expenses. Inventory should not be carried at more than net realizable value.

Perpetual inventory system Provides a continuous (perpetual) running record of the goods on hand. As goods are sold their cost is transferred to a Cost of Goods Sold account.

Physical inventory A systematic count of all goods on hand, followed by the application of unit prices to the quantities counted and development of a dollar value for ending inventory.

Retail method A method of estimating inventory in a retail store based on the assumption that the cost of goods on hand bears the same percentage relationship to retail prices as does the cost of all goods available for sale to the original retail prices. Inventory is first priced at retail and then converted to cost by application of a cost-to-retail percentage.

SEC rule on replacement cost A ruling by the SEC which requires large corporations to disclose in financial statements the replacement cost of inventories and also what cost of goods sold would be if computed on the basis of replacement cost. A step toward current value accounting as opposed to historical cost.

Specific identification method A method of pricing inventory by identifying the units in the ending inventory as coming from specific purchases.

REVIEW QUESTIONS

1 Which of the seven items listed below are used in computing the *cost of goods available for sale?*

 a Ending inventory   *e* Transportation-in
 b Sales   *f* Purchase returns and allowances
 c Beginning inventory *g* Freight-out expense
 d Purchases

2 Explain the meaning of the term *physical inventory.*

3 Through an accidental error in counting of merchandise at December 31, 1979, the Trophy Company overstated the amount of goods on hand by $8,000. Assuming that the error was not discovered, what was the effect upon net income for 1979? Upon the owner's equity at December 31, 1979? Upon the net income for 1980? Upon the owner's equity at December 31, 1980?

4 Near the end of December, Hadley Company received a large order from a major customer. The work of packing the goods for shipment was begun at once but could not be completed before the close of business on December 31. Since a written order from the customer was on hand and the goods were nearly all packed and ready for shipment, Hadley felt that this merchandise should not be included in the physical inventory taken on December 31. Do you agree? What is probably the reason behind Hadley's opinion?

5 During a prolonged period of rising prices, will the fifo or lifo method of inventory valuation result in higher reported profits?

6 Throughout several years of strongly rising prices, Company A used the lifo method of inventory valuation and Company B used the fifo method. In which company would the balance sheet figure for inventory be closer to current replacement cost of the merchandise on hand? Why?

7 Explain the usefulness of the **gross profit method** of estimating inventories.

8 Estimate the ending inventory by the gross profit method, given the following data: beginning inventory $40,000; purchases $100,000; net sales $106,667; average gross profit rate 25% of net sales.

9 Assume that a business uses the first-in, first-out method of accounting for inventories during a prolonged period of inflation and that the owner makes withdrawals equal to the amount of reported net income. Suggest a problem that may arise in continued successful operation of the business. What does this situation have to do with "inventory profits"?

10 The Securities and Exchange Commission requires large corporations to disclose the cost of replacing their inventories and to disclose what their cost of goods sold would be if computed by using replacement costs. Do you think this policy indicates that corporate profits have tended to be overstated or understated in recent years? Explain.

11 One of the items in the inventory of Grayline Stores is marked for sale at $125. The purchase invoice shows the item cost $95, but a newly issued price list from the manufacturer shows the present replacement cost to be $90. What inventory valuation should be assigned to this item if Grayline Stores follows the lower-of-cost-or-market rule?

12 You are making a detailed analysis of the financial statements and accounting records of two companies in the same industry, Adams Corporation and Bar Corporation. Price levels have been rising steadily for several years. In the course of your investigation, you observe that the inventory value shown on the Adams Corporation balance sheet is quite close to the current replacement cost of the merchandise on hand. However, for Bar Corporation, the carrying value of the inventory is far below current replacement cost. What method of inventory valuation is probably used by Adams Corporation? By Bar Corporation? If we assume that the two companies are identical except for the inventory valuation method used, which company has probably been reporting higher net income in recent years?

13 Explain the meaning of the term **market** as used in the expression "lower of cost or market."

14 Summarize the difference between the **periodic system** and the **perpetual system** of accounting for inventory. Which system would usually cost more to maintain? Which system would be most practicable for a restaurant, a retail drugstore, a new car dealer?

15 A store using the **retail inventory method** takes its physical inventory by applying current retail prices as marked on the merchandise to the quantities counted. Does this procedure indicate that the inventory will appear in the financial statements at retail selling price? Explain.

16 Identify each of the four statements shown below as true or false. In the accounting records of a company using a perpetual inventory system:

a The Inventory account will ordinarily remain unchanged until the end of an accounting period.

b The Cost of Goods Sold account is debited with the sales price of merchandise sold.

c The Inventory account and the Cost of Goods Sold account will both normally have debit balances.

d The Inventory account and the Cost of Goods Sold account will normally have equal but offsetting balances.

EXERCISES

Ex. 10-1 The condensed income statements prepared by Blaze Company for two years are shown below:

	Year 2	Year 1
Sales	$183,400	$168,000
Cost of goods sold	106,400	134,400
Gross profit on sales	$ 77,000	$ 33,600
Operating expenses	28,000	28,000
Net income	$ 49,000	$ 5,600

The inventory at the end of Year 1 was understated by $16,800, but the error was not discovered until after the accounts had been closed and financial statements prepared at the end of Year 2. The balance sheets for the two years showed owner's equity of $71,400 at the end of Year 1 and $86,800 at the end of Year 2.

Compute the correct net income figures for Year 1 and Year 2 and the gross profit percentage for each year based on corrected data. What correction, if any, should be made in owner's equity at the end of Year 1 and at the end of Year 2?

Ex. 10-2 The beginning inventory balance of item X on August 1 and the purchases of this item during August were as follows:

Aug.	1	Beginning inventory	450 units @ $1.00	$ 450
Aug.	7	Purchase	1,800 units @ $1.10	1,980
Aug.	14	Purchase	900 units @ $1.12	1,008
Aug.	22	Purchase	900 units @ $1.16	1,044
Aug.	28	Purchase	450 units @ $1.25	563
		Totals	4,500 units	$5,045

At August 31 the ending inventory consisted of 675 units.

Determine the cost of the ending inventory, based on each of the following methods of inventory valuation:

a Average cost (Compute average cost per unit to the nearest tenth of a cent.)

b First-in, first-out (Round to the nearest dollar.)

c Last-in, first-out

Ex. 10-3 Ruger Company has compiled the following information concerning items in its inventory at December 31 as shown on page 391.

Determine the total inventory value to appear on Ruger Company's balance sheet under the lower-of-cost-or-market rule, assuming (**a**) that the rule is applied to inventory as a whole, and (**b**) that the rule is applied on an item-by-item basis.

		Unit Price	
		Cost (fifo)	Market
Item	Quantity		
A	120	$192	$196
B	72	360	336
C	96	96	114
D	84	480	482

Ex. 10-4 When Ellen Sharp arrived at her store on the morning of May 29, she found empty shelves and display racks; thieves had broken in during the night and stolen the entire inventory. Sharp's accounting record showed that she had $48,000 inventory on May 1 (cost value). From May 1 to May 29, she had made sales of $192,000 and purchases of $151,200. The gross profit during the past several years had consistently averaged 30% of sales. Sharp wishes to file an insurance claim for the theft loss. What is the estimated cost of her inventory at the time of the theft? Show computations.

Ex. 10-5 Vagabond Shop wishes to determine the approximate month-end inventory using data from the accounting records without taking a physical count of merchandise on hand. From the following information, estimate the cost of the September 30 inventory by the retail method of inventory valuation.

	Cost Price	Selling Price
Inventory of merchandise, Aug. 31	$264,800	$400,000
Purchases (net) during September	170,400	240,000
Sales (net) during September		275,200

Ex. 10-6 Santa Cruz Wholesale Company uses a **perpetual inventory system.** On January 1, the Inventory account had a balance of $87,500. During the first few days of January the following transactions occurred.

Jan. 2 Purchased merchandise on credit from Bell Company for $12,500.

Jan. 3 Sold merchandise for cash, $9,000. The cost of this merchandise was $6,300.

a Prepare entries in general journal form to record the above transactions.

b What was the balance of the Inventory account at the close of business January 3?

Ex. 10-7 Stream Bicycle Shop uses the first-in, first-out method of inventory valuation. At the end of the current year the shop had exactly the same number of bicycles in stock as at the beginning of the year, and the same proportion of each model. However, the year had been one of severe inflation and the cost of the ending inventory was shown in the accounts at $12,000 whereas the cost of the beginning inventory had been only $8,000. The net income reported by the shop for the year was $15,000. Comment on the validity of the reported net income and indicate what adjustment might be reasonable to give the owner a realistic picture of the results of the year's operations.

PROBLEMS

Group A

10A-1 Cascade Ventures is being offered for sale as a going concern. Its income statements for the last three years include the following key figures.

	Year 3	Year 2	Year 1
Net sales	$520,000	$325,000	$260,000
Cost of goods sold	348,400	221,000	182,000
Gross profit on sales	$171,600	$104,000	$ 78,000
Gross profit percentage	33%	32%	30%

In discussions with prospective buyers, the owner emphasized the rising trend of the gross profit percentage as a very favorable factor.

Assume that you are retained by a prospective purchaser of the business to make an investigation of the fairness and reliability of the Cascade Ventures' accounting records and financial statements. You find everything in order except for the following: (1) The inventory was understated by $6,500 at the end of Year 1 and (2) it was overstated by $20,800 at the end of Year 3. The company uses the periodic inventory system and these errors had not been brought to light prior to your investigation.

Instructions
a Prepare a revised three-year schedule along the lines of the one illustrated above.
b Comment on the trend of gross profit percentage before and after the revision.

10A-2 Handley Corporation sells only one product, and the selling price per unit of $12 has been unchanged throughout the past year. The total sales for the year amounted to $840,000. The beginning inventory at January 1 consisted of 15,000 units valued at cost of $112,500. Purchases during the year were as follows: 20,500 units at $7.75; 33,000 units at $8.00; 23,000 units at $8.30; and 8,500 units at $8.44.

Instructions
a Compute the year-end (December 31) inventory using:
  (1) The first-in; first-out method
  (2) The last-in, first-out method
  (3) The weighted-average method (Compute average unit cost to the nearest cent.)
b Prepare partial income statements for each of the above three methods of pricing inventory. The income statements are to be carried only to the determination of gross profit on sales.
c Which of the three methods of pricing inventory would be most advantageous from an income tax standpoint during a period of rising prices? Comment on the significance of the inventory figure under the method you recommend with respect to current replacement cost.

10A-3 On May 15, Year 4, an early morning fire destroyed the entire inventory of Forest Company. The inventory was stored in a rented warehouse; the offices occupied by the company were not damaged and the accounting records were intact. Forest Company did not maintain perpetual inventory records, and the last physical inventory taken had been on December 31 of the prior year.

An estimate of the inventory value at May 15, the date of the fire, must be prepared in order to file an insurance claim. The income statement on page 393 for the prior year is available to aid you in estimating the amount of the inventory at the date of the fire.

Other data Included in the purchases figure shown in the income statement was $22,500 of office equipment which the Forest Company had acquired late in December for its own use from a competing concern which was quitting business. The bookkeeper of the Forest Company had not understood the nature of this transaction and had recorded it by debiting the Purchases account. The office equipment, however, was not included in the inventory at December 31, Year 3.

The accounting records revealed the merchandise transactions from December 31, Year 3, to the date of the fire to be: sales, $306,000; sales returns and allowances, $2,700; transportation-in, $1,800; purchases, $196,200; purchase returns and allowances, $3,600.

FOREST COMPANY

Income Statement

For the Year Ended December 31, Year 3

Net sales		$738,000
Cost of goods sold:		
Inventory, Jan. 1	$144,000	
Purchases	666,000	
Cost of goods available for sale	$810,000	
Less: Inventory, Dec. 31	234,000	576,000
Gross profit on sales		$162,000
Expenses		72,000
Net income		$ 90,000

Instructions
a Prepare a report directed to the insurance adjuster summarizing your findings. Include an estimate of the inventory value as of the date of the fire and a computation of the applicable gross profit rate.
b Explain how the gross profit method of estimating inventories may be used other than in case of a fire loss.
c Is the rate of gross profit customarily computed as a percentage of the cost of merchandise or as a percentage of sales? Show how the gross profit rate in this problem would vary if based on cost of goods sold rather than on sales.

10A-4 Denver Corporation, a retail store, carries a wide range of merchandise consisting mostly of articles of low unit price. The selling price of each item is plainly marked on the merchandise. At each year-end, the company has taken a physical count of goods on hand and has priced these goods at cost by looking up individual purchase invoices to determine the unit cost of each item in stock. Stevens, the store manager, is anxious to find a more economical method of assigning dollar values to the year-end inventory. He explains that it takes much more time to price the inventory than to count the merchandise on hand.

By analyzing the accounting records you are able to determine that the sales of Year 4, amounted to $1,625,000. During the year, net purchases of merchandise totaled $1,330,000; the retail selling price of this merchandise was $1,750,000. At the end of Year 4, a physical inventory showed goods on hand priced to sell at $375,000. This represented a considerable increase over the inventory of a year earlier. At December 31, Year 3, the inventory on hand had appeared in the balance sheet at cost of $170,000, although it had a retail value of $250,000.

Instructions
a Outline a plan whereby the inventory can be computed without the necessity of looking up individual purchase invoices. List step by step the procedures to be followed. Ignore the possibility of markups and markdowns in the original retail price of merchandise.
b Compute the cost of the inventory at December 31, Year 4, using the method described in **a**.
c Explain how the adoption of the inventory method you have described would facilitate the preparation of monthly financial statements.

10A-5 A perpetual inventory system is used by Vista Company and an inventory record card is maintained for each type of product in stock. The following transactions show the beginning inventory, the purchases, and the sales of product KR9 for the month of May.

May	1 *Balance on hand, 20 units, cost $40 each*	*$800*
	5 *Sale, 8 units, sales price $60 each*	*480*
	6 *Purchase, 20 units, cost $45 each*	*900*
	21 *Sale, 10 units, sales price $60 each*	*600*
	31 *Sale, 15 units, sales price $65 each*	*975*

Instructions
a Record the beginning inventory, the purchases, the cost of goods sold, and the running balance on an inventory record card like the one illustrated on page 385. Use the first-in, first-out method.
b Assume that all sales were made on credit. Compute the total sales and the total cost of goods sold of product KR9 for May. Prepare an entry in general journal form to record these sales and a second entry to record the cost of goods sold for the month of May.
c Compute the gross profit on sales of product KR9 for the month of May.

10A-6 The owner's equity as shown in the balance sheets prepared by Delaware Company for the last three years was as follows: December 31, Year 8, $360,000; December 31, Year 9, $672,685; and December 31, Year 10, $996,685.
The income statements for Years 9 and 10 were as follows:

	Year 10	Year 9
Net sales	$1,260,000	$1,188,000
Cost of goods sold:		
Beginning inventory	$ 455,472	$ 432,000
Net purchases	768,528	736,787
Cost of goods available for sale	$1,224,000	$1,168,787
Ending inventory	468,000	455,472
Cost of goods sold	$ 756,000	$ 713,315
Gross profit on sales	$ 504,000	$ 474,685
Expenses	180,000	162,000
Net income	$ 324,000	$ 312,685

Samuel Peterson, accountant for the Delaware Company, decided early in Year 11 to make a review of the documents and procedures used in taking the physical inventory at December 31, Year 9 and Year 10. His investigation revealed two questionable items as indicated below:
(1) Merchandise shipped to a customer on December 31, Year 9, F.O.B. shipping point, was included in the physical inventory at December 31, Year 9. The cost of the merchandise was $5,220 and the sales price was $6,480. Because of the press of year-end work, the sales invoice was not prepared until January 8, Year 10. On that date the sale was recorded as a January, Year 10, transaction in the sales journal, and the invoice was mailed to the customer.
(2) Merchandise with a cost of $12,312 which had been received on December 31, Year 9, had been included in the inventory taken on that date, although the purchase was not recorded until January 8, Year 10, when the vendor's invoice arrived. The invoice was then recorded in the purchases journal as a January transaction.

Instructions

a Prepare corrected income statements for the periods ended December 31, Year 9 and Year 10. (You may find it helpful to set up T accounts for Sales, Year 9, and Sales, Year 10; Purchases, Year 9, and Purchases, Year 10; and Inventory, December 31, Year 9.)

b Compute corrected amounts for owner's equity at December 31, Year 9 and Year 10.

Group B

10B-1 Key figures taken from the income statements of Fox Company for the last three years are shown below.

	Year 3	Year 2	Year 1
Net sales.	$720,000	$450,000	$360,000
Cost of goods sold	482,400	306,000	252,000
Gross profit on sales	$237,600	$144,000	$108,000
Gross profit percentage	33%	32%	30%

An audit of the company's affairs performed after the accounts had been closed at the end of Year 3 disclosed the following errors: (*1*) an arithmetical error in the computation of inventory at the end of Year 1 had caused a $9,000 understatement in that inventory; and (2) a duplication of figures in the computation of inventory at the end of Year 3 had caused an overstatement of $28,800 in that inventory.

Instructions

a Prepare a three-year schedule in the form illustrated above, using figures that reflect correction of the erroneous inventory amounts. Include the revised gross profit percentage for each year. (Round any fractions to the nearest full percentage point.)

b Is the president of Fox Company justified in his enthusiasm for the trend of the gross profit percentage of the company? Explain.

10B-2 Motor-Aid Company specializes in the sale of a single product. The volume of sales during Year 9 amounted to $1,470,000 and the unit selling price was unchanged at $14. The inventory at January 1, Year 9, consisted of 9,000 units valued at cost of $47,250. Purchases during the year were as follows: 22,000 units @ $6 00; 30,000 units @ $6.25; 50,000 units @ $6.60; and 9,500 units @ $7.00.

Instructions

a Compute the December 31, Year 9, inventory using (*1*) the first-in, first-out method; and (2) the last-in, first-out method.

b Prepare comparative income statement data for each of the above two methods of pricing inventory. The income statements are to be carried only to the determination of gross profit on sales.

c Which of the two methods of pricing inventory would be more advantageous from an income tax standpoint during a period of rising prices? Comment on the significance of the inventory figure under the method you recommend with respect to its reasonableness and relevance as an element of the balance sheet. What additional disclosure may be desirable in the balance sheet with respect to inventory?

10B-3 Raytown Electric uses the periodic method of inventory and maintains its accounts on a calendar-year basis. On May 10, Year 6, the entire inventory was destroyed by fire. In order to file an insurance claim, Raytown Electric had to estimate the cost of the merchandise on hand at the date of the fire. The last income statement of the company was prepared for the year ended December 31, Year 5, and appears on page 396.

RAYTOWN ELECTRIC

Income Statement

For the Year Ended, December 31, Year 5

Net sales		$960,000
Cost of goods sold:		
Inventory, Jan. 1, Year 5	$ 192,000	
Purchases	888,000	
Cost of goods available for sale	$1,080,000	
Less: Inventory, Dec. 31, Year 5	312,000	768,000
Gross profit on sales		$192,000

Included in the purchases figure shown above was $30,000 of office equipment which the company had acquired late in December of Year 5 for its own use from a competing concern which was quitting business. The bookkeeper had not understood the nature of this transaction and had recorded it by debiting the Purchases account. The office equipment, however, was not included in the inventory as of December 31, Year 5.

The sales figure of $960,000 for Year 5 did not include $24,000 sales value of merchandise packaged and ready for shipment to a customer on December 31, Year 5. This lot of merchandise was being held by Raytown Electric merely as an accommodation to the customer. The customer had originally ordered this merchandise for delivery on December 10; just prior to that date he had re-quested, because of overcrowded warehouses, that the goods be held by Ray-town Electric until January 10. It was agreed that the regular 30-day credit terms should run from December 10 per the original agreement. This merchandise had not been included in the Raytown Electric year-end inventory; the goods were delivered to the customer on January 10, Year 6, and payment of $24,000 was received the same day.

Records salvaged from the fire revealed the merchandise transactions from January 1, Year 6, to the date of the fire to be: sales, $432,000; sales returns and allowances, $3,600; transportation-in, $2,400; purchases, $264,000; purchase returns and allowances, $4,800. The sales figure for Year 6 includes the $24,000 described above.

Instructions

a Prepare a report addressed to the insurance adjuster summarizing your find-ings. Include an estimate of the inventory value as of the date of the fire and a computation of the applicable gross profit rate, after making appropriate corrections to the Year 5 income statement.

b Explain how the gross profit method of estimating inventories may be used other than in case of a fire loss.

10B-4 Golf Shop, a retail business, had net sales during January of $32,600. Purchases of merchandise from suppliers during January amounted to $20,722. Of these January purchases, invoices totaling $13,722 were paid during the month; the remaining January invoices totaling $7,000 were still unpaid at January 31. The merchandise purchased during January had a retail sales value of $29,650.

On January 1 the merchandise on hand represented a cost of $21,200 as determined by the year-end physical inventory. The retail sales value of this inventory was $32,000. The retail selling price was plainly marked on every item of merchandise in the store.

At January 31 the owner of Golf Shop wished to estimate the cost of inventory on hand without taking time to count the merchandise and look up the cost prices as shown on purchase invoices.

Instructions

a Use the retail inventory method to estimate the cost of the inventory at January

31. The possibility of markups and markdowns in the original retail price of merchandise may be ignored.

b What effect, if any, does the fact that January purchase invoices in the amount of $7,000 were unpaid at January 31 have upon the determination of the amount of inventory at January 31?

10B-5 Oaktree Wholesale Company uses a perpetual inventory system, including a perpetual inventory record card for each of the 60 types of products it keeps in stock. The following transactions show the purchases and sales of one of these products (XK3) during September.

Sept.	1	*Balance on hand, 50 units, cost $60 each*	$3,000
	4	*Purchase, 20 units, cost $65 each*	1,300
	8	*Sale, 35 units, sales price $100 each*	3,500
	9	*Purchase, 40 units, cost $65 each*	2,600
	20	*Sale, 60 units, sales price $100 each*	6,000
	25	*Purchase, 40 units, cost, $70 each*	2,800
	30	*Sale, 5 units, sales price $110 each*	550

Instructions

a Record the beginning inventory, the purchases, the cost of goods sold, and the running balance on an inventory record card like the one illustrated on page 385. Use the first-in, first-out method.

b Assume that all sales were made on credit. Compute the total sales and total cost of goods sold of product XK3 for September. Prepare an entry in general journal form to record these sales and a second entry to record the cost of goods sold for September.

c Compute the gross profit on sales of product XK3 for the month of September.

10B-6 Income statements prepared by Sunflower Paints for Year 4 and Year 5 are shown below.

	Year 5	Year 4
Net sales	$630,000	$594,000
Cost of goods sold:		
Beginning inventory	$227,736	$216,000
Net purchases	384,264	368,393
Cost of goods available for sale	$612,000	$584,393
Ending inventory	234,000	227,736
Cost of goods sold	$378,000	$356,657
Gross profit on sales	$252,000	$237,343
Expenses	90,000	81,000
Net income	$162,000	$156,343

The owner's equity as shown in the company's balance sheet was as follows: December 31, Year 3, $180,000; December 31, Year 4, $336,343; and December 31, Year 5, $498,343.

Early in Year 6, Alan Frank, accountant for Sunflower Paints, made a review of the documents and procedures used in taking the physical inventory at December 31 for both Year 4 and Year 5. His investigation disclosed the two questionable items listed below:

(*1*) Merchandise shipped to a customer on December 31, Year 4, F.O.B. shipping point, was included in the physical inventory taken that date. The cost of the merchandise was $2,610 and the sales price was $3,240. Because of the press of year-end work, the sales invoice was not prepared until January 6, Year 5.

On that date the sale was recorded as a January transaction by entry in the sales journal, and the sales invoice mailed to the customer.

(2) Merchandise costing $6,156, which had been received on December 31, Year 4, had been included in the inventory taken on that date, although the purchase was not recorded until January 8 when the vendor's invoice arrived. The invoice was then recorded in the purchases journal as a January transaction.

Instructions
a Prepare corrected income statements for the years ended December 31, Year 4 and Year 5. (You may find it helpful to set up T accounts for Sales, Year 4, and Sales, Year 5; Purchases, Year 4, and Purchases, Year 5; and Inventory, December 31, Year 4.)
b Compute corrected amounts for owner's equity at December 31, Year 4 and Year 5.

BUSINESS DECISION PROBLEM 10

You are the sales manager of Continental Motors, an automobile dealership specializing in European imports. Among the automobiles in Continental Motors' showroom are two Italian sports cars, which are identical in every respect except for color; one is red and the other white. The red car had been ordered last February, at a cost of $6,300 American dollars. The white car had been ordered early last March, but because of a revaluation of the Italian lira relative to the dollar, the white car had cost only $5,850 American dollars. Both cars arrived in the United States on the same boat and had just been delivered to your showroom. Since the cars were identical except for color and both colors were equally popular, you had listed both cars at the same suggested retail price, $9,000.

Paul Davis, one of your best salesmen, comes into your office with a proposal. He has a customer in the showroom who wants to buy the red car for $9,000. However, when Davis pulled the inventory card on the red car to see what options were included, he happened to notice the inventory card of the white car. Continental Motors, like most automobile dealerships, uses the specific identification method to value inventory. Consequently, Davis noticed that the red car had cost $6,300, while the white one had cost Continental Motors only $5,850. This gave Davis the idea for the following proposal.

"If I sell the red car for $9,000, Continental Motors makes a gross profit of $2,700. But if you'll let me discount that white car $150, I think I can get my customer to buy that one instead. If I sell the white car for $8,850, the gross profit will be $3,000, so Continental Motors is $300 better off than if I sell the red car for $9,000. Since I came up with this plan, I feel I should get part of the benefit, so Continental Motors should split the extra $300 with me. That way, I'll get an extra $150 commission, and the company still makes $150 more than if I sell the red car."

Instructions
a Prepare a schedule which shows the total revenue, cost of goods sold, and gross profit to Continental Motors if **both** cars are sold for $9,000 each.
b Prepare a schedule showing the revenue, cost of goods sold, and gross profit to Continental Motors if both cars are sold but Davis's plan is adopted and the white car is sold for $8,850. Assume the red car is still sold for $9,000. To simplify comparison of this schedule to the one prepared in part **a,** include the extra $150 commission to Davis in the cost of goods sold of the part **b** schedule.
c Write out your decision whether or not to accept Davis's proposal, and explain to Davis why the proposal either would or would not be to the advantage of Continental Motors. (*Hint:* Refer to your schedules prepared in parts **a** and **b** in your explanation.)

11   Plant and Equipment: Depreciation

PLANT AND EQUIPMENT

The term *plant and equipment* is used to describe long-lived assets acquired for use in the operation of the business and not intended for resale to customers. Among the more common examples are land, buildings, machinery, furniture and fixtures, office equipment, and automobiles. A delivery truck in the showroom of an automobile dealer is inventory; when this same truck is sold to a drugstore for use in making deliveries to customers, it becomes a unit of plant and equipment.

The term *fixed assets* has long been used in accounting literature to describe all types of plant and equipment. This term, however, has virtually disappeared from the published financial statements of large corporations. *Plant and equipment* appears to be a more descriptive term. Another alternative title used on many corporation balance sheets is *property, plant, and equipment.*

Although land used in the business is classified under plant and equipment, a tract of land acquired as a future building site and not presently being used in the business is classified under the balance sheet caption of Investments or under Other Assets. Similar reasoning indicates that a building formerly used in the business, but now idle and not required for operating purposes, should be excluded from the plant and equipment category.

Plant and equipment represent bundles of services to be received

It is convenient to think of a plant asset as a bundle of services to be received by the owner over a period of years. Ownership of a delivery truck, for example, may provide about 100,000 miles of transportation. The cost of the delivery truck is customarily entered in a plant and equipment account entitled Delivery Truck, which in essence represents payment in advance for several years of transportation service. Similarly, a building may be regarded as payment in advance for several years' supply of housing services. As the years go by, these services are utilized by the business and the cost of the plant asset is gradually transferred into depreciation expense.

An awareness of the similarity between plant assets and prepaid expenses is essential to an understanding of the accounting process by which the cost of plant assets is allocated to the years in which the benefits of ownership are received.

Major categories of plant and equipment

Plant and equipment items are often classified into one of the following groups:

1 Tangible plant assets. The term *tangible* denotes physical substance, as exemplified by land, a building, or a machine. This category may be subdivided into two distinct classifications:
   a Plant property subject to depreciation; included are plant assets of limited useful life such as buildings and office equipment.
   b Land. The only plant asset not subject to depreciation is land, which has an unlimited term of existence.
2 Intangible assets. Examples are patents, copyrights, trademarks, franchises, organization costs, leaseholds, and goodwill. Current assets such as accounts receivable or prepaid rent are not included in the intangible classification, even though they are lacking in physical substance. The term *intangible assets* is used to describe assets which are used in the operation of the business but have no physical substance, and are noncurrent.

Natural resources

Natural resources are subject to depletion rather than to depreciation. Examples are mines, oil and gas wells, and tracts of timber. The term *depletion* means the exhaustion of a natural resource through mining, pumping, cutting, or otherwise using up the deposit or growth. Accounting for natural resources and for depletion is considered in Chapter 12.

Accounting problems relating to plant and equipment

Some major accounting problems relating to plant and equipment are indicated by the following questions:

1 How is the cost of plant and equipment determined?

2 How should the costs of plant and equipment be allocated against revenue?

3 How should expenditures for repairs and maintenance be treated?

4 How does inflation affect the measurement of depreciation expense?

5 Should financial statements include disclosure of depreciation computed on the basis of replacement cost?

6 How should disposal of plant assets be recorded?

We are presently concerned with answering the first of these questions; an understanding of how the cost of plant and equipment is determined will be helpful in subsequent study of depreciation.

DETERMINING THE COST OF PLANT AND EQUIPMENT The cost of plant and equipment includes all expenditures reasonable and necessary in acquiring the asset and placing it in a position and condition for use in the operations of the business. Only *reasonable* and *necessary* expenditures should be included. For example, if the company's truck driver receives a traffic ticket while hauling a new machine to the plant, the traffic fine is *not* part of the cost of the new machine. If the machine is dropped and damaged while being unloaded, the expense of repairing the damage should *not* be added to the cost of the machine.

Cost is most easily determined when an asset is purchased for cash. The cost of the asset is then equal to the cash outlay necessary in acquiring the asset plus any expenditures for freight, insurance while in transit, installation, trial runs, and any other costs necessary to make *the asset ready for use.* If plant assets are purchased on the installment plan or by issuance of notes payable, the interest element or carrying charge should be recorded as interest expense and not as part of the cost of the plant assets.

This principle of including in the cost of a plant asset all the incidental charges necessary to put the asset in use is illustrated by the following example. A factory in Minneapolis orders a machine from a San Francisco tool manufacturer at a list price of $10,000, with terms of 2/10, n/30. A sales tax of 6% must be paid, also freight charges of $1,250. Transportation from the railroad station to the factory costs $150, and installation labor amounts to $400. The cost of the machine to be entered in the Machinery account is computed as follows:

Items **List price of machine**	**$10,000**
included in **Less: Cash discount (2% × $10,000)**	**200**
cost of **Net cash price**	**$ 9,800**
machine **Sales tax (6% × $9,800)**	**588**
Freight	**1,250**
Transportation from railroad station to factory	**150**
Installation labor	**400**
Cost of machine	**$12,188**

Why should all the incidental charges relating to the acquisition of a machine be included in its cost? Why not treat these incidental charges as expenses of the period in which the machine is acquired?

The answer is to be found in the basic accounting principle of *matching costs and revenue.* The benefits of owning the machine will be received over a span of years, 10 years, for example. During those 10 years the operation of the machine will contribute to revenue. Consequently, the total costs of the machine should be recorded in the accounts as an asset and allocated against the revenue of the 10 years. All costs incurred in acquiring the machine are costs of the services to be received from using the machine.

Land   When land is purchased, various incidental costs are generally incurred, in addition to the purchase price. These additional costs may include commissions to real estate brokers, escrow fees, legal fees for examining and insuring the title, delinquent taxes paid by the purchaser, and fees for surveying, draining, clearing, grading, and landscaping the property. All these expenditures are part of the cost of the land. Special assessments for local improvements, such as the paving of a street or the installation of sewers, should also be charged to the Land account, for the reason that a more or less permanent value is being added to the land.

Apportionment of a lump-sum purchase   Separate ledger accounts are necessary for land and buildings, because buildings are subject to depreciation and land is not. The treatment of land as a nondepreciable asset is based on the premise that land used as a building site has an unlimited life. When land and building are purchased for a lump sum, the purchase price must be apportioned between the land and the building. An appraisal may be necessary for this purpose. Assume, for example, that land and a building are purchased for a bargain price of $100,000. The apportionment of this cost on the basis of an appraisal may be made as follows:

	Value per Appraisal	Percentage of Total	Apportionment of Cost
Apportioning cost between land and building **Land**	$ 48,000	40%	$ 40,000
Building	72,000	60%	60,000
Total	$120,000	100%	$100,000

Sometimes a tract of land purchased as a building site has on it an old building which is not suitable for the buyer's use. The Land account should be charged with the entire purchase price plus any costs incurred in tearing down or removing the building. Proceeds received from sale of the materials salvaged from the old building are recorded as a credit in the Land account.

Land acquired as a future building site should be reported under Investments or Other Assets, rather than as part of Plant and Equipment, since it is not currently used in operations.

Land improvements   Improvements to real estate such as driveways, fences, parking lots, and sprinkler systems have a limited life and are therefore subject to depreciation. For this reason they should be recorded not in the Land account but in a separate account entitled Land Improvements. On the other hand, any improvements such as grading or leveling, which will last indefinitely and are not to be depreciated, are entered in the Land account.

Buildings   Old buildings are sometimes purchased with the intention of repairing them prior to placing them in use. Repairs made under these circumstances are charged to the Buildings account. After the building has been placed in use, *ordinary repairs* are considered as maintenance expense when incurred.

When a building is constructed by the business itself, rather than being purchased, cost includes the materials and labor used plus an equitable portion of overhead or other indirect costs, such as executive salaries. Any other outlays specifically relating to the construction such as architectural fees, insurance during the construction period, and building permits should also be included in the cost of the building. A building or machine constructed by a company for its own use should be recorded in the accounts at cost, not at the price which might have been paid to outsiders if the asset had been acquired through purchase.

Leasehold improvements   When buildings or other improvements are constructed on leased property by the lessee, the costs should be recorded in a Leasehold Improvements account and written off as expense during the remaining life of the lease or of the estimated useful life of the building, whichever is shorter. This procedure is usually followed even though the lessee has an option to renew the lease, because there is no assurance in advance that conditions will warrant the exercise of the renewal clause.

DEPRECIATION

Allocating the cost of plant and equipment over the years of use

Plant assets, with the exception of land, are of use to a company for only a limited number of years, and the cost of each plant asset is allocated as an expense of the years in which it is used. Accountants use the term *depreciation* to describe this gradual conversion of the cost of a plant asset into expense.

Depreciation, as the term is used in accounting, does not mean the physical deterioration of an asset. Neither does depreciation mean the decrease in market value of a plant asset over a period of time. *Depreciation means the allocation of the cost of a plant asset to the periods in which services are received from the asset.*

When a delivery truck is purchased, its cost is first recorded as an asset. This cost becomes expense over a period of years through the accounting process of depreciation. When gasoline is purchased for the truck, the price paid for each tankful is immediately recorded as expense. In theory, both outlays (for the truck and for a tank of gas) represent the acquisition of assets, but since it is reasonable to assume that a tankful of gasoline will be consumed in the accounting period in which it is purchased, we record the outlay for gasoline as an expense immediately. It is important to recognize, however, that *both the outlay for the truck and the payment for the gasoline become expense in the period or periods in which each renders services.*

A separate Depreciation Expense account and a separate Accumulated Depreciation account are generally maintained for each group of depreciable assets such as factory buildings, delivery equipment, and office equipment so that a proper allocation of depreciation expense can be made between functional areas of activity such as sales and manufacturing. Depreciation on manufacturing facilities is not necessarily an expense of the period in which it is recorded; the depreciation charge is first embodied in the inventory of finished goods manufactured, and the cost of this inventory is later deducted from revenue as an expense of the period when the goods are sold.

Depreciation differs from most expenses in that it does not require a cash payment at or near the time it is recorded. The entry to record depreciation (a debit to Depreciation Expense and a credit to Accumulated Depreciation) has no effect on current assets or current liabilities. However, when depreciable assets wear out, a large cash payment must be made in order to replace them.

Because of the noncash nature of depreciation expense and because the dollar amount is materially affected by the depreciation method selected, it is generally desirable that the total amount of depreciation expense for the year be disclosed in the income statement.

Depreciation not a process of valuation

Accounting records do not purport to show the constantly fluctuating market values of plant and equipment. Occasionally the market value of a building may rise substantially over a period of years because of a change in the price level, or for other reasons. Depreciation is continued, however, regardless of the increase in market value. The accountant recognizes that the building will render useful services for only a limited number of years, and that its full cost must be allocated as expense of those years regardless of fluctuations in market value.

The *book value* or *carrying value* of a plant asset is its cost minus the related accumulated depreciation. Plant assets are shown in the balance sheet at their book values, representing the portion of their cost which will be allocated to expense in future periods. Accumulated depreciation represents the portion of the assets' cost which has already been recognized as expense.

Causes of depreciation

There are two major causes of depreciation, physical deterioration and obsolescence.

PHYSICAL DETERIORATION Physical deterioration of a plant asset results from use, and also from exposure to sun, wind, and other climatic factors. When a plant asset has been carefully maintained, it is not uncommon for the owner to claim that the asset is as "good as new." Such statements are not literally true. Although a good repair policy may greatly lengthen the useful life of a machine, every machine eventually reaches the point at which it must be discarded. In brief, the making of repairs does not lessen the need for recognition of depreciation.

OBSOLESCENCE The term *obsolescence* means the process of becoming out of date or obsolete. An airplane, for example, may become obsolete even though it is in excellent physical condition; it becomes obsolete because better planes of superior design and performance have become available. Obsolescence relates to the capacity of a plant asset to render services to a particular company for a particular purpose.

The usefulness of plant assets may also be reduced because the rapid growth of a company renders such assets inadequate. Inadequacy of a plant asset may necessitate replacement with a larger unit even though the asset is in good physical condition and is not obsolete. Obsolescence and inadequacy are often closely associated; both relate to the opportunity for economical and efficient use of an asset rather than to its physical condition. Obsolescence is probably a more significant factor than physical deterioration in putting an end to the usefulness of most depreciable assets. Current accounting practice, however, does not usually attempt to separate the effects of physical deterioration and obsolescence.

Methods of computing depreciation

A business need not use the same method of depreciation for all its various assets. For example, a company may use straight-line depreciation on some assets and a declining-balance method for other assets. Management also has the option of using different methods of depreciation in the accounting records and financial statements than are employed in the determination of taxable income. The most widely used methods (straight-line, units-of-output, declining-balance, and sum-of-the-years'-digits) are explained and illustrated in the following sections.

STRAIGHT-LINE METHOD The simplest and most widely used method of computing depreciation is the straight-line method. This method was described in Chapter 3 and has been used repeatedly in problems throughout this book. Under the straight-line method, an equal portion of the cost of the asset is allocated to each period of use; consequently, this method is most appropriate when usage of an asset is fairly uniform from year to year.

The computation of the periodic charge for depreciation is made by deducting the estimated *residual* or *salvage value* from the cost of the asset and dividing the remaining *depreciable cost* by the years of estimated useful life. For example, if a depreciable asset has a cost of $5,200, a residual value of $400, and an estimated useful life of four years, the annual computation of depreciation expense will be as follows:

$$\frac{\text{Cost} - \text{Residual Value}}{\text{Years of Useful Life}} = \frac{\$5,200 - \$400}{4} = \$1,200$$

This same depreciation computation is shown below in tabular form.

<table>
<tr><td rowspan="6">*Computing depreciation by straight-line method*</td><td>Cost of the depreciable asset . . . .</td><td>$5,200</td></tr>
<tr><td>Less: Estimated residual value (amount to be realized by sale of asset</td><td></td></tr>
<tr><td>when it is retired from use) . . . .</td><td>400</td></tr>
<tr><td>Total amount to be depreciated (depreciable cost). . . . .</td><td>$4,800</td></tr>
<tr><td>Estimated useful life . . . .</td><td>4 years</td></tr>
<tr><td>Depreciation expense each year ($4,800 ÷ 4) . . . .</td><td>$1,200</td></tr>
</table>

The following schedule summarizes the accumulation of depreciation over the useful life of the asset. The amount to be depreciated is $4,800 (cost of $5,200 minus estimated residual value of $400).

Depreciation Schedule: Straight-Line Method

	Year	Computation	Depreciation Expense	Accumulated Depreciation	Book Value
					$5,200
Constant annual depreciation expense	First	($\frac{1}{4}$ × $4,800)	$1,200	$1,200	4,000
	Second	($\frac{1}{4}$ × $4,800)	1,200	2,400	2,800
	Third	($\frac{1}{4}$ × $4,800)	1,200	3,600	1,600
	Fourth	($\frac{1}{4}$ × $4,800)	1,200	4,800	400
			$4,800		

Depreciation rates for various types of assets can conveniently be stated as percentages. In the above example the asset had an estimated life of four years, so the depreciation expense each year was $\frac{1}{4}$ of the depreciable amount. The fraction "$\frac{1}{4}$" is of course equivalent to an annual rate of 25%. Similarly, an asset with a 20-year life would call for annual depreciation expense of $\frac{1}{20}$, or 5%. A 10-year life would require a depreciation rate of $\frac{1}{10}$, or 10%, and an eight-year life a depreciation rate of $\frac{1}{8}$, or $12\frac{1}{2}$%.

In the preceding illustration we assumed that the company maintained its accounts on a calendar-year basis and that the asset was acquired on January 1, the beginning of the accounting period. If the asset had been acquired sometime during the year, on October 1 for example, it would have been in use for only three months, or $\frac{3}{12}$ of a year. Consequently, the depreciation to be recorded at December 31 would be only $\frac{3}{12}$ of $1,200, or $300. Stated more precisely, the depreciation expense in this situation is computed as follows: $\frac{3}{12} \times 25\% \times \$4,800 = \$300$.

In practice, the possibility of residual value is sometimes ignored and the annual depreciation charge computed by dividing the total cost of the asset by the number of years of estimated useful life. This practice may be justified in those cases in which residual value is not material and is difficult to estimate accurately. Under this approach the yearly depreciation expense in the above example would be $5,200 ÷ 4, or $1,300. The percentage rate would still be 25%, since one-fourth of the depreciable amount becomes expense each year.

UNITS-OF-OUTPUT METHOD For certain kinds of assets, more equitable allocation of the cost can be obtained by dividing the cost (minus salvage value, if significant) by the estimated units of output rather than by the estimated years of useful life. A truck line or bus company, for example, might compute depreciation on its vehicles by a mileage basis. If a truck costs $11,000 and has a residual value of $1,000 and a useful life of 100,000 miles, the depreciation rate per mile of operation is 10 cents ($10,000 ÷ 100,000). This calculation of the depreciation rate may be stated as follows:

$$\frac{\text{Cost } - \text{ Residual Value}}{\text{Estimated Units of Output (Miles)}} = \frac{\text{Depreciation per}}{\text{Unit of Output (Mile)}}$$

or

$$\frac{\$11,000 - \$1,000}{100,000 \text{ miles}} = \$0.10 \text{ depreciation per mile}$$

At the end of each year, the amount of depreciation to be recorded would be determined by multiplying the 10-cent rate by the number of miles the truck had operated during the year. This method is suitable only when the total units of output of the asset over its entire useful life can be estimated with reasonable accuracy.

ACCELERATED DEPRECIATION METHODS The term *accelerated depreciation* means recognition of relatively large amounts of depreciation in the early years of use and reduced amounts in the later years. Many types of plant and equipment are most efficient when new and therefore provide more and better services in the early years of useful life. If we assume that the benefits derived from owning an asset are greatest in the early years when the asset is relatively new, then the amount of the asset's cost which we allocate as depreciation expense should be greatest in these same years. This is consistent with the basic accounting concept of matching costs with related revenue.

One reason for adoption of accelerated methods of depreciation is that the increasingly rapid pace of invention of new products is making obsolescence a factor of greater significance than physical deterioration. When an industry is in a period of rapid technological change, plant and equipment may have to be replaced within shorter periods than would be necessary in a less dynamic economy. Businesses may, therefore, reason that the acquisition of a new plant facility is justified only if most of the cost can be recovered within a comparatively short period of years. Also significant is the pleasing prospect of reducing the current year's income tax burden by recognizing a relatively large amount of depreciation expense.

Another argument for allocating a comparatively large share of the cost of a depreciable asset to the early years of use is that repair expenses tend to increase as assets grow older. The combined expense of depreciation and repairs may be more uniform from year to year under an accelerated method of depreciation than when straight-line depreciation is followed. Whether a uniform total amount of depreciation expense plus repairs expense from year to year is realistic accounting, however, depends upon whether the benefits received from owning the asset are relatively constant from year to year.

Declining-balance method   For income tax purposes one of the acceptable methods of "rapid write-off" of depreciable assets consists of doubling the normal rate of depreciation and applying this doubled rate each year to the undepreciated cost (book value) of the asset. The term *double-declining-balance* is often applied to this form of accelerated depreciation.

Assume, for example, that an automobile is acquired for business use at a cost of $8,000. Estimated useful life is four years; therefore, the depreciation rate under the straight-line method would be 25%. To depreciate the automobile by the declining-balance method, we double the straight-line rate of 25% and apply the doubled rate of 50% to the book value. Depreciation expense in the first year would then amount to $4,000. In the second year the depreciation expense would drop to $2,000, computed at 50% of the remaining book value of $4,000. In the third year depreciation would be $1,000, and in the fourth year only $500. The table on page 409 shows the allocation of cost under this method of depreciation.

If the automobile is continued in use beyond the estimated life of four years, depreciation may be continued at the 50% rate on the book value. In the fifth year, for example, the depreciation expense would be $250

Depreciation Schedule: Declining-Balance Method

	Year	Computation	Depreciation Expense	Accumulated Depreciation	Book Value
					$8,000
Accelerated	First	(50% × $8,000)	$4,000	$4,000	4,000
depreciation:	Second	(50% × $4,000)	2,000	6,000	2,000
declining-balance	Third	(50% × $2,000)	1,000	7,000	1,000
	Fourth	(50% × $1,000)	500	7,500	500

(50% × $500), and in the sixth year $125 (50% × $250). When the declining-balance method is used, the cost of a depreciable asset will never be entirely written off as long as the asset continues in use. Perhaps because of the existence of this undepreciated balance of original cost, the tax regulations do not require any deduction from original cost for residual value when this method of depreciation is used. However, if the asset has a residual value, depreciation must stop at this point. For example, if the $8,000 automobile illustrated above has a residual value of $800, the depreciation for the fourth year would be restricted to $200, which is the amount of depreciation required to reduce the carrying value of the automobile to its residual value.

If the asset in the above illustration had been acquired on April 1 rather than on January 1, depreciation for only nine months (April–December) would be recorded in the first year. The computation would be $\frac{9}{12}$ × (50% × $8,000) or $3,000. For the next calendar year the calculation would be 50% × ($8,000 − $3,000), or $2,500.

Sum-of-the-years'-digits method This is another method of allocating a large portion of the cost of an asset to the early years of its use. The depreciation rate to be used is a fraction, of which the numerator is the remaining years of useful life (as of the beginning of the year) and the denominator is the sum of the years of useful life. Consider again the example of an automobile costing $8,000, having an estimated life of four years and an estimated residual value of $800. (Present income tax regulations require that residual value be taken into account when either the straight-line method or the sum-of-the-years'-digits method of depreciation is used.) Since the asset has an estimated life of four years, the denominator of the fraction will be 10, computed as follows (1 + 2 + 3 + 4 = 10). For the first year, the depreciation will be $\frac{4}{10}$ × $7,200, or $2,880. For the second year, the depreciation will be $\frac{3}{10}$ × $7,200, or $2,160; in the third year $\frac{2}{10}$ × $7,200, or $1,440; and in the fourth year, $\frac{1}{10}$ × $7,200, or $720. In tabular form this depreciation program will appear as on page 410.

Assume that the asset being depreciated by the sum-of-the-years'-digits method was acquired on April 1 and the company maintains its accounts on a calendar-year basis. Since the asset was in use for only nine months

Depreciation Schedule: Sum-of-the-Years'-Digits Method

	Year	Computation	Depreciation Expense	Accumulated Depreciation	Book Value
					$8,000
Accelerated	First	.($\frac{4}{10}$ × $7,200)	$2,880	$2,880	5,120
deprecia-	Second	.($\frac{3}{10}$ × $7,200)	2,160	5,040	2,960
tion: sum-					
of-the-	Third	.($\frac{2}{10}$ × $7,200)	1,440	6,480	1,520
years'-	Fourth	.($\frac{1}{10}$ × $7,200)	720	7,200	800
digits					

during the first accounting period, the depreciation to be recorded in this first period will be for only $\frac{9}{12}$ of a full year, that is, $\frac{9}{12}$ × $2,880, or $2,160. For the second accounting period the depreciation computation will be:

$\frac{3}{12}$ × ($\frac{4}{10}$ × $7,200) . . . . $ 720

$\frac{9}{12}$ × ($\frac{3}{10}$ × 7,200) 1,620

  Depreciation expense, second period $2,340

A similar pattern of allocation will be followed for each accounting period of the asset's life.

DEPRECIATION FOR FRACTIONAL PERIODS In the case of depreciable assets acquired sometime during the year, it is customary to figure depreciation to the nearest month. For example, if an asset is acquired on July 12, depreciation would be computed from July 1; if the asset had been acquired on July 18 (or any other date in the latter half of July), depreciation would be recorded for only five months (August through December) for the current calendar year.

Some businesses prefer to begin depreciation on the first of the month following the acquisition of a depreciable asset. This method, or any one of many similar variations, is acceptable so long as it is followed consistently.

Revision of depreciation rates

Depreciation rates are based on estimates of the useful life of assets. These estimates of useful life are seldom precisely correct and sometimes are grossly in error. Consequently, the annual depreciation expense based on the estimated useful life may be either excessive or inadequate. What action should be taken when, after a few years of using a plant asset, it is decided that the asset is actually going to last for a considerably longer or shorter period than was originally estimated? When either of these situations arises, a revised estimate of useful life should be made and the periodic depreciation expense decreased or increased accordingly.

The procedure for correcting the depreciation program may be stated in a very few words: ***Spread the remaining undepreciated cost of the asset over the years of remaining useful life.*** The annual depreciation expense is increased or decreased sufficiently so that the depreciation program will be completed in accordance with the revised estimate of remaining useful life. The following data illustrate a revision which increases the estimate of useful life and thereby decreases the annual depreciation expense.

Data prior *Cost of asset*	*$10,000*
to revision *of depreci-* *Estimated useful life (no residual value)*	*10 years*
ation rate *Annual depreciation expense (prior to revision)*	*$ 1,000*
Accumulated depreciation at end of six years ($1,000 × 6)	*$ 6,000*

At the beginning of the seventh year, it is decided that the asset will last for eight more years. The revised estimate of useful life is, therefore, a total of 14 years. The depreciation expense to be recognized for the seventh year and for each of the remaining years is $500, computed as follows:

Revision of *Undepreciated cost at end of sixth year ($10,000 − $6,000)*	*$4,000*
depreciation *program* *Revised estimate of remaining years of useful life*	*8 years*
Revised amount of annual depreciation expense ($4,000 ÷ 8)	*$ 500*

The method described above for the revision of a depreciation program is generally used and is acceptable in the determination of taxable income. The Financial Accounting Standards Board also supports this approach for financial reporting purposes.

Depreciation and income taxes

Different methods of depreciation may be used for the purpose of preparing financial statements and the purpose of preparing income tax returns. The vast majority of businesses use straight-line depreciation in their financial statements, possibly motivated in part by a desire to report higher earnings per share of stock. For income tax purposes, however, many businesses use an accelerated depreciation method.

Accelerated methods of depreciation became quite popular some years ago when the federal government approved their use for income tax purposes. By offering businesses the opportunity of writing off as depreciation expense a large portion of the cost of a new asset during its early years of use, the government has provided a powerful incentive for investment in new productive facilities. Since an increased charge for depreciation expense will reduce taxable income, business executives may feel that by purchasing new assets and writing off a large part of the cost in the early years of use, they are in effect paying for the new assets with dollars that otherwise would have been used to pay income taxes.

In theory, the ideal depreciation policy is one that allocates the cost of a depreciable asset to the several periods of its use in proportion to the services received each period. Accelerated methods of depreciation sometimes fail to allocate the cost of an asset in proportion to the flow of services from the property and therefore prevent the determination of annual net income on a realistic basis. If annual net income figures are misleading, stockholders, creditors, management, and others who use financial statements as a basis for business decisions may be seriously injured. For income tax purposes, however, accelerated methods of depreciation may be effective in encouraging business organizations to invest in new productive facilities and thereby to raise the level of economic activity.

Accumulated depreciation does not consist of cash

Many readers of financial statements who have not studied accounting mistakenly believe that accumulated depreciation accounts (depreciation reserves) represent money accumulated for the purpose of buying new equipment when the present equipment wears out. Perhaps the best way to combat such mistaken notions is to emphasize that *a credit balance in an accumulated depreciation account represents the expired cost of assets acquired in the past.* The amounts credited to the accumulated depreciation account could, as an alternative, have been credited directly to the plant and equipment account. An accumulated depreciation account has a *credit* balance; it does not represent an asset; and it cannot be used in any way to pay for new equipment. To buy a new plant asset requires cash; the total amount of cash owned by a company is shown by the asset account for cash.

Capital expenditures and revenue expenditures

The term *expenditure* means making a payment or incurring an obligation to make a future payment for an asset or service received. The acquisition of an asset (such as an automobile) or of a service (such as repairs to the automobile) may be for cash or on credit. In either situation the transaction is properly referred to as an expenditure.

Expenditures for the purchase or expansion of plant assets are called *capital expenditures* and are recorded in asset accounts. Expenditures for ordinary repairs, maintenance, fuel, and other items necessary to the ownership and use of plant and equipment are called *revenue expenditures* and are recorded by debits to expense accounts. The charge to an expense account is based on the assumption that the benefits from the expenditure will be used up in the current period, and the payment should therefore be deducted from the revenue of the current period in determining the net income. In brief, *any expenditure that will benefit several accounting periods is considered a capital expenditure; any expenditure that will benefit only the current accounting period is referred to as a revenue expenditure.*

Careful distinction between capital and revenue expenditures is important in the determination of net income. If the cost of constructing a new building, for example, is recorded as *ordinary repairs expense* (a revenue expenditure), the net income of the current period will be understated. The net income of future periods will be overstated because of the absence of depreciation expense applicable to the unrecorded asset.

Examples We have already stressed the basic point that a careful distinction between capital expenditures and revenue expenditures is essential to a proper measurement of net income and to an accurate accounting for plant and equipment. Many companies develop formal policy statements defining capital and revenue expenditures as a guide toward consistent accounting practice in all branches and divisions and from year to year. These policy statements often set a minimum dollar limit for a capital expenditure (such as $50 or $100). Such limits are reasonable because a small expenditure will require much less time and paper work if charged to expense at the time of the transaction than if it were entered in an asset account and depreciated over a period of years. For example, the acquisition of a pencil sharpener at a cost of, say, $4 is reasonably charged to expense, despite the fact that it will probably have a useful life extending beyond the current accounting period.

Among the more common types of *capital expenditures* are:

1 Acquisition cost of plant and equipment, including freight, sales tax, and installation charges. When secondhand property is purchased, the cost of any repairs made to put the property in good operating condition *before* placing it in use is also considered as a capital expenditure and is charged to the asset account.

2 Additions. If a building is enlarged by adding a new wing or a mezzanine floor, the benefits from the expenditure will be received over a period of years, and the outlay should be debited to the asset account.

3 Betterments. The replacement of a stairway with an escalator is an example of an expenditure for a betterment or improvement which will yield benefits over a period of years and should therefore be charged to the asset account.

Among the more common types of *revenue expenditures* relating to plant and equipment are the repairs, maintenance, lubrication, cleaning, and inspection necessary to keep an asset in good working condition. The term *ordinary repairs* is often used to include all expenditures of this type. The cost of replacing small component parts of an asset (such as window panes in a building or tires and battery in an automobile) are also included in ordinary repairs.

Any expenditure made for the purpose of maintaining a plant asset in normally efficient working condition is an expense and will appear on the income statement as a deduction from the revenue of the current period. The treatment of an expenditure as a deduction from the revenue of the current period is the reason for the term revenue expenditure.

EFFECT OF ERRORS IN DISTINGUISHING BETWEEN CAPITAL AND REVENUE EXPENDITURES Because a capital expenditure is recorded by debiting an asset account, the transaction has no immediate effect upon net income. However, the depreciation of the amount entered in the asset account will be reflected as an expense in future periods. A revenue expenditure, on the other hand, is recorded by debiting an expense account and therefore represents an immediate deduction from earnings in the current period.

If a capital expenditure is erroneously recorded as a revenue expenditure, as, for example, the cost of a new typewriter charged to the Office Expense account, the result will be an understatement of the current year's net income. If the error is not corrected, the net income of subsequent years will be overstated because no depreciation expense will be recognized during the years in which the typewriter is used.

If a revenue expenditure is erroneously treated as a capital expenditure, as, for example, a payment for truck repairs charged to the asset account, Delivery Truck, the result will be an overstatement of the current year's net income. If the error is not corrected, the net income of future years will be understated because of excessive depreciation charges based on the inflated amount of the Delivery Truck account.

These examples indicate that a careful distinction between capital and revenue expenditures is essential to attainment of one of the most fundamental objectives of accounting—the determination of net income for each year of operation of a business.

Extraordinary repairs

The term *extraordinary repairs* has a specific meaning in accounting terminology; it means a reconditioning or major overhaul that will extend the useful life of a plant asset beyond the original estimate. For example, a new automobile may be depreciated on the basis of an estimated useful life of four years. Assume that after three years of use, a decision is made to install a new engine in the automobile and thereby to extend its overall useful life from the original estimate of four years to a total of six years.

An extraordinary repair of this type may be recorded by debiting the Accumulated Depreciation account. This entry is sometimes explained by the argument that the extraordinary repair cancels out some of the depreciation previously recorded. The effect of this reduction (debit entry) in the Accumulated Depreciation account is to *increase* the carrying value of the asset by the cost of the extraordinary repair. Since an extraordinary repair causes an increase in the carrying value of the asset and has no immediate direct effect upon net income, it may be regarded as a form of capital expenditure.

To expand the above example of an extraordinary repair to an automobile, assume the following data: on January 1, 1978, a new automobile was acquired at a cost of $8,000; estimated useful life, four years; salvage value, zero; annual depreciation expense, $2,000. Three years later on December 31, 1980, extraordinary repairs (a new engine) were made at a cost of $2,200. Estimated useful life of the automobile beyond this date was thereby increased from the original estimate of one year to a revised estimate of three more years. The ledger accounts will appear as follows after recording these events.

	Automobile		*Accumulated Depreciation*		

			Dec. 31, 1980 2,200	*Dec. 31, 1978* 2,000

Extraordi- | *Jan. 1, 1978* 8,000 | | *Dec. 31, 1980* 2,200 | *Dec. 31, 1978* 2,000
nary repair | | | | *Dec. 31, 1979* 2,000
charged to | | | | *Dec. 31, 1980* 2,000
Accumu-
lated De-
preciation

The carrying value of the automobile is now $4,200, and the balance sheet presentation will be as follows on Decmeber 31, 1980.

Increased **Plant and equipment:**
book value
for depre-   Automobile $8,000
ciable   Less: Accumulated depreciation 3,800 $4,200
asset

In the remaining three years of estimated life for the automobile, the annual depreciation expense will be $1,400 (carrying value $4,200 ÷ 3). Three years later at the end of 1983, the automobile will be fully depreciated, and the Accumulated Depreciation account (illustrated below) will show a credit balance of $8,000 (credits of $10,200 less debits of $2,200).

	Accumulated Depreciation		

Total de- | *Dec. 31, 1980* | 2,200 | *Dec. 31, 1978* | 2,000
preciation | | | *Dec. 31, 1979* | 2,000
equals | | | *Dec. 31, 1980* | 2,000
total cost | | | *Dec. 31, 1981* | 1,400
incurred | | | *Dec. 31, 1982* | 1,400
| | | *Dec. 31, 1983* | 1,400

The valuation account, Accumulated Depreciation, now exactly offsets the asset account and no more depreciation can be taken. Observe that the total depreciation recorded during the six years the automobile was in use amounts to $10,200; this agrees exactly with the total expended for the automobile and for the extraordinary repair. In other words, these two capital expenditures have been transformed into expense over a period of six years, during which the business was receiving the benefits from the expenditures.

Inflation and depreciation

The valuation of plant and equipment on a cost basis and the computation of depreciation in terms of cost work very well during periods of stable price levels. However, the substantial rise in the price level in recent years has led both government officials and business executives to suggest that a more realistic measurement of net income could be achieved by basing depreciation on the estimated replacement cost of plant assets rather than on the original cost of the assets presently in use.

As a specific illustration, assume that a manufacturing company purchased machinery in 1965 at a cost of $1,000,000. Estimated useful life was 15 years and straight-line depreciation was used. Throughout this 15-year period the price level rose sharply. By 1980 the machinery purchased in 1965 was fully depreciated; it was scrapped and replaced by new machinery in 1980. Although the new machines were not significantly different from the old, they cost $3,000,000, or three times as much as the old machinery. Many accountants would argue that the depreciation expense for the 15 years was in reality $3,000,000, because this was the outlay required for new machinery if the company was merely to "stay even" in its productive facilities. The recorded depreciation expense of $1,000,000 was therefore an understatement, and *an understatement of expenses causes an overstatement of net income.* In brief, reported profits will tend to be overstated during a period of rising prices if depreciation is based on the lower plant costs of some years ago. An overstatement of profit causes higher income taxes and perhaps larger demands for wage increases than are justified by the company's financial position and earnings. A more general criticism is that financial statements which show overstated earnings are misleading and do not serve as a useful basis for decisions by management, investors, or others.

Historical cost versus replacement cost

The above criticism of depreciation accounting based on the historical cost of assets is a convincing one. (*Historical cost* means the cost actually incurred by a company in acquiring an asset, as evidenced by paid checks and other documents.) However, this criticism does not mean that business enterprise in general is on the verge of abandoning the cost principle in accounting for assets and computing depreciation. To substitute estimated current replacement cost for the historical cost of plant and equipment would create many new difficulties and a great deal of confusion. Current replacement cost cannot be determined easily or with precision for many assets. For example, the cost of replacing a steel mill with its great variety of complex, made-to-order machinery would involve making many assumptions and unprovable estimates. Or, as another example, consider the difficulty of estimating the replacement cost of a large tract of timber or of a gold mine. The price level is constantly changing; consequently, estimates of replacement cost which took a long time to develop for certain complex plant assets might be out-of-date by the time they were completed.

Another difficulty in substituting replacement cost for historical cost of plant assets would be that the whole process of establishing estimated cost data would presumably need to be repeated each year. In contrast, historical cost (which we presently use as the basis of accounting for plant and equipment) is determined at the time of acquiring an asset and remains unchanged throughout the useful life of the asset.

Finally, another difficulty to be faced if we were to adopt a system of current replacement cost for plant and equipment is that financial statements could not be audited and approved by certified public accountants as readily as at present. Financial statements incapable of objective verification might be less dependable and more subject to manipulation. There is objective evidence available to support the historical cost of assets—evidence such as purchase orders, contracts, and paid checks. Certified public accountants can attest to the fairness of financial statements based on historical cost because objective evidence exists to show that the reported costs were actually incurred. On the other hand, CPA firms will face a new challenge if they are to prove with equal confidence that a company's estimate of the current replacement cost of plant and equipment is fair and reliable?

These difficulties connected with the possible adoption of replacement cost as a basis of accounting for assets do not mean that such a change cannot or should not be attempted. However, these difficulties do explain why American business has continued to use historical cost as a primary basis of accounting for assets even during continued inflation. The authors believe that accountants and business leaders should continue to search for means of making accounting data more *relevant* and should be willing to experiment with new methods. It appears probable that business organizations in the United States will increasingly make use of replacement cost in accounting for plant and equipment.

The SEC requirement for disclosure of replacement cost

The Securities and Exchange Commission in 1976 adopted a rule requiring large corporations to *disclose* the estimated current replacement cost of plant and equipment. Also required to be disclosed is depreciation expense based on the replacement cost of the assets. *This rule does not mean that replacement cost is to be used instead of historical cost, but rather that additional supplementary information is to be disclosed.* The disclosure can be made in a footnote to the financial statements or as a supplementary section accompanying the financial statements. The methods used in determining the estimated amounts must be explained. This information can be labeled as "Unaudited," since at present, methods have not been established by which a CPA firm could verify such estimates.

This action by the SEC (Accounting Series Release 190) requiring disclosure of replacement costs by large corporations is viewed by many accountants as an important first step which may eventually lead to current-value accounting on a widespread basis rather than the traditional reliance upon historical cost. The degree of inflation we experience in future years will be an important factor in determining whether such changes in accounting standards actually take place.

Price-level adjustments of accounting data

For more than 40 years, suggestions have been advanced that depreciation expense and most other accounting measurements based on cost should be adjusted each year by the change in a price index measuring general purchasing power. The purpose of these suggestions is to make year-to-year financial statements comparable.

The Financial Accounting Standards Board in 1974 circulated a proposal for a second supplementary set of historical cost financial statements expressed in units of general purchasing power rather than actual dollar costs. However, this proposal has not been adopted to date. In view of the action by the SEC to require disclosure of *current replacement cost,* it now appears probable that we shall try to cope with inflation by moving toward estimates of replacement cost rather than toward historical cost adjusted by a general price-level index.

KEY TERMS INTRODUCED OR EMPHASIZED IN CHAPTER 11

Accelerated depreciation   Methods of depreciation that call for recognition of relatively large amounts of depreciation in the early years of an asset's useful life and relatively small amounts in the later years.

Capital expenditures   A cost incurred to acquire a long-lived asset. An expenditure that will benefit several accounting periods.

Declining-balance depreciation   An accelerated method of depreciation in which the rate is a multiple of the straight-line rate, which is applied each year to the *undepreciated cost* of the asset. Most commonly used is double the straight-line rate.

Depletion   Allocating the cost of a natural resource to the units removed as the resource is mined, pumped, cut, or otherwise consumed.

Depreciable cost   The cost of an asset minus the estimated residual or salvage value.

Depreciation   The systematic allocation of the cost of an asset to expense over the years of its estimated useful life.

Double-declining-balance depreciation   The most widely used version of declining-balance depreciation. The rate is double the straight-line rate. Approved for most new assets for income tax purposes.

Extraordinary repairs   A reconditioning or major overhaul that will extend the useful life of a plant asset beyond the original estimate. Recorded by debiting the Accumulated Depreciation account.

Intangible assets   Those assets which are used in operation of the business but which have no physical substance and are noncurrent.

Obsolescence   The process of becoming out-of-date or obsolete and less efficient than newer types of equipment. A major factor limiting the useful life of most depreciable assets.

Plant and equipment (*fixed assets*) Long-lived assets used in the operation of a business.

Replacement cost The estimated cost of replacing an asset at the current balance sheet date. Disclosure of such data is required of large companies.

Residual (*salvage*) value The portion of an asset's cost expected to be recovered through sale or trade-in of the asset at the end of its useful life.

Revenue expenditures Any expenditure that will benefit only the current accounting period.

Straight-line depreciation A method of depreciation which allocates the cost of an asset (minus any residual value) equally to each year of its useful life.

Sum-of-the-years'-digits depreciation An accelerated method of depreciation. The depreciable cost is multiplied each year by a fraction of which the numerator is the remaining years of useful life (as of the beginning of the current year) and the denominator is the sum of the years of useful life.

Tangible plant assets Long-lived assets used in the operation of the business and possessing physical substance, such as land and buildings.

Units-of-output depreciation A depreciation method in which cost (minus residual value) is divided by the estimated units of lifetime output. The unit depreciation cost is multiplied by the actual units of output each year to compute the annual depreciation expense.

REVIEW QUESTIONS

1 Which of the following items should be included in the balance sheet category of "plant and equipment"?

   a A machine in good physical condition which has been used in operations in the past, but is now idle and awaiting disposal by sale or scrapping. No future use of the machine is contemplated by the company.

   b A typewriter acquired by an office supply firm for the purpose of resale to customers.

   c An item capable of use in operations of the business over several years which has recently been acquired and placed in use but has not yet been paid for. Cost is substantial and payment will probably be made in installments.

   d Cost of paving a parking lot, $10,000. Expected life of the paving five years.

   e Advertising designed to make the public aware of the air pollution control features of a new steel mill.

   f Installation of waste disposal equipment which will avoid the dumping of waste products in a river, but which will not reduce the cost of production or increase the efficiency of the manufacturing process.

2 The following expenditures were incurred in connection with a large new machine acquired by a metals manufacturing company. Identify those which should be included in the cost of the asset. (*a*) Freight charges, (*b*) sales tax on the machine, (*c*) payment to a passing motorist whose car was damaged by the equipment used in unloading the machine, (*d*) wages of employees for time spent in installing and testing the machine before it was placed in service, (*e*) wages of employees assigned to lubrication and minor adjustments of machine one year after it was placed in service.

3 Which of the following statements best describes the nature of depreciation?

   a Regular reduction of asset value to correspond to changes in market value as the asset ages.

   b A process of correlating the carrying value of an asset with its gradual decline in physical efficiency.

c Allocation of cost in a manner that will ensure that plant and equipment items are not carried on the balance sheet at amounts in excess of net realizable value.

d Allocation of the cost of a plant asset to the periods in which services are received from the asset.

4 Should depreciation continue to be recorded on a building when ample evidence exists that the current market value is greater than original cost and that the rising trend of market values is continuing? Explain.

5 Which of the following characteristics would prevent an item from being included in the classification of plant and equipment? *(a)* Intangible, *(b)* limited life, *(c)* unlimited life, *(d)* held for sale in the regular course of business, *(e)* not capable of rendering benefits to the business in the future.

6 What is the distinction between *capital expenditures* and *revenue expenditures?*

7 What connection exists between the choice of a depreciation method for expensive new machinery and the amount of income taxes payable in the near future?

8 What is an *extraordinary repair* and how is it recorded in the accounts?

9 Company A's balance sheet shows accumulated depreciation on machinery and equipment of $100,000 and Company B shows accumulated depreciation of $50,000. Both companies are considering the acquisition of new equipment costing $60,000. From the information given, can you determine which company is in a better position to purchase the new equipment for cash? Explain.

10 Criticize the following quotation:

"We shall have no difficulty in paying for new plant assets needed during the coming year because our estimated outlays for new equipment amount to only $20,000, and we have more than twice that amount in our depreciation reserves at present."

11 A factory machine acquired at a cost of $93,600 was to be depreciated by the sum-of-the-years'-digits method over an estimated life of eight years. Residual salvage value was estimated to be $1,600. State the amount of depreciation during the first year and during the eighth year.

12 After four years of using a machine acquired at a cost of $15,000, Kral Construction Company determined that the original estimated life of 10 years had been too short and that a total useful life of 12 years was a more reasonable estimate. Explain briefly the method that should be used to revise the depreciation program, assuming that straight-line depreciation has been used.

13 *a* Give some reasons why a company may change its depreciation policy for financial reporting purposes from an accelerated-depreciation method to the straight-line method.

b Is it possible for a corporation to use accelerated depreciation for income tax purposes and a straight-line depreciation for financial reporting purposes?

14 An asset costing $10,000 with an estimated useful life of four years and residual value of $1,000 is depreciated by the double-declining-balance method. What will be the amount of depreciation expense for the fourth year and the carrying value of the asset at the end of the fourth year, assuming it is still in use? Explain your answer.

15 During a period of continued severe inflation, does the computation of depreciation on the basis of the historical cost of plant and equipment lead to an *overstatement* or *understatement* of annual net income in terms of economic reality? Explain.

EXERCISES

Ex. 11-1 Identify the following expenditures as capital expenditures or revenue expenditures:
  a Purchased new battery at a cost of $40 for two-year-old delivery truck.
  b Installed an escalator at a cost of $12,500 in a three-story building which had previously been used for some years without elevators or escalators.
  c Purchased a pencil sharpener at a cost of $3.50.
  d Immediately after acquiring a new delivery truck at a cost of $5,500, paid $125 to have the name of the store and other advertising material painted on the truck.
  e Painted delivery truck at a cost of $175 after two years of use.
  f Original life of the delivery truck had been estimated as four years and straight-line depreciation of 25% yearly had been recognized. After three years' use, however, it was decided to recondition the truck thoroughly, including a new engine and transmission, at a cost of $2,000. By making this expenditure it was believed that the useful life of the truck would be extended from the original estimate of four years to a total of six years.

Ex. 11-2 New office equipment was purchased by the Barker Company at a list price of $86,400 with credit terms of 2/10, n/30. Payment of the invoice was made within the discount period; it included 5% sales tax on the net price. Transportation charges of $2,880 on the new equipment were paid by Barker Company as well as labor cost of $5,760 for installing the equipment in the appropriate locations. During the unloading and installation work, some of the equipment fell from a loading platform and was damaged. Repair of the damaged parts cost $4,320. After the equipment had been in use for three months, it was thoroughly cleaned and lubricated at a cost of $960. Prepare a list of the items which should be capitalized by debit to the Office Equipment account and state the total cost of the new equipment. (Round off figures to the nearest dollar.)

Ex. 11-3 Franklin Corporation acquired machinery with a useful life of five years at a cost of $183,900. The estimated residual salvage value was $3,900. You are to compute the annual depreciation on the machinery in each of the five years of useful life using the double-declining-balance method. (Round all computations to the nearest dollar.)

Ex. 11-4 Valley Farms paid $100,000 to acquire a herd of 100 dairy cattle with an estimated useful life of six years. At the end of six years, it is expected that the cattle can be sold for a residual or salvage value of $10,000. Compute the amount of depreciation to be recorded on the cattle in each of the six years under each of the following methods of depreciation:
  a Straight-line
  b Sum-of-the-years'-digits (Round all computations to the nearest dollar.)

Ex. 11-5 Two business executives were discussing the accounting issues involved in distinguishing between capital expenditures and revenue expenditures. A made the following statement: "A good example of a revenue expenditure is the cost of painting our factory building and of replacing broken window glass all the time. Certainly all costs of this nature should always be charged to expense."
  B replied as follows: "Your examples are good but on the other hand we recently had a rather special situation in which we capitalized the cost of repainting a building and of replacing a large number of window panes."
  "You were way off base," said A. "The Internal Revenue Service won't allow it and your CPA won't approve your financial statements."
  Evaluate these statements. What kind of special situation might B be referring to?

Ex. 11-6 David Jay, general manager of Block Company, attended an auction of used machinery. He was the successful bidder on a lot consisting of three machines for which he paid $70,500. Freight charges of $4,500 were incurred to have the three machines delivered to Block Company's plant. In anticipation of this auction the company had borrowed $75,000 in order to be able to make cash bids for the equipment being auctioned. The interest charge on the borrowing amounted to $2,500.

The estimated fair market value of the machines and the costs of installations and trial runs necessary to prepare them for regular operations were as follows:

	Machine No. 1	Machine No. 2	Machine No. 3
Fair market value	$35,000	$45,000	$20,000
Installation costs	2,000	4,000	1,500
Costs of trial runs	500	750	None

Determine the cost of each machine for accounting purposes, assuming that the auction and delivery cost is apportioned to the three machines on the basis of relative market value.

Ex. 11-7 Jewel Company acquired its plant and equipment 20 years ago at a cost of $200,000 paid in cash. After paying for the plant and equipment, the company had about $15,000 cash for use in operations. The company has consistently used straight-line depreciation based on historical cost and an estimated useful life of 20 years. Residual or salvage value was estimated to be virtually zero. The company has reported a net income each year. However, each year the owner has withdrawn an amount of cash equal to the reported net income.

The plant and equipment are now worn out and must be replaced. Replacement cost is approximately four times the cost of the original plant and equipment.

a Based solely on the above information, about how much cash would you expect Jewel Company to have today? Explain the basis for your answer. (Bear in mind that the company had $15,000 cash after paying for the plant and equipment 20 years ago and that depreciation is a noncash expense.)

b What is the prospect for Jewel Company being able to pay for the new plant and equipment it needs?

c On what grounds might the accounting measurement of net income by Jewel Company be criticized in the light of 20 years of operation in an inflationary environment?

PROBLEMS

Group A

11A-1 Hailey Corporation, a newly organized business, purchased equipment at a cost of $146,560. The estimated life of these assets is five years and the residual value $2,560. The company is considering whether to use straight-line depreciation, the sum-of-the-years'-digits method, or the double-declining-balance method. Consideration is also being given to the possibility of using one method for the preparation of income tax returns and another method for financial reporting to stockholders.

The president of Hailey Corporation informs you that the company wants to keep income taxes at a minimum during the coming year (Year 1), but to report the largest possible earnings per share in the company's first annual report to its stockholders. (Earnings per share is computed by dividing net income by the number of shares of stock outstanding; therefore, the higher the net income, the higher the earnings per share.)

Instructions

a Compute the annual depreciation expense throughout the five-year life of the equipment under each of the three methods under consideration. (Use a work sheet with three money columns headed, respectively, Straight-line, Sum-of-the-years'-digits, and Double-declining-balance. Also show the total depreciation under each method and show in footnotes how the calculations were made.) Round off depreciation calculations to the nearest dollar.

b Advise the president of Hailey Corporation which method of depreciation should be used for income tax purposes and which method for the company's financial statements in order to achieve the stated objectives of holding income taxes to a minimum in Year 1 while showing the maximum earnings per share in the company's financial statements.

11A-2 Cypress Company early in the current year purchased some hilly land with old abandoned buildings. The old buildings were removed, the land was leveled, and a new building was constructed. The company moved from its former rented quarters into the new building on October 1. Transactions relating to these events were recorded in an account entitled Property, which contained the following entries at the end of the current year.

Debit entries:

3/9	Purchase for cash of building site	$ 68,750
4/28	Payment for demolition of old building	7,500
5/15	Payment for leveling of land	25,000
9/28	Payment for insurance of building during construction	15,000
9/28	Payment for new building completed today	300,000
10/7	Payment to caterer for office party for employees, customers, and friends to celebrate the move to new building	3,750
	Total debits	$420,000

Credit entries:

4/28	Cash received from sale of materials from demolished building	$11,250	
12/31	Depreciation for the current year, computed at 4% of balance in Property account ($408,750). Debit was to Depreciation Expense	16,350	
	Total credits		27,600
12/31	Balance in Property account at year-end		$392,400

Instructions

a List the errors made in the application of accounting principles or practices by Cypress Company.

b Prepare a compound correcting journal entry at December 31 of the current year, assuming that the estimated life of the new building is 25 years and that depreciation is to be recognized for the three months the building was in use during the current year, using the straight-line method. The accounts have not been closed for the current year.

11A-3 Woods Laboratories acquired new equipment with an estimated useful life of five years. Cost of the equipment was $128,240 and the residual salvage value was estimated to be $2,240.

Instructions Compute the annual depreciation expense throughout the five-year life of the equipment under each of the following methods of depreciation:

    a Straight-line
    b Sum-of-the-years'-digits
    c Double-declining-balance (Round computations to the nearest dollar.)

11A-4 Solar Power acquired a new machine on April 1, 1977, at a cost of $528,000. The company has used the straight-line method of depreciation based on an estimated life of five years and a residual salvage value of $48,000.

    On January 2, 1980, after almost three years of use, extraordinary repairs were made on the machine at a cost of $114,000. The repairs were virtually the equivalent of rebuilding the machine, and management believed that this thorough reconditioning would extend the normal life of the machine substantially. The revised estimate of useful life was four years from January 1, 1980.

Instructions Prepare general journal entries to record the original purchase of the machine; the provision for depreciation on December 31, 1977, 1978, and 1979; the expenditure for the extraordinary repairs in 1980; and the provision for depreciation on December 31, 1980. Assume payment in cash for the machine and for the extraordinary repairs.

11A-5 In the last few years Winchester Company has acquired four machines. At the time of acquiring each machine, different personnel were employed in the accounting department; consequently, various methods of depreciation have been adopted for the several machines. Information concerning the four machines may be summarized as follows:

Machine	Date Acquired	Cost	Estimated Useful Life, Years	Estimated Residual Value	Method of Depreciation
A	Jan. 1, 1978	$ 97,200	6	None	Declining-balance
B	June 30, 1978	151,200	8	10%	Straight-line
C	Jan. 1, 1979	100,800	10	$1,800	Sum-of-the-years'-digits
D	Jan. 1, 1980	118,800	12	None	Declining-balance

Instructions
a Compute the amount of accumulated depreciation, if any, on each machine owned at December 31, 1979. For machines A and D, assume that the depreciation rate was double the rate which would be applicable under the straight-line method.
b Prepare a depreciation schedule for use in the computation of the 1980 depreciation expense. Use the following column headings:

Machine	Method of Depreciation	Date of Acquisition	Cost	Estimated Residual Value	Amount to Be Depreciated	Useful Life, Years	Accumulated Depreciation, Dec. 31, 1979	Depreciation Expense, 1980

c Prepare a journal entry to record the 1980 depreciation expense.

11A-6 Remington Company purchased new machinery on July 1, Year 7, at the advertised price of $32,400. The terms of payment were 2/10, n/30 and payment was made immediately, including a 4% state sales tax on $31,752. On July 3, the machinery was delivered; Remington Company paid freight charges of $709.92 and assigned its own employees to the task of installation. The labor costs for installing the machinery amounted to $2,268. During the process of installation, carelessness by a workman caused damage to an adjacent machine, with resulting repairs of $288.

On October 15, after more than three months of satisfactory operation, the machinery was thoroughly inspected, cleaned, and oiled at a cost of $378.

The useful life of the machinery was estimated to be 10 years and the residual scrap value to be zero. The policy of the Remington Company is to use straight-line depreciation and to begin depreciation as of the first of the month in which a plant asset is acquired. During Year 7 and Year 8, however, numerous changes in the company's accounting personnel were responsible for a number of errors and deviations from policy.

At December 31, Year 8, the unaudited financial statements of the Remington Company showed the machinery to be carried at a cost of $31,752 and the accumulated depreciation as $4,763. Net income reported for Year 7 was $89,280 and for Year 8 $99,540.

Instructions

a Prepare entries in general journal form for all the above transactions from July 1 to December 31, Year 7. Include the year-end entry for depreciation and the related closing entry.

b Compute the correct balances for the Machinery account and for accumulated depreciation at December 31, Year 8.

c Compute revised figures for net income for Year 7 and Year 8. (The only errors in the reported net income figures are those indicated by information given in the problem.) Use a separate column for each year and begin with the reported net income for each year, followed by the necessary additions and deductions to arrive at corrected net income for each year.

Group B

11B-1 Marine Gears, Inc., uses straight-line depreciation on all its depreciable assets. The accounts are adjusted and closed at the end of each calendar year. On January 2, 1977, the corporation purchased machinery for cash at a cost of $143,280. Useful life was estimated to be 10 years and residual value $6,480.

After almost three years of using the machinery, the company decided in December 1979, that, in view of technological changes in the industry, the total estimated useful life of the machinery should be revised from 10 years to six years and that the residual scrap value estimate should be lowered from $6,480 to $4,320. The revised estimate of useful life was made prior to recording depreciation for the year ended December 31, 1979.

Instructions Prepare general journal entries in chronological order for the above events, beginning with the purchase of the machinery on January 2, 1977. Show separately the depreciation for each year from 1977 to 1979, inclusive.

11B-2 The ledger of Rainbow Company contained an account entitled Property, which had been used to record a variety of expenditures. At the end of Year 5, the Property account contained the following entries:

Debit entries:

4/3	Amount paid to acquire building site	$ 62,500
4/15	Cost of removing old unusable building from site	5,000
9/30	Contract price for new building completed Sept. 30	200,000
9/30	Insurance, inspection fees, and other costs directly related to construction of new building	10,000
	Total debits	$277,500

Credit entries:

4/15 Proceeds from sale of old lumber and other material from
  demolition of old building . . . . $ 7,500

12/31 Depreciation for Year 5, computed at 5% of balance in
  Property account ($270,000). Debit was to Deprecia-
  tion Expense 13,500

  Total credits 21,000

12/31 Balance in Property account at year-end $256,500

Instructions
a List the errors made in the application of accounting principles or practices by Rainbow Company.
b Prepare a compound correcting journal entry at December 31, Year 5, assuming that the estimated life of the new building is 20 years and that depreciation is to be recognized for three months of Year 5 using the straight-line method. The accounts have not been closed for Year 5.

11B-3 New machinery was acquired by Ozark Company at a cost of $293,120. Useful life of the machinery was estimated to be five years, with residual salvage value of $5,120.

Instructions Compute the annual depreciation expense throughout the five-year life of the machinery under each of the following methods of depreciation:
a Straight-line
b Sum-of-the-years'-digits
c Double-declining-balance (Round calculations to nearest dollar.)

11B-4 During the last few years, Santa Maria Corporation has acquired four costly machines but has given little consideration to depreciation policies. At the time of acquisition of each machine, a different accountant was employed; consequently, various methods of depreciation have been adopted for the several machines. Information concerning the four machines appears below:

Machine	Date Acquired	Cost	Estimated Useful Life, Years	Estimated Residual Value	Method of Depreciation
A	Jan. 1, 1978	$145,800	6	None	Declining-balance
B	June 30, 1978	302,400	8	10%	Straight-line
C	Jan. 1, 1979	201,600	10	$3,600	Sum-of-the-years'-digits
D	Jan. 1, 1980	237,600	12	None	Declining-balance

Instructions
a Compute the amount of accumulated depreciation, if any, on each machine at December 31, 1979. For machines A and D, assume that the depreciation rate was double the rate which would be applicable under the straight-line method.
b Prepare a depreciation schedule for use in the computation of the 1980 depreciation expense. Use the following column headings:

Machine	Method of Depreciation	Date of Acquisition	Cost	Estimated Residual Value	Amount to Be Depreciated	Useful Life, Years	Accumulated Depreciation, Dec. 31, 1979	Depreciation Expense, 1980

c Prepare a journal entry to record the depreciation expense for 1980.

11B-5 On March 31, Year 1, Dawson Corporation purchased new machinery at a cost of $140,800. Depreciation has been computed by the straight-line method based on an estimated useful life of five years and residual scrap value of $12,800.

On January 2, Year 4, extraordinary repairs (which were almost equivalent to a rebuilding of the machinery) were performed at a cost of $30,400. Because of the thoroughgoing nature of these repairs, the normal life of the machinery was extended materially. The revised estimate of useful life was four years from January 1, Year 4.

Instructions Prepare journal entries to record the original purchase of the machinery; the provision for depreciation on December 31, Year 1, Year 2, and Year 3; the expenditure for the extraordinary repairs in January, Year 4; and the provision for depreciation on December 31, Year 4. Assume payment in cash for the machine and for the extraordinary repairs.

11B-6 On July 1, 1978, Electronic Gear purchased a new machine at the advertised price of $144,000. The terms of payment were 2/10, n/30 and payment was made immediately, including a 4% state sales tax. On July 3, the machine was delivered; Electronic Gear paid freight charges of $3,155.20 and assigned its own employees to the task of installation. The labor costs for installing the machine amounted to $10,080. During the process of installation, carelessness by a workman caused damage to an adjacent machine, with resulting repairs of $1,280.

On November 10, 1978, after more than four months of satisfactory operations, the machine was thoroughly inspected, cleaned, and oiled at a cost of $1,680.

The useful life of the machine was estimated to be 10 years and the residual scrap value zero. The policy of Electronic Gear is to use straight-line depreciation and to begin depreciation as of the first of the month in which a plant asset is acquired. During 1978 and 1979, however, numerous changes in the company's accounting personnel were responsible for a number of errors and deviations from policy.

At December 31, 1979, the unaudited financial statements of Electronic Gear showed the machine to be carried at a cost of $141,120 and the accumulated depreciation as $21,168. Net income reported for 1978 was $396,800 and for 1979 it was $442,400.

Instructions
a Prepare correct journal entries for all the above transactions from July 1 to December 31, 1978. Include the year-end entry for depreciation and the related closing entry. The sales tax was $5,644.80.
b Compute the correct balances for the Machinery account and for the Accumulated Depreciation: Machinery account at December 31, 1979.
c Compute revised figures for net income for 1978 and 1979. Disregard income taxes.

BUSINESS DECISION PROBLEM 11

Howard Meyers is interested in buying a manufacturing business and has located two similar companies being offered for sale. Both companies began operations three years ago, each with invested capital of $900,000. A considerable part of the assets in each company is represented by a building with an original cost of $300,000 and an estimated life of 40 years, and by machinery with an original cost of $300,000 and an estimated life of 20 years. Residual scrap value is negligible.

Company A uses straight-line depreciation and Company B uses double-declining-balance depreciation. In all other respects the accounting policies of the two companies are quite similar. Neither company has borrowed from banks or incurred any indebtedness other than normal trade payables. The nature of products and other characteristics of operations are much the same for the two companies.

Audited financial statements for the three years show net income as follows:

Year	Company A	Company B
1	$63,000	$60,000
2	69,300	66,300
3	76,200	72,900

Meyers asks your advice as to which company he should buy. They are offered for sale at approximately the same price, and he is inclined to choose Company A because of its consistently higher earnings. On the other hand, he is impressed with the fact that Company B has more cash and a stronger working capital position. The audited financial statements show that withdrawals by the two owners have been approximately equal during the three-year life of the two companies.

Instructions

a Compute the depreciation recorded by each company in the first three years. Round off depreciation expense for each year to the nearest dollar.

b Write a memorandum to Meyers advising him as to which company in your judgment represents the more promising purchase. Give specific reasons to support your recommendation.

12

Plant and Equipment, Natural Resources, and Intangibles

Disposal of plant and equipment

When depreciable assets are disposed of at any date other than the end of the year, an entry should be made to record depreciation for the fraction of the year ending with the date of disposal. In the following illustrations of the disposal of items of plant and equipment, it is assumed that any necessary entries for fractional-period depreciation have been recorded.

As units of plant and equipment wear out or become obsolete, they must be scrapped, sold, or traded in on new equipment. Upon the disposal or retirement of a depreciable asset, the cost of the property is removed from the asset account, and the accumulated depreciation is removed from the related valuation account. Assume, for example, that office equipment purchased 10 years ago at a cost of $5,000 has been fully depreciated and is no longer useful. The entry to record the scrapping of the worthless equipment is as follows:

Scrapping fully depreciated asset *Accumulated Depreciation: Office Equipment* *5,000*
  Office Equipment *5,000*
To remove from the accounts the cost and the accumulated depreciation on fully depreciated office equipment now being scrapped. No salvage value.

Once an asset has been fully depreciated, no more depreciation should be recorded on it, even though the property is in good condition and is continued in use. The objective of depreciation is to spread the *cost* of an asset over the periods of its usefulness; in no case can depreciation expense be greater than the amount paid for the asset. When a fully depreciated asset is continued in use beyond the original estimate of useful life, the asset account and the Accumulated Depreciation account should remain in the accounting records without further entries until the asset is retired.

GAINS AND LOSSES ON DISPOSAL OF PLANT AND EQUIPMENT The *book value* (or *carrying value*) of a plant asset is its cost minus the total recorded depreciation, as shown by the Accumulated Depreciation account. For a fully depreciated asset with no salvage value, the book value is zero, since the credit balance in the Accumulated Depreciation account exactly offsets the debit balance in the asset account. If a depreciable asset is discarded before it is fully depreciated and there is no salvage value, a loss results in an amount equal to the book value of the asset. Since the residual value and useful life of plant assets are only estimates, it is not uncommon for plant assets to be sold at a price which differs from their book value at the date of disposal. When plant assets are sold, any gain or loss on the disposal is computed by comparing the book value with the amount received from the sale. A sales price in excess of the book value produces a gain; a sales price below the book value produces a loss. These gains or losses, if material in amount, should be shown as a separate item in the income statement in computing the income from operations.

Disposal at a price above book value Assume that a machine originally cost $10,000 and that, after several years of use, depreciation has been recorded in the total amount of $8,000. The machine therefore has a book value (or undepreciated cost) of $2,000. Next, let us assume that this machine with a book value of $2,000 is sold for $3,000 cash. Since we are receiving $3,000 in cash, or $1,000 more than the book value of the machine, a gain of $1,000 is realized on the disposal of this asset. The entry to record this disposal of a plant asset is as follows:

Gain on disposal of plant asset	*Cash*	*3,000*	
	Accumulated Depreciation: Machinery	*8,000*	
	Machinery		*10,000*
	Gain on Disposal of Plant Assets		*1,000*
	To record sale of machinery at a price above book value.		

Disposal at a price below book value Now assume that the same machine is sold for $500. The journal entry in this case would be as follows:

Loss on disposal of plant asset	*Cash*	*500*	
	Accumulated Depreciation: Machinery	*8,000*	
	Loss on Disposal of Plant Assets	*1,500*	
	Machinery		*10,000*
	To record sale of machinery at a price below book value.		

Disposal at a price equal to book value   As a third example, assume that this same machine is sold for $2,000, the exact amount of its book value. The disposal of a depreciable asset at a price equal to book value would result in neither a gain nor a loss. The entry would be as follows:

No gain or loss when disposal price equals book value

Cash	*2,000*	
Accumulated Depreciation: Machinery	*8,000*	
Machinery		*10,000*

To record sale of machinery at a price equal to book value.

DEPRECIATION FOR FRACTIONAL PERIOD BEFORE DISPOSAL   Most disposals of plant and equipment occur at dates other than the year-end. In such cases it is necessary to record depreciation for the fraction of the year ending with the date of disposal. Assume that straight-line depreciation is being used and that the accounts showed the following balances at December 31.

Office equipment	$20,000
Accumulated depreciation: office equipment	16,000

The balance of $16,000 in the Accumulated Depreciation account was the result of eight annual credits of $2,000 each. On the following March 31, the office equipment was sold for $1,000. No depreciation had been recorded since the accounts were adjusted and closed on December 31. Two entries are necessary at the time of disposing of the office equipment: one to record depreciation for the three months ending with the date of disposal, and a second to record the sale of the equipment.

Record depreciation to date of disposal

Depreciation Expense: Office Equipment	500	
Accumulated Depreciation: Office Equipment		500

To record depreciation for the three months prior to disposal of office equipment ($2,000 × $\frac{1}{4}$).

. . . then record sale of the equipment

Cash	1,000	
Accumulated Depreciation: Office Equipment	16,500	
Loss on Disposal of Plant Assets	2,500	
Office Equipment		20,000

To record sale of office equipment at less than book value.

Trading in used assets on new

Certain types of depreciable assets, such as automobiles and office equipment, are customarily traded in on new assets of the same kind. The trade-in allowance granted by the dealer may differ materially from the book value of the old asset. If the dealer grants a trade-in allowance in excess of the book value of the asset being traded in, there is the suggestion of a gain being realized on the exchange. The evidence of a gain is not conclusive, however, because the list price of the new asset may purposely have been set higher than a realistic cash price to permit the offering of inflated trade-in allowances.

For the purpose of determining taxable income, no gain or loss is recognized when a depreciable asset is traded in on another similar asset. The tax regulations provide that *the cost of the new asset shall be the sum of the book value of the old asset traded in plus the additional amount paid or to be paid in acquiring the new asset.*

To illustrate the handling of an exchange transaction in this manner, assume that a delivery truck is acquired at a cost of $8,000. The truck is depreciated on the straight-line basis with the assumption of a five-year life and no salvage value. Annual depreciation expense is ($8,000 ÷ 5), or $1,600. After four years of use, the truck is traded in on a new model having a list price of $10,000. The truck dealer grants a trade-in allowance of $2,400 for the old truck; the additional amount to be paid to acquire the new truck is, therefore, $7,600 ($10,000 list price minus $2,400 trade-in allowance). The *cost basis* of the new truck is computed as follows:

Trade-in: cost of new equipment

Cost of old truck	$8,000
Less: Accumulated depreciation ($1,600 × 4)	6,400
Book value of old truck	$1,600
Add: Cash payment for new truck (list price, $10,000 – $2,400 trade-in allowance)	7,600
Cost basis of new truck	$9,200

The trade-in allowance and the list price of the new truck are not recorded in the accounts; their only function lies in determining the amount which the purchaser must pay in addition to turning in the old truck. The journal entry for this exchange transaction is as follows:

Entry for trade-in

Delivery Truck (new)	9,200	
Accumulated Depreciation: Delivery Truck (old)	6,400	
Delivery Truck (old)		8,000
Cash		7,600

To remove from the accounts the cost of old truck and accumulated depreciation thereon, and to record new truck at cost equal to book value of old truck traded in plus cash paid.

Note that the method used above to record the trade-in of an old productive asset for a new one is different from the usual assumption that the cost of a newly acquired asset is equal to its implied cash price. The reason (as approved by the Financial Accounting Standards Board) for not recognizing a gain on a trade-in is that revenue is not realized merely by the act of substituting a new productive asset for an old one. Revenue flows from the production and sale of the goods or services which the productive asset makes possible.[1] The nonrecognition of a suggested

---

[1] *Opinions of the Accounting Principles Board, No. 29,* "Accounting for Nonmonetary Transactions," AICPA (New York: 1973).

gain on a trade-in causes the recorded cost of the new asset to be less than if the gain were recognized. Consequently, depreciation expense will be less because of the reduced amount recorded as cost of the new asset, and the net income in future years will be correspondingly greater.

Although income tax regulations and financial accounting rules are alike in not recognizing a *gain* on a trade-in, they differ in the case of a trade-in which involves a material loss. Tax regulations do not permit recognition of the loss, but for financial statements the loss should be recognized. For example, assume that a company receives a trade-in allowance of only $10,000 for old machinery which has a book value of $100,000. A journal entry illustrating this situation follows:

Machinery (new)	*600,000*	
Accumulated Depreciation: Machinery (old)	*300,000*	
Loss on Trade-in of Plant Assets	*90,000*	
Machinery (old)		*400,000*
Cash		*590,000*

To recognize for financial reporting purposes a material loss on trade-in of machinery. Loss not recognized in determining taxable income.

If a trade-in transaction involved only a very small loss, most companies would probably follow the income tax rules and not recognize the loss. This treatment would avoid the need for a double record of depreciable assets and depreciation expense, and the departure from financial accounting rules would be permissible if the amount of the loss was not material.

Maintaining control over plant and equipment: subsidiary ledgers

Unless internal controls over plant and equipment are carefully designed, many units of equipment are likely to be broken, discarded, or stolen without any entry being made in the accounting records for their disposal. The asset accounts will then be overstated, and depreciation programs for such missing units of equipment will presumably continue. Consequently, net income will be misstated because of the omission of losses on retirement of plant assets and because of erroneous depreciation charges.

One important control device which guards against failure to record the retirement of assets is the use of control accounts and subsidiary ledgers for plant and equipment. The general ledger ordinarily contains a separate asset account and related depreciation accounts for each major classification of plant assets, such as land, buildings, office equipment, and delivery equipment. For example, the general ledger will contain the account Office Equipment, and also, the related accounts Depreciation Expense: Office Equipment, and Accumulated Depreciation: Office Equipment. The general ledger account, Office Equipment, contains entries for a variety of items: typewriters, filing cabinets, dictaphones, desks, etc. It is not possible in this one general ledger account to maintain adequate information concerning the cost of each item, its estimated useful life, book value, insured value, and other data which may be needed by management as a basis for decisions on such issues as replacement, insurance, and taxation.

A *subsidiary ledger* should therefore be established for office equipment, and for each of the other general ledger accounts which represents many separate units of plant property. The subsidiary ledger in a manual accounting system may consist of a card file, with a separate card for each unit of property, such as a typewriter or desk. Each card shows the name of the asset, identification number, and such details as date of acquisition, cost, useful life, depreciation, accumulated depreciation, insurance coverage, repairs, and gain or loss on disposal. The general ledger account, Office Equipment, serves as a control; the balance of this control account is equal to the total cost of the items in the subsidiary ledger for office equipment. The general ledger account, Accumulated Depreciation: Office Equipment, is also a control account; its balance is equal to the total of the accumulated depreciation shown on all the cards in the office equipment ledger. Every acquisition of office equipment is entered in the control account and also on a card in the subsidiary ledger. Similarly, every disposal of an item of office equipment is entered in both the control account and the subsidiary ledger.

Each card in a subsidiary ledger for plant and equipment shows an identification number which should also appear in the form of a metal tag attached to the asset itself. Consequently, a physical inventory of plant and equipment can be taken and will prove whether all units of equipment shown by the records are actually on hand and being used in operations.

Other advantages afforded by a plant and equipment ledger are the ready availability of information for the periodic computation of depreciation, and for entries to record the disposal of individual items of property. A better basis is also available for supporting the data in tax returns, for obtaining proper insurance coverage, and for supporting claims for losses sustained on insured property. In well-managed companies, it is standard practice to control expenditures for plant and equipment by preparing a budget of all planned acquisitions for at least a year in advance. A first essential to the preparation of such a budget is a detailed record showing the assets presently owned, their cost, age, and remaining useful life.

NATURAL RESOURCES

Accounting for natural resources

Mining properties, oil and gas wells, and tracts of standing timber are leading examples of natural resources or "wasting assets." The distinguishing characteristics of these assets are that they are physically consumed and converted into inventory. In a theoretical sense, a coal mine might even be regarded as an "underground inventory of coal"; however, such an inventory is certainly not a current asset. In the balance sheet, mining property and other natural resources are usually listed as a separate group of tangible assets.

Natural resources should be recorded in the accounts at cost. As the resource is removed through the process of mining, cutting, or drilling, the asset account must be proportionately reduced. The carrying value (book value) of a coal mine, for example, is reduced by a small amount for each ton of coal mined. The original cost of the mine is thus gradually transferred out of the asset account and becomes part of the cost of the coal mined and sold.

The cost of a mine or other natural resource may include not only the purchase price but also payments for surveying and various exploratory and developmental activities. Many companies in such industries as oil, gas, and mining carry on a continuous program of exploration and development as, for example, the much-discussed development of offshore oil fields. Since expenditures for exploration and development thus become normal and continuous, these payments are generally charged to expense in the year in which the exploration or development is performed. If the payments for exploration and development were reasonably certain to produce future revenue, the theoretically preferrable accounting policy would be to capitalize these costs so that they could be matched against the related revenue which they would produce in later years.

DEPLETION The term *depletion* is used to describe the pro rata allocation of cost of a natural resource to the units removed. Depletion is computed by dividing the cost of the natural resource by the estimated available number of units, such as barrels of oil or tons of coal. The depletion charge per unit is then multiplied by the number of units actually removed during the year to determine the total depletion charge for that period.

To illustrate the computation of depletion expense, assume that the sum of $2,000,000 is paid for a coal mine believed to contain 1 million tons of coal. The depletion charge per unit is $2,000,000 ÷ 1,000,000 tons, or $2 a ton. If we assume that 200,000 tons of coal were mined and sold during the first year of operation, the depletion charge for the year would be $2 × 200,000 tons or $400,000. The journal entry necessary at the end of the year to record depletion of the mine would be as follows:

Recording depletion *Depletion Expense* *400,000*
        Accumulated Depletion: Coal Mine *400,000*
To record depletion expense for the year; 200,000 tons mined
@ $2 per ton.

In reporting natural resources in the balance sheet, accumulated depletion should be deducted from the cost of the property. A recent balance sheet of Anaconda Company, for example, reports its natural resources as follows:

Natural resources in the balance sheet Mines and mining claims, water rights and lands, less accumulated
depletion of $149,874,000 . . . . $138,410,000
balance Timberlands and phosphate and gravel deposits, less accumulated
sheet depletion of $5,602,000 2,111,000

Depletion expense in a mining business might be compared with the Purchases account in the ledger of a retail store. The Purchases account represents part of the cost to the store of the goods available for sale; the Depletion Expense account in a mining company represents a part of the cost of the coal or other product available for sale. To the extent that coal produced during the year is not sold but is carried forward as inventory for sale in the following year, **the depletion charge will also be carried forward as part of the inventory value.** In other words, depletion is recorded in the year in which extraction of the product occurs but becomes a deduction from revenue in the period in which the product is sold. Of course, the cost of the inventory of coal or other extracted product on hand at the end of the year includes not only the depletion charge but also the labor cost and other expenditures incurred in bringing the coal to the surface.

PERCENTAGE DEPLETION VERSUS COST DEPLETION For the determination of taxable income, the Internal Revenue Code permits a deduction for depletion expense equal to a specified **percentage of the revenue** from production from mineral deposits such as gold, silver, lead, and zinc ore. Depletion as a percentage of revenue was formerly allowed for the oil and gas industry, but this provision of the tax laws was repealed by Congress except for certain small producers.

Depletion computed as a percentage of revenue **is used only for income tax purposes, not for financial statements.** In terms of generally accepted accounting principles, depletion is always based on the **cost** of the mine or other natural resource.

DEPRECIATION OF BUILDINGS AND EQUIPMENT CLOSELY RELATED TO NATURAL RESOURCES Assume that a building costing $205,000 and having a normal useful life of 20 years is erected at the site of a mine estimated to contain 100,000 tons of ore. Once the mine is exhausted, the building will have only scrap value, say, $5,000. Production of ore is being carried on at a rate which will probably exhaust the mine within four to six years. Consequently, the useful life of the building will be only four to six years. During the first year after construction of the building, ore is mined in the amount of 25,000 tons. How much depreciation should be recognized on the building?

In this situation, depreciation of the building should be based on the life of the mine, and computed in the same manner as depletion. Cost, $205,000, minus scrap value, $5,000, times 25,000/100,000 equals

$50,000 depreciation for the first year. The formula may be concisely stated as

$$\text{Depreciation per Year} = (\text{Cost} - \text{Scrap Value}) \times \frac{\text{Units Produced}}{\text{Estimated Total Units}}$$

INTANGIBLE ASSETS

Characteristics

As the word *intangible* suggests, assets in this classification have no physical substance. Leading examples are goodwill, leaseholds, copyrights, franchises, licenses, and trademarks. Intangible assets are classified on the balance sheet as a subgroup of plant assets. However, not all assets which lack physical substance are regarded as intangible assets; an account receivable, for example, or a short-term prepayment is of nonphysical nature but is classified as a current asset and is not regarded as an intangible. In brief, intangible assets are assets which are used in the operation of the business but which have no physical substance and are noncurrent.

The basis of valuation for intangible assets is cost. In some companies, certain intangible assets such as trademarks may be of great importance but may have been acquired without the incurring of any cost. An intangible asset should appear on the balance sheet *only* if a cost of acquisition or development has been incurred.

However, accounting for an intangible asset is rendered somewhat difficult because the lack of physical substance makes evidence of its existence more elusive, may make its value more debatable, and may make the length of its useful life more questionable. These characteristics of intangible assets suggest that realizable value may be undeterminable or even nonexistent. Perhaps because of the lack of clear support for precise valuation of intangibles, many companies choose to carry their intangible assets on the balance sheet at a nominal valuation of $1; Jantzen, Inc., and the Polaroid Corporation are prominent examples.

There is little doubt, however, that in some companies the intangible assets, such as goodwill or trademarks, may be vitally important to profitable operations. The carrying of intangible assets on the balance sheet is justified only when there is good evidence that future earnings will be derived from these assets.

Operating expenses versus intangible assets

Many types of expenditures offer at least a half promise of yielding benefits in subsequent years, but the evidence is so doubtful and the period of usefulness so hard to define that most companies treat these expenditures as expense when incurred. Another reason for charging these outlays to expense is the practical difficulty of separating them from the recurring expenses of current operations.

Examples are the expenditures for intensive advertising campaigns to introduce new products, and the expense of training employees to work with new types of machinery or office equipment. There is little doubt that some benefits from these outlays continue beyond the current period, but because of the indeterminable duration of the benefits, it is almost universal practice to treat expenditures of this nature as expense of the current period.

Amortization

The term *amortization* is used to describe the systematic write-off to expense of the cost of an intangible asset over the periods of its economic usefulness. The usual accounting entry for amortization consists of a debit to Amortization Expense and a credit to the intangible asset account. There is no theoretical objection to crediting an accumulated amortization account rather than the intangible asset account, but this method is seldom encountered in practice.

For many years some accountants argued that certain intangibles, such as trademarks, had *unlimited* useful lives and therefore should not be amortized. However, the FASB supports the view that the value of intangible assets at any one date eventually disappears, and that *all* intangible assets must be amortized over their useful lives.[2]

Although it is difficult to estimate the useful life of an intangible such as goodwill, it is highly probable that such an asset will not contribute to future earnings on a permanent basis. The cost of the intangible asset should, therefore, be deducted from revenue during the years in which it may be expected to aid in producing revenue.[3] The maximum period of amortization cannot exceed 40 years under the rules presently enforced by the Financial Accounting Standards Board.[4] The straight-line method of amortization is generally used for intangible assets.

ARBITRARY WRITE-OFF OF INTANGIBLES Arbitrary, lump-sum write-off of intangibles (leaving a nominal balance of $1 in the accounts) is a practice sometimes found in companies which have not adopted a systematic amortization program. Arguments for this practice emphasize the element of conservatism, the practical difficulty of estimating an appropriate period for amortization, and the absence of any realizable value for intangibles. Accountants generally agree that whenever any event occurs which indicates that an intangible has lost all value, immediate write-off of the entire cost is warranted regardless of whether an amortization program has previously been followed.

[2] *APB Opinion No. 17*, "Intangible Assets," AICPA (New York: 1970), par. 27.
[3] Present tax regulations do not permit the amortization of goodwill in computing taxable income.
[4] *APB Opinion No. 17, op. cit.,* par. 29.

On the other hand, arbitrary write-offs of valuable, revenue-producing intangible assets are no more in accordance with accounting theory than would be the arbitrary write-off of land or buildings.

Goodwill

Business executives and lawyers used the term *goodwill* in a variety of meanings before it became a part of accounting terminology. One of the more common meanings of goodwill in a nonaccounting sense concerns the benefits derived from a favorable reputation among customers. To accountants, however, goodwill has a very specific meaning not necessarily limited to customer relationships. It means the *present value of future earnings in excess of the earnings normally realized in the industry.* Above-average earnings may arise not only from favorable customer relations but also from such factors as location, monopoly, manufacturing efficiency, and superior management.

The existence of the intangible asset of goodwill is indicated when an entire business is sold for a price in excess of the fair market value of the other assets. The willingness of the purchasers of a going business to pay a price greater than the sum of the values of the tangible assets indicates that they are paying for intangible assets as well. If the business does not include such specific *identifiable* intangibles as patents or franchises, the extra amount paid is presumably for goodwill. Superior earnings in the past years are of significance to prospective purchasers of a going business only to the extent that they believe such earnings may continue after they acquire the business. If the prospective purchasers believe that, by purchasing a particular company with a record of superior earnings in the past, they will earn these above-average earnings in the future, they may reasonably be expected to pay a premium price for the business. The premium which they pay represents the cost of purchased goodwill and may properly be recorded in the accounting records of the new owners in a Goodwill account.

Assume that two businesses in the same line of trade are for sale and that the normal rate of earnings on capital invested in this industry is 10% a year. The relative earning power of the two companies during the past five years is indicated by the following schedule.

	Company X	Company Y
Net assets other than goodwill	$1,000,000	$1,000,000
Normal rate of earnings on invested capital	10%	10%
Average net income for past five years	$ 100,000	$ 140,000
Net income computed at normal rate (10%) on net assets other than goodwill	100,000	100,000
Annual earnings in excess of average for the industry	$ -0-	$ 40,000

Measuring superior earning power

A prospective investor would be willing to pay more for Company Y than for Company X because Company Y has a record of superior earnings which will presumably continue for some time in the future. Company Y has goodwill; Company X does not. Very few companies are able to maintain above-average earnings for more than a few years. Consequently, the purchaser of a business will usually limit the payment for goodwill to not more than four or five times the excess annual earnings.

ESTIMATING THE AMOUNT OF GOODWILL Goodwill is to be recorded in the accounts *only when paid for;* this situation usually occurs only when a going business is purchased in its entirety. When ownership of a business changes hands, any amount paid for goodwill rests on the assumption that earnings in excess of normal will continue under the new ownership. The following are methods of estimating a value for goodwill:

1 Arbitrary agreement between buyer and seller of the business may be reached on the amount of goodwill. For example, it might be agreed that the fair market value of the net tangible assets is $1,000,000 and that the total purchase price for the business will be $1,100,000, thus providing a $100,000 payment for goodwill. (We are assuming in this example that the business has no *identifiable intangible assets* such as patents.) The term *net tangible assets* may require explanation. *Net assets* means assets minus liabilities; *net tangible assets* therefore means all assets (except the intangibles) minus liabilities. Another way of computing the amount of net tangible assets is merely to deduct the intangible assets from the owners' equity.

2 Goodwill may be determined as a multiple of the average net income of past years. For example, assume that a business has earned an average annual net income of $25,000 during the past five years. The business is sold for the book value of the net tangible assets, plus two years' average net income. The payment for goodwill is, therefore, $50,000. This method may be criticized because it ignores completely the concept of *excess earnings* as a basis for estimating goodwill.

3 Goodwill may be determined as a multiple of the amount by which the average annual earnings exceed normal earnings. To illustrate, assume the following data:

Average investment in the business	$100,000
Average annual earnings (rate of 14%)	$ 14,000
Normal earnings for this industry (rate of 10%)	10,000
Average earnings in excess of normal	$ 4,000
Multiple of excess annual earnings	4
Goodwill	$ 16,000

Goodwill as multiple of excess earnings

The multiple applied to the excess annual earnings may vary widely from perhaps 1 to 10, depending on the nature of the industry and the reliance placed on the earnings projections. This method is more in accord with the concept of goodwill as earning power in *excess* of normal, whereas method 2 relates goodwill to the *total* earnings.

4 Goodwill may be determined as the capitalized value of excess earning power, using a capitalization rate considered normal in the industry. Assume that the normal rate of earnings in a given line of business is 10% and that a particular company presents the following picture:

Goodwill based on capitali- zation of excess earnings		
Average investment in the business		*$100,000*
Average annual earnings (rate of 14%)		*$ 14,000*
Normal earnings for this industry (rate of 10%)		*10,000*
Average earnings in excess of normal		*$ 4,000*
Goodwill, computed by capitalizing average excess earnings at 10%		
($4,000 ÷ .10)		*$ 40,000*

In estimating the amount of goodwill, the buyer and seller may agree to capitalize excess earnings at a rate either higher or lower than the normal earnings rate in the industry.

Leaseholds

Land, buildings, and many types of business equipment are rented under a *lease* agreement. The owner of the property is the *lessor;* the tenant or company obtaining the use of the property is the *lessee.* The rights transferred to the lessee under a lease contract are described as a *leasehold.*

Some leases merely provide for regular monthly payments of rent; in these cases a leasehold account is not used. The lessee making monthly payments to the lessor debits these payments to Rent Expense. Sometimes a lease agreement covering several years is so drawn as to require the payment in advance of the final year's rent. Rent payments for all but the final year may be made on a month-to-month basis. In this case the Leasehold account will be debited with the advance payment of the final year's rent at the time the lease is signed, and this amount will remain in the account until the final year of the lease, at which time the advance payment will be transferred to the Rent Expense account.

During periods of rising property values, a long-term lease may become extremely valuable because the agreed rental is much less than would be charged under current market conditions. Such a development is particularly likely for leases that run for 20 or 30 years or more. No entry is usually made in the accounts to reflect the increased value of the lease attributable to rising property values, because assets are accounted for on the basis of cost, not on the basis of estimated market values. However, if the lessee company should sell its rights under the lease to another company, the new tenant would record the cost to it of the lease. Assume, for example, that A Company owns a new building which it leases to B Company for 15 years at an annual rental of $12,000. After five years, during which property values and rental rates have increased sharply, B Company sells its rights under the lease to C Company for a cash payment of $10,000. The new tenant, C Company, also assumes the obligation of making the required yearly payments of $12,000 to A Company during the remaining 10 years of the lease. The annual rent expense to C Company will be $13,000, consisting of $12,000 payable in cash each year plus $1,000 in amortization of the cost incurred in acquiring the lease. By transferring $1,000 a year from the Leasehold account to the Rent Expense account, C Company will spread the cost of this favorable lease uniformly over the 10 years during which it occupies the property. The journal entry in C Company's accounts will be as follows:

Leasehold	10,000	
Cash		10,000
To record purchase of a lease with 10 years of life remaining.		
Annual cash payments of $12,000 to owner are required.		

The Leasehold account will be written off to Rent Expense by the following entry in each of the next 10 years.

Rent Expense	1,000	
Leasehold		1,000
To transfer to expense one-tenth of the cost of a lease having 10 years to		
run from date of acquisition.		

OBLIGATIONS UNDER LONG-TERM LEASES Some long-term leases cover the entire life of a building, require the tenant to bear all maintenance expenses, and are not subject to cancellation. The economic substance of such a lease contract is much the same as if the lessee had obtained a loan and purchased the property. In other words, the lease has been the means of financing the acquisition of an asset. Certain leases of this type are accounted for as though the property had been purchased. The liability under the lease is included in the balance sheet as a long-term liability and an asset is recognized (the right to use of the property). This topic is more fully explored in the *Intermediate Accounting* volume of this series.

Leasehold improvements

When buildings or other improvements are constructed on leased property by the lessee, the costs should be recorded in a Leasehold Improvements account and written off as expense during the remaining life of the lease or of the estimated useful life of the building, whichever is shorter. This procedure is usually followed even though the lessee has an option to renew the lease, because there is no assurance in advance that conditions will warrant the exercise of the renewal clause.

Patents

A patent is an exclusive right granted by the federal government for manufacture, use, and sale of a particular product. The purpose of this exclusive grant is to encourage the invention of new machines and processes. When a company acquires a patent by purchase from the inventor or other holder, the purchase price should be recorded by debiting the intangible asset account, Patents. The cost of a successful lawsuit to defend the validity of a patent is also capitalized by charge to the Patents account.

Patents are granted for a period of 17 years, and the period of amortization must not exceed that period. However, if the patent is likely to lose its usefulness in less than 17 years, amortization should be based on the shorter period of estimated useful life. Assume that a patent is purchased from the inventor at a cost of $100,000, after five years of the legal life have expired. The remaining *legal* life is, therefore, 12 years, but if the estimated *useful* life is only five years, amortization should be based on this shorter period. The entry to be made to record the annual amortization expense would be:

Entry for amortization of patent

Amortization Expense: Patents	20,000	
Patents		20,000

To amortize cost of patent on a straight-line basis and estimated life of five years.

If new information becomes available indicating a different useful life for a patent than was originally estimated, the revising of the amortization rate should be carried out in the same manner described in Chapter 11 for revising depreciation rates. In brief, spread the unamortized cost over the remaining life indicated by the new estimate, but in no case beyond the legal life of the patent.

Research and development costs

The spending of billions of dollars a year on research and development leading to all kinds of new products is a striking characteristic of American industry. In the past, some companies treated all research and development costs as expense in the year incurred; other companies in the same industry recorded these costs as intangible assets to be amortized over future years. This diversity of practice prevented the financial statements of different companies from being comparable.

The lack of uniformity in accounting for research and development was ended when the Financial Accounting Standards Board ruled that all research and development expenditures should be charged to expense when incurred.[5] The action by the FASB was favorably received because it reduced the number of alternative accounting practices and helped make financial statements of different companies more comparable. Incidentally, the FASB Statement did not apply to the development costs unique to companies developing natural resources, as discussed on page 435.

[5] *Statement of Financial Accounting Standards No. 2*, "Accounting for Research and Development Costs," (Financial Accounting Standards Board, (Stamford, Conn.: 1974), par. 12.

Copyrights

A copyright is an exclusive right granted to protect the production and sale of literary or artistic materials for a period of 28 years. The cost of obtaining a copyright is minor and therefore is chargeable to expense when paid. Only when a copyright is purchased will the expenditure be material enough to warrant capitalization and spreading over the useful life. The revenue from copyrights is usually limited to only a few years, and the purchase cost should, of course, be amortized over the years in which the revenue is expected.

Trademarks

A permanent exclusive right to the use of a trademark, brand name, or commercial symbol may be obtained by registering it. If the use of the trademark is abandoned or if its contribution to earnings becomes doubtful, immediate write-off of the cost is called for. The outlay for securing a trademark is often not consequential, and it is common practice to treat such outlays as expense when incurred.

Other intangibles and deferred charges

Many other types of intangible assets are found in the published balance sheets of large corporations. Some examples are formulas, processes, designs, franchises, name lists, and film rights.[6]

   Intangibles, particularly those with limited lives, are sometimes classified as "deferred charges" in the balance sheet. A *deferred charge* is an expenditure that is expected to yield benefits for several accounting periods, and should be amortized over its estimated useful life. Included in this category are such items as bond issuance costs, plant rearrangement and moving costs, start-up costs, and organization costs. The distinction between intangibles and deferred charges is not an important one; both represent "bundles of services" in the form of long-term prepayments awaiting allocation to those accounting periods in which the services will be consumed.

KEY TERMS INTRODUCED OR EMPHASIZED IN CHAPTER 12

Amortization   The systematic write-off to expense of the cost of an intangible asset over the periods of its economic usefulness.

Book value   The cost of a plant asset minus the total recorded depreciation, as shown by the Accumulated Depreciation account. The remaining undepreciated cost, also known as *carrying value.*

---

[6] In a recent survey of the financial statements of 600 leading corporations, 526 reportedly carried one or more types of intangible assets on their balance sheets. American Institute of Certified Public Accountants, *Accounting Trends & Techniques* (New York: 1970), p. 96.

Copyright   An exclusive right granted by the federal government to protect the production and sale of literary or artistic materials for a period of 28 years.

Deferred charge   An expenditure expected to yield benefits for several accounting periods and therefore capitalized and written off during the periods benefited.

Depletion   Allocating the cost of a natural resource to the units removed as the resource is mined, pumped, cut, or otherwise consumed.

Goodwill   The present value of expected future earnings of a business in excess of the earnings normally realized in the industry. Recorded when a business entity is purchased at a price in excess of the fair value of its tangible assets and identifiable intangible assets less liabilities.

Intangible assets   Those assets which are used in the operation of a business but which have no physical substance and are noncurrent.

Lessee   The tenant of leased property.

Lessor   The owner of leased property.

Natural resources   Mines, oil fields, standing timber, and similar assets which are physically consumed and converted into inventory.

Net assets   Assets minus liabilities. Equal to owner's equity.

Net tangible assets   Total of all assets (except the intangibles) minus liabilities.

Patent   The exclusive right granted by the federal government for the manufacture, use, and sale of a particular product.

Percentage depletion   For income tax purposes only, a deduction for depletion expense equal to a specified percentage of the revenue from a natural resource. Eliminated or reduced by recent legislation.

REVIEW QUESTIONS

1 Century Company traded in its old computer on a new model. The trade-in allowance for the old computer is greater than its book value. Should Century Company recognize a gain on the exchange in computing its taxable income or in determining its net income for financial reporting? Explain.

2 Fargo Corporation traded in an old machine on a similar new one, but received a trade-in allowance less than the book value of the old machine. The Internal Revenue Service did not permit the company to recognize any loss on the transaction in computing its taxable income. How will Fargo benefit in future years for income tax purposes as a result of the indicated loss on the trade-in not being allowed by the IRS?

3 Describe briefly three situations in which debit entries may properly be made in accumulated depreciation accounts.

4 Student A asserts that when a depreciable plant asset is to be sold a first step is to record depreciation for the fractional period to the date of sale. Student B argues that an entry for depreciation at the date of disposing of the asset is inefficient because in his opinion it is more convenient to make all depreciation entries at the end of the year. At that time he would take into consideration that certain depreciable assets had been in use for only a portion of the year prior to their disposal. Evaluate these arguments.

5 Topeka Corporation maintains a general ledger control account for office equipment. This controlling account is supported by a subsidiary ledger in the form of a card file with a card for each unit of equipment. On 30 of these cards, the accumulated depreciation is equal to the cost of the asset. Assuming that the 30 items represented by the cards are still in regular use, should additional depreciation be recorded on them? When should these 30 cards be removed from the subsidiary ledger, and the cost and accumulated depreciation be removed from the general ledger accounts?

6 What is the term used to describe the pro rata allocation of the cost of a mine or other natural resource to the units removed during the year?

7 Lead Hill Corporation recognizes $1 of depletion for each ton of ore mined. During the current year the company mined 600,000 tons but sold only 500,000 tons, as it was attempting to build up inventories in anticipation of a possible strike by employees. How much depletion should be deducted from revenue of the current year?

8 Under what circumstances does good accounting call for a mining company to depreciate a plant asset over a period shorter than the normal useful life.

9 Define *intangible assets.* Would an account receivable arising from a sale of merchandise under terms of 2/10, n/30 qualify as an intangible asset under your definition?

10 The James Electric Shop obtained its store building under a 10-year lease at $400 a month. The lease agreement required payment of rent for the tenth year at the time of signing the lease. All other payments were on a monthly basis. Give the journal entry required at the date of signing the lease when James wrote a check for $5,200, representing payment of the current month's rent and the $4,800 applicable to the tenth year of the lease. What entries, if any, are indicated for the tenth year of the lease?

11 Under what circumstances should goodwill be recorded in the accounts?

12 In reviewing the financial statements of Digital Products Co. with a view to investing in the company's stock, you notice that net tangible assets total $1 million, that goodwill is listed as $100,000, and that average earnings for the past five years have been $20,000 a year. How would these relationships influence your thinking about the company?

13 Space Research Company paid $500,000 cash to acquire the entire business of Saturn Company, a strong competitor. In negotiating this lump-sum price for the business, a valuation of $60,000 was assigned to goodwill, representing four times the amount by which Saturn Company's annual earnings had exceeded normal earnings in the industry. Assuming that the goodwill is recorded in the accounts of Space Research Company, should it remain there permanently or be amortized? What basis of amortization might be used?

14 Current accounting standards require that the cost of various types of intangible assets be amortized by regular charges against earnings. Over what period of time should amortization extend? (Your answer should be in the form of a principle or guideline rather than a specific number of years.)

15 Dell Company traded in an old machine on a similar new one. The original cost of the old machine was $30,000 and the accumulated depreciation was $24,000. The list price of the new machine was $40,000 and the trade-in allowance was $8,000. What amount must Dell pay? Compute the indicated gain or loss (regardless of whether it should be recorded in the accounts). Compute the cost basis of the new machine to be used in figuring depreciation for determination of income subject to federal income tax.

EXERCISES

Ex. 12-1 An airplane with a book value of $30,000 was traded in on a new airplane with a list price of $300,000. The trade-in allowance (not necessarily the fair market value) for the old airplane was $45,000.

a How much cash must be paid for the new airplane?

b What is the cost basis of the new airplane for income tax purposes?

c How much depreciation should be recorded on the new airplane for the first year of use, assuming a four-year life, a residual value of $33,000, and the use of straight-line depreciation?

Ex. 12-2 A tractor which cost $28,800 had an estimated useful life of five years and an estimated salvage value of $4,800. Straight-line depreciation was used. Give the entry required by each of the following alternative assumptions:

a The tractor was sold for cash of $18,000 after two years' use.

b The tractor was traded in after three years on another tractor with a list price of $36,000. Trade-in allowance was $16,200. The trade-in was recorded in a manner acceptable for income tax purposes.

c The tractor was scrapped after four years' use. Since scrap dealers were unwilling to pay anything for the tractor, it was given to a scrap dealer for his services in removing it.

Ex. 12-3 Edison Company on April 1 purchased machinery priced at $270,000 but received a trade-in allowance of $24,000 for used machinery. Cash of $60,000 was paid and a 12%, one-year note payable given for the balance. The machinery traded in had an original cost of $180,000 and had been depreciated at the rate of $18,000 a year. Residual value had been ignored on the grounds of not being material. Accumulated depreciation amounted to $144,000 at December 31 prior to the year of the exchange. No depreciation had been recorded between the closing of the accounts on December 31 and the exchange for the new machinery on April 1.

In general journal form, give the entries to record:

a Depreciation for the fraction of a year prior to the April 1 transaction

b The acquisition of the new machinery on April 1 under the rules acceptable for income tax purposes

c The acquisition of the new machinery on April 1 under the assumption that gain or loss is to be recognized and that the trade-in allowance represents the fair market value of the old machinery being traded in.

Ex. 12-4 Yellow Knife Mines started mining activities early in Year 1. At the end of the year its accountant prepared the following summary of its mining costs:

Labor	$2,380,000
Materials	245,000
Miscellaneous	539,280

These costs do not include any charges for depletion or depreciation. Data relating to assets used in mining the ore follow:

Cost of mine (*estimated deposit, 10 million tons; residual value of the mine estimated at $420,000*)	$2,100,000
Buildings (*estimated life, 15 years; no residual value*)	184,800
Equipment (*useful life, six years regardless of number of tons mined; residual value $42,000*)	336,000

During the year 800,000 tons (8%) of ore were mined, of which 600,000 tons were sold. It is estimated that it will take at least 15 years to extract the ore.

Determine the cost that should be assigned to the inventory of unsold ore at the end of Year 1.

Ex. 12-5 During the past several years the net sales of Hawthorne Company have averaged $4,500,000 annually and net income has averaged 6% of net sales. At the present time the company is being offered for sale. Its accounting records show net assets (total assets minus all liabilities) to be $1,500,000.

An investor negotiating to buy the company offers to pay an amount equal to the book value for the net assets and to assume all liabilities. In addition, the investor is willing to pay for goodwill an amount equal to net earnings in excess of 15% on net assets, capitalized at a rate of 25%.

On the basis of this agreement, what price should the investor offer for the Hawthorne Company?

PROBLEMS

Group A

12A-1 Waverly Laboratories acquired equipment on July 1, Year 4, at a cost of $103,480. Useful life was estimated to be 10 years and scrap value $4,680. Waverly Laboratories depreciates its plant assets by the straight-line method and closes its accounts annually on June 30.

On June 30, Year 7, after considerable experience with the equipment, the company decided that the estimated total life should be revised from 10 years to six years and the residual scrap value lowered from $4,680 to $3,120. This revised estimate was made prior to recording depreciation for the fiscal year ended June 30, Year 7.

On December 31, Year 8, the equipment was sold for $17,810 cash.

Instructions Prepare journal entries to record all the above transactions and the depreciation expense from July 1, Year 4, to December 31, Year 8. (Use the word "Equipment" as the title of the asset account.)

12A-2 The following summary schedule shows the entries made in the Office Equipment account during the current year by Rentals, Etc.

Debits:

Jan. 2	Acquired four identical data processing machines @ $10,500 each	$42,000
Jan. 5	Installation costs	1,400
	Total debits	$43,400

Credits:

Dec. 31	Proceeds from sale of one data processing machine	(8,050)
Dec. 31	Balance in Office Equipment account	$35,350

The company depreciates the data processing machines on a straight-line basis with an estimated useful life of five years and an estimated residual value of $1,225 per machine. The December 31 transaction for the sale of one machine was recorded by a debit to Cash for the full sales price of $8,050 and a credit to Office Equipment for $8,050.

Instructions

a Prepare one journal entry at December 31 to record depreciation for the year on all four machines.

b What was the amount of gain or loss on the sale of the machine on December 31? Show computations.

c Prepare one journal entry to **correct the accounts** at December 31. In drafting your correcting entry, give consideration to the debit and credit already entered in the accounts on December 31 to record the sale of one of the machines. Your entry should reduce the Office Equipment account and the Accumulated Depreciation account and should record the gain or loss on the disposal of the machine which was not recognized in the entry made at the time of the sale.

12A-3 The accounting policies of Harrison Climate Systems provide for adjusting and closing the accounts at the end of each calendar year. Straight-line depreciation is used for all items of plant and equipment.

On January 2, Year 1, the company purchased machinery for cash at a cost of $366,300. The useful life was estimated to be 10 years and the residual salvage value $6,300.

In December, Year 3, after almost three years of using the machinery, the company decided that because of rapid technological change, it should revise the estimated total life from 10 years to six years. The estimate of scrap value was not changed. The revised estimate of useful life was decided upon prior to recording depreciation for the year ended December 31, Year 3.

On June 30, Year 4, the company decided to lease new, more efficient machinery and the machinery described above was sold for $90,000 cash.

Instructions Prepare journal entries to record the purchase of the machinery, depreciation for Year 1 through Year 4, and the disposal. Do not prepare closing entries.

12A-4 Cycle Imports leased a store building from Builders, Inc., on July 1 for a period of 10 years for a total contractual amount of $624,000. The fiscal year used by Cycle Imports begins on July 1. Terms of the lease called for an immediate cash payment of $62,400, representing rent for the final year of the 10-year lease period. Also on July 1, Cycle Imports (the lessee) paid $5,200 for the current month's rent and agreed to pay rent monthly in advance during the first nine years of the lease. The lease also provided that Cycle Imports must pay for any repairs or improvements it wished to make.

An escalator was immediately installed by the lessee at a cost of $41,600, paid in cash. The normal life of the escalator was stated by the manufacturer to be 20 years. Some lighting fixtures were also installed at a cost of $5,200 paid in cash, for which the estimated life was five years.

Instructions Prepare journal entries to record:
a Payment of $67,600, representing $5,200 rent for July and $62,400 for the final year's rent under the 10-year lease contract.
b Payment for the escalator and lighting fixtures.
c First annual amortization of the cost of the escalator.
d First annual amortization of the cost of the lighting fixtures.
e Final disposition of the $62,400 advance payment of rent applicable to the tenth year of the lease.

12A-5 The Western Mines acquired a coal mine on January 1, 1977, for a cash price of $884,000. Estimates by the company's engineers indicated that the mine contained 1,700,000 tons of coal. The equipment required to extract the coal from the mine was purchased January 2, 1977, for $301,600 cash. The useful life of this equipment was estimated to be five years, with a residual scrap value of $28,600. The straight-line method of depreciation was used by the company on this equipment and on all its depreciable assets.

On July 1, 1977, three trucks intended for use around the mine were purchased for $75,400 cash. Depreciation was to be computed on the basis of an estimated useful life of four years, with a residual scrap value of $7,800.

Construction of a frame building to be used as a mine office was completed on July 1, 1977, at a cost of $59,800 cash. Estimated life of this building was 10 years; the residual scrap value was estimated as no more than enough to cover the cost of demolition.

An assortment of secondhand office equipment approximately five years old was purchased on July 1, 1977, for $7,020 cash. The remaining useful life of this used equipment was estimated at five years, and the residual scrap value was estimated at $1,820.

During 1977, a total of 120,000 tons of coal was mined and sold. In 1978, production increased to 190,000 tons, and again the entire output was sold. On March 31, 1979, after 70,000 tons of coal had been extracted and sold, the mine and all related property were sold for $1,084,200 cash. The contract covering the sale of the mine specified the following prices for the various assets being transferred: mine, $806,000; equipment, $200,200; trucks, $33,800; building, $41,600; and office equipment, $2,600.

Instructions
a Prepare general journal entries to record all transactions and necessary adjustments from January 1977, through March 31, 1979. Include depreciation

entries using the straight-line method. Record depreciation for the fraction of the year 1979 prior to the sale of the mine and other property. The five asset accounts to be used are Mining Property, Equipment, Trucks, Building, and Office Equipment.

b Prepare a three-column schedule showing (*1*) the sale price, (*2*) the un-depreciated cost, and (*3*) the gain or loss on the disposal of each of the five items of plant and equipment.

12A-6 Overland Trail Company, an aggressive growing company, is considering pur-chase of the assets of Saddle Company, exclusive of cash, on January 2, 1980. The Saddle Company has been in business for six years and has had average net earnings of $48,900 during this period.

The purchase plan calls for a cash payment of $150,000 and a promissory note to be issued by Overland Trail as payment for the assets including goodwill after any necessary adjustments have been made. The goodwill is to be determined as four times the average excess earnings over a normal rate of return of 8% on the present net tangible assets.

The balance sheet of Saddle Company on December 31, 1979, follows:

Assets

Cash			$ 45,000
Other current assets			75,000
Plant and equipment:			
Land		$ 90,000	
Buildings	$366,000		
Less: Accumulated depreciation	94,500	271,500	
Machinery	$285,000		
Less: Accumulated depreciation	193,500	91,500	
Equipment	$180,000		
Less: Accumulated depreciation	100,500	79,500	532,500
Patents			39,375
Goodwill			15,000
			$706,875

Liabilities & Owner's Equity

Current liabilities	$111,000
Long-term liabilities	268,500
Paul Saddle, capital	327,375
	$706,875

Other data

(*1*) Goodwill was entered in the accounts three years ago when Saddle decided that the increasing profitability of the company should be recognized.

(*2*) The patent appears at original cost. It was acquired by purchase six years ago from a competitor who had recorded amortization for two years on the basis of its legal life. The patent is highly useful to the business, and its usefulness is expected to continue.

Instructions

a Prepare any adjusting entries needed in the accounts of Saddle Company to bring the amounts shown in the balance sheet into accord with generally accepted accounting principles. (Two corrections are required.)

b Compute the amount to be paid by Overland Trail for goodwill after considering the effects of the adjusting entries in **a** above. (The reported average net earnings should be adjusted to reflect amortization of the patent.)

c Prepare a compound journal entry on Saddle Company's accounts to record the sale to Overland Trail Company. The long-term liabilities are not being transferred. The entry should record:

(1) The receipt of cash and the note receivable.

(2) The closing of the asset accounts being transferred, excluding cash. The "other current assets" of $75,000 may be treated as the title of a ledger account.

(3) The closing of the accumulated depreciation accounts.

(4) A credit to the capital account of Paul Saddle.

d Prepare a revised balance sheet for the Saddle Company at January 2, 1980, after the journal entries called for above have been posted.

Group B

12B-1 Machinery with an estimated useful life of 10 years had been acquired by Triangle Company at a cost of $108,000. Straight-line depreciation had been used with no provision for residual salvage value because the expense of dismantling and removing the machinery at the end of its useful life was expected to be as much as any salvage received.

After several years of using the machinery, Triangle Company traded it in on new machinery priced at $162,000. A trade-in allowance of $14,400 was received. The accumulated depreciation on the old machinery amounted to $86,400 at December 31 prior to the year of the trade-in. No depreciation had been recorded between the closing of the accounts at December 31 and the exchange for the new machinery on April 1. The remainder of the trade-in transaction consisted of a $36,000 cash payment and the signing of a 12% one-year note payable for the balance of the purchase price of the new machine.

Instructions Prepare entries in general journal form to record the following:

a Depreciation for the fraction of a year prior to the April 1 transaction.

b The acquisition of the new machinery on April 1 under the rules acceptable for income tax purposes.

c The acquisition of the new machinery on April 1 under the assumption that gain or loss is to be recognized and that the trade-in allowance represents the fair market value of the old machinery being traded in.

12B-2 Eastern Shore Corporation, a manufacturer, showed the following information in its ledger account for Machinery for the current year.

Jan. 2 *Acquired four identical machines @ $10,800 each*	. . . .	$43,200
Jan. 4 *Installation costs*	. . . .	1,440
Total debits	. . . .	$44,640
Dec. 31 *Less: Credit for proceeds from sale of one machine*	. . . .	(8,280)
31 *Balance in Machinery account*	. . . .	$36,360

The corporation's policy for depreciating the machines is to use the straight-line method with an estimated useful life of five years and an estimated residual value of $1,260 per machine. The December 31 transaction for the sale of one machine was recorded by a debit to Cash for the full sales price of $8,280 and a credit to Machinery for $8,280.

Instructions

a Prepare one journal entry at December 31 to record depreciation expense for the year on all four machines.

b What was the amount of the gain or loss on the sale of the machine on December 31? Show computations.

c Prepare one journal entry to **correct the accounts** at December 31. In drafting your correcting entry, give consideration to the debit and credit already entered in the accounts on December 31 to record the sale of one of the machines. Your entry should reduce the Machinery account and the Accumulated Depreciation account and should record the gain or loss on the disposal of the machine which was not recognized in the entry made at the time of the sale.

12B-3 Old Dominion Company adjusts and closes its accounts at the end of each calendar year and uses the straight-line method of depreciation on all its plant and equipment. On January 1, Year 1, machinery was purchased for cash at a cost of $427,350. Useful life was estimated to be 10 years and residual value $7,350.

Three years later in December, Year 3, after steady use of the machinery, the company decided that because of rapid technological change, the estimated total useful life should be revised from 10 years to six years. No change was made in the estimate of residual value. The revised estimate of useful life was decided upon prior to recording depreciation for the period ended December 31, Year 3.

On June 30, Year 4, Old Dominion Company decided to lease new, more efficient machinery; consequently, the machinery described above was sold on this date for $105,000 cash.

Instructions Prepare journal entries to record the purchase of the machinery, the recording of depreciation for each of the four years, and the disposal of the machinery on June 30, Year 4. Do not prepare closing entries.

12B-4 A new patent was purchased by Houston Company from the inventor immediately after its issuance on January 2, Year 2. The full price of $280,000 was paid in cash. The patented device was promptly put to use in Houston's production operations. Although the legal life of the patent was 17 years, the company estimated that technological changes in its industry would limit the economic usefulness of the patent to 10 years.

On March 1, Year 2, the company paid $157,500 in legal fees for the services of attorneys who successfully defended an infringement suit against the patent.

In December of Year 4, Houston Company decided that the **total** useful life of the patent would be limited to six years rather than the original estimate of 10 years. This decision was reached before amortization was recorded for Year 4.

Instructions Prepare journal entries to record the above events relating to the acquisition and amortization of the patent from January 2, Year 2, through December 31, Year 4.

12B-5 On January 1, Year 10, Midwest Petroleum, an established concern, borrowed $9 million from the First National Bank, issuing a note payable in five years with interest at 9%, payable annually on December 31. Also on January 1, the company purchased for $4,800,000 an undeveloped oil field estimated to contain at least 2 million barrels of oil. Movable equipment having an estimated useful life of five years and no scrap value was also acquired at a cost of $156,000.

During January the company spent $750,000 in developing the field, and several shallow wells were brought into production. The established accounting policy of the company was to treat drilling and development charges of this type as expense of the period in which the work was done.

Construction of a pipeline was completed on May 1, Year 10, at a cost of $1,440,000. Although this pipeline was physically capable of being used for 10 years or more, its economic usefulness was limited to the productive life of the wells; therefore, the depreciation method employed was based on the estimated number of barrels of oil to be produced.

Operating costs incurred during Year 10 (other than depreciation and depletion) amounted to $960,000, and 230,000 barrels of oil were produced and sold.

In January, Year 11, further drilling expense was incurred in the amount of $600,000, and the estimated total capacity of the field was raised from the original 2,000,000 barrels to 2,590,000 barrels, including oil produced to date.

Cash operating costs for Year 11 amounted to $1,500,000, in addition to the $600,000 of drilling expense mentioned above. Oil production totaled 800,000 barrels, of which all but 80,000 barrels were sold during the year.

Instructions Prepare journal entries to record the transactions of Year 10 and Year 11, including the setting up of the inventory at December 31, Year 11. Do not prepare entries for sales. The inventory valuation should include an appropriate portion of the operating costs of the year, including depreciation and depletion.

12B-6 Jane Warren, an experienced executive in retail store operation, is interested in buying an established business in the retail clothing field. She is now attempting to make a choice among three similar concerns which are available for purchase. All three companies have been in business for five years. The balance sheets presented by the three companies may be summarized as follows:

Assets	Company X	Company Y	Company Z
Cash	$ 24,000	$ 24,000	$ 40,000
Accounts receivable	185,600	190,400	217,600
Inventory	352,000	288,000	288,000
Plant assets (net)	110,400	128,000	80,000
Goodwill		4,800	
	$672,000	$635,200	$625,600

Liabilities & Owner's Equity	Company X	Company Y	Company Z
Current liabilities	$284,800	$296,000	$320,000
Owner's equity	387,200	339,200	305,600
	$672,000	$635,200	$625,600

The average net earnings of the three businesses during the past five years had been as follows: Company X, $59,200; Company Y, $51,200; and Company Z, $54,400.

With the permission of the owners of the three businesses, Warren arranged for a certified public accountant to examine the accounting records of the companies. This investigation disclosed the following information:

Accounts receivable In Company X, no provision for uncollectible accounts had been made at any time, and no accounts receivable had been written off. Numerous past-due receivables were in the accounts, and the estimated uncollectible items which had accumulated during the past five years amounted to $16,000. In both Company Y and Company Z, the receivables appeared to be carried at net realizable value.

Inventories Company Y had adopted the first-in, first-out method of inventory valuation when first organized but had changed to the last-in, first-out method after one year. As a result of this change in method of accounting for inventories, the present balance sheet figure for inventories was approximately $32,000 less than replacement cost. The other two companies had used the first-in, first-out method continuously, and their present inventories were approximately equal to replacement cost.

Plant and equipment In each of the three companies, the plant assets included a building which had cost $80,000 and had an estimated useful life of 25 years with no residual scrap value. Company X had taken no depreciation on its building; Company Y had used straight-line depreciation at 4% annually; and Company Z had depreciated its building by applying a constant rate of 4% to the undepreciated balance. All plant assets other than buildings had been depreciated on a straight-line basis in all companies. Warren believed that the book value of the plant assets of all three companies would approximate fair market value if depreciation were uniformly computed on a straight-line basis.

Goodwill The item of goodwill, $4,800, on the balance sheet of Company Y represented the cost of a nonrecurring advertising campaign conducted during the first year of operation.

   Warren is willing to pay for net tangible assets (except cash) at book value, plus an amount for goodwill equal to three times the average annual net earnings in excess of 10% on the net tangible assets. Cash will not be included in the transfer of assets.

Instructions
a Prepare a revised summary of balance sheet data after correcting all errors made by the companies. In addition to correcting errors, make the necessary changes to apply straight-line depreciation and first-in, first-out inventory methods in all three companies. Round all amounts to the nearest dollar.
b Determine revised amounts for average net earnings of the three companies after taking into consideration the correction of errors and changes of method called for in *a* above.
c Determine the price which Warren should offer for each of the businesses.

BUSINESS DECISION PROBLEM 12

Doris Bell, president of Bell Home Products Corporation, states that her company has spent nearly a half million dollars during the current year on special advertising campaigns to introduce new products. "The campaigns were begun and completed during the current year," she explains, "but I believe we will be selling these new products for many years in the future. Consequently, I wanted to show the cost of this advertising as an intangible asset on the balance sheet and amortize it over, maybe, 10 years. However, the CPA firm that audits our company insisted on treating this advertising as a charge against this year's operations."
a Is Bell's argument that benefits will be received in future years from the advertising this year to introduce new products a logical and valid one? Explain.
b What is the position of the Financial Accounting Standards Board with respect to expenditures for developing intangible assets which are not specifically identifiable?
c On balance, what is your conclusion as to whether the advertising expenditures should be an expense of the current year or listed as intangible assets on the balance sheet?

13

Payroll Accounting

Labor costs and related payroll taxes constitute a large and constantly increasing portion of the total costs of operating most business organizations. In the commercial airlines, for example, labor costs represent over 50% of total operating costs.

The task of accounting for payroll costs would be an important one simply because of the large amounts involved; however, it is further complicated by the many federal and state laws which require employers to maintain certain specific information in their payroll records not only for the business as a whole but also for each individual employee. Regular reports of total wages and amounts withheld must be filed with government agencies, accompanied by payment of the amounts withheld from employees and of the payroll taxes levied on the employer.

A basic rule in most business organizations is that every employee must be paid on time, and the payment must be accompanied by a detailed explanation of the computations involved in determining the net amount received by the employee. The payroll system must therefore be capable of processing the input data (such as employee names, social security numbers, regular hours worked, pay rates, overtime, and taxes) and producing a prompt and accurate output of paychecks, payroll records, withholding statements, and reports to government agencies. In addition, the payroll system must have built-in safeguards against overpayments to employees, the issuance of duplicate paychecks, payments to fictitious employees, and the continuance on the payroll of persons who have been terminated as employees.

Internal control over payrolls

The requirements for a payroll system as enumerated in the preceding section indicate the need for strong internal control over payrolls. The large dollar amounts involved; the need for fast, accurate processing of data; the requirement of prompt, regular distribution of payroll checks; the required reports to government—all these factors point to the need for strong internal controls, regardless of whether the business entity is a small one with a manual accounting system or a larger organization with an electronic data processing system.

Some specific characteristics of present-day payroll accounting reduce the likelihood of payroll frauds, which in the past were common and often substantial. These helpful factors include the required frequent filing of payroll data with the government, and the universal use of employer identification numbers and employees' social security numbers. For example, "padding" a payroll with fictitious names is more difficult when social security numbers must be on file for every employee, individual earnings records must be created, and quarterly reports must be submitted to the Internal Revenue Service, showing for every employee the gross earnings, social security taxes, and income tax withheld.

The repetitive nature of payroll preparation also encourages careful system design, extensive subdivision of duties relating to payroll, and automation of the processes for computation and record preparation. The records must be retained for extended periods and must be available for inspection by government agencies.

The widespread use of computers for processing payroll should not be taken as assurance that payroll fraud is no longer a threat. The separation and subdivision of duties is still essential. For the company with an EDP system, adequate internal control over payrolls demands clear separation of the functions of systems analysts, programmers, key-punch operators, computer operators, librarians, and control group personnel. If this segregation of duties is not maintained, the opportunity exists for payroll fraud on a gigantic scale. The fact that virtually all phases of payroll accounting can be handled rapidly by a computer may have induced some companies to place less emphasis on the separation of duties essential to strong internal control. One recent payroll fraud case in a huge company was linked with a well-publicized change in income tax rates. Knowing that employees expected a change in the amount of tax withheld on the officially scheduled date, a computer operator with wide latitude of duties purposely overstated each employee's tax by a few cents and diverted to himself the aggregate of these amounts. Since a very large labor force was involved, the dollar amount of the fraud was quite substantial. This irregularity would not have been possible if reasonable standards for subdivision of duties had been maintained.

In most organizations the payroll activities include the functions of (1) employing workers, (2) timekeeping, (3) payroll preparation and record keeping, and (*4*) the distribution of pay to employees. Internal control will be strengthened if each of these functions is handled by a separate department of the company.

EMPLOYMENT (PERSONNEL) DEPARTMENT The work of the employment or personnel department begins with the screening of applicants. For those applicants who appear acceptable, interviews are arranged with the line supervisor for whom they would work. If an applicant is approved by the line supervisor, the personnel department will review the applicant's former employment record. This review will include determining why the applicant left a former job and whether the former employer would re-employ the person.

For each new employee hired, the personnel department should create a record showing the date of employment, the authorized rate of pay, and payroll deductions. The new employee must sign a W-4 form (see page 461) as to number of payroll exemptions and must sign authorizations for any payroll deductions such as union dues, insurance, savings bonds, or other items. Information from these records maintained by the personnel department will be sent to the payroll department to authorize the placing of a new name on the payroll.

Subsequent changes in pay rates and the termination of employees will also be entered in personnel department records. The performance of these steps by the personnel department does not prevent job applicants from being interviewed in various departments of the company, but these steps do ensure that names and rates which appear on the payroll *will be properly authorized prior to any payment.*

The personnel department may also carry on a continuous program of job evaluation to determine that each employee's current rate of pay is in conformity with his or her qualifications, with the duties assigned, and with the terms of a union contract, if any. Such internal control procedures help avoid inequitable pay rates, management-labor disputes, and possible violations of federal wage laws or contractual agreements.

Before a person's employment is terminated, the personnel department should conduct a "termination" or "exit" interview to determine why the employee is resigning, or to explain the reasons for layoff or dismissal. Upon completion of the interview, the personnel department will give written notification to the payroll department to remove the employee's name from the payroll, thus providing a control against the continuance of former employees on the payroll. To ensure that the responsibilities involved in the employment function are carried out, it is important that someone be appointed as personnel administrator to direct these related activities.

TIMEKEEPING For employees paid by the hour, it is desirable that the hours of arrival and departure be punched on time cards, unless the business is small enough that the owner-manager can easily maintain a written record of employee hours worked. A time clock should be located at the entrance to the store or factory, along with a rack of time cards. A new time card for each employee is placed in the rack at the beginning of each week or other pay period. Each employee entering the building will remove his or her time card from the rack and insert it in the time clock to be punched. Date and time of arrival are automatically stamped on the time card. Procedures should be designed to ensure that each employee punches his or her own time card and no other. At the end of the workday, the employee punches out in the same manner. The time cards are thus *source documents* showing for each employee the hours on the job.

For salaried personnel, a weekly or monthly time report may replace the time card. The timekeeping function should be lodged in a separate department which will control the time cards and transmit these source documents to the payroll department.

THE PAYROLL DEPARTMENT The input of information to the payroll department consists of hours reported by the timekeeping department, and authorized names, pay rates, and payroll deductions received from the personnel department. The output of the payroll department includes (1) payroll checks, (2) individual employee records of earnings and deductions, and (3) regular reports to the government showing the earnings of employees and taxes withheld.

DISTRIBUTION OF PAYCHECKS The paychecks prepared in the payroll department may be transmitted to the treasurer for signature. The signed paychecks may be given to the personnel administrator for distribution to employees. In larger companies the position of paymaster may be created under the treasurer's supervision. The paymaster would then distribute paychecks to employees. Paychecks for absent employees should never be turned over to other employees or to supervisors for delivery. Instead, the absent employee should pick up the paycheck at the personnel department after presenting proper identification and signing a receipt.

Other uses of payroll records

We have already stressed that federal and state laws require the maintenance and retention of detailed payroll records. In addition, good payroll records are often useful to personnel specialists in dealing with employee grievances, authorizing vacations and sick leaves, and determining eligibility for retirement pensions. In negotiations with labor unions, the development from the records of complete information concerning total labor costs and trends in wage rates is a necessary preliminary step.

Distinction between employees and independent contractors

Every business obtains personal services from *employees* and also from *independent contractors.* The distinction between the two groups is important because payroll systems, taxes, reports, and records cover *employees* only. The employer-employee relationship exists when the business or individual paying for the services has a right to direct and supervise the performance of the person rendering the services.

Certified public accountants performing an annual audit for a company must determine independently the scope and character of their investigation; they are not controlled or supervised by the client company. Consequently, the CPA is an independent contractor and not an employee. However, if a CPA should leave the practice of public accounting and accept a position as controller of a company, he or she would become an employee. Another example of an independent contractor is a typist who types term papers for college students, using her own typewriter and supplies and working in her own office or home. The *fees* paid to independent contractors are distinct from *salaries* and *wages;* they are not included in payroll records and are not subject to withholding.

Compensation to employees on an hourly rate or on a piecework basis is usually called *wages.* Compensation on a monthly or yearly basis is usually referred to as *salary.* The *hourly payroll* for wages is often prepared separately from the *monthly salary payroll* as a matter of convenience in computation, but both are subject to the same tax rules. In practice, one often finds the terms *wages* and *salaries* used interchangeably.

Employee earnings

Employers engaged in interstate commerce are required by the Federal Fair Labor Standards Act (also known as the Wages and Hours Law) to pay overtime at a minimum rate of $1\frac{1}{2}$ times the regular rate for hours worked in excess of 40 per week. Many companies also pay overtime premium rates for night shifts and for work on Sundays and holidays. Union contracts often require the payment of double time for work on Sundays and holidays and time and one-half for hours worked in excess of eight on any single day. Since wages earned are now commonly based on hours worked at various rates, the function of timekeeping has become of increased importance. Time clocks and time cards are widely used in compiling the detailed information required for payroll purposes.

Deductions from earnings of employees

The take-home pay of most employees is considerably less than the gross earnings. Major factors explaining this difference between the amount earned and the amount received are social security taxes, federal income taxes withheld, and other deductions discussed below.

Social security taxes (FICA)

Under the terms of the Social Security Act, qualified workers in covered industries who retire after reaching a specified age receive monthly retirement payments and Medicare benefits. Benefits are also provided for the family of a worker who dies before or after reaching this retirement age. Funds for the operation of this program are obtained through taxes levied under the Federal Insurance Contributions Act, often referred to as FICA taxes, or simply as *social security taxes.*

Employers are required by the Federal Insurance Contributions Act to withhold a portion of each employee's earnings as a contribution to the social security program. A tax at the same rate is levied against the employer. For example, assume that an employee earns $10,000 subject to FICA taxes of 6%. The employer will withhold $600 ($10,000 × .06) from the employee's earnings. The employer will then pay to the government the amount of $1,200, consisting of the $600 withheld from the employee plus an additional $600 of tax on the employer.

Two factors are involved in computing the FICA tax: the *base* or amount of earnings subject to tax, and the *rate* which is applied to the base. Both the base and the rate have been increased many times in recent years and probably will continue to be changed in future years. The following table indicates that individuals were required to pay approximately 18 times as much in 1977 as they were 25 years earlier.

Year	Base (Earnings Subject to FICA Tax)	Tax Rate	Amount of Tax
1937	$ 3,000	1.0%	$ 30
1951	3,600	1.5%	54
1966	6,600	4.2%	277
1972	9,000	5.2%	468
1977	16,500	5.85%	965
1980	?	?	?

These changes in rates and in the base do not affect the accounting principles or procedures involved. For illustrative purposes in this book, we shall assume the rate of tax to be 6% on both the employee and the employer, applicable to a base of $15,000 (the first $15,000 of wages received by each employee in each calendar year). This assumption of round amounts for both the tax and the base is a convenient one for the purpose of illustrations and for the solution of problems by the student, regardless of frequent changes in the rate and base.

Federal income taxes

Our pay-as-you-go system of federal income tax requires employers to withhold a portion of the earnings of their employees. The amount withheld depends upon the amount of the earnings and upon the number of exemptions to which the employee is entitled. Each new employee is asked to file a withholding exemption certificate (Form W-4) as illustrated below:

Form **W-4**	**Employee's Withholding Allowance Certificate**	
(Rev. Dec. 1975) Department of the Treasury Internal Revenue Service	(This certificate is for income tax withholding purposes only; it will remain in effect until you change it.)	

Type or print your full name

Rita Miller

	Your social security number
	572 — 19 -4627

Home address (Number and street or rural route)

3819 Hoover Street

City or town, State and ZIP code

Los Angeles, Calif. 90007

Marital status
☐ Single   ☒ Married
(If married but legally separated, or spouse is a nonresident alien, check the single block.)

1 Total number of allowances you are claiming . . . . | *2*

2 Additional amount, if any, you want deducted from each pay (if your employer agrees) . . . . | $ —

I certify that to the best of my knowledge and belief, the number of withholding allowances claimed on this certificate does not exceed the number to which I am entitled.

Signature ▶ *Rita Miller*   Date ▶ *January 2*, 19 —

The exemption certificate (Form W-4) states the number of exemptions claimed by the employee. Each employee is entitled to one exemption for himself, and an additional exemption for each person qualifying as a dependent. The employee may file a new certificate if the number of dependents changes. Persons over sixty-five or blind are entitled to additional exemptions. (More extensive consideration of exemptions and of other aspects of federal income taxes will be discussed in Chapter 20.) The exemption certificate is given to the employing company so that it will be able to compute the proper amount of tax to be withheld. As a matter of convenience to employers, the government provides withholding tax tables which indicate the amount to withhold for any amount of earnings and any number of exemptions.

Present regulations provide a graduated system of withholding, designed to make the amount of tax withheld closely approximate the rates used in computing the individual's tax liability at the end of the year. Since persons in higher income brackets are subject to higher rates of taxation, the withholding rates are correspondingly higher for them.

States or cities which levy income taxes may also require the employer to withhold the tax from employees' earnings, but as such situations involve a variety of rates, they will not be discussed here.

OTHER DEDUCTIONS FROM EMPLOYEES' EARNINGS Programs of unemployment compensation insurance are found in every state, but they are generally financed by taxes on employers rather than on employees. In a few states unemployment insurance taxes are levied on employees and such taxes are withheld by employers from employees' earnings.

In addition to the compulsory deductions for taxes, many other deductions are voluntarily authorized by employees. Union dues, insurance premiums, and savings bond purchases have already been mentioned as examples of payroll deductions. Others include charitable contributions, supplementary retirement programs and pension plans, and repayments of payroll advances or other loans.

EMPLOYER'S RESPONSIBILITY FOR AMOUNTS WITHHELD When an employing company withholds a portion of an employee's earnings for any reason, it must maintain accounting records which will enable it to file required reports and make designated payments of the funds withheld. From the employer's viewpoint, most amounts withheld from employees' earnings represent current liabilities. In other words, the employing company must pay to the government or some other agency the amounts which it withholds from the employee's earnings. An exception would be the deductions made from an employee's pay to liquidate a previous loan to the employee. A statement of earnings and deductions is usually prepared by the employer and presented to the employee with each paycheck or pay envelope to explain how the net pay was determined.

Illustration: computation of employee's net pay

This illustration shows the deductions which typically may explain the difference between *gross earnings* for a pay period and the "take-home" pay, or net amount received by an employee. The deductions are in part based upon the two exemptions indicated in Rita Miller's Employee's Withholding Exemption Certificate illustrated previously. The pay period is for the month of May.

Computing the take-home pay	*Gross earnings of employee Miller for the month*	*$1,500.00*
	Deductions:	
	FICA tax (assume 6%) . . . . $ 90.00	
	Federal income tax 226.70	
	Retirement plan (assume 4%) 60.00	
	Group insurance 22.20	
	Total deductions from Miller's earnings	*398.90*
	Net take-home pay for the month for employee Rita Miller	*$1,101.10*

In the preceding illustration, the inclusion of the FICA deduction shows that Rita Miller's earnings thus far in the calendar year had not reached the $15,000 maximum earnings assumed to be subject to FICA taxes. Since Miller earns $1,500 a month, her take-home pay of $1,101.10 can be expected to rise by $90 after October when her gross earnings will have reached the $15,000 limitation.

The amount of federal income tax withheld, $226.70, was determined by reference to the wage bracket for a married taxpayer with two exemptions as shown in the withholding schedules published each year by the

Internal Revenue Service. The other two deductions from gross earnings (for a retirement plan and for group insurance) were voluntary and had been authorized in writing by Rita Miller.

Payroll records and procedures

Although payroll records and procedures vary greatly according to the number of employees and the extent of automation in processing payroll data, there are a few fundamental steps common to payroll work in most organizations. One of these steps taken at the end of each pay period is the preparation of a payroll showing the names and earnings of all employees. The information entered in this payroll record (often called a *payroll register*) will include the authorized rate of pay for each employee and the number of hours worked, taken from time cards or similar documents. After separating the regular hours from overtime hours and applying appropriate pay rates for each category, the total taxable earnings are determined. Federal income tax, FICA tax, and any items authorized by the employee are then deducted to arrive at the net amount payable. When the computation of the payroll sheet has been completed, the next step is to reflect the expense and the related liabilities in the ledger accounts. A general journal entry such as shown below may be made to bring into the accounts the payroll and the deductions from *employees'* earnings; this entry does not include payroll taxes on the employer.

Entry to	Sales Salaries Expense	2,200	
record	Office Salaries Expense	1,800	
payroll	FICA Taxes Payable		240
	Liability for Income Tax Withheld		830
	Group Insurance Payments Withheld		100
	Accrued Payroll		2,830

To record the payroll and related deductions for the pay period ended Jan. 15.

The two debits to expense accounts indicate that the business has incurred a total salary expense of $4,000; however, only $2,830 of this amount will be paid to the employees. The remaining $1,170 (consisting of deductions for taxes and insurance premiums withheld) is credited to liability accounts. Payment of these liabilities will be made at various later dates.

PAYMENT OF EMPLOYEES The preceding section illustrated the recording of the payroll and showed the sum of $2,830 in a current liability account entitled Accrued Payroll. The procedures for the actual payment to employees to discharge this liability will depend upon whether the company pays salaries by checks on the regular bank account, by checks drawn on a special bank account, or in cash. These payment procedures also depend on whether a voucher system is in use.

The advantages of establishing a separate payroll bank account were discussed in Chapter 8. At the close of each pay period, a check is drawn on the general bank account for the entire amount of the payroll and deposited in the payroll bank account. Paychecks to individual employees are then drawn on the payroll bank account, which is immediately reduced to zero. If the voucher system is in use, a voucher for the payroll would be prepared and recorded in the voucher register as a debit to Payroll Bank Account and a credit to Vouchers Payable in the amount of $2,830.[1] The transfer of the funds would then be carried out by issuing a check on the general bank account and recording this disbursement in the check register by a debit to Vouchers Payable and a credit to Cash.

PAYMENT OF EMPLOYEES IN CASH Payment of salaries in cash affords less internal control than the use of checks, but it is preferred by a few companies in locations where banks or other check-cashing facilities are not readily available. The recording procedures do not differ significantly from those previously described; a voucher is prepared for the amount of the payroll, and a single check drawn and cashed to obtain the cash to fill the individual pay envelopes. As previously mentioned, a statement of earnings and deductions is usually furnished to the employee each payday. When payment is made by check, this information is printed on a stub attached to the paycheck. When wages are paid in cash, the information is usually printed on the pay envelope.

WITHHOLDING STATEMENT By January 31 each year, employers are required to furnish every employee with a withholding statement (Form W-2), illustrated below. This form shows the gross earnings for the preceding calendar year and the amounts withheld for FICA tax and income

For Official Use Only		Wage and Tax Statement	1976
95-2215683 Wilton Company 690 Delta Drive Sacramento, Calif. 95841		Type or print EMPLOYER'S name, address, ZIP code and Federal identifying number.	Copy A For Internal Revenue Service Center
			Employer's State identifying number 900-0096-4

	Employee's social security number	1 Federal income tax withheld	2 Wages, tips, and other compensation	3 FICA employee tax withheld	4 Total FICA wages
21 ☐	572-19-4627	$3,750.00	$18,000.00	$895.00	$15,300.00

	Type or print Employee's name, address, and ZIP code below. (Name must aline with arrow)	5 Was employee covered by a qualified pension plan, etc.?	6 °	7 °
Name ►	Rita Miller 403 College Ave. Sacramento, Calif. 95841	Yes		
		8 State or local tax withheld	9 State or local wages	10 State or locality
		$410.40	$18,000.00	Calif.
		11 State or local tax withheld	12 State or local wages	13 State or locality

° See instructions on back of Copy D

Form **W-2** See instructions on Form W-3 and back of Copy D Department of the Treasury—Internal Revenue Service

---

[1] No vouchers need be prepared at this time for the $1,170 of liabilities resulting from deductions. Vouchers will be prepared prior to the time for payment of these liabilities.

tax. The employer sends one copy of this form to the Director of Internal Revenue and gives three copies to the employee. When the employee files a federal income tax return, he or she must attach a copy of the withholding statement. A copy must also be attached to the state income tax return.

EMPLOYER'S QUARTERLY FEDERAL TAX RETURN An employer is required to report to the government detailed information about payrolls every three months. This report, Form 941, illustrated on page 466, includes the names and social security numbers of all employees, the amount of wages earned by each, FICA taxes, and federal income taxes. The employer makes frequent deposits through a commercial bank of amounts due to the government for taxes withheld from employees and the FICA tax on the employer.

INDIVIDUAL EARNINGS RECORDS FOR EMPLOYEES At the end of each payroll period, it is essential to have available the cumulative amount of each employee's earnings for the year to date. Otherwise, the employer would not know whether FICA taxes should be withheld from the earnings by the employee during the current week or month. An Individual Employee's Earnings Record is illustrated on page 467.

This detailed record also shows for each employee the gross earnings for each pay period, the portion, if any, not subject to FICA tax, the deduction for FICA tax, the income tax withheld, other deductions authorized by the employee, and the amount of net pay. These employee earnings records are also used by employers in preparing the quarterly and annual reports which they must file with federal and state authorities. A variety of other uses may occur such as calculating bonuses, or proving compliance with the Federal Wages and Hours Law.

Payroll taxes on the employer

The discussion of payroll taxes up to this point has dealt with taxes levied on employees and withheld from their pay. From the viewpoint of the employing company, such taxes are significant because it must account for and remit the amounts withheld to the appropriate government offices. Payroll taxes are also levied on the *employer;* these taxes are expenses of the business and are recorded by debits to expense accounts, just as in the case of property taxes or license fees for doing business.

FICA TAX The employer is taxed to help finance the social security program. The tax is figured at the same rate and on the same amount of earnings used to compute FICA tax on employees. (In all problems and illustrations in this book, the tax is assumed to be 6% on the first $15,000 of gross earnings by each employee in each calendar year.)

Form **941** (Rev. Jan. 1976) Department of the Treasury Internal Revenue Service	**Employer's Quarterly Federal Tax Return**	**SSA Use Only**

Schedule A—Quarterly Report of Wages Taxable under the Federal Insurance Contributions Act—FOR SOCIAL SECURITY

List for each nonagricultural employee the WAGES taxable under the FICA which were paid during the quarter. If you pay an employee more than $15,300 in a calendar year, report only the first $15,300 of such wages. In the case of "Tip Income," see instructions on page 4. IF WAGES WERE NOT TAXABLE UNDER THE FICA, MAKE NO ENTRIES IN ITEMS 1 THROUGH 9 AND 14 THROUGH 18.

SSA Use Only:
F ☐ 2 ☐ U ☐ E ☐
S ☐ 1 ☐ L ☐ T ☐
X ☐ 0 ☐ V ☐ A ☐

1. Total pages of this return including this page and any pages of Form 941a ▶ **1**	2. Total number of employees listed ▶ **3**	3. (First quarter only) Number of employees (except household) employed in the pay period including March 12th ▶ **3**

4. EMPLOYEE'S SOCIAL SECURITY NUMBER	5. NAME OF EMPLOYEE (Please type or print)	6. TAXABLE FICA WAGES Paid to Employee in Quarter (Before deductions) Dollars / Cents	7. TAXABLE TIPS REPORTED (See page 4) Dollars / Cents
000 00 0000 ▼		▼	
562 32 4197	Janet Kay Hall	3,600.00	
560 18 8462	Robert Hale Downs	4,500.00	
572 19 4627	Rita Miller	4,500.00	

If you need more space for listing employees, use Schedule A continuation sheets, Form 941a.
Totals for this page—Wage total in column 6 and tip total in column 7 ⟶ **12,600.00** | **-0-**

8. TOTAL WAGES TAXABLE UNDER FICA PAID DURING QUARTER. $ **12,600.00** ◁
(Total of column 6 on this page and continuation sheets.) Enter here and in item 14 below.

9. TOTAL TAXABLE TIPS REPORTED UNDER FICA DURING QUARTER. $ **-0-** ◁
(Total of column 7 on this page and continuation sheets.) Enter here and in item 15 below. (If no tips reported, write "None.")

Name (as distinguished from trade name) **John Wilton**	Date quarter ended **March 31, 1977**

Employer's name, address, employer identification number, and calendar quarter. (If not correct, please change)

Trade name, if any ▶ **Wilton Company**   Employer Identification No. **95-2215683**
Address and ZIP code **690 Delta Drive, Sacramento, Calif. 95841**
Entries must be made both above and below this line; if address different from previous return, check here ☐

Name (as distinguished from trade name) **John Wilton**	Date quarter ended **March 31, 1977**

Trade name, if any ▶ **Wilton Company**   Employer Identification No. **95-2215683**
Address and ZIP code **690 Delta Drive, Sacramento, Calif. 95841**

T | FP
FF | I
FD | TOT

10. Total Wages And Tips Subject To Withholding Plus Other Compensation ⟶	12,600 00
11. Amount Of Income Tax Withheld From Wages, Tips, Annuities, etc. (See instructions)	2,600 00
12. Adjustment For Preceding Quarters Of Calendar Year	
13. Adjusted Total Of Income Tax Withheld ⟶	2,600 00
14. Taxable FICA Wages Paid (Item 8) . . $ 12,600.00 multiplied by 11.7%=TAX	1,474 20
15. Taxable Tips Reported (Item 9) . . $ multiplied by 5.85%=TAX	
16. Total FICA Taxes (Item 14 plus item 15) ⟶	1,474 20
17. Adjustment (See instructions)	
18. Adjusted Total Of FICA Taxes	1,474 20
19. Total Taxes (Item 13 plus Item 18)	4,074 20
20. TOTAL DEPOSITS FOR QUARTER (INCLUDING FINAL DEPOSIT MADE FOR QUARTER) AND OVERPAYMENT	4,074 20

Note: If undeposited taxes at the end of the quarter are $200 or more, the full amount must be deposited with an authorized commercial bank or a Federal Reserve bank. This deposit must be entered in Schedule B and included in item 20.

21. Undeposited Taxes Due (Item 19 Less Item 20—This Should Be Less Than $200). Pay To Internal Revenue Service And Enter Here ▶

22. If Item 20 Is More Than 19, Enter Excess Here ▶ $ And Check If You Want It ☐ Applied to Next Return, Or ☐ Refunded.

23. If not liable for returns in the future write "FINAL" (See instructions) ▶   Date final wages paid ▶

Under penalties of perjury, I declare that I have examined this return, including accompanying schedules and statements, and to the best of my knowledge and belief it is true, correct, and complete.
Date **April 10, 1977**   Signature _____   Title (Owner, etc) **Owner**

Form 941 (1—76)

INDIVIDUAL EMPLOYEE'S EARNINGS RECORD

Employee's Name _____ Social Security No. _____

Address _____ Date of Birth _____

_____ Date Employed _____

Position _____ Date Terminated _____

Number of Exemptions _____ Rate of Pay _____

Pay Period Ended	Total Hours	Earnings				Deductions					Net Pay
		Regular	Over-time	Total	Cumula-tive Total	FICA Tax	Federal Income Tax	Other	Total		
Total 1st Qtr											
Total for Year											

FEDERAL UNEMPLOYMENT INSURANCE TAX Unemployment insurance is another part of the national social security program designed to offer temporary relief to unemployed persons. The FUTA tax (Federal Unemployment Tax Act) is levied on *employers* only and is not deducted from the wages of employees. The FUTA tax (also known as "unemployment compensation" or UC) applies to approximately the same classes of employment as the FICA tax. Employers of one or more persons in nonexempt employment are subject to the tax. The rates of tax and the wage base subject to the tax are changed from time to time. For purposes of illustration in this book, we shall assume that employers of one or more persons are subject to federal unemployment tax at the rate of 3.2% on the first $4,200 of each employee's earnings in each calendar year. However, the employer may take a credit against this tax (not in excess of 90% of the first 3% of the federal tax) for amounts that are paid into state unemployment funds. Under this provision, the employer actually makes payment of the larger part of the FUTA tax directly to state governments which carry out the federal-state unemployment insurance program.

This arrangement means that the FUTA tax is divided into two parts: the larger part, or 2.7% (.90 × .03), of the first $4,200 of wages paid going to the state and the remainder to the federal government. Some states use a merit-rating plan enabling those employers who maintain stable work forces to pay a reduced rate of state unemployment tax. Under the merit-rating plans of some states, an employer whose employees have applied for little or no unemployment compensation may be rewarded with a rate of perhaps 1 to 2% rather than the standard 2.7%. In computing the federal unemployment compensation tax, the employer company will still receive credit for the full 2.7% it would have been required to pay the state if it had not qualified as a superior risk.

To illustrate the merit-rating plan, assume that an employee working for an employer with a favorable merit rating earns $12,000 of wages and that the employer is required by the state to pay only 1.5 rather than 2.7%. The total unemployment tax (both state and federal) would then be $84, computed as $4,200 × (.015 + .005). The $84 tax would be divided $63 to the state and $21 to the federal government. If the employer had not qualified for a favorable merit rating, the total tax would have been $134.40 with $113.40 going to the state and the same $21 to the federal government.

As a separate example, and without taking a merit-rating plan into account, consider the common situation in which an employee working for a covered employer (one or more employees) earns wages of $10,000. The employer would pay a total unemployment compensation tax of $134.40 ($4,200 × .032), of which $113.40 ($4,200 × .027) would be paid to the state and $21 ($4,200 × .005) would be paid to the federal government.

ACCOUNTING ENTRY FOR EMPLOYER'S PAYROLL TAXES The entry to record the employer's payroll taxes is usually made at the same time the payroll is recorded. To illustrate, let us use again the $4,000 payroll first used on page 463 in the discussion of amounts withheld from employees; this time, however, we are illustrating taxes levied on the *employer,* as follows:

Entry for payroll taxes on employer	*Payroll Taxes Expense* 368	
	FICA Taxes Payable ($4,000 × .06)	240
	State Unemployment Taxes Payable ($4,000 × .027)	108
	Federal Unemployment Taxes Payable ($4,000 × .005)	20
	To record payroll taxes on employer for pay period ended Jan. 15.	

None of the employees has as yet reached the $4,200 level of cumulative earnings constituting the base for federal unemployment taxes. Consequently, the illustrated entry shows all three taxes (FICA, federal unemployment taxes, and state unemployment taxes) being applied to the full $4,000 of the company's payroll for this period early in the year.

Combined entry for payroll and all related taxes and deductions

The preceding illustration shows the recording of taxes on the *employer,* whereas the entry illustrated on page 463 showed the recording of the payroll (wages earned) and the amounts withheld as taxes and other deductions from employees. Let us now combine these two illustrative entries into one entry which will record the $4,000 total payroll and all taxes and deductions applicable to both the employer and the employees.

The total	Sales Salaries Expense	2,200	
package:	Office Salaries Expense	1,800	
salaries,			
taxes on	Payroll Taxes Expense $4,000 × (.06 + .027 + .005)	368	
employer,	FICA Taxes Payable ($4,000 × .12)		480
and			
amounts	State Unemployment Taxes Payable ($4,000 × .027)		108
withheld	Federal Unemployment Taxes Payable ($4,000 × .005)		20
from			
employees	Liability for Income Tax Withheld		830
	Group Insurance Payments Withheld		100
	Accrued Payroll		2,830

To record payroll, payroll taxes expense, and amounts withheld from employees for pay period ended Jan. 15.

In studying this illustrated entry, note that the employer's basic payroll expense of $2,200 in sales salaries and $1,800 in office salaries, or $4,000 in total salaries is increased by $368 to a total payroll expense of $4,368.

Accrual of payroll taxes at year-end

The payroll taxes levied against an employer become a legal liability when wages are actually paid, rather than at the time the services by employees are rendered. If the wages earned in a given accounting period are paid in the same period, the payroll tax expense is clearly applicable to that period. However, at year-end, most businesses make an adjusting entry to accrue wages earned by employees but not payable until the following period. Should the related payroll taxes on the employer also be accrued? Logically, both wages and taxes on such wages are an expense of the period in which the wages are earned and should therefore be accrued. However, as a practical matter, many businesses do not accrue the payroll tax expense because legally the liability does not come into being until the following year when the wages are paid. In determining income subject to federal income tax, the legal concept prevails, and payroll tax cannot be deducted until the period in which paid. As a matter of convenience, many companies want their accounting records and their income tax returns to agree as closely as possible; therefore such companies prefer *not to accrue* payroll tax on employers. This conflict between the logic of accounting principles and the administrative conveniences built into income tax laws appears in many other areas of accounting apart from payroll taxes.

Presentation of payroll taxes in the financial statements

The payroll taxes levied on the employer and the taxes withheld from employees are current liabilities of the business until payment to the government is made. The following accounts are, therefore, classified in the balance sheet as current liabilities: FICA Taxes Payable, Federal Unemployment Taxes Payable, State Unemployment Taxes Payable, and Liability for Income Tax Withheld.

Payroll Taxes Expense appears in the income statement: it may be apportioned between selling expenses and general expenses on the basis of the amount of payroll originating in each functional division. Thus, payroll tax on salaries of the sales staff is classified as a selling expense, and payroll tax on office salaries is classified as a general and administrative expense.

Payment of payroll taxes

A business must use the calendar year in accounting for payroll taxes, even though it uses a fiscal year for its financial statements and its income tax returns. Four times a year, the employer is required to report to the government the amounts withheld from employees' pay for income taxes and FICA taxes. The FICA tax on the employer is also reported on the same tax form. These reports are made during the month following the close of each quarter of the year. If the amounts withheld from employees plus payroll taxes on the employer are significant in amount, they must be deposited at very frequent intervals with a Federal Reserve bank or a commercial bank. However, if the total amount involved is less than $200 at the end of a calendar quarter, it may be paid with the tax return.

The employer must file a federal unemployment tax return by January 31 of each year for the preceding calendar year. Most states require employers to make payment of the state unemployment compensation tax on a monthly basis and to file tax returns for each quarter of the year.

KEY TERMS INTRODUCED OR EMPHASIZED IN CHAPTER 13

Employee's individual earnings record A record maintained for each employee summarizing gross earnings, deductions, net pay, and other payroll information.

Employee's withholding exemption certificate (W-4) A federal form prepared by the employee and given to the employer stating the number of withholding exemptions claimed. Used in determining the amount of income tax to be withheld from the employee's pay.

Employer's quarterly federal tax return (941) A report prepared every three months by the employer to provide the federal government with a record of all wages paid, amounts withheld, and amounts of tax on both employees and employer.

Federal unemployment compensation tax (FUTA) A tax imposed on the employer by the Federal Unemployment Tax Act based on amount of payrolls. Designed to provide temporary payments to unemployed persons.

FICA tax A tax imposed by the Federal Insurance Contribution Act on both employer and employees. Used to finance the social security program.

Gross earnings Total amount earned by an employee before deductions such as social security taxes, federal income tax withheld, and any voluntary deductions.

Independent contractor A person or firm providing services to a company for a fee or commission. Not controlled or supervised by the client company. Not subject to payroll taxes.

Payroll A record listing the names of employees during a given pay period, the rates of pay, time worked, gross earnings, deductions for taxes and any other amounts withheld, and net pay.

Payroll register A form of payroll record showing for each pay period all payroll information for employees individually and in total.

Salaries Compensation on a monthly or yearly basis to employees performing administrative, managerial, or professional duties.

Social security taxes FICA and FUTA taxes based on payrolls and intended to provide funds for operation of benefit programs in which monthly retirement payments and Medicare benefits are paid to qualified workers in covered industries, as well as benefits to the family of a worker who dies prior to reaching retirement age.

State unemployment compensation tax A tax levied on employers only and based on payrolls. A part of the joint federal-state program to provide payments to unemployed persons.

Wages Compensation to employees computed at an hourly rate or on a piece-work basis.

Withholding statement (W-2) A form furnished by the employer to every employee showing the gross earnings for the calendar year and the amounts withheld for social security and income tax.

Withholding tables Tables provided by federal and state governments showing amounts of federal and state income tax to be withheld from employees' pay.

REVIEW QUESTIONS

1 Name the federal taxes that most employers are required to withhold from employees. What account or accounts would be credited with the amounts withheld?

2 Distinguish between an employee and an independent contractor. Why is this distinction important with respect to payroll accounting?

3 Explain which of the following taxes relating to an employee's wages are borne by the employee and which by the employer:
   a FICA taxes
   b Federal unemployment compensation taxes
   c State unemployment compensation taxes
   d Federal income taxes

4 List four kinds of information which constitute input to the payroll accounting system and four kinds of information included in the output of the payroll system.

5 That type of payroll fraud known as "padding" a payroll is a more difficult maneuver under today's payroll accounting practices than it was a generation or more ago. What present-day factors make the padding of payrolls a complex and more difficult type of fraud?

6 Is Salary Expense equal to "take-home" pay or to gross earnings? Why?

7 When and for what purpose is an Employee's Withholding Exemption Certificate obtained?

8 What purposes are served by maintaining a detailed earnings record for each employee?

9 Are the payroll taxes levied against employers considered a legal liability and a deductible expense in the period the wages are earned by the employees or in the period the wages are paid?

EXERCISES

Ex. 13-1 The payroll of Olympic Company may be summarized as follows:

Gross earnings of employees	$300,000
Employee earnings not subject to FICA tax	48,000
Employee earnings not subject to FUTA tax	75,000

Assuming that the payroll is subject to an FICA tax rate of 6%, a 2.7% state unemployment tax rate, and an FUTA tax rate of .5 of 1%, compute the amount of the Olympic Company's payroll tax expense for the year, showing separately the amount of each of the three taxes. (Note: Taxes on employees are not involved in this exercise.)

Ex. 13-2 Windsor Milling Company had 100 employees throughout the current year. The lowest-paid employee had gross earnings of $5,000. Assume that the Federal Unemployment Tax Act specifies a rate of 3.2% on the first $4,200 of gross earnings, and that the state unemployment tax is 2.7% of the same base. The employer is permitted to take as a credit against the federal tax the 2.7% of wages paid to the state. Compute the following:
a The state unemployment tax for the year
b The federal unemployment tax for the year
c The total unemployment tax for the year

Ex. 13-3 Martin earns a salary of $18,000 a year from Rand Corporation. FICA taxes are 6% of wages up to $15,000. Federal unemployment taxes are 3.2% of wages up to $4,200 a year, but a credit against this FUTA tax is permitted for payment to the state of 2.7% of wages up to $4,200 a year. Federal income tax of $3,600 was withheld from Martin's paychecks during the year.
a Prepare in general journal form a compound entry summarizing the payroll transactions for employee Martin for the full year. (In drafting this entry, ignore any payments of tax during the year and let the liability accounts show the totals for the year. Credit Cash for the amount paid to Martin.)
b What is the total yearly cost (including taxes) to Rand Corporation of having Martin on the payroll at an annual salary of $18,000?

Ex. 13-4 Ruth Cohen is employed at a base rate of $5 an hour by a company subject to the Fair Labor Standards Act (Wages and Hours Law). The only deductions for Cohen are FICA taxes and $39.80 for federal income taxes. During the first week in January Cohen worked 45 hours. You are to prepare a schedule showing her regular pay, overtime premium pay, gross earnings for the week, FICA tax deduction (assume a 6% rate), federal income tax deduction, and net pay.

Ex. 13-5 The payroll record of Miller Company for the week ended January 7 showed the following amounts for total earnings: sales employees $8,800; office employees $7,200. Amounts withheld consisted of FICA taxes at a 6% rate on all earnings for this period, federal income taxes $1,920, and medical insurance $600.
a After computing the amount of FICA taxes withheld, prepare a general journal entry to record the payroll. Do not include taxes on the employer.
b Prepare a general journal entry to record the payroll taxes expense to Miller

Company relating to this payroll. Assume that the federal unemployment tax rate is 3.2% of the first $4,200 paid each employee, and that 2.7% of this tax is payable to the state. No employee received more than $4,200 in this first pay period of the year.

PROBLEMS

Group A

13A-1 During January, Beverly Corporation incurred salaries expense of $11,200, classified as follows: $8,000 of salaries expense for the sales force, and $3,200 salaries expense for office personnel.

FICA taxes were withheld from employees' earnings at an assumed rate of 6%. Other amounts withheld were $1,500 for federal income taxes and $180 for group insurance premiums.

Instructions
a Prepare a general journal entry to record the payroll and the deductions from employees' earnings. Do not include payroll taxes on the employer in this journal entry.
b Prepare a general journal entry to record the payroll taxes on the *employer* as a result of the above payroll. Assume an FICA tax of 6%, a state unemployment tax of 2.7%, and a federal unemployment tax of .5% on the entire payroll.
c Prepare a combined general journal entry which will record the total payroll and all taxes and deductions applicable to both the employer and employees. This combined entry could be used instead of the entries called for in a and b above.
d What is the total payroll expense of Beverly Corporation for January? Show computations.

13A-2 Friendly Finance Company makes small loans through a network of more than 100 branch offices in several states. A branch manager is in charge of each office and the number of employees under the manager's supervision is usually from four to seven. Each branch manager prepares a weekly payroll sheet, including his or her own salary. All employees are paid from cash on hand. The employees sign the payroll sheet signifying receipt of their salaries. Hours worked by hourly personnel are inserted in the payroll sheet from time cards prepared by the employees and approved by the manager.

The weekly payroll sheets are sent to the home office along with other accounting statements and reports. The home office compiles employee earnings records and prepares all federal and state salary reports from the payroll sheets.

Salaries are established by home office job evaluation schedules. Salary adjustments, promotions, and transfers of full-time employees are approved by a home office salary committee based upon recommendations of branch managers and area supervisors. Branch managers advise the salary committee of new full-time employees and terminations. Part-time and temporary employees are hired without referral to the salary committee.

Instructions After evaluation of the company's payroll system, especially the internal control features, suggest five ways in which the branch managers might carry out payroll fraud. (AICPA adapted.)

13A-3 Because of its record of stable employment, Safety Products qualifies under a state merit-rating plan which permits a company to pay a reduced state unemployment tax rate if its employees have collected little or no unemployment insurance. Safety Products qualifies under the merit-rating plan for a rate of 1.2% rather than the usual 2.7% of gross earnings.

The employees' earnings records so far in the current year are as follows:

Employee	Cumula- tive Earnings	Employee	Cumula- tive Earnings
Axler, C. F.	$8,593	Hart, P. W.	$ 5,261
Cox, R. M.	7,121	Kelly, P. T.	19,890
Ford, G. A.	1,530	Loe, S. B.	2,358
Gamble, E. H.	3,701	Pratt, L. M.	6,039

The FICA taxes are assumed to be 6% on the first $15,000 of gross earnings. The rate of federal unemployment tax is assumed to be 3.2% on the first $4,200 of gross earnings, but with credit to the employer for a maximum of 2.7% of gross earnings for state unemployment taxes.

Instructions
a Prepare a three-column schedule showing for each employee the following amounts: cumulative earnings (as given), earnings subject to unemployment compensation tax, and earnings subject to FICA taxes. As an example, the first line of the schedule would show for Axler, C. F. the following three amounts: $8,593, $4,200, and $8,593.
b Some payroll taxes are levied on the employee and some on the employer. Use the information shown in **a** above to compute the total payroll taxes *deducted* from the earnings of the employees as a group. (Income taxes are not involved in this problem.)
c Compute the total payroll taxes levied on the employer, Safety Products, and the percentage of the total payroll represented by this payroll tax. Round amounts to the nearest tenth of a percent.

13A-4 High Tide Company adjusts and closes its accounts on a calendar-year basis. During the week ended December 31, the gross earnings of the company's office employees amounted to $120,000. Under established company policy, the payment of this payroll would be made to employees on January 3.

The federal income tax to be withheld from the earnings of employees during the last week of December amounted to $16,800. The FICA taxes (6% each on employer and employee) were applicable to only $72,000 of the $120,000 payroll, and unemployment taxes (2.7% state and .5 of 1% federal) were applicable to only $19,200 of the gross earnings for the last week of the year.

Instructions
a In making the adjusting entry for unpaid salaries at December 31, should the payroll taxes be accrued? Explain fully.
b High Tide Company, like many other concerns, prefers to have its accounting records agree with rules by the Internal Revenue Service as to the timing of expense deductions for payroll taxes in computing income taxes payable. In accordance with this company policy, what amount should appear in the balance sheet at December 31 to reflect the liability arising from salaries earned by employees during the last week of the year?
c Assume that the company wishes to accrue all payroll expenses at the year-end, regardless of the deductibility of payroll taxes under income tax rules. Draft a compound journal entry to accrue the payroll at December 31.

13A-5 Plaza Center has six employees; two are paid monthly salaries and the other four are paid an hourly rate with provision for time and one-half for overtime. The basic data for the July 31 payroll are given on page 475.

	Hours			Com- pensation to June 30	Gross Pay Due for July	Federal Income Tax Withheld
Employee	Reg	OT	Pay Rate			
Rausch	160	14	$ 5.40 hr	$ 5,580	$ 977.40	$ 96.66
Sims	160		6.30 hr	6,120	1,008.00	110.52
Tyler	160	21	3.60 hr	4,410	689.40	39.78
Ulmer	Salary		1,296.00 mo	7,776	1,296.00	172.44
Vincent	160		4.05 hr	1,296	648.00	63.72
Wayne	Salary		1,800.00 mo	10,800	1,800.00	167.94

Other data Compensation of Ulmer and Wayne is considered an administrative expense; the balance of the earnings is chargeable to Shop Wages. Payroll taxes apply as follows: FICA, 6% up to maximum of $15,000; state unemployment, 2.7% up to maximum of $4,200; federal unemployment, .5% up to maximum of $4,200. Plaza Center has group insurance and a retirement plan under which all employees contribute 7% of their gross pay and Plaza Center matches this contribution. Both employees' and employer's contributions are deposited with the National Insurance Company at the end of each month. (Round calculations to the nearest cent and disregard one-cent discrepancies due to rounding.)

Instructions
a Prepare a payroll record for July, using the following columns:

	Gross Pay	Amount Subject to		Federal Income Tax Withheld	FICA Tax Withheld	Retire- ment Deduc- tion	Net Pay Due
Employee		Unemploy- ment Taxes	FICA Taxes				

b Explain how the gross pay for Tyler was computed for the month of July.
c Explain why the federal income taxes withheld for Wayne are less than those withheld for Ulmer despite the fact that Wayne received a higher gross compensation.
d Prepare in general journal form the entry to record the payroll for the month of July and the amounts withheld from employees.
e Prepare in general journal form the entry to record the employer's payroll taxes and insurance plan contributions for the month of July.

Group B

13B-1 The payroll records of Mossberg Company for the first week in January showed total salaries earned by employees of $9,600. This total included $5,200 of salaries to sales employees and $4,400 to office employees.

The amounts withheld from employees' pay consisted of FICA taxes computed at an assumed rate of 6%, federal income taxes of $1,150, and group insurance premiums of $140.

Instructions
a Prepare a general journal entry to summarize the above payroll and the deductions from the earnings of employees. Payroll taxes on the employer are not to be included in this entry.
b Prepare a general journal entry to summarize the payroll taxes on the *employer* associated with the above payroll. Assumed tax rates are as follows: FICA tax of 6%, state unemployment tax of 2.7%, and a federal unemployment tax of .5%.

c Prepare a combined general journal entry which records the total payroll and all taxes and deductions applicable to both the employer and the employees. The effect of this entry should be the same as the two separate entries called for in *a* and *b* above.

d What is the amount of the total payroll expense of Mossberg Company for the first week in January? Show computations.

13B-2 Big Burger, a chain of ten drive-in hamburger stands, is a sole proprietorship owned by Jeanne Harris. Although Harris has other business interests, she devotes a portion of her time to management of the drive-in chain. A manager is employed at each of the ten locations and the number of employees varies from six to twelve.

The manager of each unit prepares payroll sheets each week showing hours worked as reported by the employees on time cards which are approved by the manager. Each manager's salary is also listed on the weekly payroll. Upon completion of the payroll, the manager pays all employees and him or herself in cash. Each employee acknowledges receipt of payment by signing the payroll sheet.

Employees at each branch are employed and terminated by the local managers, who also set wage rates. The salaries of the managers are authorized by Jeanne Harris.

Each week the payroll sheets are mailed by the managers to Harris, whose secretary prepares individual earnings records for each employee and compiles federal and state tax returns from the weekly payroll sheets.

Instructions

a What is your general evaluation of the adequacy of internal control over payrolls? State the specific practices, if any, which you think should be changed.

b List four specific ways in which payroll fraud could be carried on by the manager of any of the ten drive-ins.

13B-3 Wilson Company is located in a state which permits a company to pay a reduced state unemployment tax rate if the company's employees have collected little unemployment insurance. Wilson Company has an excellent record of maintaining a stable work force and therefore qualifies under the merit plan for a rate of 1.2% rather than the usual 2.7% of gross earnings.

The employees' earnings records thus far in the current year are as follows:

Employee	Cumula-tive Earnings	Employee	Cumula-tive Earnings
Arthur, D. S.	$14,322	Hamilton, A. J.	$ 8,771
Barnett, S. T.	11,868	Monday, M. D.	17,328
Darwin, E. G.	2,550	Saunders, K. U.	3,930
Greer, C. K.	6,167	Taylor, M. E.	10,065

FICA taxes are assumed to be 6% on the first $15,000 of an employee's gross earnings. The federal unemployment tax is assumed to be 3.2% of the first $4,200 of gross earnings, but with credit to the employer for a maximum of 2.7% of gross earnings for state unemployment taxes.

Instructions

a Prepare a schedule showing for each employee the cumulative earnings, the earnings subject to unemployment compensation tax, and the earnings subject to FICA taxes.

b Compute the total payroll taxes **deducted** from the earnings of employees as a group.

c Compute the total payroll taxes expense of Wilson Company, and the percentage of total payroll represented by payroll taxes expense. (Round off to the nearest tenth of a percent.)

13B-4 Gross earnings of the employees of Riverboat Travel during the week ended December 31 amounted to $80,000. Company policy provided for the payment of this payroll on January 3. The company adjusts and closes its accounts at December 31.

With respect to payroll, the income tax withholding for the last week of December amounted to $11,200. FICA taxes (6% each on employer and employee) were applicable to only $48,000 of the $80,000 payroll, and unemployment taxes (2.7% state and .5 of 1% federal) were applicable to only $12,800 of the gross earnings for this last week of the year.

Instructions

a In making the adjusting entry for unpaid wages at December 31, should the payroll taxes be accrued? Explain fully.

b Assume that the company wishes to have its accounting records agree with rules by the Internal Revenue Service as to the timing of expense deductions for payroll taxes in computing income tax returns. In accordance with this policy, what amount should appear in the balance sheet at December 31 to reflect the liability arising from wages earned by employees during the last week of the year?

c Assume that the company wishes to accrue all payroll expenses at the year-end, regardless of the deductibility of payroll taxes under income tax rules. Draft a compound journal entry to accrue the payroll at December 31.

13B-5 Two of the employees of Stone Company receive monthly salaries; the remaining four employees are paid an hourly rate with provision for time and one-half for overtime. The basic data for the July 31 payroll are given below:

Employee	Hours Reg	Hours OT	Pay Rate	Compensation to June 30	Gross Pay Due for July	Federal Income Tax Withheld
Haller	160	14	$ 7.20 hr	$ 7,440	$1,303.20	$136.00
Isley	160		8.40 hr	8,160	1,344.00	143.20
Jones	160	21	4.80 hr	3,920	919.20	56.16
Kay	Salary		1,728.00 mo	10,368	1,728.00	208.00
Len	160		6.40 hr	1,152	1,024.00	79.04
Mont	Salary		2,400.00 mo	14,400	2,400.00	188.80

Other data Compensation of Kay and Mont is considered an administrative expense; the balance of the earnings is chargeable to Shop Wages. Payroll taxes apply as follows: FICA, 6% up to maximum of $15,000; state unemployment, 2.7% up to maximum of $4,200; federal unemployment, .5% up to maximum of $4,200. Stone Company has group insurance and a retirement plan under which all employees contribute 7% of their gross pay and the company matches this contribution. Both employees' and employer's contributions are deposited with the First Insurance Company at the end of each month. (Round calculations to the nearest cent and disregard one-cent discrepancies due to rounding.)

Instructions

a Prepare a payroll record for July, using the following columns:

Employee	Gross Pay	Amount Subject to		Federal Income Tax Withheld	FICA Tax Withheld	Retire- ment Deduc- tion	Net Pay Due
		Unemploy- ment Taxes	FICA Taxes				

b Explain how the gross pay for Jones was computed for the month of July.

c Explain why the federal income taxes withheld for Mont are less than those withheld for Kay despite the fact that Mont received a higher gross compensation.

d Prepare in general journal form the entry to record the payroll for the month of July and the amounts withheld from employees.

e Prepare in general journal form the entry to record the employer's payroll taxes and insurance plan contributions for the month of July.

BUSINESS DECISION PROBLEM 13

The payroll procedures of Grill Company, a manufacturing concern with 80 factory employees, may be summarized as follows:

1 Applicants are interviewed and hired by Carl Olson, the factory superintendent. He obtains an Employee's Withholding Exemption Certificate (a W-4 form) from each new employee and writes on it the hourly rate of pay to be used. The superintendent gives this certificate to a payroll clerk as notice that a new employee has been added.

2 When hourly pay rate changes are made, the superintendent advises the payroll clerk verbally of the new rate for the employee(s) affected.

3 Blank time cards are kept in a box at the factory entrance. On Mondays each employee takes a time card, writes in his or her name, and makes pencil notations during the week of hours of arrival and departure. At the end of the week, the employee returns the card to the box.

4 The completed cards are taken from the box on Monday mornings. Two payroll clerks divide the cards alphabetically between them; compute the gross pay, deductions, and net pay; post the information to the employees' individual earning records; and prepare and number the payroll checks.

5 The payroll checks are signed by the chief accountant and given to the superintendent, who distributes them to employees and holds those for any absent employees.

6 The payroll bank account is reconciled by the chief accountant, who also prepares the quarterly and annual payroll tax reports.

Instructions With the objective of improving the system of internal control over the hiring practices and payroll procedures of Grill Company, you are to recommend any basic changes needed in organization, equipment, forms, and procedures. Then list at least six specific hiring practices and payroll procedures which you believe should be instituted.

14

Accounting Principles and Concepts; Current-Value Accounting

Throughout this book we try to explain the theoretical roots of each new accounting principle or standard as it comes under consideration. When you travel through new territory, however, you may find it useful to pause at some intermediate stage in your trip to consider what you have seen and to sort out your observations into some meaningful overall impression. This seems an appropriate point in our discussion of accounting for such a pause. You now have an overview of the accounting process and should be better prepared to understand how accounting procedures are shaped by theoretical concepts.

A basic objective of accounting

A basic objective of accounting is to provide useful information for making economic decisions. Investors, managers, economists, bankers, labor leaders, and government administrators all rely upon financial statements and other accounting reports in making the decisions which shape our economy. In determining the proper content of financial statements and other accounting reports, it is necessary to consider the *information needs* of the users of these statements and reports.

THE NEEDS OF MANAGEMENT   Managers are interested in receiving information that will aid them in making operating decisions. The area of accounting designed to meet this need is primarily concerned with producing reports and summaries for internal use by management and is known as *management accounting.*

In management accounting, theory is not a major issue, since any information that aids in making rational choices among alternative courses of action is relevant and useful. One measurement method may be used for one managerial purpose and another measurement method for a different purpose. For example, in setting the selling price of some merchandise, management may be less interested in the actual recorded cost of goods on hand than in the estimated cost of replacing these articles as they are sold. Accounting measurements of past operating results and current financial position are useful to management, but it is not necessary that all internal information be developed in accordance with any particular set of accounting principles.

THE NEEDS OF STOCKHOLDERS AND CREDITORS While management accounting provides information for use within the business, *financial accounting* deals primarily with reporting of financial information to outsiders. Measurement of periodic net income and financial position and the reporting of the results to stockholders and creditors are the key objectives of financial accounting.

In reporting to stockholders and creditors, different considerations come into play. Corporate managers, even in small companies, have always been accountable to the owners who employ them. But the responsibility for managing a large corporation carries with it a great deal of economic and social power and requires a more extensive accountability. In most large corporations, stock ownership is widely scattered. The owner of even several thousand of the nearly 300 million shares of General Motors common stock can scarcely expect to exert much influence on managerial policy. As stockholder power has diminished, managerial power and responsibility have broadened.

Modern corporate managers are accountable not only to stockholders and creditors but also to employees, customers, potential investors, and the public at large. Financial statements are the primary means by which management reports on its accountability. Such statements are used to evaluate management's performance, to measure borrowing power, to guide investment decisions, and to support arguments on taxes, development of energy sources, and other public policy issues.

In this book we are primarily concerned with the reporting of financial information to outsiders. We shall therefore concentrate on the accounting principles and reporting standards relating to general-purpose financial statements, rather than special-purpose accounting reports to management.

THE NEED FOR ACCOUNTING PRINCIPLES It is vital to the functioning of our economy that financial statements be widely used and clearly understood. Users of these statements must have confidence in the reliability of the accounting information. Also, it is important for financial statements to be prepared in a manner which permits them to be compared fairly with prior years' statements and with financial statements of other companies. In short, we need a well-defined body of accounting principles or standards to guide corporate managers in preparing financial statements which will achieve the objectives of *understandability, reliability,* and *comparability.*

Generally accepted accounting principles

The principles which constitute the "ground rules" for financial reporting are termed *generally accepted accounting principles.* The financial statements of all publicly owned corporations should be prepared in conformity with generally accepted accounting principles. To assure outsiders that financial statements have been prepared in accordance with these principles, the financial statements of publicly owned corporations are audited by independent certified public accountants.

Accounting principles are also referred to as *standards, assumptions, postulates, and concepts.* The various terms used to describe accounting principles indicate the many efforts which have been made to develop a satisfactory framework of accounting theory.[1] For example, the word *standards* was chosen rather than *principles* when the Financial Accounting Standards Board replaced the Accounting Principles Board as the top rule-making body of the accounting profession. The efforts to construct a satisfactory body of accounting theory are still in process, since accounting theory must continually change with changes in the business environment and changes in the needs of financial statement users. Accounting principles are not rooted in laws of nature, as are the laws of the physical sciences. *Accounting principles or standards are developed in relation to what we consider to be the most important objectives of financial reporting.*

For example, in recent years accountants as well as business executives have recognized that the cost to society of maintaining an economic activity, such as a manufacturing plant, includes the pollution of air and water and other damage to the environment. Research is currently being undertaken to develop accounting principles for the identification and measurement of these "social costs," and also for methods of measuring and reporting the human resources that are so important to the successful operation of a business.

Authoritative support for accounting principles

To qualify as "generally accepted," an accounting principle must usually receive "substantial authoritative support." The most influential authori-

---

[1] See, for example, *Accounting Research Study No. 1,* "The Basic Postulates of Accounting," AICPA (New York: 1961); *Accounting Research Study No. 3,* "A Tentative Set of Broad Accounting Principles for Business Enterprises," AICPA (New York: 1962); and *Objectives of Financial Statements,* AICPA (New York: 1973).

tative groups in this country include: (*1*) the American Institute of Certified Public Accountants (AICPA), the professional association of licensed CPAs; (*2*) the Financial Accounting Standards Board which includes representatives from public accounting, industry, education, and government; and (*3*) the Securities and Exchange Commission (SEC), an agency of the federal government established to administer laws and regulations relating to the publication of financial information by corporations whose stock is publicly owned.[2] Also important in the development of accounting theory has been the American Accounting Association, an organization of accounting educators.

AMERICAN INSTITUTE OF CERTIFIED PUBLIC ACCOUNTANTS (AICPA) The AICPA has long been concerned with stating and defining accounting principles because its members daily face the problem of making decisions about generally accepted principles in the performance of audits and professional work. Some years ago, the AICPA established an Accounting Principles Board, composed of practitioners, educators, and industry representatives. This Board was authorized to issue *Opinions* which would improve financial reporting and narrow areas of differences and inconsistencies in accounting practices and which would be regarded as expressions of generally accepted accounting principles. At the same time, the AICPA expanded its research efforts and sponsored a series of Accounting Research Studies to aid the APB in its work. The Accounting Principles Board issued 31 formal *Opinions* on specific accounting problems, and also issued broad *Statements* designed to improve the quality of financial reporting. For example, *Statement No. 4,* "Basic Concepts and Accounting Principles Underlying Financial Statements of Business Enterprises," was issued in 1970, with the objective of advancing the written expression of financial accounting principles.

In 1973, the AICPA replaced the Accounting Principles Board with the Financial Accounting Standards Board. However, the *Opinions* and *Statements* of the APB remain in effect.

FINANCIAL ACCOUNTING STANDARDS BOARD (FASB) The FASB was established by the AICPA as an independent body to assume the responsibilities of the former Accounting Principles Board. The FASB consists of seven full-time, well-paid members, including representatives from public accounting, industry, government and accounting education. The Accounting Principles Board had consisted of 21 part-time, unpaid members, primarily from public accounting.

Lending support to the FASB are an advisory council and a large research staff. The FASB is authorized to issue *Statements of Financial*

---

[2] Other professional organizations which have influenced the development of accounting principles are the National Association of Accountants and the Financial Executives Institute. In addition to the SEC, the following government regulatory agencies influence financial reporting of business units falling under their jurisdiction: Federal Power Commission, Interstate Commerce Commission, Civil Aeronautics Board, and Federal Communications Commission.

Accounting Standards, which represent expressions of generally accepted accounting principles.

SECURITIES AND EXCHANGE COMMISSION (SEC) The SEC has considerable opportunity to exercise its authority since it may reject corporate financial statements that do not, in the opinion of the Commission, meet acceptable standards. The views of the Commission on various accounting issues are published in the SEC's *Accounting Series Releases,* or *ASRs.* Recently in *ASR 190,* the SEC gave powerful support to the disclosure of replacement costs for certain elements of corporate financial statements.

AMERICAN ACCOUNTING ASSOCIATION (AAA) The AAA has sponsored a number of research studies and monographs in which individual authors and Association committees attempt to summarize accounting principles. These statements have no doubt had considerable influence on the thinking of accounting theorists and practitioners. However, the AAA lacks the power of the AICPA to impose its collective view on accounting practice; it therefore exercises its influence through the prestige of its authors and the persuasiveness of their views.

In addition to the foregoing, "substantial authoritative support" may include accounting practices commonly found in certain industries and in the literature of accounting, including books, journal articles, and expert testimony offered in court.

The accounting environment

The principles of accounting are to a considerable extent shaped by the environment in which the accounting process is employed. Accounting is concerned with economic activity, that is, the ownership and exchange of goods and services. Accounting systems developed in response to the need for information about business activity as an aid both to management and outsiders in making rational economic decisions. Since money is a common denominator in which the value of goods and services is measured, the accounting process is implemented in terms of a monetary unit. Most goods and services produced in our economy are distributed through exchange rather than being directly consumed by producers. It is logical, therefore, to base accounting measurements on exchange (market) prices generated by *past, present,* and *future* transactions and events.

For example, when accountants report the original cost of a plant site acquired some years ago, they are reflecting a past exchange. When they state inventory at market under the lower-of-cost-or-market rule, they are using a present exchange price (market value) as the basis for their measurement. When they record a liability for income taxes, they are measuring the present effect of a future cash outflow to the government.

Since present decisions can affect only current and future outcomes, current and future exchange prices are in general more relevant for decision making than past exchange prices. We live in a world of uncertainty, however, and estimates of future, and even current, exchange prices are often subject to wide margins of error. Where to draw the line of acceptability in the trade-off between *reliability* and *relevance* is one of the crucial issues in accounting theory. The need for reliable and verifiable data is an important constraint, particularly with respect to information reported to outsiders. This factor has led accountants to rely heavily on past exchange prices as the basis for their measurements.

In the remaining sections of this chapter we shall summarize briefly the major principles that govern the accounting process and comment on some areas of controversy. We have noted the need for accepted principles to foster confidence in the published financial statements of large publicly owned corporations. Most accounting principles are equally applicable to profit-making organizations of any size or form.

The accounting entity concept

One of the basic principles of accounting is that information is compiled for a clearly defined accounting entity. Most economic activity is carried on through entities. An individual person is an accounting entity. So is a business enterprise, whether conducted as a single proprietorship, partnership, or corporation. The estate of a deceased person is an accounting entity, as are all nonprofit clubs and organizations. The basic accounting equation, Assets = Liabilities + Owner's Equity, reflects the *accounting entity concept* since the elements of the equation relate to the particular entity whose economic activity is being metered in financial statements.

We should distinguish between accounting and legal entities. In some cases the two coincide. For example, corporations, estates, trusts, and governmental agencies are both accounting and legal entities. In other cases, accounting entities differ from legal entities. For example, the *proprietorship* is an *accounting* entity, as indicated by the fact that only the assets and liabilities of the business unit are included in its financial statements. The proprietorship is not a legal entity; the *proprietor* is a *legal* entity. He is legally liable both for his personal obligations and for those incurred in his business. For accounting purposes, the proprietor as an individual and his business enterprise are separate entities. Furthermore, a proprietor may own several businesses, each of which is treated as a separate entity for accounting purposes.

The choice of an accounting entity is somewhat flexible, as in the case of several business activities owned by one person or group of persons. The decision rests in part on the kinds and amount of information desired by management. As a general rule, we can say that any legal or economic unit which controls economic resources and is accountable for those resources is an accounting entity.

CONSOLIDATED ACCOUNTING ENTITIES A single accounting entity may also include more than one legal entity. Several corporations, for example, may be combined to form a single accounting entity. Since corporations are usually granted the power to hold title to any form of property, one corporation may own shares of stock in another. When one corporation controls another corporation through the ownership of a majority of its capital stock, the controlling corporation is called a *parent* company, and the company whose stock is owned is called a *subsidiary* company. Because both the parent and subsidiary companies are legal entities, separate financial statements may be prepared for each company. However, it may also be useful to prepare financial statements which view the *affiliated* companies (the parent company and its subsidiaries) as if they were a single unified business. Such statements are called *consolidated financial statements.*

In a *consolidated balance sheet,* the assets and liabilities of the affiliated companies are combined and reported as though only a single entity existed. Similarly, in a *consolidated income statement,* the revenue and expenses of the affiliated companies are combined, on the assumption that the results of operations for a single economic entity are being measured.

There are a number of economic, financial, legal, and tax advantages which encourage corporate enterprises to operate through subsidiaries rather than through a single business entity. As a result corporate affiliations are common in the United States. A majority of the companies with shares listed on the New York Stock Exchange or the American Stock Exchange have one or more subsidiaries and include consolidated financial statements in their annual reports.

The going-concern assumption

An underlying assumption in accounting is that an accounting entity will continue in operation for a period of time sufficient to carry out its existing commitments. This assumption leads to the concept of the *going concern.* Since most accounting entities have indefinite lives, the assumption of continuity is in accord with experience in our economic system. In general, the going-concern assumption justifies ignoring immediate liquidating values in presenting assets and liabilities in the balance sheet.

For example, suppose that a company has just purchased a five-year insurance policy for $5,000. If we assume that the business will continue in operation for five years or more, we will consider the $5,000 payment for the insurance as an asset whose services (freedom from risk) will be enjoyed by the business over a five-year period. On the other hand, if we assume that the business is likely to terminate in the near future, the insurance policy should be recorded at its cancellation value—the amount of cash which can be obtained from the insurance company as a refund on immediate cancellation of the policy, which may be, say, $4,500.

In summary, the going-concern assumption is used by nearly all companies but may be dropped when it is not in accord with the facts. Accountants are sometimes asked to prepare a statement of financial position for an enterprise that is about to liquidate. In this case the assumption of continuity is no longer valid and the accountant drops the going-concern assumption and reports assets at their current liquidating value and liabilities at the amount required to settle the debts immediately.

The time period principle

We assume an indefinite life for most accounting entities. But accountants are asked to measure operating progress and changes in economic position at relatively short time intervals during this indefinite life. Users of financial statements want periodic measurements for decision-making purposes.

Dividing the life of an enterprise into time segments, such as a year or a quarter of a year, and measuring changes in financial position for these short periods is a difficult process. A more precise measurement of net income and financial position can be made when a business has been liquidated and its resources have been fully converted into cash. At any time prior to liquidation, the worth of some assets and the amount of some liabilities are matters of speculation. Thus periodic measures of net income and financial position are at best only informed estimates.

Periodic measurements of net income are generally *tentative.* This fact should be clearly understood by those who rely on periodic accounting information. The need for periodic measurements creates many of accounting's most serious problems. For example, the attempt to measure net income over short time periods requires the selection of inventory flow assumptions and depreciation methods. The end-of-period adjustments discussed in Chapter 4 stem directly from the need to update accounting information to a particular point in time.

The monetary principle

The monetary principle means that money is used as the basic measuring unit for financial reporting. Money is the common denominator in which accounting measurements are made and summarized. The dollar, or any other monetary unit, represents a unit of value; that is, it reflects ability to command goods and services. Implicit in the use of money as a measuring unit is the *assumption that the dollar is a stable unit of value,* just as the mile is a stable unit of distance and an acre is a stable unit of area.

Having accepted money as their measuring unit, accountants freely combine dollar measures of economic transactions that occur at various times during the life of an accounting entity. They combine, for example, a $20,000 cost of equipment purchased in 1968 and the $40,000 cost of similar equipment purchased in 1978 and report the total as a $60,000 investment in equipment.

Unlike the mile and the acre, which are stable units of distance and area, the dollar *is not a stable unit of value.* The prices of goods and services in our economy change over time. When the *general price level* (a phrase used to describe the average of all prices) increases, the value of money (that is, its ability to command goods and services) decreases.

Despite the steady erosion in the purchasing power of the dollar in the United States during the last 40 years, accountants have continued to prepare financial statements in which the value of the dollar is assumed to be stable. This somewhat unrealistic assumption is one of the reasons why financial statements are viewed by some users as misleading. Restatement of accounting information for the changing value of the dollar and the preparation of supplementary statements in terms of replacement costs have received much attention in recent years. Such approaches to new financial reporting practices will be discussed in a subsequent section of this chapter. The disclosure of *replacement costs* as supplementary information to accompany financial statements expressed in historical cost became a requirement for large corporations as a result of a rule established by the SEC in 1976.

The objectivity principle

The term *objective* refers to measurements that are unbiased and subject to verification by independent experts. For example, the price established in an arm's-length transaction is an objective measure of exchange value at the time of the transaction. It is not surprising, therefore, that exchange prices established in business transactions constitute much of the raw material from which accounting information is generated.

If a measurement is objective, 10 competent investigators who make the same measurement will come up with substantially identical results. It is probably true, however, that 10 competent accountants who set out independently to measure the net income of a given business would not arrive at an identical result. In the light of the objectivity principle, why is this so? The variation would probably arise because of the existence of alternative accounting measurement methods, rather than the lack of objectivity in any given measurement method. To illustrate, in measuring the cost of goods sold one accountant might use the lifo method, and another the weighted-average method for valuing inventory. These choices could produce significant variations in net income.

Accountants rely on various kinds of evidence to support their financial measurements, but they seek always the most objective evidence available. Invoices, contracts, paid checks, and physical counts of inventory are examples of objective evidence used by accountants.

Despite the goal of objectivity, it is not possible to insulate accounting information from opinion and personal judgment. The cost of a depreciable asset can be objectively determined but not the periodic depreciation expense. To measure the cost of the asset services that have been used up during a given period requires estimates of the residual value and service life of the asset and judgment as to the depreciation method that should be used.

Objectivity in accounting has its roots in the quest for reliability. Accountants want to make their economic measurements reliable and, at the same time, as relevant to decision makers as possible. The accountant is constantly faced with the necessity of compromising between what users of financial information would like to know and what it is possible to measure with a reasonable degree of reliability.

Asset valuation: the cost principle

Both the balance sheet and the income statement are extensively affected by the cost principle. Assets are initially recorded in the accounts at cost, and no adjustment is made to this valuation in later periods, except to allocate a portion of the original cost to expense as the assets expire. At the time an asset is originally acquired, cost represents the "fair market value" of the goods or services exchanged, as evidenced by an arm's-length transaction. With the passage of time, however, the fair market value of such assets as land and buildings may vary greatly from their historical cost. These later changes in fair market value have been generally ignored in the accounts, and the assets have continued to be valued in the balance sheet at historical cost (less the portion of that cost which has been allocated to expense).

Increasing numbers of accountants believe that current market values, or *fair values,* should be used as the basis for asset valuation rather than historical cost. These accountants argue that current values would result in a more meaningful balance sheet. Also, they claim that current values should be allocated to expense to represent fairly the cost to the entity of the goods or services consumed in the effort to generate revenue.

The cost principle is derived from the principle of objectivity. Those who support the cost principle argue that it is important that users have confidence in financial statements, and this confidence can best be maintained if accountants recognize changes in assets and liabilities only on the basis of objective evidence. Objective evidence generally exists to support cost, but fair value is usually a less objective measurement.

Measuring revenue: the realization principle

When should revenue be recognized? Under the assumptions of accrual accounting, revenue should be recognized "when it is earned." However, the "earning" of revenue is an *economic process* and does not actually take place at a single point in time.

Some revenue, such as interest earned, is directly related to time periods. For this type of revenue, it is easy to determine how much revenue has been earned by computing how much of the earning process is complete. However, the earning process for sales revenue relates to *economic activity* rather than to a specific period of time. In a manufacturing business, for example, the earning process involves (*1*) acquisition of raw materials, (*2*) production of finished goods, (*3*) sale of the finished goods, and (*4*) collection of cash from credit customers.

In the manufacturing example, there is little objective evidence to indicate how much revenue has been earned during the first two stages of the earning process. Accountants therefore usually do not recognize revenue until the revenue has been *realized.* Revenue is realized (*1*) when the earning process is essentially complete and (*2*) when objective evidence exists as to the amount of revenue earned.

In most cases, the realization principle indicates that revenue should be recognized *at the time of the sale of goods or the rendering of services.* Recognizing revenue at this point is logical because the firm has essentially completed the earning process and the realized value of the goods or services sold can be objectively measured in terms of the price billed to customers. At any time prior to sale, the ultimate realizable value of the goods or services sold can only be estimated. After the sale, the only step that remains is to collect from the customer, and this is usually a relatively certain event.

Under certain special circumstances, accountants may deviate from the realization principle. In Chapter 3, we described a complete *cash basis* of income measurement whereby revenue is considered realized only when cash is collected from customers and expenses are recorded only when cash is actually paid out. Lawyers, accountants, and doctors, for example, generally use the cash basis of accounting in computing their taxable income. In computing realized revenue on the cash basis, receivables from clients or customers are ignored; only the actual cash collections are recorded as revenue.

THE INSTALLMENT METHOD Companies selling goods on the installment plan sometimes use the *installment method* of accounting. This method may be considered appropriate when collections extend over relatively long periods of time and there is a strong possibility that full collection will not be made. As customers make installment payments, the seller recognizes the gross profit on sales in proportion to the cash collected. If the gross profit on installment sales is 30%, then out of every dollar collected on installment accounts receivable, the sum of 30 cents represents *realized gross profit.* For example, assume that a retailer sells a television set in Year 1 for $400 which cost $280, or 70% of sales price. The collections and the profit earned would be recognized over a three-year period as follows:

	Year	Cash Collected	−	Cost Recovery, 70%	=	Profit Earned, 30%
Installment method illustrated	1	$150		$105		$ 45
	2	200		140		60
	3	50		35		15
	Totals	$400		$280		$120

This method of profit recognition exists largely because it is allowed for income tax purposes; it postpones the payment of income taxes until cash is collected from customers. From an accounting viewpoint, there is little theoretical justification for delaying the recognition of profit beyond the point of sale, because few if any cases exist where the realizable value of the receivable cannot be measured at that time through the establishment of an adequate allowance for doubtful accounts.

LONG-TERM CONSTRUCTION CONTRACTS There are some circumstances in which the accountant finds it appropriate to recognize revenue as realized *during production* or when production is completed. An example arises in the case of *long-term construction contracts,* such as the building of a dam over a three-year period. In this case the revenue (contract price) is known when the construction job is begun, and it would be unreason-able to assume that the entire revenue is realized in the accounting period in which the project is completed. The accountant therefore estimates the portion of the dam completed during each accounting period, and rec-ognizes revenue and profits in proportion to the work completed. This is known as the *percentage-of-completion method* of accounting for long-term contracts.

Assume, for example, that the costs to be incurred over a three-year period on a $5,000,000 contract are estimated at $4,000,000. Using the percentage-of-completion method of accounting, the profits on the con-tract would be recognized over the three-year period as follows:

	Year	Actual Cost Incurred	Actual Cost as Percentage of Estimated Total Cost	Portion of Contract Price Realized	Profit Considered Realized
Profit recognized as work progresses	1	$ 600,000	15	$ 750,000	$150,000
	2	2,000,000	50	2,500,000	500,000
	3	1,452,000	*	1,750,000 balance	298,000 balance
	Totals	$4,052,000		$5,000,000	$948,000

*Balance required to complete the contract.

The portion of the contract price realized in Years 1 and 2 is determined by taking the percentage of estimated total cost incurred in each year and applying it to the contract price of $5,000,000. Because 15% ($600,000/$4,000,000) of the total estimated cost was incurred in Year 1, 15% of the total estimated profit of $1,000,000 ($5,000,000 — $4,000,000) was considered realized; in Year 2, 50% ($2,000,000/$4,000,000) of the cost was incurred, and therefore 50% of the estimated profit was considered realized. In Year 3, however, the total actual cost is known and the profit on the contract is determined to be $948,000 ($5,000,000 — $4,052,000). Since profits of $650,000 ($150,000 + $500,000) were previously recognized in Years 1 and 2, the rest of the profit, $298,000, must be recognized in Year 3. If at the end of any accounting period it appears that a loss will be incurred on a contract in progress, *the loss should be recognized at once.*

If it is difficult to estimate the degree of contract completion or if there are extreme uncertainties involved in measuring the ultimate profit on a contract in progress, profit may be recognized when the *production is completed.* This approach is often referred to as the *completed-contract method* and is supported by many accountants because it is conservative, requires little subjective judgment, and is advantageous for income tax purposes. If the completed-contract method of accounting for long-term construction contracts had been used in the preceding example, no profit would have been recognized in Years 1 and 2; the entire profit of $948,000 would be recorded in Year 3 when the contract was completed and actual costs known.

Measuring expenses: the matching principle

Revenue, the gross increase in net assets resulting from the production or sale of goods and services, is offset by expenses incurred in bringing the firm's output to the point of sale. Examples of expenses relating to revenue are the cost of merchandise sold, the expiration of asset services, and out-of-pocket expenditures for operating costs. The measurement of expenses occurs in two stages: (*1*) measuring the *cost* of goods and services that are consumed or expire in generating revenue and (2) determining when the goods and services acquired have contributed to revenue and their cost thus *becomes an expense.* The second aspect of the measurement process is often referred to as *matching costs and revenue* and is fundamental to the *accrual basis* of accounting.

Costs are associated with revenue (and thus become expenses) in two major ways:

1 IN RELATION TO THE PRODUCT SOLD OR SERVICE RENDERED If a good or service can be related to the product or service which constitutes the output of the enterprise, its cost becomes an expense when the product is sold or the service rendered to customers. The cost of goods sold in a merchandising firm is a good example of this type of expense. Similarly, a commission paid to a real estate salesperson by a real estate brokerage office is an expense directly related to the revenue generated by the salesperson.

2 IN RELATION TO THE TIME PERIOD DURING WHICH REVENUE IS EARNED Some costs incurred by businesses cannot be directly related to the product or service output of the firm. Expired fire insurance, property taxes, depreciation on a building, the salary of the president of the company—all are examples of costs incurred in generating revenue which cannot be related to specific transactions. The accountant refers to this class of costs as *period costs,* and charges them to expense by associating them with the period of time during which they are incurred and presumably contribute to revenue, rather than by associating them with specific revenue-producing transactions.

Recognition of gains and losses

The same principles applied in recognizing revenue are applicable to the measurement of gains and losses on assets other than inventories. In general, an increase in the value of a productive asset, such as a machine or a building, is not recognized until the asset in question is sold, in which case the amount of the gain is objectively determinable.

If a productive asset increases in value while it is in service, the accountant ordinarily does not record this gain because it has not been realized. "Not realized" means that the gain in value has not been substantiated by a transaction in which an exchange price has been established.

Accountants are not so insistent on following the rules of *realization* in measuring losses. We have seen in Chapter 10, for example, that the lower-of-cost-or-market valuation of inventories results in the recognition of losses in inventory investment prior to the sale of the goods in question. Recognizing losses when inventories appear to be worth less than their cost but refusing to recognize gains when inventories appear to be worth more than their cost is logically inconsistent. This inconsistency is justified by an accounting presumption that assets should not be reported in the balance sheet in excess of the amount which can be expected to be recovered through revenue.

The consistency principle

The principle of *consistency* implies that a particular accounting method, once adopted, will not be changed from period to period. This assumption is important because it enables users of financial statements to interpret intelligently the changes in financial position and the amount of net income.

As a practical matter, management (with approval from its accountants) can change an accounting method when in its judgment a different method would better serve the needs of users of financial statements. It would hardly be a virtue to employ an improper accounting method consistently year after year. When a significant change in accounting occurs, however, the independent public accountant must report both the fact that a change in method has been made and the dollar effect of the change. In published financial statements, this disclosure is incorporated in the CPA's opinion. A typical disclosure might be as follows: "During the current year the company changed from the declining-balance method of computing depreciation to the straight-line method. This change in method had the effect of increasing net income by $210,000."

If income statements for previous years are included alongside the current statement for comparison purposes, the statements for the preceding years should be presented as previously reported. The cumulative effect of retroactive application of the new accounting principle on the owner's equity at the beginning of the period in which the change is made should be included in the net income of that period.[3]

Consistency applies to a single accounting entity and increases the comparability of financial statements from period to period. Different companies, even those in the same industry, may follow different accounting methods. For this reason, it is important to determine the accounting methods used by companies whose financial statements are being compared.

The disclosure principle

Adequate disclosure means that all *material* and *relevant facts* concerning financial position and the results of operations *are communicated to users.* This can be accomplished either in the financial statements or in the notes accompanying the statements. Such disclosure should make the statements more useful and less subject to misinterpretation.

Adequate disclosure does not require that information be presented in great detail; it does require, however, that no important facts be withheld. For example, if a company has been named as defendant in a large lawsuit, this information must be disclosed. If patents are about to expire or if accounts receivable have been pledged as collateral in obtaining a loan, the financial statements would be incomplete without disclosure of these facts. Naturally, there are practical limits to the amount of disclosure that can be made in financial statements or the accompanying notes. As a minimum, the following information should generally be disclosed:

1 Terms of major borrowing arrangements and existence of large contingent liabilities
2 Contractual provisions relating to leasing arrangements, employee pension and bonus plans, and major proposed asset acquisitions
3 Accounting methods used in preparing the financial statements
4 Changes in accounting methods made during the latest period
5 Other significant events affecting financial position, including major new contracts for sale of goods or services, labor strikes, shortages of raw materials, and pending legislation which may significantly affect operations
6 For large corporations, the estimated replacement cost of (*1*) inventories, (*2*) cost of goods sold, (*3*) plant and equipment, and (*4*) depreciation, in accordance with *ASR 190* issued by the SEC

Supplementary disclosure through footnotes, however, should not take the place of sound accounting practices in preparing financial statements. The primary information made available to readers of financial statements is derived from the accounting records, but it is not neces-

---

[3] For a full discussion of this subject, see "Accounting Changes," *Opinion No. 20* issued by the Accounting Principles Board of the AICPA (New York: 1971).

sarily limited to such information. The key point to keep in mind is that the supplementary information should be *relevant to the user.* Even significant events which occur *after* the end of the accounting period but before the financial statements are released should be disclosed.

Materiality

The term *materiality* refers to the *relative importance* of an item or event. Disclosure of relevant information is closely related to the concept of materiality; what is material is likely to be relevant. Accountants are primarily concerned with significant information and are not overly concerned with those items which have little effect on financial statements. For example, should the cost of a pencil sharpener, a wastepaper basket, or a stapler be set up as assets and depreciated over their useful lives? Even though more than one period will benefit from the use of these assets, the concept of materiality permits the immediate recognition of the cost of these items as an expense on grounds that it would be too expensive to undertake depreciation accounting for such low-cost assets and that the results would not differ significantly.

We must recognize that the materiality of an item is a relative matter; what is material for one business unit may not be material for another. Materiality of an item may depend not only on its *amount* but also on its *nature.* In summary, we can state the following rule: *An item is material if there is a reasonable expectation that knowledge of it would influence the decisions of prudent users of financial statements.*

Conservatism as a guide in resolving uncertainties

We have previously referred to the use of *conservatism* in connection with the measurement of net income and the reporting of accounts receivable and inventories in the balance sheet. Although the concept of conservatism may not qualify as an accounting principle, it has long been a powerful influence upon asset valuation and income determination. Conservatism is most useful when matters of judgment or estimates are involved. Ideally, accountants should base their estimates on sound logic and select those accounting methods which neither overstate nor understate the facts. When some doubt exists about the valuation of an asset or the realization of a gain, however, the accountant traditionally leans in the direction of caution and selects the accounting option which produces a lower net income for the current period and a less favorable financial position. Conservatism, however, may be viewed as a double-edged sword. If an asset is prematurely recognized as an expense in Year 1, for example, the balance sheet and net income for Year 1 will be conservatively stated but the net income for Year 2 will be overstated.

An example of conservatism is the traditional practice of pricing inventory at the lower of cost or market (replacement cost). Decreases in the market value of the inventory are recognized as a part of the cost of goods sold in the current period, but increases in market value of inventory are ignored. A judicious application of conservatism to the accounting process should produce more useful information; in contrast, the excessive use of conservatism or failure to apply conservatism may produce misleading information and result in losses to creditors and stockholders.

Opinion on financial statements rendered by independent CPAs

After independent certified public accountants have audited the financial statements and accounting records of a business, they attest to the reasonableness of the financial statements by issuing an *audit opinion* (sometimes called *auditors' report*). This opinion is published as part of the company's annual report to stockholders. Because of its importance, the wording of the audit opinion has been carefully considered and a standard form has been developed. Considering the extensive investigation that precedes it, the audit opinion is surprisingly short. It usually consists of two brief paragraphs, unless the CPAs comment on unusual features of the financial picture. The first paragraph describes the *scope* of the auditors' examination; the second states their *opinion* of the financial statements. A report of independent accountants might read as follows:

Typical audit opinion

We have examined the balance sheet of the Reed Company as of September 30, 19____, and the related statements of income, retained earnings, and changes in financial position for the year then ended. Our examination was made in accordance with generally accepted auditing standards, and accordingly included such tests of the accounting records and such other auditing procedures as we considered necessary in the circumstances.

In our opinion, the above financial statements present fairly the financial position of the Reed Company at September 30, 19____, and the results of its operations and the changes in its financial position for the year then ended, in conformity with generally accepted accounting principles applied on a basis consistent with that of the preceding year.

Observe that CPAs *do not guarantee* the accuracy of the financial statements. The financial statements are issued by management of the business: the CPAs render a professional opinion as to the "fairness" of the presentation. The important point to keep in mind is that the *primary responsibility for the accuracy of the financial statements rests with the management* of the business entity issuing the statements.

The phrase "in conformity with generally accepted accounting principles" in the second paragraph of the audit opinion is particularly relevant to our discussion in this chapter. *An authoritative and exhaustive list of generally accepted accounting principles does not exist.* Yet the widespread reliance upon this phrase implies that there is general consensus as to what these accounting principles are.

THE SEARCH FOR BETTER FINANCIAL REPORTING

Accounting is a man-made information system. It is an imperfect system, and constant efforts are being made to improve the precision and relevance of accounting measurements and the usefulness of the end products of the accounting process—financial statements. Because economic conditions are full of uncertainty and business transactions are often complex, the end products of the accounting process must be accepted for what they are—tentative in nature and subject to certain limitations. Accordingly, we should not expect financial statements to attain a higher level of certainty than the business transactions which they summarize.

While accounting may never become a precise science, no one can argue that further improvements are not possible in measuring and communicating financial information. Should accountants, for example, continue to adhere to the assumption that the monetary unit is stable and that historical costs are the most relevant measures of "value" for financial reporting purposes? In the remaining pages of this chapter, we shall examine the implications of this important question.

Inflation—the greatest challenge to accounting

The greatest single challenge to the accounting profession today is to develop new accounting methods that will bring financial statements into accord with economic reality. The continuing steady inflation of the last generation has accelerated in recent years and has become even more intense in some other countries than in the United States. Our traditional accounting process is based on the assumption of a stable dollar. This cost-based system works extremely well in periods of stable prices; it works reasonably well during prolonged but mild inflation; but it loses virtually all meaning if inflation becomes extreme.

We have experienced persistent inflation for almost 40 years; more importantly, the forces which have been built into our economic and political institutions almost guarantee that inflation will continue. The only question is how severe the inflationary trend will be.

Profits—fact or illusion?

As inflation has eroded the usefulness of cost-based financial statements, one consequence has been the reporting of *illusory profits* by corporations. (Fictitious inventory profits were discussed in Chapter 10.) When fictitious profits arising from the assumption of a stable dollar are reported, it follows that what we label as income taxes is in reality the taxation of capital. Moreover, dividends labeled as a distribution of earnings are in fact being paid from capital. The reporting of large, but fictitious, profits also leads to demands for higher wages consistent with the reported profits.

In summary, the real world is one of inflation. If we continue to measure profits on the assumption that price levels do not change, financial statements will be misleading and out of touch with reality. Several broad social consequences appear to follow. For one, corporate liquidity (debt-paying ability) may fall so low as to bring an economic crisis. Secondly, since we allocate economic resources in large part on the basis of financial statements, misallocation of resources may be the end consequence of ignoring inflation in our financial reporting. Finally, the overstatement of profits may lead to an unrecognized failure to maintain reasonable rates of capital formation. A nation with a declining rate of capital formation will find it difficult to hold its relative position in a competitive world economy or to achieve a rising standard of living.

Two approaches to "inflation accounting"

Two alternative approaches to modifying our accounting process to cope with inflation have received much attention. These two approaches are:

1 The adjustment of historical cost financial statements for changes in general purchasing power.

2 Current-value accounting. This approach envisions a series of transitional steps away from historical cost accounting, the first of which would be limited to requiring footnote disclosure of the current values for inventories, cost of goods sold, plant and equipment, and depreciation. A second step would involve preparing supplementary financial statements expressed in current values for most items, and a final step would call for a set of current-value financial statements to become the *primary* financial statements of a company.

The Financial Accounting Standards Board in December 1974 issued an exposure draft of a proposed Statement which would require all companies to include in their annual reports *supplemental* financial statements expressed in units of general purchasing power (GPP). This exposure draft presented much the same concepts as were set forth previously in APB Statement No. 3.[4] The GPP financial statements were not intended to replace conventional statements but to supplement them. The GNP Implicit Price Deflator was identified as the sole index to restate historical financial statements into GPP financial statements.

This exposure draft was issued in December 1974, but it has neither been acted upon nor withdrawn to this date. In view of the position taken by the SEC in 1976 requiring disclosure of *replacement costs* by large corporations, it appears probable that the FASB and the accounting profession generally may now emphasize *replacement cost* or *current-value accounting* as a means of adjusting to inflation rather than developing general purchasing power financial statements.

Many influential accountants who formerly advocated adjustment of cost-based financial statements by use of an index of general purchasing power have changed their position to urge concentration of efforts on the

---

[4] *APB Statement No. 3*, "Financial Statements Restated for General Price Level Changes," AICPA (New York: 1969).

move toward the use of current-value or replacement cost accounting. In other countries similar moves away from historical cost have occurred or are in process. Severe inflation in South American countries has led to revaluation of assets. Great Britain has taken official action to adopt a system of "current cost" accounting, and in the Netherlands some large corporations have for some years been preparing financial statements utilizing current replacement costs.

In view of the attention which has been given to both general purchasing power financial statements and to a change from historical cost to current replacement cost, we need to examine and compare these two alternative approaches to coping with the problem of how accounting can best function in a world of inflation.

General purchasing power financial statements

As previously emphasized, the general price level in the United States has been going up for many years. The general price level is the weighted average of the prices of goods and services within the economy. Generally, it is measured by an index with a base year assigned a value of 100. The reciprocal of the price index represents the purchasing power of the dollar. Thus, if Year 1 = 100 and Year 5 = 125, prices have risen 25% and purchasing power has decreased by 20% [100 − (100 ÷ 125)]. The most common measures of the general price level are the consumer price index, the wholesale price index, and the Gross National Product Implicit Price Deflator. The GNP Deflator is the most comprehensive index and is widely accepted as the best measure of the general price level.

What effect do material changes in general price levels, and thus changes in the value of money, have on accounting measurements? By combining transactions measured in dollars of varying years, the accountant in effect ignores changes in the size of the measuring unit. For example, suppose that a company purchased land early in Year 1 for $200,000 and sold this land for $400,000 late in Year 10. If prices roughly doubled during that 10-year period and the value of money was cut in half, we might say that the company was no better off as a result of these two transactions; the $400,000 received for the land in Year 10 represented approximately the same command over goods and services as $200,000 did when invested in the land in Year 1. In terms of the *dollar* as a measuring unit, however, the accountant would recognize a gain of $200,000 ($400,000 sales price − $200,000 cost) at the time the land was sold in Year 10. Thus, by comparing the Year 1 and Year 10 transactions in dollar terms to measure gains and losses, *the accountant assumes that a firm is as well off when it has recovered its original dollar investment, and that it is better off whenever it recovers more than the original number of dollars invested in any given asset.*

The question is whether financial statements prepared using historical dollars as the measuring unit are more useful than financial statements prepared on some other basis. Years ago methods were devised for making accounting measurements and presenting financial statements in terms of current dollars rather than historical dollars. Such statements have come to be known as *general purchasing power financial statements,* or *common dollar financial statements,* or *price-level financial statements,* because all historical dollar amounts are restated in terms of the current value of the dollar.

Conventional financial statements ignore changes in the purchasing power of money. General purchasing power financial statements are produced by restating the amounts taken from the accounting records through application of an index number which measures the general purchasing power of the dollar at successive dates. When both the balance sheet and income statement have been translated into units of general purchasing power at the current balance sheet date, the financial statements reflect uniform purchasing power. Financial statements of prior years can also be restated to facilitate comparison of the financial position and operating results of the business from year to year. The FASB has indicated that the GNP Implicit Price Deflator would be the only price index used to restate historical financial statements. The plan has been for these general purchasing power financial statements to be prepared as supplemental information to accompany conventional financial statements.

MONETARY ITEMS AND NONMONETARY ITEMS In discussing the changing value of the dollar, we must identify the balance sheet accounts which are affected by such changes and those which are not. Cash, notes receivable, accounts receivable, and all liabilities are *monetary items* because they represent claims to purchasing power or obligations to pay out cash. Monetary items are already stated in terms of current dollars and need not be restated. All other balance sheet accounts (inventories, investments in stock of other companies, plant and equipment, intangibles, and owners' equity accounts) are *nonmonetary items* and must be restated in current dollars in preparing common dollar financial statements.

Changes in price levels give rise to gains and losses as a result of holding monetary items. Owning cash or claims to cash (such as accounts or notes receivable) results in a loss of purchasing power when the general price level is rising; owing money during a period of rising price levels, on the other hand, gives rise to a purchasing power gain because fixed-dollar liabilities can now be paid off with dollars having less purchasing power. We can summarize this point as follows: *In a period of inflation (increasing price levels), it is better to be in debt and hold a minimum of monetary assets; in a period of deflation (decreasing price levels), it is better to hold monetary assets and avoid taking on debts.* To illustrate, assume the following condensed balance sheets, stated in terms of historical costs, for two companies:

	Company A	Company B
Cash and receivables	$500	$200
Merchandise and plant	300	600
Total assets	$800	$800
Liabilities	$150	$700
Owners' equity	650	100
Total liabilities & owners' equity	$800	$800

What effect will inflation have on each company?

If we assume that the general price level had increased by 50% since the merchandise and plant were acquired by Companies A and B, their balance sheets restated to current dollars would appear as follows:

	Company A	Company B
Cash and receivables	$500	$ 200
Merchandise and plant	450 ($300 × 1.5)	900 ($600 × 1.5)
Total assets	$950	$1,100
Liabilities	$150	$ 700
Owners' equity	975 ($650 × 1.5)	150 ($100 × 1.5)
Net purchasing power (loss) or gain	(175)*	250†
Total liabilities & owners' equity	$950	$1,100

High debt and small amount of monetary assets result in a purchasing power gain for Company B

* Loss from holding cash and receivables $250 ($500 × 50%), plus the gain on holding liabilities $75 ($150 × 50%) = $175 net purchasing power loss.

† Gain from holding liabilities $350 ($700 × 50%), reduced by the loss from holding cash and receivables $100 ($200 × 50%) = $250 net purchasing power gain.

Holding monetary assets during a period of rising prices results in a loss of purchasing power because the value of money is falling. This is illustrated by the $250 loss experienced by Company A as a result of carrying $500 in monetary assets during a period when prices increased by 50%. In contrast, the purchasing power loss for Company B as a result of holding monetary assets during the same period was only $100 (50% of $200).

Owing money during a period of rising prices results in a purchasing power gain. This gain results because the debtor company can settle its liabilities in a fixed number of dollars which have a lesser value than the dollars which represented the original amount borrowed. This is illustrated by the purchasing power gain of $75 realized by Company A as a result of owing $150 while prices were rising by 50%. In contrast, the purchasing power gain for Company B is $350 because it owed a much larger sum, $700, while prices increased by 50%. Thus, Company A shows a net purchasing power loss of $175 ($250 − $75) while Company B shows a net purchasing power gain of $250 ($350 − $100).

INCOME MEASUREMENT UNDER PURCHASING POWER ACCOUNTING As stated earlier, a business entity is assumed to be better off (that is, to have earned income) only after it has recovered the equivalent general purchasing power represented by the dollars originally invested in assets. Depreciation expense, for example, should be restated in terms of the general price index at the end of the accounting period. If a building with a useful life of 20 years was acquired for $100,000 when the general price level stood at 100, depreciation expense for the latest year when the price level stood at 170 would be $8,500 ($5,000 × 1.70). Other expense and revenue items would be similarly adjusted in terms of current general purchasing power in preparing a common dollar income statement.

GENERAL PURCHASING POWER STATEMENTS IN PRACTICE Financial statements expressed in units of general purchasing power are *not* accepted as primary reports to stockholders. A very few companies have published some version of general purchasing power financial statements in supplementary schedules included in their annual reports. The trend of thinking today is that a better approach to reporting in terms of economic reality lies in current value (replacement cost) accounting.

Current-value accounting distinguished from general purchasing power accounting

We have used the expression *general purchasing power accounting* to describe financial statements in which historical costs were adjusted to reflect changes in the general price level. General purchasing power accounting does not abandon historical cost as the basis of measurement but simply expresses cost in terms of the current value of money. Also, general purchasing power accounting does not mean that *replacement costs* (which may be assumed to approximate fair market value) are used in the preparation of financial statements. For example, a tract of land which cost $100,000 many years ago would be stated at $150,000 in common dollars if the general price level had risen by 50%. However, the replacement cost of the land might be $400,000 because land prices might have risen much more than the general price level.

    Current-value accounting on the other hand, does represent a departure from the historical cost concept and requires that accountants develop new techniques for measuring the current cost of replacing various types of assets and for converting historical operating costs into current replacement costs as of the dates sales were made. These new techniques have not yet been agreed upon. The accounting profession is now in the process of experimenting with various valuation methods and considering possible related changes in the format of financial statements.

Current-value accounting—objectives and problems

The term *current value* is used in this discussion to mean replacement cost. In *Accounting Series Release No. 190* the SEC required disclosure of certain replacement cost information for large corporations. Replacement cost means the lowest amount that would have to be paid in the normal course of business to obtain a new asset of equivalent operating or productive capability. There are of course alternative meanings which could be assigned to *current value,* such as the net realizable value, or the present value of future cash flows, but these are not considered in our present discussion.

The purpose of disclosing replacement cost is to help investors obtain an understanding of the current costs of operating the business. For example, depreciation expense computed on the basis of replacement cost of the assets in use will usually be much greater than depreciation expense computed on the basis of historical cost. In addition, the required disclosure of replacement cost may help investors determine the current value of inventories and of plant facilities, thus acquiring a new perspective on the economic value of these elements in the balance sheet.

The present SEC rule requires that the disclosure of replacement costs be included in a note to the financial statements, or in separate schedules. Keep in mind that at present the complete primary set of financial statements continues to be based on historical cost. The information on replacement costs is supplementary to the conventional financial statements and not a substitute for them.

The specific information to be disclosed on replacement costs may be summed up under five headings:

1 *Inventories.* Each annual balance sheet must disclose the current replacement cost of inventories at the year-end.
2 *Plant and equipment.* The estimated current cost of replacing new the productive facilities of the company and also the depreciated cost of such facilities.
3 *Cost of goods sold.* The cost of goods sold for the current and the preceding year must be computed as the replacement cost of the goods and services sold at the dates sales were made.
4 *Depreciation, depletion, and amortization.* Straight-line depreciation, depletion, and amortization must be computed on the basis of the current replacement cost of plant and equipment.
5 Description of the methods followed in developing the above estimates.

Disclosure of this information on replacement costs is required only at the end of the fiscal year, and not in connection with interim financial statements.

Responsibility of CPA firms for replacement cost data

The disclosure of replacement cost as part of the annual financial statements of large corporations is presented in a note or schedule labeled as "unaudited." Independent auditors are concerned with the fairness of the replacement cost information disclosed, but they cannot at present verify it and assume responsibility for it in the same manner as for historical cost data included in conventional financial statements. If current-value financial statements are to replace historical cost statements as the primary means of financial reporting, the public accounting profession will have to develop a basis for attesting to the reliability of this proposed new type of financial statements.

Since replacement costs are estimates and methods for their measurement are in an experimental stage, the liability of the corporations issuing this information is stated by the SEC to be limited if the estimates are prepared in good faith with reasonable care and the methods of calculation are explained.

Comparison of current-value accounting with general purchasing power accounting

Today's trend is toward current-value accounting, and not toward financial reporting in terms of general purchasing power. The British government has given approval to a System of Current Cost Accounting and has arranged for development of methods to implement it. In the Netherlands, large corporations are basing depreciation on replacement cost and determining cost of goods sold in terms of replacement values. In Australia the Institute of Chartered Accountants has gone on record as favoring the valuation of assets at current cost and the measurement of profit by stating both revenue and expenses at current values. In the United States, the Securities and Exchange Commission, by requiring disclosure of replacement cost for large corporations, appears to have taken a first step toward general adoption of current-value accounting. Leading CPA firms are encouraging experimentation with specific applications of current-value accounting as the most practical response to the distortion of historical cost data by continuing inflation.

Both current-value accounting and general purchasing power accounting rest on the concept that *profit should be recognized only when real capital is kept intact.* However, general purchasing power accounting leads to financial statements based on the *general price level* and not on changes in prices of individual goods and services. Any given company has inventories of specific commodities for which prices may be changing in quite a different manner from the general price level.

> *ILLUSTRATIVE CASE.* In a recent year the wholesale price of sugar declined from over 60 cents a pound to approximately 12 cents a pound although the general price level was rising strongly. A company in the sugar industry would have presented much more realistic financial statements by using current-value accounting than by adjusting its historical costs by the upward change in the general price level.

A principal problem to be solved if current-value accounting is to succeed is the development of uniform standards for measuring the current value of various types of assets and operating expenses. Consideration must also be given to the most effective methods of presenting this information. It appears likely that price index numbers will be the most objective and satisfactory means of developing much replacement cost data. However, these will be specialized indexes measuring changes in the prices of specific groups of commodities and services rather than an index of the general price level.

KEY TERMS INTRODUCED OR EMPHASIZED IN CHAPTER 14

Accounting principles   Standards or guidelines that aid in the preparation of financial statements to achieve the objectives of understandability, reliability, and comparability. Also used as criteria for judging acceptability of accounting methods.

Accounting Series Release No. 190   A pronouncement by the SEC in 1976 that large corporations must disclose in notes to their financial statements the replacement costs of inventories, cost of goods sold, plant and equipment, and depreciation computed on the basis of replacement cost. A rule designed to compensate for the distortion of financial statements caused by inflation.

Accrual basis of accounting   Recording revenue in the period in which it is earned and recording expenses in the period in which they are incurred. The effect on the business of economic events is recognized as the events occur. Thus revenue is recognized as goods are sold and services rendered rather than when cash is received.

Audit opinion   The report issued by a firm of certified public accountants after auditing the financial statements of a business. Expresses an opinion on the fairness of the financial statements and indicates the nature and limits of the responsibility being assumed by the independent auditors.

Cash basis of accounting   An accounting system in which revenue is recorded when received in cash and expenses are recorded in the period in which cash payments are made. Fails to match revenue with related expenses and does not meet generally accepted accounting principles. Used for individual income tax returns and in accounting records of many professional firms and small service-type enterprises.

Common dollar statements   Supplementary financial statements prepared by a few companies in terms of current dollars by adjusting historical cost by an index of the general price level. Also called *general purchasing power financial statements.*

Completed-contract method   A method of accounting for long-term projects under which revenue is recognized only when the contract has been completed.

Conservatism   A traditional practice of resolving uncertainties by choosing asset valuation at the lower point of the range of reasonableness. Also refers to the policy of postponing recognition of revenue to a later date when a range of reasonable choice exists. Designed to avoid overstatement of financial strength and earnings.

Consistency   An assumption that once a particular accounting method is adopted, it will not be changed from period to period. Intended to make financial statements of a given company comparable from year to year.

Consolidated financial statements   Financial statements which present the financial position and operating results of a group of affiliated corporations as though the group represented a single unified business.

Cost principle   The traditional, widely used policy of accounting for assets at their historical cost determined through arm's-length bargaining. Justified by the need for objective evidence to support the valuation of assets.

Current-value accounting   The valuation of assets and measurement of income in terms of current values rather than historical cost. An approach designed to avoid the distortion of financial statements by inflation.

Disclosure principle Financial statements should disclose all material and relevant information about the financial position and operating results of a business. The notes accompanying financial statements are an important means of disclosure.

Entity concept Any legal or economic unit which controls economic resources and is accountable for these resources may be considered an accounting entity. The resources and the transactions of the entity are not to be intermingled with those of its owner or owners.

General purchasing power (GPP) financial statements A much-discussed proposal to prepare financial statements in which historical costs are adjusted for changes in the general price level. Designed to offset the distortion of financial statements caused by inflation. Also known as *common dollar financial statements.* Currently, this proposal appears less likely of adoption than replacement cost accounting.

Generally accepted accounting principles Those accounting principles which have received substantial authoritative support, such as the approval of the FASB, the AICPA, or the SEC. Often referred to by the acronym GAAP.

GNP Implicit Price Deflator An index of the general price level prepared by the federal government to measure changes in the general purchasing power of the dollar. (GNP refers to Gross National Product.) This index is appropriate for general purchasing power financial statements.

Going-concern assumption An assumption that a business entity will continue in operation indefinitely and thus will carry out its existing commitments. If evidence to the contrary exists, then the assumption of liquidation would prevail and assets would be valued at their estimated liquidation values.

Illusory profits Profits reported on the basis of accounting for historical costs when, in fact, inflation has caused replacement costs to be significantly higher than the costs charged to cost of operations.

Installment method An accounting method used principally in the determination of taxable income. It provides for recognition of realized profit on installment contracts in proportion to cash collected.

Matching principle The revenue earned during an accounting period is compared or matched with the expenses incurred in generating this revenue in order to measure income. Fundamental to the accrual basis of accounting.

Materiality The relative importance of an amount or item. An item which is not important or significant enough to influence the decisions of prudent users of financial statements is considered as *not* material. The accounting treatment of immaterial items may be guided by convenience rather than by theoretical principles. For example, purchase of 10 gallons of gasoline is treated as the incurring of an expense rather than the acquisition of an asset.

Monetary items With respect to changes in price levels, monetary items include assets representing claims to a fixed number of dollars (such as cash and receivables) and all liabilities. Monetary items are not restated when preparing general purchasing power financial statements.

Monetary (stable-dollar) assumption In using money as a measuring unit and preparing financial statements expressed in dollars, accountants make the assumption that the dollar is a stable unit of measurement. This assumption is obviously faulty as a result of continued inflation, and strenuous efforts are being made to change to current-value accounting or to price-level-adjusted measurements.

Objectivity (objective evidence) The valuation of assets and the measurement of income are to be based as much as possible on objective evidence, such as exchange prices in arm's-length transactions. Objective evidence is subject to verification by independent experts.

Percentage-of-completion method A method of accounting for long-term construction projects which recognizes revenue and profits in proportion to the work completed, based on an estimate of the portion of the project completed each accounting period.

Realization principle The principle of recognizing revenue in the accounts only when earned. Revenue is realized when the earning process is virtually complete, which is usually at the time of sale of goods or rendering service to customers.

Replacement cost accounting The valuation of assets and measurement of cost of goods sold in terms of replacement cost rather than historical cost. Disclosure of replacement cost of certain items required as supplementary information in financial statements of large corporations. See current-value accounting.

Time period principle The concept that operating progress and financial position must be measured at relatively short intervals in order to provide financial statements for the decision-making process. The basic time period is one year but more frequent interim statements are also prepared.

REVIEW QUESTIONS

1 What is a basic objective of accounting?

2 What is the primary informational need of managers? How do the needs of creditors and owners differ from those of management?

3 To qualify as "generally accepted," accounting principles must receive substantial authoritative support. Name three groups or organizations in the United States which have been most influential in giving substantial authoritative support to accounting principles.

4 Accounting measurements are based on past, present, and future exchange transactions. Give an example of accounting measurement based on each kind of transaction.

5 Explain what is meant by the expression "trade-off between *reliability* and *relevance*" in connection with the preparation of financial statements.

6 Barker Company has at the end of the current period an inventory of merchandise which cost $500,000. It would cost $600,000 to replace this inventory, and it is estimated that the goods will probably be sold for a total of $700,000. If the firm were to terminate operations immediately, the inventory could probably be sold for $480,000. Discuss the relative reliability and relevance of each of these dollar measurements of the ending inventory.

7 Why is it necessary for accountants to assume the existence of a clearly defined accounting entity?

8 What are *consolidated financial statements?*

9 If the going-concern assumption were dropped, there would be no point in having current asset and current liability classifications in the balance sheet. Explain.

10 "The matching of costs and revenue is the natural extension of the time period principle." Evaluate this statement.

11 Define *objectivity, consistency, materiality,* and *conservatism.*

12 Is the assumption that the dollar is a stable unit of measure realistic? What alternative procedures would you suggest?

13 a Why is it important that any change in accounting methods from one period to the next be disclosed?

b Does the concept of consistency mean that all companies in a given industry follow similar accounting methods?

14 Briefly define the principle of *disclosure.* List five examples of information that should be disclosed in financial statements or in notes accompanying the statements.

15 List four stages of the productive process which might become the accountant's basis for recognizing changes in the value of a firm's output. Which stage is most commonly used as a basis for revenue recognition? Why?

16 A CPA firm's standard audit opinion consists of two major paragraphs. Describe the essential content of each paragraph.

17 Define *monetary assets* and indicate whether a gain or loss results from the holding of such assets during a period of rising prices.

18 Why is it advantageous to be in debt during an inflationary period?

19 Evaluate the following statement: "During a period of rising prices, the conventional income statement overstates net income because the amount of depreciation recorded is less than the value of the service potential of assets consumed."

20 In presenting financial information to their stockholders and the public, corporations do not report in units of general purchasing power or in *common dollar* terms, although such statements are occasionally presented in addition to regular financial statements as supplementary information. Why has the use of common dollars in financial reporting not gained general acceptance?

21 Publicly owned corporations are required to include in their annual reports a description of the accounting principles followed in the preparation of their financial statements. What advantages do you see in this practice?

22 What efforts, if any, are being made in countries other than the United States to supplement or replace historical cost in financial statements in reaction to continued inflation?

23 How does general purchasing power accounting differ from current-value accounting? For which one would the Gross National Product Implicit Price Deflator be used?

EXERCISES

Ex. 14-1 For each situation described below, indicate the concept (or concepts) of accounting that is violated, if any. You may choose among the following concepts: Conservatism, consistency, disclosure, entity, going concern, matching, materiality, objectivity.

Situations
a A pencil sharpener acquired by a small business at a cost of $5 is estimated to have a useful life of 10 years and is recorded by a debit to the Office Equipment account.

b The owner of a small business used the business bank account in writing a check to a department store in payment for personal expenditures.

c The machinery used by a car wash business was shown in the balance sheet at its estimated scrap value which was far below the book value.

d The assets of a partnership are combined with the separate assets of the partners in preparing a balance sheet.

e The cost of merchandise purchased is recognized as expense before it is sold in order to report a less favorable financial position.

f Plans to dispose of a major segment of the business are not communicated to readers of the balance sheet.

g A portion of the cost of a major television promotional campaign in the month of May is deferred and arbitrarily allocated to expense over a five-year period.

h The method of depreciation is changed every two years and the change is disclosed in financial statements.

Ex. 14-2 This exercise emphasizes the significance of accrued and deferred revenue and expenses in applying the matching principle. Naylor Company reported net income for the period of $72,000, but failed to make adjusting entries for the following items:

(1) Included in the revenue account was the amount of $8,400 which should be considered as deferred revenue, as the services for which the customer had paid would not be rendered by Naylor Company until the following year.

(2) Accrued expense relating to unpaid salaries, $5,200.

(3) Accrued revenue for services rendered, $4,100.

(4) Included in the Rent Expense account was the amount of $3,800 of rent paid applicable to the following year.

(5) A payment of $4,100 for ordinary repairs to driveways and fences had been charged to the Land account.

Compute the corrected net income. Your answer should begin with "Net income as reported . . . $72,000," and show on a separate line the increase or decrease caused by each of the five items.

Ex. 14-3 The Clinton Corporation recognizes the profit on a long-term construction project as work progresses. From the information given below, compute the profit that should be recognized each year, assuming that the original cost estimate on the contract was $6,000,000 and that the contract price is $7,200,000:

Year	Costs Incurred	Profit Considered Realized
1	$1,440,000	$?
2	3,600,000	?
3	914,280	?
Totals	$5,954,280	$1,245,720

Ex. 14-4 On September 15, Year 1, Ruth Jackson sold a piece of property which cost her $28,800 for $48,000, net of commissions and other selling expenses. The terms of sale were as follows: Down payment, $4,800, balance, $1,800 on the fifteenth day of each month for 24 months, starting October 15, Year 1. Compute the gross profit to be recognized by Jackson in Year 1, Year 2, and Year 3 (*a*) on the *accrual basis* of accounting and (*b*) on the *installment basis* of accounting.

Ex. 14-5 Three companies started business with $500,000 at the beginning of the current year when the general price index stood at 125. The First Company invested the money in a note receivable due in four years; the Second Company invested its cash in land; and the Third Company purchased a building for $2,000,000, assuming a liability for the unpaid balance of $1,500,000. The price level stood at 140 at the end of the year. Compute the purchasing power gain or loss for each company during the year.

Ex. 14-6 Samson Corporation was organized in Year 1 with total invested capital of $8 million for the purpose of acquiring land for long-term investment. At this time, the general price index was 100. In Year 5, the general price index stands at 140 but the price of all land in the area in which the Samson Corporation invested has doubled in value. Rental receipts for grazing and farming during the five-year period were sufficient to pay all carrying charges on the land.

a Does the company hold any monetary items? What is the purchasing power gain or loss, if any, for the Samson Corporation during the five-year period?

b What is the "economic" gain or loss during this period?

PROBLEMS

Group A

14A-1 After reading an article concerning the SEC's rule on the disclosure of replacement cost in financial statements, Harold Wilson, sole proprietor of Wilson
Company, instructed his newly employed accountant to utilize replacement costs
in the preparation of the year-end balance sheet and to provide footnotes disclosing all needed supplementary information. The accountant (whose experience and study of accounting had been quite limited) complied with Wilson's
instructions to the best of his ability and produced the following balance sheet.

WILSON COMPANY
Balance Sheet
December 31, 19___

$\frac{140}{100} \times 8,000$

Assets

Cash		$ 24,000
Accounts receivable (Note #1)		84,320
Inventory, at replacement cost (Note #2)		142,600
Land, buildings, and equipment (Note #3)	$190,000	
Less: Accumulated depreciation (Note #4)	80,000	110,000
Office supplies (Note #5)		1
		$360,921

Liabilities & owner's equity

Notes payable to bank	$120,000
Interest payable (Note #6)	10,000
Accounts payable (Note #7)	104,000
Mortgage payable (Note #8)	40,000
Harold Wilson, capital	86,921
	$360,921

Note 1. Accounts receivable include a receivable for $24,000 withdrawn in
cash by Harold Wilson during the current year at the rate of $2,000 per month.
Wilson has indicated that he may in the future pay this amount back to the
company.

Accounts receivable have been reduced by the amount of $8,000 due from
Murray Company because that company is both a customer and a supplier.
Wilson Company owes Murray Company $9,000 in purchase invoices and has
accounts receivable from Murray Company of $8,000. In preparing the balance
sheet, a net figure of $1,000 owing to Murray Company was computed by offset-
ting the account receivable against the account payable.

Note 2. The cost of the inventory to Wilson Company was $131,000, but
inquiries of suppliers at year-end indicated the goods in stock have a current
replacement cost of $142,600. The company has been using the fifo method.

Note 3. The land cost $20,000 but is shown at its current value of $100,000, as
estimated by a local realtor. The building, which cost $60,000, is estimated to have
a replacement cost of $80,000. The furniture in use in the business is not owned
but rented; however $10,000 of furniture in Wilson's home is included in the
company's assets because it was paid for with company funds and a monthly staff

meeting of all employees is held at Wilson's home. No depreciation has been recorded on the furniture.

Note 4. The accumulated depreciation was increased from the $40,000 balance in the accounts to $80,000 because of the estimated increased replacement cost of the building.

Note 5. Office supplies all bear the company name and would produce nothing if offered for sale. The cost of $2,400 has therefore been reduced to the nominal amount of $1 in accordance with the accounting principle of conservatism.

Note 6. A bank loan of $100,000 has been restated on the balance sheet as $120,000 to reflect the change in the price level. Also, interest payable of $8,000 per the accounting records has been increased to $10,000 to reflect the increase in the general level of interest rates since the loan was obtained from the bank.

Note 7. Accounts payable were reduced $8,000 by offsetting a receivable from Murray Company, as explained in Note #4.

Note 8. The mortgage, payable in 10 years, has been increased from the ledger figure of $30,000 to reflect the rise in the price level since it was incurred.

Instructions

a Wilson and his accountant appear to have a basic misunderstanding of the SEC position on disclosure of replacement costs. Explain the basic error or errors in their efforts to follow the SEC's official views on replacement cost.

b For each footnote and related balance sheet item which you believe represents a violation of generally accepted accounting principles, write a sentence or two stating your criticism.

c Prepare a corrected balance sheet in accordance with generally accepted accounting principles. Include footnotes only if you believe the needed information cannot be satisfactorily presented in the body of the balance sheet.

14A-2 In each of the situations described below, the question is whether generally accepted accounting principles have been properly observed. In each case state the accounting principle or concept, if any, that has been violated and explain briefly the nature of the violation. If you believe the treatment *is in accord with generally accepted accounting principles,* state this as your position and defend it.

a For a number of years the Waterman Company used the declining-balance method of depreciation both on its financial accounting records and in its income tax returns. During the current year the company decided to employ the straight-line method of depreciation in its accounting records but to continue to use the declining-balance method for income tax purposes.

b During the current year the Louis Company adopted a policy of charging purchases of small tools (unit cost less than $100) to expense as soon as they were acquired. In prior years the company had carried an asset account Small Tools which it had depreciated at the rate of 10% of the book value at the beginning of each year. The balance in the Small Tools account represented about 1% of the company's total plant and equipment, and depreciation on small tools was 0.4% of sales revenue. It is expected that purchases of small tools each year will run about the same as the depreciation that would be taken on these small tools.

c Ace Company printed a large mail-order catalog in July of each year, at a cost of $1.8 million. Customers ordered from this catalog throughout the year and the company agreed to maintain the catalog prices for 12 months after the date of issue. The controller charged the entire cost of the catalog to Advertising Expense in August when it was issued. The Ace Company's fiscal year ends on January 31 of each year. In defending this policy, the controller stated, "Once those catalogs are mailed they are gone. We could never get a nickel out of them."

14A-3 Health, Incorporated, began business early in Year 1 in a large eastern city. Its program of weight reduction and body building was received with great enthusiasm and by June of Year 1 it was selling franchises to independent business executives (franchisees) throughout the United States.

Each franchise contract was sold for $15,000, payable $1,500 down and $4,500 per year, commencing one year after the contract was sold. Even though the franchise contract provides that Health, Incorporated, must provide considerable services to the franchisees for at least three years, the company records the sale of a franchise as follows:

Cash	1,500	
Accounts Receivable from Franchise Sales	13,500	
Revenue from Franchise Sales		15,000

Information relating to franchise sales during the first three years of operations is given below:

	Year 1	Year 2	Year 3
Number of franchises sold	50	80	40
Number of franchisees going out of business	5	10	20
Cash collected from franchises	$ 75,000	$ 322,500	$577,500
Revenue recorded as realized	750,000	1,200,000	600,000
Accounts written off as worthless	67,500	103,500*	153,000†
Operating expenses related directly to franchise sales	22,500	46,500	72,000

*3 @ $13,500 and 7 @ $9,000 = $103,500
†4 @ $13,500, 6 @ $9,000, and 10 @ $4,500 = $153,000

Instructions

a Prepare a schedule summarizing the income from franchise sales of Health, Incorporated, as reported by the company (before income taxes) for the first three years of operations. Use a separate column for each year.

b Discuss fully in a separate paragraph the propriety of the company's accounting policy. Would you consider the policy conservative?

c Prepare a schedule summarizing the income from franchise sales of Health, Incorporated (before income taxes), assuming that the revenue from franchise sales is reported on a cash basis, as would be required under generally accepted accounting standards because Health, Incorporated, "must provide considerable services to the franchisees for at least three years." Use a separate column for each year.

d Discuss fully in a separate paragraph, the merits of the accounting method used in c above.

14A-4 The financial information shown below has been compiled by the owner of Sheridan Company and pertains to the current year. The information includes a variety of concepts such as depreciation based on replacement cost, depreciation based on historical cost, and increase in goodwill, some of which are not in conformity with presently accepted accounting principles. Some items needed for the preparation of an income statement are not given as specific amounts but may be computed from related data. The gross profit on sales for Sheridan Company is assumed to be constant on all items normally included in inventory.

Sales (net of returns and allowances)	$560,000
Cost of goods purchased for resale (net)	378,000
Inventory at Jan. 1 (at selling price)	70,000
Inventory at Dec. 31 (at selling price), replacement cost $81,200	140,000
Cash payments for operating expenses, including prepayments	84,000
Estimated profit on sales orders for goods not yet delivered to customers	16,940

101, 220

Depreciation expense based on actual cost	$14,000
Depreciation expense based on current replacement cost	21,000
Increase in prepaid expenses during the year	420
Estimated uncollectible accounts receivable at end of year	1,540
Increase in accrued expenses during the year	2,100
Increase in goodwill (value of the business) during the year.	35,000
Net purchasing power gain resulting from increase in	
general price level during the year	5,880

Instructions

a Prepare a schedule computing the relationship between the sales value and the cost of the merchandise purchased by Sheridan Company during the current year. (Cost of beginning inventory is purposely omitted.)

b Prepare an income statement for the current year in accordance with generally accepted accounting principles. Ending inventory is to be valued at the lower of cost or market.

c Indicate the proper disposition of any item not used in preparing the income statement.

14A-5 The management consulting firm of Ryan Associates was organized on January 1, Year 1, by Robert Ryan for the purpose of performing research studies on transportation problems of cities and business organizations. Ryan invested $80,000 of his savings to begin the business. Office space was rented at a rate of $1,600 monthly. At the end of Year 1, having kept only cash receipts and disbursement records during the year, Ryan prepared the following financial statements:

RYAN ASSOCIATES
Income Statement
Year 1

Cash received for consulting services		$312,000
Salaries and payroll taxes	$201,920	
Rent expense	20,800	
Travel expense	45,600	
Office expense	43,200	
Miscellaneous expense	24,480	336,000
Net loss for the year		$(24,000)

RYAN ASSOCIATES
Balance Sheet
December 31, Year 1

Assets

Cash	$12,800
Office equipment.	43,200
Total assets	$56,000

Capital

Robert Ryan, capital [$80,000 − $24,000 (net loss for the year)]	$56,000

Ryan was understandably discouraged by his first year's results. Before deciding whether to disband his operations, he asks you to go over his records and review the situation with him. You make the following notes as a result of your investigation:

(1) Office equipment was purchased on January 2, Year 1. Ryan paid cash of $43,200 and signed a $32,000, 8% note. The note, along with interest of $3,840, is payable on July 2, Year 2. The equipment has an average service life of 10 years and a salvage value of $4,800 (straight-line depreciation).

(2) Accounts receivable from clients at the end of Year 1 total $48,000, of which $960 is in dispute and is probably not collectible.

(3) Three research projects are in progress at the end of Year 1, on which no billings have yet been made to clients. Memorandum records indicate that the following direct charges relate to these projects and should be deferred: Salaries and payroll taxes, $19,200; travel, $4,480, miscellaneous, $3,520.

(4) Rent on the office for one month ($1,600) has been prepaid at December 31.

(5) At December 31, Ryan owed $2,400 to the Green Travel Co. and $800 to various creditors who furnished office supplies.

(6) Office supplies on hand at December 31, $5,600. Insurance premiums paid during Year 1 amounted to $3,840, of which $1,440 is applicable to Year 2. Premiums paid were recorded in the Miscellaneous Expense account.

(7) Accrued but unpaid salaries and payroll taxes at December 31, $20,000.

Instructions

a On the basis of your notes, prepare a revised balance sheet as of the end of Year 1 and an income statement for the year in accordance with generally accepted accounting principles. Use an eight-column work sheet to revise Ryan's figures and compile the necessary account balances for the statements. The following column headings are suggested: Unadjusted Balances, Adjustments, Income Statement, and Balance Sheet.

b Write a letter to Ryan commenting on the results of his first year of operations as restated, including the rate of earnings (if any) on his investment of $80,000.

Group B

14B-1 Air Services, a single proprietorship, has compiled the following information applicable to the year ended December 31, 19____.

	Balance, Jan. 1	Cash Receipts or (Payments)	Balance, Dec. 31
Accounts receivable—sale of merchandise	$17,000	$180,000	$25,500
Accounts payable	9,750	(88,200)	11,200
Prepaid supplies	1,360	(4,900)	750
Merchandise inventories	21,000		23,600
Accrued wages payable	2,500	(39,000)	6,000

Instructions

a Prepare an "income statement" for the year on a cash basis of accounting. (A more accurate title would be a "Statement of Cash Receipts and Disbursements.") Disregard the fact that companies with inventories should not use the cash basis of accounting. Cost of goods sold is to be stated at the amount of cash payments on accounts payable during the year. The beginning and ending inventories are to be ignored in the cash basis statement.

b Prepare an income statement for the year on the accrual basis of accounting required by generally accepted accounting principles for a company with these characteristics. Hint: Sales equals cash receipts ($180,000) minus beginning balance of accounts receivable ($17,000) plus ending balance of accounts receivable ($25,500). Use a similar line of reasoning for the other items, considering first the cash receipt or payment during the year and then making adjustments for the beginning and ending balances.

14B-2 In each of the situations described below, the question is whether generally accepted accounting principles have been violated. In each case state the accounting principle or concept, if any, that has been violated and explain briefly the nature of the violation. If you believe the treatment *is in accord with generally accepted accounting principles,* state this as your position and briefly defend it.

a Merchandise inventory which cost $2 million is reported in the balance sheet at $3 million, the expected sales price less estimated direct selling expenses.

b Jefferson Company reports net income for the current year of $1,300,010. In the audit report the auditors stated: "We certify that the results of operations shown in the income statement are a true and accurate portrayal of the company's operations for the current year."

c The Lynn Company has purchased a computer for $1.5 million. The company expects to use the computer for five years, at which time it will acquire a larger and faster computer. The new computer is expected to cost $3.5 million. During the current year the company debited $700,000 to the Depreciation Expense account to "provide for one-fifth of the estimated cost of the new computer."

d Bob Savage operates a mine as a single proprietorship. During the current year, geologists and engineers revised upward the estimated value of ore deposits on his property. Savage instructed his accountant to record goodwill of $2 million, the estimated value of unmined ore in excess of previous estimates. The offsetting credit was made to Bob Savage, Capital.

e The Lee Oil Company reported on its balance sheet as an intangible asset the total of all wages, supplies, depreciation on equipment, and other costs related to the drilling of a producing oil well and then amortized this asset as oil was produced from the well.

14B-3 All sales by Fire Equipment are made on credit, with terms calling for payment 90 days after the date of sale. The company pays a commission of 10% of selling price to its sales staff as soon as the customers pay their accounts.

During the first three years of operations, the company reported sales on a cash basis; that is, it did not record the sale until the cash was collected. Commissions to the sales staff were recorded only when cash was collected from customers. Net income figures computed on this basis were:

Year 1	$ 64,000
Year 2	96,000
Year 3	144,000

An accountant, called in at the end of Year 3 to review the store's accounting system, suggested that a better picture of earnings would be obtained if both sales and commissions were recorded on the accrual basis. After analyzing the company's records, the accountant reported that accounts receivable at the end of each year were as follows:

Year 1	$48,000
Year 2	76,800
Year 3	35,200

Sales commissions should be accrued at the rate of 10% of accounts receivable.

Instructions

a On the basis of this information, prepare a schedule showing the amount of net income Fire Equipment would have reported in each of the three years if it had followed accrual accounting for its sales and sales commissions.

b Comment on the differences in net income under the two methods and the significance of the trend in the net income figures as revised.

14B-4 Edward Lopez received large amounts of income from investments in mining properties and consequently was subject to a very high income tax rate. At the beginning of the current year he organized a new business entity, Lopez Engineering Company, which carried on construction work and also engaged in the purchase and sale of building materials.

Because Lopez was concerned about the large amount of income taxes he expected to pay on income from his mining investments, he gave the following instructions to his accountant: "In preparing the income statement for the first year of operations of Lopez Engineering Company, I want you to be as conservative as possible. Wherever alternative methods are available, you should choose the method which will lead to the minimum income tax this year."

The accountant followed these instructions and prepared the following income statement:

LOPEZ ENGINEERING COMPANY
Income Statement
First Year of Operations

Revenue:		
Sales—regular		$277,200
Collections on installment sales		396,000
Construction work completed		118,800
Total revenue		$792,000
Cost and expenses:		
Cost of goods sold—regular	$221,760	
Cost of goods sold—installment basis,		
80% of collections	316,800	
Cost of construction work completed	96,360	
Operating expenses	158,400	
Interest expense	64,680	
Total costs and expenses		858,000
Loss for first year of operations		$(66,000)

Lopez was pleased to know that he will be able to reduce his other taxable income as a result of the loss from his business. He was, however, concerned because his banker refused to lend him $132,000 for use in his business because, as the banker put it, "You've lost too much money in your first year of operations and I have a policy against lending money to unprofitable businesses." At this point, Lopez comes to you for advice and gives you additional information relating to the items appearing in the income statement. After reviewing this information, you suggest that the following changes be made:

(1) Installment sales amounted to $858,000; the cost of the goods sold was $686,400, or 80% of sales. The accountant reported only the cash collections as revenue and deducted a proportional amount as the cost of the goods sold on the installment basis. You recommend that the entire income on installment sales be included in the income statement.

(2) The revenue and cost of construction work include three contracts started and completed in the first year. In addition, the following data relate to the six contracts started in the first year which will be completed in the following year.

Total contract price	$1,425,600
Total estimated cost of contracts	1,188,000
Actual costs incurred in first year	396,000

You suggest that profit on these contracts be recognized on the percentage-of-completion basis.

(3) The ending inventory of goods to be sold on the regular basis was valued on the lifo basis at $67,320; this inventory on a fifo basis would have been $73,920. You propose that the first-in, first-out method be used in preparing the income statement to be resubmitted to the banker.

(4) Included in operating expense is depreciation of $21,120, computed by using an accelerated method. You recommend the use of the straight-line depreciation method, which would result in depreciation of only $15,840.

(5) Also included in operating expenses is $39,600 of expenditures which are applicable to future periods. You suggest that these items be deferred and reported in the balance sheet as assets.

Instructions

a Prepare a revised income statement for Lopez Engineering Company, giving effect to the changes in accounting you suggested to Lopez. (Ignore income taxes.) Certain key figures to appear in the revised income statement should be computed in supporting schedules. Reference to these supporting schedules should appear in the revised income statement. The appropriate supporting schedules are indicated in *b* below. (The first item of revenue, Sales—regular, means sales made on 30-day open account as opposed to sales on the installment plan.)

b Prepare the following separate schedules to support the revised income statement:

(1) A schedule showing the revenue from construction work measured on the percentage-of-completion basis

(2) A schedule showing the cost of goods sold—regular (30-day open account sales)

(3) A schedule showing the cost of construction work

(4) A schedule showing operating expenses

14B-5 The Pozzo Construction Company was organized early in Year 1 with the investment by Anthony Pozzo of $30 million in cash. He was the successful bidder on the construction of a section of highway. The bid price of the construction was $36 million. The construction will begin in Year 1 and will take almost two years to complete; the deadline for completion is near the end of Year 2.

The contract calls for payments of $7.2 million per year to Anthony Pozzo at the end of Year 1 and at the end of each of the next four years. Pozzo expects that construction costs will total $30 million, of which $12 million will be incurred in Year 1 and $18 million in Year 2.

Pozzo's accountant recognizes that there are a number of ways he might account for this contract. He might recognize income at the time the contract is completed (sales method), near the end of Year 2. Alternatively, he might recognize income during construction (production method), in proportion to the percentage of the total cost incurred in each of Years 1 and 2. Finally, he might recognize income in proportion to the percentage of the total contract price collected in installment receipts during the five-year period (installment method).

Instructions

a Assuming that the timing and cost of construction are exactly according to plan and that this contract is Pozzo's sole activity during the five-year period beginning with Year 1, prepare a comparative five-year statement (in millions of dollars) showing the amount of annual net income that would be reported each year and the balance in Pozzo's capital account (net assets) at the end of each year under each of the accounting methods considered by Pozzo's accountant. (Ignore income taxes.)

b Prepare comparative balance sheets (in millions of dollars) for Pozzo Construction Company as of the end of Year 1 and Year 2, under each of the three accounting methods.

c Explain how the measurement of Pozzo's capital (net assets) and the recognition of net income are related under each of the three accounting methods.

BUSINESS DECISION PROBLEM 14

For many years, Logan Company used the lifo method of inventory valuation and the declining-balance method of depreciation in measuring the net income of its mail-order business. In addition, Logan charged off all costs of catalogs as incurred. In Year 10, Logan changed its inventory pricing method to fifo, adopted the straight-line method of depreciation, and decided to charge off catalog costs only as catalogs are distributed to potential customers.

The following information for the last three years is taken from the accounting records:

	Year 10	Year 9	Year 8
Sales (net).	$600,000	$480,000	$420,000
Purchases (net)	360,000	264,000	240,000
Ending inventory—fifo	60,000	54,000	48,000
Ending inventory—lifo	36,000	33,600	30,000
Depreciation—declining-balance method	33,000	36,000	42,000
Depreciation—straight-line method	24,000	24,000	24,000
Operating expenses other than depreciation	144,600	111,600	96,000
Catalog costs included in operating expenses but			
considered applicable to future revenue	22,200	9,600	6,000
Net income as computed by Logan Company	120,000	72,000	44,400

At the end of Year 10, Logan Company prepared the following comparative income statement and presented it to a banker when applying for a substantial long-term loan:

LOGAN COMPANY
Comparative Income Statement
For Years Ended December 31

	Year 10	Year 9
Sales (net).	$600,000	$480,000
Cost of goods sold*	333,600	260,400
Gross profit on sales	$266,400	$219,600
Operating expenses	146,400	147,600
Net income	$120,000	$ 72,000

* Based on lifo inventory method in Year 9; inventory at end of Year 10 was valued on fifo basis.

The loan officer for the Plaza National Bank, where Logan has applied for the loan, asks your help in analyzing the earnings record of Logan Company.

Instructions

a Prepare a more detailed comparative income statement for Years 9 and 10. For the cost of goods sold section, you should use the figures listed in the three-column schedule at the beginning of this problem to show as individual items the beginning inventory, net purchases, cost of goods available for sale, ending inventory, and cost of goods sold. In the section for operating expenses, show the depreciation expense separately from other operating expenses. Summary figures should be the same as those compiled by Logan Company.

Criticize the detailed comparative income statement in terms of generally accepted accounting principles. Indicate the dollar effect on net income of any violations of accounting principles.

b Prepare two comparative income statements for Years 9 and 10. First, prepare a comparative statement on the same accounting basis as in prior years. Second, prepare a comparative income statement on the revised basis of accounting decided upon by the company.

c What good feature is common to both of the comparative income statements called for in **b** above. Comment on the *trend* of net income shown in each income statement in **b** above, and also in the comparative income statement prepared by Logan Company.

15 **Partnerships**

Three types of business organization are common to American business: the single proprietorship, the partnership, and the corporation. In this chapter we shall concentrate on the accounting problems peculiar to a partnership. The Uniform Partnership Act, which has been adopted by many states to govern the formation and operation of partnerships, defines a partnership as "an association of two or more persons to carry on, as co-owners, a business for profit."

Reasons for formation of partnerships

In the professions and in businesses which stress the factor of personal service, the partnership form of organization is widely used. The laws of the state may even deny the incorporation privilege to persons engaged in such professions as medicine, law, and public accounting, because the personal responsibility of the professional practitioner to his or her client might be lost behind the impersonal legal entity of the corporation. However, in recent years a number of states have passed legislation extending the privilege of incorporation to members of these professions.

In the fields of manufacturing, wholesaling, and retail trade, partnerships are also popular, because they afford a means of combining the capital and abilities of two or more persons. Perhaps the most common factor which impels an individual to seek a partner is the lack of sufficient capital to begin or to expand a business. A partnership is often referred to as a *firm;* the name of the firm often includes the word "company" as, for example, "Adams, Barnes, and Company."

Significant features of a partnership

Before taking up the accounting problems peculiar to partnerships, it will be helpful to consider briefly some of the distinctive characteristics of the partnership form of organization. These characteristics (such as limited life and unlimited liability) all stem from the basic point that a partnership is not a separate legal entity in itself but merely a voluntary association of individuals.

EASE OF FORMATION A partnership can be created without any legal formalities. When two persons agree to become partners, a partnership is automatically created. The voluntary aspect of a partnership agreement means that no one can be forced into a partnership or forced to continue as a partner.

LIMITED LIFE A partnership may be ended at any time by the death or withdrawal of any member of the firm. Other factors which may bring an end to a partnership include the bankruptcy or incapacity of a partner, the expiration of the period specified in the partnership contract, or the completion of the project for which the partnership was formed. The admission of a new partner or the retirement of an existing member means an end to the old partnership, although the business may be continued by the formation of a new partnership.

MUTUAL AGENCY Each partner acts as an agent of the partnership, with authority to enter into contracts for the purchase and sale of goods and services. The partnership is bound by the acts of any partner as long as these acts are within the scope of normal operations. The factor of mutual agency suggests the need for exercising great caution in the selection of a partner. To be in partnership with an irresponsible person or one lacking in integrity is an intolerable situation.

UNLIMITED LIABILITY Each partner is personally responsible for all the debts of the firm. The lack of any ceiling on the liability of a partner may deter a wealthy person from entering a partnership.

A new member joining an existing partnership may or may not assume liability for debts incurred by the firm prior to his or her admission. A partner withdrawing from membership must give adequate public notice of withdrawal; otherwise the former partner may be held liable for partnership debts incurred subsequent to his or her withdrawal. The retiring partner remains liable for partnership debts existing at the time of withdrawal unless the creditors agree to a release of this obligation.

CO-OWNERSHIP OF PARTNERSHIP PROPERTY AND PROFITS When a partner invests a building, inventory, or other property in a partnership, he or she does not retain any personal right to the assets contributed. The property becomes jointly owned by all partners. Each member of a partnership also has an ownership right in the profits.

Sometimes a store manager or other supervisory employee is allowed a certain percentage of the profits as a bonus, or in lieu of a fixed salary. This arrangement is merely a device for computing the bonus or salary; it does *not* give the employee an ownership right in the profits and does not make him a partner. Some retail stores rent their buildings under an agreement calling for a yearly rental computed as a percentage of profits. This type of rental agreement does not make the landlord a partner. To be a partner one must have an *ownership* right in the profits.

Advantages and disadvantages of a partnership

Perhaps the most important advantage and the principal reason for the formation of most partnerships is the opportunity to bring together sufficient capital to carry on a business. The opportunity to combine special skills, as, for example, the specialized talents of an engineer and an accountant, may also induce individuals to join forces in a partnership. The formation of a partnership is much easier and less expensive than the organization of a corporation. Operating as a partnership may produce income tax advantages. The partnership itself is not a legal entity and does not have to pay income taxes as does a corporation, although the individual partners pay taxes on their respective shares of the firm's income. Members of a partnership enjoy more freedom and flexibility of action than do the owners of a corporation; the partners may withdraw funds and make business decisions of all types without the necessity of formal meetings or legalistic procedures.

Offsetting these advantages of a partnership are such serious disadvantages as limited life, unlimited liability, and mutual agency. Furthermore, if a business is to require a large amount of capital, the partnership is a less effective device for raising funds than is a corporation.

The partnership contract

Although a partnership can generally be formed without any written agreement, it is highly desirable that a written contract of partnership be prepared by an attorney, setting forth the understanding between the partners on such points as the following:

1 The name, location, and nature of the business.
2 Names of the partners, and the duties and rights of each.
3 Amount to be invested by each partner. Procedure for valuing any noncash assets invested or withdrawn by partners.
4 Procedure for sharing profits and losses.
5 Withdrawals to be allowed each partner.
6 Provision for insurance on the lives of partners, with the partnership or the surviving partners named as beneficiaries.
7 The accounting period to be used.
8 Provision for periodic audit by certified public accountants.

9 Provision for arbitration of disputes.

10 Provision for dissolution. This part of the agreement may specify a method for computing the equity of a retiring or deceased partner and a method of settlement which will not disrupt the business.

Partnership accounting

An adequate accounting system and an accurate measurement of income are needed by every business, but they are especially important in a partnership because the net income is divided among two or more owners. All partners need current, accurate information on profits so that they can make intelligent decisions on such questions as additional investments, expansion of the business, or sale of their respective interests in the partnership.

Partnership accounting requires the maintenance of a separate capital account for each partner; a separate drawing account for each partner is also needed. The other distinctive feature of partnership accounting is the division of each year's net profit or loss among the partners in the proportions specified by the partnership agreement. In the study of partnership accounting, the new concepts lie almost entirely in the owners' equity section; accounting for partnership assets and liabilities follows the same principles as for other forms of business organization.

Opening the accounts of a new partnership

When a partner contributes assets other than cash, a question always arises as to the value of such assets. The valuations assigned to noncash assets should be their *fair market values* at the date of transfer to the partnership. The valuations assigned must be agreed to by all the partners.

To illustrate the opening entries for a newly formed partnership, assume that on January 1 John Blair and Richard Cross, who operate competing retail stores, decide to form a partnership by consolidating their two businesses. A capital account will be opened for each partner and credited with the agreed valuation of the *net assets* (total assets less total liabilities) he contributes. The journal entries to open the accounts of the partnership of Blair and Cross are as follows:

Entries for formation of partnership	*Cash*	*40,000*	
	Accounts Receivable	*60,000*	
	Inventory	*90,000*	
	Accounts Payable		*30,000*
	John Blair, Capital		*160,000*
	To record the investment by John Blair in the partnership of Blair and Cross.		

Cash	*10,000*	
Land	*60,000*	
Building	*100,000*	
Inventory	*60,000*	
Accounts Payable		*70,000*
Richard Cross, Capital		*160,000*

To record the investment by Richard Cross in the partnership of
Blair and Cross.

The values assigned to assets in the accounts of the new partnership may be quite different from the amounts at which these assets were carried in the accounts of their previous owners. For example, the land contributed by Cross and valued at $60,000 might have appeared in his accounting records at a cost of $20,000. The building which he contributed was valued at $100,000 by the partnership, but it might have cost Cross only $80,000 some years ago and might have been depreciated on his records to a net value of $60,000. Assuming that market values of land and buildings had risen sharply while Cross owned this property, it is no more than fair to recognize the *present market value* of these assets at the time he transfers them to the partnership and to credit his capital account accordingly. Depreciation of the building will begin anew in the partnership accounts and will be based on the assigned value of $100,000 at the date of acquisition by the partnership.

Additional investments

Assume that after six months of operation the firm is in need of more cash, and the partners make an additional investment of $10,000 each on July 1. These additional investments are credited to the capital accounts as shown below:

Entry for
additional
investment

Cash	*20,000*	
John Blair, Capital		*10,000*
Richard Cross, Capital		*10,000*

To record additional investments.

Drawing accounts

The drawing account maintained for each partner serves the same purpose as the drawing account of the owner of a single proprietorship. The transactions calling for debits to the drawing accounts of partners may be summarized as follows:

1 Cash or other assets withdrawn by a partner

2 Payments from partnership funds of the personal debts of a partner

3 Partnership cash collected on behalf of the firm by a partner but retained by the partner personally

Credits to the drawing accounts are seldom encountered; one rather unusual transaction requiring such an entry consists of the payment of a partnership liability by a partner out of personal funds.

Loans from partners

Ordinarily any funds furnished to the firm by a partner are recorded by crediting that partner's capital account. Occasionally, however, a partnership may be in need of funds but the partners do not wish to increase their permanent investment in the business, or perhaps one partner is willing to advance funds when the others are not. Under these circumstances, the advance of funds may be designated as a loan from the partner and credited to a partner's loan account. Partnership liabilities to outsiders always take precedence over any claims of partners.

Closing the accounts of a partnership at year-end

At the end of the accounting period, the balance in the Income Summary account is closed to the partners' capital accounts, in accordance with the profit-sharing provisions of the partnership contract. If the partnership contract does not mention how profits are to be divided, the law assumes that the intention of the partners was for an equal division of profits and losses. If the partnership agreement specifies a method of dividing profits but does not mention the possibility of losses, any losses are divided in the proportions provided for sharing profits.

In the previous illustration of the firm of Blair and Cross, an equal sharing of profits was agreed upon. Assuming that a profit of $60,000 was realized during the first year of operations, the entry to close the Income Summary account would be as follows:

Closing Income Summary: profits shared equally

Income Summary	60,000	
John Blair, Capital		30,000
Richard Cross, Capital		30,000

To divide net income for 19___ in accordance with partnership agreement to share profits equally.

The next step in closing the accounts is to transfer the balance of each partner's drawing account to his capital account. Assuming that withdrawals during the year amounted to $12,000 for Blair and $8,000 for Cross, the entry at December 31 to close the drawing accounts is as follows:

Closing the drawing accounts to capital accounts

John Blair, Capital	12,000	
Richard Cross, Capital	8,000	
John Blair, Drawing		12,000
Richard Cross, Drawing		8,000

To transfer debit balances in partners' drawing accounts to their respective capital accounts.

WORKING PAPERS The working papers for a partnership may include a pair of columns for each partner. These columns are placed between the Income Statement columns and the Balance Sheet columns of the work sheet. The net income or loss as shown in the Income Statement columns is also carried to the partners' capital columns and divided between them as provided in the partnership agreement. In all other aspects, the working papers for a partnership are identical to those for a single proprietorship as illustrated in Chapters 4 and 5.

INCOME STATEMENT FOR A PARTNERSHIP The income statement for a partnership differs from that of a single proprietorship in only one respect: a final section may be added to show the division of the net income between the partners, as illustrated on this page for the firm of Blair and Cross.

BLAIR AND CROSS
Income Statement
For the Year Ended December 31, 19____

Note distribution of net income

Sales			$600,000
Cost of goods sold:			
Inventory, Jan. 1		$150,000	
Purchases		310,000	
Cost of goods available for sale		$460,000	
Less: Inventory, Dec. 31		200,000	
Cost of goods sold			260,000
Gross profit on sales			$340,000
Operating expenses:			
Selling expenses		$200,000	
General & administrative expenses		80,000	280,000
Net income			$ 60,000
Distribution of net income:			
To John Blair (50%)		$ 30,000	
To Richard Cross (50%)		30,000	$ 60,000

STATEMENT OF PARTNERS' CAPITALS The partners will usually want an explanation of the change in their capital accounts from one year-end to the next. A supplementary schedule called a *statement of partners' capitals* is prepared to show this information. A statement of partners' capitals for Blair and Cross appears at the top of page 526.

The balance sheet for Blair and Cross would show the capital balance for each partner, as well as the total of $380,000.

BLAIR AND CROSS
Statement of Partners' Capitals
For the Year Ended December 31, 19___

	Blair	Cross	Total
Changes in capital accounts during the year Investment, Jan. 1, 19___	$160,000	$160,000	$320,000
Add: Additional investment	10,000	10,000	20,000
Net income for the year	30,000	30,000	60,000
Subtotals	$200,000	$200,000	$400,000
Less: Drawings	12,000	8,000	20,000
Balances, Dec. 31, 19___	$188,000	$192,000	$380,000

Partnership profits and income taxes

Partnerships are not required to pay income taxes. However, a partnership is required to file an information tax return showing the amount of the partnership net income ($60,000 in our example), and the share of each partner in the net income. Each partner must include his share of the partnership profit on his individual income tax return. Partnership net income is thus taxable to the partners individually in the year in which it is earned. In the partnership of Blair and Cross illustrated above, each would report and pay tax on $30,000 of partnership net income.

Note that partners report and pay tax on their respective shares of the profits earned by the partnership during the year and not on the amounts which they have drawn out of the business during the year. *The entire net income of the partnership is taxable to the partners each year,* even though there may have been no withdrawals. This treatment is consistent with that accorded a single proprietorship.

The nature of partnership profits

The profit earned by a partnership, like that of a single proprietorship, may be regarded as consisting of three distinct elements: (*1*) compensation for the personal services rendered by the partners, (*2*) compensation (interest) for the use of invested capital, and (*3*) a "pure" profit or reward for the entrepreneurial functions of risk taking and policy making. Recognition of these three elements of partnership profits will be helpful in formulating an equitable plan for the division of profits.

If one partner devotes full time to the business while another does not participate actively, the profit-sharing plan should give weight to this disparity in contributions of services. Any salaries authorized for partners *are regarded as a preliminary step in the division of profits, not as an expense of the business.* The partner is considered an owner, not an employee. The services which a partner renders to the firm are, therefore, considered to be rendered in anticipation of a share in profits, not in contemplation of a salary. Another reason for not treating salaries of partners as an expense of the business is that the amounts are often set arbitrarily without the arm's-length bargaining typical of employer-employee contracts. Consequently, the salary of a partner may not be closely related to the fair market value of the personal services the partner renders to the business. The net profit reported by a partnership cannot be compared directly with the profit earned by a corporation of similar size, because the corporation treats as expense any payments to owner-managers for personal services rendered.

In the solution of problems in this book, the student should record all withdrawals of assets by partners as debits to the partners' drawing accounts, regardless of whether or not the withdrawals are described as salaries. Some alternative treatments of salaries of partners can be more effectively explored in advanced accounting courses.

In the preceding illustrations of the partnership of Blair and Cross, we assumed that the partners invested equal amounts of capital, rendered equal services, and divided profits equally. We are now ready to consider cases in which the partners invest unequal amounts of capital and services.

Alternative methods of dividing profits and losses

The following alternative methods of dividing profits and losses place varying degrees of emphasis on the three elements (interest, salaries, and "pure" profit) comprising partnership profits.

1 A fixed ratio
2 A capital ratio
3 Interest on capital, salaries to partners, and remaining profits in a fixed ratio

FIXED RATIO The fixed-ratio method has already been illustrated in the example of the Blair and Cross partnership in which profits were divided equally. Partners may agree upon any fixed ratio, such as 60% and 40%, or 70% and 30%. In demonstrating the various other methods of profit sharing, the following capital accounts will be used:

	A. B. Adams, Capital			*B. C. Barnes, Capital*	
Capital accounts used in illustration	*19___*			*19___*	
	Jan. 1	*80,000*		*Jan. 1*	*20,000*
	July 1	*10,000*		*July 1*	*10,000*

During the first year of operations, Adams withdrew a total of $12,000 in cash and merchandise; Barnes made withdrawals of $24,000. These withdrawals were recorded by debits in the partners' drawing accounts. At year-end, the Income Summary account showed a credit balance of

$48,000, representing the net income for the year, before any salaries or interest to partners.

CAPITAL RATIO The division of profits on the basis of *relative capital investments* may be appropriate in a merchandising or manufacturing business if invested capital is regarded as the most important factor in the production of income. The capital ratio would generally not be a satisfactory basis for sharing profits in a partnership of professional persons, such as a law firm or public accounting firm. The technical skill and professional reputations of attorneys and accountants are usually much more significant in achieving profitable operations than is the small amount of capital required to establish a professional firm. When partners agree to base their profit-sharing plan on the factor of capital invested, the question of whether to use beginning capital balances or average capital must be decided.

Ratio of beginning capitals The beginning capitals for the firm of Adams and Barnes were as follows: A. B. Adams, $80,000, and B. C. Barnes, $20,000. Adams's beginning capital constitutes 80% ($80,000/$100,000) of the total beginning capital, and Barnes's beginning capital constitutes the other 20% ($20,000/$100,000). If the partners agreed to share profits in the ratio of their beginning capitals, the division of the first year's net income of $48,000 would be computed as follows:

		Division of Profit
Profit sharing; beginning capitals as basis	A. B. Adams ($48,000 × .80)	$38,400
	B. C. Barnes ($48,000 × .20)	9,600
	Total	$48,000

The entry to close the Income Summary account is as follows:

Income Summary	48,000	
A. B. Adams, Capital		38,400
B. C. Barnes, Capital		9,600

To close the Income Summary account by dividing the year's net income in the ratio of the beginning capitals.

The capital accounts of Adams and Barnes in this illustration will not remain in the original 80:20 proportion for two reasons: neither the additional investments made by the partners on July 1 nor the withdrawals of cash and merchandise during the year were in the proportion of the original investments. When profits are to be divided in the ratio of "beginning capitals," the partnership agreement may provide that the ratio will be set at the first of each year on the basis of the *new capital balances,* or the agreement may provide for the original ratio to remain in force regardless of subsequent changes in capital accounts.

Ratio of average capital investments Since the balances in the capital accounts may change significantly during the course of a year, the partners may prefer to use the *average* capitals rather than the beginning balances as the basis for dividing profits. To compute the average capital for a partner during the year, the first step is to multiply the capital balance at the beginning of the year by the number of months until the date of a change in the capital account. Multiply the new balance in the capital account by the number of months until the next change in the account. After carrying out this procedure for the entire year, add together the amounts thus obtained. The total represents the *dollar-months* of capital invested. Each partner's share of profits is equal to the ratio of his dollar-months to the total dollar-months for all the capital accounts.

In the partnership of Adams and Barnes the beginning capitals were $80,000 and $20,000, respectively. The only change in the capital accounts occurred on July 1 when each partner invested an additional $10,000. If we ignore the periodic withdrawals by the partners, the division of the year's profit of $48,000 would be computed as follows:

	Dollar-months
Profit A. B. Adams:	
sharing; Jan. 1 to June 30 ($80,000 × 6 months)	$ 480,000
average July 1 to Dec. 31 ($90,000 × 6 months)	540,000
capitals as	
basis Total	$1,020,000
B. C. Barnes:	
Jan. 1 to June 30 ($20,000 × 6 months)	$ 120,000
July 1 to Dec. 31 ($30,000 × 6 months)	180,000
Total	$ 300,000
Total dollar-months for both partners	$1,320,000

	Division of Profit
A. B. Adams $\left(\dfrac{1,020,000}{1,320,000} \times \$48,000 \text{ profit}\right)$	$37,091
B. C. Barnes $\left(\dfrac{300,000}{1,320,000} \times \$48,000 \text{ profit}\right)$	10,909
Total profit divided	$48,000

The entry to close the Income Summary account is:

Income Summary	48,000	
A. B. Adams, Capital		37,091
B. C. Barnes, Capital		10,909

To divide the year's net income between the partners in the ratio of average capital investments.

SALARIES, INTEREST, AND REMAINDER IN A FIXED RATIO Since partners often contribute varying amounts of personal services as well as different amounts of capital, partnership agreements often provide for partners' salaries as a factor in the division of profits.

As a first example, assume that Adams and Barnes agree that Adams will be allowed an annual salary of $12,000 and Barnes an annual salary of $24,000. Any remaining profits will be divided equally. It is agreed that the salaries will be withdrawn in cash each month and recorded by debits to the drawing accounts.[1] The authorized salaries total $36,000 a year; this amount represents a first step in the division of the year's profit and is therefore subtracted from the net income of $48,000. The remaining profit of $12,000 will be divided equally.

Distribution of Net Income

Net income to be divided		$48,000
Salaries to partners:		
A. B. Adams	$12,000	
B. C. Barnes	24,000	36,000
Remaining profit, to be divided equally		$12,000
A. B. Adams	$ 6,000	
B. C. Barnes	6,000	12,000

Profit sharing; salaries and fixed ratio as basis

Under this agreement, Adams's share of the $48,000 net income amounts to $18,000 ($12,000 + $6,000) and Barnes's share amounts to $30,000 ($24,000 + $6,000). The entry to close the Income Summary account would be:

Income Summary	48,000	
A. B. Adams, Capital		18,000
B. C. Barnes, Capital		30,000

To close the Income Summary account by crediting each partner with his authorized salary and dividing the remaining profits equally.

The preceding example took into consideration the difference in the value of personal services contributed by Adams and Barnes but ignored the disparity in capital contributions. In the next example, we shall assume that the partners agree to a profit-sharing plan providing for interest on beginning capitals as well as salaries. Salaries, as before, are authorized at $12,000 for Adams and $24,000 for Barnes. Each partner is to be allowed interest at 6% on his beginning capital balance, and any remaining profit is to be divided equally.

---

[1] Salaries may be used as a device for dividing partnership net income, even though the partners do not wish to make any withdrawals of cash whatsoever. In this illustration, however, it is assumed that cash is withdrawn by each partner in an amount equal to his or her authorized salary.

Distribution of Net Income

*Profit
sharing;
salaries, in-
terest, and
fixed ratio
as basis*

Net income to be divided			$48,000
Salaries to partners:			
A. B. Adams	$12,000		
B. C. Barnes	24,000	$36,000	
Interest on invested capital:			
A. B. Adams ($80,000 × .06)	$ 4,800		
B. C. Barnes ($20,000 × .06)	1,200	6,000	42,000
Remaining profit to be divided equally			$ 6,000
A. B. Adams		$ 3,000	
B. C. Barnes		3,000	6,000

This three-step division of the year's profit of $48,000 has resulted in giving Adams a total of $19,800 and Barnes a total of $28,200. The amounts credited to each partner may be summarized as follows:

	Adams	Barnes	Together
Salaries	$12,000	$24,000	$36,000
Interest on beginning capitals	4,800	1,200	6,000
Remaining profit divided equally	3,000	3,000	6,000
Totals	$19,800	$28,200	$48,000

The entry to close the Income Summary account will be:

Income Summary	48,000	
A. B. Adams, Capital		19,800
B. C. Barnes, Capital		28,200

To close the Income Summary account by crediting each partner with his authorized salary and with interest on his beginning capital at 6%, and by dividing the remaining profits equally.

AUTHORIZED SALARIES AND INTEREST IN EXCESS OF NET INCOME In the preceding example the total of the authorized salaries and interest was $42,000 and the net income to be divided was $48,000. Suppose that the net income had been only $30,000; how should the division have been made?

If the partnership contract provides for salaries and interest on invested capital, these provisions are to be followed even though the net income for the year is less than the total of the authorized salaries and interest. If the net income of the firm of Adams and Barnes amounted to only $30,000, this amount would be distributed as shown on page 532.

Distribution of Net Income

Net income to be divided			$30,000
Salaries to partners:			
A. B. Adams	$12,000		
B. C. Barnes	24,000	$36,000	
Interest on invested capital:			
A. B. Adams ($80,000 × .06)	$ 4,800		
B. C. Barnes ($20,000 × .06)	1,200	6,000	42,000
Residual loss to be divided equally			$12,000
A. B. Adams		$ 6,000	
B. C. Barnes		6,000	12,000

The residual loss of $12,000 must be divided equally because the
partnership contract states that profits and losses are to be divided
equally after providing for salaries and interest.

The result of this distribution of the net income of $30,000 has been to
give Adams a total of $10,800 and Barnes a total of $19,200. The entry to
close the Income Summary account will be as follows:

Income Summary	30,000	
A. B. Adams, Capital		10,800
B. C. Barnes, Capital		19,200

*To close the Income Summary account by crediting each partner with
his authorized salary and with interest on his beginning capital at
6% and by dividing the residual loss equally.*

Admission of a new partner

An individual may gain admission to an existing partnership in either of
two ways: (1) by buying an interest from one or more of the present
partners, or (2) by making an investment in the partnership. When an
incoming partner purchases an equity from a present member of the firm,
the payment goes personally to the old partner, and there is no change in
the assets or liabilities of the partnership. On the other hand, if the
incoming partner acquires an equity by making an investment in the
partnership, the assets of the firm are increased by the amount paid in by
the new partner.

BY PURCHASE OF AN INTEREST When a new partner buys an interest from
a present member of a partnership, the only change in the accounts will
be a transfer from the capital account of the selling partner to the capital
account of the incoming partner.

Assume, for example, that L has a $50,000 equity in the partnership of
L, M, and N. Partner L arranges to sell his entire interest to X for $80,000
cash. Partners M and N agree to the admission of X, and the transaction is

recorded in the partnership accounts by the following entry:

<table>
<tr><td>*Incoming partner buys interest from present partner*</td><td>L, Capital ....</td><td>50,000</td><td></td></tr>
<tr><td></td><td>   X, Capital ....</td><td></td><td>50,000</td></tr>
</table>

Incoming partner buys interest from present partner   *To record the transfer of L's equity to the incoming partner, X.*

Note that the entry in the partnership accounts was for $50,000, the recorded amount of Partner L's equity. *The amount of this entry was not influenced by the price paid the retiring partner by the new member.* The payment of $80,000 from X to L was a personal transaction between the two individuals; it did not affect the assets or liabilities of the partnership and is therefore not entered in the partnership accounting records.

As a separate but related example, assume that X is to gain admission to the firm of L, M, and N by purchasing one-fourth of the equity of each partner. The present capital accounts are as follows: Partner L, $80,000; Partner M, $80,000; and Partner N, $80,000. The payments by the incoming partner X are to go to the old partners personally and not to the partnership. The only entry required is the following:

No change in total capital

L, Capital	20,000	
M, Capital	20,000	
N, Capital	20,000	
X, Capital		60,000

To record admission of X to a one-fourth interest in the firm by purchase of one-fourth of the equity of each of the old partners.

BY AN INVESTMENT IN THE FIRM An incoming partner may acquire an equity by making an investment in the firm. In this case the payment by the new partner goes to the partnership and not to the partners as individuals; the investment therefore increases the partnership assets and also the total owners' equity of the firm. As an example, assume that Dan Phillips and Joe Ryan are partners, each having a capital account of $100,000. They agree to admit Bart Smith to a one-half interest in the business upon his investment of $200,000 in cash. The entry to record the admission of Smith would be as follows:

Investment in business by new partner

Cash	200,000	
Bart Smith, Capital		200,000

To record the admission of Bart Smith to a one-half interest in the firm.

Although Smith has a one-half equity in the net assets of the new firm of Phillips, Ryan, and Smith, he is not necessarily entitled to receive one-half of the profits. Profit sharing is a matter for agreement among the partners; if the new partnership contract contains no mention of profit sharing, the assumption is that the three partners intended to share profits and losses equally.

ALLOWING A BONUS TO FORMER PARTNERS If an existing partnership has exceptionally high earnings year after year, the present partners may demand a *bonus* as a condition for admission of a new partner. In other words, to acquire an interest of, say, $80,000, the incoming partner may be required to invest $120,000 in the partnership. The excess investment of $40,000 may be regarded as a bonus to the old partners and credited to their capital accounts in the established ratio for profit sharing.

To illustrate the recording of a bonus to the old partners, let us assume that James Rogers and Richard Steel are members of a highly successful partnership. As a result of profitable operations, the partners' capital accounts have doubled within a few years and presently stand at $100,000 each. David Taylor desires to join the firm and offers to invest $100,000 for a one-third interest. Rogers and Steel refuse this offer but extend a counteroffer to Taylor of $120,000 for a one-fourth interest in the capital of the firm and a one-fourth interest in profits. Taylor accepts these terms because of his desire to share in the unusually large profits of the business. The recording of Taylor's admission to the partnership is based on the following calculations:

Calculation of bonus to old partners	

Net assets (owners' equity) of old partnership	$200,000
Cash investment by Taylor	120,000
Net assets (owners' equity) of new partnership	$320,000
Taylor's one-fourth interest	$ 80,000

To acquire an interest of $80,000 in the net assets of $320,000, Taylor has invested $120,000. His excess investment or bonus of $40,000 will be divided equally between Rogers and Steel, since their partnership agreement called for equal sharing of profits and losses.

The entry to record Taylor's admission to the partnership follows:

Recording bonus to old partners	

Cash	120,000	
David Taylor, Capital		80,000
James Rogers, Capital		20,000
Richard Steel, Capital		20,000

To record admission of David Taylor as a partner with a one-fourth interest in capital and profits.

ALLOWING A BONUS TO NEW PARTNER An existing partnership may sometimes be very anxious to bring in a new partner who can bring needed cash to the firm. In other instances the new partner may be a person of extraordinary ability or may possess advantageous business contacts that will presumably add to the profitability of the partnership. Under either of these sets of circumstances, the old partners may offer the new member a bonus in the form of a capital account larger than the amount of the incoming partner's investment.

Assume, for example, that A. M. Bryan and R. G. Davis are equal partners, each having a capital account of $36,000. Since the firm is in desperate need of cash, they offer to admit Kay Grant to a one-third interest in the firm upon her investment of only $24,000 in cash. The amounts of the capital accounts for the three members of the new firm are computed as follows:

Total capital of old partnership:

A. M. Bryan, capital	*$36,000*	
R. G. Davis, capital	*36,000*	*$72,000*
Cash invested by Kay Grant		*24,000*
Total capital of new three-member partnership		*$96,000*
Capital of each partner in the new firm:		
A. M. Bryan ($96,000 × ⅓)	*$32,000*	
R. G. Davis ($96,000 × ⅓)	*32,000*	
Kay Grant ($96,000 × ⅓)	*32,000*	*96,000*

The following journal entry records the admission of Grant to a one-third interest in the business and also adjusts each capital account to the required level of $32,000.

Entry for	*Cash* *24,000*	
bonus to	*A. M. Bryan, Capital* *4,000*	
new partner	*R. G. Davis, Capital* *4,000*	
	Kay Grant, Capital	*32,000*
	To record admission of Grant to a one-third interest, and the	
	allowance of a bonus to her.	

Retirement of a partner

A partner interested in retirement may, with the consent of the other partners, sell his or her interest to an outsider. In this case the payment by the incoming partner goes directly to the retiring partner, and there is no change in the assets or liabilities of the partnership. The only entry required is to transfer the capital account of the retiring partner to an account with the new partner. This transaction is virtually the same as the one described on pages 532–533 for the admission of a partner by purchase of an interest.

Next, let us change our assumptions slightly and say that Carol Coe, the retiring partner, has a $100,000 interest which she sells to her fellow partners, A and B, in equal amounts. A and B make the agreed payment to Coe from their personal funds, so again the partnership assets and liabilities are not changed. Regardless of the price agreed to for Coe's interest, the transaction can be handled in the partnership accounting records merely by transferring the $100,000 balance in Coe's capital account to the capital accounts of the other two partners.

No change	*Carol Coe, Capital* *100,000*	
in total	*A, Capital*	*50,000*
capital	*B, Capital*	*50,000*
	To record the sale of Coe's interest in equal portions to A and B.	

There are other acceptable methods of handling this transaction. For example, if A and B agree to pay Coe an amount greater than the balance of her capital account, the reason for the excess payment may be that the present market values of the partnership assets are greater than the amounts shown in the accounts. Under these circumstances a revaluation of the assets may be decided upon.

PAYMENT TO RETIRING PARTNER FROM PARTNERSHIP ASSETS The retiring partner, Carol Coe, may be paid from partnership funds an amount equal to her capital account or a larger or smaller amount. The present market values of the partnership assets may be quite different from the book figures and goodwill may have been developed although not recorded in the accounts. One solution is to adjust the asset accounts to current appraised values. A corresponding increase or decrease would be made in the partners' capital accounts in the agreed ratio for sharing profits and losses.

As an alternative, any excess payment to the retiring partner may be treated as a bonus to her which must be charged against the capital accounts of the continuing partners in the agreed ratio for sharing profits and losses, as shown below:

Bonus paid to retiring partner	Carol Coe, Capital (retiring partner)	100,000	
	A, Capital	20,000	
	B, Capital	20,000	
	Cash		140,000

*To record the retirement of partner Coe, and payment of her
capital account plus a bonus of $40,000.*

As a separate example, assume that Coe is to receive a settlement smaller than her capital account balance, because she agrees to take a loss in order to expedite the settlement. If Coe surrenders her $100,000 interest for $80,000, the entry will be:

Payment to retiring part-ner of less than book equity	Carol Coe, Capital	100,000	
	Cash		80,000
	A, Capital		10,000
	B, Capital		10,000

*To record the retirement of Coe, and settlement in full for $20,000
less than the balance of her capital account.*

Death of a partner

A partnership is dissolved by the death of any member. To determine the amount owing to the estate of the deceased partner, it is usually necessary to close the accounts and prepare financial statements. This serves to credit all partners with their individual shares of the net income earned during the fractional accounting period ending with the date of *dissolution.*

The partnership agreement may prescribe procedures for making settlement with the estate of a deceased partner. Such procedures often include an audit by certified public accountants, appraisal of assets, and computation of goodwill. If payment to the estate must be delayed, the amount owed should be carried in a liability account replacing the deceased partner's capital account.

INSURANCE ON LIVES OF PARTNERS Members of a partnership often obtain life insurance policies which name the partnership as the beneficiary. Upon the death of a partner, the cash collected from the insurance company is used to pay the estate of the deceased partner. An alternative plan is to have each partner named as the beneficiary of an insurance policy covering the lives of the other partners. In the absence of insurance on the lives of partners, there might be insufficient cash available to pay the deceased partner's estate without disrupting the operation of the business.

Liquidation of a partnership

A partnership is terminated or dissolved whenever a new partner is added or an old partner withdraws. The termination or dissolution of a partnership, however, does not necessarily indicate that the business is to be discontinued. Often the business continues with scarcely any outward evidence of the change in membership of the firm. Termination of a partnership indicates a change in the membership of the firm, which may or may not be followed by liquidation.

The process of breaking up and discontinuing a partnership business is called *liquidation.* Liquidation of a partnership spells an end to the business. If the business is to be discontinued, the assets will be sold, the liabilities paid, and the remaining cash distributed to the partners.

SALE OF THE BUSINESS The partnership of X, Y, and Z sells its business to the North Corporation. The balance sheet appears as follows:

X, Y, AND Z

Balance Sheet

December 31, 19___

Cash	*$ 50,000*	*Accounts payable*		*$100,000*
Inventory	*200,000*	*X, capital*		*140,000*
Other assets	*150,000*	*Y, capital*		*120,000*
		Z, capital		*40,000*
	$400,000			*$400,000*

Partnership at time of sale

The terms of sale provide that the partnership will retain the cash of $50,000 and will pay the liabilities of $100,000. The inventory and other assets will be sold to the North Corporation for a consideration of $230,000. The entry to record the sale of the inventory and other assets is as follows:

Entries for sale of business

Accounts Receivable, North Corporation	*230,000*	
.Loss on Sale of Business	*120,000*	
Inventory		*200,000*
Other Assets		*150,000*

To record the sale of all assets other than cash to North Corporation.

Cash	*230,000*	
Accounts Receivable, North Corporation		*230,000*

Collected the receivable from sale of assets.

Division of the gain or loss from sale of the business The gain or loss from the sale of the business must be divided among the partners in the agreed profit- and loss-sharing ratio *before* any cash is distributed to them. The amount of cash to which each partner is entitled in liquidation cannot be determined until each capital account has been increased or decreased by the proper share of the gain or loss on disposal of the assets. Assuming that X, Y, and Z share profits and losses equally, the entry to allocate the $120,000 loss on the sale of the business will be as follows:

Entry to divide loss on sale

X, Capital	*40,000*	
Y, Capital	*40,000*	
Z, Capital	*40,000*	
Loss on Sale of Business		*120,000*

To divide the loss on the sale of the business among the partners in the established ratio for sharing profits and losses.

Distribution of cash The balance sheet of X, Y, and Z appears as follows after the loss on the sale of the assets has been entered in the partners' capital accounts:

X, Y, AND Z
Balance Sheet
(After the Sale of All Assets Except Cash)

Balance sheet after sale of assets

Assets		Liabilities & Partners' Equity	
Cash	$280,000	Accounts payable	$100,000
		X, capital	100,000
		Y, capital	80,000
		Z, capital	–0–
	$280,000		$280,000

The creditors must be paid in full before cash is distributed to the partners. The sequence of entries is shown on page 539.

(1) Pay	Accounts Payable	100,000	
creditors	Cash		100,000
	To pay the creditors in full.		

(2) Pay	X, Capital	100,000	
partners	Y, Capital	80,000	
	Cash		180,000 ,
	To complete liquidation of the business by distributing the		
	remaining cash to the partners according to the balances in		
	their capital accounts.		

Note that the equal division of the $120,000 loss on the sale of the business reduced the capital account of Partner Z to zero; therefore, Z received nothing when the cash was distributed to the partners. This action is consistent with the original agreement of the partners to share profits and losses equally. In working partnership liquidation problems, accounting students sometimes make the error of dividing the cash among the partners in the profit- and loss-sharing ratio. A profit- and loss-sharing ratio means just what the name indicates; it is a ratio for sharing profits and losses, ***not a ratio for sharing cash or any other asset.*** The amount of cash which a partner should receive in liquidation will be indicated by the balance in the capital account after the gain or loss from the disposal of assets has been divided among the partners in the agreed ratio for sharing profits and losses.

Treatment of debit balance in a capital account To illustrate this situation, let us change our assumptions concerning the sale of the assets by the firm of X, Y, and Z, and say that the loss incurred on the sale of assets was $144,000 rather than the $120,000 previously illustrated. Z's one-third share of a $144,000 loss would be $48,000, which would wipe out the $40,000 credit balance in his capital account and create a $8,000 debit balance. After the liabilities had been paid, a balance sheet for the partnership would appear as follows:

X, Y, AND Z

Balance Sheet

(After the Sale of All Assets Except Cash)

Z now owes	Cash	$156,000	X, capital	$ 92,000
$4,000 to	Z, capital	8,000	Y, capital	72,000
the partner-		$164,000		$164,000
ship				

To eliminate the debit balance in the capital account for Z the partnership should collect from Z $8,000 in cash. If this collection is made, the capital balance for Z will become zero, and the cash on hand will be increased to $164,000, which is just enough to pay X and Y the balances shown by their capital accounts.

If Z is unable to pay the $8,000 due to the firm, how should the $156,000 of cash on hand be divided between X and Y, whose capital accounts stand at $92,000 and $72,000, respectively? Failure of Z to pay in the debit balance means an additional loss to X and Y; according to the original partnership agreement, X and Y are to share profits and losses equally. Therefore, each must absorb $4,000 additional loss thrown on them by Z's inability to pay the $8,000 due to the partnership. The $156,000 of cash on hand should be divided between X and Y in such a manner that the capital account of each will be paid down to $4,000, their respective shares of the additional loss. The journal entry to record this distribution of cash to X and Y is as follows:

Entry to re-cord distri-bution of cash on hand	X, Capital	**88,000**
	Y, Capital	**68,000**
	Cash	**156,000**

To divide the remaining cash by paying down the capital accounts of X and Y to a balance of $4,000 each, representing the division of Z's loss between them.

After this entry has been posted the only accounts still open in the partnership records will be the capital accounts of the three partners. A trial balance of the ledger will appear as follows:

X, Y, AND Z
Trial Balance
(After Distribution of Cash)

Trial balance after cash distribution	X, capital.		$4,000
	Y, capital.		4,000
	Z, capital.	$8,000	
		$8,000	$8,000

If Z is able later to pay in the $8,000 debit balance, X and Y will then receive the additional $4,000 each indicated by the credit balances in their accounts. If Z is not able to make good the debit balance, the distribution of cash to X and Y will have been equitable under the circumstances.

KEY TERMS INTRODUCED OR EMPHASIZED IN CHAPTER 15

Bonus to former partners Portion of the investment by an incoming partner which may be credited to the capital accounts of the former partners. A premium paid to gain admission.

Bonus to new partner Excess of the capital account granted to a new partner over and above the amount of his investment. A special inducement to persuade an individual to join an existing partnership.

Co-ownership of property and profits The concept that all property of a partnership is owned by the partners as a group and that each partner has an ownership right in the profits.

Information return A partnership is not a taxable entity, but must file an information return with the IRS, showing the partnership net income and the share therein of each partner.

Limited life A partnership is legally dissolved by the death or withdrawal of any partner.

Liquidation The process of breaking up and discontinuing a partnership, including the sale of assets, payment of creditors, and distribution of remaining assets to the partners.

Mutual agency Authority of each partner to act as agent for the partnership within its normal scope of operations and to enter into contracts which bind the partnership.

Partnership An association of two or more persons to carry on as co-owners a business for profits.

Partnership contract An agreement among partners on the formation and operation of the partnership. Usually includes such points as a plan for sharing profits, amounts to be invested, and provision for dissolution.

Profit sharing A plan for division of partnership profits and losses among partners. May include salaries, allowances for interest on capital, and allowances for a fixed ratio. In the absence of an agreement on profit sharing, the law assumes an intention to share profits equally.

Purchase of an interest Transfer of all or part of the capital account of an existing partner to an incoming partner. Involves payment between individuals and not to the partnership.

Salaries to partners A method for division of a portion of partnership net income according to the agreed value of personal services rendered by individual partners. Not an expense, but a device for sharing profits.

Statement of partners' capitals An annual financial statement which shows for each partner and for the firm the amounts of beginning capitals, additional investments, net income, drawings, and ending capitals.

Uniform Partnership Act Uniform legislation enacted by most states which governs the formation, operation, and liquidation of partnerships.

Unlimited liability Personal responsibility of each partner for all debts of the partnership.

DEMONSTRATION PROBLEM FOR YOUR REVIEW

The accounts shown below and on page 542 appear in the records of the Bison Company after all revenue and expense accounts have been closed at the end of the first year of operations:

Partner B, Capital

	Jan. 1	Bal.	54,000
	Nov. 1	Investment	27,000

Partner B, Drawing

Dec. 31	Bal.	9,000	

Partner S, Capital

July 31	Excess withdrawal	12,000	Jan. 1	Bal.	54,000

Partner S, Drawing

Dec. 31 Bal.	10,800	

Income Summary

	Dec. 31 Bal.	38,000

The partnership agreement (drawn up by B's uncle) contains the following provision relative to the division of income: "Partner B shall be allowed a salary of $750 per month; Partner S shall be allowed a salary of $900 per month. Each partner shall be allowed 20% per annum on his invested capital. Any excess or deficiency shall be divided equally. Withdrawals in excess of above salary allowances in any month shall be charged against capital."

At the end of the year, the partners find they cannot agree on the division of income. Partner S maintains that 20% interest on capital as of the beginning of the year should be credited to each partner. Partner B maintains that the 20% should be applied to capital as of the end of the year and that he should be credited with $16,200 and S with $8,400 as interest. When it is apparent that agreement is impossible, the partners consent to submit their controversy to arbitration.

Instructions

a As an arbitrator, how would you settle this disagreement? How might the partnership agreement be amended to avoid this difficulty in future years?

b Assuming that your decision in *a* is adopted, make the journal entries necessary to complete the closing of the partnership accounts at December 31.

SOLUTION TO DEMONSTRATION PROBLEM

a The difficulty stems from the fact that the partnership agreement does not clearly specify the agreed meaning of the term *invested capital.* Since Partner B has added capital during the year while Partner S has withdrawn capital, neither the capital at the beginning nor that at the end of the year is representative of their investment throughout the year. A reasonable decision would be to compute the "investment allowance" by taking 20% of a weighted average of capital invested throughout the year. An average daily capital could be computed, but for the purpose at hand an average by months is sufficiently precise. The partnership agreement should be amended to specify the meaning of the term *invested capital* that the partners intend to apply in future years.

b Journal entries to complete closing as of Dec. 31:

Income Summary	19,800	
B, Capital		9,000
S, Capital		10,800
To credit each partner with salary allowance.		

Income Summary	21,500	
B, Capital		11,700
S, Capital		9,800
To credit each partner with allowance of 20% on average capital, computed as follows:		

B: ***Dollar-months***

$54,000 invested for 10 months . .	*$540,000*
$81,000 invested for 2 months . . .	*162,000*
Total dollar-months invested	*$702,000*
Average investment (divide by 12) .	*$ 58,500*
20% of average investment	*$ 11,700*

S:

$54,000 invested for 7 months . . .	*$378,000*
$42,000 invested for 5 months . . .	*210,000*
Total dollar-months invested	*$588,000*
Average investment (divide by 12) .	*$ 49,000*
20% of average investment	*$ 9,800*

B, Capital	*1,650*	
S, Capital	*1,650*	
Income Summary		*3,300*

To divide excess of salary and interest allowances over income among partners equally:

Salaries	*$19,800*
Interest on capital	*21,500*
Total	*$41,300*
Income for year . .	*38,000*
Excess	*$ 3,300*

B, Capital	*9,000*	
S, Capital	*10,800*	
B, Drawing		*9,000*
S, Drawing		*10,800*

To close partners' drawing accounts.

REVIEW QUESTIONS

1 Explain the difference between being admitted to a partnership by buying an interest from an existing partner and by making an investment in the partnership.

2 Is it possible that a partnership agreement containing interest and salary allowances as a step toward distributing income could cause a partnership net loss to be distributed so that one partner's capital account would be decreased by more than the amount of the entire partnership net loss?

3 Jane Miller is the proprietor of a small manufacturing business. She is considering the possibility of joining in partnership with Bracken, whom she considers to be thoroughly competent and congenial. Prepare a brief statement outlining the advantages and disadvantages of the potential partnership to Miller.

4 Scott has land having a book value of $5,000 and a fair market value of $8,000, and a building having a book value of $50,000 and a fair market value of

$40,000. The land and building become Scott's sole capital contribution to a partnership. What is Scott's capital balance in the new partnership? Why?

5 Allen and Baker are considering forming a partnership. What do you think are the two most important factors for them to include in their partnership agreement?

6 Partner X withdraws $25,000 from a partnership during the year. When the statements are made at the end of the year, X's share of the partnership income is $15,000. Which amount must X report on his income tax return?

7 Partner John Young has a choice to make. He has been offered by his partners a choice between no salary allowance and a one-third share in the partnership income or a salary of $6,000 per year and a one-quarter share of residual profits. Write a brief memorandum explaining the factors he should consider in reaching a decision.

8 What factors should be considered in drawing up an agreement as to the way in which income shall be shared by two or more partners?

9 Bill Bray and Carl Carter are partners who share profits and losses equally. The current balances in their capital accounts are: Bray, $20,000; Carter, $15,000. If Carter sells his interest in the firm to Deacon for $20,000 and Bray consents to the sale, what entry should be made in the partnership accounting records?

10 What is meant by the term *mutual agency?*

11 If C is going to be admitted to the partnership of A and B, why is it first necessary to determine the current fair market value of the assets of the partnership of A and B?

12 Describe how a *dissolution* of a partnership may differ from a *liquidation* of a partnership.

13 What measure can you suggest to prevent a partnership from having insufficient cash available to pay the estate of a deceased partner without disrupting the operation of the business?

14 What factors should be considered when comparing the net income figure of a partnership to that of a corporation of similar size?

15 Upon the death of Robert Bell, a partner in the firm of Bell, Cross, and Davis, Charles Bell, the son of Robert Bell, demanded that he replace his father as a member of the partnership. Can Charles Bell enforce this demand? Explain.

16 The partnership of X and Y is being dissolved. After the assets had been sold at a loss, the cash balance was $38,000. All creditors' claims, amounting to $14,000, were then paid. The capital account for X then showed a credit balance twice as large as that for Y. What must be the amount of Y's capital account? Explain.

EXERCISES

Ex. 15-1 A business owned by John Rogers was short of cash and Rogers therefore decided to form a partnership with Steve Wilson, who was able to contribute cash to the new partnership. The assets contributed by Rogers appeared as follows in the balance sheet of his business: cash, $900; accounts receivable, $18,900, with an allowance for doubtful accounts of $600; inventory, $42,000; and store equipment, $15,000. Rogers had recorded depreciation of $1,500 during his use of the store equipment in his single proprietorship.

Rogers and Wilson agreed that the allowance for doubtful accounts was inadequate and should be $1,000. They also agreed that a fair value for the inventory was its replacement cost of $46,000 and that the fair value of the store equipment was $12,000. You are to open the partnership accounts by making a general journal entry to record the investment by Rogers.

Ex. 15-2 Explain briefly the effect of each of the transactions given below on a partner's capital and drawing accounts:

a Partner borrows funds from the business.

b Partner collects a partnership account receivable while on vacation and uses the funds for personal purposes.

c Partner receives in cash the salary allowance provided in the partnership agreement.

d Partner takes home merchandise (cost $80, selling price $120) for personal use.

e Partner has loaned money to the partnership. The principal together with interest at 6% is now repaid in cash.

Ex. 15-3 On July 31, 19____, A and B agreed to combine their single proprietorships into a partnership. The partnership will take over all assets and assume all liabilities of A and B. The balance sheets for A and B are shown below:

	A's Business		*B's Business*	
	Book Value	*Fair Value*	*Book Value*	*Fair Value*
Assets				
Cash	$ 2,500	$ 2,500	$ 9,000	$ 9,000
Accounts receivable . . .	12,000	11,600	30,000	29,000
Inventory	18,000	20,400	40,000	35,000
Equipment (net)	23,000	23,500	62,000	76,200
Total	$55,500	$58,000	$141,000	$149,200
Liabilities & Owner's Capital				
Accounts payable	$20,500	$20,500	$ 39,500	$ 41,000
Accrued wages payable .	600	600	1,000	1,000
A, capital	34,400	36,900		
B, capital			100,500	107,200
Total	$55,500	$58,000	$141,000	$149,200

Accounts receivable of $1,400 are written off as uncollectible. This write-off explains the difference in amounts of accounts receivable shown in the Book Value and Fair Value column. The book value of B's accounts payable was less than fair value because liabilities of $1,500 had not been recorded.

Prepare a *classified* balance sheet in good form for the new entity of A-B Company immediately following formation of the partnership.

Ex. 15-4 Marsh and Nelson form a partnership by investing $40,000 amd $60,000, respectively. Determine how the first year's net income of $45,000 would be divided under each of the following assumptions:

a The partnership agreement does not mention profit sharing.

b Net income to be divided in the ratio of the original investments.

c Interest at 8% to be allowed on original capital investments and balance to be divided equally.

d Salaries of $18,000 to Marsh and $15,000 to Nelson, balance to be divided equally.

e Interest at 9% to be allowed on original capital investments, salaries of $18,000 to Marsh and $15,000 to Nelson, balance to be divided equally.

Ex. 15-5 Redmond and Ancil form a partnership, with Redmond investing $45,000 and Ancil $30,000. They agree to share net income as follows:
(1) Interest at 8% on beginning capital balances.
(2) Salary allowances of $24,000 to Redmond and $18,000 to Ancil.
(3) Any partnership earnings in excess of the amount required to cover the interest and salary allowances to be divided 45% to Redmond and 55% to Ancil.

    The partnership net income for the first year of operations amounted to $60,000 before interest and salary allowances. Show how this $60,000 should be divided between the two partners. Use a three-column schedule with a separate column for each partner and a total column. List on separate lines the amounts of interest, salaries, and the residual amount divided.

Ex. 15-6 Hal Jones, Carl Kent, and Dave Lawrence are partners and each has a capital account of $40,000. Kent, who owns another business, wishes to sell his equity in the partnership to his son, Charles, for $5,000 cash and a promissory note (without interest) for $15,000. Jones and Lawrence agree to the admission of Charles Kent as a partner. Prepare a general journal entry to record the transfer of Carl Kent's equity in the business.

Ex. 15-7 A and B are partners having capital balances of $60,000 and $30,000. They share profits equally. The partnership has been quite profitable and has an excellent reputation. A and B agree to admit C to a one-third interest in the partnership for an investment of $54,000. The assets of the business are not to be revalued. Explain how the bonus to the old partners is computed and prepare a general journal entry to record the admission of C.

Ex. 15-8 The capital accounts of the XYZ partnership are as follows: X, $120,000; Y, $60,000; Z, $90,000. Profits are shared equally. Partner Y is withdrawing from the partnership and it is agreed that he shall be paid $75,000 for his interest because the earnings of the business are high in relation to the assets of the firm. Assuming that the excess of the settlement over the amount of Y's capital account is to be recorded as a bonus to Y, prepare a general journal entry to record Y's retirement from the firm.

Ex. 15-9 The CDE partnership is being liquidated. After all liabilities have been paid and all assets sold, the balances of the partners' capital accounts are as follows: C, $42,000 credit balance; D, $28,000 debit balance; E, $63,000 credit balance. The partners share profits equally.
a How should the available cash (the only remaining asset) be distributed if it is impossible to determine at this date whether D will be able to pay the $28,000 he owes the firm?
b Draft the journal entries to record a partial payment of $21,000 to the firm by D, and the subsequent distribution of this cash.

PROBLEMS

Group A

15A-1 The partnership of James and Low was formed on January 1, 19___, when Ruth James and Susan Low agreed to invest equal amounts and to share profits equally. The investment by James consists of $50,400 cash and an inventory of merchandise valued at $75,600. Low is also to contribute a total of $126,000. However, it is agreed that her contribution will consist of the following assets of her business along with the transfer to the partnership of her business liabilities. The agreed value of the various items as well as their carrying values on Low's records are listed on page 547.

	Investment by Low	
	Balances on Low's Records	Agreed Value
Accounts receivable	$117,600	$117,600
Allowance for doubtful accounts	5,040	10,500
Inventory	12,600	16,800
Office equipment (net)	16,800	10,500
Accounts payable	37,800	37,800

Low also contributed enough cash to bring her capital account to $126,000.

Instructions
a Draft general journal entries to record the investments of James and Low in the new partnership.
b Prepare the beginning balance sheet of the partnership (in report form) at the close of business January 1, reflecting the above transfers to the firm.
c On the following December 31 after one year of operations, the Income Summary account had a credit balance of $168,000 and the Drawing account for each partner showed a debit balance of $42,000. Prepare journal entries to close the Income Summary and the drawing accounts at December 31.

15A-2 The accounts making up the trial balance of the partnership of Lee and Miller at the end of the current year are shown below arranged in alphabetical order.

Accounts payable	$ 34,400
Accounts receivable	62,944
Accrued liabilities	19,040
Accumulated depreciation: equipment	20,800
Administrative expenses	146,192
Allowance for doubtful accounts	3,776
Cash	43,360
Equipment	104,000
Inventory	36,480
Lee, capital	69,760
Lee, drawing	9,920
Merchandise purchases	465,760
Miller, capital	86,400
Miller, drawing	7,680
Sales	807,520
Selling expenses	131,920
Short-term prepayments	9,120
Transportation-in	24,320

Other data There were no changes in partners' capital accounts during the year. The inventory at the end of the year was $30,912. The partnership agreement provides that partners are to be allowed 10% interest on invested capital as of the beginning of the year and are to divide residual profits in the ratio of Lee 60%, Miller 40%.

Instructions
a Prepare an income statement for the year. (Round figures to nearest dollar.)
b Prepare a statement of partners' capital accounts.
c Prepare a balance sheet as of the end of the year.

15A-3 At the close of the current year, the capital accounts and the profit- and loss-sharing ratios for the partners of Western Imports are as follows. At this date, it is agreed that a new partner, Donald Fraser, is to be admitted to the firm.

	Capital	Profit-sharing Ratio
Daniel Ekert	$100,000	$\frac{5}{8}$
Nancy Townsend	80,000	$\frac{1}{4}$
Doug Patterson	60,000	$\frac{1}{8}$

Instructions For each of the following situations involving the admission of Fraser to the partnership, give the necessary journal entry to record his admission.
a Fraser purchases one-half of Townsend's interest in the firm, paying Townsend $47,500.
b Fraser buys a one-quarter interest in the firm for $70,000 by purchasing one-fourth of the present interest of each of the three partners. Fraser pays the three individuals directly.
c Fraser invests $115,000 and receives a one-quarter interest in capital and profits of the business. Give the necessary journal entries to record Fraser's admission as a partner and the division of the bonus to the old partners in their established ratio for profit sharing.

15A-4 At the end of the current year, the partnership of Hale-Dart-King Stores had the following balance sheet.

HALE-DART-KING STORES
Balance Sheet
Close of Current Year

Cash	$165,000	Liabilities	$ 99,000
Receivables	75,000	Hale, capital	132,000
Inventory	60,000	Dart, capital	90,000
Equipment (*net*)	105,000	King, capital	84,000
	$405,000		$405,000

The partners share profits and losses in the ratio of 50% to Hale, 30% to Dart, and 20% to King. It is agreed that King is to withdraw from the partnership on this date.

Instructions Listed below are a number of different situations involving the retirement of King from the firm. For each case you are to prepare the general journal entry or entries needed to record King's withdrawal.
a An analysis of the assets indicates that $12,000 of the receivables will probably prove uncollectible and that inventories are understated by $18,000 and equipment is understated by $24,000. It is agreed that the assets are to be adjusted accordingly and that King is to be paid an amount equal to the book value of his adjusted equity.
b Dart buys one-fourth of King's interest for $24,000 and Hale buys three-fourths for $72,000.
c King, with the permission of the other partners, gives his equity to his brother-in-law, Jones, who is accepted as a partner in the firm.
d King is paid $90,000 from partnership funds for his interest. The bonus indi-

cated by this payment is charged against the continuing partners ($\frac{5}{8}$ against Hale and $\frac{3}{8}$ against Dart).

e The partnership agrees to pay King $102,000 because equipment is undervalued in the accounts. King is given $48,000 cash and a two-year, 8% note for $54,000. (Prepare one entry to revalue the equipment and another for payment to King.)

f King is given $60,000 cash and equipment having a book value of $66,000. The partners agree that no revaluation of assets will be made. (Ratio for loss between Hale and Dart is 5 : 3.)

15A-5 Stuart's Mens' Shop is a single proprietorship owned by Doug Stuart. The business is in need of additional working capital and Stuart is personally in need of $21,000 in cash. To meet these needs, Stuart agreed on August 31 to join in partnership with Barry Davies. It is agreed that Stuart will contribute all noncash assets of his fashion shop to the partnership and will withdraw (from funds supplied by Davies) $21,000 in cash. Davies will invest $56,000 in the business. The partnership contract provides that income shall be divided 55% to Stuart and 45% to Davies.

Information as to the assets and liabilities of Stuart's business on August 31, 19___, and their agreed valuation is shown below. None of the receivables has been identified as definitely uncollectible.

	Per Stuart's Accounts	Agreed Valuation
Accounts receivable	$47,600	
Allowance for doubtful accounts	4,480	$39,760
Merchandise inventory	92,960	75,600
Store equipment	17,360	
Accumulated depreciation	5,880	12,600
9% note payable (dated May 1, 19___, due Apr. 30, next year) .	33,600	34,188
Accounts payable	19,600	19,600

It is agreed that the new partnership (to be called The Clothes Shop) will assume all present debts of Stuart's business.

Instructions

a Make the necessary journal entries to record the formation of The Clothes Shop partnership at August 31, 19___. (Credit Allowance for Doubtful Accounts $7,840. Do not record accumulated depreciation.)

b At the end of September, after all adjusting entries, the Income Summary account of The Clothes Shop shows a credit balance of $6,300. The partners' drawing accounts have debit balances as follows: Stuart $2,800; Davies, $1,400. Make the journal entries necessary to complete the closing of the partnership accounts at the end of September.

c Prepare a statement of partners' capitals for the month of September.

15A-6 The partnership of Carlos, Dunn, and Earl is in the process of liquidation. The assets other than cash and accounts receivable have been sold. The accounts receivable remain uncollected. The balances in the general ledger at the present time are:

Cash	$ 27,200	
Accounts receivable	116,800	
Allowance for doubtful accounts		$ 6,400
Liabilities		36,800
Carlos, capital (profit share 30%)		43,200

Dunn, capital (*profit share 50%*)	*33,600*
Earl, capital (*profit share 20%*)	*24,000*

Instructions Present in general journal form the entries necessary to record the liquidation of the partnership and the distribution of all cash under each of the circumstances shown below. Support all entries with adequate explanations showing how amounts were determined.

a Collections of $67,200 are made on receivables, and the remainder are deemed uncollectible. Use an account entitled Loss on Liquidation.

b Receivables are sold to a collection agency; the partnership receives in cash as a final settlement 30% of the gross amount of its receivables. The personal financial status of the partners is uncertain, but all available cash is to be distributed at this time. (Dunn's deficiency will be charged to Carlos and Earl in a 30:20 ratio.)

15A-7 Lawrence Company had the following balance sheet at December 31, 19____.

LAWRENCE COMPANY

Balance Sheet

End of Current Year

Cash	$ 60,000	Liabilities	$120,000
Other assets	300,000	Dee, capital	100,000
		Fay, capital	80,000
		May, capital	60,000
	$360,000		$360,000

Dee, Fay, and May share profits in a ratio of 3:2:1, respectively. At the date of the above balance sheet the partners decided to liquidate the business.

Instructions Prepare schedules showing how the liquidation of the partnership would affect the various balance sheet items and how the cash would be distributed under each of the following circumstances. Use six money columns in your schedules, as follows:

Cash	Other Assets	Lia- bilities	Dee, Capital	Fay, Capital	May, Capital

a Other assets are sold for $264,000.

b Other assets are sold for $96,000. All partners have personal assets and will contribute any necessary amounts to the partnership.

c Other assets are sold for $74,400. Fay has personal assets and will contribute any necessary amounts; Dee and May are both personally bankrupt.

d Other assets are sold for $48,000. May is personally solvent and will contribute any amount for which he is liable. Dee and Fay both have personal debts in excess of their personal assets.

Group B

15B-1 The partnership of Henry and Jensen was formed on July 1, Year 1, when William Henry and Wallace Jensen agreed to invest equal amounts and to share profits and losses equally. The investment by Henry consists of $38,400 cash and an inventory of merchandise valued at $57,600. Jensen also is to contribute a total of $96,000. However, it is agreed that his contribution will consist of the following assets of his business along with the transfer to the partnership of his business liabilities. The agreed values of the various items as well as their carrying values on Jensen's records are listed below. Jensen also contributes enough cash to bring his capital account to $96,000.

	Investment by Jensen	
	Balances on Jensen's Records	Agreed Value
Accounts receivable	$89,600	$89,600
Allowance for doubtful accounts	3,840	8,000
Inventory	9,600	12,800
Office equipment (net)	12,800	8,000
Accounts payable	28,800	28,800

Instructions
a Draft entries (in general journal form) to record the investments of Henry and Jensen in the new partnership.
b Prepare the beginning balance sheet of the partnership (in report form) at the close of business July 1, reflecting the above transfers to the firm.
c On the following June 30 after one year of operation, the Income Summary account showed a credit balance of $128,000 and the Drawing account for each partner showed a debit balance of $32,000. Prepare journal entries to close the Income Summary account and the drawing accounts at June 30.

15B-2 At the end of the current year, the ledger accounts of Steel-Harding, a partnership, contained the balances shown below. The accounts are listed in alphabetical order.

Accounts payable	$ 38,520
Accounts receivable	81,000
Accrued liabilities	2,880
Accumulated depreciation	18,000
Administrative expenses	91,620
Cash	37,020
Equipment	90,000
Harding, capital (beginning of year)	74,400
Harding, drawing	10,080
Inventory (beginning of year)	27,360
Notes payable	9,600
Purchases (including transportation-in)	391,800
Sales	648,960
Selling expenses	112,380
Short-term prepayments	3,900
Steel, capital (beginning of year)	60,000
Steel, drawing	7,200

There were no changes in partners' capital accounts during the year. The inventory at the end of the year was $28,200. The partnership agreement provided that partners are to be allowed 10% interest on invested capital as of the beginning of the year and that the residual net income is to be divided equally.

Instructions
a Prepare an income statement for the current year, showing the distribution of net income as illustrated on page 525.
b Prepare a statement of partners' capitals for the current year.
c Prepare a balance sheet at the end of the current year.

15B-3 Mountain Trails has three partners—A, B, and C. During the current year their average capital balances were as follows: A, $280,000; B, $200,000; and C, $120,000. The partnership agreement provides that partners shall receive an annual allowance of 6% of their average capital balance and a salary allowance as follows: A, none; B, $48,000; and C, $40,000. Partner B, who manages the business, is to receive a bonus of 25% of income in excess of $72,000 after partners' interest and salary allowances. Residual profits are to be divided: A, $\frac{1}{2}$; B, $\frac{1}{3}$; and C, $\frac{1}{6}$.

Instructions Prepare separate schedules showing how income will be divided among the three partners in each of the following cases. The figure given is the annual income available for distribution among the partners.
a Loss of $44,000
b Income of $76,000
c Income of $260,000

15B-4 A condensed balance sheet for the partnership of the Mark-Tyler Company at September 30 is shown below. On this date the two partners agreed to admit a new partner, Wells. Mark and Tyler have been dividing profits in a ratio of 3 : 2 (that is, 60% and 40%), and this ratio will continue between the two of them after the admission of Wells.

MARK-TYLER COMPANY

Balance Sheet

September 30

Current assets	$180,000	Liabilities	$160,000
Plant & equipment		Mark, capital	280,000
(net)	420,000	Tyler, capital	160,000
	$600,000		$600,000

Instructions Described below are four different situations under which Wells might be admitted to partnership. Considering each independently, prepare the journal entries necessary to record the admission of Wells to the firm.
a Wells purchases a one-half interest (50% of the entire ownership equity) in the partnership from Mark for $260,000. Payment is made to Mark as an individual.
b Wells purchases one-half of Mark's interest and one-half of Tyler's interest, paying Mark $168,000 and Tyler $96,000.
c Wells invests $300,000 in the partnership and receives a one-half interest in capital and income. It is agreed that there will be no change in the valuation of the present net assets. (Bonus to Wells is charged against Mark and Tyler in a 3 : 2 ratio.)
d Wells invests $560,000 in the partnership and receives a one-half interest in capital and income. It is agreed that the allowance for doubtful accounts is currently overstated by $20,000. All other assets are carried at amounts approximating current fair value; therefore, no further revaluation is to be made. The bonus to the old partners indicated by the amount of the investment by

Wells for a one-half interest will be divided between Mark and Tyler in the 3:2 ratio. Prepare one journal entry for the adjustment of the Allowance for Doubtful Accounts and another entry to record the investment by Wells.

15B-5 In the partnership of Hart, Smith, & Davis, the partners' capital accounts at the end of the current year were as follows: Hart, $224,000; Smith, $148,000; and Davis, $60,000. The partnership agreement provides that profits will be shared 40% to Hart, 50% to Smith, and 10% to Davis. At this time, Hart decides to retire from the firm.

Instructions Below are described a number of independent situations involving the retirement of Hart. In each case prepare the journal entries necessary to reflect the withdrawal of Hart from the firm.

a Davis buys three-fourths of Hart's interest for $208,000 and Smith buys one-fourth for $64,000, paying Hart out of their personal funds.

b The partners agree that certain assets are carried at amounts which do not represent their current value. Land is undervalued by $44,000; a building purchased five years ago for $320,000 and depreciated on a 20-year basis should have been depreciated on a 40-year basis. A patent having a book value of $100,000 is currently worth at least $220,000. It is agreed that these adjustments will be made in the accounts and that Hart will receive in cash from the partnership an amount equal to the adjusted book value of his interest.

c Hart accepts $80,000 in cash and all rights in a patent having a book value of $100,000 in full payment for his interest. The remaining partners agree that a revaluation of remaining assets is not warranted. (Round off to the nearest dollar.)

d Hart receives $100,000 in cash and a 10-year, 9% note for $188,000 in payment for his interest. Assets are not to be revalued. The bonus to Hart is to be charged against the capital accounts of the continuing partners. (Round the amounts to the nearest dollar.)

15B-6 The J-K Agency, a partnership, had the following account balances, among others, at December 31 of the current year. The revenue and expense accounts have been closed to the Income Summary account.

	December 31 Balance	
	Debit	*Credit*
Partner J, capital		$120,800
Partner J, drawing	$29,225	
Partner K, capital		93,125
Partner K, drawing	24,650	
Income summary		31,025

Other data

(1) During the year Partner K took out of stock for his personal use merchandise which cost the company $1,725 and had a retail value of $2,875. The bookkeeper credited Sales and charged Miscellaneous Expense for the retail value of all merchandise taken by K.

(2) Partner J paid $1,500 from his personal funds on November 18 to an attorney for legal services. Of this amount $625, which was for services relating to partnership business, should be treated as an additional investment by J.

(3) Partner K borrowed $13,500 from the partnership on September 1 of the current year, giving a six-month note with interest at 8%. The only record made of this transaction was a charge to K's drawing account for $13,500 at the time of the loan. K intends to repay the loan with interest at maturity.

(4) Partner J had the full-time use of a company-owned car. All operating expenses were paid by the partnership. It was agreed that J's drawing account

would be charged 12½ cents per mile for all miles driven for personal use. At the end of the year J reported that he had driven 6,000 miles for personal reasons, but the bookkeeper filed this information and made no entry.

(5) On March 31 Partner J invested an additional $25,000 in the business. Other than this, no changes in partners' capital accounts have been recorded during the year.

Instructions

a On the basis of the above information, make any adjusting or correcting entries necessary on December 31. The portion of any entry affecting revenue or expense accounts may be charged or credited directly to Income Summary.

b Prepare a schedule showing how the adjusted partnership income would be divided between the partners. The partnership agreement calls for salary allowances of $1,250 per month to J and $2,000 per month to K. The balance of profits is to be shared in a 3:2 ratio.

c What effect did the adjustments have on J's share of the partnership income for the year? Determine the amount and explain briefly.

d Prepare a statement of changes in partners' capitals for the year.

BUSINESS DECISION PROBLEM 15

Mike and Joe are considering the formation of a partnership to engage in the business of aerial photography. Mike is a licensed pilot, is currently employed at a salary of $24,000 a year, and has $64,000 to invest. Joe is a recent college graduate who has been earning $11,200 a year working in a photographic shop; he has just inherited $160,000 which he plans to put into the business. The partners, after a careful study of their requirements, conclude that $96,000 additional funds will be required, and they have been assured by a local investor, A. W. Thomas, that he will lend them this amount on a five-year, 8% note.

Both partners will devote full time to the business. They have prepared a careful estimate of their prospects and expect that revenue during the first year will just cover expenses, with the exception of the interest expense on the $96,000 loan from Thomas. During the second year the estimates indicate that revenue should exceed expenses (other than the interest expense on the loan) by $32,000 For the third year it is believed that revenue will exceed expenses (other than the interest expense on the loan) by $72,000.

Instructions

a On the basis of the above information, draw up a brief statement of the income-sharing agreement you would recommend that the partners adopt, explaining the basis for your proposal.

b Assuming that the income expectations of the partners are reasonable, draw up a schedule for each of the three years showing how the partners will share in income under the arrangement you have proposed in *a*. No significant change has occurred in capitals of partners. (This simplifying assumption makes it possible to ignore the possibility of capital account changes resulting from the division of profits or losses, or from drawings and investments. Any such influences are assumed to counterbalance. In other words, it is arbitrarily assumed that the original capital balances for both partners remained unchanged throughout the first three years of operations.) Write a brief statement defending the results of the profit-sharing plan you have devised.

16 Corporations: Organization and Operation

The corporation has become the dominant form of business organization on the American economic scene, probably because it gathers together large amounts of capital more readily than single proprietorships or partnerships. Because of its efficiency as a device for pooling the savings of many individuals, the corporation is an ideal means of obtaining the capital necessary for large-scale production and its inherent economies. Virtually all large businesses are corporations.

There are still many more single proprietorships and partnerships than corporations, but in terms of dollar volume of output, the corporations hold an impressive lead. In the field of manufacturing, more than three-quarters of the total value of goods produced comes from corporations. Corporations account for over 90% of the goods and services supplied in such industries as public utilities, banking, transportation, and mining. The rise of the corporation to this commanding position has been inseparably linked with the trend toward larger factories and stores, organized research and development of new products, nationwide marketing areas, and the professionalization of business management.

Definition of corporation

A corporation has been defined as "an artificial being, invisible, intangible, and existing only in contemplation of the law." A corporation is regarded as a legal entity having a continuous existence apart from that of its owners. By way of contrast, a partnership is a relatively unstable type of organization which is dissolved by the death or retirement of any one of its members, whereas the continuous existence of a corporation is not interrupted by the death of a stockholder.

Ownership in a corporation is evidenced by transferable shares of stock, and the owners are called *stockholders* or *shareholders.* To administer the affairs of the corporation, the stockholders elect a *board of directors.* The directors in turn select a president and other corporate officers to carry on active management of the business.

Advantages of the corporate form of organization

The corporation offers a number of advantages not available in other forms of organization. Among these advantages are the following:

1 *Greater amounts of capital can be gathered together.* Some corporations have a half million or more stockholders. The sale of stock is a means of obtaining funds from the general public; both small and large investors find stock ownership a convenient means of participating in ownership of business enterprise.

2 *Limited liability.* Creditors of a corporation have a claim against the assets of the corporation only, not against the personal property of the owners of the corporation. Since stockholders have no personal liability for the debts of the corporation, they can never lose more than the amount of their investment.

3 *Shares of stock in a corporation are readily transferable.* The ease of disposing of all or part of one's stockholdings in a corporation makes this form of investment particularly attractive.

4 *Continuous existence.* A corporation is a separate legal entity with a perpetual existence. The continuous life of the corporation despite changes in ownership is made possible by the issuance of transferable shares of stock.

5 *Centralized authority.* The power to make all kinds of operating decisions is lodged in the president of a corporation. The president may delegate to others limited authority for various phases of operations but retains final authority over the entire business.

6 *Professional management.* The person who owns a few shares of stock in a large corporation usually has neither the time nor the knowledge of the business necessary for intelligent participation in operating problems. For this reason the functions of management and of ownership are sharply separated in the corporate form of organization, and the corporation is free to employ as executives the best managerial talent available.

Disadvantages of the corporate form of organization

Among the disadvantages of the corporation are:

1 *Heavy taxation.* A corporation must pay a high rate of taxation on its income. Furthermore, when its net income is distributed to the owners in the form of dividends, the dividends are considered to be personal income to the stockholders and are subject to personal income tax. This practice of first taxing corporate income to the corporation and then taxing dividends to the stockholder is often referred to as *double taxation.*

2 *Greater regulation.* Corporations come into existence under the terms of state laws and these same laws may provide for considerable regulation of the

corporation's activities. For example, the withdrawal of funds from a corporation is subject to certain limits set by law. Large corporations, especially those with securities listed on stock exchanges, must make extensive public disclosure of their affairs.

3 *Separation of ownership and control.* The separation of the functions of ownership and management may be an advantage in some cases but a disadvantage in others. On the whole, the excellent record of growth and earnings in most large corporations indicates that the separation of ownership and control has benefited rather than injured stockholders. In a few instances, however, a management group has chosen to operate a corporation for the benefit of insiders (for example, paying excessive executive salaries and bonuses). The stockholders may find it difficult in such cases to take the concerted action necessary either to change corporate policies or to oust the officers.

Formation of a corporation

To form a corporation, an application signed by at least three incorporators is submitted to the corporation commissioner (or other designated official) of the state in which the company is to be incorporated. The approved application contains the *articles of incorporation* and becomes the company *charter.* The incorporators (who have subscribed for capital stock and therefore are now stockholders) hold a meeting to elect *directors* and to pass *bylaws* as a guide to the company's affairs. The directors in turn hold a meeting at which officers of the corporation are appointed. Capital stock certificates are then issued and the formation of the corporation is complete.

ORGANIZATION COSTS The formation of a corporation is a much more costly step than the organization of a partnership. The necessary costs include the payment of an incorporation fee to the state, the payment of fees to attorneys for their services in drawing up the articles of incorporation, payments to promoters, and a variety of other outlays necessary to bring the corporation into existence. These costs are charged to an asset account called Organization Costs.

The incurring of these organization costs leads to the existence of the corporate entity; consequently, the benefits derived from these costs may be regarded as extending over the entire life of the corporation. Since the life of a corporation may continue indefinitely, organization costs may be carried at the full amount until the corporation is liquidated. Because present income tax law permits organization costs to be written off over a period of five years or more, most companies elect to write off organization costs over a five-year period. Accountants have been willing to accept this practice, despite the lack of theoretical support, on the grounds that such costs are not material in relation to other assets. Unnecessary detail on the balance sheet is always to be avoided, and there seems to be little reason for carrying indefinitely organization costs of modest amount.

RIGHTS OF STOCKHOLDERS The ownership of stock in a corporation usually carries the following basic rights:

1 To vote for directors, and thereby to be represented in the management of the business. The approval of a majority of stockholders may also be required for such important corporate actions as mergers and acquisitions, the selection of independent auditors, the incurring of long-term debts, the establishment of stock option plans, or the splitting of capital stock into a larger number of shares.

2 To share in profits by receiving dividends declared by the board of directors.

3 To share in the distribution of assets if the corporation is liquidated. When a corporation ends its existence, the creditors of the corporation must first be paid in full; any remaining assets are divided among stockholders in proportion to the number of shares owned.

4 To subscribe for additional shares in the event that the corporation decides to increase the amount of stock outstanding. This ***preemptive right*** entitles stockholders to maintain their percentages of ownership in the company by subscribing, in proportion to their present stockholdings, to any additional shares issued. Corporations organized in certain states do not grant preemptive rights to their stockholders. In other cases stockholders sometimes agree to waive their preemptive rights in order to grant more flexibility to management in negotiating mergers.

The ownership of stock does not give a stockholder the right to intervene in the management of a corporation or to transact business in its behalf. Although the stockholders as a group own the corporation, they do not personally own the assets of the corporation; neither do they personally owe the debts of the corporation. The stockholders have no direct claim on income earned; income earned by a corporation does not become income to the stockholders unless the board of directors orders the distribution of the income to stockholders in the form of a cash dividend.

Stockholders' meetings are usually held once a year. Each share of stock is entitled to one vote. In large corporations, these annual meetings are usually attended by relatively few persons, often by less than 1% of the stockholders. Prior to the meeting, the management group will request stockholders who do not plan to attend in person to send in ***proxy statements*** assigning their votes to the existing management. Through this use of the proxy system, management may secure the right to vote as much as, perhaps, 90% or more of the total outstanding shares.

FUNCTIONS OF THE BOARD OF DIRECTORS The primary functions of the board of directors are to manage the corporation and to protect the interests of the stockholders. At this level, management may consist principally of formulating policies and reviewing acts of the officers. Specific duties of the directors include declaring dividends, setting the salaries of officers, authorizing officers to arrange loans from banks, and authorizing important contracts of various kinds.

The extent of active participation in management by the board of directors varies widely from one company to another. In some corporations the officers also serve as directors and a meeting of directors may differ only in form from a conference of operating executives. In other corporations the board may consist of outsiders who devote little time to the corporation's affairs and merely meet occasionally to review and approve policies which have been formed and administered by the officers. In recent years increased importance has been attached to the inclusion on the boards of large corporations individuals who were not officers of the company and who could thus have a view independent of that of active managers.

The official actions of the board are recorded in minutes of their meetings. The **minutes book** is the source of many of the accounting entries affecting the owners' equity accounts.

FUNCTIONS OF CORPORATE OFFICERS Corporate officers usually include a president, one or more vice-presidents, a controller, a treasurer, and a secretary. A vice-president is often made responsible for the sales function; other vice-presidents may be given responsibility for such important functions as personnel, finance, production, and research and development.

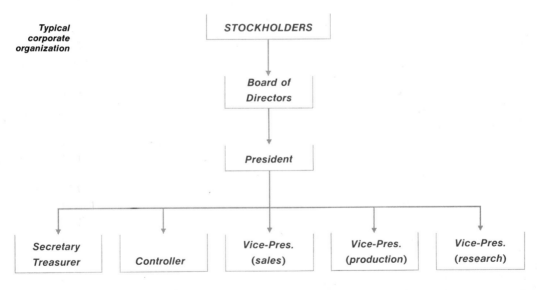

The responsibilities of the controller, treasurer, and secretary are most directly related to the accounting phase of business operation. The **controller,** or chief accounting officer, is responsible for the maintenance of adequate internal control and for the preparation of accounting records and financial statements. Such specialized activities as budgeting, tax planning, and preparation of tax returns are usually placed under the controller's jurisdiction. The **treasurer** has custody of the company's funds and is generally responsible for planning and controlling the company's cash position. The **secretary** represents the corporation in many contractual and legal matters and maintains minutes of the meetings of directors and stockholders. Another responsibility of the secretary is to coordinate the preparation of the annual report, which includes the financial statements and other information relating to corporate activities. In small corporations, one officer frequently acts as both secretary and treasurer. The organization chart on page 559 indicates lines of authority extending from stockholders to the directors to the president and other officers.

SOURCES OF CORPORATE CAPITAL   The sections of a balance sheet showing assets and liabilities are much the same for a corporation as for a single proprietorship or partnership. The owner's equity section is the principal point of contrast. In a corporation the term **stockholders' equity** is used instead of owner's equity. The capital of a corporation, as for other types of business organizations, is equal to the excess of the assets over the liabilities. However, the capital of a corporation may be divided into several segments. In succeeding chapters, these various classifications of corporate capital will be considered in some detail, but at this point we are concerned with a simplified model in which the capital of a corporation is carried in only two ledger accounts and shown on the balance sheet in two separate portions. These two classifications are (1) the capital invested by the stockholders (paid-in capital), and (2) the capital accumulated and retained through profitable operations.

The capital paid in by stockholders is regarded as permanent capital not ordinarily subject to withdrawal.[1] The unit of corporate ownership is a **share of stock,** and the balance of the Capital Stock account is always equal to the total number of shares of stock issued, multiplied by a stipulated amount (par value or stated value) per share.

The second major type of corporate capital is **retained earnings.** At the end of the year the balance of the Income Summary account is closed into the Retained Earnings account, as shown by the following entry.

Income Summary *70,000*
    Retained Earnings *70,000*
To close the Income Summary account by transferring the year's net
income into the Retained Earnings account.

If the company operates at a loss of, say, $25,000, the Income Summary account will have a debit balance. The account must then be credited to close it. The closing entry will be:

Retained Earnings *25,000*
    Income Summary *25,000*
To close the Income Summary account by transferring the year's net
loss into the Retained Earnings account.

---

[1] For legal reasons, the contributed capital may be divided into two portions: (1) legal capital, equal to par or stated value times the number of shares issued, and (2) excess of contributed capital over and above legal capital.

Any dividends distributed to stockholders serve to reduce the Retained Earnings account. (The journal entries for the declaration and payment of a cash dividend are illustrated later in this chapter.) The amount of the Retained Earnings account at any balance sheet date represents the accumulated earnings of the company since the date of incorporation, minus any losses and minus all dividends distributed to stockholders. (Various types of dividends are discussed in Chapter 17.) An alternative name for the Retained Earnings account is Earned Surplus. This is an older term which has gradually been replaced by Retained Earnings.

STOCKHOLDERS' EQUITY ON THE BALANCE SHEET For a corporation with $100,000 of capital stock and $40,000 of retained earnings, the stockholders' equity section of the balance sheet will appear as follows:

Paid-in capital and earned capital

Stockholders' equity:		
Capital stock	*$100,000*	
Retained earnings	*40,000*	*$140,000*

If this same company had been unprofitable and had incurred losses aggregating $30,000 since its organization, the stockholders' equity section of the balance sheet would be as follows:

Paid-in capital reduced by losses incurred

Stockholders' equity:		
Capital stock	*$100,000*	
Less: Deficit	*30,000*	*$70,000*

This second illustration tells us that $30,000 of the original $100,000 invested by stockholders has been lost. Note that the capital stock in both illustrations remains at the fixed amount of $100,000, the stockholders' original investment. The accumulated profits or losses since the organization of the corporation are shown as *retained earnings* or as a *deficit* and are not intermingled with the paid-in capital. The term *deficit* indicates a negative amount of retained earnings.

INCOME TAXES IN CORPORATE FINANCIAL STATEMENTS A corporation is a legal entity subject to corporation income tax; consequently, the ledger of a corporation should include accounts for recording income taxes. No such accounts are needed for a business organized as a single proprietorship or partnership.

Income taxes are based on a corporation's earnings. At year-end, before preparing financial statements, income taxes are recorded by an adjusting entry such as the following:

Recording corporate income taxes

Income Taxes Expense	*45,650*	
Income Taxes Payable		*45,650*

To record the income taxes payable for the year ended Dec. 31, 19____.

The account debited in this entry, Income Taxes Expense, is an expense account and usually appears as the very last deduction in the income statement as follows:

Final step in income statement	*Income before income taxes*	*$100,000*
	Income taxes	*45,650*
	Net income	*$ 54,350*
	Earnings per share	*$2.17*

The liability account, Income Taxes Payable, will ordinarily be paid within a few months and should, therefore, appear in the current liability section of the balance sheet. More detailed discussion of corporation taxes is presented in Chapter 20.

Authorization and issuance of capital stock

The articles of incorporation specify the number of shares of capital stock which a corporation is authorized to issue and the par value, if any, per share. The corporation may choose not to issue immediately all the authorized shares; in fact, it is customary to secure authorization for a larger number of shares than presently needed. In future years, if more capital is needed, the previously authorized shares will be readily available for issue; otherwise, the corporation would be forced to apply to the state for permission to increase the number of authorized shares.

Par value

In an earlier period of the history of American corporations, all capital stock had par value, but in more recent years state laws have permitted corporations to choose between par value stock and no-par value stock. The corporate charter always states the par value, if any, of the shares to be issued.

Par value may be $1 per share, $5, $100, or any other amount decided upon by the corporation. The par value of the stock is no indication of its market value; the par value merely indicates the amount per share to be entered in the Capital Stock account. The par value of most common stocks is relatively low. Polaroid Corporation common stock, for example, has a par value of $1; General Motors Corporation common stock has a par of $1⅔; Avon Products common stock has a par value of 50 cents per share. The market value of all these securities is far above their par value.

The chief significance of par value is that it represents the *legal capital* per share, that is, the amount below which stockholders' equity cannot be reduced except by (*1*) losses from business operations, or (*2*) legal action taken by a majority vote of stockholders. A dividend cannot be declared by a corporation if such action would cause the stockholders' equity to fall below the par value of the outstanding shares. Par value, therefore, may be regarded as a minimum cushion of capital existing for the protection of creditors.

Issuance of capital stock

Mere authorization of a stock issue does not bring an asset into existence, nor does it give the corporation any capital. The obtaining of authorization from the state for a stock issue merely affords a legal opportunity to obtain assets through the sale of stock.

When par value stock is *issued,* the Capital Stock account is credited with the par value of the shares issued, regardless of whether the issuance price is more or less than par. Assuming that 10,000 shares of $10 par value stock have been authorized and that 6,000 of these authorized shares are issued at a price of $10 each, Cash would be debited and Capital Stock would be credited for $60,000. When stock is sold for more than par value, the Capital Stock account is credited with the par value of the shares issued, and a separate account, Paid-in Capital in Excess of Par Value, is credited for the excess of selling price over par. If, for example, the issuance price is $15, the entry is as follows:

Stock-	*Cash* *90,000*	
holders'		
investment	*Capital Stock*	*60,000*
in excess of	*Paid-in Capital in Excess of Par Value*	*30,000*
par value	*Issued 6,000 shares of $10 par value stock at a price of $15*	
	a share.	

An alternative title for the account, Paid-In Capital in Excess of Par Value, is Premium on Capital Stock. The premium or amount received in excess of par value does not represent a profit to the corporation. It is part of the invested capital and it will be added to the capital stock on the balance sheet to show the total paid-in capital. The stockholders' equity section of the balance sheet is illustrated below. (The existence of $10,000 in retained earnings is assumed in order to have a complete illustration.)

Corpora-	*Stockholders' equity:*	
tion's	*Capital stock, $10 par value, authorized 10,000 shares, issued and*	
capital		
classified	*outstanding 6,000 shares*	*$ 60,000*
by source	*Paid-in capital in excess of par value*	*30,000*
	Total paid-in capital	*$ 90,000*
	Retained earnings	*10,000*
	Total stockholders' equity	*$100,000*

If stock is issued by a corporation for less than par, the account Discount on Capital Stock should be debited for the difference between the issuance price and the par value. The issuance of stock at a discount is seldom encountered; it is illegal in many states. In planning the issuance of capital stock, the corporation is free to set the par value as low as it pleases, and a par value of $1 a share is not uncommon. Consequently, the question of a discount on capital stock is no longer of much practical importance.

Capital stock outstanding

The unit of stock ownership is the share, but the corporation may issue stock certificates in denominations of 10 shares, 100 shares, or any other number. The total capital stock outstanding at any given time represents 100% ownership of the corporation. Outstanding shares are those in the hands of stockholders. Assume, for example, that the Draper Corporation is organized with authorization to issue 100,000 shares of stock. However, only 50,000 shares are issued, because this amount of stock provides all the capital presently needed. The holders of the 50,000 shares of stock own the corporation in its entirety.

If we assume further that Thomas Draper acquires 5,000 shares of the 50,000 shares outstanding, we may say that he has a 10% interest in the corporation. Suppose that Draper now sells 2,000 shares to Evans. The total number of shares outstanding remains unchanged at 50,000, although Draper's percentage of ownership has declined to 6% and a new stockholder, Evans, has acquired a 4% interest in the corporation. The transfer of 2,000 shares from Draper to Evans had no effect upon the corporation's assets, liabilities, or amount of stock outstanding. The only way in which this transfer of stock affects the corporation is that the list of stockholders must be revised to show the number of shares held by each owner.

Cash dividends

The term *dividend,* when used by itself, is generally understood to mean a distribution of cash by a corporation to its stockholders. Dividends are stated as a specific amount per share, as, for example, a dividend of $1 per share. The amount received by each stockholder is in proportion to the number of shares owned. A stockholder who owns 100 shares will receive a check for $100.

Dividends are paid only through action by the board of directors. The board has full discretion to declare a dividend or to refrain from doing so. Once the declaration of a dividend has been announced, the obligation to pay the dividend is a current liability of the corporation and cannot be rescinded.

Because a dividend is declared on one date by the board of directors and paid at a later date, two separate journal entries are necessary. To illustrate the entries for declaration and payment of a cash dividend assume that a corporation declares a dividend of $1 a share on 100,000 shares of outstanding stock. The dividend is declared on December 15 and payable on January 25. The two entries would be as follows:

Dec. 15   *Retained Earnings* *100,000*

                 Dividends Payable *100,000*

                 To record declaration by the board of directors of a cash

                 dividend of $1 per share on the 100,000 shares of

                 stock outstanding.

Jan. 25   *Dividends Payable* *100,000*

                 Cash *100,000*

                 To record payment of the $1 per share dividend declared

                 December 15 on the 100,000 shares of stock

                 outstanding.

The account **Dividends Payable,** which was credited at the date of declaring the dividend, is a current liability. Some companies in recording the declaration of a dividend will debit an account entitled Dividends instead of debiting the Retained Earnings account. In this case, a closing entry will be required at the end of the year to transfer the debit balance in the Dividends account into the Retained Earnings account. Under either method the end result is a reduction in retained earnings for the amount of the dividends declared.

Preferred and common stock

In order to appeal to as many investors as possible, a corporation may issue more than one kind of stock, just as an automobile manufacturer may make sedans, convertibles, and station wagons in order to appeal to various groups of car buyers. When only one type of stock is issued, it is called **common stock.** Common stock has the four basic rights previously mentioned. Whenever these rights are modified, the term **preferred stock** (or sometimes Class B Common) is used to describe this second type of stock. A few corporations issue two or three classes of preferred stock, each class having certain distinctive features designed to interest a particular type of investor. In summary, we may say that every business corporation has common stock; a good many corporations also issue preferred stock; and some companies have two or more types of preferred stock.

Common stock may be regarded as the basic, residual element of ownership. It carries voting rights and, therefore, is the means of exercising control over the business. Common stock has unlimited possibilities of increase in value; during periods of business expansion the market prices of common stocks of some leading corporations may rise to two or three times their former values. On the other hand, common stocks lose value more rapidly than other types of securities when corporations encounter periods of unprofitable business.

The following stockholders' equity section illustrates the balance sheet presentation for a corporation having both preferred and common stock; note that the item of retained earnings is not apportioned between the two groups of stockholders.

Balance sheet presentation

Stockholders' equity:

Preferred stock, 8% cumulative, $100 par value, authorized and issued	
100,000 shares	*$10,000,000*
Common stock, $5 par value, authorized and issued 1 million shares .	*5,000,000*
Retained earnings	*3,500,000*
Total stockholders' equity	*$18,500,000*

CHARACTERISTICS OF PREFERRED STOCK Most preferred stocks have the following distinctive features:

1 Preferred as to dividends
2 Preferred as to assets in event of the liquidation of the company
3 Callable at the option of the corporation
4 No voting power

Another very important but less common feature is a clause permitting the **conversion** of preferred stock into common at the option of the holder. Preferred stocks vary widely with respect to the special rights and privileges granted. Careful study of the terms of the individual preferred stock contract is a necessary step in the evaluation of any preferred stock.

Stock preferred as to dividends Stock preferred as to dividends is entitled to receive each year a dividend of specified amount before any dividend is paid on the common stock. The dividend is usually stated as a dollar amount per share. For example, the balance sheet of General Motors Corporation shows two types of preferred stock outstanding, one paying $5.00 a year and the other $3.75 a year, as shown below:

Dividend stated as dollar amount

Capital stock:

Preferred, without par value (authorized 6 million shares):	
$5.00 series; stated value $100 per share, redeemable at $120	
per share (issued 1,875,366 shares; in treasury 39,722 shares;	
outstanding 1,835,644 shares)	*$183,564,400*
$3.75 series; stated value $100 per share, redeemable at $101	
per share (issued and outstanding 1,000,000 shares)	*100,000,000*

Some preferred stocks state the dividend preference as a percentage of par value. For example, a 9% preferred stock with a par value of $100 per share would mean that $9 must be paid yearly on each share of preferred stock before any dividends are paid on the common. An example of the percentage method of stating the dividend on a preferred stock is found in the balance sheet of Georgia-Pacific Corporation:

Dividend stated as percentage

Capital stock:

Preferred, $5\frac{1}{2}$% cumulative, par value $100 per share	*$10,000,000*

The holders of preferred stock have no assurance that they will always receive the indicated dividend. A corporation is obligated to pay dividends to stockholders only when the board of directors declares a dividend. Dividends must be paid on preferred stock before anything is paid to the common stockholders, but if the corporation is not prospering, it may decide not to pay dividends on either preferred or common stock. For a corporation to pay dividends, profits must be earned and cash must be available. However, preferred stocks in general offer more assurance of regular dividend payments than do common stocks.

Cumulative preferred stock   The dividend preference carried by most preferred stocks is a *cumulative* one. If all or any part of the regular dividend on the preferred stock is omitted in a given year, the amount in arrears must be paid in a subsequent year before any dividend can be paid on the common stock. Assume that a corporation was organized January 1, 1977, with 10,000 shares of $4 cumulative preferred stock and 10,000 shares of common stock. Dividends paid in 1977 were at the rate of $4 per share of preferred stock and $3 per share of common. However, in 1978 earnings declined sharply and the only dividend paid was $1 per share on the preferred stock. No dividends were paid in 1979. What is the status of the preferred stock as of December 31, 1979? Dividends are in arrears in the amount of $7 a share ($3 omitted during 1978 and $4 omitted in 1979). On the entire issue of 10,000 shares of preferred stock, the dividends in arrears amount to $70,000.

In 1980, we shall assume that the company earned large profits and wished to pay dividends on both the preferred and common stocks. Before paying a dividend on the common, the corporation must pay the $70,000 in arrears on the cumulative preferred stock plus the regular $4 a share applicable to the current year. The preferred stockholders would, therefore, receive a total of $110,000 in dividends in 1980; the board of directors would then be free to declare dividends on the common stock.

Dividends in arrears *are not listed among the liabilities of a corporation,* because no liability exists until a dividend is declared by the board of directors. Nevertheless, the amount of any dividends in arrears on preferred stock is an important factor to investors and should always be disclosed. This disclosure is usually made by a note accompanying the balance sheet such as the following:

"As of December 31, 1979, dividends on the $4 cumulative preferred stock were in arrears to the extent of $7 per share, and amounted in total to $70,000."

For a *noncumulative preferred stock,* any unpaid or omitted dividend is lost forever. Because of this factor, investors view the noncumulative feature as an unfavorable element, and very few noncumulative preferred stocks are issued.

Participating clauses in preferred stock   Since participating preferred stocks are very seldom issued, discussion of them will be brief. A fully participating preferred stock is one which, in addition to the regular specified dividend, is entitled to participate in some manner with the common stock in any additional dividends paid. For example, a $5 participating preferred stock would be entitled to receive $5 a share before the common stock received anything. After $5 a share had been paid to the preferred stockholders, a $5 dividend could be paid on the common stock. If the company desired to pay an additional dividend to the common, say, an extra $3 per share, the preferred stock would also be entitled to receive an extra $3 dividend. In brief, a fully participating preferred stock participates dollar for dollar with the common stock in any dividends paid in excess of the stated rate on the preferred stock.

Stock preferred as to assets   Most preferred stocks carry a preference as to assets in the event of liquidation of the corporation. If the business is terminated, the preferred stock is entitled to payment in full of a stated liquidation value (or par value) before any payment is made on the common stock. This priority also includes any dividends in arrears.

Callable preferred stock   Most preferred stocks are callable at the option of the corporation at a stipulated price, usually slightly above the issuance price. The *call price* or *redemption price* for a $100 par value preferred stock is often $103 or $104 per share.

In the financing of a new or expanding corporation, the organizers usually hold common stock, which assures them control of the company because only the common stock has voting rights. However, it is often necessary to obtain outside capital. One way of doing this, without the loss of control or any serious reduction in possible future earnings on the common stock, is to issue a callable preferred stock.

It may be argued that the position of the holders of a callable preferred stock is more like that of creditors than that of owners. They supply capital to the company for an agreed rate of return, have no voice in management, and may find their relationship with the company terminated at any time through the calling in of their certificates. If a company is so fortunate as to enter upon a period of unusually high earnings, it will probably increase the dividend payments on its common stock, but it will not consider increasing the income of the preferred stockholders. On the contrary, the corporation may decide that this era of prosperity is a good time to eliminate the preferred stock through exercise of the call provision.

Regardless of the fact that preferred stock lacks many of the traditional aspects of ownership, it is universal practice to include all types of preferred stock in the stockholders' equity section of the balance sheet.

Convertible preferred stock   In order to add to the attractiveness of preferred stock as an investment, corporations sometimes offer a conversion privilege which entitles the preferred stockholders to exchange their shares for common stock in a stipulated ratio. If the corporation prospers, its common stock will probably rise in market value, and dividends on the common stock will probably be increased. The investor who buys a convertible preferred stock rather than common stock has greater assurance of regular dividends. In addition, through the conversion privilege, the investor is assured of sharing in any substantial increase in value of the company's common stock.

As an example, assume that the Remington Corporation issued a 5%, $100 par, convertible preferred stock on January 1, at a price of $100 a share. Each share was convertible into four shares of the company's $25 par value common stock at any time. The common stock had a market price of $20 a share on January 1, and an annual dividend of 60 cents a share was being paid. The yield on the preferred stock was 5% ($5 ÷ $100); the yield on the common stock was only 3% ($0.60 ÷ $20).

During the next few years, the Remington Corporation's earnings increased, the dividend on the common stock was raised to an annual rate of $1.50, and the market price of the common stock rose to $40 a share. At this point the preferred stock would have a market value of at least $160, since it could be converted at any time into four shares of common stock with a market value of $40 each. In other words, the market value of a convertible preferred stock will tend to move in accordance with the price of the common. When the dividend rate is increased on the common stock, some holders of the preferred stock may convert their holdings into common stock in order to obtain a higher cash return on their investments.

If the holder of 100 shares of the preferred stock presented these shares for conversion, the Remington Corporation would make the following entry:

Conversion of preferred stock into common	*5% Convertible Preferred Stock*	*10,000*
	Common Stock	*10,000*
	To record the conversion of 100 shares of preferred stock, par $100, into 400 shares of $25 par value common stock.	

The preceding illustration was based on the assumption that the Remington Corporation enjoyed larger earnings after the issuance of its convertible preferred. Let us now make a contrary assumption and say that shortly after issuance of the convertible preferred stock, the company's profits declined and the directors deemed it necessary to cut the annual dividend on the common stock from 60 cents a share to 20 cents a share. Stockholders who acquired common stock at a cost of $20 a share now find that their dividend income has dropped to a rate of 1% ($0.20 ÷ $20 cost). The dividend on the preferred stock remains at $5 a share.

These two illustrations indicate that the convertible preferred stock has two important advantages from the viewpoint of the investor: It increases in value along with the common stock when the company prospers, and it offers greater assurance of steady dividend income during a period of poor earnings.

The underwriting of stock issues

When a large amount of stock is to be issued, the corporation will probably utilize the services of an investment banking firm, frequently referred to as an *underwriter.* The underwriter guarantees the issuing corporation a specific price for the stock and makes a profit by selling the stock to the investing public at a higher price. For example, an issue of 1,270,000 shares of $1 par value common stock might be sold to the public at a price of $47 a share, of which $2.35 a share is retained by the underwriter and $44.65 represents the net proceeds to the issuing corporation.[2] The corporation would enter in its accounts only the net amount received from the underwriter ($44.65) for each share issued. The use of an underwriter assures the corporation that the entire stock issue will be sold without delay, and the entire amount of funds to be raised will be available on a specific date.

Market price of common stock

The preceding sections concerning the issuance of stock at prices above and below par value raise a question as to how the market price of stock is determined. The price which the corporation sets on a new issue of stock is based on several factors including (1) an appraisal of the company's expected future earnings, (2) the probable dividend rate per share, (3) the present financial position of the company, and (4) the current state of the investment market.

After the stock has been issued, the price at which it will be traded among investors will rise and fall in response to all the forces of the marketplace. The market price per share will tend to reflect the progress of the company, with primary emphasis being placed on earnings and dividends per share. *Earnings per share* of common stock, for example, is computed by dividing the annual net income available to the common stock by the number of shares outstanding. At this point in our discussion, the significant fact to emphasize is that market price is not related to par value, and that it tends to reflect current and future earnings and dividends. (Earnings per share is discussed in some detail in Chapter 17.)

---

[2] These figures are taken from a prospectus issued by Levi Strauss & Co. covering the issuance of 1,070,000 shares by the corporation and 200,000 shares by stockholders in an initial public offering by the corporation. Figures taken from the face of the prospectus follow:

	Price to Public	Underwriting Discounts and Commissions*	Proceeds to the Company†	Proceeds to Selling Stockholders
Per Share	$47.00	$2.35	$44.65	$44.65
Total	$59,690,000	$2,984,500	$47,775,500	$8,930,000

*The Company has agreed to indemnify the Underwriters against certain liabilities under the Securities Act of 1933.
†Before deducting expenses payable by the Company estimated at $200,000.

Stock issued for assets other than cash

Corporations generally sell their capital stock for cash and use the cash obtained in this way to buy the various types of assets needed in the business. Sometimes, however, a corporation may issue shares of its capital stock in a direct exchange for land, buildings, or other assets. Stock may also be issued in payment for services rendered by attorneys and promoters.

When a corporation issues capital stock in exchange for services or for assets other than cash, a question arises as to the proper valuation of the property or services received. For example, assume that a corporation issues 1,000 shares of its $1 par value common stock in exchange for a tract of land. A problem may exist in determining the fair market value of the land, and consequently in determining the amount of paid-in capital. If there is no direct evidence of the value of the land, we may value it by using indirect evidence as to the alternative amount of cash for which the shares might have been sold. Assume that the company's stock is listed on a stock exchange and is presently selling at $90 a share. The 1,000 shares which the corporation exchanged for the land could have been sold for $90,000 cash, and the cash could have been used to pay for the land. The direct exchange of stock for land may be considered as the equivalent of selling the stock for cash and using the cash to buy the land. It is therefore logical to say that the cost of the land to the company was $90,000, the market value of the stock given in exchange for the land. *Note that the par value of the stock is not any indication of the fair value of the stock or of the land.*

Once the valuation question has been decided, the entry to record the issuance of stock in exchange for noncash assets can be made as follows:

How were dollar amounts determined?	Land 90,000	
	Common Stock	1,000
	Paid-in Capital in Excess of Par Value	89,000

To record the issuance of 1,000 shares of $1 par value common stock in exchange for land. Current market value of stock ($90 a share) used as basis for valuing the land.

No-par stock

An understanding of no-par stock can best be gained by reviewing the reasons why par value was originally required in an earlier period of American corporate history. The use of the par value concept in state laws was intended for the protection of creditors and of public stockholders. In some states stock could not be issued at less than par value; in most states if stock *was* issued at less than par value the purchaser was contingently liable for the discount below par. A corporation was thus discouraged from selling its stock to the public at, say, $100 a share and concurrently to insiders or promoters at, say, $50 a share.

Protection was also afforded to creditors by laws prohibiting a corporation from paying any dividend which would "impair its capital" (reduce its capital to an amount less than the par value of the outstanding shares). Because of these statutes concerning par value, a creditor of a corporation could tell by inspection of the balance sheet the amount which owners had invested permanently in the corporation. This permanent investment of ownership capital (par value times the number of outstanding shares) represented a buffer which protected the corporation creditor from the impact of any losses sustained by the corporation. Such protection for creditors was considered necessary because stockholders have no personal liability for the debts of the corporation.

The par value device proved rather ineffective in achieving its avowed objective of protecting creditors and stockholders, and most states later enacted legislation permitting corporations to issue stock without par value.

With the advent of no-par stock, state legislatures attempted to continue the protection of corporate creditors by designating all or part of the amount received by the corporation for its no-par shares as *stated capital* not subject to withdrawal.

Assume that a corporation is organized in a state which permits the board of directors to establish a *stated value* on the 100,000 shares authorized, and that the board passed a resolution setting the stated value per share at $5. If a total of 80,000 shares were issued at $12, the journal entry to record the issuance would be:

Note stated value per share	*Cash*	*960,000*	
	Common Stock		*400,000*
	Paid-in Capital in Excess of Stated Value		*560,000*

Issued 80,000 shares of no-par value common stock at $12 each. Stated value set by directors at $5 per share.

If in the foregoing example the company reported a net income of $25,000 during the first month, the stockholders' equity section of the balance sheet would be as follows:

Only part of paid-in capital in Common Stock account	*Stockholders' equity:*	
	Common stock, no par value, stated value $5 per share, authorized 100,000 shares, issued and outstanding 80,000 shares	*$400,000*
	Paid-in capital in excess of stated value	*560,000*
	Total paid-in capital	*$960,000*
	Retained earnings	*25,000*
	Total stockholders' equity	*$985,000*

In the absence of a stated value, the entire proceeds on the sale of stock ($960,000) would be credited to the Common Stock account and would be viewed as legal capital. However, most companies which issue no-par capital stock do establish a stated value per share.

Subscriptions to capital stock

Small corporations sometimes sell stock on a subscription plan, in which the investor agrees to pay the subscription price at a future date or in a series of installments. For example, Subscriptions Receivable: Common would be debited and Common Stock Subscribed would be credited when the subscription contract was signed. Collections would be credited to Subscriptions Receivable: Common; when the entire subscription price had been collected and the stock issued, Common Stock Subscribed would be debited and Common Stock would be credited. The following illustration demonstrates the accounting procedures for stock subscriptions.

In this example, 10,000 shares of $10 par value stock are subscribed at a price of $15. Subscriptions for 6,000 shares are collected in full. A partial payment is received on the other 4,000 shares.

Sub- *Subscriptions Receivable: Common*	*150,000*	
scription *Common Stock Subscribed*		*100,000*
price above		
par *Paid-in Capital in Excess of Par Value*		*50,000*
Received subscriptions for 10,000 shares of $10 par value stock at price of $15 a share.		

When the subscriptions for 6,000 shares are collected in full, certificates for 6,000 shares will be issued. The following entries are made:

Certificates *Cash*	*90,000*	
issued for *Subscriptions Receivable: Common*		*90,000*
fully paid		
shares *Collected subscriptions in full for 6,000 shares at $15 each.*		
Common Stock Subscribed	*60,000*	
Common Stock		*60,000*
Issued certificates for 6,000 fully paid $10 par value shares.		

The subscriber to the remaining 4,000 shares paid only half of the amount of the subscription but promised to pay the remainder within a month. Stock certificates will not be issued until the subscription is collected in full, but the partial collection is recorded by the following entry:

Partial col- *Cash*	*30,000*	
lection of *Subscriptions Receivable: Common*		*30,000*
subscription *Collected partial payment on subscription for 4,000 shares.*		

From the corporation's point of view, Subscriptions Receivable is a current asset, which ordinarily will be collected within a short time. If financial statements are prepared between the date of obtaining subscriptions and the date of issuing the stock, the Common Stock Subscribed account will appear in the stockholders' equity section of the balance sheet.

Special records of corporations

The financial page of today's newspaper reports that the most actively traded stocks on the New York Stock Exchange today were the following:

		Number of Shares Sold	Closing Price
Today's stock market	Texaco	340,200	$26\frac{3}{8}$
	General Electric	282,500	$51\frac{1}{2}$
	General Motors	179,300	69

Several significant facts concerning capital stock transactions are implicit in this brief news item. In the first place, the three corporations listed did not necessarily buy or sell any shares of their stock today. The quantities of shares listed above were probably sold by existing stockholders to other investors. When a corporation first issues its stock, the transaction is between the corporation and the investor; once the stock is outstanding, most further stock transactions are between individuals and do not affect the corporation which issued the stock.[3] However, the corporation must be informed of each such stock transaction so that it can correct its records of stock ownership by eliminating the name of the former owner and adding the name of the new owner.

A second observation which might be made from the above news item is that a great volume of trading occurs each business day in the stocks of large corporations listed on the nation's stock exchanges. The availability of a ready market which permits individual investors to convert their stockholdings into cash at any time is one of the principal reasons that corporations have become the dominant form of business organization.

STOCK CERTIFICATES Ownership of a corporation is evidenced by stock certificates. A large corporation with stock listed on an organized stock exchange usually has many millions of shares outstanding and may have several hundred thousand stockholders. The number of shares changing hands on a typical business day may be as many as 200,000 to 300,000 shares. Exxon Corporation, for example, has over 200 million shares of stock outstanding. These shares are owned by approximately 700,000 investors. (The term *investor* as used in this discussion is meant to include investment groups or entities such as pension funds, investment clubs, and similar organizations, as well as individual investors.)

Even a small corporation is apt to have a considerable number of stock certificates to account for. It is essential, therefore, that detailed records be maintained showing exactly how many shares are outstanding and the names and addresses of the shareholders. These capital stock records

---

[3] A corporation may reacquire some of its own shares by purchase in the open market. Shares reacquired by a corporation are called *treasury stock* (see Chap. 17).

are in a process of continual change to reflect the purchase and sale of shares among the army of public investors.

A small corporation may order blank stock certificates from a printer, usually in a bound book with stubs similar to a checkbook. The certificates and the stubs are serially numbered by the printer, which aids the corporation in maintaining control over both the outstanding and the unissued certificates. At the time of issuance, a certificate is signed by the president and the secretary of the corporation, the number of shares represented by the certificate is filled in, and the certificate is delivered to a stockholder.

A stock certificate and the related stub are shown below. This certificate is ready to be detached from the stub and delivered to the shareholder, Richard Warren. Note that the certificate has been signed by the officers of the company and that the following information is listed on both the certificate and the stub:

Certificate number *901*
Name of shareholder . . . . *Richard Warren*
Number of shares *100*
Date issued . . . . *January 10, 1978*
Type of stock . . . . *Common*

The certificate is now detached from the stub and delivered to Richard Warren. The open stubs in the certificate book (stubs without any certificates attached) represent outstanding certificates. If a stockholder sells his or her shares, the certificate is returned to the company, canceled, and attached to the corresponding stub in the stock certificate book. The total number of shares of stock outstanding at any time can be determined by adding up the number of shares listed on all the open stubs.

Certificate No. .... 901 ....

For .... −100− .... Shares
Of the Common Stock of
The Gold Cup Corporation

ISSUED TO:
.... Richard Warren ....

Date ..... January 10, 1974 ....

FROM WHOM TRANSFERRED:

.... −−Original issue−− ....

| No. of Original Certificate | No. of Original Shares | No. of Shares Transferred |

Certificate No. ...... 901 .... −100− .... Shares

THE GOLD CUP CORPORATION

Par Value $5 per Share Common Stock
Incorporated under the Laws of the State of California

THIS IS TO CERTIFY that ...... Richard Warren ...... is the owner of ..... −one hundred− ..... fully paid and non-assessable shares of the common capital stock of The Gold Cup Corporation, transferable only on the books of this corporation by the said owner hereof in person or by attorney, upon surrender of this certificate properly endorsed.

Witness the seal of the corporation and the signatures of its duly authorized officers on this ...... −10th− ...... day of ...... −January− ...... , 1974

Murray Whitehall
President

Byron Bannock
Secretary

THE GOLD CUP CORPORATION
INCORPORATED
1967

STOCKHOLDERS' LEDGER For a company with a large number of stock-holders, it is not practicable to include in the general ledger an account with each stockholder. Instead a single controlling account entitled Common Stock is carried in the general ledger and a subsidiary stock-holders' ledger with individual stockholders is maintained. In this stock-holders' ledger, each stockholder's account shows the number of shares which he or she owns, the certificate numbers, and the dates of acquisition and sale. Entries are not made in dollars but in number of shares.

The stockholders' ledger contains essentially the same information as the stock certificate book, but the arrangement of the information is in an alphabetical listing of stockholders rather than in the sequence of stock certificate numbers. One stockholder may own a number of certificates, acquired at various dates. The entire holdings of any one stockholder would be summarized in one account in the stockholders' ledger.

STOCK TRANSFER AGENT AND STOCK REGISTRAR The large corporation with thousands of stockholders and a steady flow of stock transfers usually turns over the function of maintaining capital stock records to an independent stock transfer agent and a stock registrar. A bank or trust company serves as stock transfer agent and another bank acts as the stock registrar. When certificates are to be transferred from one owner to another, the certificates are sent to the transfer agent, who cancels them, makes the necessary entries in the stockholders' ledger, and signs new certificates which are forwarded to the stock registrar. The function of the registrar is to prevent any improper issuance of stock certificates. To accomplish this objective, the bank acting as registrar maintains records showing the total number of shares outstanding at all times. The use of an independent stock transfer agent and a stock registrar is an excellent control device, which eliminates the possibility that a dishonest officer or employee of a corporation might issue stock certificates for cash without making any entry in the records.

MINUTES BOOK A corporate minutes book consists of a narrative record of all actions taken at official meetings of the corporation's board of directors and of its stockholders. Typical of the actions described in the minutes book are the declaration of dividends by the board of directors, the authorization of important transactions such as the obtaining of bank loans or the purchase of plant and equipment, the setting of officers' salaries, and the adoption of retirement plans or pension agreements.

Balance sheet for a corporation illustrated

A fairly complete corporation balance sheet is presented on page 577. In studying this balance sheet, the student should bear in mind that current practice includes many alternatives in the choice of terminology and the arrangement of items in financial statements. Some of these alternatives are illustrated in the Appendix at the end of this book.

TABLE CORPORATION
Balance Sheet
December 31, Year 10

Assets

Current assets:

Cash	$ 305,600
U. S. government securities, at cost (market value $812,800)	810,000
Accounts receivable (net of allowance for doubtful accounts)	1,165,200
Subscriptions receivable: preferred stock	50,000
Inventories (lower of fifo cost or market)	1,300,800
Short-term prepayments	125,900
Total current assets	$3,757,500

Investments: Common stock of Price Corporation			444,900
Plant and equipment:			
Land		$ 500,000	
Buildings	$2,482,100		
Less: Accumulated depreciation	400,000	2,082,100	
Equipment	$1,800,000		
Less: Accumulated depreciation	800,000	1,000,000	3,582,100
Intangibles: Patents and trademarks			110,000
Total assets			$7,894,500

Liabilities & Stockholders' Equity

Current liabilities:

Accounts payable	$1,037,800
Income taxes payable	324,300
Dividends payable	70,000
Interest payable	20,000
Total current liabilities	$1,452,100
Long-term liabilities: Bonds payable, 8%, due Oct. 1, Year 20	1,000,000
Total liabilities	$2,452,100

Stockholders' equity:

Cumulative 5% preferred stock, $100 par, authorized 10,000 shares:		
8,000 shares issued	$ 800,000	
2,000 shares subscribed	200,000	$1,000,000
Common stock, $1 par, authorized		
1,000,000 shares: 600,000 shares issued	600,000	
Paid-in capital in excess of par: common	2,200,000	
Total paid-in capital	$3,800,000	
Retained earnings	1,642,400	
Total stockholders' equity		5,442,400
Total liabilities & stockholders' equity		$7,894,500

KEY TERMS INTRODUCED OR EMPHASIZED IN CHAPTER 16

Board of directors Persons elected by common stockholders to direct the affairs of a corporation.

Call price The price to be paid by a corporation for each share of callable preferred stock if the corporation decides to call (redeem) the preferred stock.

Capital stock Transferable units of ownership in a corporation. A broad term which may refer to common stock, preferred stock, or both.

Common stock A type of capital stock which possesses the basic rights of ownership including the right to vote. Represents the residual element of ownership in a corporation.

Convertible preferred stock Preferred stock which entitles the owner to exchange his or her shares for common stock in a specified ratio.

Corporation A business organized as a legal entity separate from its owners. Chartered by the state with ownership divided into shares of transferable stock. Stockholders are not liable for debts of the corporation.

Cumulative preferred stock A class of stock with a provision that if dividends are reduced or omitted in any year, this amount accumulates and must be paid prior to payment of dividends on the common stock.

Deficit Accumulated losses incurred by a corporation. A negative amount of retained earnings.

Dividend A distribution of cash by a corporation to its stockholders.

Limited liability An important characteristic of the corporate form of organization. The corporation as a separate legal entity is responsible for its own debts; the stockholders are not personally liable for the corporation's debts.

Minutes book Formal record of official actions taken in meetings of stockholders and of the board of directors.

No-par stock Stock without par value. Usually has a stated value which is similar to par value.

Organization costs Costs incurred to form a corporation.

Paid-in capital The amounts invested in a corporation by its stockholders.

Par value The legal capital of a corporation. Also the face amount of a share of capital stock. Represents the minimum amount per share to be invested in the corporation when shares are originally issued.

Preferred stock A class of capital stock usually having preferences as to dividends and in the distribution of assets in event of liquidation.

Retained earnings That portion of stockholders' equity resulting from profits earned and retained in the business.

Stated capital That portion of capital invested by stockholders which cannot be withdrawn. Provides protection for creditors. Also called *legal capital.*

Stock certificate A document issued by a corporation as evidence of the ownership of the number of shares stated on the certificate.

Stock registrar An independent fiscal agent, usually a large bank, retained by a corporation to control the issuance of stock certificates and provide assurance against overissuance.

Stock transfer agent A bank or trust company retained by a corporation to maintain its records of capital stock ownership and make transfers from one investor to another.

Stockholders' ledger A subsidiary record showing the number of shares owned by each stockholder.

Subscriptions to capital stock Formal promises to buy shares of stock from a corporation with payment at a later date. Stock certificates delivered when full payment received.

Underwriter An investment banking firm which handles the sale of a corporation's stock to the public.

REVIEW QUESTIONS

1 Distinguish between corporations and partnerships in terms of the following characteristics:
   a Owners' liability
   b Transferability of ownership interest
   c Continuity of existence
   d Federal taxation on income

2 The corporate form of organization is usually considered advantageous for large enterprises. Why do you suppose large firms of certified public accountants, attorneys, or architects generally do not incorporate?

3 Describe three kinds of expenses that may be incurred in the process of organizing a corporation. How are such expenditures treated for accounting purposes? Why?

4 What are the basic rights of the owner of a share of corporate stock? In what way are these basic rights commonly modified with respect to the owner of a share of preferred stock?

5 Describe the usual nature of the following features as they apply to a share of preferred stock: (**a**) cumulative, (**b**) participating, (**c**) convertible, and (**d**) callable.

6 Why is noncumulative preferred stock considered a very unattractive form of investment?

7 Smith owns 200 of the 8,000 shares of common stock of X Company issued and outstanding. The company issues 2,000 additional shares of stock. What is Smith's position with respect to the new issue if he is entitled to preemptive rights?

8 In theory, a corporation may sell its stock for an amount greater or less than par value; in practice, stock is seldom if ever issued for less than par. Explain the significance of par value and why it is impractical to issue shares for less than par.

9 When stock is issued by a corporation in exchange for assets other than cash, the accountant faces the problem of determining the dollar amount at which to record the transaction. Discuss the factors to consider and explain their significance.

10 State the classification (asset, liability, stockholders' equity, or expense) of each of the following accounts:
   a Subscriptions receivable: common
   b Organization costs
   c Capital stock, common
   d Retained earnings
   e Capital stock subscribed: preferred
   f Premium on common stock
   g Discount on preferred stock
   h Federal and state income taxes

11 Explain the following terms:
   a Stock transfer agent
   b Stockholders' ledger
   c Underwriter
   d Minutes book
   e Stock registrar

12 Distinguish between *paid-in capital* and *retained earnings* of a corporation. Why is such a distinction useful?

EXERCISES

Ex. 16-1 McGee Corporation was organized on September 1, 19___. The corporation was authorized to issue 10,000 shares of $100 par value, 8% cumulative preferred stock, and 100,000 shares of $5 par value common stock.

All the preferred stock was issued at par and 80,000 shares of the common stock were sold for $22 per share. Prepare a statement of stockholders' equity for McGee Corporation immediately after the sale of the securities but prior to any operation of the company.

Ex. 16-2 Tower Corporation has outstanding two classes of $100 par value stock: 1,000 shares of 6% cumulative preferred and 5,000 shares of common. The company had a $20,000 deficit at the beginning of the current year, and preferred dividends had not been paid for two years. During the current year, the company earns $100,000. What will be the balance in retained earnings at the end of the current year, if the company pays a dividend of $2 per share on common stock?

Ex. 16-3 The year-end balance sheet of Jamestown Corporation included the following stockholders' equity section:

Stockholders' equity:
  Capital stock:

$5.50 dividend cumulative preferred stock; no-par value, 300,000 shares authorized, 180,000 shares outstanding, stated at	*$ 18,000,000*
Common stock; no-par value, 5,000,000 shares authorized, 4,300,000 shares issued, stated at	*32,250,000*
Retained earnings	*75,800,000*
Total retained earnings	*$126,050,000*

Instructions From this information, compute answers to the following questions:
a What is the stated value per share of the preferred stock?
b What was the average issuance price of a share of common stock?
c What is the amount of the total legal capital and the amount of the total paid-in capital?
d What is the total amount of the annual dividend requirement on the preferred stock issue?
e Total dividends of $5,200,000 were declared on the preferred and common stock during the year, and the balance in retained earnings at the beginning of the year amounted to $67,800,000. What was the amount of net income for the year?

Ex. 16-4 A portion of the stockholders' equity section from the balance sheet of Barnes Corporation appears below:

Stockholders' equity:

Preferred stock, 6% cumulative, $50 par, 40,000 shares authorized and issued	*$2,000,000*
Preferred stock, 9% noncumulative, $100 par, 8,000 shares authorized and issued	*800,000*
Common stock, $5 par, 400,000 shares authorized and issued	*2,000,000*
Total paid-in capital	*$4,800,000*

Instructions Assume that all the stock was issued on January 1, 19___ , and that no dividends were paid during the first two years of operations. During the third year, Barnes Corporation paid total cash dividends of $532,000.

a Compute the amount of cash dividends paid during the third year to each of the three classes of stock.

b Compute the dividends paid **per share** during the third year for each of the three classes of stock.

Ex. 16-5 Orange Corporation has only one issue of capital stock, consisting of 50,000 outstanding shares of $5 par value. The net income in the first year of operations was $88,000. No dividends were paid in the first year. On January 15 of the second year, a dividend of 80 cents per share was declared by the board of directors payable February 15.

a Prepare the journal entry at December 31 of Year 1 to close the Income Summary account.

b Prepare the journal entries for declaration of the dividend on January 15 and payment of the dividend on February 15.

c Assuming that operations for Year 2 resulted in a net loss of $25,000, prepare the journal entry to close the Income Summary account at December 31, Year 2.

d Compute the balance of the Retained Earnings account as it would appear in the balance sheet at December 31, Year 2.

Ex. 16-6 Janet Harris owns 500 shares of convertible preferred stock of Bell Corporation. Each share is convertible into 1.5 shares of common stock. The preferred stock is selling at $80 per share and pays a dividend of $2.50 per year. The common stock is selling for $50 and pays an annual dividend of $2 per share.

Harris is considering converting the preferred stock in order to increase her total dividend income from $1,250 of preferred dividends to $1,500 a year in common dividends. However, an accounting student suggests that she sell her 500 preferred shares at the current market price of $80 and then buy 750 shares of common stock at the current market price of $50.

Harris objects to the student's suggestion on the grounds that she would have to pay income taxes at the rate of 25% on the gain from the sale of preferred stock, which she had acquired at $68 per share a year ago. Harris also points out that the conversion of preferred stock into common would involve no commissions expense but that the sale of preferred stock and purchase of common would require paying two commissions.

Prepare a schedule showing the results under the two alternatives. Disregard the question of commissions on the sale and purchase.

PROBLEMS

Group A

16A-1 The two cases described below are independent of each other.

(1) Fence Corporation was organized early in Year 3 with authorization to issue 80,000 shares of $5 par value common stock. All the shares were issued at par. The operations of the company resulted in a net loss of $20,000 for Year 3 and a net loss of $52,000 in Year 4. In Year 5 net income was $1.60 per share.

(2) Royal Corporation was formed early in Year 1. Authorization was obtained to issue 100,000 shares of $10 par value common stock and 4,000 shares of cumulative preferred stock. All the preferred and 80,000 shares of common were issued at par. The preferred stock was callable at 105% of its $100 par value and was entitled to dividends of 6% before any dividends were paid to common. During the first five years of its existence, the corporation earned a

total of $560,000 and paid dividends of 20 cents per share each year on common stock.

Instructions For each of the situations described above, prepare in good form the stockholders' equity section of the balance sheet as of December 31, Year 5. Include a supporting schedule for each case showing your determination of the balance of retained earnings that should appear in the balance sheet.

16A-2 In January, Year 10, Marsh Corporation was organized with authorization to issue both preferred stock and common stock. The preferred stock consisted of 50,000 authorized shares of $100 par value and a cumulative annual dividend of 8%. The common stock had a par value of $1 and 400,000 shares were authorized. Since Marsh Corporation planned to sell its stock for cash to a small number of investors and to issue the shares without delay, subscription contracts were not used. The following transactions (among others) occurred during Year 10.

Jan. **6** Issued for cash 50,000 shares of common stock at $8 a share.

Jan. **7** Issued 5,000 shares of preferred stock for cash of $500,000.

June **1** Acquired land as a building site in exchange for 1,000 shares of Marsh Corporation preferred stock and 10,000 shares of the common stock. In view of the appraised value of the land and the progress of Marsh Corporation, the parties agreed that the preferred stock was to be valued for purposes of this transaction at $100 a share and the common stock at $10 a share. The shares were issued.

Dec. **20** The first annual dividend of $8 per share was declared on the preferred stock to be paid January 20 of Year 11.

Dec. **31** After the revenue and expenses (except income taxes) were closed into the Income Summary account, that account showed a before-tax profit of $90,000. Income taxes were determined to be $32,000.

Instructions

a Prepare journal entries for Year 10 in general journal form to record the above transactions. Include entries at December 31 to (*1*) record the income tax liability; (*2*) close the income tax expense into the Income Summary account; and (*3*) close the Income Summary account.

b Prepare the stockholders' equity section of the balance sheet at December 31, Year 10.

16A-3 Greenhead Company, a partnership, is owned by three members of a family. The three partners decided on December 31, Year 5, to change the business into a corporation in order to limit their personal liability. The balance sheet of the partnership was as follows:

GREENHEAD COMPANY

Balance Sheet

December 31, Year 5

Various assets	*$520,000*	*Accounts payable*	*$130,000*
		B. Wallace, capital	*195,000*
		C. Wallace, capital	*117,000*
		D. Wallace, capital	*78,000*
	$520,000		*$520,000*

Other data The partners filed an application for incorporation under the name Greenhead Corporation. Authorization was received to issue 65,000 shares of $10 par value common stock and 5,200 shares of $100 par value 6% cumulative preferred stock. Organization costs were $7,800. On January 1, Year 6, the corporation was formed, and each partner was issued, at par, common stock for one-half of his capital interest and preferred stock for the remaining half. The organization costs were paid on January 1 and were not amortized during the year.

During Year 6 the corporation earned $130,000 before income taxes. Accounts payable increased by $52,000 during Year 6; the only other liability at year-end was income taxes payable. The provision for income taxes was 22% of the first $50,000 of income and 48% of income in excess of $50,000. Dividends were paid on preferred stock, and dividends of $1 per share were paid on common stock.

Instructions Prepare the balance sheet of the Greenhead Corporation as of December 31, Year 6. Show in two separate supporting schedules how you arrive at (*a*) the amounts of stock issued and (*b*) the amount of retained earnings at December 31, Year 6.

16A-4 On July 1, Year 6, Clearwater Corporation was organized by Helen Farmer with authorized stock of 250,000 shares of $5 par value common and 12,500 shares of $100 par value, 6% preferred stock. John Troon was given 250 shares of preferred and 2,500 shares of common for his work and expenses in organizing and promoting the corporation. Attorneys' fees of $2,250 in connection with the formation of the corporation have been billed but not paid.

Near the end of July, 200,000 shares of common were sold at par for cash, $150,000 of which was used to buy land and $750,000 applied to the price of a building. The building cost $1,675,000; the balance was represented by a 9% mortgage due in 10 years.

John Troon transferred assets from a previous business in exchange for 7,500 shares of preferred. The current fair value of these assets was as follows: notes receivable, $450,000; inventories, $75,000; equipment, $225,000.

The business did not begin operation until after July 31, but interest of $1,875 accrued on the notes receivable between the time they were turned over to the corporation and July 31. Interest on the mortgage payable did not begin until August 1. (Ignore income taxes.)

Instructions Prepare in good form the balance sheet of the Clearwater Corporation as of July 31, Year 6.

16A-5 At the close of the current year, the stockholders' equity section of the Rockhurst Corporation's balance sheet appeared as follows:

1000,000

Stockholders' equity:

$1.50 preferred stock, $25 par value, authorized 1,500,000 shares:		
Issued $10,800,000		
Subscribed............................ 5,400,000		$16,200,000
Common stock, no par, $5 stated value, authorized		
6,000,000 shares		12,300,000
Paid-in capital in excess of par or stated value:		
On preferred stock .... $ 810,000		
On common stock 7,626,000		8,436,000
Retained earnings (deficit)		(600,000)
Total stockholders' equity		$36,336,000

Among the assets of the corporation appears the following item: Subscriptions Receivable: Preferred, $1,123,200.

Instructions On the basis of this information, write a brief answer to the following questions, showing any necessary supporting computations.
a How many shares of preferred and common stock have been issued?
b How many shares of preferred stock have been subscribed?

c What was the average price per share received (including stock subscribed) by the corporation on its preferred stock?

d What was the average price per share received by the corporation on its common stock?

e What is the average amount per share that subscribers of preferred stock have yet to pay on their subscriptions?

f What is the total paid-in capital including stock subscribed?

g What is the total legal or stated value of the capital stock including stock subscribed?

16A-6 The two cases presented below are independent of each other.

Case A On July 31, Year 4, the Stake Corporation had outstanding 280,000 of 480,000 authorized shares of $20 par value common stock, and also 24,000 of 80,000 authorized shares of $7 preferred stock, cumulative, par value $100. The preferred stock was entitled to liquidation preference of par, plus any dividends in arrears. No dividends had ever been declared. The company had been in existence for three years and had lost money in each year, accumulating a deficit of $236,800 as of July 31, Year 4. On that date, all assets (other than cash on hand of $147,200) were sold for 80% of their book value, and the liabilities of $1,280,000 were paid in full.

Instructions Prepare a schedule showing the amount of assets available for distribution to stockholders, and the amount per share that would be received in liquidation on each of the two kinds of stock at July 31, Year 4.

Case B Line Corporation was organized on January 31, Year 5, and was authorized to issue 320,000 shares of $10 par value common stock and 40,000 shares of $2 cumulative preferred stock, par value $40 per share. The corporation sold 136,000 shares of common stock for cash at $12 per share, and also issued 16,000 shares of common stock to promoters and attorneys for their services in organizing the corporation.

During Year 5, the first year of operation, Line Corporation incurred a loss of $160,000. At the beginning of Year 6, the company needed cash. In order to sell its preferred stock at par, the company added a convertible feature to the preferred stock by making it convertible into four shares of common stock. With this feature added, 19,200 shares of preferred stock were sold at par early in Year 6.

During Year 6, the company earned $608,000. The market price of the common stock rose, and holders of 16,000 shares of preferred stock converted these preferred shares, receiving in exchange 64,000 shares of common stock. A semiannual dividend of $1 per share had been declared and paid on all 19,200 shares of preferred stock prior to the conversion of any shares.

Late in Year 6, the company paid the second semiannual dividend of $1 on the preferred stock still outstanding and also declared a dividend of $1.50 per share on the common stock. All the 216,000 shares of common stock outstanding on December 31, Year 6, received the $1.50 dividend.

Instructions Prepare in good form the stockholders' equity section of the balance sheet at December 31, Year 6. Show in a separate supporting schedule how you arrived at the balance of retained earnings at that date.

Group B

16B-1 The two cases described below are independent of each other.

(1) Early in Year 3 Campus Corporation was formed with authorization to issue 160,000 shares of $5 par value common. The stock was issued at par, and the corporation reported a net loss of $48,000 for Year 3 and a net loss of $112,000 in Year 4. In Year 5 net income was $2.10 per share.

(2) Landers Corporation was organized early in Year 1 and authorized to issue 200,000 shares of $10 par value common and 16,000 shares of cumulative preferred stock. All the preferred and 192,000 shares of common were issued at par. The preferred stock was callable at 105% of its $100 par value and was entitled to dividends of 6% before any dividends were paid to common. During the first five years of its existence, the corporation earned a total of $1,152,000 and paid dividends of 25 cents per share each year on the common stock.

Instructions For each of the independent situations described, prepare in good form the stockholders' equity section of the balance sheet as of December 31, Year 5. Include a supporting schedule for each case showing your determination of the balance of retained earnings that should appear in the balance sheet.

16B-2 (1) Douglas Corporation, a successful, family-owned company, is in the process of acquiring a tract of land suitable for the construction of a factory. The Douglas Corporation has agreed to offer 52,000 shares of common stock in exchange for the land, which has an agreed fair market value of $1,300,000, based on an independent appraisal.

Instructions Give the journal entry that should be made to record this transaction under each of the following assumptions:
a The stock has a $25 par value.
b The stock has a $2 par value.
c The stock has a $30 par value. (Disregard possible violation of state laws.)
d The stock is no par, with a stated value of $5.

(2) Hale Corporation, a well-established company, issued 5,200 shares of its $15 par value common stock in exchange for certain patents. The patents were entered in the accounts at $78,000. At this time, Hale common stock was quoted on the over-the-counter market at "25 bid and 27 asked"; that is, sellers were offering a given quantity of the stock at $27 per share, and buyers were offering to buy certain quantities at $25 per share.

Instructions Comment on the company's treatment of this transaction. Write a brief statement explaining whether you agree or disagree, and why. What is the essential difference between the evidence available to the accountant as a basis for the record of Douglas Corporation and the evidence available for Hale Corporation?

16B-3 On December 31, Year 2, the three partners of Paradise Cove agreed to incorporate their business. The balance sheet of the partnership on this date was as follows:

Assets	*$800,000*	*Accounts payable*	*$200,000*
		Axlee, capital	*300,000*
		Temkin, capital	*180,000*
		Gerrard, capital	*120,000*
	$800,000		*$800,000*

Articles of incorporation were approved under the name Paradise Cove, Inc., and authorization received for 160,000 shares of $10 par value common stock and 16,000 shares of $100 par value 6% cumulative preferred stock. Organization costs amounted to $13,120. On January 1, Year 3, the corporation was formed, and each partner was issued, at par, common stock for one-half of his capital interest and preferred stock for the remaining half. The organization costs were paid on January 1 and were not amortized during the year.

During Year 3, the corporation earned $200,000 before income taxes. Accounts payable increased by $39,680 during Year 3; the only other liability at year-end was income taxes payable. Income taxes are 40% of taxable income.

Regular quarterly dividends were paid on preferred stock, and a dividend of $1.50 per share was paid on common stock.

Instructions Prepare the balance sheet of Paradise Cove, Inc., as of December 31, Year 3. Show in two separate supporting schedules how you arrive at:
a The amount of stock issued
b The amount of retained earnings at December 31, Year 3

16B-4 The net assets (assets minus liabilities) of Dunleer, Incorporated, at January 1, Year 4, amounted to $4,500,000, represented by 450,000 shares of $5 par value common and 6,000 shares of 6%, $100 par value, cumulative preferred stock. All shares had been issued at par. The preferred stock is convertible into common at any time on the basis of one share of preferred for 20 shares of common. Income before income taxes is expected to be 20% of net assets during Year 4. The company is subject to income taxes at an average rate of 40%.

Instructions Assuming that earnings are as forecast,
a Compute the amount of net income in Year 4 that is allocable to common stock, assuming that none of the preferred shares is converted during the year.
b Compute the net income for Year 4 available per share of common stock, assuming that all preferred shares are converted at the beginning of Year 4. Round off to the nearest cent.
c Determine the maximum legal dividend per share of common that could be paid at the end of Year 4, assuming that all shares of preferred were converted at the beginning of Year 4 and that no part of paid-in capital is available for dividends. Prepare a journal entry to record the declaration on December 31 of a dividend of $1 per share on the common stock payable on February 1, Year 5. The shares receiving this dividend include the new common shares issued when the preferred stock was converted.

16B-5 Shown below is the stockholders' equity section of the balance sheet of Reno Corporation at the end of the current year.

RENO CORPORATION
Stockholders' Equity
December 31, Current Year

$2.75 preferred stock, $50 par value, authorized 40,000 shares:		
Issued	$720,000	
Subscribed	360,000	$1,080,000
Common stock, no par, $5 stated value, authorized 320,000 shares:		
Issued	$680,000	
Subscribed	140,000	820,000
Paid-in capital in excess of par or stated value:		
On preferred	$108,000	
On common	164,000	272,000
Retained earnings (deficit)		(300,000)
Total stockholders' equity		$1,872,000

Among the assets of the corporation appear the following items: Subscriptions Receivable: Preferred, $180,000; Subscriptions Receivable: Common, $91,000.

Instructions On the basis of this information, write a brief answer to the following questions, showing any necessary supporting computations.

a How many shares of preferred and common have been issued?
b How many shares of preferred and common have been subscribed?
c What was the average price per share received by the corporation on its preferred stock including preferred stock subscribed?
d What was the average price per share received by the corporation on its common stock including common stock subscribed?
e What is the average amount per share that subscribers of preferred stock have yet to pay on their subscriptions?
f What is the total contributed capital of the Reno Corporation?
g What is the total legal or stated value of its capital stock?
h What is the average amount per share that common stock subscribers have already paid on their subscriptions? (Assume common subscribed at $6.)

16B-6 Presented below are three separate cases requiring preparation of the stock-holders' equity section of a corporate balance sheet.

Case A Artists Corporation was organized January 1, Year 3, and was authorized to issue 320,000 shares of $5 par value common stock. All shares were issued at a price of $8 per share. The corporation reported a net loss of $96,000 for Year 3 and a net loss of $224,000 in Year 4. In Year 5, the net income was $1.80 per share. No dividends were declared during the three-year period.

Case B Builders Corporation was organized in Year 1. The company was authorized to issue 400,000 shares of $10 par value common stock and 32,000 shares of cumulative preferred stock. All the preferred stock was issued at par and 384,000 shares of the common stock were issued at $12. The preferred stock was callable at 105% of its $100 par value and was entitled to dividends of 8% before any dividends were paid on the common stock. During the first five years of its existence, the corporation earned a total of $2,304,000 and paid dividends of 35 cents per share each year on the common stock, in addition to regular dividends on the preferred stock.

Case C Crafts Corporation was organized in Year 2, issuing at $22 per share one-half of the 320,000 shares of $20 par common stock authorized. On January 1, Year 3, the company sold at par the entire 16,000 authorized shares of $100 par value, 7% cumulative preferred. On January 1, Year 4, the company issued 16,000 shares of an authorized 32,000 shares of $6 no-par, cumulative, participating preferred stock for $1,760,000. The $6 preferred stock provided that after common stockholders had received $3 per share in a given year, the $6 preferred stock would participate in additional dividends on a share-for-share basis up to $5 more per share. The company suffered losses in Year 2 and Year 3, reporting a deficit of $480,000 at the end of Year 3. During Year 4 and Year 5 combined, the company earned a total of $2,400,000. Dividends of $1 per share were paid on the common stock in Year 4 and $4.25 in Year 5. Thus in Year 5, the $6 preferred stock participated to the extent of $1.25 per share with common stockholders in dividends.

Instructions For each of the independent cases described, prepare in good form the stockholders' equity section of the balance sheet at December 31, Year 5. Include a supporting schedule for each case showing your determination of the balance of retained earnings at December 31, Year 5.

BUSINESS DECISION PROBLEM 16

Northern Electric and Western Power are two utility companies with very stable earnings. Northern Electric consistently has a net income of approximately $48 million per year, and Western Power's net income consistently approximates $42 million per year. Northern Electric has 5,400,000 shares of 6% preferred stock, $50 par value, and 7,950,000 shares of $50 par value common stock outstanding.

Western Power has 2,400,000 shares of 6% preferred stock, $100 par value, and 5,520,000 shares of $10 par value common stock outstanding. Assume that both companies distribute all net income as dividends every year, and will continue to do so. Neither company plans to issue additional shares of capital stock.

Instructions

a Compute the annual dividend which would be paid on the common stock of each company, assuming that Northern Electric has a net income of $48 million and Western Power has a net income of $42 million.

b Which company's common stock would you expect to have the higher *market price per share?* Support your answer with information provided in the problem.

17 Corporations: Earnings Per Share, Retained Earnings, and Dividends

The most important aspect of corporate financial reporting, in the view of most stockholders, is the determination of periodic net income. Both the market price of common stock and the amount of cash dividends per share depend to a considerable extent on the current level of earnings. The amount of *earnings per share* of common stock for a year, or an *interim* period such as three months, is of particular interest to stockholders and financial analysts. Even more important than the absolute amount of earnings per share is the *trend* of such earnings. Are earnings per share in an upward or downward trend? The common stocks of those companies which regularly achieve higher earnings per share year after year become the favorite securities of the investment community. Such stature helps greatly in raising new capital, in attracting and retaining highly competent management, and in many other ways.

Extraordinary items

An income statement tells us a great deal about the performance of a company over the past year. For example, study of the income statement makes clear the rate of gross profit on sales, the net income for the year, the percentage of profit per dollar of sales, and the net income earned on each share of common stock. Can we expect the income statement for next year to indicate about the same level of performance? If the transactions summarized in the income statement for the year just completed were of a normal recurring nature, such as selling merchandise, buying office equipment, and paying employees, we can reasonably assume that the operating results were typical and that somewhat similar results can reasonably be expected in the following year. However, in any business, *extraordinary gains and losses* may sometimes occur as a result of events and transactions that are of a very unusual nature and are unlikely to occur again in the foreseeable future. An example would be a major loss from an earthquake. If an extraordinary item is segregated on the income statement; that is, shown separately from the normal recurring operations of the business, it will be easier for us to use the income statement as a measure of normal typical performance.

There has long been agreement that an event or transaction must be *material* to warrant separate disclosure as an extraordinary item. However, for many years there was much argument over what kinds of events should be considered extraordinary. The definition was narrowed considerably by *APB Opinion No. 30.*[1] Extraordinary items are now defined as material transactions and events that are both *unusual in nature and occur infrequently* in the operating environment of the business. To illustrate these criteria, consider the case of a farming enterprise located along river bottomland subject to severe flood damage every few years. A large loss from a flood would not qualify as an extraordinary item in the income statement of this agricultural business, because it is not unusual and infrequent in the environment in which this particular business operates.

In order to be considered unusual in nature, the underlying event or transaction should be abnormal and clearly unrelated to the ordinary and typical activities of the entity. The scope of operations, lines of business, operating policies, and the environment in which an entity operates should be considered in applying this criterion. The environment of a business includes such factors as the characteristics of the industry, the geographic location of activities, and the degree of government regulation.

If an event or a transaction is not reasonably expected to take place in the foreseeable future, it is considered to occur infrequently. Past experience of the entity is generally a helpful guide in determining the frequency of an event or transaction.

Thus only those events which are both *unusual and infrequent* lead to extraordinary gains and losses. However, these qualitative standards are difficult to apply in practice, and differences of opinion still exist as to what is and what is not an extraordinary item. Listed below and on page 591 are some examples of gains or losses which are viewed as extraordinary and some which are not.

Extraordinary Items	**Not Extraordinary Items**
1 *Effects of major casualties such as earthquake (if rare in the area)*	1 *Write-down or write-off of receivables, inventories, or intangible assets*

---

[1] *APB Opinion No. 30,* "Reporting the Results of Operations—Reporting the Effects of Disposal of a Segment of a Business, and Extraordinary, Unusual and Infrequently Occurring Events and Transactions," AICPA (New York: 1973).

2 *Expropriation of assets by foreign governments*

3 *Effects of a prohibition under a newly enacted law or regulation*

2 *Gains or losses on disposal of a segment of a business or from sale or abandonment of plant assets*

3 *Effects of labor strikes or shortages of raw materials*

4 *Changes in estimates of accumulated depreciation, accrued expenses, and profits or losses on long-term construction contracts*

Few extraordinary items currently appear in corporate income statements as a result of the rigorous criteria established in *APB Opinion No. 30.* The presentation of extraordinary items in the income statement is illustrated below.

ATLANTA CORPORATION
Income Statement
For the Year Ended December 31, 19___

Net sales		$10,000,000
Cost of goods sold		6,000,000
Gross profit on sales		$ 4,000,000
Operating expenses:		
Selling expenses	$1,200,000	
General and administrative expenses	600,000	
Loss from suspension of operations during strike	200,000	2,000,000
Income before income taxes		$ 2,000,000
Deduct: Income taxes		800,000
Income before extraordinary item		$ 1,200,000
Extraordinary item: Loss from earthquake, net of reduction in income		
taxes		700,000
Net income		$ 500,000
Earnings per share of common stock:		
Income before extraordinary item		$1.20
Extraordinary item		.70
Net income		$0.50

|In studying the illustrated income statement of Atlanta Corporation, note that the nonoperating loss of $200,000 resulting from a strike was disclosed separately in the income statement but was not listed as an extraordinary item. This strike loss was important enough to bring to the attention of readers of the financial statements; but strikes do occur with some frequency in many industries. However, the loss from earthquake of $700,000 was considered both unusual in nature and infrequent in occurrence and therefore was presented as an extraordinary item. At the

bottom of the income statement, the net income is shown on a per-share basis. Earnings per share of common stock amounted to $1.20 per share before the extraordinary loss of 70 cents per share and 50 cents per share after considering the earthquake loss. Presumably the $1.20 per-share earnings before extraordinary items is a better indication of what may be expected next year than is the amount of earnings per share after deduction of the earthquake loss.

Note also that the amount of the earthquake loss is stated at the net after-tax amount of $700,000. The actual amount of the loss was greater, but because the loss reduced the income subject to income tax there was a reduction in income taxes. This tax saving was deducted from the total loss from the earthquake to show the after-tax loss of $700,000.

Discontinued operations of a segment of a business

Assume that a corporation sells a major segment of its operations to another company late in the current year. A problem would arise in making the income statements comparable for this year and next year since the operations would be of different scope and magnitude after disposal of a segment of the business.

Current accounting standards include rather precise guidelines for measuring and reporting the operating results of discontinued segments of a business. This topic was covered in *APB Opinion No. 30* along with the rules concerning extraordinary items. A *segment of a business* is "a component of a company whose activities represent a major line of business or class of customer."[2] The assets and operating results of a segment of a business should be clearly identifiable from the other assets and results of operations of the company. Several examples of segments of a business are listed below:

1 An electronics division of a highly diversified manufacturing company
2 A professional sports team owned by a newspaper publishing company
3 A wholesale milk distributorship owned by a retail food chain

The income statement is probably more useful if the results from the *continuing and ordinary operations* of a business entity are reported separately from the results of unusual transactions or events of material amount. Thus, the operating results of a discontinued segment of a business (including any gain or loss on the disposal of the segment) for the current period should be reported separately in the income statement in arriving at the income *before* extraordinary items. The purpose of such separate disclosure is to enable users of financial statements to make better predictive judgments as to the future earnings performance of the company.

For example, assume that the Childs Company reported a net income of

2 Ibid., par. 13.

$10 million for Year 10, including $4 million net income earned on sales of $100 million by an exporting division which was sold near the end of the year. Would the Childs Company be able to earn $10 million in Year 11 without the exporting business? Before answering this question, let us make an alternative assumption, that is, that the exporting division lost $8 million (after income taxes) in Year 10 instead of earning $4 million. What income might the Childs Company be expected to earn in Year 11 without the drain on earnings from the exporting business? The following partial income statement would be helpful to investors contemplating answers to these two questions:

CHILDS COMPANY
Partial Income Statement
For Year 10

		Assuming Exporting Division Earned $4 Million	Assuming Exporting Division Lost $8 Million
Income or	Income from continuing operations	$ 6,000,000	$18,000,000
loss from discon-	Income (or loss) from discontinued		
tinued	operations*	4,000,000	(8,000,000)
operations in the	Net income	$10,000,000	$10,000,000
income			
statement	Earnings per share of common stock:		
	Income from continuing operations	$1.50	$4.50
	Income (or loss) from discontinued		
	operations	1.00	(2.00)
	Net income	$2.50	$2.50

*The revenue in Year 10 from the discontinued segment was $100 million.

The income from continuing operations is a logical starting point in forecasting the probable earnings of the Childs Company for Year 11. However, other variables (such as price changes, increase in sales volume, and the acquisition of new lines of business) may cause the income from continuing operations in Year 11 to change materially under either assumption above.

The *revenue* and *expenses* shown in an income statement for the year in which a segment of a business is eliminated should consist only of the *revenue and expenses from continuing operations.* The net income or loss from discontinued operations is reported separately in the income statement, and the revenue from the discontinued segment is disclosed in the notes to the financial statements. Any gain or loss on the disposal of a segment should be reported with or near the results of the discontinued operations and *not as an extraordinary item.*

Public misconceptions of the rate of corporate earnings

Numerous public opinion surveys indicate that most people mistakenly believe that corporate earnings generally amount to somewhere between 20 and 50% of sales. College and university students should be better informed, but the authors have found, from questioning numerous classes at the beginning of the first course in accounting, that college students in guessing at the average rate of corporate earnings usually suggest far higher rates than actually exist. If you will look at the published annual reports of leading corporations, you will find that earnings (net income) usually fall somewhere between 2 and 10% of sales. Remember that these financial statements have been audited by independent CPA firms, and also reviewed by the SEC. For all manufacturing companies a representative rate of earnings in recent years has been around 4 to 5%. Of course, there are exceptions. In the airline industry, for example, American Airlines, TWA, and Pan American each operated at a net loss for several years during the early and mid-1970s. This question of the rate of corporate earnings will be considered more fully in Chapter 22.

Earnings per share (EPS)

Perhaps the most widely used of all accounting statistics is *earnings per share* of common stock. To compute earnings per share, the annual net income available to the common stock is divided by the average number of shares outstanding. The amount of quarterly and annual earnings per share is used especially in making investment decisions. Since a purchase or sale of common stock is executed on the basis of the market price per share, it is helpful to know the amount of earnings applicable to a single share.

Investors use earnings per share in evaluating the past performance of a company and in forming an opinion as to its potential for future performance. By computing the *price-earnings ratio* (the market price of a share of common stock divided by the annual earnings per share), investors can determine whether the market price of the stock appears reasonable or whether it may be unreasonably high or unreasonably low. Because of the wide publicity given to earnings per share data in newspapers and business journals, it is important that these data be computed in a consistent and logical manner.

AVERAGE NUMBER OF SHARES OUTSTANDING The simplest example of computing earnings per share is found when a company has issued common stock only and the number of shares outstanding has not changed during the year. In this situation, the net income for the year divided by the number of shares outstanding at the year-end equals earnings per share.

In many companies, however, the number of shares of stock outstanding is changed one or more times during the year. A **weighted-average** number of shares outstanding during the year must be computed when additional shares **were sold or issued in exchange for assets** during the year. (A different treatment of an increase in the number of shares outstanding resulting from the **conversion** of preferred stock into common shares will be discussed later in this chapter.) The weighted-average number of shares for the year is determined by multiplying the number of shares outstanding by the fraction of the year that said number of shares out-standing remained unchanged. For example, assume that 100,000 shares of common stock were outstanding during the first three months of Year 1 and 140,000 shares during the last nine months. Assume also that the increase in shares outstanding resulted from the sale of 40,000 shares for cash. The weighted-average number of shares outstanding during Year 1 would be 130,000, determined as follows:

100,000 shares × $\frac{1}{4}$ *of a year*	**25,000**
140,000 shares × $\frac{3}{4}$ *of a year*	**105,000**
Weighted-average number of common shares outstanding	**130,000**

This procedure gives more meaningful earnings per share data than if the actual number of shares outstanding **at the end** of the year were used in the calculations. The increased significance arises because the proceeds from the sale of the 40,000 shares were available to generate earnings only during the last nine months of the year. These 40,000 shares were outstanding for three-fourths of a year and are, therefore, equivalent to 30,000 shares for a full year. In other words, the weighted-average num-ber of shares outstanding consists of 100,000 shares outstanding during the entire year plus 30,000 full-year equivalent shares sold during the year.[3]

PRIMARY AND FULLY DILUTED EARNINGS PER SHARE The computation of earnings per share is easily done for companies with common stock only, that is, companies not having convertible securities, stock options, or other rights capable of being converted into additional common shares. In companies with such **simple capital structures** there is no risk of conver-sion which would increase the number of common shares and probably **dilute** (reduce) earnings per share of common stock. If only one class of stock is outstanding, earnings per share is computed by dividing the net income for the period by the weighted-average number of shares out-standing during the period. When nonconvertible preferred stock is outstanding, earnings per share of common stock may be determined as shown on page 596.

---

[3] When the number of shares outstanding changes as a result of a stock split or a stock dividend (discussed later in this chapter), the computation of the weighted-average number of shares outstanding should be adjusted retroactively rather than weighted for the period the new shares were outstanding. Earnings per share data for prior years thus will be consistently stated in terms of the current capital structure.

Net income	*$280,000*
Less: Dividend on preferred stock for current period	*20,000*
Income available for common stock	*$260,000*
Weighted-average number of common shares outstanding	*130,000*
Earnings per share of common stock, $260,000 ÷ 130,000 shares	*$2.00*

Many corporations have **complex capital structures** including various securities convertible into common stock. Some of these convertible securities are considered to be common stock equivalents; others are not. If a significant part of the value of the convertible security at the time it is issued lies in the conversion right rather than in the specified dividend or interest rate, it is considered to be a **common stock equivalent.** Stock options are always treated as common stock equivalents in computing earnings per share. A **dual presentation** is sometimes necessary: **primary earnings per share,** based on the weighted-average number of common shares actually outstanding plus common stock equivalents and **fully diluted earnings per share,** based on the maximum potential number of shares outstanding.[4]

To illustrate, let us assume that a company with a net income of $100,000 for Year 1 has 5,000 shares of $2 convertible preferred stock and 40,000 shares of common stock outstanding. The preferred stock is convertible into two shares of common stock and did not qualify as a common stock equivalent. Primary and fully diluted earnings per share of common stock would be computed as follows:

	Primary	*Fully Diluted*
Net income	*$100,000*	*$100,000*
Less: Dividends on preferred stock, 5,000 × $2	*10,000*	*–0–*
Earnings available for common stock	*$ 90,000*	*$100,000*
Number of shares of common stock outstanding:		
In computing primary earnings per share	*40,000*	
In computing fully diluted earnings per share, 40,000 +		
(5,000 × 2)		*50,000*
Earnings per share of common stock	*$2.25*	*$2.00*

The existence of convertible securities usually poses the threat of diluting (reducing) earnings per common share, but this general rule is subject to exceptions. For example, assume that the dividend rate on the preferred stock had been at the annual rate of $6 per share rather than $2 per share as illustrated above. The primary earnings per share would then have been $1.75 (net income of $100,000 less dividends on preferred stock of $30,000 and divided by 40,000 shares of common stock currently outstanding). In this case, only primary earnings per share would be reported in the income statement because earnings per share would be

---

[4] *APB Opinion No. 15,* "Earnings per Share," AICPA (New York: 1969), p. 221.

increased rather than *diluted* if we assume the conversion of the preferred stock into common shares.

The assumptions and computations for determining primary and fully diluted earnings per share are often quite complex. A detailed discussion of this topic is more appropriately included in the *Intermediate Accounting* volume of this series.

PRESENTATION OF EARNINGS PER SHARE IN THE INCOME STATEMENT
Earnings per share for a company with a complex capital structure which also had extraordinary items is illustrated below:

Primary and fully diluted earnings per share in the income statement

	Year 2	Year 1
Income before extraordinary items	$15,090,600	$12,640,000
Extraordinary loss, net of related income tax effect . . .	(2,080,000)	(6,100,000)
Net income	$13,010,600	$ 6,540,000
Earnings per share of common stock:		
Primary:		
Earnings before extraordinary loss	$3.77	$3.33
Extraordinary loss	(0.52)	(1.61)
Net earnings for the year	$3.25	$1.72
Fully diluted:		
Earnings before extraordinary loss	$3.51	$3.16
Extraordinary loss	(0.48)	(1.53)
Net earnings for the year	$3.03	$1.63

Income statement for a corporation illustrated

A comparative income statement which includes losses from discontinued operations and extraordinary losses is illustrated on page 598 for California Industries, Inc. Fully diluted earnings per share are not given because the company has a simple capital structure which does not create a potential for dilution of earnings per common share.

Cash dividends

The prospect of receiving cash dividends is a principal reason for investing in the stocks of corporations. An increase or decrease in the established rate of dividends will usually cause an immediate rise or fall in the market price of the company's stock. Stockholders are keenly interested in prospects for future dividends and as a group are generally strongly in favor of more generous dividend payments. The board of directors, on the other hand, is primarily concerned with the long-run growth and financial strength of the corporation; it may prefer to restrict dividends to a minimum in order to conserve cash for purchase of plant and equipment or for

CALIFORNIA INDUSTRIES, INC.
Comparative Income Statement
For Years Ended September 30

Income statement with loss from discontinued operations and extraordinary items

	Year 2	Year 1
Net sales	$81,853,000	$57,167,000
Cost of goods sold	68,649,000	46,114,000
Gross profit on sales	$13,204,000	$11,053,000
Expenses:		
Selling, administrative, and general expenses	$10,072,000	$ 8,493,000
Interest expense	1,504,000	1,325,000
Other expense, net of miscellaneous income	66,000	101,000
Total expenses	$11,642,000	$ 9,919,000
Income (before income taxes) from continuing operations	$ 1,562,000	$ 1,134,000
Federal and state income taxes	658,000	505,000
Income from continuing operations	$ 904,000	$ 629,000
Loss from discontinued operations, net of income tax benefit of $80,000 in Year 2 and $362,000 in Year 1	(94,000)	(342,000)
Income before extraordinary items	$ 810,000	$ 287,000
Extraordinary items: expropriation loss, net of taxes	–0–	(203,000)
Net income	$ 810,000	$ 84,000
Net income (loss) per share of common stock:		
Income from continuing operations	$0.39	$0.27
Loss from discontinued operations	(0.04)	(0.15)
Income before extraordinary items	$0.35	$0.12
Extraordinary items	–0–	(0.08)
Net income	$0.35	$0.04

other needs of the company. Many of the so-called "growth companies" plow back into the business most of their earnings and pay only very small cash dividends.

The preceding discussion suggests three requirements for the payment of a cash dividend. These are:

1 **Retained earnings.** Since dividends represent a distribution of earnings to stockholders, the theoretical maximum for dividends is the total net income of the company. As a practical matter, many corporations limit dividends to somewhere near 40% of earnings, in the belief that a major portion of the net income must be retained in the business if the company is to grow and to keep pace with its competitors.

2 **An adequate cash position.** The fact that the company reports large earnings does not mean that it has a large amount of cash on hand. Earnings may have been invested in new plant and equipment, or in paying off debts, or in acquiring a larger inventory. There is no necessary relationship between the balance

in the Retained Earnings account and the balance in the Cash account. The traditional expression of "paying dividends out of retained earnings" is misleading. Cash dividends can be paid only "out of" cash.

3 Dividend action by the board of directors. Even though the company's net income is substantial and its cash position seemingly satisfactory, dividends are not paid automatically. A positive action by the directors is necessary to declare a dividend.

Regular and special dividends

Many corporations establish a regular quarterly or annual dividend rate and pay this same amount for a period of years regardless of the year-to-year changes in earnings. Such a policy gives a higher investment quality to a company's stock. A strong cash position is necessary if a company is to be prepared to make regular dividend payments in the face of irregular earnings.

If earnings increase but the increase is regarded as a temporary condition, the corporation may decide to pay a *special dividend* in addition to the *regular dividend.* The implication of a special dividend is that the company is making no commitments as to a permanent increase in the amount of dividends to be paid. Of course, even a regular dividend may be reduced or discontinued at any time, but well-financed companies which have long-established regular dividend rates are not likely to omit or reduce regular dividend payments except in extreme emergencies.

Dividend dates

Four significant dates are involved in the distribution of a dividend. These dates are:

1 Date of declaration. On the day on which the dividend is declared by the board of directors, a liability to make the payment comes into existence. The journal entries to record the declaration and the later payment of a cash dividend were illustrated on page 565.

2 Date of record. The date of record always follows the date of declaration, usually by a period of two or three weeks, and is always stated in the dividend declaration. In order to be eligible to receive the dividend, a person must be listed as the owner of the stock on the date of record.

3 Ex-dividend date. The ex-dividend date is significant for investors in companies with stocks traded on the stock exchanges. To permit the compilation of the list of stockholders as of the record date, it is customary for the stock to go "ex-dividend" three business days before the date of record. A stock is said to be selling ex-dividend on the day that it loses the right to receive the latest declared dividend. A person who buys the stock before the ex-dividend date is entitled to receive the dividend; conversely, a stockholder who sells shares in the period between the date of declaration and the ex-dividend date does not receive the dividend.

4 Date of payment. The declaration of a dividend always includes announcement of the date of payment as well as the date of record. Usually the date of payment comes from two to four weeks after the date of record.

The journal entries to record the declaration and payment of a cash dividend were illustrated in Chapter 16 but are repeated here with emphasis on the date of declaration and date of payment.

```
June  1 Retained Earnings . . . . . . . . . . . . . . . . . . . . . . . . . .100,000
             Dividends Payable . . . . . . . . . . . . . . . . . . . . .      100,000
          To record declaration of a cash dividend of $1 per
          share on the 100,000 shares of common stock
          outstanding. Payable July 10 to stockholders of
          record on June 20.

July 10 Dividends Payable . . . . . . . . . . . . . . . . . . . . . . . . .100,000
             Cash . . . . . . . . . . . . . . . . . . . . . . . . . . . . .      100,000
          To record payment of $1 per share dividend
          declared June 1 to stockholders of record on
          June 20.
```

If a company has one or more issues of preferred stock as well as common stock, it will use separate dividend accounts for each issue. The account debited when a dividend is declared may have a title such as Dividends on Preferred Stock; such an account would be closed to Retained Earnings at the end of the year.

Dividends on preferred stock

As indicated in Chapter 16, a preferred stock carries a stated annual dividend rate, such as $9 per share, or 9% of par value. Under no circumstances does a corporation pay more than the stated dividend on preferred stock. This policy of not permitting the preferred stockholder to share in any unusually large earnings suggests that the corporation views the preferred stockholder only as a supplier of capital rather than as a full-fledged owner in the traditional sense of the word.

Dividends on preferred stocks are not paid unless declared by the board of directors. Since most preferred stocks are of the cumulative variety, any omitted dividend must be made up before any payment can be made to the common. Dividends in arrears on preferred stock do not constitute a liability of the corporation but should be disclosed by a footnote to the balance sheet. Separate accounts are used to record the declaration of preferred and common dividends.

Liquidating dividends

Most dividends are paid in cash, but occasionally a dividend declaration calls for payment in assets other than cash. A large distillery once paid a dividend consisting of a bottle of whiskey for each share of stock. When a corporation goes out of existence (particularly a small corporation with only a few stockholders), it may choose to distribute noncash assets to its owners rather than to convert all its assets into cash.

A *liquidating* dividend occurs when a corporation returns to stockholders all or part of their paid-in capital investment. Liquidating dividends are usually paid only when a corporation is going out of existence or is making a permanent reduction in the size of its operations. Normally dividends are paid as a result of profitable operations, and the recipients of a dividend are entitled to assume that the dividend represents a distribution of income unless they are specifically notified that the dividend is a return of invested capital.

Stock dividends

Stock dividend is an important but confusing term which requires close attention. It is confusing because all dividends are distributions to stockholders and "stock dividend" may suggest to some people merely a dividend on capital stock. *A stock dividend is a pro rata distribution of additional shares to a company's stockholders in proportion to their present holdings.* In brief, the dividend consists of shares of stock rather than cash. Perhaps a better term for a stock dividend would be a "dividend payable in capital stock," but the expression "stock dividend" is too firmly entrenched to be easily replaced. Most stock dividends consist of additional shares of common stock distributed to holders of common stock, and our discussion will be limited to this type of stock dividend.

What is the effect of a stock dividend on the company's financial position? Why does a corporation choose to pay a dividend in shares of stock rather than in cash? Would you as an investor prefer to receive a stock dividend or a cash dividend? These questions are closely related, and a careful analysis of the nature of a stock dividend should provide a basis for answering them.

A cash dividend reduces the assets of a corporation and reduces the stockholders' equity by the same amount. A stock dividend, on the other hand, causes no change in assets and no change in the *total* amount of the stockholders' equity. The only effect of a stock dividend on the accounts is to transfer a portion of the retained earnings into the Common Stock and Paid-in Capital from Stock Dividends accounts. In other words, a stock dividend merely "reshuffles" the stockholders' equity accounts, increasing the permanent capital accounts and decreasing the Retained Earnings account. A stockholder who receives a stock dividend will own an increased number of shares, but his total ownership equity in the company will be no larger than before.

An example may make this fundamental point clear. Assume that a corporation with 800 shares of stock is owned equally by James Davis and Frank Miller, each owning 400 shares of stock. The corporation declares a stock dividend of 25% and distributes 200 additional shares (25% of 800 shares), with 100 shares going to each of the two stockholders. Davis and Miller now hold 500 shares apiece, but each still owns one-half of the business. The corporation has not changed; its assets and liabilities and its total stockholders' equity are exactly the same as before the dividend. From the stockholder's viewpoint, the ownership of 500 shares out of a total of 1,000 outstanding shares represents no more than did the ownership of 400 shares out of a total of 800 shares previously outstanding.

Assume that the fair market value of this stock was $10 per share prior to the stock dividend. Total market value of all the outstanding shares was, therefore, 800 times $10, or $8,000. What would be the market value per share and in total after the additional 200 dividend shares were issued? The 1,000 shares now outstanding should have the same total market value as the previously outstanding 800 shares, because the "pie" has merely been divided into more but smaller pieces. The value per share should have dropped from $10 to $8, and the aggregate market value of outstanding shares would consequently be computed as 1,000 shares times $8, or $8,000. Whether the market price per share will, in all cases, decrease in proportion to the change in number of outstanding shares is another matter. The market prices of stocks listed on a stock exchange are subject to many conflicting influences, some as unpredictable as the state of mind of investors.

REASONS FOR DISTRIBUTION OF STOCK DIVIDENDS Many reasons have been given for the popularity of stock dividends; for example:

1 To conserve cash. When the trend of profits is favorable but cash is needed for expansion, a stock dividend may be an appropriate device for "passing along the earnings" to stockholders without weakening the corporation's cash position.[5]

2 To reduce the market price of a corporation's stock to a more convenient trading range by increasing the number of shares outstanding. This objective is usually present in large stock dividends (25 to 100% or more).

3 To avoid income tax on stockholders. For income tax purposes, stock dividends are not considered as income to the recipients; therefore, no income tax is levied.

Some critics of stock dividends argue that a stock dividend is not really a dividend at all. These critics say that a company which cannot afford to pay a cash dividend should declare no dividends, rather than trying to deceive stockholders by increasing the number of outstanding shares. The popularity of stock dividends, according to such critics, is based on a lack of understanding on the part of stockholders.

Regardless of the merit of the arguments for and against stock dividends, most stockholders welcome these distributions. In many cases a small stock dividend has not caused the market price per share to decline appreciably; consequently, the increase in the number of shares in the

[5] For example, the Standard Oil Company of California, in a letter to its stockholders, gave the following reason for the "payment" of a 5% stock dividend: "Payment of this stock dividend recognizes the continuing increase in your stockholder's equity in the Company's assets, resulting from reinvestment of part of the Company's earnings. Reinvestment of earnings has helped to sustain the Company's long-range program of capital and exploratory expenditures and investments aimed to increase future income and enhance further the value of your shareholding."

hands of each stockholder has, regardless of logic, resulted in an increase in the total market value of his or her holdings.

ENTRIES TO RECORD STOCK DIVIDENDS Assume that a corporation had the following stockholders' equity accounts on December 15, Year 1, just prior to declaring a 10% stock dividend:

Stockholders' equity before stock dividend

Stockholders' equity:

Common stock, $10 par value, 300,000 shares authorized, 100,000	
shares issued and outstanding	*$1,000,000*
Paid-in capital in excess of par	*500,000*
Retained earnings	*2,000,000*
Total stockholders' equity	*$3,500,000*

Assume also that the closing market price of the stock on December 15, Year 1, was $30 a share. The company declares and distributes a 10% stock dividend, consisting of 10,000 common shares (10% × 100,000 = 10,000). The entry to record the **declaration** of the dividend is as follows:

Stock dividend declared; note use of market price of stock

Year 1

Dec. 15	*Retained Earnings*	*300,000*	
	Stock Dividend to Be Distributed		*100,000*
	Paid-in Capital from Stock Dividends		*200,000*
	To record declaration of a 10% stock dividend		
	consisting of 10,000 shares of $10 par value common		
	stock. To be distributed on February 9, Year 2, to		
	stockholders of record on January 15, Year 2. Amount		
	of retained earnings transferred to permanent capital		
	is based on market price of $30 a share on		
	December 15, Year 1.		

The entry to record **distribution** of the dividend shares is as follows:

Stock dividend distributed

Year 2

Feb. 9	*Stock Dividend to Be Distributed*	*100,000*	
	Common Stock		*100,000*
	To record distribution of stock dividend of 10,000 shares.		

Note that the amount of retained earnings transferred to permanent capital accounts by the above entries is not the par value of the new shares, but the **market value,** as indicated by the market price prevailing at the date of declaration. The reasoning behind this practice is simple: Since stockholders tend to measure the "worth" of a small stock dividend (say, 20 to 25% or less) in terms of the market value of the additional shares issued, then Retained Earnings should be reduced by this amount. Large stock dividends (for example, those in excess of 20 to 25%)

should be recorded by transferring only the par or stated value of the dividend shares from the Retained Earnings account to the Common Stock account. Large stock dividends generally have the effect of proportionately reducing the market price of the stock. For example, a 100% stock dividend would reduce the market price by about 50%, because twice as many shares would be outstanding. A 100% stock dividend is very similar to the 2 for 1 stock split discussed on page 605.

To illustrate the accounting for a large stock dividend, let us assume that Randall Company on May 1 declared a 100% stock dividend on the 100,000 shares of $5 par value common stock outstanding. The journal entries to record the declaration and distribution of the stock dividend are shown below:

Declaration and distribution of 100% stock dividend

May 1	*Retained Earnings*	*500,000*	
	Stock Dividend to Be Distributed		*500,000*
	To record 100% stock dividend declared on 100,000		
	shares of $5 par value common stock outstanding.		
	To be distributed June 1, 19___, to stockholders of		
	record on May 15, 19___.		
June 1	*Stock Dividend to Be Distributed*	*500,000*	
	Common Stock		*500,000*
	To record distribution of 100,000 shares of $5 par		
	value common stock as a 100% stock dividend.		

The Stock Dividend to Be Distributed account is not a liability, because there is no obligation to distribute cash or any other asset. If a balance sheet is prepared between the date of declaration of a stock dividend and the date of distribution of the shares, this account, as well as Paid-in Capital from Stock Dividends, should be presented in the stockholders' equity section of the balance sheet.

Stock splits

Most large corporations are interested in as wide as possible a distribution of their securities among the investing public. If the market price reaches very high levels as, for example, $150 per share, the corporation may feel that, by splitting the stock 5 for 1 and thereby reducing the price to $30 per share, the number of shareholders may be increased. The bulk of trading in securities occurs in 100-share lots and an extra commission is charged on smaller transactions. Many investors with limited funds prefer to make their investments in 100-share lots of lower-priced stocks. The majority of leading American corporations have split their stock; some have done so several times. Generally the number of shareholders has increased noticeably after the stock has been split.

A stock split consists of increasing the number of outstanding shares and reducing the par or stated value per share in proportion. For example, assume that a corporation has outstanding 1 million shares of $10 par value stock. The market price is $90 per share. The corporation now reduces the par value from $10 to $5 per share and increases the number of shares from 1 million to 2 million. This action would be called a 2 for 1 stock split. A stockholder who formerly owned 100 shares of the $10 par old stock would now own 200 shares of the $5 par new stock. Since the number of outstanding shares has been doubled without any change in the affairs of the corporation, the market price will probably drop from $90 to approximately $45 a share.

   A stock split does not change the balance of any ledger account; consequently, the transaction may be recorded merely by a memorandum notation in the general journal and in the Common Stock account.

DISTINCTION BETWEEN STOCK SPLITS AND LARGE STOCK DIVIDENDS

What is the difference between a 2 for 1 stock split and a 100% stock dividend? Both will double the number of outstanding shares without changing total stockholders' equity, and both will serve to cut the market price of the stock in half. The stock dividend, however, will cause a transfer from the Retained Earnings account to the Common Stock account equal to the par or stated value of the dividend shares, whereas the stock split does not change the dollar balance of any account. After an increase in the number of shares as a result of a stock split or stock dividend, earnings per share are of course computed in terms of the increased number of shares. In presenting five- or ten-year summaries, the earnings per share for earlier years are retroactively revised to reflect the increased number of shares currently outstanding and thus make the trend of earnings per share from year to year a valid comparison.

Retained earnings

Throughout this book the term *retained earnings* is used to describe that portion of stockholders' equity derived from profitable operations. Retained earnings is a historical concept, representing the accumulated earnings (including prior period adjustments) minus dividends declared from the date of incorporation to the present. If we assume that there are no prior period adjustments, the major sources of entries in the Retained Earnings account will be (1) the periodic transfer of net income (or loss) from the Income Summary account and (2) the debit entries for dividend declarations.

Prior period adjustments to Retained Earnings account

As previously stated, extraordinary items are included in the income statement, but prior period adjustments are recorded directly in the Retained Earnings account and reported in the statement of retained earnings. Prior period adjustments are relatively rare because they must be material in amount and must also meet the following four criteria:

1 Must be directly related to the activities of a prior period

2 Could not have been measured with reasonable accuracy in the prior period

3 Must not be attributable to an economic event of the current period

4 Must result from decisions and determinations by persons other than management of the reporting corporation, such as a government agency or a court of law

Examples of prior period adjustments include additional income tax assessments for prior years, settlement of litigation based on events of earlier periods, and settlement of rate disputes which affect the income previously reported by public utility companies. To illustrate a prior period adjustment, assume that an additional income tax assessment of $1,950,000 for Year 2 was levied against the Benson Corporation in Year 4. The assessment would be recorded in Year 4 as follows:

Recording a prior period adjustment	*Retained Earnings*	*1,950,000*
	Income Tax Assessment Payable	*1,950,000*

*To record income tax assessment applicable to Year 2 as a
prior period adjustment.*

The presentation of this prior period adjustment in the statement of retained earnings for Benson Corporation is illustrated on page 608.

The Financial Accounting Standards Board in 1976 issued an exposure draft of a proposed new Statement on Financial Standards entitled **Prior Period Adjustments.** The proposed **Statement** would abandon the former criteria and limit the use of prior period adjustments principally to correction of errors contained in financial statements of prior years.

Appropriations and restrictions of retained earnings

A few corporations transfer a portion of their retained earnings into separate accounts called **appropriations.** The purpose of such appropriations is to indicate to users of financial statements that a portion of retained earnings is not available for the declaration of cash dividends. The limitation on cash dividends may be established voluntarily by the board of directors (perhaps to provide for some contingency) or it may be required by law or contract. An appropriation of retained earnings is recorded by a debit to Retained Earnings and a credit to the appropriation account such as Retained Earnings Appropriated for Contingencies. Appropriation accounts are still a part of total retained earnings, as indicated by the following partial stockholders' equity section which appeared in a recent balance sheet of Wm. Wrigley Jr. Company:

Appropriations in the balance sheet	*Stockholders' equity:*
	Capital stock, no par value—authorized and issued—2,000,000
	shares . . . . *$ 19,200,000*
	Accumulated earnings retained for use in the business *109,130,000*
	Accumulated earnings appropriated for guarantees under
	employment assurance contracts *2,000,000*

When the restriction on retained earnings is no longer needed, the appropriation account is eliminated by transferring its balance back to the Retained Earnings account.

Instead of establishing appropriations of retained earnings, most corporations disclose restrictions on the declaration of cash dividends in notes accompanying the financial statements.[6] Two examples of such disclosure are shown below.

Alternative disclosure of restrictions placed on retained earnings

Rockwell International Corporation:
Among other covenants, certain of the long-term debt agreements contain limitations on creation of additional long-term debt and restrictions on payment of dividends and acquisition of treasury stock. Retained earnings . . . not so restricted amounted to approximately $117,000,000.

Ethyl Corporation:
The Corporation's articles of incorporation and note agreements contain restrictions, among others, against the payment of cash dividends. . . . $28,658,000 of retained earnings is free of such restriction under the agreement presently most restrictive.

Since the only purpose of appropriating retained earnings is to inform readers of the financial statements that a portion of the retained earnings is "reserved" for a specific purpose and is not available for declaration of cash dividends, this information can be conveyed more directly, with less danger of misunderstanding, by a note accompanying the financial statements.

Statement of retained earnings

In addition to the balance sheet and the income statement, most corporations include a statement of retained earnings and a statement of changes in financial position in their annual reports to stockholders. If a company is audited by a CPA firm, all four of these basic financial statements are covered by the audit report. A simple example of a statement of retained earnings follows:

SHORE LINE CORPORATION
Statement of Retained Earnings
For the Year Ended December 31, 19____

Retained earnings at beginning of year	$620,000
Net income for the year	280,000
Subtotal	$900,000
Less: Dividends	100,000
Retained earnings at end of year	$800,000

---

[6] According to a recent issue of *Accounting Trends & Techniques* published by the AICPA, very few of the 600 annual reports surveyed showed appropriated retained earnings while a large majority of the annual reports referred to restrictions on retained earnings.

In the published annual reports of publicly owned corporations, the statement of retained earnings is usually presented in comparative form covering two years. This format and the treatment of a *prior period adjustment* are illustrated below for Benson Corporation.

BENSON CORPORATION
Statement of Retained Earnings
For Years Ended June 30

	Year 4	Year 3
Retained earnings at beginning of year:		
As originally reported	$15,400,000	$14,850,000
Prior period adjustment—additional income taxes,		
applicable to Year 2	(1,950,000)	(1,950,000)
As restated	$13,450,000	$12,900,000
Net income	5,500,000	2,350,000
Subtotal	$18,950,000	$15,250,000
Less: Cash dividends on common stock:		
$2.40 per share in Year 4	(2,400,000)	
$1.80 per share in Year 3		(1,800,000)
Retained earnings at end of year	$16,550,000	$13,450,000

Statement of retained earnings shows prior period adjustments, net income, and dividends

The additional income tax applicable to Year 2 was assessed in Year 4 and is shown as a correction to the beginning balance in retained earnings for both years, since both beginning amounts were overstated. The statement of retained earnings thus provides a useful vehicle for the disclosure of prior period adjustments and for the reconciliation of changes in retained earnings resulting from net income (or net loss) and dividends declared.

An alternative presentation of net income and retained earnings is used by some companies. The reconciliation of retained earnings may be shown in the body of a *combined statement of income and retained earnings,* as illustrated on page 609 for Lacey Corporation.

The statement for the Lacey Corporation emphasizes the close relationship of operating results and retained earnings. Some readers of financial statements, however, object to the fact that net income (or loss) is "buried" in the body of a combined statement of income and retained earnings rather than being prominently displayed as the final figure before reporting earnings per share.

LACEY CORPORATION
Combined Statement of Income and Retained Earnings
For Years Ended December 31

	Year 10	Year 9
Net sales	$2,900,000	$2,700,000
Cost of goods sold	1,730,000	1,650,000
Gross profit on sales	$1,170,000	$1,050,000
Operating expenses	620,000	590,000
Income before income taxes	$ 550,000	$ 460,000
Income taxes	260,000	215,000
Net income	$ 290,000	$ 245,000
Retained earnings at beginning of year	730,000	665,000
	$1,020,000	$ 910,000
Dividends: $1 per share in Year 10 and		
$.90 per share in Year 9	210,000	180,000
Retained earnings at end of year	$ 810,000	$ 730,000
Earnings per share of common stock	$1.38	$1.22

TREASURY STOCK

Corporations frequently reacquire shares of their own capital stock by purchase in the open market. The effect of reacquiring shares is to reduce the assets of the corporation and to reduce the stockholders' equity by the same amount. One reason for such purchases is to have stock available to reissue to officers and employees under bonus plans. Other reasons may include a desire to increase the reported earnings per share, to support the market price of the stock, and to have shares available for the acquisition of other companies.

Treasury stock may be defined as a corporation's own capital stock which has been issued, fully paid, and reacquired but not canceled. Treasury shares may be held indefinitely or may be issued again at any time. Shares of capital stock held in the treasury are not entitled to receive dividends, vote, or receive cash or other assets upon dissolution of the company.

Recording purchases and reissuance of treasury stock

Purchases of treasury stock should be recorded by debiting the Treasury Stock account with the cost of the stock. For example, if a corporation reacquires 100 shares of its own $10 par stock at a price of $150 per share, the entry is as follows:

Treasury
stock
recorded at
cost

Treasury Stock	15,000	
Cash		15,000
Purchased 100 shares of $10 par treasury stock at $150 per share.		

Treasury stock is customarily recorded *at cost* regardless of whether it is par value stock or no-par stock. When the treasury shares are reissued, the Treasury Stock account is credited for *the cost* of the shares reissued, and Paid-in Capital from Treasury Stock Transactions is debited or credited for the difference between cost and reissuance price.

To illustrate the reissuance of treasury stock at a price above cost, assume that the 100 shares acquired at a cost of $15,000 are reissued for a higher price, $18,000. The entry is:

Reissued at a price above cost	*Cash* *18,000*	
	Treasury Stock	*15,000*
	Paid-in Capital from Treasury Stock Transactions	*3,000*

Sold 100 shares of treasury stock, which cost $15,000, at a price of $180 each.

If treasury stock is reissued at a price below cost and a paid-in capital account exists as a result of previous treasury stock transactions, this account may be debited. If there is no paid-in capital as a result of previous treasury stock transactions, the excess of the cost of the treasury shares over reissuance price could be recorded as a debit in any other paid-in capital account. If the company had no paid-in capital in excess of par from any source, the debit would be entered in the Retained Earnings account.

Treasury stock not an asset

Corporations sometimes list treasury stock among the assets, on the grounds that the shares could be sold for cash just as readily as shares owned in another corporation. The same argument could be made for treating unissued shares as assets. Treasury shares are basically the same as unissued shares, and an unissued share of stock is definitely not an asset.

When treasury stock is purchased, the corporation is eliminating a part of the stockholders' equity by paying off one or more stockholders. It is, therefore, reasonable to think of the purchase of treasury stock not as the acquisition of an asset, but as the returning of capital to stockholders. For this reason treasury stock should appear in the balance sheet *as a deduction in the stockholders' equity section.*

Conversely, if the treasury shares are later reissued, this is a separate transaction in which the corporation is securing additional invested capital. Assume, for example, that a corporation pays $10 to acquire a share of treasury stock and later reissues this share for $15. Has the corporation made a $5 profit on this transaction with its owners? Definitely not; *there is no profit or loss on treasury stock transactions.* When the treasury share was reissued for $15, the corporation was merely receiving a larger amount of invested capital than was previously withdrawn when a stockholder surrendered the share to the company. A corporation earns profits by selling goods and services to outsiders at a price above cost, not by issuing or reissuing shares of its own stock.

Restriction of retained earnings when treasury stock is acquired

If a corporation is to maintain its paid-in capital intact, it must not pay out to its stockholders any more than it earns. As previously stated in the section dealing with dividends, the amount of dividends to be paid must not exceed the corporation's accumulated earnings, or the corporation will be returning a portion of the stockholders' original investment to them.

The payment of cash dividends and the acquisition of treasury stock have a good deal in common. In both transactions, the corporation is disbursing cash to its stockholders. Of course, the dividend payment is spread out among all the stockholders, whereas the payment to purchase treasury stock may go to only a few stockholders, but this does not alter the fact that the corporation is turning over some of its assets to its owners. The total amount which a corporation may pay to its stockholders without reducing paid-in capital is shown by the balance in the Retained Earnings account. Consequently, it is important that a corporation keep track of the total amount disbursed in payment for treasury stock and make sure that this amount plus any dividends paid does not exceed the company's accumulated earnings. This objective is conveniently accomplished by restricting the availability of retained earnings for dividends to the extent of the cost of treasury stock purchased. The restriction should be disclosed in a note accompanying the financial statements.

BOOK VALUE PER SHARE OF COMMON STOCK

Earlier in this chapter, we emphasized that most stockholders are much interested in earnings per share and dividends per share. Another accounting measurement of interest to stockholders is *book value per share of common stock.* In a corporation which has issued common stock only, the book value per share is computed by dividing total stockholders' equity by the number of shares of stock outstanding. Thus book value per share is equal to the *net assets* represented by one share of stock. The term *net assets* means total assets minus total liabilities; in other words, the total net assets are equal to the total stockholders' equity.

Book value is usually computed only for common stock. If a company has both preferred and common stock outstanding, the computation of book value per share of common stock requires two steps. First the redemption value or call price of the entire preferred stock issue and any dividends in arrears are deducted from total stockholders' equity. Secondly, the remaining amount of stockholders' equity is divided by the number of common shares outstanding to determine book value per common share. This procedure reflects the fact that the common stockholders are the residual owners of the corporate entity.

For example, assume that a corporation has 4,000 shares of capital stock outstanding and the stockholders' equity section of the balance sheet is as follows:

How much is book value per share?	*Capital stock, $1 par value*	*$ 4,000*
	Paid-in capital in excess of par value	*40,000*
	Retained earnings	*76,000*
	Total stockholders' equity	*$120,000*

The book value per share is $30; it is computed by dividing the stockholders' equity of $120,000 by the 4,000 shares of outstanding stock. In computing book value, we are not concerned with the number of authorized shares but merely with the outstanding shares, because the total of the outstanding shares represents 100% of the stockholders' equity.

Book value does *not* indicate the amount which the holder of a share of stock would receive if the corporation were to be dissolved. In liquidation, the assets would probably be sold at prices quite different from their carrying values in the accounts, and the stockholders' equity would go up or down accordingly.

The concept of book value is of vital importance in many contracts. For example, a majority stockholder might obtain an option to' purchase the shares of the minority stockholders at book value at a specified future date. Many court cases have hinged on definitions of book value.

Book value is also used in judging the reasonableness of the market price of a stock. However, it must be used with great caution; the fact that a stock is selling at less than its book value does not necessarily indicate a bargain. The disparity between book value and market price per share is indicated by the following data currently available for three well-known corporations: Texaco, Inc., book value $32, market price $28; Eastman Kodak, book value $23, market price $101; General Motors, book value $44, market price $68. Earnings per share, dividends per share, and prospects for future earnings are usually more important factors affecting market price than is book value.

Book value when company has both preferred and common stock

How is book value per common share computed when a company has both preferred and common stock? Assuming that there are no dividends in arrears on the preferred stock, book value per common share is equal to the total stockholders' equity (exclusive of the redemption value of the preferred stock) divided by the number of common shares outstanding. To illustrate, assume that the stockholders' equity is as follows:

Two classes of stock	*8% preferred stock, $100 par, callable at $110*	*$1,000,000*
	Common stock, no-par; $5 stated value; authorized 100,000 shares issued	
	and outstanding 80,000 shares	*400,000*
	Paid-in capital in excess of par value	*800,000*
	Retained earnings	*900,000*
	Total stockholders' equity	*$3,100,000*

All the capital belongs to the common stockholders, except the $1.1 million applicable to the preferred stock (and any dividends in arrears on the preferred stock). This reasoning is supported by the general practice of making the preferred stock callable at or near its issuance price, so that the eventual elimination of the preferred stock is not at all improbable. The calculation of book value per share of common stock can therefore be made as follows:

Compute book value per share of common stock	*Total stockholders' equity*	*$3,100,000*
	Less: Preferred stock (at call price of $110 per share)	*1,100,000*
	Equity of common stockholders	*$2,000,000*
	Number of shares of common stock outstanding	*80,000*
	Book value per share of common stock $\dfrac{\$2,000,000}{80,000}$	*$25*

The computation of book value is made in the same way for par value and no-par value stock. The basic concept is the net assets per share.

Illustration of stockholders' equity section

The following illustration of a stockholders' equity section of a balance sheet shows a fairly detailed classification by source of the various elements of corporate capital:

Stockholders' Equity

Compare with published financial statements	*Capital stock:*		
	9% preferred stock, $100 par value, authorized and issued		
	1,000 shares	*$100,000*	
	Common stock, no-par, stated value $5 a share, authorized		
	100,000 shares, issued 60,000 shares, of which 1,000 are		
	held in treasury	*300,000*	
	Common stock subscribed, 6,000 shares	*30,000*	*$430,000*
	Additional paid-in capital:		
	Paid-in capital from stock dividends	*$ 50,000*	
	Paid-in capital in excess of stated value: common stock ..	*290,000*	
	Paid-in capital from treasury stock transactions	*5,000*	*345,000*
	Total paid-in capital		*$775,000*
	Retained earnings (of which $12,000, an amount equal to the cost		
	of treasury stock purchased, is unavailable for dividends)		*162,000*
			$937,000
	Less: Cost of 1,000 shares of treasury stock		*12,000*
	Total stockholders' equity		*$925,000*

The published financial statements of leading corporations indicate that there is no one standard arrangement for the various items making up the stockholders' equity section. Variations occur in the selection of titles, in the sequence of items, and in the extent of detailed classification. Many companies, in an effort to avoid excessive detail in the balance sheet, will combine several related ledger accounts into a single balance sheet item. An example of published financial statements appears in the Appendix.

KEY TERMS INTRODUCED OR EMPHASIZED IN CHAPTER 17

Appropriation of retained earnings The transfer of a portion of retained earnings to a separate account by order of the board of directors to indicate its unavailability for dividends. A practice now largely replaced by footnote disclosure of restrictions on retained earnings.

Book value per share The net assets per share of common stock, computed by dividing stockholders' equity by the number of common shares outstanding.

Date of record The date on which a person must be listed as a shareholder in order to be eligible to receive a dividend. Follows the date of declaration of a dividend by two or three weeks.

Discontinued operations The operations (revenue and expenses) of a segment of a company which has been or is being sold.

Dividends The distribution of cash, other assets, or additional shares of stock by a corporation to its stockholders.

Earnings per share (EPS) Net income available to the common stock divided by the average number of common shares outstanding during the year.

Ex-dividend date A date three days prior to the date of record specified in a dividend declaration. A person buying a stock prior to the ex-dividend date also acquires the right to receive the dividend. The three-day interval permits the compilation of a list of stockholders as of the date of record.

Extraordinary items Transactions and events that are both unusual in nature and occur infrequently; for example, a large earthquake loss.

Fully diluted earnings per share Net income available to the common stock divided by the average number of common shares outstanding during the year, plus common stock equivalents plus any other securities convertible into common (if conversion would decrease EPS).

Liquidating dividend A return to shareholders of all or part of their paid-in capital investment. To be distinguished from a distribution of earnings.

Price-earnings ratio Market price of a share of common stock divided by annual earnings per share.

Primary earnings per share Net income available to the common stock divided by average number of common shares outstanding plus any common stock equivalents (if conversion would reduce EPS).

Prior period adjustments Gains or losses of material amount which constitute adjustment of prior years' reported earnings and are recorded directly in the Retained Earnings account.

Rate of corporate earnings Usually expressed as the percentage relationship of net income to sales. Can also be reflected by comparing net income with total assets or stockholders' equity.

Restrictions of retained earnings Action by the board of directors to classify a portion of retained earnings as unavailable for dividends.

Segment of a business A component of a business. The activities of the component represent a major line of business or class of customer.

Statement of retained earnings A basic financial statement showing the change in retained earnings during the year.

Stock dividend A distribution of additional shares to common stockholders in proportion to their holdings.

Stock split An increase in the number of shares outstanding with a corresponding decrease in par value per share. Distributed proportionately to all common shareholders. Purpose is to reduce market price per share and encourage wider public ownership of the company's stock. A 2 for 1 stock split will give each stockholder twice as many shares as previously owned.

Treasury stock Shares of a corporation's own stock which have been issued, fully paid, and reacquired but not canceled.

REVIEW QUESTIONS

1 Why is the reporting of the results of operations so important to users of financial statements?

2 Define a **segment of a business** and **extraordinary items** for purposes of reporting the results of operations.

3 Give some examples of **segments of a business** and **extraordinary losses.**

4 Briefly describe how each of the following should be reported in the income statement:
   a Write-off of a large account receivable from a bankrupt customer
   b Large loss from sale of a major segment of a business
   c Large gain from sale of one of many investments in common stock
   d Large write-off of obsolete inventory
   e Large uninsured loss from earthquake
   f Large damages payable as result of unfavorable settlement of a lawsuit applicable to an earlier year

5 How should the effect of a material event or transaction which is either unusual in nature or occurs infrequently, but not both, be disclosed?

6 Briefly define each of the following:
   a Price-earnings ratio
   b Common stock equivalents
   c Primary earnings per share
   d Fully diluted earnings per share

7 Explain the significance of the following dates relating to dividends: date of declaration, date of record, date of payment, ex-dividend date.

8 Distinguish between a **stock split** and a **stock dividend.** Is there any reason for the difference in accounting treatment of these two events?

9 If the Retained Earnings account has a debit balance, how is it presented in the balance sheet and what is it called?

10 Favorable settlement of a lawsuit relating to events which occurred several years ago brought the Betty Company a court award during the current year. What special accounting term is used to describe transactions of this type? What four criteria must be met in order for such transactions to be excluded from the income statement? What account should be credited to record receipt of the large cash settlement?

11 What is the purpose of an appropriation of retained earnings? What are the arguments for and against the use of such appropriations?

12 What type of transaction most frequently appears as a deduction in a statement of retained earnings?

13 What is *treasury stock?* Why do corporations purchase their own shares? Is treasury stock an asset? How should it be reported in the balance sheet?

14 In many states, the corporation law requires that retained earnings be restricted for dividend purposes to the extent of the cost of treasury shares. What is the reason for this legal rule?

15 What would be the effect, if any, on book value per share of common stock as a result of each of the following independent events: a corporation (*a*) obtains a bank loan, (*b*) is assessed additional income taxes applicable to prior years, and (*c*) distributes a 5% stock dividend?

EXERCISES

Ex. 17-1 Grain Corporation declared a cash dividend of $500,000 on its common stock on September 15, payable on October 20 to stockholders of record on October 1. Prepare journal entries in general journal form (if an entry is needed) on each of the three dates.

Ex. 17-2 Tom Jones purchased 100 shares of stock in Mills Corporation at the time it was organized. At the end of the first year's operations, the corporation reported earnings (after taxes) of $6 per share, and declared a dividend of $3 per share. Jones complains that he is entitled to the full distribution of the amount earned on his investment. Is there any reason why a corporation that earns $6 per share may not be able to pay a dividend of this amount? Are there any advantages to Jones in the retention by the company of one-half of its earnings?

Ex. 17-3 Martin Corporation has a total of 20,000 shares of common stock outstanding and no preferred stock. The net assets of the Martin Corporation at the end of the current year are $400,000 and the market value of the stock is $48 per share. At year-end, the company declares a stock dividend of one share for each five shares held. If all parties concerned clearly recognized the nature of the stock dividend, what would you expect the market price per share of Martin's common stock to be on the ex-dividend date?

Ex. 17-4 Glass Corporation has 1 million shares of $5 par value capital stock outstanding. You are to prepare the journal entries to record the following transactions:

June 1 Declared a cash dividend of 20 cents per share.
July 1 Paid the 20-cent cash dividend to stockholders.
Aug. 1 Declared a 5% stock dividend. Market value of stock was $18 per share.
Sept. 10 Issued 50,000 shares pursuant to the 5% stock dividend.
Dec. 1 Declared a 50% stock dividend. Market value of stock was $30 per share.

Ex. 17-5 San Lorenzo Corporation has been in existence for three years and at the end of Year 3 intends to report earnings per share for each of the three years on a *comparable basis.* During Years 1 and 2 the common stock outstanding remained unchanged at 2,000,000 shares. In Year 3, the stock was split 3 for 1 on March 1, and 1,200,000 new shares were sold for cash on July 1. (Note that the company had the use of additional funds paid in by stockholders for the last half of Year 3.) The corporation had 7,200,000 shares outstanding at the end of Year 3.

a Compute the *weighted-average number* of shares outstanding for each year that should be used in reporting *comparative earnings per share data* in the financial statements at the end of Year 3.

b Assuming that net earnings were $4,500,000 in Year 1, $600,000 in Year 2, and $9,900,000 in Year 3, compute the earnings per share for each year to be reported on a comparable basis at the end of Year 3.

Ex. 17-6 F owns 1,000 out of a total of 20,000 outstanding common shares of McNerney

Corporation. The McNerney Corporation reports total assets of $1,360,000 and total liabilities of $480,000 at the end of the current year, and at that time the board declares a stock dividend of one share for each 10 shares held. Compute the book value *per share* of F's stock and the total book value of F's investment in the corporation: (*a*) before the stock dividend; (*b*) after the stock dividend.

Ex. 17-7 In Year 5, Torrance Company had net sales of $1,200,000; costs and other expenses (including income taxes) of $720,000, a tax refund of $96,000 applicable to Year 3, and an extraordinary loss (net of income tax) of $200,000. Prepare a condensed income statement (including earnings per share) for Year 5, assuming that an average of 100,000 shares of common stock were outstanding during Year 5.

Ex. 17-8 Lee Company has 180,000 shares of $10 par common stock and 10,000 shares of $6.60 cumulative preferred stock outstanding at the end of the current year. Each share of preferred stock is convertible into four shares of common stock. The preferred stock did *not* qualify as a common stock equivalent on the date of issue. Net income for the current year is $660,000. Show how the primary and fully diluted earnings per share should appear in the income statement for the current year.

Ex. 17-9 The following information was compiled from the accounting records of Jefferson Corporation.

Total liabilities	$423,000
7% cumulative preferred stock, $10 par (liquidation value, $210,000)	200,000
Treasury stock, 1,500 shares, at cost	19,500
Deficit	55,000
Organization costs	10,000
Dividends in arrears on preferred stock, 2 full years	
Paid-in capital from treasury stock transactions	11,500
Common stock, no par, 101,500 shares issued, 1,500 shares held in treasury	940,000

Instructions
a Compute the amount of net assets (stockholders' equity).
b If all assets are sold for 90% of book value, how much would each share of common stock receive as a liquidating dividend?

PROBLEMS

Group A

17A-1 After several years of unprofitable operations, Starlight Corporation decided to cease business, sell its assets, pay its debts, and distribute whatever cash remained to its stockholders. The position of the company prior to liquidation is indicated by the following partial list of ledger accounts:

Cash	$ 6,000
Account receivable: U.S. government	12,000
Treasury stock, common, 1,500 shares at cost	23,400
9% cumulative preferred stock (liquidation value $126,000)	120,000
Common stock, no par, 51,500 shares issued, 1,500 in treasury	768,000
Paid-in capital from treasury stock transactions	1,800

Dividends in arrears on preferred stock	....	$ 25,200
Deficit	....	132,000
Total liabilities	....	465,600

Instructions

a Compute the amount of net assets (stockholders' equity).

b Compute the amount of total assets.

c The account receivable, U.S. government, is collected in full. The remaining assets (except Cash) are sold for 80% of book value. Compute the amount that each share of common stock will receive as a liquidating dividend. Round off to the nearest cent.

17A-2 Katherine Woods, accountant for Barker Corporation, was injured in a skiing accident at year-end, and a temporary employee was assigned responsibility for completing the financial statements. The temporary employee had only a limited knowledge of accounting but managed to prepare the following combined statement of income and retained earnings.

BARKER CORPORATION

Combined Statement of Income and Retained Earnings

For the Year Ended December 31, 19____

Sales	....	$3,500,000
Cost of goods sold	....	$2,450,000
Income taxes	....	320,000	2,770,000
Income before extraordinary items	....	$ 730,000
Extraordinary items:		
Gain from settlement of litigation begun five years ago	....	200,000
Income from operations	....	$ 930,000
Selling expenses	....	$ 225,000	
Administrative & general expenses	....	175,000	400,000
Net income	....	$ 530,000
Retained earnings at beginning of year	....	1,150,000
		$1,680,000
Dividends: 80 cents per share	....	240,000
Retained earnings at end of year	....	$1,440,000
Earnings per share	....	$4.80

The dollar amounts in this income statement that represent specific ledger accounts such as Sales, Income Taxes, Dividends, etc. are to be assumed correct, because the regular accountant had made all necessary adjustments and developed all account balances before her accident. However, the classification and arrangement of items and any totals or subtotals in the financial statements as well as the computation of earnings per share were carried out by the temporary employee and may require correction. It is the company's policy to use the "multiple-step" form of income statement for the upper portion of the combined statement of income and retained earnings.

a How was the earnings per share amount of $4.80 computed? Do you agree with this amount?

b Prepare a list of specific defects in the financial statement as presented.

c Prepare a revised combined statement of income and retained earnings in good form. Include the earnings per share.

17A-3 The board of directors of Santa Rosa Corporation held a meeting on December 31, Year 5, and obtained from the controller the following information on the financial position of the company and the operating results for the year just ending.

Current ratio	1.4 to 1
Sales (as compared with prior year)	+20%
Net income (as compared with prior year)	+18%
Market price per share of common stock	$32
Selected ledger account balances:	
Common Stock, par $2, issued and outstanding 100,000 shares	$ 200,000
Paid-in Capital in Excess of Par	1,800,000
Retained Earnings, beginning of year	900,000
Income Summary (credit)	310,000
Dividends (declared and paid in cash during the year)	100,000

After hearing the controller's report, the board of directors declared a 5% stock dividend to be distributed February 15, Year 6, to stockholders of record on January 10, Year 6. After this action Director Jones made the following statement: "I want my opposition to this 5% stock dividend to appear in the minutes of this meeting. Although our earnings are good, our current ratio is weak, and this dividend action will weaken us further."

The controller responded: "I should also have advised you that the litigation begun by the company early this year has just been successfully concluded, and we received today a cashier's check for $100,000 which has not yet been entered in the account balances reported to you." No receivable had been recorded with respect to this settlement.

Instructions

a Prepare journal entries in general journal form to record the declaration of the 5% stock dividend and the settlement received on December 31 from the successful outcome of the lawsuit. No entry should be made for distribution of the stock dividend because this distribution will not take place in the current year.

b Prepare journal entries to close the Income Summary account and the Dividends account. (Assume that declaration of cash dividends had been debited to a Dividends account and that the declaration of the 5% stock dividend had been debited directly to the Retained Earnings account.)

c Prepare the stockholders' equity section of the balance sheet at December 31, Year 5.

d Comment on the logic underlying Director Jones's objection to the 5% stock dividend.

17A-4 The income statement shown on page 620 was not satisfactorily prepared.

At the beginning of Year 3, the audited financial statements of the company show unappropriated retained earnings of $3,900,000 and a balance in Retained Earnings Appropriated for Purchase of Treasury Stock account of $1,200,000. The treasury stock transaction is not taxable, and the earthquake loss is fully deductible in computing taxable income. Income tax expense has been properly estimated by a tax adviser. The earthquake loss should be reported in the income statement as an extraordinary item *net of income taxes.*

12/100

COASTAL RESOURCES, INC.

Income Statement

For Year 3

Net sales	$10,800,000
Sale of treasury stock in Year 3 (cost, $780,000	
proceeds $960,000)	180,000
Excess of proceeds over par value of common stock issued	
in Year 3	1,152,000
Reduction in appropriation for purchase	
of treasury stock	780,000
Total revenue	$12,912,000
Less:	

Cost of goods sold	$5,940,000	
Operating expenses	2,448,000	
Loss from earthquake (before tax reduction of $216,000) .	504,000	
Dividends declared on capital stock	360,000	
Estimated income tax expense, after reduction of $216,000		
as a result of loss from earthquake	804,000	10,056,000
Net income		$ 2,856,000

Instructions

a Prepare a corrected income statement for Year 3. Show data for earnings per share of common stock in the income statement. Coastal Resources, Inc., had a weighted average of 240,000 shares of a single class of common stock outstanding during the year.

b Prepare a statement of retained earnings for Year 3. (Use three columns as follows: Retained Earnings Appropriated for Purchase of Treasury Stock, Unappropriated, and Total Retained Earnings.)

17A-5 Cargill Corporation was organized early in Year 1 and was authorized to issue 160,000 shares of $10 par value common stock and 80,000 shares of $50 par value 7% preferred stock. During Year 1 the company sold 112,000 shares of common stock, at an average price of $30 per share, and issued an additional 16,000 shares of common stock in exchange for patents valued at $512,000. The company earned a net income of $168,000 in Year 1 and paid dividends of 40 cents per share of common stock at the end of Year 1.

On January 1 of Year 2, the company issued 32,000 shares of preferred stock in exchange for land valued at $1,616,000. Quarterly dividends were declared and paid on preferred shares in March, June, and September of Year 2. On December 28, Year 2, the company declared the fourth quarterly dividend on preferred stock and a 10% stock dividend to be distributed in Year 3 to common stockholders. Net income for Year 2 was $572,800. The market price of common stock at the end of Year 2 was $40 per share.

Instructions Prepare the stockholders' equity section of the balance sheet at

a December 31, Year 1

b December 31, Year 2

17A-6 On January 1 of the current year, Hickman Mills Corporation showed the following amounts in the stockholders' equity section of the balance sheet.

Stockholders' equity:

8% cumulative preferred stock, $100 par, 80,000 shares authorized, 9,600 shares issued	$ 960,000
Common stock, $5 par, 800,000 shares authorized, 307,200 shares issued	1,536,000
Paid-in capital in excess of par:	
Preferred stock	96,000
Common stock	1,228,800
Total paid-in capital	$3,820,800
Retained earnings	2,496,000
Total stockholders' equity	$6,316,800

The transactions relating to the stockholders' equity accounts during the current year are shown below:

Jan. 18 Paid regular semiannual dividend on preferred stock and $1 per share cash dividend on common stock. Both dividends were declared in December of the prior year and properly recorded at that time.

June 5 Declared semiannual dividend on preferred stock to stockholders of record on July 12, payable on July 26. (Debit Dividends on Preferred Stock.)

July 26 Paid preferred dividend declared on June 5.

Oct. 14 Declared 5% stock dividend on common stock to stockholders of record on October 31, to be distributed November 15; market price, $14 a share.

Nov. 15 Distributed 5% stock dividend declared on October 14.

Nov. 30 Sold 29,440 shares of common stock for $16 per share.

Dec. 23 Declared regular semiannual dividend on preferred stock and a dividend of $1 per share on common stock of record at January 10, payable on January 21.

Dec. 31 Net income for the current year amounted to $672,000. (Debit Income Summary and credit Retained Earnings.)

Dec. 31 Closed dividend accounts to Retained Earnings account.

Instructions

a Prepare in general journal form the entries necessary to record these transactions.

b Comment on whether Hickman Mills Corporation increased or decreased the total amount of cash dividends *declared* on the common stock during the current year in comparison with the dividends declared in the past year.

c Prepare a balance sheet for Hickman Mills Corporation at the end of the current year, assuming that total assets amount to $9.6 million. (Hint: Prepare the stockholders' equity section of the balance sheet and "plug" the amount of other liabilities after computing the amount of dividends payable.)

17A-7 On January 1 of the current year the Cedar Company had retained earnings of $7,104,000. On July 31, the company declared and paid a cash dividend of 50 cents per share.

At November 30 of the current year, the stockholders' equity was as follows:

Capital stock, $10 par value, authorized 1,200,000 shares, issued and outstanding 840,000 shares	$ 8,400,000
Paid-in capital in excess of par value	5,040,000
Retained earnings	8,148,000
Total stockholders' equity	$21,588,000

During December the company earned net income of $159,048, and on December 30 the board of directors declared a cash dividend of 60 cents per share. The equity accounts were also affected during December by the company's action in reacquiring 12,000 shares of its own capital stock for $354,000. Later in the month (and prior to the December 30 dividend declaration), the company sold 7,200 shares of the treasury stock at $32 per share.

Instructions
a Prepare the stockholders' equity section of the balance sheet at December 31.
b Prepare a statement of retained earnings for the year.
c Compute book value per share at November 30 and at December 31. [Net assets at November 30 − (cost of treasury stock acquired and dividends) + (proceeds from sale of treasury stock and December earnings) = net assets at December 31.]

Group B

17B-1 Whaleboat Company has been operating at a loss and is in a weak financial position, as indicated by the following selected ledger balances:

Deficit	*$154,000*
Account receivable: U.S. government	*14,000*
Total liabilities	*543,200*
Treasury stock, common, 1,500 shares at cost	*27,300*
7% preferred stock, cumulative (liquidation value $147,000)	*140,000*
Common stock, no par, 51,500 shares issued, 1,500 in treasury	*896,000*
Paid-in capital from treasury stock transactions	*2,100*
Dividends in arrears on preferred stock	*29,400*
Cash	*4,000*

Instructions
a Compute the total amount of net assets (stockholders' equity).
b Compute the amount of total assets.
c The company is to be liquidated. The account receivable, U.S. government, is collected in full. All other assets (except cash) are sold for 70% of book value. Compute the amount that each share of common stock will receive as a liquidating dividend. Round off to the nearest cent.

17B-2 The outstanding stock of Palisades Corporation consists of 10,000 shares of common stock, which was issued at par value of $10 per share. On January 1, Year 5, the book value of the stock was $48. During Year 5, the following transactions were completed by the corporation:

Jan. 14 An additional 2,000 shares of stock were sold to investors at $72 per share.
Mar. 3 The corporation acquired 1,000 shares of its own stock for $60,800.
Nov. 27 A cash dividend of 96 cents per share was declared by the board of directors.
Dec. 31 A net income of $61,600 was reported for Year 5.

Instructions Compute the successive book values per share of Palisades Corporation stock after each transaction.

17B-3 Transactions affecting the stockholders' equity section of Hickory Lane, Inc., from the date of its incorporation have been as follows:
(1) Received from investors $378,000 in payment for 6,000 shares of $50 par value 8% preferred stock. The total preferred stock authorized was 18,000 shares.

(2) The company has received from stockholders $825,000 in exchange for 30,000 outstanding shares of no-par value common stock having a stated value of $10 per share (authorized: 150,000 shares).

(3) Total net income since the date of incorporation has been $573,000.

(4) Cash dividends paid since the date of incorporation, $234,000.

(5) Stock dividends declared (but not yet distributed to stockholders) amount to 3,000 shares of common. The market value of the common at the date of record was $40 per share.

(6) Certain land having an assessed valuation of $30,000 was donated to the corporation by the city as a site for a manufacturing plant. The fair market value of the land at the time of the gift was $96,000. The company properly credited Donated Capital for $96,000.

(7) The amount of $60,000 was recently transferred by order of the board of directors from the Retained Earnings account to Retained Earnings Appropriated for Contingencies.

Instructions On the basis of this information, prepare in good form the stockholders' equity section of the Hickory Lane, Inc., balance sheet at the end of the current year.

17B-4 South Bay Company presented the following balance sheet at September 30 of the current year.

Assets		Liabilities & Stockholders' Equity	
Cash	$ 36,000	Notes payable	$ 24,000
Accounts receivable	132,000	Accounts payable	60,000
Other assets	360,000	Common stock, $5 par	156,000
		Paid-in capital in excess of	
		par	120,000
		Retained earnings	168,000
	$528,000		$528,000

On September 20 a decision was made to dissolve the business. The transactions listed below were carried out for this purpose.

On September 21 all the accounts receivable were collected, and all the "other assets" were sold for $504,000 cash. A liability for income taxes in the amount of $43,200 was incurred because of the gain on the sale of the "other assets."

On September 21 all liabilities were paid, including the $43,200 liability for income taxes resulting from the sale of the "other assets."

On September 22 all remaining cash was distributed to stockholders. The shareholders surrendered their stock certificates, and all ledger accounts were closed.

Instructions

a Prepare general journal entries to record the events from September 21 to September 22, inclusive. Assume that the gain (net of income taxes) is credited to Gain on Sale of Other Assets before being closed to Retained Earnings.

b South Bay Company had paid a total of $780,000 in cash dividends from the date of its organization to September 20 of the current year. It had also issued a 30% stock dividend consisting of 7,200 shares three years ago. Compute the total amount of net income earned by South Bay Company over its entire life (including the gain on sale of "other assets" net of income tax).

17B-5 The general ledger accounts for assets, liabilities, and stockholders' equity of Marine Development, Inc., at December 31 of the current year are shown on page 624 in alphabetical order. The revenue and expense accounts have been closed.

Accounts payable	$ 124,800
Accounts receivable (net)	180,072
Accrued miscellaneous liabilities	31,752
Accumulated depreciation: buildings	432,000
Accumulated depreciation: equipment	383,040
Buildings	1,464,000
Cash	85,272
Common stock, no par, $5 stated value	768,000
Dividends payable	36,000
Equipment	1,263,120
Income taxes payable	81,600
Inventories	348,000
Land (held for future plant site)	24,000
Land (used in operations)	120,000
Long-term notes payable, due July 1, 1987	600,000
Notes receivable	122,520
Patents	48,000
Paid-in capital from treasury stock transactions . . . . : .	31,200
Paid-in capital in excess of stated value: common	76,800
Paid-in capital in excess of par: preferred	24,000
8% preferred stock, $100 par	480,000
Retained earnings, Dec. 31	766,992
Short-term prepayments	15,600
Trademarks	21,600
Treasury stock (24,000 shares of common stock at cost)	144,000

The company was authorized to issue 48,000 shares of 8%, $100 par value preferred stock and 240,000 shares of no-par common stock, stated value $5.

Instructions Prepare the December 31 balance sheet in a form suitable for publication. (Use the illustrated balance sheet on page 577 as a guide.)

17B-6 The accountant for Greentree Corporation prepared the following income statement for Year 8.

GREENTREE CORPORATION
Income Statement
For Year 8

Sales (net)		$5,736,000
Cost of goods sold		4,272,000
Gross profit on sales		$1,464,000
Operating expenses		1,398,720
Income before extraordinary items		$ 65,280
Extraordinary items:		
Loss from discontinued operations	$(432,000)	
Damages collected on contract dispute (applicable		
to Year 6)	216,000	
Flood loss	(48,000)	(264,000)
Net loss		$ (198,720)

The stockholders' equity section of the balance sheet at December 31, Year 8, consisted of the following items.

Stockholders' equity:

6% cumulative preferred stock, $10 par; 240,000 shares authorized,	
120,000 shares issued and outstanding	$1,200,000
Common stock, no par, $1 stated value; 1,200,000 shares authorized,	
600,000 shares issued and outstanding	600,000
Paid-in capital in excess of stated value: common	4,890,000
Retained earnings (deficit)	(60,000)
Total stockholders' equity	$6,630,000

The company did not declare any dividends in Year 8. An audit at the end of Year 8 disclosed the following: On July 1, Year 8, the company purchased equipment for $79,200 which was debited to an operating expense account by mistake. The equipment has an estimated service life of 10 years and an estimated salvage value of $7,200. On March 1, Year 8, the company paid a three-year insurance premium in the amount of $4,320, which was debited to an expense account.

Instructions

a Prepare the necessary journal entries at December 31 to correct the errors discovered in the audit. Record straight-line depreciation expense for one-half year on the equipment acquired July 1. Any adjustments of revenue or expense for Year 8 should be made by debiting or crediting the Income Summary account because the individual revenue and expense accounts have been closed.

b Prepare a corrected income statement for Year 8, showing extraordinary items and earnings per share.

c Prepare a corrected statement of retained earnings for Year 8. (Deficit of $60,000 at December 31, combined with the reported net loss of $198,720, indicates a balance of $138,720 in the Retained Earnings account at January 1, Year 8.)

17B-7 The stockholders' equity of Timberline Corporation at November 30 of the current year consisted of the following elements:

Common stock, $10 par value, authorized 2,000,000 shares, issued and	
outstanding 980,000	$ 9,800,000
Paid-in capital in excess of par value	5,880,000
Retained earnings	9,506,000
Total stockholders' equity	$25,186,000

Net income earned by the company during the month of December amounted to $185,556. On December 5 the company acquired 14,000 shares of its own common stock by a purchase from the estate of a deceased stockholder for $413,000 cash. On December 22 the company sold 8,400 shares of the newly acquired treasury stock for $268,800. On December 31 a cash dividend of 60 cents per share was declared with the payment date set 60 days later.

The Retained Earnings account at the beginning of the current year showed a credit balance of $8,288,000. On July 31 the company had declared a cash dividend totaling $490,000; payment of this dividend was made on September 30.

Instructions

a Prepare a statement of retained earnings for the year.

b Prepare the stockholders' equity section of the balance sheet at December 31 of the current year.

c Determine the book value per share at November 30 and at December 31. Suggestion: [Net assets at November 30 − (cost of treasury shares and dividends declared in December) + (proceeds from sale of treasury stock in December and December net income) = net assets at December 31.]

BUSINESS DECISION PROBLEM 17

Near the end of the current year, the board of directors of the Ridge Corporation is presented with the following statement of stockholders' equity:

Capital stock (120,000 shares issued)	*$2,400,000*
Paid-in capital in excess of par	*1,440,000*
Retained earnings	*1,920,000*
Total stockholders' equity	*$5,760,000*

Ridge Corporation has paid dividends of $3.60 per share in each of the last five years. After careful consideration of the company's cash needs, the board of directors declared a stock dividend of 24,000 shares. Shortly after the stock dividend had been distributed and before the end of the year, the company declared a cash dividend of $3 per share.

John Joseph owned 10,000 shares of Ridge Corporation's stock which he acquired several years ago. The market price of this stock before any dividend action in the current year was $60 per share.

Instructions Based on the information given above, answer each of the following questions, showing all relevant computations.

a What is Joseph's share (in dollars) of the net assets as reported in the balance sheet of the Ridge Corporation before the stock dividend action? What is his share after the stock dividend action? Explain why there is or is not any change as a result of the 20% stock dividend.

b What are the probable reasons why the market value of Joseph's stock differs from the amount of net assets per share shown in the accounting records?

c How does the amount of cash dividends that Joseph received in the current year compare with dividends received in prior years?

d On the day the stock went ex-dividend (with respect to the 20% stock dividend), its quoted market price fell from $60 to $50 per share. Did this represent a loss to Joseph? Explain.

e If the Ridge Corporation had announced that it would continue its regular cash dividend of $3.60 per share on the increased number of shares outstanding after the 20% stock dividend, would you expect the market price of the stock to react in any way different from the change described in **d?** Why?

18 Corporations: Bonds Payable and Investments in Corporate Securities

One of the most important functions of management is providing the funds required to operate the business. Several alternatives are generally available in meeting the temporary and the more permanent cash and working capital needs of a business. Management evaluates the cost and availability of each form of financing and selects the type most advantageous to the company and to its stockholders.

Inventories needed to meet seasonal peaks of activity may be obtained on account from trade creditors. Accounts payable, however, seldom constitute a sufficient source. Cash needed for seasonal peaks of activity may be obtained through borrowing from banks. For example, a six-month bank loan might be arranged in order to buy merchandise for the peak selling season. The sale of the merchandise would provide cash with which to repay the bank loan.

If funds are needed for long-term purposes such as the construction of a new factory building, the borrowing may take the form of long-term mortgage notes or bonds. This will allow time for the increased earnings from the new plant facilities to be used in retiring the debt. A small business in need of permanent financing will often issue a long-term note secured by a mortgage on its plant assets; a large corporation in need of permanent financing will probably consider the issuance of bonds or additional shares of capital stock.

BONDS PAYABLE

A corporation may obtain money for a long-term purpose, such as construction of a new plant, by issuing long-term mortgage notes or bonds payable. Usually the amount of money needed is greater than any single lender can supply. In this case the corporation may sell bonds to the investing public, thus splitting the loan into a great many units, usually of $1,000 each. An example of corporation bonds is the 8% sinking fund debentures of The Singer Company due January 15, 1999, by which The Singer Company borrowed $100 million.

Characteristics of a bond

A bondholder is a creditor of the corporation; a stockholder is an owner. From the viewpoint of the issuing corporation, bonds payable constitute a long-term liability. Throughout the life of this liability the corporation makes semiannual payments of interest to the bondholders for the use of their money.

Formal approval of the board of directors and of the stockholders is usually required before bonds can be issued. The contract between the corporation and the *trustee* (usually a bank) representing the bondholders may place some limitation on the payment of dividends to stockholders during the life of the bonds. For example, dividends may be permitted only when working capital is above specified amounts. In the event that the corporation encounters financial difficulties and is unable to make the required payments of interest or principal, the bondholders may force the corporation into bankruptcy.

Some but not all bonds are secured by the pledge of specific assets. An unsecured bond is called a *debenture bond;* its value rests upon the general credit of the corporation. A debenture bond issued by a very large and strong corporation may have a higher investment rating than a secured bond issued by a corporation in less satisfactory financial condition.

Some bonds have a single fixed maturity date for the entire issue. Other bond issues, called *serial bonds,* provide for varying maturity dates to lessen the problem of accumulating cash for payment. For example, serial bonds in the amount of $10 million issued in 1975 might call for $1 million of bonds to mature in 1985, and an additional $1 million to become due in each of the succeeding nine years. Almost all bonds are *callable,* which means that the corporation has the right to pay off the bonds in advance of the scheduled maturity date. The call price is usually somewhat higher than the face value of the bonds.

As an additional attraction to investors, corporations sometimes include a conversion privilege in the bond indenture. A *convertible bond* is one which may be exchanged for common stock at the option of the bondholder. The advantages to the investor of the conversion feature in the event of increased earnings for the company were described in Chapter 17 with regard to convertible preferred stock.

REGISTERED BONDS AND COUPON BONDS Most corporation bonds is- sued in recent years have been *registered* bonds; that is, the name of the owner is registered with the issuing corporation. Payment of interest is made by semiannual checks mailed to the registered owner. *Coupon* bonds were more popular some years ago and many are still outstanding. Coupon bonds have interest coupons attached; each six months during the life of the bond one of these coupons becomes due. The bondholder detaches the coupon and deposits it with a bank for collection. The names of the bondholders are not registered with the corporation.

TRANSFERABILITY OF BONDS Corporation bonds, like capital stocks, are traded daily on organized securities exchanges. The holders of a 25-year bond issue need not wait 25 years to convert their investment into cash. By placing a telephone call to a broker, an investor may sell bonds within a matter of minutes at the going market price. This quality of liquidity is one of the most attractive features of an investment in corporation bonds.

QUOTATIONS FOR BONDS Corporate bond prices are quoted at a given amount per $100 of face value. For example, assume that a bond of $1,000 face amount (par value) is quoted at 106. The total price for the bond is 10 times 106, or $1,060. Market quotations for corporate bonds use an eighth of a dollar as the minimum variation. The following line from the financial page of a daily newspaper summarizes the previous day's trading in bonds of Sears, Roebuck and Co.

	Bonds	Sales	High	Low	Close	Net Change
What is the market value of this bond?	Sears R $8\frac{5}{8}$ 95	45	103	102	$102\frac{1}{2}$	−1

This line of condensed information indicates that 45 of Sears, Roebuck and Co.'s $8\frac{5}{8}$, $1,000 bonds maturing in 1995 were traded. The highest price is reported as 103, or $1,030 for a bond of $1,000 face value. The lowest price was 102 or $1,020 for a $1,000 bond. The closing price (last sale of the day) was $102\frac{1}{2}$, or $1,025. This was one point below the closing price of the previous day, a decrease of $10 in the price of a $1,000 bond.

Effect of bond financing on holders of capital stock

Interest payments on bonds payable are deductible as an expense by the issuing company in determining the income subject to corporation in- come tax, but dividends paid on capital stock are not. High tax rates on corporate earnings thus encourage the use of bonds to obtain long-term capital.

Assume that a growing and profitable corporation with 100,000 shares of capital stock outstanding is in need of $10 million cash to finance a new plant. The management is considering whether to issue an additional 100,000 shares of stock or to issue 8% bonds. Assume also that after acquisition of the new plant, the annual earnings of the corporation, before deducting interest expense or income taxes, will amount to $2 million. From the viewpoint of the stockholders, which financing plan is preferable? The following schedule shows the earnings per share of capital stock under the two alternative methods of financing:

	If Capital Stock Is Issued	If 8% Bonds Are Issued
Which financing plan is better? Annual earnings before bond interest and income taxes . .	$2,000,000	$2,000,000
Less: Interest on bonds (8% of $10,000,000)		800,000
Earnings before income taxes	$2,000,000	$1,200,000
Less: Income taxes (assume 50% rate)	1,000,000	600,000
Net income	$1,000,000	$ 600,000
Number of shares of capital stock outstanding	200,000	100,000
Earnings per share of capital stock	$5.00	$6.00

Financing through issuance of additional capital stock rather than issuance of bonds saves $400,000 (after taxes) but results in *lower earnings per share* because of the *dilution* caused by doubling the number of shares outstanding.

The use of borrowed capital by business firms is referred to as *leverage* or *trading on the equity;* this concept is discussed further in Chapter 22.

Management planning of the bond issue

A corporation wishing to borrow money by issuing bonds faces months of preliminary work. Decisions must be made on such points as the amount to be borrowed, the interest rate to be offered, the conversion privilege, if any, the maturity date, and the property to be pledged, if any.

In forecasting the company's cash position for future periods, consideration must be given to the new requirement of semiannual bond interest payments as well as to the long-range problem of accumulating the cash required to pay the bonds at maturity. If the borrowed funds are to be invested in new plant facilities, will this expansion produce an increase in the cash inflow sufficient to meet the interest payments? If the bond issue includes a call provision, the company may plan to call in bonds in small amounts each year as cash becomes available. Perhaps the bond issue should be of the convertible variety; this feature might attract investors even though the interest rate were set at a relatively low level. In addition, if the bonds are convertible, the company may not have to accumulate cash for repayment of the entire issue. Effective long-range planning of the company's financial needs will greatly reduce the cost of securing capital and will leave the door open to issuing additional securities in the future on advantageous terms.

AUTHORIZATION OF A BOND ISSUE   After the board of directors has decided upon the details of a bond issue, the proposal is presented to stockholders for their approval. Once this approval has been gained, the *deed of trust* is drawn and the bonds are printed. If the company's present financial requirements are for less than the amount of bonds authorized, only a portion of the bonds may be issued at this time.

No formal entry in the accounts is required for the act of authorization; however, a memorandum notation may be made in the Bonds Payable ledger account indicating the total amount of bonds authorized. The total authorized amount of a bond issue should be disclosed in the balance sheet.

THE ROLE OF THE UNDERWRITER IN MARKETING A BOND ISSUE   An investment banker or underwriter is usually employed to market a bond issue, just as in the case of capital stock. The corporation turns the entire bond issue over to the underwriter at a specified price (say, 98); the underwriter sells the bonds to the public at a slightly higher price (say, 100). By this arrangement the corporation is assured of receiving the entire proceeds on a specified date. The calculation of the bond discount or bond premium is based on the net amount which the issuing corporation receives from the underwriter, not on the price paid by investors for the bonds.

Accounting entries for a bond issue

Assume that Wells Corporation on January 1, 1979, after proper authorization by the board of directors and approval by the stockholders, issues $1,000,000 of 20-year, 9% bonds payable. All the bonds bear the January 1, 1979 date, and interest is computed from this date. Interest on the bonds is payable semiannually, each July 1 and January 1. If all the bonds are sold at par value (face value), the sale will be recorded by the following entry:

Jan. 1	Cash	1,000,000	
	Bonds Payable.		1,000,000
	To record issuance of 9%, 20-year bonds at par on		
	the interest date.		

The first semiannual interest payment of $45,000 would be due on July 1. The computation is ($1,000,000 × .09) ÷ 2 = $45,000. The interest payment would be recorded by the entry shown on page 632.

```
July 1   Bond Interest Expense . . . . . . . . . . . . . . . . . . . . . . .    45,000
             Cash . . . . . . . . . . . . . . . . . . . . . . . . . . .                     45,000
         Paid semiannual interest on 9% 20-year bonds with face
         amount of $1,000,000.
```

When the bonds mature 20 years later on January 1, 1999, the entry to record payment of the principal amount will be:

```
Jan. 1   Bonds Payable . . . . . . . . . . . . . . . . . . . . . . .    1,000,000
             Cash . . . . . . . . . . . . . . . . . . . . . . . . . . . .              1,000,000
         Paid face amount of bonds at maturity.
```

RECORDING THE ISSUANCE OF BONDS BETWEEN INTEREST DATES The semiannual interest dates (such as January 1 and July 1, or April 1 and October 1) are printed on the bond certificates. However, bonds are often issued between the specified interest dates. The investor is then required to pay the interest accrued to date of issuance in addition to the stated price of the bond. This practice enables the corporation to pay a full six months' interest on all bonds outstanding at the semiannual interest payment date. The accrued interest collected from investors purchasing bonds between interest payment dates is thus returned to them on the next interest payment date. To illustrate, let us modify our previous example for Wells Corporation and assume that the $1,000,000 face value of 9% bonds were issued at par and accrued interest, *two months after the interest date printed on the bonds.* The entry will be:

Bonds issued between interest dates
```
Cash . . . . . . . . . . . . . . . . . . . . . . . . . . . . . . . . . . .    1,015,000
    Bonds Payable . . . . . . . . . . . . . . . . . . . . . . .                   1,000,000
    Bond Interest Payable . . . . . . . . . . . . . . . . . .                        15,000
Issued $1,000,000 face value of 9%, 20-year bonds at 100
plus accrued interest for two months.
```

Four months later on the regular semiannual interest payment date, a full six months' interest ($45 per each $1,000 bond) will be paid to all bondholders, regardless of when they purchased their bonds. The entry for the semiannual interest payment is illustrated below:

What is the net interest expense?
```
Bond Interest Payable . . . . . . . . . . . . . . . . . . . . . . . . . .    15,000
Bond Interest Expense . . . . . . . . . . . . . . . . . . . . . . . . . .    30,000
    Cash . . . . . . . . . . . . . . . . . . . . . . . . . . . . . . . . . . .              45,000
Paid semiannual interest on $1,000,000 face value of 9% bonds.
```

Now consider these interest transactions from the standpoint of the investors. They paid for two months' accrued interest at the time of purchasing the bonds, and they received checks for six months' interest after holding the bonds for only four months. They have therefore, been reimbursed properly for the use of their money for four months.

At first glance, it may seem strange for a corporation to charge investors for the accrued interest when the investors purchase bonds, since this amount will be returned to them as part of the next interest payment. However, good reason exists for this practice. For example, assume that a corporation sells portions of its bond issue to different investors on different dates. If the corporation does not collect the accrued interest from each investor when the bonds are sold, it must maintain records of the individual bondholders and dates on which they bought their bonds. Then, at the next interest date, the corporation would need to compute separately the interest due to each bondholder.

A much more efficient plan is to charge each bondholder the accrued interest up to the date of his or her purchase of the bonds; then the corporation need not maintain these detailed records of purchase dates. A full period's interest may be paid to each bondholder. Regardless of the date that individual bondholders acquired their bonds, each bondholder will receive a return of the accrued interest he or she was charged, plus the exact interest earned since the date of purchase.

When bonds are subsequently sold by one investor to another, they sell at the quoted market price *plus accrued interest* since the last interest payment date. This practice enables the issuing corporation to pay all the interest for an interest period to the investor owning the bond at the interest date. Otherwise, the corporation would have to make partial payments to every investor who bought or sold the bond during the interest period.

The amount which investors will pay for bonds is the *present value* of the principal and interest payments they will receive. Before going further in our discussion of bonds payable, it will be helpful to review the concepts of present value and effective yield.

The concept of present value

The concept of present value is based upon the "time value" of money—the idea that receiving money today is preferable to receiving money at some later date. Assume, for example, that a bond has a maturity value of $1,000 in five years but pays no interest in the meantime. Investors would not pay $1,000 for this bond today, because they would receive no return on their investment over the next five years. There are prices less than $1,000, however, at which investors would buy the bond. For example, if the bond could be purchased for $600, the investor could expect a return (interest) of $400 from the investment over the five-year period.

The present value of a future cash receipt is the amount that a knowledgeable investor would pay *today* for the right to receive that future payment. The exact amount of the present value depends upon (1) the amount of the future payment, (2) the length of time until the payment will be received, and (3) the rate of return required by the investor. However, the present value will always be less than the future amount. This is because money received today can be invested to earn interest and thereby become equivalent to a larger amount in the future.

The rate of interest which will cause a given present value to grow to a given future amount is called the discount rate or *effective interest rate.* The effective interest rate required by investors at any given time determines the going market rate of interest.

The present value concept and bond prices

The price at which bonds will sell is the present value to investors of the future principal and interest payments. If the bonds sell at par, the effective interest rate is equal to the contract interest rate printed on the bonds. The higher the effective interest rate investors require, the less they will pay for bonds with a given contract rate of interest. For example, if investors insist upon a 9% return, they will pay less than $1,000 for an 8%, $1,000 bond. Thus, if investors require an effective interest rate greater than the contract rate of interest for the bonds, the bonds will sell at a *discount* (price less than face value). On the other hand, if investors require an effective interest rate of less than the contract rate, the bonds will sell at a *premium* (price above face value).

A corporation wishing to borrow money by issuing bonds must pay the going market rate of interest. On any given date, the going market rate of interest is in reality a whole schedule of rates corresponding to the financial strength of different borrowers. Since market rates of interest are constantly fluctuating, it must be expected that the *contract rate* of interest printed on the bonds will seldom agree with the *market rate* of interest at the date the bonds are issued.

Bonds sold at a discount

If the interest rate carried by an issue of bonds is lower than the market rate for bonds of this grade, the bonds can be sold only at a discount. For example, assume that on May 1, 1978, a corporation issues $100,000 face value of 7%, 10-year bonds.[1] Each bond will pay the holder $70 interest (7% × $1,000) each year, consisting of two semiannual payments of $35 each. If the market rate of interest were exactly 7%, the bonds would sell at par, but if the market rate of interest is above 7%, no one will be willing to pay $1,000 for a bond which will return only $70 a year. The price at which the bonds can be sold will, therefore, be less than par. Assume that the bonds sell for $93,205; this price results in an effective yield to bondholders of 8%. The issuance of the bonds on May 1, 1978, at this price will be recorded by the entry on page 635.

---

[1] For illustrative purposes, this bond issue is for an unusually small amount.

Issuing bonds at discount

Cash	93,205
Discount on Bonds Payable	6,795
Bonds Payable	100,000

Issued $100,000 face value of 7%, 10-year bonds at a discount.

If a balance sheet is prepared immediately after the issuance of the bonds, the liability for bonds payable will be shown as follows:

Liability shown net of discount

Long-term liabilities:

7% bonds payable, due May 1, 1988	$100,000	
Less: Discount on bonds payable	6,795	$93,205

The amount of the discount is deducted from the face value of the bonds payable to show the present value or *carrying value* of the liability. At the date of issuance, the carrying value of bonds payable is equal to the amount for which the bonds were sold. In other words, the amount of the company's liability at the date of issuing the bonds is equal to the amount of money borrowed. Over the life of the bonds, however, we shall see that this carrying value gradually increases until it reaches the face value of the bonds at the maturity date.

BOND DISCOUNT AS PART OF THE COST OF BORROWING   Whenever bonds are issued at a discount, the total interest cost over the life of the bonds is equal to the regular cash interest payments *plus the amount of the discount.* In our example, the corporation received $93,205 for the bonds, but it will have to pay bondholders $100,000 when the bonds mature. Since the amount to be repaid exceeds the amount borrowed, the corporation will incur an additional cost of $6,795. This additional cost, equal to the discount on the bonds, is incurred because the contract rate of interest is less than the market rate required by bondholders. Although this cost will not be paid until the bonds mature, the corporation benefits from this cost during each period that it has the use of the bondholders' money. Thus, the cost represented by the discount should be allocated over the life of the bonds; this allocation follows the familiar concept of matching expenses with the related benefits.

Amortization of the discount

The process of allocating a bond discount to expense is termed *amortization* of the discount. The simplest method of amortizing a discount is the straight-line method, which allocates an equal portion of the discount to Bond Interest Expense in each interest period. If our $6,795 discount were amortized by the straight-line method, the amount of $339.75 ($6,795 ÷ 20 interest periods) would be allocated to Bond Interest Expense at each semiannual interest date. The entries to be made each six months to record bond interest expense are as follows (rounded to the nearest dollar):

Bond Interest Expense 3,500	
Cash	3,500

Paid semiannual interest on $100,000 of 7% 10-year bonds.

Bond Interest Expense 340	
Discount on Bonds Payable	340

Amortized $\frac{1}{20}$ of discount on 10-year bond issue.

The two entries shown above to record the cash payment of bond interest and to record the amortization of bond discount can conveniently be combined into one compound entry, as follows:

Bond Interest Expense 3,840	
Cash	3,500
Discount on Bonds Payable	340

To record payment of semiannual interest on $100,000 of 7% 10-year bonds ($100,000 × 7% × $\frac{1}{2}$) and to amortize $\frac{1}{20}$ of the discount on the 10-year bond issue.

Regardless of whether the cash payment of interest and the amortization of bond discount are recorded in separate entries or combined in one entry, the amount recognized as Bond Interest Expense is the same.

Note that the additional interest expense resulting from amortization of the discount does not involve any additional cash payment. The credit portion of the entry is to the contra-liability account, Discount on Bonds Payable, rather than to the Cash account. Crediting this contra-liability account *increases the carrying value of bonds payable.* The Discount on Bonds Payable will be completely written off by the end of the tenth year, and the net liability (carrying value) will be the full face value of the bonds.

Although straight-line amortization causes the full cost of borrowing to be recognized over the life of the bonds, the method has one conceptual weakness: the same amount of interest expense is recognized each year. Since the carrying value of the net liability increases every year, the interest expense shown in the financial statements will be a decreasing percentage of the liability. Straight-line amortization could therefore distort the annual cost of capital as portrayed in a company's financial statements. For this reason, the FASB supports the effective interest method of amortization and permits the straight-line method to be used only when it produces results not materially different from those produced by the effective interest method.

EFFECTIVE INTEREST METHOD OF AMORTIZATION The effective interest method of amortization causes interest expense to be a *constant percentage of the carrying value of the liability.* The interest expense for each period is determined by multiplying the carrying value of the bonds at the beginning of each period by the effective rate of interest for the bond issue. The amount of discount to be amortized each period is the difference between the interest expense computed in this manner and the amount of interest to be paid to bondholders for the period. The computation of effective interest expense and discount amortization can be made in advance on a schedule called an *amortization table.* An amortization table for our $100,000 bond issue is shown below (amounts of interest expense have been rounded to the nearest dollar).

This amortization table can be used to illustrate the concepts underlying the effective interest method of determining interest expense and

$E =$

Amortization Table for Bonds Sold at a Discount

($100,000, 10-year bonds, 7% interest payable semiannually,
sold at $93,205, to yield 8% compounded semiannually)

Six-Month Interest Period	(A) Interest Paid Semiannually (3½% of face value)	(B) Effective Semiannual Interest Expense (4% of bond carrying value)	(C) Discount Amortization (B − A)	(D) Bond Discount Balance	(E) Carrying Value of Bonds, End of Period ($100,000 − D)
				$6,795	$93,205 +228=
1	$3,500	$3,728 = .04(93,205) $228	$228	6,567	93,433 +237=
2	3,500	3,737	237	6,330	93,670
3	3,500	3,747	247	6,083	93,917
4	3,500	3,757	257	5,826	94,174
5	3,500	3,767	267	5,559	94,441
6	3,500	3,778	278	5,281	94,719
7	3,500	3,789	289	4,992	95,008
8	3,500	3,800	300	4,692	95,308
9	3,500	3,812	312	4,380	95,620
10	3,500	3,825	325	4,055	95,945
11	3,500	3,838	338	3,717	96,283
12	3,500	3,851	351	3,366	96,634
13	3,500	3,865	365	3,001	96,999
14	3,500	3,880	380	2,621	97,379
15	3,500	3,895	395	2,226	97,774
16	3,500	3,911	411	1,815	98,185
17	3,500	3,927	427	1,388	98,612
18	3,500	3,944	444	944	99,056
19	3,500	3,962	462	482	99,518
20	3,500	3,982*	482	−0−	100,000

*In the last period, interest expense is equal to interest paid to bondholders plus the remaining balance of the bond discount. This compensates for the accumulated effects of rounding amounts.

discount amortization. Note that the "interest periods" in the table are the semiannual (six-month) interest periods. Thus, the interest payments (Column A), interest expense (Column B), and discount amortization (Column C) are for six-month periods. Similarly, the balance of the Discount on Bonds Payable account (Column D) and the carrying value of the liability (Column E) are shown as of each semiannual interest payment date.

The original issuance price of the bonds ($93,205) is entered at the top of Column E. This represents the carrying value of the liability throughout the first six-month interest period. The semiannual interest payment, shown in Column A, is $3\frac{1}{2}$% (one-half of the annual contract rate) of the $100,000 face value of the bond issue. The semiannual cash interest payment does not change over the life of the bonds. The interest expense shown in Column B, however, *changes every period.* This expense is always a constant percentage of the carrying value of the liability as of the end of the preceding period. The "constant percentage" is the effective interest rate of the bond issue. The bonds have an effective annual interest rate of 8%, indicating a semiannual rate of 4%. Thus, the effective interest expense for the first six-month period is $3,728 (4% of $93,205). The discount amortization for period 1 is the difference between this effective interest expense and the contract rate of interest paid to bondholders.

Note that after the discount is reduced by $228 at the end of period 1, the carrying value of the bonds in Column E *increases* by $228 (from $93,205 to $93,433). In period 2, the effective interest expense is determined by multiplying the effective semiannual interest rate of 4% by this new carrying value of $93,433 (4% × $93,433 = $3,737).

Semiannual interest expense may be recorded every period directly from the data in the amortization table. For example, the entry to record bond interest expense at the end of the first six-month period is:

Bond Interest Expense	3,728	
Discount on Bonds Payable		228
Cash		3,500

To record semiannual interest payment and amortize discount for six months.

Similarly, interest expense at the end of the fifteenth six-month period would be recorded by:

Bond Interest Expense	3,895	
Discount on Bonds Payable		395
Cash		3,500

To record semiannual interest payment and amortize discount for six months.

When a bond discount is amortized, the carrying value of the liability for bonds payable *increases* every period toward the maturity value. Since the effective interest expense in each period is a constant percentage of this increasing carrying value, the interest expense also increases from one period to the next. This is the basic difference between the effective interest method and straight-line amortization.

Bonds sold at a premium

Bonds will sell above par if the contract rate of interest specified on the bonds is higher than the current market rate for bonds of this grade. Let us now change our basic illustration by assuming that the $100,000 issue of 7%, 10-year bonds is sold at a price of $107,443, resulting in an effective interest rate of 6% annually (3% per six-month interest period). Assume also that the bonds are sold on their issuance date of May 1, 1978, with interest dates of November 1 and May 1. The entry to record the sale is:

Issuing bonds at premium

Cash *107,443*	
Bonds Payable	*100,000*
Premium on Bonds Payable	*7,443*

Issued $100,000 face value of 7%, 10-year bonds at a premium.

If a balance sheet is prepared immediately following the sale of the bonds, the liability will be shown as follows:

Carrying value increased by premium

Long-term liabilities:		
7% bonds payable, due May 1, 1988	*$100,000*	
Add: Premium on bonds payable	*7,443*	*$107,443*

The amount of any unamortized premium is added to the par value of the bonds payable to show the carrying value of the liability. Over the life of the bonds, the carrying value will be reduced toward the maturity value of $100,000.

When bonds are issued at a premium, the total interest cost over the life of the issue is equal to the regular cash interest payments *minus the amount of the premium.* In our example, the corporation received $107,443, but it will have to repay only $100,000 of this amount at the maturity date. The difference, equal to the $7,443 premium, is not a gain but a *reduction in the cost of borrowing.* This cost reduction should be allocated over the life of the bonds to reduce the amount of interest expense recognized each period.

Amortization of the premium

As in the amortization of a discount, the FASB supports the effective interest method rather than straight-line amortization. An amortization table for this bond issue is shown on page 640 (amounts rounded to the nearest dollar).

Amortization Table for Bonds Sold at a Premium

($100,000, 10-year bonds, 7% interest payable semiannually,
sold at $107,443, to yield 6% compounded semiannually)

Six-Month Interest Period	(A) Interest Paid Semiannually (3½% of face value)	(B) Effective Semiannual Interest Expense (3% of bond carrying value)	(C) Premium Amortization (A − B)	(D) Bond Premium Balance	(E) Carrying Value of Bonds, End of Period ($100,000 + D)
		.03(107,443)		$7,443	$107,443 −277=
1	$3,500	$3,223 =	$277	7,166	107,166
2	3,500	3,215	285	6,881	106,881
3	3,500	3,206	294	6,587	106,587
4	3,500	3,198	302	6,285	106,285
5	3,500	3,189	311	5,974	105,974
6	3,500	3,179	321	5,653	105,653
7	3,500	3,170	330	5,323	105,323
8	3,500	3,160	340	4,983	104,983
9	3,500	3,149	351	4,632	104,632
10	3,500	3,139	361	4,271	104,271
11	3,500	3,128	372	3,899	103,899
12	3,500	3,117	383	3,516	103,516
13	3,500	3,105	395	3,121	103,121
14	3,500	3,094	406	2,715	102,715
15	3,500	3,081	419	2,296	102,296
16	3,500	3,069	431	1,865	101,865
17	3,500	3,056	444	1,421	101,421
18	3,500	3,043	457	964	100,964
19	3,500	3,029	471	493	100,493
20	3,500	3,007*	493	−0−	100,000

* In the last period, interest expense is equal to interest paid to bondholders minus the remaining balance of the bond premium. This compensates for the accumulated effects of rounding amounts.

In this amortization table, the interest expense for each six-month period is equal to 3% of the carrying value at the beginning of that period. This amount of interest expense is less than the amount of cash being paid to bondholders, illustrating that the effective interest rate is less than the contract rate.

Based upon this amortization table, the entry to record the interest payment and amortization of the premium for the first six months of the bond issue is:

Amortization of premium decreases interest expense

Bond Interest Expense	3,223
Premium on Bonds Payable	277
Cash	3,500

To record semiannual interest payment and amortization of premium.

Note that the amortization of the premium reduces the amount of interest expense recognized during the period below the $3,500 cash payment. Similar entries will be made at the end of each six-month period, recognizing decreasing amounts of interest expense and increasing amounts of premium amortization. As the premium is amortized, the net amount of the liability is reduced year by year, until, at the maturity date of the bonds, the premium will have been completely written off and the liability will stand at the face amount of the bond issue.

Year-end adjustments for bond interest expense

Frequently, the end of a corporation's accounting period does not coincide with an interest payment date for bonds payable. In such cases, it is necessary to make adjusting entries at year-end to accrue interest and amortize any discount or premium for the period of time since the last interest date. To illustrate, consider our example of the bonds sold at a premium on May 1, 1978. The entry to record interest and amortization of the premium through November 1, 1978, was shown on page 640. If the company keeps its accounts on a calendar-year basis, two months' interest has accrued as of December 31, 1978, and the following adjusting entry is made (amounts rounded to nearest dollar): ·

Bond Interest Expense	1,072	
Premium on Bonds Payable	95	
Bond Interest Payable		1,167

To record two months' accrued interest and amortize one-third of the premium for the interest period.

This adjusting entry covers one-third (two months) of the second interest period. Consequently, the amounts shown as bond interest expense and amortization of premium are one-third of the amounts shown in the amortization table for the second interest period. Similar adjusting entries must be made at the end of every accounting period while the bonds are outstanding. The dollar amounts of these adjusting entries will vary, however, since the amounts of interest expense and premium amortization change in every interest period. The amounts applicable to any given adjusting entry will be the appropriate fraction of the amounts for the interest period then in progress.

Following the year-end adjusting entry illustrated above, the interest expense and premium amortization on May 1, 1979, are recorded as follows (rounded to nearest dollar):

Bond Interest Expense	2,143	
Bond Interest Payable	1,167	
Premium on Bonds Payable	190	
Cash		3,500

To record semiannual interest payment, a portion of which had been accrued, and amortize remainder of premium applicable to interest period.

Retirement of bonds payable

Bonds are sometimes retired before the scheduled maturity date. Most bond issues contain a call provision, permitting the corporation to redeem the bonds by paying a specified price, usually a few points above par. Even without a call provision, the corporation may retire its bonds before maturity by purchasing them in the open market. If the bonds can be purchased by the issuing corporation at less than their carrying value, a gain is realized on the retirement of the debt. If the bonds are reacquired by the issuing corporation at a price in excess of their carrying value, a loss must be recognized. In *Statement No. 4*, the FASB ruled that these gains and losses, if *material* in amount, should be shown separately in the income statement as extraordinary items.[2]

For example, assume that the Briggs Corporation has outstanding a $1 million bond issue with unamortized premium in the amount of $20,000. The bonds are callable at 105 and the company exercises the call provision on 100 of the bonds, or 10% of the issue. The entry would be as follows:

Bonds called at price above carrying value	*Bonds Payable*	*100,000*	
	Premium on Bonds Payable	*2,000*	
	Loss on Retirement of Bonds	*3,000*	
	Cash		*105,000*

To record retirement of $100,000 face value of bonds called at 105.

The carrying value of each of the 100 called bonds was $1,020, whereas the call price was $1,050. For each bond called the company incurred a loss of $30, or a total loss of $3,000. Note that when 10% of the total issue was called, 10% of the unamortized premium was written off.

By the maturity date of the bonds, the discount or premium will have been completely amortized and the accounting entry to retire the bonds (assuming that interest is paid separately) will consist of a debit to Bonds Payable and a credit to Cash.

One year before the maturity date, the bonds payable may be reclassified from long-term debt to a current liability in the balance sheet if payment is to be made from current assets rather than from a bond sinking fund.

Conversion of bonds payable into common stock

Convertible bonds represent a popular form of financing, particularly during periods when common stock prices are rising. The conversion feature gives bondholders an opportunity to profit from a rise in the market price of the issuing company's common stock despite the fact that

---

[2] Financial Accounting Standards Board, *Statement No. 4*, "Reporting Gains and Losses from Extinguishment of Debt," FASB (Stamford, Conn.: 1975).

they still maintain the status of creditors. Because of this potential gain, convertible bonds generally carry lower interest rates than nonconvertible bonds.

The conversion ratio is typically set at a price above the current market price of the common stock. For example, if common stock with a par value of $10 a share has a current market price of $42 a share, the conversion price might be set at $50 per share, thus enabling a holder of a $1,000 par value convertible bond to exchange the bond for 20 shares of common stock.[3] Let us assume that $5 million of such bonds are issued at par, and that some time later when the common stock has risen in price to $60 per share, the holders of 100 bonds decide to convert their bonds into common stock. The conversion transaction would be recorded as follows:

Conversion of bonds into common stock	*Convertible Bonds Payable*	*100,000*
	Common Stock, $10 par	*20,000*
	Paid-in Capital in Excess of Par	*80,000*
	To record the conversion of 100 bonds into 2,000 shares of common stock.	

No gain or loss is recognized by the issuing corporation upon conversion of bonds; the carrying value of the bonds is simply assigned to the common stock issued in exchange. If the bonds had been issued at a price above or below par, the unamortized premium or discount relating to the bonds would be written off at the time of conversion in order to assign the carrying value of the bonds to the common stock.

Bond sinking fund

To make a bond issue attractive to investors, corporations may agree to create a sinking fund, exclusively for use in paying the bonds at maturity. A bond sinking fund is created by setting aside a specified amount of cash at regular intervals. The cash is usually deposited with a trustee, who invests it and adds the earnings to the amount of the sinking fund. The periodic deposits of cash plus the earnings on the sinking fund investments should cause the fund to equal approximately the amount of the bond issue by the maturity date. When the bond issue approaches maturity, the trustee sells all the securities in the fund and uses the cash proceeds to pay the holders of the bonds. Any excess cash remaining in the fund will be returned to the corporation by the trustee.

A bond sinking fund is not included in current assets because it is not available for payment of current liabilities. The cash and securities comprising the fund are usually shown as a single amount under Investments, placed just below the current asset section. Interest earned on sinking fund securities constitutes revenue to the corporation.

[3] $1,000 ÷ $50 conversion price = 20 shares of common stock.

Mortgages payable

Mortgages are usually payable in equal monthly installments. A portion of each payment represents interest on the unpaid balance of the loan and the remainder of the monthly payment reduces the amount of the unpaid balance (principal). Since the principal is being reduced each month, the portion of each successive payment representing interest will decrease and the portion of the payment going toward retirement of the principal will increase. This process is illustrated by the following schedule of payments for a three-month period on a 6.6% mortgage note with an unpaid balance of $100,000 at September 11 of the current year.

Monthly payments on a mortgage note

	Monthly Payment	Interest for One Month at 6.6% on Unpaid Balance	Reduction in Principal	Unpaid Principal Balance
Sept. 11				$100,000.00
Oct. 11	$1,000.00	$550.00	$450.00	99,550.00
Nov. 11	1,000.00	547.53	452.47	99,097.53
Dec. 11	1,000.00	545.04	454.96	98,642.57

On December 31 of the current year, the portion of the unpaid principal balance of $98,642.57, due within one year, should be classified as a current liability and the remainder as a long-term liability. In addition, the accrued interest for 20 days, amounting to $361.69 ($98,642.57 × 6.6% × $\frac{20}{360}$), would be included under current liabilities.

Leases

A company may purchase the assets needed for use in its business or it may choose to lease them. Examples of assets often acquired by lease include buildings, office equipment, automobiles, and factory machinery. A *lease* is a contract in which the *lessor* gives the *lessee* the right to use an asset in return for periodic rental payments. Accounting for the many forms of lease transactions and the disclosure of lease obligations by lessees are among the more important issues facing accountants today. When the lessor gives the lessee the right to use the leased property but retains the usual risks and rewards of ownership, the periodic rentals are recorded as revenue by the lessor and as rental expense by the lessee. Such a contract is known as an *operating lease* and does not require the recognition of a liability in the records of the lessee, other than for any accrued monthly rentals.

When the objectives of the lease contract are to provide financing to the lessee for the eventual purchase of the property and to transfer the usual risks and rewards of ownership to the lessee, the contract is referred to as a *financing lease.* Some financing leases are essentially equivalent to a sale of an asset by the lessor and a purchase of an asset by the lessee. A lease which is equivalent to a sale and purchase should be recorded as an installment sale by the lessor and as a purchase by the lessee. The asset and related liability should be recorded by the lessee at an amount equal to the present value of the future rental payments. The present value is determined by discounting the rental payments at a fair rate of interest. The lessee should depreciate the asset over its estimated useful life rather than over the period of the lease.

Opinion No. 31 of the APB required that notes to the financial statements of the lessee make full disclosure of the terms of all noncancelable leases.[4] Otherwise, major obligations to make cash payments would not be disclosed in the financial statements.

Pension plans

A *pension plan* is a contract between a company and its employees under which the company agrees to pay retirement benefits to eligible employees. An employer company generally meets its obligations under a pension plan by making regular payments to an insurance company or other outside agency. As pension obligations accrue, the employer company records them by a debit to Pension Expense and a credit to Cash. If all required payments are made promptly to the pension fund trustee, no liability need appear on the employer company's financial statements. When employees retire, their retirement benefits are paid by the insurance company. This type of arrangement is called a *funded pension plan.*

The Retirement Security Act of 1974 (ERISA) was a most complex piece of legislation requiring extensive reporting of pension plans to the federal government. The objectives included assuring that the enormous amounts of money in pension plans were properly accounted for, audited regularly, and available to meet obligations to retiring employees. The FASB is currently studying the need for new accounting standards to meet the requirements imposed by ERISA. Pension plans are considered in some detail in *Intermediate Accounting* of this series.

INVESTMENTS IN CORPORATE SECURITIES

Securities transactions from the viewpoint of investors

In the preceding section, the issuance of securities and such related transactions as the payment of dividends and interest have been considered primarily from the viewpoint of the issuing corporation. Now we shall consider these transactions from the viewpoint of the investor.

The stocks and bonds of most large corporations are listed on the New York Stock Exchange or on other organized exchanges. Among the investors in these securities are trust funds, pension funds, universities, banks, insurance companies, industrial corporations, and great numbers of individuals. The stocks and bonds of many smaller companies are not listed on an organized exchange but are bought and sold *over the counter.*

[4] *APB Opinion No. 31,* "Disclosure of Lease Commitments by Lessees," AICPA (New York: 1973), pp. 576–577

At the time of issuance of bonds or stocks, the transaction is between the investor and the issuing corporation (or its underwriting agent). The great daily volume of transactions, however, consists of the sale of stocks and bonds by investors to other investors. Virtually all these transactions are made through a stockbroker acting as intermediary.

LISTED CORPORATIONS REPORT TO A MILLION OWNERS When a corporation invites the public to purchase its stocks and bonds, it accepts an obligation to keep the public informed on its financial position and the profitability of operations. This obligation of disclosure includes public distribution of financial statements. The Securities and Exchange Commission is a government agency responsible for seeing that corporations make full and fair disclosure of their affairs so that investors have a basis for intelligent investment decisions. The flow of corporate accounting data distributed through newspapers and financial advisory services to millions of investors is a vital force in the functioning of our economy; in fact, the successful working of a profit-motivated economy rests upon the quality and dependability of the accounting information being reported.

LISTED CORPORATIONS ARE AUDITED BY CERTIFIED PUBLIC ACCOUNT-ANTS Corporations with securities listed on organized stock exchanges are required to have regular audits of their accounts by certified public accountants. The financial statements distributed each year to stockholders are accompanied by a report by a firm of certified public accountants indicating that an audit has been made and expressing an opinion as to the fairness of the company's financial statements. It is the *independent status* of the auditing firm that enables investors to place confidence in audited financial statements.

Marketable securities as current assets

A recent balance sheet of International Business Machines Corporation shows the following items listed first in the current asset section.

Current assets:

Cash	$ 183,869,340
Marketable securities, at lower of cost or market	4,584,445,162

The large investment by IBM in marketable securities is in no way unusual. The published balance sheets of many corporations show large holdings of marketable securities. Often these holdings include government bonds, corporation bonds, and both preferred and common stocks. Marketable securities are usually listed immediately after the asset, Cash, because these securities are almost as liquid as cash itself. In the event that cash is needed for any operating purpose, the marketable securities can be quickly sold and thus transformed into cash. The most recent balance sheet of Gulf Oil Corporation shows as the very first current asset: "Cash and marketable securities. . . . $1,837,000, 000." This practice of lumping together cash and marketable securities reflects the general attitude that these two assets are essentially similar. From the viewpoint of creditors, it is often said in appraising a company's financial strength that "cash and marketable securities" amount to so many dollars. To a loan officer in a bank reviewing an application for a loan, there is no more impressive or reassuring asset on the balance sheet of a prospective borrower than a large amount of high-quality marketable securities.

Valuation of marketable securities

The FASB presently requires, in *Statement of Financial Accounting Standards No. 12,* that marketable securities be shown in financial statements at the lower of the aggregate cost or market value determined at the balance sheet date.[5] In applying the lower-of-cost-or-market rule, the FASB considers the possibility that a company may choose to separate its investments in marketable securities into two groups: one group considered as temporary investments and classified as current assets, and the other group considered to be permanent investments and classified as non-current assets. In practice, however, this distinction is seldom made. Most published balance sheets show marketable securities as one group in the current asset section. (The balance sheet of Johnson & Johnson shown in the Appendix of this book is an exception.) If a company has a definite intention to hold certain marketable securities on a long-term basis, it can justifiably show them on the balance sheet as Investments below the current asset section. More realistically, however, management usually stands ready to sell marketable securities whenever company needs require it, or whenever favorable stock market movements make such action appropriate. Consequently, marketable securities are generally viewed as current assets.

LOWER OF AGGREGATE COST OR MARKET It is apparent from a glance at the financial pages of a newspaper that the market prices of stocks and bonds fluctuate from day to day. Therefore, we can expect that a company owning a number of marketable securities will find on a given balance sheet date that some of its investments presently have a market value above cost and that the market value of others has dropped below cost. The aggregate cost of all marketable securities regarded as current assets is compared with the total market value of these securities as a group and the lower of the two amounts is used as the balance sheet valuation.

For example, assume the following facts for marketable securities owned by Eagle Corporation at December 31.

[5] *Statement of Financial Accounting Standards No. 12,* "Accounting for Certain Marketable Securities," Financial Accounting Standards Board (Stamford, Conn.: 1975).

	Cost	Market Value
Bonds of Adams Company	$100,000	$102,000
Common stock of Barnes Company	60,000	56,000
Preferred stock of Alpha Corporation	200,000	192,000
Other marketable securities	25,000	25,000
Totals	$385,000	$375,000

Since the total market value of the securities in our example is less than their cost to Eagle Corporation, the proper balance sheet valuation would be the lower amount of $375,000. This downward adjustment of $10,000 means that an unrealized loss of $10,000 will be included in the determination of the year's net income. The accounting entry might be as follows:

Unrealized Loss on Marketable Securities	10,000	
Valuation Allowance for Marketable Securities		10,000
To reduce the carrying value of the investment in marketable securities to the lower of cost or market.		

Next, let us assume that in the following year the marketable securities owned by Eagle Corporation rose in market value, so that by year-end, the aggregate market value was in excess of cost. The valuation allowance would no longer be needed. An entry to eliminate or reduce the valuation allowance results in a credit to Unrealized Gain on Marketable Securities and is included in the determination of the year's net income. In brief, when marketable securities have been written down to the lower of cost or market, they can be written back up to original cost if the market prices recover. However, current rules of the FASB do not permit recognition of a market rise above the aggregate cost of the securities owned. One of the weaknesses of the position taken by the FASB is that a company may be required to recognize increases in market prices of some securities while ignoring others.

INCOME TAX RULES FOR MARKETABLE SECURITIES The FASB rules described above are not acceptable in determining income subject to income tax. The only gains or losses recognized for income tax purposes are realized gains and losses resulting from sale of an investment.

PRESENTATION OF MARKETABLE SECURITIES IN FINANCIAL STATEMENTS The financial statements should include a footnote disclosure of both the cost and market value of marketable securities. Realized gains and losses from sale of marketable securities should be reported as well as the unrealized amounts from establishing or changing a valuation allowance to value investments at the lower of cost or market. The basis of measuring cost (such as first-in, first-out, average cost, etc.) should also be disclosed.

The argument for valuation at market value

Many accountants believe that investments in marketable securities should be valued in the balance sheet at *current market price* regardless of whether this price is above or below cost. Increases and decreases in market value would then be recognized as gains or losses as these changes occur. Several strong arguments exist for valuing marketable securities at market value: (*1*) current market value is more relevant for decision making than the value which existed in the past; (*2*) creditors are primarily concerned with the present market value of securities; (*3*) current market quotations are available, which definitely establish market values for this type of asset; and (*4*) investments in marketable securities can be sold at any time without interfering with the normal operation of the business.

INVESTMENTS FOR PURPOSE OF CONTROL Some corporations buy stocks of other corporations in sufficient quantity that a degree of control or influence may be exercised over the issuing corporation. Sometimes a substantial investment in stock of a customer company may be helpful in maintaining good business relations. Investments of this type cannot be sold without disturbing established policies; therefore, such investments are not current assets. In this chapter we are not considering investments which enable the investor to exercise influence or control.

Determining the cost of investments in stocks and bonds

An investment in marketable securities is recorded in the accounts at cost, including any commissions paid to stockbrokers and any transfer taxes.

The principal distinction between the recording of an investment in bonds and an investment in stocks is that interest on bonds accrues from day to day. The interest accrued since the last semiannual interest payment date is paid for by the purchaser and should be recorded separately from the cost of the bond itself. Dividends on stock, however, do not accrue and the entire purchase price paid by the investor in stocks is recorded in the account, Investment in Marketable Securities.

INCOME ON INVESTMENTS IN STOCKS Dividends are seldom recorded as income until received. The entry upon receipt of a dividend check consists of a debit to Cash and a credit to Dividends Earned.

Dividends in the form of additional shares of stock are not income to the stockholder, and only a memorandum entry needs to be made to record the increase in the number of shares owned. The *cost basis per share* is decreased, however, because of the larger number of shares comprising the investment after distribution of a stock dividend. As an example, assume that an investor paid $72 a share for 100 shares of stock, a total cost of $7,200. Later the investor received 20 additional shares as a stock dividend. The cost per share is thereby reduced to $60 a share, computed by dividing the total cost of $7,200 by the 120 shares owned after the 20% stock dividend.

PURCHASE OF BONDS BETWEEN INTEREST DATES When bonds are pur-. chased between interest dates, the purchaser pays the agreed price for the bonds plus the interest accrued since the last interest payment date. By this arrangement the new owner becomes entitled to receive in full the next semiannual interest payment. An account entitled Accrued Bond Interest Receivable should be debited for the amount of interest purchased. For example, assume the purchase of a 9%, $1,000 bond at a price of 100 (100% of par value) and two months' accrued interest of $15. The entry is as follows:

Separate account for accrued bond interest purchased

Investment in Bonds	*1,000*	
Accrued Bond Interest Receivable	*15*	
Cash		*1,015*
Purchased 9% bond of XYZ Co. at 100 and accrued interest.		

Four months later at the next semiannual interest payment date, the investor will receive an interest check for $45, which will be recorded as follows:

Note portion of interest check earned

Cash	*45*	
Accrued Bond Interest Receivable		*15*
Bond Interest Revenue		*30*
Received semiannual interest on XYZ Co. bond.		

The $30 credit to Bond Interest Revenue represents the amount actually earned during the four months the bond was owned.

ENTRIES TO RECORD BOND INTEREST EARNED EACH PERIOD If the investor in bonds is to determine bond interest earned each year on an accrual basis, an adjusting entry will be necessary at the balance sheet date for any interest earned but not yet received. This procedure is similar to that used in accounting for interest on notes receivable. The following series of entries illustrates the accounting for bond interest earned by a company on a calendar-year basis of accounting. The investment consists of $100,000 face value of 6% bonds (purchased at par) with interest dates of February 28 and August 31.

Allocating bond interest earned by years

Year 1

Dec. 31 Accrued Bond Interest Receivable	*2,000*	
Bond Interest Revenue		*2,000*
To accrue four months' interest earned on $100,000 face value of 6% bonds.		

Year 2

Feb. 28	*Cash*	*3,000*	
	Accrued Bond Interest Receivable		*2,000*
	Bond Interest Revenue		*1,000*
	Received semiannual bond interest.		
Aug. 31	*Cash*	*3,000*	
	Bond Interest Revenue		*3,000*
	Received semiannual bond interest.		
Dec. 31	*Accrued Bond Interest Receivable*	*2,000*	
	Bond Interest Revenue		*2,000*
	To accrue four months' interest earned on $100,000 face value of 6% bonds.		

Acquisition of bonds at premium or discount

In the discussion of bonds *payable* from the viewpoint of the issuing corporation, emphasis was placed on the point that the issuing company *must* amortize the premium or discount over the life of the bonds. The position of the *individual investor in bonds,* however, is very different with respect to the significance of premium or discount. Many investors purchasing bonds above or below par do *not* amortize the premium or discount on these investments, because they do not expect to hold the bonds until maturity. Since bond issues often run for 25 years or more, it is the exception rather than the rule for an individual investor to hold the bond until it matures. If the investor sells the bond before it matures, the price received may be either above or below the cost, according to the current state of the bond market. Under these circumstances there is no assurance that amortization of premium or discount would give any more accurate measurement of investment income than would be obtained by carrying the bonds at cost.

Companies making long-term investments in bonds are required by *APB Opinion No. 21* to amortize the difference between the cost of the investment and its maturity value over the life of the bonds. This amortization should follow the effective interest method, which results in a constant rate of return over the life of the investment.[6] Investments in bonds usually are recorded at cost in a single account, that is, the investing company does not use separate accounts to record the face value of the investment and any related discount or premium. Thus, amortization of the difference between cost and maturity value results in a direct adjustment to the Investments account.

AMORTIZATION OF PREMIUM ON BONDS OWNED When a bond reaches maturity, only the face value of $1,000 will be paid by the issuing corporation. The value of a bond purchased at a premium will, therefore, tend to

---

[6] *APB Opinion No. 21,* "Interest on Receivables and Payables," AICPA (New York: 1971), p. 423.

decrease toward par as the maturity date approaches, and the carrying value of the bonds can logically be reduced in each successive year. When a corporation buys bonds at a premium, the effective rate of interest earned on the investment will be less than the contract rate of interest stated on the bonds. The investing company should determine the interest earned each period by applying the effective rate of interest to the carrying value of the investment at the beginning of the period. The difference between the interest revenue determined in this manner and the amount of the semiannual interest payment received is the amount of premium to be amortized. This process is the same as that used by the issuing corporation to determine the effective interest expense and amortization of the premium on the liability.

For example, assume that on July 1, 1978, Standard Corporation purchased $100,000 of 8% bonds of Fox Corporation payable January 1, 1988. Interest is payable July 1 and January 1. The purchase price was $106\frac{1}{2}$ and the broker's commission $500, making a total cost of $107,000. At this price the investor will earn an effective interest rate of approximately 7% ($3\frac{1}{2}$% semiannually). Every semiannual interest payment received may be regarded as consisting of two parts: (1) interest revenue equal to $3\frac{1}{2}$% of the carrying value of the bonds at the beginning of the period, and (2) a recovery of part of the premium. Thus, the $7,000 excess of cost over maturity value is to be written off against the interest received during the 10 years the bonds will be held. The amount of premium amortized each period will be the difference between the interest revenue recognized and the $4,000 cash received. The journal entries to record the purchase of the bonds and the first receipt of interest are:

NOT ON TEST

Investor's entries showing amortization of premium

1978			
Jan. 1	Investment in Bonds	107,000	
	Cash		107,000
	Purchased 100 8% bonds of Fox Corporation at $106\frac{1}{2}$		
	plus commission of $500. Bonds mature Jan. 1, 1988.		
July 1	Cash	4,000	
	Bond Interest Revenue		3,745
	Investment in Bonds		255
	Received semiannual bond interest payment and amortized		
	portion of premium on investment in Fox Corporation		
	bonds.		

The amount of interest revenue recognized in the July 1 entry was determined by multiplying the $107,000 carrying value of the investment by the effective semiannual interest rate of $3\frac{1}{2}$% (.035 × $107,000 = $3,745); the amount of premium amortization is the difference between the $4,000 cash received and the amount of interest revenue recognized. As of July 1, 1978, the carrying value of the investment in bonds has been reduced to $106,745 ($107,000 − $255). Thus, the entries required at year-end are as shown on page 653.

NOT ON TEST

Investor's entries at year-end	**1978**	

Investor's entries at year-end

1978

Dec. 31 Accrued Bond Interest Receivable *4,000*

               Bond Interest Revenue *3,736*

               Investment in Bonds *264*

         To accrue bond interest receivable at year-end and amortize

         portion of premium.

Dec. 31 Bond Interest Revenue *7,481*

               Income Summary *7,481*

         To close Bond Interest Revenue account ($3,745 + $3,736).

The accrued bond interest receivable of $4,000 at December 31 will appear in the balance sheet as a current asset, which will be collected January 1 upon receipt of the bond interest check. The bonds will appear in the Investments section of the balance sheet at $106,481, which represents the cost of $107,000 minus the $519 of premium amortized during the year.

The two essential ideas portrayed by this series of entries may be stated as follows: (1) The carrying value of the bonds is gradually being reduced to par by amortizing the premium; and (2) the net interest earned each year is equal to the interest received minus the amount of premium amortized. Note that the amount of bond interest earned in the second six-month period is less than that earned during the first six months. This is because the interest earned is always a *constant percentage* ($3\frac{1}{2}$% in this example) of the decreasing carrying value of the investment. The carrying value of the investment and the amount of interest earned will continue to decrease over the life of the bonds.

AMORTIZATION OF DISCOUNT ON BONDS OWNED The value of a bond purchased for *less than its face value* will tend to increase to par as the maturity date approaches. Amortization of the discount on an investment in bonds means writing up the carrying value of the bonds each year with an offsetting credit to the Bond Interest Revenue account. The revenue from a bond purchased at a discount and held until maturity is equal to the total of the interest payments received plus the amount of the discount.

When bonds are purchased at a discount, the effective rate of interest earned by the investing company is greater than the contract rate of interest on the bonds. The investor should determine the amount of interest revenue by applying the effective interest rate to the carrying value of the bonds at the beginning of the interest period. The difference between this interest revenue and the amount of the semiannual interest payment received is the amount of discount to be amortized in the period.

As an example of the periodic entries for amortization of discount on bond investments, assume that on January 1, 1978, an investor purchased $200,000 face value 7% bonds of the Bay Corporation payable January 1, 1988. Interest is payable July 1 and January 1. The purchase price was 92¾ and the broker's commission $1,000, making a total cost of $186,500. At this price, the investor will earn an effective interest rate of approximately 8% (4% semiannually).

The journal entries for the first year the bonds are owned will be as follows:

<table>
<tr><td rowspan="4">Investor's
entries
showing
amortization
of discount</td><td colspan="5">1978</td></tr>
<tr><td>Jan.</td><td>1</td><td>Investment in Bonds . . . .</td><td align="right">186,500</td><td></td></tr>
<tr><td></td><td></td><td>Cash . . . .</td><td></td><td align="right">186,500</td></tr>
<tr><td></td><td></td><td>Purchased 200 7% bonds of Bay Corporation at 92¾
plus commission of $1,000. Bonds mature Jan. 1, 1988.</td><td></td><td></td></tr>
</table>

July 1 Cash *7,000*
    Investment in Bonds *460*
       Bond Interest Revenue *7,460*
    To record six months' interest on investment in bonds.
    Computations:
      Interest earned (.04× $186,500) *$7,460*
      Interest payment received *7,000*
    Amortization of discount . . . .   *$ 460*

Dec. 31 Accrued Bond Interest Receivable *7,000*
    Investment in Bonds *478*
       Bond Interest Revenue *7,478*
    To record six months' interest on investment in bonds.
    Computations:
      Interest earned (.04 × $186,960) *$7,478*
      Interest payment accrued *7,000*
    Amortization of discount . . . .   *$ 478*

Dec. 31 Bond Interest Revenue *14,938*
          Income Summary *14,938*
    To close Bond Interest Revenue account ($7,460 + $7,478).

The fact that a bond will be paid at par at a distant maturity date does not ensure that its price will move closer to par during each year of its life; bond prices fluctuate with changes in market rates of interest, business activity, and other elements of the economic environment.

Gains and losses from sale of investments in securities

The sale of an investment in stocks is recorded by debiting Cash for the amount received and crediting the Investment account for the carrying value of the stocks sold. Any difference between the proceeds of the sale and the carrying value of the investment is recorded by a debit to Loss on Sale of Investments or by a credit to Gain on Sale of Investments.

At the date of sale of an investment in bonds, any interest accrued since the last interest payment date should be recognized as interest revenue. For example, assume that 10 bonds of the Elk Corporation carried in the accounts of an investor at $9,600 are sold at a price of 94 and accrued interest of $90. The commission on the sale is $50. The following entry should be made:

Investment in bonds sold at a loss	*Cash*	*9,440*	
	Loss on Sale of Investments	*250*	
	Investment in Bonds		*9,600*
	Bond Interest Revenue		*90*
	Sold 10 bonds of Elk Corporation at 94 and accrued interest of $90		
	less broker's commission of $50.		

How should investors measure their performance?

The return on an investment includes both the periodic cash receipts of interest or dividends and the gain or loss when the investment is sold.

The earnings rate for the periodic dividends or interest received may be computed as a percentage of cost or of current market value. Assume, for example, that an individual investor, Jane Morgan, bought 100 shares of Standard Company stock at $40 a share. The annual dividend was $2.40 a share, and therefore provided a yield of 6% on cost ($240 yearly dividend ÷ $4,000 cost = 6% return on cost). The market price of the stock then rose to $80 without any change in the annual dividend. Although Morgan is still receiving a return of 6% on the cost of her investment ($4,000), the return expressed as a percentage of the present market value of her shares has dropped to 3% (computed as $240 ÷ $8,000). The return based on current market value is more useful as a basis for making investment decisions. Morgan may wish to sell her stock in Standard Company for $8,000 and invest this amount in some other stock which is currently paying dividends at a rate of 6% on its present market value. This would cause her investment income to rise from $240 a year to a higher level of $480, that is, $8,000 × 6%.

KEY TERMS INTRODUCED OR EMPHASIZED IN CHAPTER 18

Amortization of discount or premium on bonds payable The process of systematically writing off a portion of bond discount to increase interest expense or writing off a portion of bond premium to decrease interest expense each period the bonds are outstanding.

Bond A formal certificate (or debt instrument) issued by a corporation to borrow money on a long-term basis.

Bond sinking fund Money set aside by the corporation at regular intervals (usually with a trustee) to be used to pay the bonds at maturity.

Callable bonds May be called in (redeemed) at the option of the issuing corporation at specified prices within specified periods.

Carrying value of bonds The face amount of the bonds plus any unamortized premium or minus any unamortized discount.

Convertible bonds Bonds which can be exchanged for a specified amount of common stock of the issuing corporation at the option of the bondholder.

Coupon bonds Semiannual interest coupons are attached to the bonds, each coupon bearing a different date. Coupons can be detached as they come due and collected through a bank. Also called ***bearer bonds*** because they are transferred by delivery. The holder of the bond is assumed to be the owner.

Debenture bond An unsecured bond, the value of which rests on the general credit of the corporation. Not secured by pledge of specific assets.

Discount on bonds payable Amount by which the face amount of the bond exceeds the price received by the corporation at the date of issuance. Indicates that the contractual rate of interest is lower than the market rate of interest.

Effective interest method of amortization Discount or premium on bonds is amortized by the difference between the contractual cash interest payment each period and the amount of interest computed by applying the effective interest rate to the carrying value of the bonds at the beginning of the current interest period. Causes bond interest expense to be a constant percentage of the carrying value of the liability.

Effective interest rate The actual rate of interest expense to the borrowing corporation, taking into account the contractual cash interest payments and the discount or premium to be amortized.

Leverage The practice of borrowing money at a given rate of interest and using the borrowed money in the business to earn a higher rate of return. This practice enhances the earnings of stockholders. Also known as ***trading on the equity.***

Lower of aggregate cost or market The total cost of marketable securities owned is compared with the market value determined at the balance sheet date. The lower of these two aggregate figures is the amount used to value the asset in the balance sheet. The method presently required by FASB rules for valuation of marketable securities.

Marketable securities A highly liquid type of investment which can be sold at any time without interfering with normal operation of the business. Usually classified as a current asset second only to cash in liquidity.

Premium on bonds payable Amount by which the issuance price of a bond exceeds the face value. Indicates that the contractual rate of interest is higher than the market rate.

Present value concept Based on the time value of money. The basic premise is that a dollar today is worth more than receiving a dollar at some future date. The present value of a future sum is the amount an investor would pay for it today based on an assumed rate of interest. Used in determining bond prices.

Registered bond Name of the owner of a registered bond is registered with the corporation. Interest payments are mailed directly to the bondholder. Transfer of the bond requires endorsement and notification of the issuing corporation.

Secured bonds Secured by a prior claim against specific assets of the issuing corporation in the event interest or principal is not paid as agreed. Also called ***mortgage bonds.***

Serial bonds An issue of bonds that matures in installments rather than at a single maturity date.

Unrealized losses and gains An unrealized loss results from writing down marketable securities to a market value below cost. An unrealized gain results from restoring a former write-down because of a recovery in market price. Securities cannot be written up above aggregate cost. Unrealized losses and gains on marketable securities classified as current assets are included in the determination of the year's net income.

Valuation allowance for marketable securities Used to reduce the carrying value of marketable securities from cost to a market value below cost. Adjusted at each balance sheet date.

REVIEW QUESTIONS

1 Distinguish between the two terms in each of the following pairs:
  a Long-term notes; bonds
  b Mortgage bonds; debenture bonds
  c Fixed-maturity bonds; serial bonds
  d Coupon bonds; registered bonds

2 K Company has decided to finance expansion by issuing $10 million of 20-year debenture bonds and will ask a number of underwriters to bid on the bond issue. Discuss the factors that will determine the amount bid by the underwriters for these bonds.

3 What is a *convertible bond?* Discuss the advantages and disadvantages of convertible bonds from the standpoint of (*a*) the investor and (*b*) the issuing corporation.

4 The Computer Sharing Co. has paid-in capital of $10 million and retained earnings of $3 million. The company has just issued $1 million in 20-year, 8% bonds. It is proposed that a policy be established of appropriating $50,000 of retained earnings each year to enable the company to retire the bonds at maturity. Evaluate the merits of this proposal in accomplishing the desired result.

5 The following excerpt is taken from an article in a leading business periodical: "In the bond market high interest rates mean low prices. Bonds pay out a fixed percentage of their face value, usually $1,000; a 5% bond, for instance, will pay $50 a year. In order for its yield to rise to $6\frac{1}{4}$%, its price would have to drop to $800." Give a critical evaluation of this quotation.

6 A recent annual report of Lear Siegler, Inc., contained the following note accompanying the financial statements: "The loan agreements . . . contain provisions as to working capital requirements and payment of cash dividends. At June 30, retained earnings of approximately $13,400,000 were available for payment of cash dividends." What is the meaning of this note and why is it considered necessary to attach such a note to financial statements? (The total retained earnings of Lear Siegler, Inc., at this date amounted to $77.5 million; working capital amounted to $100 million; and total liabilities amounted to $142 million.)

7 Discuss the advantages and disadvantages of a call provision in a bond contract from the viewpoint of (*a*) the bondholder and (*b*) the issuing corporation.

8 When the effective interest method is used to amortize bond discount or premium, the amount of bond interest expense will differ in each period from that of the preceding period. Explain how the amount of bond interest expense changes from one period to another when the bonds are issued (*a*) at a discount and (*b*) at a premium.

9 Can a company owning an investment in listed corporate bonds with a maturity date 10 years in the future properly classify these marketable securities as current assets? Explain.

10 Writing down securities to market value when market is below cost, but refusing to write up securities to market prices above cost, is inconsistent procedure. What arguments may be given in favor of this treatment?

11 "To substitute present market value for cost as a basis for valuing marketable securities would represent a departure from traditional accounting practice." Discuss the case for and against using market value consistently as the basis of valuation in accounting for marketable securities.

12 If an investor buys a bond between interest dates he or she pays, as a part of the purchase price, the accrued interest since the last interest date. On the other hand, if the investor buys a share of common or preferred stock, no "accrued dividend" is added to the quoted price. Explain why this difference exists.

13 John Lee buys a $1,000, 8% bond for 106, five years from the maturity date. After holding the bond for four years, he sells it for 102. Lee claims that he has a loss of $40 on the sale. A friend argues that Lee has made a gain on the sale. Explain the difference in viewpoint. With whom do you agree? Why?

14 *Statement on Financial Accounting Standards No. 12,* issued by the FASB, requires that marketable securities classified as current assets be valued at the lower of aggregate cost or market. What effect, if any, does this practice have upon the determination of net income?

15 How does the financial reporting requirement of valuing marketable securities at the lower of aggregate cost or market value compare with income tax rules concerning marketable securities?

EXERCISES

Ex. 18-1 On December 31, Year 10, Wayne Corporation received authorization to issue $15,000,000 of 10%, 30-year debenture bonds. Interest payment dates were June 30 and December 31. The bonds were all issued at par on January 31, Year 11, one month after the interest date printed on the bonds.

Instructions
a Prepare the journal entry at January 31, Year 11, to record the sale of the bonds.
b Prepare the journal entry at June 30, Year 11, to record the semiannual bond interest payment.

Ex. 18-2 Basin Corporation has issued $1,000,000 of 10-year, 7% bonds payable on the date printed on the bonds and has received proceeds of $932,050. Interest is payable semiannually. The effective interest method is to be used to amortize the bond discount.

Instructions
a Prepare a journal entry to record the issuance of the bonds.
b Prepare a journal entry to record the payment of interest and amortization of discount at the first semiannual interest payment date. (See the amortization table for bonds sold at a discount on page 637.) Round the interest expense for the period to the nearest $10.
c Prepare a journal entry to record the payment of interest and amortization of discount at the end of the fifth six-month interest period. (See table as in **b**.) Round interest expense for the period to the nearest $10.

Ex. 18-3 Crown Point Corporation issued $1,000,000 of 10-year, 7% bonds payable with interest payable semiannually and received proceeds of $1,074,430. The premium is to be amortized by the effective interest method.

Instructions
a Show how the liability for the bonds would appear on a balance sheet prepared immediately after issuance of the bonds.
b Show how the liability for the bonds would appear on a balance sheet prepared after 16 semiannual interest periods (two years prior to maturity). Refer to the amortization table for bonds sold at a premium on page 640. Round unamortized premium to the nearest $10.
c If these 7% bonds were sold by Crown Point Corporation to yield 6% and interest is paid semiannually, show the necessary *calculations* to determine: interest expense by the effective interest method for the first six-month period, the premium amortized at the end of that first period, and the cash interest

payment. Your calculations should include use of the effective interest rate and also the contractual rate.

Ex. 18-4 Brand Corporation issued $1,000,000 of 7%, 10-year convertible bonds dated December 31, Year 8, at a price of 98. Semiannual interest payment dates were June 30 and December 31. The conversion rate was 20 shares of $10 par common stock for each $1,000 bond. Four years later on December 31, Year 12, bond-holders converted $250,000 face value of bonds into common stock. Assume that unamortized discount on this date amounted to $12,000 for the entire bond issue. Prepare a journal entry to record the conversion of the bonds.

Ex. 18-5 Yamato Company purchased as a short-term investment $10,000 face value of the 9% bonds of Lorenzo, Inc., on March 31 of the current year, at a total cost of $10,125, including interest accrued since January 1. Interest is paid by Lorenzo, Inc., on June 30 and December 31. On July 31, four months after the purchase, Yamato Company sold the bonds and interest accrued since July 1 for a total price of $10,105.

Prepare all entries required in the accounting records of Yamato Company relating to the investment in Lorenzo, Inc., bonds. (Commissions are to be ignored.)

Ex. 18-6 Companies A and B have the same amount of operating income, but different capital structures. Determine the amount earned per share of common stock for each of the two companies and explain the source of any difference.

	Company A	Company B
5% debenture bonds payable	$500,000	$ 200,000
6% cumulative preferred stock, $100 par	500,000	300,000
Common stock, $50 par value	500,000	1,000,000
Retained earnings	250,000	250,000
Operating income, before interest and income taxes		
(assume a 40% tax rate)	300,000	300,000

PROBLEMS

Group A

18A-1 Birch Corporation obtained all necessary approvals to issue $10,000,000 face value of 9%, 10-year bonds, dated December 31, Year 4. Interest payment dates were June 30 and December 31. The bonds were not issued, however, until four months later, May 1, Year 5. On this date the entire issue was sold at a price of 100 plus accrued interest.

Instructions Prepare journal entries in general form on:
_a_ May 1, Year 5, to record the issuance of the bonds.
_b_ June 30, Year 5, to record the first semiannual interest payment on the bond issue.
_c_ December 31, Year 5, to record the semiannual bond interest payment and to close the Bond Interest Expense account at year-end.

18A-2 Marlin Corporation maintains its accounts on a calendar-year basis. On June 30, 1978, the company issued $6,000,000 face value of 7.6% bonds at a price of $97\frac{1}{4}$, resulting in an effective rate of interest of 8%. Semiannual interest payment dates are June 30 and December 31. The bonds mature on June 30, 1988.

Instructions
_a_ Prepare the required journal entries (with explanations) on:
(_1_) June 30, 1978, to record the sale of the bonds.

(2) December 31, 1978, to pay interest and amortize the discount.

(3) June 30, 1988, to pay interest, amortize the discount, and retire the bonds. As of the beginning of this last interest period, the carrying value of the bonds is $5,988,461. (Use a separate journal entry to show the retirement of the bonds.)

b Explain how the accounts, Bonds Payable and Discount on Bonds Payable, should appear on the balance sheet at December 31, 1978.

18A-3 Roan Antelope, Inc., on September 1, Year 1, issued $9,000,000 par value, $8\frac{1}{2}$%, 10-year bonds payable with interest dates of March 1 and September 1. The company maintains its accounts on a calendar-year basis and follows the policy of amortizing bond discount and bond premium by the effective interest method at the semiannual interest payment dates as well as at the year-end adjusting of the accounts.

Instructions

a Prepare the necessary journal entries to record the following transactions, assuming that the bonds were sold for $8,700,000, a price resulting in an effective annual interest rate of 9%.

(1) Sale of the bonds on September 1, Year 1.

(2) Adjustment of the accounts at December 31, Year 1, for accrued interest and amortization of discount.

(3) Payment of bond interest and amortization of discount on March 1, Year 2.

b Assume that the sales price of the bonds on September 1, Year 1 had been $9,300,000, resulting in an effective annual interest rate of 8%. Prepare journal entries parallel to those called for in **a** above at the dates of September 1, Year 1; December 31, Year 1; and March 1, Year 2.

c State the amounts of bond interest expense for Year 1 and the **net** amount of the liability for the bonds payable at December 31, Year 1, under the independent assumptions set forth in both **a** and **b** above. Show your computations.

18A-4 On December 31, Year 4, Rawlins Corporation sold an $8,000,000, $9\frac{1}{2}$%, 12-year bond issue to an underwriter at a price of $103\frac{1}{4}$. This price results in an effective annual interest rate of 9%. The bonds were dated December 31, Year 4, and the interest payment dates were June 30 and December 31. Rawlins Corporation follows a policy of amortizing the bond premium by the effective interest method at each semiannual payment date.

Instructions

a Prepare an amortization table for the first two years (four interest periods) of the life of this bond issue. Round all amounts to the nearest dollar and use the following column headings:

Six-Month Interest Period	(A) Interest Paid Semi-annually ($8,000,000 × 4¾%)	(B) Effective Semi-annual Interest Expense (carrying value × 4½%)	(C) Premium Amortization (A − B)	(D) Bond Premium Balance	(E) Carrying Value of Bonds, End of Period ($8,000,000 + D)

b Using the information in your amortization table, prepare all journal entries necessary to record the bond issue and the bond interest expense during Year 5.

c Show the proper balance sheet presentation of the liability for bonds payable at December 31, Year 6.

18A-5 John Rider made an investment by purchasing $800,000 of 7%, 10-year bonds at 94. The bonds mature eight years from the date of purchase. Rider sold the bonds for 95 four years after the date of purchase. (Assume no commissions are involved.)

Instructions

a Assume that at the time of purchase Rider had no intention of holding the bonds to maturity and did not amortize the discount. You are to compute the total interest earned during the four-year period he owned the bonds, the gain or loss on disposal, and the total revenue derived from the investment including the gain or loss on sale of the bonds.

b Assume that at the time of purchase Rider intended to hold the bonds until maturity and followed a policy of amortizing the discount. When the bonds were sold, the investment had a carrying value in Rider's accounting records of $774,000. You are to compute the total interest revenue recorded during the four-year period of actual ownership, the gain or loss on disposal, and the total revenue (including the gain or loss) derived from the investment over the four-year period.

c Will the amortization of discount or premium on an investment in bonds always give an individual investor a more realistic and useful measure of the annual results achieved on the investment? Explain.

18A-6 Carson Jones, a substantial investor in marketable securities, purchased 2,000 shares of Davis Products common stock for $36 a share plus a broker's commission of $800 on February 28. During the year the following events occurred relating to this investment.

Mar. 15 Davis Products paid a cash dividend of 50 cents per share which had been declared on February 20 payable on March 15 to stockholders of record on March 6.

May 31 Davis Products distributed a 20% stock dividend.

Nov. 15 Davis Products distributed additional shares as the result of a 2 for 1 stock split.

Dec. 10 Davis Products paid a cash dividend of 25 cents per share. Dividend was declared November 20 payable December 10 to stockholders of record on November 30.

Dec. 10 Carson Jones sold 1,200 shares of his Davis Products stock to a friend at $21 per share. No commission was involved.

Instructions Prepare the journal entries to be made in the accounting records of Carson Jones. Include memorandum entries when appropriate even though dollar amounts are not involved. For journal entries involving computations, the explanation portion of the entry should include the computation.

18A-7 The following securities were owned by Lisa Manning, an investor, throughout the current year.

960 shares of North Star $4.50 convertible preferred stock, $1 par value. Purchased for $108,000, market price at end of current year 130½. Received regular dividends on March 1 and September 1 of current year.

1,200 shares of Pomona Corporation common stock, cost $98 per share, market value at December 31, $192,000. Received dividends of $3.10 per share on March 1, 10% stock dividend on June 1, and $2.50 per share on December 31 of current year.

$60,000 face value of 8% Mark Corporation bonds. Purchased for $61,800; market price at end of current year, 101¾. Received two regular semiannual interest payments during current year.

$24,000 face value of 6% Columbia Corporation bonds. Purchased for $22,128, market price on December 31, 94½. Received two regular semiannual interest payments during the current year.

Instructions

a Prepare a schedule showing the amount received by Manning during the current year on each of these investments and this amount stated as a percentage of cost and as a percentage of market value at the end of the year.

(Round to the nearest tenth of a percent.) Manning does not amortize premium or discount on investments in bonds. The schedule should be in columnar form with the following column headings:

Name of Security	Original Cost	End-of-Year Market Value	Income Received This Year	Rate Earned on Cost, %	Rate Earned on Market Value, %

b In a discussion with a business associate, Manning commented on her average rate of return for the year on the total cost of her investments. Her friend replied that the rate earned on market value was a better measure of earning perform-ance. Discuss the merits of the rate earned on cost and the rate earned on market value as measures of investment performance.

Group B

18B-1 A bond issue of $12,000,000 in 8%, 20-year bonds was authorized by Bayview Company on December 31, Year 9. The semiannual interest payment dates were June 30 and December 31. Issuance of the bonds did not take place until March 1, Year 10. On this date all the bonds were sold at a price of 100 plus accrued interest.

Instructions
a Prepare entries in general journal form on the following dates:
(1) March 1, Year 10, to record the issuance of the bonds.
(2) June 30, Year 10, to record the first semiannual interest payment on the bond issue.
(3) December 31, Year 10, to record the semiannual bond interest payment and also to close the Bond Interest Expense account.
b Assume that you had purchased 12 of Bayview Company's bonds on March 1, Year 10, at par plus accrued interest. Compute the amount of interest earned on your investment for the year ended December 31, Year 10.

18B-2 On June 30, 1978, King Cotton Company issued $4,800,000 par value of $7\frac{1}{2}$% bonds payable at a price of $103\frac{1}{2}$, resulting in an effective annual rate of interest of 7%. The semiannual interest payment dates are June 30 and December 31, and the company maintains its accounts on a calendar-year basis. The maturity date of the bonds is June 30, 1988.

Instructions
a Prepare the required journal entries (with explanations) on:
(1) June 30, 1978, to record the sale of the bonds.
(2) December 31, 1978, for payment of interest and amortization of premium on bonds. (Use one compound entry.)
(3) June 30, 1988, for payment of interest, amortization of the remaining premium, and to retire the bonds. As of the beginning of this last six-month interest period, the carrying value of the bonds is $4,811,594.
b Show how the accounts, Bonds Payable and Premium on Bonds Payable, would appear on the balance sheet at December 31, 1978.

18B-3 On November 1, 1978, Landers Company issued $11,900,000 face value of $8\frac{1}{2}$% 10-year bonds with interest dates of May 1 and November 1. The bonds were purchased by an underwriter for $11,500,000, resulting in an effective interest rate to Landers Company of 9%. Company policy calls for amortizing bond discount at each interest payment date as well as for year-end adjustment of the accounts. The accounting records are maintained on a calendar-year basis.

Instructions
a Prepare the journal entries required to:
(1) Record the sale of the bonds on November 1, 1978.

(2) Adjust the accounts at December 31, 1978, for accrued bond interest and amortization of discount. (Use one compound entry.)

(3) Record the semiannual payment of bond interest on May 1, 1979, and amortize the bond discount. (Use one compound entry.)

b State the amounts to be reported on the financial statements at the end of 1978 for:

(1) Bonds payable (face amount)

(2) Unamortized discount on bonds payable

(3) Net amount of liability for bonds payable

(4) Interest expense for 1978

18B-4 On December 31, 1978, Apache Corporation sold a $4,000,000 face value, 6%, 12-year bond issue to an underwriter at a price of 92. This price results in an effective annual interest rate of 7%. Interest is payable semiannually on June 30 and December 31.

Instructions

a Prepare an amortization table for the first two years (four interest periods) of this bond issue. Round all amounts to the nearest dollar and use the following column headings for your table:

(A) Six-Month Interest Period	(B) Interest Paid Semi- annually ($4,000,000 × 3%)	(C) Effective Semi- annual Interest Expense (carrying value × 3½%)	(D) Discount Amortization (B − A)	(E) Bond Discount Balance	Carrying Value of Bonds, End of Period ($4,000,000 − D)

b Using the information from your amortization table, prepare all journal entries necessary to record issuance of the bonds and bond interest for the year 1979. (Use a compound entry for interest payment and amortization of bond discount at each semiannual interest payment date.)

c Show the proper balance sheet presentation of Bonds Payable and Discount on Bonds Payable at December 31, 1980.

18B-5 Marie De Graf invested in $420,000 face value of 9%, 10-year bonds at a price of 95. The investment was made at the date of original issuance of the bonds and consequently neither accrued interest nor a broker's commission was involved. Shortly after this transaction, the market price of the bonds dropped to 90. After holding the bonds exactly six years, De Graf sold them at a price of 102. The broker's commission charged was $1,500. There was no accrued interest at the date of sale because the sale occurred immediately after receipt of the semiannual interest payment.

Instructions

a Assume that De Graf at the date of purchase had no intention of holding the bonds to maturity and did not amortize the discount. Determine the total interest earned during the six-year period and the gain or loss on disposal.

b Assume that De Graf did intend to hold the bonds until maturity and did amortize the discount. When De Graf sold the bonds six years later, her carrying value for the investment was $411,600. Determine the total interest earned during the six-year period and the gain or loss on disposal.

c What is the most probable reason for the price of the bonds being above their face value at the date De Graf disposed of them? Would amortization of discount on the bonds have produced a more realistic measurement of yearly income in this case? Explain.

18B-6 On March 31, Ruth Windsor purchased 1,000 shares of Torch Company common stock at $63 per share plus broker's commission of $300. The company had declared a cash dividend of 60 cents per share on March 18, payable on April 18 to stockholders of record on April 7.

On June 30 the company distributed a 20% stock dividend. On December 1, the shares were split 2 for 1 and the additional shares distributed to stockholders. On December 5, a cash dividend of 50 cents per share was declared, payable on December 30 to stockholders of record on December 20. Windsor sold 600 shares of the stock at $40 a share on December 31. Commission charges on the sale amounted to $250.

Instructions Prepare journal entries to record the above events in Windsor's accounts. Include memorandum entries when appropriate, even though ledger accounts are not affected. For journal entries involving computations, the explanation portion of the entry should include the computations.

18B-7 June Jensen owned the following investments in marketable securities throughout the current year. She does not amortize discounts and premiums on bonds owned.

$140,000 in 10% Melton Corporation bonds, due four years and two months from date of purchase. Purchased at cost of $143,500, market value at end of current year, $142,500. Received two regular semiannual interest payments during current year.

$84,000 in 6% Chapel City bonds maturing eight years from date of purchase. Purchased for $78,568, market price on December 31 of current year, $94\frac{1}{2}$. Received regular semiannual interest payments during year.

2,240 shares of Webber Corporation $6 convertible preferred stock, $100 par value. Purchased for $223,720, market price at end of current year $102\frac{3}{8}$ per share. (Market prices are customarily stated in eighths of a dollar. The fraction $\frac{3}{8}$ is expressed as .375 for purposes of computation.) Received regular dividends on March 1 and September 1 of current year.

1,400 shares of Lee Corporation common stock: cost $170 per share, market price at December 31, $290 per share. Received dividends of $5 per share on March 1, a 10% stock dividend on June 1, and $4 per share in cash on December 31 of current year.

Instructions
a Prepare a schedule showing the amount earned during the current year on each of these investments and the rate of return as a percentage of cost and of market value at the end of the year. Calculate the rate of return to the nearest hundredth of a percent. This schedule may be in columnar form with the following column headings:

Name of Security	Original Cost	Year-end Market Value	Earnings This Year	Rate Earned on Cost, %	Rate Earned on Market Value, %

b In a discussion with a business associate, Jensen commented on her average return for the year on the total cost of her investment. Her friend replied that return on market value was a better measure of earning performance. Discuss the merits of the percentage earned on cost and the percentage earned on market value as measures of investment success.

BUSINESS DECISION PROBLEM 18

Tide Corporation reported the balances given below at the end of the current year:

Total assets	$14,800,000
Current liabilities	3,600,000
Long-term liabilities	400,000

Stockholders' equity:

Capital stock, $10 par value	$4,000,000
Paid-in capital in excess of par	3,000,000
Retained earnings	3,800,000

The company is planning an expansion of its plant facilities, and a study shows that $12 million of new funds will be required to finance the expansion. Two proposals are under consideration:

Stock Financing   Issue 200,000 shares of capital stock at a price of $60 per share.

Bond Financing   Borrow $12 million on a 20-year bond issue, with interest at 7%.

The assets and liabilities of Tide Corporation have remained relatively constant over the past five years, and during this period the earnings *after* income taxes have averaged 10% of the stockholders' equity as reported at the end of the current year. The company expects that its earnings *before* income taxes will increase by an amount equal to 12% of the new investment in plant facilities.

Past and future income taxes for the company may be estimated at 40% of income before income taxes.

Instructions
a Prove that the company's average income before income taxes during the past five years was $1,800,000.
b Prepare a schedule showing the expected earnings per share of capital stock during the first year of operations following the completion of the $12 million expansion, under each of the two proposed means of financing.
c Evaluate the two proposed means of financing from the viewpoint of a major stockholder of Tide Corporation.

Corporations: Consolidated Financial Statements

Since corporations are usually granted the power to hold title to any form of property, one corporation may own shares of stock in another. When one corporation **controls** another corporation through the ownership of a majority of its capital stock, the controlling corporation is called a **parent** company, and the company whose stock is owned is called a **subsidiary** company. Because both the parent and subsidiary companies are legal entities, separate financial statements are prepared for each company. However, it may also be useful to prepare financial statements for the **affiliated** companies (the parent company and its subsidiaries) as if they were a single unified business. Such statements are called **consolidated financial statements.**

In a **consolidated balance sheet,** the assets of the affiliated companies are combined and reported as though only a single entity existed. For example, the amount shown as Cash on a consolidated balance sheet is the total of the cash owned by all the affiliated companies. Liabilities of the various companies are also combined. Similarly, in a **consolidated income statement,** the revenue and expenses of the affiliated companies are combined, on the assumption that the results of operations for a single economic entity are being measured.

Although we tend to think of Sears or Texaco or General Motors or IBM as single companies, each of these organizations is really a group of affiliated corporations. Each such business presents consolidated financial statements in its annual report to shareholders. However, since the parent company in each case controls its subsidiaries, it is logical for us to consider an affiliated group such as IBM as one economic entity.

There are a number of economic, financial, legal, and tax advantages which encourage large business organizations to operate through subsidiaries rather than through a single business entity. As a result corporate affiliations are common in the United States. Almost all the companies whose stock is listed on the New York Stock Exchange and the American Stock Exchange have one or more subsidiaries and include **consolidated** financial statements in their annual reports. Thus anyone using published financial statements to make business decisions will find it useful to know something about the basic principles used in preparing consolidated financial statements for the parent company and its subsidiaries.

Nature of business combinations

There are several ways in which a corporation can acquire or control another corporation. Two or more corporations may, for example, transfer their assets and liabilities to a newly organized corporation and conduct business as a new single unit; this type of transaction is called a **consolidation.** In other cases, one corporation may buy all the stock of another corporation; the parent company can then control the operations of the subsidiary. If the parent company wishes, it can liquidate the subsidiary and simply take over its assets and liabilities. The capital stock of the subsidiary would be canceled and the combined resources of the two companies would then be operated as a single legal and economic entity; this type of transaction is called a **merger.** Mergers and consolidations are frequently referred to as **business combinations.**

If a parent company acquires less than 100% of the stock in a subsidiary, the subsidiary must be maintained as a separate legal entity unless outside stockholders in the subsidiary are willing to sell their stock to the parent company. This form of business combination is also called a merger.

When subsidiaries are operated as separate legal entities, each subsidiary keeps a set of accounting records and prepares separate financial statements. However the parent company and its subsidiaries are in effect an integrated business unit controlled by the board of directors of the parent company, and consolidated statements are needed for such a unit. Only consolidated financial statements can give a fair presentation of the overall financial position and results of operations of a group of affiliated companies.

An ownership of a majority of the voting shares in a subsidiary gives the parent company a **controlling** interest in the subsidiary's net assets. If the parent company owns less than 100% of the subsidiary's stock, outside stockholders will own a **minority interest** in the subsidiary's net assets. For example, if a parent owns 80% of the stock in a subsidiary, the minority interest will be 20%. This relationship is illustrated below:

Note the
key role of
board of
directors of
parent

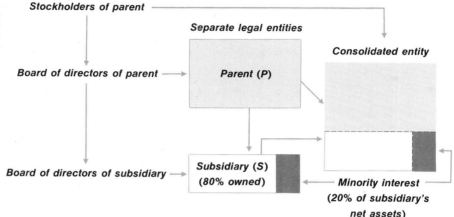

The stockholders of the parent (P) company elect the board of directors of P, who in turn appoint the corporate officers of P. The officers of P manage and control all assets owned by P. Included in P's assets is 80% of the capital stock of the subsidiary (S). Therefore when the time comes to vote these shares, officers of P can determine how these votes should be cast and can elect the board of directors of S. Through the board of directors of S, the parent company controls the resources and actions of S. In effect, P and S are operating under the unified control of the board of directors of the parent company, control which is exercised through stock ownership.

Consolidation at date of acquisition

A consolidated balance sheet is prepared by combining the accounts that appear in the separate balance sheets of the parent and subsidiary companies. In the combining process, certain adjustments are made to eliminate the duplication of accounts and to reflect the assets, liabilities, and stockholders' equity from the viewpoint of a *single economic entity.*

To illustrate the process of consolidation, we shall start with a very simple case involving P Company. A highly condensed balance sheet for P Company at the beginning of Year 1 is given below:

P COMPANY
Balance Sheet
At Beginning of Year 1

*Balance
sheet for P
Company*

Cash	$200,000	Liabilities	$150,000
Other assets	300,000	Capital stock, $5 par value .	300,000
		Retained earnings	50,000
	$500,000		$500,000

At this time, P Company organizes a fully owned subsidiary, S Company, which issues all its capital stock (12,000 shares, with a par value of $10 per share) to P Company for $120,000 in cash. The journal entries to record this transaction for each company are:

	P Company's Records		S Company's Records

S Company issues stock to P Company

P Company's Records

Investment in		
S Company	120,000	
Cash		120,000
Acquired 12,000		
shares of stock issued		
by S Company.		

S Company's Records

Cash	120,000	
Capital Stock .		120,000
Sold 12,000 shares		
of stock to		
P Company.		

This transaction has not changed the total assets of P Company; cash in the amount of $120,000 has simply been replaced by the investment in S Company. The cash invested in S Company, however, is now legally owned by S Company. Since S Company is 100% owned by P Company, we can conclude that the amount of economic resources controlled by P Company has not changed. If we combine the balance sheets of the two companies at the beginning of Year 1 into a single balance sheet, we would expect that the resulting consolidated balance sheet would be identical to the balance sheet of P Company before the investment in S Company was made. A set of working papers is often helpful in visualizing the "consolidating" process:

P AND S COMPANIES
Working Papers—Consolidated Balance Sheet
At Beginning of Year 1 (Date of Acquisition)

	P Company	S Company	Intercompany Eliminations Debit	Intercompany Eliminations Credit	Consolidated Balance Sheet
Cash	80,000	120,000			200,000
Other assets	300,000				300,000
Investment in S Company	120,000			(1) 120,000	
Totals	500,000	120,000			500,000
Liabilities	150,000				150,000
Capital stock—P Company	300,000				300,000
Capital stock—S Company		120,000	(1) 120,000		
Retained earnings—					
P Company	50,000				50,000
Totals	500,000	120,000	120,000	120,000	500,000

Explanation of elimination:
(1) To eliminate the Investment in S Company account against the subsidiary's Capital Stock account. These are reciprocal accounts without significance when the two companies are viewed as a single economic entity. This elimination entry appears only in the working papers; it is not recorded in the accounts of either the parent or the subsidiary.

Note that the Consolidated Balance Sheet column shows the same amounts found in the separate balance sheet of P Company before it organized S Company as a 100%-owned subsidiary. One of the important points to keep in mind at this stage of our discussion is that *the stockholders' equity of the parent company is also the stockholders' equity which appears in the consolidated balance sheet.*

The Investment in S Company and the Capital Stock of S Company are eliminated because these accounts were set up by transferring cash of $120,000 from P Company to S Company, which is fully owned by P Company. To include both of these accounts (the Investment in S Company, $120,000, and S Company's Cash, $120,000) in the consolidated balance sheet would mean that the same asset would be included twice. Similarly, there would be a double counting of stockholders' equity. From the consolidated viewpoint, the $120,000 capital stock of S Company is already included in the stockholders' equity of P Company because P Company's stockholders own 100% of P Company's assets, which include the shares of S Company. By eliminating the investment account in the books of P Company against the Capital Stock account of S Company, *we have a consolidated statement of assets, liabilities, and stockholders' equity* as shown below:

P AND S COMPANIES

Consolidated Balance Sheet

At Beginning of Year 1 (Date of Acquisition)

This is the	Cash	$200,000	Liabilities	$150,000
same as the	Other assets	300,000	Capital stock, $5 par value .	300,000
separate			Retained earnings	50,000
balance				
sheet for P		$500,000		$500,000
Company				
shown on				
page 668				

Consolidation after date of acquisition

If the parent company and a 100%-owned subsidiary operate profitably after affiliation, the stockholders' equity (net assets) of both companies will increase. The parent company carries its investment in the subsidiary on the *equity method.* Under the equity method, the earnings of the subsidiary are debited to the Investment in S Company account and credited to the earnings of the parent; cash dividends received from the subsidiary are recorded by a debit to Cash and a credit to the Investment in S Company account. A loss reported by a subsidiary is recorded by the parent as a reduction in earnings and a credit to the Investment in S Company account.

To illustrate this procedure, let us assume that P Company and S Company, discussed in the preceding section, reported net income and paid cash dividends for Year 1 as follows:

		P Company	*S Company*

<table>
<tr><td>**Net income
and cash
dividends
for Year 1**</td><td>*Net income (P's net income does not
include any earnings of S Company)* ....
Cash dividends paid. ....</td><td>$60,000

None</td><td>$20,000

5,000</td></tr>
</table>

For the sake of simplicity, let us assume that the net income for each company results in an increase in Other Assets and in the Retained Earnings accounts. Using the equity method, the entries to record the activities for Year 1 in the accounts of each company would be:

	Events	*P Company's Records*		*S Company's Records*	

**Recording
changes in
net assets
for both
companies
for Year 1**
	*Net income
	reported by
	P Co.*
		Other Assets . . . 60,000
		  Retained
		    Earnings . . . .
			
			60,000
				None	

	*Net income
	reported by
	S Co.*
		Investment in
		  S Co 20,000
		  Retained
		    Earnings . . . .
			
			20,000
				Other Assets . 20,000
				  Retained
				    Earnings . .
					
					20,000

	*Dividends
	paid by
	S Co.*
		Cash 5,000
		  Investment in
		    S Co. . . . . . .
			
			5,000
				Retained
				  Earnings 5,000
				  Cash . . . . .
					
					5,000

When these entries are combined with the information appearing on the separate balance sheets for each company at the date of acquisition, we have the balance sheets for each company as shown in the first two columns of the working papers shown on page 672. For example, P Company's cash balance of $85,000 now consists of the beginning balance on its separate balance sheet, $80,000, plus dividends received from S Company, $5,000; the Investment in S Company, $135,000, now consists of the beginning balance, $120,000, plus the earnings of S Company for Year 1 not distributed in the form of cash dividends, $15,000 ($20,000 − $5,000). These working papers also show the elimination entry required to arrive at the consolidated balance sheet figures shown in the last column.

In preparing a consolidated balance sheet after the date of acquisition, the assets (other than the Investment in S Company account) and the liabilities of the parent and subsidiary *at statement date* are combined and the investment account is eliminated against the stockholders' equity of S Company. Since the parent company has already recorded the net income and dividends of the subsidiary in the Investment in S Company account, this account increased by $15,000 during the year (net income of the subsidiary, $20,000, less dividends paid by the subsidiary, $5,000), an amount equal to the total increase in the stockholders' equity of S Company. In other words, the balance in the Investment in S Company account, $135,000, is equal to the total stockholders' equity of S Company

P AND S COMPANIES

Working Papers—Consolidated Balance Sheet

At End of Year 1 (One Year after Acquisition)

	P Company	S Company	Intercompany Eliminations Debit	Intercompany Eliminations Credit	Consolidated Balance Sheet
Cash	85,000	115,000			200,000
Other assets	360,000	20,000			380,000
Investment in S Company .	135,000			(1) 135,000	
Totals	580,000	135,000			580,000
Liabilities	150,000				150,000
Capital stock—P Company .	300,000				300,000
Capital stock—S Company .		120,000	(1) 120,000		
Retained earnings—					
P Company	130,000				130,000
Retained earnings—					
S Company		15,000	(1) 15,000		
Totals	580,000	135,000	135,000	135,000	580,000

Explanation of elimination:
(1) To eliminate the investment in S Company against the subsidiary's stockholders' equity accounts one year after acquisition of 100% of S Company's capital stock by P Company.

consisting of capital stock, $120,000, and retained earnings, $15,000. After these "reciprocal" balances are eliminated, the remaining accounts are extended to the Consolidated Balance Sheet column and are used to prepare a formal balance sheet for the two affiliated companies. Note that the consolidated stockholders' equity consists of P Company's capital stock, $300,000, and P Company's retained earnings, $130,000, as adjusted for P Company's share of S Company's earnings for Year 1.

Less than 100% ownership in subsidiary

If a parent company owns a controlling interest in a subsidiary but less than 100% of the outstanding shares, a new kind of ownership equity known as the *minority interest* will appear in the consolidated balance sheet. The consolidated balance sheet will include all the assets and liabilities of the affiliated companies (other than the parent's investment in subsidiary, which is eliminated). Only a portion of the ownership equity in these net assets is represented by the equity of the parent company stockholders because some of the equity interest in the subsidiary's net assets is held by the minority stockholders of the subsidiary. We might conceivably prepare a consolidated balance sheet which included only the parent company's share of the assets of the subsidiary. A more complete and useful financial picture of the consolidated entity results, however, if we include all the subsidiary's assets and allocate the ownership equity in these assets between the controlling and minority interests.

To illustrate, assume that at the end of Year 4 the Park Company **purchased** 75% of the outstanding capital stock of Sims Company for $150,000 in cash, **an amount equal to the book value of the stock acquired.** The working papers to prepare a consolidated balance sheet on the date that control of Sims Company is acquired appear on page 674.

In the eliminating entry on the working papers, the stockholders' equity of Sims Company (capital stock, $125,000, and retained earnings, $75,000) is eliminated. Of this stockholders' equity, $50,000 (25% of $200,000) is shown as **minority interest,** and the remaining 75% is offset against the $150,000 Investment in Sims Company account which appears in Park Company's accounts.

On the consolidated balance sheet for Park and Sims Companies, the minority interest appears in the stockholders' equity section as illustrated below:

PARK AND SIMS COMPANIES

Consolidated Balance Sheet

At End of Year 4 (Date of Acquisition)

Minority	Cash	$250,000	Liabilities		$310,000
interest: an	Other assets	710,000	Stockholders' equity:		
element of			Minority interest . .	$ 50,000	
stockhold-			Capital stock	500,000	
ers' equity			Retained earnings .	100,000	650,000
		$960,000			$960,000

The consolidated stockholders' equity consists of two elements, the minority interest and the controlling interest: The minority interest amounts to $50,000 (25% of the $200,000 total stockholders' equity in Sims Company) and represents the equity in consolidated net assets held by the stockholders of Sims Company; the controlling interest of $600,000 is owned by the stockholders of Park Company and is represented by Park Company's capital stock, $500,000, and retained earnings, $100,000. In practice, minority interest is frequently reported between liabilities and stockholders' equity, on the questionable premise that it represents claims by "outsiders" against consolidated net assets. Once we assume that the parent and subsidiary are a single entity, the minority interest is as much an ownership claim against consolidated net assets as is the equity of the controlling group.

Acquisition of subsidiary stock at more (or less) than book value

When a parent corporation purchases a controlling interest in a subsidiary it will probably pay a price for the shares that differs from their underlying book value. In consolidating the financial statements of two affiliated corporations, we cannot ignore a discrepancy between the cost

PARK AND SIMS COMPANIES
Working Papers—Consolidated Balance Sheet
At End of Year 4 (Date of Acquisition)

	Park Company	Sims Company	Intercompany Eliminations Debit	Intercompany Eliminations Credit	Consolidated Balance Sheet
Cash	200,000	50,000			250,000
Other assets	500,000	210,000			710,000
Investment in Sims Company	150,000			(1) 150,000	
Totals	850,000	260,000			960,000
Liabilities	250,000	60,000			310,000
Capital stock—Park Company	500,000				500,000
Capital stock—Sims Company		125,000	(1) 125,000		
Retained earnings—Park Company	100,000				100,000
Retained earnings—Sims Company		75,000	(1) 75,000		
Minority interest (25% of $200,000)				(1) 50,000	50,000
Totals	850,000	260,000	200,000	200,000	960,000

Explanation of elimination:
(1) To eliminate Park Company's investment in Sims Company's stockholders' equity, and to establish the 25% minority interest in Sims Company (25% of total stockholders' equity of Sims Company)

of the parent company's investment in subsidiary shares and the book value of these shares on the statements of the subsidiary company. In consolidation, the parent's investment is offset against the appropriate stockholders' equity accounts of the subsidiary, and if the two amounts are not equal, we must determine what the difference between them represents.

To illustrate, suppose that at the end of the current year, C Company purchased *all* the outstanding shares of D Company for $120,000. At the date of acquisition, D Company reported on its balance sheet total stockholders' equity of $95,000, consisting of capital stock of $50,000 and retained earnings of $45,000. In preparing the elimination entry on the working papers for a consolidated balance sheet at the date of acquisition, we must determine what to do with the $25,000 discrepancy between the price paid, $120,000, and the stockholders' equity of D Company, $95,000.

If we ask ourselves why C Company paid $120,000 for the stock of D Company, the answer must be that the management of C Company considered the net assets of D Company to be worth $120,000 rather than their book value of $95,000. C's management may believe that the fair market value of certain specific assets of D Company is in excess of book value, or they may believe that D Company's future earnings prospects are so favorable as to justify paying $25,000 for D Company's unrecorded goodwill. Since C Company paid $120,000 for a 100% interest in D Company in an arm's-length market transaction, the accountant has objective evidence that certain assets of D Company are undervalued, or that unrecorded goodwill of $25,000 exists. This evidence provides a basis for making the following eliminating entry *on the working papers* for a consolidated balance sheet on date of acquisition:

D Com-	*Capital Stock—D Company*	*50,000*
pany's	*Retained Earnings—D Company*	*45,000*
assets are		
understated	*Specific Assets (or Goodwill) of D Company*	*25,000*
	Investment in D Company (on C's records)	*120,000*

To eliminate the cost of C Company's 100% interest in D Company against the appropriate stockholders' equity accounts and to restate undervalued assets of D Company (or establish unrecorded goodwill of D Company).

The $25,000 in increased valuation assigned to specific assets (or goodwill) of D Company will be carried over as an asset in the consolidated balance sheet. In practice this amount is often described in the consolidated balance sheet as Excess of Cost over Book Value of Investment in Subsidiary and is amortized over a period of years, depending on the type of asset to which it is assigned.[1]

---

[1] For example, a recent annual report of Hilton Hotels Corporation included the following note accompanying its financial statements: "The $13,680,000 . . . cost of investment in excess of the net book value was attributable to the land and buildings. The portion allocated to the buildings is being amortized over the lives of the buildings." See also Accounting Principles Board, *Opinion No. 17,* "Intangible Assets," AICPA (New York: 1970).

If the parent company *pays less than book value* for its interest in a subsidiary, a similar problem of interpretation exists. For example, suppose in the previous case that C Company had paid only $85,000 for all the outstanding shares of D Company, which have a book value of $95,000. In this case we may assume that the management of C Company considered that D Company's assets were overvalued by $10,000. The eliminating entry on the working papers to consolidate the financial statements of the two companies on the date of acquisition would be:

Capital Stock—D Company	*50,000*	
Retained Earnings—D Company	*45,000*	
Investment in D Company (on C's records)		*85,000*
Specific Assets of D Company		*10,000*

D Company's assets are overstated

To eliminate investment in D Company against appropriate stockholders' equity accounts, and to record the indicated reduction in D Company's assets.

The credit excess of $10,000 should be reported in the consolidated balance sheet as a reduction in the book value of specific assets of D Company. As an alternative, this item may be reported below total liabilities as Excess of Book Value over Cost of Investment in Subsidiary. Placement of this item between liabilities and stockholders' equity indicates its unusual and complicated nature. Discussion of the arguments for and against inclusion on the balance sheet of an element other than assets, liabilities, and owners' equity are presented in the *Modern Advanced Accounting* volume of this series.

Intercompany receivables and payables

If one affiliated company (either a parent or subsidiary) owes money to another there will be an asset (receivable) on the individual balance sheet of the creditor firm and a liability (payable) on the balance sheet of the debtor company. When the financial statements of the two companies are consolidated, however, *both the asset and liability should be eliminated.* Neither a receivable nor a liability exists from the viewpoint of the consolidated entity.

On consolidating working papers an eliminating entry is made to cancel out any intercompany debt between affiliated companies. Suppose, for example, that a parent company has borrowed $10,000 from its subsidiary and at the balance sheet date owes this amount plus $500 accrued interest. On consolidating working papers for a consolidated balance sheet, the following elimination entry would be made:

Notes Payable—(Parent's balance sheet)	*10,000*	
Interest Payable—(Parent's balance sheet)	*500*	
Notes Receivable—(Subsidiary's balance sheet)		*10,000*
Interest Receivable—(Subsidiary's balance sheet)		*500*

To cancel intercompany debt on working papers

To eliminate intercompany payables and receivables.

The elimination entry shown above appears *only* on consolidating working papers; it would *not appear on the accounting records* of either the parent company or the subsidiary.

Consolidated income statement

A consolidated income statement is prepared by combining the revenue and expense accounts of the parent and subsidiary. Revenue and expenses arising from *intercompany transactions* are eliminated because they reflect transfers of assets from one affiliated company to another and do not change the net assets from a consolidated viewpoint. Some of the more common examples of intercompany items that should be eliminated in preparing a consolidated income statement are:

1 Sales to affiliated companies
2 Purchases from affiliated companies
3 Interest paid on loans from affiliated companies
4 Interest received on loans made to affiliated companies
5 Rent or other revenue received for services rendered to affiliated companies
6 Rent or other expenses paid for services received from affiliated companies

To illustrate the procedure, consider the following income statement data for X Company and its 90%-owned subsidiary, Y Company, several years after control was achieved. X Company has not yet recorded its share of Y Company's earnings for Year 10.

X AND Y COMPANIES
Year 10 Income Statements

	X Company	Y Company	Total
Sales	$600,000	$300,000	$900,000
Other revenue	50,000	25,000	75,000
Total revenue	$650,000	$325,000	$975,000
Cost of goods sold	$400,000	$225,000	$625,000
Expenses (including income taxes)	190,000	60,000	250,000
Total expenses	$590,000	$285,000	$875,000
Net income	$ 60,000	$ 40,000	$100,000

Does the total reflect consolidated results?

The Total column would represent the consolidated income statement *only if there were no intercompany transactions and if X Company owned 100% of the stock in Y Company.* Any revenue and expenses arising from transactions between the two companies must be eliminated when the affiliated companies are viewed as a single economic entity. Assume, for example, that the intercompany transactions on page 678 had taken place during Year 10 between X Company and Y Company.

1 All the goods sold by Y Company were acquired from X Company for $225,000. Y Company has no inventory at the end of the year.

2 Other revenue of X Company include rental revenue of $45,000 received from Y Company.

Keep in mind that X Company has not recorded its 90% share of Y Company's net income. The intercompany eliminations necessary to arrive at a consolidated income statement for Year 10 are shown in the working papers below:

X AND Y COMPANIES
Working Papers—Consolidated Income Statement
Year 10

	X Company	Y Company	Intercompany Eliminations		Consolidated Income Statement
			Debit	Credit	
Sales (credit)	600,000	300,000	(1) 225,000		675,000
Other revenue (credit) . . .	50,000	25,000	(2) 45,000		30,000
Total revenue	650,000	325,000			705,000
Cost of goods sold (debit) .	400,000	225,000		(1) 225,000	400,000
Expenses, including income					
taxes (debit)	190,000	60,000		(2) 45,000	205,000
Net income (credit)	60,000	40,000	(3) 4,000		96,000
Minority interest in net					
income of Y Company					
(10% of $40,000)				(3) 4,000	4,000
Totals	650,000	325,000	274,000	274,000	705,000

Explanations of eliminations:
(1) To eliminate intercompany sales and purchases, included in the cost of goods sold.
(2) To eliminate rental revenue and rental expense.
(3) To recognize minority interest in net income of Y Company, 10% of $40,000.

COMMENTS ON WORKING PAPER ELIMINATIONS Entry (1) This entry eliminated the intercompany sales and purchases. In other words, the sale recorded by X Company was recorded as a purchase by Y Company at the same dollar amount, $225,000. In preparing a consolidated income statement, this transaction (sale and purchase) is viewed as an *internal transfer* between affiliated units of a single entity and is eliminated.

Entry (2) This entry eliminates the intercompany rental revenue and rent expense accounts. Rent paid by Y Company to X Company is included in X Company's revenue and Y Company's expenses. The debit portion of the eliminating entry cancels the revenue recorded by X Company and the credit portion cancels the expense recorded by Y Company. This eliminating entry has no effect on consolidated net income, because we are simply offsetting an item recorded as revenue by one company in the affiliated structure against the expense recorded by the other affiliated company.

Entry (3) The purpose of this eliminating entry in the working papers is to recognize the share of the net income of Y Company accruing to the minority stockholders of Y Company. The net income of Y Company amounts to $40,000 and X Company owns 90% of the stock of Y Company, therefore $36,000 (90% × $40,000) of Y Company's net income accrues to X Company and becomes a part of *consolidated net income;* the other $4,000 (10% × $40,000) of Y Company's net income accrues to the minority interest. This is recognized in the working papers by debiting (reducing) net income of Y Company (a credit balance) and crediting Minority Interest in Net Income for $4,000. This minority interest in net income is generally shown as a deduction from "income before minority interest" in arriving at "net income" in the consolidated income statement.

When the various income statement items are combined, after the effect of the eliminating entries on the working papers has been taken into account, the figures in the last column of the working papers provide the basis for the preparation of a consolidated income statement. A condensed consolidated income statement of X and Y Companies for Year 10 is shown below:

X AND Y COMPANIES

Consolidated Income Statement

For Year 10

Sales and other revenue		*$705,000*
Less:		
Cost of goods sold	*$400,000*	
Expenses (including income taxes)	*205,000*	*605,000*
Income before minority interest		*$100,000*
Less: Minority interest in net income of subsidiary		*4,000*
Net income		*$ 96,000*

Minority stockholders' equity in earnings of subsidiary is deducted in computing net income

Observe that the net income of the consolidated entity for Year 10 actually amounts to $100,000, of which $96,000 is allocated to the controlling interest and $4,000 is allocated to the minority interest. The income accruing to the controlling interest is usually labeled "net income," although it is sometimes referred to as "consolidated net income." Instead of showing "income before minority interest" as illustrated above, some companies include the minority interest in net income under the Expenses caption in the income statement.[2]

---

[2] In a recent study of 600 annual reports by the AICPA, 209 companies reported minority interests in their consolidated statements. Of these, 53 companies listed the minority interest in earnings among expenses and 59 companies listed the minority interest as a deduction from income after income taxes. The remaining 97 companies did not disclose the minority stockholders' share of income.

Consolidated statement of retained earnings

The net income reported in the consolidated income statement also appears in the consolidated statement of retained earnings. Assume, for example, that the retained earnings appearing in the consolidated balance sheet at the end of Year 9 for X and Y Companies in the previous illustration amounted to $345,000 and that X Company declared cash dividends of $47,500 in Year 10. The consolidated statement of retained earnings would appear as follows:

X AND Y COMPANIES
Consolidated Statement of Retained Earnings
For Year 10

Only dividends declared by parent company appear in consolidated statement of retained earnings

Retained earnings, beginning of year	$345,000
Add: Net income for year	96,000
Total	$441,000
Less: Cash dividends declared (by parent company)	47,500
Retained earnings, end of year	$393,500

It is important to remember that the consolidated statement of retained earnings includes only the net income accruing to the controlling interest and the dividends declared by the parent company. Any dividends received by the parent from the subsidiary would be eliminated in preparing a consolidated income statement; dividends paid to minority stockholders by the subsidiary simply reduce the amount of minority interest reported in the consolidated balance sheet.

Unrealized profits on intercompany sales

Assume that a subsidiary company sells to its parent for $1,000 goods which cost the subsidiary $700. From the viewpoint of the subsidiary as a legal entity, a gross profit of $300 has been realized on this transaction. From the viewpoint of a single entity, however, goods have been transferred from one division of the economic entity to another, and no gain will be realized until the goods have been sold to someone outside the consolidated entity. If these goods are in the parent company's inventory at the time a consolidated balance sheet is prepared, the goods should be valued at $700, the cost to the consolidated entity. Therefore, in the process of consolidation, it would be necessary to remove $300 from the inventory account of the parent company and $300 from the retained earnings account of the subsidiary company.

The problem of eliminating unrealized increases in inventory valuation as a result of intercompany sales should be distinguished from that of eliminating the dollar amount of intercompany sales and purchases. When one affiliated company sells goods to another, and the second affiliate in turn sells these goods to outsiders, there is no *unrealized* intercompany profit. The profit recognized by each affiliate on the sale of these goods has been realized by the sale of the goods to outsiders. For example, suppose that a subsidiary sells goods which cost $40,000 to the parent for $50,000, and the parent in turn sells these goods to outsiders for $65,000. Both the $10,000 gross profit recognized by the subsidiary and the $15,000 gross profit recognized by the parent are fully realized, since none of the goods remain in inventory within the consolidated entity. In preparing a consolidated income statement for these companies, however, it would be necessary to eliminate $50,000 from the sales of the subsidiary and $50,000 from the purchases (or cost of goods sold) of the parent. This elimination would have no effect on consolidated assets or net income, since its purpose is simply to remove the *double counting* of revenue and expenses resulting from the transfer of goods from one affiliate to another.

The procedures necessary to remove unrealized profits in transactions between affiliates are somewhat complicated. However, familiarity with the technical procedure is not necessary to understand consolidated financial statements; the reader of such statements may assume that unrealized profits on transfers of assets between affiliates have been eliminated.

Consolidated statements on a pooling-of-interests basis

In recent years the acquisition of a subsidiary corporation has often been carried out by an *exchange of stock,* and the preparation of consolidated statements has followed a "pooling-of-interests" method. A key aspect of such acquisitions is that the stockholders of the subsidiary company being acquired become stockholders of the parent corporation. The stockholders of the two companies are said to have *pooled their interests,* rather than one ownership group having sold its equity to the other.[3]

If we accept the view that no ownership interests have been severed (in other words no purchase or sale occurred), then there is no reason to revalue the assets of the acquired company, regardless of the market value of the securities exchanged. When the acquisition is treated as a pooling of interests, the investment account in the accounts of the parent can be established at the par or stated value of the shares issued by the parent regardless of the current market price of the stock issued. Furthermore, if the parent acquired 100% of the stock of the subsidiary late in the year, the earnings (revenue and expenses) of the subsidiary *for the entire year* can be included in consolidated earnings.

To illustrate, let us assume that P Company acquired 100% of S Company's stock on November 1, Year 1, and that each company earned

---

[3] For a more complete discussion of the differences between a purchase and a pooling of interests, see Accounting Principles Board, *Opinion No. 16,* "Business Combinations," AICPA (New York: 1970).

$60,000 during Year 1. The consolidated net income for the two companies on a pooling basis would be $120,000, even though $50,000 ($^{10}/_{12}$ of $60,000) of the earnings of S Company were earned before the two companies became affiliated on November 1.

The following brief summary emphasizes some of the points of contrast between treating a corporate acquisition as a *purchase* or as a *pooling of interests.*

Purchase Method	Pooling-of-Interests Method
1 *Parent records its investment in subsidiary at amount of cash paid or at market value of shares issued by parent in exchange for shares of subsidiary. Excess of cost over book value (or book value over cost) may result.*	*Parent records its investment in subsidiary at par (or stated) value of shares issued; the market value of shares issued (or assets acquired) is ignored.*
2 *Retained earnings of subsidiary at date of acquisition do not become part of consolidated retained earnings.*	*Retained earnings of subsidiary at date of acquisition generally become part of consolidated retained earnings.*
3 *Earnings of subsidiary are combined with the earnings of the parent only from the date of the affiliation.*	*Earnings of subsidiary for the entire year in which the affiliation occurs are included in the consolidated income statement.*

The popularity of the pooling concept in recent years can be attributed largely to two factors. The first is the opportunity for the parent company to acquire valuable assets and to record these assets at relatively low values as shown in the accounting records of the subsidiary company. As a result the consolidated earnings will not be penalized through amortization of higher (current) asset values against revenue. A second reason for the popularity of the pooling concept is that it permits a company whose stock sells at a high price-earnings multiple to show an *instant increase* in its earnings per share by issuing additional stock to acquire companies whose stock customarily sells at a low price-earnings multiple. A "growth" company may thus be able to maintain its reputation for reporting higher per-share earnings each year by continually acquiring other companies and accounting for such acquisitions on a pooling-of-interests basis.

The preparation of a consolidated balance sheet using the pooling-of-interests approach will be illustrated for the Parent and Sub companies. Assume that at the end of Year 1, the Parent Company issues 10,000 shares of its stock ($10 par) in exchange for the 12,500 shares of Sub Company stock. The market value of Parent Company's stock at this time is $35 per share. The Parent Company records the shares issued at par value, $100,000; the market value of Parent Company's stock, $350,000, is not considered relevant and is ignored for accounting purposes under the pooling concept. The working papers to develop a consolidated balance sheet on a pooling basis are shown below:

PARENT AND SUB COMPANIES
Working Papers—Consolidated Balance Sheet (Pooling Basis)
End of Year (Date of Acquisition)

	Parent Company	Sub Company	Intercompany Eliminations		Consolidated Balance Sheet
			Debit	Credit	
Various assets	700,000	400,000			1,100,000
Investment in Sub Company	100,000			(1) 100,000	
Totals	800,000	400,000			1,100,000
Liabilities	200,000	75,000			275,000
Capital stock, $10 par	390,000	125,000	(1) 125,000		390,000
Retained earnings . . .	200,000	200,000			400,000
Paid-in capital in excess of par	10,000			(1) 25,000	35,000
Totals	800,000	400,000	125,000	125,000	1,100,000

A pooling combines retained earnings of both companies on date of acquisition

Explanation of elimination:
(1) To eliminate investment in subsidiary account, $100,000, and subsidiary's capital stock, $125,000; the excess, $25,000, is recognized as paid-in capital in excess of par.

The eliminating entry on the working papers cancels the balance in the investment account, $100,000 (par value of stock issued to acquire control of Sub Company), and the capital stock of the Sub Company, $125,000. Since the par value of the stock issued, $100,000, is less than the par value of the acquired company's stock, $125,000, the excess of $25,000 is recorded as a credit to Paid-in Capital in Excess of Par. Note that the retained earnings balances of the two companies ($200,000 for each company) are combined in the consolidated balance sheet even though the retained earnings of Sub Company were earned *before* Parent Company acquired control of Sub Company. The consolidated balance sheet on a pooling basis is shown below:

PARENT AND SUB COMPANIES
Consolidated Balance Sheet (Pooling Basis)
End of Year 1 (Date of Acquisition)

A pooling may increase the paid-in capital in excess of par

Various assets	$1,100,000	Liabilities	$ 275,000
		Capital stock, $10 par . .	390,000
		Paid-in capital in excess	
		of par	35,000
		Retained earnings	400,000
	$1,100,000		$1,100,000

If the Parent Company had issued 13,500 shares of $10 par value stock in exchange for all the capital stock of Sub Company, the excess of the $135,000 par value of stock issued over the $125,000 par value of Sub Company stock acquired would be debited to Paid-in Capital in Excess of Par. If the Parent Company had no paid-in capital in excess of par, the $10,000 charge could be made against retained earnings.

When should consolidated statements be prepared?

Accounts of some subsidiary companies may not be included in consolidated statements. Consolidation of accounts is deemed appropriate only when effective control over the subsidiary is *present* and *continuing* and when the consolidated statements *give a meaningful picture of financial position and results of operations.* For example, a subsidiary's accounts should not be consolidated with those of the parent if control is likely to be temporary or if the subsidiary is facing bankruptcy. Similarly, if the assets of a foreign subsidiary cannot be withdrawn by the parent because of restrictions placed on such assets by foreign governments, consolidation of accounts should be avoided.

In other instances, consolidation of accounts may not be appropriate because the activities of the subsidiary are significantly different from those of the parent. For example, General Motors Corporation does not consolidate its wholly owned General Motors Acceptance Corporation, which is engaged in the financing and insurance business; American Telephone and Telegraph Company (a public utility) does not consolidate Western Electric Company, which manufactures telephones and other electronic equipment.

When the parent company controls a subsidiary but consolidation is not considered appropriate, the question arises as to how the investment in the *unconsolidated subsidiary* should be reported in the separate financial statements of the parent. For many years, both the *cost* and the *equity* method of accounting for the investment were widely used. The equity method *is now required.*[4] Under the *equity method,* the parent company "accrues" its share of the subsidiary's net income by debiting the Investment in Subsidiary account and crediting Earnings of Unconsolidated Subsidiary; losses are debited to Loss of Unconsolidated Subsidiary and credited to the Investment in Subsidiary account. Dividends received are debited to Cash and credited to the Investment in Subsidiary account. Under the *cost method,* earnings of the subsidiary would be recognized only to the extent of cash dividends received from the subsidiary; earnings not distributed in the form of dividends and losses incurred by the subsidiary would be ignored.

---

[4] Accounting Principles Board, *Opinion No. 18,* "The Equity Method of Accounting for Investments in Common Stock," AICPA (New York: 1971), p. 354.

In *Opinion No. 18,* the Accounting Principles Board recommended that the equity method of accounting for an investment in common stock be followed by companies whose investment in voting stock gives them the ability "to exercise significant influence over operating and financial policies of an investee even though the investor holds 50% or less of the voting stock."[5] An investment of 20% or more of the voting stock is considered sufficient to exercise "significant influence" over the company whose voting stock is owned. Net income earned and losses incurred by companies in which 20% or more stock is owned are reported in the income statement of the investor corporation. *Only cash dividends received from companies less than 20% owned are reported in the income of the investor corporation.*

The accounting requirements for investments in subsidiaries and significant investments in other corporations are summarized below:

Situation	*General Practice*
1 *Controlled subsidiary (more than 50% owned)*	*Consolidate, except in situations where activities of subsidiary are significantly different from those of the parent or where assets of a foreign subsidiary cannot be withdrawn by the parent company. The equity method of accounting for unconsolidated subsidiaries would generally be used.*
2 *Ownership of between 20% and 50% of voting stock*	*The use of the equity method by investor corporation is generally required.*
3 *Ownership of less than 20% of voting stock*	*Cost method must be used; only cash dividends received on stock owned is included in net income of investor corporation.*

Who uses consolidated financial statements?

Millions of people invest in the securities of major corporations listed on the stock exchanges. All these people receive consolidated financial statements regularly informing them of the progress of the companies in which they have invested. The tabulation on page 686 of stock ownership in IBM gives some idea of the diversity of the groups which need an understanding of consolidated financial statements. Incidentally, note that more women than men are owners of IBM stock.

---

[5] Ibid, p. 355.

Who owns IBM

Type of Stockholder	Number of Accounts	Number of Shares	Average Per Stockholder	Percent of Total Shares
Men	120,239	12,711,524	106	8.5
Women	134,308	14,993,727	112	10.0
Joint tenants	84,435	2,537,055	30	1.7
Fiduciaries	94,732	5,228,291	55	3.5
Brokers	819	9,965,190	12,168	6.6
Bank nominees	3,722	88,292,185	23,722	58.8
Partnerships and corporations	3,681	3,748,864	1,018	2.5
Insurance companies	672	4,623,492	6,880	3.1
Investment organizations	847	165,235	195	.1
Banks and trust companies . .	205	632,140	3,084	.4
Other organizations and associations	8,336	2,504,064	300	1.7
Employees and directors	132,517	4,737,871	36	3.1
Scrip	—	15,637	—	—
Totals	584,513	150,155,275		100.0

Capital stock as of the record date for the annual meeting, March 8, 1976

The stockholders, managers, and members of the board of directors of the parent company have the primary interest in consolidated statements. The managers and directors are responsible for the entire resources under their control and for managing these resources profitably. Similarly, the stockholders of the parent company will prosper as the consolidated entity prospers. Their ownership interest is controlling, and they stand to benefit from strength anywhere in the entity and to suffer from weakness.

Long-term creditors of the parent company may find consolidated statements useful in assessing the general strength or weakness of the economic entity. In the long run, earning power is the primary source of safety for creditors. The operating performance of the affiliated group may be a significant safety index for creditors of the parent company.

Consolidated statements are not significant to the minority stockholders or creditors of a subsidiary company. A strong financial position shown in a consolidated balance sheet may conceal a very weak situation in the particular subsidiary company in which a creditor or minority stockholder has a legal interest. These groups should rely on the individual financial statements of the affiliate in which they have a legal claim.

Additional uses of consolidated financial statements and more complex problems encountered in preparing them are discussed in the **Modern Advanced Accounting** volume of this series.

KEY TERMS INTRODUCED OR EMPHASIZED IN CHAPTER 19

Affiliated companies   A parent company and one or more subsidiary companies.

Consolidated financial statements   A set of statements presenting the combined financial position and operating results of affiliated corporations.

Equity method   The method of accounting used when the investment by one corporation in another is large enough to influence the policies of the investee. The investor recognizes as investment income its proportionate share of the investee's net income, rather than considering dividends received as income.

Intercompany receivables and payables   Amounts owed by one member of an affiliated group of corporations to another member of the group.

Minority interest   The shares of a subsidiary company owned by persons other than the parent corporation.

Parent company   A corporation which owns a controlling interest in another company.

Pooling of interests   A method of accounting for a business combination in which assets and liabilities of the separate entities are combined at their existing carrying values. The stockholders of the combining companies are considered to have "pooled their interests," as opposed to an outright sale.

Purchase method   A method of accounting for a business combination by recording assets at current market values as indicated by the price paid in the acquisition.

Subsidiary company   A corporation in which a controlling stock interest is held by another corporation (the parent).

REVIEW QUESTIONS

1 Define each of the following: (**a**) merger, (**b**) consolidation, (**c**) consolidated balance sheet, and (**d**) consolidated income statement.

2 Alexander Corporation owns 80% of the outstanding common stock of Benton Company. Explain the basis for the assumption that these two companies constitute a single economic entity operating under unified control.

3 The following item appears on a consolidated balance sheet: "Minority interest in subsidiary . . . $620,000." Explain the nature of this item, and where you would expect to find it on the consolidated balance sheet.

4 The annual report of the Standard Oil Company (Indiana) and Subsidiaries included the following note: "Accounts of all subsidiaries in which the Company directly or indirectly owns more than 50 per cent of the voting stock are included in the consolidated financial statements, with three exceptions: Imperial Casualty and Indemnity Company and Amoco Credit Corporation, which are accounted for on an equity basis, and Amoco Argentina Oil Company, which is accounted for on a cost basis."

   Explain what is meant by the **equity basis** and the **cost basis** and give a possible reason for not consolidating the three subsidiaries.

5 The Excelsior Corporation "purchased" 80% of the stock of the Acme Co. on July 1, 1978, when the retained earnings of the Acme Co. amounted to $100,000. The retained earnings of the Acme Co. now amount to $750,000. Show how much of the retained earnings of the Acme Co. would be reported on the latest consolidated balance sheet and what disposition would be made of any portion of Acme's retained earnings not reported on the consolidated balance sheet.

6 Explain why the price paid to acquire a controlling interest in a subsidiary company may be different from the book value of the equity acquired.

7 Explain why intercompany sales, rents, interest, etc., should be eliminated in preparing consolidated income statements in order to avoid double counting of revenue and expenses. Do these eliminations have any effect on consolidated net income? Why?

8 Indiana Company owns an 85% interest in Jin Company. During Year 1, Jin Company sold to Indiana Company for $300,000 merchandise which cost Jin Company $210,000. At the end of Year 1, Indiana Company has in its ending inventory goods purchased from Jin Company at a cost of $75,000. What amount of intercompany profit should be eliminated in preparing consolidated statements? When will this profit be realized by the consolidated entity?

9 Briefly explain the differences found in consolidated financial statements when the merger of two companies is viewed as a *pooling of interests* rather than as a *purchase.*

10 The 19＿＿ annual report of the Fedders Corporation stated that its consolidated statement of income for the year ended August 31, 19＿＿, included sales of $19,500,000 and net income of $120,000 from the Norge Division purchased on July 1, 19＿＿. The division was acquired for approximately $45 million in cash, notes, and common stock. The balance sheet reported total assets of $129 million compared to only $61 million for the previous year. Would any of the foregoing amounts be reported differently if only common stock was issued in acquiring the Norge Division and the transaction was treated as a pooling of interests?

11 As a general rule, when should consolidated financial statements be prepared?

12 a How should the investment in an unconsolidated subsidiary be reported on the balance sheet of the parent company?
b Explain the generally accepted accounting procedures for an investment representing 20% or more of the voting stock held in another corporation.

13 What groups of persons are likely to be primarily interested in consolidated financial statements? Why?

14 A creditor of Great Mining Company is concerned because the company is in financial difficulty and has reported increasingly large losses in the past three years. Great Mining Company is a 75%-owned subsidiary of Hannah Company. When creditors examine the consolidated statements of the two companies they find that the earnings are satisfactory and that the consolidated entity is in a sound financial position. To what extent should the creditors be reassured by the consolidated statements, assuming that the information contained in them fairly presents the financial position of the consolidated entity?

EXERCISES

Ex. 19-1 Jax Company paid $456,000 for all the capital stock of Mac Company. At the date of acquisition, Jax Company's total stockholders' equity of $1.2 million is composed of $960,000 in capital stock and $240,000 of retained earnings. Mac Company has $480,000 in capital stock and a deficit of $24,000 at the date of acquisition. What is the total amount of stockholders' equity that will appear on a consolidated balance sheet prepared for these two affiliated companies at date of acquisition?

Ex. 19-2 A Company has purchased all the outstanding shares of B Company for $2,700,000. At the date of acquisition, the B Company balance sheet showed total assets of $3,900,000 and total liabilities of $1,500,000. Assuming that B Company's retained earnings at date of acquisition are one-third the amount of its stated capital, prepare the eliminating entry necessary on the working papers to consolidate the balance sheets of these two companies.

Ex. 19-3 On June 30 of Year 1, P Company ***purchased*** 80% of the stock of S Company for $480,000 in cash. The separate condensed balance sheets immediately after the purchase are shown below:

	P Company	S Company
Other assets	*$2,320,000*	*$800,000*
Investment in S Company (80%)	*480,000*	*–0–*
	$2,800,000	*$800,000*
Liabilities	*$ 600,000*	*$200,000*
Capital stock, $5 par value	*1,200,000*	*480,000*
Retained earnings	*1,000,000*	*120,000*
	$2,800,000	*$800,000*

Prepare a consolidated balance sheet immediately after P Company acquired control of S Company.

Ex. 19-4 The separate balance sheets of Adams Co. and its 80%-owned Baker Corp. show the following account balances.

	Adams Co.	Baker Corp.	Consolidated
Accounts receivable	*$ 400,000*	*$ 160,000*	*$*
Interest receivable—bonds of Adams Co.		*4,000*	
Investment in stock of Baker Corp. 80%	*1,240,000*		
Investment in bonds of Adams Co. (at par)		*200,000*	
Accounts payable	*320,000*	*120,000*	
Interest payable—bonds	*16,000*		
Bonds payable	*800,000*		
Capital stock	*2,000,000*	*1,000,000*	

Adams Co. owes Baker Corp. $40,000 for purchase of merchandise and Baker Corp. owes Adams Co. $20,000 for services rendered. In the Consolidated column, show the amounts that should appear in the consolidated balance sheet for each account.

Ex. 19-5 The Parent Co. acquired all the stock of Sun Co. at the beginning of Year 1. The acquisition is treated as a ***purchase*** for accounting purposes. Relevant information for Year 1 is given below:

	Parent Co.	Sun Co.
Retained earnings, beginning of Year 1	*$800,000*	*$400,000*
Net income for Year 1 (including dividends from Sun Co.)	*320,000*	*160,000*
Dividends declared during Year 1	*240,000*	*80,000*

Prepare a statement of consolidated retained earnings for the two companies covering the activities of Year 1. (The equity method was not used.)

Ex. 19-6 Given below are selected accounts appearing on the balance sheets of the Parent and its 100%-owned Subsidiary shortly after affiliation:

	Parent	Subsidiary
Investment in Subsidiary (at par value of Parent stock issued		
to former stockholders of Subsidiary)	*$1,000,000*	
Capital stock	*2,500,000*	*$1,000,000*

Premium on capital stock	$ 750,000	$ 50,000
Retained earnings	3,000,000	975,000

Prepare the stockholders' equity section of the consolidated balance sheet on a *pooling-of-interests* basis.

PROBLEMS

Group A

19A-1 Below are the liabilities and stockholders' equity sections of the balance sheets of Post Company and Sand Company at the end of the current year:

Liabilities & Stockholders' Equity	Post Company	Sand Company
Liabilities	$ 600,000	$ 360,000
Capital stock, $10 par value	1,800,000	960,000
Retained earnings	840,000	300,000
Total liabilities & stockholders' equity	$3,240,000	$1,620,000

Instructions For each of the following independent fact situations, prepare the liabilities and stockholders' equity section of the consolidated balance sheet as of the end of the current year:

a Post Company acquired all the outstanding capital stock of Sand Company just prior to the date of the above statements, in exchange for 84,000 shares of Post Company capital stock. The consolidated statements are prepared on a *pooling-of-interests* basis.

b Post Company *purchased* for cash all the outstanding capital stock of Sand Company, at the time of the latter's organization. The Post Company carries its investment in Sand Company on the equity method.

19A-2 The following data relate to P Company and S Company, several years after P Company acquired control of S Company for $1,170,000 in cash:

Assets	P Company	S Company	Consolidated
Investment in S Company stock (at			
equity)	$1,710,000		
Other assets	5,100,000	$3,090,000	$7,500,000
Total assets	$6,810,000	$3,090,000	$7,500,000

Liabilities & Stockholders' Equity	P Company	S Company	Consolidated
Bonds payable	$1,500,000		$1,050,000
Other liabilities	840,000	$ 990,000	1,590,000
Capital stock, no par	1,800,000	600,000	1,800,000
Retained earnings	2,670,000	1,500,000	2,670,000
Minority interest			210,000
Excess of book value over cost of			
investment in subsidiary			180,000
Total liabilities & stockholders'			
equity	$6,810,000	$3,090,000	$7,500,000

The excess of book value over cost of investment in subsidiary has not been amortized since acquisition. Additional stock has not been issued by either company.

Instructions
a Compute the percentage of stock in S Company owned by P Company.
b Compute the par value of bonds issued by P Company now held by S Company.
c If S Company owes P Company $210,000 on open account, how much does P Company apparently owe to S Company?
d How much of the retained earnings of $1,500,000 currently reported by S Company is included in the $2,670,000 retained earnings figure appearing on the consolidated balance sheet?
e Compute S Company's retained earnings balance on the date that P Company acquired control of S Company.

19A-3 At the beginning of Year 10, the High Corporation acquired all the capital stock of the Low Corporation for $365,000 in cash and $160,000 in notes, payable at the rate of $20,000 per month. The balance sheets of the two companies at the end of Year 10 are given below:

Assets	*High Corporation*	*Low Corporation*
Cash	$ 35,000	$ 18,000
Note receivable from Low Corporation	50,000	
Accounts receivable	90,000	50,000
Inventories	100,000	45,000
Investment in Low Corporation stock (equity method) . . .	475,000	
Plant and equipment	350,000	550,000
Accumulated depreciation	(140,000)	(83,000)
Total assets	$960,000	$580,000

Liabilities & Stockholders' Equity		
Notes payable	$100,000	$ 50,000
Accounts payable	120,000	60,000
Accrued liabilities	30,000	20,000
Capital stock, $5 par	400,000	200,000
Retained earnings	310,000	250,000
Total liabilities & stockholders' equity	$960,000	$580,000

Additional information
(*1*) A summary of the Investment in Low Corporation Stock account for Year 10 on the records of High Corporation follows:

Cost of 40,000 shares (100%), beginning of Year 10	$525,000
Less: 100% of net loss incurred by Low Corporation during Year 10 . . .	50,000
Balance, end of Year 10	$475,000

(*2*) At the beginning of Year 10, the Low Corporation had $200,000 in capital stock and $300,000 in retained earnings.
(*3*) The excess of cost over book value of investment in Low Corporation cannot be allocated to any specific asset and should be reported at "Excess of Cost

over Book Value of Investment in Subsidiary'' in the consolidated balance sheet.

(*4*) Late in Year 10, the Low Corporation borrowed $50,000 from High Corporation for a one-year period.

Instructions Prepare working papers for a consolidated balance sheet at the end of Year 10. Use the form illustrated on page 672. Include at the bottom of the working papers explanations of the elimination entries.

19A-4 X Company owns 100% of the stock of Y Company. The income statements for each company for Year 1 appear below.

	X Company	Y Company
Sales	$600,000	$300,000
Cost of goods sold	400,000	210,000
Gross profit on sales	$200,000	$ 90,000
Operating expenses	(83,000)	(30,000)
Interest expense	(5,000)	(8,000)
Interest earned	8,000	
Income taxes	(50,000)	(18,500)
Net income	$ 70,000	$ 33,500

Y Company sold merchandise to X Company for $30,000 which cost $24,000. One-half of this merchandise has not been sold by X Company to its customers and is included in its ending inventory at $15,000. Y Company paid $8,000 interest to X Company in Year 1 on a long-term loan. X Company has not recorded its share of Y Company's net income.

Instructions

a Prepare a consolidated income statement for Year 1 for X Company and its subsidiary, Y Company. You need not use working papers.

b Prepare a consolidated income statement for the two companies, assuming the same facts as above except that X Company owns only 80% of the stock of Y Company and that all the merchandise acquired by X Company from Y Company has been sold by X Company. You need not use working papers.

19A-5 The Clark Corporation plans to acquire the Davis Corporation on a *pooling-of-interests* basis by issuing 100,000 shares of its $1 par value capital stock for the 50,000 shares of stock of Davis Corporation outstanding. Given below are selected figures taken from the financial statements of the two corporations for Year 1:

	Clark Corporation	Davis Corporation
Total assets, net of accumulated depreciation	$3,350,000	$1,500,000
Total liabilities	1,000,000	650,000
Capital stock, $1 par	500,000	50,000
Retained earnings	1,850,000	800,000
Net income for latest year	600,000	300,000
Market price per share of stock	$30	$60
Earnings per share	$1.20	$6.00

Instructions

a Prepare a consolidated balance sheet for the two companies on a *pooling-of-interests* basis, after Clark Corporation issues 100,000 additional shares of its capital stock in exchange for the 50,000 shares of Davis Corporation's capital stock.

b What would be the amount of net income for the two corporations on a consolidated basis if the *pooling of interests* is completed on the last day of Year 1? What would be the earnings per share of Clark Corporation's stock after the pooling?

c Assuming that the stock of Clark Corporation continues to sell at 25 times earnings ($1.20 × 25 = $30), at what price should its stock sell shortly after the *pooling* is effected?

Group B

19B-1 Condensed balance sheets of Wheat and Pine Companies at the end of Year 1 are shown below:

Assets	Wheat Company	Pine Company
Current assets	$1,680,000	$240,000
Other assets	1,920,000	660,000
Total assets	$3,600,000	$900,000

Liabilities & Stockholders' Equity		
Current liabilities	$ 840,000	$120,000
Long-term debt	600,000	84,000
Capital stock	1,200,000	360,000
Retained earnings	960,000	336,000
Total liabilities & stockholders' equity	$3,600,000	$900,000

Instructions Assume that, at the end of Year 1, Wheat Company purchased (using current assets) all the outstanding capital stock of Pine Company for $768,000. Prepare a consolidated balance sheet for Wheat and Pine Companies at the date of acquisition. (Use the title "Excess of cost over book value of investment in subsidiary" as an asset in the consolidated balance sheet.)

19B-2 The following information is given to you relating to Major Company and its subsidiary, the Minor Company:

Assets	Major Company	Minor Company	Consolidated
Cash	$ 120,000	$ 75,000	$ 195,000
Accounts receivable	180,000	90,000	150,000
Merchandise inventory	360,000	240,000	600,000
Investment in Minor Company (at equity)	900,000		
Other assets	1,200,000	600,000	1,800,000
Excess of cost over book value of investment in subsidiary			30,000
Total assets	$2,760,000	$1,005,000	$2,775,000

Liabilities & Stockholders' Equity

Accounts payable	$ 165,000	$ 90,000	$ 135,000
Accrued liabilities	30,000	45,000	75,000
Capital stock	1,500,000	300,000	1,500,000
Paid-in capital in excess of par	315,000	120,000	315,000
Retained earnings	750,000	450,000	750,000
Total liabilities & stockholders' equity	$2,760,000	$1,005,000	$2,775,000

The excess of cost over book value of investment in subsidiary has not been amortized since Major Company acquired control of Minor Company. The Major Company issued notes valued at $660,000 for the stock of Minor Company.

Instructions

a What percentage of the outstanding stock of Minor Company is held by Major Company?

b What is the amount of intercompany accounts receivable and accounts payable?

c Was the consolidation of the accounts of the two companies effected as a purchase or as a pooling of interests? Why?

d How much of the retained earnings of Minor Company are included in the consolidated retained earnings figure of $750,000?

e What was the amount of retained earnings reported by Minor Company on the date Major Company acquired control of Minor Company?

19B-3 Given below are the balance sheet accounts for the London Company and the Pub Company at the end of Year 1:

Assets	London Company	Pub Company
Cash	$ 50,000	$ 20.000
Accounts receivable	85,000	30,000
Inventories	60,000	40,000
Investment in Pub Company stock (equity method)	162,000	
Plant and equipment	250,000	180,000
Accumulated depreciation	(50,000)	(40,000)
Total assets	$557,000	$230,000

Liabilities & Stockholders' Equity	London Company	Pub Company
Accounts payable	$ 40,000	$ 40,000
Accrued liabilities	25,000	10,000
Capital stock, $1 par	300,000	100,000
Retained earnings	192,000	80,000
Total liabilities & stockholders' equity	$557,000	$230,000

Additional information

(1) The entries in Investment in Pub Company Stock account in the accounts of London Company are given on page 695.

Cost of 90,000 shares (90%) acquired on Jan. 2, Year 1	*$135,000*
Add: 90% of net income of Pub Company	*36,000*
Less: 90% of dividend paid by Pub Company	*(9,000)*
Balance, end of Year 1	*$162,000*

(2) On January 2, Year 1, the Pub Company had 100,000 shares of capital stock outstanding and retained earnings of $50,000.

(3) Pub Company owes London Company $25,000 for purchases of merchandise. All the merchandise purchased by Pub Company from London Company has been sold.

Instructions Prepare working papers for a consolidated balance sheet at the end of Year 1. Use the form illustrated on page 674.

19B-4 The Weaver Company owns 70% of the capital stock of Small Company. The income statements for each company for Year 1 are presented below:

	Weaver Company	*Small Company*
Sales	*$1,500,000*	*$800,000*
Cost of goods sold	*1,000,000*	*650,000*
Gross profit on sales	*$ 500,000*	*$150,000*
Operating expenses	*(200,000)*	*(60,000)*
Interest expense	*(20,000)*	*(10,000)*
Interest earned	*10,000*	
Income taxes	*(140,000)*	*(32,000)*
Net income	*$ 150,000*	*$ 48,000*

Weaver Company sold merchandise costing $300,000 to Small Company for $420,000. All this merchandise was sold by Small Company to its customers during Year 1. The interest expense incurred by Small Company represents interest at 8% on a $125,000 note payable to Weaver Company. Weaver Company has not recorded its share of Small Company's net income.

Instructions
a Prepare working papers for a consolidated income statement for Weaver Company and its subsidiary. Use the format illustrated on page 678.
b Prepare a consolidated income statement for Year 1.

19B-5 Sam Company and Tab Company are planning to *pool* their activities into a single company. Data relating to the two companies follow:

	Sam Company	*Tab Company*
Total assets, net of accumulated depreciation	*$1,500,000*	*$2,800,000*
Total liabilities	*500,000*	*800,000*
Capital stock, $5 par (80,000 shares)	*400,000*	*400,000*
Retained earnings	*600,000*	*1,600,000*
Net income for latest year	*240,000*	*240,000*
Annual earnings per share	*$3.00*	*$3.00*
Price per share of stock	*$60*	*$30*
Price-earnings ratio	*20 times*	*10 times*

Instructions

a Assuming that Sam Company issues 40,000 additional shares of its capital stock in exchange for all the stock of Tab Company, prepare a consolidated balance sheet on a *pooling-of-interests* basis. You need not use working papers.

b If Sam Company issues 40,000 additional shares in exchange for all the stock of Tab Company and the earnings for the two companies remain unchanged, compute the earnings per share on Sam Company stock after the *pooling* of the two companies.

c Assuming that Sam Company stock continues to sell at 20 times earnings, what would be the price of its stock after the *pooling* of the two companies?

BUSINESS DECISION PROBLEM 19

On March 1, Year 1, Milton Paper Co. invested $1,590,000 cash in the capital stock of Travis Book Company. This represents 58% (58,000 shares) of the outstanding capital stock of Travis Book Company. The balance sheets of Travis Book Company at date of acquisition and at the end of Year 10 include the following:

	December 31 Year 10	March 1 Year 1
Current assets	$13,500,000	$7,500,000
Current liabilities	9,000,000	3,900,000
Other assets	15,000,000	9,000,000
Long-term liabilities	2,400,000	4,500,000
Capital stock, $5 stated value	3,000,000	3,000,000
Retained earnings	14,100,000	5,100,000

The balance sheet of the Milton Paper Co. at December 31, Year 10, is shown below:

MILTON PAPER CO.

Balance Sheet

December 31, Year 10

Assets

Current assets	$22,500,000
Investment in capital stock of Travis Book Company (58%, at cost)	4,770,000
Other assets	17,730,000
Total assets	$45,000,000

Liabilities & Stockholders' Equity

Current liabilities		$12,000,000
Bonds payable		9,000,000
Total liabilities		$21,000,000
Stockholders' equity:		
Capital stock, no par	$ 7,500,000	
Retained earnings	16,500,000	
Total stockholders' equity		24,000,000
Total liabilities & stockholders' equity		$45,000,000

The accounts receivable of Milton Paper Co. include $7,500,000 due from Travis Book Company. The accounts of the two companies have never been consolidated because one manufactures a variety of paper products and the other publishes childrens' books. However, if a consolidated balance sheet were prepared at December 31, Year 10, the current assets would be $28,500,000 and the current liabilities would be $13,500,000.

Bonnie Bent, a director of Milton Paper Co., suggests that a consolidated balance sheet be prepared for the two companies in order to show a more meaningful financial position. She also suggests that the increase in the new assets of the Travis Book Company since acquisition, $5,220,000 [58% × ($14,100,000 − $5,100,000)], be included in the separate balance sheet of Milton Paper Co.

Louis Joseph another director of Milton Paper Co., objects to Bent's suggestion in view of the poor working capital position of Travis Book Company and the low percentage of stock held in Travis Book Company. "Why should we hide our strong working capital position in consolidated statements? We only own 58% of the stock in Travis and I hate to see us show a liability to minority stockholders of $7,182,000 on our balance sheet. Besides, Travis is not in our kind of business, and I don't even want us to take up the profits of Travis earned since we made our investment because we haven't realized that profit and it violates the accounting principle of conservatism."

Instructions Carefully evaluate the points made by Louis Joseph and give your recommendation whether or not the preparation of consolidated statements for the two companies would be appropriate.

20

Income Taxes and Business Decisions

"A penny saved is a penny earned" according to an old saying credited to Benjamin Franklin. However, now that corporations (as well as some individuals) are subject to approximately a 50% income tax rate, we can modify this bit of folklore to read: "A dollar of income tax saved is worth two dollars of income earned."

In other words, about half of what a corporation earns, and half of what some individuals earn, must be paid to the federal government as income taxes. If advance tax planning will enable a corporation or an individual to save a dollar of income taxes, that dollar saved may be the equivalent of two dollars of before-tax earnings. Furthermore, there are a good many perfectly legal actions which can be taken to save or at least to postpone income taxes.

The critical importance of income taxes

Taxes levied by federal, state, and local governments are a significant part of the cost of operating a typical household, as well as a business enterprise. The knowledge required to be expert in taxation has made it a field of specialization among professional accountants. However, every manager who makes business decisions, and every individual who makes personal investments, urgently needs some knowledge of income taxes to be aware of the tax implications of these decisions. A general knowledge of income taxes will help any business manager or owner to benefit more fully from the advice of the professional tax accountant.

Some understanding of income taxes will also aid the individual citizen in voting intelligently, because a great many of the issues decided in every election have tax implications. Such issues as pollution, inflation, foreign policy, and employment are inextricably linked with income taxes. For example, the offering of special tax incentives to encourage businesses to launch massive programs to reduce pollution is one approach to protection of the environment.

In terms of revenue generated, the four most important kinds of taxes in the United States are *income taxes, sales taxes, property taxes,* and *excise taxes.* Income taxes probably exceed all others in terms of the amounts involved, and they also exert a pervasive influence on all types of business decisions. For this reason we shall limit our discussion to the basic federal income tax rules applicable to individuals, partnerships, and corporations.

Income taxes are usually determined from information contained in accounting records. The amount of income tax is computed by applying the appropriate tax rates (as set by federal, state, and some local governments) to *taxable income.* As explained more fully later in this chapter, taxable income is not necessarily the same as accounting income even though both are derived from the accounting records. Although taxes are involuntary and often unrelated to benefits received, some degree of control over the amount of tax is usually attainable. Business managers may legally alter the amount of taxes they pay by their choice of form of business organization, methods of financing, and alternative accounting methods. Thus income taxes are inevitably an important factor in arriving at business decisions.

The federal income tax: history and objectives

The present federal income tax dates from the passage of the Sixteenth Amendment to the Constitution in 1913.[1] This amendment, only 30 words in length,[2] removed all questions of the constitutionality of income taxes and paved the way for the more than 50 revenue acts passed by Congress since that date. In 1939 these tax laws were first combined into what is known as the Internal Revenue Code. The administration and enforcement of the tax laws are duties of the Treasury Department, operating through a division known as the Internal Revenue Service. The Treasury Department publishes its interpretation of the tax laws in Treasury regulations; the final word in interpretation lies with the federal courts.

Originally the purpose of the federal income tax was simply to obtain revenue for the government. And at first, the tax rates were quite low—by today's standards. In 1913 a married person with taxable income of

---

[1] A federal income tax was proposed as early as 1815, and an income tax law was actually passed and income taxes collected during the Civil War. This law was upheld by the Supreme Court, but it was repealed when the need for revenue subsided after the war. In 1894 a new income tax law was passed, but the Supreme Court declared this law invalid on constitutional grounds.

[2] It reads: "The Congress shall have power to lay and collect taxes on incomes, from whatever source derived, without apportionment among the several States, and without regard to any census or enumeration."

$15,000 would have been subject to a tax rate of 1%, resulting in a tax liability of $150. Today, a married person with a $15,000 taxable income (worth far less in purchasing power) would pay over $3,000 in federal income tax. The maximum federal income tax rate in 1913 was 7%. Today it is 70%.

The purpose of federal income tax today includes a number of goals in addition to raising revenue. Among these other goals are to combat inflation or deflation, to influence the rate of economic growth, to encourage full employment, to favor small businesses, and to redistribute national income on a more equal basis.

The effect of income taxes on business decisions

To minimize income taxes is the goal of tax planning. Almost every business decision is a choice among alternative courses of action. For example, should we lease or buy business automobiles; should we obtain needed capital by issuing bonds or preferred stock; should we use straight-line depreciation or an accelerated method? Some of these alternatives will lead to much lower income taxes than others. Tax planning, therefore, means *determining in advance the income tax effect* of every proposed business action and then making business decisions which will lead to the smallest tax liability. Tax practice is an important element of the services furnished to clients by CPA firms. This service includes not only the computing of taxes and preparing of tax returns, but also tax planning.

Classes of taxpayers

In the eyes of the income tax law, there are four major classes of taxpayers: *individuals, corporations, estates,* and *trusts.* Proprietorships and partnerships are not taxed as business units; their income is taxed directly to the individual proprietor or partners, *whether or not actually withdrawn from the business.* A single proprietor reports his or her business income on an individual tax return; the members of a partnership include on their individual tax returns their respective shares of the partnership net income. An individual taxpayer's income tax return must include not only any business income from a proprietorship or partnership, but also any salary or other income and any deductions affecting the tax liability. A partnership must file an *information return* showing the computation of total partnership net income and the allocation of this income to each partner.

A corporation is a separate taxable entity; it must file a tax return and pay a tax on its annual taxable income. In addition, individual stockholders must report dividends received as part of their personal taxable income. The taxing of corporate dividends has led to the charge that there is "double taxation" of corporate income—once to the corporation and again when it is distributed to stockholders.

The income before taxes earned by a corporation may be subject to a federal corporate income tax rate of 48%. If the 52 cents remaining after taxes is distributed as dividends to individual stockholders, it is taxed to them personally at rates varying from 14 to 70%, depending on their individual tax brackets. Thus, the 52 cents of after-tax income to the corporation could be reduced by 70%, or 36 cents of individual income tax, leaving 16 cents of the original dollar for the shareholder. In summary, federal income taxes can take as much as 84 cents out of a dollar earned by a corporation and distributed as a dividend to a shareholder. The remaining 16 cents could be further reduced by state income taxes.

Special and complex rules apply to the determination of taxable income for estates and trusts. These rules will not be discussed in this chapter.

Cash basis of accounting for individual tax returns

Almost all individual tax returns are prepared on the cash basis of measuring income. Revenue is recognized when collected; expenses are recognized when paid. The cash basis is advantageous for the individual taxpayer because it is simple, requires a minimum of record keeping, and often permits tax saving by shifting the timing of revenue and expense transactions from one year to another. For example, a dentist whose taxable income is higher than usual in the current year may decide in December to delay billing patients until January 1, and thus postpone the receipt of gross income to the next year. The timing of expense payments near the year-end is also controllable by a taxpayer using the cash basis. A taxpayer who has received a bill for a deductible expense item in December may choose to pay it before or after December 31 and thereby influence the amount of taxable income in each year. Further comparison of the cash basis with the accrual basis of income measurement is presented later in this chapter.

Tax rates

All taxes may be characterized as progressive, proportional, or regressive with respect to any given base. A *progressive* tax becomes a larger portion of the base as that base increases. Federal income taxes are *progressive* with respect to income, since a higher tax rate applies as the amount of taxable income increases. A *proportional* tax remains a constant percentage of the base no matter how that base changes. For example, a 6% sales tax remains a constant percentage of sales regardless of changes in the sales figure. A *regressive* tax becomes a smaller percentage of the base as the base increases. A business license tax of $500, for example, is regressive with respect to income, since the larger the income the smaller the license tax as a percentage of income.

INDIVIDUAL TAX RATES Different tax rate schedules apply to individual taxpayers, married taxpayers who file *joint returns,* married taxpayers filing separate returns, and single taxpayers who qualify as the **head of a house-hold.** In computing the amount of the tax, the tax rates are applied to taxable income, the computation of which is discussed in a later section of this chapter. The rate schedules below show the personal income tax rates in effect at the time this was written. These rates are frequently changed by Congress.

Unmarried Individuals

Taxable Income	Tax on Column 1	% on Excess	Taxable Income	Tax on Column 1	% on Excess
$	$	14	$ 20,000	$ 5,230	38
500	70	15	22,000	5,990	40
1,000	145	16	26,000	7,590	45
1,500	225	17	32,000	10,290	50
2,000	310	19	38,000	13,290	55
4,000	690	21	44,000	16,590	60
6,000	1,110	24	50,000	20,190	62
8,000	1,590	25	60,000	26,390	64
10,000	2,090	27	70,000	32,790	66
12,000	2,630	29	80,000	39,390	68
14,000	3,210	31	90,000	46,190	69
16,000	3,830	34	100,000	53,090	70
18,000	4,510	36	200,000	123,090	70

Tax table for single taxpayers

Example: Find the tax for a *single person* having taxable income of $9,200.

Answer:
Tax on $8,000 as shown on the rate schedule $1,590
Tax on $1,200 excess at 25% 300

Tax on $9,200 for a single person $1,890

Married Individuals Filing Joint Returns

Taxable Income	Tax on Column 1	% on Excess	Taxable Income	Tax on Column 1	% on Excess
$	$	14	$ 40,000	$ 12,140	48
1,000	140	15	44,000	14,060	50
2,000	290	16	52,000	18,060	53
3,000	450	17	64,000	24,420	55
4,000	620	19	76,000	31,020	58
8,000	1,380	22	88,000	37,980	60
12,000	2,260	25	100,000	45,180	62
16,000	3,260	28	120,000	57,580	64
20,000	4,380	32	140,000	70,380	66
24,000	5,660	36	160,000	83,580	68
28,000	7,100	39	180,000	97,180	69
32,000	8,660	42	200,000	110,980	70
36,000	10,340	45	300,000	180,980	70

Tax table for joint returns

Example: Find the tax for a *married couple filing a joint return* and having a taxable income of $35,000.

Answer:
Tax on $32,000 as shown on the rate schedule $8,660
Tax on $3,000 excess at 42% 1,260

Tax on $35,000 for a married couple filing a joint return $9,920

Note that different and lower tax rates are applicable to the taxable income of married taxpayers who combine their income and deductions on a joint return. Certain persons who qualify as the head of a household are entitled to use still another schedule of tax rates. The schedules for heads of households and for married taxpayers filing separate returns are not shown in this chapter.

MARGINAL VERSUS AVERAGE TAX RATES In any analysis of tax costs, it is important to distinguish the *marginal* rate of tax from the *average* rate. This distinction may be illustrated as follows: If a single person has a taxable income of $26,000, his or her income tax will be $7,590, an average tax rate of about 29% of taxable income. On the next dollar of income, however, the tax is 45 cents since the individual is subject to a marginal tax rate of 45% on all income over $26,000.

As another example, assume Jose Sanchez, an unmarried executive having a taxable income of $26,000, is considering a change to a job that pays $6,000 more per year in salary. Using the illustrative tax rates, Sanchez now pays federal income taxes of $7,590, an average of 29% of his taxable income. His *marginal* tax rate on the $6,000 salary increase, however, is 45%. His decision with respect to the new position may well be affected by the fact that he will be able to keep only slightly more than half ($3,300) of the $6,000 increase in his salary. Assume that Sanchez lives in a state with a relatively high state income tax. California, for example, has an income tax rate of 11% on income above $15,500 earned by a single person. Thus, Sanchez would be able to keep less than half of the proposed salary increase of $6,000.

MAXIMUM TAX ON EARNED INCOME The maximum federal tax on *earned income* is limited to 50%. Wages, salaries, and other compensation for personal services are defined as earned income. For example, an unmarried individual with an earned income of $100,000 is subject to a marginal tax rate of 50%. However, an individual who received the same amount of income from investments would be subject to a marginal tax rate of 70%.

Income taxes and inflation

As salaries and prices in general have risen sharply in recent years, people find themselves in higher income tax brackets even though their higher salaries represent no increase in purchasing power. Since income tax rates are steeply progressive, this means that many people must pay a *higher percentage* of their earnings as income taxes merely as a result of inflation. Thus, income taxes are actually being increased in each year of inflation even though the schedule of tax rates remains unchanged. A $14,000 salary may buy no more today than a $7,000 salary some years ago, but a $14,000 salary is taxed at a much higher rate.

INCOME TAX FORMULA FOR INDIVIDUALS

The federal government supplies standard income tax forms on which taxpayers are guided to a proper computation of their taxable income and the amount of the tax. It is helpful to visualize the computation in terms of an income tax formula. The general formula for the determination of taxable income for all taxpayers (other than corporations, estates, and trusts) is outlined on page 705.

The actual sequence and presentation of material on income tax forms differs somewhat from the arrangement in this formula. However, it is easier to understand the structure and logic of the federal income tax and to analyze tax rules and their effect by referring to the tax formula.

TOTAL AND GROSS INCOME Total income is an accounting concept; gross income is a tax concept. *Total income* includes, in the words of the law, "all income from whatever source derived." To determine whether an amount received by an individual taxpayer should be included in total income, one need only ask, "Is it income or is it a return of capital?"

Gross income for tax purposes is all income not excluded by law. To determine whether any given income item is included in taxable gross income, one must ask, "Is there a provision in the tax law excluding this item of income from gross income?" To identify legal exclusions from gross income, it is necessary to refer to the tax law and sometimes to Treasury regulations and court decisions.

Among the items presently *excluded from gross income* by statute are interest on state and municipal bonds, gifts and inheritances, life insurance proceeds, workmen's compensation and sick pay, social security benefits and the portion of receipts from annuities that represent return of cost, pensions to veterans, compensation for damages, and the first $100 of dividends from corporations ($200 on a joint tax return).

CAPITAL GAINS AND LOSSES Certain kinds of property are defined under the tax law as *capital assets*.[3] Gains or losses from the sale or exchange of such assets are granted special treatment for income tax purposes. Because long-term capital gains generally are taxed at *one-half or less* than the rates applicable to *ordinary income,* there is a strong incentive for taxpayers to arrange their business and personal affairs so that income will be realized in the form of *capital gains.* The government's efforts to keep such arrangements within bounds have been exceeded only by the collective ingenuity of taxpayers and tax advisers in making income appear in the form of capital gains.

---

[3] Capital assets are defined by exclusion. The Internal Revenue Code states that capital assets include all items of property *except* (a) trade accounts and notes receivable; (b) inventories in a trade or business; (c) real or depreciable property in a trade or business; (d) copyrights, literary, musical, or artistic compositions in the hands of their creator; (e) letters or similar property in the hands of original recipient; (f) government obligations issued on a discount basis and due within one year without interest.

KNOW P. 705

General Federal Income Tax Formula for Individuals

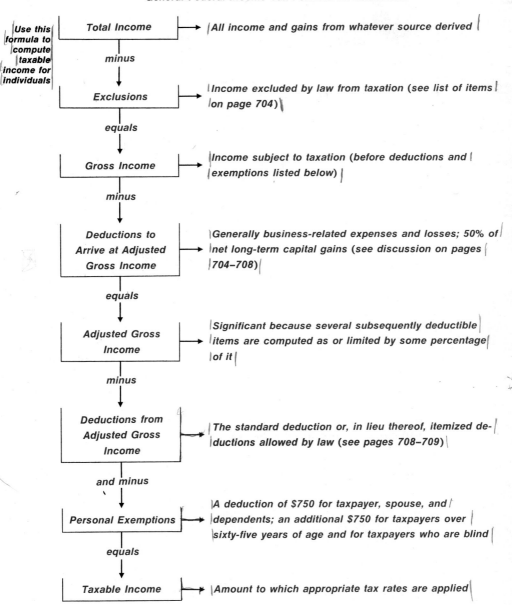

Use this formula to compute taxable income for individuals

Total Income → |All income and gains from whatever source derived |

minus

Exclusions → |Income excluded by law from taxation (see list of items on page 704)|

equals

Gross Income → |Income subject to taxation (before deductions and exemptions listed below) |

minus

Deductions to Arrive at Adjusted Gross Income → |Generally business-related expenses and losses; 50% of net long-term capital gains (see discussion on pages 704–708)|

equals

Adjusted Gross Income → |Significant because several subsequently deductible items are computed as or limited by some percentage of it |

minus

Deductions from Adjusted Gross Income → |The standard deduction or, in lieu thereof, itemized deductions allowed by law (see pages 708–709)|

and minus

Personal Exemptions → |A deduction of $750 for taxpayer, spouse, and dependents; an additional $750 for taxpayers over sixty-five years of age and for taxpayers who are blind|

equals

Taxable Income → |Amount to which appropriate tax rates are applied|

Amount of gain or loss The tax gain (or loss) from the sale or exchange of capital assets is the difference between the selling price and the *basis* of property sold. Basis rules are complicated; tax basis depends, among other things, on how the property was acquired (purchase, gift, or inheritance), whether it is personal or business property, and in some cases whether it is sold at a gain or at a loss. In general, the basis of purchased property is its cost, reduced by any depreciation that has been allowed in computing taxable income.

Long term versus short term Long and short are relative terms: in income taxation the dividing line was traditionally six months but was changed to nine months for the year 1977 and to one year in 1978 and thereafter. Long-term capital gains or losses result from the sale or exchange of capital assets held *for more than the specified period* (one year, in 1978); short term from those held one year or less.

The term *net short-term gain* means short-term gains in excess of short-term losses. Net short-term gains must be reported in full and are taxed as ordinary income. Only one-half of long-term gains, reduced by any net short-term losses, are included in adjusted gross income, and the maximum rate of tax on the total gain is generally 25% of gains up to $50,000.[4] For example, suppose that Bob Savage, a taxpayer subject to a marginal tax rate of 30%, has a $1,000 net long-term capital gain and no net short-term capital loss. He would include only $500 in adjusted gross income and pay a $150 (30% of $500) tax on the gain. The tax rate applicable to his $1,000 long-term gain is 15%, one-half of his marginal rate.

On the other hand, suppose that the same taxpayer has a marginal tax rate of 70%. If he were to include $500 (one-half of the $1,000 net long-term gain) in adjusted gross income and apply the 70% marginal rate, his tax would be $350, or 35% of the total $1,000 net long-term gain. Instead, he would be entitled to compute his tax on the long-term capital gain at $250 (25% of $1,000). In this case the rate of tax applicable to the long-term capital gain would be *less* than one-half of the taxpayer's marginal rate of tax on other income.

In general, capital *losses,* either long-term or short-term, are deductible only against capital gains. If total capital losses exceed gains, however, individual taxpayers (but not corporations) may deduct capital losses against other gross income up to a maximum of $2,000 in 1977 or $3,000 in 1978. For example, if an individual incurred a capital loss of $100,000 in 1978 but also had a salary of $50,000, he or she would have gross income subject to taxation of $47,000. The unused capital loss could be carried forward and offset against capital gains, if any, in future years, or against other income at the rate of $3,000 a year. Thus, a great many years would be required to offset the $50,000 capital loss against other income.

Critics of our present tax laws point out that persons who save and invest are taxed in a similar manner to those who gamble on horse races. Gains from investment are taxed heavily and losses from investments are

---

[4] The effective maximum tax on net long-term gains in excess of $50,000 may be 35% or more for taxpayers in the highest tax bracket.

generally not permitted as deductions if they exceed gains. This policy may be inconsistent with the national goal of encouraging investment. Although the United States formerly had worldwide recognition for its high productivity, the ratio of capital investment to gross national product has now fallen far below many other nations. The tax laws of some other countries are more conducive to investment, for example, no tax on capital gains.

Only 50% of a net long-term capital loss can be used in arriving at the maximum which can be offset against other income in a single year. In other words, a net long-term capital loss of $4,000 would be required to entitle the taxpayer to take a $2,000 deduction. Although capital losses not deductible in any given year may be carried forward to future tax years, it is apparent that a large capital loss as in the preceding example will not be fully utilized in future years unless the taxpayer is fortunate enough to have a large capital gain.

BUSINESS PLANT AND EQUIPMENT Real or depreciable property used in a trade or business is not a capital asset under the tax law. This means that a net loss realized on the sale or disposal of such property is fully deductible. However, gains on such property held more than one year may be granted capital gains treatment under certain complex conditions. Gains on the sale of assets used in business and held six months or less are taxable as ordinary income.

DEDUCTIONS TO ARRIVE AT ADJUSTED GROSS INCOME The *deductions from gross income* allowed in computing adjusted gross income are discussed below.

1 Business expenses These include all ordinary and necessary expenses of carrying on a trade, business, or profession (other than as an employee). In the actual tax computation, business expenses are deducted from business revenue, and net business income is then included in adjusted gross income.

2 Employees' expenses Some expenses incurred by employees in connection with their employment are allowed as a deduction if the employee is not reimbursed by the employer. These include, for example, travel and transportation expenses, expenses of "outside salespersons," and certain moving expenses.

3 Expenses attributable to rents and royalties Expenses, such as depreciation, depletion, property taxes, repairs, maintenance, interest on indebtedness related to property, and any other expense incurred in connection with the earning of rental or royalty income, are allowed as a deduction. This means that only the *net income* derived from rents and royalties is included in adjusted gross income. (See page 715 for a discussion of statutory depletion allowances on certain royalties.)

4 Losses from the sale of property used in a trade or business The loss resulting from the sale of property used in a trade or business may be deducted against other items of gross income.[5]

5 Net capital losses Up to $2,000 of net capital losses may be deducted in 1977 and $3,000 in 1978 and later years to arrive at adjusted gross income. (See pages 706–707.)

6 Long-term capital gain deduction One-half of the excess of net long-term capital gains over net short-term capital losses is a deduction to arrive at adjusted gross income.

7 Net operating loss carry-over Taxable income may be either positive or negative. If positive income were taxed and no allowance made for operating losses, a taxpayer whose business income fluctuated between income and loss would pay a relatively higher tax than one having a steady income averaging the same amount. Therefore, the tax law allows the carry-back and carry-over of net operating losses as an offset against the income of other years. At the present time a loss must be carried back against the income of the three preceding years, and then forward against the income of the next five years.

DEDUCTIONS FROM ADJUSTED GROSS INCOME Individual taxpayers have an option with respect to *deductions from adjusted gross income.* They may choose to take a lump-sum standard deduction, or they may choose to itemize their deductions, in which case they may deduct a number of expenses specified in the tax law as itemized deductions.

The standard deduction In recent years the standard deduction has been 16% of adjusted gross income but not in excess of $2,800 for persons filing jointly or a surviving spouse. The maximum is $2,400 for single individuals, or $1,400 for married individuals filing separately. For example, if David Chow, a married person filing a joint return had adjusted gross income of $14,000, his standard deduction would be $2,240 (16% of $14,000). If his adjusted gross income were $25,000, his standard deduction would be $2,800, the legal maximum.

Also affecting the standard deduction is a *low income allowance* of $2,100 for certain taxpayers who are eligible to deduct this amount if it is larger than the standard deduction computed at 16%.

Deductions *to arrive at adjusted gross income* do not affect the decision to elect the standard deduction. However, itemized deductions (discussed

---

[5] Losses arising from the sale of personal property, such as a home or personal automobile, are not deductible. On the other hand, gains from the sale of personal property are taxable. This appears inconsistent, until one realizes that a loss on the sale of personal property usually reflects depreciation through use, which is a personal expense.

below) are relinquished if the standard deduction is taken. This explains why it is important to know whether a given deduction comes before or after adjusted gross income in the income tax formula.

Itemized deductions Instead of taking a standard deduction, a taxpayer may elect to itemize deductions. The major categories of itemized deductions allowable under the law are described below:

1 *Interest.* Interest on any indebtedness, within certain limits.

2 *Taxes.* State and local real and personal property taxes; state income taxes, all sales taxes, and state and local gasoline taxes are deductible by the person on whom they are imposed. No federal taxes qualify as itemized deductions.

3 *Contributions.* Contributions by individuals to charitable, religious, educational, and certain other nonprofit organizations are deductible, within certain limits.

4 *Medical expenses.* Medical and dental expenses of the taxpayer and his or her family are deductible to the extent that they exceed 3% of adjusted gross income, subject to certain maximum limits, and limits on the deductibility of drugs and medicines. A taxpayer may deduct one-half of the medical insurance costs up to $150 without regard to the 3% exclusion.

5 *Casualty losses.* Losses in excess of $100 from any fire, storm, earthquake, shipwreck, theft, or other sudden, unexpected, or unusual causes are deductible.

6 *Expenses related to the production of income.* In this category are included any necessary expenses in producing income or for the management of income-producing property, other than those deductible to arrive at adjusted gross income. Some examples of *miscellaneous deductible expenses* are union dues, work clothes, professional dues, subscriptions to professional periodicals, investment advisers' fees, legal fees relating to investments, and fees for income tax advice and for preparation of tax returns. Examples of *miscellaneous nondeductible expenses* are the cost of going to and from work, gifts to needy friends, most living expenses, baby-sitting expenses, the cost of school tuition, and gambling losses in excess of gambling winnings.

PERSONAL EXEMPTIONS In addition to itemized deductions, a deduction from adjusted gross income is allowed for *personal exemptions.* One exemption each is allowed for the taxpayer, his spouse, and each person who qualifies as a dependent of the taxpayer. Recently the amount of each personal exemption has been $750. The amount of the personal exemption may be changed by Congress at any time. Proposals for an increase to $1,000 or more have been much discussed in recent years.

The term *dependent* has a particular meaning under law. Briefly but incompletely stated, a dependent is a person who (*1*) receives over one-half of his or her support from the taxpayer, (*2*) is either closely related to the taxpayer or lives in the taxpayer's home, and (*3*) has gross income during the year of less than the current exemption amount unless he or she is a child of the taxpayer and is under nineteen years of age or is a full-time student.[6]

---

[6] A child under nineteen or a full-time student who qualifies as a dependent in all other respects but who earns over the current exemption amount in any one year has, in effect, two personal exemptions. One may be taken by the taxpayer who claims him or her as a dependent; the other he will claim for himself on his own personal income tax return.

A taxpayer and his spouse may each claim an additional exemption if he or she is blind, and another exemption if either is sixty-five years of age or over. These additional exemptions do not apply to dependents.

TAX RETURNS AND PAYMENT OF THE TAX Every individual who has gross income in excess of the amount of his or her own personal exemption (or two exemptions in the case of persons over sixty-five) must file an income tax return within $3\frac{1}{2}$ months after the close of the taxable year. On the calendar-year basis, applicable to most taxpayers, the due date is April 15.

Currently, the payment of federal income taxes is on a "pay as you go" basis. The procedure by which employers withhold income taxes from the wages of employees has been discussed previously in Chapter 13. Without the withholding feature, the present income tax system would probably be unworkable. The high rate of income taxes would probably pose an impossible collection problem if employees received their total earnings in cash and were then called upon to pay to the government a major portion of a year's wages at the end of the year.

To equalize the treatment of employees and self-employed persons, the tax law requires persons who have taxable income in excess of a given amount, from which no withholdings have been made, to file a declaration of estimated income tax and to pay estimated income taxes in quarterly installments. Any under- or overpayment is adjusted when the tax return is filed.

When the tax liability on taxable income has been computed, the final step in computing the amount of tax due is to deduct any allowable *credits* against the tax. Examples of tax credits are: (*1*) taxes withheld or paid on declared estimates; (*2*) retirement income credit for taxpayers over 62 years of age; (*3*) taxes paid to foreign countries on income also taxed by the United States; and (*4*) the *investment tax credit* on purchase of certain depreciable assets.

The investment tax credit is an example of efforts to provide tax incentives as a means of stimulating investment. When a business buys certain types of new long-lived equipment, it can take a credit of from 4 to 10% of the cost of the new property as a deduction from the income tax for the year.

COMPUTATION OF INDIVIDUAL INCOME TAX ILLUSTRATED The computation of the federal income tax for Mary and John Reed is illustrated on page 711.

In this example it is assumed that the Reeds provide over one-half the support of their two children. John Reed is a practicing attorney who received $56,000 in gross fees from his law practice, and incurred $30,000 of business expenses. Mary Reed earned $24,400 during the year as a CPA working for a national firm of accountants. During the year, $4,460 was withheld from her salary for federal income taxes. The Reeds received $700 interest on municipal bonds, and $320 on savings accounts.

Dividends received on stock jointly owned amounted to $25,800 during the year. During the year, stock purchased several years ago by John Reed for $1,600 was sold for $2,400, net of brokerage fees, thus producing an $800 long-term capital gain.

The Reeds have allowable itemized expenses (contributions, interest expense, taxes, medical costs, etc.) of $8,720. They paid a total of $18,000 on their declaration of estimated income tax during the year.

On the basis of these facts, the taxable income for the Reeds is shown to be $65,000. Since they file a joint return, the tax on this amount of taxable income may be computed from the rate table for married couples, and is $24,970. Taking withholdings and payments on declared estimates into account, the Reeds have already paid income taxes of $22,460 and thus owe $2,510 at the time of the filing of their tax return. If their credits had amounted to $25,000, for example, they would be entitled to a refund of $30.

MARY AND JOHN REED
Illustrative Federal Income Tax Computation
For the Year 19____

Compare with tax formula on page 705

Gross income (excluding $700 interest on municipal bonds):		
Gross fees from John Reed's law practice	$56,000	
Dividends ($25,800 less $200 exclusion)	25,600	
Mary Reed's salary	24,400	
Interest revenue on savings accounts	320	
Long-term capital gain (on stock held more than six months)	800	$107,120
Deductions to arrive at adjusted gross income:		
Operating expenses of John Reed's law practice	$30,000	
Long-term capital gain deduction (50% of $800)	400	30,400
Adjusted gross income		$ 76,720
Deductions from adjusted gross income:		
Itemized deductions	$ 8,720	
Personal exemptions (4 × $750)	3,000	11,720
Taxable income		$ 65,000
Computation of tax (using rates shown on page 702):		
Tax on $64,000 (joint return)	$24,420	
Tax on $1,000 × 55%	550	$ 24,970
Less: Tax credits:		
Withheld from Mary Reed's salary	$ 4,460	
Payments by Reeds on declaration of estimated tax	18,000	22,460
Amount of tax remaining to be paid		$ 2,510

PARTNERSHIPS

Partnerships are not considered taxable entities by income tax statutes. Under the federal income tax law, partnerships are treated as a conduit through which taxable income flows to the partners. An information return must be filed by all partnerships, showing the determination of net income and the share of each partner. However, certain items of partnership income and deductions are segregated, and all partners are required to treat their share of each of these items as if they had received or paid them personally. In general, segregated items are those granted special tax treatment; they include tax-exempt interest, capital gains and losses, charitable contributions, and cash dividends received. Any salaries actually paid to partners may be deducted in arriving at partnership income, but they must be reported as salaries by the individual partners on their personal income tax returns.

CORPORATIONS

A corporation is a separate taxable entity and is subject to a tax at special rates on its taxable income. Every corporation, unless expressly exempt from taxation, must file an income tax return whether or not it has taxable income or any tax is due.

CORPORATION TAX RATES The corporate tax rate schedule is much simpler than the schedule for individuals. The rates in effect at the time this was written for most types of corporations are shown below. These rates are also frequently changed by Congress. A slight change in rates applicable to the year 1977 only was approved by Congress late in 1976. This temporary change was originally scheduled to expire on December 31, 1977 but was extended by Congress to include the year 1978.*

Corporation tax rates

Rate for first $50,000 of taxable income	22%
Rate for taxable income over $50,000	48%

In computing the tax, it is often convenient to multiply the entire taxable income by 48% and then deduct $13,000 (26% of the first $50,000 of taxable income which is taxed at only 22%). For example, the tax on $100,000 of taxable income may be determined as follows:

Computation of income tax for corporation illustrated

	Method 1	Method 2
Rate for first $50,000 of taxable income, 22%	$11,000	
Rate for taxable income over $50,000, 48% of $50,000	24,000	
Tax on entire taxable income of $100,000 at 48%		$48,000
Less: 26% of $50,000 which is taxed at only 22%		(13,000)
Total income tax	$35,000	$35,000

Corporate taxable income is computed in much the same manner as for individuals, with the following major differences:

---

* The change in rates effective through 1978 reduced the tax rate on the first $25,000 of corporate taxable income from 22% to 20%.

1 The concept of adjusted gross income is not applicable to a corporation, since there is no standard deduction or itemized deduction.

2 Corporations are not entitled to the dividend exclusion of $100 allowed to individual taxpayers. Instead a corporation may deduct 85% of any dividends received from other domestic corporations. This means in effect that only 15% of dividends is taxed to the receiving corporation.

3 Corporations may deduct capital losses only to the extent of capital gains. If capital losses exceed gains, the net loss may be offset against net capital gains of the preceding three years (carry-back) or the following five years (carry-forward).

4 Corporations are subject to a maximum tax rate of 30% on net long-term capital gains. A corporation is not entitled to the 50% long-term capital gain deduction. If corporate taxable income (including any long-term capital gain) is below $50,000, a corporation pays the 22% normal tax on the long-term capital gain, rather than the 30% maximum capital gain tax rate.

5 Corporations may deduct charitable contributions only to the extent of 5% of taxable income, computed before the deduction of any contributions. Contributions in excess of the limit may be carried forward for five succeeding years if contributions (including those carried forward) in those years are within the 5% limit.

6 Corporations may deduct organization costs over a period of five years or more.

To illustrate some of the features of the income tax law as it applies to corporations, a tax computation for the Luis Perez Corporation is shown below:

LUIS PEREZ CORPORATION
Illustrative Tax Computation

Note difference between income per accounting records ($84,000) and taxable income ($80,000)	**Revenue:**		
	Sales		$400,000
	Dividends received from domestic corporations		20,000
	Total revenue		$420,000
	Expenses:		
	Cost of goods sold	$236,000	
	Other expenses (includes capital loss of $6,000)	100,000	336,000
	Income per accounting records		$ 84,000
	Add back (items not deductible for tax purposes):		
	Capital loss deducted as part of operating expenses*		6,000
	Charitable contributions in excess of 5% limit		7,000
			$ 97,000
	Special deductions:		
	Dividends received credit (85% or $20,000)		17,000
	Taxable income		$ 80,000
	Tax computation:		
	Tax on first $50,000 of taxable income at 22%	$ 11,000	
	Tax on taxable income over $50,000 ($30,000 × 48%)	14,400	
	Total tax†		$ 25,400

* Can be carried back three years and offset against capital gains if any.
† Alternate computation: $80,000 × 48%, or $38,400, less $13,000 = $25,400.

Accounting income versus taxable income

The accountant's objective in determining accounting income is to measure business operating results as accurately as possible, in accordance with the generally accepted accounting principles summarized in Chapter 14. Taxable income, on the other hand, is a legal concept governed by statute. In setting the rules for determining taxable income, Congress is interested not only in meeting the revenue needs of government but in achieving certain public policy objectives. Since accounting and taxable income are determined with different purposes in mind, it is not surprising that they often differ by material amounts.

CASH VERSUS ACCRUAL BASIS OF INCOME MEASUREMENT The *accrual basis* of measuring income has been discussed throughout the preceding chapters of this book, because it is the method used by most business enterprises. Revenue is recognized when it is realized, and expenses are recorded when they are incurred, without regard to the timing of receipt or payment. Any taxpayer who maintains a set of accounting records may elect to use the accrual basis for tax purposes. When the production, purchase, or sale of merchandise is a significant factor in a business, the accrual method is mandatory.

The *cash basis* of measuring income does not reflect income in the accounting sense. Revenue is recognized when cash is received, and expenses are recorded when they are paid. This method is allowed for tax purposes because it is simple, requires a minimum of records, and produces reasonably satisfactory results for individuals not engaged in business and for businesses in which receivables, payables, and inventories are not a major factor.

The cash basis allowed for income tax purposes and used on nearly all tax returns by individuals varies in two important ways from a simple offsetting of cash receipts and disbursements.

1 On the revenue side, a cash basis taxpayer must report revenue when it has been *constructively received,* even though the cash is not yet in his or her possession. Constructive receipt means that the revenue is so much within the control of the taxpayer as to be equivalent to receipt. For example, if a taxpayer has a savings account, for income tax purposes the interest on that account is considered to be constructively received even though the taxpayer does not draw it out. Similarly, a check received on December 31 is considered to be constructively received even though it is not cashed until January 2.

2 On the expenditure side, the cost of acquiring depreciable property having a service life of more than one year is not deductible in the year of purchase. The taxpayer must treat such a purchase as an asset and deduct depreciation in appropriate years. A similar treatment must be given to major prepayments, such as rent paid in advance or insurance premiums which cover more than one year.

The choice between the cash and accrual method, where permitted, rests on the question of tax timing. Taxpayers are motivated to elect the cash basis because it permits postponing the recognition of taxable income and the payment of the tax. In this way they have the interest-free use of funds that would otherwise be paid in taxes.

SPECIAL TAX TREATMENT OF REVENUE AND EXPENSE Even when the accrual method is used for tax purposes, differences between taxable and accounting income may occur. Some differences result from special tax rules which are unrelated to accounting principles.

1 Some items included in accounting income are not taxable. For example, interest on state or municipal bonds is excluded from taxable income.

2 Some business expenses are not deductible. For example, donations to political parties are generally not deductible.

3 Special deductions in excess of actual business expenses are allowed some taxpayers. For example, depletion deductions in excess of actual cost are allowed taxpayers in some mining industries. However, the *statutory depletion* (or *percentage depletion*) allowance which formerly existed for income derived from oil and gas operations has been eliminated.

4 Some business expenses must be treated as capital expenditures for income tax purposes. For example, goodwill may be amortized for accounting purposes; for income tax purposes goodwill is a permanent asset and amortization is not a deductible expense.

In addition, the *timing* of the recognition of certain revenue and expenses under tax rules differs from that under accounting principles. Some items of income received in advance may be taxed in the year of receipt while certain accrued expenses may not be deductible for income tax purposes until they are actually paid in cash.

ALTERNATIVE ACCOUNTING METHODS Various accounting methods result in different net income figures, largely because of differences in the timing of revenue and expense recognition. The tax law permits taxpayers, in some cases, to adopt for income tax purposes accounting methods which differ from those used for financial reporting. For example, it may be advantageous to use accelerated depreciation in the income tax return and straight-line depreciation in the accounting records and financial statements. Business executives are therefore faced with the problem of choosing an accounting method for income tax purposes that will result in minimizing their tax burdens—usually by postponing the tax.

The choice of inventory pricing methods will affect the timing of net income recognition, as we have seen in Chapter 10. One of the reasons for the popularity of the lifo pricing method is that it results in lower net income during periods of rising prices. A peculiarity of the *lifo* tax rules is that *this method must be used in published financial statements if it is elected for income tax purposes.*

The tax law allows the adoption of a variety of depreciation methods in computing taxable income. It will generally be advantageous for a taxpayer to adopt the depreciation method for income tax purposes which results in the largest amount of cumulative depreciation over the shortest period of time.

There are a number of other less common examples of elective methods which postpone taxes. Taxpayers who sell merchandise on the **installment basis** may elect to report income in proportion to the cash received on the installment contract, rather than at the time of sale. The cost of drilling oil wells and preparing wells for production may be charged off as incurred, or may be capitalized and depreciated.

TAXES AND FINANCIAL REPORTING; INTERPERIOD INCOME TAX ALLOCATION When there are differences between accounting principles and income tax rules, many businesses choose to keep their accounting records on a tax basis as a matter of convenience. In other words, accounting principles give way to tax laws. If the differences are not material, there is no objection to this practice as a means of simplifying the keeping of tax records. When the differences between tax rules and accounting principles are material, however, the result of following the tax law would be to distort financial statements. It is clearly preferable to maintain accounting records to meet the need for relevant information about business operations and to adjust such data to arrive at taxable income.

When a corporation follows different accounting methods for accounting and tax purposes, a financial reporting problem arises. The difference in method will usually have the effect of postponing the recognition of income (either because an expense deduction is accelerated or because revenue recognition is postponed). The question is whether the income tax expense should be accrued when the income is recognized in the accounting records, or when it is actually subject to taxation.

To illustrate the problem, let us consider a very simple case. Suppose the Pryor Company has before-tax accounting income of $200,000 in each of two years. However, the company takes as a tax deduction in Year 1 an expense of $80,000 which is reported for accounting purposes in Year 2. The company's accounting and taxable income, and the actual income taxes due (assuming a tax rate of 40%) are shown below:

	Year 1	Year 2
Accounting income (before income taxes)	$200,000	$200,000
Taxable income	120,000	280,000
Actual income taxes due each year, at assumed rate of 40% of		
taxable income	48,000	112,000

Following one approach, the Pryor Company might simply report in its income statement in each year the amount of income taxes due for that year as computed on the company's income tax returns. The effect on reported net income would be as follows:

	Year 1	Year 2
Accounting income (before income taxes)	$200,000	$200,000
Income taxes actually due	48,000	112,000
Net income	$152,000	$ 88,000

Company reports actual taxes

The reader of the Pryor Company's income statement might well wonder why the same accounting income before income taxes in the two years produced such widely varying tax expense and net income figures.

To deal with this distortion between pre- and after-tax income, an accounting policy known as *interperiod income tax allocation* has been devised, which is required for financial reporting purposes.[7] Briefly, the objective of the tax allocation procedure is to accrue income taxes in relation to accounting income, whenever differences between accounting and taxable income are caused by differences in the *timing* of revenue or expenses. In the Pryor Company example, this means we would report in the Year 1 income statement a tax expense on the $80,000 ($200,000 − $120,000) of income which was reported for accounting purposes in Year 1 but which will not be taxed until Year 2. The effect of this accounting procedure is demonstrated by the following journal entries to record the income tax expense in each of the two years:

Entries to record income tax allocation

Year 1	*Income Taxes Expense*	*80,000*	
	Current Income Tax Liability		*48,000*
	Deferred Income Tax Liability		*32,000*

To record current and deferred income taxes at 40% of accounting income of $200,000.

Year 2	*Income Taxes Expense*	*80,000*	
	Deferred Income Tax Liability	*32,000*	
	Current Income Tax Liability		*112,000*

To record income taxes at 40% of accounting income of $200,000 and to record actual income taxes due.

Using tax allocation procedures, the Pryor Company would report its net income during the two-year period as follows:

Company uses tax allocation procedure

	Year 1	Year 2
Income before income taxes	*$200,000*	*$200,000*
Income taxes expense (tax allocation basis)	*80,000*	*80,000*
Net income	*$120,000*	*$120,000*

In this simple example, the difference between taxable and accounting income (caused by the accelerated deduction of an expense) was fully offset in a period of two years. In practice, differences between accounting and taxable income may persist over extended time periods and deferred tax liabilities may accumulate to significant amounts. For example, in a recent balance sheet of Sears, Roebuck and Co., deferred taxes of $690 million were reported as a result of the use of the installment sales method for income tax purposes while reporting net income in financial statements on the usual accrual method.

In contrast to the example for the Pryor Company in which income taxes were deferred, income taxes *may be prepaid* when taxable income

---

[7] For a more complete discussion of tax allocation procedures, see *APB Opinion No. 11*, "Accounting for Income Taxes," AICPA (New York: 1967).

exceeds accounting income because of timing differences. The portion of taxes paid on income deferred for accounting purposes would be reported as prepaid taxes in the balance sheet. When the income is reported as earned for accounting purposes in a later period, the *prepaid taxes are recognized as tax expense* applicable to the income currently reported but *taxed in an earlier period.*[8]

TAX PLANNING

Federal income tax laws have become so complex that detailed tax planning has become a way of life for most business firms. Almost all businesses today engage professional tax specialists to review the tax aspects of major business decisions and to develop plans for legally minimizing income taxes.

Tax avoidance and tax evasion

Newspaper stories tell us each year of some taxpayers who have deliberately understated their taxable income by failing to report a portion of income received or by claiming fictitious deductions such as an excess number of personal exemptions. Such purposeful understatement of taxable income is called *tax evasion* and is, of course, illegal. On the other hand, *tax avoidance* (the arranging of business and financial affairs in a manner that will minimize tax liability) is entirely legal. Because it is important for everyone to recognize areas in which tax savings may be substantial, a few of the major opportunities for tax planning are discussed in the following sections of this chapter.

Form of business organization

Tax factors should be carefully considered at the time a business is organized. As a single proprietor or partner, a business owner will pay taxes at individual rates, ranging currently from 14 to 70%, on the business income earned in any year *whether or not it is withdrawn from the business.* Corporations, on the other hand, are taxed on earnings at average rates varying from 22 to 48%. Corporations may deduct salaries paid to owners for services but may not deduct dividends paid to stockholders. Both salaries and dividends are taxed to their recipients.

These factors must be weighed in deciding in any given situation whether the corporate or noncorporate form of business organization is

---

[8] A good example of this treatment is found in the annual report of the Ford Motor Company. A recent balance sheet showed "Income Taxes Allocable to the Following Year," $206.5 million, as a current asset. This large prepaid tax came about as a result of estimated car warranty expense being deducted from revenue in the period in which cars were sold; for income tax purposes, this expense is deductible only when it is actually incurred.

preferable. There is no simple rule of thumb, even considering only these basic differences. To illustrate, suppose that Able, a married man, starts a business which he expects will produce, before any compensation to himself and before income taxes, an average annual income of $80,000. Able plans to withdraw $20,000 yearly from the business. The combined corporate and individual taxes under the corporate and single proprietorship form of business organization are summarized below.

At first glance this comparison suggests that the corporate form of organization is favorable from an income tax viewpoint. It must be noted, however, that the $44,200 ($60,000 — $15,800) of earnings retained in the corporation will be taxed to Able as ordinary income when and if distributed as dividends. On the other hand, if Able later sells his business and realizes these earnings in the form of the increased value of the capital stock, any gain may be taxed at a maximum of, say, 25%. In either case Able can postpone the payment of tax on retained earnings so long as these earnings remain invested in the business.

Form of Business Organization

	Corporate	Single Proprietorship
Business income	$80,000	$80,000
Salary to Able	20,000	
Taxable income	$60,000	$80,000
Corporate tax:		
22% of $50,000 .... $11,000		
48% on excess of $10,000 4,800	15,800	
Net income	$44,200	$80,000
Combined corporate and individual tax:		
Corporate tax on $60,000 income (above)	$15,800	
Individual tax—joint return:*		
On Able's $20,000 salary	4,380	
On Able's $80,000 share of business income		$33,340
Total tax on business income	$20,180	$33,340

Which form of business organization produces a lower tax?

* Able's personal exemptions and deductions have been ignored, on the assumption that his other income equals personal exemptions and deductions.

If Able decided to withdraw all net income from the business each year, the total tax on corporate net income and on the $44,200 that he would receive in dividends would amount to $40,330, compared to only $33,340 tax paid on the $80,000 of earnings from the single proprietorship. The amount of $40,330 consists of $15,800 corporate tax plus $24,530 tax on personal income of $64,200.

Under this assumption the income tax results under the single proprietorship form of organization are preferable. It is clear that both the marginal rate of tax to which individual business owners are subject and the extent to which profits are to be withdrawn from the business must be considered in assessing the relative advantages of one form of business organization over another.

Under certain conditions, small, closely held corporations may elect to be "tax-option" corporations, in which case the corporation pays no tax but the individual shareholders are taxed directly on the corporation's earnings.

Planning business transactions to minimize income taxes

Business transactions may often be arranged in such a way as to produce favorable tax treatment. For example, when property is sold under an installment contract, the taxable gain may be prorated over the period during which installment payments are received by the seller. To qualify for this treatment, payments received during the first year must not exceed 30% of the selling price. By arranging the transaction to meet these conditions, a substantial postponement of tax payments may be secured. For this reason farms, apartment buildings, and some other types of real estate are often offered for sale with a down payment of 29%.

Sometimes sellers try to arrange a transaction one way to their tax benefit and the buyers try to shape it another way to produce tax savings for them. Income tax effects thus become a part of price negotiations. For example, in buying business property, the purchasers will try to allocate as much of the cost of the property to the building and as little to the land as possible, since building costs can be depreciated for tax purposes. Similarly, in selling a business, the sellers will try to allocate as much of the selling price as possible to goodwill, since this is a capital asset. The buyers of the business, however, will want the purchase price to be attributable to inventories or depreciable assets, because the cost of goods sold and depreciation are deductible against ordinary income. Goodwill cannot be amortized for tax purposes. The point is, *any failure to consider the tax consequences of major business transactions can be costly.*

Some examples of provisions of the federal tax laws clearly designed to affect business decisions include (*1*) accelerated depreciation, (*2*) additional first-year depreciation of 20% on assets of tangible personal property costing up to $10,000, (*3*) rapid depreciation on assets "critical to the public interest" such as pollution-control facilities and coal-mine safety equipment, (*4*) tax-free exchanges of certain types of assets or securities pursuant to a corporate merger, and (*5*) *investment tax credits* when certain types of depreciable assets are acquired.

Tax planning in the choice of financial structure

Different forms of business financing produce different tax expense. Interest on debt, for example, is *fully deductible* while dividends on preferred or common stocks are not. This factor operates as a strong incentive to finance expansion by borrowing.

Suppose that a company needs $100,000 to invest in productive assets on which it can expect to earn a 12% annual return. If the company issues $100,000 in 6% preferred stock, it will earn after taxes, assuming a 48% marginal tax rate, $6,240 ($12,000 less taxes at 48% of $12,000). This is barely enough to cover the $6,000 preferred dividend. If, on the other hand, the company borrowed the $100,000 at 6% interest, its taxable income would be decreased $6,000 ($12,000 earnings less $6,000 interest expense). The tax on this amount at 48% would be $2,880, leaving income of $3,120 available for common stockholders or for reinvestment in the business. A similar analysis should be made in choosing between debt and common stock financing.

Budgeting

Taxable income computed on the accrual basis is not necessarily matched by an inflow of cash. A healthy profit picture accompanied by a tight cash position is not unusual for a rapidly growing company. Income taxes are a substantial cash drain and an important factor in preparing cash budgets. In other words, a profitable growing business may find itself without the cash needed to pay its tax liability.

Tax shelters

A tax shelter is an investment which produces a loss for tax purposes in the near term but hopefully proves profitable in the long run. Near the close of each year, many newspaper advertisements appear offering an opportunity to invest in a program which promises to reduce the investor's present tax liability yet produce future profits. These programs have a particular appeal to persons in very high tax brackets who face the prospect of paying most of a year's net income as taxes.

A limited partnership organization is often used, so that each investor may claim his or her share of the immediate losses. Typical of the types of ventures are oil and gas drilling programs and real estate investments offering high leverage and accelerated depreciation. Unfortunately, many so-called tax shelters have proved to be merely unprofitable investments, in which the investors saved taxes but lost larger amounts of capital. A sound approach to tax shelters should probably be based on the premise that if an investment does not appear worthwhile without the promised tax benefits, it should be avoided.

Some tax shelters, on the other hand, are not of a high risk nature. State and municipal bonds offer a modest rate of interest which is tax-exempt. Investment in real property with deductions for mortgage interest, property taxes, and depreciation will often show losses which offset other taxable income, yet eventually prove profitable because of rising market value, especially in periods of inflation.

KEY TERMS INTRODUCED OR EMPHASIZED IN CHAPTER 20

Adjusted gross income A subtotal in an individual's tax return computed by deducting from gross income business-related expenses and other deductions authorized by law. A key figure to which many measurements are linked.

Capital asset Stocks, bonds, and rental property not used in a trade or business.

Capital gain and loss The difference between the cost basis of a capital asset and the amount received from its sale.

Gross income All income and gains from whatever source derived unless specifically excluded by law, such as interest on state and municipal bonds.

Interperiod tax allocation Allocation of income tax expense among accounting periods because of timing differences between accounting income and taxable income. Causes income tax expense reported in financial statements to be in logical relation to accounting income.

Itemized deductions Personal expenses deductible from adjusted gross income, such as interest, taxes, contributions, medical expenses, casualty losses, and expenses incurred in production of income.

Long-term capital gains and losses Gains and losses resulting from sale of capital assets owned for more than a specified period (nine months in 1977 and one year thereafter). A net long-term capital gain qualifies for a special tax rate.

Personal exemption A deduction (presently $750) from adjusted gross income for the taxpayer, the taxpayer's spouse, and each dependent.

Standard deduction Instead of itemizing deductions from adjusted gross income, taxpayers may deduct an amount equal to 16% of adjusted gross income but not more than $2,800 on a joint return.

Tax credit An amount to be subtracted from the tax itself. Examples are withheld taxes, payments of estimated tax, and the investment tax credit.

Tax shelters Investment programs designed to show losses in the short term to be offset against other taxable income, but offering the hope of long-run profits.

Taxable income The computed amount to which the appropriate tax rate is to be applied to arrive at the tax liability.

DEMONSTRATION PROBLEM FOR YOUR REVIEW

Robert Sandison has been engaged in various businesses for many years and has always prepared his own income tax return. In Year 11 Sandison decided to ask a certified public accountant to prepare his income tax returns.

Early in Year 12, Sandison presented the following tax information for Year 11 to his CPA:

Personal revenue:

Salary from Sandi Construction Company, after withholding of $3,168 and social security taxes of $772	$ 15,060
Dividends from Sandi Construction Company (jointly owned)	16,875
Drawings from Northwest Lumber Company	6,000
Drawings from S & S Business Advisers	9,600
Interest income—City of Norwalk bonds	800
Interest income—savings account	950
Proceeds on sale of stock:	
Sale of stock acquired two years ago for $6,200	14,200
Sale of stock held for three months, cost $4,100	3,400
Sale of stock held for over six years, cost $3,500	1,800

Personal expenses:

Contribution to St. Jerome's Church	$ 610
Interest on mortgage, $3,820; on personal note, $900	4,720
Property taxes, including $400 on vacant land in Arizona and a special assessment of $500 on residence for street widening	3,980
Sales taxes, including $580 paid on purchase of new automobile for personal use	850
Income taxes paid to state	1,900
Medical expenses	1,100
Subscription to investment advisory service	385

Single proprietorship—wholesale lumber, doing business as Northwest Lumber Company:

Sales	$118,000
Cost of goods sold	82,000
Operating expenses	38,800
Drawings by Sandison	6,000

Partnership—engaged in business consulting under the name of S & S Business Advisers:

Fees earned	$ 76,300
Gain on sale of vacant lot acquired four years ago	4,400
Professional salaries and other wages paid	32,400
Supplies expense	3,500
Contributions to charity	1,000
Rent expense	4,800
Miscellaneous business expenses	7,100
Drawings (Sandison, $9,600 and Sims, $6,400)	16,000

Corporation—engaged in construction under the name of Sandi Construction Company:

Customer billings	$230,000
Materials used	70,000
Construction labor	60,000
Officers' salaries expense	25,000
Legal and professional expense	3,500
Advertising expense	2,000
Other business expenses	19,800
Loss on sale of equipment	4,200
Cash dividends paid	22,500

Sandison has a 60% share in the profits of S & S Business Advisers and John Sims has a 40% share. Sandison owns 75% of the stock of Sandi Construction Company. Because of his controlling interest, he is responsible for the preparation of the income tax returns for these organizations.

Sandison is married, has five children, and supports his seventy-nine-year-old mother. He is fifty-five years old and his wife is younger but will not give her date of birth. The oldest child, Bill, is twenty years old and attends school full time. Sandison provides all of his son's support, even though Bill earns approximately $1,400 per year from odd jobs and from investments inherited from his grandfather.

In April of Year 11, Sandison paid $3,100 balance due on his federal income tax return for Year 10. In addition to the income taxes withheld by the Sandi Construction Company, Sandison made four equal payments of $2,000 each on his estimated tax for Year 11.

Instructions Using the income tax table on page 702, prepare the joint return for Mr. and Mrs. Sandison for last year, showing the amount of tax due (or refund coming). You should also prepare in summary form the information on the partnership tax return for S & S Business Advisers and the corporation income tax return for the Sandi Construction Company. Assume that a personal exemption is $750, that the corporate tax rate is 22% on the first $50,000 of taxable income and 48% on any income in excess of $50,000, and that Sandi Construction Company has not paid any part of its income tax for Year 11.

SOLUTION TO DEMONSTRATION PROBLEM

S & S BUSINESS ADVISERS (a partnership)
Computation of Ordinary Income
For Year Ended December 31, Year 11

Fees earned		$76,300
Operating expenses:		
Professional salaries and other wages	$32,400	
Supplies expense	3,500	
Rent expense	4,800	
Miscellaneous business expenses	7,100	47,800
Ordinary income		$28,500

Ordinary income and other items are to be included in partners' individual tax returns as follows:

	Sandison (60%)	Sims (40%)
Ordinary income, $28,500	$17,100	$11,400
Gain on sale of vacant lot, long-term capital gain, $4,400	2,640	1,760
Contributions to charity, $1,000	600	400

SANDI CONSTRUCTION COMPANY
Income Tax Return
For Year Ended December 31, Year 11

Customer billings		$230,000
Operating expenses:		
Materials used	$70,000	
Construction labor	60,000	
Officers' salaries expense	25,000	
Legal and professional expenses	3,500	
Advertising expense	2,000	
Other business expenses	19,800	
Loss on sale of equipment	4,200	184,500
Taxable income		$ 45,500
Income tax due: ($45,500 × 22%)		$ 10,010

MR. AND MRS. SANDISON
Joint Income Tax Return
For Year 11

Gross income:

Salary from Sandi Construction Company ($15,060 + $3,168 + $772)		$19,000
Dividends from Sandi Construction Company ($16,875, less $200 exclusion)		16,675
Interest on savings account		950
Income from S & S Business Advisers, a partnership		17,100

Net long-term capital gain:

Stock acquired two years ago	$8,000		
Stock held over six years	(1,700)		
Gain on sale of vacant lot—from partnership return	2,640		
Total long-term capital gain	$8,940		
Less: Short-term loss on stock held for three months	700	8,240	$61,965

Deductions to arrive at adjusted gross income:

Loss incurred by Northwest Lumber Company, a single proprietorship ($118,000 − $82,000 − $38,800)	$ 2,800	
Long-term capital gain deduction (50% of $8,240)	4,120	6,920

Adjusted gross income $55,045

Deductions from adjusted gross income:

Itemized deductions:

Contributions ($600 from partnership return and $610 to St. Jerome's Church)	$ 1,210	
Interest paid	4,720	
Property taxes ($3,980 − $500)	3,480	
Sales taxes	850	
Income taxes paid to state	1,900	
Subscription to investment advisory service	385	
Total itemized deductions	$12,545	
Personal exemptions (8 × $750)	6,000	18,545

Taxable income for Year 11 . . . . $36,500

Computation of tax for Year 11:

Tax on $36,000 on joint return (see page 702)	$10,340	
Tax on $500 excess at 45%	225	$10,565

Less tax credits:

Withheld from Mr. Sandison's salary	$ 3,168	
Payments on declaration of estimated tax ($2,000 × 4)	8,000	11,168

Overpayment of tax for Year 11 . . . . $ 603

Notes:
(1) The loss from single proprietorship is properly deducted in arriving at adjusted gross income despite the fact that Sandison withdrew $6,000 from the business.
(2) Sandison's share of ordinary income from the partnership (S & S Business Advisers), $17,100, is fully taxable despite the fact that Sandison withdrew only $9,600 from the partnership.
(3) Sandison's salary from the Sandi Construction Company is included in gross income as $19,000, the gross salary before any deductions.
(4) The ordinary income for the partnership is determined without taking into account the contribution to charity of $1,000 or the long-term capital gain of $4,400. These items are reported by the partners on their personal income tax return on the basis of the profit- and loss-sharing ratio agreed upon by the partners.
(5) The special assessment on residence for street widening, $500, is not deductible in arriving at taxable income.
(6) Medical expenses are less than 3% of adjusted gross income, and therefore none is deductible.
(7) Sandison's son, Bill, qualifies as a dependent even though he earned $1,400 because he is a full-time student.
(8) Interest on City of Norwalk bonds, $800, is not taxable.

REVIEW QUESTIONS

1 List several ways in which business owners may legally alter the amount of taxes they pay.

2 What is meant by the expression "tax planning"?

3 What are the four major classes of taxpayers under the federal income tax law?

4 It has been claimed that corporate income is subject to "double taxation." Explain the meaning of this expression.

5 Taxes are characterized as *progressive, proportional,* or *regressive* with respect to any given base. Describe an income tax rate structure that would fit each of these characterizations.

6 During the current year, John Dennison, a bachelor, expects a taxable income of $20,000. Using the tables on page 702 determine how much federal income tax Dennison would save were he to get married before the end of the year, assuming that his bride had no taxable income or itemized deductions and that the personal exemption is $750.

7 State in equation form the federal income tax formula for individuals, beginning with total income and ending with taxable income.

8 In computing income taxes, why does it make any difference whether a given deduction may be taken before or after computing adjusted gross income? Explain.

9 List some differences in the tax rules for corporations in contrast to those for individuals.

10 Helen Bame, M.D., files her income tax return on a cash basis. During the current year she collected $12,600 from patients for medical services rendered in prior years, and billed patients $77,000 for services rendered this year. She has accounts receivable of $16,400 relating to this year's billings at the end of the year. What amount of gross income from her practice should Bame report on her tax return?

11 Gilmore files his income tax return on a cash basis. During the current year $300 of interest was credited to him on his savings account; he withdrew this interest on January 18 of the following year. Gilmore purchased a piece of business equipment having an estimated service life of five years in December of the current year. He also paid a year's rent in advance on certain business property on December 29 of the current year. Explain how these items would be treated on Gilmore's current year's income tax return.

12 From an individual taxpayer's viewpoint it is better to have a $10,000 net long-term capital gain than $10,000 of ordinary income; however, ordinary losses are usually more advantageous than net capital losses. Explain.

13 Even when a taxpayer uses the accrual method of accounting, taxable income may differ from accounting income. Give four examples of differences between the tax and accounting treatment of items that are included in the determination of income.

14 Under what circumstances is the accounting procedure known as *income tax allocation* appropriate? Explain the purpose of this procedure.

15 List some tax factors to be considered in deciding whether to organize a new business as a corporation or as a partnership.

16 Explain how the corporate income tax makes debt financing in general more attractive than financing through the issuance of preferred stock.

EXERCISES

Ex. 20-1 From the tax tables on page 702, compute the tax for each of the following. (Assume that the 50% limitation on earned income does not apply.)

	Taxable Income
a *Unmarried individual*	$ 16,200
b *Unmarried individual*	144,000
c *Married couple filing joint return*	16,200
d *Married couple filing joint return*	144,000

Ex. 20-2 From the following information for Bob Joseph, a married man, compute his taxable income for Year 4:

Total income, including gifts, inheritances, interest on municipal bonds, etc.	$49,200
Exclusions (gifts, inheritances, interest on municipal bonds, etc.)	17,520
Deductions to arrive at adjusted gross income	1,680
Itemized deductions	6,690
Personal exemptions ($750 each)	5,250
Income taxes withheld from salary	4,320

Ex. 20-3 Twin Bridges, Inc., reports the following income during Year 1:

Operating income (income before extraordinary items and income taxes)	$550,000
Long-term capital gain	250,000
Extraordinary item:	
Loss (fully deductible)	50,000

Assume that corporate tax rates are as follows:

On first $50,000 of taxable income	22%
On taxable income over $50,000	48%
On long-term capital gains	30%

Compute the total tax liability for Twin Bridges, Inc., for Year 1.

Ex. 20-4 Robert and Jodi Collins, a married couple, file a joint return and claim one exemption each plus two exemptions for dependents. They have gathered the following information in getting ready to prepare their tax return.

Taxes withheld from salaries	$ 9,400
Estimated tax payments	5,400
Itemized deductions	2,480
Total income (including $800 interest on municipal bonds)	60,000
Business-related expenses	5,200

Compute (*a*) gross income, (*b*) adjusted gross income, (*c*) taxable income, and (*d*) amount of tax remaining to be paid. (Use the tax table for married individuals filing joint returns, page 702.)

Ex. 20-5 Mission Bay Corporation deducted on its tax return for Year 5 an expense of $100,000 which was not recognized as an expense for accounting purposes until Year 6. The corporation's accounting income before income taxes in each of the two years was $425,000. The company uses tax allocation procedures.

    a Prepare the journal entries required at the end of Year 5 and Year 6 to record income tax expense. Use corporate tax rates of 22% for the first $50,000 of taxable income and 48% for taxable income over $50,000.

    b Prepare a two-column schedule showing the net income to appear on the financial statements for Years 5 and 6, assuming tax allocation procedures are used. Also prepare a similar schedule on the assumption that tax allocation procedures are not used.

PROBLEMS

Group A

20A-1 *a* You are to consider the income tax status of each of the items listed below. List the numbers 1 to 15 on your answer sheet. For each item state whether it is *included in gross income* or *excluded from gross income* for federal income tax on individuals.

    (*1*) Cash dividends received on stock of General Motors Corporation.
    (*2*) Value of a color TV set won as a prize in a quiz contest.
    (*3*) Gain on the sale of an original painting.
    (*4*) Inheritance received on death of a rich uncle.
    (*5*) Interest received on Kansas City municipal bonds.
    (*6*) Proceeds of life insurance policy received on death of husband.
    (*7*) Tips received by a waitress.
    (*8*) Value of U.S. Treasury bonds received as a gift from aunt.
    (*9*) Rent received on personal residence while on extended vacation trip.
    (*10*) Share of income from partnership in excess of drawings.
    (*11*) Amount received as damages for injury in automobile accident.
    (*12*) Salary received from a corporation by a stockholder who owns directly or indirectly all the shares of the company's outstanding stock.
    (*13*) Gain on sale of Signal Companies capital stock.
    (*14*) Taxpayer owed $1,000 on a note payable. During the current year the taxpayer painted a building owned by the creditor, and in return the creditor canceled the note.
    (*15*) Las Vegas vacation given by employer as reward for outstanding service.

    b Consider the deductibility status of each of the items listed below for the purpose of preparing an individual's income tax return. List the numbers 1 to 11 on your answer sheet. For each item state whether the item is *deducted to arrive at adjusted gross income; deducted from adjusted gross income;* or *not deductible.*

(1) Dave Carter uses his vacation to paint a house (not his residence) which he owns and rents to others. A professional painter had bid $1,200 to do the job.

(2) Cost of commuting between home and place of employment.

(3) State sales tax paid on purchase of sailboat.

(4) Damage to roof of house caused by tornado.

(5) Interest paid on gambling debts.

(6) Capital loss on sale of investment in securities sold three months after purchase.

(7) Gambling losses. No gambling gains during the year.

(8) Expenses incurred in moving across country to accept position with different employer. Not reimbursed.

(9) Travel expense incurred by sales personnel in calling on various customers. Not reimbursed.

(10) Fee paid to CPA for services in contesting assessment of additional income taxes by IRS.

(11) Net operating loss carry-over by single proprietor.

20A-2 The following two cases are independent of each other. See the instructions following the second case.

Case A The following information relates to the income tax situation of David White for the current year.

Total income	*$96,000*
Personal exemptions	*6,000*
Deductions to arrive at adjusted gross income	*7,680*
Itemized deductions	*9,840*
Exclusions from gross income	*1,920*

Case B Ruth Monday, a psychiatrist, uses the accrual basis of accounting in maintaining accounting records for her business and in preparing financial statements, but uses cash basis accounting in determining her income subject to federal income tax. For the current year, her business net income (computed on an accrual basis) was $90,480. A comparison of the current balance sheet for the business with a balance sheet prepared a year earlier showed an increase of $14,400 in accounts receivable from clients during the current year. Current liabilities for rent, salaries owed to employees, and other operating expenses were $8,160 less at year-end than they were one year ago. The business income of $90,480 included $1,440 of interest received on municipal bonds.

Apart from the business, Monday has a personal savings account to which $864 was credited during the year, none of which was withdrawn. In addition to business expenses taken into account in computing net income of her business, Monday has $1,632 in deductions to arrive at adjusted gross income. Her personal exemptions amount to $4,500, and her itemized deductions are $2,266.

Instructions For each of the situations described above, determine the amount of the taxpayer's adjusted gross income and the taxable income for the year. Assume that the maximum limit for the standard deduction is $2,800.

20A-3 Carl and Judy Rogers, a married couple with four minor children, had the items of income and expense for the year just ended shown on page 730.

Instructions Compute the taxable income and the income tax for Mr. and Mrs. Rogers. Use the tax table for married individuals filing joint returns on page 702. Assume that the personal exemption is $750, that the maximum standard deduction is $2,800, and that both Mr. and Mrs. Rogers are fifty years of age.

Salary from C & R Corporation	$35,000
Consulting fees (net of applicable expenses)	4,200
Dividends (jointly owned)	840
Interest on bonds of State of Maine	252
Casualty loss, interest, taxes, and other expenditures (see list below)	22,400
Long-term capital gains	6,720
Short-term capital losses	2,800
Unused capital loss carry-over from previous year	2,100
Proceeds on insurance policy on life of uncle	7,000
Casualty loss, interest, taxes, and other expenditures:	
Theft of furniture on July 20 while on vacation	$ 2,100
Interest paid on loans to buy stocks	2,520
Medical expenses	1,120
Insurance on home	252
Income taxes withheld from salary	6,300
Miscellaneous deductible expenses	210
Sales taxes	476
Property taxes on home	1,148
State income taxes	980
Clothes, food, and other living expenses	7,294
Total (as listed above)	$22,400

20A-4 In preliminary calculations the chief accountant of Hill Corporation computed income before income taxes to be $350,000 for the first year of operations. Some of the steps included in arriving at this figure are listed below.

(1) Depreciation of $21,000 was recognized under the straight-line method.

(2) The direct charge-off method of measuring uncollectible accounts expense was followed. Accounts receivable of $4,550 were identified as uncollectible and were written off.

(3) The cost of ending inventories was determined on a first-in, first-out basis and amounted to $185,500.

The accountant pointed out to the president of the company that alternative accounting methods could be selected which would result in a smaller amount of taxable income. After some discussion it was agreed to make the following changes in accounting methods.

(1) Accelerated depreciation was adopted and the revised figure for depreciation expense was $40,250.

(2) The allowance method of estimating uncollectible accounts expense was adopted. An aging of accounts receivable led to the conclusion that an allowance for uncollectible accounts of $14,000 was required with respect to customers' accounts other than the $4,550 of receivables which had already been written off as worthless.

(3) The last-in, first-out method of measuring inventory cost was adopted. Ending inventories amounted to $140,000 under this method.

Instructions

a Determine the taxable income of the Hill Corporation on the revised basis.

b If the tax rates for corporations are 22% on the first $50,000 of taxable income and 48% on any taxable income in excess of $50,000, compute the reduction in the current year's income tax liability for the Hill Corporation resulting from the accounting changes.

20A-5 Campbell Company, a sole proprietorship owned by Jane Campbell, purchased for $200,000 a machine having an estimated life of four years and no salvage value. Campbell wants you to depreciate the machine on a straight-line basis for income tax purposes but you suggest that she use the sum-of-the-years'-digits method. You also suggest that she invest any amount saved as a result of the postponement of income taxes with a local businessman who pays 10% interest on unsecured loans.

Instructions Prepare a four-column work sheet showing for each of the four years (1) the depreciation by the sum-of-the-years'-digits method, (2) the depreciation by the straight-line method, (3) the difference in depreciation expense between the two methods each year, and (4) the tax deferral (or payment of deferral) computed at the 50% rate.

Complete the work sheet by determining the interest for each year on the fund saved and invested at 10%, and finally show the total interest earned as a result of deferring income taxes by use of the sum-of-the-years'-digits method of depreciation.

20A-6 The accounting records of Wayside Corporation included the following information for the current year:

Net sales	$7,500,000
Cost of goods sold	5,400,000
Dividends received from a domestic corporation	300,000
Dividends declared by board of directors on common stock of Wayside	
Corporation	600,000
Selling expenses	720,000
Administrative expenses	780,000
Earthquake loss (fully deductible for income tax purposes)	150,000

In December of the current year, Wayside Corporation spent $225,000 to move its corporate headquarters from one city to another. This expenditure was deducted in computing taxable income, but the company chose to defer it in the accounting records and charge it against revenue of the two subsequent years. The deferral was considered to achieve a better matching of costs with the benefits to revenue arising from the move. The company will follow income tax allocation procedures in reporting income taxes on the income statement during the current year.

Instructions
a Prepare an income statement for the Wayside Corporation for the current year. At the bottom of the income statement show earnings per share data, including the effect of the extraordinary item. The company has 300,000 shares of capital stock outstanding. In a separate schedule show your computation of federal income taxes for the year, using the following rate schedule:

First $50,000 of taxable income	22%
On excess over $50,000	48%

b Prepare the journal entry which should be made to record the income taxes expense and income tax liability (both current and deferred) at the end of the current year. Any tax credit resulting from the full deductibility of the earthquake loss should be offset against the Earthquake Loss account.

Group B

20B-1 **a** You are to consider the income tax status of each of the items listed on page 732. List the numbers 1 to 15 on your answer sheet. For each item state whether it is *included in gross income* or *excluded from gross income* for federal income tax on individuals.

(1) Trip to Hawaii given by employer as reward for outstanding service.

(2) Taxpayer owed $1,500 on a note payable. During the current year the taxpayer painted a building owned by the creditor, and in return the creditor canceled the note.

(3) Gain on sale of Bart Corporation capital stock, held for five months.

(4) Salary received from a corporation by a stockholder who owns directly or indirectly all the shares of the company's outstanding stock.

(5) Amount received as damages for injury in automobile accident.

(6) Share of income from partnership in excess of drawings.

(7) Rent received on personal residence while on extended vacation trip.

(8) Value of U.S. Treasury bonds received as a gift from uncle.

(9) Tips received by a waitress.

(10) Proceeds of life insurance policy received on death of husband.

(11) Interest received on River City municipal bonds.

(12) Inheritance received on death of a rich uncle.

(13) Gain on the sale of an original painting.

(14) Value of a color TV set won as a prize in a quiz contest.

(15) Cash dividends received on stock of American Oil Company.

b You are to determine the deductibility status, for federal income tax purposes, of each of the items listed below. List the numbers 1 to 10 on your answer sheet. For each item state whether the item *is deducted to arrive at adjusted gross income; deducted from adjusted gross income;* or *not deductible.*

(1) Interest paid on mortgage covering personal residence.

(2) Carry-forward of an unused operating loss from previous year.

(3) Capital loss on the sale of securities.

(4) Damage in storm to motorboat used for pleasure.

(5) State sales tax paid on purchase of family automobile.

(6) Expenses incurred in moving from Arlington to Houston to accept a new position with a different company, not reimbursed by employer.

(7) Travel expenses incurred by employee in connection with job, not reimbursed.

(8) Cost of traveling to and from home to place of employment.

(9) Fee paid to accountant for assistance in successfully contesting additional personal income taxes assessed by Internal Revenue Service.

(10) Taxpayer does maintenance work on rental property which he owns. This work would cost $500 if the taxpayer hired someone to do it.

20B-2 John and Jill Todd own a hardware business and an apartment building. They file a joint federal income tax return. Mr. and Mrs. Todd furnish over one-half the support of their son who attends college and who earned $2,560 in part-time jobs and summer employment. They also support Mr. Todd's father, who is seventy-two years old and has no income of his own.

The depreciation basis of the apartment building is $160,000; depreciation is recorded at the rate of 4% per year on a straight-line basis. During the current year the Todds had the following cash receipts and expenditures.

Cash receipts:

Cash withdrawn from hardware business (*sales, $384,800; cost of goods sold, $284,800; operating expenses, $52,000*)	$36,000
Gross rentals from apartment building	28,800
Cash dividends on stock owned jointly	2,960
Interest on River County bonds	976
Received from sale of stock purchased two years ago for $9,792	13,472
Received from sale of stock purchased four months previously for $6,656	4,832

*Received from sale of motorboat purchased three years ago for $4,792 and
used entirely for pleasure* . . . . $ 2,712

Cash expenditures:

Mortgage interest on residence . . . . $ 1,827

Property taxes on residence 1,573

Insurance on residence 224

State income tax paid 1,728

State sales and gasoline taxes 656

Charitable contributions 2,264

Medical expenses 1,376

Contribution to governor's political campaign (assume nondeductible) 400

Payments on declaration of estimated tax for current year 8,672

Expenditures relating to apartment building:

Interest on mortgage 7,200

Property taxes 4,720

Insurance (one year) 560

Utilities 2,368

Repairs and maintenance 3,872

Gardening 640

Instructions

a Determine the amount of taxable income Mr. and Mrs. Todd would report on their federal income tax return for the current year. Assume that the personal exemption is $750.

b Compute the income tax liability for Mr. and Mrs. Todd using the rate schedule on page 702. Indicate the amount of tax due (or refund to be received).

20B-3 Taylor Corporation is completing its first year of operation. The company has been successful and a preliminary calculation by the controller indicated an income before taxes of $250,000 for the year. Among the items entering into the calculation of the taxable income were the following:

(1) Inventories were reported on a first-in, first-out basis and amounted to $132,500 at year-end.

(2) Accounts receivable of $3,250 were written off and recorded as uncollectible accounts expense.

(3) Depreciation of $15,000 was recorded using the straight-line method.

Officers of the corporation are concerned over the large amount of income taxes they must pay on the $250,000 of taxable income and decide to restate taxable income as follows:

(1) Inventories on a last-in, first-out basis would amount to $100,000.

(2) An acceptable allowance for uncollectible accounts, after the write-off of $3,250, would be $10,000.

(3) Use of accelerated methods of depreciation would increase depreciation expense from $15,000 to $28,750.

Instructions

a Determine the taxable income of the Taylor Corporation on the revised basis.

b If the tax rates for corporations are 22% on the first $50,000 of taxable income and 48% on any taxable income in excess of $50,000, compute the reduction in the current year's income tax liability for the Taylor Corporation resulting from the accounting changes.

20B-4 Don and Harriet Tracey own a successful small company, Tracey Corporation. The outstanding capital stock consists of 1,000 shares of $100 par value, of which

400 shares are owned by Don and 600 by Harriet. In order to finance a new branch operation, the corporation needs an additional $100,000 cash. Don and Harriet have this amount on deposit with a savings and loan association and intend to put these personal funds into the corporation in order to establish the new branch. They will either arrange for the corporation to issue to them at par an additional 1,000 shares of stock, or they will make a loan to the corporation at an interest rate of 9%.

Income before taxes of the corporation has been consistently averaging $150,000 a year, and annual dividends of $64,000 have been paid regularly. It is expected that the new branch will cause *income before taxes* to increase by $30,000. If new common stock is issued to finance the expansion, the total annual dividend of $64,000 will be continued unchanged. If a loan of $100,000 is arranged, the dividend will be reduced by $9,000, the amount of annual interest on the loan.

Instructions

a From the standpoint of the individual income tax return which Don and Harriet file jointly, would there be any saving as between the stock issuance and the loan? Explain.

b From the standpoint of getting their money out of the corporation (assuming that the new branch is profitable), should Don and Harriet choose capital stock or a loan for the infusion of new funds to the corporation?

c Prepare a two-column schedule showing under each proposed method of financing: (*1*) the present corporate income *before taxes;* (*2*) the corporate income *before taxes* after the expansion; (*3*) the corporate income taxes after the expansion, and (*4*) the corporate net income after the expansion.

20B-5 Jack Cohen files a joint federal income tax return with his wife. Cohen owns and operates a small business. Mrs. Cohen manages an apartment house which she received as a gift from her mother. Mr. and Mrs. Cohen furnish over one-half the support of their son, Kirt, who attends college and who earned $1,100 in part-time jobs and summer work, and of Mrs. Cohen's mother, who lives with the Cohens and who has no income of her own.

During the current year the Cohens had the following cash receipts and expenditures pertinent to the preparation of their income tax return:

From Mr. Cohen's records:

Cash receipts:

Cash withdrawn from business (sales, $145,000; cost of goods sold, $83,500; operating expenses, $31,200)	$16,875
Cash dividends on stock owned	980
Interest on California state bonds	450
Received from sale of stock purchased two years ago for $4,000	5,300
Received from sale of stock purchased four months previously for $2,800	2,100
Received from sale of motorboat purchased three years ago for $3,200	1,500

Cash disbursements:

Interest on mortgage on residence	930
Property taxes on residence	640
Insurance on residence	135
State income tax paid	870
State sales and gasoline taxes	280
Repair windstorm damage to residence, $750; less insurance recovery of $550	200

Charitable contributions	$ 1,120
Medical expenses	510
Contribution to governor's political campaign	100
Payments on declaration of estimated tax	6,400

From Mrs. Cohen's records:

Cash receipts:

Apartment rental revenue	$12,650
Dividends on stocks owned	300
Sale of stock purchased five months previously for $1,900	2,150

Cash disbursements:

Relating to apartment building:

(Depreciation basis is $80,000; depreciation rate 4%)

Interest on mortgage	875
Property taxes	1,300
Insurance (one year)	190
Heat, light, and water	1,870
Repairs and maintenance	1,240
Charitable contributions	300

Instructions
a Determine the amount of taxable income Mr. and Mrs. Cohen would report on their federal income tax return for the current year.
b Prepare a list of any items you omit as not deductible. Explain.
c Compute the Cohen's income tax liability, using the rate schedule on page 702. Round all computations to the nearest dollar.

20B-6 The following information appears in the accounting records of the Chung Corporation for the current year:

Net sales	$978,000
Cost of goods sold	697,200
Dividend revenue (on stock of domestic subsidiary corporation)	20,000
Dividends declared on common stock	50,000
Selling expenses	98,900
Administrative expenses	86,250
Gain on sale of capital asset acquired five years ago	8,800

During the current year the Chung Corporation incurred $30,000 of sales promotion expenses which may be deducted in computing taxable income, but which the company has chosen to defer on its accounting records and charge against revenue during the two subsequent years when the benefits of the sales promotion are reflected in revenue. The controller will follow tax allocation procedures in reporting the income taxes expense on the income statement during the current year.

Instructions
a Prepare an income statement for the Chung Corporation for the current year. In a separate supporting schedule show your computation of the provision for federal income taxes for the year, using the corporation rate schedule on page 702.
b Prepare the journal entry which should be made to record the company's income taxes expense and income tax liability as of the end of the year.

BUSINESS DECISION PROBLEM 20

Gary Allen is in the process of organizing a business which he expects will produce, before any compensation to himself and before income taxes, an income of $72,000 per year. In deciding whether to operate as a single proprietorship or as a corporation, Allen is willing to make the choice on the basis of the relative income tax advantage under either form of organization.

Allen is married, files a joint return with his wife, has no other dependents, and has itemized deductions that average around $7,800 per year.

If the business is operated as a single proprietorship, Allen expects to withdraw the entire income of $72,000 each year.

If the business is operated as a corporation, Allen and his wife will own all the shares; he will pay himself a salary of $42,000 and will withdraw as dividends the entire amount of the corporation's net income after income taxes.

It may be assumed that the accounting income and the taxable income for the corporation would be the same and that the personal exemption is $750. Mr. and Mrs. Allen have only minor amounts of nonbusiness income, which may be ignored.

Instructions
a Determine the relative income tax advantage to Gary Allen of operating either as a single proprietorship or as a corporation, and make a recommendation as to the form of organization he should adopt. Use the individual (joint return) and corporate tax rate schedules given on page 702.
b Suppose that Gary Allen planned to withdraw only $42,000 per year from the business, as drawings from a single proprietorship or as salary from a corporation. Would this affect your recommendation? Explain.

21

Statement of Changes in Financial Position: Cash Flows

The heartbeat of any profit-making enterprise is reflected in the pulsing rhythm of its operating cycle. The business obtains cash from various sources and invests it in inventories. These inventories are in turn sold to customers, often on credit. When customers pay their accounts, the company again has cash to apply against its debts and begin the operating cycle anew.

The balance sheet portrays the overall financial position of the business at a specific date during this recurring cycle of investment, recovery of investment, and reinvestment. The income statement shows the growth in the amount of resources as a result of operations. In a sense, the fate of any given business enterprise is read in the income statement, since it tells whether revenue is larger or smaller during any period than the cost of the resources used up in generating this revenue. In this chapter we introduce a third major financial statement, the **statement of changes in financial position**[1] and a related summary of cash movements, the **cash flow statement.**

---

[1] In *Opinion No. 19,* "Reporting Changes in Financial Position," the Accounting Principles Board of the AICPA concluded (p. 373) that "information concerning the financing and investing activities of a business enterprise and the changes in its financial position for a period is essential for financial statement users, particularly owners and creditors, in making economic decisions. When financial statements purporting to present both financial position (balance sheet) and results of operations (statement of income and retained earnings) are issued, a statement summarizing changes in financial position should also be presented as a basic financial statement for each period for which an income statement is presented."

STATEMENT OF CHANGES IN FINANCIAL POSITION

A statement of changes in financial position helps us understand how and why the financial position of a business has changed during the course of a year. With this understanding of how funds have flowed into the business and how funds have been used, we can answer such practical questions as the following: How many dollars of new funds flowed into the business this year as a result of profitable operations, that is, from selling goods to our customers at prices in excess of our costs and operating expenses? What use did we make of funds during the year: for example, did we pay out as dividends most of the funds provided by operating at a profit? Is the business becoming more or less solvent? And most puzzling of all questions: how can we explain the fact that our working capital has increased more or less than the amount of profit earned during the year? Perhaps our current assets have decreased and our current liabilities have increased in spite of operations having been profitable. If this situation occurs, many people will be demanding an answer.

The statement of changes in financial position gives us *answers* to these questions, because it shows in detail the amount of funds we received from each source and the amount of funds we used for each purpose throughout the year. In fact, this financial statement used to be called a *Statement of Sources and Applications of Funds.* Many people still call it simply a *Funds Statement.* However, the name officially recommended by the AICPA is the *Statement of Changes in Financial Position.*

"Funds" defined as working capital

In ordinary usage, the term *funds* usually means cash. Accountants and financial executives, however, think of "funds" in a broader sense. They view the funds available to a company as its *working capital*—the difference between current assets and current liabilities.

Short-term credit is often used as a substitute for cash; notes and accounts payable as well as various accrued liabilities are used to meet the short-term financing needs of a business. Current assets are constantly being converted into cash, which is then used to pay current liabilities. The net amount of short-term liquid resources available to a business firm at any given time, therefore, is represented by its working capital—the difference between current assets and current liabilities. This explains why it is natural to think of working capital as a "fund" of liquid resources on hand at any given time.

If the amount of working capital increased during a given fiscal period, this means that more working capital was generated than was used for various business purposes; if a decrease in working capital occurred, the reverse is true. One of the key purposes of the statement of changes in financial position is to explain fully the increase or decrease in working capital during a fiscal period. This is done by showing where working capital originated and how it was used.

Sources and uses of working capital

Any transaction that increases the amount of working capital is a *source of working capital.* For example, the sale of merchandise at a price greater than its cost is a source of working capital, because the increase in cash or receivables from the sale is greater than the decrease in inventories.

Any transaction that decreases working capital is a *use of working capital.* For example, either incurring a current liability to acquire a non-current asset or using cash to pay expenses represents a decrease in working capital.

On the other hand, some transactions affect current assets or current liabilities but do not change the amount of working capital. For example, the collection of an account receivable (which increases cash and decreases an account receivable by an equal amount) is not a source of working capital. Similarly, the payment of an account payable (which decreases cash and decreases an account payable by an equal amount) does not change the amount of working capital.

The principal sources and uses of working capital are listed below:

Sources of working capital:

1 *Current operations.* If the inflow of funds from sales exceeds the outflow of funds to cover the cost of merchandise purchases and expenses of doing business, current operations will provide a net source of funds. If the inflow of funds from sales is less than these outflows, operations will result in a net use of funds. Not all expenses require the use of funds in the current period; therefore, the amount of funds provided by operations is *not* the same as the amount of net income earned during the period. Differences between the amount of working capital provided by operations and the amount of net income will be discussed later in the chapter.

In the long run, operations must result in a net source of funds if the business is to survive. A business cannot obtain funds through other sources indefinitely if those funds will only be consumed by business operations.

2 *Sale of noncurrent assets.* A business may obtain working capital by selling noncurrent assets, such as plant and equipment or long-term investments, in exchange for current assets. As long as current assets are received, the sale is a source of funds *regardless of whether the noncurrent assets are sold at a gain or a loss.* For example, assume that a company sells land which cost $40,000 for $30,000 in cash. Although the land was sold at a loss, the company has increased its current assets by $30,000. Thus, the transaction is a source of working capital.

3 *Long-term borrowing.* Long-term borrowing, such as issuing bonds payable, results in an increase in current assets, thereby increasing working capital. *Short-term borrowing,* however, does *not* increase working capital. When a company borrows cash by signing a short-term note payable, working capital is unchanged because the increase in current assets is offset by an increase in current liabilities of the same amount.

4 *Issuing additional shares of stock.* The sale of capital stock results in an inflow of current assets, thereby increasing working capital. In a similar manner, additional investments of current assets by owners represent sources of funds to single proprietorships and partnerships.

Uses of working capital:

1 *Declaration of cash dividends.* The declaration of a cash dividend results in a current liability (dividend payable) and is therefore a use of funds. Note that it

is the *declaration* of the dividend, rather than the payment of the dividend, which is the use of funds. Actual payment of the dividend reduces current assets and current liabilities by the same amount and thus has no effect upon the amount of working capital.

2 **Purchase of noncurrent assets.** The purchase of noncurrent assets, such as plant and equipment, usually reduces current assets or increases current liabilities. In either case, working capital is reduced. Special situations in which noncurrent assets are acquired in exchange for other noncurrent assets or long-term liabilities are discussed later in this chapter.

3 **Repayment of long-term debt.** Working capital is decreased when current assets are used to repay long-term debt. However, repayment of short-term debt is not a use of funds, since current assets and current liabilities decrease by the same amount.

4 **Repurchase of outstanding stock.** When cash is paid out to repurchase outstanding shares of stock, working capital is reduced.

Simple illustration

Suppose that John Claire started a business, Claire Company, as a single proprietorship on April 30 by investing $30,000 cash; the company rented a building on May 1 and completed the transactions shown below during the month of May.

(1) Claire invested an additional $10,000 cash in the business.

(2) Purchased merchandise costing $40,000 on credit and sold three-fourths of this, also on credit, for $58,000.

(3) Collected $45,000 on receivables; paid $32,000 on accounts payable.

(4) Paid $15,500 cash for operating expenses.

(5) Purchased land for the construction of a store. Gave $15,000 cash and a six-month note for $12,000 in payment for the land.

(6) Withdrew $2,000 from the business for personal use.

The financial statements at the end of May are shown below and on page 741.

CLAIRE COMPANY

Income Statement

For Month of May

Sales		*$58,000*
Cost of goods sold:		
Purchases	*$40,000*	
Less: Ending inventory (one-fourth of purchases)	*10,000*	*30,000*
Gross profit on sales		*$28,000*
Operating expenses		*15,500*
Net income for month of May		*$12,500*

Statements covering one month's operations of single proprietorship

CLAIRE COMPANY
Comparative Balance Sheet

Assets	May 31	May 1
Cash	$20,500	$30,000
Accounts receivable	13,000	
Inventory	10,000	
Land	27,000	
Total assets	$70,500	$30,000

Liabilities & Owner's Equity		
Note payable	$12,000	
Accounts payable	8,000	
John Claire, capital	50,500	$30,000
Total liabilities & owner's equity	$70,500	$30,000

The working capital amounted to $30,000 (consisting entirely of cash) on May 1 but was only $23,500 ($43,500 − $20,000) on May 31, a decrease of $6,500. In analyzing the six transactions completed during the month of May, we see that working capital was increased and decreased as follows:

CLAIRE COMPANY
Effect of Transactions on Working Capital
For Month of May

Land and the owner's capital accounts were increased as a result of these transactions

Increases:		
Additional investment by owner		$10,000
Sale of merchandise for more than cost ($58,000 − $30,000)		28,000
Total increases in working capital		$38,000
Decreases:		
Payment of operating expenses	$15,500	
Payment of cash for purchase of land	15,000	
Issuance of current note payable for purchase of land	12,000	
Withdrawal by owner	2,000	44,500
Decrease in working capital during May		$ 6,500

A complete list of transactions for a fiscal period may not be readily available, and even if it were, analysis of such a list would be a laborious process. In practice, the statement of changes in financial position is generally prepared in summary form by analyzing the **changes that occurred in the noncurrent accounts** during a fiscal period. An analysis of the comparative balance sheet for Claire Company indicates that the Land account increased by $27,000. This increase indicates that land, a noncurrent asset, was purchased during the period. Purchase of a noncurrent asset is a use of funds. Claire's capital account increased by $20,500 as a result of (1) additional investment of $10,000 (a source of funds), (2) net income of $12,500 (a source of funds), and (3) a withdrawal of $2,000 (a use of funds). We can therefore prepare the following statement of changes in financial position, including the composition of working capital, for the month of May:

CLAIRE COMPANY
Statement of Changes in Financial Position
For Month of May

A simple statement of changes in financial position

Sources of working capital:		
Operations (net income)		*$12,500*
Additional investment by owner		*10,000*
Total sources of working capital		*$22,500*
Uses of working capital:		
Purchase of land	*$27,000*	
Withdrawal by owner	*2,000*	
Total uses of working capital		*29,000*
Decrease in working capital		*$ 6,500*

	End of May	Beginning of May	Increase or (Decrease) in Working Capital
Composition of working capital:			
Current assets:			
Cash	*$20,500*	*$30,000*	*$ (9,500)*
Accounts receivable	*13,000*	*-0-*	*13,000*
Inventory	*10,000*	*-0-*	*10,000*
Total current assets	*$43,500*	*$30,000*	
Current liabilities:			
Note payable	*$12,000*	*$ -0-*	*(12,000)*
Accounts payable	*8,000*	*-0-*	*(8,000)*
Total current liabilities	*$20,000*	*$ -0-*	
Working capital	*$23,500*	*$30,000*	
Decrease in working capital			*$ (6,500)*

The differences between net income, net cash flow, and the change in working capital should be carefully noted in the foregoing example. Although Claire Company's net income for May was $12,500, its cash account *decreased* by $9,500 and its working capital *decreased* by $6,500.

Effect of transactions on working capital

In preparing a statement of changes in financial position, it is convenient to view all business transactions as falling into three categories:

1 Transactions which affect *only current asset or current liability accounts.* These transactions produce changes in working capital accounts but do not change the amount of working capital. For example, the purchase of merchandise increases inventory and accounts payable but has no effect on working capital; it may therefore be ignored in preparing a statement of changes in financial position.

2 Transactions which affect a *current asset or current liability account and a non-working capital account.* These transactions bring about either an increase or a decrease in the amount of working capital. The issuance of long-term bonds, for example, increases current assets and increases bonds payable, a non-working capital account; therefore, the issuance of bonds payable is a source of working capital. Similarly, when the bonds approach maturity they are transferred to the current liability classification in the balance sheet. This causes a reduction (a use) of working capital. If changes in non-working capital accounts are analyzed, these events are brought to light, and their effect on working capital will be reported in the statement of changes in financial position.

3 Transactions which affect *only noncurrent accounts* and therefore have no direct effect on the amount of working capital. The entry to record depreciation is an example of such a transaction. Other transactions in this category, such as the issuance of capital stock in exchange for plant assets, are called *exchange transactions* and are viewed as *both a source and use of working capital,* but do not change the amount of working capital.

EXCHANGE TRANSACTIONS Suppose that a building worth $105,000 is acquired in exchange for 10,000 shares of $5 par value capital stock. The entry to record this purchase would be:

An exchange transaction	*Building*	*105,000*
	Capital Stock	*50,000*
	Paid-in Capital in Excess of Par . . . . :	*55,000*
	Exchange of 10,000 shares of $5 par value capital stock for building worth $105,000.	

It is quite clear that this exchange transaction did not increase or decrease any current asset or current liability account and for that reason had no *direct* effect on working capital. An *exchange transaction* of this type, however, may be viewed as consisting of two transactions: (*1*) the issuance of capital stock for $105,000, and (*2*) the use of the proceeds to purchase a building for $105,000. Instead of ignoring an *exchange transaction* of this type in analyzing the flow of working capital, it is possible for us to view the exchange as both a source of working capital (issuance of capital stock) and a use of working capital (purchase of the building). This treatment is more informative for purposes of the statement of changes in financial position because it shows more completely the movement of the company's *financial resources* during the year.

The acquisition of plant assets by issuing long-term debt and the conversion of bonds payable or preferred stock into common stock are other examples of exchange transactions affecting only noncurrent accounts. In the statement of changes in financial position, such transactions should be shown as both a source and a use of working capital.

**EFFECT OF DEPRECIATION ON WORKING CAPITAL PROVIDED BY OPERA-
TIONS** Some expenses, such as depreciation, deferred income tax expense (which will not be paid within one year), amortization of intangibles,
and amortization of discount on bonds payable, reduce net income but
have no immediate effect on the amount of working capital provided by
normal operations. Such expenses should be *added back to net income* in
measuring the increase in working capital as a result of operations.

To illustrate the reason for this, assume the following: City Express
starts business as a delivery service on January 2, with three trucks
costing a total of $30,000; it has no other assets or liabilities at this time. It
does business on a cash basis and during the year collects $40,000 in
revenue and pays out $22,000 in expenses, thus showing an $18,000
increase in cash, which is its only working capital account. The company
then records depreciation expense of $6,000 on its trucks, resulting in a
net income of $12,000 for the year. The recording of depreciation expense
did not change any current account for City Express, and the increase
in working capital remains at $18,000. Thus, in order to measure this
increase in working capital from operations, we can either take the
income figure *before depreciation expense,* $18,000, or take the net income
of $12,000 and *add back* depreciation expense of $6,000.

Obviously, the depreciation expense itself is *not* a source of working
capital. The net income figure, however, understates the amount of
working capital provided by operations. The depreciation expense recorded during the period is therefore shown as an *addition to net income* in
measuring the working capital actually provided by operations.

We have seen that some expenses do not reduce working capital.
Similarly, some items in the income statement increase net income without increasing working capital and should be *deducted* from net income in
arriving at working capital provided by operations. An example of such an
item is the amortization of premium on bonds payable, which causes
annual interest expense to be less than the cash payments of interest to
bondholders.[2]

Extraordinary and nonoperating gains and losses, if material in amount,
should be eliminated from net income in order to show the working capital
generated from recurring activities (operations). For example, if land
costing $100,000 is sold at a net gain of $50,000, the net proceeds
received on the sale, $150,000, should be reported as "working capital
provided through sale of land," and the nonoperating gain should be
deducted from net income. As a separate example, assume that the same
land is sold for $70,000; then the nonoperating loss of $30,000 should be
added to net income in arriving at the income from operations, and the
working capital provided through sale of land should be reported at

---

[2] The treatment of this item in the working paper and in the statement of changes in financial position is illustrated in the
Demonstration Problem on pages 757–760.

$70,000. The foregoing discussion relating to the measurement of working capital provided by operations can be summarized as follows:

Computation of Working Capital Provided by Operations

Impact of operations on working capital

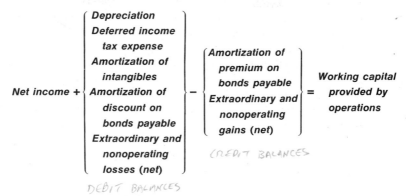

Preparation of more complex statement of changes in financial position

To illustrate the points just discussed, we shall prepare a statement of changes in financial position for the Allison Corporation from the comparative balance sheet and the condensed income statement shown below and on page 746. Note that the balance sheet is not classified, except for current assets and current liabilities.

ALLISON CORPORATION
Comparative Balance Sheet
At December 31

Assets	Year 4	Year 3
Can you give the reasons for the increase of $57,500 in working capital? Current assets:		
Cash	$ 15,000	$ 35,000
Accounts receivable (net)	105,000	85,000
Inventory	200,000	120,000
Short-term prepayments	25,000	12,000
Total current assets	$345,000	$252,000
Land	140,000	50,000
Equipment	290,000	230,000
Less: Accumulated depreciation	(107,500)	(80,000)
Total assets	$667,500	$452,000

Liabilities & Stockholders' Equity

Current liabilities:		
Notes payable to merchandise creditors	$ 60,000	$ 40,000
Accounts payable	85,000	50,000
Accrued liabilities	22,500	42,000
Total current liabilities	$167,500	$132,000
Notes payable, due Jan. 1, Year 17	15,000	10,000
Bonds payable, due June 30, Year 20	160,000	100,000
Capital stock, $5 par	160,000	110,000
Paid-in capital in excess of par	50,000	30,000
Retained earnings	115,000	70,000
Total liabilities & stockholders' equity	$667,500	$452,000

ALLISON CORPORATION

Condensed Income Statement

For Year Ended December 31, Year 4

Sales (net)		$900,000
Cost of goods sold		585,000
Gross profit on sales		$315,000
Operating expenses and income taxes	$255,000	
Gain on sale of land	(20,000)	235,000
Net income		$ 80,000

A summary of the transactions completed by the Allison Corporation which resulted in changes in *noncurrent accounts* during Year 4 follows:

1 Changes in noncurrent assets:
a Land costing $10,000 was sold for $30,000. Another parcel of land was acquired in exchange for bonds payable of $100,000.
b Equipment was purchased for $60,000; the invoice was paid within ten days.
c Depreciation of $27,500 was recorded.

2 Changes in noncurrent liabilities:
a An additional $5,000 was borrowed on long-term notes due in Year 17.
b Bonds payable of $40,000 were retired at a price equal to par value and additional bonds of $100,000 were issued in exchange for land.

3 Changes in stockholders' equity accounts:
a In February, 10,000 shares of $5 par value stock were sold at $7 per share, thus increasing Capital Stock by $50,000 and Paid-in Capital in Excess of Par by $20,000.
b Cash dividends of $35,000 were declared.
c The net income for the year, $80,000 (including the nonoperating gain of $20,000), was transferred to the Retained Earnings account.

From the comparative balance sheets, the income statement, and the summary of the transactions during the year which changed noncurrent accounts, we can prepare a statement of changes in financial position by completing the following three steps:

Follow these steps **1** Compute the change in working capital during the period.

2 Prepare a working paper for analysis of changes in noncurrent accounts.

3 Prepare the statement of changes in financial position.

COMPUTATION OF INCREASE IN WORKING CAPITAL DURING THE PERIOD
The first step in preparing a statement of changes in financial position is to determine the net increase or decrease in working capital during the period covered by the statement.

The working capital of the Allison Corporation increased by $57,500 during Year 4, determined as follows:

ALLISON CORPORATION
Computation of Increase in Working Capital during Year 4

	Dec. 31, Year 4	Dec. 31, Year 3
Current assets	$345,000	$252,000
Less: Current liabilities	167,500	132,000
Working capital	$177,500	$120,000
Increase in working capital during Year 4		57,500
	$177,500	$177,500

Sources of working capital exceed uses by $57,500

The purpose of the statement of changes in financial position is to explain the reasons for the change in working capital. This is accomplished by listing the specific sources and uses of working capital during the period. Since the working capital for the Allison Corporation increased by $57,500, the sources of working capital during Year 4 exceeded the uses by this amount. But before a statement of changes in financial position can be prepared, it is generally useful to analyze the changes in noncurrent accounts which took place during the year by preparing a working paper.

PREPARATION OF WORKING PAPER FOR ANALYSIS OF CHANGES IN NON-CURRENT ACCOUNTS A working paper showing the analysis of changes in noncurrent accounts for the Allison Corporation is illustrated on page 750. The amount of working capital and the balances in noncurrent accounts at the beginning of the period are listed in the first column of the working paper; balances at the end of the year are listed in the last (right-hand) column. The two middle columns are used to *explain the changes* in each noncurrent account during the year and to indicate whether each change corresponds to a source or a use of funds. Transactions for the year (in summary form) are recorded in these middle columns and an offsetting entry is made in the lower section of the working papers indicating the effect of each transaction upon working capital.

Explanation of transactions in working paper By studying the changes in the noncurrent accounts during Year 4, we are able to find the specific reasons for the $57,500 increase in working capital. As previously stated, only changes in the noncurrent accounts represent sources and uses of working capital. The analyses of the transactions completed by the Allison Corporation during Year 4 are explained below:

(1) The net income of $80,000 is credited to the Retained Earnings account and is shown under "sources of working capital: operations." Net income represents an increase in stockholders' equity and is one of the major sources of working capital for most businesses. Net income, however, is only a tentative measure of the increase in working capital from operations because not all revenue and expense items represent sources and uses of working capital (depreciation, for example). Furthermore, any extraordinary and nonoperating items are eliminated from net income because the transactions giving rise to such items are reported separately if they generate or use working capital.

(2) Since depreciation expense does not reduce a current asset or increase a current liability, it has no effect on working capital. Therefore, the depreciation expense of $27,500 for the year is shown as an increase to net income in the working paper and is credited to Accumulated Depreciation. The net income, $80,000, plus depreciation expense, $27,500, or a total of $107,500, represents a *tentative* increase in working capital as a result of profitable operations. This $107,500 figure is viewed as tentative because it will be reduced in adjustment (3) by the amount of the gain on the sale of land ($20,000) which was included in the net income of $80,000; this gain will be included in the $30,000 source of working capital on the sale of land.

(3) The sale of land is recorded as a source of working capital of $30,000 because cash was generated when the land was sold. The cost of the land, $10,000, is credited to the Land account and the gain, $20,000, is shown as a reduction to the net income in order that the net proceeds on the sale of the land ($30,000) can be listed as a source of working capital. This adjustment gives us net "working capital provided by operations," $87,500, consisting of income *before the gain on the sale of land,* $60,000, plus depreciation, $27,500.

(4) The issuance of $100,000 par value bonds in exchange for land is an exchange transaction, representing both a source and a use of funds. First, an entry is made in the top portion of the working papers explaining the $100,000 increase in the Bonds Payable account and an offsetting entry is made below showing a $100,000 source of funds. Next, a debit entry is made in the upper portion of the working papers explaining the $100,000 increase in the Land account and an offsetting entry is made below showing the $100,000 use of funds.

(5) The sale of capital stock in February for $70,000 is recorded in the upper portion of the working papers by credits to Capital Stock, $50,000 (10,000 shares with a $5 par value), and to Paid-in Capital in Excess of Par, $20,000. The issuance of capital stock is a source of funds; therefore, the offsetting entry in the lower section of the working papers is entered in the Sources column.

(6) An increase in long-term debt is a source of funds. Therefore, the borrowing of $5,000 on long-term notes payable is recorded in the working paper as a credit to Notes Payable and a source of working capital.

(7) Equipment was purchased for $60,000, causing a reduction in working capital. This is recorded in the working paper by a debit to Equipment and an offsetting entry describing the use of funds.

(8) During Year 4, Allison Corporation retired $40,000 of bonds payable at par. A reduction in long-term debt represents a use of working capital. The transaction is recorded in the working paper by a debit to Bonds Payable and an offsetting entry describing the use of funds. If a retirement of bonds payable results in a material loss or gain, the loss or gain would be reported in the income statement and would be eliminated from net income in the same manner as the gain on sale of land in transaction (3) above.

(9) Cash dividends declared on capital stock outstanding reduce both working capital and stockholders' equity and should be listed on a statement of changes in financial position as a use of working capital. The required working paper entry is a debit to Retained Earnings and an offsetting entry showing the use of funds. A cash dividend need not be paid in order to represent a reduction in working capital. The *declaration* of the cash dividend establishes a current liability and thus reduces working capital. The actual payment of the cash dividend has no effect on working capital because the payment merely reduces a current liability (Dividends Payable) and a current asset (Cash) by the same amount; *a transaction which changes only current accounts cannot be a source or use of working capital.*

(x) After all changes in noncurrent accounts are analyzed in the working paper, the gross sources, $312,500, and uses, $255,000, of working capital are totaled. At this point, the increase in working capital during the year, $57,500, should be entered as a debit to Working Capital on the first line of the second column in the working paper and also as a balancing figure on the next to the last line of the third column in the working paper. The account balances at December 31, Year 4, can now be determined and totals obtained for the debits and credits in the top portion of the working paper. If the totals agree, we know that our analysis is correct, at least so far as the mechanics are concerned.

PREPARATION OF STATEMENT OF CHANGES IN FINANCIAL POSITION The foregoing working paper analysis explained all changes in noncurrent accounts that took place during Year 4. In making this analysis, we listed the sources and uses of working capital in the lower section of the working paper on page 750. The increase of $57,500 in working capital has been confirmed and a statement of changes in financial position, including changes in the composition of working capital, can now be prepared as shown below:

ALLISON CORPORATION

Statement of Changes in Financial Position

For Year Ended December 31, Year 4

Statement of changes in financial position shows sources and uses of working capital

Sources of working capital:		
Operations:		
Income before gain on sale of land		$ 60,000
Add: Expense not requiring the use of current funds—depreciation		27,500
Total working capital provided by operations		$ 87,500
Sale of land		30,000
Issuance of bonds payable		100,000
Sale of capital stock		70,000
Borrowed on long-term notes payable, due Jan, 1, Year 17		5,000
Total sources of working capital		$292,500
Uses of working capital:		
Purchase of land in exchange for bonds payable	$100,000	
Purchase of equipment	60,000	
Retirement of bonds payable	40,000	
Declaration of cash dividends	35,000	
Total uses of working capital		235,000
Increase in working capital		$ 57,500

ALLISON CORPORATION
Working Paper for Statement of Changes in Financial Position
For Year Ended December 31, Year 4

Debits	Account Balances, Jan. 1, Year 4	Analysis of Transactions for Year 4 Debit		Analysis of Transactions for Year 4 Credit		Account Balances, Dec. 31, Year 4
Working capital	120,000	(x)	57,500			177,500
Land...	50,000	(4)	100,000	(3)	10,000	140,000
Equipment....................................	230,000	(7)	60,000			290,000
Total	400,000					607,500

Credits						
Accumulated depreciation	80,000			(2)	27,500	107,500
Notes payable, due Jan. 1, Year 17......................................	10,000			(6)	5,000	15,000
Bonds payable, due June 30, Year 20.......................................	100,000	(8)	40,000	(4)	100,000	160,000
Capital stock, $5 par	110,000			(5)	50,000	160,000
Paid-in capital in excess of par	30,000			(5)	20,000	50,000
Retained earnings..........................	70,000	(9)	35,000	(1)	80,000	115,000
Total	400,000		292,500		292,500	607,500

		Sources		Uses		
Sources of working capital:						
Operations–net income..................		(1)	80,000			(From
Add: Depreciation......................		(2)	27,500			operations,
Less: Gain on sale of land............				(3)	20,000	$87,500)
Sale of land..............................		(3)	30,000			
Issuance of bonds payable		(4)	100,000			
Sale of capital stock		(5)	70,000			
Borrowed on notes payable, due Jan. 1, Year 17		(6)	5,000			
Uses of working capital:						
Purchase of land in exchange for bonds payable......................				(4)	100,000	
Purchase of equipment..................				(7)	60,000	
Retirement of bonds payable..........				(8)	40,000	
Cash dividends declared................				(9)	35,000	
Total sources and uses of working capital......................			312,500		255,000	
Increase in working capital during Year 4				(x)	57,500	
			312,500		312,500	

Explanation of transactions for Year 4:
(1) Net income $80,000 (including a gain of $20,000 on sale of land) is transferred to Retained Earnings. This is a tentative source of working capital to be adjusted in (2) and (3) below.
(2) Depreciation for the year, $27,500, is added to net income in arriving at the working capital provided by operations because it did not reduce a current asset or increase a current liability.
(3) Sale of land for $30,000; the gain of $20,000 is deducted from net income in order that entire proceeds can be reported separately as a source of working capital.
(4) Issuance of $100,000 of bonds payable in exchange for land.
(5) Sale of capital stock, providing working capital of $70,000.
(6) Working capital was provided by borrowing $5,000 on long-term notes.
(7) Working capital was reduced through purchase of equipment, $60,000.
(8) Working capital of $40,000 was used to retire bonds payable.
(9) Cash dividends declared, $35,000; this is a use of working capital.
(x) Balancing figure—increase in working capital during Year 4.

Changes in Composition of Working Capital

	End of Year 4	End of Year 3	Increases or (Decreases) in Working Capital
Composition of working capital:			
Current assets:			
Cash	$ 15,000	$ 35,000	$(20,000)
Accounts receivable (net)	105,000	85,000	20,000
Inventory	200,000	120,000	80,000
Short-term prepayments	25,000	12,000	13,000
Total current assets	$345,000	$252,000	
Current liabilities:			
Notes payable to merchandise creditors .	$ 60,000	$ 40,000	(20,000)
Accounts payable	85,000	50,000	(35,000)
Accrued liabilities	22,500	42,000	19,500
Total current liabilities	$167,500	$132,000	
Working capital	$177,500	$120,000	
Increase in working capital			$ 57,500

We can see that the $87,500 of working capital provided by operations exceeds the income before the gain on the sale of land because depreciation expense was added to net income; another $205,000 of working capital came from nonoperating sources (sale of land, sale of additional capital stock, and long-term borrowing). Working capital totaling $235,000 was used to purchase land and equipment, retire bonds payable, and declare cash dividends. These sources and uses resulted in a net increase of $57,500 in working capital. The statement of changes in financial position thus provides a concise view of the way in which the Allison Corporation generated and used its working capital during the year.

Investors and creditors find the statement of changes in financial position helpful not only in evaluating the past performance of a company but also in projecting its future movements of working capital and in evaluating probable *liquidity* (the ability to pay debts as they become payable).

A statement of changes in financial position for a large listed corporation appears in the Appendix of this book.

CASH FLOW ANALYSIS

While the statement of changes in financial position reports the inflow and outflow of working capital during an accounting period, management is often more concerned with having enough cash to meet its operating needs and to pay maturing liabilities. Cash is the most liquid asset, and the efficient use of cash is one of the most important tasks of management. A *cash flow statement* is often prepared in order to give a full and complete picture of cash receipts and disbursements for an accounting period. Such a cash flow statement may also be useful in preparing a cash budget.

A cash flow statement is definitely not a substitute for an income statement. Income statements, as we have shown in prior chapters, are prepared on an accrual basis. Accrual accounting was developed to overcome the limitations of cash movements as indicators of business performance. Cash outlays simply represent investments which may or may not prove sound. Cash receipts represent disinvestment and, taken by themselves, tell nothing about whether the inflow is beneficial or not. The accountant's measurement of net income is designed to tell something about the fate of a company's overall investment and disinvestment activities during a given period of time. Despite its imperfections, the income statement is still the best means we have for reporting operating performance of business enterprises.

However, there are occasions when one may wish to reverse the accrual process and determine the amount of cash generated by operations. Reports of past cash flow may reveal a good deal about the financial problems and policies of a company. Forecasts of cash flows and cash budgets are useful managerial planning tools. The measurement of past and future cash flows from all sources, including operations, provides valuable information.

Cash flow from operations

Suppose we wish to convert a company's income statement into a report of its cash flow from operations. How should we go about adjusting the data on the income statement to convert it into cash flow information?

To answer this question, we must consider the relationship between accrual basis income statement amounts and cash movements within the firm. For illustrative purposes, consider the income statement of the Allison Corporation for Year 4, which was presented earlier in this chapter.

ALLISON CORPORATION
Condensed Income Statement
For Year Ended December 31, Year 4

Condensed income statement: accrual basis

Sales (net)		$900,000
Cost of goods sold		585,000
Gross profit on sales		$315,000
Operating expenses and income taxes	$255,000	
Gain on sale of land	(20,000)	235,000
Net income		$ 80,000

From the statement of changes in financial position presented on page 749, we already know that cash was received from the sale of land ($30,000), from the sale of capital stock ($70,000), and from borrowing on long-term notes ($5,000). We also know that cash was paid to acquire equipment ($60,000), to retire bonds payable ($40,000), and to pay cash dividends ($35,000). The remaining cash movements must consist of cash receipts from customers and cash payments for purchases and expenses, including income taxes.

CASH RECEIPTS FROM CUSTOMERS Sales on account are an important factor in most companies. The relationship between the amount of cash collected from customers and the net sales reported in the income statement depends on the change in accounts receivable between the beginning and end of any period. The relationship may be stated as follows:

Converting sales to cash basis

$$Net\ sales \begin{cases} -\ increase\ in\ accounts\ receivable \\ or \\ +\ decrease\ in\ accounts\ receivable \end{cases} = \begin{matrix} cash\ receipts\ from \\ customers \end{matrix}$$

In the Allison Corporation example, a glance at the comparative balance sheet on pages 745–746 tells us that net accounts receivable increased from $85,000 to $105,000 during Year 4, an increase of $20,000. Therefore, the cash receipts from customers during Year 4 can be determined as follows:

Net sales on cash basis

Net sales	$900,000
Less: Increase in net accounts receivable during the year	20,000
Cash receipts from customers	$880,000

CASH PAYMENTS FOR PURCHASES The relationship between the cost of goods sold for a period and the cash payments for the purchase of merchandise depends both on the change in inventory and the change in notes and accounts payable to merchandise creditors during the period. The relationship may be stated, in two stages, as follows:

Converting cost of goods sold to cash basis

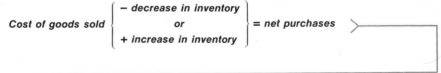

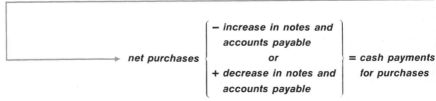

Again referring to the Allison Corporation example, we can see that the company increased its inventory by $80,000 and that notes and accounts payable to merchandise creditors increased by $55,000 during the year. The cash payments for purchases during Year 4 would be computed as follows:

Cost of goods sold on cash basis	*Cost of goods sold*	*$585,000*
	Add: Increase in inventory	*80,000*
	Net purchases (accrual basis)	*$665,000*
	Less: Increase in notes and accounts payable to creditors	*55,000*
	Cash payments for purchases	*$610,000*

The result of this computation makes sense. If a company is increasing its inventory, it will be buying more merchandise than it sells during the period; furthermore, if the company is increasing its notes and accounts payable to merchandise creditors, it is not paying for all its current purchases.

CASH PAYMENTS FOR EXPENSES Expenses in the income statement arise from three major sources: cash expenditures, the write-off of prepayments, and incurring obligations for accrued expenses. The relationship between operating expenses and cash payments, therefore, depends on changes in asset accounts representing the prepayment of expenses, and on changes in accrued liability accounts. These relationships may be stated as follows:

Converting an expense on accrual basis to cash basis

$$Expense \begin{cases} - \textit{increase in related accrued liability} \\ \qquad\qquad\qquad or \\ + \textit{decrease in related accrued liability} \\ - \textit{decrease in related prepayment} \\ \qquad\qquad\qquad or \\ + \textit{increase in related prepayment} \end{cases} = \begin{array}{l} \textit{cash payments for} \\ \textit{expense} \end{array}$$

In the case of a noncash expense such as depreciation, the decrease in the book value of a depreciable asset is exactly equal to the expense recorded, and the resultant cash payment is zero.

Using the information for the Allison Corporation, we can summarize the relationship between the operating expenses and income taxes reported in the income statement and cash payments for these expenses during Year 4 as follows:

Expenses on cash basis	*Total operating expenses and income taxes in the income statement*	*$255,000*
	Add: Decrease in accrued liabilities	*19,500*
	Increase in short-term prepayments	*13,000*
	Less: Depreciation, a noncash expense	*(27,500)*
	Cash payments for operating expenses and income taxes	*$260,000*

CONVERSION OF AN INCOME STATEMENT TO CASH BASIS The conversion of the income statement of the Allison Corporation from an accrual to a cash basis is summarized below. Note that this schedule incorporates the adjustments discussed in the preceding paragraphs.

The cash flow from operations for the Allison Corporation, $10,000, is lower than the amount of income before the gain on the sale of land, $60,000, during Year 4. This difference is caused by a series of variations between revenue and expense transactions on the accrual basis and the related cash inflows and outflows during the year.

In the past, some financial analysts added back depreciation to net income and referred to the total as "cash flow from operations." In our example, such an approach would lead to the figure of $107,500, that is, $80,000 net income plus depreciation of $27,500. However, the actual cash flow from operations for the Allison Corporation is only $10,000, and not $107,500.

ALLISON CORPORATION

Conversion of Income Statement from Accrual to Cash Basis

For Year Ended December 31, Year 4

	Income Statement (Accrual Basis)	Add (Deduct)	Cash Basis
Net sales.	$900,000		
Less: Increase in accounts receivable . . .		$(20,000)	$880,000
Cost of goods sold	585,000		
Add: Increase in inventory		80,000	
Less: Increase in notes and accounts payable to merchandise creditors		(55,000)	610,000
Gross profit on sales	$315,000		$270,000
Operating expenses and income taxes . . .	255,000		
Add: Decrease in accrued liabilities		$ 19,500	
Increase in short-term prepayments . .		13,000	
Less: Depreciation expense		(27,500)	260,000
Income before gain on sale of land (accrual basis)	$ 60,000		
Cash flow from operations			$ 10,000

How much is "cash flow" for Year 4?

CASH FLOW STATEMENT The cash flow from operations computed above for the Allison Corporation does not tell the complete story of cash movements during the period. Let us now combine the $10,000 cash flow from operations with the information relating to cash receipts and payments obtained from the comparative balance sheet by way of the statement of changes in financial position. The result will be a statement that explains in full the $20,000 decrease in the cash balance during Year 4.

Such a cash flow statement for the Allison Corporation is shown below:

ALLISON CORPORATION
Cash Flow Statement
For Year Ended December 31, Year 4

<table>
<tr><td rowspan="12" style="text-align:right">Complete
summary of
cash
movements
for Year 4</td><td colspan="3">Cash payments:</td></tr>
<tr><td>Purchase of equipment . . . .</td><td></td><td style="text-align:right">$ 60,000</td></tr>
<tr><td>Retirement of bonds payable . . . .</td><td></td><td style="text-align:right">40,000</td></tr>
<tr><td>Payment of cash dividends . . . .</td><td></td><td style="text-align:right">35,000</td></tr>
<tr><td style="text-align:right">Total cash payments . . . .</td><td></td><td style="text-align:right">$135,000</td></tr>
<tr><td colspan="3">Cash receipts:</td></tr>
<tr><td style="text-align:right">Cash generated from operations (see schedule on page 755)</td><td style="text-align:right">$10,000</td><td></td></tr>
<tr><td style="text-align:right">Sale of land . . . .</td><td style="text-align:right">30,000</td><td></td></tr>
<tr><td style="text-align:right">Sale of capital stock . . . .</td><td style="text-align:right">70,000</td><td></td></tr>
<tr><td style="text-align:right">Borrowing on long-term notes . . . .</td><td style="text-align:right">5,000</td><td></td></tr>
<tr><td style="text-align:right">Total cash receipts . . . .</td><td></td><td style="text-align:right">115,000</td></tr>
<tr><td>Decrease in cash during the year . . . .</td><td></td><td style="text-align:right">$ 20,000</td></tr>
</table>

The Allison Corporation example was sufficiently simple that we could develop cash flow information from a direct inspection of the income statement and comparative balance sheets. In more complex situations, the accountant will usually use a working paper to convert the income statement from an accrual to a cash basis and to develop cash flow information in a systematic fashion. Familiarity with these working paper procedures is not necessary in order to be able to understand and interpret cash flow information; therefore, discussion of this process is reserved for the **Intermediate Accounting** volume in this series.

KEY TERMS INTRODUCED OR EMPHASIZED IN CHAPTER 21

Cash basis A method of measuring operating results in terms of cash receipts and cash payments rather than revenue earned and expenses incurred.

Cash flow statement A statement showing the sources of cash receipts and purpose of cash payments during an accounting period. This statement is useful for explaining changes in the balance of the Cash account, but it is not a substitute for an income statement.

Exchange transaction In the context of a statement of changes in financial position, exchange transactions are financing or investing activities which do not directly affect working capital accounts. An example of such a transaction is the purchase of plant assets by issuing common stock. Such transactions should be shown in a funds statement as both a source and a use of working capital.

Funds In the context of a statement of changes in financial position, "funds" are usually defined as working capital.

Noncurrent account Any balance sheet account **other than** a current asset or a current liability. Noncurrent accounts include long-term investments, plant assets, intangible assets, long-term liabilities, and stockholders' equity accounts.

Statement of changes in financial position A financial statement showing the sources and uses of working capital during the accounting period. In addition, this statement shows financing and investing activities, such as exchange transactions, which do not directly affect working capital.

Working capital Current assets minus current liabilities. Working capital represents the net amount of liquid resources available to a business.

DEMONSTRATION PROBLEM FOR YOUR REVIEW

The comparative financial data for Liquid Gas Company for the last two years are shown below:

	December 31	
Debits	**Year 2**	**Year 1**
Cash	$ 39,220	$ 15,800
Receivables (net of allowance for doubtful accounts)	41,400	24,000
Inventories, lower of cost or market	27,600	36,800
Short-term prepayments	4,180	4,400
Land	9,000	19,000
Buildings	270,000	250,000
Equipment	478,600	450,000
Total debits	$870,000	$800,000

	December 31	
Credits	**Year 2**	**Year 1**
Accumulated depreciation: buildings	$ 95,000	$ 77,000
Accumulated depreciation: equipment	153,000	120,000
Accounts payable	59,200	30,000
Accrued liabilities	20,000	10,000
Bonds payable	90,000	90,000
Premium on bonds payable	2,800	3,000
Preferred stock ($100 par)	70,000	100,000
Common stock ($25 par)	250,000	250,000
Paid-in capital in excess of par	40,000	40,000
Retained earnings	90,000	80,000
Total credits	$870,000	$800,000

Other data
(1) Cash dividends of $6,000 were declared and paid on the preferred stock, and cash dividends of $50,000 were declared and paid on the common stock.
(2) During Year 2, 300 shares of preferred stock were retired at par value.
(3) The only entries recorded in the Retained Earnings account were for dividends and to close the Income Summary account, which had a credit balance of $66,000 after the loss on the sale of the land.
(4) There were no sales or retirements of buildings and equipment during the year; land was sold for $8,000, resulting in a loss of $2,000.

Instructions
a Compute the change in working capital during Year 2. You may use totals for current assets and current liabilities.

b Prepare a working paper for a statement of changes in financial position for Year 2.

c Prepare a statement of changes in financial position for Year 2, without showing the composition of working capital.

d Prepare a cash flow statement, with a supporting schedule converting the net income from the accrual basis to the cash basis.

SOLUTION TO DEMONSTRATION PROBLEM

a Computation of decrease in working capital:

	As of December 31	
	Year 2	*Year 1*
Current assets	$112,400	$81,000
Less: Current liabilities	79,200	40,000
Working capital	$ 33,200	$41,000
Decrease in working capital during Year 2	7,800	
	$ 41,000	$41,000

b See working paper on page 759.

c

LIQUID GAS COMPANY

Statement of Changes in Financial Position

For Year 2

Sources of working capital:		
Operations:		
Income before loss on sale of land		$ 68,000
Add: Expense not requiring the use of working capital—		
depreciation	$51,000	
Less: Increase in net income which did not provide working		
capital—amortization of premium on bonds		
payable	200	50,800
Total working capital provided by operations		$118,800
Sale of land		8,000
Total sources of working capital		$126,800
Uses of working capital:		
Declaration of cash dividends	$56,000	
Purchase of buildings	20,000	
Purchase of equipment	28,600	
Retirement of preferred stock	30,000	
Total uses of working capital		134,600
Decrease in working capital		$ 7,800

b

LIQUID GAS COMPANY
Working Paper for Statement of Changes in Financial Position
For Year 2

Debits	Account Balances Dec. 31, Year 1	Analysis of Transactions for Year 2 Debit		Analysis of Transactions for Year 2 Credit		Account Balances Dec. 31, Year 2
Working capital	41,000			(x)	7,800	33,200
Land	19,000			(4)	10,000	9,000
Buildings	250,000	(5)	20,000			270,000
Equipment	450,000	(6)	28,600			478,600
Total	760,000					790,800
Credits						
Accumulated depreciation: buildings	77,000			(2)	18,000	95,000
Accumulated depreciation: equipment	120,000			(2)	33,000	153,000
Bonds payable	90,000					90,000
Premium on bonds payable	3,000	(7)	200			2,800
Preferred stock, $100 par	100,000	(8)	30,000			70,000
Common stock, $25 par	250,000					250,000
Paid-in capital in excess of par	40,000					40,000
Retained earnings	80,000	(3)	56,000	(1)	66,000	90,000
Total	760,000		134,800		134,800	790,800

		Sources		Uses		
Sources of working capital:						
Operations—net income		(1)	66,000			
Add: Depreciation		(2)	51,000			(From
Loss on sale of land		(4)	2,000			operations,
Less: Amortization of premium						$118,800)
on bonds payable				(7)	200	
Sale of land		(4)	8,000			
Uses of working capital:						
Payment of cash dividends				(3)	56,000	
Purchase of buildings				(5)	20,000	
Purchase of equipment				(6)	28,600	
Retirement of preferred stock				(8)	30,000	
Total sources and uses of						
working capital			127,000		134,800	
Decrease in working capital		(x)	7,800			
			134,800		134,800	

Explanation of transactions for Year 2:
(1) Net income, $66,000, including a loss of $2,000 on sale of land, transferred to Retained Earnings.
(2) Depreciation for the year, $51,000 (buildings, $18,000, and equipment, $33,000) is added to net income because it is an expense which did not reduce working capital.
(3) Cash dividends declared, $56,000 (preferred stock, $6,000, and common, $50,000).
(4) To record sale of land for $8,000; the loss of $2,000 is added to net income because the loss reduced net income but had no effect on working capital.
(5) To record working capital used for purchase of buildings.
(6) To record working capital used for purchase of equipment.
(7) To record amortization of premium on bonds payable; the amortization increased net income but had no effect on working capital.
(8) To record working capital applied to retirement of preferred stock.
(x) Balancing figure—decrease in working capital during Year 2.

d

LIQUID GAS COMPANY
Cash Flow Statement
For Year 2

Cash receipts:

Cash generated from operations (see Schedule A below)		*$150,020*
Sale of land		*8,000*
Total cash receipts		*$158,020*

Cash payments:

Payment of cash dividends	*$56,000*	
Purchase of buildings	*20,000*	
Purchase of equipment	*28,600*	
Retirement of preferred stock	*30,000*	
Total cash payments		*134,600*
Increase in cash during the year		*$ 23,420*

Schedule A—Cash generated from operations:

Working capital provided by operations—part c		*$118,800*
Add: Decrease in inventories	*$ 9,200*	
Decrease in short-term prepayments	*220*	
Increase in accounts payable	*29,200*	
Increase in accrued liabilities	*10,000*	*48,620*
Less: Increase in receivables		*(17,400)*
Cash generated from operations		*$150,020*

REVIEW QUESTIONS

1 Why is working capital viewed as a "fund of liquid resources"?

2 What are the primary ways in which a firm generates working capital and the primary ways in which a firm uses working capital?

3 What information can a reader gain from a statement of changes in financial position that is not apparent from reading an income statement?

4 In preparing a statement of changes in financial position, business transactions may be classified into three categories. List these categories and indicate which category results in changes in working capital.

5 Give examples of expenses, other than depreciation expense, which reduce net income but which do not result in the use of working capital during the period.

6 Give an example of an increase in net income which does not result in an increase in working capital during the period.

7 The following quotation appeared in a report issued by a major investment banking firm: "Depreciation, depletion, and amortization charges, etc., which supply the funds for the new facilities that sustain the competitive competence of our leading companies, are increasing at a faster rate than is net income." Evaluate this quotation.

8 Although extraordinary and nonoperating gains and losses may be included in net income in measuring the working capital generated by operations, can you give a reason for excluding such gains and losses from net income? Use the following facts to illustrate your point: Net income including gain on sale of land, $100,000; sale of land, with a book value of $70,000, for $150,000.

9 What is the major difference between the statement of changes in financial position and a cash flow statement?

10 The president of a small corporation was puzzled by the following statement made by the accountant: "Our cash flow, net income plus depreciation, amounted to $85,000 last year but our cash generated from operations was only $10,000 because of the increases in our inventory and receivables and the decrease in our accounts payable." Explain what the accountant meant.

11 An outside member of the board of directors of a small corporation made the following comment after studying the comparative financial statements for the past two years: "I have trouble understanding why our cash has increased steadily during the past two years, yet our profits have been negligible; we have paid no dividends; and inventories, receivables, payables, cost of plant and equipment, long-term debt, and capital stock have remained essentially unchanged." Write a brief statement explaining how this situation might occur.

EXERCISES

Ex. 21-1 Indicate the amount of the increase or decrease (if any) in working capital as a result of each of the following events:
a Purchase and retirement of bonds payable, $1,000,000, at 96. The unamortized premium on bonds payable at the time of the retirement was $50,000.
b Declaration of a 25% stock dividend on $600,000 of par value capital stock outstanding.
c Purchase of equipment costing $400,000 for $100,000 cash and $75,000 (plus interest) payable every six months over the next two years.
d A $40,000 write-down of inventory to a market value below cost.

Ex. 21-2 Briefly explain how each of the following situations should be reported in the statement of changes in financial position.
a Depreciation of $100,000 was recorded in Year 1; however, $25,000 of this amount is included in the ending inventory of finished goods.
b In July of Year 1, the 10,000 shares of $50 par value capital stock were split 3 for 1 and in November of Year 1, a 10% stock dividend was distributed.
c Cash of $10,000 was paid and capital stock with a market value of $90,000 was issued to acquire land worth $100,000.

Ex. 21-3 The Ridgeway Corporation reports a net loss of $20,000 on its income statement. In arriving at this figure, the following items among others were included:

Amortization of patents	$ 4,000
Amortization of premium on bonds payable	2,500
Gain on sale of land	10,000
Depreciation expense	12,500
Uninsured fire damage to building	22,100

What was the working capital increase or decrease as a result of *operations*?

Ex. 21-4 A summary of the comparative financial position for the Barber Corporation for the current year appears on page 762.

	End of Current Year	Beginning of Current Year
Working capital	$160,000	$165,000
Land	80,000	50,000
Buildings	120,000	100,000
Less: Accumulated depreciation	(50,000)	(45,000)
	$310,000	$270,000
Notes payable, due in 5 years	$ 30,000	$ -0-
Capital stock, no par value	200,000	200,000
Retained earnings	80,000	70,000
	$310,000	$270,000

The net income was $22,000 and included no nonoperating gains or losses. Depreciation expense for the current year was $5,000. A cash dividend was declared at the end of the current year.

Prepare a statement of changes in financial position for the current year without using a working paper.

Ex. 21-5 The data below are taken from the records of the Ferraro Company:

	End Of Year	Beginning Of Year
Accounts receivable	$ 20,200	$10,200
Inventories	32,000	40,000
Short-term prepayments	2,300	1,500
Accounts payable (merchandise creditors)	28,000	25,000
Miscellaneous current liabilities (accrued expenses)	1,000	1,200
Net sales	300,000	
Cost of goods sold	180,000	
Operating expenses (includes depreciation of $10,000)	80,000	

From the foregoing information, compute the following:
a Cash collected from customers during the year.
b Cash paid to merchandise creditors during the year.
c Cash paid for operating expenses during the year.

Ex. 21-6 The information below is taken from comparative financial statements for the Mulvey Corporation:

	Year 10	Year 9
Net income (there were no extraordinary items)	$60,000	$37,000
Depreciation expense	42,500	31,800
Inventory at end of year	15,000	28,000
Accounts receivable at end of year	9,000	12,000
Accounts payable at end of year	8,000	6,000
Cash dividends declared in December of each year payable Jan. 15 of following year	22,500	15,000

From the data above, determine the following:
a The working capital provided by operations in Year 10.
b The cash generated by operations in Year 10.
c Working capital used for dividends in Year 10.

PROBLEMS

Group A

21A-1 Below is given a list of business transactions and adjustments. For each item you are to indicate the effect first on working capital, and second on cash. In each case the possible effects are an increase, a decrease, or no change.
  (1) Machinery sold for cash in excess of its carrying value
  (2) Warehouse destroyed by fire; one-half of its carrying value covered by insurance and recorded as a receivable from the insurance company
  (3) Amortization of discount on bonds payable
  (4) Premium paid for a three-year insurance policy
  (5) Declaration of a cash dividend
  (6) Payment of previously declared cash dividend on common stock
  (7) Payment of an account payable
  (8) Depreciation recorded for the period
  (9) Sale of long-term investment at a loss
  (10) Payment of the current year's income tax liability, which was previously recorded in the accounting records
  (11) Exchange of convertible bonds for the company's common stock
  (12) An uncollectible account receivable written off against the Allowance for Doubtful Accounts

Instructions
a List the numbers 1 to 12 on your answer sheet, and set up two columns headed "working capital effect" and "cash effect." For each transaction, write the words *increase, decrease,* or *no change* in the appropriate column to indicate the effect of the transaction on working capital and cash.
b Are any of the transactions listed above considered "exchange transactions" which would be listed as both a source and use of working capital in a statement of changes in financial position? Explain.

21A-2 The following information is taken from the annual report of Villanova, Inc.:

	Year 2	Year 1
Current assets	*$240,000*	*$162,000*
Equipment	*360,000*	*252,000*
Less: Accumulated depreciation	*(120,000)*	*(72,000)*
Investments	*48,000*	*60,000*
Current liabilities	*138,000*	*48,000*
Capital stock	*120,000*	*120,000*
Retained earnings	*270,000*	*234,000*

Cash dividends declared amounted to $42,000; no equipment items were sold; investments were sold at a gain of $6,000; and net income (including nonoperating gain) for Year 2 was $78,000.

Instructions From the information given, prepare a statement of changes in financial position for Year 2, without using working papers.

21A-3 Comparative balance sheets for Redhill Corporation at the end of Year 1 and Year 2 are shown on page 764.

	Year 2	Year 1
Cash	$ 36,000	$ 60,000
Accounts receivable (net)	90,000	105,000
Merchandise inventory	195,000	150,000
Land for future expansion	45,000	
Plant and equipment (see accumulated depreciation below) . . .	480,000	375,000
Patents (net of amortization)	54,000	60,000
	$900,000	$750,000
Accumulated depreciation	$157,500	$120,000
Accounts payable	91,500	45,000
Dividends payable	6,000	
Notes payable due in Year 5	15,000	
Capital stock, $10 par	600,000	525,000
Retained earnings	30,000	60,000
	$900,000	$750,000

Additional data
(1) The net loss for Year 2 amounted to $24,000.
(2) Cash dividends of $6,000 were declared.
(3) Land for future expansion was acquired.
(4) Equipment costing $105,000 was purchased for cash; $15,000 was borrowed for three years in order to pay for this equipment.
(5) Additional shares of capital stock were sold at par value.
(6) Other changes in noncurrent accounts resulted from the usual transactions recorded in such accounts.

Instructions
a Prepare a schedule computing the change in working capital during Year 2.
b Prepare working papers for a statement of changes in financial position for Year 2.
c Prepare a formal statement of changes in financial position for Year 2.

21A-4 A condensed balance sheet at January 1, Year 10, and the statement of changes in financial position for Year 10 for Intruder Alert, Inc., are shown below and on page 765.

INTRUDER ALERT, INC.
Balance Sheet
January 1, Year 10

Assets

Current assets	$ 86,000
Land	40,000
Equipment	96,000
Less: Accumulated depreciation	(30,000)
Patents (net of accumulated amortization)	10,000
Total assets	$202,000

Liabilities & Stockholders' Equity

Current liabilities	$ 36,000
Capital stock, no-par value	94,000
Retained earnings	72,000
Total liabilities & stockholders' equity	$202,000

INTRUDER ALERT, INC.
Statement of Changes in Financial Position
For Year 10

Working capital, Jan. 1, Year 10		$ 50,000
Sources of working capital:		
Operations:		
Net income	$48,000	
Add: Depreciation expense	20,000	
Amortization of patents	2,000	
Less: Gain on disposal of equipment	(8,000)	
Working capital provided by operations		62,000
Issuance of capital stock		22,000
Disposal of equipment		14,000
Subtotal		$148,000
Uses of working capital:		
Dividends paid	$16,000	
Purchase of land	28,000	
Purchase of equipment	62,000	106,000
Working capital, Dec. 31, Year 10		$ 42,000

Accumulated depreciation on the equipment sold in Year 10 was $12,000 and total assets at December 31, Year 10, were $278,000.

Instructions Using the information above, prepare a condensed balance sheet at December 31, Year 10. Supporting schedules should be in good form.

21A-5 Comparative post-closing trial balances for Home Port, Inc., are shown below and on page 766.

Debits	Year 2	Year 1
Cash . . . . $	72,000	$ 78,000
Marketable securities		96,000
Accounts receivable	120,000	228,000
Inventories	132,000	180,000
Prepaid expenses	36,000	24,000
Land	120,000	
Buildings	600,000	
	$1,080,000	$606,000

Credits

Allowance for doubtful accounts . . . . $	6,000	$ 12,000
Accounts payable	138,000	102,000
Accrued liabilities	102,000	78,000
Long-term notes payable	300,000	60,000
Capital stock, $10 par	396,000	246,000
Retained earnings	138,000	108,000
	$1,080,000	$606,000

During Year 1 Home Port, Inc., operated in rented space. Early in Year 2 the company acquired suitable land and made arrangements to borrow funds from a local bank on long-term notes to finance the construction of new buildings. The company also sold additional stock at par and all its marketable securities at book value. Construction of the buildings was completed near the end of Year 2. The only entries in the company's Retained Earnings account during the two-year period were the closing of the annual net income and the declaration of cash dividends of $36,000 in Year 1 and $48,000 in Year 2.

Instructions
a Prepare a schedule of changes in working capital during Year 2. The schedule should show the balances of each current account at the beginning and at the end of Year 2 and the effect of the change in the account balance on working capital.
b Prepare working papers for a statement of changes in financial position. (Determine net income by analysis of the Retained Earnings account.)
c Prepare a formal statement of changes in financial position for Year 2, showing first the uses of working capital followed by sources of working capital.

21A-6 When the controller of Avanti Corporation presented the following condensed comparative financial statements to the board of directors at the close of Year 2, the reaction of the board members was very favorable.

AVANTI CORPORATION
Comparative Income Statements
(in thousands of dollars)

	Year 2	Year 1
Net sales.	$970	$680
Cost of goods sold	590	480
Gross profit on sales	$380	$200
Operating expenses, including depreciation	(180)	(140)
Income taxes	(90)	(25)
Net income	$110	$ 35

AVANTI CORPORATION
Comparative Financial Position
As of December 31
(in thousands of dollars)

Current assets	$ 410	$395
Less: Current liabilities	200	225
Working capital	$ 210	$170
Plant and equipment (net)	970	650
Total assets minus current liabilities	$1,180	$820
Financed by following sources of long-term capital:		
Long-term liabilities	$ 250	
Capital stock ($50 par value)	500	$500
Retained earnings	430	320
Total sources of long-term capital	$1,180	$820

Noting that net income rose from $3.50 per share of capital stock to $11 per share, one member of the board proposed that a substantial cash dividend be paid. "Our working capital is up by $40,000; we should be able to make a distribution to stockholders," he commented. To which the controller replied that the company's cash position was precarious and pointed out that at the end of Year 2, a cash balance of only $15,000 was on hand, a decline from $145,000 at the end of Year 1. The controller also reminded the board that the company bought $400,000 of new equipment during Year 2. When a board member asked for an explanation of the increase of $40,000 in working capital, the controller presented the following schedule (in thousands of dollars):

		Effect on *Working Capital*
Increase in working capital:		
Accounts receivable increased by		$ 83
Inventories increased by		45
Prepaid expenses increased by		17
Accounts payable were reduced by		62
Accrued expenses payable were reduced by		28
Total increases in working capital		$235
Decreases in working capital:		
Cash decreased by	$130	
Income tax liability increased by	65	195
Increase in working capital during Year 2		$ 40

After examining this schedule, the board member shook his head and said, "I still don't understand how our cash position can be so tight in the face of a tripling of net income and a substantial increase in working capital!"

Instructions
a Prepare a statement converting Avanti Corporation's income statement to a cash basis, determining the cash generated by operations during Year 2.

b From the information in **a** and an inspection of the comparative statement of financial position, prepare a cash flow statement for Year 2, explaining the $130,000 decrease in the cash balance.

c Prepare a statement accounting for the increase in working capital (statement of changes in financial position) for Avanti Corporation in a more acceptable form.

d Write a brief note of explanation to the board member.

Group B

21B-1 Below is given a list of business transactions and adjustments. For each item you are to indicate the effect first on working capital, and second on cash. In each case the possible effects are an increase, a decrease, or no change.

(1) Purchase of patent, giving 200 shares of the company's common stock in exchange

(2) Merchandise sold for cash at a price below cost

(3) Prior period adjustment made to reflect additional income taxes due on income of a prior period

(4) Marketable securities sold for cash at a price above cost

(5) Amortization of premium on bonds payable

(6) Declaration of a cash dividend

(7) Payment of a previously declared cash dividend

(8) Three-year fire insurance policy paid in advance

(9) Inventory destroyed by fire; one-half of its carrying value covered by insurance and recorded as a receivable from the insurance company

(10) Amortization of the portion of prepaid insurance expense which expired during the current year

(11) An uncollectible account receivable written off against the Allowance for Doubtful Accounts

(12) Plant assets sold for cash at a price below their carrying values

Instructions

a List the numbers 1 to 12 on your answer sheet, and set up two columns headed "working capital effect" and "cash effect." For each transaction, write the words *increase, decrease,* or *no change* in the appropriate column to indicate the effect of the transaction on working capital and cash.

b Are any of the transactions listed above considered "exchange transactions" which would be listed as both a source and use of working capital in a statement of changes in financial position? Explain.

21B-2 During Year 6 Marine Corporation showed the following *changes* in amount for the groups of accounts listed below. For example, current assets increased by $80,000 during Year 6, and this amount therefore appears in the "Debit" change column.

	Changes during Year 6	
	Debit	Credit
Current assets	$ 80,000	
Plant and equipment	160,000	
Accumulated depreciation		$ 40,000
Current liabilities	48,000	
Capital stock, $10 par		128,000
Paid-in capital in excess of par		32,000
Retained earnings		88,000
	$288,000	$288,000

During Year 6 the company issued 12,800 shares of capital stock and applied the proceeds to the purchase of equipment. There were no retirements of plant and equipment items in Year 6. Dividends of $64,000 were declared and paid during Year 6.

Instructions Prepare a statement of changes in financial position for Year 6, without using working papers.

21B-3 The balances of the accounts of Clemente Corporation at the end of Years 9 and 10 are listed below:

	Year 10	Year 9
Cash	$ 60,000	$ 100,000
Accounts receivable (net)	150,000	175,000
Merchandise inventory	325,000	250,000
Land for future expansion	75,000	
Plant and equipment (see accumulated depreciation below) .	800,000	625,000
Patents (net of amortization)	90,000	100,000
	$1,500,000	$1,250,000
Accumulated depreciation	$ 262,500	$ 200,000
Accounts payable	152,500	75,000
Dividends payable	10,000	
Notes payable due in Year 14	25,000	
Capital stock, $10 par	1,000,000	875,000
Retained earnings	50,000	100,000
	$1,500,000	$1,250,000

The following additional information is available for your consideration:
(1) The net loss for Year 10 amounted to $40,000.
(2) Cash dividends of $10,000 were declared.
(3) Land for future expansion was acquired.
(4) Equipment costing $175,000 was purchased for cash; $25,000 was borrowed for three years in order to pay for this equipment.
(5) Additional shares of capital stock were sold at par value.
(6) Other changes in noncurrent accounts resulted from the usual transactions recorded in such accounts.

Instructions
a Prepare a schedule computing the change in working capital during Year 10.
b Prepare working papers for a statement of changes in financial position for Year 10.
c Prepare a formal statement of changes in financial position for Year 10.

21B-4 The following balance sheet data for Year 5 were obtained from the records of Anacapa Corporation:

	Dec. 31	Jan. 1
Current assets	$298,700	$202,500
Plant and equipment (net)	334,000	319,000
Goodwill (amortized over 10 years)	8,500	10,000
Current liabilities	150,000	81,500
Bonds payable, 7%	200,000	–0–
Discount on bonds payable	3,800	–0–

Preferred stock, $10 par	$ -0-	$200,000
Common stock, no par	150,000	150,000
Retained earnings	145,000	100,000

Additional data

(1) The statement of retained earnings for Year 5 follows:

Beginning balance		$100,000
Add: Net income, including gain on disposal of land		80,000
Subtotal		$180,000
Less: Amount paid to retire preferred stock in excess of		
carrying (book) value	$10,000	
Cash dividends declared	25,000	35,000
Ending balance		$145,000

(2) Ten-year bonds of $200,000 face value were issued on July 1 at 98; the proceeds and some additional cash were used to retire the entire issue of preferred stock at 105.

(3) Land having a cost of $60,000 was exchanged at its fair value of $100,000 for equipment with a value of $120,000; the balance of $20,000 was paid in cash. A $40,000 gain was recognized on the exchange.

(4) Depreciation for the year was $45,000, amortization of goodwill was $1,500, and amortization of discount on bonds payable was $200.

Instructions

a Prepare a working paper for a statement of changes in financial position.

b Prepare a statement of changes in financial position. Report working capital provided from operations in a single amount as determined in the working paper.

21B-5 The accounting records of Liberty Corporation showed the following balances at the end of Year 4 and Year 5:

	Year 5	Year 4
Cash	$ 93,000	$ 120,000
Accounts receivable	165,000	105,000
Merchandise inventory	285,000	450,000
Long-term investments	45,000	
Equipment	1,170,000	675,000
Accumulated depreciation	(240,000)	(180,000)
Land	240,000	105,000
	$1,758,000	$1,275,000
Accounts payable	$ 135,000	$ 60,000
Notes payable (current)	15,000	90,000
Bonds payable, due in Year 10	300,000	240,000
Unamortized premium on bonds payable	5,400	5,700
Capital stock, $1 par	600,000	450,000
Premium on capital stock	240,000	150,000
Retained earnings	462,600	279,300
	$1,758,000	$1,275,000

Net income for Year 5 amounted to $258,000. Cash dividends of $74,700 were declared and paid during Year 5. Additional purchases of investments, equipment, and land were completed during Year 5, financed in part through the sale of bonds at par and 150,000 shares of capital stock. Equipment costing $75,000 was sold at a price equal to its book value of $30,000.

Instructions
a Prepare a schedule of changes in working capital during Year 5.
b Prepare working papers for a statement of changes in financial position for Year 5. See the solution to the demonstration problem in this chapter for proper handling of the premium on bonds payable.
c Prepare a formal statement of changes in financial position for Year 5.

21B-6 The following information is presented to you by Linda Kahn, owner of Linda's Fashion Boutique:

Balance Sheet

Assets	Year 2	Year 1
Cash	$ 10,000	$ 40,000
Marketable securities	15,000	20,000
Accounts receivable (net)	100,000	35,000
Inventory	80,000	60,000
Equipment (net of accumulated depreciation)	35,000	45,000
Total assets	$240,000	$200,000

Liabilities & Owner's Capital	Year 2	Year 1
Accounts payable	$ 37,000	$ 40,000
Accrued liabilities	8,000	2,500
Note payable to bank (due early in Year 2)		12,500
Linda Kahn, capital	195,000	145,000
Total liabilities & owner's capital	$240,000	$200,000

Income Statement for Year 2

Sales (net)		$400,000
Cost of goods sold		300,000
Gross profit on sales		$100,000
Operating expenses (including $10,000 depreciation)	$60,000	
Loss on sale of marketable securities	500	60,500
Net income		$ 39,500
Drawings by owner		22,500
Increase in owner's capital as a result of operations		$ 17,000

Kahn is concerned over the decrease in her cash position during Year 2, particularly in view of the fact that she invested an additional $33,000 in the business and had a net income of $39,500 during the year. She asks you to prepare a statement which will explain the decrease in the Cash account. You point out that while cash decreased by $30,000, the working capital increased by $60,000. You conclude that a statement of cash receipts and cash disbursements, showing cash collected from customers, cash paid to merchandise creditors, cash paid for operating expenses, etc., would give her the information she needs.

Instructions
a Prepare a schedule showing the conversion of the income statement from an accrual to a cash basis, thus determining the net cash outflow from operations.
b Prepare a cash flow statement which explains the decrease of $30,000 in cash during Year 2.
c Prepare a statement of changes in financial position without using a working paper.

BUSINESS DECISION PROBLEM 21

Maverick Corporation has working capital of $6,150,000 at the beginning of Year 5. Restrictions contained in bank loans require that working capital not fall below $6,000,000. The following projected information is available for Year 5:
(*1*) Budgeted net income (including nonoperating items) is $7,500,000. The following items were included in estimating net income: depreciation, $2,100,000; amortization of premium on bonds payable, $150,000; uncollect-ible accounts expense, $180,000; and income taxes, $6,300,000. The estimate of net income also included the nonoperating items described below.
(*2*) Sale of plant assets with a carrying value of $1,200,000 is expected to bring $1,500,000 net of income taxes.
(*3*) Additional plant assets costing $15,000,000 will be acquired. Payment will be as follows: 20% cash, 20% short-term note, and 60% through issuance of capital stock.
(*4*) Long-term investment will be sold at cost, $300,000.
(*5*) Bonds payable in the amount of $1,500,000, bearing interest at 11%, will be redeemed at 105 approximately 10 years prior to maturity in order to eliminate the high interest expense of $165,000 per year. The elimination of this interest and the gain or loss on the retirement of bonds payable were taken into account in estimating net income for Year 5. These bonds had been issued at par.
(*6*) Tentative planned cash dividend, $4,500,000.

Instructions
a Consider all the information given above and prepare a projected statement of changes in financial position (without showing the composition of working capital) in order to determine the estimated increase or decrease in working capital for Year 5. Some of the information given may be irrelevant.
b Cash dividends of $4,500,000 have been paid in recent years. The company would like to maintain dividends at this level. Does it appear likely that the past dividend policy can be maintained in Year 5? What factors other than working capital position should be considered in determining the level of cash dividends declared by the board of directors?

22 | Analysis and Interpretation of Financial Statements

Financial statements are the instrument panel of a business enterprise. They constitute a report on managerial performance, attesting to managerial success or failure and flashing warning signals of impending difficulties. In reading a complex instrument panel, one must understand the gauges and their calibration to make sense out of the array of data they convey. Similarly, one must understand the inner workings of the accounting system and the significance of various financial relationships to interpret the data appearing in financial statements. To a reader with a knowledge of accounting, a set of financial statements tells a great deal about a business enterprise.

The financial affairs of a business may be of interest to a number of different groups: management, creditors, investors, politicians, union officials, and government agencies. Each of these groups has somewhat different needs, and accordingly each tends to concentrate on particular aspects of a company's financial picture.

What is your opinion of the level of corporate profits?

As a college student who has completed (or almost completed) a course in accounting, you have a much better understanding of corporate profits than do people who have never studied accounting. The level of earnings of large corporations is a controversial topic, a favorite topic in many political speeches and at many cocktail parties. Many of the statements one reads or hears from these sources are emotional rather than rational, and fiction rather than fact. Public opinion polls show that the public believes the average manufacturing company has an after-tax profit of about 30% of sales, when in fact, such profit has been about 5% of sales in recent years. A widespread public belief that profits are 6 times the actual rate may lead to some unwise legislation.

An in-depth knowledge of accounting does not enable you to say at what level corporate earnings *should be;* however, a knowledge of accounting does enable you to read audited financial statements that show what the level of corporate earnings *actually is.* Moreover, you are aware that the information in published financial statements of corporations has been audited by CPA firms and has been reviewed in detail by government agencies, such as the Securities and Exchange Commission and the IRS. Consequently, you know that the profits reported in these published financial statements are reasonably reliable; they have been determined in accordance with generally accepted accounting principles and verified by independent experts.

When such troublesome problems as severe unemployment and rising prices for consumer goods and services affect so many people, it is not surprising that some political leaders look for a scapegoat to hold responsible. Often, the blame has been laid on corporate profits, which sometimes have been labeled as "outrageous," "scandalous," and even "obscene." Usually the speaker who uses these emotional adjectives cites an absolute dollar amount of profits without relating it in any way to the volume of sales or the amount of assets necessary to produce the quoted profit figure.

As a specific example, let us look at the profits of one of the world's largest and most successful corporations, Exxon. The oil industry has been particularly subject to criticism for so-called "excessive" profits, and Exxon is the world's largest oil company. The latest annual report of Exxon Corporation (audited by Price Waterhouse & Co.) shows that profits amounted to about $2\frac{1}{2}$ billion dollars. Standing alone, that figure seems enormous, but we need to look a little further. Total revenue was a little under 50 billion dollars, so net income amounted to approximately **5% of sales.** Let us assume that Exxon's profits on gasoline are in line with its overall 5% profit rate and that gasoline is selling for, say, 60 cents a gallon. Even if our assumption that profit on gasoline is about the same as on fuel oil and other products is not entirely true, we could still safely say that the elimination of all profits by Exxon would not cause the price of gasoline to drop significantly.

The audited income statement of Exxon also shows that *income taxes and other taxes* were over $15 billion, or about six times as much as the company's profits. (A major portion of these taxes was paid to foreign governments.) Would you say that it is corporate profits or taxation which contributed significantly to high gasoline prices?

Another favorite tactic in attacking profits of corporations is to use percentages in a misleading manner. For example, assume that a corporation has net income in Year 1 of $1,000,000; that in Year 2 net income drops to $100,000; and that in Year 3 net income rises to $1,000,000. Clearly, Year 3 is no more profitable than Year 1, but a critic of corporate profits might say: "This company's profits in Year 3 rose by 900%, an unbelievable and unjustifiable increase." What needs to be added is that the 900% increase in Year 3 exactly offset the 90% decline in Year 2. Few people seem to realize that a 90% decline in earnings must be followed by a 900% increase just to get back to the starting point.

There are many ways of appraising the adequacy of corporate earnings; certainly, earnings should be compared with total assets and with invested capital as well as with sales. In this chapter we shall look at a number of ways of evaluating corporate profits and solvency.

Sources of financial information

For the most part, the discussion in this chapter will be limited to the kind of analysis that can be made by "outsiders" who do not have access to internal accounting records. Investors must rely to a considerable extent on financial statements in published annual and quarterly reports. In the case of large publicly owned corporations, additional information that must be filed with the Securities and Exchange Commission, is available. Financial information for most corporations is also published by Moody's Investors Service, Standard & Poor's Corporation, and stock brokerage firms.

Bankers are usually able to secure more detailed information by requesting it as a condition for granting a loan. Trade creditors may obtain financial information for businesses of almost any size from credit-rating agencies such as Dun & Bradstreet, Inc.

COMPARATIVE FINANCIAL STATEMENTS The change in financial data over time is best exhibited in statements showing data for two or more years placed side by side in adjacent columns. Such statements are called *comparative financial statements.* A highly condensed comparative balance sheet is shown below and on page 776.

BENSON CORPORATION
Comparative Balance Sheet
As of December 31
(in thousands of dollars)

	Year 3	Year 2	Year 1
Assets:			
Current assets	$180	$150	$120
Plant and equipment (net)	450	300	345
Total assets	$630	$450	$465

Condensed three-year balance sheet

Liabilities & Stockholders' Equity:

Current liabilities	$ 60	$ 80	$120
Long-term liabilities	200	100	
Capital stock	300	300	300
Retained earnings (deficit)	70	(30)	45
Total liabilities & stockholders' equity	$630	$450	$465

The usefulness of comparative financial statements covering two or more years is well recognized. Published annual reports often contain comparative financial statements covering a period as long as 10 years. By observing the change in various items period by period, the analyst may gain valuable clues as to growth and other important trends affecting the business.

Tools of analysis

Few figures in a financial statement are highly significant in and of themselves. It is their relationship to other quantities, or the amount and direction of change since a previous date, that is important. Analysis is largely a matter of establishing significant relationships and pointing up changes and trends. There are three widely used analytical techniques: (1) dollar and percentage changes, (2) component percentages, and (3) ratios.

DOLLAR AND PERCENTAGE CHANGES The dollar amount of change from year to year is of some interest; reducing this to percentage terms adds perspective. For example, if sales this year have increased by $100,000, the fact that this is an increase of 10% over last year's sales of $1 million puts it in a different perspective than if it represented a 1% increase over sales of $10 million for the prior year.

The dollar amount of any change is the difference between the amount for a *base* year and for a *comparison* year. The percentage change is computed by dividing the amount of the change between years by the amount for the base year. This is illustrated in the tabulation below, using data from the comparative balance sheet on pages 775–776.

		In Thousands			Increase or (Decrease)			
					Year 3 over Year 2		Year 2 over Year 1	
		Year 3	Year 2	Year 1	Amount	%	Amount	%
Dollar and percentage changes	Current assets	$180	$150	$120	$30	20%	$30	25%
	Current liabilities	$ 60	$ 80	$120	($20)	(25%)	($40)	(33.3%)

Although current assets increased $30,000 in both Year 2 and Year 3, the percentage of change differs because of the shift in the base year from Year 1 to Year 2. These calculations present no problems when the figures for the base year are positive amounts. If a negative amount or a zero amount appears in the base year, a percentage change cannot be computed. For example, in the above comparative balance sheet, there were no long-term liabilities in Year 1; therefore the percentage change to Year 2 for this liability cannot be calculated.

COMPONENT PERCENTAGES   The phrase "a piece of pie" is subject to varying interpretations until it is known whether the piece represents one-sixth or one-half of the total pie. The percentage relationship between any particular financial item and a significant total that includes this item is known as a *component percentage;* this is often a useful means of showing relationships or the relative importance of the item in question. Thus if inventories are 50% of total current assets, they are a far more significant factor in the current position of a company than if they are only 10% of total current assets.

One application of component percentages is to express each item on the balance sheet as a percentage of total assets. This shows quickly the relative importance of current and noncurrent assets, and the relative amount of financing obtained from current creditors, long-term creditors, and stockholders.

COMPARATIVE INCOME STATEMENT   Another application is to express all items on an income statement as a percentage of net sales. Such a statement is sometimes called a *common size* income statement. A highly condensed income statement in dollars and in common size form is illustrated below.

Income Statement

	Dollars		Component Percentages	
	Year 2	*Year 1*	*Year 2*	*Year 1*
How successful was Year 2? Net sales	$500,000	$200,000	100.0%	100.0%
Cost of goods sold	350,000	120,000	70.0	60.0
Gross profit on sales	$150,000	$ 80,000	30.0%	40.0%
Expenses (including income taxes) .	100,000	50,000	20.0	25.0
Net income	$ 50,000	$ 30,000	10.0%	15.0%

Looking only at the component percentages, we see that the decline in the gross profit rate from 40 to 30% was only partially offset by the decrease in expenses as a percentage of net sales, causing net income to decrease from 15 to 10% of net sales. The dollar amounts in the first pair of columns, however, present an entirely different picture. It is true that net sales increased faster than net income, but net income improved significantly in Year 2, a fact not apparent from a review of component percentages alone. This points out an important limitation in the use of component percentages. Changes in the component percentage may result from a change in the component, in the total, or in both. Reverting to our previous analogy, it is important to know not only the relative size of a piece of pie, but also the size of the pie; 10% of a large pie may be a bigger piece than 15% of a smaller pie.

RATIOS A ratio is a simple mathematical expression of the relationship of one item to another. Ratios may be expressed in a number of ways. For example, if we wish to clarify the relationship between sales of $800,000 and net income of $40,000, we may state: (1) The ratio of sales to net income is 20 to 1 (or 20:1); (2) for every $1 of sales, the company has an average net income of 5 cents; (3) net income is $\frac{1}{20}$ of sales. In each case the ratio is merely a means of describing the relationship between sales and net income in a simple form.

In order to compute a meaningful ratio, there must be a significant relationship between the two figures. A ratio focuses attention on a relationship which is significant, but a full interpretation of the ratio usually requires further investigation of the underlying data. Ratios are an aid to analysis and interpretation; they are not a substitute for sound thinking.

Standards of comparison

In using dollar and percentage changes, component percentages, and ratios, financial analysts constantly search for some standard of comparison against which to judge whether the relationships that they have found are favorable or unfavorable. Two such standards are (1) the past performance of the company and (2) the performance of other companies in the same industry.

PAST PERFORMANCE OF THE COMPANY Comparing analytical data for a current period with similar computations for prior years affords some basis for judging whether the position of the business is improving or worsening. This comparison of data over time is sometimes called *horizontal* or *dynamic* analysis, to express the idea of reviewing data for a number of periods. It is distinguished from *vertical* or *static* analysis, which refers to the review of the financial information for only one accounting period.

In addition to determining whether the situation is improving or becoming worse, horizontal analysis may aid in making estimates of future prospects. Since changes may reverse their direction at any time, however, projecting past trends into the future is always a somewhat risky statistical pastime.

A weakness of horizontal analysis is that comparison with the past does not afford any basis for evaluation in absolute terms. The fact that net income was 2% of sales last year and is 3% of sales this year indicates improvement, but if there is evidence that net income *should be* 5% of sales, the record for both years is unfavorable.

INDUSTRY STANDARDS   The limitations of horizontal analysis may be overcome to some extent by finding some other standard of performance as a yardstick against which to measure the record of any particular firm.[1] The yardstick may be a comparable company, the average record of several companies in the same industry, or some predetermined standard.

Suppose that Y Company suffers a 5% drop in its sales during the current year. The discovery that the sales of all companies in the same industry fell an average of 20% would indicate that this was a favorable rather than an unfavorable performance. Assume further that Y Company's net income is 2% of net sales. Based on comparison with other companies in the industry, this would be substandard performance if Y Company were an automobile manufacturer; but it would be a satisfactory record if Y Company were a grocery chain.

When we compare a given company with its competitors or with industry averages, our conclusions will be valid only if the companies in question are reasonably comparable. Because of the large number of diversified companies formed in recent years, the term *industry* is difficult to define, and companies that fall roughly within the same industry may not be comparable in many respects. One company may engage only in the marketing of oil products; another may be a fully integrated producer from the well to the gas pump, yet both are said to be in the "oil industry."

Differences in accounting methods may lessen the comparability of financial data for two companies. For example, companies may employ different depreciation methods or estimates of the useful life of substantially similar assets; inventories may be valued by different methods; and the timing of revenue recognition may differ significantly among companies engaged in certain industries. Despite these limitations, studying comparative performances is a useful method of analysis if carefully and intelligently done.

---

[1] For example, the Robert Morris Associates publishes *Annual Statement Studies* which contains detailed data obtained from 27,000 annual reports grouped in 223 industry classifications. Assets, liabilities, and stockholders' equity are presented as a percentage of total assets; income statement amounts are expressed as a percentage of net sales; and key ratios are given (expressed as the median for each industry, the upper quartile, and the lower quartile). Measurements, within each of the 223 industry groups, are grouped according to the size of the firm. Similarly, Dun & Bradstreet, Inc., annually publishes *Key Business Ratios* in 125 lines of business divided by retailing, wholesaling, manufacturing, and construction. A total of 14 ratios are presented for each of the 125 industry groups.

Objectives of financial analysis

Business decisions are made on the basis of the best available estimates of the outcome of such decisions. The purpose of financial analysis is to provide information about a business unit for decision-making purposes, and such information need not be limited to accounting data. While ratios and other relationships based on *past performance* may be helpful in predicting the future earnings performance and financial health of a company, we must be aware of the inherent limitations of such data. Financial statements are essentially summary records of the past, and we must go beyond the financial statements and look into the nature of the company, its competitive position within the industry, its product lines, its research expenditures, and, above all, the quality of its management.

The key objectives of financial analysis are to determine the company's earnings performance and the soundness and liquidity of its financial position. We are essentially interested in financial analysis as a predictive tool; accordingly, we want to examine both quantitative and qualitative data in order to ascertain the *quality of earnings* and the *quality and protection of assets.* In periods of recession when business failures are common, the balance sheet takes on increased importance because the question of liquidity is uppermost in the minds of many in the business community. When business conditions are good, the income statement receives more attention as people become absorbed in profit possibilities.

QUALITY OF EARNINGS   Profits are the lifeblood of a business entity. No entity can survive for long and accomplish its other goals unless it is profitable. Continuous losses drain assets from the business, consume owners' equity, and leave the company at the mercy of creditors. For this reason, we are interested not only in the total *amount* of earnings but also in the *rate* of earnings on sales, on total assets, and on owners' equity. In addition, we must look to the *stability* and *source* of earnings. An erratic earnings performance over a period of years, for example, is less desirable than a steady level of earnings. A history of increasing earnings is preferable to a "flat" earnings record.

A breakdown of sales and earnings by major product lines is useful in evaluating the future performance of a company. In recent years many publicly owned companies have broadened their reporting to include sales and profits by product lines, and the Securities and Exchange Commission now requires such reporting from most companies.

Financial analysts often express the opinion that the earnings of one company are of higher quality than earnings of other similar companies. This concept of *quality of earnings* arises because each company management can choose from a wide variety of accounting principles and methods, all of which are considered generally acceptable. The financial analyst should ascertain whether the accounting principles and methods selected by management lead to a conservative measurement of earnings or tend to inflate current reported earnings by deferring certain costs and anticipating certain revenue. A company's management is often under heavy pressure to report rising earnings, and accounting policies may be tailored toward this objective. We have already pointed out the impact on current reported earnings of the choice between the lifo and fifo methods of inventory valuation and the choice of depreciation policies. In judging the quality of earnings, other appropriate questions are: What has been the effect on earnings of any accounting changes? How much of the net income is attributable to nonrecurring or nonoperating items? The very existence of a concept of *quality of earnings* is evidence that accountants still have some distance to travel in developing a body of accounting standards which will ensure a reasonable comparability of earnings reported by different companies.

QUALITY OF ASSETS AND THE RELATIVE AMOUNT OF DEBT Although a satisfactory level of earnings may be a good indication of the company's long-run ability to pay its debts and dividends, we must also look at the composition of assets, their condition and liquidity, the relationship between current assets and current liabilities, and the total amount of debt outstanding. A company may be profitable and yet be unable to pay its liabilities on time; sales and earnings may be satisfactory but plant and equipment may be deteriorating because of poor maintenance policies; valuable patents may be expiring; substantial losses may be in prospect from slow-moving inventories and past-due receivables. Extensive use of credit and a liberal dividend policy may result in a low owners' equity and thus expose stockholders to substantial risks in case of a downturn in business.

IMPACT OF INFLATION

During a period of inflation, financial statements which are prepared in terms of historical costs do not fully reflect the economic resources or the *real income* (in terms of purchasing power) of a business enterprise. We have already noted that the SEC requires that large corporations disclose in footnotes the replacement cost of inventories, cost of goods sold, plant and equipment, and depreciation. Financial analysts should therefore attempt to evaluate the impact of inflation on the financial position and results of operations of the company being studied. They should raise such questions as: How much of the net income can be attributed to the increase in the general price level? Is depreciation expense understated in terms of current price levels? Are profits exaggerated because the replacement cost of inventories is higher than the cost of units charged to cost of goods sold? Is the company gaining or losing from inflation because of the composition of its assets and because its liabilities will be liquidated with "cheaper" dollars? Will the company be able to keep its "physical capital" intact by paying the higher prices necessary to replace plant assets as they wear out? The fundamental issues of modifying accounting to cope with the impact of inflation were discussed in Chapter 14.

Illustrative analysis for Weaver Company

Keep in mind the above discussion of analytical principles as you study the illustrative financial analysis which follows. The basic information for our discussion is contained in a set of condensed two-year comparative financial statements for the Weaver Company shown on the following pages. Summarized statement data, together with computations of dollar increases and decreases, and component percentages where applicable, have been compiled.

Using the information in these statements, let us consider the kind of analysis that might be of particular interest to: (1) common stockholders, (2) long-term creditors, (3) preferred stockholders, and (4) short-term creditors. Organizing our discussion in this way emphasizes the differences in the viewpoint of these groups; all of them have, of course, a considerable common interest in the performance of the company as a whole. This approach should be viewed as only one of many that may be used in analyzing financial statements. Furthermore, the ratios and other measurements illustrated here are not exhaustive; the number of measurements that may be developed for various analytical purposes is almost without limit.

WEAVER COMPANY
Condensed Comparative Balance Sheet*
December 31

Assets	Year 2	Year 1	Increase or (Decrease) Dollars	%	Percentage of Total Assets Year 2	Year 1
Current assets	$390,000	$288,000	$102,000	35.4	41.1	33.5
Plant and equipment (net)	500,000	467,000	33,000	7.1	52.6	54.3
Other assets (loans to officers).	60,000	105,000	(45,000)	(42.9)	6.3	12.2
Total assets	$950,000	$860,000	$ 90,000	10.5	100.0	100.0

Liabilities & Stockholders' Equity

Liabilities:						
Current liabilities	$147,400	$ 94,000	$ 53,400	56.8	15.5	10.9
Long-term liabilities.	200,000	250,000	(50,000)	(20.0)	21.1	29.1
Total liabilities	$347,400	$344,000	$ 3,400	1.0	36.6	40.0
Stockholders' equity:						
6% preferred stock, $100 par, callable at $105	$100,000	$100,000			10.5	11.6
Common stock, $50 par	250,000	200,000	$ 50,000	25.0	26.3	23.2
Paid-in capital in excess of par . . .	70,000	40,000	30,000	75.0	7.4	4.7
Retained earnings	182,600	176,000	6,600	3.8	19.2	20.5
Total stockholders' equity	$602,600	$516,000	$ 86,600	16.8	63.4	60.0
Total liabilities & stockholders' equity.	$950,000	$860,000	$ 90,000	10.5	100.0	100.0

* In order to focus attention on important subtotals, this statement is highly condensed and does not show individual asset and liability items. These details will be introduced as needed in the text discussion. For example, a list of the Weaver Company's current assets and current liabilities appears on page 793.

WEAVER COMPANY
Comparative Income Statement
Years Ended December 31

	Year 2	Year 1	Increase or (Decrease) Dollars	%	Percentage of Net Sales Year 2	Year 1
Net sales	$900,000	$750,000	$150,000	20.0	100.0	100.0
Cost of goods sold	585,000	468,800	116,200	24.8	65.0	62.5
Gross profit on sales	$315,000	$281,200	$ 33,800	12.0	35.0	37.5
Operating expenses:						
Selling expenses	$117,000	$ 75,000	$ 42,000	56.0	13.0	10.0
Administrative expenses	126,000	94,500	31,500	33.3	14.0	12.6
Total operating expenses	$243,000	$169,500	$ 73,500	43.4	27.0	22.6
Operating income	$ 72,000	$111,700	$(39,700)	(35.5)	8.0	14.9
Interest expense	12,000	15,000	(3,000)	(20.0)	1.3	2.0
Income before income taxes	$ 60,000	$ 96,700	$(36,700)	(38.0)	6.7	12.9
Income taxes	23,400	44,200	(20,800)	(47.1)	2.6	5.9
Net income	$ 36,600	$ 52,500	$(15,900)	(30.3)	4.1	7.0
Earnings per share of common stock	$6.12	$11.63	$(5.51)	(47.4)		

WEAVER COMPANY
Statement of Retained Earnings
Years Ended December 31 ·

	Year 2	Year 1	Increase or (Decrease) Dollars	%
Balance, beginning of year	$176,000	$149,500	$26,500	17.7
Net income . . . . ·	36,600	52,500	(15,900)	(30.3)
	$212,600	$202,000	$10,600	5.2
Less: Dividends on common stock	$ 24,000	$ 20,000	$ 4,000	20.0
Dividends on preferred stock	6,000	6,000		
	$ 30,000	$ 26,000	$ 4,000	15.4
Balance, end of year	$182,600	$176,000	$ 6,600	3.8

Analysis by common stockholders

Common stockholders and potential investors in common stock look first at a company's earnings record. Their investment is in shares of stock, so *earnings per share and dividends per share* are of particular interest.

EARNINGS PER SHARE OF COMMON STOCK As indicated in Chapter 17, earnings per share of common stock are computed by dividing the income available to common stockholders by the number of shares of common stock outstanding. Any preferred dividend requirements must be subtracted from net income to determine income available for common stock, as shown in the following computations for Weaver Company:

Earnings per Share of Common Stock

		Year 2	Year 1
Earnings related to number of common shares outstanding	Net income	$36,600	$52,500
	Less: Preferred dividend requirements	6,000	6,000
	Net income available for common stock . . . . (a)	$30,600	$46,500
	Shares of common outstanding, end of year . . . . (b)	5,000	4,000
	Earnings per share of common stock (a ÷ b)	$6.12	$11.63

Earnings per share of common stock are shown in the income statement below the net income figure. When the income statement includes operations discontinued during the period, the earnings per share of common stock may be reported in the income statement in three amounts as follows: (*1*) income from continuing operations, (*2*) income (or loss) from discontinued operations, and (*3*) net income. Similar treatment may be appropriate for extraordinary items. The Weaver Company had no discontinued operations or extraordinary items and therefore the amount earned per share is computed by dividing the net income available for the common stock by the number of common shares outstanding at the end of each year. The computation of earnings per share in more complicated situations was illustrated in Chapter 17.

DIVIDEND YIELD AND PRICE-EARNINGS RATIO The importance of dividends varies among stockholders. Earnings reinvested in the business should produce an increase in the net income of the firm and thus tend to make each share of stock more valuable. Because the federal income tax rates applicable to dividend income are much higher than the rate of tax on capital gains from the sale of shares of stock, some stockholders may prefer that the company reinvest most of its earnings. Others may be more interested in dividend income despite the tax disadvantage.

If we compare the merits of alternative investment opportunities, we should relate earnings and dividends per share to market value of stock. Dividends per share divided by market price per share determines the *yield* rate of a company's stock. Net income per share divided by market price per share determines the *earnings rate* of a company's stock.

Earnings performance of common stock is often expressed as a *price-earnings ratio* by dividing the price per share by the net income per share. Thus, a stock selling for $60 per share and earning $3 per share may be said to have a price-earnings ratio of 20 times earnings ($60 ÷ $3). The price-earnings ratio of the 30 stocks included in the Dow-Jones Industrial Average has varied widely in recent years, ranging from a low of about 6 for the group to a high of about 20.

Assume that the 1,000 additional shares of common stock issued by Weaver Company early in Year 2 received the full dividend of $4.80 paid in Year 2. When these new shares were issued, Weaver Company announced that it planned to continue indefinitely the $4.80 dividend per common share currently being paid. With this assumption and the use of assumed market prices of the common stock at December 31, Year 1 and Year 2, the earnings per share and dividend yield may be summarized as follows:

Earnings and dividends related to market price of common stock

Earnings and Dividends per Share of Common Stock

Date	Assumed Market Value per Share	Earnings per Share	Price-Earnings Ratio	Dividends per Share	Dividend Yield, %
Dec. 31, Year 1	$125	$11.63	11	$5.00	4.0
Dec. 31, Year 2	$100	$ 6.12	16	$4.80	4.8

The decline in market value during Year 2 presumably reflects the decrease in earnings per share. Investors appraising this stock at December 31, Year 2, would consider whether a price-earnings ratio of 16 and a dividend yield of 4.8% represented a satisfactory situation in the light of alternative investment opportunities. They would also place considerable weight on estimates of the company's prospective future earnings and the probable effect of such estimated earnings on the market price of the stock and on dividend payments.

BOOK VALUE PER SHARE OF COMMON STOCK   The procedures for computing book value per share were fully described in Chapter 17 and will not be repeated here. We will, however, determine the book value per share of common stock for the Weaver Company:

Book Value per Share of Common Stock

	Year 2	Year 1
Total stockholders' equity	*$602,600*	*$516,000*
Less: Equity of preferred stockholders (1,000 shares at call price of $105)	*105,000*	*105,000*
Equity of common stockholders ....(a)	*$497,600*	*$411,000*
Shares of common stock outstanding ....(b)	*5,000*	*4,000*
Book value per share of common stock (a ÷ b).........	*$99.52*	*$102.75*

Why did book value per share decrease?

Book value per share was reduced by $9.35 in Year 2 as a result of dividend payments and the issuance of 1,000 additional shares of common stock at $80 per share, a figure significantly below the book value of $102.75 per share at the end of Year 1; book value was increased by earnings of $6.12 per share in Year 2, thus causing a net decrease of $3.23 in the book value per share.

REVENUE AND EXPENSE ANALYSIS   The trend of earnings of the Weaver Company is unfavorable and stockholders will want to know the reasons for the decline in net income. The comparative income statement on page 783 shows that despite a 20% increase in net sales, net income fell from $52,500 in Year 1 to $36,600 in Year 2, a decline of 30.3%. The **net income as a percentage of net sales** went from 7.0% to only 4.1%. The primary causes of this decline were the increases in selling expenses (56.0%), in general and administrative expenses (33.3%), and in the cost of goods sold (24.8%), all exceeding the 20% increase in net sales.

These observations suggest the need for further investigation. Suppose we find that the Weaver Company cut its selling prices in Year 2. This fact would explain the decrease in **gross profit rate** from 37.5 to 35% and would also show that sales volume in physical units rose more than 20%, since it takes proportionally more sales at lower prices to produce a given increase in dollar sales. Since the dollar amount of gross profit increased $33,800 in Year 2, the strategy of reducing sales prices to increase volume would have been successful if there had been little change in operating expenses. Operating expenses, however, rose by $73,500, resulting in a $39,700 decrease in operating income.

The next step would be to find which expenses increased and why. An investor may be handicapped here, because detailed operating expenses are not usually shown in published statements. Some conclusions, however, can be reached on the basis of even the condensed information available in the comparative income statement for the Weaver Company shown on page 783.

The substantial increase in selling expenses presumably reflects greater selling effort during Year 2 in an attempt to improve sales volume. However, the fact that selling expenses increased $42,000 while gross profit increased only $33,800 indicates that the cost of this increased sales effort was not justified in terms of results. Even more disturbing is the increase in general and administrative expenses. Some growth in administrative expenses might be expected to accompany increased sales volume, but because some of the expenses are fixed, the growth should be less than proportional to any increase in sales. The increase in general and administrative expenses from 12.6 to 14% of sales would be of serious concern to informed investors.

Management generally has greater control over operating expenses than over revenue. The *operating expense ratio* is often used as a measure of management's ability to control its operating expenses. The unfavorable trend in this ratio for the Weaver Company is shown below:

Operating Expense Ratio

		Year 2	Year 1
Operating expenses	(a)	$243,000	$169,500
Net sales	(b)	$900,000	$750,000
Operating expense ratio (a ÷ b)		27.0%	22.6%

Does a higher operating expense ratio indicate higher net income?

If management were able to increase the sales volume while at the same time increasing the gross profit rate and decreasing the operating expense ratio, the effect on net income could be quite dramatic. For example, if the Weaver Company increased its sales in Year 3 by 11% to $1,000,000, increased its gross profit rate from 35 to 38%, and reduced the operating expense ratio from 27 to 24%, its operating income would increase from $72,000 to $140,000 ($1,000,000 − $620,000 − $240,000), an increase of over 94%.

Return on investment (ROI)

The rate of return on investment (often called ROI) is a test of management's efficiency in using available resources. Regardless of the size of the organization, capital is a scarce resource and must be used efficiently. In other words, management has a limited amount of dollars to work with, and a good manager is the one who can get the most out of the resources which are available. In judging the performance of branch managers or of company-wide management, it is reasonable to raise the question: What rate of return have you earned on the resources under your control? The concept of return on investment can be applied to a number of situations: for example, evaluating a branch, a total business, a product line, or an individual investment. A number of different ratios have been developed for the ROI concept, each well-suited to a particular situation. We shall consider the return on total assets and the return on common stockholders' equity as examples of the return on investment concept.

RETURN ON TOTAL ASSETS An important test of management's ability to earn a return on funds supplied from all sources is the rate of return on total assets.

The income figure used in computing this ratio should be *income before deducting interest expense,* since interest is a payment to creditors for money used to *acquire assets.* Income before interest reflects earnings throughout the year and therefore should be related to the average investment in assets during the year. The computation of this ratio for the Weaver Company is shown below:

Percentage Return on Total Assets

			Year 2	Year 1
Earnings related to investment in assets	*Net income*		$ 36,600	$ 52,500
	Add back: Interest expense		12,000	15,000
	Income before interest expense	*(a)*	$ 48,600	$ 67,500
	Total assets, beginning of year		$860,000	$820,000
	Total assets, end of year		950,000	860,000
	Average investment in assets	*(b)*	$905,000	$840,000
	Return on total assets (a ÷ b)		5.4%	8.0%

This ratio shows that earnings per dollar of assets invested have fallen off in Year 2. If the same ratios were available for other companies of similar kind and size, the significance of this decline could be better appraised.

Management's effectiveness in employing assets can be measured by dividing sales for the year by the average assets used in producing these sales. In computing this *asset turnover* rate, those assets not contributing directly to sales (such as long-term investments and loans to officers) should be excluded. A higher asset turnover suggests that management is making better use of assets, and if the earnings rate on sales remains relatively constant, a higher rate of return on total assets will result.[2]

---

[2] In order to show that the return on total assets is dependent on both the asset turnover rate and the earnings rate on sales, we can develop the following formula:

$$\frac{Sales}{Assets} \times \frac{Net\ Income}{Sales} = Return\ on\ Assets$$

If we assume sales of $100, assets of $50, and net income of $10, the formula yields the following result:

$$\frac{\$100}{\$50} \times \frac{\$10}{\$100} = 20\%$$

The asset turnover (2 times) multiplied by earnings rate on sales (10%) results in a 20% return on assets. Assume that management is able to improve the asset turnover by increasing sales to $200 without increasing total assets and that the earnings rate on sales actually declines to 8%. Then the formula yields:

$$\frac{\$200}{\$50} \times \frac{\$16}{\$200} = 32\%$$

Despite a lower earnings rate on sales (8%), the return on total assets increased dramatically because assets were more effectively utilized, as indicated by the higher asset turnover rate of 4 times ($200 ÷ $50).

RETURN ON COMMON STOCKHOLDERS' EQUITY Because interest and dividends paid to creditors and preferred stockholders are fixed in amount, a company may earn a greater or smaller return on the common stockholders' equity than on its total assets. The computation of return on stockholders' equity for the Weaver Company is shown below:

Return on Common Stockholders' Equity

		Year 2	Year 1
Does Net income . . . . :		$ 36,600	$ 52,500
trading on Less: Preferred dividend requirements . . . . : . .		6,000	6,000
the equity			
benefit Net income available for common stock . . . .(a)		$ 30,600	$ 46,500
common Common stockholders' equity, beginning of year		$416,000	$389,500
stock-			
holders? Common stockholders' equity, end of year		502,600	416,000
Average common stockholders' equity . . . .(b)		$459,300	$402,750
Return on common stockholders' equity (a ÷ b) . . . . :		6.7%	11.5%

In both years the rate of return to common stockholders was higher than the return on total assets, because the average combined rate of interest paid to creditors and dividends to preferred stockholders was less than the rate earned on each dollar of assets used in the business

LEVERAGE Financing with fixed-return securities is often called *leverage,* or *trading on the equity.* Results may be favorable or unfavorable to holders of common stock:

1 If the rate of return on total assets is *greater* than the average rate of payment to creditors and preferred stockholders, the common stockholders will *gain* from the leverage factor. This was the case in the Weaver Company.

2 If the rate of return on total assets is *smaller* than the average rate of payments to creditors and preferred stockholders, the common stockholders will *lose* from their use of leverage.

The use of leverage is a means of maximizing the profits to common stockholders in a business which is profitable and in a growth phase. However, the use of leverage also increases the risk born by common stockholders. If the company enters a period of operating losses, these losses will be magnified by the existence of a leveraged capital structure. Since leverage offers an opportunity for increasing profits but carries the threat of disastrous losses, we may conclude that companies noted for stable earnings (such as telephone and other utility companies) may safely use more leverage than companies with earnings that fluctuate widely from year to year.

EQUITY RATIO The equity ratio measures the proportion of the total assets financed by stockholders, as distinguished from creditors. It is computed by dividing total stockholders' equity by total assets (or the sum of liabilities and stockholders' equity, which is the same). The equity ratio for the Weaver Company is determined as shown on page 790.

Equity Ratio

		Year 2	Year 1
Total assets . . . . (a)		$950,000	$860,000
Total stockholders' equity . . . . (b)		$602,600	$516,000
Equity ratio (b ÷ a)		63.4%	60.0%

Proportion of assets financed by stockholders

The Weaver Company has a higher equity ratio in Year 2 than in Year 1. Is this favorable or unfavorable?

From the common stockholder's viewpoint, a low equity ratio (that is, a large proportion of financing supplied by creditors) will produce maximum benefits if management is able to earn a rate of return on assets greater than the rate of interest paid to creditors. However, a low equity ratio can be very unfavorable if the rate of return on total assets falls below the rate of interest paid to creditors. Furthermore, if a business incurs so much debt that it is unable to meet the required interest or principal payments, creditors may force liquidation or reorganization of the business, to the detriment of stockholders.

Because of these factors, the equity ratio is usually judged by stockholders in the light of the probable stability of the company's earnings, as well as the rate of earnings in relation to the rate of interest paid to creditors.

As we saw earlier in our analysis, the use of leverage from the common stockholder's viewpoint can also be accomplished through the issuance of preferred stock. Since preferred stock dividends are not deductible for income tax purposes, however, the advantage gained in this respect will usually be much smaller than in the case of debt financing.

Analysis by long-term creditors

Bondholders and other long-term creditors are primarily interested in three factors: (1) the rate of return on their investment, (2) the firm's ability to meet its interest requirements, and (3) the firm's ability to repay the principal of the debt when it falls due.

YIELD RATE ON BONDS The yield rate on bonds or other long-term indebtedness cannot be computed in the same manner as the yield rate on shares of stock, because bonds, unlike stocks, have a definite maturity date and amount. The ownership of a 6%, 10-year bond represents the right to receive $1,000 at the end of 10 years and the right to receive $60 per year during each of the next 10 years. If the market price of this bond is $950, the yield rate on an investment in the bond is the rate of interest that will make the present value of these two contractual rights equal to $950. *The yield rate varies inversely with changes in the market price of the bond.* If the price of a bond is above maturity value, the yield rate is less than the bond interest rate; if the price of a bond is below maturity value, the yield rate is higher than the bond interest rate.

NUMBER OF TIMES INTEREST EARNED Long-term creditors have learned from experience that one of the best indications of the safety of their investment is the fact that, over the life of the debt, the company has sufficient income to cover its interest requirements by a wide margin. A failure to cover interest requirements may have serious repercussions on the stability and solvency of the firm.

A common measure of debt safety is the ratio of income available for the payment of interest to the annual interest expense, called *times interest earned.* This computation for the Weaver Company would be:

Number of Times Interest Earned

		Year 2	Year 1
Operating income (before interest and income taxes) . . . . *(a)*		*$72,000*	*$111,700*
Annual interest expense . . . . *(b)*		*$12,000*	*$ 15,000*
Times interest earned (a ÷ b)		6.0	7.4

Long-term creditors watch this ratio

The decline in the ratio during Year 2 is unfavorable, but a ratio of 6.0 times interest earned for that year would still be considered quite strong in many industries. In the electric utilities industry, for example, the interest coverage ratio for the leading companies presently averages about 3, with the ratio for individual companies varying from 2 to 6.

Since business executives and investors are strongly conditioned to an after-tax view of corporate affairs, the times interest earned ratio is often computed by a more conservative method of taking net income (after taxes) plus interest expense and dividing this total by the annual interest expense.

DEBT RATIO Long-term creditors are interested in the amount of debt outstanding in relation to the amount of capital contributed by stockholders. The *debt ratio* is computed by dividing total liabilities by total assets, shown below for the Weaver Company.

Debt Ratio

		Year 2	Year 1
Total liabilities . . . . *(a)*		*$347,400*	*$344,000*
Total assets (or total liabilities & stockholders' equity) . . . *(b)*		*$950,000*	*$860,000*
Debt ratio (a ÷ b)		36.6%	40.0%

What portion of total assets is financed by debt?

From a creditor's viewpoint, the lower the debt ratio (or the higher the equity ratio) the better, since this means that stockholders have contributed the bulk of the funds to the business, and therefore the margin of protection to creditors against a shrinkage of the assets is high.

Analysis by preferred stockholders

If preferred stock is convertible, the interests of preferred stockholders are similar to those of common stockholders, previously discussed. If preferred stock is not convertible, the interests of preferred stockholders are more closely comparable to those of long-term creditors.

Preferred stockholders are interested in the yield on their investment. The yield is computed by dividing the dividend per share by the market value per share. The dividend per share of Weaver Company preferred stock is $6. If we assume that the market value at December 31, Year 2, is $80 per share, the yield rate at that time would be 7.5% ($6 ÷ $80).

The primary measurement of the safety of an investment in preferred stock is the ability of the firm to meet its preferred dividend requirements. The best test of this ability is the ratio of the net income available to pay the preferred dividend to the amount of the annual dividend, as shown below.

Times Preferred Dividends Earned

		Year 2	Year 1
Net income available to pay preferred dividends . . . .(a)		*$36,600*	*$52,500*
Annual preferred dividend requirements . . . .(b)		*$ 6,000*	*$ 6,000*
Times dividends earned (a ÷ b)		*6.1*	*8.8*

Is the preferred dividend safe?

Although the margin of protection declined in Year 2, the annual preferred dividend requirement appears well-protected.

Analysis by short-term creditors

Bankers and other short-term creditors share the interest of stockholders and bondholders in the profitability and long-run stability of a business. Their primary interest, however, is in the current position of the firm—its ability to generate sufficient funds (working capital) to meet current operating needs and to pay current debts promptly. Thus the analysis of financial statements by a banker considering a short-term loan, or by a trade creditor investigating the credit status of a customer, is likely to center on the working capital position of the prospective debtor.

AMOUNT OF WORKING CAPITAL The amount of working capital is measured by the *excess of current assets over current liabilities.* Thus, working capital represents the amount of cash, near-cash items, and cash substitutes (prepayments) on hand after providing for payment of all current liabilities. The details of the working capital of the Weaver Company are shown on page 793.

This schedule shows that current assets increased $102,000, while current liabilities rose by only $53,400, with the result that working capital increased $48,600. There was a shift in the composition of the current assets and current liabilities; cash decreased from 13.9 to 9.7% of current assets, and inventory rose from 41.6 to 46.2%. Inventory is a less liquid resource than cash. Therefore, although the amount of working capital increased in Year 2, the quality of working capital is not as liquid as in

Year 1. Although creditors want to see large amounts of high-quality working capital, management must consider that excess amounts of cash are not productive and do not generate a high return.

WEAVER COMPANY
Comparative Schedule of Working Capital
As of December 31

	Year 2	Year 1	Increase or (Decrease) Dollars	%	Percentage of Total Current Items Year 2	Year 1
Current assets:						
Cash	$ 38,000	$ 40,000	$ (2,000)	(5.0)	9.7	13.9
Receivables (net)	117,000	86,000	31,000	36.0	30.0	29.9
Inventories	180,000	120,000	60,000	50.0	46.2	41.6
Prepaid expenses	55,000	42,000	13,000	31.0	14.1	14.6
Total current assets	$390,000	$288,000	$102,000	35.4	100.0	100.0
Current liabilities:						
Notes payable to creditors	$ 50,000	$ 10,000	$ 40,000	400.0	33.9	10.7
Accounts payable	66,000	30,000	36,000	120.0	44.8	31.9
Accrued liabilities	31,400	54,000	(22,600)	(41.9)	21.3	57.4
Total current liabilities	$147,400	$ 94,000	$ 53,400	56.8	100.0	100.0
Working capital	$242,600	$194,000	$ 48,600	25.0		

THE CURRENT RATIO   One means of further evaluating these changes in working capital is to observe the relationship between current assets and current liabilities, a test known as the *current ratio.* The current ratio for the Weaver Company is computed below:

Current Ratio

		Year 2	Year 1
Does this	Total current assets . . . . (a)	$390,000	$288,000
indicate sat-isfactory	Total current liabilities . . . . (b)	$147,400	$ 94,000
debt-paying ability?	Current ratio (a ÷ b)	2.6	3.1

Despite the increase of $48,600 in the amount of working capital in Year 2, current assets per dollar of current liabilities declined. The margin of safety (current ratio), however, still appears satisfactory.

In interpreting the current ratio, a number of factors should be kept in mind:

1 Creditors tend to feel that the larger the current ratio the better; however, from a managerial view there is an upper limit. Too high a current ratio may indicate that capital is not productively used in the business.

2 Because creditors tend to stress the current ratio as an indication of short-term solvency, some firms may take conscious steps to improve this ratio just before statements are prepared at the end of a fiscal period for submission to bankers or other creditors. This may be done by postponing purchases, pressing collections on accounts receivable, and using the cash collected to pay off current liabilities.

3 The current ratio computed at the end of a fiscal year may not be representative of the current position of the company throughout the year. Since many firms arrange their fiscal year to end during a low point in the seasonal swing of business activity, the current ratio at year-end is likely to be more favorable than at any other time during the year.

Use of both the current ratio and the amount of working capital helps to place debt-paying ability in its proper perspective. For example, if Company X has current assets of $20,000 and current liabilities of $10,000 and Company Y has current assets of $2,000,000 and current liabilities of $1,990,000, each company has $10,000 of working capital, but the current position of Company X is clearly superior to that of Company Y. The current ratio for Company X is quite satisfactory at 2 to 1, but Company Y's current ratio is very low—only slightly above 1 to 1.

As another example, assume that Company A and Company B both have current ratios of 3 to 1. However, Company A has working capital of $20,000 and Company B has working capital of $200,000. Although both companies appear to be good credit risks, Company B would no doubt be able to qualify for a much *larger* bank loan than would Company A.

A widely used rule of thumb is that a current ratio of 2 to 1 or better is satisfactory. Like all rules of thumb this is an arbitrary standard, subject to numerous exceptions and qualifications.

QUICK RATIO Because inventories and prepaid expenses are further removed from conversion into cash than other current assets, a ratio known as the *quick ratio* or *acid-test ratio* is sometimes computed as a supplement to the current ratio. This ratio compares the highly liquid current assets (cash, marketable securities, and receivables) with current liabilities. The Weaver Company has no marketable securities; its quick ratio is computed as follows:

Quick Ratio

		Year 2	Year 1
A measure of liquidity Quick assets (cash and receivables) ....(a)		$155,000	$126,000
Current liabilities ....(b)		$147,400	$ 94,000
Quick ratio (a ÷ b)................................		1.1	1.3

Here again the analysis reveals an unfavorable trend. Whether the quick ratio is adequate depends on the amount of receivables included among quick assets and the average time required to collect receivables as compared to the credit period extended by suppliers. If the credit periods extended to customers and granted by creditors are roughly equal, a quick ratio of 1.0 or better would be considered satisfactory.

Some financial analysts compute a *liquidity ratio* as a measure of immediate ability to pay short-term debts. This ratio is computed by dividing the total of cash and government securities owned by the total current liabilities outstanding.

INVENTORY TURNOVER   The cost of goods sold figure on the income statement represents the total cost of all goods that have been transferred out of inventories during any given period. Therefore the relationship between cost of goods sold and the average balance of inventories maintained throughout the year indicates the number of times that inventories "turn over" and are replaced each year.

Ideally we should total the inventories at the end of each month and divide by 12 to obtain an average inventory. This information is not always available, however, and the nearest substitute is a simple average of the inventory at the beginning and at the end of the year. This tends to overstate the turnover rate, since many companies choose an accounting year that ends when inventories are at a minimum.

Assuming that only beginning and ending inventories are available, the computation of inventory turnover for the Weaver Company may be illustrated as follows:

Inventory Turnover

		Year 2	Year 1
What does inventory turnover mean? Cost of goods sold	(a)	$585,000	$468,800
Inventory, beginning of year		$120,000	$100,000
Inventory, end of year		180,000	120,000
Average inventory	(b)	$150,000	$110,000
Average inventory turnover per year (a ÷ b)		3.9 times	4.3 times
Average days to turn over (divide 365 days by inventory turnover)		94 days	85 days

The trend indicated by this analysis is unfavorable, since the average investment in inventories in relation to the cost of goods sold is rising. Stating this another way, the company required on the average 9 days more during Year 2 to turn over its inventories than during Year 1. Furthermore, the inventory status *at the end of the year* has changed even more: At the end of Year 1 there were 94 days' sales in the ending inventory ($120,000/$468,800 × 365 days) compared to 112 days' sales in the ending inventory at the end of Year 2 ($180,000/$585,000 × 365 days).

The relation between inventory turnover and gross profit per dollar of sales may be significant. A high inventory turnover and a low gross profit rate frequently go hand in hand. This, however, is merely another way of saying that if the gross profit rate is low, a high volume of business is necessary to produce a satisfactory return on total assets. Although a high inventory turnover is usually regarded as a good sign, a rate that is high in relation to that of similar firms may indicate that the company is losing sales by a failure to maintain an adequate stock of goods to serve its customers promptly.

ACCOUNTS RECEIVABLE TURNOVER The turnover of accounts receivable is computed in a manner comparable to that just described for inventories. The ratio between the net sales for the period and the average balance in accounts receivable is a rough indication of the average time required to convert receivables into cash. Ideally, a monthly average of receivables should be used, and only *sales on credit* should be included in the sales figure. For illustrative purposes, we shall assume that Weaver Company sells entirely on credit and that only the beginning and ending balances of receivables are available:

Accounts Receivable Turnover

		Year 2	Year 1
Net sales on credit . . . . (a)		$900,000	$750,000
Receivables, beginning of year		$ 86,000	$ 80,000
Receivables, end of year		117,000	86,000
Average receivables . . . . (b)		$101,500	$ 83,000
Receivable turnover per year (a ÷ b)		8.9 times	9.0 times
Average age of receivables (divide 365 days by receivable turnover)		41 days	41 days

Are customers paying promptly?

There has been no significant change in the average time required to collect receivables. The interpretation of the average age of receivables would depend upon the company's credit terms and the seasonal activity immediately before year-end. If the company grants 30-day credit terms to its customers, for example, the above analysis indicates that accounts receivable collections are lagging. If the terms were for 60 days, however, there is evidence that collections are being made ahead of schedule. On the other hand, if the sales in the last month of the year were unusually large, the average age of receivables as computed above can be misleading.

The *operating cycle* in Year 2 was approximately 135 days (computed by adding the 94 days required to turn over inventory and the average 41 days required to collect receivables). This compares to an operating cycle of only 126 days in Year 1, computed as 85 days to dispose of the inventory plus 41 days to collect the resulting receivables. The operating cycle measures the time interval required to convert inventory to accounts receivable and then accounts receivable to cash. A trend toward a longer operating cycle suggests that inventory and receivables are increasing relative to sales and that profits may be hurt because of lower sales volume and an increasing investment in current assets.

Summary of analytical measurements

The basic ratios and other measurements discussed in this chapter and their significance are summarized below and on page 798.

Ratio or Other Measurement	Method of Computation	Significance
1 Earnings per share on common stock	$$\frac{\text{Net income} - \text{preferred dividends}}{\text{Shares of common outstanding}}$$	Gives the amount of earnings applicable to a share of common stock.
2 Dividend yield	$$\frac{\text{Dividend per share}}{\text{Market price per share}}$$	Shows the rate earned by stockholders based on current price for a share of stock.
3 Price-earnings ratio	$$\frac{\text{Market price per share}}{\text{Earnings per share}}$$	Indicates whether price of stock is in line with earnings.
4 Book value per share of common stock	$$\frac{\text{Common stockholders' equity}}{\text{Shares of common outstanding}}$$	Measures the recorded value of net assets behind each share of stock.
5 Operating expense ratio	$$\frac{\text{Operating expenses}}{\text{Net sales}}$$	Indicates management's ability to control expenses.
6 Return on total assets	$$\frac{\text{Net income} + \text{interest expense}}{\text{Average investment in assets}}$$	Measures the productivity of assets regardless of capital structures.
7 Return on common stockholders' equity	$$\frac{\text{Net income} - \text{preferred dividends}}{\text{Average common stockholders' equity}}$$	Indicates the earning power of common stockholders' equity.
8 Equity ratio	$$\frac{\text{Total stockholders' equity}}{\text{Total assets}}$$	Shows the protection to creditors and the extent of trading on the equity.
9 Number of times interest earned	$$\frac{\text{Operating income}}{\text{Annual interest expense}}$$	Measures the coverage of interest requirements, particularly on long-term debt.
10 Debt ratio	$$\frac{\text{Total liabilities}}{\text{Total assets}}$$	Indicates the percentage of assets financed through borrowing; it shows the extent of trading on the equity.
11 Times preferred dividends earned	$$\frac{\text{Net income}}{\text{Annual preferred dividends}}$$	Shows the adequacy of current earnings to pay dividends on preferred stock.
12 Current ratio	$$\frac{\text{Current assets}}{\text{Current liabilities}}$$	Measures short-run debt-paying ability.
13 Quick (acid-test) ratio	$$\frac{\text{Quick assets}}{\text{Current liabilities}}$$	Measures the short-term liquidity of a firm.

ASSET TURNOVER

$$\frac{SALES}{TOTAL\ ASSETS}$$

| 14 Inventory turnover | $\dfrac{\text{Cost of goods sold}}{\text{Average inventory}}$ | Indicates management's ability to control the investment in inventory. |
| 15 Accounts receivable turnover | $\dfrac{\text{Net sales on credit}}{\text{Average receivables}}$ | Indicates reasonableness of accounts receivable balance and effectiveness of collections. |

The student should keep in mind the fact that the full significance of any of the foregoing ratios or other measurements depends on the *direction of its trend* and on its *relationship to some predetermined standard* or industry average.

LIST OF KEY TERMS INTRODUCED OR EMPHASIZED IN CHAPTER 22

Common size financial statements   All items are stated in percentages rather than dollar amounts. In the balance sheet each item is expressed as a percentage of total assets; in the income statement each item is expressed as a percentage of net sales.

Comparative financial statements   Financial statement data for two or more successive years placed side by side in adjacent columns to facilitate study of changes.

Component percentage   The percentage relationship of any financial statement item to a total including that item. For example, each type of asset as a percentage of total assets.

Horizontal analysis   Comparison of the change in a financial statement item such as inventories during two or more accounting periods.

Quality of assets   The concept that some companies have assets of better quality than others, such as well-balanced composition of assets, well-maintained plant and equipment, and receivables that are all current. A lower quality of assets might be indicated by poor maintenance of plant and equipment, slow-moving inventories with high danger of obsolescence, past-due receivables, and patents approaching an expiration date.

Quality of earnings   Earnings are said to be of high quality if they are stable, the source seems assured, and the methods used in measuring income are conservative. The existence of this concept suggests that the range of alternative but acceptable accounting principles may still be too wide to produce financial statements that are comparable.

Rate of return on investment (ROI)   The overall test of management's ability to earn a satisfactory return on the assets under its control. Numerous variations of the ROI concept are used such as return on total assets, return on total equities, etc.

Ratios   See pages 797–798 for list of ratios, methods of computation, and significance.

Vertical analysis   Comparison of a particular financial statement item to a total including that item, such as inventories as a percentage of current assets, or operating expenses in relation to net sales.

REVIEW QUESTIONS

1 a What groups are interested in the financial affairs of publicly owned corporations?

b List some of the more important sources of financial information for investors.

2 In financial statement analysis, what is the basic objective of observing trends in data and ratios? What is an alternative standard of comparison?

3 In financial analysis, what information is produced by computing a ratio that is not available in a simple observation of the underlying data?

4 Explain the distinction between *percentage change* and *component percentages.*

5 "Although net income declined this year as compared with last year, it increased from 3% to 5% of net sales." Are sales increasing or decreasing?

6 Differentiate between *horizontal* and *vertical* analysis.

7 Assume that the Chemco Corporation is engaged in the manufacture and distribution of a variety of chemicals. In analyzing the financial statements of this corporation, why would you want to refer to the ratios and other measurements of companies in the chemical industry? In comparing the financial results of the Chemco Corporation with another chemical company, why would you be interested in the accounting procedures used by the two companies?

8 What is the objective of financial analysis? What types of information may be relevant in evaluating the future profitability of a company?

9 What single ratio do you think should be of greatest interest to:
a a banker considering a short-term loan?
b a common stockholder?
c an insurance company considering a long-term mortgage loan?

10 Modern Company earned (after taxes) an 8% return on its total assets. Current liabilities are 10% of total assets and long-term bonds carrying a $6\frac{1}{2}$% coupon rate are equal to 30% of total assets. There is no preferred stock. Would you expect the rate of return on stockholders' equity to be greater or less than 8%? Explain.

11 In deciding whether a company's equity ratio is favorable or unfavorable, creditors and stockholders may have different views. Why?

12 Company A has a current ratio of 3 to 1. Company B has a current ratio of 2 to 1. Does this mean that A's operating cycle is longer than B's? Why?

13 An investor states, "I bought this stock for $50 several years ago and it now sells for $100. It paid $5 per share in dividends last year so I'm earning 10% on my investment." Criticize this statement.

14 Company C experiences a considerable seasonal variation in its business. The high point in the year's activities comes in November, the low point in July. During which month would you expect the company's current ratio to be higher? If the company were choosing a fiscal year for accounting purposes, how would you advise them?

15 Both the inventory turnover and accounts receivable turnover increased from 10 times to 15 times from Year 1 to Year 2, but net income decreased. Can you offer some possible reasons for this?

16 Is the rate of return on investment (ROI) intended primarily to measure liquidity, solvency, or some other aspect of business operations? Explain.

17 Mention three financial amounts to which corporate profits can logically be compared in judging their adequacy or reasonableness.

18 Under what circumstances would you consider a corporate net income of $1,000,000 for the year as being unreasonably low? Under what circumstances would you consider a corporate profit of $1,000,000 as being unreasonably high?

EXERCISES

Ex. 22-1 Selected information taken from the balance sheets of Young Company for two successive years is shown below. Compute the percentage change from the base year to the following year whenever possible.

	Year 2	Year 1
a Cash	$ 36,000	$ 30,000
b Sales	325,000	250,000
c Retained earnings (deficit)	20,000	(10,000)
d Current liabilities	120,000	80,000
e Notes payable	60,000	–0–
f Accounts receivable	80,000	50,000
g Marketable securities	20,000	25,000

Ex. 22-2 Prepare *common size* income statements for Top Company, a single proprietorship, for the two years shown below by converting the dollar amounts into percentages. In each year, sales will appear as 100%, and other items will be expressed as a percentage of sales. Round the figures to the nearest tenth of one percent. (Income taxes are not involved since the business is not incorporated.)

TOP COMPANY

Comparative Income Statements

For the Years Ended December 31, Years 1 and 2

	Year 2	Year 1
Sales	$500,000	$400,000
Cost of goods sold	330,000	256,000
Gross profit	$170,000	$144,000
Operating expenses	139,500	128,000
Net income	$ 30,500	$ 16,000

Ex. 22-3 Given below is a condensed balance sheet for the Walnut Company:

Assets		Liabilities & Stockholders' Equity	
Cash	$ 30,000	Current liabilities	$ 75,000
Accounts receivable . . . . ,	60,000	Long-term liabilities	150,000
Inventory	135,000	Capital stock, $10 par . . .	300,000
Prepaid expenses	45,000	Retained earnings	75,000
Plant assets (net)	300,000		
Other assets	30,000	Total liabilities &	
Total assets	$600,000	stockholders' equity . .	$600,000

During the latest year, the company earned a gross profit of $480,000 on sales of $1,200,000. Accounts receivable, inventory, and plant assets remained relatively constant during the year. From this information, compute the following:
a Current ratio
b Acid-test ratio
c Equity ratio
d Asset turnover

    e Accounts receivable turnover (all sales are on credit)
    f Inventory turnover
    g Book value per share of capital stock

Ex. 22-4 The information below relates to the activities of a retail store:

	Year 2	Year 1
Sales (terms 2/10, n/30)	$480,000	$360,000
Cost of goods sold	312,000	252,000
Inventory at end of year	57,000	63,000
Accounts receivable at end of year	96,000	30,000

Compute the following for Year 2:
a Gross profit percentage
b Inventory turnover
c Accounts receivable turnover

Ex. 22-5 The following information is available for the Lung Company:

	Year 2	Year 1
Total assets (40% of which are current)	$400,000	$325,000
Current liabilities	$ 80,000	$100,000
Bonds payable, 7%	100,000	50,000
Capital stock, $10 stated value	150,000	150,000
Retained earnings	70,000	25,000
Total liabilities & stockholders' equity	$400,000	$325,000

The income tax rate is 50% and dividends of $6,000 were declared and paid in Year 2. Compute the following:
a Current ratio for Year 2 and Year 1
b Debt ratio for Year 2 and Year 1
c Earnings per share for Year 2

Ex. 22-6 Figures for two companies engaged in the same line of business are presented below for the latest year:

	A Company	B Company
Sales (all on credit)	$1,600,000	$1,200,000
Total assets	800,000	400,000
Total liabilities	100,000	100,000
Average receivables	200,000	100,000
Average inventory	240,000	140,000
Gross profit as a percentage of sales	40%	30%
Operating expenses as a percentage of sales	37%	25%
Net income as a percentage of sales	3%	5%

Compute the following for each company (Round all answers to the nearest percent):
a Net income
b Net income as a percentage of total assets
c Net income as a percentage of stockholders' equity
d Accounts receivable turnover
e Inventory turnover

PROBLEMS

Group A

22A-1 The following information was developed from the financial statements of Flagstone, Inc.

	Year 11	Year 10
Net income	$ 46,000	$ 38,000
Net income as a percentage of sales	5%	4%
Gross profit on sales	$322,000	$342,000
Income taxes as a percentage of income before		
income taxes	20%	20%

Instructions
a Compute the net sales for each year.
b Compute the cost of goods sold in dollars and as a percentage of sales for each year.
c Compute the federal income taxes for each year.
d Prepare a condensed comparative income statement for Years 10 and 11. Show the following items; Sales, cost of goods sold, gross profit on sales, operating expenses, income before income taxes, income taxes, and net income.
e What favorable trends and unfavorable trends do you see in this year-to-year comparison of the income statement data of Flagstone, Inc.?

22A-2 In the schedule below, certain items taken from the income statements of the Vincent Company for two fiscal years ending January 31 have been expressed as a percentage of net sales:

	Percentage of Net Sales	
	Year 2	Year 1
Net sales.	100%	100%
Beginning inventory	10	16
Net purchases	68	60
Ending inventory	8	12
Selling expenses	13	15
Administrative expenses	8	9
Income taxes	4	5

Net sales were $1 million in Year 1 and increased by 20% in Year 2.

Instructions Did the net income increase or decrease in Year 2 as compared with Year 1? By how much? Prepare a comparative income statement to support your answer.

22A-3 Listed in the left-hand column below is a series of business transactions and events relating to the activities of the Blue Corporation. Opposite each transaction is listed a particular ratio used in financial analysis:

Transaction	*Ratio*
(1) Purchased inventory on open account.	*Quick ratio*
(2) A larger physical volume of goods was sold at smaller unit prices.	*Gross profit percentage*

(3) *Corporation declared a cash*
dividend.   *Current ratio*

(4) *An uncollectible account receivable*
was written off against the allow-
ance account.   *Current ratio*

(5) *Issued additional shares of common*
stock and used proceeds to retire
long-term debt.   *Rate of earnings on total assets*

(6) *Paid stock dividend on common*
stock, in common stock.   *Earnings per share*

(7) *Operating income increased*
25%; interest expense increased
10%.   *Times interest charges earned*

(8) *Appropriated retained earnings.*   *Rate of return on stockholders' equity*

(9) *During period of rising prices, com-*
pany changed from fifo to lifo
method of inventory pricing.   *Inventory turnover*

(10) *Paid previously declared cash*
dividend.   *Debt ratio*

(11) *Purchased factory supplies on open*   *Current ratio (assume that ratio is*
account.   *greater than 1:1)*

(12) *Issued shares of capital stock in*
exchange for patents.   *Equity ratio*

Instructions What effect would each transaction or event have on the ratio listed opposite to it; that is, as a result of this event would the ratio increase, decrease, or remain unchanged? Why?

22A-4 At the end of the first year of operations of Crest Corporation, the following information was taken from the accounting records.

Sales (all on credit)	*$800,000*
Cost of goods sold	*480,000*
Average inventory (fifo method)	*80,000*
Average accounts receivable	*133,300*
Net income	*24,000*
Total assets	*300,000*
Total liabilities	*150,000*

The corporation did not declare dividends during the year and capital stock was neither issued nor retired. The liabilities consisted of accounts payable and accrued items. No interest expense was incurred.

Instructions From the information given, compute the following for Year 1: (Any answers expressed in percentages are to be rounded to the nearest percent.)
a Inventory turnover
b Accounts receivable turnover
c Total operating expenses, assuming that income taxes amounted to $5,500
d Gross profit percentage
e Rate earned on average stockholders' equity
f Rate earned on total assets (Use end-of-year total.)
g Considering the information given about this company, is it reasonable to

expect that the rate earned on average stockholders' equity (*e*) would be higher or lower than the rate earned on total assets (*f*)? Give specific reasons supporting your answer.

22A-5 John Gale, the accountant for Bay Corporation, prepared the financial statements for Year 1, including all ratios, and agreed to bring them along on a hunting trip with the executives of the corporation. To his embarrassment, he found that he had only placed certain fragmentary information in his briefcase and had left the completed statements in his office. One hour before he was to present the financial statements to the executives, he was able to come up with the following information:

BAY CORPORATION

Balance Sheet

End of Year 1

(in thousands of dollars)

Assets			*Liabilities & Stockholders' Equity*		
Current assets:			*Current liabilities*	$	?
Cash	$	?	*Long-term debt, 8% interest* . . .		?
Accounts receivable (net) . . .		?	*Total liabilities*	$	?
Inventory		?	*Stockholders' equity:*		
Total current assets	$	?	*Capital stock, $5 par* . . . $300		
Plant assets:			*Retained earnings* . . . . . _100_		
Machinery and equipment $580			*Total stockholders' equity*		400
Less: Accumulated					
depreciation . . . . _80_		_500_	*Total liabilities &*		
Total assets	$	?	*stockholders' equity*	$	?

BAY CORPORATION

Income Statement

For Year 1

(in thousands of dollars)

Net sales	$	?
Cost of goods sold		?
Gross profit on sales (25% of net sales)	$	?
Operating expenses		?
Operating income (10% of net sales)	$	?
Interest expense		28
Income before income taxes	$	?
Income taxes—40% of income before income taxes		?
Net income		$60

Additional information

(*1*) The equity ratio was 40%; the debt ratio was 60%.

(*2*) The only interest expense paid was on the long-term debt.

(3) The beginning inventory was $150,000; the average inventory turnover was 4.8 times. (Inventory turnover = cost of goods sold ÷ average inventory.)

(4) The current ratio was 2 to 1; the acid-test ratio was 1 to 1.

(5) The beginning balance in accounts receivable was $80,000; the average accounts receivable turnover for Year 1 was 12.8 times. All sales were made on account. (Average receivable turnover = net sales ÷ average accounts receivable.)

Instructions Using only the information available, the accountant asks you to help him complete the financial statements for the Bay Corporation. Present supporting computations and explanations for all amounts appearing in the balance sheet and the income statement. Hint: In completing the income statement, start with the net income figure (60% of income before income taxes) and work up.

22A-6 Certain financial information relating to two companies, Tell Company and Rex Company, as of the end of the current year, is shown below. All figures (except market price per share of stock) are in *thousands of dollars.*

Assets	*Tell Company*	*Rex Company*
Cash	$ 126.0	$ 180.0
Marketable securities, at cost	129.0	453.0
Accounts receivable, net	145.0	167.0
Inventories	755.6	384.3
Prepaid expenses	24.4	15.7
Plant and equipment, net	1,680.0	1,570.0
Intangibles and other assets	140.0	30.0
Total assets	$3,000.0	$2,800.0

Liabilities & Stockholders' Equity		
Accounts payable	$ 344.6	$ 304.1
Accrued liabilities, including income taxes	155.4	95.9
Bonds payable, 7%, due in 10 years	200.0	500.0
Capital stock ($10 par)	1,000.0	600.0
Capital in excess of par	450.0	750.0
Retained earnings	910.0	550.0
Treasury stock (1,000 shares, at cost)	(60.0)	–0–
Total liabilities & stockholders' equity	$3,000.0	$2,800.0

Analysis of retained earnings:		
Balance, beginning of year	$ 712.0	$ 430.0
Add: Net income	297.0	240.0
Less: Dividends	(99.0)	(120.0)
Balance, end of year	$ 910.0	$ 550.0
Market price per share of stock, end of year	$50	$40

Instructions Tell Company and Rex Company are in the same industry and are generally comparable in the nature of their operations and accounting procedures used. Write a short answer to each of the following questions, using whatever analytical computations you feel will best support your answer. Show the amounts used in calculating all ratios and percentages. Carry per-share computations to the nearest cent and percentages one place beyond the decimal point, for example, 9.8%.

a What is the book value per share of stock for each company?

b From the viewpoint of creditors, which company has a more conservative capital structure? Determine the percentage of total assets financed by each group.

c What are the price-earnings ratios and the dividend yield on the stock of each company?

d Which company is covering its bond interest by the greater margin?

e Which company has a more liquid financial position?

Group B

22B-1 The information listed below was taken from the financial statements of Harding Corporation. At the beginning of Year 5, the company began buying merchandise from a new supplier.

	Year 5	Year 4
Gross profit on sales	$292,500	$231,000
Net income as a percentage of sales	2%	3%
Net income	$ 15,000	$ 21,000
Income taxes as a percentage of income before income taxes	25%	25%

Instructions

a Compute the net sales for each year.

b Compute the cost of goods sold in dollars and as a percentage of sales for each year.

c Compute the federal income taxes for each year.

d Prepare a condensed comparative income statement for Years 4 and 5. Include the following items: Sales, cost of goods sold, gross profit on sales, operating expenses, income before income taxes, income taxes and net income.

e What favorable trends and unfavorable trends do you see in this year-to-year comparison of the income statement data of Harding Corporation? Comment on any unusual changes.

22B-2 The Apex Company manufactures and distributes a full line of farm machinery. Given below for Year 1 is the income statement for the company and a common size summary for the industry in which the company operates:

	Apex Company	Industry Average
Sales (net)	$2,000,000	100%
Cost of goods sold	1,440,000	68
Gross profit on sales	$ 560,000	32%
Operating expenses:		
Selling	$ 160,000	7%
General and administrative	180,000	10
Total operating expenses	$ 340,000	17%
Operating income	$ 220,000	15%
Income taxes	100,000	6
Net income	$ 120,000	9%

Instructions

a Prepare a common size income statement comparing the results for the Apex Company for Year 1 with the average for the farm machinery industry.

b Explain the significance of the results obtained in the comparative common size income statement prepared in part *a.*

22B-3 Listed below is the working capital information for the Washington Corporation at the end of Year 1:

Cash	*$225,000*
Temporary investments in marketable securities	*120,000*
Notes receivable—current	*180,000*
Accounts receivable	*300,000*
Allowance for doubtful accounts	*15,000*
Inventory	*240,000*
Prepaid expenses	*30,000*
Notes payable within one year	*90,000*
Accounts payable	*247,500*
Accrued liabilities	*22,500*

The following transactions are completed early in Year 2:

 (*0*) Sold inventory costing $36,000 for $30,000.
 (*1*) Declared a cash dividend, $120,000.
 (*2*) Declared a 10% stock dividend.
 (*3*) Paid accounts payable, $60,000.
 (*4*) Purchased goods on account, $45,000.
 (*5*) Collected cash on accounts receivable, $90,000.
 (*6*) Borrowed cash on short-term note, $150,000.
 (*7*) Issued additional shares of capital stock for cash, $450,000.
 (*8*) Sold temporary investments costing $30,000 for $27,000 cash.
 (*9*) Acquired temporary investments, $52,500. Paid cash.
(*10*) Wrote off uncollectible accounts, $9,000.
(*11*) Sold inventory costing $37,500 for $48,000.
(*12*) Acquired plant and equipment for cash, $240,000.

Instructions

a Compute the following at the end of Year 1: (*1*) Current ratio, (*2*) acid-test ratio, and (*3*) working capital.

b Indicate the effect (increase, decrease, none) of each transaction listed above for Year 2 on the current ratio, acid-test ratio, and working capital. Use the following four-column format (item *0* is given as an example):

	Effect on		
Item	*Current Ratio*	*Acid-Test Ratio*	*Working Capital*
0	*Decrease*	*Increase*	*Decrease*

22B-4 The following information is taken from the records of Frost Corporation at the end of Year 1:

Sales (all on credit)	*$600,000*
Cost of goods sold	*360,000*
Average inventory (fifo method)	*60,000*
Average accounts receivable	*100,000*
Net income for Year 1	*24,000*

Total assets	$250,000
Total liabilities	140,000

The corporation did not declare dividends during the year and capital stock was neither issued nor retired. The liabilities consisted of accounts payable and accrued items; no interest expense was incurred.

Instructions From the information given, compute the following for Year 1: (Any answers expressed as percentages should be rounded to the nearest percent.)
a Inventory turnover
b Accounts receivable turnover
c Total operating expenses, assuming that income taxes amounted to $6,000
d Gross profit percentage
e Rate earned on average stockholders' equity
f Rate earned on total assets (Use end-of-year total.)
g Frost Corporation has an opportunity to obtain a long-term loan at an annual interest rate of 8% and could use this additional capital at the same rate of profitability as indicated above. Would obtaining the loan be desirable from the viewpoint of the stockholders? Explain.

22B-5 Given below are selected balance sheet items and ratios for the Central Corporation at June 30, 1978:

Total stockholders' equity (includes 100,000 shares of no-par value capital stock issued at $6 per share)	$1,000,000
Plant and equipment (net)	470,000
Asset turnover rate per year (sales ÷ total assets)	3 times
Inventory turnover rate per year	6 times
Average accounts receivable collection period (assuming a 360-day year)	30 days
Gross profit percentage	30%
Ratio of current liabilities to stockholders' equity (there is no long-term debt)	1.2 to 1
Acid-test ratio (quick ratio)	0.8 to 1

Assume that balance sheet figures represent average amounts and that all sales are made on account.

Instructions From the foregoing information, construct a balance sheet for the Central Corporation as of June 30, 1978, in as much detail as the data permit.

22B-6 The financial information given below and on page 809 for Bar Company and Todd Company (except market price per share of stock) is stated in thousands of dollars. The figures are as of the end of the current year. The two companies are in the same industry and are quite similar as to products, facilities, and accounting methods.

Assets	Bar	Todd
Current assets	$ 97,450	$132,320
Plant and equipment	397,550	495,680
Less: Accumulated depreciation	(55,000)	(78,000)
Total assets	$440,000	$550,000

Liabilities & Stockholders' Equity

Current liabilities	$ 34,000	$ 65,000
Bonds payable, 8%, due in 15 years	120,000	100,000
Capital stock, no par*	150,000	200,000
Retained earnings	136,000	185,000
Total liabilities & stockholders' equity	$440,000	$550,000

Analysis of retained earnings:

Balance, beginning of year	$125,200	$167,200
Net income for the year	19,800	37,400
Dividends	(9,000)	(19,600)
Balance, end of year	$136,000	$185,000
Market price of capital stock, per share	$30	$61
*Number of shares of capital stock outstanding	6 million	8 million

Instructions

a Although market prices for the bonds are not stated, which company's bonds do you think will sell at the higher price per $1,000 bond? Which company's bonds will probably yield the higher rate of return? (You may assume that the safer the bonds, according to your analysis, the lower the yield rate.)

b What are the dividend yield, the price-earnings ratio, and book value per share for the stock of each company? Which company's stock is a better investment?

BUSINESS DECISION PROBLEM 22

Condensed comparative financial statements for Pacific Corporation appear below and on page 810.

PACIFIC CORPORATION
Comparative Balance Sheets
As of May 31
(in thousands of dollars)

Assets	Year 3	Year 2	Year 1
Current assets	$ 3,960	$ 2,610	$ 3,600
Plant and equipment (net of depreciation)	21,240	19,890	14,400
Total assets	$25,200	$22,500	$18,000

Liabilities & Stockholders' Equity			
Current liabilities	$ 2,214	$ 2,052	$ 1,800
Long-term liabilities	4,716	3,708	3,600
Capital stock ($10 par)	12,600	12,600	8,100
Retained earnings	5,670	4,140	4,500
Total liabilities & stockholders' equity	$25,200	$22,500	$18,000

PACIFIC CORPORATION
Comparative Income Statements
For Years Ended May 31
(in thousands of dollars)

	Year 3	Year 2	Year 1
Net sales.	$90,000	$75,000	$60,000
Cost of goods sold	58,500	46,500	36,000
Gross profit on sales	$31,500	$28,500	$24,000
Operating expenses	28,170	25,275	21,240
Income before income taxes	$ 3,330	$ 3,225	$ 2,760
Income taxes	1,530	1,500	1,260
Net income	$ 1,800	$ 1,725	$ 1,500
Cash dividends paid (plus 20% in stock in Year 2) .	$270	$465	$405
Cash dividends per share	$0.63	$1.11	$1.50

Instructions
a Prepare a three-year comparative balance sheet in percentages rather than dollars, using Year 1 as the base year.
b Prepare common size comparative income statements for the three-year period, expressing all items as percentage components of net sales for each year.
c Comment on the significant trends and relationships revealed by the analytical computations in *a* and *b*. These comments should cover current assets and current liabilities, plant and equipment, capital stock, retained earnings, and dividends.
d If the capital stock of this company were selling at $11.50 per share, would you consider it to be overpriced, underpriced, or fairly priced? Consider such factors as book value per share, earnings per share, dividend yield, trend of sales, and trend of the gross profit percentage. Also consider the types of investors to whom the stock would be attractive or unattractive.

23 Responsibility Accounting: Departments and Branches

In most of our discussion thus far, we have viewed accounting as a system for information processing and measurement of assets, liabilities, and net income for a business unit as a whole. Considerable attention has been given to meeting the informational needs of outsiders, such as investors and creditors. In this and succeeding chapters, we shall focus closer attention on the *uses of accounting information by management* in planning and controlling the activities of a business unit.

Planning and control involve the formulation of plans, the taking of action, reporting the results of the action, and finally the evaluation of the action. This process can be illustrated as follows:

Managers need information to plan, act, report, and evaluate performance

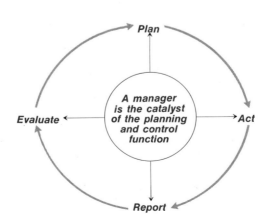

The key to this process is the manager, because each step requires decisions to be made based on relevant information. The outcome of management decisions must then be measured, reported, and evaluated on a regular basis. To be useful to management, an effective accounting system should yield information which is useful not only in arriving at decisions, but also in evaluating decisions and in making managers more accountable for their actions.

Responsibility accounting

Operating a business unit is a complex undertaking. Even in a single proprietorship the owner will benefit by setting goals such as expected sales volume, the expected amounts of related costs, and the planned amount of net income. The existence of these goals makes it possible to evaluate performance and identify trouble spots. In larger enterprises, with perhaps hundreds of managers and thousands of employees, the officers of the corporation must assign specific organizational responsibilities to different managers. An information system designed to measure the performance of that segment of a business for which a given manager is responsible is often referred to as a *responsibility accounting system.*

A responsibility accounting system attempts to fit the functions of information gathering and internal reporting to the organizational structure of the business. In this way, the effectiveness of managers can be judged on the basis of expenses incurred (or revenue earned) which are *directly under their control.* To illustrate, assume that a grocery chain operates stores at six different locations and that each store is divided into four departments. A diagram depicting a *partial* responsibility accounting system for sales salaries incurred by this grocery chain might appear as shown on page 813.

This diagram indicates that the head of the grocery department is responsible for only the sales salaries incurred in that department; the manager of Store No. 6 is accountable for all salaries paid within the store; and the vice-president in charge of sales has responsibility for all sales salaries for the company. In a responsibility accounting system all expenses and contributions to net income can be similarly traced from the income statement down through the various levels of responsibility.

A responsibility accounting system should reflect the plans and performance of each segment or activity of a business organization. It is designed to provide timely information for decision making and for the evaluation of performance. In addition to being timely, such information should highlight deviations of actual performance from planned performance so that appropriate corrective action can be taken.

All items of expense are the responsibility of some individual and should be charged to that individual at the *point of origin.* In other words, expenses should be viewed as the responsibility of the manager of the organizational unit where costs originate. The manager at this level is

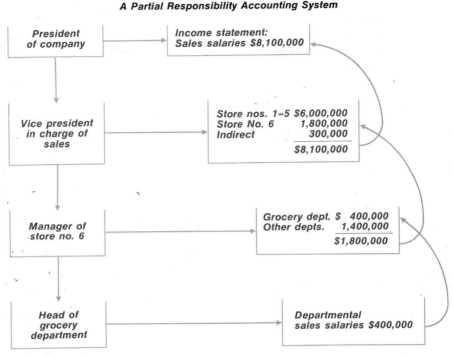

A Partial Responsibility Accounting System

authorized to incur expenses and is in a position to exercise direct control over them. A department head, for example, is generally in the best position to exercise control over the expenses incurred in the department. When a responsibility accounting system is used, the amount of expenses the department head incurred in generating sales or in providing services to other segments of the business would be clearly reported. In this way the department head is held accountable for a specific area of responsibility without being able to pass the blame for poor overall company performance to other people.

Responsibility accounting systems may be developed at all levels of an organization where specific areas of authority and responsibility can be reasonably identified. Top management has the ultimate responsibility for overall profitability of a business enterprise; vice-presidents and different levels of "middle management" are responsible for generating revenue from various products or territories and for controlling costs incurred in generating such revenue; at lower levels, managers are charged with the responsibility of reaching the revenue goals and controlling costs incurred within the units which they supervise. In the remaining pages of this chapter we shall direct our attention to two types of accountability units—departments and branches.

THE NEED FOR DEPARTMENTAL INFORMATION

If a business entity includes two or more segments, each providing a different service or handling different classes of merchandise, organization along departmental lines is a natural development. For example, a company consisting of a car rental service and an automobile repair shop could reasonably be operated as a two-department business. Departments are found in businesses of all sizes but are more likely to be found in larger companies; they are useful to service companies as well as to merchandising and manufacturing firms. A manager is usually put in charge of each department, and resources are assigned to enable the manager to carry out necessary responsibilities. In addition, a department manager may draw upon the general resources and staff talent of the entity for such services as accounting, financing, hiring, legal advice, advertising, transportation, and storage.

This kind of organizational subdivision creates a need for internal information about the operating results of each department. Top management can then determine the relative profitability of the various departments and evaluate the performance of department heads. Departmental accounting information also provides a basis for intelligent planning and control, as well as for assessing the effect of new ideas and procedures. To serve these managerial needs, accountants have to refine their measurement process. In addition to determining the revenue and expenses of the business as a whole, accountants face the problem of measuring the revenue and expenses attributable to each subdivision of the business.

Departments may be cost centers or profit centers

For information processing and control purposes, subdivisions of a business may be organized as either cost centers or profit centers. A *cost center* is a unit of a business which incurs expenses (or costs) but which does not directly generate revenue. Examples of cost centers include such *service departments* as personnel, accounting, and public relations, which provide services to other departments. A *profit center,* on the other hand, is a segment of a business which not only incurs expenses (or costs) but also produces revenue that can be identified with such a segment. A profit center is expected to make a profit contribution to the business by earning a fair rate of return on the assets it employs. Examples of profit centers include a furniture department of a large retail store, a branch of a large bank, and the Chevrolet Motor Division of General Motors Corporation.

Cost and profit centers represent control or responsibility units and are extensively used in business. Managers of cost centers are typically evaluated in terms of their ability to keep costs and expenses within budgeted allowances; managers of profit centers are most frequently judged on their ability to generate earnings. In this chapter we are primarily concerned with units of a retail business (departments and branches) which are organized as profit centers for accounting purposes.

The managerial viewpoint

The details of departmental revenue and expenses are not usually made available to the public, on the grounds that such information would be of considerable aid to competitors. Departmental accounting information, therefore, is designed to serve the needs of internal management. Among the major uses of such information are the following:

1 *As a basis for planning and allocating resources.* Management wants to know how well various departments are performing in order to have a guide in planning future activities and in allocating the resources and talent of the firm to those areas that have the greatest profit potential. If one department is producing larger profits than another, this may indicate that greater effort should be made to expand and develop the activities in the more profitable department.

2 *As a basis for corrective action.* A well-designed accounting system will throw a spotlight on troubled areas. A manager who is not doing a good job should be replaced; costs that are out of line should be more closely controlled; an unsuccessful department should be revamped or perhaps dropped altogether. Pointing up the areas that need managerial attention is an important function of responsibility accounting.

3 *As a basis for pricing decisions.* The idea that product prices are determined by finding costs and adding a required margin of profit contains only a grain of truth. For the average firm, prices are set by the market; and management's ability to exercise control over prices is severely limited by the prices of substitute products and by the actions of competitors. Nevertheless, over the long run, a firm must either set its prices high enough to cover all operating expenses plus a reasonable return on its investment or face extinction. If we are careful not to attribute too much to the statement, it may be said that departmental cost information is useful in making pricing decisions.

This is not a complete list of the uses that might be made by management of departmental accounting information. It serves to indicate, however, that we must keep the decision-making objective in mind in allocating revenue and expenses among departments.

Collecting information on departmental revenue and expenses

Two basic approaches may be used in developing departmental information for a business engaged in merchandising activities:

1 *Establish separate departmental accounts for each item of revenue and expense and identify each item with a particular department.* This method is easily adapted for accounts such as sales, purchases, and inventories. For example, a business having three departments would use a sales account, a purchase account, and an inventory account for each department. In large companies most of this data gathering would be computerized. Department stores, for example, may use *punched tags* such as the one illustrated on page 816.

Punched tag used by department store

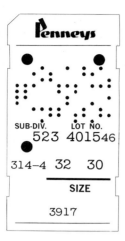

When the item is sold, the tag is removed and processed in order to generate departmental sales and inventory information.

2 *Maintain only one general ledger account for a particular item of revenue or expense, and distribute the total amount among the various departments at the end of the accounting period.* When this procedure is used, distribution by departments is made on a work sheet at the end of the accounting period rather than in the ledger accounts. For example, rent might be recorded in a single expense account and the total allocated among departments. A simple departmental expense allocation sheet is illustrated on page 820.

Some companies carry departmentalization of operating results only as far as gross profit on sales; others extend the process to include certain direct operating expenses such as wages; a few go so far as to apportion *all* expenses among departments and compute net income on a departmental basis.

Departmental gross profit on sales

In a merchandising business a figure of extreme interest to management is the total gross profit realized over and above the cost of merchandise sold in any department. Gross profit on sales is a function of two variables: (*1*) the volume of goods sold and (*2*) the gross profit earned on each dollar of sales. The same total gross profit may be realized from a large volume of sales made at a low rate of gross profit, or from a smaller volume of sales made at a higher rate of gross profit.

Within any given business, department managers are constantly making decisions that affect the gross profit rate, in the hope of maintaining a sales volume that will maximize the total dollar gross profit realized by their departments. This is not to say that operating expenses may be ignored; obviously a prime objective is to earn a satisfactory level of net income, the figure often referred to as the "bottom line."

DEPARTMENTAL REVENUE The first step in arriving at departmental gross profit is to departmentalize all revenue. To illustrate, assume that the Day Corporation maintains in its general ledger separate departmental accounts for sales, sales returns and allowances, and sales discounts. As a convenient means of accumulating departmental revenue data, special columns may be added to the various journals. For example, the Day Corporation's sales journal and cash receipts journal for a typical month might appear as shown below.

Sales Journal

Date	Invoice No.	Account Debited	LP	Accounts Receivable Dr	Cash Dr	Sales Dept. A Cr	Sales Dept. B Cr
19—							
Aug. 1	100	Abar Co.	√	700		700	
		Cash sales			1,180	470	710
31		Totals		50,200	4,900	32,600	22,500
				(5)	(√)	(200)	(300)

Cash Receipts Journal

Date	Account Credited	LP	Other Accounts Cr	Cash Sales Cr	Accounts Receivable Cr	Sales Discounts Dept. A Dr	Sales Discounts Dept. B Dr	Cash Dr
19—								
Aug. 1	Cash sales			1,180				1,180
	High Co.	√			1,000	15	5	980
2	Sale of equipment							
	at cost	206	800					800
31	Totals		8,600	4,900	34,800	520	270	47,510
			(x)	(5)	(201)	(301)		(1)

The amount of credit sales applicable to each department may be computed from the original sales invoices. If cash registers are used, the division of cash sales by departments may be made at the time each sale is rung up; daily totals by departments will thus be available on the cash register tapes.

In the illustrative journals, cash sales have been recorded in both the sales and cash receipts journals. This procedure makes it possible to omit departmental sales columns in the cash receipts journal, since the distribution of sales by departments is made in the sales journal. The totals of the Cash debit column in the sales journal ($4,900) and the Cash Sales credit column in the cash receipts journal ($4,900) exactly offset and need not be posted.

If a business is divided into a large number of departments, the use of a separate journal column for each departmental account would result in journals of unmanageable size. In such cases it is more efficient to analyze duplicate copies of sales invoices by departments, posting the totals directly to the departmental accounts in the ledger. The trend in modern accounting systems is to avoid journals with numerous columns by using various machine methods of sorting, classifying, and summarizing original data prior to recording in journals.

Regardless of the system used, the basic procedures are: (*1*) See that operating data are classified by departments on original invoices, credit memorandums, cash register tapes, etc.; (*2*) sort and accumulate these individual transaction figures to arrive at subtotals for each departmental account; (*3*) enter this information in ledger accounts.

Since separate departmental accounts for sales, sales returns and allowances, and sales discounts are used by the Day Corporation, the net sales (as reported in the income statement on page 819) can be determined directly from the balances in these accounts.

DEPARTMENTAL COST OF GOODS SOLD We shall assume that the Day Corporation keeps separate departmental accounts for each element of cost of goods sold. Inventories, purchases, and purchase returns are readily identified by department. Purchase discounts and transportation-in must also be classified by department to determine the cost of goods sold by each department. This classification may be made at the time of each transaction, or the total purchase discounts and total transportation-in may be allocated to individual departments at the end of the accounting period. The cost of goods sold by departments for the current year is shown in the income statement illustrated in the following section.

INCOME STATEMENT: GROSS PROFIT BY DEPARTMENTS An income statement for the Day Corporation, departmentalized only through the gross profit on sales, is shown on page 819. Note that the gross profit as a percentage of net sales is given for the business as a whole and by departments.

If the number of departments were large, a horizontal expansion of the income statement in this fashion might become unwieldy, in which case separate statements of gross profit on sales for each department might be prepared and attached to the income statement for the business as a whole.

It is evident that Department A contributes a much higher rate of gross profit than Department B. By studying the reasons for this difference, management may be led to make changes in buying policies, selling prices, or the personnel of Department B in an effort to improve its performance. Whether Department A contributes more than B to the net income of the business, however, depends on the amount of operating expenses attributable to each department.

DAY CORPORATION

Income Statement

Current Year

	Total	Dept. A	Dept. B
Sales	$500,000	$320,000	$180,000
Less: Sales returns and allowances	(5,000)	(2,300)	(2,700)
Sales discounts	(8,000)	(6,000)	(2,000)
Net sales	$487,000	$311,700	$175,300
Cost of goods sold:			
Beginning inventory	$ 70,000	$ 28,000	$ 42,000
Purchases	360,000	205,200	154,800
Transportation-in	17,000	4,800	12,200
Purchase returns	(10,000)	(5,700)	(4,300)
Purchase discounts	(6,100)	(3,000)	(3,100)
Merchandise available for sale	$430,900	$229,300	$201,600
Less: Ending inventory	90,000	36,000	54,000
Cost of goods sold	$340,900	$193,300	$147,600
Gross profit on sales	$146,100	$118,400	$ 27,700
Gross profit as percentage of net sales (30%			
combined)		38%	16%
Operating expenses (details omitted)	125,500		
Operating income	$ 20,600		
Income taxes, 22%	4,532		
Net income	$ 16,068		
Net income per share	$0.12		

Allocating operating expenses to departments

An analysis of expenses by departments provides information about the cost of departmental operations and makes it possible to prepare an income statement showing departmental net income. Two steps are generally involved in allocating operating expenses to departments: First, identify the expenses which are considered *direct* expenses of certain departments, and second, identify the expenses which are considered *indirect* departmental expenses and allocate these to the respective departments on some basis which would properly recognize the benefits received by each department.

Direct expenses are those which may be identified by department, in the sense that if the department did not exist, the expense would not be incurred. *Indirect expenses* are incurred for the benefit of the business as a whole; they cannot be identified readily with the activities of a given department. These would, for the most part, continue even though a particular department were discontinued.

Some direct expenses may be charged to separate departmental expense accounts at the time they are incurred. Other expenses, even though they are direct in nature, may be more conveniently charged to a single account and allocated to departments at the end of the accounting period.

Indirect expenses, by their very nature, can be assigned to departments only by a process of allocation. For example, the salary of the president of the company is an expense not directly related to the activities of any particular department. If it is to be divided among the departments, some method of allocation is necessary which would charge each department with the approximate cost of the benefits it received.

Operating expenses may be allocated to departments through the use of a *departmental expense allocation sheet* similar to the one illustrated below for the Day Corporation:

Departmental Expense Allocation Sheet
Current Year

		Total Operating Expenses	Department A		Department B	
			Direct	Indirect	Direct	Indirect
Sales force expense	(1)*	$ 27,000	$16,900		$10,100	
Advertising expense	(2)	18,000	5,000	$ 6,250	3,000	$ 3,750
Building expense	(3)	16,000		9,600		6,400
Buying expense	(4)	26,800	14,000	2,850	7,800	2,150
Delivery expense	(5)	12,000		3,000	2,000	7,000
Administrative expense	(6)	25,700	3,100	12,800	2,600	7,200
Totals—direct and indirect . . .		$125,500	$39,000	$34,500	$25,500	$26,500
Total for each department . . .			$73,500		$52,000	

*See explanations on page 821.

In order to keep this example short and simple, we have assumed that the Day Corporation grouped its operating expenses into various functions or activities performed. For example, sales force expense includes all compensation and payroll-related costs of the sales staff and sales executives; delivery expense includes all costs of operating delivery trucks, wages of drivers, and all other costs relating to shipping merchandise to customers. The allocation of operating expenses in the departmental expense allocation sheet prepared by the Day Corporation is explained in the following sections.

1 **Sales force expense.** Day Corporation's salespeople work exclusively in either Department A or Department B. This is an example of a direct expense clearly identified with the departments involved and thus charged to departments on the basis of the personnel involved. The expense allocation sheet shows that direct sales force expense incurred was $16,900 for Department A and $10,100 for Department B.

2 **Advertising expense.**   The Day Corporation advertises primarily through newspapers, with occasional spot advertisements on radio and television. Direct advertising expense amounts to $8,000 and represents the cost of newspaper space and time purchased to advertise specific products identified with each department. Indirect advertising expense amounts to $10,000 and includes the cost of administering the advertising program, plus advertising applicable to the business as a whole. Indirect advertising expense is allocated in proportion to the direct advertising expense:

	Direct Advertising Expense	% of Total	Indirect Advertising Expense	Total Direct and Indirect
Department A	$5,000	62.5	$ 6,250	$11,250
Department B	3,000	37.5	3,750	6,750
Total	$8,000	100.0	$10,000	$18,000

3 **Building expense.**   This includes all costs relating to the occupancy of the building. The Day Corporation allocates the building expense on the basis of square feet occupied by each department, 60% by Department A and 40% by Department B. Thus $9,600 (60% of $16,000) was allocated to Department A and $6,400 (40% of $16,000) was allocated to Department B. If the value of the floor space varies (as, for example, between the first floor and the second floor) then the allocation would be made on the basis of **value of space** rather than square footage.

4 **Buying expense.**   The compensation of departmental buyers, their travel expenses, and certain merchandise handling costs, a total of $21,800, were considered direct expenses and assigned to the two departments on the basis of the personnel involved. Department A was charged with $14,000 of this direct expense and Department B absorbed $7,800. The indirect buying expense of $5,000 was allocated on the basis of total departmental purchases of $360,000 as follows: Department A, $205,200/$360,000 × $5,000, or $2,850; Department B, $154,800/$360,000 × $5,000, or $2,150. The possible defects of purchases as an allocation basis are obvious; there is no necessary reason why the cost of buying or handling an item of large dollar value is significantly greater than for a less costly item.

5 **Delivery expense.**   Department B shipped certain merchandise by common carrier at a cost of $2,000, a direct expense of this department. The $10,000 balance of the cost of maintaining a delivery service applies to both departments. A study covering several months of typical operation showed that on the average 70% of all delivery requests originated in Department B; therefore 30% ($3,000) of the indirect delivery expense was charged to Department A, and 70% ($7,000) to Department B.

6 **Administrative expense.**   Two direct expenses were included in the administrative expense category; the remainder were indirect:

	Total	Department A	Department B
Direct administrative expense:			
Uncollectible accounts expense	$ 3,700	$ 2,300	$1,400
Insurance on inventories	2,000	800	1,200
Total direct expenses	$ 5,700	$ 3,100	$2,600
Indirect administrative expense (allocated			
on basis of net sales)	20,000	12,800	7,200
Total administrative expense	$25,700	$15,900	$9,800

The division of the $3,700 uncollectible accounts expense was made on the basis of an analysis of accounts charged off during the period. If this had not been feasible, allocation on the basis of credit sales in each department would have been reasonable. Insurance on inventories of $2,000 was charged to the departments on the basis of the average inventory in each department ($32,000 and $48,000, respectively), or a 40:60 ratio. Indirect administrative expense of $20,000 was allocated on the basis of net sales, for want of a more reasonable basis.

Department A, $311,700/$487,000 × $20,000	$12,800
Department B, $175,300/$487,000 × $20,000	7,200
Total	$20,000

The following summary of operating expenses for the Day Corporation will be useful to us in discussing the possibility of discontinuing Department B, which appears to be losing money:

	Total	Department A	Department B
Operating expenses:			
Direct . . . :	$ 64,500	$39,000	$25,500
Indirect	61,000	34,500	26,500
Total	$125,500	$73,500	$52,000

Departmental income statement

On the basis of departmental data developed thus far, we can now prepare a statement showing the net income of the business and of each department, as shown on page 823.

For the sake of simplicity, we are assuming that income taxes are paid by the Day Corporation at the flat rate of 22%. To reflect clearly the relationship between income taxes and operating results, the income tax expense charged to Department A is 22% of the income before income taxes of that department, and this is offset by a credit of $5,346 equal to 22% of the loss before income taxes of $24,300 reported in Department B.

DAY CORPORATION
Departmental Income Statement
Current Year

	Total	Department A	Department B
Net sales.	$487,000	$311,700	$175,300
Cost of goods sold	340,900	193,300	147,600
Gross profit on sales	$146,100	$118,400	$ 27,700
Operating expenses (see depart-			
mental expense allocation sheet			
on page 820):			
Sales force expense	$ 27,000	$ 16,900	$ 10,100
Advertising expense	18,000	11,250	6,750
Building expense	16,000	9,600	6,400
Buying expense	26,800	16,850	9,950
Delivery expense	12,000	3,000	9,000
Administrative expense	25,700	15,900	9,800
Total operating expenses	$125,500	$ 73,500	$ 52,000
Income (or loss) before income taxes . . .	$ 20,600	$ 44,900	$(24,300)
Income taxes (or credit), 22%	4,532	9,878	(5,346)
Net income (or loss)	$ 16,068	$ 35,022	$(18,954)
Net income per share	$0.12		

Should De-partment B be closed?

WHEN IS A DEPARTMENT UNPROFITABLE? The first reaction of management, confronted with the departmental income statement shown above,
might be that the corporation would be better off if Department B were
dropped. The income statement appears to indicate that net income
would have been $35,022 rather than $16,068 were it not for the existence
of Department B. Is this true?

If we could, with a wave of the hand, blot Department B out of existence, the income statement of the Day Corporation for the current year
would probably appear as shown on page 824.

Instead of improving the company's showing, the result is a *decrease* in
income of $1,716 ($16,068 − $14,352). Apparently the information in the
departmental income statement is misleading. The answer to this paradox
is that *the elimination of Department B would eliminate the entire gross profit on
sales earned in that department but not any of the indirect expenses that were
allocated to Department B.* An explanation of the estimated decline in net
income of $1,716 shown above ($16,068 − $14,352), is summarized on
page 824.

It is apparent from this summary that reducing direct expenses by
$25,500 and eliminating $484 in income taxes are not sufficient to offset
the decrease in gross profit on sales of $27,700 that would follow from the
elimination of Department B. If we compare the effect on expenses shown
on this summary with the expenses allocated to Department B as shown

DAY CORPORATION
Income Statement Reflecting Elimination of Department B
Current Year

<table>
<tr><td rowspan="13" style="text-align:right">Effect of eliminating Depart-ment B</td><td>Net sales . . . .</td><td></td><td>$311,700</td></tr>
<tr><td>Cost of goods sold . . . .</td><td></td><td>193,300</td></tr>
<tr><td>Gross profit on sales . . . .</td><td></td><td>$118,400</td></tr>
<tr><td>Operating expenses:</td><td></td><td></td></tr>
<tr><td>Direct expenses of Department A (see departmental allocation</td><td></td><td></td></tr>
<tr><td>sheet on page 820) . . . .</td><td>$39,000</td><td></td></tr>
<tr><td>Indirect expenses (total originally allocated to both departments,</td><td></td><td></td></tr>
<tr><td>$34,500 + $26,500) . . . .</td><td>61,000</td><td>100,000</td></tr>
<tr><td>Income before income taxes . . . .</td><td></td><td>$ 18,400</td></tr>
<tr><td>Income taxes (22%) . . . .</td><td></td><td>4,048</td></tr>
<tr><td>Net income . . . .</td><td></td><td>$ 14,352</td></tr>
<tr><td>Net income per share . . . .</td><td></td><td>$0.11</td></tr>
</table>

on page 820, we see that only direct expenses of $25,500 were assumed to be eliminated as a result of the elimination of this department. This is no coincidence, since direct expenses were defined as those relating to the activities of a particular department that would be eliminated if the department did not exist. Thus compensation of sales and buying personnel, cost of direct advertising space, outbound transportation paid to carriers, uncollectible accounts expense, and insurance on inventories would presumably disappear along with Department B.

DAY CORPORATION
Estimated Effect of Elimination of Department B
Current Year

			Assuming Elimination of Department B		
		Depart-ment B's share	Not Eliminated (Indirect)	Eliminated (Direct)	Effect on Net Income
Is Depart-ment B un-profitable?	Gross profit on sales	$27,700		$27,700	$(27,700)
	Operating expenses	52,000	$26,500	25,500	25,500
	Effect on income before				
	income taxes				$ (2,200)
	Reduction in income taxes				
	(22% of $2,200)				484
	Reduction in net income if				
	Department B is				
	eliminated				$ (1,716)

The $26,500 of operating expenses that would *not* be eliminated is the amount of indirect expenses assigned to Department B. The assumption that indirect expenses are inescapable (fixed) and that they would remain unchanged is a convenient assumption but, realistically, some reduction in indirect expenses would probably occur if Department B were eliminated. The change in indirect expenses that follows from departmental changes will depend to some extent on the alternatives that are being considered. For example, the indirect expense, building expense, would continue largely unchanged whether Department B existed or not, since the Day Corporation owns the entire building. However, if the Day Corporation were to drop Department B and reduce the scale of its activities, it might rent the surplus space to outsiders and thus reduce building expense. On the other hand, if the question were whether Department B should be reorganized or a new kind of operation substituted for it, building expenses and other indirect expenses would probably not change by an amount large enough to influence the decision.

There is considerable wisdom in the phrase "different costs for different purposes." The allocation of costs for one purpose may not produce results that are significant for a different kind of decision; special cost studies are often necessary to answer particular questions. Some of these will be discussed in subsequent chapters.

Departmental contribution to indirect expenses (overhead)

We have seen that the gross profit on sales by departments can be determined with good assurance that the results are meaningful and useful. We have seen also that the division of direct expenses among departments is a fairly straightforward process. Sales revenue, cost of goods sold, and direct expenses are all operating elements that, in general, relate clearly to the existence of a given department and its activities.

On the other hand, most indirect expenses (*overhead*) are costs associated with the business as a whole, and in general they lie outside the control of department managers. Because of their indirect relationship to departmental activities, any basis of allocation used is somewhat arbitrary and the proper interpretation of the results is often in doubt.

Some accountants argue that the important benefits of departmental accounting can be gained by stopping short of a full allocation of all expenses to departments. They urge that each department be credited with revenues and charged with expenses that, in the opinion of management, would disappear if the department did not exist. This approach leads to a departmental income statement showing the **contribution of each department to the indirect expenses of the business.** Such a statement, using figures previously developed for the Day Corporation, is illustrated on page 826.

DAY CORPORATION
Departmental Income Statement Showing Contribution to Indirect Expenses
Current Year

	Total	Department A	Department B
Net sales	$487,000	$311,700	$175,300
Cost of goods sold	340,900	193,300	147,600
Gross profit on sales	$146,100(30%)	$118,400(38%)	$ 27,700(16%)
Direct departmental expenses			
(see page 820):			
Sales force expense	$ 27,000	$ 16,900	$ 10,100
Advertising expense	8,000	5,000	3,000
Buying expense	21,800	14,000	7,800
Delivery expense	2,000		2,000
Administrative expense . . .	5,700	3,100	2,600
Total direct expenses . . .	$ 64,500	$ 39,000	$ 25,500
Contribution to indirect			
expenses	$ 81,600	$ 79,400	$ 2,200

Indirect expenses		
(see page 820):		
Advertising		
expense.	$10,000	
Building		
expense.	16,000	
Buying		
expense.	5,000	
Delivery		
expense.	10,000	
Administrative		
expense.	20,000	
Total indirect expenses . .		61,000
Income before income taxes .		$ 20,600
Income taxes, 22%.		4,532
Net income		$ 16,068
Net income per share		$0.12

In contrast to the departmental net income statement on page 823, which shows that Department B suffered a net loss of $18,954, this statement shows that Department B contributed $2,200 (before income taxes) to the indirect expenses of the business. This figure agrees with the estimated reduction in net income *before income taxes* (see page 824) if Department B were discontinued.

The performance of department managers can be better judged by their contribution to indirect expenses than by the *net income* or *loss* for a department, because indirect expenses are generally outside the control

of department managers. Furthermore, so long as a department is covering its direct expenses, it is probably contributing to the profitability of the
business as a whole.

WORKING PAPERS FOR DEPARTMENTAL OPERATIONS A work sheet,
similar to the one illustrated in Chapter 5, may still be used when operating expenses are allocated among departments. Each revenue and expense item is extended into the proper departmental columns, as illustrated in the solution to the Demonstration Problem for Your Review at the
end of this chapter. The difference between the departmental Debit and
Credit columns in the income statement section is the contribution to
indirect expenses for each department.

A separate departmental expense allocation sheet, similar to the one
illustrated on page 820, is usually prepared to support the amount of each
departmental expense item shown on the work sheet and the departmental income statement.

ACCOUNTING SYSTEMS FOR BRANCH OPERATIONS

Merchandising companies often do business in more than one location by
opening **branch stores.** As a business grows it may open branches in order
to market its products over a larger territory and thus increase its profits.
A branch is typically located at some distance from the **home office** and
generally carries a stock of merchandise, sells the merchandise, makes
collection on receivables, and pays some of its operating expenses. A
branch is not a separate legal entity; it is simply a segment of a business
which may be a single proprietorship, a partnership, or a corporation.
From an accounting standpoint, a branch is a clearly identifiable **profit
center** and offers an opportunity to implement the principles of responsibility accounting discussed earlier in this chapter.

An accounting system for a branch should generate information
needed to measure the profitability of the branch and to ensure strong
control over branch assets. Management needs information to answer
questions such as: Is the branch yielding a satisfactory rate of return on
the capital invested in it? Should the branch be expanded or closed? Are
prices on merchandise sold by the branch too low? How much of a bonus
should the branch manager receive? How much merchandise does the
branch have in stock?

The home office may provide the branch with a cash **working fund** to be
used for the payment of branch expenses. The merchandise handled by a
branch may be obtained solely from the home office or a portion may be
purchased from outside suppliers. Bills for merchandise purchases and
certain operating expenses, such as wages and insurance, may be paid
by the home office, or from the branch working fund. Cash receipts of the
branch may be deposited either in a branch or a home office bank

account. When a branch is authorized to have its own bank account, it will also generally pay its bills and remit any unneeded cash to the home office. The amount of operating independence given to a branch varies among companies and even among branches within the same company. Branch accounting systems are either *centralized* in the home office or *decentralized* at the branches.

Branch records centralized in home office

In a *centralized* accounting system, the branch is provided with a small working fund (similar to a petty cash fund which is replenished periodically) to pay for small items of expense. The home office keeps most of the accounting records relating to the branch. Records of branch assets, liabilities, revenue, payrolls, and other expenses are maintained in the home office which processes the business documents (sales slips, deposit slips, invoices, etc.) received from the branch. The branch keeps very few accounting records and is generally instructed to deposit cash receipts in a home office account with a local bank. A centralized system is particularly appropriate when data processing equipment is located in the home office or when the branch is too small to hire a full-time accountant.

Separate records of revenue and expenses for each branch are maintained in the accounting records of the home office. In this way the operating results for each branch can be readily determined. Thus the three important features of a centralized accounting system for a branch are: (*1*) A working fund for the branch is established and is replenished as needed; (*2*) all business documents originating at the branch are transmitted to the home office; and (*3*) a separate record of branch assets, liabilities, revenue, and expenses is maintained by the home office.

Records decentralized at the branch

As an alternative to centralizing all accounting work in the home office, a company may decide that a branch should maintain its own complete set of accounting records. Under such a *decentralized* accounting system, the branch accountant will prepare complete financial statements for the branch and forward them to the home office. The number and type of accounts, the system of internal control, the form and content of financial statements, and the accounting policies are generally prescribed by the home office. As a minimum, the transactions recorded by the branch include the expenses under the control of the branch manager and the revenue generated at the branch. At the end of the accounting period, the home office may notify the branch that certain expenses incurred at the home office have been allocated to the branch. Records of certain assets purchased by the home office and assigned to the branch, such as furniture and equipment and the related depreciation accounts, are often

maintained at the home office. Bank loans may be negotiated and recorded by the home office; the proceeds on such loans are advanced to
the branch, or simply deposited in the branch bank account.

TYPICAL BRANCH TRANSACTIONS ILLUSTRATED In order to illustrate the
basic features of a decentralized branch accounting system, assume that
on March 1, Homer & Company (a single proprietorship) opens a branch
in the city of Brady. The company rents a fully equipped store and
transfers cash of $10,000 and store supplies of $1,500 to the branch. The
entries in the accounts of the Brady Branch and the home office to record
this transfer, along with other *branch* transactions during March, are
shown in summary form on page 830.

   Only transactions (*1*), (*4*), and (*8*) are recorded in the home office
accounting records, because these three transactions involve both the
branch and the home office and thus require the use of the *reciprocal*
accounts as follows:

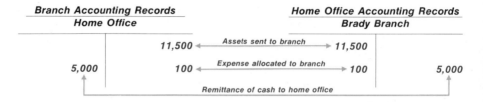

Branch Accounting Records		Home Office Accounting Records	
Home Office		**Brady Branch**	
	11,500 ← Assets sent to branch → 11,500		
5,000	100 ← Expense allocated to branch → 100		5,000
	Remittance of cash to home office		

Note that the credit balance in the Home Office account, $6,600, is equal
to the debit balance in the Brady Branch account, $6,600.

BRANCH RECORDS The Home Office account in the branch accounting
records may be viewed as a "proprietorship" account which shows the
net investment in the branch made by the home office. It is credited for
assets transferred to the branch and for expenses allocated to the branch
by the home office; it is debited when cash or other assets are remitted to
the home office by the branch. At the end of the accounting period when
the branch closes its accounts, the branch income or loss is closed into
the Home Office account. A branch net income is debited to the Income
Summary account and credited to the Home Office account; a loss
reported by the branch would be debited to the Home Office account and
credited to Income Summary.

HOME OFFICE RECORDS The net investment in the branch is recorded in
the Brady Branch account in the accounting records of the home office.
This account is debited when assets are transferred to the branch or
when expenses incurred at the home office are allocated to the branch; it
is credited when cash or other assets are received from the branch.
Income reported by the branch is debited to the Brady Branch account

Summary of Transactions for March

	Branch Accounting Records		Home Office Accounting Records	
(1) Home office opened Brady Branch and transferred cash and store supplies to the branch	Cash .... Store Supplies ... Home Office	10,000 1,500 11,500	Brady Branch....... Cash .... Store Supplies	11,500 10,000 1,500
(2) Merchandise purchased by branch. Branch uses a perpetual inventory system.[1]	Inventory .... Accounts Payable ...	18,000 18,000	No entry	
(3) Expenses incurred by branch.	Selling Expense ...... General Expense ...... Cash .... Accounts Payable ...... Store Supplies	2,500 1,900 3,200 1,000 200	No entry	
(4) General expense incurred by home office allocated to branch.	General Expense ...... Home Office......	100 100	Brady Branch........ General Expense	100 100
(5) Sales made by branch.	Cash .... Accounts Receivable ...... Sales	3,000 17,000 20,000	No entry	
(6) Collections by branch on accounts receivable.	Cash .... Accounts Receivable	13,000 13,000	No entry	
(7) Payments by branch to merchandise creditors.	Accounts Payable...... Cash	14,500 14,500	No entry	
(8) Branch remits cash to home office at end of month.	Home Office ...... Cash	5,000 5,000	Cash ...... Brady Branch........	5,000 5,000
(9) To record the cost of goods sold by branch during the month.	Cost of Goods Sold ...... Inventory	12,000 12,000	No entry	

[1] See pp. 384–385 for a description of a perpetual inventory system.

and credited to Income—Brady Branch; branch losses would be debited to Loss—Brady Branch and credited to the Brady Branch account.

STATEMENTS FOR THE BRANCH After the transactions illustrated on page 830 are recorded and summarized, the accountant for the Brady Branch submits the following statements to the home office:

<table>
<tr><td colspan="2" align="center">*BRADY BRANCH*</td></tr>
<tr><td colspan="2" align="center">*Income Statement*</td></tr>
<tr><td colspan="2" align="center">*For Month of March*</td></tr>
<tr><td>Sales ....</td><td>$20,000</td></tr>
<tr><td>Cost of goods sold ....</td><td>12,000</td></tr>
<tr><td>Gross profit on sales ......</td><td>$ 8,000</td></tr>
<tr><td>Less: Selling expense. . $2,500</td><td></td></tr>
<tr><td>General expense . 2,000</td><td>4,500</td></tr>
<tr><td>Net income ....</td><td>$ 3,500</td></tr>
</table>

<table>
<tr><td colspan="2" align="center">*BRADY BRANCH*</td></tr>
<tr><td colspan="2" align="center">*Balance Sheet*</td></tr>
<tr><td colspan="2" align="center">*March 31*</td></tr>
<tr><td>Cash ....</td><td>$ 3,300</td></tr>
<tr><td>Accounts receivable.......</td><td>4,000</td></tr>
<tr><td>Inventory..............</td><td>6,000</td></tr>
<tr><td>Store supplies ....</td><td>1,300</td></tr>
<tr><td></td><td>$14,600</td></tr>
<tr><td>Accounts payable ....</td><td>$ 4,500</td></tr>
<tr><td>Home office ($6,600 +</td><td></td></tr>
<tr><td>net income of $3,500) ....</td><td>10,100</td></tr>
<tr><td></td><td>$14,600</td></tr>
</table>

WORKING PAPERS FOR COMBINED STATEMENTS FOR HOME OFFICE AND BRANCH When the accountants for the home office receive the branch statements for March, they can prepare *combined statements* through the use of working papers similar to those illustrated on page 832. The branch figures are taken from the statements submitted by the branch and the home office figures are assumed.

The figures in the Combined column are used to prepare the income statement and the balance sheet for Homer & Company. Because there is nothing unusual about these statements, they will not be illustrated.

CLOSING ENTRIES At the end of the accounting period, the revenue and expense accounts at the branch are closed and the income of $3,500 is transferred to the Home Office account. The home office records the branch income in the Income—Brady Branch account; the balance in this account is then closed to Income Summary when the home office ac-

HOMER & COMPANY
Working Papers for Combined Statements
For Month Ended March 31

	Adjusted Trial Balances		Eliminations		
	Home Office	Branch	Debit	Credit	Combined
Debit balances:					
Cash	9,100	3,300			12,400
Accounts receivable	26,000	4,000			30,000
Inventory	34,000	6,000			40,000
Store supplies	3,000	1,300			4,300
Land	25,000				25,000
Buildings and equipment	60,000				60,000
Brady Branch	6,600			(1) 6,600	
Cost of goods sold	50,000	12,000			62,000
Selling expense	6,500	2,500			9,000
General expense	5,800	2,000			7,800
Interest expense	300				300
Total debits	226,300	31,100			250,800
Credit balances:					
Notes payable	40,000				40,000
Accounts payable	22,500	4,500			27,000
Accrued liabilities	2,800				2,800
Home office		6,600	(1) 6,600		
John Homer, capital	75,000				75,000
Sales	85,000	20,000			105,000
Purchase discounts	1,000				1,000
Total credits	226,300	31,100	6,600	6,600	250,800

Explanation of elimination:
(1) Reciprocal accounts maintained by the home office and branch are eliminated. These accounts have no significance since the home office and the branch are a single entity. This elimination entry is made only on the working papers; it is not recorded in the accounting records of either the home office or the branch.

counts are closed. These entries are illustrated below and on page 833.

Branch Accounting Records		**Home Office Accounting Records**	
Sales 20,000		Brady Branch 3,500	
Cost of Goods Sold .	12,000	Income—Brady Branch .	3,500
Selling Expense . . .	2,500	To record branch income.	
General Expense . .	2,000		
Income Summary . .	3,500	Income—Brady Branch . . 3,500	
To close revenue and		Income Summary	3,500
expense accounts.		To close branch income	
		to Income Summary.	

Income Summary . . . .   *3,500*   -

    Home Office *3,500*

To transfer balance in

Income Summary ac-

count to Home Office

account.

Interdepartmental and interbranch pricing policies

In order to obtain a better measure of departmental or branch profit performance, some companies bill the merchandise transferred to departments or branches at prices above cost. Of course, a company does not "make a profit" by simply transferring merchandise to one of its departments or branches; a profit on such transfers can only be realized when the merchandise is sold to customers. When end-of-period statements for the company as a whole are prepared, the **unrealized profits** on intracompany transfers of merchandise are eliminated. The **actual** cost of merchandise sold is deducted from revenue and the actual cost of merchandise on hand is included among the current assets in the balance sheet.

KEY TERMS INTRODUCED OR EMPHASIZED IN CHAPTER 23

Centralized accounting system A system in which the branches of a company send information on daily transactions to the home office which maintains the accounting records for the entire company.

Cost center A unit of a business which incurs expenses or costs but does not directly generate revenue; for example, the personnel department.

Decentralized accounting system A system in which each branch of a company maintains its own complete set of accounting records.

Departmental contribution to overhead The excess of the gross profit of a given department over the operating expenses which would be eliminated if the department were discontinued. Even though a department is unprofitable when all expenses have been properly allocated, discontinuance of the department would cause the company's net income to decline if the department is making a contribution toward meeting overhead expenses.

Departmental expense allocation The process of allocating indirect expenses of a business among departments in order to measure the performance of each department. For example, building occupancy expense may be allocated on the basis of the square feet of space used by each department.

Departmental income statement An income statement showing the revenue, expenses, and net income of the business and of each department.

Profit center A unit of a business which produces revenue which can be identified with the unit; for example, the meat department of a supermarket.

Reciprocal accounts Offsetting accounts maintained by the home office and a branch. The home office maintains an account (with a debit balance) summarizing its investment in the branch. The branch maintains a Home Office account (with a credit balance) similar to a proprietorship account.

Responsibility accounting A system designed to measure performance of each segment of a business for which a supervisor is responsible.

DEMONSTRATION PROBLEM FOR YOUR REVIEW

The summarized adjusted trial balance of the Suburb Outlet Company for the fiscal year ending on September 30 is shown below. (Note that the items are listed in alphabetical order for the objectives of this problem.)

SUBURB OUTLET COMPANY
Adjusted Trial Balance
September 30, Current Year

Accumulated depreciation		$ 72,000
Administrative expense	$ 43,600	
Advertising expense	40,600	
Buildings and equipment	167,000	
Building occupancy expense	18,000	
Buying expense	25,600	
Capital stock		50,000
Cost of goods sold	368,500	
Current assets	166,000	
Current liabilities		84,400
Goodwill	25,000	
Interest earned		1,200
Interest expense	5,500	
Land	42,000	
Long-term notes payable		80,000
Net sales		578,600
Retained earnings		70,600
Sales salaries	35,000	
	$936,800	$936,800

Revenue and expenses are analyzed below:

	Total	Direct Expenses Dept. A	Direct Expenses Dept. B	Indirect Expenses
Net sales	$578,600	$360,000	$218,600	
Interest earned	1,200	500	700	
Administrative expense	43,600	12,300	5,900	$25,400
Advertising expense	40,600	12,400	12,200	16,000
Building occupancy expense	18,000	2,800	4,000	11,200
Buying expense	25,600	10,300	5,600	9,700
Cost of goods sold	368,500	218,500	150,000	
Sales salaries	35,000	18,000	9,000	8,000

No provision has been made for corporate income taxes, which are 22% on the first $50,000 of income and 48% on income in excess of $50,000.

Instructions Prepare year-end working papers (10-column) from which a departmental income statement and a balance sheet could be prepared. The Suburb Outlet Company is interested in knowing the contribution that each department makes toward the indirect expenses of the business.

Since all adjustments other than for income taxes have been made, the working papers may start with the adjusted trial balance. Allow two columns each for the following: Income Statement, Department A; Income Statement, Department B; Unallocated (for indirect expenses and total departmental contribution to indirect expenses); and Balance Sheet.

SOLUTION TO DEMONSTRATION PROBLEM

SUBURB OUTLET COMPANY
Working Papers
September 30, Current Year

| | Adjusted Trial Balance | | Income Statements | | | | | | Balance Sheet | |
| | | | Department A | | Department B | | Unallocated | | | |
	Dr	Cr	Dr	Cr	Dr	Cr	Dr	Cr	Dr	Cr
Accumulated depreciation		72,000								72,000
Administrative expense	43,600		12,300		5,900		25,400			
Advertising expense	40,600		12,400		12,200		16,000			
Buildings and equipment	167,000								167,000	
Bldg. occupancy expense	18,000		2,800		4,000		11,200			
Buying expense	25,600		10,300		5,600		9,700			
Capital stock		50,000								50,000
Cost of goods sold	368,500		218,500		150,000					
Current assets	166,000								166,000	
Current liabilities		84,400								84,400
Goodwill	25,000								25,000	
Interest earned		1,200		500		700				
Interest expense	5,500						5,500			
Land	42,000								42,000	
Long-term notes payable		80,000								80,000
Net sales		578,600		360,000		218,600				
Retained earnings		70,600								70,600
Sales salaries	35,000		18,000		9,000		8,000			
	936,800	936,800	274,300	360,000	186,700	219,300				
Departmental contribution to indirect expenses			86,200		32,600			118,800		
			360,500	360,500	219,300	219,300	75,800	118,800		
Income taxes*							9,460			9,460
Net income for current year							33,540			33,540
							118,800	118,800	400,000	400,000

* Computation of income taxes:

Departmental contribution to indirect expenses	$118,800
Less: Unallocated expenses	75,800
Income before income taxes	$ 43,000
Income taxes ($43,000 × 22%)	$ 9,460

REVIEW QUESTIONS

1 What is a *responsibility accounting* system?

2 Distinguish between a *cost center* and a *profit center*.

3 What are some uses that management may make of departmental accounting information?

4 The College Bookstore has employed Kay Barton as its new manager. In the past the income statement of the bookstore has shown only total revenue and operating expenses. The new manager wants to introduce procedures for measuring gross profits for each of three departmental areas: textbooks, general books, and merchandise. Explain what changes in the accounting system will be required and what benefits Barton may expect to gain from the departmental information.

5 Jill Stone, the manager of a retail store, states that the selling prices in her business are established by adding 50% to merchandise cost.
  a If this statement is factual, what rate of gross profit per dollar of gross sales should the company realize?
  b Assuming that the actual gross profit for one department of this firm for a given period is 28% of *net* sales, what reasons can you give to explain this?

6 What two steps are generally involved in allocating operating expenses to departments?

7 Explain the distinction between direct expenses and indirect expenses as these terms are used in relation to expense allocation among departments.

8 Atwood Hardware has three operating departments. In its departmental income statement, building occupancy expenses are allocated among departments on the basis of sales. Explain why you do or do not agree that this procedure will produce useful information for management.

9 After examining an income statement showing net income by departments, James Wood, the manager of one department, complains that the amount of income taxes allocated to his department is greater than the amount the business as a whole will have to pay, and he feels this is entirely unreasonable. Explain how this could happen, and whether or not you agree with the department manager's view.

10 What is meant by the term *contribution to indirect expenses?* Explain why management may find information about the contribution to overhead of each department more useful than departmental net income figures.

11 Briefly describe the type of information that management should obtain from a branch accounting system.

12 Differentiate between a *centralized* and a *decentralized* accounting system for branch operations.

13 Describe the nature of the Home Office account which appears in the records of the branch and the Branch account which appears in the records of the home office. Why are these two accounts referred to as *reciprocal* accounts?

14 What is the reason for preparing working papers for combined statements of the home office and branch?

EXERCISES

Ex. 23-1 The floor space on the first floor is twice as valuable as the floor space on the second floor. Each of the two floors has 60,000 square feet and total monthly rental paid on the building is $7,500. How much of the monthly rental expense should be allocated to a department which occupies 24,000 square feet on the second floor?

Ex. 23-2 The president of Beaver Company wants to eliminate Department B "because it's losing money." The operating results for the latest year appear below:

	Total	Dept. A	Dept. B
Sales	$900,000	$600,000	$ 300,000
Operating expenses (40% of which remain			
constant at all levels of sales)	810,000	360,000	450,000
Operating income	$ 90,000	$240,000	$(150,000)

What advice would you give the president, assuming that the indirect operating expenses of $324,000 would remain unchanged if Department B is eliminated?

Ex. 23-3 The Feltham Company allocates indirect operating expenses to its two departments on the basis of sales. In Year 1, the following allocation was made:

	Total	Dept. A	Dept. B
Sales	$500,000	$300,000	$200,000
Indirect operating expenses	140,000	84,000	56,000

Assume that the sales price of the products sold in Department B are increased by 100% in Year 2 resulting in total sales of $400,000 for Department B. Assume also that indirect operating expenses remain unchanged at $140,000. How much of these expenses will be allocated to each department in Year 2? Is the result logical?

Ex. 23-4 A given department shows an annual operating loss of $36,000 after deducting $54,000 of operating expenses. If $24,000 of the operating expenses allocated to this department are fixed and cannot be avoided, what would be the effect on the company's operating income if this particular department is closed?

Ex. 23-5 Given below are the reciprocal interbranch accounts at the end of Year 1:

Branch Records
Home Office

Date	Transaction	Dr	Cr	Balance
12/1	Balance			91,600
12/10	Cash remitted	14,000		77,600
12/20	Merchandise received		10,000	87,600
12/31	Net income		6,500	94,100

Home Office Records
Jersey Branch

Date	Transaction	Dr	Cr	Balance
12/1	Balance			91,600
12/12	Cash received		14,000	77,600
12/19	Merchandise shipped	10,000		87,600
12/29	Equipment sent	2,000		89,600

Prepare the entries required to bring each set of accounts up to date at the end of Year 1.

Ex. 23-6 Refer to Ex. 23-5 on page 838.

a What is the ***correct*** balance in each account at the end of Year 1?

b Give the elimination entry that would be required on the working papers at the end of Year 1 in preparing combined statements for the home office and the branch.

PROBLEMS

Group A

23A-1 A preliminary summary of the operating results for the Dart Company for Year 1 follows:

	Total	Department C	Department D
Net sales	$1,600,000	$640,000	$960,000
Operating income	160,000	90,000	70,000
Advertising expense (allocated on basis of net sales)	200,000	80,000	120,000

Advertising expense consists of $120,000 in direct product advertising (70% of which was applicable to Department C and 30% to Department D) and $80,000 in general advertising which promoted the image of the company. Bill Jay, the manager of Department D, thinks that his department was actually more profitable than Department C and argued that he was charged with an unreasonable amount of advertising expense. He maintains that the direct product advertising should be assigned to the departments on the basis of actual expenditures and that only the $80,000 of general (indirect) advertising should be allocated in proportion to net sales.

Instructions Prepare a departmental income statement for Year 1, following the expense allocation procedure suggested by the manager of Department D. Which department was more profitable? Why?

23A-2 Western Shop offers its customers a 2% cash discount on all cash sales and adds a financing charge of 1% per month to all account balances that are not paid within 30 days of the invoice date. Cash discounts are allocated directly to its three operating departments at the time of sale. Revenue from financing charges are allocated to the departments on the basis of net credit sales.

These data are taken from the Western Shop accounts for the current year:

	Total	Department X	Department Y	Department Z
Sales	$1,236,000	$367,200	$652,000	$216,800
Revenue from financing charges	75,000			
Sales returns (all from credit sales)	(36,000)	(7,200)	(12,000)	(16,800)
Cash discounts on sales	(9,000)	(2,000)	(5,800)	(1,200)
Net revenue from sales	$1,266,000			

Instructions

a Determine the amount of net credit sales for each of the three departments.

b Determine the amount of financing charges that will be allocated to each department by the accountant of the Western Shop.

c Comment on the validity of the method used by this company in allocating financing charges to departments. Explain why you think it will or will not produce accurate results.

23A-3 Martin Company has four operating departments. At the end of the current year the controller has computed departmental results in three ways, showing net income by departments, the departmental contribution to indirect expenses, and the gross profit on sales for each department as shown below.

	Total	Dept. One	Dept. Two	Dept. Three	Dept. Four
Departmental net income	$ 21,200	$ 68,300	$(4,000)	$(13,100)	$(30,000)
Departmental contribution					
to indirect expenses	88,800	98,000	14,000	(2,000)	(21,200)
Departmental gross					
profit on sales	184,000	128,000	36,000	22,000	(2,000)
Gross profit as a percent-					
age of sales	23%	40%	20%	10%	$(2\frac{1}{2}\%)$

Note: Parentheses indicate a loss.

Instructions

a On the basis of the above information, prepare a departmental income statement for the Martin Company. It will be necessary to compute the following amounts: net sales, cost of goods sold, direct expenses, and indirect expenses. Hint: Gross profit on sales is given for the company as a whole and for each department. Net sales can be computed from this information.)

b What conclusions would you reach about the operations of Departments Two, Three, and Four on the basis of the statement prepared in **a**? Should any of these departments be discontinued? Explain your reasoning.

23A-4 John Cross operates a retail business having three departments. Departmental expense accounts are maintained for some expenses, with the rest being allocated to the departments at the end of each accounting period. The operating expenses and other departmental data for the current year are shown below:

	Dept. K	Dept. L	Dept. M	Indirect Expenses
Departmental operating expenses:				
Sales salaries (direct)	$ 30,000	$ 25,750	$19,250	
Indirect salaries				$25,000
Building rental				9,600
Advertising (direct and indirect)	1,800	1,200	600	1,500
Supplies used (direct)	600	700	500	
Payroll taxes (5% of salaries)				5,000
Insurance expense				900
Depreciation on equipment (direct)	375	530	695	
Miscellaneous expense (direct and indirect) . .	300	200	100	2,400

Other departmental data:

Net sales	$212,500	$127,500	$85,000
Cost of goods sold	158,500	82,950	48,550
Equipment (original cost)	3,640	3,900	5,460
Average inventory	15,860	19,500	29,640
Value of floor space	50%	30%	20%
Floor space (square feet)	1,600	1,600	800

Indirect expenses are allocated among the departments on the bases given below.

Indirect Expense	*Basis of Allocation*
Indirect salaries	Amount of gross profit
Building rental	Value of floor space occupied
Advertising	Direct departmental advertising
Payroll taxes	Salaries, both direct and indirect
Insurance expense	Sum of equipment (original cost) and average inventory
Miscellaneous expense	Net sales

Instructions

a Prepare a schedule showing the allocation of operating expenses among the three departments. Use four money columns headed: Total, Department K, Department L, and Department M. Give schedules for each expense item in support of the amounts allocated to departments. Round all expense allocations to the nearest dollar.

b Prepare a summarized departmental income statement for John Cross's business, using the same column headings as in part *a*. Show summary figures for both total and departmental operating expenses, using totals from the schedule in *a*. Disregard income taxes.

23A-5 Auto Tune, Inc., operates several sales and service outlets (branches) throughout the metropolitan area of a large city. A decentralized accounting system is used by each branch. At the end of October, the following reciprocal accounts appear in the accounting records of the Central branch and the home office:

Branch Records	*Home Office Records*
Home Office (credit balance) . . $17,970	*Central Branch (debit balance)* . $17,210

The reason for the discrepancy in the amounts shown in the two accounts is that the branch net income for October, $1,800, and a cash deposit made by the branch to the account of the home office, $1,040, have not been recorded by the home office. Both the branch and the home office use a perpetual inventory system.

During November, the following transactions affected the two accounts:

Nov. 6 Home office shipped merchandise to branch, $7,250. Debit Inventory account on branch books; credit Inventory account on home office books.

Nov. 12 Branch transferred $4,950 from its bank account to the bank account of the home office.

Nov. 19 Branch returned shop supplies costing $610 to the home office. Shop supplies are carried in the Shop Supplies account in both sets of accounts.

Nov. 30 Home office notified branch that operating expenses of $1,100 which had been recorded in the accounts of the home office in the Operating Expense account were chargeable to the Central branch.

Nov. 30 The Income Summary account in the accounts of the branch showed a debit balance of $590 at the end of November.

Instructions

a Record the transactions listed above in the accounts of the Central branch. (Explanations may be omitted for all journal entries in this problem.)

b Record the two transactions relating to the month of October and all transactions for November in the accounts of the home office.

c Determine the balances in the Home Office account and the Central Branch account at the end of November.

Group B

23B-1 Given below are the results for the two departments operated by West Mart during Year 1:

	Dept. X	Dept. Y
Sales	$622,000	$350,000
Sales returns and allowances	12,000	20,000
Direct departmental expenses	120,000	80,000
Indirect departmental expenses (not allocated), $90,000		
Interest earned (not allocated), $10,000		
Gross profit percentage (on net sales)	40%	30%

Instructions Prepare a departmental income statement for Year 1 showing contribution to indirect expenses. Use three columns as follows: Total, Dept. X, and Dept. Y. Disregard income taxes.

23B-2 Parkway Company operates a retail business in a three-story building. Each floor has usable space of 20,000 square feet. The occupancy cost for the building per year averages $128,400. There are a number of separate departments in the store, and departmental income statements are prepared each year. Department no. 4 occupies 10,000 square feet of space on the first floor. Department no. 8 occupies 12,500 square feet of space on the third floor.

In allocating occupancy cost among the various departments, the accountant has determined that the average annual occupancy cost per square foot is $2.14 ($128,400 ÷ 60,000); therefore Department no. 4 has been charged with $21,400 of occupancy cost and Department no. 8 with $26,750, on the basis of space occupied.

Ellen Ward, the manager of Department no. 8, feels that this allocation is unreasonable. She has made a study of rental prices being charged for similar property in the area and finds the following:

**Average Yearly Rental
per Square Foot**

First-floor space	$5.00
Second-floor space	3.00
Third-floor space	2.00

On the basis of this evidence, Ward argues that the charge to her department should be made on the *relative value* of space on each floor.

Instructions
a Comment on the validity of Ward's position.
b On the basis of Ward's findings, how much occupancy cost per year should be charged to Department no. 4 and to Department no. 8? Show computations.

23B-3 Joe Miller owns an apple orchard, from which he harvested and sold during the current year 200,000 pounds of apples. The price received varied in accordance with the grade of apple, as shown in the table below:

Grade of Apple	Pounds	Price per Pound	Receipts
Superior	40,000	$0.24	$ 9,600
Medium	100,000	0.108	10,800
Cooking	60,000	0.06	3,600
	200,000		$24,000

Miller's expenses for the year, as taken from his accounting records, are given below:

	Dollars	Per Pound
Growing expenses	$ 6,000	$0.03
Harvesting expenses	4,000	0.02
Packing and shipping:		
Superior (40,000 pounds)	$2,000	0.05
Medium (100,000 pounds)	4,000	0.04
Cooking (60,000 pounds)	1,800 7,800	0.03
Total expenses	$17,800	

Miller asked a friend, who was taking an accounting course at a nearby university, to determine his income from each grade of apple. The friend gave him the following statement:

	Total	Superior	Medium	Cooking
Sales	$24,000	$9,600	$10,800	$ 3,600
Expenses:				
Growing	$ 6,000	$1,200	$ 3,000	$ 1,800
Harvesting	4,000	800	2,000	1,200
Packing and shipping	7,800	2,000	4,000	1,800
Total expenses	$17,800	$4,000	$ 9,000	$ 4,800
Net income (or loss)	$ 6,200	$5,600	$ 1,800	$(1,200)

After studying this statement, Miller remarked to a neighbor, "I made a lot of money on my superiors and a little bit on the mediums, but I should have dumped the cooking apples in the river; they cost me more than I got for them!"

Instructions
a Do you agree with Miller's remark to his neighbor? Discuss.
b Prepare an income statement in a form that will show the contribution of each grade of apples to overhead (indirect expenses of growing and harvesting). Packing and shipping expenses should be considered direct expenses. Use separate columns for Total, Superior, Medium, and Cooking. Comment on the conclusion to be drawn as to the contribution of the cooking apples.
c Prepare an income statement showing *net income* for each grade of apple by allocating growing and harvesting expenses on the basis of the *relative sales value* of each grade.

23B-4 The summarized adjusted trial balance shown below was prepared from the records of Hyde & Rogers, a retailing partnership, at the end of July of the current year. The partnership keeps separate departmental accounts for sales and cost of goods sold.

	Debit	Credit
Accumulated depreciation		$ 447,900
Administrative expense	$ 69,900	
Advertising expense	52,800	
Buildings and equipment	1,014,300	
Buying expense	60,000	
Cost of goods sold: Dept. A	297,000	
Cost of goods sold: Dept. B	243,000	
Current assets	321,000	
Current liabilities		128,100
Hyde, capital, June 30		258,000
Interest expense	1,800	
Land	75,000	
Mortgage payable		360,000
Net sales: Dept. A		540,000
Net sales: Dept. B		360,000
Occupancy expense	66,000	
Rogers, capital, June 30		192,000
Selling expense	85,200	
	$2,286,000	$2,286,000

An analysis of operating expenses during July indicates that the following amounts in each class of expense are directly chargeable to the departments. (The allocation basis of the indirect portion of each class of expense is shown in brackets.)

	Direct Expenses		Indirect Expenses
	Dept. A	Dept. B	
Administrative expense (8 to 5 ratio)	$18,000	$ 9,000	$42,900
Advertising expense (on basis of net sales)	21,000	15,000	16,800
Buying expense (on basis of cost of goods sold) . .	21,900	16,500	21,600
Occupancy expense (equally)	1,500	3,000	61,500
Selling expense (on basis of net sales)	35,400	21,600	28,200

The partnership agreement provides that net income shall be divided as follows: Hyde, 60%; Rogers, 40%. The partners made no withdrawals during July.

Instructions
a Prepare a departmental expense allocation sheet for the month of July. Use the form illustrated on page 820.
b Prepare a departmental income statement for July showing contribution to indirect expenses. Use the form illustrated on page 823. Show the division of

net income among the partners below the net income figure in the income statement.

c Prepare a condensed income statement for July, assuming that both direct and indirect expenses are allocated to the departments. Show a single figure for operating expenses. Does this statement suggest that Department B should be eliminated?

23B-5 For many years the Contour Furniture Company has operated a store near downtown Los Angeles. Early in Year 10, the company decided to open a branch store in Fresno and to use a decentralized accounting system for the branch. Both the branch and the home office use a perpetual inventory system. During the month of February the following transactions (given in summary form) were completed by the branch:

Feb.   **1** The home office sent $10,000 cash to the branch to be used as a working fund and authorized the branch manager to sign a lease on a store.

Feb.   **2** The branch manager signed the lease and paid rent for February, $2,000 (debit Operating Expense on branch records).

Feb.   **3** Received merchandise from home office, $14,400 (debit Inventory on branch records; credit inventory on home office records).

Feb.   **5** Purchased merchandise on credit from local factory, $13,600 (debit Inventory on branch records).

Feb. **10** Received office equipment from home office, $3,000. The Office Equipment account is carried on the records of the home office.

Feb. **12** Borrowed $6,000 from local bank and deposited balance in branch checking account.

Feb. **28** Sales during February: cash, $8,400; credit, $24,200.

Feb. **28** Payments to merchandise creditors, $8,000.

Feb. **28** Collections on accounts receivable, $11,500.

Feb. **28** Paid operating expenses, $3,300.

Feb. **28** Sent cash of $9,000 to home office. Returned to home office damaged sofa, which had been billed to the branch at $350.

Feb. **28** Home office notified branch that operating expenses allocated to the branch for the month of February amounted to $840. This included depreciation on office equipment and other expenses (such as advertising) paid by the home office. These expenses were originally recorded by the home office in the Operating Expense account.

Feb. **28** Cost of goods sold by the Fresno Branch during February amounted to $22,400.

Instructions

a Record the foregoing transactions in journal entry form in the records of the branch. (Explanations may be omitted from all journal entries in this problem.) Also prepare closing entries. Compute the balance at February 28 in the Home Office account which appears in the accounts of the branch.

b Select the transactions which should be recorded in the records of the home office (including entry to record branch net income) and prepare entries to record them. Ignore closing entries. Compute the balance in the Fresno Branch account at February 28 which appears in the accounts of the home office.

BUSINESS DECISION PROBLEM 23

Brit Dalby, owner of Dalby Drug Company, is considering the advisability of dropping all services in his store that are not pharmaceutical in nature and concentrating on the drug business. At the present time, in addition to drugs, Dalby has a fountain and handles various general merchandise such as magazines, candy, toys, and cosmetics. During the past year, the sales and cost of goods sold for his store were as follows:

	Total	Drugs	Fountain	General Merchandise
Sales (net)	$637,200	$480,000	$54,000	$103,200
Cost of goods sold	360,600	240,000	43,200	77,400

Dalby has studied trade association studies summarizing the reports of other store owners who have made similar decisions. They report that after dropping fountain operations, drug sales declined an average of 10% and sales of general merchandise fell 8%. Reports from store owners who discontinued general merchandise operation, but continued to operate a fountain, indicate that drug sales fell by an average of 4% and fountain sales declined by $7\frac{1}{2}$%. If Dalby Drug Company discontinued general merchandise operation it could lease the surplus floor space for $3,000 per month to another business which would use it as a storage facility.

At the present time Dalby employs three pharmacists at combined annual salaries of $90,000, and a fountain man at $12,000 per year. It is a rule of the trade that one pharmacist is required for every $160,000 of annual drug sales. The fountain man spends about 40% of his time stocking shelves and selling general merchandise items. If he were not there, a pharmacist would have to do this work and Dalby estimates that drug sales would decline an additional 2% (of present sales) as a result of inconvenience to customers.

The pharmacists have stated they would not be willing to take over the fountain operation, but Dalby believes that he could employ student help at a cost of $6,000 per year if the general merchandise sales were dropped. Dalby estimates that if the fountain were discontinued he might realize about $4,800 from the sale of fountain equipment, but he would have to spend about this amount in remodeling. He also considers that the effect on indirect operating expenses as a result of dropping either department would be negligible.

Instructions

a Determine the departmental contribution to indirect expenses during the past year.

b Prepare an analysis of the estimated dollar benefit or loss that might be expected to result if Dalby discontinued the fountain. Prepare a similar analysis assuming discontinuance of the general merchandise operation. What would be your advice to Dalby?

24 Accounting for Manufacturing Operations

In preceding chapters we have considered accounting principles and procedures applicable to nonmanufacturing businesses—firms engaged in buying and selling merchandise, or in furnishing services. Another large and important category of business operation is *manufacturing.* All of the accounting principles and most of the accounting procedures we have discussed are equally applicable to manufacturers. Firms engaged in manufacturing, however, face some special accounting problems and require additional accounting procedures to measure, control, and report factory production costs.

Accounting problems of manufacturers

A typical manufacturing firm buys raw materials and parts and converts them into a finished product. The raw materials and parts purchased by an aircraft manufacturer, for example, include sheet aluminum, jet engines, and a variety of electronic gear and control instruments. The completed airplanes assembled from these components are the *finished goods* of the aircraft manufacturer. The terms *raw materials* and *finished goods,* as used in accounting, are defined from the viewpoint of each manufacturing firm. Sheet aluminum, for example, is a raw material from the viewpoint of an aircraft company, but it is a finished product of an aluminum company.

In converting raw materials into finished goods, the manufacturer employs factory labor, uses machinery, and incurs many other manufacturing costs, such as heat, light, and power, machinery repairs, and supervisory salaries. These production costs are added to the cost of raw materials to determine the cost of the finished goods manufactured during any given period. The accounting records of a manufacturing firm must be expanded to include ledger accounts for these various types of factory costs. Financial statements must also be changed to reflect the costs of manufacturing and several new classes of inventories. At any given moment, a manufacturer will have on hand a stock of raw materials, finished goods awaiting shipment and sale, and partially completed products in various stages of manufacture. Inventories of each of these classes of items must be taken at the end of each accounting period in order to measure the cost of goods that have been completed and sold during the period.

The accounting records of a manufacturer are more complex than those of the merchandising or service business because an additional function is involved. The merchandising firm is engaged in distributing goods or services. The manufacturer has two major functions: the production of finished goods and the sale of the goods produced. Many of the accounting problems of a manufacturer relate to the production function; however, manufacturing firms also incur selling and administrative expenses comparable to those of merchandising companies.

DETERMINING THE COST OF GOODS SOLD   The principal difference in accounting for a merchandising business and for a manufacturing business is found in computing the cost of goods sold. In a merchandising business the cost of goods sold is computed as follows:

$$\text{Beginning Inventory of Merchandise} + \text{Purchases of Merchandise} - \text{Ending Inventory of Merchandise} = \text{Cost of Goods Sold}$$

In a manufacturing business the cost of goods sold is determined by a parallel computation, as follows:

$$\text{Beginning Inventory of Finished Goods} + \text{Cost of Goods Manufactured} - \text{Ending Inventory of Finished Goods} = \text{Cost of Goods Sold}$$

Comparison of these two similar computations shows that the *cost of goods manufactured* in a manufacturing company is in a sense the equivalent of *purchases of merchandise* in a merchandising business. This point is further emphasized by comparing the income statements of a merchandising company and a manufacturing company.

COMPARISON OF INCOME STATEMENTS FOR MANUFACTURING AND MERCHANDISING COMPANIES   The treatment of sales, selling expenses, general administrative expenses, and income taxes is the same on the income statement of a manufacturing company as for a merchandising company.

The only difference in the two partial income statements shown below lies in the cost of goods sold section. In the income statement of the manufacturing company, Cost of Goods Manufactured replaces the item labeled Purchases in the income statement of the merchandising company.

A MERCHANDISING COMPANY
Partial Income Statement
For the Current Year

Sales		$1,000,000
Cost of goods sold:		
Beginning inventory of merchandise	$300,000	
Purchases.	600,000	
Cost of goods available for sale	$900,000	
Less: Ending inventory of merchandise	250,000	
Cost of goods sold.		650,000
Gross profit on sales		$ 350,000

A MANUFACTURING COMPANY
Partial Income Statement
For the Current Year

Sales		$1,000,000
Cost of goods sold:		
Beginning inventory of finished goods	$300,000	
Cost of goods manufactured (Exhibit A)	600,000	
Cost of goods available for sale	$900,000	
Less: Ending inventory of finished goods	250,000	
Cost of goods sold.		650,000
Gross profit on sales		$ 350,000

STATEMENT OF COST OF GOODS MANUFACTURED   The principal new item in the illustrated income statement for a manufacturing company is the item: "Cost of goods manufactured . . . $600,000." This amount was determined from the Statement of Cost of Goods Manufactured, a statement prepared to accompany and support the income statement. This statement is illustrated in condensed form on page 850.

Observe that the final amount of $600,000 on the statement of cost of goods manufactured shown on page 850 is carried forward to the income statement and is used in determining the cost of goods sold, as illustrated in the income statement for the manufacturing company above.

		A MANUFACTURING COMPANY	*Exhibit A*

Statement of Cost of Goods Manufactured

For the Current Year

Goods in process inventory, beginning of year	. . . .		$ 70,000
Raw materials used:			
Beginning raw materials inventory		$ 50,000	
Purchases of raw materials	$100,000		
Less: Purchase returns and allowances	3,000	97,000	
Transportation-in		5,000	
Cost of raw materials available for use		$152,000	
Less: Ending raw materials inventory		42,000	
Cost of raw materials used		$110,000	
Direct labor		230,000	
Factory overhead (detail omitted)		250,000	
Total manufacturing costs			590,000
Total cost of goods in process during the year			$660,000
Less: Goods in process inventory, end of year			60,000
Cost of goods manufactured			$600,000

Manufacturing costs

To gain a better understanding of how the cost of goods manufactured is determined, we must now examine the nature of the costs incurred in a manufacturing plant. To paint a clear picture of the major elements of manufacturing costs and to distinguish clearly between manufacturing costs on the one hand and administrative and selling expenses on the other, assume that our hypothetical manufacturing company owns five separate buildings, each used exclusively for a single function of the business. These five buildings, as shown in the sketch on page 851, consist of (1) a raw materials warehouse, (2) a factory building, (3) a finished goods warehouse, (4) a general office building, and (5) a building housing the sales division of the company.

    The raw materials received from suppliers are first placed in the raw materials warehouse; as these raw materials are needed in the production process they are moved into the factory, as shown by the arrow connecting these two buildings. In the factory building the raw materials are converted (cut up, processed, and assembled) into finished goods. Each unit of finished product is moved immediately upon completion out of the factory into the finished goods warehouse. As sales orders are obtained from customers, shipments are made from the finished goods warehouse.

    Each unit of finished goods leaving the factory includes three elements of manufacturing cost. Each of the three cost elements will now be discussed in some detail.[1]

[1] The Committee on Terminology of the American Institute of Certified Public Accountants has recommended that ". . . items entering into the computation of cost of manufacturing, such as material, labor and overhead, should be described as *costs* and not as *expenses.*"

Functional divisions of a manufacturing company

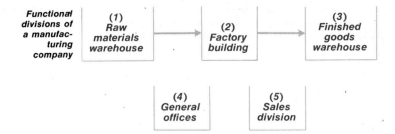

First let us concentrate our attention upon the factory building, for it is here that all manufacturing costs are incurred. These costs are classified into three groups:

1 Raw materials used

2 Direct labor

3 Factory overhead

RAW MATERIALS The cost of raw materials (also called **direct materials**) represents the delivered cost of materials and parts which enter into and become part of the finished product. In thinking about the elements of manufacturing cost during a given period, we are interested in the cost of raw materials **used** rather than the amount of raw materials purchased. Purchases of raw materials flow into the raw materials warehouse, but the consumption or use of raw materials consists of the materials moved from the raw materials warehouse into the factory to be processed. The computation of the cost of raw materials used was illustrated in the statement of cost of goods manufactured on page 850. The raw materials section of that statement is presented again at this point to emphasize the flow of cost for materials.

Computing the cost of raw materials used

Raw materials used:		
Beginning raw materials inventory		$ 50,000
Purchases of raw materials	$100,000	
Less: Purchase returns and allowances	3,000	97,000
Transportation-in		5,000
Cost of raw materials available for use		$152,000
Less: Ending raw materials inventory		42,000
Cost of raw materials used		$110,000

Since the cost of raw materials used is computed by subtracting the amount of raw materials on hand at the end of the period from the total of the beginning inventory plus the purchases of raw materials during the period, any raw materials which were stolen, spoiled, or lost will be included in the residual amount labeled "cost of raw materials used." Inability to spotlight shortages or wastage of materials is one of the weaknesses inherent in the periodic inventory system.

In order to have the information for computing the cost of raw materials used readily available in the accounting records, the following ledger accounts are maintained:

<table>
<tr><td></td><td colspan="2">Raw Materials Inventory</td><td colspan="2">Transportation-in</td></tr>
<tr><td>Ledger accounts for raw materials</td><td>50,000</td><td></td><td>5,000</td><td></td></tr>
<tr><td></td><td colspan="2">Purchases of Raw Materials</td><td colspan="2">Raw Materials Returns and Allowances</td></tr>
<tr><td></td><td>100,000</td><td></td><td></td><td>3,000</td></tr>
</table>

The Raw Materials Inventory account is used only at the end of the year, when a physical count of raw materials on hand is made, and the cost of these materials on hand is recorded by a debit to the Raw Materials Inventory account. The offsetting credit is made to the Manufacturing account, which will be explained later in this chapter. The other three accounts illustrated are used throughout the year to accumulate (1) the purchases of raw materials, (2) the transportation charges on inbound shipments of raw materials, and (3) the returns to suppliers of unsatisfactory or excessive raw materials.

DIRECT LABOR COST   The second major element of manufacturing costs is called *direct labor* and consists of the wages paid to factory employees who work directly on the product being manufactured. Direct labor costs include the payroll costs of machine operators, assemblers, and those who work on the product by hand or with tools, but not the wages of indirect workers such as plant watchmen, janitors, timekeepers, and supervisors.

What is the reason for separating the costs of direct labor and indirect labor? Direct labor is expended in converting raw materials into finished goods. If factory output is to be increased, it will be necessary to employ more direct workers and direct labor costs will rise. If factory output is to be reduced, any existing hours of overtime will be reduced and workers may be discharged. Direct labor costs vary directly with changes in the level of output; consequently, in planning operations for future periods, management can estimate the direct labor cost required for any desired volume of production.

Indirect labor, on the other hand, is much less inclined to rise and fall with changes in factory output. An increase or decrease of 10%, for example, in the number of units being produced will ordinarily not cause any change in the salary of the factory superintendent or in the number of janitors or guards. A large change in the volume of production will, of course, have some impact upon indirect labor costs.

FACTORY OVERHEAD   *Factory overhead* includes all costs incurred in the factory other than the costs of raw materials and direct labor. Included in factory overhead are such costs as the following:

1 *Indirect labor*
  a Supervision
  b Timekeeping
  c Janitorial and maintenance
  d Production scheduling and quality control
  e Plant security service

2 *Occupancy cost*
  a Depreciation of buildings
  b Insurance on buildings
  c Property taxes on land and buildings
  d Repairs and maintenance of buildings
  e Heat, light, and power

3 *Machinery and equipment costs*
  a Depreciation of machinery and equipment
  b Insurance on machinery and equipment
  c Property taxes on machinery and equipment
  d Repairs and maintenance of machinery and equipment
  e Small tools used in the factory

This is not a complete list of factory overhead costs; in fact, it is the impossibility of preparing a complete list that leads accountants to define factory overhead as *all costs incurred in the factory other than raw material and direct labor.* A significant characteristic of factory overhead is that these costs cannot be directly related to units of product as can the costs of direct labor and direct material. In a factory producing two different products such as radios and television sets, it is possible to measure fairly accurately the costs of raw material and direct labor applied to each product, but the nature of factory overhead costs (such as insurance and repairs to buildings) is such that they cannot be associated directly with the particular articles being produced. For this reason, raw materials and direct labor are sometimes referred to as the *direct costs* or *prime costs* of manufacturing in contrast to factory overhead, which may be regarded as an *indirect cost.* Alternative titles for factory overhead include *indirect manufacturing cost, factory burden, manufacturing burden,* and *manufacturing overhead.* The total of direct labor and factory overhead costs is frequently referred to as *processing costs* or *conversion costs.*

Certain costs such as insurance, property taxes, telephone, and salaries of executives may be applicable in part to factory operations and in part to administrative and selling functions of the company. In such cases the costs may be apportioned among factory overhead, general administrative expense, and selling expense accounts at the time incurred; or as an alternative, the costs may be recorded in a single ledger account and the apportionment made later through the use of working papers.

The flow of costs in a manufacturing business

The sketch shown below emphasizes the flow of costs in a manufacturing business and some of the principal concepts appearing in the financial statements.

Raw materials warehouse

The cost of raw materials used consists of:
    Beginning inventory of raw materials
    Plus the delivered cost of net purchases
    Minus the ending inventory of raw materials

Factory

Manufacturing costs consist of:
    Cost of raw materials used
    Direct labor
    Factory overhead

The cost of goods manufactured, which refers to the cost of units completed and moved out of the factory, consists of:
    Beginning inventory of goods in process
    Plus manufacturing costs
    Minus ending inventory of goods in process

Finished goods warehouse

The cost of goods sold consists of:
    Beginning inventory of finished goods
    Plus cost of goods manufactured
    Minus ending inventory of finished goods

Shipments of finished goods to customers are made from the finished goods warehouse.

PRODUCT AND PERIOD COSTS Costs that become a part of goods in process and finished goods inventories are called *product costs.* In theory, product costs include all costs associated with the production and flow of manufactured goods up to the point where the goods are completed and ready for sale. Product costs become a part of the asset valuations assigned to inventories at the end of each accounting period. They are deducted from revenue as the cost of goods sold in the period when the goods to which they attach are sold.

Costs that are charged to expense in the period in which they are incurred are called *period costs.* Such costs are not related to the production and flow of product but are deducted from revenue immediately, on the assumption that the associated benefits expire in the same period as the expenditures are made.

The exact dividing line between product and period costs is not always clear. Traditionally, expenditures relating to the manufacturing function are considered product costs, and those relating to the selling and administrative functions are considered period costs. In some cases it is difficult to determine whether a particular cost relates to manufacturing or administrative functions. For example, the cost of maintaining a cost accounting department, or a personnel department, or a plant guard service may be treated by some companies as factory overhead (product costs) and by other firms as administrative expense (period cost). These variations in accounting practice, however, stem more from differences of interpretation than from lack of agreement as to theoretical distinctions.

FULL (ABSORPTION) COSTING AND VARIABLE (DIRECT) COSTING The process of treating as product costs all costs relating to the manufacturing function of a business is known as *full* or *absorption costing.* In recent years an alternative concept, called *variable,* or *direct costing,* has received considerable attention and some support. Under this procedure, product costs are limited to raw materials, direct labor, and that portion of factory overhead that *varies directly* with changes in the volume of products manufactured. The *fixed* portion of factory overhead, that is, manufacturing costs that continue regardless of changes in the volume of output, are not included in inventories but are deducted from revenue in the period in which they are incurred. It is apparent that when variable costing is used inventory valuations will be lower and reported net income will differ period by period, since many costs normally converted into inventory values will be charged to expense immediately. We shall discuss variable costing and its implications in more detail in Chapter 28. Throughout this chapter the full costing concept is used; that is, all elements of factory overhead are included as a part of the cost of goods manufactured, and thus are included in the valuation assigned to inventories of goods in process and finished goods.

Additional accounts needed by a manufacturing firm

A considerable number of ledger accounts is required by a manufacturing firm in order to measure and report costs of production. Accounts relating to sales, selling expenses, administrative expenses, ownership equity, and many common kinds of assets and liabilities are handled in the same manner as in a merchandising or service business. However, manufacturing involves some additional asset accounts, and a number of new income statement accounts.

CURRENT ASSET ACCOUNTS In place of the single inventory account found on the balance sheet of a retail or wholesale business, a manufacturing firm has three separate inventory accounts:

1 *Raw materials inventory.* This account represents the unused portion of the raw materials purchased. The amount is determined at year-end by taking a physical count of the raw materials which have not yet been placed in production. In our earlier example of the company with five buildings, this inventory would be located in the raw materials warehouse. As a matter of convenience, *factory supplies* on hand (oil, grease, sweeping compounds) acquired for use in maintaining and servicing the factory building and machinery are often merged with raw materials.

2 *Goods in process inventory.* This inventory consists of the partially completed goods on hand in the factory at year-end, determined by a physical count. The cost of these partially manufactured goods is determined by estimating the costs of the raw materials, direct labor, and factory overhead associated with these units. The goods in process inventory appears on the balance sheet as a current asset and also appears on the statement of cost of goods manufactured (page 850).

3 Finished goods inventory. This account shows the cost of finished goods on hand and awaiting sale to customers as of the end of the year. The cost of these finished units is composed of the costs of raw material used, direct labor, and factory overhead. The method of pricing finished goods will be discussed later in this chapter. In the balance sheet, the finished goods inventory appears as a current asset; it is also used in computing the cost of goods sold in the income statement.

PLANT AND EQUIPMENT ACCOUNTS Manufacturing companies generally invest a large part of their total capital in plant and equipment, including tools, dies, conveyors, etc. In recent years the trend toward automation of production has led to particularly heavy investment in manufacturing facilities. Depreciation of the plant and equipment is one of the costs included in factory overhead; the cost of the plant and equipment is thereby gradually transformed into the cost of goods manufactured. If a company rents or leases its plant and equipment, the monthly rentals paid would be included in factory overhead.

Because of the great variety of items of manufacturing equipment, it is customary to maintain a subsidiary plant ledger as described in Chapter 12. On the balance sheet the caption of Plant and Equipment, or Machinery and Equipment, is often used to summarize all types of productive facilities.

RESEARCH AND DEVELOPMENT EXPENDITURES (R & D) Most manufacturing companies find that continuous operation of an extensive program of research and development is essential merely to maintain a competitive position in their industry. Especially in recent years, success in the field of manufacturing seems to have been closely related to leadership in research and development of new products. As explained in Chapter 12, a diversity of accounting practice prevailed in the past, with some companies accumulating research and development costs in intangible asset accounts and other similar companies treating these expenditures as period costs to be deducted from revenue in the year incurred. Fortunately, this diversity of practice was ended by action of the Financial Accounting Standards Board, which ruled that all research and development expenditures must be charged to expense in the year incurred.[2]

RAW MATERIAL, DIRECT LABOR, AND FACTORY OVERHEAD The accounts required for recording the three major elements of production cost have already been discussed. In recording factory overhead a separate account must be created for each type of indirect manufacturing cost (Depreciation of Machinery, Repairs, Timekeeping, etc.) as indicated on page 853. If there are a great many of these factory overhead accounts, it is convenient to transfer them to a subsidiary ledger which will be controlled by a general ledger account entitled Factory Overhead.

[2] *Statement of Financial Accounting Standards No. 2,* "Accounting for Research and Development Costs," Financial Accounting Standards Board (Stamford, Conn.: 1974), par. 12.

THE MANUFACTURING ACCOUNT Last in our list of ledger accounts peculiar to a manufacturing business is a summary account called **Manufacturing,** which is used at the end of each period to summarize the various elements of factory cost and to determine the cost of goods manufactured. The balance of this account represents the cost of goods manufactured during the period. The Manufacturing account is closed by transferring its $600,000 debit balance to the Income Summary account, as shown in the illustration below. This $600,000 is the cost of the units completed during the year. It is entered as a debit in the Income Summary account so that we can compare the costs and revenue for the year.

Manufacturing

Note kinds of costs summarized in Manufacturing account						
	19—			19—		
	Dec. 31	Beginning goods in process inventory	70,000	Dec. 31	Ending goods in process inventory	60,000
	31	Beginning raw materials inventory	50,000	31	Ending raw materials inventory	42,000
	31	Purchases of raw materials	100,000	31	Raw materials purchase returns and allowances	3,000
	31	Transportation-in	5,000	31	Cost of goods manufactured, to Income Summary	600,000
	31	Direct labor	230,000			
	31	Factory overhead (total)	250,000			
			705,000			705,000

Income Summary

	19—			19—		
	Dec. 31	Beginning finished goods inventory	300,000	Dec. 31	Ending finished goods inventory	250,000
	31	Cost of goods manufactured	600,000			

It is important to distinguish between the terms **cost of goods manufactured** and **total manufacturing costs.** Cost of goods manufactured means the cost of the units of finished product completed during the period and transferred from the factory to the warehouse for finished goods. Total manufacturing costs, on the other hand, include the cost of raw materials used, direct labor, and factory overhead for the period, whether the units worked on have been completed or are still in process at the end of the period. As an extreme example, consider a manufacturing plant engaged in the construction of a single huge airplane. During the first year of work on the plane the manufacturing costs are as follows:

Compare	Cost of raw materials used	$ 300,000
"total man-	Direct labor	700,000
ufacturing		
costs" with	Factory overhead	1,000,000
"cost of	Total manufacturing costs	$2,000,000
goods man-		
ufactured"	Less: Goods in process inventory, ending	2,000,000
	Cost of goods manufactured	$ –0–

The cost of goods manufactured is zero in the above illustration because no products (airplanes) were completed during the year, and we have defined the term *cost of goods manufactured* to mean the manufacturing cost of units that have been *completed and moved out* of the factory during the year.

Working papers for a manufacturing business

The work sheet for a merchandising business illustrated in Chapter 5 can be adapted for use in a manufacturing company merely by adding a pair of columns for the data which will appear in the statement of cost of goods manufactured. Illustrative working papers for the Chemical Manufacturing Corporation are presented on page 861. As a means of simplifying the illustration, it is assumed that all adjusting entries were made before the trial balance was entered on the work sheet and that numerous factory overhead and operating expense accounts have been combined. The adjustments columns are, therefore, omitted and the illustration begins with an Adjusted Trial Balance. Adjusting entries for a manufacturing business do not differ significantly from those previously described for a merchandising business.

TREATMENT OF INVENTORIES IN THE WORKING PAPERS Since the Manufacturing columns are the distinctive feature of this work sheet, they require close study, especially the handling of the inventory accounts.

1 The beginning inventory of raw materials and the beginning inventory of goods in process have become part of the cost of goods manufactured and are, therefore, carried from the Adjusted Trial Balance debit column to the Manufacturing debit column.

2 The ending inventories of raw materials and of goods in process must be recorded as assets and must be shown as a deduction in determining the cost of goods manufactured. This step requires the listing of the two inventories as debits in the Balance Sheet columns and as credits in the Manufacturing columns.

The nature of the Manufacturing columns may be clarified by a brief summary of the items placed in each column. The debit column includes the beginning inventories of raw materials and goods in process, plus all the manufacturing costs of the period. The credit column contains credits for the ending inventories of raw materials and goods in process. The total of the amounts in the debit column exceeds the total of the credit column by $371,800. This debit balance represents the cost of goods manufactured and is extended as a debit to the Income Statement columns.

Note that the beginning and ending inventories of finished goods appear in the Income Statement columns but not in the Manufacturing columns. The illustration earlier in this chapter (A Manufacturing Company), involving separate buildings for factory operations and for the storage of finished goods was designed to emphasize that changes in the finished goods inventory are not a factor in computing the cost of goods that are manufactured in the factory.

Financial statements

Four statements for the Chemical Manufacturing Corporation prepared from the illustrated work sheet on page 861 are presented on pages 863 to 865. These statements are the balance sheet (Exhibit A, page 863), statement of retained earnings (Exhibit B, page 864), income statement (Exhibit C, page 864), and statement of cost of goods manufactured (Exhibit D, page 865).

Closing the accounts at the end of the period

The entries to close the accounts of a manufacturing company can be taken directly from the work sheet. A Manufacturing account is opened by debiting it with the total of all the amounts listed in the Manufacturing debit column of the work sheet. A second entry is made crediting the Manufacturing account with the total of all the accounts listed in the Manufacturing credit column. These two entries serve to close out all the operating accounts used in computing the cost of goods manufactured. The next step in the closing procedure is to transfer the balance of the Manufacturing account to the Income Summary. Note that this balance is the cost of goods manufactured. Inventories of finished goods and all expenses are closed to the Income Summary account. Finally, the balances in the Income Summary and Dividends accounts are closed to Retained Earnings. The closing entries at December 31, Year 2, for the Chemical Manufacturing Corporation are illustrated below and on page 860.

Closing entries for a manufacturing firm	***Manufacturing***	***403,800***
	Goods in Process Inventory (beginning)	*18,000*
	Raw Materials Inventory (beginning)	*10,000*
	Purchases of Raw Materials (net)	*101,000*
	Direct Labor	*171,750*
	Indirect Labor	*67,250*
	Rent on Plant Facilities	*12,000*
	Other Factory Overhead Costs	*23,800*

To close manufacturing accounts having debit balances.

Goods in Process Inventory (ending)	20,000	
Raw Materials Inventory (ending)	12,000	
Manufacturing		32,000

To record ending inventories of goods in process and raw
materials.

Income Summary	542,260	
Finished Goods Inventory (beginning)		55,000
Advertising		14,000
Sales Salaries		32,000
Other Selling Expenses		3,400
Administrative Salaries		40,000
Uncollectible Accounts Expense		2,700
Other General and Administrative Expenses		11,900
Interest Expense		5,000
Income Taxes		6,460
Manufacturing		371,800

To close beginning inventory of finished goods, all expense
accounts, and Manufacturing account to Income Summary.

Sales (net)	500,000	
Finished Goods Inventory (ending)	62,800	
Income Summary		562,800

To close Sales account and to record ending finished goods
inventory.

Income Summary	20,540	
Retained Earnings		20,540

To transfer balance in Income Summary (net income) to retained
earnings.

Retained Earnings	16,000	
Dividends		16,000

To close the Dividends account.

Valuation of inventories in a manufacturing business

Under the periodic inventory system described in this chapter, a manufacturing business determines inventory amounts on the basis of a physical count of raw materials, goods in process, and finished goods at the
end of each accounting period. When the physical quantity of raw materials on hand has been established, the cost of the raw materials inventory
is determined in the same manner as an inventory of merchandise in a
trading company. Cost is readily determinable by reference to purchase
invoices. If the raw materials inventory is to be priced at the lower of cost
or market, the "market" prices to be used are the current replacement
costs for the materials on hand.

CHEMICAL MANUFACTURING CORPORATION
Working Papers
For the Year Ended December 31, Year 2

	Adjusted Trial Balance		Manufacturing		Income Statement		Retained Earnings		Balance Sheet	
	Dr	Cr	Dr	Cr	Dr	Cr	Dr	Cr	Dr	Cr
Cash	20,600								20,600	
Accounts receivable	40,000								40,000	
Allowance for doubtful accounts		1,000								1,000
Inventories, beginning:										
Finished goods	55,000				55,000					
Goods in process	18,000		18,000							
Raw materials	10,000		10,000							
Machinery and equipment	136,000								136,000	
Accum. depr.: mach. and equip.		40,000								40,000
Furniture and fixtures	14,000								14,000	
Accum. depr.: furn. and fix.		4,200								4,200
Patents	8,000								8,000	
Franchises and trademarks	12,000								12,000	
Accounts payable		40,200								40,200
Accrued factory payroll		800								800
Income taxes payable		6,460								6,460
Notes payable, 9%, due Year 5		80,000								80,000
Capital stock, $10 par value		100,000								100,000
Retained earnings, beginning		48,200						48,200		
Dividends	16,000						16,000			
Sales (net)		500,000				500,000				
Purchases of raw materials (net)	101,000		101,000							
Direct labor	171,750		171,750							
Indirect labor	67,250		67,250							
Rent on plant facilities	12,000		12,000							
Other factory overhead costs	23,800		23,800							
Advertising	14,000				14,000					
Sales salaries	32,000				32,000					
Other selling expenses	3,400				3,400					
Administrative salaries	40,000				40,000					
Uncollectible accounts expense	2,700				2,700					
Other general and adm. expenses	11,900				11,900					
Interest expense	5,000				5,000					
Income taxes	6,460				6,460					
	820,860	820,860								
Inventories, ending:										
Finished goods						62,800			62,800	
Goods in process				20,000					20,000	
Raw materials				12,000					12,000	
Cost of goods manufactured				371,800	371,800					
			403,800	403,800						
Net income					20,540			20,540		
					562,800	562,800				
Retained earnings, ending							52,740			52,740
							68,740	68,740	325,400	325,400

Determining the cost of an inventory of goods in process and an inventory of finished goods is usually a more difficult process. Cost cannot be derived merely by pulling a purchase invoice out of the files. If a manufacturing plant produces only a single product, the cost per unit for the finished goods inventory can be computed by dividing the cost of goods manufactured by the number of units produced. For example, if the cost of goods manufactured were $100,000 in a given year, during which the factory turned out 1,000 identical units, the cost per unit would be $100. Most factories, however, produce more than one product, and the unit cost of each product must be determined by deriving from the accounting records the approximate amount of raw materials, direct labor, and factory overhead applicable to each unit. In this situation the determination of cost of a unit of the work in process at the year-end requires the following steps:

1 Estimate the cost of the raw materials in the partially completed units.
2 Add the estimated direct labor cost incurred.
3 Add an appropriate amount of factory overhead.

This same procedure of computing a total cost by combining the three elements of manufacturing cost is followed in pricing the finished goods inventory.

The raw material cost included in a unit of goods in process or a unit of finished goods may be established by reference to the engineering specification for the article. The cost of the direct labor embodied in each unit may be estimated on the basis of tests and observations by supervisors of the direct labor time required per unit of output. In other words, both raw material cost and direct labor cost *are directly associated* with units of product.

The third element of manufacturing cost to be included in pricing the inventory of goods in process is factory overhead, and this cost element *is not directly related* to units of output. Factory overhead, however, is usually related to the amount of direct labor. A factory overhead rate may, therefore, be computed by dividing the total factory overhead for the period by the total direct labor cost for the same period. The resulting factory overhead rate is then applied to the direct labor cost of the goods in process to determine the amount of factory overhead to be included in the inventory cost. In the illustrated statement of cost of goods manufactured of the Chemical Manufacturing Corporation shown on page 865, *direct labor cost* is *$171,750* and *factory overhead* is *$103,050.*

The *factory overhead rate* is $103,050 ÷ $171,750, or 60% of direct labor cost. This 60% rate was used in determining the factory overhead cost in the ending inventories of goods in process and of finished goods, as shown at the bottom of page 865.

CHEMICAL MANUFACTURING CORPORATION   Exhibit A
Balance Sheet
December 31, Year 2

Assets

Current assets:

Cash		$ 20,600
Accounts receivable	$40,000	
Less: Allowance for doubtful accounts	1,000	39,000
Inventories:		
Finished goods	$62,800	
Goods in process.....	20,000	
Raw materials	12,000	94,800
Total current assets		$154,400

Plant and equipment:

	Cost	Accumulated Depreciation	Book Value	
Machinery and equipment	$136,000	$40,000	$96,000	
Furniture and fixtures.....	14,000	4,200	9,800	
	$150,000	$44,200		105,800

Intangible assets:		
Patents	$ 8,000	
Franchises and trademarks	12,000	20,000
Total assets		$280,200

Liabilities & Stockholders' Equity

Current liabilities:		
Accounts payable		$ 40,200
Accrued factory payroll		800
Income taxes payable		6,460
Total current liabilities		$ 47,460
Notes payable, 9%, due Year 5		80,000
Total liabilities		$127,460
Stockholders' equity:		
Capital stock, $10 par value; authorized and issued 10,000		
shares	$100,000	
Retained earnings (Exhibit B)	52,740	152,740
Total liabilities & stockholders' equity.....		$280,200

CHEMICAL MANUFACTURING CORPORATION   *Exhibit B*

Statement of Retained Earnings

For the Year Ended December 31, Year 2

Retained earnings, beginning of year	$48,200
Net income for the year (Exhibit C)	20,540
Subtotal	$68,740
Less: Dividends	16,000
Retained earnings, end of year	$52,740

CHEMICAL MANUFACTURING CORPORATION   *Exhibit C*

Income Statement

For the Year Ended December 31, Year 2

Net sales			$500,000
Cost of goods sold:			
Beginning finished goods inventory		$ 55,000	
Cost of goods manufactured (Exhibit D)		371,800	
Total cost of finished goods available for sale		$426,800	
Less: Ending finished goods inventory		62,800	
Cost of goods sold			364,000
Gross profit on sales			$136,000
Operating expenses:			
Selling expenses:			
Advertising	$14,000		
Sales salaries	32,000		
Other selling expenses	3,400		
Total selling expenses		$ 49,400	
General and administrative expenses:			
Administrative salaries	$40,000		
Uncollectible accounts expense	2,700		
Other general and administrative expenses	11,900		
Total general and administrative expenses		54,600	
Total operating expenses			104,000
Income from operations			$ 32,000
Less: Interest expense			5,000
Income before income taxes			$ 27,000
Income taxes			6,460
Net income			$ 20,540
Earnings per share of capital stock			$2.05

CHEMICAL MANUFACTURING CORPORATION *Exhibit D*
Statement of Cost of Goods Manufactured
For the Year Ended December 31, Year 2

Goods in process inventory, beginning of year			$ 18,000
Raw materials used:			
Beginning raw materials inventory		$ 10,000	
Purchases of raw materials (net)		101,000	
Cost of raw materials available for use		$111,000	
Less: Ending raw materials inventory		12,000	
Cost of raw materials used		$ 99,000	
Direct labor		171,750	
Factory overhead:			
Indirect labor	$67,250		
Rent on plant facilities	12,000		
Other factory overhead costs	23,800		
Total factory overhead		103,050	
Total manufacturing costs			373,800
Total cost of goods in process during the year			$391,800
Less: Goods in process inventory, end of year			20,000
Cost of goods manufactured			$371,800

CHEMICAL MANUFACTURING CORPORATION
Valuation of Ending Inventories
December 31, Year 2

	Prime Costs per Unit		Factory Overhead, 60% of Direct Labor Cost	Total Unit Cost	Units in Inventory	Total Cost of Inventory
Inventory	**Raw Materials**	**Direct Labor**				
Goods in process:						
Product D-3	$8	$10	$ 6	$24	500	$12,000
Product D-4	2	5	3	10	800	8,000
Total						$20,000
Finished goods:						
Product D-3	$8	$20	$12	$40	820	$32,800
Product D-4	6	15	9	30	1,000	30,000
Total						$62,800

Note the three cost elements in ending inventories

Cost accounting and perpetual inventories

The periodic system of inventory and the related accounting procedures described in this chapter are used by many small manufacturing companies, but these procedures have serious deficiencies and *they do not constitute a cost accounting system.* The shortcomings inherent in the use of periodic inventories by a manufacturing company include the following:

1 The estimates used in computing the inventories of goods in process and finished goods are rough and inexact. Any inaccuracy in pricing the inventories causes a corresponding error in net income for the period.

2 Taking and pricing inventories is so time-consuming that it usually is done only once a year; consequently, operating statements are not available to management at sufficiently frequent intervals.

3 Cost data available to management are not sufficiently detailed to afford a sound basis for control of operations.

The greater the number of products being manufactured, the more critical these deficiencies become. Management needs detailed day-to-day information on the costs of each product being manufactured. Decision making with respect to possible discontinuance of certain products or increases in the output of other articles requires current detailed reporting of cost data. An accurate determination of costs for individual products is also very useful in setting selling prices. Many progressive manufacturing companies achieve control of costs and operations by the preparation of budgets which indicate far in advance what the outlays for material, labor, and factory overhead *should* be.[3] The accounting records and procedures are so designed as to provide a steady flow of reports summarizing actual cost results for comparison with the budgeted figures. A key step in providing the cost information needed by management for planning and controlling manufacturing operations with optimum efficiency is the maintenance of perpetual inventories.

Cost accounting is a specialized field of accounting, with the objective of providing management with means of planning and controlling manufacturing operations. A cost accounting system is characterized by the maintenance of perpetual inventories and by the development of cost figures for each unit of product manufactured. An introduction to the subject of cost accounting is presented in the following chapter.

KEY TERMS INTRODUCED OR EMPHASIZED IN CHAPTER 24

Cost of goods manufactured Cost of units of finished product completed during the period. Beginning inventory of goods in process, plus cost of raw material used plus direct labor and factory overhead and minus ending inventory of goods in process, equals cost of goods manufactured during the period.

Direct labor Wages paid to factory employees who work directly on the products being manufactured.

Factory overhead All costs incurred in the manufacturing process other than the cost of raw materials and direct labor (for example, insurance, depreciation of machinery, and supervisors' salaries).

Finished goods inventory The completed units which have emerged from the manufacturing process and are on hand ready for sale to customers at year-end or any other specific date.

---

[3] See Chap. 26 for a more detailed discussion of budgeting.

Full (absorption) costing All manufacturing costs are treated as product costs, including the fixed portion of factory overhead. Results in higher values for inventories than does variable (direct) costing.

Goods in process inventory The inventory of partially completed goods in the process of manufacture as determined by a physical count at the year-end or other specific date.

Indirect labor Wages of employees in manufacturing operations who do not work directly with the product. Examples are wages of security guards and maintenance employees.

Manufacturing account A summary account used in closing the accounts of a manufacturing business. All costs used in computing the cost of goods manufactured are transferred into the account, which is then closed to the Income Summary.

Period costs Costs which are charged to expense in the period in which they are incurred. Generally include costs associated with selling and administrative functions.

Product costs Costs which become part of the inventory value of goods in process and finished goods. Deductible from revenue in the period the products in which they are included are sold.

Raw (direct) materials inventory The raw materials or purchased parts which are on hand and ready to be placed in production. Eventually become part of the units to be manufactured. Also includes factory supplies.

Research and development (R&D) Expenditures intended to lead to new products or to improve existing products. Required by the FASB to be charged to expense in the year incurred. Formerly, some companies accumulated these costs in intangible assets accounts.

Statement of cost of goods manufactured A financial statement to support the income statement of a manufacturing company. Shows the various types of costs included in the cost of goods produced and becoming available for sale during the period.

Total manufacturing costs The total amount of the costs of raw materials used, direct labor, and factory overhead costs for a given period without regard to whether products are completed.

Variable (direct) costing A concept under which only raw materials, direct labor, and the portion of factory overhead which varies directly with the volume of production are treated as product costs. The fixed portion of factory overhead (depreciation on the building, for example) is considered a period cost.

REVIEW QUESTIONS

1 What are the three major components of the cost of manufactured goods?

2 A manufacturing firm has four inventory control accounts. Name each of the accounts, and describe briefly what the balance in each at the end of any accounting period represents.

3 Into which of the three elements of manufacturing cost would each of the following be classified?
   a Wages of the factory payroll clerk
   b Briar used in the manufacture of pipes
   c Wages paid to employees who test-drive completed automobiles
   d Cost of making duplicate copies of blueprints in engineering department
   e Cost of glue used to bind layers of plywood
   f Property taxes on machinery
   g Small tools used in the factory

4 Explain the distinction between *product* and *period costs* under the full costing concept. Why is this distinction important?

5 During a given period the cost of raw materials used by a manufacturing firm was $22,000. The raw material inventory decreased by $4,500 during the period, and purchase returns amounted to $1,200. What was the delivered cost of raw materials purchased?

6 Distinguish between *total manufacturing costs* and the *cost of goods manufactured.*

7 What does the balance in the Manufacturing account represent, before the account is closed?

8 What is meant by the term *factory overhead rate?*

9 Explain how the cost of the ending inventory of goods in process is determined under the physical inventory system at the end of the period.

10 What are the major shortcomings of the periodic inventory system when used by a manufacturing company?

11 Explain how the content of the income statement of a manufacturing company differs from the items usually found in the income statement of a merchandising company.

12 A manufacturing company has more than one kind of inventory. Do all the types of inventories of a manufacturing company appear on its income statement? Explain.

EXERCISES

Ex. 24-1 The information below is taken from the financial statements of Joe Trevino, Inc., at the end of Year 1:

Goods in process inventory, ending	$ 30,000
Cost of raw materials used	156,000
Cost of goods manufactured	372,000
Factory overhead, 75% of direct labor cost	90,000

Compute the cost of the goods in process inventory at January 1.

Ex. 24-2 Factory overhead is 30% of cost of goods manufactured. Direct labor is 20% of sales and 40% of cost of goods manufactured. Ending raw materials inventory is $4,000 more than beginning raw materials inventory. Sales totaled $100,000 for the year. Compute the net cost of raw materials purchased during the year.

Ex. 24-3 From the following account balances, prepare the entries required to close the manufacturing accounts at the end of Year 1. Include an entry to close the Manufacturing account to the Income Summary account:

	End of Year	Beginning of Year
Raw materials inventory	$ 45,000	$52,500
Goods in process inventory	70,500	57,600
Purchases of raw materials (net)	240,000	
Direct labor	216,000	
Factory overhead (detail omitted)	119,400	

Ex. 24-4 From the following account balances for the Dell Products Corporation, determine the factory overhead rate based on direct labor cost:

Raw materials used	$288,000
Direct labor	240,000
Indirect labor	58,800
Factory maintenance	31,200
Depreciation on factory plant and machinery	23,400
Other factory overhead costs	30,600
Selling expenses (balance in controlling account)	48,000
General expenses (balance in controlling account)	72,000
Interest expense	12,000

Ex. 24-5 Monroe Company produces a single product. At the end of the current year, the inventories of goods in process and finished goods are summarized below:

	Units	Raw Materials per Unit	Direct Labor per Unit	OH
Goods in process (75% finished).	500	$6	$3	3.30
Finished goods	600	8	4	4.40

Factory overhead is applied to units produced at the rate of 110% of direct labor cost. Compute the cost of the ending inventory of goods in process and finished goods.

Ex. 24-6 From the following information, determine the cost which would be assigned to the ending inventory of finished goods, assuming that variable (direct) costing is used to value inventories:

			Costs per Unit	
			Factory Overhead	
	Units	Prime Costs*	Variable	Fixed
Finished goods inventory:				
Item X	200	$10.00	$5.00	$2.00
Item Y	600	6.00	3.50	1.50
Item Z	500	8.00	4.50	2.50

*Raw materials and direct labor.

PROBLEMS

Group A

24A-1 Medallion Company prepared journal entries to close its accounts at December 31, Year 5. Two of these year-end closing entries are shown below:

Manufacturing	508,500	
Raw Materials Inventory (beginning)		51,500
Goods in Process Inventory (beginning)		27,250
Purchases of Raw Materials		225,500
Transportation-in		5,750
Direct Labor		96,500
Indirect Labor		53,500
Factory Lease Rental		10,750

(Journal entry continued on next page.)

Occupancy Cost	8,000
Machinery Repairs and Maintenance	11,250
Taxes and Insurance	4,750
Depreciation Expense: Machinery	8,750
Miscellaneous Factory Expense	5,000

To close manufacturing accounts having debit balances.

Purchase Returns and Allowances	7,500	
Purchase Discounts	6,750	
Raw Materials Inventory (ending)	56,250	
Goods in Process Inventory (ending)	24,500	
Manufacturing		95,000

To record ending inventories of raw materials and goods in process
and to close manufacturing accounts with credit balances.

Instructions Prepare a statement of cost of goods manufactured for Year 5.

24A-2 An automobile accident which injured Ann Riley, chief accountant for Coast Manufacturing Company, interrupted the preparation of the company's financial statements for the year ended December 31, Year 10. You are given the partially completed working papers and asked to finish the task.

You find that Riley had completed a Statement of Cost of Goods Manufactured which showed the cost of products completed during the year as $600,000. The following account balances also appeared in the working papers.

Raw materials used in production	$216,000
Direct labor	270,000
Indirect labor	82,080
Heat, light, and power.	8,640
Depreciation: factory building and machinery	23,520
Miscellaneous factory costs	27,480
Sales	852,000
Sales returns and allowances	6,000
Finished goods inventory, ending	62,400
Goods in process inventory, ending	60,720
Selling expenses (control account)	51,600
General and administrative expenses (control account)	88,800
Income taxes: 22% on income up to $50,000 and	
48% on income above that amount	?

The beginning inventories consisted of the following:

Raw materials	$50,400
Goods in process	33,000
Finished goods	48,000

Instructions

a Prepare an income statement for the year ended December 31, Year 10. The income statement should include the $600,000 figure computed by Riley as the cost of goods manufactured. In computing earnings per share, assume that 10,000 shares of capital stock are outstanding.

b Prepare a supporting schedule showing the computation of the cost of goods manufactured as $600,000.

c Prepare a supporting schedule showing the computation of income taxes.

24A-3 The adjusted trial balance and other records of Gate Corporation at the end of May included the items listed below:

Goods in process inventory, May 1	$ 73,600
Direct labor	680,000
Indirect labor	254,000
Raw materials inventory, May 1	264,800
Raw materials inventory, May 31	236,800
Raw materials purchases	994,880
Maintenance and repairs	24,000
Heat, light, and power	34,400
Property taxes: factory buildings and equipment	30,400
Depreciation: factory buildings and equipment	76,320
Insurance on manufacturing operations	9,600
Amortization of patents on products manufactured	19,680
Other factory overhead costs	27,600

The factory superintendent reports that raw materials costing $48,000 and direct labor of $80,000 are applicable to uncompleted goods in process at the close of business on May 31.

Instructions
a Compute the factory overhead rate for the month of May based on direct labor cost.
b Determine the cost of the May 31 inventory of goods in process.
c Prepare a statement of cost of goods manufactured for May. Show one amount for factory overhead as computed in **a**.

24A-4 The operations of Conway Manufacturing Company for the month of March were reported as follows:

Cost of goods manufactured	$209,760
Cost of goods sold	206,280
Net income	53,520

The company auditor, after reviewing the records, reports that he has discovered the following errors:
(1) The inventory of raw materials on hand at March 31 did not include materials costing $960 which were on hand but were inadvertently missed in taking the inventory.
(2) The following expenses incurred in March, which apply in part to selling and administrative functions, were charged entirely to factory overhead:

	Total	Manufacturing	Selling	Administrative
Building occupancy	$44,640	$33,480	$2,520	$8,640
Taxes and insurance	6,360	4,680	360	1,320

(3) Sales returns of $2,760 were treated as a part of factory overhead for the month of March.
(4) Factory supplies of $6,000, charged to factory overhead during the month of March, are unused and available for use in future periods.

(5) As the result of the above errors, the goods in process inventory at March 31 was overstated by $3,240, and the finished goods inventory was overstated by $3,960.

Instructions

a Determine the proper amount of the cost of goods manufactured, the cost of goods sold, and the net income for the month of March. Set up a schedule with three columns headed: Cost of Goods Manufactured, Cost of Goods Sold, and Net Income, and enter the amounts of each as determined by the accountant. In the space below, explain the effect of each of the above errors, and show the amount that should be added to or subtracted from the accountant's figures to arrive at the corrected totals.

b Did the company's finished goods inventory, as corrected, increase or decrease during March, and by what amount? Show computations.

24A-5 Shown below is the adjusted trial balance of Green Bay Corporation at June 30, Year 5, the end of the company's fiscal year.

GREEN BAY CORPORATION

Adjusted Trial Balance

June 30, Year 5

Cash	$ 101,750	
Accounts receivable	148,000	
Allowance for doubtful accounts		$ 7,250
Raw materials inventory, July 1, Year 4	38,250	
Goods in process inventory, July 1, Year 4	34,500	
Finished goods inventory, July 1, Year 4	18,750	
Prepaid expenses	8,000	
Factory machinery	607,500	
Accumulated depreciation: factory machinery		182,000
Sales and office equipment	355,750	
Accumulated depreciation: sales and office equipment		118,500
Patents	35,500	
Accounts payable		76,500
Miscellaneous current payables		14,250
Income taxes payable		116,360
Capital stock, $5 par value		500,000
Additional paid-in capital		125,000
Retained earnings, July 1, Year 4		111,750
Dividends	55,000	
Sales		1,981,000
Sales returns	14,250	
Purchases of raw materials	416,750	
Purchase returns		20,750
Transportation-in	69,500	
Direct labor	588,500	
Factory overhead (control)	303,750	
Selling expenses (control)	181,000	
Administrative expenses (control)	160,250	
Income taxes	116,360	
	$3,253,360	$3,253,360

Inventories at June 30, Year 5, are as follows:

Raw materials inventory	*$40,250*
Goods in process inventory	*36,250*
Finished goods inventory	*16,750*

Instructions Prepare:

a Working papers (Include a pair of columns for adjusted trial balance, manufacturing, income statement, retained earnings, and balance sheet.)

b Statement of cost of goods manufactured.

c Income statement. Include earnings per share. (There was no change in number of shares outstanding during the year.)

d Balance sheet in report form.

Group B

24B-1 The information listed below was taken from the adjusted trial balance and other records of Norfleet Corporation at June 30, Year 10.

	June 1	June 30
Inventories		
Raw materials	*$88,550*	*$68,600*
Finished goods	*72,450*	*94,500*
Goods in process	*54,950*	*70,000*

Month of June	
Purchases of raw materials	*$802,200*
Transportation-in on raw materials	*97,300*
Factory overhead (*control account*)	*295,750*
Direct labor	*356,300*
Selling expense (*control account*)	*135,100*
Raw material purchase discounts	*8,050*
Raw material purchase returns	*8,400*
General expense (*control account*)	*268,800*

Instructions

a Prepare a statement of cost of goods manufactured for the month of June.

b Compute the cost of goods sold for the month of June.

24B-2 The income statement on page 874 of Maxwell Company, prepared by an employee with a limited understanding of accounting, is unsatisfactory in several respects.

You are asked to help management prepare a corrected income statement for the first year of operations. Management informs you that 60% of rent, insurance, and utilities is applicable to the factory and that correct ending inventories consist of the following: Raw materials, $35,000; finished goods, $56,000; goods in process, none. The company has 35,000 shares of capital stock outstanding.

Instructions

a Prepare a statement of cost of goods manufactured.

b Prepare a corrected income statement. Assume that income taxes are 22% on the first $50,000 of taxable income and 48% on taxable income in excess of $50,000.

MAXWELL COMPANY
Income Statement
For First Year of Operations

Sales (net)		$910,000
Cost of goods sold:		
Purchases of raw materials	$245,000	
Transportation-in	11,200	
Direct labor	350,000	
Indirect labor	84,000	
Depreciation on machinery—factory	28,000	
Rent	25,200	
Insurance	5,600	
Utilities	16,800	
Miscellaneous factory overhead	44,800	
Other operating expenses	122,500	
Dividends declared on capital stock	35,000	
Cost of goods sold		968,100
Loss for year		$(58,100)

24B-3 The accounting records of Mars Corporation contain the following information: Inventories July 1, Year 5:

Raw materials	$132,000
Goods in process	97,200
Finished goods	144,600

Inventories at December 31, Year 5:

	Raw Materials	Goods in Process	Finished Goods
Raw materials	$144,000	$38,700	$130,500
Direct labor		24,000	90,000
Factory overhead		?	72,000
Totals	$144,000	$?	$292,500

Data for the six months ended December 31, Year 5:

Cost of goods manufactured	$2,430,000
Factory overhead, 80% of direct labor	535,200

The company also paid transportation costs of $90,000 on materials purchased; it received credit of $48,900 for materials returned to suppliers.

Instructions Prepare a statement of cost of goods manufactured for the six months ended December 31, Year 5. Some information needed for this statement is not listed above but can be computed from the data given. Show supporting computations for (1) goods in process inventory at December 31; (2) total cost of goods in process during the six months; (3) direct labor; (4) cost of raw materials used; (5) cost of raw materials available for use; and (6) purchases of raw materials (gross).

24B-4 Marathon Motors manufactures three different models of outboard motors. During the month of January, the following information on unit costs was applicable to these three models.

Product	Raw Material Cost	Direct Labor Cost
Model 100	$45	$ 75
Model 200	65	100
Model 300	80	125

The manufacturing costs for January were as follows:

Raw materials used	$2,545,500
Direct labor	2,660,000
Factory overhead	2,128,000

The inventories of Marathon Motors at the beginning and end of January were as follows:

Raw materials, Jan. 1	$229,500
Raw materials, Jan. 31	213,000
Goods in process, Jan. 1	65,500
Goods in process, Jan. 31 (fully complete as to materials, and 50% complete as to direct labor and factory overhead):	
Model 100	1,000 units
Model 200	750 units
Model 300	500 units
Finished goods, Jan. 1	$419,000
Finished goods, Jan. 31:	
Model 100	2,500 units
Model 200	3,000 units
Model 300	2,000 units

Factory overhead is allocated to products on the basis of its relation to direct labor cost.

Instructions
a Determine the cost of the inventories of finished goods and goods in process at January 31. (For each of the three models, determine the raw materials cost per unit, the direct labor cost per unit, the factory overhead cost per unit, and the total unit cost. Then multiply total unit cost by the number of units in inventory at January 31. Follow this same procedure for finished goods and for goods in process.)
b Compute the cost of goods manufactured for January. (Begin with cost of raw materials used, as given, $2,545,500.)
c Compute the cost of goods sold for January.

24B-5 At September 30, Year 10, the following adjusted trial balance was prepared for Bridgeport Company.

BRIDGEPORT COMPANY
Adjusted Trial Balance
September 30, Year 10

Cash . . . .$	92,000	
Accounts receivable	236,800	
Allowance for doubtful accounts		$ 11,600
Raw materials inventory, Oct. 1, Year 9	61,200	
Goods in process inventory, Oct. 1, Year 9	55,200	
Finished goods inventory, Oct. 1, Year 9	30,000	
Prepaid expenses	12,800	
Factory machinery	972,000	
Accumulated depreciation: factory machinery		291,200
Sales and office equipment	569,200	
Accumulated depreciation: sales and office equipment		189,600
Patents	56,800	
Accounts payable		122,400
Miscellaneous current payables		94,000
Income taxes payable		125,816
Capital stock, $2 par value		800,000
Additional paid-in capital		200,000
Retained earnings, Oct. 1, Year 9		178,800
Dividends	88,000	
Sales (net)		3,004,800
Purchases of raw materials	666,800	
Purchase returns		33,200
Transportation-in	111,200	
Direct labor	941,600	
Factory overhead (control)	486,000	
Selling expenses (control)	289,600	
Administrative expenses (control)	256,400	
Income taxes	125,816	
	$5,051,416	$5,051,416

Inventories at September 30, Year 10, are shown below:

Raw materials inventory	$64,400
Goods in process inventory	58,000
Finished goods inventory	26,800

Instructions Prepare the following:
a Working papers (Include pairs of columns for an adjusted trial balance, manufacturing, income statement, retained earnings, and balance sheet.)
b Statement of cost of goods manufactured.
c Income statement. Include earnings per share. (No change occurred in the number of shares outstanding during the year.)
d Balance sheet in report form.

BUSINESS DECISION PROBLEM 24

John Hall, a recent college graduate, is employed as assistant to the controller of Artcraft, Inc., a manufacturer of wood products. Manufacturing operations are carried on in the main plant in a large southern city and in two smaller plants in the nearby towns of Davis and Kingston. Each of the three plants manufactures a different line of products and each maintains a complete set of accounting records and determines its own cost of goods manufactured.

In studying the company's manufacturing costs, John Hall finds that certain factory overhead costs incurred in the main plant have not been allocated to the Davis and Kingston plants although these costs by their nature are clearly applicable to the two smaller plants. The costs in question include property taxes and insurance paid by the main plant and a portion of the salary of the production manager who regularly makes trips to Davis and Kingston to solve production problems. John Hall recommends that the portion of factory overhead costs incurred at the main plant which are applicable to operations at the Davis and Kingston plants be allocated as manufacturing costs of the two smaller plants. In support of this recommendation, Hall emphasizes that the ending inventories of all three plants are incorrectly stated at the end of the current year, as was the case in prior years.

The controller is reluctant to adopt Hall's recommendation and argues as follows: "We have been handling these costs in the same way for fifteen years. All overhead costs have been charged to one plant or another, and it all ends up in cost of goods sold eventually anyway. Furthermore, for control purposes we want to record the indirect costs where the responsibility for their control lies, and the responsibility for the costs in question rests in the main plant."

In presenting his recommendation to the controller, John Hall had accumulated the following information:

Factory overhead costs incurred in main plant during current year which are

    allocable to Davis and Kingston plants **$200,000**

Percentage of current year's output included in ending inventories of finished

    goods and goods in process:

    Main plant **30%**

    Davis plant **10%**

    Kingston plant **5%**

Instructions

a Assuming that John Hall's recommendation is carried out for the current year, what would be the dollar effect on total ending inventories? Show computations.

b Evaluate the positions taken by John Hall and by the controller, and suggest a solution to the dispute.

25

Cost Accounting Systems

In Chapter 24 the financial statements for a manufacturing business were introduced. Among the matters emphasized were the cost of goods manufactured schedule and the several asset and factory cost accounts not found in the ledger of a merchandising business. In this chapter we are concerned with the more complex task of determining the *cost of activities and products* through the use of cost accounting systems.

Cost accounting systems

A cost accounting system is a method of developing cost information within the framework of general ledger accounts. Because cost accounting systems are more widely used in manufacturing industries, we shall focus our attention on manufacturing costs. The need for cost information, however, is much broader than this. Many of the procedures used to obtain manufacturing costs are applicable to a variety of business situations and have been used by retailers, wholesalers, governmental agencies, and such service organizations as hospitals, public utilities, banks, and accounting firms to determine the cost of performing various service functions.

Cost accounting serves two important managerial objectives: (1) to determine product costs, and (2) to control the cost of business operations. *Product costs* are determined by relating prices paid for materials, labor, and factory overhead to some unit of output such as tons of steel produced. Product cost information has some influence on pricing decisions; it also provides a basis for inventory valuation needed to measure periodic net income and for bidding on contracts. *Control of costs* is a part of management's general responsibility for carrying on the functions of a business efficiently and economically. Knowing the cost of making a product, performing a manufacturing operation, or carrying on some other function of a business is a starting point in control. By comparing actual costs with budgets, standards, or other yardsticks, management finds a basis for controlling costs and planning future operations.

Problems of cost determination

A common misconception about accounting figures is that the cost of any product or unit of output can be measured with precision.

There are two reasons for the difficulty in measuring accurately *the cost* of anything: First, the relationship between the costs incurred and the output produced is often difficult to establish. Secondly, a number of different relationships may be found, each useful for different purposes, but none of which can really claim to be *the cost*. Let us consider these two problems briefly.

RELATING COSTS TO OUTPUT Costs are related to units of output in two stages. The first stage, common to all phases of accounting, is to measure the cost of resources used up in the total productive effort of a given accounting period. Dividing the cost of assets or services among accounting periods is more a matter of judgment than arithmetic. For example, raw materials are purchased at different unit prices. Determining which prices are applicable to materials used and which to materials and supplies on hand for future use requires some rather arbitrary assumptions (such as fifo, lifo, or weighted average). The services of long-lived assets, such as plant and equipment, are purchased in "bundles" and used up over a number of accounting periods. Both the total service life of such assets and the relative amount and value of services withdrawn from the bundle each period are uncertain. The portion of the total cost of the asset to be charged against the production of any given accounting period is therefore, at best, an educated guess.

The second stage in cost accounting is to relate total manufacturing cost to the output of any given accounting period. This, also, is a process fraught with difficulties. Almost all total cost figures include some joint costs which cannot be traced directly to any given unit of output. These costs must therefore be assigned or allocated on some reasonable, but necessarily arbitrary, basis. For example, a part of the cost of a barrel of crude oil is clearly a part of the cost of each product (gasoline, fuel oil, lubricating oil) that emerges from the refinery, but no one can determine exactly how the cost of crude oil should be divided among these products. Similarly, some part of the salary of the plant manager is a cost of operating each department within the plant, but the precise portion cannot be determined for any particular department. Is the cost of training a new employee chargeable to production during the training period, or to production after the employee is fully trained? Resolving these issues and assigning such costs to products or processes is the distinguishing feature of cost accounting.

DIFFERENT COSTS FOR DIFFERENT PURPOSES The second reason it is confusing to talk about *the cost* of anything is that *for different purposes different costs may be useful.* In reporting on the overall position and progress of a business, cost information is needed primarily to determine the valuation of raw materials, goods in process, and finished goods inventories in the balance sheet, and the cost of goods sold figure in the income statement. For these purposes total manufacturing costs are usually associated with the flow of products through the factory to determine the "full" cost of products sold and those on hand at the end of the accounting period.

Cost information is also used, however, as a *basis for managerial decisions.* For these purposes certain portions of the total cost figure may not be relevant. For example, consider the cost of heating a factory building. In arriving at inventory valuation and cost of goods sold, some portion of the total heating cost should be allocated to the various operations and in turn to the production of the period. In a study of the operating efficiency of factory supervisors, the cost of heating the building should be ignored because it is not subject to their control. If we are planning the addition of a wing to the building, the *change* in the heating cost as a result of the addition is the relevant cost figure. Thus for some purposes the entire heating cost is useful, for some only a part of the heating cost is relevant, and for still other purposes this cost may be omitted altogether.

If cost information is to be used intelligently, the user must understand that any cost figure has inherent limitations and that no single method of arriving at cost will serve equally well all the varied purposes for which such information is needed. Most cost systems are designed to meet the general purpose of income determination and to develop in the accounts the basic information from which cost studies for special purposes can be derived. In the balance of this chapter two basic cost systems will be briefly described.

Flow of costs through perpetual inventory accounts in cost systems

In Chapter 24 we saw that even when periodic inventories are used, certain overall cost information can be obtained. Under the periodic inventory system, however, much potentially useful information is buried in totals; cost data are available only at infrequent intervals; and the details of product or departmental costs are not available. The first step in setting up a cost system, therefore, is to establish *perpetual* inventories.

The cost elements that enter into the valuation of inventories are called

product costs; costs that are not included in inventories but are deducted from revenue in the period in which they are incurred are called ***period costs.***

Product costs typically consist of manufacturing costs, as distinguished from selling and general administrative expenses. The flow of costs through perpetual inventories is therefore usually limited to direct materials, direct labor, and factory overhead.

Three perpetual inventory accounts are used to trace the flow of costs through the manufacturing operations and to associate costs with output:

1 Materials Inventory (raw materials and factory supplies)
2 Goods In Process Inventory (product in the process of manufacture)
3 Finished Goods Inventory (completed product)

To visualize basic cost flows, look at the diagram below. The arrows show the flow of costs through the perpetual inventory accounts; arrows connecting two items indicate the two sides of an accounting entry. Thus *Arrows show flow of costs* the use of raw materials reduces the Materials Inventory account and increases the Goods in Process Inventory.

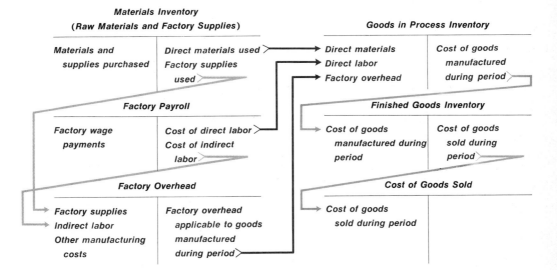

Note that when all the indicated entries have been made, the balances in the Materials Inventory, Goods in Process Inventory, and Finished Goods Inventory accounts represent the dollar valuation of these inventories. When a perpetual inventory system is used, the cost of goods sold can be taken directly from the ledger and placed in the income statement.

Even under a perpetual inventory system it is essential to take a physical inventory at various times to verify the accuracy of the ledger amounts and to disclose losses due to waste, theft, or breakage that were not recorded in the accounts.

Two basic types of cost accounting systems

There are two distinct types of cost accounting systems: a job order cost system and a process cost system. In both systems the end product is the average unit cost of physical output.

Under a *job order cost system,* the key point of costing is a particular quantity of finished product known as a *job* or *lot.* The cost of raw materials, direct labor, and factory overhead applicable to each job is compiled and divided by the number of finished units in the job to arrive at average unit cost.

A job order cost sheet for a completed job is illustrated below:

Job Order Cost Sheet

Cost sheet for one job

Job Number: __1101__	*Date Started:* __3/10/—__
Product: __Model P Hand Drill__	*Date Completed:* __4/15/—__
Units Completed: __2,000__	

Raw materials used	*$ 7,500*
Direct labor cost applicable to this job	*10,000*
Factory overhead applicable to this job, 125% of direct labor cost	*12,500*
Total cost of job no. 1101	*$30,000*
Average cost per unit ($30,000 ÷ 2,000)	*$15*

Under a *process cost system,* the key points in costing are the various departments or processes in the production cycle. First the cost of raw materials, direct labor, and factory overhead applicable to each department or process for *a given period of time* is compiled. Then the average cost of running a unit of product through each department is determined by dividing the total departmental cost by the number of units processed in that department during the period.

When a product moves through two or more departments, the total unit cost of finished product is accumulated by tracing the costs incurred in each department to the product as it moves from process to process. The process cost accounts for two departments are illustrated at the top of page 883.

Each kind of cost accounting system (job order and process) has advantages in particular manufacturing situations. Both are widely used. In the sections that follow we shall examine briefly the basic structure of the two cost accounting systems.

Buildup of costs in two departments (processes)

Goods in Process, Mixing Department

Raw material	4,000	Transferred to Packing Dept.	
Direct labor	5,000	1,000 units @ $12	
Factory overhead applicable to mixing process	3,000	($12,000 ÷ 1,000)	12,000

Goods in Process, Packing Department

From Mixing Dept. (1,000 units @ $12)	12,000	Transferred to finished goods inventory, 1,000 units @	
Materials added	2,000	$28 ($28,000 ÷ 1,000)	28,000
Direct labor	6,000		
Factory overhead applicable to packing process	8,000		

JOB ORDER COST SYSTEM

In general, a job order cost system is applicable when each product or batch of product is significantly different. A job order cost system is used in the construction industry, for example, since each construction project is to some extent unique. Job order cost systems are also used in the aerospace, machine tool, job printing, motion picture, and shipbuilding industries for similar reasons.

An essential requirement of a job order cost system is that each product or batch of product can be identified in each step of the manufacturing operation. Through the use of various subsidiary cost records, the cost of raw materials, direct labor, and factory overhead applicable to each job is recorded on a *job cost sheet,* so that when the job is finished the total and the average unit cost of the job can be computed.

Job order cost flow chart

A flow chart showing the accounts used in a simple job order cost system, together with lines indicating the flow of costs from one account to another, appears on pages 884 and 885.

The flow chart contains figures representing one month's operations for the Job Manufacturing Company. The company makes three products, identified as product A, product B, and product C. Two kinds of raw materials (materials Y and Z) are used. Each of the three perpetual inventory accounts (Materials Inventory, Goods in Process Inventory, and Finished Goods Inventory) is supported by subsidiary ledger records in which the details of the flow of costs are recorded.

Job order cost flow chart

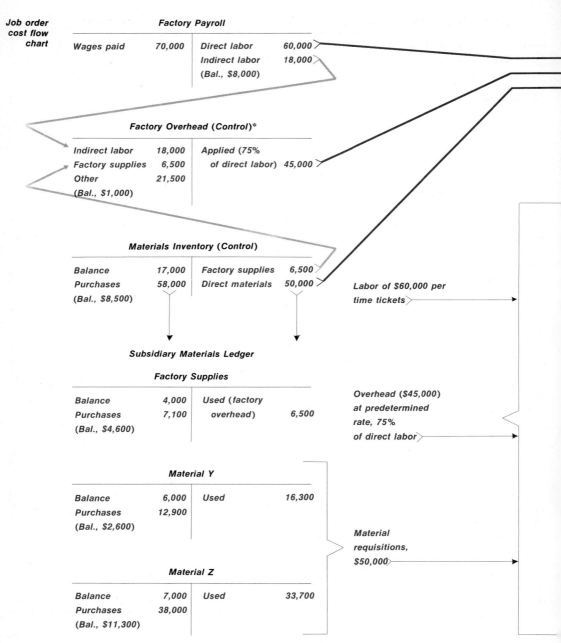

Factory Payroll

Wages paid	70,000	Direct labor	60,000
		Indirect labor	18,000
		(Bal., $8,000)	

Factory Overhead (Control)*

Indirect labor	18,000	Applied (75%	
Factory supplies	6,500	of direct labor)	45,000
Other	21,500		
(Bal., $1,000)			

Materials Inventory (Control)

Balance	17,000	Factory supplies	6,500
Purchases	58,000	Direct materials	50,000
(Bal., $8,500)			

Labor of $60,000 per time tickets

Subsidiary Materials Ledger

Factory Supplies

Balance	4,000	Used (factory	
Purchases	7,100	overhead)	6,500
(Bal., $4,600)			

Overhead ($45,000) at predetermined rate, 75% of direct labor

Material Y

Balance	6,000	Used	16,300
Purchases	12,900		
(Bal., $2,600)			

Material requisitions, $50,000

Material Z

Balance	7,000	Used	33,700
Purchases	38,000		
(Bal., $11,300)			

*Debit balance of $1,000 in this account represents underapplied factory overhead for the month.

Goods in Process Inventory (Control)

Balance	20,000	Completed	
Direct labor	60,000	(Job 101 & 102)	130,000
Factory overhead	45,000		
Raw materials	50,000		
(Bal., $45,000)			

Finished Goods Inventory (Control)

Balance	25,000	Sold	125,000
Completed	130,000		
(Bal., $30,000)			

Subsidiary Job Ledger

Job No. 101   **Product A**

Balance	20,000
Direct labor	24,000
Factory overhead	18,000
Raw materials	8,000
	70,000

Subsidiary Finished Stock Ledger

Product A

Balance	3,000	Sold	66,000
Completed	70,000		
(Bal., $7,000)			

Job No. 102   **Product B**

Direct labor	20,000
Factory overhead	15,000
Raw materials	25,000
Total	60,000

Product B

Completed	60,000	Sold	40,000
(Bal., $20,000)			

Job No. 103   **Product C**

Direct labor	16,000
Factory overhead	12,000
Raw materials	17,000
	Unfinished

($45,000-ending inventory
of Product C in process
agrees with balance
in control account)

Product C

Balance	22,000	Sold	19,000
(Bal., $3,000)			

Cost of Goods Sold

125,000

MATERIALS Accounting for the purchase and use of raw materials and factory supplies is a straightforward application of the use of perpetual inventories. The summary entries in the Materials Inventory control account are matched by detailed entries in the subsidiary ledger accounts as follows:

1 The $17,000 beginning balance in the Materials Inventory control account is equal to the beginning balances in the subsidiary ledger accounts for Factory Supplies, $4,000, Material Y, $6,000, and Material Z, $7,000.

2 The record in the subsidiary ledger accounts for the quantity and cost of materials purchased is made from information on suppliers' invoices. The cost of materials purchased, $58,000, was posted in total from the cash payments journal (or the voucher register if one is used).

3 Materials and factory supplies are issued on the basis of *requisitions,* which show the quantity needed and the identity of the job on which raw materials are to be used or the Factory Overhead account to which supplies should be charged. The *direct materials cost* is the cost of raw materials identified with specific jobs; *indirect materials* refers to materials or supplies charged to the Factory Overhead account.

4 The materials clerk refers to individual materials ledger cards to get the cost of each item requisitioned, and enters this on the requisition form. Since purchases are at different prices, the costing of materials used requires some systematic cost flow assumption such as lifo, fifo, or weighted average. A summary of the materials requisitions for the month becomes the basis for the entries crediting Materials Inventory ($56,500) and debiting Goods in Process Inventory ($50,000) for the cost of direct materials used and Factory Overhead ($6,500) with the cost of factory supplies used.

In the flow chart on pages 884 and 885 subsidiary materials ledger accounts are shown in T-account form only as a matter of convenience; in practice they would contain more detailed unit cost information and dates of entries. An illustrative materials ledger card, showing the record for material Y during the month, appears below:

Materials Ledger Card
Material Y

	Ref*	Received			Issued			Balance	
		Quantity, lb	Unit Cost	Amount	Quantity, lb	Unit Cost†	Amount	Quantity, lb	Balance
Subsidiary ledger record for material Y	Balance at beginning of month							6,000	$ 6,000
	Inv. no. 47	7,500	$1.20	$9,000				13,500	15,000
	Req. no. 3				6,000	$1.00	$6,000		
					4,000	1.20	4,800	3,500	4,200
	Inv. no. 98	3,000	1.30	3,900				6,500	8,100
	Req. no. 6				3,500	1.20	4,200		
					1,000	1.30	1,300	2,000	2,600

* Identifying number of invoice or requisition from which data were taken.
† fifo basis.

FACTORY LABOR Payment of factory employees usually occurs after the services have been performed. During the pay period, detailed records of time, rates of pay, and the jobs on which employees worked must be kept in order to compile the necessary cost information. The wages earned by employees who work directly on job production are referred to as *direct labor* and are charged to each job. The wages earned by employees whose work is not directly associated with any particular job, known as *indirect labor,* are charged to Factory Overhead.

A number of mechanical and computerized means have been devised for compiling payroll information. A common system is to prepare *time tickets* for each employee, showing the time worked on each job, the rates of pay, and the total cost chargeable to each job. These tickets, summarized periodically, become the basis for preparing the payroll and paying factory employees. They also become the basis for entries on various job cost sheets showing the direct labor cost incurred.

In the flow chart on pages 884 and 885, $60,000 of direct labor was charged to the three jobs in process and $18,000 of indirect labor was charged to Factory Overhead. Of the total wage cost of $78,000, only $70,000 was actually paid during the month. The balance of $8,000 in the Factory Payroll account represents the liability for unpaid wages at the end of the month.

FACTORY OVERHEAD Included in factory overhead are all manufacturing costs other than *prime costs* (direct materials and direct labor). Direct labor and factory overhead costs are often referred to as *processing* or *conversion costs.* The Factory Overhead account is usually a control account; details of individual factory overhead costs are kept in a subsidiary ledger. The source of individual overhead charges varies: indirect labor charges are summarized from payroll records; factory supplies used are summarized from materials requisitions; charges for such current services as electricity and water are posted from the cash payments journal (or the voucher register); depreciation on plant assets, the expiration of prepaid expenses, and overhead costs resulting from accrued liabilities (for example, property taxes) are recorded as adjusting entries at the end of the period.

Determining the total factory overhead cost for a given accounting period is relatively easy. The major problem is to relate overhead cost to physical output. The nature of factory overhead is such that the direct relation between cost and output, which exists in the case of direct labor and materials, is lacking. We might determine an average overhead cost per unit by dividing the total overhead for a given period by the units of output produced in that period. Most manufacturing firms, however, produce several different products (or different models of the same product). A meaningful average factory overhead cost figure is not possible where the units of output are significantly different.

This problem is usually solved by relating factory overhead costs to some other cost factor which *can* be directly identified with units or lots of output. Many factory overhead costs either are a function of the passage of time (for example, building rent, foreman's salary) or tend to vary with the amount of labor or machine time involved in manufacture. For these reasons, charging factory overhead against units of output in proportion to the amount of *direct labor cost, direct labor hours,* or *machine-hours* involved in production is a reasonable and widely used procedure.

PREDETERMINED OVERHEAD RATES Since many overhead costs tend to remain relatively fixed (constant) from month to month, total monthly overhead does not vary in proportion to seasonal or cyclical variations in factory output. Examples of *fixed costs* are property taxes and insurance on plant assets, straight-line depreciation on plant assets, and the monthly salary of the plant superintendent. *Variable costs* are those which change in direct proportion to output. If we allocate actual overhead costs incurred each month to the output of that month, the unit cost of production is likely to vary widely month by month. In months of high output, unit overhead costs would be low; in months of low output, unit overhead costs would be high. We can illustrate this for a company with a capacity to produce 10,000 units per month:

Overhead Costs per Unit at Different Levels of Output

		Level of Output			
		*100% of Capacity**	*75% of Capacity*	*50% of Capacity*	*25% of Capacity*
Overhead unit costs increase as volume decreases	*Fixed overhead costs (constant at all levels)*	$ 60,000	$ 60,000	$ 60,000	$60,000
	Variable overhead costs	100,000	75,000	50,000	25,000
	Total overhead costs	$160,000	$135,000	$110,000	$85,000
	Number of units produced	10,000	7,500	5,000	2,500
	Overhead cost per unit	$16	$18	$22	$34

*100% = normal level of output.

Note that the *fixed cost per unit increases as the level of output decreases* and that the variable cost remains constant at $10 per unit. For most business purposes, it is more confusing than helpful to have product cost figures that vary widely in response to short-run variations in the volume of output. Management needs product cost information for long-range product pricing decisions, income determination, and inventory valuation. For these purposes it is more useful to use what might be called "normal" costs than to have unit cost figures that reflect short-run variations in volume. For example, if we were determining the cost of two identical units of product in the finished goods inventory, it would not seem reasonable to say that one unit cost $30 because it was produced in a low-volume month and the other cost $20 because it was produced in a high-volume month.

The solution to this problem is to predetermine overhead application rates for an entire year in advance. To do this we first make an estimate of the total overhead costs for the year. This is called the **budgeted overhead.** Then we estimate the machine-hours, or direct labor hours, or direct labor cost, whichever is to be used as the **overhead application base** for the year. The predetermined overhead rate used in costing units of production is the budgeted overhead divided by the application base. For example, if factory overhead is budgeted at $600,000 for the coming year and it is estimated that the direct labor cost will amount to $500,000, the factory overhead rate would be determined as follows:

Pre-determined factory overhead rate | *Budgeted factory overhead for year* . . . . | *$600,000*
| *Budgeted direct labor cost for year* . . . . | *500,000*
| *Predetermined factory overhead rate ($600,000 ÷ $500,000)* . . . . | *120%*

The use of predetermined overhead rate has another advantage. Because the rate is estimated at the beginning of the year, "normal" product costs can be determined as various jobs are completed. It is not necessary to wait until the end of any period to know the factory overhead chargeable against goods produced.

Assume that we are using direct labor cost as the overhead application base and that the predetermined application rate is 75% of direct labor cost. The actual overhead cost for any given period will be accumulated in the Factory Overhead control account. As production takes place and the direct labor cost is charged against jobs, overhead will also be applied to jobs at the predetermined rate of 75% of direct labor cost. As soon as a job is completed, we can determine the total cost and the unit cost of that job order. In the accounting records, the total amount of overhead applied to jobs during the period will be debited to Goods in Process and credited to Factory Overhead.[1] In the flow chart on pages 884 and 885, for example, the total direct labor charged against the three jobs worked on during the month was $60,000 and 75% of this amount, or $45,000, was applied as the overhead cost applicable to these three jobs.

OVER- OR UNDERAPPLIED OVERHEAD We should not expect that applied overhead will ever exactly equal actual overhead, since the predetermined overhead rate was based on estimates. A debit balance in the Factory Overhead account at the end of a period indicates that actual overhead exceeded the overhead applied to jobs; a credit balance shows that overhead applied was greater than the actual overhead costs incurred.

---

[1] Some accountants feel that actual overhead charges and applied overhead credits should not be mixed in the same account. Therefore, they credit applied overhead to a special account called Applied Factory Overhead, which has a credit balance until closed at the end of an accounting period.

At the end of the year, if the amount of overapplied or underapplied overhead is material, it should be apportioned among the Goods in Process Inventory, the Finished Goods Inventory, and Cost of Goods Sold on some reasonable basis to restate them at a more realistic cost. If the amount of over- or underapplied overhead is not material it should be closed into Cost of Goods Sold, on the ground that most of the error applied to goods sold during the period.

The bases (such as direct labor cost) used in applying overhead vary with production but many elements of overhead do not. Therefore, overhead will tend to be *underapplied* during months of low production and *overapplied* during months of high production. The difference between actual and applied overhead is usually carried forward from month to month, and the overapplied overhead of one month is offset against the underapplied overhead of another. At the end of the year, any net balance of over- or underapplied overhead is then handled as described above.

GOODS IN PROCESS INVENTORY The Goods in Process Inventory account is charged with the cost of direct materials, direct labor, and an estimate of the factory overhead costs applicable to all jobs. The supporting subsidiary ledger records for this control account are the job cost sheets relating to each job in process during the period. In the flow chart on pages 884 and 885, note that the balance in the goods in process inventory at the beginning of the month, $20,000, represents the cost incurred on job no. 101 during the previous month. During the current month additional costs of $155,000 were incurred. The flow of costs through subsidiary cost sheets and the Goods in Process Inventory control account is illustrated on page 891.

Note that the only job in process at the end of the month is job 103, and the cost of this job to date, $45,000, is equal to the balance in the control account, Goods in Process Inventory. The Goods in Process Inventory account includes all the information needed to prepare a statement of cost of goods manufactured at the end of an accounting period.

FINISHED GOODS INVENTORY When a job is completed, the information on the job cost sheet is summarized and the total cost of that job becomes the basis for an entry crediting Goods in Process Inventory and debiting Finished Goods Inventory. Stock ledger cards are maintained as subsidiary ledger records for each type of finished product. When finished product is sold, Cash (or Accounts Receivable) is debited and Sales is credited. In addition, information on the stock ledger cards becomes the basis for removing the cost of these products from the Finished Goods Inventory account and charging the Cost of Goods Sold account. Once more some flow assumption (such as fifo or lifo) is required.

The relation between entries in the Finished Goods Inventory control

Subsidiary Job Order Cost Sheets

	Job 101	Job 102	Job 103	Total (Control Account)
Flow of costs through job order cost sheets and control account Goods in process inventory, beginning of month	$20,000			$ 20,000
Direct labor	24,000	$20,000	$16,000	60,000
Raw materials.	8,000	25,000	17,000	50,000
Factory overhead.	18,000	15,000	12,000	45,000
Total costs incurred	$70,000	$60,000	$45,000	$175,000
Less: Cost of jobs completed— transferred to Finished Goods Inventory account	(70,000)	(60,000)		(130,000)
Goods in process inventory, end of month (job 103)				$ 45,000

account and the subsidiary finished stock ledger, as shown on the flow chart on pages 884 and 885, is summarized in the following schedule:

Finished Goods Inventory, Control Account		**Subsidiary Finished Stock Ledger**	
Stock ledger supports entries in control account Beginning balance	$ 25,000	{ Product A Balance	$ 5,000
		{ Product C Balance.	20,000
Completed during period	130,000	{ Product A (job 101)	70,000
Total goods available for sale .	$155,000	{ Product B (job 102)	60,000
			$155,000
Less: Cost of goods sold during the period	(125,000)	{ Product A	$66,000
		{ Product B	40,000
		{ Product C	19,000 (125,000)
Balance on hand at end of period	$ 30,000	{ Product A	$ 7,000
		{ Product B	20,000
		{ Product C	3,000 $ 30,000

PROCESS COST SYSTEM

In many industries the production of a large volume of standard products on a relatively continuous basis is the typical situation. The natural focus of cost measurement in such situations is a *cost center* such as a manufacturing operation, a department, or a process. A process cost system is a method of accumulating cost information in the accounts for such cost centers.

Process costs are particularly suitable for mass-production operations of all types. They are used in such industries as appliances, cement, chemicals, dairy products, lumber, and petroleum. The process cost approach also may be used in the analysis of nonmanufacturing costs. Distribution activities, for example, may be divided into such functions as sales visits, receipt of orders, filling orders, packing and shipping, and the cost per unit sold computed for any given period of time.

Characteristics of a process cost system

In a process cost system, no attempt is made to determine the cost of particular lots of product as they move through the factory. Instead the costs of materials, labor, and factory overhead during any given time period (such as a month) are traced to various manufacturing processes (or departments). The costs incurred in each process are accumulated in separate goods in process accounts, and a record is kept of the units produced in that process in each period. The *cost report* of each process shows the average per unit cost of processing output during the period, and this figure becomes the basis for tracing the flow of costs through the various goods in process accounts and finally to Finished Goods Inventory and to Cost of Goods Sold.

In a very simple situation, only one product is processed in each department. Process costs can be used, however, when more than one product is involved. In such cases, charges for materials and direct labor are identified with individual products or models and accumulated separately in each department's cost reports. Since all products utilize departmental machinery and other indirect services, these costs may be divided among various products on the basis of their relative usage of departmental facilities. To simplify our illustrations, we shall assume that only a single product is manufactured.

Direct and indirect process costs

Direct process costs are those associated with the operations of a particular process; *indirect process costs* are common to several processes and are treated as a part of factory overhead.

MATERIALS AND LABOR The cost of materials and supplies used, and the wages of production line workers can usually be traced directly to the operations of each process; if not, they are recorded as factory overhead. Note that direct departmental or process costs are not necessarily variable in relation to output. For example, a department superintendent's salary is a direct cost of the department, but his or her salary is a fixed cost in relation to variations in the output of that department.

FACTORY OVERHEAD The simplest method of handling factory overhead in a process cost system is to allocate *actual* overhead costs among the various processes at the end of each period. If this is done, goods produced during any given period are charged with the actual overhead costs incurred and there is no balance in the factory overhead account at the end of the period.

Alternatively, factory overhead rates may be predetermined by setting up a factory overhead budget for each department or process at the beginning of the period. Overhead is then charged to the department or process in proportion to labor cost, machine hours, or some other basis. When predetermined rates are used in applying factory overhead, a balance of under- or overapplied factory overhead will usually appear in the Factory Overhead account at the end of the period. This represents the difference between actual factory overhead costs incurred and factory overhead allocated to the units produced during the period. The problem of disposing of this balance was discussed earlier in connection with the job order cost system; the same concepts apply for a process cost system.

A refinement in overhead accounting is to set up special overhead cost accounts for one or more *service departments,* that is, departments that do not actually process raw materials or work directly on the units produced. For example, a power department might be established, and all costs of producing power for the factory would be charged to this department. A maintenance department is another example of a service department. The cost of operating a service department would in turn be charged to *productive departments* in proportion to their relative use of the service.

To illustrate, suppose that a maintenance department is set up, a record is kept of maintenance work done for three productive departments (A, B, and C), and an hourly charge is made to each productive department. The Maintenance Department account for a month might appear as follows:

Maintenance Department (a Service Department)

Use of service department to allocate costs to productive departments	*Wages*	2,000	*Allocated to productive departments:*	
	Supplies	900	*Dept. A, 250 hr @ $8*	*2,000*
	Portion of various factory costs		*Dept. B, 150 hr @ $8*	*1,200*
	applicable to maintenance		*Dept. C, 100 hr @ $8*	*800*
	department	1,100		
		4,000		4,000

A total of 500 hours of maintenance work was done during the month for three productive departments (A, B, and C) at a total cost of $4,000. Each productive department is therefore charged with an average hourly cost of $8 per hour ($4,000 ÷ 500 hours). Alternatively, a predetermined hourly rate for maintenance work might have been set and used to charge the productive departments as maintenance services were performed.

Flow of costs in a process cost system illustrated

To illustrate the main features of a process cost system, let us assume a very simple manufacturing situation. The Process Manufacturing Company makes a standard-size steel container. The company has two processing departments: In the Cutting Department, the metal is cut and shaped to required uniform specifications; in the Assembly Department, the metal parts are welded, ground, and sprayed with a chemical coating. Finished containers are stored in the warehouse and shipped to customers as orders are received.

The cost flow diagram on page 895 shows the basic process cost accounts and a summary of the journal entries for the month of July. A careful study of the diagram will show that the Goods in Process account for each department contains the information needed to prepare a statement of cost of goods manufactured. When perpetual inventories are used, it is unnecessary to show the beginning and ending inventories and the purchases of materials in the statement of cost of goods manufactured; only the cost of materials transferred to production need be shown. Each major step in the process will now be examined briefly to demonstrate the process cost accounting under these relatively simple conditions.

MATERIALS There was a $4,000 balance in the Materials Inventory control account at the beginning of July. During the month of July purchases of materials were charged to the Materials Inventory account in the amount of $34,000. All material needed to complete a unit in each department is placed in process at the beginning of production. At the end of July a summary of direct materials requisitioned by each department and factory supplies used by all departments became the basis for the following entry:

<table>
<tr><td>End-of-</td><td>Goods in Process: Cutting Department</td><td>. . . . .</td><td>29,400</td><td></td></tr>
<tr><td>month
entry:</td><td>Goods in Process: Assembly Department</td><td>. . . . .</td><td>3,460</td><td></td></tr>
<tr><td>materials</td><td>Factory Overhead</td><td>. . . . .</td><td>2,000</td><td></td></tr>
<tr><td>used</td><td>   Materials Inventory</td><td>. . . . .</td><td></td><td>34,860</td></tr>
<tr><td></td><td colspan="4">To record materials used in July.</td></tr>
</table>

FACTORY LABOR On the basis of departmental payroll records, the total cost of direct labor used in each department during July was determined. The wages of personnel (such as the factory superintendent, cost accountant, general maintenance employees) whose work is applicable to all departments were charged to Factory Overhead. The entry summarizing the payroll (ignoring various withholdings from wages) would be:

End-of-
month
entry:
factory
payroll

Goods in Process: Cutting Department	......	24,600	
Goods in Process: Assembly Department	......	12,000	
Factory Overhead	......	5,100	
Factory Payroll	......		41,700

To record factory labor used in July.

Cost flow
diagram for
process
costing—
compare
with job
order flow
chart on
pages 884
and 885 Total factory labor cost incurred amounted to $41,700 and payments to employees during the month amounted to $37,800, leaving a credit balance of $3,900 in the Factory Payroll account, which represents wages payable at the end of July.

FACTORY OVERHEAD The Process Manufacturing Company prepares a departmental factory overhead budget at the beginning of each year, and

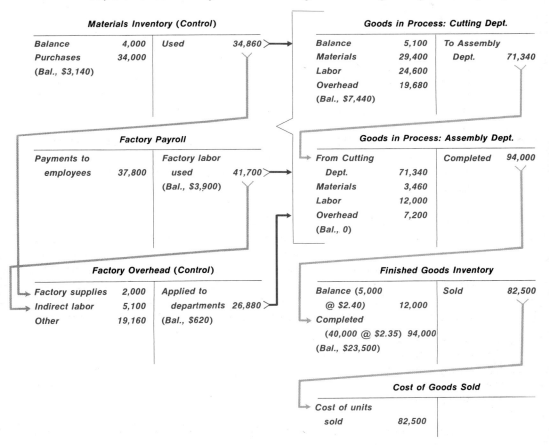

factory overhead is applied to departmental goods in process accounts
Pre-
determined
overhead
rates for our
example on the basis of departmental direct labor cost at the following rates:

| Cutting Department | ...... | 80% of direct labor cost |
| Assembly Department | ...... | 60% of direct labor cost |

The entry charging the departmental goods in process accounts for their share of factory overhead, at these predetermined rates, may be summarized as follows:

End-of-
month
entry:
factory
overhead
applied

Goods in Process: Cutting Department (80% of $24,600) 19,680
Goods in Process: Assembly Department (60% of $12,000) 7,200
  Factory Overhead 26,880
To record factory overhead applied to production on basis of
direct labor cost.

Actual overhead for July totaled $26,260, leaving a credit balance of $620 in the Factory Overhead account, representing overapplied over-head for the month. This amount would be carried forward month to month, and any balance at the end of the year would be apportioned between ending inventories of goods in process and finished goods and the cost of goods sold during the year, or, if not material, simply closed out to the Cost of Goods Sold account.

Determining unit costs for inventory valuation and control

If all units of product in any particular department are completely proc-essed during the period, computing unit costs is a simple matter of dividing departmental costs by the number of units processed. In some cases, however, there may be unfinished units of product on hand at the beginning as well as at the end of an accounting period. The total costs incurred in each department during the period, plus the cost of any partially completed units at the beginning of the period, must then be allocated between the units that have been completed and the units that are left in various stages of completion at the end of the period. Obviously, total costs cannot be divided by the total number of units worked on during the period, some of which are complete and some of which are only partly finished. If completed and partly completed units of product are expressed in *equivalent full units* of completed product, however, this difficulty is overcome and a meaningful unit cost can be determined by dividing total costs by the equivalent full units produced. This computa-
A key
step in
process
cost
accounting
tion can be illustrated for materials as follows:

$$\text{Cost per unit of materials} = \frac{\text{total cost of materials for current month}}{\text{equivalent full units produced in current month}}$$

Equivalent full units is a measure of the productive effort for a given ac-counting period. This measure of unit output is used to obtain separate unit costs for material, labor, and factory overhead; the unit cost of goods produced can then be used to assign a value to ending inventories and to units sold. Unit costs are also useful for other management purposes.

When materials and processing costs (direct labor and factory overhead) are applied uniformly to the units being produced, the equivalent full units of work done will be identical for all three cost elements. If the materials are placed in process at various stages (such as 100% at the beginning, or 60% at the beginning and 40% when most of the processing has been completed), the equivalent unit figure for material will differ from that for processing costs. In such situations, the equivalent-unit computation must be determined separately for each cost element.

The computation of equivalent full units for a hypothetical company for the month of March is illustrated below:

Computation of Equivalent Full Units

	Units	×	Portion Completed during March	=	Equivalent Full Units Completed (All Costs)
Beginning inventory in process (3/1), 80% completed in February but finished in March	*20,000*	×	*20%*	=	*4,000*
Units started and completed in March	*50,000*	×	*100%*	=	*50,000*
Units completed and transferred to storage	*70,000*				
Ending inventory in process (3/31), 40% completed in March	*25,000*	×	*40%*	=	*10,000*
Output in March in terms of equivalent full units					*64,000*

Equivalent full units— an index of productive effort for a period

Equivalent full units should be viewed as a physical measure of production activity for a period. Although 70,000 units were completed and transferred to storage in our example, the actual measure of work accomplished during March was only 64,000 units. These units consist of 54,000 equivalent full units of work (4,000 + 50,000) on the 70,000 units transferred to storage and 10,000 equivalent full units (40% of 25,000) on the 25,000 units still in process at the end of March.

The computation of unit cost and the assignment of departmental costs to goods completed and goods in process at the end of the period will now be illustrated using the information for the Cutting Department and the Assembly Department for the Process Manufacturing Company which appears on the cost flow chart on page 895. The costs incurred in the two processing departments during July appear in the departmental goods in process accounts. A *production report* for the Process Manufacturing Company shows the units of product processed in each department for July, as shown on page 898.

Production Report for July

	Cutting Dept.	Assembly Dept.
Units in process on July 1	4,000	None
Add: Units placed in production during July	42,000	40,000
Total units worked on during July	46,000	40,000
Less: Units in process on July 31	6,000	none
Units completed during July	40,000	40,000

Production report shows units only

Using this information, we can now determine unit costs in each of the two departments.

CUTTING DEPARTMENT In the Cutting Department, we have both begin-ning and ending inventories in process which are 100% completed as to material and 50% completed as to labor and overhead. On the basis of cost information and the production report above, a *cost report* for the Cutting Department for July may be prepared as illustrated on page 899.

The total cost inputs in the Cutting Department during July amounted to $78,780, including the cost of $5,100 applicable to the beginning goods in process inventory carried forward from June. This total cost of $78,780 was incurred on the 46,000 units worked on during the month. We could not, however, divide the total cost by 46,000 to determine the cost per unit. Not all of these units were entirely produced in July: 4,000 units were carried forward from June with all material cost and 50% of processing costs (labor and overhead) included, while another 6,000 units in process at the end of July were 100% complete as to material cost but only 50% completed as to processing costs. We first had to compute the equivalent full units of work for material and for processing costs.

The reasoning behind the computation of equivalent full units in the Cutting Department may be stated as follows: The equivalent full units of work in the beginning inventory of goods in process must be subtracted from units completed during the period, because the cost of these goods is included in the $5,100 carried forward from the previous month. The equivalent finished units in the ending inventory must then be added, because the cost of this productive effort is included in the costs for the current period. The result is the equivalent production in terms of finished units during July, and this is divided into the costs incurred during July to derive a unit production cost for July. Applying this procedure, it was determined that 42,000 equivalent full units of material and 41,000 equiv-alent full units of labor and overhead were completed during July. Dividing the cost of material, $29,400, by the equivalent full units of material used, 42,000, gives us a unit cost for material of $0.70; dividing the direct labor cost, $24,600, by the equivalent full units of direct labor, 41,000, gives us

CUTTING DEPARTMENT
Cost Report for July

Cost report
for July.
Note how
unit costs
were
computed
and then
used to
assign
value to the
outputs

	Total Units	Total Costs ÷	Equivalent Full Units* =	Unit Cost
Inputs:				
Units in process at beginning of month (100% complete as to materials and 50% as to processing)	4,000	$ 5,100		
Materials requisitions	.42,000	29,400	42,000	$0.70
Direct labor		24,600	41,000	0.60
Factory overhead		19,680	41,000	0.48
Total inputs—units and costs	.46,000	$78,780		
Unit cost for July				$1.78
Outputs (see Exhibit A on page 900 for supporting computations):				
Transferred to Assembly Department, $1.7835 per unit	.40,000	$71,340		
Units in process at end of month (100% complete as to materials and 50% as to processing)	6,000	7,440		
Total outputs—units and costs	.46,000	$78,780		

*Computation of equivalent full units:

	Materials	Labor and Overhead
Units completed during July	40,000	40,000
Less: Units in process at start of month (4,000):		
Material equivalent (4,000 × 100%)	(4,000)	
Labor and overhead equivalent (4,000 × 50%)		(2,000)
Add: Units in process at end of month (6,000):		
Material equivalent (6,000 × 100%)	6,000	
Labor and overhead equivalent (6,000 × 50%)		3,000
Equivalent full units (expressed in finished units)	42,000	41,000

a unit cost for direct labor of $0.60; dividing factory overhead, $19,680, by the equivalent full units of factory overhead, 41,000, gives us a unit cost for factory overhead of $0.48.[2] The total of these three cost elements gives a unit cost per container of $1.78 in the Cutting Department for the month of July.

Once unit costs for materials, direct labor, and factory overhead are determined, the total cost inputs of $78,780 can be assigned to units completed and transferred to the Assembly Department and to the units still in process in the Cutting Department at the end of July as shown at the top of page 900.

[2] The unit cost of factory overhead can also be computed by taking 80% of $0.60, the direct labor cost per unit, because factory overhead is applied at the rate of 80% of direct labor cost. See bottom of page 895.

CUTTING DEPARTMENT   *Exhibit A*

Assignment of Cost Inputs—Month of July

Total cost inputs assigned to units completed and to units in process	Beginning inventory in process (4,000 units):	
	Cost brought forward from previous month	$5,100
	Cost to complete during July:	
	Materials	—
	Labor (4,000 × 50% × $0.60).	1,200
	Overhead (4,000 × 50% × $0.48)	960
	Total cost of first 4,000 units finished	$ 7,260
	Goods started and finished during July (36,000 units):	
	Materials, labor, and overhead (36,000 × $1.78)	64,080
	Cost of goods transferred to Assembly Department (40,000 units @ $1.7835)	$71,340
	Cost of units in process at end of month (6,000 units):	
	Materials (6,000 × 100% × $0.70)	$4,200
	Labor (6,000 × 50% × $0.60)	1,800
	Overhead (6,000 × 50% × $0.48)	1,440
	Cost of ending goods in process inventory (6,000 units)	$ 7,440

In computing the cost of the 40,000 units transferred to the Assembly Department, it is necessary to make some assumption as to which units are involved. A *first-in, first-out* assumption has been used in this illustration. This means that the 40,000 units transferred out consist of 4,000 units which were in process at the beginning of the period, and 36,000 units which were *started and finished* during the period. The cost allocated to these 40,000 units is $71,340, or $1.7835 each,[3] and the cost allocated to the 6,000 units in process at the end of July is $7,440. Thus, the total cost inputs of $78,780 have been assigned to goods completed and transferred to the Assembly Department and to the ending goods in process inventory. The entry to transfer the cost of the units completed in the Cutting Department to the Assembly Department is illustrated below:

Transfer of cost to next department	Goods in Process: Assembly Department	71,340
	Goods in Process: Cutting Department	71,340
	To transfer cost of 40,000 units completed in July from	
	Cutting Department to Assembly Department.	

ASSEMBLY DEPARTMENT There was neither a beginning nor an ending inventory of goods in process in the Assembly Department. Therefore, the unit cost in this department may be determined by dividing each cost element by the 40,000 units started, completed, and transferred to Finished Goods Inventory during July. The cost report for the Assembly Department appears on page 901.

---

[3] Actually the first 4,000 units cost $7,260, or $1.815 per unit, and the other 36,000 units cost $64,080, or $1.78 per unit. It would be possible to carry these slightly different unit costs forward to the Assembly Department, but such refinement is generally considered unnecessary.

ASSEMBLY DEPARTMENT
Cost Report for July

	Total Units	Total Costs	÷	Equivalent Full Units	=	Unit Cost
Inputs:						
Transferred from Cutting Department	40,000	$71,340		40,000		$1.7835
Materials added in Assembly						
Department		3,460		40,000		0.0865
Direct labor		12,000		40,000		0.3000
Factory overhead		7,200		40,000		0.1800
Total inputs—units and costs	40,000	$94,000				
Unit cost for July						$2.3500
Outputs:						
Transferred to Finished Goods						
Inventory, $2.35 per unit	40,000	$94,000				

Cost report—no goods in process inventories

The $2.35 unit cost of the steel container completed in the Assembly Department includes $1.7835 incurred in the Cutting Department and $0.5665 incurred in the Assembly Department. It is important to keep in mind that this is an *average cost* and that it includes both variable costs (direct materials, direct labor, and variable factory overhead) and fixed costs (fixed portion of factory overhead). If the variable cost per unit amounted to only $2, for example, the Process Manufacturing Company might accept a special order for 1,000 units at $2.25 per unit and thereby recover all variable cost assigned to these units and have $250 available to help defray the total fixed costs for the period.

Given below is the entry to transfer the cost of goods completed in the Assembly Department during July to the Finished Goods Inventory account:

Transfer of cost to finished goods inventory

Finished Goods Inventory	94,000	
Goods in Process: Assembly Department		94,000

To transfer cost of 40,000 units completed in Assembly Department during July to Finished Goods Inventory.

The entries to record the sale of goods by the Process Manufacturing Company during July appear below:

Entries to record sales and cost of goods sold

Accounts Receivable	120,000	
Sales		120,000

To record sales on account during July.

Cost of Goods Sold	82,500	
Finished Goods Inventory		82,500

To record the cost of containers sold in July.

Summary of job order and process cost systems

Several simplifying assumptions have been made in developing the illustrations of job order and process cost systems; nevertheless, the essential features of the two types of cost systems were included. Both the job order and the process cost systems are essentially devices for collecting cost information. A job order cost system produces information about the cost of manufacturing a particular product or a batch of a given product; a process cost system produces information about the *average cost* of putting a homogeneous unit of product through various manufacturing operations for a given time period. A job order cost system usually involves more detailed cost accounting work and in return gives more specific cost information. A process cost system involves less detailed accounting work and accumulates costs in terms of major production sequences (processes) or departmental cost centers. Both systems provide the information required to prepare a statement of cost of goods manufactured, to arrive at unit costs, and to formulate business decisions.

KEY TERMS INTRODUCED OR EMPHASIZED IN CHAPTER 25

Equivalent full units   The number of equivalent fully completed units of product manufactured during an accounting period after giving consideration to the beginning and ending inventory of goods in process.

Factory labor   Wages earned by factory employees who work directly on the products being manufactured.

Factory overhead   All costs incurred in the manufacturing process other than the cost of raw materials and direct labor. Included in factory overhead are, for example, insurance, depreciation of machinery, and supervisors' salaries.

Job order cost system   A cost accounting system under which the focal point of costing is a quantity of product known as a *job* or *lot*. Costs of raw materials, direct labor, and factory overhead applicable to each job are compiled to arrive at average unit cost.

Materials   Raw materials which become part of the finished product.

Over- or underapplied overhead   The difference between the actual factory overhead incurred during the period and the amount applied to goods in process by use of a predetermined factory overhead rate. A physical measure of production activity.

Predetermined overhead rate   A rate estimated at the beginning of the year as the probable relationship of factory overhead expenses to a correlated factor such as direct labor cost, direct labor hours, or machine-hours. This predetermined rate is used to allocate factory overhead to goods in process, thus making it possible to determine the approximate complete cost of finished units as quickly as possible.

Process cost system   A cost accounting system used mostly in industries such as petroleum or chemicals characterized by continuous mass production. Costs are not assigned to specific units but to a manufacturing process or department.

DEMONSTRATION PROBLEM FOR YOUR REVIEW

The Diversified Mfg. Company started operations early in January with two production departments, Foundry and Blending. The Foundry Department produces special castings to customer specifications and the Blending Department produces an industrial compound which is sold by the pound. The company uses a job order cost system in the Foundry and a process cost system in the Blending Department.

The following schedule summarizes the operations for January:

	Total Costs Incurred	Foundry	Blending	Inventory at Jan. 31
Materials	$40,000	$13,000	$23,000	$4,000
Direct labor	56,800	20,000	36,800	
Factory overhead	43,600	16,000	27,600	

Shown below is the schedule of the jobs in process in the Foundry at January 31:

	Materials	Direct Labor
Job no. 9	$600	$400
Job no. 10	580	500

All other jobs were shipped to customers at a billed price of $60,000. The factory overhead in the Foundry is applied on the basis of direct labor cost.

The January production report for the Blending Department shows the following:

	Pounds
Placed in production	95,000
Completed	80,000
In process at Jan. 31, 80% complete as to materials and conversion costs . . .	15,000

Of the units completed, 70,000 were sold for $92,500 and the other 10,000 are stored in the warehouse. Selling expenses for January amounted to $14,250 and general and administrative expenses amounted to $12,500.

Instructions

a Prepare the journal entries to record (1) materials purchases and the requisitions for the Foundry and Blending departments and (2) the labor and overhead costs (including allocation to the two departments).

b Determine the cost of the jobs in process in the Foundry at the end of January and prepare journal entries (1) to transfer the cost of jobs completed to Finished Goods Inventory and (2) to record the sales and cost of goods sold for the month.

c Prepare a cost report for the Blending Department and prepare journal entries (1) to transfer the cost of the finished product to the Finished Goods Inventory account and (2) to record the sales and cost of goods sold for the month.

d Prepare a condensed income statement for January. (Ignore income taxes.)

SOLUTION TO DEMONSTRATION PROBLEM

a (1) Materials Inventory 40,000

           Accounts Payable   40,000

    To record purchase of materials.

    Goods in Process: Foundry Department 13,000

    Goods in Process: Blending Department 23,000

           Materials Inventory   36,000

    To record requisitions of materials.

(2) Factory Payroll 56,800
Factory Overhead 43,600
      Cash, Accounts Payable, etc.   100,400
To record factory payroll and overhead costs.

Goods in Process: Foundry Department 36,000
Goods in Process: Blending Department 64,400
      Factory Payroll   56,800
      Factory Overhead   43,600
To allocate factory payroll and overhead costs to
productive departments.

b   Cost of jobs in process in Foundry Department at January 31:

	Total	Job No. 9	Job No. 10
Materials	$1,180	$ 600	$ 580
Direct labor	900	400	500
Factory overhead, 80% of direct labor	720	320	400
	$2,800	$1,320	$1,480

(1) Finished Goods Inventory   46,200
      Goods in Process: Foundry Department . . .   46,200
To record cost of jobs completed: Total debits to
Foundry Department, $49,000, less cost of jobs in
process, $2,800 = $46,200.

(2) Accounts Receivable   60,000
      Sales   60,000
To record sale of goods completed in Foundry
Department.

Cost of Goods Sold   46,200
      Finished Goods Inventory   46,200
To record cost of goods sold from Foundry
Department.

c

BLENDING DEPARTMENT
Cost Report for January

	Total Units	Total Costs ÷	Equivalent Full Units* =	Unit Cost
Inputs:				
Materials	95,000	$23,000	92,000	**$0.25**
Direct labor		36,800	92,000	**0.40**
Factory overhead		27,600	92,000	**0.30**
Total inputs—units and costs	95,000	$87,400		
Unit cost for January				**$0.95**
Outputs:				
Transferred to Finished Goods				
Inventory ($0.95 per unit)	80,000	$76,000		
Units in process at end of month				
(80% complete as to materials and				
conversion costs), 12,000 @ $.95	15,000	11,400		
Total outputs—units and costs	95,000	$87,400		

* Computation of equivalent full units:

Units completed during January	80,000
Add: Full units of work done in January on ending inventory in process	
(15,000 × 80%)	12,000
Output in January in terms of equivalent full units	92,000

(1) Finished Goods Inventory	76,000	
Goods in Process: Blending Department		76,000
To record cost of finished product.		
(2) Accounts Receivable	92,500	
Sales		92,500
To record sales from Blending Department.		
Cost of Goods Sold	66,500	
Finished Goods Inventory		66,500
To record cost of goods sold from Blending Department,		
70,000 units @ $0.95 per unit.		

d

DIVERSIFIED MFG. COMPANY
Income Statement
For January

Sales ($60,000 + $92,500)		$152,500
Cost of goods sold ($46,200 + $66,500)		112,700
Gross profit on sales		$ 39,800
Operating expenses:		
Selling expenses	$14,250	
General and administrative expenses	12,500	26,750
Operating income		$ 13,050

REVIEW QUESTIONS

1 What is a cost accounting system?

2 What are the two major objectives of cost accounting?

3 Why is it difficult to measure the precise cost of a product or a service produced by a business enterprise?

4 What is meant by the phrase, "different costs for different purposes"? Illustrate by explaining how a factory superintendent's salary might be treated differently, as a cost, for different purposes.

5 Differentiate between *product costs* and *period costs.*

6 What factors should be taken into account in deciding whether to use a job order cost system or a process cost system in any given manufacturing situation?

7 Describe the three kinds of charges on a job cost sheet. For what general ledger control account do job cost sheets constitute supporting detail?

8 Explain why it is advantageous to use predetermined overhead rates in associating factory overhead with output.

9 Define each of the following: *Prime costs, conversion costs, fixed costs,* and *variable costs.*

10 Gerox Company applies factory overhead on the basis of machine-hours, using a predetermined overhead rate. At the end of the current year the factory overhead account has a credit balance. What are the possible explanations for this? What disposition should be made of this balance?

11 What are the characteristics of a process cost system?

12 Define *direct* and *indirect* or departmental costs.

13 What is the purpose of service department cost accounts? Give some examples of service departments in a factory.

14 What is meant by the term *equivalent full units?* How is this concept used in computing average unit costs?

15 Briefly describe a *cost report* as it might be prepared for a department using a process cost system.

EXERCISES

Ex. 25-1 The information below is taken from the job order cost system used by the Gate Company:

Job Number	Balance, July 1	Production Costs in July
101	$1,400	
102	1,080	
103	300	$ 650
104	750	1,300
105		1,900
106		1,210

Jobs no. 103 and 104 were completed and jobs no. 101, 102, and 103 were delivered to customers in July. From the foregoing information, compute the following:

a The goods in process inventory at July 1
b The finished goods inventory at July 1

c The cost of goods sold during July
d The goods in process inventory at July 31
e The finished goods inventory at July 31

Ex. 25-2 The Patio Floorings Company uses a process cost accounting system but does not use a predetermined overhead rate. Its records show the following information for the month of June:

	June 30	*June 1*
Inventories:		
Raw materials	*$ 24,000*	*$30,000*
Goods in process	*22,500*	*12,000*
Finished goods	*39,000*	*36,000*
Purchases of raw materials	*90,000*	
Direct labor	*120,000*	
Factory overhead	*75,000*	

Compute the following:
a Overhead rate based on direct labor cost
b Cost of goods manufactured in June
c Cost of goods sold in June

Ex. 25-3 The following information appears in the Goods in Process account of Bar Stools, Inc., for the month of January:

Debits to account:	
Raw materials	*$ 48,000*
Direct labor	*80,000*
Factory overhead (applied to jobs at 120% of direct labor cost)	*96,000*
Total debits to account	*$224,000*
Credits to account:	
Transferred to Finished Goods Inventory account	*192,000*
Balance in account, end of January	*$ 32,000*

If the cost of raw materials relating to the jobs in process on January 31 amounts to $14,400, determine the amount of direct labor and factory overhead which has been charged to the jobs still in process at January 31.

Ex. 25-4 The Snowplow Company, which used a job order cost system, completed the following transactions during the month of November:
a Direct labor, $18,000, and indirect labor, $6,000, were transferred from the Factory Payroll account to other appropriate accounts.
b Other factory overhead costs of $13,800 were incurred (credit Miscellaneous Accounts).
c Factory overhead costs were applied to goods in process at the rate of 80% of direct labor cost.
d Raw materials identified with specific jobs amounted to $9,840.
e Jobs with total accumulated costs of $36,000 were finished.
f The cost of units sold during the month amounted to $34,560; the sales price of units sold is $48,000.
Prepare entries in journal form to record the foregoing transactions. Explanations may be omitted.

Ex. 25-5 The following relates to the Assembly Department which manufactures product Y:

Units in process at beginning of period (60% completed)	*2,000*
Additional units placed in production during the period	*20,000*
Units in process at end of period (80% completed)	*5,000*

Determine the equivalent full units of production during the period, assuming that all costs are incurred uniformly as the units move through the production line.

Ex. 25-6 Given below are the production data for Department no. 1 for the first month of operation:

Inputs to department:

Material, 1,000 units	$10,000
Direct labor	19,000
Factory overhead	14,250

During the first month, 800 units were completed and the remaining 200 units are 100% completed as to material and 75% completed as to direct labor and factory overhead.

You are to determine:

a Unit cost of material used
b Equivalent full units of production for direct labor and factory overhead
c Unit cost of direct labor
d Unit cost of factory overhead
e Total cost of 800 units completed
f Total cost of 200 units in process at end of month

PROBLEMS

Group A

25A-1 Neilson Company uses a predetermined rate in applying factory overhead to individual production orders. Overhead is applied in Department C on the basis of machine-hours, and in Department D on the basis of direct labor hours. At the beginning of the current year, management made the following budget estimates:

	Department C	Department D
Direct labor	$110,000	$384,000
Factory overhead	$216,000	$240,000
Machine-hours	72,000 √	900
Direct labor hours	25,000	100,000 √

Production order no. 399 for 2,000 units was started in the middle of January and completed two weeks later. The cost records for this job show the following information:

	Department C	Department D
Job no. 399 (2,000 units of product):		
Cost of materials used on job	$6,000	$14,180
Direct labor cost	$8,000	$16,000
Direct labor hours	1,000	1,800
Machine-hours	2,500	100

Instructions
a Determine the overhead rate that should be used for each department in applying overhead costs to job no. 399.
b What is the total cost of job no. 399, and the unit cost of the product manufactured on this production order?
c Assume that actual overhead costs for the year were $215,000 in Department C and $236,400 in Department D. Actual machine-hours in Department C were

75,000, and actual direct labor hours in Department D were 90,000 during the year. On the basis of this information, determine the over- or underapplied overhead in each department for the year.

25A-2 Below is a summary of the cost flow relating to production orders in process in the Lexington Company during the month of June:

	Production Order 22	Production Order 23	Production Order 24	Production Order 25	Production Order 26
In process on June 1	$11,400	$ 2,920			
Costs in June:					
Direct materials	1,200	8,600	$12,500	$15,800	$ 4,700
Direct labor	3,300	9,700	15,800	20,300	6,400
Overhead applied, 110% .	3,630	10,670	17,380	22,330	7,040
Total cost	$19,530	$31,890	$45,680	$58,430	$18,140

Other data At the beginning of June, the following inventories appeared on the records of the company: materials $24,100, goods in process $14,320, finished goods $24,600. During June production orders numbered 22, 23, and 24 were completed and production was transferred to finished goods inventory. All finished product in the beginning inventory was sold, and 90% of June's production was sold, for $200,000. All sales were on open account. Below is a summary of other transactions during June:

(1) In addition to direct labor, the accrued payroll for indirect labor during the month was $28,200, and for selling and administrative salaries was $40,000. Credit Accrued Payroll for $123,700.

(2) Raw materials and supplies purchased on open account during June amounted to $49,000.

(3) Depreciation on buildings and equipment was $6,000 (75% related to manufacturing and 25% to selling and administrative functions).

(4) Additional factory costs amounting to $27,700 were incurred. Credit Materials Inventory, $18,850, and Accounts Payable, $8,850.

(5) Other selling and administrative expenses incurred totaled $7,040. Credit Prepaid Expenses, $3,240, and Accounts Payable, $3,800.

Instructions

a Prepare general journal entries summarizing the transactions of the Lexington Company for the month of June. Use a single control account for factory overhead and for selling and administrative expenses.

b Set up ledger control accounts in three-column form for Materials Inventory, Goods in Process Inventory, and Finished Goods Inventory accounts, and for the Factory Overhead account, and enter the June 1 balances and transactions relating to these accounts for the month of June.

c Prepare in condensed form an income statement for the month of June. Assume that over- or underapplied overhead is closed to the Cost of Goods Sold account at the end of each month.

25A-3 Dynamics, Inc., manufactures a standard subassembly which it sells to another division of the company at $50 per unit. The plant manager has prepared a budget for the current year which calls for the production and delivery of 32,000 units at an average unit cost of $38 per unit; this is composed of material cost $12, direct labor cost $15, and factory overhead $11. The manager estimates that income before taxes will be $6.50 per unit delivered, after allowing for operating expenses.

The plant had no inventory of goods in process at the beginning of the year. During the current year 42,000 units of product were put into production, and 30,000 units were completely finished. The 12,000 units in process at the end of the year were fully complete as to materials but were only 50% complete, on the average, as to labor and factory overhead.

The cost data shown below were taken from the accounting records at the close of the current year:

Materials used	*$483,000*
Direct labor	*576,000*
Factory overhead	*270,000*
Operating expenses	*160,000*

The plant had beginning finished goods inventory of 4,000 units carried at a cost of $152,000. During the current year 32,000 finished units were delivered and billed at $50 each to the sister division of the company.

Instructions
a Compute the per-unit material, labor, and overhead cost of production during the year. (Hint: First determine equivalent full units produced.)
b Determine the cost of the ending inventories of goods in process and finished goods. (Assume fifo flow of costs.)
c Prepare a comparative statement showing the actual income (before income taxes) and the income which was anticipated by the manager on the basis of the budget estimates. Comment on the differences between the two income figures.

25A-4 The Haley Mfg. Company uses a process cost accounting system for all three of its departments. The following information was prepared by the company's cost accountant, summarizing the activities of the Finishing Department for the current month:

Cost inputs—Finishing Department:	
Beginning goods in process inventory, 200 units, all materials included,	
80% completed as to processing costs	*$ 2,606*
Direct materials placed in production, sufficient to produce 8,000 units	
(includes costs transferred from preceding department)	*80,400*
Direct labor and factory overhead incurred during the month	*38,808*
Total cost inputs	*$121,814*
Cost inputs assigned to:	
Units completed, 7,700 @ $15.82	*$121,814*
Ending goods in process inventory, 500 units, all materials included,	
60% completed as to processing costs	*none*
Total cost inputs assigned	*$121,814*

The beginning inventory of finished goods consisted of 2,000 units costing $24,000 (on a fifo basis). A total of 6,700 units were sold during the current month. The company's cost accountant computed the cost of goods sold and the ending inventory of finished goods as follows:

Cost of goods sold:	
2,000 units @ $12.00	*$24,000*
4,700 units @ $15.82	*74,354*
Total cost of goods sold	*$98,354*
Finished goods inventory, 3,000 units @ $15.82	*47,460*

No value was assigned to ending goods in process.

Instructions

a Compute the equivalent full units of work done during the month relating to direct materials and processing costs and determine the cost per unit. Do not prepare a formal cost report.

b Prepare a schedule showing the assignment of the cost inputs to the 7,700 units completed during the month and to the 500 units in process at the end of the month.

c Assuming that the accounts are still open, prepare a correcting entry to restate the Cost of Goods Sold and the Finished Goods Inventory accounts and to establish the appropriate balance in the Goods in Process account. The inventory of finished goods should be valued at the average manufacturing cost for the current month ($15).

25A-5 One of the primary products of Camera, Inc., is Photorex, a product which is processed successively in Department A and Department B, and then transferred to the company's sales warehouse. After having been shut down for three weeks as a result of a material shortage, the company resumed production of Photorex on May 1. The flow of product through the departments during May is shown below.

Department A		*Department B*	
Goods in Process		*Goods in Process*	
Input—	*To Dept. B—*	*From Dept. A—*	*To warehouse—*
30,000 units	*25,000 units*	*25,000 units*	*21,000 units*

Departmental manufacturing costs applicable to Photorex production for the month of May were as follows:

	Department A	*Department B*
Raw materials.	$11,200	$ 4,680
Direct labor	9,800	7,020
Factory overhead.	7,000	14,040
Total manufacturing costs	$28,000	$25,740

Unfinished goods in each department at the end of May were on the average 60% complete, with respect to both raw materials and processing costs.

Instructions

a Determine the present status of the 30,000 units put into production in Department A during May.

b Determine the equivalent full units of production in each department during May.

c Compute unit production costs in each department during May.

d Prepare the necessary journal entries to record the transfer of product out of Departments A and B during May.

Group B

25B-1 Niles Company applies a predetermined overhead rate to production on the basis of direct labor hours in Department One and on the basis of machine—hours in Department Two. The budget estimates for the current year are shown on page 912.

	Department One	Department Two
Direct labor cost	$200,000	$150,000
Direct labor hours	40,000	37,500
Shop overhead (fixed and variable)	$120,000	$ 60,000
Machine-hours	10,000	15,000

Production of a batch of custom furniture ordered by the City Furniture Chain (job no. 58) was started early in the year and completed three weeks later on January 29. The records for this job show the following cost information:

	Department One	Department Two
Job order for City Furniture Chain (job no. 58):		
Direct materials cost	$10,100	$ 4,600
Direct labor cost.	$16,000	$10,200
Direct labor hours	3,100	2,600
Machine-hours	750	880

Selected additional information for January is given below:

	Department One	Department Two
Direct labor hours—month of January	3,700	3,000
Machine-hours—month of January	1,000	1,400
Shop overhead incurred in January	$10,800	$6,100

Instructions
a Compute the predetermined overhead rate for each department.
b What is the total cost of the furniture produced for the City Furniture Chain?
c Prepare the entries required to record the shipment of the furniture to the City Furniture Chain. The sales price of the order was "cost plus 20%."
d Determine the over- or underapplied overhead for each department at the end of January.

25B-2 The information below relates to a production department operated by the Springfield Company:

Units in process at beginning of May—40% complete as to materials and 60% complete as to conversion costs	2,000
Cost of units in process at beginning of May	$20,000
Units placed in production during May	11,000
Cost of materials placed in production	$91,600
Direct labor cost incurred	$56,000
Factory overhead costs incurred (applied at 120% of direct labor cost) . . .	$67,950
Units in process at end of May—75% complete as to materials and 80% complete as to conversion costs	3,000

Underapplied factory overhead amounts to $750 at the end of May.

Instructions
a Compute the equivalent full units completed during May. Use one column for materials and one for conversion costs.
b Prepare a cost report for May, as illustrated on page 899. Prepare a separate

schedule (Exhibit A) showing the assignment of cost inputs to the units completed during May and to the units in process at the end of May.

c Prepare journal entries to record the costs allocated to production and the cost of goods completed during May.

25B-3 The owner of Bel Air Company has requested your assistance in preparing a summary of operations during June for a job order cost system. Inventories at June 1 are shown below:

Raw materials inventory	$30,000
Factory supplies inventory	1,000
Goods in process (Foundry, $8,000; Machine Shop, $12,000)	20,000
Finished goods inventory	15,000

Purchases and factory requisitions of raw materials and factory supplies during June are summarized as follows:

	Purchases	Requisitions
Raw materials	$20,000	$39,500
Factory supplies	2,150	2,500

After reviewing the work done up to June 1, you accumulate the following cost information for the month of June:

		Service Depts.		Productive Depts.	
Costs	Total	Power Plant	General Plant	Foundry	Machine Shop
Direct departmental					
labor	$26,150	$2,300	$1,350	$12,500	$10,000
Raw materials	39,500	500	1,000	23,500	14,500
Depreciation	1,100	140	80	350	530
Property taxes	250	40	20	70	120
Insurance	500	100	25	150	225
Repairs	200	200			
Miscellaneous factory					
costs	2,800	130	205	630	1,835
Factory supplies	2,500	150	1,100	500	750
Totals	$73,000	$3,560	$3,780	$37,700	$27,960

The overhead costs in the Foundry and the Machine Shop are allocated to individual jobs on the basis of direct labor costs. The following direct costs have been incurred on the four production orders in process at the end of June:

	Foundry	Machine Shop
Raw materials	$3,000	$1,200
Direct departmental labor	1,800	900

Instructions

a Prepare a work sheet showing the distribution of factory overhead costs to the departments for the month of June. Power Plant costs are allocated equally to the two productive departments and the costs of the General Plant are allocated to the Foundry and Machine Shop in a 2:1 ratio. Determine the factory overhead rate for the Foundry and the Machine Shop.

b Determine the total cost to be assigned to the four production orders in process at the end of June.

c Determine the cost of goods completed in June in each of the two departments. You need not prepare a formal statement of cost of goods manufactured.

25B-4 The White River Company manufactures a chemical XPO-2 in four sequential processes. The Fourth Process is the last step before the chemical is transferred to the warehouse as finished inventory.

All material needed to complete XPO-2 is added at the beginning of the Fourth Process. The company accumulated the following cost information for the Fourth Process during the month of April:

Costs assigned to the 40,000 units in process on April 1:	
Costs from Third Process transferred to Fourth Process in March	*$ 152,000*
Costs added in Fourth Process in March:	
Materials (100% or total requirement)	*86,000*
Direct labor (75% of total requirement)	*156,000*
Factory overhead (75% of total requirement)	*168,000*
Cost of goods in process inventory, April 1	*$ 562,000*
Cost inputs in the Fourth Process during April:	
From Third Process (140,000 units)	*$ 560,000*
Materials requisitions	*280,000*
Direct labor added	*625,000*
Factory overhead costs incurred	*750,000*
Total inputs during April	*$2,215,000*

During April, 130,000 units of XPO-2 were completed and transferred to the warehouse. The 50,000 units in process at the end of April were 50% completed as to direct labor and factory overhead and 100% completed as to materials.

Instructions

a Compute the equivalent full units completed during April. Use one column for materials and one for labor and overhead.

b Prepare a cost report for the month of April. Prepare a separate Exhibit A showing the assignment of cost inputs completed and goods in process.

c Prepare journal entries to record:

(1) Costs incurred in the Fourth Process during April.

(2) Transfer of the 130,000 units completed from the Fourth Process to the Finished Goods Inventory account.

25B-5 Files, Inc., produces a line of metal filing cabinets. The company has been divided into a number of departments, one of which is the Lock Assembly Department. The company uses a process cost system. The following information pertains to the goods in process in the Lock Assembly Department during the month of April:

Beginning inventory	*$ 22,000*
Materials used	*79,000*
Direct labor	*155,000*
Applied factory overhead (80% of direct labor cost)	*124,000*
Total cost inputs	*$380,000*

Production Report for April

Units in process April 1 (100% complete as to materials, 75% complete as to labor and factory overhead)	3,000
Units put into process during April	40,000
Total units to account for	43,000
Units transferred to the Painting Department	38,000
Units in process April 30 (90% complete as to materials; 60% complete as to labor and factory overhead)	5,000
Total units accounted for	43,000

Instructions

a Compute the unit costs for materials, direct labor, and factory overhead for the Lock Assembly Department for the month of April. You should first compute the equivalent full units of work completed.

b Make the journal entry necessary to transfer the product from the Lock Assembly Department to the Painting Department for the month of April. Show how you determined the cost of the units transferred. (You may use the first-in, first-out assumption.)

c Prepare a schedule showing the computation of the cost of the ending inventory of goods in process in the Lock Assembly Department.

BUSINESS DECISION PROBLEM 25

The demand for the product made by Hart Benton Products fluctuates seasonally. Units costs are computed quarterly on the basis of actual material, labor, and factory overhead costs charged to goods in process at the end of each quarter. At the close of the current year, Benton received the following cost report, by quarters, for the year. (Fixed factory overhead represents items of manufacturing costs that remain relatively constant month by month; variable factory overhead includes those costs that tend to move up and down in proportion to changes in the volume of production.)

	First Quarter	Second Quarter	Third Quarter	Fourth Quarter
Direct materials	$ 9,200	$ 37,200	$ 26,500	$ 19,900
Direct labor	21,000	80,000	60,000	39,000
Fixed factory overhead	25,000	25,000	25,000	25,000
Variable factory overhead	14,800	47,000	38,500	25,700
Total manufacturing cost	$70,000	$189,200	$150,000	$109,600
Units produced	10,000	40,000	30,000	20,000
Unit costs	$ 7.00	$ 4.73	$ 5.00	$ 5.48

Benton is concerned about the wide variation in quarterly unit costs. He notes that his unit product cost was $7.00 in the first quarter of the year but only $4.73 in the second quarter. He asks you to study the problem and see whether the method of computing unit costs could be improved.

You point out that the primary reason for the quarterly variation in unit costs is the seasonal fluctuation in volume of production and suggest that the company change its costing system.

Instructions

a What change in the company's costing procedure would you recommend? Redetermine the unit cost for each quarter using the procedure you recommend.

b At the end of the first quarter of the year, the company had received an offer from an exporter to buy 8,000 units at a special price of $4.70 per unit. The company's normal selling price is $8 per unit. Since the company's total unit costs had bever been as low as $4.70, and amounted to $7.00 in the first quarter, Benton refused the offer. On the basis of the information that you have, would you have made the same decision? Why?

26

Managerial Control: Standard Costs and Budgeting

One of the primary functions of management is to control the operations of the organization for which it is responsible. In a broad sense, managerial control includes: (*1*) *planning*—setting organizational objectives, standards of performance, and choosing among alternative courses of action; (*2*) *action*—seeing that plans are put into effect and that policies are followed; (*3*) *reporting*—measuring the results of actions taken; and (*4*) *evaluation*—assessing the quality of performance and taking necessary steps to correct deviations from plans. In a nutshell, the function of managerial control is to see that what is intended to be done is in fact done.

Management needs information to implement control

Accounting information is useful in all four areas of managerial control. However, the information needed by management frequently differs materially from the data collected in the accounting records. The primary purpose of most accounting systems is to provide information for the preparation of financial statements. Management's internal needs for information, however, extend beyond the data contained in financial statements. To exercise effective control, management must estimate future costs and revenue, measure the effect of alternative actions, and compare past performance with predetermined standards. In developing information for its own internal use, management is not tied to generally accepted accounting principles. Estimates may be incorporated freely into the data and whatever measurement rules prove most useful and relevant may be adopted.

An accounting system that serves all possible external and internal informational needs is a dream that will probably never become a reality. Too many different ways of measuring and relating costs and benefits can be devised that are useful and relevant in making business decisions. Therefore, anyone who depends on accounting data for control purposes should know how to rearrange and modify the informational output of an accounting system to meet varying decision-making needs.

In this chapter we discuss two important concepts that have proved useful to managers in planning and controlling operations—standard costs and budgeting.

STANDARD COSTS FOR PRODUCT COSTING AND CONTROL

In the preceding chapter it was stated that one of the objectives of cost accounting is to determine the unit cost of production. We saw that *actual* costs are determined through *process cost* or *job order cost* systems, and that such actual costs are used to compute the cost of goods sold, to value ending inventories, and to control factory operations.

If a process or job order cost system is to be of maximum value to management, however, *predetermined* cost estimates for material, labor, and factory overhead should be introduced into such a system in order to have a bench mark against which actual costs can be compared. These predetermined costs are called *standard costs.* A standard cost is the cost that *should be* incurred to produce a given product or to perform a particular operation under relatively ideal conditions. The use of such costs in the accounting records is known as a *standard cost system.*

As stated previously, an effective managerial control system calls for the setting of standards of performance, measuring actual performance, and taking corrective action when necessary. Standard costs can be used to establish cost goals and to direct management's attention to areas requiring corrective action. This is known as *management by exception* because managers should not spend time on areas of activity which are running according to plans. Effective managers focus attention on those activities which are "off target," that is, those not meeting the established standards of performance. For example, if a standard cost to produce a given product is set at $10 per unit and the actual cost is $12.50 per unit, management would want to know why actual cost exceeded standard cost by such a large margin and would strive to attain tighter control over production costs.

Establishing and revising standard costs

In establishing a standard cost for a manufactured product, for example, factory conditions and prices for materials, labor, and factory overhead must be studied. The most efficient methods for the use of materials, labor, and machinery should be selected before cost standards for each operation or product can be established.

Once cost standards are set, they should be periodically reviewed and changed only when production methods change, when products are redesigned, or when prices paid for materials, labor, and factory overhead change. Standard costs should not be changed simply because actual costs are excessive. If standard costs are too low and actual costs regularly exceed standard costs by a large margin, the standards should be revised upward; if standard costs are too high, they may be easily achieved and much of the potential benefit of using a standard cost system as a control instrument may be lost.

A standard cost for materials, for example, would not be changed if 10% of material placed in production has been spoiled because of carelessness by employees; the standard cost for material would be changed, however, if the price for materials is reduced by suppliers. Similarly, the standard cost for labor would not be changed if too many hours of labor are wasted; but the standard cost for labor would be changed if labor-saving equipment is installed or if new contracts with labor unions call for increased wage rates.

Cost variances

Even though standard costs may be carefully set and revised as conditions change, actual costs will still vary from standard costs. The differences between standard costs and actual costs are known as *cost variances.* Cost variances for materials, direct labor, and factory overhead result from a wide variety of causes which must be carefully measured and analyzed. As might be expected, different individuals within an organization are responsible for different cost variances.

It is possible to use standard costs only for cost control purposes and for the preparation of various internal reports for management's use. In most cases, however, standard costs and cost variances are recorded in the accounts. Under standard cost procedures, the costs charged to Goods in Process, Finished Goods, and Cost of Goods Sold are the standard costs of materials, direct labor, and factory overhead, not the actual costs. Any differences between the actual costs and the standard costs of goods produced are accumulated in a number of *variance accounts.*

In order to illustrate the application of standard cost procedures, assume that the Standard Manufacturing Company has a normal monthly capacity to work 10,000 direct labor hours and to produce 10,000 units of product M. The standard cost for a unit of product M is shown at the top of page 920.

Standard cost for a unit of product M	Materials, one pound at $5 per pound		$ 5
	Direct labor, one hour at $4 per hour		4
	Factory overhead, based on direct labor hours:		
	Fixed ($20,000 ÷ 10,000 labor hours of monthly capacity)	$2	
	Variable ($10,000 ÷ 10,000 labor hours of monthly capacity)	1	3
	Standard cost per unit of product M		$12

During the month of March, the following actual costs were incurred in producing 9,500 units of product M. There was no work in process either at the beginning or at the end of March.

Were standard cost targets achieved?	Materials, 9,400 pounds at $5.20 per pound		$ 48,880
	Direct labor, 9,600 hours at $4.10 per hour		39,360
	Factory overhead:		
	Fixed	$20,000	
	Variable, 9,600 hours at $1.30 per hour	12,480	32,480
	Total actual costs incurred in March		$120,720

Even though the company "saved" 100 pounds of materials, (9,500 − 9,400), its total actual costs were $6,720 in excess of costs that *should have been incurred* in producing 9,500 units of product M. This is the *total cost variance,* determined as follows:

Who is responsible for the apparent waste of $6,720?	Total actual costs (see above)	$120,720
	Total standard costs for units produced, 9,500 units at $12 per unit	114,000
	Total cost variance (excess of actual over standard costs)	$ 6,720

MATERIAL PRICE AND MATERIAL QUANTITY VARIANCES In establishing the standard material cost for each unit of product, two factors were considered: (*1*) the quantity of material that should have been used in making a unit of finished product, and (*2*) the prices that should have been paid in acquiring this quantity of material. Therefore, the total material cost variance may result from differences between standard and actual material usage, or between standard and actual prices paid for materials, or from a combination of these two factors. This can be illustrated by the following diagram:

Material variances illustrated

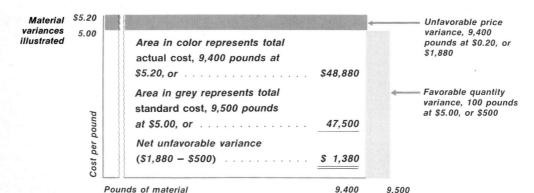

$5.20
5.00

Area in color represents total actual cost, 9,400 pounds at $5.20, or $48,880

Area in grey represents total standard cost, 9,500 pounds at $5.00, or 47,500

Net unfavorable variance ($1,880 − $500) .... $ 1,380

Cost per pound

Pounds of material   9,400   9,500

Unfavorable price variance, 9,400 pounds at $0.20, or $1,880

Favorable quantity variance, 100 pounds at $5.00, or $500

The variances for materials and the journal entry required to record the cost of material incurred by the Standard Manufacturing Company in the month of March may be summarized as follows:

Material Price and Quantity Variances

Why was actual material cost higher than standard?

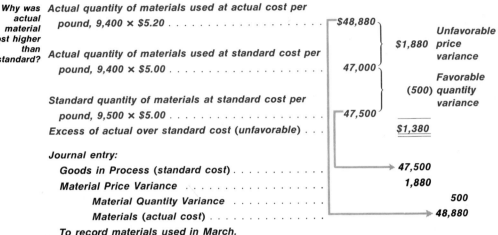

Actual quantity of materials used at actual cost per pound, 9,400 × $5.20 . . . . $48,880

Actual quantity of materials used at standard cost per pound, 9,400 × $5.00 47,000

Unfavorable $1,880 price variance

Favorable (500) quantity variance

Standard quantity of materials at standard cost per pound, 9,500 × $5.00 47,500

Excess of actual over standard cost (unfavorable) . . . $1,380

Journal entry:

Goods in Process (standard cost) 47,500

Material Price Variance 1,880

Material Quantity Variance 500

Materials (actual cost) 48,880

To record materials used in March.

The excess of actual cost of materials over standard cost was caused by two factors: The unfavorable *material price variance* of $1,880 resulted from the fact that each pound of material used cost 20 cents more than the standard price of $5; this portion of the total material variance is the responsibility of the person placing orders for materials. The favorable *material quantity variance* of $500 resulted from using 100 fewer pounds of materials than the standard allowed; this variance indicates that the shop supervisors are doing a good job because they are responsible for seeing that materials are not wasted or spoiled.

Note that in the example above the Goods in Process account is debited for the standard cost of materials used and that the Materials account is reduced by an amount equal to the actual cost of materials used. An alternative procedure would be to record materials purchased in the Materials account at standard cost, thus recording the price variance at the time of purchase. The unfavorable material price variance is recorded as a debit (a loss) and the favorable material quantity variance is recorded as a credit (a gain).

LABOR RATE AND LABOR USAGE VARIANCES Labor cost standards are also a product of two factors: (1) the hours of labor that should be used in making a unit of product, and (2) the wage rate that should be paid for that labor. An analysis of the total labor variance will indicate whether the variance was due to the fact that more (or less) than standard time was required in production, or that more (or less) than standard wage rates were paid, or some combination of these two factors. The computation of the labor variances for the Standard Manufacturing Company and the journal entry required to record the direct labor cost for March are illustrated below.

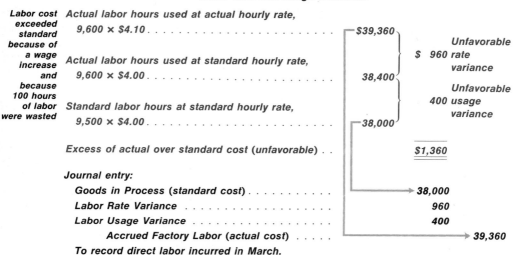

Labor Rate and Usage Variances

Labor cost exceeded standard because of a wage increase and because 100 hours of labor were wasted

Actual labor hours used at actual hourly rate,
9,600 × $4.10 . . . . $39,360

Unfavorable $ 960 rate variance

Actual labor hours used at standard hourly rate,
9,600 × $4.00 38,400

Unfavorable 400 usage variance

Standard labor hours at standard hourly rate,
9,500 × $4.00 38,000

Excess of actual over standard cost (unfavorable) . . $1,360

Journal entry:
Goods in Process (standard cost) 38,000
Labor Rate Variance 960
Labor Usage Variance 400
   Accrued Factory Labor (actual cost) 39,360
To record direct labor incurred in March.

The foregoing tabulation indicates that both the *labor rate variance* and the *labor usage variance* are unfavorable. The causes of these variances should be carefully investigated. If the rate increase of 10 cents per labor hour resulted from a new union contract, nothing much can be done; however, if the increase resulted from using higher-rated employees on the production line or from unnecessary overtime work, corrective action on the part of the shop foreman may be in order. The supervisor should also be asked to explain the reason why 100 hours of labor in excess of standard were used during the month.

FACTORY OVERHEAD VARIANCES The difference between actual factory overhead costs incurred and the standard factory overhead costs charged to the units produced during the period is called the *overhead variance.* The standard factory overhead cost is applied to goods in process by the Standard Manufacturing Company on the basis of a predetermined factory overhead rate of $3 per direct labor hour.

The association of factory overhead with production depends on estimates of factory overhead costs for the normal volume of production. *Normal volume* is the expected average utilization of plant capacity over many years. The presence of fixed costs in factory overhead means that the amount of factory overhead per unit of output will differ depending on the *actual* production volume attained. It is not surprising, therefore, that the analysis of the factory overhead variance is a complicated undertaking.

One possible approach is to take the difference between actual factory overhead incurred and standard factory overhead and divide it into two variances: (*1*) the difference between actual factory overhead and the factory overhead budgeted for the level of output attained (called the ***controllable factory overhead variance***), and (2) the difference between factory overhead budgeted for the volume of output attained and the standard factory overhead for the volume of output attained (called the ***factory overhead volume variance***). The computation of these two variances for the Standard Manufacturing Company and the journal entry required to record factory overhead for March follow:

Factory Overhead Variances

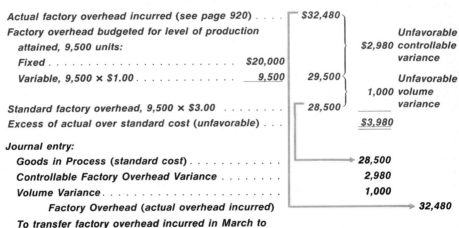

Actual factory overhead exceeded standard. Can you explain why this happened?

Actual factory overhead incurred (see page 920)	$32,480	
Factory overhead budgeted for level of production attained, 9,500 units:		Unfavorable
		$2,980 controllable
Fixed	$20,000	variance
Variable, 9,500 × $1.00	9,500	29,500
		Unfavorable
		1,000 volume
Standard factory overhead, 9,500 × $3.00	28,500	variance
Excess of actual over standard cost (unfavorable) . . .		$3,980
Journal entry:		
Goods in Process (standard cost)	28,500	
Controllable Factory Overhead Variance	2,980	
Volume Variance	1,000	
Factory Overhead (actual overhead incurred)		32,480

To transfer factory overhead incurred in March to goods in process and variance accounts.

The major reason for the large unfavorable factory overhead variance is that variable factory overhead incurred amounted to $1.30 per hour compared to the standard variable factory overhead of $1.00 per hour. This increase accounted for $2,880 (9,600 hours × $0.30) of the ***controllable factory overhead variance.*** The excess of hours worked (9,600) over standard hours (9,500) accounted for the other $100 of the controllable factory overhead variance. This is determined by multiplying the 100 excess hours worked by the standard variable factory overhead rate of $1.00. The reason this variance is "controllable" is that the two factors which are responsible for it, variable factory overhead costs incurred and the actual hours worked, can both be heavily influenced by an effective cost control system.

The unfavorable ***volume variance*** of $1,000 is the portion of the total fixed factory overhead not applied to production, 500 units not produced × $2.00 (fixed factory overhead rate per unit). Since the Standard Manufacturing Company produced only 9,500 units of product M, it fell 5% short of its monthly capacity of 10,000 units. Therefore, 5% of the total capacity (fixed) costs of $20,000, or $1,000, was *not applied* to units produced. In other words, this was the *idle capacity loss* for the month of March.

TRANSFER OF COST OF UNITS COMPLETED TO FINISHED GOODS INVENTORY At the end of March, the entry to record the transfer of cost of goods completed from the Goods in Process account to the Finished Goods Inventory account is shown below:

Entry to record goods completed
Finished Goods Inventory (*at standard cost*) 114,000
     Goods in Process (*at standard cost*) 114,000
To transfer cost of units completed to finished goods inventory.

Disposition of variance accounts

Under a standard cost system, monthly inventories of goods in process and finished goods may be priced at standard cost. Cost variances are allowed to accumulate from month to month; hopefully, only a small total variance will remain because unfavorable variances in one month are offset by favorable variances in other months. At the end of the fiscal year, however, a net unfavorable cost variance would be added to Cost of Goods Sold, as illustrated below:

RAQUEL MFG. COMPANY
Partial Income Statement
Year 1

Unfavorable cost variance is added to cost of goods sold

Sales (*net*)		$450,000
Cost of goods sold, at standard	$300,000	
Add: Net unfavorable cost variance	3,000	
Cost of goods sold and net unfavorable cost variance		303,000
Gross profit on sales		$147,000

A net favorable cost variance would be deducted from Cost of Goods Sold at the end of the fiscal year.

However, if the total cost variance (either favorable or unfavorable) for the year is large, it would be more appropriate to prorate the total cost variance between Goods in Process, Finished Goods, and Cost of Goods Sold in order to restate these accounts to *actual cost.* This would be particularly appropriate when the cost variance is caused by unrealistic standards rather than from outright waste or idle capacity losses. A large cost variance representing both inefficiency and idle capacity losses generally would be charged off in the period in which it was incurred.

Summary of advantages of standard cost system

Among the advantages accruing to management from the use of a standard cost system are the following:

1 The setting of standards requires a thorough analysis of operations; this tends to uncover inefficiencies and helps management maximize profits.

2 A standard cost system assists in the establishment of clearly defined organizational lines of authority and responsibility; this may result in less day-to-day confusion and higher employee morale.

3 Analysis of variances from standard costs helps management control costs in future periods.

4 Standard cost information is often useful in formulating pricing decisions concerning products and services.

5 Standard costs are useful in designing an effective system of responsibility accounting and budgetary controls throughout the organization.

BUDGETING AS AN AID TO PLANNING AND CONTROL

A *budget* is a summary statement of plans expressed in quantitative terms; it guides individuals or an accounting entity in reaching financial or operational goals. If standard costs are used in the accounting system for a company engaged in manufacturing activities, such costs are also used in the preparation of budgets.

Most college students have at one time or another drawn up plans for the effective use of their time to secure a balance between academic and extracurricular activities. This is a *time budget* expressed in days or hours. Similarly, students with limited financial resources find it helpful to write down a plan for spending available money which will see them through a semester or year of schooling. This is an *expenditure budget* expressed in monetary terms.

The problem that plagues college students—planning the efficient use of limited resources—also faces managers of organizations of every type. Business executives must plan to attain profit objectives and meet their financial obligations as they become due. Administrators of nonprofit organizations and government agencies must plan to accomplish objectives of programs with the resources available to them. Budgets are as universal as the concept of planning; as a matter of fact, a budget is often viewed as a comprehensive *financial plan*—a kind of compass designed to guide managers through the turbulent waters of business activity.

The purpose of budgeting

Every budget is a forecast of future events. Business budgets show anticipated revenue, expenses, and the financial position of the company at some future point in time, assuming that the budget estimates are met.

Systematic forecasting serves the control function in two major ways:

First, by showing what results will be if present plans are put into effect, a budget discloses areas that require attention or **corrective action.** For example, the college student whose budget shows potential expenditures of $3,000 for the year and who has only $2,000 in financial resources is forewarned. By knowing this in advance, the student may be able to find ways of augmenting resources or reducing expenses. Similarly, a business budget showing that profit objectives will not be met or that working capital will not be sufficient may enable management to act in advance to alter the revenue and cost picture or to obtain additional financing.

The second use of budgets for control purposes is in **evaluating performance.** Organizational plans are carried out by people. Control is thus exercised not over operations, revenue, and costs, but over the persons responsible for various business functions and the revenue and expense results attained. Budgets provide a yardstick against which a manager's actual performance may be compared.

It is this latter feature—performance evaluation—that accounts for the general unpopularity of budgets. Managers are human, and few of us are overjoyed about techniques which enable our boss to check our performance. Furthermore, budgets often restrict freedom of action, since they are designed to motivate personnel to follow a plan. Unbridled freedom is generally more fun than following an orderly plan of action. Therefore, budgets are regarded by some business managers as penny-pinching, restrictive devices designed to harass them and prevent them from doing their job as they would like to do it.

The largest part of effective budgeting is the delicate task of dealing with its **human relations** aspects. Budgets themselves are inanimate and mechanical. They will be effective only if those who are responsible for carrying out plans and whose performance will be measured against planned results participate fully in the development of the budget. The greater the participation in the planning process, the greater the awareness of a company's objectives and problems throughout the organization. Meaningful participation in the preparation of a budget by managers at all levels of the organization is an important prerequisite to successful budgeting.

The budget period

As a general rule, the period covered by a budget should be long enough to show the effect of managerial policies but short enough so that estimates can be made with reasonable accuracy. This suggests that different types of budgets should be made for different time spans.

A **master budget** is an overall financial and operating plan for a forthcoming fiscal period and the coordinated program for achieving the plan. It is usually prepared on a quarterly or an annual basis. Long-range budgets, called **capital budgets,** which incorporate plans for major expenditures for plant and equipment or the addition of product lines, might be prepared to cover plans for as long as 5 to 10 years. *Responsibility budgets,* which are segments of the master budget relating to the aspect of the business that is the responsibility of a particular manager, are often prepared monthly. *Cash budgets* may be prepared on a day-to-day basis. Some companies follow a *continuous budgeting* plan whereby budgets are constantly reviewed and updated. The updating is accomplished, for example, by extending the annual budget one additional month at the end of each month. A review of the budget may also suggest that the budget be changed as a result of changing business and operating conditions.

Preparing a master budget

The major steps in developing a master budget may be outlined as follows:

1 Establish basic goals and long-range plans for the company.

2 Prepare a sales forecast for the budget period. The sales forecast, of course, will be based on the forecast of general business and economic conditions antici-pated during the budget period. This is a starting point because to a significant extent production or purchases, inventory levels, cash requirements, and operating expenses are governed by the expected volume of sales.

3 Estimate the cost of goods sold and operating expenses. These estimates will depend directly on the sales budget and a thorough knowledge of the relation between costs and volume of activity. Production costs used to estimate cost of goods sold are often based on standard costs for the products manufactured.

4 Determine the effect of budgeted operating results on asset, liability, and ownership equity accounts. The cash budget is the largest part of this step, since changes in many asset and liability accounts will depend on cash flow forecasts.

5 Summarize the estimated data in the form of a projected income statement for the budget period and a projected (sometimes called a *pro forma*) balance sheet as of the end of the budget period.

Master budget illustrated

Master budgets are the culmination of the entire planning process throughout an organization. The detailed mechanics of a master budget may become quite complex. To illustrate master budgeting in an intro-ductory fashion, it is necessary to assume a very simple budgeting situa-tion and to condense detail as much as possible.

We shall assume a manufacturing company that makes and sells a single product. The balance sheet for the Berg Company as of January 1 is shown on page 928. Management has asked for a master budget that will provide an estimate of net income for the first and second quarters of the coming year and a projected balance sheet at the end of each of the first two quarters. The company has notes payable of $160,000 due in quarterly installments of $40,000, starting on March 31 of the current year. Sales of the company's product are seasonal; sales during the second quarter are expected to exceed first-quarter sales by 50%. However, the economy of stabilizing production and a very tight labor supply have led management to plan for stable production of 120,000 units during the first and second quarters. This will require an increase in inventory during the first quarter to meet second-quarter sales demand. Management is concerned about its ability to finance the inventory buildup during the first quarter and meet the quarterly payments on the bank loan.

BERG COMPANY

Actual Balance Sheet

January 1, Current Year

Current assets:			
Cash			$ 75,000
Receivables			82,000
Inventories:			
Materials		$ 25,000	
Finished goods (fifo method)		52,000	77,000
Prepayments			21,000
Total current assets			$255,000
Plant and equipment:			
Buildings and equipment		$970,000	
Less: Accumulated depreciation		420,000	
Total plant and equipment			550,000
Total assets			$805,000

Liabilities & Stockholders' Equity

Current liabilities:			
Notes payable, 8% ($40,000 payable quarterly)			$160,000
Other current payables			78,000
Income taxes payable			50,000
Total current liabilities			$288,000
Stockholders' equity:			
Capital stock, no par, 100,000 shares		$350,000	
Retained earnings		167,000	517,000
Total liabilities & stockholders' equity			$805,000

OPERATING BUDGET ESTIMATES The operating data estimates needed to prepare a budgeted income statement for each of the first two quarters are shown on page 929.

Estimates of unit sales and sales price per unit (Schedule A1) are based on marketing plans and pricing policy in the light of past experience. The production budget (Schedule A2) reflects not only the decision to stabilize production, but the decision to reduce the inventory of finished goods from its January 1 level of 30,000 units to 20,000 units at the end of June

BERG COMPANY
Operating Budget Estimates
First and Second Quarters of Current Year

Schedule		1st Quarter	2d Quarter
A1	**Sales budget:**		
	Selling price per unit	$ 3.00	$ 3.00
	Sales forecast in units	100,000	150,000
	Budgeted sales	$300,000	$450,000
A2	**Production budget (in units):**		
	Planned production	120,000	120,000
	Inventory at beginning of quarter	30,000	50,000
	Units available for sale.	150,000	170,000
	Estimated sales (A1)	100,000	150,000
	Inventory at end of quarter	50,000	20,000

Both 1st and 2d quarters
(120,000 units each quarter)

A3	**Cost estimates:**	
	Variable costs:	
	Per unit manufactured:	
	Materials	$ 0.50
	Direct labor	0.60
	Variable factory overhead	0.30
	Per unit sold:	
	Selling and administrative expense	0.30
	Fixed costs (per quarter):	
	Factory overhead	$ 42,000
	Selling and administrative expense	70,000
A4	**Budgeted cost of goods manufactured (120,000 units):**	
	Materials used ($0.50 per unit)	$ 60,000
	Direct labor ($0.60 per unit)	72,000
	Variable factory overhead ($0.30 per unit)	36,000
	Fixed factory overhead	42,000
	Total cost of goods manufactured	$210,000
	Cost per unit ($210,000 ÷ 120,000 units)	$1.75

Schedule		1st Quarter	2d Quarter
A5	**Ending finished goods inventory:**		
	50,000 units at $1.75	$ 87,500	
	20,000 units at $1.75		$ 35,000
A6	**Selling and administrative expense budget:**		
	Variable expenses ($0.30 × units sold)	$ 30,000	$ 45,000
	Fixed expenses	70,000	70,000
	Total selling and administrative expense	$100,000	$115,000

to minimize funds tied up in finished goods and thus help meet the second-quarter loan repayment. The cost estimates (Schedule A3) provide the basis for attaching dollars to production and for budgeting operating expenses. Details of operating expenses are omitted. *Note that variable factory overhead is stated in terms of units manufactured, and variable selling and administrative expenses in terms of units sold.* Schedules A4 and A6 show the determination of budgeted costs of goods manufactured and operating expenses. The ending finished goods inventory is computed in Schedule A5.

PROJECTED INCOME STATEMENT The projected income statement shown below is based on the operating budget estimates in Schedules A1 to A6. Schedule numbers are indicated parenthetically on the statement. Two items need further comment:

BERG COMPANY
Projected Income Statement
First Two Quarters of Current Year

	1st Quarter	*2d Quarter*
Sales	$300,000	$450,000
Cost of goods sold:		
Finished goods, beginning inventory	$ 52,000	$ 87,500
Cost of goods manufactured (A4)	210,000	210,000
Cost of goods available for sale	$262,000	$297,500
Less: Finished goods, ending inventory (A5)	87,500	35,000
Cost of goods sold	$174,500	$262,500
Gross profit on sales	$125,500	$187,500
Expenses:		
Selling and administrative expense (A6)	$100,000	$115,000
Interest expense	3,200	2,400
Total expenses	$103,200	$117,400
Income before income taxes	$ 22,300	$ 70,100
Income taxes (50% of income before income taxes)	11,150	35,050
Net income	$ 11,150	$ 35,050
Earnings per share	$0.11	$0.35

Here is what quarterly income should be

Interest on the $160,000 bank loan is estimated on the assumption that the $40,000 installment will be paid at the end of the first quarter. Interest at 8% per year, or 2% per quarter, is computed on the outstanding balance of $160,000 during the first quarter and on $120,000 during the second quarter.

Income tax expense is budgeted on the assumption that combined federal and state income taxes will amount to 50% of income before income taxes. We shall assume that last year's tax liability of $50,000 will be paid in two equal installments in the first two quarters of the current year.

FINANCIAL BUDGET ESTIMATES The estimates and data necessary to prepare a cash budget and projected balance sheet for each quarter are shown on pages 932 and 933. A forecast of the Berg Company's financial position at the end of each quarter requires that the account balances on the January 1 balance sheet be adjusted to reflect projected revenue and expenses and the resulting changes in assets and liabilities. Since cash is the most active financial account in a business, the key to preparing a financial budget is a forecast of cash flows, leading to a cash budget by quarters.

The starting point in this process is to convert the operating budget data into cash flows and changes in financial accounts. We begin by scheduling the source of budgeted operating costs (Schedule B2). It is first necessary to convert the materials used figure in the cost of goods manufactured statement into materials purchased, which requires an estimate of the materials inventories at the end of each quarter. The production supervisor feels that the January 1 materials inventory of $25,000 is too low. To meet the production schedule, the supervisor would like to have on hand at the end of the first quarter and throughout the second quarter about two-thirds of the materials usage for the second quarter. The desired ending inventory in Schedule B1 is therefore set at $40,000, which is two-thirds of the $60,000 projected materials usage in the second quarter.

The three primary sources of operating costs are current payables (accounts payable and accrued liabilities), the write-off of prepaid expenses, and depreciation of plant and equipment. The analysis of the source of manufacturing, selling, and administrative costs in Schedule B2 provides the key to estimates of the required outlays for current payables in Schedule B3. The estimate of the ending balance of current payables ($98,500 at the end of the first quarter and $85,500 at the end of the second quarter) has been made by the company treasurer on the basis of past experience and knowledge of suppliers' credit terms and the wage payment policies of the company.

The Berg Company sells to customers entirely on account. Therefore, the sole source of cash receipts for this company during the two quarters is the collection of accounts receivable.Losses from uncollectible accounts and cash discounts are ignored in this example. The credit manager estimates that two-thirds of the sales in any quarter will be collected in that quarter, and the remaining one-third of the quarter's sales will be collected in the following quarter. The forecast of cash collections (B6) and estimated balance of receivables (B7) are based on these estimates.

BERG COMPANY
Financial Budget Estimates
First and Second Quarters of Current Year

Schedule		1st Quarter	2d Quarter
B1	Budgeted materials purchases and inventory:		
	Materials used (A4)	$ 60,000	$ 60,000
	Desired ending inventory	40,000	40,000
	Materials available for use	$100,000	$100,000
	Less: Inventory at beginning of quarter.	25,000	40,000
	Budgeted material purchases.	$ 75,000	$ 60,000

B2   Source of budgeted operating costs:

	Total	Current Payables	Prepayment Write-off	Depre-ciation
First quarter:				
Material purchases (B1)	$ 75,000	$ 75,000		
Direct labor (A4).	72,000	72,000		
Factory overhead (A4) .	78,000	64,000	$ 4,400	$ 9,600
Selling and administra-				
tive expense (A6) . . .	100,000	94,600	3,000	2,400
Total	$325,000	$305,600	$ 7,400	$ 12,000
Second quarter:				
Material purchases (B1)	$ 60,000	$ 60,000		
Direct labor (A4).	72,000	72,000		
Factory overhead (A4) .	78,000	64,400	$ 4,000	$ 9,600
Selling and administra-				
tive expense (A6) . . .	115,000	109,500	3,100	2,400
Total	$325,000	$305,900	$ 7,100	$ 12,000

		1st Quarter	2d Quarter
B3	Payments on current payables:		
	Balance at beginning of quarter	$ 78,000	$ 98,500
	Increase in payables during quarter (B2) . . .	305,600	305,900
	Total payables during quarter	$383,600	$404,400
	Estimated balance at end of quarter (given). .	98,500	85,500
	Payments on current payables during quarter	$285,100	$318,900

CASH BUDGET   The information derived in the financial budget schedules forms the basis for the quarterly cash budget for the Berg Company which appears on page 934.

Note that the quarterly payments of $40,000 on the bank loan, plus $3,200 interest in the first quarter and $2,400 interest in the second quarter, are included in the cash budget. In many cases a cash budget becomes the basis for determining a company's short-term borrowing

Schedule		1st Quarter	2d Quarter
B4	*Prepayments budget:*		
	Balance at beginning of quarter	$ 21,000	$ 15,600
	Estimated cash expenditure during quarter . . .	2,000	5,000
	Total prepayments	$ 23,000	$ 20,600
	Write-off of prepayments (B2)	7,400	7,100
	Prepayments at end of quarter	$ 15,600	$ 13,500
B5	*Budgeted income taxes:*		
	Income tax liability at beginning of quarter . . .	$ 50,000	$ 36,150
	Estimated income taxes for the quarter		
	(income statement)	11,150	35,050
	Total accrued income tax liability	$ 61,150	$ 71,200
	Cash outlay (one-half of last year's tax liability)	25,000	25,000
	Income tax liability at end of quarter	$ 36,150	$ 46,200
B6	*Estimated cash collections on receivables:*		
	Balance of receivables at beginning of year . .	$ 82,000	
	Collections on first-quarter sales of $300,000		
	($\frac{2}{3}$ in first quarter and $\frac{1}{3}$ in second)	200,000	$100,000
	Collections on second-quarter sales of		
	$450,000 ($\frac{2}{3}$ in second quarter)		300,000
	Total cash collections by quarter	$282,000	$400,000
B7	*Budgeted accounts receivable:*		
	Balance at the beginning of the quarter	$ 82,000	$100,000
	Sales on open account during quarter (A1) . .	300,000	450,000
	Total accounts receivable	$382,000	$550,000
	Less: Estimated collections on accounts		
	receivable (B6)	282,000	400,000
	Estimated accounts receivable balance at end		
	of quarter	$100,000	$150,000

needs and in establishing a reasonable repayment schedule for loans. In this example the loan was already in existence and only the scheduled repayments are included in the budget.

PROJECTED BALANCE SHEET We now have the necessary information to forecast the financial position of the Berg Company at the end of each of the next two quarters. The projected balance sheets are shown on page 935. Budget schedules from which various figures on the balance sheet have been derived are indicated parenthetically on the statement.

In this simple budget example, the balance sheets may be prepared directly from the budget schedules. In a more complex budgeting case, it might be desirable to set up the beginning balance sheet amounts on a work sheet and trace through the budgeted transactions for each quarter.

BERG COMPANY

Cash Budget

First Two Quarters of Current Year

	1st Quarter	2d Quarter
Cash balance at beginning of quarter	$ 75,000	$ 1,700
Receipts:		
Collections on receivables (B6)	282,000	400,000
Total cash available	$357,000	$401,700
Disbursements:		
Payment of current payables (B3)	$285,100	$318,900
Income tax payments (B5)	25,000	25,000
Prepayments (B4)	2,000	5,000
Payments on notes (interest included)	43,200	42,400
Total disbursements	$355,300	$391,300
Cash balance at end of the quarter	$ 1,700	$ 10,400

Projected cash flow and ending cash balance

Using budgets effectively

The process of systematic planning would probably be of some value even if a budget, once prepared, were promptly filed away and forgotten. In preparing a budget managers are forced to look into all aspects of a company's activity, and this in itself will often enable them to do a better job of managing. The primary benefits of budgeting, however, stem from uses made of budgeted information after it is prepared. We have noted three ways in which budgets serve management: (*1*) as a plan or blueprint for accomplishing a set of objectives, (*2*) as a warning system for antici-pating conditions that require advance remedial action, and (*3*) as a means of evaluating the performance of company personnel.

Let us consider briefly how the master budget we have just demon-strated might serve these three functions.

A PLAN FOR ACCOMPLISHING OBJECTIVES A number of operating ob-jectives were incorporated in the budget estimates of the Berg Company. A primary objective was to achieve management's profit goals. Secondary objectives were to stabilize production throughout the first two quarters and to reduce the inventory of finished goods by the end of the second quarter. The operating budget is a set of plans for doing these things.

The budgeted income statement (page 930) shows an improved net income during the second quarter, reflecting the favorable effect of increased sales volume in relation to the existence of certain fixed costs. The responsibility for securing the volume of sales revenue budgeted in each quarter rests with the sales department. The problem of scheduling the production of 120,000 units each quarter and of seeing that produc-tion costs do not exceed budget estimates is the responsibility of the manufacturing department. General management is responsible for maintaining control over administrative expenses.

BERG COMPANY
Projected Balance Sheet
As of the End of First Two Quarters of Current Year

	1st Quarter	2d Quarter
Assets		
Current assets:		
Cash (per cash budget)	$ 1,700	$ 10,400
Receivables (B7)	100,000	150,000
Inventories:		
Materials (B1)	40,000	40,000
Finished goods (A5)	87,500	35,000
Prepayments (B4)	15,600	13,500
Total current assets	$244,800	$248,900
Plant and equipment:		
Buildings and equipment	$970,000	$970,000
Less: Accumulated depreciation (B2)	(432,000)	(444,000)
Total plant and equipment	$538,000	$526,000
Total assets	$782,800	$774,900
Liabilities & Stockholders' Equity		
Current liabilities:		
Notes payable (8%, $40,000 due quarterly)	$120,000	$ 80,000
Other current payables (B3)	98,500	85,500
Income taxes payable (B5)	36,150	46,200
Total current liabilities	$254,650	$211,700
Stockholders' equity:		
Capital stock, no par, 100,000 shares issued and		
outstanding	$350,000	$350,000
Retained earnings, beginning of quarter	167,000	178,150
Net income for the quarter	11,150	35,050
Total stockholders' equity	$528,150	$563,200
Total liabilities & stockholders' equity	$782,800	$774,900

Projected quarterly balance sheet

In order to relate budgeted information to these various responsibilities, it is desirable to rearrange the overall master budget figures in terms of responsibility centers. In broad outline, such a rearrangement might be accomplished by preparing quarterly budget estimates for major centers of responsibility, such as sales by territories, factory overhead costs, cash receipts and disbursements, personnel requirements, research expenditures, etc.

Dividing the total budget plan into responsibility segments ensures that each executive knows the goals and his or her part in achieving them. The use of responsibility budgets requires a carefully designed system of *responsibility accounting* in order that the results of a given responsibility center can be compared with the budget plan.

AN ADVANCE WARNING OF POTENTIAL TROUBLE   One of the major concerns of the management of the Berg Company was the ability of the company to meet the quarterly payments on its loan obligation. The cash budget for the first two quarters of the year indicates that the cash position of the company at the end of each quarter will be precariously low. A cash balance of $1,700 is forecast at the end of the first quarter, and a balance of $10,400 at the end of the second quarter (see page 934). This indicates that if all goes well the payments *can* be met, but there is little margin for error in the estimates.

Management, when confronted with such a forecast, should take steps in advance to prevent the cash balance from dropping as low as the budgeted amounts. It may be possible to obtain longer credit terms from suppliers and thus reduce payments on accounts payable during the first two quarters. The company may decide to let inventories fall below scheduled levels in order to postpone cash outlays. An extension of the terms of the note payable might be sought, or the possibility of long-term financing might be considered. If any or all of these steps were taken, it would be necessary to revise the budget estimates accordingly. The fact that management is *forewarned* of this condition several months before it happens, however, illustrates one of the prime values of budgeting.

A YARDSTICK FOR APPRAISING PERFORMANCE   The effective use of budgets in gauging performance is not an easy task. It is not feasible to discuss all facets of this problem here, but let us consider briefly two points:

1 The heart of successful responsibility budgeting is to hold supervisors accountable for the costs and revenue over which they can exercise significant control, and for which they are responsible.[1]

For example, Mike Jones, the foreman of a manufacturing department, can influence labor costs in his department through his control over idle time, overtime hours, and the number of employees to be hired. He may also exert some control over such overhead costs as equipment maintenance, supplies used, and power expenses. On the other hand, Jones probably has no influence on either the salary of the plant superintendent or the amount of building depreciation, some portion of which might be charged to his department.

The view that a manager should not be charged with costs over which he or she has no control is widely used in modern budgeting practice, with the result that responsibility budgets commonly include only *controllable costs.* An alternative is to segregate noncontrollable costs in a separate section of a manag-

---

[1] See Chap. 23 for a discussion of responsibility accounting, which serves as a basis for the preparation of responsibility budgets.

er's budget and to use only the figures that are in the "controllable" section of the budget in appraising the manager's performance.

2 The problem does not end here, however. Even controllable costs may be affected by factors over which a manager has little influence. A primary example is the effect of significant differences between the volume of sales or production budgeted and the volume actually attained. The fact that attainment varied from budgeted volume will, of course, show up in comparisons with the overall budget. However, the effect of volume variations may lead to confusion when actual and budgeted results are compared for various responsibility centers. This confusion can be avoided through the use of a flexible budget.

Flexible budget—a more effective control tool

Suppose, for example, that Harold Stone, production manager of Berg Company, is presented with the following schedule of budgeted and actual results at the end of the first quarter's operations:

BERG COMPANY

Production Costs—Budgeted and Actual for First Quarter

(Master Budget)

	Budgeted	Actual	Over or (under) Budget
Production costs			
Materials used	$ 60,000	$ 63,800	$ 3,800
Direct labor	72,000	76,500	4,500
Variable factory overhead	36,000	38,000	2,000
Fixed factory overhead	42,000	42,400	400
Total production costs	$210,000	$220,700	$10,700

Is this a good or a bad performance?

At first glance it appears that the production manager's cost control performance is bad, since his production costs are $10,700 in excess of budget. However, one piece of information has been deliberately omitted from the above schedule. *Instead of the 120,000 units of production planned for the first quarter, 130,000 units were actually manufactured.*

Under these circumstances, the above comparison of budgeted and actual costs becomes meaningless as a measure of the production manager's performance. There is no point in comparing actual costs for one level of output with budgeted cost performance at a different level of output.

One solution is to base performance evaluation on a *flexible budget.* A flexible budget consists of advance estimates of costs and expenses for *each of several possible levels of activity,* such as 100,000 units, 120,000 units, and 130,000 units. As the year progresses, the actual level of production will become known and the *estimated costs for that level* will be compared with the *actual costs* to determine how well management has performed. On this basis, a comparison of the production manager's budgeted and actual performance might be made as shown on page 938.

BERG COMPANY
Production Costs—Budgeted and Actual for First Quarter
(Flexible Budget)

	Originally Budgeted	Flexible Budget	Actual Costs	Actual Costs over or (under) Flexible Budget
Units of production	120,000	130,000	130,000	
Production costs:				
Materials used	$ 60,000	$ 65,000	$ 63,800	$(1,200)
Direct labor	72,000	78,000	76,500	(1,500)
Variable factory overhead . .	36,000	39,000	38,000	(1,000)
Fixed factory overhead	42,000	42,000	42,400	400
Total production costs	$210,000	$224,000	$220,700	$(3,300)

Flexible budget shows a different picture

This comparison gives quite a different picture of the production manager's cost performance. On the basis of actual volume, Stone has done better than budgeted costs in all categories except fixed factory overhead, most of which is probably outside his control.

Many well-managed companies prepare a flexible budget for different levels of production and sales. A flexible budget is in reality a series of budgets for *different levels of activity.* The preparation of a flexible budget rests on the ability to predict the probable cost behavior at different activity levels. The installation of a standard cost system is generally quite useful for this purpose.

KEY TERMS INTRODUCED OR EMPHASIZED IN CHAPTER 26

Budget A plan or forecast for a future period expressed in quantitative terms. Intends to establish objectives and aid in achieving these objectives with the resources available.

Capital budget Plans for major expenditures for plant and equipment or product lines for perhaps 5 to 10 years in the future.

Cash budget A forecast of expected cash receipts, payments, and periodic balances.

Controllable factory overhead variance The difference between actual factory overhead and the budgeted factory overhead for the level of output achieved.

Factory overhead volume variance The difference between the factory overhead budgeted for the volume of output obtained and the standard factory overhead for this volume of output.

Fixed costs Those costs which do not change with changes in volume of output.

Flexible budget A series of budgets for different possible levels of production. Facilitates evaluation of performance.

Idle capacity loss The portion of total capacity (fixed costs) not fully utilized and not applied to units produced.

Labor rate variance The difference between the standard labor rate and actual rate multiplied by the actual hours.

Labor usage variance The difference between standard labor hours and actual labor hours used multiplied by the standard hourly rate.

Management by exception The concept of directing the attention of management to trouble spots, such as variations between standard costs and actual costs.

Master budget An overall financial and operating plan, including a sales forecast, estimated cost of goods sold, operating expenses, and projected financial statements.

Material price variance The difference between the standard price and actual price of material used multiplied by the standard quantity.

Material quantity variance The difference between standard quantity and actual quantity of material used multiplied by the standard price of the material.

Standard costs Predetermined costs that should be incurred to produce a unit of product or perform a particular operation under ideal conditions.

Variable costs Costs that vary proportionately with volume of output.

REVIEW QUESTIONS

1 What are the four primary elements of the managerial control function?

2 To what extent may generally accepted accounting principles be ignored in developing information for managerial control and decision-making purposes?

3 Define *standard costs* and briefly indicate how they may be used by management in planning and control.

4 What is meant by the expression *management by exception?*

5 What is wrong with the following statement: "There are three basic kinds of cost systems: job order, process, and standard."

6 Once standard costs are established, what conditions would require that standards be revised?

7 List the variances from standard cost that are generally computed for materials, direct labor, and factory overhead.

8 Define each of the following terms: *normal volume, fixed costs,* and *idle capacity loss.*

9 "The cost of waste and inefficiency cannot be regarded as an asset." Explain how this statement supports the use of standard costs in the valuation of goods in process and finished goods inventories.

10 Briefly list some of the advantages of using a standard cost system.

11 What would be the purposes of preparing a budget for a business of any size?

12 An article in *Business Week* stated that approximately one-third of the total federal budget (which exceeds $200 billion dollars by a substantial margin) is considered "controllable." What is meant by a budgeted expenditure being controllable? Give two examples of government expenditures that may be considered "noncontrollable."

13 Describe the five major steps in the preparation of a master budget.

14 Describe three ways in which budgets serve management.

15 What is a *flexible budget?* Explain how a flexible budget increases the usefulness of budgeting as a means of evaluating performance.

EXERCISES

Ex. 26-1 The standard for materials in manufacturing item Z is one pound at $4.00. During the current month, 5,000 units of Item Z were produced and 5,100 pounds of materials costing $21,420 were used. Analyze the $1,420 variance between actual cost and standard cost in such a way as to show how much of it was attributable to price change and how much to excess quantity of materials used. Indicate whether the variances are favorable or unfavorable.

Ex. 26-2 From the following information for the Fitch Corporation, compute the controllable factory overhead variance and the volume variance and indicate whether the variances are favorable or unfavorable.

Standard factory overhead based on direct labor hours at normal capacity:

Fixed ($80,000 ÷ 10,000 hours)	$ 8.00	
Variable ($120,000 ÷ 10,000 hours)	12.00	$20.00
Direct labor hours actually worked.		9,000 hours
Actual factory overhead costs incurred (including $80,000 fixed)		$184,400

Ex. 26-3 The standard costs and variances for direct materials, direct labor, and factory overhead for the month of April are given below:

		Variances	
	Standard Cost	*Unfavorable*	*Favorable*
Direct materials	$ 60,000		
Price variance			$3,000
Quantity variance			1,800
Direct labor	120,000		
Rate variance.		$1,200	
Usage variance			5,400
Factory overhead.	180,000		
Controllable variance		2,400	
Volume variance		3,600	

Determine the actual costs incurred during the month of April for direct materials, direct labor, and factory overhead.

Ex. 26-4 The flexible budget at the 70 and 80% levels of activity is shown below:

	At 70%	*At 80%*	*At 90%*
Sales	$315,000	$360,000	$
Cost of goods sold	231,000	264,000	
Gross profit on sales	$ 84,000	$ 96,000	$
Operating expenses ($36,000 fixed)	78,000	84,000	
Operating income	$ 6,000	$ 12,000	$
Income taxes, 30%.	1,800	3,600	
Net income	$ 4,200	$ 8,400	$

Complete the flexible budget at the 90% level of activity.

Ex. 26-5 Sales on account for the first quarter are budgeted as follows:

January	$200,000
February	250,000
March.	300,000

All sales are made on terms of 2/10, n/30; collections on accounts receivable are typically made as follows:

In month of sale:	
Within discount period	50%
After discount period	20%
In month following sale:	
Within discount period	15%
After discount period	10%
Returns, allowances, and uncollectibles	5%
Total	100%

Compute the estimated cash collections on accounts receivable for the month of March.

Ex. 26-6 The cost accountant for the Modern Molding Co. prepared the following monthly report relating to the Grinding Department:

			Variances	
	Budget *(10,000 hours)*	*Actual* *(11,000 hours)*	*Unfavorable*	*Favorable*
Direct materials	$30,000	$32,000	$2,000	
Direct labor	20,000	21,500	1,500	
Variable factory overhead	25,000	27,850	2,850	
Fixed factory overhead	15,000	14,950		$50

Prepare a revised report of production costs in which the variances are computed by comparing the actual costs incurred with estimated costs *using a flexible budget* for 11,000 hours. Assume that direct materials, direct labor, and variable factory overhead would all be 10% higher when 11,000 hours are worked than when only 10,000 hours are worked.

PROBLEMS

Group A

26A-1 Cabinet Company uses a standard cost system in accounting for its production costs. The standard cost for a certain product for the normal volume of 1,000 units is as follows:

Lumber, 100 feet at $300 per 1,000 feet		$30.00
Direct labor, 5 hours at $8.00 per hour		40.00
Factory overhead (applied at $22.00 per unit produced):		
Fixed ($10,000 ÷ 1,000 units)	$10.00	
Variable	12.00	22.00
Total standard unit cost		$92.00

The actual unit cost for a given month in which 800 units were produced is shown below.

Lumber, 110 feet at $280 per 1,000 feet	$30.80
Direct labor 5½ hours at $7.80 per hour	42.90
Factory overhead, $18,000 ÷ 800 units	22.50
Total actual unit cost	$96.20

At the end of the month, the company's accountant submitted the following cost report to management relating to the 800 units produced:

	Total	Per Unit
Excess lumber used in production	$ 640	$0.80
Excess labor cost incurred	2,320	2.90
Actual factory overhead in excess of standard:		
$18,000 − (800 × $22.00)	400	0.50
Actual cost in excess of standard	$3,360	$4.20

Instructions Prepare a schedule which would give management a better understanding of the reasons for the $3,360 excess cost incurred. This schedule should include the following:
a Material price variance and material quantity variance
b Labor rate variance and labor usage variance
c Controllable factory overhead variance and volume variance
Indicate whether each variance is favorable or unfavorable.

26A-2 Coast Company manufactures a product which is first refined and then packed for shipment to customers. The standard direct labor cost per 100 pounds in each process follows:

Process	Direct Labor Hours per 100 Pounds	Standard Direct Labor Cost per Hour
Refining	2	$6.00
Packing	1	4.80

The budget for October calls for the production of 100,000 pounds of product. The expected labor cost in the refinery is expected to be 8% above standard for the month of October as a result of higher wage rates and inefficiencies in the scheduling of work. The expected cost of labor in the packing room is expected to be 5% below standard because of a new arrangement of equipment.

Instruction Prepare a budget for direct labor costs for October. Use column headings as follows: Total, Refining, and Packing.

26A-3 Mavis Company processes an insecticide and uses a standard cost accounting system. The process requires preparation and blending of materials in 400-pound batches. You are engaged to explain any differences between standard and actual costs incurred in producing 100 batches during the first month of operation. The following additional information is available:
(1) The standard costs for a 400-pound batch are as follows:

	Quantity	Price	Total Cost
Materials:			
Different grades of chemicals	400 pounds	$0.30	$120
Direct labor:			
Preparation, blending, etc.	20 hours	5.00	100
Factory overhead:			
Variable costs	20 hours	3.00	60
Fixed costs	20 hours	1.00	20
Total standard cost per 400-pound batch			$300

(2) During the first month, 41,000 pounds of chemicals were purchased for

$11,480, an average cost of $0.28 cents per pound. All the chemical was used during the month, resulting in a price variance of $820 and a quantity variance of $300.

(3) Average wage paid for 1,900 hours of direct labor was $4.80 per hour and amounted to $9,120. The labor rate variance was $380 and the labor usage variance was $500.

(4) The standards were established for a normal production volume of 125 batches per month. At this level of production, variable factory overhead was budgeted at $7,500 per month and fixed factory overhead was budgeted at $2,500 per month. During the first month, actual factory overhead amounted to $8,800, including $2,500 fixed costs. The controllable factory overhead variance was $300 and the volume variance was $500.

Instructions

a Prepare schedules showing how the variances from standard for materials, labor, and factory overhead were computed. Indicate whether the variances are favorable or unfavorable.

b Prepare journal entries to record the variances and costs incurred (at standard) in the Goods in Process account for (1) materials, (2) labor, and (3) factory overhead.

26A-4 Helen Barnes, owner of the Barnes Company, is negotiating with her bank for a $100,000, 6%, 90-day loan effective July 1 of the current year. If the bank grants the loan, the proceeds will be $98,500, which Barnes intends to use on July 1 as follows: pay accounts payable, $75,000; purchase equipment, $8,000; add to bank balance, $15,500.

The current position of the Barnes Company, according to financial statements as of June 30, is as follows:

Cash in bank	$ 10,000
Receivables (net of allowance for doubtful accounts)	80,000
Merchandise inventory	45,000
Total current assets	$135,000
Accounts payable (including accrued operating expenses)	75,000
Working capital	$ 60,000

The bank loan officer asks Barnes to prepare a forecast of her cash receipts and disbursements for the next three months, to demonstrate that the loan can be repaid at the end of September.

Barnes has made the following estimates, which are to be used in preparing a three-month cash budget: Sales (all on open account) for July, $150,000; August, $180,000; September, $135,000; and October, $100,000. Past experience indicates that 80% of the receivables generated in any month will be collected in the month following the sale, 19% in the second month following the sale, and 1% will prove uncollectible. Barnes expects to collect $60,000 of the June 30 receivables in July, and the remaining $20,000 in August.

Cost of goods sold has averaged consistently about 65% of sales. Operating expenses are budgeted at $18,000 per month plus 8% of sales. With the exception of $2,200 per month depreciation expense, all operating expenses and purchases are on open account and are paid in the month following their incurrence.

Merchandise inventory at the end of each month should be sufficient to cover the following month's sales.

Instructions

a Prepare a monthly cash budget showing estimated cash receipts and disbursements for July, August, and September, and the cash balance at the end of each month. Supporting schedules should be prepared for estimated collections on receivables, estimated merchandise purchases, and estimated payments for operating expenses and of accounts payable for merchandise purchases.

b On the basis of this cash forecast, write a brief report to Barnes explaining whether she will be able to pay the $100,000 loan at the bank at the end of September.

26A-5 After several years of unprofitable operations, Jefferson Corporation retained a CPA firm to design better cost controls. The following flexible budget was prepared for the current year:

	Yearly Fixed Expenses	Variable Expenses per Sales Dollar
Cost of merchandise sold		$0.700
Selling and promotion expense	$ 70,000	0.082
Building occupancy expense	62,000	0.022
Buying expense	50,000	0.052
Delivery expense	37,000	0.034
Credit and collection expense	24,000	0.002
Administrative expense	49,000	0.003
Totals	$292,000	$0.895

Management expected to attain a sales level of $4 million during the current year. At the end of the year the actual results achieved by the company were as follows:

Net sales	$3,500,000
Cost of goods sold	2,380,000
Selling and promotion expense	340,000
Building occupancy expense	140,000
Buying expense	240,000
Delivery expense	145,000
Credit and collection expense	30,000
Administrative expense	60,000

Instructions

a Prepare a statement comparing the actual and budgeted revenues and expenses for the current year, showing variations between actual and budgeted amounts. Use a flexible budget procedure to determine budgeted revenues and expenses.

b Write a brief statement evaluating the company's performance in relation to planning as reflected in the flexible budget.

Group B

26B-1 The accountants for Cedar Company have developed the information shown on page 945 for the standard cost and the actual cost of a product manufactured last month.

The normal capacity level is 10,000 units per month. Last month 8,000 units were manufactured.

Instructions Compute the following cost variances for last month and indicate whether each variance is favorable or unfavorable:

a Material price variance and material quantity variance *b* Labor rate variance and labor usage variance

c Controllable factory overhead variance and volume variance

	Standard Cost	Actual Cost
Materials:		
Standard: 10 ounces at $0.15 per ounce	$1.50	
Actual: 11 ounces at $0.16 per ounce		$1.76
Direct labor:		
Standard: .50 hour at $4.00 per hour	2.00	
Actual: .45 hour at $4.20 per hour.		1.89
Factory overhead:		
Standard: $5,000 fixed cost and $5,000 variable cost for 10,000 units budgeted to be produced	1.00	
Actual: $5,000 fixed cost and $4,600 variable cost for 8,000 units actually produced		1.20
Total unit cost.	$4.50	$4.85

26B-2 Mossberg Company produces a machine part. Each part must move through Department X and Department Y and factory overhead is applied on the basis of machine-hours. The number of machine-hours required to produce a unit and the factory overhead rate per machine-hour are shown below:

Department	Standard Machine-Hours	Factory Overhead Rate per Machine-Hour
X	5	$2.10
Y	3	1.80

The factory overhead rate is based on a normal volume of production of 1,000 units per month; the rate for each department includes $0.80 of fixed costs. The variable factory overhead cost per unit for January is expected to be 5% above standard. The company plans to produce 800 units during January.

Instructions Prepare a budget for factory overhead costs for January. Use column headings as follows: Total, Department X, and Department Y.

26B-3 Safari Gear uses standard costs in its Assembly Department. At the end of the current month, the following information is prepared by the company's cost accountant:

	Materials	Direct Labor	Factory Overhead
Actual costs incurred	$96,000	$82,500	$123,240
Standard costs	90,000	84,000	115,500
Material price variance	2,400		
Material quantity variance	8,400		
Labor rate variance		3,000	
Labor usage variance		1,500	
Controllable factory overhead variance			3,240
Volume variance			4,500

The total standard cost per unit of finished product is $30. During the current month, 9,000 units were completed and transferred to the finished goods inventory and 8,800 units were sold. The inventory of goods in process at the end of the month consists of 1,000 units which are 65% completed. There was no inventory in process at the beginning of the month.

Instructions

a Prepare journal entries to record all variances and the costs incurred (at standard) in the Goods in Process account. Prepare separate compound entries for (1) materials, (2) direct labor, and (3) factory overhead.

b Prepare journal entries to record (1) the transfer of units finished to the Finished Goods Inventory account and (2) the cost of goods sold (at standard) for the month.

c Assuming that the company operated at 90% of its normal capacity during the current month, what is the amount of the fixed factory overhead per month?

26B-4 Rogers Company wants a projection of cash receipts and disbursements for the month of November. On November 28, a note will be payable in the amount of $40,400, including interest. The cash balance on November 1 is $18,100. Accounts payable to merchandise creditors at the end of October were $77,500.

The company's experience indicates that 60% of sales will be collected during the month of sale, 30% in the month following the sale, and 8% in the second month following the sale; 2% will be uncollectible. The company sells various products at an average price of $8 per unit. Selected sales figures are shown below:

	Units
September—actual	20,000
October—actual	30,000
November—estimated	40,000
December—estimated	25,000
Total estimated for Year 1	400,000

Because purchases are payable within 15 days, approximately 50% of the purchases in a given month are paid in the following month. The average cost of units purchased is $5 per unit. Inventories at the end of each month are maintained at a level of 1,000 units plus 10% of the number of units that will be sold in the following month. The inventory on October 1 amounted to 4,000 units.

Budgeted operating expenses for November are $85,000. Of this amount, $30,000 is considered fixed (including depreciation of $12,000). All operating expenses, other than depreciation, are paid in the month in which they are incurred.

The company expects to sell fully depreciated equipment in November for $9,500 cash.

Instructions Prepare a cash budget for the month of November, supported by schedules of cash collections on accounts receivable and cash disbursements for purchases of merchandise.

26B-5 The Parker Gun Corporation employs departmental budgets and performance reports in planning and controlling its manufacturing operations. The budget for Year 1 called for the production of 15,000 guns.

The following performance report for the production department for Year 1 was presented to the president of the company:

	Budgeted Costs	Actual Costs	Over or (under)
Variable manufacturing costs:			
Direct materials	$150,000	$161,500	$11,500
Direct labor	240,000	255,000	15,000
Indirect labor	75,000	92,500	17,500
Indirect materials, supplies, etc.	45,000	43,500	(1,500)
Total variable manufacturing costs .	$510,000	$552,500	$42,500
Fixed manufacturing costs:			
Lease rental	$ 45,000	$ 45,000	None
Salaries of foremen	120,000	125,000	$ 5,000
Depreciation and other	75,000	77,500	2,500
Total fixed manufacturing costs . . .	$240,000	$247,500	$ 7,500
Total manufacturing costs	$750,000	$800,000	$50,000

The production and shipping count for Year 1 is shown below:

	Units
Guns completed and transferred to warehouse	17,000
Guns shipped to customers	15,000
Guns in process of production	None

The corporation does not close its accounts on a monthly basis. In preparing monthly financial statements, however, a predetermined factory overhead rate based on direct labor cost is used. This rate for Year 1 was 150% ($360,000 ÷ $240,000).

After a quick glance at the performance report showing an unfavorable manufacturing cost variance of $50,000, the president said to the accountant: "Fix this thing so it makes sense. It looks as though our production people really blew the budget. Remember that we exceeded our budgeted production schedule by a significant margin. I want this performance report to show a better picture of our ability to control costs."

Instructions

a Prepare a revised performance report on a flexible budget basis for Year 1. Show the budgeted costs for 15,000 guns in the first column, the budgeted figures for the actual level of production (17,000 guns) in the second column, and the actual costs incurred in the third column. In the fourth column show the difference between amounts in columns 2 and 3, and indicate whether the differences are favorable or unfavorable.

b In a few sentences compare the original performance report with the revised report.

c What is the amount of over- or underapplied factory overhead for Year 1? (Note that a standard cost system is not used.)

BUSINESS DECISION PROBLEM 26

North Company has for many years used the standard cost data shown on page 948 in manufacturing a product called Kylex.

	Prime Cost	Factory Overhead	Cumulative Cost
Material X-1, one component	$13		$13
Material X-2, one pound	6		19
Direct labor:			
Shaping and Assembly Department	12	$6	37
Packing Department	2	1	40
Totals	$33	$7	40

There were no inventories at the beginning of Year 1. During Year 1, 1,000 units of Kylex were produced and 600 units were sold. The factory overhead rate was determined by dividing budgeted factory overhead for Year 1 by the 1,000 units scheduled to be produced in Year 1.

Actual costs incurred during Year 1 are:

Material X-1 purchased, 1,200 components @ $9		$10,800
Material X-2 purchased, 1,150 pounds @ $6		6,900
Direct labor:		
Shaping and Assembly Department	$13,200	
Packing Department	2,200	15,400
Factory overhead		7,000
Total production costs incurred in Year 1		$40,100

At the end of Year 1, the following variance accounts appear on the accounting records of the North Company:

Favorable price variance on all material X-1 purchased,	
1,200 components (credit)	$(4,800)
Unfavorable material quantity variance, 50 pounds of material	
X-2 spoiled in production (debit)	300
Unfavorable direct labor rate variance because of 10% wage	
increase early in Year 1 (debit)	1,400
Net favorable variance	$ 3,100

The total inventory at end of Year 1, at standard cost, consists of the following:

Materials:		
Material X-1, 200 components @ $13 per component	$2,600	
Material X-2, 100 pounds @ $6 per pound	600	$ 3,200
Finished goods:		
Kylex shaped and packed, 400 units @ $40		16,000
Total inventory at end of Year 1 at standard cost		$19,200

The independent certified public accountant, who has been engaged to audit the company's financial statements, wants to adjust this inventory to "a revised standard cost" which would take into account the favorable price variance on material X-1 ($4 per component) and the 10% wage increase at the beginning of Year 1. The president of the company objects on the following grounds: "Such a revision is not necessary because the cost of material X-1 already shows signs of going up and the wage increase was not warranted because the productivity of workers did not increase one bit. Furthermore, if we revise our inventory figure of $19,200, our operating income will be reduced from the current level of $10,000." You are called in by the president to help resolve the controversy.

Instructions Do you agree with the president? Assuming that you conclude that the standards for July should be revised, what value should be assigned to the inventory at the end of Year 1?

27

Cost-Revenue Analysis for Decision Making

In addition to standard costs and budgeting discussed in Chapter 26, management uses many other aids to plan and control the activities of a business. One of the more important analytical tools used by management is cost-revenue analysis. *Cost-revenue analysis* is a means of learning how revenue and costs behave in response to changes in the level of business activity. It is a *predictive* rather than a historical concept and is primarily concerned with the possible outcomes of various business decisions contemplated by management.

Uses of cost-revenue analysis

Cost-revenue analysis may be used by management to answer questions such as the following:

1 What level of sales must be reached to cover all expenses, that is, to break even?

2 How many units of a product must be sold to earn a given net income per year?

3 What will happen to our net income if we expand capacity and thereby add $50,000 to our annual fixed costs?

4 What will be the effect of changing compensation of sales personnel from fixed monthly salaries to a straight commission of 10% on sales?

5 If we increase our spending on advertising to $100,000 per month, what increase in sales volume will be required to maintain our current level of net income?

Cost and revenue relationships are useful not only to management but also to creditors and investors. The ability of a business to pay its debts and to increase dividend payments, for example, depends largely on its ability to generate earnings. Thus the level of earnings is important to creditors and investors, and earnings depend on selling prices, number of units sold, the amount of variable and fixed costs, and the mix of different products sold. All these variables are used in analyzing cost and revenue relationships and in predicting the profitability of a business under various assumptions and management strategies.

To illustrate one possible use of cost-revenue analysis by an investor, assume that the shares of each of two companies (A and B) are selling at $10 a share. The annual earnings for each company amount to $1 per share, resulting in a price-earnings ratio of 10 times earnings. Company A has large fixed costs and is operating near full capacity, while Company B has low fixed costs and is operating at less than 50% of capacity. At full capacity, Company B is capable of earning over $8 per share. The demand for the products sold by both companies is strong and should increase. Which stock would you buy?

Obviously, the prospects for an increase in the earnings per share for Company A (with existing facilities) are rather dim, and the price of its stock is not likely to increase. On the other hand, the earnings of Company B "have room to grow" without additional investment in plant and equipment (which would increase fixed costs). For example, if the sales for Company B should double, the earnings could reach $8 per share and the price of its stock might increase spectacularly. Without knowledge of the cost and revenue structure for the two companies, you would not be able to make an intelligent decision.

Keep in mind that cost-revenue analysis may be used not only for the business as a whole, but also for a segment of a business such as a division, a branch, a department, or a given product line.

A nonbusiness example—operating a personal automobile

An important first step in cost-revenue analysis is to know how costs behave in response to changes in the level of activity. Understanding cost behavior is particularly important in planning to meet objectives, in evaluating past performance, and in taking corrective action to control costs. To illustrate this point we shall first consider cost behavior in a simple and familiar setting, the cost of operating a personal automobile.

THE VOLUME INDEX Suppose that someone told you it cost $1,900 a year to own and operate an automobile. If you thought about this statement a bit, you would soon conclude that it was too ambiguous to be very enlightening. One reason is that a year's automobile ownership is not an operational description of the quantity of service provided by this asset during a year. Ignoring psychological and status benefits, an automobile provides transportation measured in miles. The cost of X miles of automobile transportation during a year would be a more useful cost concept for analytical purposes.

In studying cost behavior, we first look for some measurable concept of volume or activity that is meaningful to the person responsible for controlling the cost, and then try to find out how the cost changes with changes in volume. The volume index may be measured in terms of cost *inputs,* such as tons of raw peaches processed, hours of labor used, or machine-hours worked; or volume may be measured in terms of *outputs,* such as units of services rendered, units of physical products produced, or the dollar value of sales revenue generated. Student credit hours is a significant volume index in analyzing educational costs; seat miles flown is a useful volume index in airline operations; dollar sales is an important volume measure for a department store.

In our example, we shall use *miles driven* as the volume index of operating a personal automobile. Once an appropriate volume index has been found, we can classify all costs into three general categories:

VARIABLE COSTS   A *variable* cost increases and decreases directly and proportionately with changes in volume. If, for example, volume increases 10%, a variable cost will also increase by approximately 10%. Gasoline is an example of a variable automobile cost, since fuel consumption is directly related to miles driven.

SEMIVARIABLE (OR MIXED) COSTS   Costs which change in response to changes in volume but by less than a proportionate amount are called *semivariable* or *mixed* costs. A 10% increase in volume, for example, may result in a 6% increase in a semivariable cost. Automobile maintenance and repair costs rise as miles driven increase, but a certain amount of such costs will be incurred without regard to mileage. For example, tire and battery deterioration occurs in response to both miles driven and the passage of time.

FIXED (OR NONVARIABLE) COSTS   Costs which remain unchanged despite changes in volume are called *fixed* or *nonvariable.* Usually such costs are incurred as a function of some other factor such as time. For example, the annual insurance premium and license fee on an automobile are fixed costs since they are independent of the number of miles driven.

Automobile costs—graphic analysis   To illustrate automobile cost-volume behavior, we shall assume the following somewhat simplified data to describe the cost of owning and operating a small automobile:

	Type of Cost	*Amount*
Three classes of automobile costs	*Variable costs:*	
	Gasoline, oil, and servicing	*3 cents per mile*
	Semivariable costs:	
	Maintenance and repairs	*$100 per year plus 1 cent per mile*
	Depreciation	*$500 per year plus 1 cent per mile*

Fixed costs:

Insurance . . . . *$260 per year*

License fee . . . . *$40 per year*

We can express these cost-volume relationships graphically. The relation between volume (miles driven per year) and the three types of cost both separately and combined is shown in the diagrams below:

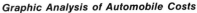

Graphic Analysis of Automobile Costs

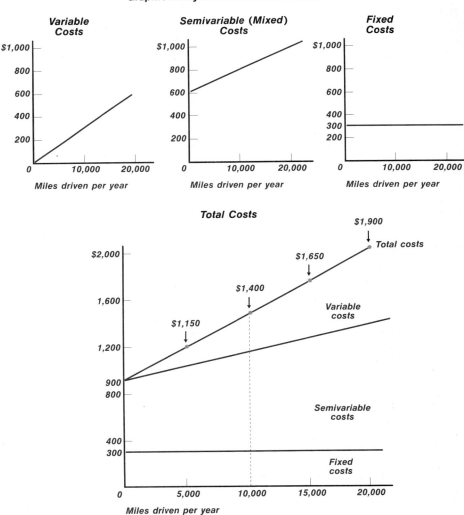

We can read from the total costs graph the estimated annual automobile cost for any assumed mileage. For example, an owner who expects to drive 10,000 miles in a given year may estimate the total cost at $1,400, or

14.0 cents per mile. By combining all the fixed and variable elements of cost, we can generalize the cost-volume relationship and state simply that the cost of owning an automobile is $900 per year plus 5 cents per mile driven during the year.

The effect of volume on unit (per-mile) costs can be observed by converting total cost figures to average unit costs as follows:

Cost per Mile of Owning and Using an Automobile

	5,000	10,000	15,000	20,000
Miles driven	5,000	10,000	15,000	20,000
Costs:				
Fully variable	$ 150	$ 300	$ 450	$ 600
Semivariable:				
Variable portion	100	200	300	400
Fixed portion	600	600	600	600
Completely fixed	300	300	300	300
Total costs	$1,150	$1,400	$1,650	$1,900
Cost per mile	$ 0.23	$ 0.14	$ 0.11	$0.095

Note rapid decrease in cost per mile as use increases

It should be noted that the variable portion of the costs incurred in operating an automobile increases in total as miles driven increase but *remains constant on a per-mile basis* (5 cents per mile). In contrast, total fixed costs remain the same regardless of the number of miles driven but *decrease on a per-mile basis* as miles driven increase. The average unit-cost behavior of operating an automobile may be presented graphically as shown on page 955.

Measuring capacity of a business unit

In analyzing cost-revenue relationships of a business, reference is often made to the *capacity* of a plant, a store, or a company as a whole. For example, a refinery may be able to process a maximum of 50,000 barrels of crude oil per month, or a factory may be capable of assembling 1,000 cars per day. These measures of capacity represent the number of units of input or the units of output that may be processed under ideal conditions, that is, *theoretical capacity.* Under ideal conditions there would be no curtailment in production for any reason, such as holidays, material shortages, strikes, machine breakdowns, etc. Deducting from theoretical capacity the losses in output because of these factors gives us *practical capacity,* which is the maximum level of output if all goods produced can be sold.[1] Needless to say, such a blissful condition is seldom encountered, and a more realistic measure of capacity for cost accounting

---

[1] In a recent year, for example, manufacturing companies in the United States were operating at 73% of practical capacity, whereas manufacturers of durable goods were operating at 68% of practical capacity.

Unit cost behavior

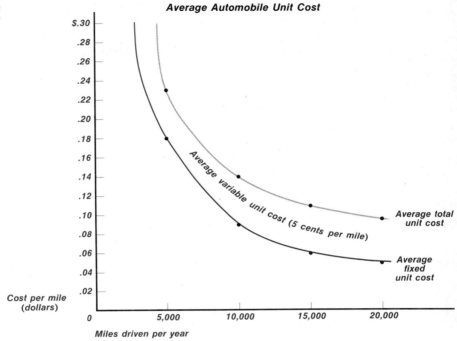

Average Automobile Unit Cost

Average variable unit cost (5 cents per mile)

Average total unit cost

Average fixed unit cost

Cost per mile (dollars)

Miles driven per year

purposes is based on existing factory conditions and the level of demand expected over a relatively long period of time; we shall refer to such a realistic measure of capacity as **normal capacity** or **normal volume.**

Cost behavior in businesses

As pointed out in earlier chapters, cost relationships in a business are seldom as simple as those in our automobile example. Given a suitable index of volume (or activity), however, the operating costs of all businesses exhibit variable, semivariable, and fixed characteristics.

Some business costs increase in lump-sum steps rather than continuous increments, as shown in graph (**a**) on page 956. For example, when production reaches a point where another supervisor and crew must be added, a lump-sum addition to labor costs occurs at this point. Other costs may vary along a curve rather than a straight line, as in graph (**b**) on page 956. For example, when overtime must be worked to increase production, the labor cost per unit may rise more rapidly than volume because of the necessity of paying overtime premium to employees.

Taking all the possible vagaries of cost behavior into account would add greatly to the complexity of cost-volume analysis. How far from reality are the assumed straight-line relationships? Fortunately, there are two factors that make straight-line approximations of cost behavior useful for analytical purposes.

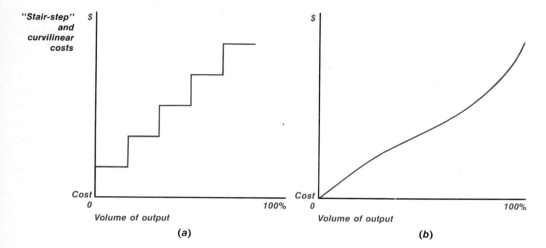

"Stair-step" and curvilinear costs

(a)

(b)

First, unusual patterns of cost behavior tend to offset one another. If we were to plot actual total costs incurred by a business over a time period in which volume changes occurred, the result might appear as in the cost-volume graph (*a*) below:

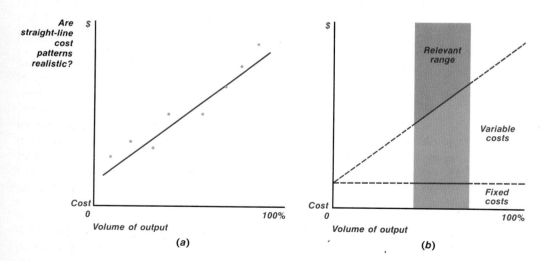

Are straight-line cost patterns realistic?

(a)

(b)

Total cost often moves in close approximation to a straight-line pattern when the various "stair-step" and curvilinear cost patterns of individual costs are combined.

Second, and more important, is the fact that the relevant range of volume variation is usually quite narrow. *Relevant volume range* is the span of output over which the assumptions made about cost behavior are generally valid. In making decisions, management may consider the effect of fairly wide swings in volume, but the range from zero to maximum capacity shown on the cost-volume graph is seldom realistic. An extreme decline in volume might involve shutting down plants and extensive layoffs, but such an extreme reversal is unlikely in any given year. Variable costs may curve sharply upward at the upper limits of capacity, but full-capacity volume is seldom attained. In short, the probability that volume will vary outside a fairly narrow range is usually remote. The significant area of a cost-volume graph is likely to be the normal or relevant range of volume (say, 45 to 75% of capacity for a given company) as shown in graph (*b*). Within this relevant range, the assumption that costs are composed of fixed and variable elements that vary in straight-line relation to changes in volume is reasonably realistic for most companies.

Cost-volume-earnings analysis

In our discussion thus far we have not given much attention to the dollar value of output (volume) or the direct effect of volume on the earnings of a business. Managers continually study the effect of internal decisions and external conditions on revenue, expenses, and ultimately on net income. Revenue is affected by the actions of competitors, by a firm's pricing policies, and by changes in the market demand for a firm's products or services. Expenses are affected by the prices paid for inputs, the volume of production or business activity, and the efficiency with which a firm translates input factors into salable output.

An important aspect of planning to meet given profit objectives is the analysis of the effect of volume changes on net income. The study of business profit-volume relationships is sometimes called **break-even analysis,** in honor of the point at which a business moves from a loss to a profit position. Since the objective of business endeavor is to earn a fair rate of return on investment, the break-even point (that is, the point of zero income) is of course not a planned goal. However, the knowledge of revenue and cost behavior necessary to determine the break-even point carries with it valuable insights that are useful in planning and control.

COST-VOLUME-EARNINGS ANALYSIS—AN ILLUSTRATION A simple business situation will be used to illustrate the kinds of information that can be derived from cost-volume-earnings analysis. The Percy Ice Cream Company (a single proprietorship) has a chain of stores located throughout a large city, selling ice cream in various flavors. Although the company sells to customers in packages of different size, we shall assume that volume of business is measured in gallons of ice cream sold. The company buys its ice cream from a dairy at a price of $1.10 per gallon. Retail sales prices vary depending on the quantity purchased by a customer, but revenue per gallon of ice cream sold *averages* $2 per gallon and does not vary significantly from store to store or from period to period. Monthly operating statistics for a typical store are shown below.

PERCY ICE CREAM COMPANY
Monthly Operating Data—
Typical Retail Store

		Variable Expenses per Gallon	Variable Expenses as Percentage of Sales Price
Average selling price		$2.00	100%
Cost of ice cream (including delivery)		$1.10	55.0%
	Fixed Expenses		
Monthly operating expenses:			
Manager's salary	$1,100		
Wages	2,100 +	.07	3.5
Store rent	800		
Utilities	90 +	.02	1.0
Miscellaneous	410 +	.01	.5
Total expenses	$4,500 +	$1.20	60.0%
Contribution to fixed expenses		$ .80	40.0%

Note variable and fixed expense elements

GRAPHIC ANALYSIS A *profit-volume* (or *break-even*) graph for the typical retail store of the Percy Ice Cream Company, based on the above data, is shown on page 959. The horizontal scale represents volume in thousands of gallons of ice cream per month. Since none of the company's stores sells more than 10,000 gallons per month, this is assumed to be the upper limit of the relevant volume range. The vertical scale is in dollars of revenue or expenses. The steps in plotting this profit-volume graph are as follows:

1 First the revenue line is plotted, running from $0 at zero volume of sales to $20,000, representing 10,000 gallons of sales per month at $2 per gallon.

2 The fixed (nonvariable) monthly operating expenses are plotted as a horizontal line at the level of $4,500 per month.

3 Starting at the $4,500 fixed expense line, the variable expense of $1.20 per gallon is plotted. Note that this line also becomes the total expense line since it is added on top of the fixed expense line.

The monthly profit or loss that may be expected at any sales volume level per store may be read from the profit-volume graph. For example, the break-even point (zero profit) is 5,625 gallons per month, or $11,250 of sales per month. Sales below 5,625 gallons per month will result in a net loss, and sales above 5,625 gallons per month will result in net income.

Income taxes are not relevant in our example because the Percy Ice Cream Company is a single proprietorship.

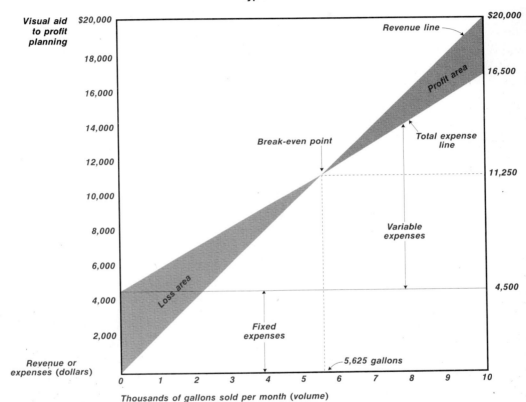

PERCY ICE CREAM COMPANY
Monthly Profit—Volume Graph
Typical Retail Store

PROFIT-VOLUME FORMULA A formula may be developed for general use in analyzing profit-volume behavior. The formula is based on the factors that make up the computation of net income.

Sales (S) = Variable Expense (V) + Fixed Expense (F) + Net Income (I)

We are usually looking for a "target volume" in profit-volume analysis. For example, we want to know the volume necessary to break even, or the volume necessary to earn a given net income, or the effect of a change in variable or fixed expenses on the volume necessary to produce a given net income. The target volume in any given case is represented by sales (S).

To illustrate, in computing the break-even point for a Percy Ice Cream

Company store, we want to know the sales volume (either dollars or gallons) at which net income will be zero. Fixed expenses (*F*) and net income (*I*) are given in dollars, and variable expenses (*V*) can be expressed as a function of sales (*S*). Thus we have one unknown, *S*, and can solve our equation, expressed either in dollars or gallons, as follows:

Break-even Sales Volume **(in dollars)**	**Break-even Sales Volume** **(in gallons)**

Two ways of computing break-even sales volume

$S = V + F + I$	$S = V + F + I$
$S = .60S + \$4,500 + \$0$	$\$2S = \$1.20S + \$4,500 + \$0$
$.40S = \$4,500$	$\$.80S = \$4,500$
$S = \$11,250$ to break even	$S = 5,625$ gallons to break even

Determining the break-even volume in dollars is a more practical approach, because volume is most often expressed in terms of revenue dollars rather than physical units. This is particularly true in the usual situation where a company sells more than one product. We shall therefore express volume in sales dollars in subsequent illustrations.

CONTRIBUTION MARGIN APPROACH The *contribution margin,* in profit-volume analysis, is the excess of sales (in dollars) over variable expenses. The *contribution margin ratio* is the percentage of sales (in dollars) available to cover fixed expenses and yield a net income. The contribution margin ratio is computed as follows:

A key to profit-volume analysis

$$\text{Contribution Margin Ratio} = \frac{\text{Sales (in dollars)} - \text{Variable Expenses}}{\text{Sales (in dollars)}}$$

The contribution margin ratio does not vary with changes in sales volume; it represents the average contribution that each dollar of sales makes to the recovery of fixed expenses and toward generating a net income. Therefore, we can simplify our profit-volume formula by expressing dollar volume (*S*) in terms of the contribution margin ratio as follows:

Simplified profit-volume formula

$$\text{Dollar Sales Volume } (S) = \frac{\text{Fixed Expenses} + \text{Net Income}}{\text{Contribution Margin Ratio}}$$

To illustrate, in terms of our ice cream store example, suppose that we want to know the sales volume per store necessary to produce a monthly net income of $700. The contribution margin ratio is 40% ($.80 ÷ $2.00), as shown in the operating data on page 958. Therefore, the sales volume necessary to produce $700 in monthly net income may be computed as follows:

$$\text{Dollar Sales Volume } (S) = \frac{\$4,500 + \$700}{.40} = \$13,000 \text{ per month}$$

(or 6,500 gallons
@ $2 per gallon)

PROFIT-VOLUME PLANNING Once profit-volume relationships have been established, it is possible to provide planning information that is useful in arriving at a variety of decisions. To illustrate the process, consider a number of different questions that might be raised by the management of the Percy Ice Cream Company:

1 *Question.* To increase volume, management is considering a policy of giving greater discounts on gallon and half-gallon packages of ice cream. It is estimated that the effect of this pricing policy would be to reduce the average selling price per gallon by 8 cents (that is, from $2 per gallon to $1.92). Management is interested in knowing the effect of such a price reduction on the monthly break-even volume per store.
Analysis. The proposed change in average sales price changes the contribution margin from .40 to .375, as shown below:

$$\frac{\$1.92 - \$1.20}{\$1.92} = .375 \text{ (or } 37\tfrac{1}{2}\%)$$

The cost of ice cream and fixed operating expenses remain unchanged by this pricing decision. Therefore, the target monthly sales volume to break even under the new pricing situation would be:

$$\text{Dollar Sales Volume } (S) = \frac{\$4,500 + \$0}{.375} = \$12,000 \text{ per month}$$

In terms of gallons sold per month, the break-even volume would be $12,000 ÷ $1.92 = 6,250 gallons, or more than 11% higher than the present 5,625 gallon break-even volume. Thus management should be advised that the proposed pricing policy is desirable only if the unit sales volume per store can be expected to increase more than 11% per month as a result of the lower sales prices on gallon and half-gallon packages.

2 *Question.* Management is considering a change in the method of compensating store managers. Instead of a fixed salary of $1,100 per month, it is proposed that managers be put on a salary of $330 per month plus a commission of 12 cents per gallon of sales. The present average monthly net income per store is $1,200 on sales of $14,250 ($14,250 × 40% − $4,500 = $1,200). What sales volume per store will be necessary to produce the same monthly net income under the proposed incentive compensation arrangement?
Analysis. This proposal involves a change in both the contribution margin ratio and the fixed monthly operating expenses. Adding 12 cents per gallon to variable costs raises the total variable cost to $1.32 per gallon and reduces the contribution margin ratio to 34%, as computed below:

$$\frac{\$2.00 - \$1.32}{\$2.00} = 34\%$$

Cutting the manager's salary from $1,100 to $330 per month will reduce monthly fixed expenses from $4,500 to $3,730. The sales volume required to produce a monthly net income of $1,200 may be computed as follows:

$$\text{Required Sales Volume } (S) = \frac{\$3,730 + \$1,200}{.34} = \$14,500 \text{ per month}$$

To produce the same $1,200 per month net income under the new compensation plan, sales volume per store would have to be increased by $250 (or 125 gallons) over the current monthly sales volume of $14,250. The issue thus boils down to whether the incentive compensation arrangement will induce store managers to increase volume by more than 125 gallons per month.

Profit-volume analysis does not answer this question, but it provides the information which enables management to exercise its judgment intelligently.

3 Question. The Percy Ice Cream Company stores are now open 12 hours each day (from 9 A.M. to 9 P.M.). Management is considering a proposal to decrease store hours by opening two hours later each morning. It is estimated that this policy would reduce sales volume by an average of 500 gallons per month and would cut fixed expenses (utilities and wages) by $500 per month. Assuming a present average net income of $1,200 per store, would it pay the company to change its store hours?

Analysis. The loss of 500 gallons of sales per month would decrease revenue by $1,000 (500 × $2). This would result in the loss of contribution margin of $400 ($1,000 × 40%). Therefore, whether the reduction in store hours would increase net income per store may be determined by direct *incremental analysis* as follows:

Reduction in fixed operating expenses	*$500*
Less: Loss of contribution margin ($1,000 × 40%)	*400*
Prospective increase in monthly net income per store	*$100*

Note that the present average monthly net income of $1,200 per store is not considered relevant in making this analysis. Incremental analysis indicates that reducing store hours will decrease any net loss by $100 or add $100 to any net income figure. The incremental approach to cost and revenue analysis is discussed in more detail in Chapter 28.

Other uses of a profit-volume graph

The profit-volume graph is a flexible planning and control tool; its form can be changed to meet various decision-making needs of management. Two examples are presented below.

SALES VOLUME REQUIRED TO RECOVER CASH EXPENDITURES Management may wish to determine a cash (or funds) break-even point by excluding depreciation and other noncash expense items from total expenses.[2] For example, if total fixed expenses for accounting purposes amount to $10,000 per month and the contribution margin ratio is 40%, the monthly sales volume necessary to break even would be $25,000 ($10,000 ÷ .40). However, if $3,000 of the monthly fixed expenses consists of depreciation (a noncash expense) computed on the straight-line basis, the sales volume required to recover all variable expenses and the "out-of-pocket" fixed expenses would be only $17,500 ($7,000 ÷ .40). *Out-of-pocket* expenses are those requiring the use of current funds. When a sales volume of $17,500 is reached, the loss from operations would be $3,000 (the unrecovered portion of fixed expenses), and the funds provided by operations would be zero, as illustrated on page 963.

---

[2] See Chap. 21 for a complete discussion of funds flow as reported in a statement of changes in financial position.

Sales	*Sales*		*$17,500*
volume required to recover	*Less: Fixed expenses, including depreciation of $3,000*	*$10,000*	
	Variable expenses ($17,500 × 60%)	*10,500*	*20,500*
cash outlays	*Loss from operations*		*$(3,000)*
	Add: Depreciation, a noncash expense		*3,000*
	Funds provided by operations		*$ –0–*

PROFIT-VOLUME GRAPH SHOWING TOTAL CONTRIBUTION MARGIN AND MARGIN OF SAFETY A profit-volume graph may be prepared in such a way that it shows the total contribution margin at any level of activity (sales volume) and the margin of safety sales volume. For example, assume that Dash Company has total fixed expenses of $180,000 per year, that the contribution margin ratio is 45%, and that sales at full capacity would be $800,000 per year. A profit-volume graph may be prepared as follows:

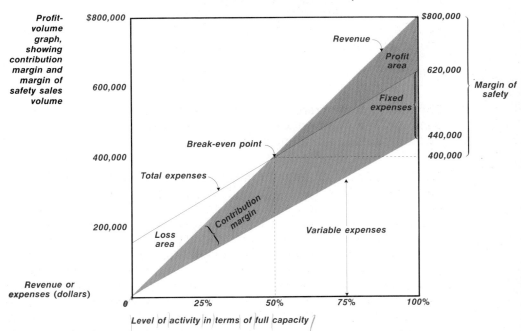

DASH COMPANY
Annual Profit–Volume Graph

When the profit-volume graph is prepared in this form, it is easy to determine the total contribution margin (the difference between total revenue and variable expenses) at any level of activity. We can see that at the break-even point the total contribution margin is equal to total fixed expenses ($180,000); at any level beyond the break-even point, the profit area is equal to the difference between the total contribution margin and total fixed expenses. For example, at full capacity the profit is equal to $180,000, which is the excess of the contribution margin, $360,000 ($800,000 − $440,000), over total fixed expenses, $180,000.

The *margin of safety* is the dollar amount by which actual sales exceed break-even sales volume. It measures the amount by which sales can decrease (assuming that expense relationships remain unchanged) without producing a loss. In the graph illustrated above, the margin of safety sales volume at 100% level of activity is $400,000; at the 75% level, the margin of safety sales volume is $200,000 ($600,000 − $400,000). If you study the graph carefully, you will see that the net income may be determined as follows:

Margin of Safety Sales Volume × Contribution Margin Ratio = Net Income

This relationship gives us a quick tool in projecting net income at various levels of sales. For example, if sales are expected to be $500,000 and the break-even point is $400,000, the net income will be $45,000 when the contribution margin ratio is 45%. This is determined by simply multiplying the margin of safety sales volume, $100,000 ($500,000 − $400,000), by the contribution margin ratio, 45%.

Assumptions underlying profit-volume analysis

In preparing a profit-volume graph, accountants assume the following:

1 Sales price per unit remains constant.
2 If more than one product is sold, the proportion of the various products sold (sales mix) is assumed to be constant.
3 Fixed expenses remain constant at all levels of sales within the assumed relevant range of activity.
4 Variable expenses remain constant as a percentage of sales revenue.
5 For a business engaged in manufacturing, the number of units produced is assumed to be equal to the number of units sold.

These assumptions simplify profit-volume analysis. In actual practice, however, some of these assumptions may not hold true. However, profit-volume analysis is still a useful planning and control tool for management. As changes take place in selling prices, sales mix, expenses, and production levels, management should incorporate such changes into profit-volume analysis and revise any previous estimates of probable results. The assumptions underlying profit-volume analysis suggest that this management tool should be continuously monitored and revised as conditions change.

Importance of sales mix in profit-volume analysis and management decisions

In our example for the Percy Ice Cream Company, we assumed that the contribution margin ratio *averaged* 40% of sales expressed in dollars and that the *average* selling price was $2 per gallon of ice cream sold. Let us now change our example and assume that a detailed analysis indicates that ice cream is actually sold in three packages as follows:

	Quart	Half-Gallon	Gallon
Sales price per package	$0.60	$1.00	$1.80
Less: Variable expense per package	0.42	0.55	0.90
Contribution margin per package.	$0.18	$0.45	$0.90
Contribution margin ratio (contribution margin ÷ sales price).	30%	45%	50%
Break-even sales volume, assuming that only the one size package was sold (fixed expenses, $4,500, divided by contribution margin ratio) . . .	$15,000	$10,000	$9,000

Why would you prefer to sell only the gallon size?

Earlier in this chapter we stated that the Percy Ice Cream Company is now selling a certain *mix* of the three sizes and that a sales volume of $11,250 is required to break even ($4,500 ÷ .40). If ice cream were sold exclusively in quarts, sales of $15,000 would be required to break even; if only half-gallon packages were sold, the break-even sales volume would be $10,000; if only gallon packages were sold, the break-even sales volume would be $9,000. The reason the break-even sales volume differs for each size is because each size yields a different contribution margin per dollar of sales (contribution margin ratio). *The larger the contribution margin ratio, the lower the sales volume that is required to cover a given amount of fixed expenses.*

The amount of net income earned by a business unit depends not only on the volume of sales and the ability to control expenses, but also on the quality of sales. Sales yielding a high contribution margin are more profitable than sales yielding a low contribution margin. Thus, sales with a high contribution margin percentage are said to be *high-quality sales.* A shift from low-margin sales to high-margin sales can materially increase net income even though total sales decrease; on the other hand, a shift from high-margin to low-margin sales can turn a net income into a loss despite an increase in total sales.

Contribution margin per unit of scarce resource

The contribution margin approach is useful to management in deciding what products to manufacture (or purchase for resale) and what products to eliminate when certain factors of production are available only in limited quantity. One of the important functions of management is to develop the most profitable uses of such scarce resources as raw materials, skilled labor, high-cost equipment, and factory floor space.

Assume that you are offered two equally satisfactory jobs, one paying $4 per hour and one paying $6 per hour. Since your time is scarce and you wish to maximize the pay that you receive for an hour of your time, you would naturally choose the job paying $6 per hour. For the same reason, if a company has a plant capacity of only 100,000 direct labor hours, management would want to use this capacity in such a way as *to produce the maximum contribution margin per hour of direct labor.* To illustrate this concept, assume that the Maximus Corporation is considering the production of three products. The contribution margin per direct labor hour required to produce each of the three products is estimated as follows:

MAXIMUS CORPORATION
Contribution Margin per Hour of Direct Labor

	Product	Sales Price per Unit	−	Variable Costs per Unit	=	Contribution Margin per Unit	÷	Direct Labor Hours Required to Produce One Unit	=	Contribution Margin per Hour of Direct Labor
Should	A	$100		$60		$40		10		$ 4
production of product	B	80		50		30		5		6
C be	C	60		40		20		2		10
expanded?										

Even though a unit of product A yields the highest contribution margin ($40) and the highest contribution margin ratio (40%), it is **the least profitable product in terms of contribution margin per hour of direct labor.** If sales of products B and C do not depend on the sales of product A and there are no operational problems involved in varying the production mix of the three products, the production of product A should be kept to a minimum. This would be particularly appropriate if the Maximus Corporation could not meet the demand for all three products because of inability to expand plant capacity beyond 100,000 direct labor hours.

We can see that a unit of product A requires 10 hours of direct labor and generates $40 in contribution margin; a unit of product B requires only 5 hours of direct labor and yields $30 in contribution margin; and a unit of product C requires only 2 hours of direct labor and yields $20 in contribution margin. In summary, 10 hours of effort on product A yields $40 in contribution margin while 10 hours of effort on product B yields $60 in contribution margin, and 10 hours of effort on product C generates a whopping $100 in contribution margin. If the entire capacity of 100,000 direct labor hours were used to produce **only a single product,** the total contribution margin shown at the top of page 967 would result:

	Product	Total Capacity (hours)	×	Contribution Margin per Hour of Direct Labor	=	Total Contribution Margin if Only One Product Is Manufactured
Why should	A	*100,000*		*$ 4*		*$ 400,000*
we continue	B	*100,000*		*6*		*600,000*
to produce	C	*100,000*		*10*		*1,000,000*
product A?						

This schedule does not mean that the production of product A can be discontinued. While product C is clearly the most profitable, perhaps the demand for it is not enough to keep the plant working at full capacity; or the sales of product C may to some extent depend on sales of products A and B. In most cases, a company is not in a position to manufacture only the product which yields the highest contribution margin and let other less alert business executives manufacture the low-margin products. A company should, however, try to sell as much of the high-margin products as possible in order to maximize its net income.

One of the key functions of business organizations is to employ scarce economic resources in ways which will best serve the needs of society. The net income earned by a business is, in a way, a reward for producing the goods needed by a society at the lowest possible cost. Sales mix and contribution margin analyses are useful in realizing the twin goals of producing goods at low cost and at the same time earning a satisfactory net income in order for a business unit to survive and thus to continue to meet social needs.

Summary of cost-revenue analysis

In this chapter we limited our discussion to a few key ideas which will be further developed in Chapter 28. For example, cost behavior patterns, the contribution margin concept, sales mix data, and the amount of idle plant capacity are often useful in developing quantitative information in arriving at answers to some puzzling problems facing management.

The important point to keep in mind is that cost-revenue analysis rests on assumptions which give management useful, but rough, estimates of *probable* results of future courses of action.

KEY TERMS INTRODUCED OR EMPHASIZED IN CHAPTER 27

Break-even point The level of sales and output at which a company neither earns a profit or incurs a loss. Revenue exactly covers expenses.

Contribution margin Sales minus variable expenses.

Contribution margin ratio The percentage of sales available to cover fixed expenses and yield a net income.

Cost-revenue analysis The study of how revenue and costs respond to changes in the level of business activity.

Fixed (or nonvariable) costs Costs that remain unchanged despite changes in volume of output.

Margin of safety Amount by which actual sales exceed the break-even point.

Profit-volume formula Sales = variable expenses + fixed expenses + net income.

Relevant volume range The span or range of output over which assumptions about cost behavior are generally valid. Excludes extreme volume variations.

Semivariable costs Costs that respond to change in volume of output by less than a proportionate amount.

Variable costs Costs that increase and decrease directly and proportionately to changes in volume of output.

REVIEW QUESTIONS

1 Why is it important for management to focus attention on cost-revenue relationships?

2 What is a *volume index* and why is it important in analyzing cost behavior?

3 List and briefly explain two general ways in which the capacity of a business unit may be measured.

4 Explain what is meant by the *normal volume* of operations.

5 A is a variable cost; B is a fixed (nonvariable) cost; and C is a semivariable cost. How would you expect each of these total dollar costs to vary with changes in production volume? How would they vary with changes in production if they were expressed in *dollars per unit* of production?

6 The simplifying assumption that costs and volume vary in straight-line relationships makes the analysis of cost behavior much easier. What factors make this a reasonable and useful assumption in many cases?

7 What important relationships are shown on a profit-volume (break-even) graph?

8 Kris Company has an average contribution margin of 35%. What target sales volume per month is necessary to produce a monthly operating income of $22,000, if fixed (nonvariable) expenses are $118,000 per month?

9 Why is the profit-volume formula a more flexible analytical tool than a profit-volume graph?

10 Define *margin of safety* and *relevant range* of activity.

11 A top executive of a major steel company was recently quoted as follows: "The industry finds itself at the highest break-even point in our history. In the past we could make a profit at a 50% operating rate, but now that has gone up 20 points." List some reasons why the break-even point probably increased to 70% of capacity for the steel industry.

12 An executive of the U.S. Steel Corporation put the blame for lower net income for a recent fiscal period on the "shift in product mix to higher proportion of export sales." Sales for the period increased slightly while net income declined by 28%. Explain how a change in product (sales) mix to a higher proportion in export sales would result in a lower level of net income.

13 Why is it helpful to know the approximate amount of contribution margin generated from the use of a scarce resource such as a machine-hour or an hour of direct labor?

14 The president of an airline blamed a profit squeeze on "unwise and unjustifiable promotional fares." He pointed out that 50% of the company's revenue came from "discount fares." Explain why discount fares tend to reduce net income and point out circumstances in which a discount from the regular price of a plane fare could possibly increase net income.

15 An economist writing in the **Wall Street Journal** stated that inflation is caused by a shortage of supply in relation to demand. The article suggested that business executives should try to maintain profits by increasing sales and reducing prices rather than by increasing prices. Evaluate this argument.

16 In a recent report to stockholders, the management of a large corporation stated that lower sales volume, coupled with higher material and labor costs, resulted in a first-quarter loss of $131,292, compared with a profit of $506,258 in the first quarter of the preceding year. In order to keep costs and expenses in line with anticipated volume, budgeted fixed costs and expenses for the current year were reduced from $28.3 million to $25 million, thus reducing the break-even sales level from $80.4 million to "a more comfortable $76 million." According to the report, variable costs and expenses amounted to 64% of each sales dollar in the original budget.

List some ways that fixed costs and expenses can be reduced and mention several other actions which were probably taken by management to attain a lower break-even point.

EXERCISES

Ex. 27-1 The following information relates to the single product manufactured by the Portland Manufacturing Company:

Selling price per unit		*$12.00*
Variable cost per unit:		
Direct materials	*$2.40*	
Direct labor	*2.40*	
Factory overhead and selling expenses	*1.20*	*6.00*
Contribution margin per unit		*$ 6.00*

a Assuming that the sales volume at the break-even point stands at $24,000 per month, what are total fixed costs for the year?

b What increase in selling price is necessary to cover a 15% increase in direct labor cost per unit and still maintain the current contribution margin ratio at 50%?

Ex. 27-2 Information concerning a product manufactured by Ames Brothers appears below:

Sales price per unit	*$70.00*
Variable cost per unit	*$42.00*
Total fixed production and operating costs	*$280,000*
Maximum capacity with present facilities	*20,000 units*

Determine the following:
a The contribution margin per unit
b The number of units that must be sold to break even
c The sales level that must be reached in order to earn $224,000 before income taxes

Ex. 27-3 Lake Corporation has a break-even sales volume of $60,000 per month. Because of an increase of $3,600 in fixed expenses, the sales volume required to break even increased to $72,000. The sales price and the variable expenses of the single product produced did not change. Based on the foregoing information compute:
a Variable expenses as a percentage of sales.
b Total fixed expenses before the $3,600 increase.

c From the facts given in this exercise, we can conclude that a ____ % increase in total fixed expenses increases the break-even sales volume by ____ %.

Ex. 27-4 Malibu Corporation has fixed expenses of $30,000 per month. It sells two products as follows:

	Sales Price	Variable Expense	Contribution Margin
Product no. 1	$10	$4	$6
Product no. 2	10	7	3

600
240,000
280

a What sales volume is required to break even if two units of product no. 1 are sold with one unit of product no. 2?

b What sales volume is required to break even if one unit of product no. 1 is sold with two units of product no. 2?

Ex. 27-5 For each of the six independent situations below, compute the missing amounts:

a Only one product is manufactured:

13(4,000)-24,000=)

	Sales	Variable Expenses	Contribution Margin per Unit	Fixed Expenses	Income (before taxes)	Units Sold
(1)	$192,000	$120,000	$18	$48,000	$24,000	4,000
(2)	180,000	105,000	15	45,000	30,000	5,000
(3)	600,000	360,000	30	150,000	90,000	8,000

150,000+90,000 → 8,000
30

b Many products are manufactured:

	Sales	Variable Expenses	Contribution Margin, %	Fixed Expenses	Income (before taxes)
(1)	$900,000	$720,000	20%	$162,000	$78,000
(2)	600,000	366,000	40%	195,000	45,000
(3)	450,000	315,000	30%	105,000	30,000

165,000 + 36,000
.3

F.E. + N.I.
─────── =
SALES

PROBLEMS

CONTRIBUTION
MARGIN

Group A

27A-1 Harper Industries, Inc., produces two models of binoculars. Information for each model is shown below:

	Model 100	Model 101
Sales price per unit	$180	$120
Costs and expenses per unit:		
Direct materials	$51	$33
Direct labor	33	30
Factory overhead (applied at the rate of 18 per machine-hour)	36	18
Variable selling expenses	30	15
Total costs and expenses per unit	150	96
Profit per unit	$ 30	$ 24

Total factory overhead amounts to $180,000 per month, one-third of which is fixed. The demand for either product is sufficient to keep the plant operating at full capacity of 10,000 machine-hours per month. Assume that *only one product is to be produced, in the future.*

a Prepare a schedule showing the contribution margin per machine-hour for each product.

b Explain your recommendation as to which of the two products should be discontinued.

27A-2 Service Systems operates a downtown parking lot containing 800 parking spaces. The lot is open 2,500 hours per year. The parking charge per car is 40 cents per hour; the average customer parks two hours. Service Systems rents the lot for $6,250 per month. The lot supervisor is paid $12,000 per year. Five employees who handle the parking of cars are paid $150 per week for 50 weeks, plus $300 each for the two-week vacation period. Employees rotate vacations during the slow months when four employees can handle the reduced load of traffic. Lot maintenance, payroll taxes, and other fixed expenses amount to $3,000 per month, plus 4 cents per parking hour sold.

Instructions

a Draw a profit-volume graph for Service Systems on an annual basis. Use parking-space hours as the measure of volume of activity and show fixed expenses on the bottom of the graph.

b What is the contribution margin ratio? What is the annual break-even point in dollars of parking revenue?

c Suppose that the five employees were taken off the hourly wage basis and paid 12 cents per car parked, with the same vacation pay as before. (*1*) How would this change the contribution margin per parking-space hour sold and total fixed expenses? (*2*) What annual sales revenue would be necessary to produce $25,500 per year income before taxes under these circumstances?

27A-3 Eastern Gear operates its production department only when orders are received for its one product, a metal disc. The manufacturing process begins with the cutting of "rings" from strips of sheet metal; these rings are then pressed into discs. The sheets of metal, each 4 feet long and weighing 33.2 ounces (2.075 pounds), are purchased for $6.32 each.

The following information is available for the first year of operations:

(*1*) Five thousand 4-foot pieces of metal were used to produce 30,000 discs, each weighing 5 ounces and selling for $3.10 each.

(*2*) The company has been operating at 50% of capacity and has had no spoilage in the cutting step of the process. The skeletons remaining after the rings have been cut are sold for scrap at $1.60 per pound. The proceeds on the sale of scrap have been improperly credited to Sales.

(*3*) The variable conversion cost of each disc is 130% of the direct material cost (metal), after deducting the proceeds from the sale of scrap. Variable conversion cost is the sum of direct labor and variable factory overhead.

(*4*) Fixed costs amount to $40,000 per year.

Instructions

a Prepare schedules computing the following for the first year of operations: (*1*) Cost of metal per disc (after deducting the proceeds from the sale of scrap), (*2*) variable conversion cost per disc, (*3*) contribution margin on each disc, and (*4*) total contribution margin for all units sold.

b Compute the number of discs that must be sold per year to break even.

c Management of Eastern Gear thinks that they could sell 50,000 discs if the price were reduced to $2.60 per disc. Would you advise them to reduce the price? Why?

27A-4 James Denny is considering investing in a vending machine operation involving 50 vending machines located in various plants around the city. The machine manufacturer reports that similar vending machine routes have produced a sales volume ranging from 500 to 1,000 units per machine per month. The following information is made available to Denny in evaluating the possible profitability of the operation.

(1) An investment of $25,000 will be required, $7,000 for merchandise and $18,000 for the 50 machines.

(2) The machines have a service life of five years and no salvage value at the end of that period. Depreciation will be computed on the straight-line basis.

(3) The merchandise (candy and soft drinks) retails for an average of 15 cents per unit and will cost Denny an average of 6 cents per unit.

(4) Owners of the buildings in which the machines are located are paid a commission of 3 cents per unit of candy and soft drinks sold.

(5) One man will be hired to service the machines. He will be paid $700 per month.

(6) Other expenses are estimated at $200 per month. These expenses do not vary with the number of units sold.

Instructions

a Determine the break-even volume in dollars and in units per month.

b Draw a monthly profit-volume graph for sales volume up to 1,000 units per machine per month. The graph should be similar to the one illustrated on page 959 which shows the total contribution margin and the margin of safety.

c What sales volume per month will be necessary to produce a return of 12% (before taxes) on Denny's investment during his *first year* of operation?

d Denny is considering offering the building owners a flat rental of $15 per machine per month in lieu of the commission of 3 cents per unit sold. What effect would this change in commission arrangement have on his *monthly* break-even volume in terms of units?

27A-5 Sound Shack manufactures tape decks and currently sells 9,250 units annually to producers of sound reproduction systems. Jay Shack, the owner, anticipates a 15% increase in the cost per unit of direct labor on January 1 of next year. He expects all other costs and expenses to remain unchanged. The owner has asked you to assist him in developing the information he needs to formulate a reasonable product strategy for next year.

You are satisfied that volume is the primary factor affecting costs and expenses and have separated the semivariable costs and expenses into their fixed and variable segments. Beginning and ending inventories generally remain at a level of 1,000 units.

Below are the current-year data assembled for your analysis:

Selling price per unit		$200.00
Variable costs and expenses per unit:		
Materials	$60.00	
Direct labor	40.00	
Factory overhead and selling and administrative expenses	20.00	120.00
Contribution margin per unit (40%)		$ 80.00

Fixed costs and expenses (factory and other), $400,000

Instructions

a What increase in the selling price is necessary to cover the 15% increase in direct labor cost and still maintain the current contribution margin ratio of 40%?

b How many tape decks must be sold to maintain the current operating income of $340,000 if the sales price remains at $200 and the 15% wage increase goes into effect? Disregard income taxes.

c The owner believes that an additional $600,000 of machinery (to be depreciated at 20% annually) will increase present capacity (10,000 units) by 40%. If all tape decks produced can be sold at the present price of $200 per unit and the wage increase goes into effect, how would the estimated operating income before capacity is increased compare with the estimated operating income after capacity is increased? Prepare schedules of estimated operating income at full capacity *before* and *after* the expansion. Disregard income taxes.

Group B

27B-1 Richard Bolt recently began a manufacturing business. He leased plant facilities capable of producing 10,000 units per year of a new product. The following information has been developed on estimated costs and revenue.

	Amount	Total per Unit	Variable per Unit
Estimated costs and expenses (except selling):			
Direct materials	$30,000	$3.00	$3.00
Direct labor	10,000	1.00	1.00
Factory overhead (60% of total is fixed)	20,000	2.00	0.80
Administrative expense (all fixed)	15,000	1.50	
Total	$75,000	$7.50	$4.80

Selling expenses are expected to be 12% of sales and profit before income taxes is projected at $1.30 per unit at the current sales level of 10,000 units.
a Compute the selling price per unit.
b What is the margin of safety in terms of sales dollars?

27B-2 Mini-Serve, Inc., is a gasoline retailer operating three self-service gasoline stations. The stations sell one grade of gasoline purchased from an independent oil company. No mechanical or other major services are offered. Miscellaneous revenue from vending machine sales and other sources are so negligible that for planning purposes they are treated as an offset against fixed expenses.

The president is studying the advisability of opening another station. His estimate of monthly expenses for the proposed location are:

Fixed expenses:	
Rent	$1,500
Wages	3,500
Other (net of miscellaneous revenue)	1,300
Variable expense	$0.27 per gallon

The planned sales price of gasoline is 36 cents per gallon.

Instructions
a What is the break-even point for the proposed station, in dollars of sales volume per month, and in gallons?
b Draw a monthly profit-volume graph for the proposed station, assuming 120,000 gallons per month as the maximum sales potential. Show fixed expenses on the bottom of the graph.
c The president thinks that the monthly volume at 36 cents per gallon will average 90,000 gallons and that, if the price of gasoline is reduced to 34 cents per gallon, the monthly volume will average 110,000 gallons. How much income (before taxes) would be earned per month at each sales volume?

27B-3 Capistrano Company budgeted the following costs for the production and sale of 40,000 units of a fishing rod.

	Total Annual Costs	Unit Costs and Expenses	Percentage of Total Annual Costs and Expenses That Are Variable
Direct materials	$400,000	$10	100%
Direct labor	320,000	8	100
Factory overhead (fixed and			
variable)	160,000	4	40
Administrative expenses	80,000	2	20
Totals	$960,000	$24	

The unit will be sold by manufacturer's representatives who will receive a commission of 10% of the gross sales price. Management wants to price the product to realize a 15% profit (before income taxes) on gross sales price.

Instructions
a Compute the gross sales price per unit that would result in a pretax profit of 15% on sales if sales amount to 40,000 units.
b Assuming that the gross sales price per unit is set at $40, compute the number of units that must be sold annually in order to break even.

27B-4 Landry Knife Company manufactures four products in four different departments. The estimated demand for the products for Year 4 is such that production will not be able to keep pace with incoming orders. Some pertinent data for each product are listed below:

Product	Estimated Sales for Year 4, Units	Sales Price	Direct Material Cost	Direct Labor Cost	Variable Factory Overhead
A	8,000	$11.00	$3.00	$4.00	$1.00
B	1,200	9.00	2.00	4.00	1.00
C	4,000	6.50	1.00	2.00	1.00
D	6,000	4.25	0.25	1.00	1.20

Direct labor costs an average of $4.00 per hour.

Instructions
a Prepare a schedule showing the contribution margin per one unit of each product and also the contribution margin per one hour of direct labor applied to the production of each class of product.
b If you were to reduce the production of one of the products in order to meet the demand for the others, what would that product be? Why? Assume that direct labor hours represent the scarce resource.
c Assume that the 8,000 hours of direct labor hours now used to produce product A are used to produce additional units of product C. What would be the effect on total contribution margin?

27B-5 Lava Company manufactures two products from a single raw material. The company's plant has a capacity to process 150,000 pounds of raw material per month. The cost inputs and the outputs from the various processing operations are summarized below and on page 975.

Inputs	*Outputs*
1 100 pounds of raw material at 40 cents per pound	1 60 pounds of product X, which sells for $1.60 per pound

2 Variable processing costs, 60 cents per pound

3 Fixed processing costs per month, $16,000

2 40 pounds of product Y, which sells for $2.60 per pound

The finished product is shipped from the plant daily; therefore, ending inventories of goods in process and finished product are negligible. Fixed selling and administrative expenses are estimated at $32,000 per month. Variable selling and administrative expenses are budgeted at 18% of dollar sales.

Instructions

a Compute the contribution margin ratio and the monthly sales volume (in pounds) which must be sold in order to break even.

b Prepare a budgeted income statement for the month of June, Year 1, showing the operating income that should be forecast if the plant operated at 80% of capacity. Ignore income taxes.

BUSINESS DECISION PROBLEM 27

Blue Star Company operates a chain of drive-ins selling only ice cream products. The following information is taken from the records of a typical drive-in now operated by the company:

Average selling price of ice cream per gallon		$ 3.20
Number of gallons sold per month		15,000
Variable expenses per gallon:		
Ice cream	$1.80	
Supplies (cups, cones, toppings, etc.)	0.60	
Total variable expenses per gallon		$ 2.40
Fixed expenses per month:		
Rent on building and parking lot		$1,200.00
Utilities and upkeep		760.00
Wages, including payroll taxes		4,540.00
Manager's salary, including payroll taxes but excluding any bonus		1,800.00
Other fixed expenses		700.00
Total fixed expenses per month		$9,000.00

Based on these data, the monthly break-even sales volume is determined as follows:

$$\frac{\$9,000 \text{ (Fixed Expenses)}}{\$0.80 \text{ (Contribution Margin per Unit)}} = 11,250 \text{ Gallons (or \$36,000)}$$

Instructions

a Assuming that the manager has a contract calling for a bonus of 10 cents per gallon for each gallon sold beyond the break-even point, compute the number of gallons of ice cream that must be sold per month in order to earn $2,800 per month. Disregard income taxes.

b In order to increase monthly income, the company is considering the following two alternatives:

(*1*) Reduce the selling price to $3.00 per gallon. This action is expected to increase the number of gallons sold by 40%. The manager would be paid a salary of $1,800 per month without a bonus.

(*2*) Spend $1,000 per month on advertising without any change in selling price. This action is expected to increase the number of gallons sold by 20%. The manager would be paid a salary of $1,800 per month without a bonus.

Which of these two alternatives would be more profitable for a typical drive-in store now selling 15,000 units? How many gallons must be sold per month under each alternative in order to break even? Give complete schedules in support of your answers and indicate to management which of the two alternatives it should adopt.

28

Capital Budgeting and Other Aids to Managerial Decisions

Deciding among alternatives

All business decisions involve a choice among alternative courses of action. The criteria for such choices may be subjective, such as attitudes of employees, or the criteria may be objective, such as dollars of cost and revenue. Most decisions are influenced by a combination of both subjective and objective factors. In most situations it is possible to analyze some of the consequences of alternative actions in quantitative terms and to use the results of this analysis in making a decision.

If two alternative actions are under consideration, quantitative analysis will generally show which action will lead to the higher profit, or if an investment is involved, to the higher return on investment. *Return on investment* may be expressed as the ratio of income per period to the average investment for the period. Since income is influenced by both revenue and cost (expenses), any expected change either in revenue or in cost (expenses) is relevant to the decision.

If a decision involves a new investment that will be recovered through increased net revenue or cost savings over a period of several years, an analysis of cash flows over time is appropriate, an analysis which requires the use of present value computations.

OUTLINE OF AN ALTERNATIVE-CHOICE PROBLEM The solution to most alternative-choice problems is formulated through the following steps:

1 Define the problem and identify the alternative solutions to be considered.

2 Measure and compare the consequences of each alternative, insofar as these consequences can be expressed quantitatively.

3 Evaluate the subjective factors and consider the extent to which they offset quantitative considerations.

4 Arrive at a decision.

Often the existence of an alternative choice comes to light through a proposal to change what is now being done. Once the issue is raised, however, the alternatives to consider may be more numerous than simply making a choice between what is now being done and the specific proposed change. For example, suppose that the installation of a certain computer for data processing has been proposed. If we are seriously considering this computer, the alternatives may be to: (*1*) continue our present data processing system; (*2*) buy the computer in question; (*3*) buy some other type of computer; (*4*) lease the computer selected; or (*5*) improve the present data processing system by eliminating unnecessary steps. If too many alternatives are considered, the analysis becomes hopelessly complex. Fortunately, it is usually possible to rule out certain choices on the basis of a rough analysis, leaving only a few alternatives for serious consideration.

Measuring the outcome or consequences of alternative courses of action involves a forecast of the future, and some degree of error is always present. We may decide to estimate what will probably happen and proceed with our analysis on the assumption that our expectations will be fully realized. On the other hand, we may formulate two or more possible outcomes, assess the *probability* of each and arrive at an expected outcome which is a weighted average of the probability of a number of outcomes. It is clearly advantageous to express as many consequences of a decision in quantitative terms as possible because it is easy to find the net effect of quantitative factors. *Costs* and *cost additions* can be subtracted from *revenue* and *cost savings* to produce a net numerical representation of the advantage or disadvantage associated with a given course of action.

A few of the more common applications of alternative-choice decisions are discussed in the following sections.

Illustration of an alternative-choice decision: unprofitable product line

The Suncraft Company manufactures household mixers in three models: Deluxe, Standard, and Economy. The overall profit margins for the last few years have been unsatisfactory, and the issue has been raised as to whether one or more of the models should be dropped from production. An income statement showing product results for last year is shown on page 979.

SUNCRAFT COMPANY
Income Statement—Last Year

	Total	Deluxe Model	Standard Model	Economy Model
Sales (units)	34,000	4,000	20,000	10,000
Sales revenue	$960,000	$160,000	$600,000	$200,000
Manufacturing costs	730,000	138,000	412,000	180,000
Gross profit on sales	$230,000	$ 22,000	$188,000	$ 20,000
Operating expenses	223,200	38,200	125,000	60,000
Income or (loss) before taxes	$ 6,800	$(16,200)	$ 63,000	$(40,000)
Income or (loss) per unit	$0.20	$(4.05)	$3.15	$(4.00)

Should the Deluxe and Economy models be dropped?

This information suggests that if the company were to drop both the Deluxe and Economy models and produce only the Standard model it might expect earnings of around $63,000 per year—a striking improvement. On the other hand, it might be argued that the Deluxe model contributes $22,000 of gross profit and the Economy model $20,000, and that they should be continued since this is a positive contribution to operating expenses. The trouble with both these conclusions is that they are based on irrelevant information. The fact that a given expense is *allocated* to a particular product, for example, does not mean that this cost would disappear if the product were dropped.

A first step in obtaining information more useful for decision-making purposes is to determine the contribution margin of each product. *Contribution margin* per unit is the difference between unit sales price and all variable costs per unit. The contribution margin per unit, based on the Suncraft Company data, is shown below:

SUNCRAFT COMPANY
Per-Unit Contribution Margin by Models—Last Year

	Deluxe Model	Standard Model	Economy Model
Selling price per unit	$40	$30	$20
Variable costs per unit:			
Variable manufacturing costs	$30	$18	$15
Variable operating expenses	6	4	4
Total variable costs per unit	$36	$22	$19
Contribution margin per unit	$ 4	$ 8	$ 1

All models are covering their variable costs

This per-unit data may be reconciled with the income statement figures as shown at the top of page 980.

SUNCRAFT COMPANY

Income Statement—Last Year

	Total	Deluxe Model	Standard Model	Economy Model
Total contribution margin by products: Number of units sold . . . (a)	34,000	4,000	20,000	10,000
Contribution margin per unit (b)		$4	$8	$1
Total contribution margin (a × b). .$186,000		$ 16,000	$160,000	$ 10,000
Less: All fixed costs.	179,200	32,200	97,000	50,000
Income or (loss) before taxes . .	$ 6,800	$(16,200)	$ 63,000	$(40,000)

The contribution margin analysis begins to sharpen the picture. Apparently each of the three models makes some contribution to fixed costs. Dropping the Deluxe model would reduce income by $16,000 and dropping the Economy model would reduce income by $10,000. Before accepting this conclusion, however, we should ask ourselves whether the assumptions used in dividing costs into their fixed and variable components are sound.

Two assumptions, inherent in the fixed and variable cost data, are important to our tentative conclusions. First, we have assumed that the variable and fixed relationship of cost to volume holds for variations in output all the way down to zero for a particular model. In our discussion of cost-volume relationships in Chapter 27, we noted that the division of costs into fixed and variable components is usually valid for variations in output somewhat above and below the normal scale of production. If manufacture of a product is discontinued entirely, however, the nature of operations may be changed so that some fixed costs can be eliminated in their entirety.

Secondly, the use of contribution margin data rests on the assumption that the sales of any particular model are independent of the sales of the other two models. It is entirely possible that dropping either the Deluxe or Economy model *will result in an increase in sales of the other models;* it is also possible that dropping one model *may adversely affect the sale of the other models.*

Let us see how these two factors might affect our analysis. In view of its low contribution margin, the Economy model seems the most likely candidate for elimination. Assume that a careful study of fixed costs is made and indicates that the elimination of this model would enable the Suncraft Company to reduce certain fixed costs by $7,000.

It seems likely that some buyers of the Economy model might shift to the Standard model if the Economy model were no longer offered. When asked for an estimate of this factor, the sales manager presented the report shown on page 981.

	Number of Economy Model Sales That Might Shift to Standard Model (per Year)	×	My Estimate of the Probability That This Many Would Shift	=	Expected Shift in Sales
Sales manager's estimate of shift in sales	1,000		.05		50
	2,000		.10		200
	3,000		.30		900
	4,000		.40		1,600
	5,000 or more		.15		750
					3,500 units

Note: The fact that we did not maintain a full line of mixers may be expected to result in the loss of the entire business of some dealers, especially those who put special emphasis on the low-priced Economy model. *I would expect a reduction of 10% in our present sales of Deluxe and Standard models due to this factor.*

By incorporating the expected reduction in fixed costs and shift in sales into our analysis, we can prepare the schedule shown below:

SUNCRAFT COMPANY
Estimate of Annual Change in Income from Dropping Economy Model

Complete analysis of decision variables

Increase in annual income from dropping Economy model:

Estimated reduction in costs presently classified as fixed . . . . $ 7,000

Gain in contribution margin because of shift in sales from Economy model to Standard model:

Sales manager's expected sales shift to Standard model	3,500	
Contribution margin per unit of Standard model	×$8	28,000
Total increase in annual income		$35,000

Less: Reduction in annual income from dropping Economy model:

Contribution margin on Economy models now sold: 10,000 units × $1 contribution margin per unit $10,000

Contribution margin on 10% reduction in sales of Standard and Deluxe models as a result of elimination of Economy model:

2,000 units of standard model × $8 contribution margin per unit 16,000

400 units of Deluxe models × $4 contribution margin per unit 1,600

Total reduction in annual income 27,600

Estimated net increase in annual income if Economy model is dropped . . . . $ 7,400

We have now finally isolated the data relevant to the decision. If our assumptions and estimates are realized, we can increase the annual income of the Suncraft Company to $14,200 ($6,800 + $7,400) by dropping the Economy model from the line.

Accepting special orders

In many business decisions, the relevant factors are the **differences** between the costs incurred and the revenue earned under alternative courses of action. These differences are often called **incremental (or differential)** costs and revenue. Costs which do not vary among alternative courses of action are not relevant in making alternative-choice decisions.

The decision of whether to accept an order for an additional volume of business at special terms may be used to illustrate the concept of incremental analysis. Assume, for example, that Sports Supply Company estimates its production of golf balls for the coming year at 400,000 dozen, although its plant capacity is approximately 525,000 dozen golf balls per year. The company receives an order from a foreign company for 100,000 dozen golf balls to be used for sales promotion efforts. The foreign company would pay all shipping costs and wants a special imprint on the ball. The company normally sells golf balls for $6 per dozen and the foreign company's offer is for $4 per dozen. If the order is accepted, the company will have to spend $15,000 in cash to design and set up the special imprint on the golf balls. A summary of estimated results for the coming year is presented below:

	Planned Output (400,000 Dozen)	With Special Order (500,000 Dozen)	Incremental (or Differential) Analysis
A special Sales: $6 per dozen	$2,400,000	$2,400,000	
order is $4 per dozen		400,000	$400,000
profitable if			
revenue Variable costs:			
from it $3 per dozen	(1,200,000)	(1,500,000)	(300,000)
exceeds			
incremental Fixed costs	(900,000)	(900,000)	
costs Special imprint costs		(15,000)	(15,000)
Estimated income	$ 300,000	$ 385,000	$ 85,000

Note that the average cost of producing golf balls without the special order is $5.25 per dozen [($1,200,000 + $900,000) ÷ 400,000 dozen]. If a decision were made based on this average cost, the special order would probably be rejected. Incremental analysis, however, shows that incremental revenue from accepting the special order amounts to $400,000, while the incremental cost is only $315,000. Thus, accepting the special order will increase Sports Supply Company's net income by $85,000.

The relevant factors in this type of decision are the incremental revenue that will be earned and the additional (incremental) cost that will be incurred by accepting the special order. The average cost of production is **not relevant** to the decision.

In evaluating the merits of a special order such as the one received by the Sports Supply Company, we must give particular attention to the effect that such an order may have on the company's regular sales volume and selling prices. Obviously, it would not be wise for the Sports Supply

Company to sell 100,000 dozen golf balls to a domestic company which might try to sell the golf balls to the regular customers of Sports Supply Company for, say, $5 per dozen.

Make or buy decisions

In many manufacturing situations, companies are often faced with decisions whether (1) to produce a certain component part required in the assembly of its finished products or (2) to buy the part from outside suppliers. If a company produces a part which can be purchased at a lower cost, it may be more profitable for the company to buy the part and utilize its productive resources for other purposes.

For example, if a company can buy a part for $5 per unit which costs the company $6 per unit to produce, the choice seems to be clearly in favor of buying. But the astute reader will quickly raise the question, "What is included in the cost of $6 per unit?" Assume that the $6 unit cost of producing 10,000 units was determined as follows:

	Cost of Part
Direct materials	*$ 8,000*
Direct labor	*12,500*
Variable factory overhead	*10,000*
Fixed factory overhead	*29,500*
Total costs	*$60,000*
Cost per unit ($60,000 ÷ 10,000 units)	*$6*

What is the variable cost per unit for this company?

A careful review of operations indicates that if the production of this part were discontinued, all the cost of direct materials and direct labor and $9,000 of the variable factory overhead would be eliminated. In addition, $2,500 of the fixed factory overhead can be eliminated. These, then, are the relevant costs in producing the 10,000 parts, and we can summarize them as follows:

Incremental costs ($32,000) exceed the variable cost ($30,500); however, it would cost $50,000 to buy the part from outside suppliers

	Make the Part	*Buy the Part*	*Incremental (or Differential) Analysis*
Manufacturing costs for 10,000 units:			
Direct materials	*$ 8,000*		*$ 8,000*
Direct labor	*12,500*		*12,500*
Variable factory overhead	*10,000*	*$ 1,000*	*9,000*
Fixed factory overhead	*29,500*	*27,000*	*2,500*
Purchase price of part, $5 per unit		*50,000*	*(50,000)*
Totals	*$60,000*	*$78,000*	*$(18,000)*

It appears that the company should continue to produce this part. The incremental cost per unit is only $3.20 [($8,000 + $12,500 + $9,000 + $2,500) ÷ 10,000 units], and it would cost the company $1.80 per unit (or $18,000) *more* to buy the part than it is costing to produce. If, however, in place of this particular part, the company had an opportunity to manufacture another product which would produce a contribution margin greater than $18,000, then the part should be purchased.

Note that, in the foregoing analysis, not all the variable factory overhead costs incurred in producing the part would be eliminated if the part were not produced and that only $2,500 of fixed factory costs would be eliminated. We have assumed these facts in order to illustrate that not all variable costs are necessarily incremental and that *some fixed costs may be incremental* in a given situation.

Sunk costs and opportunity costs

The only costs relevant to a decision are those costs which vary among the alternative courses of action being considered. A *sunk cost* is one which has been irrevocably incurred by past actions. Sunk costs are not relevant to decisions because they cannot be changed regardless of what decision is made. The term *out-of-pocket cost* is often used to describe costs which have not yet been incurred and which may vary among the alternative courses of action. Out-of-pocket costs, therefore, are relevant in making decisions.

SCRAP OR REBUILD DEFECTIVE UNITS   To illustrate the irrelevance of sunk costs, assume that 1,000 television sets which cost $80,000 to manufacture are found to be defective and management must decide what to do with them. These sets may be sold "as is" for $30,000, or they can be rebuilt and placed in good condition at an additional out-of-pocket cost of $60,000. If the sets are rebuilt, they can be sold for the regular price of $100,000. Should the sets be sold "as is" or rebuilt?

Regardless of whether the sets are sold or rebuilt, the $80,000 sunk cost has already been incurred. The relevant considerations in the decision to sell the sets "as is" or rebuild are the incremental revenue and the incremental cost. By rebuilding the sets, the company will realize $70,000 more revenue than if the sets are sold "as is." The incremental cost necessary to obtain this incremental revenue is the $60,000 cost of rebuilding the sets. Thus, the company will be $10,000 ($70,000 − $60,000) better off if it rebuilds the sets.

OPPORTUNITY COSTS   At this stage, we should give consideration to the concept of *opportunity costs.* An opportunity cost is the benefit which could be obtained by pursuing another course of action. As a simple illustration, assume that a student passes up a summer job that pays $1,800 in order to attend summer school. The $1,800 may be viewed as an opportunity cost of attending summer school.

Opportunity costs are not recorded in the accounting records, but they are an important factor in many business decisions. Ignoring opportunity costs is a common source of error in making cost analyses. In our example involving the defective television sets, we determined that the company could earn an additional $10,000 by rebuilding the sets rather than by selling them "as is." Suppose, however, that rebuilding the sets would require the use of production facilities which would otherwise be used to manufacture new sets worth $20,000 in excess of their cost. Obviously, the company should not forgo a $20,000 profit in order to earn $10,000. When this $20,000 opportunity cost is considered, it becomes evident that the company should sell the defective sets "as is" and use its production facilities for the manufacture of new sets.

CAPITAL BUDGETING

Perhaps the most common alternative-choice problems involve decisions for replacement of plant assets or expansion of productive facilities. The process of planning and evaluating proposals for investment in plant assets is called *capital budgeting.* Capital budgeting decisions are complicated by the fact that the decision must be made from estimates of future operating results, which by their nature involve a considerable degree of uncertainty. Yet these decisions are crucial to the long-run financial health of a business enterprise. Not only are large amounts of money committed for long periods of time, but many capital budgeting decisions are difficult or impossible to reverse once the funds have been committed and the project has begun. Thus, companies may benefit from good capital budgeting decisions and suffer from poor ones for many years.

Many nonfinancial factors are considered in making capital budgeting decisions. For example, many companies give high priority to creating new jobs and avoiding layoffs. However, it is also essential that investments in plant assets earn a satisfactory return on the funds invested. Without this return, investors will not be willing to make funds available to finance the project and the company will not be able to generate sufficient funds for future investment projects.

Capital budgeting is a broad field, involving many sophisticated techniques for evaluating the financial and nonfinancial considerations. We shall limit our discussion in this area to three of the most common techniques of evaluating investment opportunities: payback period, return on average investment, and discounted cash flow analysis.

To illustrate these techniques, let us assume that Tanner Corporation is considering several alternative investments, including the purchase of equipment to produce a new product. The equipment costs $40,000, has an eight-year service life, and no estimated salvage value. Tanner Corporation estimates that production and sale of the new product will increase the company's net income by $3,000 per year, computed as shown at the top of page 986.

Estimated sales of new product		*$40,000*
Deduct estimated expenses:		
Depreciation on new equipment	*$ 5,000*	
Manufacturing costs other than		
depreciation	*22,000*	
Additional selling and general expenses	*7,000*	*34,000*
Estimated increase in before-tax income		*$ 6,000*
Less: Additional income taxes (50%)		*3,000*
Estimated increase in net income		*$ 3,000*

Most capital budgeting techniques involve analysis of the estimated annual net cash flows pertaining to the investment. Annual net cash flow is the excess of cash receipts over cash payments in a given year. In our example, assume that all revenue is received in cash and all expenses other than depreciation are paid in cash. Tanner Corporation should expect an annual net cash flow of $8,000 ($40,000 − $22,000 − $7,000 − $3,000) from sales of the new product. Note that annual net cash flow exceeds estimated net income ($3,000) by the amount of the depreciation expense ($5,000). This is because none of the cash received as revenue is paid out as depreciation expense. Other differences which may exist between net income and net cash flow were discussed in Chapter 21.

Payback period

The *payback period* is the length of time necessary to recover the entire cost of an investment from the resulting annual net cash flow. In our example, the payback period is computed as follows:

$$\frac{\text{Amount to Be Invested}}{\text{Estimated Annual Net Cash Flow}} = \frac{\$40,000}{\$8,000} = 5 \text{ years}$$

In selecting among alternative investment opportunities, a short payback period is considered desirable because the sooner the amount of the investment is recovered, the sooner the funds may be put to other use. A short payback period also reduces the risk that changes in economic conditions will prevent full recovery of the investment. Before an investment can be considered profitable, the life of the investment must exceed the payback period. However, the payback period ignores the total life and, therefore, the total profitability of the investment. For this reason, the payback period should never be the only factor considered in a major capital budgeting decision.

Return on average investment

The *rate of return on average investment* is the average annual net income from an investment expressed as a percentage of the *average* amount invested. Tanner Corporation will have to invest $40,000 in the new equipment, but each year depreciation will reduce the carrying value of this asset by $5,000. Since the annual net cash flow will exceed net income by this amount, we may view depreciation expense as providing for the recovery of the amount originally invested. Thus, the amount invested in the equipment at any given time is represented by the carrying value (cost less accumulated depreciation) of the asset.

When straight-line depreciation is used, the carrying value of an asset decreases uniformly over the asset's life. Thus, the average carrying value is equal to an amount halfway between the asset's original cost and its salvage value. Mathematically, the average amount invested over the life of an asset may be determined as follows:

$$\text{Average Investment} = \frac{\text{Original Cost} + \text{Salvage Value}}{2}$$

When the expected salvage value is zero, the average investment is simply one-half of the original investment. Thus, Tanner Corporation will have an average investment in the new equipment of $20,000 ($40,000 ÷ 2). We may compute the expected rate of return on this average investment as follows:

$$\frac{\text{Average Estimated Net Income}}{\text{Average Investment}} = \frac{\$3,000}{\$20,000} = 15\%$$

In deciding whether 15% is a satisfactory rate of return, Tanner Corporation should consider such factors as the rate of return available from alternative investment opportunities, the risk involved in actually realizing the expected rate of return, the corporation's cost of capital, and the nonfinancial factors relating to the investment. In comparing alternative investment opportunities, management usually prefers the investment with the lowest risk, highest rate of return, and shortest payback period. Of course, the same investment is seldom superior to all others in every respect. Thus, managers must consider many subjective factors in making their decisions.

The expected rate of return technique for comparing investment opportunities does not give consideration to the *timing* of net income. In computing the *average* annual net income, we ignore whether the income was received early or late in the life of the investment. (In the Tanner Corporation example, net income was constant at $3,000 a year, but in other cases net income will vary from year to year.) A technique which does take into account the timing of cash flows is called *discounting future cash flows.*

Discounting future cash flows

As explained in Chapter 18, the present value of a future cash flow is the amount that a knowledgeable investor would pay today for the right to receive that future amount. The exact amount of the present value depends upon (*1*) the amount of the future payment, (*2*) the length of time until the future amount will be received, and (*3*) the rate of return required by the investor. **Discounting** is the process of determining the present value of future cash flows.

To illustrate the discounting of a future amount, assume that a specific investment results in a $1,000 cash flow at the end of one year. A business requiring a 6% annual return would be willing to invest $943.40 ($1,000 ÷ 1.06) to receive this future amount. This computation may be verified as follows:

Amount invested (present value)	$ 943.40
Required earnings on investment ($943.40 × .06)	56.60
Amount to be received in one year (future value)	$1,000.00

If the $1,000 is to be received two years in the future, the business would invest only $890 today [($1,000 ÷ 1.06) ÷ 1.06]. This computation also may be verified as follows:

Amount invested (present value of $1,000 in two years)	$ 890.00
First year's earnings ($890 × .06)	53.40
Amount of investment after one year	$ 943.40
Second year's earnings ($943.40 × .06)	56.60
Amount to be received in two years	$1,000.00

The amount to be invested, $890, is the present value of $1,000 to be received in two years, **discounted at an annual rate of 6%.**

Although we can compute the present value of future amounts by a series of divisions as illustrated above, a more convenient method is available. We can use a **table of present values** to find the present value of $1 at the specified discount rate and then multiply that value by the future amount. For example, in the table shown below, the present value of $1 to

Present Value of $1 at Compound Interest

Years	6%	8%	10%	12%	15%
1	.943	.926	.909	.893	.870
2	.890	.857	.826	.797	.756
3	.840	.794	.751	.712	.658
4	.792	.735	.683	.636	.572
5	.747	.681	.621	.567	.497
6	.705	.630	.565	.507	.432
7	.665	.584	.513	.452	.376
8	.627	.540	.467	.404	.327
9	.592	.500	.424	.361	.284
10	.558	.463	.386	.322	.247

be received two years from now, discounted at 6% a year, appears as .890. Therefore we multiply .890 by the future amount of $1,000 and get an answer of $890, the same amount produced by the series of two divisions in our illustration.

The discount rate may be viewed as the investor's required rate of return. The present value of the future cash flows is the maximum amount that the investor may pay for the investment and still expect to earn the required rate of return. Therefore, an investment is considered desirable when its cost is less than the present value of the expected future cash flows. Conversely, an investment is undesirable when its cost is greater than the present value of expected future cash flows.

The interest rate used in discounting future cash flows may be viewed as the investor's required rate of return. When a higher discount rate is used, the resulting present value will be lower and the investor, therefore, will be interested in the investment only at a lower price. The "appropriate" discount rate for determining the present value of a specific investment depends upon the nature of that investment, the alternative investment opportunities available, and the investor's cost of capital.

Let us now apply the concept of discounting cash flows to our continuing example of the Tanner Corporation. The $40,000 investment in new equipment is expected to produce annual net cash flows of $8,000 for eight years. If Tanner Corporation requires a 10% annual rate of return on investments of this type, the present value of the expected cash flows may be determined as follows:

Year	Net Cash Flows	Present Value of $1 at 10%	Present Value of Net Cash Flows
1	$8,000	.909	$ 7,272
2	8,000	.826	6,608
3	8,000	.751	6,008
4	8,000	.683	5,464
5	8,000	.621	4,968
6	8,000	.565	4,520
7	8,000	.513	4,104
8	8,000	.467	3,736

Present value of future cash flows	$42,680
Amount to be invested	40,000
Net present value of proposed investment	$ 2,680

This analysis indicates that the present value of the expected net cash flows from the investment, discounted at an annual rate of 10%, amounts to $42,680. This is the maximum amount which Tanner Corporation could afford to invest in the project and still expect to earn the required 10% annual rate of return. Since the actual cost of the investment is only $40,000, Tanner Corporation can expect to earn more than 10%.

The **net present value** of the proposal is the difference between the total present value of the net cash flows and the cost of the investment. When the net present value is equal to zero, the investment provides a rate of return exactly equal to the rate used in discounting the cash flows. A **positive** net present value means that the investment provides a rate of return **greater than the discount rate;** a **negative** net present value means that the investment yields a return of **less** than the discount rate. Since the discount rate is usually the minimum rate of return required by the investor, proposals with a positive net present value are considered acceptable and those with a negative net present value are viewed as unacceptable.

DISCOUNTING UNIFORM ANNUAL CASH FLOWS In our preceding example, we multiplied each of the annual $8,000 cash flows by the present value of $1 in the appropriate future period, discounted at 10%. The present value of each annual cash flow was then added to determine the total present value of future cash flows. Since the annual cash flows are uniform in amount, there are two easier ways to compute this total present value. One way is to add the eight decimal figures representing the present values of $1 in the successive years and then to multiply this total (5.335) by the $8,000 annual cash flow. This approach produces the same result ($8,000 × 5.335 = $42,680) as we obtained by determining the present value of each year's cash flow separately and adding the results.

An even easier approach to determining the total present value of uniform annual cash flows is to refer to an **annuity table,** which shows the present value of $1 received annually for a given number of years, discounted at various discount rates. An annuity table is shown below:

Present Value of $1 Received Annually for a Number of Years

Years	6%	8%	10%	12%	15%
1	0.943	0.926	0.909	0.893	0.870
2	1.833	1.783	1.736	1.690	1.626
3	2.673	2.577	2.487	2.402	2.283
4	3.465	3.312	3.170	3.037	2.855
5	4.212	3.993	3.791	3.605	3.352
6	4.917	4.623	4.355	4.111	3.764
7	5.582	5.206	4.868	4.564	4.160
8	6.210	5.747	5.335	4.968	4.487
9	6.802	6.247	5.759	5.328	4.772
10	7.360	6.710	6.145	5.650	5.019

Note that the present value of $1 received annually for eight years, discounted at 10%, is 5.335. Thus, $8,000 received annually for eight years, discounted at 10%, is $42,680 ($8,000 × 5.335).

Replacement of old equipment

A problem often facing management is whether it should buy new and more efficient equipment or whether it should continue to use existing equipment. Assume, for example, that the Ardmore Company is meeting increasing competition in the sale of product Q. The sales manager believes the source of the trouble is that competitors have installed more efficient equipment, which has enabled them to reduce prices. The issue raised therefore is whether Ardmore Company should: (*1*) buy new equipment at a cost of $60,000, or (2) continue using its present equipment. We will make the simplifying assumption that both the new and present equipment have a remaining useful life of five years and neither will have any residual value. The new equipment will produce substantial savings in direct labor, direct materials, and factory overhead costs. The company does not believe the use of new equipment will have any effect on sales volume, so the decision rests entirely on whether cost savings are possible.

The old equipment has a book value of $45,000 but can be sold for only $5,000 if it is replaced. At first glance, the resulting $40,000 loss on disposal appears to be a good reason for not replacing the old equipment. However, the cost of the old equipment is a *sunk cost* and is not relevant to the decision. If the old machinery is sold, its book value contributes to the amount of the loss; if the old machinery is retained, its book value will be recognized as expense through future charges to depreciation. Thus, this cost cannot be avoided by Ardmore Company regardless of which decision is made. From a present value standpoint, there is some benefit to recognizing this sunk cost as a loss in the current period inasmuch as the related tax reduction will occur this year rather than over the remaining life of the equipment.

In deciding whether to replace the old equipment, Ardmore Company should determine the present value of the incremental net cash flows resulting from replacement of the old machinery. This present value may then be compared with the cost of the new equipment to determine whether the investment will provide the required rate of return. To compute the incremental annual net cash flow from replacing the old equipment, management must consider both the annual cash savings in manufacturing costs and the difference in annual income taxes. Income taxes will differ under the alternative courses of action because of differences in (*1*) variable manufacturing costs and (2) annual depreciation expense.

Let us assume that the new machinery will result in an $18,000 annual cash savings in variable manufacturing costs. However, annual depreciation on the new equipment will be $12,000 ($60,000 ÷ 5 years), whereas annual depreciation on the old equipment is $9,000 ($45,000 ÷ 5 years). This $3,000 increase in depreciation expense means that purchase of the new equipment will *increase* taxable income by $15,000 ($18,000 cost savings less $3,000 additional depreciation). Assuming a tax rate of 40%, purchase of the new equipment will increase annual income tax expense by $6,000 ($15,000 × .40). The incremental annual net cash flow from owning the new machinery, therefore, amounts to $12,000 ($18,000 − $6,000).

We shall assume that Ardmore Company requires a 10% return on investments in plant assets. Referring to the annuity table on page 990, we see that the present value of $1 received annually for five years is 3.791. Therefore, $12,000 received annually for five years, discounted at an annual rate of 10%, has a present value of $45,492 ($12,000 × 3.791). In addition to the present value of the annual net cash flows, however, we must consider two other factors: (1) the proceeds from sale of the old equipment and (2) the tax savings resulting from the loss on disposal.

The $5,000 proceeds from sale of the old equipment will be received immediately and, therefore, have a present value of $5,000. The $40,000 loss on disposal results in a $16,000 reduction ($40,000 × .4) in income taxes payable at the end of the first year. The present value of $16,000 one year hence discounted at 10% is $14,544 ($16,000 × .909), as determined from a present value table.

We may now determine the net present value of the proposal to replace the old equipment with new as follows:

Present value of incremental annual cash flows	$45,492
Present value of proceeds from sale of old equipment	5,000
Present value of tax savings from loss on disposal	14,544
Total present value	$65,036
Amount to be invested	60,000
Net present value	$ 5,036

Since the total present value of all future cash flows from acquiring the new equipment exceeds the cost of the investment, Ardmore Company should replace the old equipment with new.

VARIABLE (DIRECT) COSTING AS AN AID TO MANAGEMENT

The discussion in Chapter 25 dealing with job order and process cost systems was based on the assumption that the actual manufacturing costs incurred in any given period are assigned to the units produced in that period. Manufacturing costs (fixed and variable) were ultimately associated with the goods in process inventory, the finished goods inventory, and the cost of goods sold. This procedure is known as **full costing** or **absorption costing**. An alternative costing assumption which can be useful to management, **variable costing** (or **direct costing**), was briefly described on page 855.

The three basic features of variable costing are:

1 All manufacturing costs are first divided into those which are variable and those which are fixed.

2 Variable manufacturing costs are treated as **product costs** and are assigned to the goods produced. Some of the goods produced are found in ending inventories (goods in process and finished goods) and the rest become a part of cost of goods sold during the current period.

3 Fixed manufacturing costs, along with all selling and administrative expenses, are treated as **period costs** and are charged to revenue of the period in which they are incurred.

The flow of costs under variable and full costing is illustrated in the diagram below:

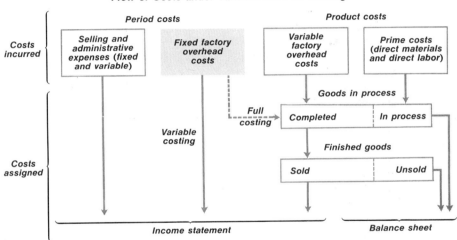

Flow of Costs under Variable and Full Costing

The diagram shows that selling and administrative expenses and fixed factory overhead costs are charged to revenue of the current period when variable costing is used. As a result, the Goods in Process account is charged only with variable manufacturing costs, and the ending inventories of goods in process and finished goods include only variable manufacturing costs. When full costing is used, fixed factory overhead costs are treated as product costs, a portion of which is assigned to the ending inventories of goods in process and finished goods.

Illustration of variable costing

The differences between variable costing and full costing may be illustrated by preparing an income statement under each method, using the following information for the Hamilton Corporation:

Data for Year 1 Production—Year 1 (assume no goods in process)	*40,000 units*
Sales—Year 1	*30,000 units*
Sales price per unit	*$10*

Variable manufacturing costs per unit $4

Variable selling and administrative expenses per unit $1

Fixed costs:

    Manufacturing $40,000

    Selling and administrative expenses $30,000

A partial[1] income statement based on this information, using the variable cost assumption, appears below:

HAMILTON CORPORATION

Partial Income Statement—Variable Costing

Year 1

Fixed factory overhead costs excluded from inventory— Year 1	Sales (30,000 units @ $10)		$300,000
	Cost of goods sold (30,000 units @ $4 variable manufacturing costs)		120,000
	Manufacturing margin		$180,000
	Variable selling and administrative expenses (30,000 units @ $1)		30,000
	Contribution margin		$150,000
	Fixed costs:		
	Manufacturing	$40,000	
	Selling and administrative expenses	30,000	70,000
	Income from operations		$ 80,000

(Ending inventory of finished goods, 10,000 units @ $4 = $40,000)

In the partial income statement using variable costing, the variable manufacturing costs of the units sold are deducted from sales in arriving at the **manufacturing margin.** When variable selling and administrative expenses are deducted from the manufacturing margin we have the **contribution margin** which is available to cover all fixed (or period) costs. Income from operations is then determined by subtracting all fixed costs from the contribution margin.

A partial income statement using the same information but following the traditional full cost assumption is presented on page 995.

Effect of variable costing on income and inventory

Comparing the partial income statements above and on page 995 shows that the income from operations using full costing exceeds by $10,000 the income using variable costing. This difference is explained by analyzing the disposition of fixed manufacturing costs under the two costing methods. Under variable costing the fixed manufacturing costs, $40,000, are recognized as expenses in the current period; under full costing, fixed

[1] The income statements illustrated here are not complete because they do not include income taxes and earnings per share.

manufacturing costs are apportioned between the ending inventory of finished goods and the cost of goods sold. Since only 75% of units produced were sold, only $30,000 of the fixed manufacturing costs were included in the cost of goods sold figure.

HAMILTON CORPORATION
Partial Income Statement—Full Costing
Year 1

Fixed factory overhead costs included in inventory— Year 1 *Sales (30,000 units @ $10)*	**$300,000**
*Cost of goods sold**	*150,000*
Gross profit on sales	*$150,000*
Selling and administrative expenses (fixed and variable)	*60,000*
Income from operations	*$ 90,000*

* Computation of cost of goods sold:

Variable manufacturing costs (40,000 units @ $4)		$160,000
Fixed manufacturing costs		40,000
Full cost of production (40,000 units @ $5)		$200,000
Less: Ending inventory of finished goods (10,000 units @ $5)		50,000
Cost of goods sold (30,000 units)		$150,000

When *inventories are increasing* (that is, units produced exceed units sold), the use of variable costing will result in a smaller net income than when full costing is used because under variable costing fixed manufacturing costs are charged immediately to expense. Under full costing, fixed manufacturing costs are included in inventories. As inventories increase, some fixed costs expensed under variable costing will remain in inventories under full costing. When *inventories are decreasing* (that is, units sold exceed units produced), the income under variable costing will be larger than the income under full costing, because the decrease in inventory will be charged against revenue at less than full cost.

To illustrate one possible case (an increase in inventories), assume that the sales volume for the Hamilton Corporation in Year 2 remained unchanged at 30,000 units at $10 per unit, and that the level of production increased to 50,000, thus increasing the ending inventory of finished goods from 10,000 units to 30,000 units. The following information is available for Year 2. **(Note that unit variable costs and total fixed costs are exactly the same as in Year 1.)**

Data for Year 2	*Production—Year 2 (assume no goods in process)*	*50,000 units*
	Sales—Year 2	*30,000 units*
	Sales price per unit	*$10*
	Variable manufacturing costs per unit	*$4*
	Variable selling and administrative expenses per unit	*$1*
	Fixed costs:	
	Manufacturing	*$40,000*
	Selling and administrative expenses	*$30,000*

A partial income statement for Year 2, using the variable cost assumption, is illustrated below:

HAMILTON CORPORATION
Partial Income Statement—Variable Costing
Year 2

Fixed factory overhead excluded from inventory— Year 2	Sales (30,000 @ $10)	$300,000
	Cost of goods sold (30,000 units @ $4 variable manufacturing costs)	120,000
	Manufacturing margin	$180,000
	Variable selling and administrative expenses (30,000 units @ $1)	30,000
	Contribution margin	$150,000
	Fixed costs:	
	Manufacturing $40,000	
	Selling and administrative expenses 30,000	70,000
	Income from operations	$ 80,000

(Ending inventory of finished goods, 30,000 units @ $4 = $120,000)

A full costing partial income statement for Year 2 appears below:

HAMILTON CORPORATION
Partial Income Statement—Full Costing
Year 2

Fixed factory overhead costs included in inventory— Year 2	Sales (30,000 @ $10)	$300,000
	Cost of goods sold*	146,000
	Gross profit on sales	$154,000
	Selling and administrative expenses (fixed and variable)	60,000
	Income from operations	$ 94,000

*Computation of cost of goods sold:

Beginning inventory, 10,000 units (from Year 1)	$ 50,000
Add: Variable manufacturing costs (50,000 units @ $4)	200,000
Fixed manufacturing costs, Year 2	40,000
Goods available for sale (60,000 units)	$290,000
Less: Ending inventory on fifo basis, 30,000 units @ $4.80	
($240,000 ÷ 50,000 units)	144,000
Cost of goods sold (30,000 units)	$146,000

Briefly, we can summarize the results for the two years using variable costing and full costing as follows:

			Income from Operations		**Ending Inventory**		
Results using variable and full costing compared		Sales	Variable Costing	Full Costing	Variable Costing	Full Costing	Difference
	Year 1	$300,000	$80,000	$90,000	$ 40,000	$ 50,000	$10,000*
	Year 2	300,000	80,000	94,000	120,000	144,000	24,000†

*Income for the first year was $10,000 higher under full costing because ending inventory is higher by this amount.
†Two-year income in total is $24,000 higher under full costing because cumulative ending inventory is higher by this amount.

When variable costing is used, the income from operations for Year 2 remained unchanged at $80,000—a perfectly logical result since sales volume, selling price, variable costs per unit, and fixed costs were all unchanged. Using full costing, however, the income from operations increased from $90,000 in Year 1 to $94,000 in Year 2, *despite the fact that the sales volume remained at the same level* as in Year 1. This apparently illogical result probably represents a strong argument in favor of the use of variable costing for decision-making purposes by management; *when variable costing is used, income from operations changes in concert with changes in sales volume rather than with changes in production volume.*

Proponents of variable costing also argue that fixed manufacturing costs are not a part of the cost of goods produced during a given period but are the *costs of having the capacity to produce.* They believe that fixed manufacturing costs are *period* or *capacity* costs which should be charged against the revenue of the period in which they are incurred, without regard to the level of production. Critics of variable costing, however, point out that fixed manufacturing costs *add value to the goods produced* and are no less essential in the production of goods than variable costs. They argue that a profit on the sale of any product emerges only after recovery of the total cost of bringing that product to the point of sale.

Segregating variable and fixed costs in the accounts produces data that are useful to management in studying cost-volume-earnings relationships and in arriving at decisions involving pricing, production planning, and cost control. On the other hand, exclusion of fixed manufacturing costs from inventory valuation understates the full cost of inventories and makes variable costing of doubtful validity for income measurement purposes. For this reason, *variable costing is not an accepted procedure for income determination.*[2] When variable costing is used for internal decision-making purposes, inventory costs must be restated on a full cost basis for external reporting and for income tax purposes.

Summary of advantages and disadvantages of variable costing

Some of the advantages and disadvantages generally associated with the use of variable costing procedures may be summarized as follows:

Advantages	*Disadvantages*
1 Installation of a variable costing system requires a careful analysis of costs and this may result in more effective planning and cost control throughout the entire organization.	*1 Financial statements prepared on the variable costing basis are not acceptable for financial reporting or income tax purposes.*
2 Information needed for cost-volume-earnings analysis is readily available	*2 Inventories, working capital, and stockholders' equity tend to be understated*

---

[2] American Institute of Certified Public Accountants, *Accounting Research and Terminology Bulletins,* Final Edition (New York: 1961), pp. 28–29.

Advantages	*Disadvantages*
from statements prepared on a variable costing basis.	when variable costing is used for financial reporting purposes.
3 Because variable and fixed costs are segregated, the variable costing income statement may be more useful to management in arriving at certain decisions.	3 Segregation of factory overhead costs into fixed and variable components is often difficult.
4 Since fixed costs are not allocated to departments or products under variable costing, it is easier for management to determine the contribution margin on product lines and sales territories.	4 Exclusion of fixed factory overhead costs from inventory tends to make long-run pricing decisions less effective because prices may be set at a level sufficient to recover the variable costs but not all the fixed costs. Net income can only result after all costs are recovered.
5 Operating income under variable costing will generally increase when sales increase and decrease when sales decrease; this may not be true when full costing is used.	

Concluding comments

The information needed by managers is sometimes significantly different from that collected in the ordinary processes of financial accounting. Managers are primarily concerned with the possible outcomes of future courses of action. This means that they must have reliable estimates of costs which will be incurred and revenue which will be earned as a result of a business decision. Effective decision making generally includes the following steps:

1 A clear definition of the problem or proposed action is prepared, and the relevant information (both quantitative and subjective) is gathered.
2 The decision is made and the actions and resources required to carry out the decision are spelled out.
3 A feedback system is designed which will evaluate the decision against actual results.

Although managers are responsible for making decisions, accountants provide inputs needed to implement each of these steps. Examples of business decisions which would not require some form of accounting information are not easy to find.

We have merely scratched the surface in discussing the possible kinds of analyses that might be prepared in making decisions. The brief treatment in this chapter, however, has been sufficient to establish the basic principles that lie behind such analyses. The most profitable course of action is determined by studying the costs, revenue, and investments that are incremental to the particular alternatives under consideration. The relevant information is often difficult to obtain and always involves making estimates about the future. As a result, such information is generally subject to some degree of error. Finally, there are always important intangible factors that defy quantification which should be brought into the decision picture only after the quantitative analysis has been made.

KEY TERMS INTRODUCED OR EMPHASIZED IN CHAPTER 28

Capital budgeting The process of planning and evaluating proposals for investments in plant assets.

Discount rate The required rate of return used by an investor to discount future cash flows to their present value.

Discounted cash flows The present value of expected future cash flows.

Full (absorption) costing The traditional method of product costing in which both fixed and variable manufacturing costs are treated as product costs and charged to inventories.

Incremental (differential) cost The difference between the total cost of alternative courses of action.

Net present value The excess of the present value of the net cash flows expected from an investment over the amount to be invested. Net present value is one method of ranking alternative investment opportunities.

Opportunity cost The benefit foregone by not pursuing an alternative course of action. Opportunity costs are not recorded in the accounting records, but are important in making many types of business decisions.

Payback period The length of time necessary to recover the cost of an investment through the cash flows generated by that investment. Payback period is one criterion used in making capital budgeting decisions.

Present value The amount of money today which is considered equivalent to a cash inflow or outflow expected to take place in the future. The present value of money is always less than the future amount, since money on hand today can be invested to become the equivalent of a larger amount in the future.

Relevant cost A cost which should be given consideration in making a specific decision.

Return on average investment The average annual net income from an investment expressed as a percentage of the average amount invested. Return on average investment is one method of ranking alternative investment opportunities according to their relative profitability.

Sunk cost A cost which has irrevocably been incurred by past actions. Sunk costs are irrelevant to decisions regarding future actions.

Variable costing The technique of product costing in which variable manufacturing costs are charged to inventories produced and fixed manufacturing costs are treated as period expenses.

REVIEW QUESTIONS

1 Comment on the following position taken by a business executive: "Since relevant quantitative information is difficult to obtain and is subject to some degree of error, I'd rather make decisions on the basis of subjective factors and my many years of business experience."

2 What is the difference between a *sunk cost* and an *out-of-pocket cost?*

3 Define *opportunity costs* and explain why they represent a common source of error in making cost analyses.

4 Briefly discuss the type of information you would want before deciding to discontinue the production of a major line of products.

5 Explain why the book value of existing equipment is not relevant in deciding whether the equipment should be scrapped (without realizing any proceeds) or continued in use.

6 The Calcutta Corporation produces a large number of products. The costs per unit of one of its products, Maxad, is shown below:

Prime costs (direct materials and direct labor)	*$7.00*
Variable factory overhead	*4.00*
Fixed factory overhead	*2.00*

The company recently decided to buy 10,000 Maxads from another manufacturer for $12.50 per unit because "it was cheaper than our cost of $13.00 per unit." Evaluate the decision only on the basis of the cost data given.

7 A company regularly sells 100,000 washing machines at an average price of $250. The average cost of producing these machines is $180. Under what circumstances might the company accept an order for 20,000 washing machines at $175 per machine?

8 What is *capital budgeting?* Why are capital budgeting decisions crucial to the long-run financial health of a business enterprise?

9 A company invests $100,000 in plant assets with an estimated 20-year service life and no salvage value. These assets contribute $10,000 to annual net income when depreciation is computed on a straight-line basis. Compute the payback period and explain your computation.

10 What is the major shortcoming of using the payback period as the only criterion in making capital budgeting decisions?

11 What factors should an investor consider in appraising the adequacy of the rate of return from a specific investment proposal?

12 Discounting a future cash flow at 15% results in a lower present value than does discounting the same cash flow at 10%. Explain why.

13 What factors determine the present value of a future cash flow?

14 Discounting cash flows takes into consideration one characteristic of the earnings stream which is ignored in the computation of return on average investment. What is this characteristic and why it is important?

15 List the three basic features of *variable (direct) costing.*

16 During the current year the inventory of finished product of a manufacturing firm declined. In which case would the company's reported income be larger: if it used variable costing, or if it used full costing? Explain your reasoning.

17 The Bombay Company reports an amount labeled *manufacturing margin* in its income statement. The income statement is stamped "for management's use only." Explain what is meant by "manufacturing margin" and why the income statement containing this term is not issued to outsiders.

18 List three advantages and three disadvantages of using variable (direct) costing.

EXERCISES

Ex. 28-1 The controller of Hyde Park, Inc., presents the following statement (in thousands of dollars) to the president and suggests that the Beach Division be eliminated:

	All Other Divisions	Beach Division	Total
Sales	$120,000	$ 6,000	$126,000
Cost of goods sold:			
Variable	(42,000)	(3,600)	(45,600)
Fixed	(12,000)	(1,200)	(13,200)
Gross profit on sales	$ 66,000	$ 1,200	$ 67,200
Operating expenses:			
Variable	(30,000)	(1,800)	(31,800)
Fixed	(18,000)	(2,400)	(20,400)
Income or (loss)	$ 18,000	$(3,000)	$ 15,000

Do you agree with the controller? Prepare a schedule in support of your answer. You may assume that fixed costs and expenses would not be affected by the elimination of the Beach Division.

Ex. 28-2 The Magic Game Company sells 600,000 game sets per year at $9.00 each. The current unit cost of the game sets is broken down as follows:

Direct materials	$1.50
Direct labor	2.70
Variable factory overhead	0.60
Fixed factory overhead	1.20
Total	$6.00

At the beginning of the current year the company receives a special order for 10,000 game sets per month *for one year only* at $5.40 per unit. A new machine with an estimated life of five years would have to be purchased for $30,000 to produce the additional units. Management thinks that it will not be able to use the new machine beyond one year and that it will have to be sold for approximately $19,500. Compute the estimated gain or loss that the company would realize if the special order is accepted.

Ex. 28-3 Auto Parts Company has 20,000 units of a defective product on hand which cost $43,200 to manufacture. The company can either sell this product as scrap for $1.08 per unit or it can sell the product for $4.20 per unit by reworking the units and correcting the defects at a cost of $26,400. What should the company do? Prepare a schedule in support of your recommendation.

Ex. 28-4 Bowman Corporation is considering an investment in special-purpose equipment to enable the company to obtain a four-year government contract for the manufacture of a special item. The equipment costs $300,000 and would have no salvage value when its use is discontinued at the end of the four years. Estimated annual operating results of the project are:

Revenue from contract sales		$325,000
Expenses other than depreciation	$225,000	
Depreciation (straight-line basis)	75,000	300,000
Increase in net income from contract work		$ 25,000

All revenue and all expenses other than depreciation will be received or paid in cash in the same period as recognized for accounting purposes. Compute for the proposal to undertake the contract work the following:

a Payback period

b Return on average investment

c Net present value of proposal to undertake contract work, discounted at an annual rate of 12% (Refer to annuity table on page 990.)

Ex. 28-5 The cost to Ellis Company of manufacturing 10,000 units of item X is $240,000, including both fixed and variable costs. Fixed factory overhead is 50% of total variable costs. The company can buy the part from an outside supplier for $18.00 per unit, although the regular price of the part is $23.00 per unit. If the company buys the part, the fixed factory overhead now allocated to the part will remain unchanged, and another product would be produced which would bring in $48,000 of contribution margin. Should the company buy the part or continue to manufacture it? Prepare a comparative schedule in good form.

Ex. 28-6 Given below are the production and sales data for the Aluminum Products Company at the end of its first year of operations:

Sales (6,000 units × $77)	*$462,000*
Production costs (10,000 units):	
Variable	*350,000*
Fixed	*210,000*
Selling and administrative expenses (all fixed)	*70,000*

Compute income from operations for the year using (**a**) full costing and (**b**) variable costing.

Ex. 28-7 Using the tables on pages 988 and 990, determine the present value of the following cash flows, discounted at an annual rate of 8%:

a $35,000 to be received 8 years from today

b $12,000 to be received annually for 5 years

c $42,000 to be received annually for 7 years, with an additional $30,000 salvage value due at the end of the seventh year

d $30,000 to be received annually for the first 3 years, followed by $20,000 received annually for the next 2 years (total of 5 years in which cash is received)

PROBLEMS

Group A

28A-1 A partial income statement for the Platte River Company for the first year of its operations, prepared in conventional (full costing) form, is shown on page 1003.

Instructions

a Revise the statement using the variable (direct) costing approach. Briefly explain the difference in the income from operations reported in the two statements.

b Prepare a schedule showing whether it would be profitable for the Platte River Company to accept an offer from a foreign customer to purchase 25,000 units for $72 per unit. This special order would have no effect on fixed factory overhead or on operating expenses.

PLATTE RIVER COMPANY
Income Statement
For First Year of Operations (in thousands)

Sales (100,000 units at $120 per unit)		$12,000
Cost of goods sold:		
Direct material	$ 4,200	
Direct labor	3,300	
Variable factory overhead	300	
Fixed factory overhead	2,400	
Total manufacturing costs	$10,200	
Less: Ending finished goods inventory (25,000 units)	2,040	
Cost of goods sold ($61.80 per unit)		8,160
Gross profit on sales		$ 3,840
Less: Operating expenses:		
Variable	$1,200	
Fixed	1,440	
Total operating expenses		2,640
Income from operations		$ 1,200

28A-2 Rothmore Appliance Company is planning to introduce a built-in blender to its line of small home appliances. Annual sales of the blender are estimated at 10,000 units at a price of $35 per unit. Variable manufacturing costs are estimated at $16 per unit, incremental fixed manufacturing costs (other than depreciation) at $30,000 annually, and incremental selling and general expenses relating to the blenders at $50,000 annually.

To build the blenders, the company must invest $240,000 in molds, patterns, and special equipment. Since the company expects to change the design of the blender every four years, this equipment will have a four-year service life with no salvage value. Depreciation will be computed on a straight-line basis. All revenue and expenses other than depreciation will be received or paid in cash. The company's combined state and federal income tax rate is 50%.

Instructions
a Prepare a schedule showing the estimated annual net income from the proposal to manufacture and sell the blenders.
b Compute the annual net cash flow expected from the proposal.
c Compute for this proposal (*1*) payback period (round to the nearest tenth of a year), (*2*) return on average investment (round to the nearest tenth of a percent), and (*3*) net present value, discounted at an annual rate of 15%.

28A-3 The Exposition Corporation opened its new Jefferson Plant at the beginning of the current year to manufacture a burglar alarm. During the year the Jefferson Plant sold 50,000 burglar alarms at an average price of $54 per unit. At the end of the year, there were 10,000 finished burglar alarms on hand. There was no goods in process inventory at the end of the year. During the year the Jefferson Plant reported the following costs charged to the Goods in Process account:

Direct materials	$810,000
Direct labor	648,000
Variable factory overhead	270,000
Fixed factory overhead	540,000

Operating expenses for the year are analyzed at the top of page 1004.

	Fixed	Variable (per Unit Sold)
Selling expenses	$270,000	$4.05
Administrative expenses	180,000	1.80

The plant manager prepared an income statement for the current year showing an income from operations for the plant of $67,500, based on a full costing assumption. The company controller, who is an advocate of variable costing, insists that on a variable costing basis the plant did not cover the fixed costs incurred for the year.

Instructions

a Prepare an income statement under the full (absorption) costing assumption as it must have been made by the plant manager.

b Prepare an income statement such as the controller had in mind, using the variable (direct) costing assumption.

28A-4 The Road Equipment Company requests your assistance in deciding whether it should continue to manufacture valves or whether it should purchase this part. The annual requirement for valves is 5,000 units and the part is currently available from Axel Corporation at $21.00 per unit.

The following information is available for your consideration:

(1) If the valves were purchased, some of the machinery used to produce valves would be used to help out in the production of other products now being manufactured and some of the machinery would be idle for the time being because it has no current resale value. The machinery used to produce valves cost $60,000, has a book value of $27,000, and has a remaining life of five years (no residual value) based on the existing depreciation schedule. Property taxes and insurance on this machinery amount to $1,200 per year.

(2) The company has devoted approximately 10% of its factory capacity to the production of valves. Direct material and labor costs could be reduced without affecting other operations if valves were purchased.

(3) During the latest year, in which 5,000 valves were produced, the total factory costs and the portion of these costs allocated to valves were as follows:

	Total Factory Costs	Costs Allocated to Valves
Direct materials	$270,000	$55,200
Direct labor (including payroll taxes)	300,000	39,000
Indirect labor (including payroll taxes)	90,000	9,000
Heat and light (allocated on basis of capacity devoted to production of valves)	30,000	?
Depreciation (straight-line method)	84,000	9,600
Property taxes and insurance	36,000	3,600
Factory supplies used	18,000	3,000
Total	$828,000	$?

(4) Direct materials, direct labor, and factory supplies used may be considered variable costs. One-half of the indirect labor cost allocated to valves is variable and the other one-half is fixed; all other costs are completely fixed.

(5) If the valves were purchased, the Road Equipment Company would incur added costs of $1.20 per unit for freight and $2,400 per year for receiving, handling, and inspection.

Instructions

a Prepare a three-column schedule showing (*1*) the total annual cost now allocated to valves, (*2*) the annual *incremental* cost that has been incurred in producing valves, and (*3*) the estimated annual cost of purchasing valves from the Axel Corporation.

b *List* some other factors that management of the Road Equipment Company should take into account in arriving at a decision whether to purchase valves or continue to manufacture them. *You need not discuss the factors listed.*

28A-5 Cardiff Corporation is considering two alternative proposals for modernizing its production facilities. To provide a basis for selection, the cost accounting department has developed the following data regarding the expected annual operating results for the two proposals:

	Proposal 1	Proposal 2
Required investment in equipment	$360,000	$350,000
Estimated service life of equipment	8 years	7 years
Estimated salvage value	–0–	$ 14,000
Estimated annual cost savings (net cash flow) . . . . :	$ 75,000	$ 76,000
Depreciation on equipment (straight-line basis)	$ 45,000	$ 48,000
Estimated increase in annual net income	$ 30,000	$ 28,000

Instructions

a For each proposal, compute the (*1*) payback period, (*2*) return on average investment, and (*3*) net present value, discounted at an annual rate of 12%. (Round the payback period to the nearest tenth of a year and the return on investment to the nearest tenth of a percent.)

b Based on your analysis in part *a,* state which proposal you would recommend and explain the reasons for your choice.

Group B

28B-1 The Rocket Corporation manufactures a single product and has a normal capacity of 100,000 units per year. Variable manufacturing costs are $18 per unit. Fixed factory overhead is $600,000 per year. Variable selling and administrative expenses are $9 per unit and fixed selling and administrative expenses are $450,000 per year. The unit sales price is $45.

The operating results for Year 1 are sales, 80,000 units, and production, 100,000 units. The beginning inventory amounted to 10,000 units at a total cost of $240,000, including $60,000 of fixed manufacturing costs.

Instructions

a Prepare formal income statements (through income from operations) for Year 1 using:

(*1*) Variable (direct) costing

(*2*) Full costing

b Briefly explain the difference in the income from operations between the two income statements.

28B-2 The owner of Multi-Products presents you with the comparison of the performance for two salesmen who are paid a commission of 6% of gross sales:

	Jack Green	Bill White
Gross sales	$1,700,000	$820,000
Sales returns	100,000	20,000

Cost of goods sold, excluding returns	$1,120,000	$480,000
Reimbursed entertainment and other direct expenses	30,000	12,000
Samples distributed	24,800	4,400
Allocated indirect expenses	20,000	10,000

Both salesmen handle similar products in comparable territories in the same state. Each is given authority to offer discounts to customers within broad guidelines established by the owner.

Instructions

a Compute the contribution margin generated by each salesman (after commissions) and compute the percentage that the contribution margin generated by each salesman bears to net sales.

b What percentage of contribution margin (before commissions) is paid out to each salesman in the form of commissions?

c Briefly evaluate the relative performance of the two salesmen and suggest possible reasons why Green's performance may be viewed as favorable or unfavorable from the owner's standpoint.

28B-3 The directors of the Southern Company have been studying the income statements for 1978 and 1979 in which pretax income (income from operations) of $104,000 and $88,000 are shown. The directors do not understand how income could decrease by $16,000 when sales increased by 50%. The cost accountant explains that underapplied fixed factory overhead of $96,000 was charged to 1979 operations because the plant worked at only $66\frac{2}{3}$% of normal capacity. His income statement was based on the following information:

	1979	1978
Sales ($25.60 per unit)	$768,000	$512,000
Total fixed factory overhead	288,000	288,000
Selling and administrative expenses (all fixed)	56,000	56,000
Inventory of finished goods (10,000 units at standard cost) . . .	None	176,000
Unit-cost information (at standard):		
Variable manufacturing cost	$8.00	$8.00
Fixed factory overhead	9.60	9.60

In 1979, the plant produced 20,000 units and in 1978, a total of 30,000. There was no inventory of finished goods at the beginning of 1978.

Instructions

a Prepare a comparative income statement for the two years using full (absorption) costing. Inventory should be valued at standard cost and the idle capacity cost of $96,000 should be added to the cost of goods sold.

b Prepare a comparative income statement for the two years using variable (direct) costing.

c Comment on the results obtained in parts *a* and *b*.

28B-4 Management of Power Tools, Inc., has asked for your assistance in arriving at a decision whether to continue manufacturing a small motor called Topper or to buy it from an outside supplier. The Topper is used by Power Tools, Inc., in assembling a line of spraying and pruning equipment.

Your investigation yields the following data as being typical of the company's operations:

(1) The annual requirement for Toppers is 6,000 units. The lowest bid received from an outside supplier is for a price of $21.00 per unit.

(2) Toppers have been manufactured by Power Tools, Inc., in its machine shop. If Toppers are purchased from an outside supplier, certain machinery will be sold at book value.

(*3*) Following are the total costs of the machine shop during the year when 6,000 Toppers were manufactured:

Direct materials	$160,000
Direct labor	120,000
Indirect labor	80,000
Heat, light, and power	18,000
Depreciation on building and machinery	20,000
Property taxes and insurance	16,000
Payroll taxes and other fringe benefits—15% of total labor costs	30,000
Other factory overhead costs	9,600

(*4*) The following costs of the machine shop were directly identified with the production of Toppers: direct materials, $60,000; direct labor, $54,000; indirect labor, $20,000; power, $800; other factory overhead costs, $1,600. The sale of the equipment used in the manufacture of Toppers would reduce the fixed factory overhead by $4,000 for depreciation and $600 for property taxes and insurance.

(*5*) The following additional costs would be incurred if Toppers were purchased from an outside supplier: freight, $1.00 per unit; indirect labor for receiving, handling, and inspection (before payroll taxes and fringe benefits), $4,400.

Instructions Prepare a schedule showing whether Toppers, should continue to be manufactured by Power Tools, Inc., or should be purchased from an outside supplier.

28B-5 Ortega Company is evaluating two alternative investment opportunities. The controller of the company has prepared the following analysis of the two investment proposals:

	Proposal A	Proposal B
Required investment in equipment	$220,000	$240,000
Estimated service life of equipment	5 years	6 years
Estimated salvage value	$ 10,000	–0–
Estimated annual net cash flow	$ 60,000	$ 60,000
Depreciation on equipment (straight-line basis)	$ 42,000	$ 40,000
Estimated annual net income	$ 18,000	$ 20,000

Instructions

a For each proposed investment, compute the (*1*) payback period, (*2*) return on average investment, and (*3*) net present value, discounted at an annual rate of 12%. (Round the payback period to the nearest tenth of a year and the return on investment to the nearest tenth of a percent.)

b Based upon your computations in part *a*, which proposal do you consider to be the best investment? Explain.

BUSINESS DECISION PROBLEM 28

Cornbelt Cereal Company is engaged in manufacturing a breakfast cereal. You are asked to advise management on sales policy for the coming year.

Two proposals are being considered by management which will (*1*) increase the volume of sales, (*2*) reduce the ratio of selling expense to sales, and (*3*) decrease manufacturing cost per unit. These proposals are as follows:

Proposal no. 1: Increase advertising expenditures by offering premium stamps
It is proposed that each package of cereal will contain premium stamps which will be redeemed for cash prizes. The estimated cost of this premium plan for a sales volume of over 500,000 boxes is estimated at $60 per 1,000 boxes sold. The new advertising plan will take the place of all existing advertising expenditures and the current selling price of 70 cents per unit will be maintained.

Proposal no. 2: Reduce selling price of product
It is proposed that the selling price of the cereal be reduced by 5% and that advertising expenditures be increased over those of the current year. This plan is an alternative to Proposal no. 1, and only one will be adopted by management.

Management has provided you with the following information as to the current year's operations:

Quantity sold	*500,000 boxes*
Selling price per unit	*$0.70*
Manufacturing cost per unit	*$0.40*
Selling expenses, 20% of sales (one-fourth of which was for newspaper advertising)	
Administrative expenses, 6% of sales	

Estimates for the coming year for each proposal are shown below:

	Proposal No. 1	Proposal No. 2
Increase in unit sales volume	*50%*	*30%*
Decrease in manufacturing cost per unit	*10%*	*5%*
Newspaper advertising	*None*	*10% of sales*
Other selling expenses	*8% of sales*	*8% of sales*
Premium plan expense	*$.06 per box*	*None*
Administrative expenses	*5% of sales*	*10% of sales*

Instructions Which of the two proposals should management select? In support of your recommendation, prepare a statement comparing the income from operations for the current year with the anticipated income from operations for the coming year under Proposal no. 1 and under Proposal no. 2. In preparing the statement use the following column headings: Current Year, Proposal No. 1, and Proposal No. 2.

Appendix

Financial Statements of a Publicly Owned Company

The financial statements of Johnson & Johnson, a company listed on the New York Stock Exchange, are presented on the following pages. These financial statements have been audited by Coopers & Lybrand, an international firm of certified public accountants. The audit report is attached. This particular company was selected because its financial statements provide realistic illustrations of many of the financial reporting issues discussed in this book.

Johnson & Johnson and Subsidiaries

Consolidated Balance Sheet at December 28, 1975 and December 29, 1974
(Dollars in Thousands Except Per Share Figures)

ASSETS	1975	1974
Current Assets		
Cash and certificates of deposit	$ 38,300	31,387
Marketable securities, at cost which approximates market value	199,921	77,952
Receivables, less allowance for collection losses and discounts $11,320 (1974 $9,711)	288,465	273,017
Inventories (Notes 1 and 4)	396,940	432,108
Expenses applicable to future operations	23,350	21,036
Total current assets	946,976	835,500
Marketable Securities Maturing After One Year, at cost		
(market value at December 28, 1975—$29,536) (Note 3)	34,147	62,030
Property, Plant and Equipment, at cost less accumulated		
depreciation and amortization (Notes 1 and 5)	528,252	467,009
Other Assets	42,129	41,138
Total assets	$1,551,504	1,405,677

LIABILITIES AND STOCKHOLDERS' EQUITY	1975	1974
Current Liabilities		
Loans and notes payable (Note 7)	$ 27,575	40,372
Accounts payable	99,424	109,000
Federal and international taxes on income	61,620	55,332
Other accrued liabilities	127,531	102,973
Total current liabilities	316,150	307,677
Loans and Notes Payable After One Year (Note 7)	30,832	35,229
Capitalized Long-Term Lease Obligations	8,570	8,640
Certificates of Extra Compensation	28,579	27,549
Deferred Investment Tax Credit	11,654	8,399
Reserve for International Exchange Losses (Notes 1 and 2)	—	12,302
Minority Interests in International Subsidiaries	4,882	6,516
Stockholders' Equity (Note 8)		
Preferred Stock—without par value (authorized and unissued 2,000,000 shares)	—	—
Common Stock—par value $2.50 per share		
(authorized 63,000,000 shares; issued 58,136,616 and 57,945,336 shares)	145,342	144,863
Additional capital	68,545	52,959
Retained earnings	938,181	803,546
	1,152,068	1,001,368
Less common stock held in treasury, at cost (101,883 and 161,512 shares)	1,231	2,003
Total stockholders' equity	1,150,837	999,365
Total liabilities and stockholders' equity	$1,551,504	1,405,677

See Notes to Consolidated Financial Statements

Johnson&Johnson and Subsidiaries

Consolidated Statement of Earnings and Retained Earnings

For the 52 Weeks Ended December 28, 1975 and December 29, 1974
(Dollars in Thousands Except Per Share Figures)

	1975	1974
Revenues		
Sales to customers	$2,224,680	1,937,211
Other revenues		
Interest income	11,779	14,756
Royalties and miscellaneous	15,606	15,918
	27,385	30,674
Total revenues	2,252,065	1,967,885
Costs and Expenses		
Cost of products sold	1,169,454	1,044,357
Selling, distribution and administrative expenses (Note 6)	755,237	632,782
Losses on translation of assets and liabilities into U.S. Dollars (Note 2)	3,893	—
Other expenses	13,336	10,078
Total costs and expenses	1,941,920	1,687,217
Earnings before provision for taxes on income	310,145	280,668
Federal and international taxes on income (Note 6)	126,327	119,048
Net Earnings	183,818	161,620
Retained Earnings At Beginning Of Period	803,546	683,719
Cash dividends paid (per share: 1975, $.85; 1974, $.725)	(49,183)	(41,793)
Retained Earnings At End Of Period	$ 938,181	803,546
Net Earnings Per Share (Note 1)	$3.18	2.80

Consolidated Statement of Common Stock, Additional Capital and Treasury Stock

For the 52 Weeks Ended December 28, 1975
(Dollars in Thousands)

	Common Stock Issued		Additional Capital	Treasury Stock	
	No. Shares	Amount	Amount	No. Shares	Amount
Balance, December 29, 1974	57,945,336	$144,863	$52,959	161,512	$2,003
Stock issued to employees under options exercised, stock compensation agreements, and awards	191,280	479	12,300	—	—
Other changes	—	—	3,286	(59,629)	(772)
Balance, December 28, 1975	58,136,616	$145,342	$68,545	101,883	$1,231

See Notes to Consolidated Financial Statements

Johnson & Johnson and Subsidiaries

Consolidated Statement of Changes in Financial Position

For the 52 Weeks Ended December 28, 1975 and December 29, 1974
(Dollars in Thousands)

Resources Provided	1975	1974
Net Earnings	$ 183,818	161,620
Expenses not requiring the outlay of cash:		
Depreciation and amortization of property, plant and equipment	68,605	59,906
Other charges against net earnings	7,518	3,066
Provided from operations	259,941	224,592
Increase (decrease) in long-term debt	(4,397)	3,370
Proceeds from the sales of capital stock under option	7,337	6,362
Proceeds from the sales of property, plant and equipment	7,275	3,062
	270,156	237,386

Resources Used		
Marketable securities maturing after one year	(27,883)	(4,270)
Additions to property, plant and equipment	135,952	157,580
Cash dividends paid	49,183	41,793
Other items—net	9,901	2,378
	167,153	197,481
Increase in Consolidated Working Capital	$ 103,003	39,905

Changes in Components of Consolidated Working Capital:

Current Assets		
Cash and marketable securities	$ 128,882	(97,483)
Receivables	15,448	49,762
Inventories	(35,168)	162,848
Expenses applicable to future operations	2,314	(4,270)
	111,476	110,857
Current Liabilities		
Loans and notes payable	(12,797)	25,033
Accounts payable	(9,576)	22,513
Federal and international taxes on income	6,288	(2,187)
Other accrued liabilities	24,558	25,593
	8,473	70,952
Increase in Consolidated Working Capital	$ 103,003	39,905

See Notes to Consolidated Financial Statements

Johnson&Johnson and Subsidiaries

Notes to Consolidated Financial Statements

Note 1   **Summary of Significant Accounting Policies**

Principles of Consolidation

The consolidated financial statements include the accounts of Johnson & Johnson and subsidiaries. All material intercompany accounts are eliminated.

Assets and liabilities of international subsidiaries are translated at approximate year-end rates of exchange except for property, plant and equipment accounts which are translated at the approximate rates of exchange at dates of acquisition. Operating accounts, except for depreciation, are translated at approximate annual average rates. Gains on translation of asset and liability accounts not offset by losses are deferred and included in the Reserve for International Exchange Losses.

Inventories

Inventories are valued at the lower of cost or market. Effective with the year ended December 29, 1974, the Company adopted the last-in, first-out (LIFO) method of inventory valuation for certain of its domestic companies. Prior to 1974 inventories were primarily on the first-in, first-out (FIFO) method of inventory valuation.

The following inventory amounts have been valued using the methods noted:

	December 28, **1975**	December 29, **1974**
LIFO Method	$124,198,000	130,852,000
FIFO Method	272,742,000	301,256,000
Total	$396,940,000	432,108,000

If all inventories were valued on the FIFO basis (which approximates replacement cost), total inventories would have been $442,641,000 and $472,892,000 at December 28, 1975 and December 29, 1974 respectively.

Depreciation and Amortization

Depreciation and amortization of property, plant and equipment are determined generally for book and tax purposes by an accelerated method for domestic companies and principally on a straight-line basis for international companies.

Research

Research costs are charged directly against income in the year in which incurred and amounted to $97,859,000 and $83,565,000 for years 1975 and 1974 respectively.

Income Taxes

Domestic investment tax credits are amortized over the lives of related assets.

The Company plans to continue to reinvest its undistributed international earnings in expanding its international operations and, therefore, makes no tax provision to cover the repatriation of such undistributed earnings. At December 28, 1975, the cumulative amount of undistributed international earnings on which the Company has not provided for United States income taxes was approximately $193,000,000.

Earnings per Share

Earnings per share are calculated on the average number of shares outstanding during each year.

Annual Closing Date

Since 1968 Johnson & Johnson has followed the concept of a fiscal year which ends on the Sunday nearest to the end of the calendar month of December. In 1976 the Sunday closest to the end of December is January 2, 1977, and Johnson & Johnson's 1976 fiscal year will end on that date. Normally, each fiscal year consists of 52 weeks, but every five or six years, as is the case in 1976, the fiscal year consists of 53 weeks.

Note 2   International Subsidiaries

The following amounts are included in the consolidated financial statements for subsidiaries located outside of the United States:

	December 28, 1975	December 29, 1974
Current assets	$392,209,000	366,501,000
Current liabilities	193,557,000	193,037,000
Net property, plant and equipment	202,634,000	177,906,000
Parent company equity in net assets	360,539,000	291,947,000
Excess of equity of parent company over investment	286,568,000	223,984,000
Sales to customers	956,720,000	799,085,000
Net earnings (after elimination of minority interests)	93,287,000	81,525,000

Analysis of the Reserve for International Exchange Losses:

	52 Weeks Ended	
	December 28, 1975	December 29, 1974
Balance beginning of period	$12,302,000	7,517,000
Gains on translation of assets and liabilities into U.S. Dollars	515,000	9,397,000
Losses on translation of assets and liabilities into U.S. Dollars	(16,710,000)	(4,612,000)
Net increase (decrease)	(16,195,000)	4,785,000
Sub-total	(3,893,000)	12,302,000
Losses on translation of assets and liabilities into U.S. Dollars charged to earnings	3,893,000	—
Balance end of period	$ —	12,302,000

Beginning with the year 1976, the Financial Accounting Standards Board Statement No. 8 requires certain changes to the Company's international currency translation policy and related reporting of international exchange gains and losses. The effect of earlier application of this statement in 1975 or any preceding year is not material and, therefore, will not require restatement of the consolidated financial statements for such years.

Note 3   Marketable Securities Maturing After One Year

Marketable securities maturing after one year and preferred stock held for long-term investment are classified as non-current investments.

The Financial Accounting Standards Board Statement No. 12 states that certain marketable equity securities must be written down to market value if market value is lower than cost. The difference between market value and cost of the securities covered by this statement was not material and, therefore, no write down has been taken.

Note 4   Inventories

	December 28, 1975	December 29, 1974
Raw materials and supplies	$124,152,000	158,322,000
Goods in process	79,432,000	81,756,000
Finished goods	193,356,000	192,030,000
	$396,940,000	432,108,000

Note 5 **Property, Plant and Equipment**

	December 28, 1975	December 29, 1974
Land and land improvements	$ 56,052,000	47,529,000
Building and building equipment	334,674,000	280,014,000
Machinery and equipment	399,520,000	338,622,000
Construction in process	58,900,000	79,124,000
	849,146,000	745,289,000
Less accumulated depreciation and amortization	320,894,000	278,280,000
	$528,252,000	467,009,000

Note 6 **Income Taxes**

Income tax expense consists of:
(Dollars in Thousands)

Year 1975	U.S. Federal	International	Total Federal and International	Domestic State and Local*
Currently Payable	$54,760	64,246	119,006	8,677
Net Tax Effect— Timing Differences	(683)	4,749	4,066	
Net Deferred Investment Tax Credit	3,255	—	3,255	
	$57,332	68,995	126,327	8,677
Effective Tax Rate	38.8%	42.5%	40.7%	

Year 1974				
Currently Payable	$54,411	57,367	111,778	6,714
Net Tax Effect— Timing Differences	(125)	5,827	5,702	
Net Deferred Investment Tax Credit	1,568	—	1,568	
	$55,854	63,194	119,048	6,714
Effective Tax Rate	41.1%	43.7%	42.4%	

*Reflected in Selling, Distribution and Administrative Expenses.

The Company's effective income tax rate was 40.7% in 1975 and 42.4% in 1974. This compares to the federal statutory rate of 48% and the major components causing such differences were as follows:

	% of Pre-Tax Income	
	1975	1974
Computed statutory tax rate	48.0%	48.0%
Difference in effective tax rate of international operations	(2.9)	(2.2)
Tax exempt Puerto Rico operations	(2.5)	(.5)
Tax exempt income on marketable securities	(.6)	(1.0)
Amortization of deferred investment tax credit	(.6)	(.5)
Internal Revenue Service audit adjustments	(.3)	(.7)
All other	(.4)	(.7)
Effective tax rate	40.7%	42.4%

Note 7   Loans and Notes Payable

Loans and notes payable are principally related to the international subsidiaries. The maximum aggregate and average short-term debt outstanding during the year were $38,122,000 and $29,709,000, respectively. The interest rates on such loans and notes vary from 5% to 20% according to local conditions. Aggregate maturities of long-term loans and notes payable for each of the next five years are $10,820,000, $5,005,000, $4,080,000, $3,427,000 and $12,013,000.

Note 8   Capital Stock

Stock compensation agreements and options with employees were outstanding at December 28, 1975 under which the Company may be required to deliver shares of common stock. For details see page 29. Common stock equivalents have no material dilutive effect on earnings per share.

During 1975 no shares of the Company were issued under the Johnson & Johnson United Kingdom Executive Share Purchase Plan. As of December 28, 1975, 13,425 shares of the 100,000 maximum authorized under the Plan have been issued.

Note 9   Retirement and Pension Plans

The Company has various retirement and pension plans which cover substantially all of its domestic operations. Certain international subsidiaries have retirement plans for their personnel. The Company's policy generally is to fund accrued pension costs. The total cost of all plans in effect amounted to approximately $21,298,000 in 1975 and $15,683,000 in 1974. The amounts funded under these plans exceeded the actuarially computed value of vested benefits at December 28, 1975.

Based on the Company's present evaluation of the Employee Retirement Security Act of 1974, compliance with the Act for 1976 and thereafter will not have a significant effect on the annual provision for pension expense, and will not require an increase in the funding of pension costs because of minimum funding standards prescribed by the Act.

Note 10   Rental Expense and Lease Commitments

Rentals of space, vehicles, and office and data processing equipment amounted to approximately $33,395,000 in 1975 and $25,840,000 in 1974. The approximate minimum rental commitments under noncancellable leases for 1976 and thereafter are as follows:

1976	—	$10,948,000	1981-1985 —	$5,508,000
1977	—	9,166,000	1986-1990 —	2,692,000
1978	—	6,323,000	1991-1995 —	1,806,000
1979	—	4,647,000	After 1995 —	8,379,000
1980	—	2,053,000		

Commitments under noncapitalized financing leases are not significant.

Note 11   Pending Legal Proceedings

The Company is involved in a number of legal proceedings. Management believes that the liability, if any, resulting from such proceedings, in the aggregate will not have a material adverse effect on the consolidated operations or financial position. For further details see page 28.

Accountants' Report

To the Stockholders and Board of Directors of Johnson & Johnson

We have examined the consolidated balance sheet of Johnson & Johnson and subsidiaries as of December 28, 1975 and December 29, 1974, and the related consolidated statements of earnings and retained earnings, common stock, additional capital and treasury stock, and changes in financial position for the fifty-two week periods then ended. Our examination was made in accordance with generally accepted auditing standards and accordingly included such tests of the accounting records and such other auditing procedures as we considered necessary in the circumstances.

In our opinion, the aforementioned financial statements present fairly the financial position of Johnson & Johnson and subsidiaries at December 28, 1975 and December 29, 1974, and the results of their operations and the changes in their financial position for the fifty-two week periods then ended, in conformity with generally accepted accounting principles applied on a consistent basis.

New York, New York
February 23, 1976

Coopers & Lybrand

Common Stock: Listed New York and Toronto Stock Exchanges
Stock Symbol   JNJ

Transfer Agents: Morgan Guaranty Trust Company of New York
30 West Broadway, New York, New York 10015

Canada Permanent Trust Company
Canada Permanent Tower
20 Eglinton Avenue West
Yonge Eglinton Center, Toronto, Ontario, Canada

Registrars: Morgan Guaranty Trust Company of New York
30 West Broadway, New York, New York 10015

Bank of Montreal, Toronto Branch
50 King Street West, Toronto, Ontario, Canada

Index

(continued from front cover)

15B-2 (a) Net income, $54,000;
(c) total assets, $222,120
15B-3 (a) Distributed to B, $4,000; distributed to C, $19,200
15B-4 (d) Bonus, $50,000
15B-5 No key figure
15B-6 (b) Adjusted net income, $33,235;
(d) K's capital, $101,944
Bus. Dec. Prob. 15:   No key figure

16A-1 Stockholders' equity,   (1) $456,000;
(2) $1,560,000
16A-2 (b) Stockholders' equity, $1,110,000
16A-3 Retained earnings, $49,400
16A-4 Total assets, $2,716,625
16A-5 No key figure
16A-6 Case A: to common, $11; Case B: stockholders' equity, $2,693,600
16B-1 Stockholders' equity,   (1) $976,000;
(2) $3,952,000
16B-2 No key figure
16B-3 Retained earnings, Dec. 31, $57,000
16B-4 (c) $3.84 per share
16B-5 No key figure
16B-6 Stockholders' equity, Case A, $2,816,000;
Case B, $8,160,000; Case C, $7,412,000
Bus. Dec. Prob. 16:   (a) Dividends on common paid by Northern Electric, $31,800,000

17A-1 (c) Amount received as liquidating dividend, $6.94 per share
17A-2 (c) Earnings per share, $1.10
17A-3 (c) Stockholders' equity, $3,210,000
17A-4 (a) Net income, $1,104,000
17A-5 (b) Stockholders' equity, $6,065,600
17A-6 (c) Retained earnings, $2,524,160
17A-7 (a) Stockholders' equity, $21,122,328
17B-1 (c) Amount received as liquidating dividend, $5.32 per share
17B-2 Book value, Dec. 31, $55.84
17B-3 Stockholders' equity, $1,638,000
17B-4 (b) Total lifetime income, $1,084,800
17B-5 Total assets, $2,877,144
17B-6 (b) Net loss, $336,000
17B-7 (b) Stockholders' equity, $24,642,716
Bus. Dec. Prob. 17:   (a) Joseph's share of net assets, $480,000

18A-1 No key figure
18A-2 (b) Net long-term liabilities, $5,840,400
18A-3 (c) Interest expense, issued at discount, $261,000; issued at premium, $248,000
18A-4 (c) Net long-term liabilities, $8,248,341
18A-5 (a) Total revenue, $232,000
18A-6 No key figure
18A-7 (a) Income received, $17,580
18B-1 (b) Interest earned, $800

18B-2 (b) Net long-term liabilities, $4,961,880
18B-3 (b) (4) Interest expense, $172,500
18B-4 (c) Net long-term liabilities, $3,717,092
18B-5 (b) Gain on sale of bonds, $15,300
18B-6 No key figure
18B-7 (a) Earnings, $45,640
Bus. Dec. Prob. 18:   (b) Earnings per share, stock financing, $3.24

19A-1 Retained earnings: (a) $1,140,000;
(b) $840,000
19A-2 (d) $540,000
19A-3 Excess of cost over book value, $25,000
19A-4 Net income: (a) $100,500; (b) $96,800
19A-5 (a) Stockholders' equity, $3,200,000;
(c) $37.50
19B-1 Total assets, $3,804,000
19B-2 (e) $210,000
19B-3 Minority interest, $18,000
19B-4 (b) Net income (after min. interest), $183,600
19B-5 (a) Stockholders' equity, $3,000,000;
(c) $80
Bus. Dec. Prob. 19:   Current ratio (consolidated basis). 2.1 to 1

20A-1 No key figure
20A-2 Taxable income, Case A, $70,560;
Case B, $58,412
20A-3 Taxable income, $28,916
20A-4 (a) Taxable income, $271,250
20A-5 Total interest earned, $5,515
20A-6 (a) Net income, $525,400
20B-1 No key figure
20B-2 (a) Taxable income, $43,680
20B-3 (a) Taxable income, $193,750
20B-4 (c) Net income if loan is used, $101,920
20B-5 (a) Taxable income, $28,540
20B-6 (a) Net income, $87,898
Bus. Dec. Prob. 20:   (a) Tax advantage under proprietorship form, $2,996

21A-1 No key figure
21A-2 Decrease in working capital, $12,000
21A-3 (c) Decrease in working capital, $46,500
21A-4 Total assets, $278,000
21A-5 (c) Decrease in working capital, $300,000
21A-6 (a) Cash flow from operations, $20,000
21B-1 No key figure
21B-2 Increase in working capital, $128,000
21B-3 (c) Decrease in working capital, $77,500
21B-4 (a) Increase in working capital, $27,700
21B-5 (c) Decrease in working capital, $132,000
21B-6 (a) Cash outflow from operations, $32,500
Bus. Dec. Prob. 21:   (a) Projected decrease in working capital, $1,050,000